From the Library of
Carolyn M. Roll
Original illustration by Lynn Bywaters Ferris
© 1987 Sunrise Publications, Inc.

The Illustrated Bible Dictionary
Part Three: Parable-Zuzim

The Illustrated Bible Dictionary

INTER-VARSITY PRESS

Co-ordination
Derek Wood

Research
Tessa Clowney (pictures)
Caroline Masom (diagrams)

Editorial
Mary Gladstone (copy-editing and proofs)
Norman Hillyer (proofs)
Rhona Pipe (proofs)
Jo Bramwell (copy-editing)
Sue Mills (copy-editing)
Derek Wood (copy-editing)
Marie Cross (secretarial)

Maps preparation
Min Topliss
Elisabeth Pearce

Production
Michael Sims (managing)
Joanne Battisson (assistant)

Indexing
Norman Hillyer

The Illustrated Bible Dictionary

PART 3
Parable-Zuzim

Organizing Editor of *The New Bible Dictionary:*

J. D. Douglas, M.A., B.D., S.T.M., Ph.D.
Editor-at-large, *Christianity Today.*

Revision Editor:

N. Hillyer, B.D., S.Th., A.L.C.D.
Formerly Librarian, Tyndale House, Cambridge.

Consulting Editors:

F. F. Bruce, M.A., D.D., F.B.A.
Emeritus Rylands Professor of Biblical Criticism and Exegesis, University of Manchester.

J. I. Packer, M.A., D.Phil., D.D.
Professor of Systematic Theology, Regent College, Vancouver.

R. V. G. Tasker, M.A., D.D.
Formerly Professor of New Testament Exegesis, University of London.

D. J. Wiseman, O.B.E., M.A., D.Lit., F.B.A., F.S.A.
Professor of Assyriology, University of London.

Additional Consulting Editors for the revised edition:

D. Guthrie, B.D., M.Th., Ph.D.
Vice-Principal, London Bible College.

A. R. Millard, M.A., M.Phil., F.S.A.
Rankin Senior Lecturer in Hebrew and Ancient Semitic Languages, University of Liverpool.

Consulting Editor for illustrations:

D. J. Wiseman,
in association with:

A. R. Millard.

J. P. Kane, Ph.D., Dip.Ed.,
Lecturer in Hellenistic Greek, University of Manchester.

K. A. Kitchen, B.A., Ph.D.,
Reader in Egyptian and Coptic, University of Liverpool.

INTER-VARSITY PRESS

TYNDALE HOUSE PUBLISHERS

First published 1980

Reprinted 1986

Inter-Varsity Press,
38 De Montfort Street,
Leicester LE1 7GP, England.

Published and sold in the USA
and Canada by
Tyndale House Publishers,
336 Gundersen Drive, Box 80,
Wheaton, Illinois 60187, USA.

First published in Australia
in 1980 by
Hodder & Stoughton (Australia)
Pty Limited, 2 Apollo Place,
Lane Cove, NSW 2066.

Part Three

UK ISBN 0 85110 629 3
US ISBN 0 8423 1568 3
US ISBN (set) 0 8423 7575 2
US Library of Congress Catalog
Card Number 79–92540
Australia ISBN 0 340 25921 3

Typeset by Monophoto Lasercomp
in Times New Roman by
Richard Clay (The Chaucer Press)
Limited, Bungay,
Suffolk NR35 1ED, England.

Designed by
Thumb Design Partnership Limited,
20–21 D'Arblay Street,
London W1V 3FN, England.

Cartography by
George Philip and Son Limited,
12–14 Long Acre,
London WC2E 9LP, England.

Colour reproduction by
Vauvelle (Photo-litho) Limited,
Clayton Wood Close, West Park,
Leeds LS16 6QE, England.

Printed by
Tien Wah Press (Pte) Ltd
Singapore

Contents

Preface

The Illustrated Bible Dictionary is based on the text of **The New Bible Dictionary,** first published in 1962, which has now been completely revised using the Revised Standard Version of the Bible. While a few of the original articles have been omitted as superfluous and others amalgamated for easier reference, many new articles have been added. A large number have been completely re-written. Bibliographies have been brought up-to-date, cross references revised and a comprehensive index added at the end of the last volume.

In its original form **The New Bible Dictionary** has proved itself to be a steady bestseller through two decades. It came to be regarded by many throughout the world, echoing the verdict of the late Professor William F. Albright, as 'the best one-volume Bible dictionary in the English language'. The revised text is now published in an entirely new form, in three parts, with every advantage that accrues from extensive colour illustrations, photographs, diagrams and maps.

The illustrations have been chosen, not as mere decoration, but with a view to enhancing the value of the Dictionary, by increasing its scope as a source of information. If they make the work more attractive to a wider range of readers, a further advantage has been gained.

The New Bible Dictionary is a major product of the Tyndale Fellowship for Biblical Research, which was founded in close association with the Inter-Varsity Fellowship (now the Universities and Colleges Christian Fellowship) to foster evangelical biblical scholarship. The contributors to **The Illustrated Bible Dictionary,** as to its predecessor, are not, however, drawn exclusively from the ranks of the (mainly British) Tyndale Fellowship; we are deeply indebted to academic colleagues in many parts of the world for their generous co-operation.

The aim of the editors and contributors has continued to be to produce a work of reference, written in a spirit of unqualified loyalty to Holy Scripture, which will substantially further the understanding of God's Word to mankind. That loyalty to Holy Scripture involves treating as true and trustworthy all its statements of fact, theological, physical and historical, is an assumption basic to the whole Dictionary. We do not apologize for the fact that this book reflects the credal, confessional and evangelical convictions for which the Tyndale Fellowship stands—the triunity of God, the deity, atoning death, bodily resurrection and approaching return of Jesus Christ, the divine inspiration and authority of the Bible, the supernatural life of the Christian church, and all that these articles of faith bring with them. No attempt, however, has been made to impose a rigid uniformity upon the work as a whole, or to exclude the occasional expression of different viewpoints within the bounds of this basic loyalty. Nor, of course, are our contributors bound to endorse all the opinions expressed by their colleagues, whether in the Dictionary itself or elsewhere.

The task of organizing this huge revision has fallen on the shoulders of the Rev. Norman Hillyer, whose care, application and courtesy have been instrumental in bringing to birth the text as it now appears.

All who have been involved in the revision are conscious of our continuing debt to Dr J. D. Douglas, the Organizing Editor of the original work, and to Mr Ronald Inchley, the former Publications Secretary of the Inter-Varsity Fellowship. The new Dictionary builds upon their foundation.

As Consulting Editors we are the first to recognize that a major enterprise such as this is possible only because of the enthusiastic and dedicated effort of a large team of people. We wish to record our gratitude to the staff of the Inter-Varsity Press, including those specially engaged for this project, and to the typesetters, colour reproduction specialists, cartographers and printers. Considerable assistance in the preparation of the maps was given by Dr Colin Hemer and Dr John Bimson. A fully illustrated work owes a great deal to its designer, and we are glad to acknowledge here the skilful contribution of Philip Miles and his colleagues at Thumb Design Partnership Ltd.

Our hope is that **The Illustrated Bible Dictionary** will enable many to reach a deeper understanding of the Bible and a richer appreciation of its message.

F.F.B.

D.G.

A.R.M.

J.I.P.

D.J.W.

How to use this Dictionary

The work is divided into three parts and gives the reader the simplest possible access to the most comprehensive information.

Cross references

There are two methods of cross reference:

1. An asterisk before a word indicates that further relevant information will be found in the article under that title and is equivalent to the abbreviation *q.v.*
2. References in the margin provide a list of topics which do not carry articles under their own heading, but the relevant information can be found under another heading, *e.g.*

■ ADVOCATE
See Counsellor, Part 1.

Index

A comprehensive index, containing every significant reference to each topic, is to be found at the end of Part Three. This includes locations on maps and an index to illustrations.

Abbreviations

A full list of abbreviations used in the Dictionary will be found on pages xii–xvi.

Authorship of articles

The authors and co-authors of articles are indicated by their initials at the foot of each article. A full index of contributors is to be found on pages viii–xi. The entries are listed in alphabetical order of initials, not of surnames.

Bibliographies

To assist those wishing to study subjects in greater detail, bibliographies appear at the end of most of the longer articles. These usually provide references to the recent general works on the subject and may include detailed studies or books which take up a position different from that of the contributor.

Picture acknowledgments

The source and/or holder of copyright for the illustrations is indicated by initials in brackets at the end of the picture caption. The full list of sources to which these initials refer is to be found at the end of this volume.

Bible versions

The Bible translation adopted for this Dictionary is the Revised Standard Version. In a few cases contributors have selected quotations from the King James (Authorized) Version, or, when available at the time of writing, the New International Version.

Maps

There is no map supplement in the Dictionary, but maps are to be found alongside the articles themselves for easy reference.

Names of regions, provinces, kingdoms, *etc.*, are printed in large roman capitals, *e.g.* BABYLONIA

Tribes and ethnic groups: large italic capitals, *e.g. AMORITES*

Towns and villages: lower case roman, *e.g.* Jerusalem

Geographical features such as mountains, rivers, lakes, seas, *etc.*: lower case italic, *e.g. Great Sea*

Modern place-names: as above but in brackets, *e.g.* (*Mediterranean Sea*). Absolute consistency has not been possible but, in general, where the modern name is clearly derived from the ancient (*e.g.* Creta = Crete, Italia = Italy) or where it would be pedantic to place modern names in brackets (*e.g.* Egypt, Jerusalem) brackets have been omitted. In a few other cases, where nearly all the place-names are modern, the principle has been abandoned for the sake of simplicity.

Features to be noted particularly, such as the subject of the article concerned, are underlined, *e.g.* Ashdod.

Where a site was known by two or more alternative names they are divided by an oblique stroke, *e.g.* Ezion-geber/Elath.

The word 'or' indicates uncertainty about the name or the location, as does a question mark.

Transliteration

The following systems have been adopted throughout the volume. In fairness to our contributors it should be said that some have disagreed on philological grounds with our transliteration of Hebrew words generally and of the divine name *Yahweh* in particular, but have graciously subordinated their convictions to editorial policy.

Hebrew

א = '	ד = ḏ	י = y	ס = s	ר = r
בּ = b	ה = h	כּ = k	ע = '	שׂ = ś
ב = ḇ	ו = w	כ = ḵ	פּ = p	שׁ = š
גּ = g	ז = z	ל = l	פ = p̄	תּ = t
ג = ḡ	ח = ḥ	מ = m	צ = ṣ	ת = ṯ
דּ = d	ט = ṭ	נ = n	ק = q	

Long vowels		Short vowels	Very short Vowels
(ה)ָ = â	ָ = ā	ַ = a	ֲ = ^{a}
ֵי = ê	ֵ = ē	ֶ = e	ֱ = ^{e}
ִי = î		ִ = i	ְ = ^{e} (if vocal)
וֹ = ô	ֹ = ō	ָ = o	ֳ = ^{o}
וּ = û		ֻ = u	

Greek

α = a	ι = i	ρ = r	ῥ = rh
β = b	κ = k	σ,ς = s	' = h
γ = g	λ = l	τ = t	γξ = nx
δ = d	μ = m	υ = y	γγ = ng
ε = e	ν = n	φ = ph	αυ = au
ζ = z	ξ = x	χ = ch	ευ = eu
η = ē	ο = o	ψ = ps	ου = ou
θ = th	π p	ω = ō	υι = yi

Arabic

ا = '	خ = ḫ	ش = š	غ = ġ	ن = n
ب = b	د = d	ص = ṣ	ف = f	ه = h
ت = t	ذ = ḏ	ض = ḍ	ق = ḳ	و = w
ث = t	ر = r	ط = ṭ	ك = k	ي = y
ج = ǧ	ز = z	ظ = ẓ	ل = l	ة = t
ح = ḥ	س = s	ع = '	م = m	

List of Contributors

A.A.J. A. A. Jones, M.A., B.D., Ph.D., formerly Head of Department of Religious Studies, Avery Hill College, London.

A.C. R. A. Cole, B.A., B.D., M.Th., Ph.D., Federal Secretary, Church Missionary Society (Australia) and Lecturer in Old Testament Language and Literature, University of Sydney.

A.E.C. A. E. Cundall, B.A., B.D., Principal, Bible College of Victoria, Australia.

A.E.W. A. E. Willingale, B.A., B.D., M.Th., Romford, Essex.

A.F. A. Flavelle, B.A., B.D., Minister of Finaghy Presbyterian Church, Belfast.

A.F.W. A. F. Walls, M.A., B.Litt., Professor of Religious Studies, University of Aberdeen.

A.G. A. Gelston, M.A., Senior Lecturer in Theology, University of Durham.

A.J.M.W. A. J. M. Weddeburn, M.A., B.D., Ph.D., Lecturer in New Testament Language and Literature, University of St Andrews.

A.K.C. A. K. Cragg, M.A., D.Phil., D.D., Assistant Bishop of Wakefield and formerly Vicar of Helme, Huddersfield.

A.R. The late A. Ross, M.A., B.D., D.D., formerly Professor of New Testament, Free Church College, Edinburgh.

A.R.M. A. R. Millard, M.A., M.Phil., F.S.A., Rankin Reader in Hebrew and Ancient Semitic Languages, University of Liverpool.

A.S. A. Stuart, M.Sc., Dip.R.M.S., Emeritus Professor of Geology, University of Exeter.

A.S.W. A. S. Wood, B.A., Ph.D., F.R.Hist.S., formerly Principal, Cliff College, Calver, Derbyshire.

A. van S. A. van Selms, Th.D., Emeritus Professor of Semitic Languages, University of Pretoria.

B.A.M. B. A. Milne, M.A., B.D., Ph.D., Lecturer in Biblical and Historical Theology and Christian Ethics, Spurgeon's College, London.

B.F.C.A. The late B. F. C. Atkinson, M.A., Ph.D., formerly Under-Librarian, University of Cambridge.

B.F.H. B. F. Harris, B.A., M.A., B.D., Ph.D., Associate Professor of History, Macquarie University, New South Wales.

B.L.S. B. L. Smith, B.D., Th.Schol., Classics Teacher, Sydney Grammar School; Visiting Lecturer, Moore Theological College, Sydney.

B.O.B. B. O. Banwell, B.A., M.A., formerly Lecturer in Old Testament, Rhodes University; Methodist Minister, Fort Beaufort, S. Africa.

C.D.W. C. de Wit, Docteur en philologie et histoire orientales; Conservateur honoraire Musées Royaux d'Art et Histoire, Brussels; Emeritus Professor of the University of Louvain.

C.F.P. The late C. F. Pfeiffer, B.A., B.D., Ph.D., formerly Associate Professor of Old Testament, Gordon Divinity School, Beverly Farms, Massachusetts.

C.H.D. C. H. Duncan, M.A., B.D., Ph.D., Th.D., Lecturer in Philosophy, State College of Victoria, Australia; Canon of St Paul's Cathedral, Melbourne.

C.J.D. C. J. Davey, B.Sc., M.A., Inspector of Mines, Victoria, Australia.

C.J.H. C. J. Hemer, M.A., Ph.D., Librarian, Tyndale House, Cambridge.

C.L.F. C. L. Feinberg, A.B., A.M., Th.B., Th.M., Ph.D., Emeritus Professor of Semitics and Old Testament and Dean of Talbot Theological Seminary, Los Angeles.

D.A.H. D. A. Hubbard, B.A., B.D., Th.M., Ph.D., D.D., L.H.D., President and Professor of Old Testament, Fuller Theological Seminary, Pasadena, California.

D.B.K. D. B. Knox, B.A., B.D., M.Th., D.Phil, A.L.C.D., Principal, Moore Theological College, Sydney; Senior Canon of St Andrew's Cathedral, Sydney.

D.F. D. Freeman, B.A., Th.B., Th.M., Ph.D., Professor, Rhode Island Junior College.

D.F.P. D. F. Payne, B.A., M.A., Academic Registrar, London Bible College.

D.G. D. Guthrie, B.D., M.Th., Ph.D., formerly Vice-Principal, London Bible College.

D.G.S. D. G. Stradling, Magdalen College, Oxford.

D.H.F. D. H. Field, B.A., Vice-Principal, Oak Hill College, London.

D.H.T. D. H. Tongue, M.A., formerly Lecturer in New Testament, Trinity College, Bristol.

D.H.W. D. H. Wheaton, M.A., B.D., Vicar of Christ Church, Ware; formerly Principal, Oak Hill College, London; Canon of St Alban's Cathedral.

D.J.A.C. D. J. A. Clines, M.A., Senior Lecturer, Department of Biblical Studies, University of Sheffield.

D.J.V.L. D. J. V. Lane, Ll.B., B.D., Overseas Director, Overseas Missionary Fellowship, Singapore.

D.J.W. D. J. Wiseman, O.B.E., M.A., D.Lit., F.B.A., F.K.C., F.S.A., Emeritus Professor of Assyriology, University of London.

D.K.I. D. K. Innės, M.A., B.D., Rector of Alford and Loxwood, West Sussex.

D.O.S. D. O. Swann, B.A., B.D., Minister of Ashford Evangelical Congregational Church, Middlesex.

D.R. de L. D. R. de Lacey, M.A., Ph.D., Lecturer in New Testament, Ridley Hall, Cambridge.

D.R.H. D. R. Hall, M.A., M.Th, Superintendent Minister of the North of Scotland Mission Circuit of the Methodist Church, Aberdeen.

D.T. D. H. Trapnell, M.A., M.D., F.R.C.P., F.R.C.R., Consultant Radiologist, Westminster Hospital, London.

D.W. D. Wenham, M.A., Ph.D., Lecturer in New Testament, Wycliffe Hall, Oxford.

D.W.B. D. W. Baker, A.B., M.C.S., M.Phil., Part-time Lecturer in Hebrew, Regent College, Vancouver, BC.

D.W.B.R. D. W. B. Robinson, M.A., Bishop in Parramatta, New South Wales; formerly Head of New Testament Department, Divinity School, University of Sydney.

D.W.G. D. W. Gooding, M.A., Ph.D., M.R.I.A., formerly Professor of Old Testament Greek, The Queen's University, Belfast.

E.A.J. E. A. Judge, M.A., Professor of History, Macquarie University, New South Wales.

E.E.E. E. E. Ellis, Ph.D., Research Professor of New Testament Literature, New Brunswick Theological Seminary, New Jersey.

E.J.Y. The late E. J. Young, B.A., Th.M., Ph.D., formerly Professor of Old Testament, Westminster Theological Seminary, Philadelphia.

E.M.B. The late E. M. Blaiklock, O.B.E., M.A., Litt.D., formerly Professor of Classics, University of Auckland.

E.M.B.G. E. M. B. Green, M.A., B.D., Rector of St Aldate's Church, Oxford; Canon of Coventry Cathedral. Formerly Principal, St John's College, Nottingham.

E.M.Y. E. M. Yamauchi, B.A., M.A., Ph.D., Director of Graduate Studies and Professor of History, Miami University, Oxford, Ohio.

F.C.F. F. C. Fensham, M.A., Ph.D., D.D., Professor in Semitic Languages, University of Stellenbosch.

F.D.K. F. D. Kidner, M.A., A.R.C.M., formerly Warden, Tyndale House, Cambridge.

F.F. F. Foulkes, B.A., B.D., M.A., M.Sc., Lecturer in Biblical Studies, St John's College, Auckland, and Lecturer in Biblical History and Literature, University of Auckland.

F.F.B. F. F. Bruce, M.A., D.D., F.B.A., Emeritus Rylands Professor of Biblical Criticism and Exegesis, University of Manchester.

F.H.P. F. H. Palmer, M.A., Diocesan Missioner and Minister of St Matthew's Church, Walsall, West Midlands.

F.N.H. F. N. Hepper, F.I.Biol., B.Sc., F.L.S., Assistant Keeper, The Herbarium, Royal Botanic Gardens, Kew.

F.R.S. F. R. Steele, A.B., M.A., Ph.D., Assistant Director North America for the North Africa Mission; formerly Assistant Professor of Assyriology, University of Pennsylvania.

F.S.F. F. S. Fitzsimmonds, B.A., B.D., M.Th., formerly Vice-Principal, Spurgeon's College, London.

G.C.D.H. The late G. C. D. Howley, formerly Consulting Editor of *The Witness*.

G.G.G. G. G. Garner, B.A., B. D., Director, Australian Institute of Archaeology, Melbourne.

G.I.D. G. I. Davies, M.A., Ph.D., Lecturer in Old Testament and Intertestamental Studies, University of Cambridge.

G.I.E. Mrs G. I. Emmerson, M.A., Dip.Or.Lang., Lecturer, Department of Theology, University of Birmingham.

G.O. The late G. Ogg, M.A., B.Sc., D.D., D.Litt., formerly Minister at Anstruther Easter, Fife.

G.R.B.-M. G. R. Beasley-Murray, M.A., Ph.D., D.D., James Buchanan Harrison Professor of New Testament Interpretation, Southern Baptist Theological Seminary, Louisville, Kentucky.

G.S.C. G. S. Cansdale, B.A., B.Sc., F.L.S., Consultant Biologist.

G.S.M.W. The late G. S. M. Walker, M.A., B.D., Ph.D., formerly Lecturer in Church History, University of Leeds.

G.T.M. The late G. T. Manley, M.A., sometime Fellow, Christ's College, Cambridge.

G.W. G. Walters, B.A., B.D., Ph.D., Professor of Ministry, Gordon-Conwell Theological Seminary, South Hamilton, Massachusetts.

G.W.G. G. W. Grogan, B.D., M.Th., Principal, Bible Training Institute, Glasgow.

H.A.G.B. H. A. G. Belben, M.A., B.D., formerly Principal, Cliff College, Calver, Derbyshire.

H.D.McD. H. D. McDonald, B.A., B.D., Ph.D., D.D., formerly Vice-Principal, London Bible College.

H.G.M.W. H. G. M. Williamson, M.A., Ph.D., Assistant Lecturer in Hebrew and Aramaic, University of Cambridge.

H.L.E. The late H. L. Ellison, B.A., B.D., formerly Senior Tutor, Moorlands Bible College.

H.M.C. H. M. Carson, B.A., B.D., Minister of Knighton Evangelical Free Church, Leicester.

H.R. H. N. Ridderbos, D. Theol., Emeritus Professor of New Testament, Kampen Theological Seminary, The Netherlands.

I.H.M. I. H. Marshall, B.A., M.A., B.D., Ph.D., Professor of New Testament Exegesis, University of Aberdeen.

J.A.M. J. A. Motyer, M.A., B.D., Minister of Christ Church, Westbourne, Dorset; formerly Principal, Trinity College, Bristol.

J.A.T. J. A. Thompson, M.A., M.Sc., B.D., B.Ed., Ph.D., formerly Reader in Department of Middle Eastern Studies, University of Melbourne.

J.B.J. J. B. Job, M.A., B.D., Minister on the Rugby and Daventry Methodist Circuit; formerly Tutor in Old Testament, Cliff College, Calver, Derbyshire.

J.B.P. The late J. B. Payne, Ph.D., formerly Professor of Old Testament, Covenant Theological Seminary, St Louis, Missouri.

J.B.T. J. B. Torrance, M.A., B.D., Professor of Systematic Theology, University of Aberdeen.

J.B.Tr. J. B. Taylor, M.A., Bishop of St Albans.

J.C.C. J. C. Connell, B.A., M.A., formerly Director of Studies and Lecturer in New Testament Exegesis, London Bible College.

J.C.J.W. J. C. J. Waite, B.D., Minister of Wycliffe Independent Chapel, Sheffield; formerly Principal, South Wales Bible College.

J.C.W. J. C. Whitcomb, Jr, Th.D., Professor of Theology and Director of Postgraduate Studies, Grace Theological Seminary, Winona Lake, Indiana.

J.D.D. J. D. Douglas, M.A., B.D., S.T.M., Ph.D., Editor-at-large, *Christianity Today*.

J.D.G.D. J. D. G. Dunn, M.A., B.D., Ph.D., Professor of Divinity, University of Durham.

J.E.G. J. E. Goldingay, B.A., Registrar and Lecturer in Old Testament, St John's College, Nottingham.

J.G.B. Miss J. G. Baldwin, B.A., B.D., formerly Dean of Women, Trinity College, Bristol.

J.G.G.N. The late J. G. G. Norman, B.D., M.Th., formerly Pastor of Rosyth Baptist Church, Fife.

J.G.S.S.T. J. G. S. S. Thomson, B.A., M.A., B.D., Ph.D., Minister at Wigtown, Scotland.

J.H. J. W. L. Hoad, M.A., Clinical Supervisor, Princeton, New Jersey.

J.H.H. J. H. Harrop, M.A., formerly Lecturer in Classics, Fourah Bay College, University of Sierra Leone.

J.H.P. J. H. Paterson, M.A., Emeritus Professor of Geography, University of Leicester.

J.H.S. J. H. Skilton, B.A., M.A., M.Div., Ph.D., Director of the Robert H. Skilton and Margaret B. Skilton House, Philadelphia; formerly Dean of the Reformed Bible Institute of the Delaware Valley and Lecturer in New Testament, Westminster Theological Seminary, Philadelphia.

J.H.Sr. The late J. H. Stringer, M.A., B.D., formerly Tutor, London Bible College.

J.I.P. J. I. Packer, M.A., D.Phil., D.D., Professor of Systematic Theology, Regent College, Vancouver, BC.

J.J.H. J. J. Hughes, B.A., M.Div., Assistant Professor of Religious Studies, Westmont College, Santa Barbara, California.

J.L.K. The late J. L. Kelso, B.A., Th.M., M.A., Th.D., D.D., Ll.D., formerly Professor of Old Testament History and Biblical Archaeology, Pittsburgh Theological Seminary, Pennsylvania.

J.M. The late J. Murray, M.A., Th.M., formerly Professor of Systematic Theology, Westminster Theological Seminary, Philadelphia.

J.M.H. J. M. Houston, M.A., B.Sc., D.Phil., Chancellor, formerly Principal, Regent College, Vancouver, BC.

J.N.B. J. N. Birdsall, M.A., Ph.D., F.R.A.S., Professor of New Testament and Textual Criticism, University of Birmingham.

J.N.G. The late J. N. Geldenhuys, B.A., B.D., Th.M.

J.P. J. Philip, M.A., Minister of Holyrood Abbey, Edinburgh.

J.P.B. J. P. Baker, M.A., B.D., Rector of Newick, East Sussex.

J.P.K. J. P. Kane, Ph.D., Dip.Ed., Lecturer in Hellenistic Greek, University of Manchester.

J.P.U.L. J. P. U. Lilley, M.A., F.C.A., Magdalen College, Oxford.

J.R. J. Rea, M.A., Th.D., Professor of Old Testament, Melodyland School of Theology, Anaheim, California.

J.Ru. J. Ruffle, M.A., Keeper, Gulbenkian Museum of Oriental Art, University of Durham.

J.S.W. The late J. S. Wright, M.A., formerly Principal, Tyndale Hall, Bristol; Canon of Bristol Cathedral.

J.T. J. A. Thompson, B.A., M.Div., Th.M., Ph.D., Research Consultant, American Bible Society.

J.T.W. J. T. Whitney, M.A., L.C.P., Ph.D., Head of Religious Studies, South East Essex Sixth Form College.

J.W.C. J. W. Charley, M.A., Warden of Shrewsbury House and Rector of St Peter's, Everton, Liverpool.

J.W.D. J. W. Drane, M.A., Ph.D., Lecturer in Religious Studies, University of Stirling.

J.W.M. J. W. Meiklejohn, M.B.E., M.A., formerly Secretary of the Inter-School Christian Fellowship in Scotland.

K.A.K. K. A. Kitchen, B.A., Ph.D., Reader in Egyptian and Coptic, University of Liverpool.

K.L.McK. K. L. McKay, B.A., M.A., Reader in Classics, The Australian National University, Canberra.

L.C.A. L. C. Allen, M.A., Ph.D., Professor of Old Testament, Fuller Theological Seminary, Pasadena, California.

L.M. L. L. Morris, M.Sc., M.Th., Ph.D., formerly Principal, Ridley College, Melbourne; Canon of St Paul's Cathedral, Melbourne.

M.A.M. M. A. MacLeod, M.A., Director, Christian Witness to Israel.

M.B. Mrs M. Beeching, B.A., B.D., M.Ed., formerly Principal Lecturer and Head of Department of Divinity, Cheshire College of Education, Alsager.

M.G.K. M. G. Kline, Th.M., Ph.D., Professor of Old Testament, Gordon-Conwell Theological Seminary, South Hamilton, Mass.

M.H.C. M. H. Cressey, M.A., Principal of Westminster College, Cambridge.

M.J.S. M. J. Selman, B.A., M.A., Ph.D., Lecturer in Old Testament, Spurgeon's College, London.

M.J.S.R. M. J. S. Rudwick, M.A., Ph.D., Sc.D., Professor of History of Science, The Free University, Amsterdam.

M.R.G. M. R. Gordon, B.D., Minister of the Church of England, in South Africa; formerly Principal, Bible Institute of South Africa.

M.R.W.F. M. R. W. Farrer, M.A., Vicar of St Paul's Church, Cambridge.

M.T.F. M. T. Fermer, B.A., B.Sc., A.R.C.S., Rector of Old Brampton and Loundsley Green, Derbyshire.

N.H. N. Hillyer, B.D., S.Th., A.L.C.D., formerly Librarian, Tyndale House, Cambridge; Vicar of Hatherleigh, Devonshire.

N.H.R. N. H. Ridderbos, D.D., Emeritus Professor of Old Testament, The Free University, Amsterdam.

P.A.B. P. A. Blair, M.A., Rector of Barking, Essex.

P.E. P. Ellingworth, B.A., M.A., Ph.D., Translation Consultant to the United Bible Societies, London.

P.E.H. P. E. Hughes, M.A., B.D., Th.D., D.Litt., Visiting Professor at Westminster Theological Seminary, Philadelphia; Associate Rector of St John's Episcopal Church, Huntingdon Valley, Pennsylvania.

P.H.D. P. H. Davids, B.A., M.Div., Ph.D., Head of Department of Biblical Studies and Language, Trinity Episcopal School for Ministry, Ambridge, Pennsylvania.

P.W. P. Woolley, B.A., Th.M., D.D., Emeritus Professor of Church History, Westminster Theological Seminary, Philadelphia.

R.A.F. R. A. Finlayson, M.A., Emeritus Professor of Systematic Theology, Free Church College, Edinburgh.

R.A.H.G. R. A. H. Gunner, B.A., M.Th., Lecturer in Charge of Modern Languages and Lecturer in Religious Studies, Brooklands Technical College, Weybridge, Surrey.

R.A.S. R. A. Stewart, M.A., B.D., M.Litt., formerly Church of Scotland Minister.

R.E.N. The late R. E. Nixon, M.A., formerly Principal, St John's College, Nottingham.

R.H.M. R. H. Mounce, B.A., B.D., Th.M., Ph.D., President, Whitworth College, Spokane, Washington State.

R.J.A.S. R. J. A. Sheriffs, B.A., B.D., Ph.D., formerly Lecturer in Old Testament, Rhodes University, Grahamstown, Cape Province.

R.J.B. R. J. Bauckham, M.A., Ph.D., Lecturer in the History of Christian Thought, University of Manchester.

R.J.C. The late R. J. Coates, M.A., sometime Warden, Latimer House, Oxford.

R.J.McK. R. J. McKelvey, B.A., M.Th., D.Phil., Principal, The Congregational College, Manchester.

R.J.T. R. J. Thompson, M.A., B.D., Th.M., D. Theol., Lecturer in Biblical and Historical Theology and Christian Ethics, Spurgeon's College, London; formerly Principal, New Zealand Baptist Theological College, Auckland.

R.J.W. R. J. Way, M.A., Minister of St Columba's United Reformed Church, Leeds.

R.K.H. R. K. Harrison, M.Th., Ph.D., D.D., Professor of Old Testament, Wycliffe College, University of Toronto.

R.N.C. R. N. Caswell, M.A., Ph.D., Head of Religious Education, The Academical Institution, Coleraine, Northern Ireland.

R.P.G. R. P. Gordon, M.A., Ph.D., Lecturer in Old Testament, University of Cambridge.

R.P.M. R. P. Martin, M.A., Ph.D., Professor of New Testament, Fuller Theological Seminary, Pasadena, California.

R.S.W. R. S. Wallace, M.A., B.Sc., Ph.D., formerly Professor, Columbia Theological Seminary, Decatur, Georgia.

R.T.B. R. T. Beckwith, M.A., Warden, Latimer House, Oxford.

R.T.F. R. T. France, M.A., B.D., Ph.D., Vice-Principal of London Bible College.

R.V.G.T. The late R. V. G. Tasker, M.A., D.D., formerly Professor of New Testament Exegesis, University of London.

S.S.S. S. S. Smalley, M.A., B.D., Ph.D., Canon Residentiary and Precentor of Coventry Cathedral.

T.C.M. T. C. Mitchell, M.A., Deputy Keeper, Department of Western Asiatic Antiquities, British Museum.

T.H.J. T. H. Jones, M.A., B.D., A.M.B.I.M., Rector of the Langtons, Leicestershire and Chaplain for Ministry of Deliverance, Diocese of Leicester.

W.G.P. W. G. Putman, B.A., B.D., Methodist Minister, High Wycombe, Bucks.

W.H.G. W. H. Gispen, D.Theol., Doctorandus Semitic Languages, Emeritus Professor of Hebrew and Old Testament, The Free University, Amsterdam.

W.J.C. W. J. Cameron, M.A., B.D., Professor of New Testament Language, Literature, Exegesis and Theology, Free Church of Scotland College, Edinburgh.

W.J.M. The late W. J. Martin, M.A., Th.B., Ph.D., formerly Head of the Department of Hebrew and Ancient Semitic Languages, University of Liverpool.

W.O. W. Osborne, M.A., M.Phil., Lecturer in Old Testament, The Bible College of New Zealand.

W.W.W. W. W. Wessel, M.A., Ph.D., Professor of New Testament, Bethel College, St Paul, Minnesota.

Abbreviations

I. Books and Journals

AASOR
Annual of the American Schools of Oriental Research

AB
Anchor Bible

ACA
Sir Moses Finley, *Atlas of Classical Archaeology*, 1977

AfO
Archiv für Orientforschung

AJA
American Journal of Archaeology

AJBA
Australian Journal of Biblical Archaeology

AJSL
American Journal of Semitic Languages and Literatures

AJT
American Journal of Theology

ALUOS
Annual of the Leeds University Oriental Society

ANEP
J. B. Pritchard, *The Ancient Near East in Pictures*, 1954; ²1965

ANET
J. B. Pritchard, *Ancient Near Eastern Texts*, 1950; ²1965; ³1969

ANT
M. R. James, *The Apocryphal New Testament*, 1924

AOTS
D. W. Thomas (ed.), *Archaeology and Old Testament Study*, 1967

ARAB
D. D. Luckenbill, *Ancient Records of Assyria and Babylonia*, 1926

ARE
J. H. Breasted, *Ancient Records of Egypt*, 5 vols., 1906–7

Arndt
W. F. Arndt and F. W. Gingrich, *A Greek–English Lexicon of the New Testament and Other Early Christian Literature*, 1957

ARV
American Revised Version (see ASV)

AS
Anatolian Studies

ASAE
Annales du Service des Antiquités de l'Égypte

ASV
American Standard Version, 1901 (American version of RV)

ATR
Anglican Theological Review

AV
Authorized Version (*King James'*), 1611

BA
Biblical Archaeologist

BANE
G. E. Wright (ed.), *The Bible and the Ancient Near East*, 1961

BASOR
Bulletin of the American Schools of Oriental Research

BC
F. J. Foakes-Jackson and K. Lake, *The Beginnings of Christianity*, 5 vols., 1920–33

BDB
F. Brown, S. R. Driver and C. A. Briggs, *Hebrew and English Lexicon of the Old Testament*, 1906

Bib
Biblica

BibRes
Biblical Research

BIES
Bulletin of the Israel Exploration Society

BJRL
Bulletin of the John Rylands Library

BNTC
Black's New Testament Commentaries

BO
Bibliotheca Orientalis

BRD
W. M. Ramsay, *The Bearing of Recent Discovery on the Trustworthiness of the New Testament*, 1914

BS
Bibliotheca Sacra

BSOAS
Bulletin of the School of Oriental and African Studies

BTh
Biblical Theology

BZ
Biblische Zeitschrift

BZAW
Beiheft, Zeitschrift für die alttestamentliche Wissenschaft

CAH
Cambridge Ancient History, 12 vols., 1923–39; revised ed. 1970–

CB
Century Bible

CBP
W. M. Ramsay, *Cities and Bishoprics of Phrygia*, 1895–7

CBQ
Catholic Biblical Quarterly

CBSC
Cambridge Bible for Schools and Colleges

CD
Qumran Damascus Document

CDC
Cairo Geniza Documents of the Damascus Covenanters

CE
Chronique d'Égypte

CGT
Cambridge Greek Testament

CIG
Corpus Inscriptionum Graecarum

CIL
Corpus Inscriptionum Latinarum

CQ
Classical Quarterly; *Crozer Quarterly*

CRE
W. M. Ramsay, *The Church in the Roman Empire before AD 170*, 1903

CTJ
Calvin Theological Journal

DAC
J. Hastings (ed.), *Dictionary of the Apostolic Church*, 2 vols., 1915–18

DBS
Dictionnaire de la Bible, Supplément, 1928–

DCG
J. Hastings (ed.), *Dictionary of Christ and the Gospels*, 2 vols., 1906–08

DOTT
D. W. Thomas (ed.), *Documents of Old Testament Times*, 1958

EAEHL
M. Avi-Yonah (ed.), *Encyclopaedia of Archaeological Excavations in the Holy Land*, 4 vols., 1975–8

EB
Expositor's Bible

EBi
Encyclopaedia Biblica

EBr
Encyclopaedia Britannica

EBT
J. B. Bauer (ed.), *Encyclopaedia of Biblical Theology*, 3 vols., 1970

EEP
K. Lake, *The Earlier Epistles of St Paul*, 1911

EGT
W. R. Nicoll, *The Expositor's Greek Testament*[6], 1910

EIs
Encyclopaedia of Islam, 1954–

EJ
C. Roth (ed.), *Encyclopaedia Judaica*, 15 vols., 1971

EQ
Evangelical Quarterly

ERE
J. Hastings (ed.), *Encyclopaedia of Religion and Ethics*, 13 vols., 1908–26

ExpT
Expository Times

FRLANT
Forschungen zur Religion und Literatur des Alten und Neuen Testaments

FT
Faith and Thought (formerly *JTVI*)

GB
Ginsburg's Bible (New Masoretico-Critical Text of the Hebrew Bible), 1896

GNB
Good News Bible (= TEV)

GTT
J. Simons, *Geographical and Topographical Texts of the Old Testament*, 1959

HAT
Handbuch zum Alten Testament

HDB
J. Hastings (ed.), *Dictionary of the Bible*, 5 vols., 1898–1904

HES
Harvard Expedition to Samaria, 1924

HHT
J. Lightfoot, *Horae Hebraicae et Talmudicae*, 1658–64

HJ
Hibbert Journal

HJP
E. Schürer, *A History of the Jewish People in the Time of Christ*, 2 vols., E.T. 1885–1901; revised ed., M. Black, G. Vermes and F. Millar (eds.), 3 vols., 1973–

HNT
H. Lietzmann, *Handbuch zum Neuen Testament*

HSS
Harvard Semitic Series

HTKNT
Herders Theologischer Kommentar zum Neuen Testament

HTR
Harvard Theological Review

HUCA
Hebrew Union College Annual

IB
G. A. Buttrick *et al.* (eds.), *Interpreter's Bible*, 12 vols., 1952–7

IBA
D. J. Wiseman, *Illustrations from Biblical Archaeology*, 1958

ICC
International Critical Commentary

IDB
G. A. Buttrick *et al.* (eds.), *The Interpreter's Dictionary of the Bible*, 4 vols., 1962

IDBS
IDB, Supplement vol., 1976

IEJ
Israel Exploration Journal

IG
Inscriptiones Graecae

IGRR
Inscriptiones Graecae ad res Romanas pertinentes

Int
Interpretation

INT
Introduction to the New Testament

IOSCS
International Organization for Septuagint and Cognate Studies

IOT
Introduction to the Old Testament

ISBE
International Standard Bible Encyclopaedia, 5 vols., [2]1930

JAOS
Journal of the American Oriental Society

JB
Jerusalem Bible, 1966

JBL
Journal of Biblical Literature

JCS
Journal of Cuneiform Studies

JEA
Journal of Egyptian Archaeology

JEH
Journal of Ecclesiastical History

JewE
I. Singer *et al.* (eds.), *Jewish Encyclopaedia*, 12 vols., 1901–06

JHS
Journal of Hellenic Studies

JJS
Journal of Jewish Studies

JNES
Journal of Near Eastern Studies

JNSL
Journal of Northwest Semitic Languages

JPOS
Journal of the Palestine Oriental Society

JQR
Jewish Quarterly Review

JRAS
Journal of the Royal Asiatic Society

JRS
Journal of Roman Studies

JSOT
Journal for the Study of the Old Testament

JSS
Journal of Semitic Studies

JTS
Journal of Theological Studies

JTVI
Journal of the Transactions of the Victoria Institute (now *FT*)

JWH
Journal of World History

KAT
Kommentar zum Alten Testament

KB
L. Köhler and W. Baumgartner, *Hebräisches und aramäisches Lexicon zum Alten Testament*[3], 1967

KEK
H. A. W. Meyer (ed.), *Kritisch-exegetischer Kommentar über das Neue Testament*

KJV
King James' Version (= AV)

LA
Liber Annus (Jerusalem)

LAE
A. Deissmann, *Light from the Ancient East*[4], 1927

LBC
Layman's Bible Commentary

LOB
Y. Aharoni, *The Land of the Bible*, 1967

LOT
S. R. Driver, *Introduction to the Literature of the Old Testament*[9], 1913

LSJ
H. G. Liddell, R. Scott and H. S. Jones, *Greek–English Lexicon*[9], 1940

MM
J. H. Moulton and G. Milligan, *The Vocabulary of the Greek Testament illustrated from the Papyri and other non-literary sources*, 1930

MNTC
Moffatt New Testament Commentary

Moffatt
J. Moffatt, *A New Translation of the Bible*[2], 1936

NASB
New American Standard Bible, 1963

NBC
F. Davidson (ed.), *The New Bible Commentary*, 1953

NBCR
D. Guthrie *et al.* (eds.), *The New Bible Commentary Revised*, 1970

NCB
New Century Bible

NClB
New Clarendon Bible

NEB
New English Bible: NT, 1961; OT, Apocrypha, 1970

Nestle
Nestle's Novum Testamentum Graece[22], 1956

NIC
New International Commentary

NIDNTT
C. Brown (ed.), *The New International Dictionary of New Testament Theology*, 3 vols., 1975–8

NIV
New International Version: NT, 1974; complete Bible, 1978

NLC
New London Commentary

NovT
Novum Testamentum

NTD
Das Neue Testament Deutsch

NTS
New Testament Studies

OCD
M. Cary *et al.* (eds.), *The Oxford Classical Dictionary*, 1949

ODCC
F. L. Cross and E. A. Livingstone (eds.), *The Oxford Dictionary of the Christian Church*[2], 1974

Or
Orientalia

OTL
Old Testament Library

OTMS
H. H. Rowley (ed.), *The Old Testament and Modern Study*, 1951

OTS
Oudtestamentische Studiën

Pauly-Wissowa
See *RE*

PEQ
Palestine Exploration Quarterly

PG
J. P. Migne, *Patrologia Graeca*

Phillips
J. B. Phillips, *The New Testament in Modern English*, 1958; revised ed. 1972

PJB
Palästina-Jahrbuch

PL
J. P. Migne, *Patrologia Latina*

POTT
D. J. Wiseman (ed.), *Peoples of Old Testament Times*, 1973

P.Oxy.
Papyrus Oxyrhynchus

PRU
Le Palais Royal d'Ugarit

PTR
Princeton Theological Review

RA
Revue d'Assyriologie

RAC
T. Klausner *et al.* (eds.), *Reallexicon für die Antike und Christentum*, 1941–

RAr
Revue d'Archéologie

RB
Revue Biblique

RE
A. F. Pauly, G. Wissowa *et al.* (eds.), *Real-Encyclopädie der klassischen Altertumwissenschaft*, 1893–

RGG
K. Galling (ed.), *Die Religion in Geschichte und Gegenwart*[3], 7 vols., 1957–65

RHR
Revue de l'Histoire des Religions

RQ
Revue de Qumran

RSV
Revised Standard Version: NT, 1946; OT, 1952; *Common Bible*, 1973

RTR
Reformed Theological Review (Australia)

RV
Revised Version: NT, 1881; OT, 1885

SB
H. L. Strack and P. Billerbeck, *Kommentar zum Neuen Testament aus Talmud und Midrasch*, 6 vols., 1926–61

SBL
Society of Biblical Literature

SBT
Studies in Biblical Theology

Schürer See *HJP*

SHERK
The New Schaff-Herzog Encyclopaedia of Religious Knowledge[2], 1949–52

SIG
W. Dittenberger (ed.), *Sylloge Inscriptionum Graecarum*, 1915–24

SJT
Scottish Journal of Theology

SP
Samaritan Pentateuch

SPEM
G. S. Duncan, *St Paul's Ephesian Ministry*, 1929

SPT
W. M. Ramsay, *St Paul the Traveller and Roman Citizen*[4], 1920

ST
Studia Theologica

Strack-Billerbeck See *SB*

TB
Babylonian Talmud

TBC
Torch Bible Commentary

TCERK
The Twentieth Century Encyclopaedia of Religious Knowledge, 1955

TDNT
G. Kittel and G. Friedrich (eds.), *Theologisches Wörterbuch zum Neuen Testament*, 1932–74; E.T. *Theological Dictionary of the New Testament*, ed. G. W. Bromiley, 10 vols., 1964–76

TDOT
G. J. Botterweck and H. Ringgren (eds.), *Theologisches Wörterbuch zum Alten Testament*, 1970– ; E.T. *Theological Dictionary of the Old Testament*, trans. by J. T. Willis, 1974–

TEV
Today's English Version[4], 1976 (= GNB)

Th
Theology

THAT
E. Jenni and C. Westermann (eds.), *Theologisches Handwörterbuch zum Alten Testament*, 2 vols., 1971–6

THB
Tyndale House Bulletin (now *TynB*)

Them
Themelios

ThL
Theologische Literaturzeitung

THNT
Theologische Handbuch zum Neuen Testament

TJ
Jerusalem Talmud

TNT
Translators' New Testament (Bible Society)

TNTC
Tyndale New Testament Commentary

TOTC
Tyndale Old Testament Commentary

TR
Theologische Rundschau

TS
Texts and Studies

TSFB
Theological Students' Fellowship Bulletin

TU
Texte und Untersuchungen zur Geschichte der altchristlichen Literatur

TWBR
A. Richardson (ed.), *A Theological Word Book of the Bible*, 1950

TynB
Tyndale Bulletin (formerly *THB*)

TZ
Theologisches Zeitschrift

UF
Ugarit-Forschungen: Internationales Jahrbuch für die Altertumskunde Syrien-Palästinas

VC
Vigiliae Christianae

VT
Vetus Testamentum

VT Supp.
Vetus Testamentum, Supplementary vol.

WC
Westminster Commentary

WDB
Westminster Dictionary of the Bible, 1944

Wett.
J. J. Wettstein, *Novum Testamentum Graecum*, 1751–2

Weymouth
R. F. Weymouth, *The New Testament in Modern Speech*, 1903

WH
B. F. Westcott and F. J. A. Hort, *The New Testament in Greek*, 1881

WTJ
Westminster Theological Journal

ZA
Zeitschrift für Assyriologie

ZAW
Zeitschrift für die alttestamentliche Wissenschaft

ZDMG
Zeitschrift der deutschen morgenländischen Gesellschaft

ZDPV
Zeitschrift des deutschen Palästina-Vereins

ZNW
Zeitschrift für die neutestamentliche Wissenschaft

ZPEB
M. C. Tenney (ed.), *The Zondervan Pictorial Encyclopaedia of the Bible*, 5 vols., 1975

ZTK
Zeitschrift für Theologie und Kirche

Editions are indicated by small superior figures: *LOT*[9]

II. Classical Works

ad Fam.
Cicero, *Epistulae ad Familiares*

Adv. Haer.
Irenaeus, *Adversus Haereses*

Ann.
Tacitus, *Annales*

Ant.
Josephus, *Antiquities of the Jews*

Apol.
Justin Martyr, *Apologia*
Tertullian, *Apologia*

BJ
Josephus, *Jewish Wars*

Clem. Recog.
Rufinus, *Clementine Recognitions*

Contra Pelag.
Jerome, *Contra Pelagium*

Eccles. Hist.
Sozomen, *History of the Church*

EH
Eusebius, *Ecclesiastical History*

Epig.
Martial, *Epigrammaticus Latinus*

Ep. Mor.
Seneca, *Epistulae Morales ad Lucilium*

Eus.
Eusebius

Ev. Petr.
Gospel of Peter (apocryphal)

Exc. Theod.
Clement of Alexandria, *Excerpta ex Theodoto*

Geog.
Ptolemy, *Geography*; Strabo, *Geography*

Hist.
Dio Cassius, *History*; Tacitus, *History*

Hypot.
Clement of Alexandria, *Hypotyposes*

Il.
Homer, *Iliad*

Iul.
Suetonius, *C. Julius Caesar* (*Lives of the Caesars*)

In Verr.
Cicero, *In Verrem Actio*

Jos.
Josephus

Juv.
Juvenal

Lk. Hom.
Origen, *Homily on Luke*

Magn.
Ignatius, *Magnesians*

NH
Pliny, *Natural History*

Od.
Horace, *Odes*

Onom.
Eusebius, *Onomasticon de Locis Hebraicis*

Philad.
Ignatius, *Philadelphians*

Praep. Ev.
Eusebius, *Praeparatio Evangelica*

Quaest.
Seneca, *Quaestiones Naturales*

Sat.
Juvenal, *Satires*; Persius, *Satires*

Strom.
Clement of Alexandria, *Stromateis*

Trall.
Ignatius, *Trallians*

Vesp.
Suetonius, *Vespasian* (*Lives of the Caesars*)

Vit. Mos.
Philo, *De Vita Mosis* (*Life of Moses*)

III. Biblical Books

Books of the Old Testament
Gn., Ex., Lv., Nu., Dt., Jos., Jdg., Ru., 1, 2 Sa., 1, 2 Ki., 1, 2 Ch., Ezr., Ne., Est., Jb., Ps. (Pss.), Pr., Ec., Ct., Is., Je., La., Ezk., Dn., Ho., Joel, Am., Ob., Jon., Mi., Na., Hab., Zp., Hg., Zc., Mal.

Books of the New Testament
Mt., Mk., Lk., Jn., Acts, Rom., 1, 2 Cor., Gal., Eph., Phil., Col., 1, 2 Thes., 1, 2 Tim., Tit., Phm., Heb., Jas., 1, 2 Pet., 1, 2, 3 Jn., Jude, Rev.

IV. General Abbreviations

ad loc.	*ad locum* (Lat.), at the place
Akkad.	Akkadian
Apoc.	Apocrypha(l)
Aq.	Aquila's Gk. tr. of OT, *c.* AD 140
Arab.	Arabic
Aram.	Aramaic
Assyr.	Assyrian
b.	*bar/ben* (Aram./Heb.), son of
Bab.	Babylonian
BM	British Museum
c.	*circa* (Lat.), about, approximately
ch.(chs.)	chapter(s)
cf.	*confer* (Lat.), compare
Copt.	Coptic
D	Deuteronomist
DSS	Dead Sea Scrolls
E	East, eastern; Elohist
eccl. Lat.	ecclesiastical Latin
Ecclus.	Ecclesiasticus (Apoc.)
ed. (eds.)	edited by, edition, editor(s)
Egyp.	Egyptian
Eng.	English
E.T.	English translation
et al.	*et alii* (Lat.), and others
Eth.	Ethiopic
EVV	English versions
f. (ff.)	and the following (verse(s), *etc.*)
fig.	figuratively
Ger.	German
Gk.	Greek
H	Law of Holiness
Heb.	Hebrew
ibid.	*ibidem* (Lat.), the same work
idem	*idem* (Lat.), the same author
J	Yahwist
Lat.	Latin
lit.	literally
L.L.	Late Latin
loc. cit.	*loco citato* (Lat.), in the place already quoted
LXX	Septuagint (Gk. version of OT)
Macc.	Maccabees (Apoc.)
mg.	margin
mod.	modern
MS (MSS)	manuscript(s)
MT	Massoretic text
N	North, northern
n.f.	*neue Folge* (Ger.), new series
n.s.	new series
NT	New Testament
OE	Old English
OL	Old Latin
op.cit.	*opere citato* (Lat.), in the work cited above
OT	Old Testament
P	Priestly Narrative
par.	and parallel(s)
Pent.	Pentateuch
Pesh	Peshitta
Phoen.	Phoenician
pl.	plate (illustration)
Q	*Quelle* (Ger.), source thought to be behind sayings of Jesus common to Mt. and Lk.
q.v.	*quod vide* (Lat.), which see
R.	Rabbi
Rom.	Roman
S	South, southern
Sem.	Semitic
Suppl.	supplementary volume
s.v.	*sub verbo* (Lat.), under the word
Symm.	Symmachus' Gk. tr. of OT, 2nd century AD
Syr.	Syriac
Targ.	Targum
Theod.	Theodotion's Gk. tr. of OT, 2nd century AD
TR	Textus Receptus
tr.	translated, translation
Turk.	Turkish
v. (vv.)	verse(s)
v.l.	*varia lectio* (Lat.), variant reading
vol.	volume
VSS	versions
Vulg.	Vulgate
W	West, western

PARABLE.

I. Parables and allegories

'Parable' is ultimately derived from Gk. *parabolē*, literally 'putting things side by side'. Etymologically it is thus close to 'allegory', which by derivation means 'saying things in a different way'. Both parables and allegories have usually been regarded as forms of teaching which present the listener with interesting illustrations from which can be drawn moral and religious truths; 'parable' is the somewhat protracted simile or short descriptive story, usually designed to inculcate a single truth or answer a single question, while 'allegory' denotes the more elaborate tale in which all or most of the details have their counterparts in the application. Since 'truth embodied in a tale shall enter in at lowly doors', the value of this method of instruction is obvious.

The line between parables and allegories is obviously a fluid one, and both forms are found in the Gospels. There is, however, a more basic difference than that of amount of detail present. While the developed allegory is essentially illustrative, so that one might almost say that the details of the story have been derived from the application, many of the parables of Jesus are not merely illustrations of general principles; rather they embody messages which cannot be conveyed in any other way. The parables are the appropriate form of communication for bringing to men the message of the kingdom, since their function is to jolt them into seeing things in a new way. They are means of enlightenment and persuasion, intended to bring the hearers to the point of decision. Jesus, as it were, stands where his hearers stand, and uses imagery familiar to them to bring new and unfamiliar insights to them. Just as a lover finds himself restricted by the language of prose and must resort to poetry to express his feelings, so Jesus expresses the message of the kingdom in the appropriate forms of language.

II. The interpretation of the parables

In the NT the actual word 'parable' is used with the same broad variety of meaning as Heb. *māšāl* to refer to almost any kind of non-literal utterance. What we should normally call a *proverb can be termed a parable (Lk. 4:23, Gk.; RSV has 'proverb'). The 'parable' in Mt. 15:15 has almost the nature of a conundrum. The simple illustration, that leaves on a tree are signs of the approach of summer, is a 'parable' (Mk. 13:28). The more elaborate comparison between children at play and the reaction of Jesus' contemporaries to John the Baptist and himself is usually spoken of as 'the *parable* of the children's game' (Lk. 7:31f.). On the other hand, the parables of the sower and the tares are both given detailed allegorical interpretations (Mt. 13:18–23, 36–43), and the parables of the drag-net (Mt. 13:47–50), the wicked husbandmen (Mk. 12:1–12), the marriage feast (Mt. 22:1–14) and the great supper (Lk. 14:16–24) obviously contain details with allegorical significance.

Christian preachers in all ages have striven, for homiletic purposes, to express their message afresh for their own audiences. This is obviously an entirely legitimate procedure; it is justified by the nature of the parables themselves as art-forms and it is already to be seen in the NT itself (*cf.* perhaps Paul's use of the 'sower' motif in Col. 1:6). Unfortunately a tendency developed to allegorize small details in the parables so as to teach truths not in the least obvious in the stories themselves, and irrelevant to the context in which they are found. As a result, the inevitable critical reaction set in. Scholars, such as A. Jülicher, asserted that the parables were intended to illustrate one truth only; and they regarded the allegorical interpretations of the parables of the sower and the tares as early examples of the dangerous process of allegorization which had done so much harm in the Christian church. But it is in reality impossible to draw a clear-cut distinction between parable and allegory in the stories told by Jesus; some of his stories were clearly intended to illustrate *several* lessons, as in the parable of the prodigal son, where stress is laid on the joy which God as Father has in forgiving his children, the nature of repentance, and the sin of jealousy and self-righteousness (Lk. 15:11–32).

It was the mistake of Jülicher to reduce the messages of the parables to moral platitudes. More recent scholars have rightly recognized that they formed part of Jesus' proclamation of the kingdom of God. In an effort to define more precisely their meaning, J. Jeremias and other scholars have insisted that the parables must be understood in their original historical settings within the ministry and teaching of Jesus. In some cases, according to Jeremias, the parables have been re-worded by those who transmitted them in the early church in order to bring out their abiding significance for fresh generations of hearers; in order to hear them again in their pristine freshness as they fell from the lips of Jesus we must attempt to remove any secondary elements which they have acquired and free the original, comparatively simple lessons taught by Jesus from the more elaborate meanings added by early Christian teachers. While some valuable light can be shed on the parables in this way, such analysis of primary and secondary elements tends to be subjective. It is certainly the case that the Evangelists did not always know the occasion on which a particular parable was first spoken or the persons to whom it was originally addressed. In the case of the parables of the good Samaritan (Lk. 10:25), the two debtors (Lk. 7:41), the children's game (Lk. 7:31f.) and the pounds (Lk. 19:11), the context is given and provides a clue to the interpretation. Often, however, it would seem that the stories of Jesus were remembered long after the circumstances that gave rise to them were forgotten; and the Evangelists have fitted them into their narratives in suitable places, sometimes suggesting the original motive for their utterance (Lk. 18:9). On occasion collections of parables, detached from their original contexts, were made (Mt. 13).

Recent scholars have claimed that the parables constitute an art-form whose interpretation is not entirely dependent on a reconstruction of their original content and form; as parables, the stories told by Jesus are capable of showing fresh facets of meaning. It is clear, however, that exposition of the parables for today must be based on as careful an understanding of what Jesus meant by the parables as is possible; otherwise we fall back into the error of regarding them as illustrations of general truths.

The study of the parables with the aid of insights from modern linguistics and semantics has shown that they are not simply ways of conveying information in an attractive form. They have a variety of logical forms and functions. Very often their aim is to jolt the audience into seeing things from a new point of view and to be the actual means of bringing them into a new situation. The parables were meant to force people to *decide* about their attitude to Jesus and his message and thus to bring them into a new relationship with him. They have been described (by E. Fuchs) as 'language-events': *i.e.* they are the form which the kingdom of God takes in the sphere of language. Through the parables the kingly rule of God comes to men with its promises, judgments, demands and gifts.

It is on these points that interpretation of the parables must concentrate. We should not expect to find the whole of the gospel in any given parable: 'It is, for example, misleading to say that the parable of the prodigal son contains "the gospel within the Gospels" and to deduce from it that no doctrine of atonement is vital to Christianity; or to suppose from the story of the good Samaritan that practical service to our fellow men is the be-all and end-all of Christianity' (R. V. G. Tasker, *The Nature and Purpose of the Gospels*, 1957, pp. 57f.). Nor should we attempt to bring ethical and economic considerations to bear upon the interpretation of the parables when these are in fact irrelevant. The parable of the unjust steward (Lk. 16:1–9) teaches that men must prepare themselves for the future; but the morality of the steward (if he was in fact acting immorally—see J. D. M. Derrett, cited below) has no bearing on this lesson. It is futile to suggest that the parable of the labourers in the vineyard (Mt. 20:1–16) is meant to throw light on the problem of wages; it illustrates the goodness of God, who deals with men generously and not strictly in accordance with their merits.

III. Characteristics of the parables

Jesus took the illustrations for his parables sometimes from nature, as in the various parables about seeds and their growth (Mt. 13:24–30; Mk. 4:1–9, 26–29, 30–32); sometimes from familiar customs and incidents of everyday life, as in the parables of the leaven (Mt. 13:33), the lost sheep and the lost coin (Lk. 15:3–10), the importunate man (Lk. 11:5–8) and the ten virgins (Mt. 25:1–13); sometimes from recent events (Lk. 19:14); and sometimes from what might be regarded as occasional happenings or not improbable contingencies, as in the parables of the unjust judge (Lk. 18:2–8), the unjust steward (Lk. 16:1–9) and the prodigal son (Lk. 15:11–32). The style varies from the brief simile or metaphor (Mk. 2:21f.; 3:23) to the description of a typical event or a full-scale short story of a particular happening.

Sometimes the lesson of a parable is quite obvious from the story itself, as in the story of the rich fool, where the rich man dies at the very moment when he has completed his preparations to retire in security and comfort (Lk. 12:16–21), but even here the story is 'capped' with the dictum: 'So is he who lays up treasure for himself, and is not rich toward God'. On other occasions the point is elicited by means of a question, *e.g.* 'Now which of them will love him more?' (Lk. 7:42). A parable itself may be told in the form of a question which invites the hearer to think how he would act, and then to make the application (Lk. 11:5–8; 14:28–32). Jesus may draw out the point himself, either at the conclusion of a story (*e.g.* Mt. 18:23) or in response to a subsequent request for elucidation (*e.g.* Mt. 15:15). But more often the story is told without additions, and the hearers are left to draw their own deductions from it. Thus in Mk. 12:12 it is clear that the religious leaders knew that Jesus had spoken the parable of the wicked husbandmen against them.

IV. The kingdom of God

Many of the parables of Jesus are specifically related to the *kingdom of God (*e.g.* Mk. 4:26, 30), and in general the parables are related to its nature, its coming, its value, its growth, the sacrifices it calls for, and so on. Very naturally the interpretation of the parables is dependent on the view of the kingdom held by individual interpreters, and vice versa. Theologians of the 'thoroughgoing' school of eschatology, such as A. Schweitzer, who believed that Jesus envisaged the coming of the kingdom of God as a supernatural event which would take place suddenly and catastrophically in the near future, found here the clue to the meaning of the parables of the kingdom. They referred to the imminent crisis prophesied by Jesus. Even parables which implied growth or progress were regarded in this way. It was, for example, in the suddenness of the rising of leaven, not in its slow working, that the meaning of the parable was to be found (Mt. 13:33). Theologians of the school of 'realised' eschatology, such as C. H. Dodd, who argued that the kingdom had fully arrived in the ministry of Jesus, interpreted the parables in terms of fulfilment. The harvest prepared for in past ages had already come; the mustard seed planted long ago had now become a tree (Mk. 4:26–32).

Both of these interpretations are one-sided and fail to do justice to the undoubted elements of future hope (Mk. 13:28–37) and present fulfilment (Mt. 9:37f.; Jn. 4:35) in the teaching of Jesus. While Jesus regarded the kingdom or kingship of God as present indeed in his own words and actions, he also anticipated a period, the length of which he did not know (Mk. 13:32), during which that kingship would be a reality in the society of his followers who would constitute his world-wide church, and he predicted that the kingdom would not come in its fullness until he himself came as the Son of man in glory. The contrast between the apparent lack of response with which his teaching was at first received and the final outcome of it is suggested in the parables recorded in Mk. 4. Many of the parables are concerned with the grace shown by God through Jesus in the present time and indicate that the new age has dawned. Others are concerned with how men are to live in the light of the kingdom until its final consummation: they are to be persistent in prayer, to forgive others, to serve their neighbours, to use the gifts God has given them, to be free from covetousness, to remain alert, to be faithful stewards, and to remember that their final judgment is being determined by their present conduct.

V. The purpose of the parables

Some have found Mk. 4:10–12 very difficult to understand, for it seems to suggest that Jesus' purpose in the parables was not to enlighten the unenlightened, but that the unbeliever might become hardened in his unbelief. It is possible, however, that what seems to be a clause of purpose in Mk. 4:12 is in fact a clause of consequence (so Mt. 13:13). The parables of Jesus may have the effect of hardening the unbeliever, just as Isaiah prophesied with regard to the effects of preaching the Word of God. The truth is that Jesus' parables are unique. The parables of other teachers can to some extent be separated from the teachers themselves, but Jesus and his parables are inseparable. To fail to understand *him* is to fail to understand his parables. 'For those outside everything is in parables' (Mk. 4:11); the *whole* of Jesus' ministry, not merely the parables, remains on the level of earthly stories and portents devoid of any deeper significance. Here 'parables' has virtually come to mean 'riddles'. It is, therefore, possible for men to decline the invitation to understanding and commitment found in the parables, and in them Isaiah's prophecy (Is. 6:9f.) is fulfilled (*cf.* Jn. 12:40 where the same prophecy is cited with reference to the disbelief of the Jews in the face of Jesus' mighty works).

VI. Parables in John's Gospel

In Jn. 10:6 the word *paroimia* (a variant translation of *māšāl*, usually rendered 'proverb', *e.g.* Pr. 1:1) is used to describe the allegory of the true and false shepherds. In Jn. 16:25 the same word is closer to its OT sense of a difficult saying which needs further explanation. The Gospel of John is apparently lacking in parables of the kind found in the other Gospels, but C. H. Dodd and A. M. Hunter have drawn attention to a number of brief parables which lie almost hidden in this Gospel (Jn. 3:8, 29; 4:35–38; 5:19f.; 8:35; 10:1–5; 11:9f.; 12:24, 35f.; 16:21). Nor should we overlook the many 'figurative' descriptions which Jesus uses of himself in this Gospel, *e.g.* 'the good shepherd', 'the true vine', 'the door', 'the light of the world', and 'the way, and the truth, and the life'.

BIBLIOGRAPHY. F. Hauck, *TDNT* 5, pp. 744–761; C. H. Dodd, *The Parables of the Kingdom*², 1961; C. W. F. Smith, *The Jesus of the Parables*, 1948; A. M. Hunter, *Interpreting the Parables*, 1960; *idem, The Parables Then and Now*, 1971; H. Thielicke, *The Waiting Father*, 1960; J. Jeremias, *The Parables of Jesus*², 1963; G. V. Jones, *The Art and Truth of the Parables*, 1964; E. Linnemann, *Parables of Jesus*, 1966; J. D. M. Derrett, *Law in the New Testament*, 1970; D. O. Via, Jr., *The Parables: Their Literary and Existential Dimension*, 1967; J. D. Crossan, *In Parables: The Challenge of the Historical Jesus*, 1973; N. Perrin, *Jesus and the Language of the Kingdom*, 1976. On parables in Jn. see C. H. Dodd, *Historical Tradition in the Fourth Gospel*, 1963; A. M. Hunter, *According to John*, 1968. On hermeneutics and the parables, see A. C. Thiselton, *SJT* 23, 1970, pp. 437–468. R.V.G.T.
I.H.M.

PARADISE. Paradise is a loanword from ancient Iranian (*pairidaēza-*) and means a garden with a wall. The Gk. word *paradeisos* is used for the first time by Xenophon for the gardens of the Persian kings. LXX translates *gan 'ēḏen* of Gn. 2:8 by *paradeisos.*

a. In the Old Testament

The word paradise (Heb. *pardēs*) appears in Ne. 2:8; Ec. 2:5; Ct. 4:13. RSV renders it by 'king's forest' in Ne., 'park' in Ec. and 'orchard' in Ct. The actual word is thus nowhere used in the OT in an eschatological sense, which meaning developed in the later Jewish world. The following trends can be discerned. The word paradise (Aram. *pardēsā'*) was used to give expression to the meaning of primeval times (German *Urzeit*) and then expanded to include fantastic speculations on the glory and bliss of those times. This was connected with the expectations of a wonderful Messianic time in the future. This coming age of glory would be identical with the garden of Eden of ancient times. The Jews believed also that paradise was present in their own time, but concealed. This concealed paradise was the place to which the souls of the Patriarchs, the chosen and the righteous people, were taken. The ancient, future and present paradise were regarded as being identical.

b. In the New Testament

The word paradise (Gk. *paradeisos*) occurs in only three instances in the NT (Lk. 23:43; 2 Cor. 12:3; Rev. 2:7). The context shows that the predominating sense is that of the later development of the word. In Lk. 23:43 the word 'paradise' is used by Jesus for the place where souls go immediately after death, *cf.* the concealed paradise in later Jewish thought. The same idea is also present in the parable of the rich man and Lazarus (Lk. 16:19–31).

In 2 Cor. 12:2–4 Paul wrote in the third person of his experience of being caught up into paradise where he heard unspeakable words (Gk. *arrhēta rhēmata*). In this case paradise is the 'third *heaven' with its glory, perhaps the same as in Lk. 23. The only place where paradise is used in an eschatological sense is in Rev. 2:7. The promise is made by Christ that he will give paradise as a gift to the one who overcomes. The present paradise will come in its full glory with the final consummation. The idea of a garden of God in the world to come is strongly emphasized in the last chapters of Revelation. The symbols of the tree of life, of life-giving water, and of the twelve kinds of fruit are all witnesses to the glory of the coming paradise (Rev. 22). F.C.F.

PARAN. A wilderness situated in the E central region of the Sinai peninsula, NE from the traditional Sinai and SSE of Kadesh, with the

PARABLES ON PRAYER
See Prayer, Part 3.

The location of 'the wilderness of Paran'.

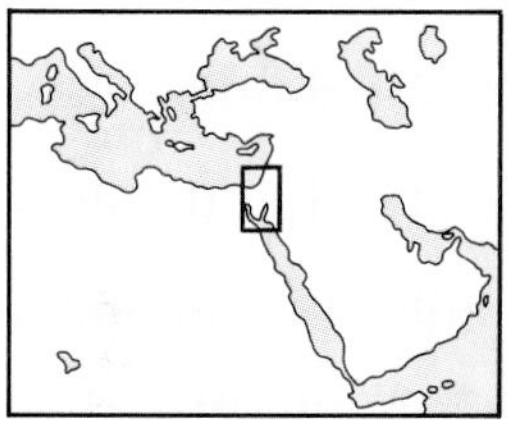

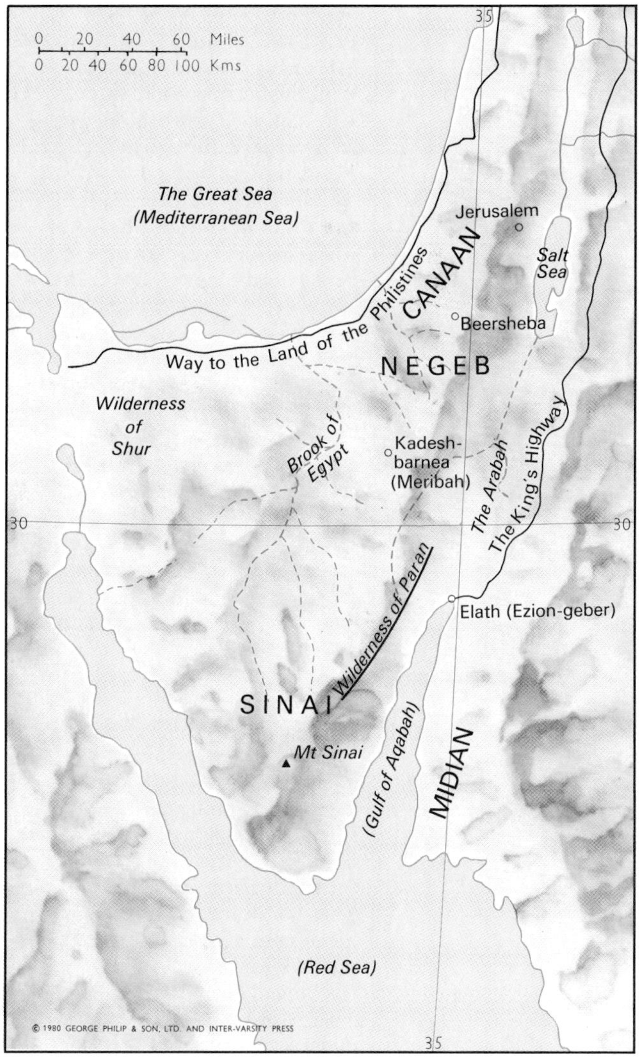

Arabah and the Gulf of Aqabah as its E border. It was to this wilderness that Hagar and Ishmael went after their expulsion from Abraham's household (Gn. 21:21) It was crossed by the Israelites following their Exodus from Egypt (Nu. 10:12; 12:16), and from here Moses despatched men to spy out the land of Canaan (Nu. 13:3, 26). The wilderness was also traversed by Hadad the Edomite on his flight to Egypt (1 Ki. 11:18).

1 Sa. 25:1 records that David went to the wilderness of Paran on the death of the prophet Samuel, but in this instance we may read with the Greek 'wilderness of Maon'.

El-paran, mentioned in Gn. 14:6 as on the border of the wilderness, may have been an ancient name for Elath. Mt Paran of the Song of Moses (Dt. 33:2) and of Hab. 3:3 was possibly a prominent peak in the mountain range on the W shore of the Gulf of Aqabah. (*ZIN.)

R.A.H.G.

PARBAR. A room or partly-roofed gateway or courtyard building to W of the Temple where gatekeepers were stationed (1 Ch. 26:18), perhaps used for disposal of sacrificial waste. It may correspond with the 'building' seen by Ezekiel (41:12) and with the word in 2 Ki. 23:11 which has been associated with Pers. *parwār* ('having light'; LXX *pharoureim*). The location of Nathan-melek's house is given as 'in *parwārim*'. RV 'precincts', AV 'suburbs', follow Targ. and Mishnah, for the city suburbs contained 'summer' or veranda-houses.

The precise meaning of the non-Heb. word is uncertain. It has been associated with an Aram.-Lydian *parbar* which describes an open anteroom of a tomb at Sardis. The suggested emendation to *p*^{e}*rāḏīm* ('who was over the mules') and any link with Iranian *frabada* remain unsupported.

D.J.W.

PARCHED GRAIN
See Grain, Part 2.

PARDON
See Forgiveness, Part 1.

PARTRIDGE
See Animals, Part 1.

PASCHAL FEAST
See Lord's supper, Part 2.

PARTHIANS. Parthia, a district SE of the Caspian Sea, was part of the Persian empire conquered by Alexander the Great. In the middle of the 3rd century BC Arsaces led the Parthians in revolt against their Seleucid (Macedonian) rulers, and his successors eventually extended their empire from the Euphrates to the Indus. Their exclusive use of cavalry-bowmen made them a formidable enemy, as the Romans discovered to their cost. In the 1st century AD the Parthians changed their capital from Ecbatana to Ctesiphon and sought to revive the Iranian elements of their civilization at the expense of the Greek.

Seal (and its impression) depicting a Parthian horseman making a characteristic 'Parthian shot'. Chalcedony. Height 2·5 cm. Achaemenid. 5th cent. BC. (BM)

The Parthians were governed by a land-owning aristocracy, and controlled the lucrative trade with the Far East. Their own religion was Iranian Mazdaism, but they were generally tolerant of other peoples' religions.

Parthia was one of the districts in which the deported Israelites had been settled, and according to Josephus their descendants continued to speak an Aram. dialect and to worship the true God, sending tribute to the Temple at Jerusalem. Consequently the Parthians in Jerusalem on the Day of Pentecost (Acts 2:9) may have been only Israelites from that district ('language' in v. 8 could equally well be 'dialect'), but there may have been Parthian proselytes with them.

BIBLIOGRAPHY. N. C. Debevoise, *Parthia*, 1938; M. A. R. Colledge, *The Parthians*, 1967.

K.L.McK.

PARVAIM. The place which produced the gold used for ornamenting Solomon's Temple (2 Ch. 3:6). The location is obscure. Some suggest Farwa in Yemen. Gesenius, identifying it with Sanskrit *parvam*, understands it to be a general term for the E regions. (*OPHIR.)

J.D.D.

Silver drachm *of Arsaces I (247–c. 211 BC) who led the Parthians in revolt against their Seleucid rulers. Diameter 24 mm.* (RG)

PASHHUR. This name is probably of Egyptian origin: Heb. *paš-ḥûr* from Egyp. *p(') š(ri n) Ḥr*, 'the son (of) (the god) Horus'; *cf.* S. Ahituv, *IEJ* 20, 1970, pp. 95–96.

1. Pashhur son of Immer. A priest, the chief officer of the house of the Lord, in the reign of Zedekiah or earlier, who put Jeremiah in the stocks and whose fate Jeremiah prophesied as exile in Babylon (Je. 20:1–6).

2. Pashhur son of Malchijah. Sent by King Zedekiah to inquire of Jeremiah (Je. 21:1), he was among those who incarcerated the prophet in the slimy pit-dungeon of the king's son Malchijah (the father of this Pashhur?) (Je. 38:1–13). He is possibly identical with the head of a priestly family of which some members were exiled to Babylonia. Some later members of this family returned to Jerusalem with Zerubbabel (Ezr. 2:38 = Ne. 7:41), six of them having to put away foreign wives there (Ezr. 10:22). Others volunteered for the fuller reoccupation of Jerusalem under Nehemiah (Ne. 11:12; probably the same Adaiah as in 1 Ch. 9:12).

3. Pashhur father of Gedaliah. His son Gedaliah was among those who imprisoned Jeremiah in Malchijah's dungeon (Je. 38:1–13); see **2** above. This Pashhur may possibly be identical with **1** or **2** above.

4. Pashhur, a priest, was among those who set their seal to the covenant under Nehemiah which followed Ezra's reading of the law (Ne. 10:3).

K.A.K.

PASSION. 1. In Acts 1:3 'passion' translates *pathein* and refers to Christ's suffering and death. This use of the term is still current. Elsewhere the same word is translated 'suffer' (*e.g.* Lk. 17:25; 24:26; Acts 17:3; Heb. 13:12, *etc.*).

2. In Acts 14:15 and Jas. 5:17 AV uses 'passion' to translate *homoiopathēs*. RSV 'of like nature' gives the sense of the Greek.

3. In its bad sense 'passion' translates *pathos* in Rom. 1:26; Col. 3:5; 1 Thes. 4:5 (in the NT this word always has the meaning 'evil desire'), and *pathēmata* in Rom. 7:5 and Gal. 5:24 (a word which usually has the sense of 'sufferings'). RSV also uses it 15 times to translate *epithymia*, 'desire' (usually in the plural) in the bad sense of that word. (* LUST.) P.E.

PASSOVER. The Passover of Ex. 12 concerns (1) the original historic event of Israel's deliverance from Egyp. bondage; (2) the later recurrent institutional commemoration of that event (*Mishnah Pesaḥim* 9:5). Closely conjoined, though separate, are (3) the prohibition of * leaven, symbolizing the haste of that unforgettable night of exodus, and (4) the later dedication of the * first-born, with statutory offerings, commemorating those first-born divinely spared in the blood-sprinkled houses. Moses quite possibly adapted more ancient ceremonials, Unleavened Bread being an agricultural festival, Passover nomadic and pastoral (*EBr*, 1974, Makropaedia, vol. 10, pp. 219f.). Passover may have had original links with circumcision, demonism, fertility cult or the first-born oblation (*cf.* H. H. Rowley, *Worship in Ancient Israel*, 1967, pp. 47ff.). Until AD 70, Passover was celebrated in Jerusalem, in any house within the city bounds, and in small companies; the lamb was ritually slaughtered in the Temple precincts. When Temple and Palestinian nation were both destroyed by war, Passover inevitably became a domestic ceremony.

The * Samaritans still meticulously observe their ancient N Israelite Passover ritual annually on Mt * Gerizim, in close conformity to the Pentateuch, keeping Passover and Unleavened Bread entirely separate entities. Unlike the Jews, they still employ a lamb. The slopes of Gerizim are now used, as the summit is ritually defiled by a Muslim cemetery (*EBr*, Mikropaedia, vol. 4, p. 494). They buttress their claims by the variant reading 'Gerizim' in place of 'Ebal' in Dt. 27:4, also by referring Dt. 12:5, 14; 16:16 to Gerizim, not Zion. There was for some time a rival Samaritan temple on Gerizim (*cf.* R. de Vaux, *Ancient Israel*, E.T. 1961, pp. 342f.), though its precise dates of functioning are disputed (*cf.* also John Macdonald, *The Theology of the Samaritans*, 1964, *passim*).

I. In the Old Testament

Ex. 12, the natural starting-point of study, suggests the following principal considerations.

1. Passover (Heb. *pesaḥ*) comes from a verb meaning 'to pass over', in the sense of 'to spare' (Ex. 12:13, 27, *etc.*). This affords excellent sense; there is no need to jettison the time-honoured view that God literally passed over the blood-sprinkled Israelite houses, whilst smiting the Egyptian ones. The term is used both for the ordinance and for the sacrificial victim. *BDB* note another verb with the same radicals, meaning 'to limp', which has suggested alternative theories (*cf.* T. H. Gaster, *Passover: Its History and Traditions*, 1949, pp. 23–25); but *KB* modify this conclusion.

2. Abib, later called Nisan, the month of the ripening ears and of the first Passover, was made by signal honour the first month of the Jewish year (Ex. 12:2; Dt. 16:1; *cf.* Lv. 23:5; Nu. 9:1–5; 28:16).

3. Was the Paschal victim customarily a lamb, as popularly conceived? In Dt. 16:2 the choice of animal is unquestionably wider; in Ex. 12 it depends on exegesis. The Heb. word *śeh* (v. 3) is restricted by *BDB* to the sheep and goat categories, irrespective of age; *KB* restrict it further to lamb or kid. There is some controversy as to the meaning of the phrase *ben-šānâ* (v. 5), lit. 'son of a year'. Some take this to signify a yearling, 12–24 months in age, *i.e.* a full-grown animal (*cf.* Gesenius–Kautzsch–Cowley, *Hebrew Grammar*, section 128 v; G. B. Gray, *Sacrifice in the OT*, 1925, pp. 345–351). But the traditional exegesis, which takes 12 months as the upper, not the lower, age-limit, is by no means disproved. Talmudic evidence seems to limit the legitimacy of the Passover victim to the sheep and goat families, following Exodus rather than Deuteronomy (*cf.* *Menaḥoth* 7:6, with Gemara). The choice of lamb or kid, lamb or goat, is several times asserted (*Pesaḥim* 8:2; 55b; 66a), yet the over-all evidence does suggest a certain preference for the lamb (*Shabbath* 23:1; *Kelim* 19:2; *Pesaḥim* 69b; *etc.*). One ruling excludes a female animal, or a male which has passed the age of 2 years—which would lend tacit support to the yearling interpretation (*Pesaḥim* 9:7). Yet a contradictory passage declares categorically that a Passover offering is valid from the eighth day of its life (*Parah* 1:4). If the universal use of a lamb cannot be certainly demonstrated from Scripture or Talmud, it is at least clear that this acquired strong consuetudinary sanction. It is of interest and significance that the Samaritans, following age-old precedents, sacrifice a lamb on the slopes of Mt Gerizim to this very day.

4. On the Passover night in Egypt, the lintels and side-posts of all Israelite doors were smeared (apotropaically, some suggest) with the victim's blood. This was carried in a basin, Heb. *sap̄*, v. 22 (which could also, with slight change of exegesis, mean 'threshold'), applied therefrom with hyssop, the foliage of the marjoram plant, a common emblem of purity. See further N. H. Snaith, *The Jewish New Year Festival*, 1947, pp. 21ff.

5. The phrase 'between the two evenings' in Ex. 12:6 (also Ex. 16:12; Lv. 23:5; Nu. 9:3, 5, 11) has been accorded two variant interpretations, according to variant community practice—either between 3 p.m. and sunset, as the Pharisees maintained and practised (*cf.* *Pesaḥim* 61a; Josephus, *BJ* 6. 423); or, as the Samaritans and others argued, between sunset and dark. The earlier time, as Edersheim points out, allows more leeway for the slaughtering of the innumerable lambs, and is probably to be preferred.

6. Ex. 12:43–49 excludes Gentiles from participating in the Passover, but not of course proselytes, who were expected, even obliged, to conform fully.

The whole drama and inner meaning of Ex. 12 is concentrated into seventeen pregnant Gk. words in Heb. 11:28.

The Passover of Dt. 16 differs in important minor respects from that of Ex. 12. The blood emphasis has disappeared; an essentially domestic ceremony has become a more formal sacrifice at a central sanctuary with a wider choice of victim; v. 7 stipulates boiling, not roasting, the animal; Passover and Unleavened Bread, here termed the bread of affliction, are integrated more thoroughly than in Exodus. This is development, event changing to institution, not contradiction; moreover it approximates better to the NT evidence concerning Passover. It is not necessary to assume a great time-gap between the passages; the changed circumstances could have been prophetically foreseen in the wilderness period. It is further recorded that a second Passover, celebrated a month later, was instituted for the benefit of those who had been levitically unclean at the time of the first (Nu. 9:1–14).

Passover was celebrated in the plains of Jericho during the Conquest (Jos. 5:10f.). In the observances of Hezekiah (2 Ch. 30:1–27) and Josiah (2 Ch. 35:1–19), the proper place is considered to be the Jerusalem Temple. Hezekiah's ceremony takes advantage of the legitimate second Passover mentioned above, because the people are not gathered in Jerusalem, and the priests are not in a state of levitical purity, at the earlier date. The brief reference of Ezekiel (45:21–24) deals with Passover in the ideal Temple of his conceiving. The three points of interest are the fuller participation of the secular leader, the fact of a sin-offering, and the complete change-over from family celebration to public ceremony. The victims specified include bullocks, rams and kids. The prescriptions of Deuteronomy are considerably extended, though not in any new thought-pattern.

Jewish usage in the last days of the Herodian Temple is reflected in the Mishnah tractate *Pesaḥim*. The people gathered in the outer Temple court in companies to slaughter the Passover victims. The priests stood in two rows; in one row each man had a golden, in the other each man a silver, basin. The basin which caught the blood of the expiring victim was passed from hand to hand in continuous exchange to the end of the line, where the last priest tossed the blood in ritual manner on the altar. All this was done to the singing of the *Hallel* (Pss. 113–118). The celebrating companies were generally family units, but other common ties were possible, such as that which bound our Lord to his disciples.

II. In the New Testament

In NT times, all Israelite males were expected to appear in Jerusalem thrice annually, for the Feasts of Passover, of Weeks or Pentecost and of Tabernacles. Even Dispersion Jews sometimes conformed; the temporary population of the Holy City (*cf.* the Pentecost gathering of Acts 2) could swell to almost 3,000,000 according to Josephus (*BJ* 6. 425)—a figure reduced to the more realistic 180,000 by J. Jeremias (*Jerusalem in the Time of Jesus*, 1969, pp. 83f.). After candlelight search for the forbidden leaven, and other careful preparations (*cf.* Mk. 14:12–16 and parallels), the Paschal supper proper was taken reclining. It included the symbolic elements of roasted lamb, unleavened bread, bitter herbs, some minor condiments and four cups of wine at specified points. The stipulated ritual hand-washings were carefully observed. The table (more probably the floor) was cleared before the second cup of wine, the story of the Egyp. Passover and Exodus recounted in a dialogue between father and son (or some suitable substitutes). The dishes of food were then brought back, part of the Hallel was sung, the second cup of wine followed. Then came the breaking of bread. In the Last Supper, it was probably at this point that Judas received the sop, and departed into the night to betray his Master (Jn. 13:30). On that fateful night, it may be assumed that the institution of the Lord's Supper or Eucharist was associated with the third cup of wine. The singing of the Hallel was completed with the fourth cup—doubtless the hymn of Mt. 26:30. It is assumed here that the Last Supper did coincide with the statutory Passover, despite the denials of certain expositors. A. Plummer, *e.g.* (*Luke, ICC*, 1896, pp. 491f.), postulates an ante-dated Passover, 20 hours before the lambs were slaughtered, maintaining that at the proper time Jesus was dying or dead. Others suggest a Passover Qiddush, or ritual purification meal in anticipation. J. N. Geldenhuys argues at length that the Last Supper was itself the Passover, that it was held on the 14th of Nisan, the day before the crucifixion, that there is no contradiction whatever between Synoptics and Fourth Gospel, when the relevant passages are correctly expounded. The Passion, he says, is to be dated on or about 6 April, AD 30. Variant views will be found in other standard commentaries.

The symbolism, 'Christ our Passover', 'Lamb of God', is familiar from NT usage. We have seen that the traditional lamb, if not provable in all instances, has widespread precedent. It is laid down in Ex. 12:46 and Nu. 9:12 that no bone of the Passover victim is to be broken. This small detail is typologically fulfilled when it is reverently applied to the crucified One (Jn. 19:36).

After the destruction of the Jerusalem Temple in AD 70, any possibility of slaughtering a victim in ritual manner utterly ceased, and the Jewish Passover reverted to the family festival it had been in the earliest days—the wheel had turned full circle. Whilst church and synagogue eventually went their separate ways, the habit of celebrating Passover would continue for some time among certain Christians, particularly those of Jewish or proselyte background. But the Lord's Supper came to replace the Jewish ordinance, just as baptism came to replace circumcision.

BIBLIOGRAPHY. See lit. cited in article; also J. Jeremias, *TDNT* 5, pp. 896–904; *SB*, 4.1, pp. 41–76; B. Schaller, *NIDNTT* 1, pp. 632–635; R. A. Stewart, 'The Jewish Festivals', *EQ* 43, 1971, pp. 149–161; G. B. Gray, *Sacrifice in the OT*, 1925, pp. 337–397; A. Edersheim, *The Temple: Its Ministry and Services as they were in the Time of Jesus Christ*; J. B. Segal, *The Hebrew Passover from Earliest Times to A.D. 70*, 1963; A. Guilding, *The Fourth Gospel and Jewish Worship*, 1960; J. Jeremias, *Jerusalem in the Time of Jesus*, 1969.

R.A.S.

PASTORS
See Ministry, Part 2.

PASTORAL EPISTLES. The three Epistles, 1 and 2 Timothy and Titus, were first called the Pastoral Epistles in the 18th century, and the name has become generally used to denote them as a group. The title is only partially an accurate description of their contents, for they are not strictly pastoral in the sense of giving instruction on the care of souls.

D.G.

PATARA. A seaport of SW *Lycia, in the Xanthus valley. Besides local trade it was important as being a suitable starting-point for a sea passage direct to Phoenicia (*SHIPS AND BOATS). According to the commonly accepted Alexandrian text of Acts 21:1, Paul transshipped at Patara on his way to Jerusalem. The Western Text, possibly influenced by Acts 27:5–6, adds 'and *Myra', which would imply that he coasted farther E before trans-shipment. There is reason to believe that the prevailing winds made Patara the most suitable starting-point for the crossing, and Myra the regular terminal for the return journey.

Patara was also celebrated for its oracle of Apollo. K.L.McK.

PATHROS, PATHRUSIM. Classed under Mizraim (Egypt), Gn. 10:14; 1 Ch. 1:12. Pathros is Egyp. *p' t'-rs(y)*, 'the Southland', *i.e.* Upper Egypt, the long Nile valley extending N–S between Cairo and Aswan; the name is attested in Assyr. inscriptions as Paturisi. Thus, the terms Mizraim for Egypt, especially Lower Egypt, Pathros for Upper Egypt and *Cush for 'Ethiopia' (N Sudan) occur in this significantly geographical order both in a prophecy of Isaiah (11:11) and in a subsequent inscription of Esarhaddon, king of Assyria, who also boasts himself 'king of Muṣur, Paturisi and Cush'. Jeremiah similarly identifies Pathros with Egypt (Je. 44:15) and specifically Upper Egypt as distinct from the cities (and land) of Lower Egypt (Je. 44:1). Pathros also appears as Upper Egypt and as the homeland of the Egyp. people in Ezk. 29:14; 30:14. K.A.K.

PATIENCE. Biblical patience is a God-exercised, or God-given, restraint in face of opposition or oppression. It is not passivity. The initiative lies with God's love, or the Christian's, in meeting wrong in this way. In the OT, the concept is denoted by Heb. *'ārēḵ*, meaning 'long'. God is said to be 'long' or 'slow' to anger, *'ereḵ 'appayim* (see Ex. 34:6; Nu. 14:18; Ne. 9:17; Pss. 86:15; 103:8; 145:8; Joel 2:13; Jon. 4:2). This idea is exactly represented in the Gk. *makrothymia*, often translated in AV as 'long-suffering', and defined by Trench as 'a long holding out of the mind' before it gives room to anger.

Such patience is characteristic of God's dealings with sinful men, who are fully deserving of his wrath (Is. 48:9; Ho. 11:8). His protecting mark on the murderer Cain (Gn. 4:15), his providential rainbow sign to a world that had forfeited its existence (Gn. 9:11–17; *cf.* 1 Pet. 3:20), his many restorations of disobedient Israel (Ho. 11:8–9), his sparing of Nineveh (Jonah), his repeated pleadings with Jerusalem (Mk. 12:1–11; Lk. 13:1–9, 34; Rom. 9:22), his deferment of Christ's second coming (2 Pet. 3:9)—these are all expressions of his patience. Christians are to show a like character (Mt. 18:26, 29; 1 Cor. 13:4; Gal. 5:22; Eph. 4:2; 1 Thes. 5:14). In Proverbs the practical value of patience is stressed; it avoids strife, and promotes the wise ordering of human affairs especially where provocation is involved.

The patience of God is a 'purposeful concession of space and time' (Barth). It is opportunity given for repentance (Rom. 2:4; 9:22; 2 Pet. 3:9). God's forbearance has been a 'truce with the sinner' (Trench, on *anochē*, Rom. 2:4; 3:25), awaiting the final revelation and redemption in Christ (Acts 17:30). Prayer may prolong the opportunity for repentance (Gn. 18:22ff.; Ex. 32:30; 1 Jn. 5:16).

The Christian's patience in respect of persons (*makrothymia*) must be matched by an equal patience in respect of things (*hypomonē*), that is, in face of the afflictions and trials of the present age (Rom. 5:3; 1 Cor. 13:7; Jas. 1:3; 5:7–11; Rev. 13:10). God is the God who gives such Christlike patience (Rom. 15:5; 2 Thes. 3:5), and Jesus is the great Exemplar of it (Heb. 12:1–3). He who thus endures to the end, by his patience will gain his soul (Mk. 13:13; Lk. 21:19; Rev. 3:10).

BIBLIOGRAPHY. R. C. Trench, *Synonyms of the New Testament*[9], 1880, pp. 195ff.; Karl Barth, *Church Dogmatics*, 2. 1, 1957, sect. 30, pp. 406ff.: 'The Patience and Wisdom of God'; U. Falkenroth, C. Brown, W. Mundle, in *NIDNTT* 2, pp. 764–776. J.H.

PATMOS. An island of the Dodecanese, lying some 55 km off the SW coast of Asia Minor, at 37° 20′ N, 26° 34′ E. To this island the apostle John was banished from Ephesus, evidently for some months about the year AD 95, and here he wrote his Revelation (Rev. 1:9). The island is about 12 km long, with a breadth of up to 7 km, and it has been suggested that the scenery of its rugged volcanic hills and surrounding seas find their

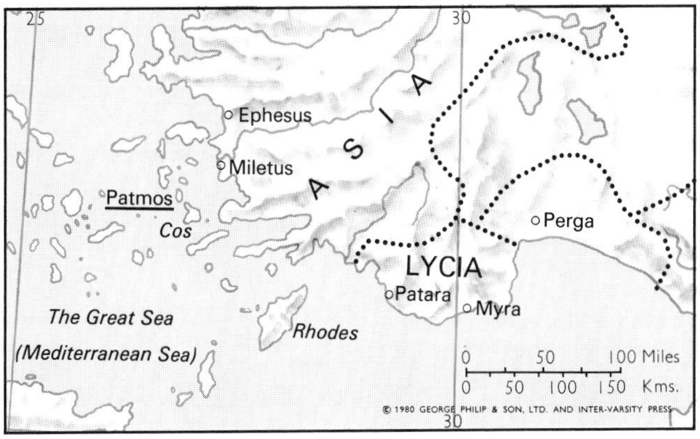

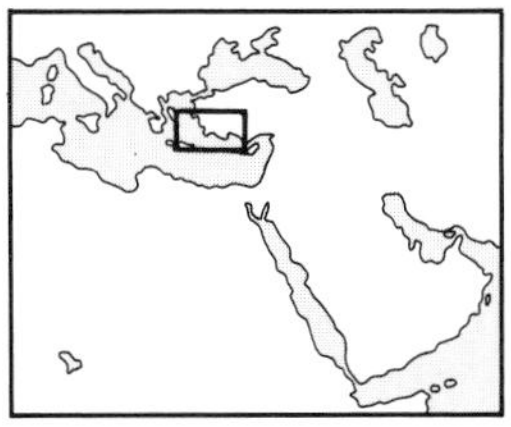

The island of Patmos off the coast of Turkey.

PATH
See Travel, Part 3.

View of the island of Patmos showing the narrow isthmus joining the two halves of the island at the harbour of Phora (modern La Scala). (JGM)

reflection in the imagery of the Apocalypse. See Pliny, *Nat. Hist.* 4. 69. The island now belongs to Greece. J.H.P.

PATRIARCHAL AGE.

I. The biblical picture

The patriarchal age covering the life-spans of Abraham, Isaac and Jacob is described in Gn. 12–50, although chs. 39–50 are concerned more with Joseph. It is extremely difficult to give a date for the patriarchal period and scholars hold widely differing views within a range of about 1900 BC to 1500 BC. Biblical data is insufficient to settle the matter and we are forced to propose tentative dates by comparing data within the patriarchal stories in Gn. with extra-biblical data from the first part of the 2nd millennium BC. There is a further difficulty in drawing a general picture of the patriarchal age because Gn. concentrates on only a few individuals. The total group which made up the kinspeople of this narrowly defined family was probably quite extensive, all of them having originated in lands to the NE of Palestine. Further, the biblical writers must have selected their own material from a wide range of traditions which were available to them in order to stress important religious and theological points. Hence, if we restrict ourselves to the biblical narratives alone there are severe limitations for the historian.

The Patriarchs are depicted in Gn. as moving across a wide canvas from Mesopotamia to Egypt. Among the towns referred to in the biblical narratives which modern archaeology has shown to have been occupied from early in the 2nd millennium are Ur (Gn. 11:28, 31; 15:7), Harran (Gn. 11:31–32; 12:4–5; 27:43; 28:10; 29:4), Shechem (Gn. 12:6; 33:18), Salem (Jerusalem, Gn. 14:18), Gerar (Gn. 20:1; 26:1, 6, *etc.*), Dothan (Gn. 37:17), and probably Hebron (Gn. 13:18; 23:2, 19; 35:27) and Bethel (Gn. 12:8). The *Ebla documents (*c.* 2300 BC) attest the existence of Sodom, Gomorrah, Admah, Zeboiim, Bela (Gn. 14:2) at an early date. Significant towns not referred to in the Bible which were flourishing in the patriarchal era were Megiddo, Hazor, Lachish, Gezer and Jericho. The Mesopotamian town of Ur at this period was not the city of great political importance that it had been at the end of the 3rd millennium BC, although it retained a considerable influence in religion and literature. The town of *Mari on the Euphrates also flourished in this period and, although not mentioned in the Bible, has produced some 20,000 tablets which throw considerable light on the age.

In some passages in Gn. lists of towns are given, *e.g.* Ashteroth-karnaim, Ham and Shaveh-kiriathaim, towns along the road traversed by the invading kings of the E (Gn. 14:5); the 'cities of the valley' (Gn. 13:12; 19:25, 29); the towns which Jacob passed through on his way back to Bethel (Gn. 35:5), and towns in Egypt (Gn. 41:35, 48; 47:21 mg.). It is clear that from Mesopotamia to Egypt there were centres of settlement, either open villages or walled towns, both small and large. In Palestine proper most of the towns were to be found in the lowlands or along the highways.

Outside the settled areas the semi-nomads moved about with their flocks forming one part of a dimorphic society in which urban dwellers and semi-nomadic pastoralists lived side by side. The latter group frequently camped in the vicinity of the towns (Gn. 12:6–9; 13:12–18; 33:18–20; 35:16–21; 37:12–17), occasionally practised agriculture (Gn. 26:12f.), were able to engage in social and economic exchange with townspeople (Gn. 21:25–34; 23:1–20; 26:17–33; 33:18–20) and even dwelt in towns as 'resident aliens' for various periods of time (Gn. 12:10; 15:13; 17:8; 20:1; 21:23, 34; 26:3; 28:4; 32:4; 35:27; 36:7; 37:1; 47:4–5). Thus when Lot and Abraham separated, Lot took up residence in the town of Sodom and pitched his tent 'toward Sodom' and 'was sitting in the gate'. The two figures of Jacob and Esau present contrasting yet complementary ways of life (Gn. 25:27–34) and Jacob and his sons at Shechem settled for a time and entered into the society of the town-dwellers (Gn. 33:18–34:31).

We gain glimpses of the semi-nomadic life of shepherds living in tents, moving with their flocks, sometimes over considerable distances, seeking pasture-lands and wells and sometimes clashing with other people (Gn. 13:5–11; 18:1–8; 21:25–31; 24:62–67; 26:1–33; 29–31; 33:12–17; 36:6–8). The valued possessions of the Patriarchs were sheep, asses, oxen, flocks and herds, and even *camels (Gn. 12:16; 13:5, 7; 20:14; 21:27–30; 30:29; 31:1–10, 38; 32:13–16; 34:28; 46:32; 47:16–18). The term *'cattle' (*b^e^hēmâ*) in some passages is a comprehensive one for small beasts, although the Patriarchs did have cattle in one sense of the word, 'oxen', *bāqār* (Gn. 12:16; 20:14; 21:27; 34:28).

*Travel seems to have been common. Abraham moved from Ur in Mesopotamia to Egypt in the course of his life; Jacob travelled from Palestine to Harran and back (Gn. 28; 35) and later to Egypt. Probably there were well-trodden trade-routes used by merchants, a group of whom took Joseph to Egypt (Gn. 37:28–36).

The patriarchal narratives make references to contemporary rulers, the pharaoh of Egypt (12:15, 17, 20), certain 'kings' (Heb. *meleḵ*) from the E, Amraphel of Shinar, Arioch of Ellasar, Chedorlaomer of Elam and Tidal king of the Goiim (14:1), petty rulers of the Sodom and Gomorrah region (14:2), *Melchizedek king of Salem (14:18), Abimelech king of Gerar (20:2; 26:1, *etc.*), certain 'chiefs' of Edom (Heb. *'allûp̄*) and later kings of Edom (Gn. 36:19, 31), 'chiefs' of the Horites (Gn. 36:29) and the chiefs of Esau (Gn. 36:40–43). None of these personalities can be identified in any historical records to date. Some of them must have been very insignificant rulers indeed and the semi-nomadic patriarchal families paid attention to them only as they were required for reasons of pasture or watering places. In some cases they entered into a covenant with them (Gn. 14:13; 21:27; 26:28f.), but for the most part they moved about freely in the dimorphic society of the day.

The daily life of the Patriarchs was governed by a variety of customs of long standing and widespread usage. The Patriarchs and their kinspeople were tribally organized into inter-related social units comprising extended families or clans (Gn. 12:1–5; 24:1–9; 28:1–5). The system was patriarchal. We read of the 'paternal house' (*bêṯ 'āḇ*) in Gn. 12:1; 24:38–40, or simply the 'house of the patriarch' (Gn. 24:2; 31:14, 43; 36:6; 46:26–27, 31; 47:12; 50:8). In such a society the father, as head of the family, had wide powers. Normally the eldest son succeeded him as heir to his position and his property. In the absence of a natural heir a slave might become heir (Gn. 15:2f.) or the son of a slave-girl who had become a subsidiary wife (Gn. 16:1ff.). In the latter case if a son was born he was regarded as the son of the true wife who had presented the slave-girl to her husband. The arrangement arose out of the wife's consent and not when the husband took a secondary wife of his own accord. The marriages of Abraham with Hagar (Gn. 16:1–4) and Keturah (Gn. 25:1–6) provide examples of these two types of union (*cf.* Gn. 30:3, 9). Problems arose if the true wife gave birth to a son after the birth of a son to the secondary wife. In patriarchal society the true son seems to have become heir (Gn. 15:4; 17:19), although Gn. 21:10 suggests that this may not have been automatic. Sarah had to insist that Ishmael should not be heir along with her own son Isaac.

Marriage was a complex affair. In the society of the times the rich and the powerful could take more than one wife but mostly marriage was monogamous. In practice, however, a husband could take a concubine or secondary wife relatively easily either through his own initiative or, if the couple could not produce the desired heir, the wife might provide a slave-girl. In patriarchal society Jacob and Esau had more than one wife of equal status (Gn. 26:34f.; 29). Abraham remarried after Sarah's death (Gn. 25:1f.) and Nahor had children by a concubine (Gn. 22:20ff.).

It would seem that there was a preference for endogamous marriage, that is, within the family, *e.g.* Abraham and Sarah, Nahor and Milcah (Gn. 11:27–30), Jacob and Rachel, Jacob and Leah, Isaac and Rebekah, Esau and Ishmael's daughter.

It is clear also that some of the patriarchal customs were forbidden in later Mosaic law, *e.g.* marriage to two sisters (*cf.* Lv. 18:18), and marriage to one's half-sister (Gn. 20:12; *cf.* Lv. 18:9, 11; Dt. 27:22).

In the case of Jacob we learn that he was required to render service to his prospective father-in-law in return for his wife (Gn. 29:18f., 27f.). We have no means of knowing whether this practice was common or not. It may have been an Aramaean custom or have been confined to an area in N Mesopotamia. Probably the practice was more widespread than our evidence allows us to say.

In at least one case further marriage was forbidden to a man (Gn. 31:50).

The patriarchal blessing was important and once given could not be revoked (Gn. 27; 48–49). In Gn. 27 the eldest son surrendered the birthright and the younger son received the blessing (vv. 22–29). It would have been normal, however, for the eldest son to receive the blessing, though not automatic.

We shall discuss below possible comparisons with other ancient Near Eastern documents. There are certain parallels between the patriarchal customs and contemporary practices, but there are also a number of features not paralleled elsewhere which seem to be specific to the patriarchal customs portrayed in the Gn. records.

In matters of religion few details are given. It is clear that the Patriarchs knew the need for a personal faith in God who guided them through life and who encouraged them with his promises (Gn. 12:1–3; 15:4f.; 17; 28:11–22, *etc.*). In the matter of guidance God was not restricted to a particular place but was active in Ur, Harran, Canaan or Egypt (*cf.* Gn. 35:3). Once God's will became known to the Patriarchs the only course was to believe and obey (Gn. 22). Prayer and the offering of sacrifices were part of the regular worship of the Patriarchs (Gn. 12:8; 13:4, 18; 26:25; 35:1, 3, 7). Circumcision was a religious rite to mark those who were in the covenant family. An intense awareness of God's activity among them caused the Patriarchs to name places and children according to some evidence of God's dealings with them (Gn. 16:11, 14, all the names of Jacob's children in Gn. 29:31ff.; *cf.* Gn. 32:30; 35:15, *etc.*). Each Patriarch seems to have had his own special name for God, which suggests a sense of special personal relationship, the 'Fear', or as W. F. Albright suggested, the 'Kinsman' (*paḥaḏ*) of Isaac (Gn. 31:42, 53) the 'Mighty One' (*'ᵃḇîr*) of Jacob (Gn. 49:24). This sense of personal relationship, the knowledge of God's promises and the awareness that obedience to the will of God is of the essence of true faith, may be said to form the heart of patriarchal religion.

Two features of patriarchal society should be stressed, namely the concepts of covenant and election. Either directly (Gn. 15:18; 27:7, 10–11, 13, 19) or indirectly, God's covenant with Abraham, Isaac and Jacob is deeply significant in patriarchal religion. In the covenant God bound himself to Abraham and his descendants and bound them to himself in a most solemn engagement which involved the divine promise to, and the divine election of, Abraham and his descendants (Gn. 12:1–3; 13:14–17; 15:18–21; 17:5–8, *etc.*). Through Abraham and his descendants God would reach out to all mankind (Gn. 12:3; 18:18; 22:17–18; 26:4; 28:14). And it was specifically through this elect family that God would act in this way (Gn. 17:18–19; 21:12). The twin concepts of covenant and election are powerful motifs in the Gn. picture of patriarchal religion.

II. Modern discovery and the patriarchal age

The precise date of the patriarchal age is difficult to determine, but there are strong reasons for placing it in the Middle Bronze Age, *c.* 1850–1570 BC (*ABRAHAM). This is based on the assumption that archaeological and epigraphic knowledge can give us contemporary information. This view is widely held today, although some writers like T. L. Thompson and J. van Seters assign the patriarchal traditions in their entirety to the Iron Age on the assumption that they are late literary inventions. For such writers archaeology cannot reconstruct a 'historical' background for the contents of the patriarchal age, since by their definition there is none. We shall return to the point below. The following outline will give an idea of the more important of the discoveries of recent years. It should be recognized that the great collections of ancient documents recovered represent only a tiny proportion of all that was written in ancient times, and are largely accidental survivors.

a. Peoples

There is a variety of peoples mentioned in the patriarchal narratives—Egyptians, Amorites, Elamites, Canaanites, Horites, Edomites, Hittites. Gn. 14 appears to refer to four specific groups. It is not possible to identify all the groups mentioned. Thus the Horites may not be the same as the Hurrians. Indeed they are connected with Edom and S Palestine in Gn. 36:20f. Nor need the Hittites of Gn. 23 be the Hittites of Anatolia. They are rather a group of indigenous people related to Canaanites (Gn. 10:15). It is true that in the early part of the 2nd millennium there were considerable movements of peoples in the ancient Near East and one might expect to find all kinds of people in Canaan. To that extent the patriarchal narratives reflect the circumstances of the period in a general way.

Two groups of people may be of particular interest, the Hapiru and the Binyaminites of Mari. The Hapiru were widely known both geographically and over a long period of time. Abraham is called a Hebrew in Gn. 14:13. This may mean that he was recognizable as being like one of the ubiquitous Hapiru people. The Binyaminites were semi-nomadic elements in the dimorphic society in the region of Mari and there is much to be gained by studying what may be known about this group from the Mari documents. There are numerous parallels on the sociological level with patriarchal society.

b. Cities

Excavation has shown that in the first part of the 2nd millennium BC the ancient Near East was heir to an ancient civilization and that several of the towns in the patriarchal records were already in existence (see **I,** above). Details of the life lived in these towns may be learnt from the ruins of the houses, the pottery and art work, the tools and weapons, and in some cases from the written records left behind in the ruins. The town of Harran (Gn. 11:31–32), for example, is known on clay tablets found in *Mari. The *Ebla tablets refer to a number of towns in Canaan which were within the ambit of its trading interest. The important Egyp. records known as the Execration Texts, dating to the 19th century BC, refer to several which were in existence in Canaan at the time, including Jerusalem (Gn. 14:18). Certainly it could be claimed that a number of the towns of the patriarchal narratives were in existence in the early part of the 2nd millennium. In Canaan itself the great Middle Bronze Age cities like Megiddo, Hazor, Lachish, Gezer, Jericho and Shechem, among others, had already been established. Outside Canaan were great towns like Mari on the Euphrates, whose written records are of considerable significance in depicting the society of the region. Despite this wealth of material we are no nearer to determining the exact date of the Patriarchs, since these cities were in existence over many centuries. Probably all we can claim with certainty is that the patriarchal stories could not refer to a period earlier than when the cities referred to came into existence.

c. Personal names

The numerous names in the patriarchal records enable a comparison with name systems which are known from the tablet records. Numerous comparisons can be made. Thus the name Abram is known in a number of variant forms, such as *A-ba-am-ra-am*, *A-ba-am-ra-ma*, *A-ba-ra-ma*, on a variety of texts in W Semitic areas over a long period of time, so that the name is of little use for specific dating. Names like *Ya'qub-ilu* (Jacob-el) occur both early and late in the 2nd millennium. Some of the names of the twelve tribes such as Simeon, Ashur, Benjamin, may also be attested. The names Ishmael and Israel consist of a verbal element plus the name for deity, El. Other names like Isaac are probably hypocoristic (a special or pet name) formed from verbal elements only, *e.g.* Isaac (*yiṣḥāq*), 'he laughs', 'mocks', 'plays' or 'fondles' (Gn. 17:17; 18:12; 21:6). Extensive studies of W Semitic names, Amorite names, Mari names, *etc.*, have been undertaken and it may be claimed that the patriarchal name system has many parallels, certainly in the early part of the 2nd millennium, but also over a longer period, so that while we gain valuable insight into the patriarchal name system as such, we are not assisted in dating the Patriarchs.

d. Travel, trade and commerce

There was a good deal of *trade and *travel all over the Near East at this time. Clay tablets from Cappadocia indicate that as early as 2000 BC there was trade in copper and wool between Asia Minor and Assyria. Other records tell of movements of armies and the transport of booty, *etc.*, all over the Near East. Great routes crossed from Mesopotamia to Asia Minor and Palestine, and others down into Egypt. That a great road traversed Transjordan (the *King's Highway, Nu. 20:17) is clear from the line of ancient towns strung out along the route not far from the modern highway. Pictures from Beni-hasan in Egypt dating to about 1900 BC depict travelling nomads, possibly metal-workers, from the general area of Palestine. From these we gain a good idea of the dress and the possessions of these people in Abraham's time. Their main beasts of burden seem to have been asses and donkeys. Finally, the *Ebla tablets of *c.* 2300 BC introduce us to the vast trading area over which the Ebla merchants ranged and point to wide activities in travel, trade and commerce well before the period we are proposing for the patriarchal age.

e. The customs of the age

These have come to light from the tens of thousands of clay tablets which represent the documents of everyday life, legal, commercial, religious and private. There are in addition some important lists of laws, such as the Laws of Hammurapi (about 1750 BC), the Code of the town of Eshnunna (19th or 18th century BC), and the fragmentary Sumerian Codes of the kings of Lipit-Ishtar and Ur-nammu (21st–19th centuries BC). Of the private and personal documents, those of *Nuzi (15th and 14th centuries BC), *Mari (18th century BC), Ras Shamra (*Ugarit, 14th century BC) and *Alalaḫ (17th and 15th centuries BC) should be mentioned. These combine to give a picture of the life in N Mesopotamia in the period 2000–1500 BC and form a body of information against which we can study the patriarchal customs. Clearly documents from the 15th and 14th centuries take us beyond what we are proposing as the patriarchal age, so that they have to be used with some caution. Customs change in the course of time, but they often reflect earlier practices and it would not be impossible to find helpful clues to life in the 18th century BC by reading documents from the 15th century BC. In general, however, documents from the same age are the most reliable source of data.

Shortly after the discovery of the Nuzi documents in the years 1925 to 1931 scholars proposed many parallels between the customs at Nuzi and the patriarchal customs. With the discovery of an increasing number of documents from other sites and from earlier centuries the Nuzi texts can now be seen to be not quite so relevant to the patriarchal narratives as was once thought. Parallels in the areas of adoption, marriage, inheritance, wife–sister marriages, sistership adoption, the 'dying words' of a patriarch, the performance of a period of service before a man could claim a wife, the giving of a slave-girl as a marriage gift and several other customs, were all sought for and found in Nuzi. Writers like C. H. Gordon and E. A. Speiser were strong proponents of the view that the Nuzi documents provided a kind of quarry for patriarchal parallels. It has now become clear that of the 4,000 cuneiform tablets from Nuzi no more than a dozen have been quoted. A concomitant of this view is that the patriarchal age was sought in the 14th century BC on the basis of links with the customs portrayed in the Ugarit, the el-Amarna and the Nuzi documents.

In fact, with a growing volume of tablet evidence parallels are more easily discovered in earlier material. Thus the most suitable example of adoption is found on an old Babylonian letter from Larsa where it is stated that a childless man could adopt his own slave, an aspect of adoption not found at Nuzi. The adoption of the son of the wife's slave-girl is found in only one Nuzi text. It was more common for the husband to marry a second wife or take his own slave-girl as a concubine. But most of the practices concerning secondary wives are known in texts from other ancient Near Eastern sites. The dying words of a patriarch are not paralleled in Nuzi and the wife–sister marriage proposed by E. A. Speiser lacks any real foundation either in Nuzi or in Gn. 12–50. It would seem that no special relationship exists between the Nuzi tablets and the patriarchal narratives. Yet such a search for parallels is not without value. One senses in a general way that the customs of the patriarchal narratives belong to a society not unlike the one we know from the tablet records of the early part of the 2nd millennium BC. However, many of the customs were current for several centuries and are not sufficiently precise for chronological purposes, though they may be useful for sociological purposes. One of the most fruitful lines of investigation is a study of nomadism and sedentarization in the ancient Near Eastern dimorphic societies such as that at Mari. If such a study is combined with a continued search for parallels in customs we may be able to gain a better idea both of patriarchal society and of the period of the patriarchal age. It is also important to realize that there may not be a specific parallel in extra-biblical material to a particular patriarchal custom, since it was peculiar to the patriarchal group.

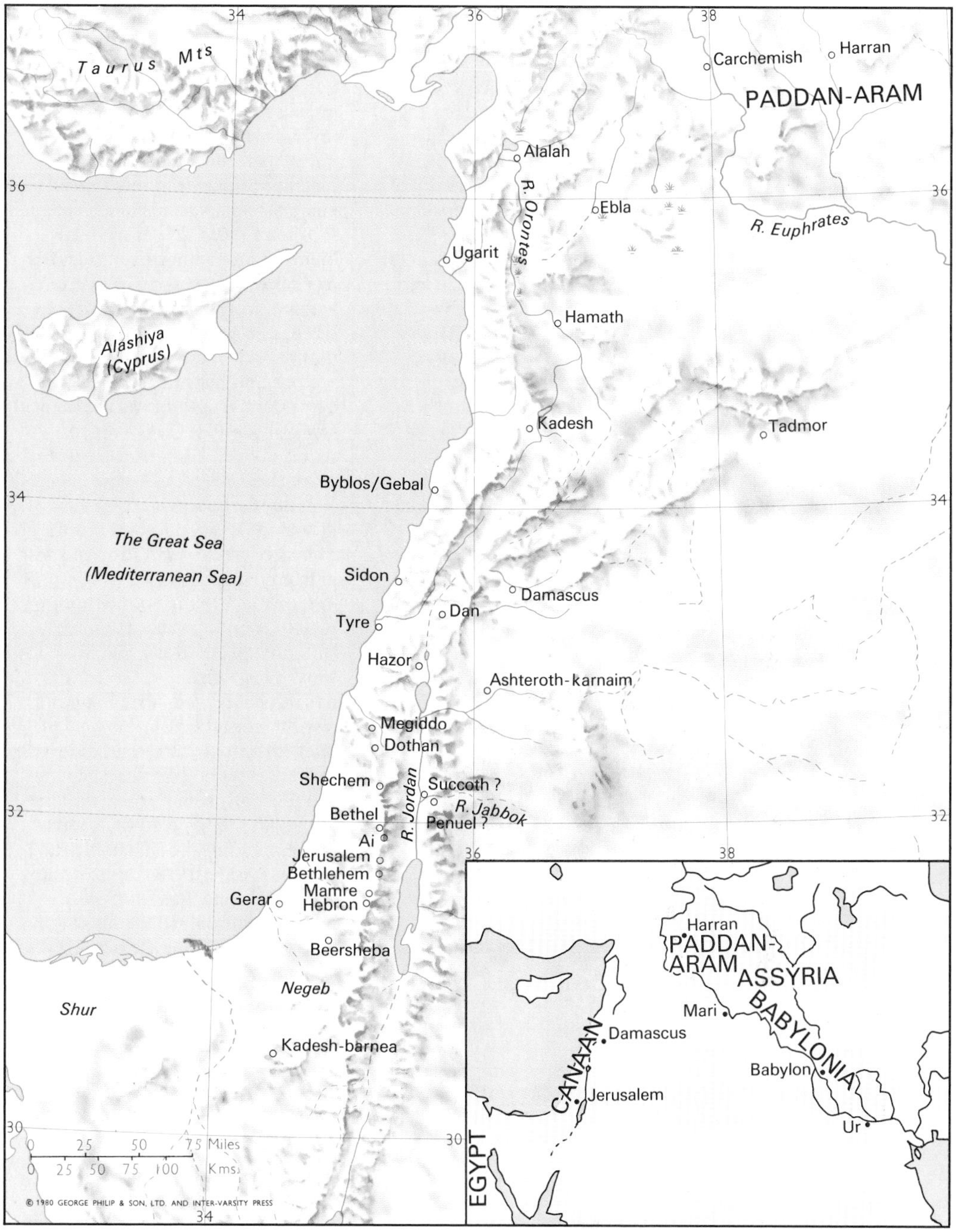

Map to illustrate the patriarchal narratives, where locations are known.

III. The historical value of the patriarchal records

It may be claimed that in general a notable change has come over scholarship since the days of J. Wellhausen at the end of the 19th century. His view was that we can attain to no historical knowledge of the Patriarchs from the biblical records, but that these are rather a reflection of the times of those men who wrote the stories in a much later day. The view is not quite forgotten and has been brought forward again by Thomas L. Thompson (1974) and J. van Seters (1975). Van Seters has raised questions about the degree to which oral tradition lies behind the stories in Gn. and is inclined to minimize its influence. He argues that it is impossible to identify specifically the personal names, places, peoples and customs of the patriarchal narratives. He can find no specific place for the Patriarchs in world events and holds that archaeology contributes very little, if anything, in elucidating their background. He also makes much of the so-called anachronisms like camels and Philistines. Hence he calls into question the whole scholarly search for parallels with the 2nd millennium and suggests instead that the traditions were largely moulded by and for the social and religious community of a later date, including the period of the Exile. This later literary activity must take priority in discussing the Gn. records. The themes of the divine promise to Abraham and the covenant were used by writers to support the dynastic ideology of the Monarchy, but they were late inventions. Thompson follows a somewhat similar line, although there are differences in detail between his approach and that of van Seters. There have been severe criticisms of these two writers. Other modern writers who have questioned the historical value of the patriarchal records are A. Alt and M. Noth, although both appear to admit that there may well be important elements of tradition which are of historical value, carried over from earlier times.

It may be agreed that a generation of scholars in recent years has made some excessive claims about several aspects of the patriarchal narratives. But it is an over-reaction to deny to these narratives any historical value. Even if we recognize them as literary-theological documents woven together from the traditions which were handed down from past centuries, there is no good reason to deny that they contain a good deal of archaic and historical material. The very strength of the theological ideas of promise and covenant required that the Patriarchs were more than mere literary inventions.

Many historical issues remain unsolved. Exact dating is impossible and precise definition of the patriarchal society and its customs in terms of a related contemporary society is not possible at present. But most present-day scholars show a disposition to treat the patriarchal records with far more respect from the point of view of their historical value than did some earlier scholars. The wisest course to follow at present is to await further evidence from all the sources. More research should enable the scholars to synthesize more accurately the biblical and the non-biblical material. In the meantime great theological doctrines like covenant, election, faith, obedience, promise, remain unobscured. Such doctrines have been the foundation of Israel's faith over the centuries and have also played a significant role in the faith of Christians. Few writers would disagree with this latter statement, whatever their view about the historicity of the Gn. narratives.

BIBLIOGRAPHY. J. Bright, *A History of Israel*[2], 1972, ch. 2; H. Cazelles, *DBS*, fasc. 36, cols. 81–156; W. G. Dever, 'Palestine in the Second Millennium BCE: the Archaeological Picture', in J. H. Hayes and J. M. Miller, *Israelite and Judaean History*, 1977, pp. 70–120; N. Glueck, 'The Age of Abraham in the Negeb', *BA* 18, 1955, pp. 2ff.; *BASOR* 149, Feb. 1958, pp. 8ff.; 152, Dec. 1958, pp. 18ff.; *idem*, *The Other Side of Jordan*, 1940; *idem*, *Rivers in the Desert*, 1959; C. H. Gordon, 'Biblical Customs and the Nuzu Tablets', *BA* 3, 1940, pp. 1ff.; K. M. Kenyon, 'Palestine in the Middle Bronze Age', *CAH*, 2/1, pp. 77–116; J. R. Kupper, *Les Nomads en Mésopotamie au temps des rois de Mari*, 1957; J. T. Luke, 'Abraham and the Iron Age, Reflections on the New Patriarchal Studies', *JSOT* 4, 1977, pp. 35–47; H. H. Rowley, 'Recent Discovery and the Patriarchal Age', *BJRL* 32, 1949–50, pp. 44ff.; M. J. Selman, 'The Social Environment of the Patriarchs', *TynB* 27, 1976, pp. 114–136; E. A. Speiser, *JBL* 74, 1955, pp. 252ff.; *idem*, *Genesis*, *AB*, 1964; T. L. Thompson, *The Historicity of the Patriarchal Narratives*, 1974; R. de Vaux, *Histoire ancienne d'Israel*, 1971, pp. 157–273; J. van Seters, *Abraham in History and Tradition*, 1975; C. J. Mullo Weir, 'Nuzi', in D. W. Thomas (ed.), *Archaeology and Old Testament Study*, 1967, pp. 73–86; D. J. Wiseman, *BS* 134, 1977, pp. 123–130; 137, 1977, pp. 228–237. J.A.T.

The Patriarchs made provision for men without heirs to adopt a slave (Gn. 15:2f.). This early Ancient Near Eastern custom is illustrated by this Old Babylonian contract. From Larsa. Width 55 mm. c. 1800 BC. (MC)

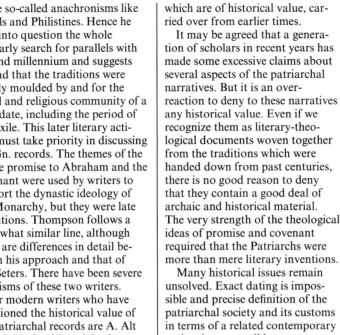

PATRISTIC LITERATURE. The importance for many branches of NT study of the extra-canonical early Christian literature, both the fragments from unorthodox writings and *NT Apocrypha, on the one hand, and the patristic writings (*i.e.* the non-apocryphal and non-sectarian ancient Christian writings), on the other, is widely recognized. For the history of the *Canon of the NT and the establishment of its text (*TEXTS AND VERSIONS, **IV**) the patristic allusions and quotations from biblical books are obviously indispensable. In exegesis, also, the Gk. Fathers in particular have to be taken into account and what writers such as Irenaeus, Clement of Alexandria and, above all, Origen say about unwritten traditions demands attention. But, in a wider aspect, the 2nd-century Gk.- and Lat.-speaking church, with all its differences in ethos from the apostolic age, is the outcome of the Jerusalem Pentecost assembly, and any illumination of the path between them is likely to cast its light backwards as well as forwards.

Unfortunately, at present a very ill-lit tunnel extends from the later apostolic age to the great apologists of the middle and later 2nd century. It is a period of intensified persecution and pernicious propaganda (as predicted in 2 Tim. 3 and elsewhere); the church is widely spread through and (in the E) beyond the Roman empire; Israel has been repudiated in AD 70, and with it any effective primacy of the

Jerusalem church has ended. The name 'Apostolic Fathers', originally meant to designate men in contact with, or appointed by, the apostles, has long been given to writings associated with this period; but lists of the Apostolic Fathers vary considerably. To three—Clement of Rome, Ignatius, Polycarp—this title is regularly applied, though only for Polycarp is there unmistakable evidence of direct contact with the apostles. All these early writings are practical, not scholarly or speculative. If one senses the immediate drop from the NT, the contrast of their directness with the tortuous intellectualism of, say, the *Gospel of Truth*, their contemporary, or with the fetid atmosphere of the apocrypha is also marked.

The works listed below represent some earlier patristic writings.

'Asiatic' soldiers of the 'patriarchal age' depicted on an Egyptian tomb-painting at Beni Hasan. Sesostris I. c. 1950 BC.

I. Clement of Rome

A long Gk. letter addressed from the church of God sojourning in Rome to that in Corinth has come down under the name of Clement (*1 Clement*). There is no ground for identifying him with the Clement of Phil. 4:3, or with Flavius Clemens, Domitian's cousin. He is doubtless the person who appears third in Roman episcopal succession lists, but the term 'bishop of Rome' in the usual sense would be an anachronism, for in the letter 'bishop' is equivalent to 'presbyter'.

The occasion is a disturbance in the church at Corinth in which legitimately appointed presbyters have been ejected. Clement, on behalf of his church, appeals for peace and order, and asks them to remember the analogy of the ordered worship of old Israel and the apostolic principle of appointing a continuance of reputable men.

The date is almost certainly about the time of Domitian's persecution, AD 95–96, *i.e.* within the NT period.

The so-called second Epistle of Clement (*2 Clement*) is a homily of unknown (though 2nd-century) date and authorship. *Cf.* K. P. Donfried, *The Setting of Second Clement in Early Christianity*, 1974.

II. Ignatius

Ignatius, bishop of Antioch, was on his way to martyrdom in Rome in Trajan's reign (AD 98–117, probably late in that period) when he wrote seven letters which were gathered into a corpus: to the Asian churches at Ephesus, Magnesia, Tralles, Philadelphia and Smyrna, to his friend Polycarp, bishop of Smyrna, and to the Roman church, asking them not to intervene to prevent his martyrdom.

Ignatius approaches nearer than any other 2nd-century writer to sublimity as he speaks of the mysteries of incarnation and salvation. But he writes hurriedly and often obscurely: and he is consumed with the desire for martyrdom and obsessed with the necessity for close adhesion to the bishop. Some have taken this to imply that government by a single bishop, as distinct from presbyters, was still fairly new in Asia. Ignatius mentions no bishop when writing to Rome.

The letters were heavily interpolated and others added by forgers, usually dated in the 4th-century (but see J. W. Hannah, *JBL* 79, 1960, pp. 221ff.). On the setting see V. Corwin, *St. Ignatius and Christianity in Antioch*, 1960.

III. Polycarp

Polycarp was one of the most revered figures of Christian antiquity. He was bishop of Smyrna when Ignatius wrote: at a great age he was martyred. The date of his martyrdom, of which a moving early account survives, is disputed: AD 155/6 and AD 168 are canvassed (see W. Telfer, *JTS* n.s. 3, 1952, pp. 79ff.). He had known the apostles, and John in particular, and he taught Irenaeus (Irenaeus, *Adv. Haer.* 3. 3. 4; Eusebius, *EH* 5. 20). He thus links the apostolic age and the late 2nd-century church. A letter to the Philippians survives, earnest and gracious. Ch. 13 is written without news of Ignatius' fate. P. N. Harrison (*Polycarp's Two Epistles to the Philippians*, 1936) argues that it is a separate early letter, and that chs. 1–12 were written *c.* AD 135–7 and conflated with it.

IV. The Didache

The *Didache* is a problematical work, consisting of teaching (which appears in other works) on the ways of life and of death, a brief church order, dealing with baptism, fasting, prayer, eucharist, ministers and prophets, and closing with an apocalypse. It has many peculiar features, according exactly neither with church order in the NT nor with what we know of the 2nd-century church. It has been argued that it is a genuine early work (*e.g.* J. P. Audet, *La Didachè*, 1958, dates it AD 60), that it is a late-2nd-century reconstruction, or that it represents a church out of the main stream. It seems to be Syrian.

V. Papias

Papias was bishop of Hierapolis in the early 2nd century and devoted much care to a five volume 'Exposition of the Oracles of the Lord', which survives only in tantalizing fragments in Irenaeus and Eusebius. Its date is uncertain: nothing later than AD 130 is likely. At all events he was in contact with hearers of the apostles (* MARK, GOSPEL OF; * MATTHEW).

VI. Barnabas

The *Epistle of Barnabas* is probably Alexandrine, from the early 2nd century. It is strongly anti-Jewish in tone, and marked by forced allegorical exegesis. It includes a form of the 'Two Ways'. The work is anonymous; its attribution to Barnabas (if the apostle is meant) is doubtless an early guess. It may, however, have led to its being read for a time in some churches (*cf.* Eusebius, *EH* 3. 25). See further P. Prigent, *L'Epître de Barnabé 1–16*, 1962.

VII. Hermas

The *Shepherd* of Hermas is a symbolic work intended to rouse a lax church and call to repentance Christians who had sinned: making clear—obviously a disputed point—that post-baptismal sin was not necessarily unforgivable. It is divided, rather artificially, into Visions, Tractates and Mandates.

Critical and historical problems abound. The Muratorian Fragment says it was written recently, by the brother of bishop Pius of Rome (*c.* AD 140), but there are some marks of earlier date, and, inferior work as it seems now, it had a period of reception as Scripture in some churches. It appears in Codex Sinaiticus of the NT. See H. Chadwick, *JTS* n.s. 8, 1957, pp. 274ff. *Cf.* also J. Reiling, *Hermas and Christian Prophecy*, 1973, for a study of the eleventh Mandate.

BIBLIOGRAPHY. J. B. Lightfoot, *The Apostolic Fathers*, 5 vols. (a mine of information and judicious comment, with texts of Clement, Ignatius and Polycarp); J. B. Lightfoot–J. R. Harmer, *The Apostolic Fathers*, 1891 (handy texts and translations); K. Lake, *The Apostolic Fathers* (texts and translations), 1917–19; J. A. Kleist, *Ancient Christian Writers* 1, 4, 1946–8; C. C. Richardson, *Early Christian Fathers*, 1953; R. M. Grant (ed.), *The Apostolic Fathers*, 1–6, 1964–8; T. F. Torrance, *The Doctrine of Grace in the Apostolic Fathers*, 1948; J. Quasten (ed.), *Patrology*, 1950; B. Altaner, *Patrology*, 1960; J. Lawson, *A Theological and Historical Introduction to the Apostolic Fathers*, 1961; L. W. Barnard, *Studies in the Apostolic Fathers and their Background*, 1966. A.F.W.

PAUL.

I. Life

a. Background

From Paul's birth until his appearance in Jerusalem as a persecutor of Christians there is little information concerning his life. Although of the tribe of Benjamin and a zealous member of the Pharisee party (Rom. 11:1; Phil. 3:5; Acts 23:6), he was born in Tarsus a Roman citizen (Acts 16:37; 21:39; 22:25ff.). Jerome cites a tradition that Paul's forbears were from Galilee. It is not certain whether they migrated to Tarsus for commercial reasons or were settled there as colonists by a Syrian ruler. That they were citizens suggests that they had resided there for some time.

Sir William Ramsay and others have shown that Tarsus truly was 'no mean city'. It was a centre of learning, and scholars generally have assumed that Paul became acquainted with various Gk. philosophies and religious cults during his youth there. Van Unnik has challenged this assumption. He argues that the relevant texts (Acts 22:3; 26:4f.) place Paul in Jerusalem as a very small child; Acts 22:3 is to be read in sequence: (i) born in Tarsus; (ii) brought up at my mother's knee (*anatethrammenos*) in this city; (iii) educated at the feet of Rabban * Gamaliel the elder. As a 'young man' (Acts 7:58; Gal. 1:13f.; 1 Cor. 15:9) Paul was given official authority to direct the persecution of Christians and as a member of a synagogue or Sanhedrin council 'cast my vote against them' (Acts 26:10). In the light of Paul's education and early prominence we may presume that his family was of some means and of prominent status; his nephew's access to the Jerusalem leaders accords with this impression (Acts 23:16, 20).

Of Paul's personal appearance the canonical account suggests only that it was not impressive (1 Cor. 2:3f.; 2 Cor. 10:10). A more vivid picture, which Deissmann (p. 58) and Ramsay (*CRE*, pp. 31f.) incline to credit, occurs in the apocryphal *Acts of Paul and Thecla*: 'And he saw Paul coming, a man little of stature, thin-haired upon the head, crooked in the legs, of good state of body, with eyebrows joining, and nose somewhat hooked, full of grace: for sometimes he appeared like a man, and sometimes he had the face of an angel.'

b. Conversion and early ministry

While there is no evidence that Paul was acquainted with Jesus during his earthly ministry (2 Cor. 5:16 means only to 'regard from a human point of view'), his Christian kinsmen (*cf.* Rom. 16:7) and his experience of the martyrdom of Stephen (Acts 8:1) must have made

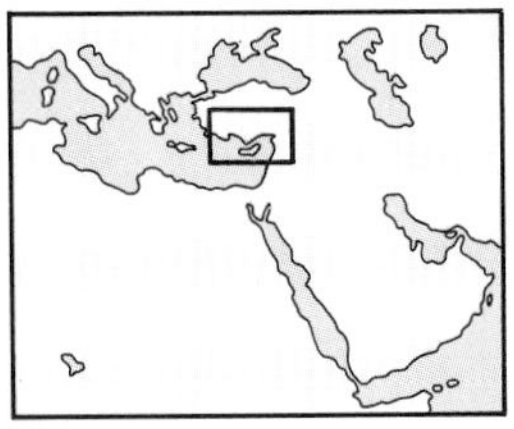

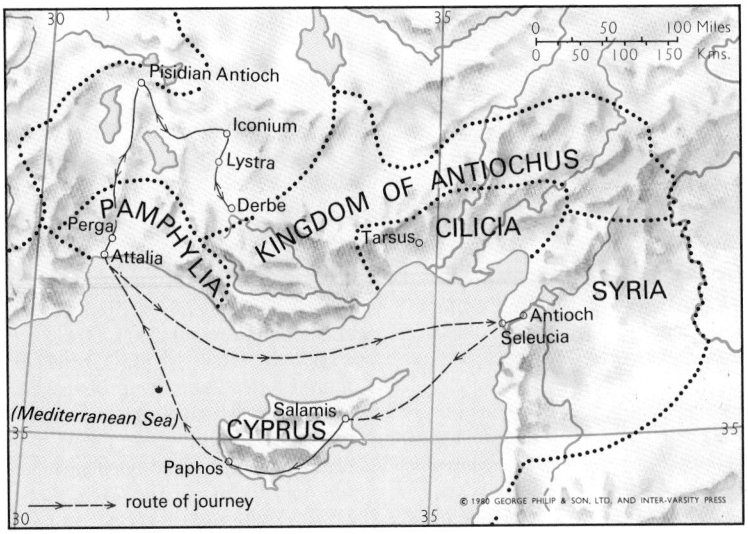

Paul's first missionary journey.

an impact upon him. The glorified Jesus' question in Acts 26:14 implies as much. The result of Paul's encounter with the risen Christ gives ample assurance that it was an experience of a healthy mind; and it can be adequately interpreted, as indeed Luke does interpret it, only as a miraculous act, which transformed Christ's enemy into his apostle. The three accounts in Acts (chs. 9, 22, 26) attest not only the significance of Paul's conversion for Luke's theme (*cf. CBQ* 15, 1953, pp. 315–338), but also, as J. Dupont and M. E. Thrall have suggested in the Bruce *Festschrift*, its essential importance for Paul's Christology and his interpretation of his ministry to the Gentiles. *Cf.* Kim, pp. 135–138, 170ff., 338.

Apart from an interval in the Transjordan desert, Paul spent the 3 years following his baptism preaching in Damascus (Gal. 1:17; Acts 9:19ff.). Under pressure from the Jews he fled to Jerusalem, where Barnabas ventured to introduce him to leaders of the understandably suspicious Christians. His ministry in Jerusalem lasted scarcely 2 weeks, for again certain Hellenistic Jews sought to kill him. To avoid them, Paul returned to the city of his birth, spending there a 'silent period' of some 10 years. No doubt it is silent only to us. Barnabas, hearing of his work and remembering their first meeting, requested Paul to come to Antioch to help in a flourishing Gentile mission (Gal. 1:17ff.; Acts 9:26ff.; 11:20ff.). These newly named 'Christians' soon began their own missionary work. After a year of notable blessing Paul and Barnabas were sent on a 'famine visit' to help stricken colleagues in Judaea.

c. Mission to Galatia—the Council of Jerusalem—mission to Greece

Upon their return from Jerusalem —about AD 46—Paul and Barnabas, commissioned by the church in Antioch, embarked on an evangelistic tour. It took them across the island of Cyprus and through 'S Galatia' (Acts 13–14). Their strategy, which became a pattern for the Pauline missions, was to preach first in the synagogue. Some Jews and Gentile 'Godfearers' accepted the message and became the nucleus for a local assembly. When the mass of Jews rejected the gospel, sometimes with violence, the focus of the preaching shifted to the Gentiles (*cf.* Acts 13:46f.). Despite these perils and the defection at Perga of their helper, John Mark, the mission succeeded in establishing a Christian witness in Pisidian Antioch, Iconium, Lystra, Derbe and possibly Perga.

Meanwhile the influx of Gentiles into the church raised serious questions concerning their relations to Jewish laws and customs. A number of Jewish Christians were insisting that Gentiles must be circumcised and observe the Mosaic law if they were to be received 'at par' in the Christian community. Upon his return to Antioch (*c.* AD 49), Paul, seeing in this Judaizing movement a threat to the very nature of the gospel, expressed his opposition in no uncertain terms. First, he rebuked Peter publicly (Gal. 2:14), after the latter, to avoid a breach with certain Judaizers, had separated himself from Gentile Christians. Secondly, hearing that the Judaizing heresy was infecting his recently established churches, Paul wrote a stinging letter of warning to the Galatians in which the Pauline *credo*, 'Salvation by grace through faith', was forcefully presented.

These events in Antioch gave rise to the first great theological crisis in the church. To resolve the problems which it raised, the church in Antioch sent Paul and Barnabas to confer with the 'apostles and elders' in Jerusalem (*c.* AD 50, Acts 15). The ensuing council gave the judgment that Gentiles should have 'no greater burden' than to abstain from food offered to idols, bloodmeat, meat from strangled animals and unchastity (or incest marriage). The effect of this decision was to sustain Paul's contention that Gentiles were under no obligation to keep the Mosaic law. The restrictions mentioned seem to have been principally for local application (*cf.* 1 Cor. 8) and as an aid to Jewish–Gentile relations.

Because of differences with Barnabas (over taking John Mark with them again) Paul took a new companion, Silas, on his 2nd missionary tour (Acts 15:40–18:22). From Antioch they travelled overland to the churches of 'S Galatia' and at Lystra added young Timothy to the party. Forbidden by the Holy Spirit to evangelize W, they journeyed N through 'N Galatia', where some converts may have been made (*cf.* Acts 16:6; 18:23). At Troas Paul in a vision saw a 'man of Macedonia' beckoning to him. Thus his evangelization of Greece began. In Macedonia missions were established in Philippi, Thessalonica and Beroea; in Achaia, or S Greece, Athens and Corinth were visited. In the latter city Paul remained almost 2 years founding a Christian fellowship that was to be the source of both joy and trial in the future. Through his co-workers (Luke the physician joined the party in Troas) and by correspondence (the Epistles to the Thessalonians) he kept in touch also with the struggling young churches in Macedonia. The Holy Spirit now moved Paul to turn his eyes once more upon the earlier forbidden province of Asia. Departing from Corinth, he stopped briefly at Ephesus, the commercial metropolis of Asia, and left as an advance party his Corinthian colleagues Priscilla and Aquila. In a quick trip back to Antioch—*via* Jerusalem—Paul completed his 'second missionary journey' and, after a final sojourn in Antioch, prepared to move his base of operation W to Ephesus.

d. The Aegean ministry

In many ways the Aegean period (*c.* AD 53–58; Acts 18:23–20:38) was the most important of Paul's life. The province of Asia, so important for the later church, was evangelized; and the Christian outposts in Greece secured. During these years he wrote the Corinthian letters, Rom. and perhaps one or more of the Prison Epistles (Eph., Phil., Col., Phm.), which in the providence of God were to constitute a holy and authoritative Scripture for all generations. For the apostle this was a time of triumph and defeat, of gospel proclamation and threatening heresies, of joy and frustration, of activity and prison meditation. The risen Christ used all these things to mould Paul into his image and to speak through Paul his word to the church.

From Antioch Paul travelled overland through the familiar Galatian region to Ephesus. There he met certain 'disciples', including Apollos, who had known John the Baptist and, presumably, Jesus (Acts 18:24ff.). On this foundation the church grew, and God performed such extraordinary miracles that certain Jewish exorcists began, without success, to use the name of 'Jesus whom Paul preaches'. Opposition from devotees of the city's patron goddess, Artemis (Diana), was soon aroused; and Demetrius, a prosperous idol-maker, succeeded (from motives other than piety) in inciting the people to riot. Paul doubtless had made a number of short trips from Ephesus; he took this occasion, some 3 years after his arrival, to make a final visit to the churches in the Aegean area. Through Troas he came to Macedonia, where he wrote 2 Cor. and, after a time, travelled S to Corinth. There he spent the winter and wrote a letter to the 'Romans' before retracing his steps to Miletus, a port near Ephesus. After a touching farewell Paul, 'bound in the Spirit' and under threatening clouds, sailed towards Jerusalem and almost certain arrest. This did not deter him, for Asia had been conquered and he had visions of Rome.

e. The Caesarean and Roman imprisonment—Paul's death

Paul disembarked at Caesarea and, with a collection for the poor, arrived at Jerusalem at Pentecost (Acts 21:23f.; *cf.* 1 Cor. 16:3f.; 2 Cor. 9; Rom. 15:25ff.). Although he was careful to observe the Temple rituals, Jewish pilgrims from Ephesus, remembering 'the apostle to the Gentiles', accused him of violating the Temple and incited the crowds to riot. He was placed under arrest but was permitted to address the crowd and later the Sanhedrin.

To prevent his being lynched, Paul was removed to Caesarea, where *Felix, the Roman governor, imprisoned him for 2 years (*c.* AD 58–60, Acts 23–26). At that time Festus, Felix's successor, indicated that he might give Paul to the Jews for trial. Knowing the outcome of such a 'trial', Paul, as a Roman citizen, appealed to Caesar. After a moving interview before the governor and his guests, King Agrippa and Bernice, he was sent under guard to Rome. Thus, under circumstances hardly anticipated, the risen Christ fulfilled the apostle's dream and his own word to Paul: 'You must bear witness also at Rome' (Acts 23:11). Paul had a stormy sea-voyage and, after being wrecked, spent the winter on Malta (*c.* AD 61). He reached Rome in the spring and spent the next 2 years under house-arrest 'teaching about the Lord Jesus Christ quite openly' (Acts 28:31). Here the story of Acts ends, and the rest of Paul's life must be pieced together from other sources. (A helpful survey of the apostolic age, and Paul's place in it, is F. F. Bruce, *New Testament History*, 1969.)

Most probably Paul was released in AD 63 and visited Spain and the Aegean area before his re-arrest and death at the hands of Nero (*c.* AD 67). *1 Clement* (5. 5–7; ?AD 95), the Muratorian Canon (*c.* AD 170), and the apocryphal (Vercelli) *Acts of Peter* (1. 3; *c.* AD 200) witness to a journey to Spain; and the Pastoral Epistles appear to involve a post-Acts ministry in the East. To the end Paul fought the good fight, finished the course and kept the faith. His crown awaits him (*cf.* 2 Tim. 4:7f.).

II. Chronology

a. General reconstruction

The book of Acts, augmented with data from the Epistles and from Jewish and secular sources, continues to serve as the chronological framework of most scholars. Its essential compatibility with the sequence of Paul's mission, detectable (in part) in his letters, is evident (*cf.* T. H. Campbell, *JBL* 74, 1955, pp. 80–87). However, its sketchiness and chronological vagueness, even in those periods treated, is increasingly conceded; and there is a growing willingness to interpolate (*e.g.* an Ephesian imprisonment) into the framework from other data or reconstructions. Fixed dates with secular history are not numerous. The most certain is the proconsulship of Gallio (*cf.* Acts 18:12), which may be fixed in AD 51–2 (Deissmann) or AD 52–3 (Jackson and Lake; *cf.* K. Haacker, *BZ* 16, 1972, pp. 252–255). If in Acts 18:12 Gallio had only recently assumed office (Deissmann), Paul's sojourn in Corinth may be dated between the end of AD 50 and the autumn AD 52. This accords with the 'recent' expulsion of Priscilla and Aquila from Rome (Acts 18:2), which may be dated *c.* AD 50 (Ramsay, *SPT*, p. 254).The accession of Festus (Acts 24:27) is often placed in AD 59 or 60. But the lack of any clear evidence leaves the matter uncertain (*cf.* C. E. B. Cranfield, *Romans*, *ICC*, 1975, pp. 14f.; Robinson, pp. 43–46).

Besides the three dates above, the mention of King Aretas of Nabatea (2 Cor. 11:32), the famine in Judaea (Acts 11:28) and Paul's trip to Spain and martyrdom in Rome under Nero (Rom. 15:28; *1 Clement* 5; Eus., *EH* 2. 25–3. 1) provide some less specific chronological data as follows. First, Damascus coins showing Roman occupation are present until AD 33, but from AD 34 to 62 they are lacking; this places a *terminus a quo* for Paul's conversion at AD 31 (*i.e.* AD 34 minus 3; *cf.* Gal. 1:18; *ICC* on 2 Cor. 11:32). (But the Nabateans apparently took control at the accession of Caligula in AD 37; *cf.* A. H. M. Jones, *The Cities of the Eastern Roman Provinces*², 1971.) Secondly, Josephus (*Ant.* 20. 101) notes a severe famine *c.* AD 44–48, probably to be located in AD 46. Thirdly, from tradition Paul's death may be dated with some probability in the latter years of Nero, *c.* AD 67.

b. The relation of Acts and Galatians

The only fully satisfying chronology is one in which there is a consensus of Acts, the Epistles and extra-biblical sources. One continuing problem for such a synthesis has been the relation between Acts and Galatians. The identification of Paul's visit to Jerusalem in Gal. 1:18 with Acts 9:26ff. is seldom questioned: the second visit in Gal. 2:1ff. poses the basic problem. Three views are current: Gal. 2 equals Acts 15, or Acts 11: 27–30, or Acts 11 and 15. In the past the first view has commanded the largest advocacy (*cf.* E. de W. Burton, *The Epistle to the Galatians*, 1921, pp. 115ff.), and it continues to attract some commentators (*cf.* H. Schlier, *An die Galater*, 1951, pp. 66ff.; H. Ridderbos, *Galatians*, 1953, pp. 34f.). The following objections, among others, have combined to undermine it: Gal. 2 pictures a second visit and a private meeting without reference to any document; Acts 15 is a third visit involving a public council and culminating in an official decree. Many scholars regard it as incredible that Gal. would, in a highly relevant context, omit mention of the Apostolic Council and decree.

The second view, often associated with the S Galatian theory, revives an interpretation of Calvin and removes a number of these objections. Acts 11 is a second visit, by revelation, and concerned with the poor (*cf.* Gal. 2:1–2, 10); the Apostolic Council in Acts 15 occurs after the writing of Gal. and, therefore, is not germane to the problem. Advanced in modern times by Ramsay (*SPT*, pp. 54ff.) and recently advocated by Bruce (*BJRL* 51, 1968–9, pp. 305ff.; 54, 1971–2, pp. 266f.), it is probably the prevailing view among British scholars (*cf.* C. S. C. Williams, *The Acts of the Apostles*, 1957, pp. 22ff.).

Dissatisfied with both alternatives, most Continental writers (*e.g.* Goguel, Jeremias), followed by a number in Britain and America (*e.g.* K. Lake, A. D. Nock), regard Acts 11 and Acts 15 as duplicate accounts of Gal. 2, which Luke, using both sources, failed to merge (*cf.* Haenchen, pp. 64f., 377). Against Ramsay, Lake urges that if the Judaizing problem is settled in Acts 11 (= Gal. 2), Acts 15 is superfluous. Gal. 2:9, however, pictures not a settlement but only a private, tacit approval of Paul's gospel and is incidental to the purpose of the visit which, as Lake admits, is the 'care of the poor' (*BC*, 5, pp. 201f.). Haenchen (p. 377) rejects Ramsay's 'crucial' application of Gal. 2:10 to the famine visit. He may be correct in identifying the 'poor' with the Gentile mission (Gal. 2:9), but it scarcely has the vital significance which he attributes to it. Ramsay's reconstruction, even with some exegetical gnats, remains the more probable alternative. Basically the view identifying Acts 11 and Acts 15 arises from the traditional equation of Gal. 2 and Acts 15, and also from an excessively negative estimate of Luke's acquaintance with and interpretation of the primary sources. Since Gal. 2 = Acts 11 provides 'a perfectly clear historical development' (W. L. Knox, *The Acts of the Apostles*, 1948, p. 49), the other is unnecessarily complex. Other views of the problem are expressed by T. W. Manson (*BJRL* 24, 1940, pp. 58–80), who identifies Gal. 2 with a visit prior to Acts 11, and M. Dibelius (*Studies in Acts*, 1956, p. 100), whose excessive *tendenz* criticism denies to both Acts 11 and 15 any claim to historicity.

c. A new reconstruction

Convinced that the Acts framework is unreliable, John Knox (*Chapters in a Life of Paul*, 1950, pp. 74–88) offers an imaginative chronological reconstruction from the evidence of the letters. A 14-year 'silent period' (AD 33–47) is impossible; therefore, the apostle's missionary activities and some letters are largely to be placed between his first (AD 38; Gal. 1:18) and second (AD 51; Gal. 2 = Acts 15) visits to Jerusalem. The final tour ends with his 'collection visit' and arrest (AD 51–3; Rom. 15:25; 1 Cor. 16:3f.). Why a silent period (which means simply that it yields no extant letters and did not fit Luke's theme) is so impossible is not readily apparent; and the traditional equation of Acts 15 and Gal. 2 also is open to question. Knox's fertile mind has found here more admirers than followers, for 'it is difficult to exchange tradition with imagination (as we find it in Acts) for imagination (however reasonable) without tradition' (Davies, *TCERK*, p. 854). Nevertheless, further attempts have been made to reconstruct the Pauline mission solely from the letters. *Cf.* Kümmel, *INT*, pp. 253f.; G. Lüdemann, *Paulus der Heidenapostel*, 1979.

III. History of criticism

a. Early developments

In a brilliant historical survey Albert Schweitzer (*Paul and his Interpreters*; *cf.* also Feine, *Paulus*, pp. 11–206; Ridderbos, *Paul*, 1976, pp. 13–43) traces the development of critical studies in Germany following the Reformation. For the orthodox, Scripture sometimes was little more than a mine of credal proof texts; exegesis became the servant of dogma. The 18th century witnessed a reaction by pietists and rationalists, who, each for his own purpose, sought to distinguish exegesis from credal conclusions. Philological exegesis and the interpretation of Scripture by Scripture became normative for scientific interpretation.

This development perhaps finds its most important expression in J. S. Semler, who, with J. D. Michaelis, pioneered the development of literary–historical criticism. His 'Prolegomena' to theological hermeneutics, 'Paraphrases' of Rom. and Cor., and other writings emphasize that the NT is a temporally conditioned document in which the purely cultural references are to be distinguished and/or eliminated. Philology exists to serve historical criticism. Our copies of Paul's letters have a 'church liturgy' format and we must, then, face the possibility that they originally had a different form. Specifically, Semler suggests that Rom. 15 and 16; 2 Cor. 9; 12:14–13:14 were separate documents, later incorporated into the larger Epistles. Foreshadowing the conclusions of F. C. Baur, Semler contrasts Paul's non-Jewish ideas with the Jewish-Christian party whom the apostle opposed; the General Epistles reflect an effort to mediate in this conflict. On questions of authorship a trend appeared in J. E. C. Schmidt (1805), who, on literary grounds, doubted the authenticity of 1 Tim. and 2 Thes. Schleiermacher (1807), Eichhorn (1812), and De Wette (1826) brought 2 Tim., Tit. and Eph. under question.

b. The Tübingen School

In 19th-century Germany exegesis was fully transformed from the 'servant of dogma' to the 'servant of scientific philosophy' (*cf.* Kümmel, *Problems*, pp. 130–143; S. Neill, *The Interpretation of the New Testament, 1861–1961*, 1964, pp. 10–28). Most significant in this regard for Pauline studies was F. C. Baur of Tübingen. He was not content merely to test the authenticity of ancient documents, a popular practice since the Renaissance. His was a 'positive criticism' which sought to find the documents' true historical setting and meaning. In *Symbolik und Mythologie*, the book which brought about his faculty appointment, he revealed the set of his mind and of his future work with the declaration that 'without philosophy history seems to me for ever dead and mute' (1. xi). In this matter Baur found in Hegelian dialectic—which viewed all historical movement as a series of theses (advance), antitheses (reaction) and syntheses (= a new thesis)—an appropriate key to interpret the history of the apostolic age (*cf.* Ellis, *Prophecy*, pp. 86–89; Haenchen, pp. 15–24). He had argued earlier (1831) that 1 Cor. 1:12 depicted a conflict between Pauline–Gentile and Petrine–Jewish Christianity. He later saw in Acts and the smaller Pauline Epistles and in the 'Gnostic' opponents of 'the so-called Pastoral letters' (1835) a more developed stage of the conflict in which, in the fight against Gnosticism, the original Pauline 'thesis' and Petrine 'antithesis' were finally resolved by the late 2nd century into an early Catholic 'synthesis'. In this 'tendency criticism' all NT writings which 'tended' towards compromise between Paul and the original apostles were viewed as later attempts to read back a subsequent unity into the apostolic period. After Baur's thoroughgoing scything only five NT documents remained uncontested witnesses from the apostolic period. Apart from Rev. all were Paul's: Rom., Cor. and Gal. The then current literary analysis of Paul's letters favoured Baur's reconstruction and, in turn, the latter accentuated and confirmed the suspicions of the more extreme literary critics. The Tübingen school rapidly became the dominant factor in NT criticism.

Using Baur's logic and sparked by Bruno Bauer's commentary on Acts (1850), an ultra-radical school questioned the genuineness of all Pauline literature. First, Acts knows no Pauline letters, and its simple picture of the apostle may be more primitive than the letters; disagreements even within Rom. and Gal. suggest several hands and a later time. Secondly, if Pauline thought (Paulinism) is the Hellenization of Christianity, as Baur thought, is it possible that this was accomplished so quickly and by one man? Could anti-Jewish feeling or Paul's high Christology have developed in a Palestinian-based church so soon after Jesus' death? No; the conflict itself is the climax of a long development, and Paulinism is to be identified with a 2nd-century Gnostic party who used the apostle's 'letters' as an authoritative vehicle for their own ideas. Why letters? Because apostolic letters already had a position of authority. Why Paul? This is impossible to say.

For all their logic the radicals succeeded only in convincing themselves. The citation of Paul in *1 Clement* (?AD 95) and Ignatius (AD 110), and the neglect of Paulinism and lack of any anti-Jewish conflict in the post-apostolic literature were fatal to their argument. The omission in Acts of Pauline literary activity was a (not very strong) argument from silence. The net result of the 'ultra-Tübingen school' was to undermine Tübingen itself. For, within their common assumption that Paul was the Hellenizer of Christianity and that Hegel supplied the key to history, the radicals had the better argument.

Baur's views came under attack from the conservatives (*e.g.* J. C. K. von Hofmann) and the followers of Schleiermacher (*e.g.* Ewald); perhaps the cruellest and most telling blow was from A. Ritschl, a former disciple. Both Ritschl and von Hofmann rejected the alleged hostility between Paul and the original disciples. The latter's emphasis upon the unity of apostolic teaching was in the next century to find renewed expression in the writings of P. Feine and A. Schlatter and in the kerygmatic theology of C. H. Dodd. A moderating literary criticism, even among Baur's disciples (*e.g.* Pfleiderer), revised the estimate of genuine Pauline Epistles sharply upward. Apart from the Pastorals, the majority excluded only 2 Thes. and Eph., and their acceptance (*e.g.* by Harnack, Jülicher) was no longer a mark of conservatism.

With its literary and philosophical presuppositions undermined, the influence of Tübingen waned. Nevertheless, by tying literary analysis to an imaginative philosophical synthesis Baur, whom Godet called Semler *redivivus*, dominated NT criticism (as Semler never did) for half a century. Again, although his own exegesis proved to have a philosophical bias unacceptable to later historians (and to all committed to a theistic interpretation of history), Baur brought into prominence an inductive historical approach to earliest Christianity and freed research from a tradition which came to much of the data with its conclusions already assumed. For this, all students can appreciate his labours. Finally, because Baur's reconstruction placed in bold relief the problems facing historians of the apostolic age, he largely set the course of future studies. What was the relationship between Paul and Jesus? What was the influence of Jewish and Hellenistic thought in the apostolic church? What are the proper philosophical presuppositions for a study of Christian origins? The Tübingen school died, and there is no apparent sign of an early resurrection. (Its airing in S. G. F. Brandon's *The Fall of Jerusalem and the Christian Church*, 1951, does not appear to have imparted life.) But the forces which gave it birth continued fecund and, for a corpse, Tübingen retained a remarkable familiarity with the following generations.

c. British contributions in the 19th century

British (and American) scholars interacted with the Tübingen reconstruction; but, with one or two exceptions (*e.g.* S. Davidson), they did not find it persuasive. Likewise, the Pauline Corpus (minus Heb.) continued to find acceptance. In America some rejected the Pastorals (*e.g.* B. W. Bacon, A. C. McGiffert); Britain, following J. B. Lightfoot (*Biblical Essays*, 1904, pp. 397–410), generally accepted them in a post-Acts setting. Nevertheless, with characteristic caution, British scholars influenced future criticism more than is generally realized by solid historical exegesis (*e.g.* Lightfoot, Ramsay) and by relating Paul to contemporary Jewish thought (*e.g.* F. W. Farrar, H. St J. Thackeray). W. M. Ramsay's espousal of the Lucan authorship of Acts after thoroughgoing archaeological and historical research was particularly influential for the critical reconstruction of Paul's life (*cf. SPT*, pp. 20ff.; W. K. Hobart's conclusions regarding *The Medical Language of St Luke*, 1882, also remain, with qualifications, a valid contribution in this area). With the advocacy of the German scholars Harnack and Deissmann this conclusion has been strengthened, although some recent students, as Haenchen, have argued anew against the tradition.

d. Trends in the 20th century

Literary criticism in the present century has focused upon: (i) a continuing effort towards a general historical reconstruction (*cf.* **IV**, below); (ii) the publication of the Pauline corpus; (iii) the provenance and date of the Prison Epistles; (iv) authorship; and (v) other questions concerning individual Epistles.

(i) *Historical reconstructions.* In spite of the demise of the Tübingen school its historical reconstruction, and some of its literary foibles, have continued to be assumed in much contemporary critical study. Johannes Munck (pp. 70–77) has rightly objected that when the literary conjectures failed, the dependent historical conjectures ought to have been revised ('It was not enough merely to transfer the problem from the two centuries to the three decades'; p. 70). Munck himself proposes such a revision. (1) The Jerusalem church, *i.e.* the original disciples, even as Paul, had no interest in excluding or 'Judaizing' Gentiles. (2) It was Paul's conviction, and his sole difference with the Jerusalem church, that Gentiles must *first* be won. Thus, as *the* apostle to the Gentiles (Gal. 2:7) he restrains antichrist (2 Thes. 2:7), by evangelism brings in (representatively) the 'fullness of the Gentiles' (Rom. 11:25; 15:19) and, as a decisive eschatological act, initiates Israel's redemption by making her jealous (Rom. 11:11) in taking the 'Gentile' collection to Jerusalem (Acts 20:4; 1 Cor. 16:3). Israel's 'No' issues in Paul's arrest and death, but Paul dies, as did Jesus, knowing God will yet save 'all Israel' in the fullness of time. In interpreting Paul's ministry within the framework of his initial call and of his eschatology, Munck gives due heed to critical emphases; on balance, his work marks a constructive advance.

Like F. C. Baur and W. Schmithals, E. E. Ellis (*Prophecy*, pp. 69ff., 78f., 104–128) also interprets Paul's mission in terms of his conflict with opponents: (1) Because the Hebraists (= 'the circumcision party', Acts 11:2f.; Gal. 2:12) and the Hellenists of Acts 6:1 had respectively a strict and a loose attitude towards the ritual law, they pursued somewhat separate missions in the Diaspora. (2) There a faction of the Hebraists, the Judaizers, sought to impose circumcision on Gentile believers. After the Council of Jerusalem they apparently subordinated their judaizing interests to a boastful triumphalism, licentious tendencies and a claim to mediate divine *gnōsis* through visions of angels. (3) Seeking to maintain the unity of the church, Paul counselled with Hebraist leaders (Gal. 2), worked with Hebraist colleagues (Col. 4:11) and took offerings to the Hebraist church of Jerusalem. (4) Against the opponents and their sympathizers he emphasized justification apart from works together with judgment according to one's works (Gal., Rom., Pastorals), the cruciform model of Christian ministry (Cor., Phil.), the Christocentric character of divine *gnōsis* and of all the charisms (Cor., Col.) and, at length, a church order that would protect the congregations from the false teachers (Pastorals).

(ii) *The Pauline corpus.* E. J. Goodspeed, departing from Harnack and earlier authorities, drew fresh attention to the formation of the Pauline corpus. He conjectured that about AD 90 an admirer of Paul in Ephesus published the apostle's letters (excepting the Pastorals) and wrote Eph. himself as an 'Introduction'. J. Knox (*Philemon*, pp. 98ff.) took the hypothesis a step further and identified that admirer with Onesimus the slave, and later bishop of Ephesus. While receiving considerable acceptance (*cf.* C. L. Mitton, *The Formation of the Pauline Corpus of Letters*, 1955), the theory has been unpersuasive to many. (1) The text demands some addressee, and the primitive omission of such points to a circular letter, hardly suitable for a corpus introduction. (2) Eph. never introduces or ends the Pauline corpus in any ancient MS. (3) It is very doubtful that the content of Eph. can be properly described as a non-Pauline summation of Pauline thought. (4) G. Zuntz (pp. 14ff., 276–279), while recognizing the possibility of an earlier pre-corpus collection in Ephesus, finds that the textual and other evidence points to *c.* AD 100 and to 'the scholarly Alexandrian methods of editorship'. C. F. D. Moule suggests that Luke may be the collector of Paul's letters (*BJRL* 47, 1964–5, pp. 451f.).

(iii) *The provenance and date of the Prison Epistles.* The provenance of Paul's prison letters (Eph., Phil., Col., Phm.), traditionally assigned to Rome, has been a matter of increasing interest since G. S. Duncan, following Lisco and Deissmann, located them in *St Paul's Ephesian Ministry* (1929). Although Acts mentions no Ephesian imprisonment, Paul's letters imply it (*e.g.* 1 Cor. 15:32; 2 Cor. 1:8; 6:5; 11:23); also the setting, journeys and personages of the prison letters fit Ephesus better than distant Rome (*cf.* Phm. 22; Phil. 2:24 with Rom. 15:24ff.; *NTS* 3, 1956–7, pp. 211–218). J. Knox (*Philemon*, p. 33), Michaelis (pp. 205ff., 220), and as to Phil., Bruce (*Acts*, English text, p. 341) and T. W. Manson (*BJRL* 22, 1939, pp. 182ff.) are sympathetic to Duncan. C. H. Dodd (*Studies*, pp. 85–108) and Percy (pp. 473f.) object. (1) The tradition apart from Marcion's Prologue is unanimous for Rome, and such probably (though not certainly) is the meaning of Phil. 4:22. (2) Such references as 1 Cor. 15:32 are to be taken metaphorically. (3) The 'developed theology' of the captivity Epistles suggests the later Roman date. On balance, the Ephesian provenance is inviting and, at least in the case of Phil., may prove to be a permanent advance. However, a Caesarean provenance is advocated by Reicke (in the Bruce *Festschrift*) and by J. A. T. Robinson (*Redating the New Testament*, 1976, pp. 60f.).

(iv) The *authorship* of Paul's letters has been regarded traditionally as the individual enterprise of the apostle. On this assumption it is thought that the 'authentic' letters can be identified in terms of vocabulary, style, idiom and subject-matter and, on the same basis, that they can be divided into Pauline and 'interpolated' sections (*cf.* Schweitzer, pp. 141–150; Schmithals, *Gnosticism*, pp. 302–325; J. C. O'Neill, *Galatians*, 1972; *Romans*, 1975).

However, the effort to determine

Paul's second missionary journey.

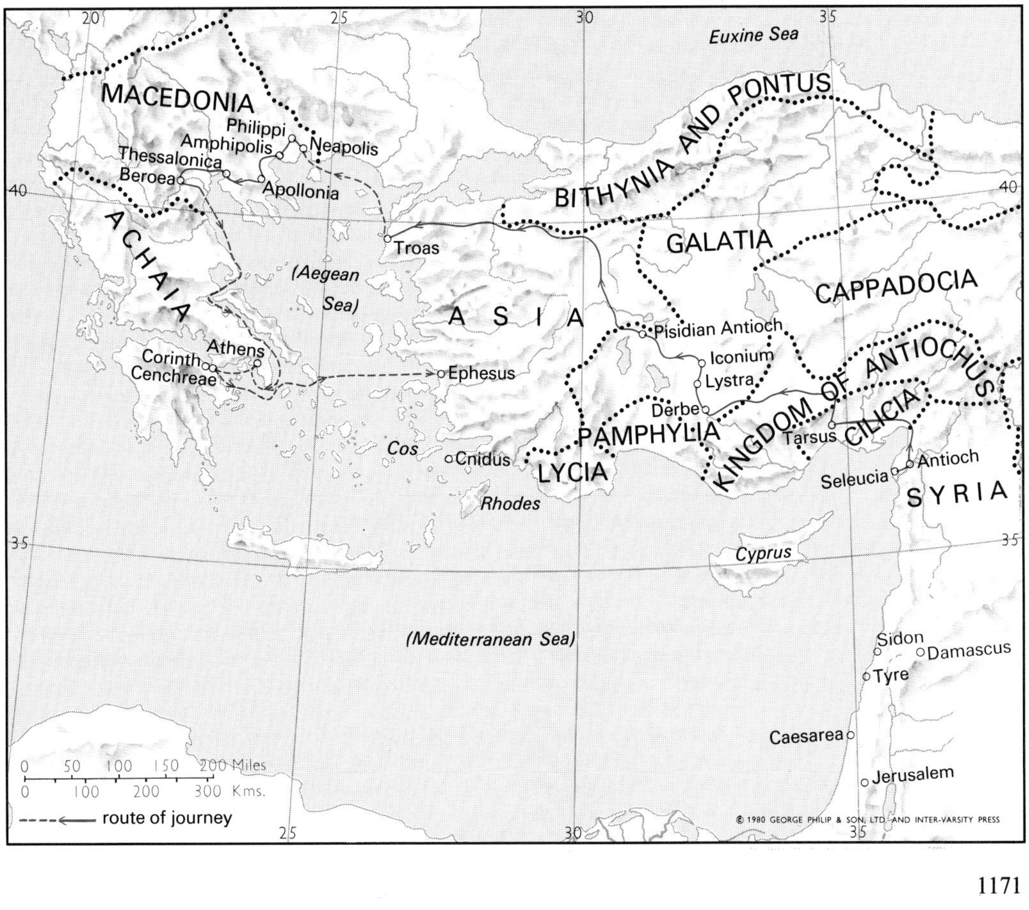

authorship on the basis of literary criteria has now been brought into question by several factors. (1) As Otto Roller showed, *the role of the amanuensis* in ancient letter-writing included an influence on the vocabulary and style of the letter. The hand of such secretaries is clearly present in the Pauline letters—even in the brief note to Philemon (Rom. 16:22; Gal. 6:11; 2 Thes. 3:17; Phm. 19). (2) The *role of the co-senders* of some letters is not entirely clear but, as H. Conzelmann (*NTS* 12, 1965–6, p. 234n.; *cf.* Roller, pp. 153–187) has observed, it probably involved some influence on their composition. (3) Paul worked within a circle of prophets and teachers (*cf.* Acts 13:1; Rom. 16:21f.; Col. 4:10–14), and the work of these colleagues is sometimes incorporated into his letters (*cf.* Ellis, *Prophecy*, pp. 25f., 213). It is reflected in the *many pre-formed pieces* that are used by the apostle —hymns (*e.g.* Phil. 2:5–11; 1 Tim. 3:16), expositions (*e.g.* 1 Cor. 2:6–16; 2 Cor. 6:14–7:1) and creeds (*e.g.* Rom. 1:3f.; 1 Cor. 15:3–7)—a phenomenon widely recognized today, and shows that even the undisputed Pauline letters are not a literary unity.

Paul is the author of the letters under his name in the sense that they were written under his supervision and in part by his hand or dictation, and they were sent out under his authority. But they are not, as a whole, solely his *de novo* compositions. Consequently, the literary criteria traditionally used to determine Pauline authorship can be given little weight in their present form, for they were devised under mistaken assumptions about the Pauline mission praxis and about the process by which the letters were composed.

(v) *Individual Epistles.* Critical emphases within the individual letters have shifted, except in the case of Eph. and the Pastorals, from authorship to other matters. (See separate articles on the various Epistles.) Many British and American scholars favour an early date for *Galatians* (*c.* AD 49 from Antioch) and a S Galatia destination, *i.e.* to the churches founded on Paul's first mission tour. On the Continent, N Galatia, *i.e.* the ethnic region (Acts 16:6; 18:23), and a post-Acts 15 chronology remain popular. The order of *1* and *2 Thessalonians* is reversed by T. W. Manson. Differences of style and subject-matter caused Harnack to suppose that 2 Thes. was written to the Jewish Christians but, more likely, it was directed to Paul's Thessalonian co-workers (Ellis, *Prophecy*, pp. 19ff.). Munck (pp. 36ff.; contrast *NIC*), following Cullmann, identifies the restraining power in 2 Thes. 2:6f. with Paul himself.

The *Corinthians correspondence* includes, in addition to the canonical Epistles, a letter prior to 1 Cor. (5:9) and a 'painful letter' (*cf.* 2 Cor. 2:4; 7:8) which are identified by some scholars with 2 Cor. 6:14–7:1 and 2 Cor. 10–13 respectively. C. K. Barrett (*Second . . . Corinthians*, 1973) and R. V. G. Tasker (*TNTC*) argue for the unity of our second Epistle. A more plausible case for the combination of two letters occurs in *Romans*, where the concluding doxology occurs after 14:23 and 15:33 in a number of MSS, and the addressees in Rom. 1:7, 15 are missing in a few. Of several explanations the one given by T. W. Manson (pp. 225–241), among others, is quite attractive: Rom. 1–15 was a circular letter to which ch. 16, an introduction of Phoebe to the Ephesians, was attached in the Ephesus copy. Nevertheless, the traditional view continues to find wide support (*e.g.* C. E. B. Cranfield, *ICC*, 1975; K. P. Donfried, *The Romans Debate*, 1977).

A 'circular letter' appears to be indicated in the case of *Ephesians* by: (1) the currency of the practice in the 1st century (*cf.* Zuntz, p. 228), and (2) the necessity for, and yet manuscript omission of, an addressee. Such a view would militate against Goodspeed's corpus introduction theory, but it would leave open Sanders' view (*cf.* F. L. Cross, below) that Ephesians is not an Epistle but Paul's 'spiritual testament'. It might also explain the title 'to the Laodiceans', which, according to Tertullian, Marcion gave the letter (*cf.* Col. 4:16). E. Percy, M. Barth and A. van Roon have given the most recent arguments for Pauline authorship; C. L. Mitton in *Epistle to the Ephesians* (1951) argues against it. A more popular 'pro and con' is found in F. L. Cross's symposium, *Studies in Ephesians* (1956). 'Which is more likely,' asks H. J. Cadbury (*NTS* 5, 1958–9, p. 101), 'that an imitator of Paul in the 1st century composed a writing 90 or 95% in accordance with Paul's style or that Paul himself wrote a letter diverging 5 or 10% from his usual style?' With the increased tendency to allow for variation in Pauline

Paul's third missionary journey.

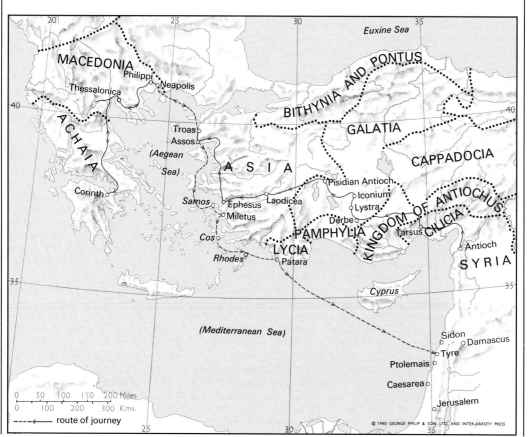

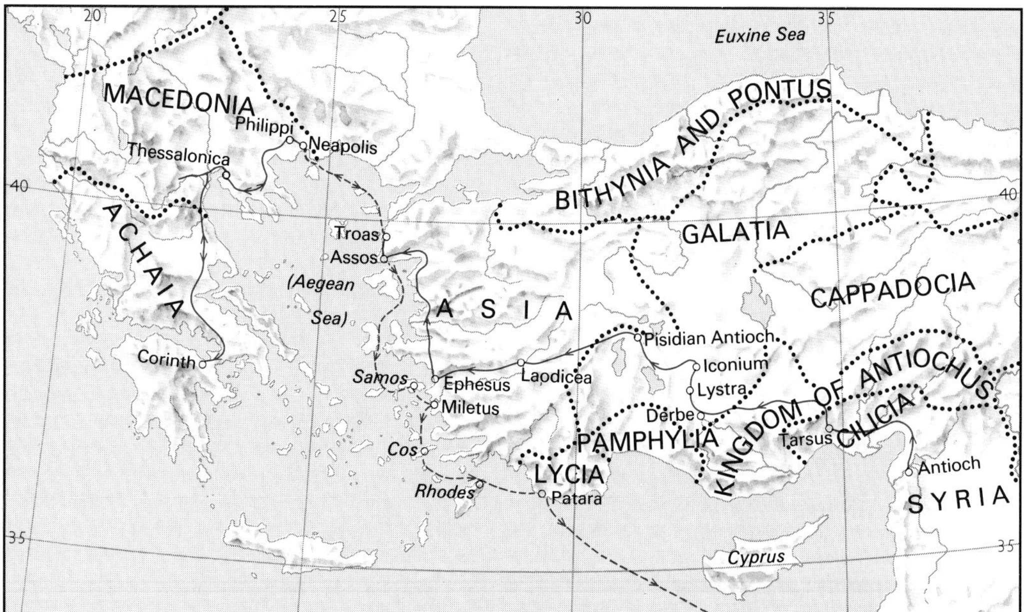

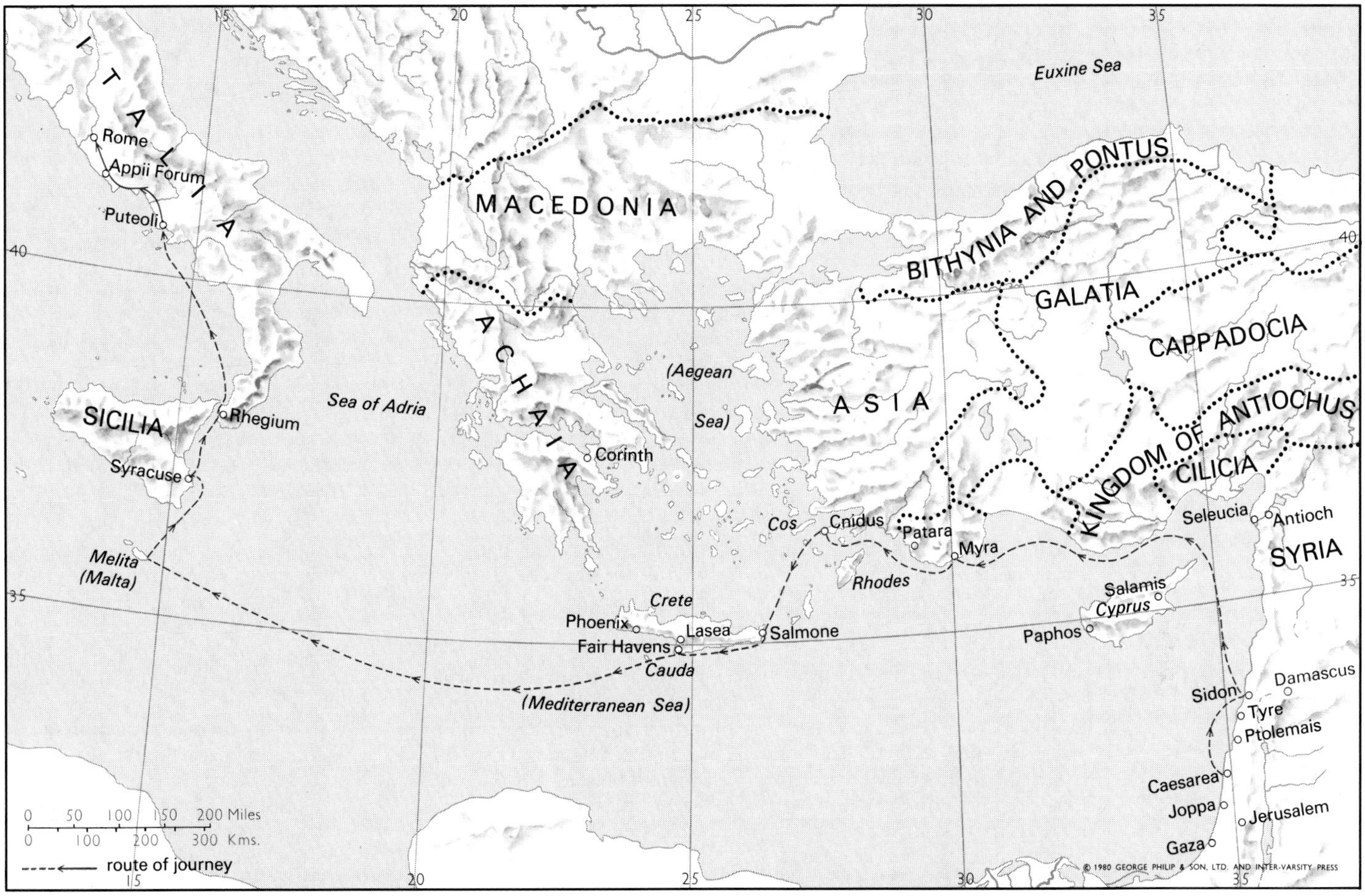

Paul's journey to Rome.

literary and theological expression and a different perception of the nature of authorship (above) the arguments against genuineness become less convincing; they are weakened even further by the Dead Sea Scrolls parallels (*cf.* Flusser, p. 263; Murphy-O'Connor, pp. 115–131, 159–178).

Outside Germany most students consider the 19th-century 'non-Pauline' verdicts valid only for the Pastorals. (In recent years Pauline authorship of the Epistle to the Hebrews has been seriously argued only by the Roman Catholic scholar William Leonard.) Anglo-American opinion (and also Schmithals, *Gnostics*) has tended to agree with P. N. Harrison's 'fragment hypothesis', *i.e.* Pauline fragments supplemented and edited; most Continentals who reject the Pastorals favour, with Kümmel (*INT*), a later Paulinist author. The case for genuineness has found support in Roller's 'secretary hypothesis', *i.e.* that stylistic variations stem from Paul's amanuensis, whom some suggest to be Luke (*e.g.* C. F. D. Moule, *BJRL* 47, 1965, pp. 430–452); the traditional view has been argued anew by Spicq and Michaelis. The growing dissatisfaction with Harrison's hypothesis expressed, *e.g.*, in Guthrie (*TNTC*), Kelly and Metzger (*ExpT* 70, 1958–9, pp. 91ff.) may represent a general re-appraisal of the prevailing view (*cf. EQ* 32, pp. 151–161). But see M. Dibelius and H. Conzelmann, *The Pastoral Epistles*, 1972. See also *Timothy and Titus, Epistles to (**IV**).

IV. Pauline thought

a. Background

The Reformation emphasis upon righteousness or justification by faith (Rom. 1:17) continued in the following centuries to be the controlling factor in the interpretation of Paul's doctrine. With the rise of literary criticism the absence of this motif became sufficient reason to suspect or even reject a 'Pauline' letter; and in the incipient development of Paulinism, *i.e.* the system of Pauline thought, 'righteousness' was regarded as the key to the apostle's mind. (In the following sketch compare especially Schweitzer, *Interpreters*.)

(i) *Paul's doctrine of redemption.* L. Usteri (1824) and A. F. Daehne (1835) sought to explain the whole of Pauline thought in terms of the imputed righteousness of Romans (*e.g.* 3:21ff.). In contrast, the rationalist H. E. G. Paulus, starting from texts stressing the 'new creation' and sanctification (*e.g.* 2 Cor. 5:17; Rom. 8:29), insisted that Pauline righteousness was an ethical, moral concept; faith in Jesus meant ultimately the faith of Jesus. These two ideas and their relationship had a continuing significance through the 19th century.

F. C. Baur, within the framework of Hegelian idealism, sought at first (1845) to explain Paul in terms of the Spirit given through union with Christ by faith. Later, however, Baur reverted to the Reformation pattern, a compartmentalized presentation of the various Pauline doctrines without any attempt to view them from a unified concept. This *loci* approach was followed by succeeding writers who gave minute descriptions of Pauline doctrine, innocently supposing 'that in the description they possessed at the same time an explanation' (Schweitzer, *Interpreters*, p. 36).

Nevertheless, some writers pressed towards the discovery of a unifying concept for Pauline thought. R. A. Lipsius (1853) had recognized two views of redemption in Paul, the juridical (justification) and the ethical ('new creation'). Hermann Luedemann, in his book *The Anthropology of the Apostle Paul* (1872), concluded that the two views of redemption actually rested on two views of the nature of man. In Paul's earlier 'Jewish' view (Gal.; Rom. 1–4) redemption was a juridical verdict of acquittal; for the mature Paul (Rom. 5–8) it was an ethical–physical transformation from 'flesh' to 'spirit' through communion with the Holy Spirit. The source of the first idea was Christ's death; the second, his resurrection. On the other hand, Richard Kabisch concluded that Pauline redemption essentially meant deliverance from coming judgment, and its significance, therefore, was to be found in the eschatology of the apostle. The Christian must walk in newness of life to show that he actually shared Christ's resurrection. 'Spiritual' life and death in the modern religious sense are unknown to Paul; both concepts are, *e.g.* in Rom. 6, always physical; and the new life is a mystical union with Christ. Thus, future deliverance from satanic powers is anticipated by the possession of the Holy Spirit, who manifests the new age in the present and inseminates our corporal being with a super-earthly substance.

For both Luedemann and Kabisch: (1) Paul's doctrine of redemption emanates from one fundamental concept. (2) It is a physical redemption to be understood in terms of Pauline anthropology. (3) To be redeemed means to share Christ's death and resurrection, which involves union with Christ and the abolition of the 'flesh'. (4) Although future, this redemption is mediated in the present by the Holy Spirit.

But questions remained. In what sense can Christ's death and resurrection be repeated in the believer? In what sense can the Christian be 'a new creation' and yet outwardly appear unchanged? Albert Schweitzer, building upon the interpretations of Luedemann and Kabisch, sought an answer in the following synthesis. (1) Paul, as did Jesus, interpreted Jesus' death and resurrection to be eschatological, *i.e.* an end of the world event, bringing the kingdom of God and the resurrection life to all the elect. (2) But the world did not end, and believers did not in fact enter into resurrection life; in time the temporal separation between Christ's resurrection and the (anticipated) resurrection of believers became the chief problem for Paul's teaching. (3) To answer it Paul posits a 'physical mysticism': through the sacraments the Holy Spirit mediates in the present time Christ's resurrection to the 'last generation' believers. (4) This present union with Christ in the Spirit ensures to the believer a share in the 'Messianic resurrection' at the parousia.

(ii) *Pauline eschatology*. Thus, Schweitzer set the stage for 20th-century discussions of Pauline eschatology. It was his great merit that he sought to understand Paul's thought in terms of one fundamental concept, that he recognized the central importance of eschatology and (Jewish) anthropology in the apostle's doctrine of redemption, and that he recognized the Holy Spirit and the *en Christō* union as the realization of the new age in the present. But Schweitzer's interpretation of Paul's eschatology as a makeshift expedient (and as a sacramental mysticism) is questionable, to say the least. For, as Hamilton's critique has pointed out (pp. 50ff.), the exalted Christ, not the 'delay' in the parousia, determines Paul's eschatology. Also, if Paul's thought patterns are Jewish (as Schweitzer rightly recognized), sacramental mysticism is a rather awkward explanation of the realism of the 'new creation' in Christ.

(iii) *Paul's thought patterns*. In addition to eschatology as the key to Paulinism, a closely related question important for the future also had its rise in the 19th century. Are Paul's thought patterns Jewish or Hellenistic? Kabisch and Schweitzer insisted that Pauline thought was Jewish to the core. Others, following F. C. Baur's reconstruction of Paul as the 'Hellenizer of Christianity', interpreted Pauline anthropology and eschatology from the standpoint of a modified Platonic dualism. The antithesis between 'flesh' and 'spirit' in Rom. 6–8 was an ethical dualism, and 'dying' and 'rising' a spiritual transformation. This has its roots in an anthropological dualism; thus, in the future, redemption involves the deliverance of the 'soul' from its house of clay. But Paul also speaks of the resurrection of the whole man from death (1 Thes. 4; 1 Cor. 15). Otto Pfleiderer (*Paulinism*, 1877, I, p. 264) concluded that Paul held Jewish and Gk. views simultaneously, 'side by side, without any thought of their essential inconsistency'. In interpreting Pauline eschatology elsewhere (*cf.* Schweitzer, *Interpreters*, p. 70) he posits a development from 1 Thes. 4 through 1 Cor. 15 to 2 Cor. 5. The first is simply Jewish resurrection eschatology; in 2 Cor. 5 the believer goes to the heavenly realms at death.

b. The origin of Paul's religion: Hellenism

20th-century studies of Pauline thought have devoted themselves primarily to three questions. What is the relation between Paul and Jesus? What are the sources for Pauline thought? What is the role of eschatology in the mind of Paul?

(i) *Paul's relation to Jesus*. The distinction raised a half century earlier between 'juridical' (Rom. 1–4) and 'ethical' (Rom. 5–8) righteousness had borne much fruit, and the latter came to be regarded as the more central and decisive Pauline concept. A. Deissmann (pp. 148ff.) viewed 'in Christ' as an intimate spiritual communion with Christ, a Christ mysticism; more often the 'mysticism' was interpreted as a sacramental reality based upon Jewish eschatology (Schweitzer) or the pagan mysteries (J. Weiss, *Earliest Christianity*, 1959 (1937), 2, pp. 463f.). Somewhat later J. S. Stewart (*A Man in Christ*, 1935, pp. 150ff.) reflected this trend in British scholarship, regarding union with Christ as the central element in Paul's thought. This emphasis had important consequences for the course of Pauline studies in the 20th century.

The contrast between the 'liberal Jesus' and Paul's indwelling and yet transcendent Christ called forth at the turn of the century a spate of books on the relationship of Jesus and Paul (*cf.* P. Feine, *Paulus*, pp. 158ff.). W. Wrede's influential *Paulus* (1905) put the matter in the starkest terms: Paul was not truly a disciple of Jesus; he was actually the second founder of Christianity. The individual piety and future salvation of the Rabbi Jesus had been transformed by the theologian Paul into a present redemption through the death and resurrection of a christ-god. Paul's ideas could not, of course, be accepted at face value. To do so would, as Weinel (*St Paul*, 1906, p. 11) remarked, 'stifle the claims of reason for the sake of Christianity, for reason is ever-repeating . . . that the modern conception of the world is the right one'. Nevertheless, the historian's task remained. If Paul's doctrines did not arise from and build upon Jesus' mind, what was their origin?

(ii) *Sources of Pauline thought.* F. C. Baur sought to explain the mind of Paul in the context of church controversy: Paul was the champion of Gentile freedom. For Schweitzer the origin of Paul's thought was his peculiar eschatological problem forged in the mental cauldron of late Judaism. However, the rising 'History of Religion' (*Religionsgeschichte*) school found no evidence to ground Paul's sacramental mysticism in Judaism. While recognizing the eschatological problem, it built upon Baur's 'Gentile' Paul and developed still another elaborate reconstruction of the apostolic age. Represented most notably by R. Reitzenstein and W. Bousset, it interpreted Paulinism in the framework of Oriental–Hellenistic mystery religions. The Mysteries spoke, as did Paul, of a dying-rising god, of 'Lord', of sacramental redemption, of 'mysteries', *gnōsis* and 'spirit'. As a boy in Tarsus and later as a missionary the apostle came under the influence of these ideas, and they exerted a profound influence on his theology. Schweitzer (*Interpreters*, pp. 179–236), H. A. A. Kennedy, G. Wagner and J. G. Machen (pp. 255–290) subjected this reconstruction to a thorough critique, pointing out that, in ignoring the OT–Judaism background of the parallels (which Kennedy showed to be quite plausible) and the late date of its sources, the theory reflected a weakness in method. (*Cf.* also R. E. Brown, *The Semitic Background of the Term 'Mystery'* . . ., 1968). The principal contribution of the History of Religion school was to raise the important question of Paul's theological relation to the Gentile religious world. The 'mystery religion' reconstruction did not win general approval, but in a more recent gnostic dress its general outlines continue to be strongly advocated.

The mystery religion parallels paled; nevertheless, the conviction remained strong that Paul's thought was substantially influenced by the Greek world of ideas. R. Bultmann (1910) had shown the affinity of Paul's literary style with the Stoic diatribe. Others regarded Paul's doctrine of the 'corporate body' (*cf.* W. L. Knox, *Gentiles*, pp. 160ff.), his natural theology in Rom. 1 (*cf.* Acts 17) and his concept of conscience (E. Norden, *Agnostos Theos*, 1913) as rooted in Stoicism. The inadequacy of these conclusions was pointed out, respectively, by E. Best (pp. 83ff.), B. Gaertner (pp. 133–169) and C. A. Pierce (pp. 16ff.). Gaertner argues that Paul's 'natural theology' is thoroughly OT–Jewish; however, Pierce (pp. 22ff., 57ff.) concludes that the NT adopts in the case of 'conscience' a general usage of popular Gk. thought.

To determine the relationship of Paul to pagan religious thought, the area currently receiving most attention is Gnosticism. This religious–philosophical movement stressed a metaphysical dualism, deliverance from 'matter' through a divine gift and power of *gnōsis*, *i.e.* a special knowledge of God, and mediating angels to assist one to salvation. Long ago J. B. Lightfoot (*Colossians and Philemon*, 1886, pp. 71–111) detected elements of Gnosticism in the Colossian heresy. Early in the 20th century Bousset and J. Weiss (*op. cit.*, 2, pp. 650f.) urged that aspects of Paul's own thought lay in this direction. R. Bultmann and his pupil W. Schmithals became the chief representatives and developers of Bousset's reconstruction today. From existentialist considerations Bultmann again made 'justification' a central Pauline motif, although it was far from a return to Baur or to the Reformers; for the same reasons Paul's anthropology was given a thorough exposition (*Theology* 1, pp. 190–227). But the real clue to Bultmann's understanding of Paulinism is his grounding of Pauline thought in a syncretistic Judaism and Christianity. From this background Paul obtained a number of concepts, *e.g.* sacramental redemption and ethical dualism, which were Gnostic or gnosticized in some degree (*Theology* 1, pp. 63ff., 124ff., 151–188). While Paul opposed the Gnostics, *e.g.* at Colossae, in the process he modified not only his terminology but also his concepts, particularly his Christology (Messiah Jesus becomes a heavenly Lord; *cf.* Bousset) and cosmogony (the demon-controlled world is redeemed by a heavenly man; *cf.* W. L. Knox, *Gentiles*, pp. 220ff.; but see G. B. Caird, *Principalities and Powers*, 1956; W. Foerster, *TDNT* 2, pp. 566–574).

Schweitzer (*Interpreters*, p. 231) predicted that a 'Hellenized' Paulinism was a half-way house which must carry its conclusions even to the genesis of Christianity. His prediction was more than fulfilled by the discovery in 1947 of the Dead Sea Scrolls with their ethical dualism and emphasis on 'knowledge'. The Scrolls were an embarrassment for Bultmann's reconstruction, for 'pre-Gnostic' was about the closest identification most scholars cared to make for them. Also, there is little reason to believe that Paul reflects, *e.g.*, 'an earlier Gnostic doctrine about the descent of a redeemer, especially since there is no evidence that such a doctrine existed' (R. M. Grant, *Gnosticism*, p. 69; *cf.* pp. 39–69; R. McL. Wilson, pp. 27f., 57f.). Almost all else Bultmann chose to refer to Gnostic influences likewise suffered from the same chronological strictures. Grant, looking back to Schweitzer, interprets Gnosticism as arising from a failure of the apocalyptic hope; unlike Schweitzer, Grant views Paul as a man whose spiritual world lies somewhere between Jewish apocalyptic and the fully developed Gnosticism of the 2nd century (p. 158). Grant sees the latter tendency in Paul's interpretation of Christ's resurrection as a realized (eschatological) victory over the cosmic powers. More cautiously R. McL. Wilson, in a valuable assessment (*The Gnostic Problem*, 1958, pp. 75–80, 108, 261), concludes that Paul adopts a contemporary cosmogony and terminology only to oppose Gnosticism and to interpret Jesus' authority over the (Gnostic) 'powers'; the apostle rejects the gnosticizing interpretation. However, J. Dupont (*Gnosis: La Connaissance Religieuse dans les Épîtres de Saint Paul*[2], 1960) and Ellis (*Prophecy*, pp. 45–62) argue that Pauline *gnōsis* is strictly OT–Jewish.

All the 'Greek' reconstructions of Paul have their root in Baur's interpretation of Paul as the exponent of Gentile Christianity. When W. Wrede and others recognized the redemptive–eschatological character of Pauline thought, the apostle was set in opposition not only to Jewish Christianity but to the 'liberal' Jesus himself. But, as Schweitzer had shown, the 'liberal' Jesus was not the Jesus of the Gospels. Bultmann (*Theology* 1, pp. 23, 30ff.) accepted Schweitzer's 'apocalyptic' Jesus but insisted that God's demand for man's decision, not the apocalyptic window-dressing, was the essence of Jesus' eschatology. The suffering, resurrected and returning Son of man was a 'mythologized' picture of the later 'Hellenized' Christology. The mind of Paul remained far distant from the mind of the earthly Jesus or of his earliest disciples. One's estimate of Paulinism is closely tied, therefore, to one's estimate of the Gospels' picture of Jesus.

A number of mediating scholars, taking their cue from B. Weiss, see 'development' as the key to Paul's thought. In view of fading parousia hopes Paul's anthropology and eschatology move towards a Platonic dualism (Dodd) and his cosmogony towards Gnosticism (R. M. Grant).

In its present *religionsgeschichtliche* format the interpretation of Paul in terms of pagan religious ideas is subject to a number of criticisms. There is a tendency to convert parallels into influences and influences into sources. Some of its 'sources' for Pauline thought come from a period considerably later than the apostle's lifetime. (Bultmann's Paul may have more than a casual relation to the Gnostic 'Paul' of the ultra-Tübingen school.) Also, its historical inquiry has sometimes been compromised by an inadequate world-view. For example, Bultmann, like Weinel, views the natural world as a 'self-subsistent unity immune from the interference of supernatural powers' (*Kerygma and Myth*, ed. H. W. Bartsch, 1953, p. 7; *cf.* pp. 5–8, 216, 222).

Perhaps the most basic questions are these: Is Paulinism best understood as an amalgam, gathered here and there, or as the expansion and application of a central tradition rooted in the mind of Jesus Christ and the earliest church? Is Paul's mind most adequately explained within a religious syncretism or within the context of apocalyptic Judaism and the primitive church? Does the 'gnosticizing' of Christian thought begin in Paul and pre-Pauline Christianity (Bultmann) or in Paul's opponents and wayward converts; and does it arise from a failure of the primitive eschatology in Paul (Grant) or from a misunderstanding of it (and of Paul) in his churches? *Cf.* Ellis, *Prophecy*, pp. 45–62, 101–115.

c. The origin of Paul's religion: Judaism

(i) *Paul's link with the earliest church.* Both Ritschl and von Hofmann had argued, *contra* Baur, for the unity of Paul's teaching with that of the earliest church. A. Resch, in the 'Jesus or Paul' debate, upheld this view. His thorough investigation of *Der Paulinismus und die Logia Jesu* (1904) concluded that the words of Jesus were a primary source of Pauline thought. But could not rather Paul be the source of the Synoptic Jesus? The research of several writers (*e.g.* Dungan; F. F. Bruce, *BJRL* 56, 1973–4, pp. 317–335) has substantiated the priority argued by Resch.

C. H. Dodd (*Preaching*, p. 56) established that a *kerygma*, *i.e.* a gospel-core proclamation, underlay both the Gospels and Paul, 'a tradition coeval with the Church itself'. The same writer (*According to the Scriptures*, 1952, pp. 108ff.), building upon Rendel Harris' *Testimonies* (1916, 1920), found a 'substructure of NT theology' to which Paul was indebted and whose origin pointed to Christ himself. E. E. Ellis, examining the hermeneutical principles of *Paul's Use of the Old Testament* (pp. 97f., 107–112; *idem*, *Prophecy*, *passim*), suggested that some common (pre-Pauline) exegetical tradition originated with 'prophets' of the earliest church. E. Lohmeyer (*Kyrios Jesus*, 1928) interprets Phil. 2:5ff. as a primitive Christian hymn probably arising in Aram. circles (*cf.* L. Cerfaux, pp. 283ff.; R. P. Martin, *Carmen Christi*, 1967; E. G. Selwyn, *First Epistle of St Peter*, 1946, pp. 365–369, 458–466). Similarly, the pre-Pauline character of the *Primitive Christian Catechism* (1940) was demonstrated by P. Carrington.

O. Cullmann ('Tradition', pp. 69–99), K. H. Rengstorf (*TDNT* 1, pp. 413–443), H. Riesenfeld (*The Gospel Tradition*, 1969, pp. 1–29) and B. Gerhardsson point to a rationale for this understanding of Christian origins. The NT concept of apostle has a similar origin to that of the rabbinic *šālîaḥ*, an authorized agent equivalent to the sender himself. The apostles witnessed to a tradition or *paradosis*, given to them by Christ. 'But since everything has not been revealed to each individual apostle, each one must first pass on his testimony to another (Gal. 1:18; 1 Cor. 15:11), and only the entire *paradosis*, to which all the apostles contribute, constitutes the *paradosis* of Christ' (Cullmann, 'Tradition', p. 73). Thus, as an 'apostle' Paul's message is defined in terms of what he has received: his catechesis, kerygma, and the wider 'tradition' should be, and critical study finds them to be, rooted in the earliest church and ultimately in the teaching of Jesus. This teaching of Jesus seems to have included not merely moral instruction or apocalyptic warning, but also biblical exposition (Ellis, *Prophecy*, pp. 240–253) and a creative, theological synthesis which envisaged a post-resurrection ministry by his disciples (*cf.* J. Jeremias, *Jesus' Promise to the Nations*, 1958). If these writers are correct, the dichotomy between Paul and the primitive Jewish church, which has been urged from Baur to Bultmann, is an assumption which must be abandoned.

(ii) *Paul's background.* To understand a writer it would seem to be proper to give priority to that milieu to which he appeals and to which he presumably belongs. In interpreting Pauline concepts it is not the categories of a 2nd-century Gnosticism (however easily they may be 'read back') but the categories of 1st-century rabbinic/apocalyptic Judaism which demand first claim upon the critical historian's mind.

The nature of 1st-century Judaism is complex, and it is easy to overdraw or wrongly define the contrast between the 'syncretistic' and 'orthodox', terms not to be equated with 'Hellenist' and 'Hebraist' or with '*diaspora*' and 'Palestinian' (*cf.* Acts 6:1; Ellis, *Prophecy*, pp. 106f., 125f., 245ff.; Davies, pp. 1–8). Nevertheless, considerable research relates the thought of Paul, the Pharisee and 'Hebrew of the Hebrews' (Phil. 3:5), with Palestinian rabbinism and apocalypticism rather than with a syncretistic Judaism. Van Unnik has raised at least the probability that Paul's early youth was passed not in Tarsus but in Jerusalem. Certainly Paul used the Septuagint, but this translation has now been found among the DSS. He preached among the *diaspora*, and he may have been acquainted with the syncretistic Judaism exemplified by Philo. But with the doubtful exception of the Wisdom of Solomon, his relationship to the *diaspora* literature is not direct and probably reflects only traditions which both had in common. His more significant relationships lie in another direction. W. D. Davies and others have shown that Qumran and Rabbinic Judaism form the background of many Pauline concepts formerly labelled 'Hellenistic'. Likewise, the literary form of Paul's biblical exposition agrees with rabbinic models. The Dead Sea Scrolls have confirmed in remarkable fashion the Jewishness of Pauline and NT backgrounds. (*Cf.* Bruce, *Qumran Texts*, pp. 66–77; Flusser; M. Black, *The Scrolls and Christian Origins*, 1961; Ellis, *Prophecy*, pp. 35, 57ff., 213–220; Murphy-O'Connor.)

(iii) *Specific Pauline concepts.* Passing to specific Pauline concepts, anthropology and the nature of the 'in Christ' relationship have had a central importance since the days of F. C. Baur. It is widely recognized today that Paul views man in an OT–Jewish framework and not in the Platonic dualism of the Hellenistic world (*cf.* *LIFE; Bultmann, *Theology* 1, pp. 209f.; Cullmann, *Immortality*, pp. 28–39; J. A. T. Robinson, *The Body*, 1952). The corporate 'body of Christ' also is best understood not in terms of a Gnostic mythology (Käsemann) nor a Stoic metaphor (W. L. Knox) but as the OT–Jewish concept of corporate solidarity. Davies (*Judaism*, pp. 53ff.) has related Paul's thought here to the rabbinic speculations on the body of Adam. R. P. Shedd's *Man in Community* (1958) correctly finds Paul's ultimate rationale in the realism of Semitic thought patterns, as they are applied to Messiah and his people (*cf.* J. A. T. Robinson, *The Body*, 1953, pp. 56ff.; Kümmel, *Man*; J. deFraine, *Adam and the Family of Man*, 1965, pp. 245–270; Ellis, *Prophecy*, pp. 170ff.). R. Gundry (pp. 228–241) falls short of this realism in viewing the concept metaphorically. D. R. G. Owen, in *Body and Soul* (1956), offers an illuminating comparison of biblical anthropology with the modern scientific view of man. The study of D. Cox (*Jung and St Paul*, 1959) seeks to define in other areas the relevance of Paul for current faith and practice.

Whether Paul's eschatology is rooted in Jewish or Greek concepts is a matter of continuing debate. The importance of this question for Paulinism requires that some detailed attention now be given to it.

d. The eschatological essence of Pauline thought

C. A. A. Scott's well-written *Christianity according to Saint Paul* (1927), over against Albert Schweitzer's eschatological interpretation, identifies salvation as the fundamental concept of Paulinism. But what is the factor determining the character of Paul's 'already but not yet' redemption theology? Not grasping Schweitzer's real question, Scott did not really pose an alternative: he found a motif to describe Paul, not a key to explain him. (*Cf.* also Christological approaches, *e.g.* L. Cerfaux, *Christ in the Theology of St Paul*, 1959.) Schweitzer may not have stated the problem, or the solution, satisfactorily; but his identification of the key concept remains valid.

(i) *The views of Schweitzer and Dodd.* Until recently discussion of NT eschatology has revolved about the views of Schweitzer and C. H. Dodd. (For Bultmann, eschatology has nothing to do with the future or with history; it is the realm of existential living. Like F. C. Baur, Bultmann uses NT language to clothe an imposing philosophy of religion; exegesis becomes the servant of existentialism. *Cf.* N. Q. Hamilton's *The Holy Spirit and Eschatology in Paul*, 1957, pp. 41–90, for a lucid summation and critique of the eschatology of Schweitzer, Dodd and Bultmann.) Schweitzer argued that Paul's '*en Christō*' concept arose from the failure of the kingdom of God, *i.e.* the end of the world, to arrive at Christ's death and resurrection. Against Schweitzer, Dodd contended that in Christ's death the 'age to come' did arrive; eschatology was 'realized' as much as it ever would be in history. The believer already participates in the kingdom (*e.g.* Col. 1:13), and at death he fully enters the eternal, *i.e.* eschatological, realm. Eschatology, therefore, does not refer to an end-of-the-world event; in Platonic fashion it is to be understood 'spatially' rather than temporally, eternity over against time. How, then, is Paul's anticipation of a future parousia to be accounted for? Believing it to be a hangover from apocalyptic Judaism (and quite alien to the central message of Jesus), Dodd goes back to Pfleiderer for an answer: in 1 Thes. 4 Paul has a strictly Jewish eschatology but in 1 Cor. 15 modifies it with the concept of a 'spiritual' body; 2 Cor. 5, which then places the believer in heaven at death, expresses the view of the mature (and 'Greek') Paul. J. A. T. Robinson's *Jesus and His Coming* (1958, pp. 160ff.) is essentially an elaboration of Dodd's thesis.

It is Dodd's great merit that he saw, as Schweitzer did not, the essential meaning for NT thought (and for the relevance of the gospel in the present world) of the 'realized' aspect of the kingdom of God. But in adopting an unbiblical Platonic view of time Dodd failed to do justice to the futurist and temporal character of eschatological redemption. Also, his development of Pauline eschatology involved an un-Pauline anthropological dualism and, in part, reflected a misunderstanding of the texts. Both Schweitzer and Dodd made admirable attempts to achieve a comprehensive interpretation of NT eschatology. Although 'futurist or realized' has now been recognized as an improper either/or, the contributions of Schweitzer and Dodd remain fundamental landmarks in the progress of the research.

The important monographs of W. G. Kümmel (*Promise and Fulfilment*, 1957, pp. 141–155; and *NTS* 5, 1958–9, pp. 113–126) argued convincingly that both 'present' and 'future' eschatology are equally and permanently rooted in the teaching of Jesus and of Paul. Oscar Cullmann's most significant publications, *Christ and Time* (1951) and *Salvation in History* (1967), contrasted the Platonic idea of redemption, *i.e.* to escape the time 'circle' at death, with the biblical concept that redemption is tied to resurrection in future 'linear' time, *i.e.* at the parousia. These works, plus a proper appreciation of Paul's OT–Jewish anthropology and of the Semitic concept of corporate solidarity, form a proper foundation for understanding Paul's eschatology—and thus his total doctrine of redemption.

(ii) *The pre-eminence of a theology of redemption.* Historical research since the Reformation has recognized that Pauline theology is above all a theology of redemption. The 19th century witnessed a growing emphasis upon the present 'union with Christ' (rather than imputed righteousness) as the central aspect of this redemption. Since Albert Schweitzer two eschatological *foci*, Christ's death and resurrection and the parousia, have been recognized as the key to the meaning of 'union with Christ'.

Jesus Christ in his death and resurrection defeated for all time the 'powers' of the old aeon—sin, death and the demonic 'rulers of this darkness' (Eph. 6:12; Col. 2:15). Now Christians were crucified, resurrected, glorified and placed at God's right hand with Christ (Gal. 2:20; Eph. 2:5f.). 'In Christ' Christians have entered the resurrection age; the solidarity with the first Adam in sin and death has been replaced by the solidarity with the eschatological Adam in righteousness and immortal life. (* LIFE.)

This corporate redemption in and with Jesus Christ, this 'new age' reality, which the believer enters at conversion (*cf.* Rom. 6), finds an individual actualization in the present and the future (*cf.* Ellis, *NTS* 6, 1959–60, pp. 211–216). In the present life it means a transformation through the indwelling Spirit, the firstfruits of the new resurrection life (Rom. 8:23; 2 Cor. 5:5), of one's ethic (Col. 2:20; 3:1, 9f., 12) and of one's total world view (Rom. 12:1ff.). However, in the midst of moral–psychological renewal the Christian remains, in his mortality, under the death claims of the old age. But this too is to be understood no longer in terms of 'in Adam', but as a part of the 'in Christ' reality; for 'the sufferings of Christ abound to us' (2 Cor. 1:5; *cf.* Phil. 3:10; Col. 1:24), and the Christian dead have fallen asleep 'in Jesus' (1 Thes. 4:14; *cf.* Phil. 2:17; 2 Tim. 4:6). The individual actualization of Christ's sufferings is, of course, in no way a self-redemption process; rather, it means to be identified with Christ 'in the likeness of his death' (Rom. 6:5). The 'likeness of his resurrection' awaits its actualization at the parousia, when the individual Christian, raised to immortal life, shall be 'conformed to the image of his Son, that he might be the first-born among many brethren' (Rom. 8:29; *cf.* 1 Cor. 15:53ff.).

Thus, Pauline redemption is not a 'spiritual' deliverance culminating in the escape of the 'soul' at death (Dodd); it is a physical redemption culminating in the deliverance of the whole man at the parousia (Cullmann). It is to be understood not in terms of a Platonic dualism but in the framework of an OT–Jewish view of man as a unified being and as one who lives not only as an individual but in 'corporate solidarities'. The future that has become present in the resurrection of Jesus Christ is a future which the Christian realizes now only corporately, as the 'body of Christ'. However, at the parousia faith shall become sight, 'away' shall become 'at home', and the solidarities of the new age shall become individually actualized in all their glory, both in man and in the whole created order (Rom. 8:19–21). This is the living hope of Paul's heart; it is also the meaning of his theology.

BIBLIOGRAPHY. M. Barth, *Ephesians*, 2 vols., 1974; E. Best, *One Body in Christ*, 1955; G. Bornkamm, *Early Christian Experience*, 1969; *idem*, *Paul*, 1971; W. Bousset, *Kurios Christos*, 1913, E.T. 1970; F. F. Bruce, *The Acts of the Apostles*, 1951 (*NLC*, 1954); *idem*, *Biblical Exegesis in the Qumran Texts*, 1959; *idem*, *Paul and Jesus*, 1974; *idem*, *Paul*, 1978; R. Bultmann, *Theology of the New Testament*, 2 vols., 1952; H. C. C. Cavallin, *Life after Death . . . in 1 Cor. 15*, 1974; O. Cullmann, *Immortality of the Soul or Resurrection of the Dead?*, 1958; *idem*, 'The Tradition', *The Early Church*, 1956, pp. 57–99; N. A. Dahl, *Studies in Paul*, 1977; W. D. Davies, *Paul and Rabbinic Judaism*, 1955; A. Deissmann, *Paul*, 1927; C. H. Dodd, *New Testament Studies*, 1953; *idem*, *The Apostolic Preaching and its Development*, 1936; K. P. Donfried (ed.), *The Romans Debate*, 1977; J. W. Drane, *Paul, Libertine or Legalist?*, 1976; D. L. Dungan, *The Sayings of Jesus in the Churches of Paul*, 1971; E. E. Ellis, *Paul's Use of the Old Testament*, 1957; *idem*, *Prophecy and Hermeneutic*, 1978; D. Flusser, 'The Dead Sea Scrolls and Pre-Pauline Christianity', *Aspects of the Dead Sea Scrolls*, ed. C. Rabin and Y. Yadin, 1958, pp. 215–266; F. J. Foakes-Jackson and K. Lake, *BC*, 5 vols., 1933; J. Friedrich (ed.), *Rechtfertigung*, 1976; V. P. Furnish, *Theology and Ethics in Paul*, 1968; B. Gaertner, *The Areopagus Speech and Natural Revelation*, 1955; W. W. Gasque and R. P. Martin, *Apostolic History and the Gospel* (F. F. Bruce *Festschrift*), 1970; B. Gerhardsson, *Die Anfänge der Evangelien Tradition*, 1977; E. J. Goodspeed, *The Meaning of Ephesians*, 1933; R. M. Grant, *Gnosticism and Early Christianity*, 1959; R. H. Gundry, *Soma*, 1974; E. Haenchen, *Acts*, 1971; A. T. Hanson, *Studies in Paul's . . . Theology*, 1974; P. N. Harrison, *The Problem of the Pastoral Epistles*, 1921; H. Hübner, *Das Besetz bei Paulus*, 1978; E. Käsemann, *Perspectives on Paul*, 1971; J. N. D. Kelly, *The Pastoral Epistles*, 1963; H. A. A. Kennedy, *Saint Paul and the Mystery Religions*, 1913; S. Kim, *An Exposition of Paul's Gospel* (Diss., Manchester), 1977; J. Knox, *Philemon among the Letters of Paul*, 1959 (1935); W. L. Knox, *Saint Paul and the Church of the Gentiles*, 1939; W. G. Kümmel, *INT*, 1975; *idem*, *Man in the New Testament*, 1963; *idem*, *The New Testament . . . Problems*, 1972; *idem*, *The Theology of the New Testament*, 1973; U. Luz, *Das Geschichtsverständnis bei Paulus*, 1968; G. Machen, *The Origin of Paul's Religion*, 1947 (1925); T. W. Manson, *Studies in the Gospels and Epistles*, 1962; I. H. Marshall, *The Origins of New Testament Christology*, 1976; B. M. Metzger, *Index to Periodical Literature on the Apostle Paul*, 1960; W. Michaelis, *Einleitung in das Neue Testament*, 1954; C. F. D. Moule, *The Origin of Christology*, 1977; J. Munck, *Paul and the Salvation of Mankind*, 1960; J. M. Murphy-O'Connor, *Paul and Qumran*, 1968; E. Pagels, *The Gnostic Paul*, 1975; E. Percy, *Probleme der Kolosser- und Epheserbriefe*, 1946; C. A. Pierce, *Conscience in the New Testament*, 1955; W. M. Ramsay, *CRE*, 1893; *idem*, *SPT*, 1895; R. Reitzenstein, *Die hellenistischen Mysterienreligionen*, 1927 (E.T. 1977); K.H. Rengstorf (ed.), *Das Paulusbild in der neueren deutschen Forschung*, 1969; H. Ridderbos, *Paul and Jesus*, 1958; *idem*, *Paul*, 1976; B. Rigaux, *S Paul et ses lettres*, 1962 (E.T. 1968); O. Roller, *Das Formular der Paulinischen Briefe*, 1933; E. P. Sanders, *Paul and Palestinian Judaism*, 1977; W. Schmithals, *Gnosticism in Corinth*, 1971; *idem*, *Paul and the Gnostics*, 1972; *idem*, *Paul and James*, 1965; H. J. Schoeps, *Paul*, 1961; A. Schweitzer, *The Mysticism of Paul the Apostle*, 1931; *idem*, *Paul and his Interpreters*, 1912; H. M. Shires, *The Eschatology of Paul*, 1966; K. Stendahl (ed.), *The Scrolls and the New Testament*, 1957; W. C. van Unnik, *Tarsus or Jerusalem?*, 1962; G. Wahner, *Pauline Baptism and the Pagan Mysteries*, 1967; D. E. H. Whiteley, *The Theology of St Paul*, 1964; R. McL. Wilson, *Gnosis and the New Testament*, 1968; G. Zuntz, *The Text of the Epistles*, 1953.

E.E.E.

PAUL, ACTS OF
See New Testament apocrypha, Part 2.

PAULUS, SERGIUS, more correctly **PAULLUS,** was the proconsul (Gk. *anthypatos*) of *Cyprus in AD 47/8 when the apostle Paul visited that island (Acts 13:7). His name suggests that he was a member of an old Roman senatorial family: if he was the L. Sergius Paullus mentioned in *CIL*, 6. 31545, he was one of the Curators of the Banks of the Tiber under Claudius. Another inscription (*IGRR*, 3. 930; *cf. EGT*, 2, 1900, p. 286) found in Cyprus refers to the proconsul *Paulos*, while an inscription discovered at Pisidian Antioch in honour of a L. Sergius Paullus, propraetor of Galatia in AD 72–4, is possibly a commemoration of his son.

B. van Elderen (in W. W. Gasque and R. P. Martin (eds.), *Apostolic History and the Gospel*, 1970, pp. 151–156) considers that the inscription *IGRR*, 3. 935 is more likely to refer to this proconsul. Commentators are divided over the reality of Paullus' profession of Christian faith. D.H.W.

PAVILION (Heb. *sōḵ*, *sukkâ*). A covered place, tent, booth or shelter, where a person or beast may hide or be sheltered. The same word is translated in AV as den (Ps. 10:9), tabernacle (Ps. 76:2), covert (Je. 25:38), booth (Jon. 4:5) and lodge (Is. 1:8), and thus represents something used by beasts, worshippers, travellers and soldiers. It is translated only six times in the AV as pavilion. In 1 Ki. 20:12, 16 it refers to the army tents in which Ben-hadad and his soldiers were resting and drinking when they were campaigning against Ahab. Such tents are illustrated on the sculptured reliefs of the Assyr. kings Shalmaneser III and Sennacherib (BM). The other uses of the word are metaphorical. It represents the place of divine protection in the day of trouble (Pss. 27:5; 31:20), or the place where God is hidden with dark waters and thick clouds for his pavilion (Ps. 18:11; 2 Sa. 22:12).

RSV translates a difficult phrase in Jb. 36:29 as 'the thunderings of his pavilion' (*sukkâ*, AV 'tabernacle'). NEB takes it differently: as the sky is sometimes described as God's tent, clouds, viewed from the earth, might appear as carpeting on the tent floor.

The term is also used for the bough shelters erected at the Feast of Booths (Tabernacles) commemorating the shelters in which Israel dwelt in the wilderness. In Ps. 19:5 the reference is to the canopy (RSV 'tent') under which a bridegroom stands with his bride on their wedding day.

For Egyp. data, *cf.* K. A. Kitchen, *THB* 5–6, 1960, pp. 7–11. J.A.T.

PEACE. Basically the OT word for peace, *šālôm*, means 'completeness', 'soundness', 'well-being'. (See *BDB*.) It is used when one asks of or prays for the welfare of another (Gn. 43:27; Ex. 4:18; Jdg. 19:20), when one is in harmony or concord with another (Jos. 9:15; 1 Ki. 5:12), when one seeks the good of a city or country (Ps. 122:6; Je. 29:7). It may mean material prosperity (Ps. 73:3) or physical safety (Ps. 4:8). But also it may mean spiritual well-being. Such peace is the associate of righteousness and truth, but not of wickedness (Ps. 85:10; Is. 48:18, 22; 57:19–21).

Because of the world's chaos through man's sin, and because peace comes only as God's gift, the Messianic hope was of an age of peace (Is. 2:2–4; 11:1–9; Hg. 2:7–9), or of the advent of the Prince of peace (Is. 9:6f.; *cf.* Je. 33:15f.; Ezk. 34:23ff.; Mi. 5:5; Zc. 9:9f.). The NT shows the fulfilment of this hope. In Christ peace has come (Lk. 1:79; 2:14, 29f.). By him it is bestowed (Mk. 5:34; Lk. 7:50; Jn. 20:19, 21, 26), and his disciples are its messengers (Lk. 10:5f.; Acts 10:36).

In classical Greek *eirēnē* had a

PAVED STREETS
See Travel, Part 3.

The royal pavilion of Shalmaneser III of Assyria, set up during a campaign in Syria in 858 BC. Bronze relief from the Balawat gates. c. 845 BC. (BM)

primarily negative force; but by way of the LXX, the word in the NT has the full content of the OT *šālôm*, and nearly always carries a spiritual connotation. The breadth of its meaning is especially apparent from its linking with such keywords as grace (Rom. 1:7, *etc.*), life (Rom. 8:6), righteousness (Rom. 14:17), and from its use in benedictions such as 1 Thes. 5:23 and Heb. 13:20f. (*cf.* 2 Pet. 3:14).

For sinful man there must first be peace with God, the removal of sin's enmity through the sacrifice of Christ (Rom. 5:1; Col. 1:20). Then inward peace can follow (Phil. 4:7), unhindered by the world's strife (Jn. 14:27; 16:33). Peace between man and man is part of the purpose for which Christ died (Eph. 2) and of the Spirit's work (Gal. 5:22); but man must also be active to promote it (Eph. 4:3; Heb. 12:14), not merely as the elimination of discord, but as the harmony and true functioning of the body of Christ (Rom. 14:19; 1 Cor. 14:33).

BIBLIOGRAPHY. W. Foerster, G. von Rad, *TDNT* 2, pp. 400–420; D. Gillett, *Them* 1, 1976, pp. 80ff.; H. Beck, C. Brown, *NIDNTT* 2, pp. 776–783. F.F.

PEACOCK
See Animals, Part 1.

PEARL
See Jewels, Part 2.

PECULIAR TREASURE
See Treasure, Part 3.

PEDAGOGUE
See Schoolmaster, Part 3.

PEDAIAH ('Yahweh has redeemed'). **1.** Father of Joel, ruler (under David) of Manasseh, W of the Jordan (1 Ch. 27:20). **2.** Grandfather of King Jehoiakim (2 Ki. 23:36). **3.** Third son of King Jehoiachin (1 Ch. 3:18). According to 1 Ch. 3:19, he was called the father of Zerubbabel, who elsewhere is named as the son of Shealtiel, brother of Pedaiah. **4.** A son of Parosh, who helped to repair the wall of Jerusalem (Ne. 3:25). **5.** One who stood on Ezra's left when he read the law to the people (Ne. 8:4); perhaps identical with **4** above. **6.** A Levite appointed by Nehemiah to assist in distributing the tithes (Ne. 13:13). **7.** A Benjaminite (Ne. 11:7). J.D.D.

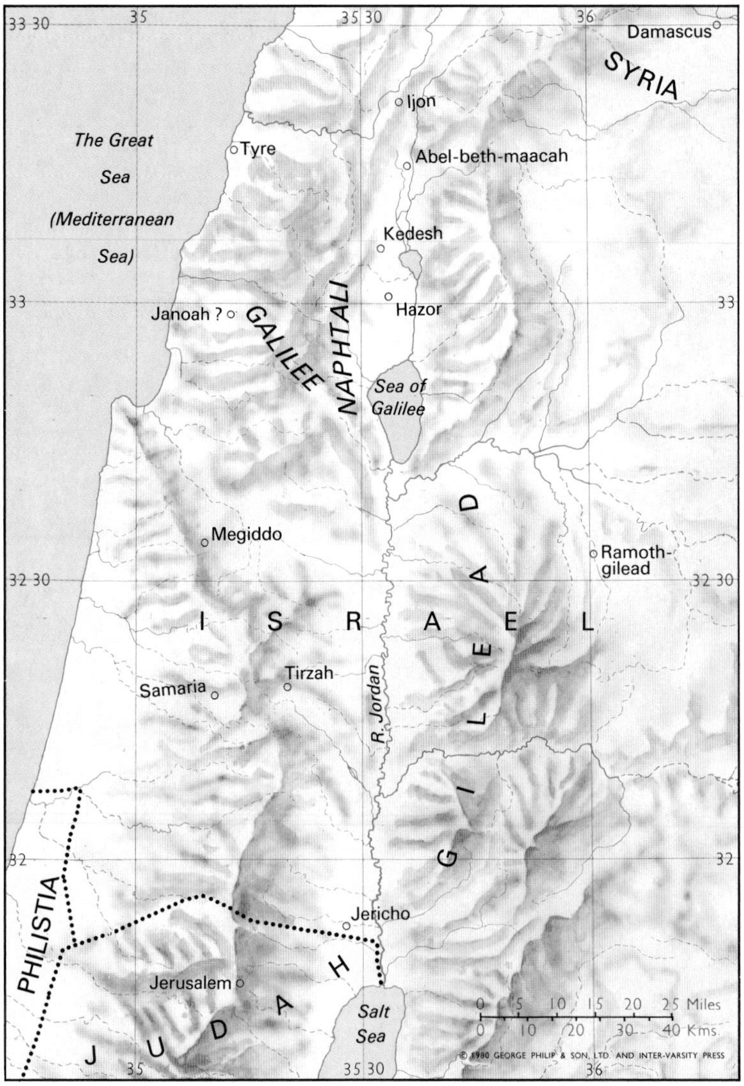

Map to illustrate the reign of Pekah of Israel (c. 737–732 BC).

PEKAH (Heb. *peqaḥ*, 'opening'). Pekah, the son of Remaliah, was the 'third man' (Heb. *šālîšâ*) in Pekahiah's war chariot. With the help of Gileadites he murdered Pekahiah, successor of Menahem, at Samaria (2 Ki. 15:21ff.). He then seized the throne and reigned as king of Israel from *c.* 737 to 732 BC. His accession was in the 52nd year of Uzziah of Judah (v. 27), and in his 2nd year Jotham succeeded Uzziah (v. 32).

Pekah adopted an anti-Assyrian policy and allied himself to *Rezin of Syria. Together they brought pressure on Jotham of Judah, probably to join them (v. 37). Isaiah, however, advised him and his successor Ahaz to be neutral. Pekah moved in force against Jerusalem, which was unsuccessfully besieged (2 Ki. 16:5; Is. 7:1). His Syrian allies took Elath, while Pekah fought the Judaeans, slaying many and taking many prisoners from the Jericho district back to Samaria (2 Ch. 28:7–8). These were later released on the intercession of the prophet Oded (vv. 8–15).

Faced with this invasion Ahaz appealed for help to Tiglath-pileser III of Assyria, who was campaigning in Syria. In 732 BC the Assyrians captured Damascus and invaded N Israel. A list of the places invaded, as far S as Galilee, is given in 2 Ki. 15:25–29 and is partly paralleled by Tiglath-pileser's own Annals. Excavation at Hazor confirms the Assyrian destruction there at this time. A wine-jar inscribed *lpqḥ*, 'belonging to Pekah', was found among the objects from the period of Pekah's occupation.

Following the swift Assyrian invasion of more than half of Israel, Hoshea, son of Elah, conspired against Pekah, whom he slew. Since Tiglath-pileser claims in his Annals to have replaced Pekah (*Paqaḫa*) by Hoshea (*'Ausi*), it is clear that this act was approved, if not instigated, by the Assyrians. Pekah's reign was considered to have followed the evil tradition of Jeroboam (2 Ki. 15:28). D.J.W.

PEKAHIAH (Heb. *pᵉqaḥyâ*, 'Yahweh has opened [his eyes]'). Son of *Menahem, king of Israel, whom he succeeded *c.* 742/1 BC (2 Ki. 15:23–26; *CHRONOLOGY OF THE OT). His assassination in the

2nd year of his reign suggests that he continued his father's policy of submission to Assyria. The revolutionaries, led by *Pekah son of Remaliah, may have been in league with *Rezin, king of Damascus, for they came from Gilead, adjacent to his territory. The king was killed while in the keep (Heb. *'armôn*) of the palace at *Samaria. The words 'with *Argob and Arieh' (2 Ki. 15:25) seem to have been transposed from v. 29. A.R.M.

PEKOD. A small *Aramaean tribe E of the lower Tigris. Akkadian sources record the temporary subjugation of *Puqūdu* under *Tiglath-pileser III (747–727 BC), *Sargon II (722–705 BC) and *Sennacherib (705–681 BC). Mentioned in Jeremiah's oracle against Babylon (50:21), Pekod is also among other Mesopotamian peoples who, though formerly lovers of Israel, will rise against Jerusalem (Ezk. 23:23). Eponymous for a city and irrigation system mentioned in TB (*Beṣah* 29a, *Kethuboth* 27b, *Ḥullin* 127a).

BIBLIOGRAPHY. S. Parpola, *Neo-Assyrian Toponyms*, 1970, pp. 280–281; M. Dietrich, *Die Aramäer Südbabyloniens*, 1970. D.W.B.

PELATIAH (Heb. *p^{e}laṭyāh(û)*, 'Yahweh delivers'; Gk. *Phaltias*, *Phalettia*). **1.** A witness to the covenant in Ne. 10:22. This may well be the same man as the grandson of Zerubbabel, a descendant of Solomon (1 Ch. 3:21). **2.** A Simeonite captain who occupied ex-Amalekite territory (1 Ch. 4:42). **3.** A leader whom Ezekiel pictured as devising mischief and giving wicked counsel in Jerusalem. He fell dead while Ezekiel prophesied (Ezk. 11:1–13).

Names composed with element *plṭ* are attested from the Amorite period and were common at Ugarit (*RAS SHAMRA) in the 13th century BC as well as in later Aramaic (*e.g.* F. Gröndahl, *Personnamen der Texte aus Ugarit*, 1967, p. 173. D.J.W.

PELEG (Heb. *peleḡ*, 'water-course, division'). The son of Eber, brother of Yoqtan (*JOKTAN), and grandson of Shem (Gn. 10:25). In his time the earth was 'divided', the word used (*nip̄l^{e}ḡâ*) being a play on, or explanation of, his name. This is commonly held to refer to the splitting up of the world's population into various geographical and linguistic groups (Gn. 11:1–9). It may equally well mark the development by the semi-nomad sons of *Ebel of cultivation, using artificial irrigation canals (Assyr. *plagu*); *peleḡ* is used in this sense in Is. 30:25, 32:2; Jb. 29:6; 38:25. Alternatively it may be a reference to division of territory by borders (Akk. *pulukku*; *JCS* 18, 1964, p. 69; *palāku*, 'to divide at borders'). Peleg was father of Reu (Gn. 11:19). D.J.W.

PELONITE. The name given to two of David's mighty men, Helez and Ahijah (1 Ch. 11:27, 36; 27:10). The former is described as the *Paltite in the parallel text, 2 Sa. 23:26, and the Syriac has this reading in 1 Ch. 11:27. In view of 2 Sa. 23:34 some commentators prefer to emend 1 Ch. 11:36b to 'Eliam the son of Ahithophel the Gilonite'. R.A.H.G.

PENTATEUCH. The first five books of the OT (Gn., Ex., Lv., Nu., Dt.) constitute the first and most important section of the threefold Jewish *Canon. Usually called by the Jews *sēp̄er hattôrâ*, 'the book of the law', or *hattôrâ*, 'the law' (see *KB*, p. 403, for suggested derivations of the word, which seems to mean basically 'teaching' or 'instruction'), the Pentateuch (Gk. *pentateuchos*, 'five-volumed [*sc.* book]') is also known as the 'five-fifths of the law'. For the past century or so, many higher critics, following the lead of Alexander Geddes (*c.* 1800), have tended to disregard the traditional five-book division in favour of a Hexateuch comprising the Pentateuch and Joshua (*cf.* J. Wellhausen, *Die Composition des Hexateuchs*, 1876–7). On the other hand, I. Engnell has suggested the word 'Tetrateuch' to separate Deuteronomy from the first four books (*Gamla Testamentet*, 1, 1945). The critical presuppositions which underlie these suggestions are evaluated below.

The antiquity of the fivefold division is attested by the Samaritan Pentateuch and the LXX, which gave the books their traditional names; the Jews identify them by the first word or phrase. The divisions between the books were determined both by topical and practical considerations: papyrus scrolls could contain only about one-fifth

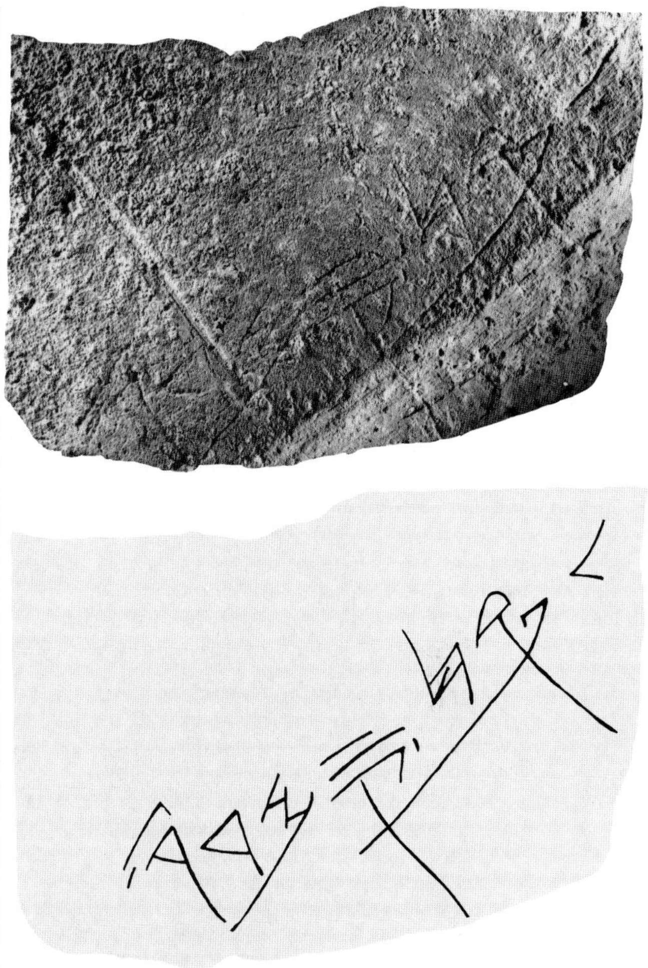

The Hebrew inscription on this fragment of a store-jar from Hazor reads 'For Peqah, Semader', probably a reference to Pekah, king of Israel, and to a type of oil. Stratum V A. 740–732 BC. (YY)

of the *tôrâ*. Jewish tradition prescribes that a section of the Law be read weekly in the synagogue. Three years were required for the completion of the Pentateuch in Palestine; the modern lectionary, in which the Pentateuch is read through in one year, is derived from that used in Babylonia. It may well be that a psalm was read along with the traditional reading from the prophetic writings (*hap̄ṭārâ*). The five books of the Psalter are probably patterned after the Pentateuch (*cf.* N. H. Snaith, *Hymns of the Temple*, 1951, pp. 18–20).

References to the Pentateuch in the OT are largely restricted to the writings of the Chronicler, who uses several designations: the law (Ezr. 10:3; Ne. 8:2, 7, 14; 10:34, 36; 12:44; 13:3; 2 Ch. 14:4; 31:21; 33:8); the book of the law (Ne. 8:3); the book of the law of Moses (Ne. 8:1); the book of Moses (Ne. 13:1; 2 Ch. 25:4; 35:12); the law of the Lord (Ezr. 7:10; 1 Ch. 16:40; 2 Ch. 31:3; 35:26); the law of God (Ne. 10:28–29); the book of the law of God (Ne. 8:18); the book of the law of the Lord (2 Ch. 17:9; 34:14); the book of the law of the Lord their

PELAGIANISM
See Fall, Part 1.

PELICAN
See Animals, Part 1.

PENITENCE
See Sackcloth, Part 3.

PENNY
See Money, Part 2.

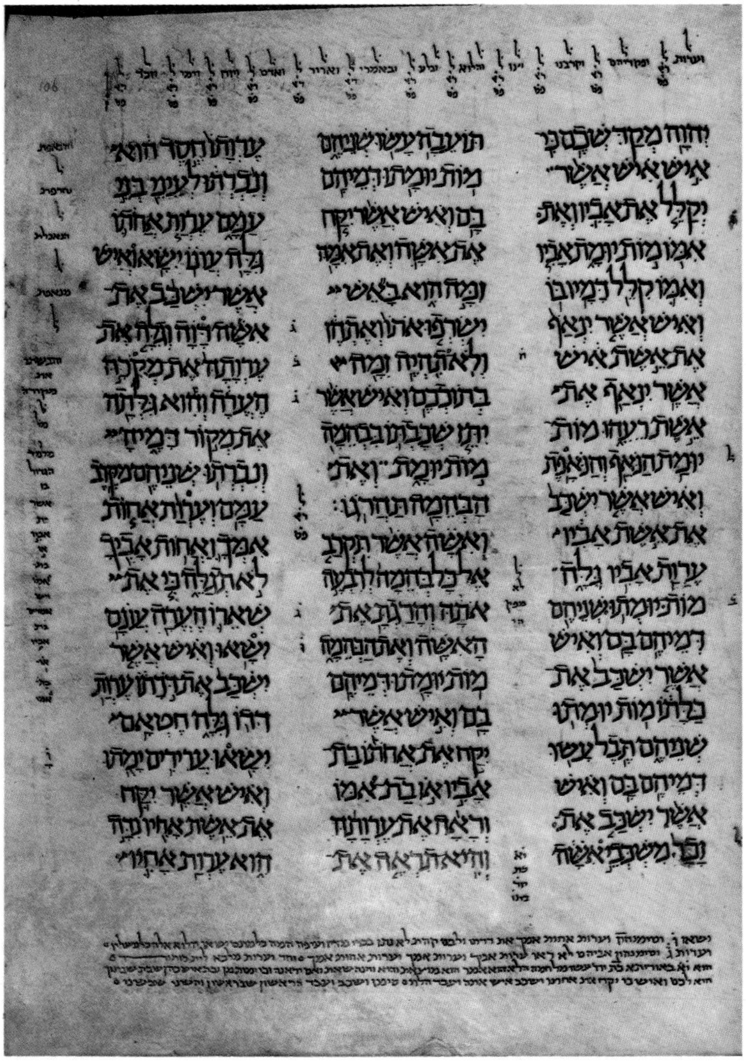

A page from one of the earliest copies of the traditional ('Massoretic') Hebrew text of the Pentateuch (Lv. 20:8–21). Mid-9th cent. AD. (BL)

God (Ne. 9:3); the law of Moses the servant of God (Dn. 9:11; *cf.* Mal. 4:4). One cannot say for certain whether references to the law in the historical writings refer to the Pentateuch as a whole or to parts of the Mosaic legislation, *e.g.* the law (Jos. 8:34); the book of the law (Jos. 1:8; 8:34; 2 Ki. 22:8); the book of the law of Moses (Jos. 8:31; 23:6; 2 Ki. 14:6); the book of the law of God (Jos. 24:26).

The NT uses similar designations: the book of the law (Gal. 3:10); the book of Moses (Mk. 12:26); the law (Mt. 12:5; Lk. 16:16; Jn. 7:19); the law of Moses (Lk. 2:22; Jn. 7:23); the law of the Lord (Lk. 2:23–24). The descriptions of the Pentateuch in both Testaments serve to emphasize its divine and human authorship, its binding authority as *the law*, and its inscripturated form in *the book*.

I. Contents

The Pentateuch narrates God's dealings with the world, and especially the family of Abraham, from creation to the death of Moses. There are six main divisions. First, the origin of the world and of the nations (Gn. 1–11). This section describes the *creation, the Fall of man, the beginnings of civilization, the Flood, the Table of the Nations and the tower of Babel. Secondly, the patriarchal period (Gn. 12–50) depicts the call of Abraham, the initiation of the Abrahamic covenant, the lives of Isaac, Jacob and Joseph, and the settling of the covenant-clan in Egypt. Thirdly, Moses and the Exodus from Egypt (Ex. 1–18). Fourthly, legislation at Sinai (Ex. 19:1–Nu. 10:10), which includes the giving of the law, the building of the tabernacle, the establishment of the levitical system and the final preparations for the journey from Sinai to Canaan. Fifthly, the wilderness wanderings (Nu. 10:11–36:13). This section describes the departure from Sinai, the acceptance of the majority report of the spies, God's consequent judgment, the encounter with Balaam, the appointment of Joshua as Moses' successor and the apportionment of the land to the twelve tribes. Sixthly, the final speeches of Moses (Dt. 1–34) recapitulate the Exodus events, repeat and expand the Sinaitic commandments, clarify the issues involved in obedience and disobedience, and bless the tribes, who are poised to enter Canaan. This section ends with the cryptic description of Moses' death and burial.

II. Authorship and unity

For centuries both Judaism and Christianity accepted without question the biblical tradition that Moses wrote the Pentateuch. Ben-Sira (Ecclus. 24:23), Philo (*Life of Moses* 3. 39), Josephus (*Ant.* 4. 326), the Mishnah (*Pirqê Abôth* 1. 1), and the Talmud (*Baba Bathra* 14b) are unanimous in their acceptance of the Mosaic authorship. The only debate centred in the account of Moses' death in Dt. 34:5ff. Philo and Josephus affirm that Moses described his own death, while the Talmud (*loc. cit.*) credits Joshua with eight verses of the *tôrâ*, presumably the last eight.

a. Pentateuchal criticism before AD *1700*

The tradition expressed in 2 Esdras 14:21–22, that the scrolls of the Pentateuch, burned in Nebuchadrezzar's siege of Jerusalem, were rewritten by Ezra, was apparently accepted by a number of the early church Fathers, *e.g.* Irenaeus, Tertullian, Clement of Alexandria, Jerome. They did not, however, reject the Mosaic authorship of the original law. The first recorded instance of such a rejection is the statement of John of Damascus concerning the Nasaraeans, a sect of Jewish Christians (*cf. PG* 94. 688–689). The *Clementine Homilies* teach that diabolical interpolations were made in the Pentateuch to try to put Adam, Noah and the Patriarchs in a bad light. Any passage out of harmony with the Ebionite assumptions of the author was suspected in this early attempt at higher criticism. Among the stumbling-blocks to the faith which Anastasius the Sinaite, patriarch of Antioch (7th century AD), attempted to remove were questions dealing with the Mosaic authorship of, and alleged discrepancies in, Genesis (*cf. PG* 89. 284–285).

During the mediaeval era, Jewish

and Muslim scholars began to point out supposed contradictions and anachronisms in the Pentateuch. For instance, Ibn Ezra (d. 1167), following a suggestion of Rabbi Isaac ben Jasos (d. 1057) that Gn. 36 was written not earlier than Jehoshaphat's reign because of the mention of Hadad (*cf.* Gn. 36:35; 1 Ki. 11:14), maintained that such passages as Gn. 12:6; 22:14; Dt. 1:1; 3:11 were interpolations.

The Reformer A. B. Carlstadt (1480–1541), observing no change in the literary style of Deuteronomy before and after Moses' death, denied that Moses wrote the Pentateuch. A Belgian Roman Catholic, Andreas Masius, produced a commentary on Joshua (1574) in which he credited Ezra with certain pentateuchal interpolations. Similar positions were maintained by two Jesuit scholars, Jacques Bonfrère and Benedict Pereira. Two famous philosophers helped to pave the way for modern higher critics by voicing in their widely circulated writings some of the contemporary criticisms of the unity of the law: Thomas Hobbes (*Leviathan*, 1651) credited Moses with everything attributed to him in the Pentateuch, but suggested that other parts were written more about Moses than by him; Benedict Spinoza (*Tractatus Theologico-politicus*, 1670) carried the observations of Ibn Ezra farther by noting doublets and alleged contradictions, and concluding that Ezra, who himself wrote Deuteronomy, compiled the Pentateuch from a number of documents (some Mosaic). 17th-century criticism of the Pentateuch was climaxed in the works of the Roman Catholic Richard Simon and the Arminian Jean LeClerc in 1685. LeClerc replied to Simon's view that the Pentateuch was a compilation based on many documents, both of divine and human origin, by asserting that the author must have lived in Babylonia between 722 BC and Ezra's time.

b. Pentateuchal criticism from AD 1700 to 1900

(i) *The question of Mosaic authorship.* Despite the questions raised by Catholics, Protestants and Jews in the period discussed above, the vast multitude of scholars and laymen clung firmly to belief in the Mosaic authorship. A milestone in pentateuchal criticism was reached in 1753, when the French physician Jean Astruc published his theory that Moses had composed Genesis from two main ancient *mémoires* and a number of shorter documents. The clue to the identification of the two *mémoires* was the use of the divine names: one employed *Elohim*; the other, *Yahweh.* Astruc maintained the Mosaic authorship of Genesis, but posited his theory of multiple sources to account for some of the repetitions and alleged discrepancies which critics had noted. J. G. Eichhorn (*Einleitung*, 1780–83) expanded Astruc's views into what is called 'the early documentary theory'. Abandoning the Mosaic authorship, he credited the final editing of the Elohistic and Yahwistic documents of Genesis and Ex. 1–2 to an unknown redactor. K. D. Ilgen (*Die Urkunden des Jerusalemischen Tempelarchivs in ihrer Urgestalt*, 1798) carried the documentary theory a step farther when he discovered in Gn. 17 independent sources traceable to three authors, two of whom use *Elohim* and the other *Yahweh.*

A Scottish Roman Catholic priest, Alexander Geddes, pursued Astruc's identification of several *mémoires* and developed (between 1792 and 1800) the *fragmentary theory* which holds that the Pentateuch was composed by an unknown redactor from a number of fragments which had originated in two different circles—one Elohistic, the other Yahwistic. Two German scholars embraced and expanded the fragmentary theory: J. S. Vater (*Commentar über den Pentateuch*, 3 vols., 1802–5) tried to trace the growth of the Pentateuch from over thirty fragments; W. M. L. De Wette (*Beiträge zur Einleitung in das Alte Testament*, 1807) stressed the comparatively late nature of much of the legal material and, significantly for later research, identified Josiah's book of the law as Deuteronomy (in this identification he had been anticipated by Jerome 1,400 years earlier).

De Wette's emphasis on one basic document augmented by numerous fragments was developed by H. Ewald, who in 1831 suggested that the chief document was the Elohistic source which carried the narrative from the creation into the book of Joshua and was supplemented by the account of the Yahwist, who was also the final redactor. Though Ewald later retreated from this 'supplementary theory', it survived in the writings of F. Bleek (*de libri Geneseos origine*, 1836) and F. Tuch (*Genesis*, 1838).

The 'new documentary theory' was fathered by H. Hupfeld (*Die Quellen der Genesis und die Art ihrer Zusammensetzung*, 1853), who, like Ilgen, found three separate sources in Genesis—the original Elohist (E^1), the later Elohist (E^2), and the Yahwist (J). A year later, when E. Riehm published his *Die Gesetzgebung Mosis im Lande Moab* in 1854, which purported to demonstrate the independent character of Deuteronomy, the four major documents had been isolated and dated in the order E^1, E^2, J, D.

K. H. Graf (in 1866) developed the suggestion of E. G. Reuss, J. F. L. George and W. Vatke and affirmed that E^1 (called P for Priestly Code by modern scholars), rather than being the earliest of the documents, was the latest. The debate then centred in the question as to whether E^2(E)JDP(E^1) or JEDP was the proper chronological order. A. Kuenen's work, *The Religion of Israel* (1869–70), assured the triumph of the latter order and set the stage for the appearance of the star actor in the drama of pentateuchal criticism, Julius Wellhausen.

(ii) *Wellhausen's views.* Wellhausen's important publications from 1876 to 1884 gave the documentary theory its most cogent and popular setting. Stated simply, this theory holds that J (*c.* 850 BC) and E (*c.* 750 BC) were combined by a redactor (R^{JE}) about 650 BC. When D (the Deuteronomic laws, *c.* 621) was added by R^D (*c.* 550) and P (*c.* 500–450) by R^P *c.* 400 BC, the Pentateuch was basically complete. In Wellhausen's presentation more was involved than mere documentary analysis. He linked his critical studies to an evolutionary approach to Israel's history which minimized the historicity of the patriarchal period and tended to detract from Moses' prominence. The religion of Israel advanced from the simple sacrifices on family altars in the days of the settlement to the intricately legalistic structure of Leviticus (P), which stemmed from Ezra's era (*PRIESTS AND LEVITES). Similarly, Israel's concept of God evolved from the animism and polytheism of the patriarchal days, through the henotheism of Moses' time and the ethical monotheism of the 8th-century prophets to the sovereign Lord of Is. 40ff.

So fundamental for later scholarship were Wellhausen's ideas that his influence in biblical studies has frequently been likened to Darwin's in the natural sciences. Largely through the writings of W. Robertson Smith and S. R. Driver, Wellhausen's documentary analysis gained a widespread acceptance throughout the English-speaking world. The following summary (somewhat oversimplified) outlines the basic characteristics of the pentateuchal documents according to the Wellhausenian school.

The *Yahwist's narrative* (J) is said to date from early in the Monarchy (*c.* 950–850 BC). Allusions to territorial expansion (Gn. 15:18; 27:40) and the ascendancy of Judah (Gn. 49:8–12) allegedly point to a Solomonic date. The J document tells the story of God's dealings with man from the creation of the universe to Israel's entry of Canaan. The combination of majesty and simplicity found in J marks it as an outstanding example of epic literature worthy of comparison with Homer's *Iliad.* Originating in Judah, the Yahwist document has some distinctive literary traits in addition to the preference for the name Yahweh: *šip̄ḥâ*, 'maidservant', is preferred to *'āmâ* (E); Sinai is used instead of Horeb (E); popular etymologies occur frequently, *e.g.* Gn. 3:20; 11:9; 25:30; 32:27.

Intensely nationalistic, the J narrative records in detail the exploits of the patriarchal families, even those that are not particularly praiseworthy. Theologically J is noted for its anthropopathisms and anthropomorphisms. God in quasi-human form walks and talks with men, although his transcendence is never doubted. The transparent biographies of the Patriarchs, deftly and simply narrated, are an outstanding feature of J.

The *Elohist's narrative* (E) is usually dated about a century after J, *i.e.* 850–750 BC. A N (Ephraimitic) origin for E has been suggested on the basis of the omission of the stories of Abraham and Lot, which centre in Hebron and the Cities of the Plain, and the special emphasis given to Bethel and Shechem (Gn. 28:17; 31:13; 33:19–20). Joseph, the ancestor of the N tribes Ephraim and Manasseh, plays a prominent role. More fragmentary than J, E nevertheless has its own stylistic peculiarities: 'the River' is the Euphrates; repetition is used in direct address (*cf.* Gn. 22:11: Ex. 3:4); 'Here am I' (*hinnēnî*) is used in replies to the Deity.

Though less noteworthy as a literary composition than J, the E document is noted for its moralistic and religious emphases. Sensitive to the sins of the Patriarchs, E attempts to rationalize them, while the anthropomorphisms of J are replaced by divine revelations through dreams and angelic mediation. An outstanding contribution of E is the story of God's testing of Abraham in the command to sacrifice Isaac (Gn. 22:1–14). With powerful simplicity the picture of conflict between love of family and obedience to God is painted, and with prophetic force the lesson concerning the inwardness of true sacrifice is conveyed.

The *Deuteronomist document* (D), in Pentateuchal studies, corresponds roughly with the book of *Deuteronomy. Essential to the documentary hypothesis is the view that Josiah's book of the law (2 Ki. 22:3–23:25) was part, at least, of Dt. The correspondences between D and the terms of Josiah's reformation are noteworthy: the worship is centralized at Jerusalem (2 Ki. 23:4ff.; Dt. 12:1–7); acts of false worship are specifically forbidden (2 Ki. 23:4–11, 24; Dt. 16:21, 22; 17:3; 18:10, 11). D lays great stress on God's love for Israel and her obligation to respond, a philosophy of history which spells out the terms of God's blessing and judgment, and the necessity for a vigorous sense of social justice under the terms of the covenant. A collection of sermons rather than narratives, D is a collection of legal and hortatory materials compiled during the exigencies of Manasseh's reign and combined with JE after the time of Josiah.

The *Priestly document* (P) draws together laws and customs from various periods of Israel's history and codifies them in such a way as to organize the legal structure of post-exilic Judaism. P contains some narratives, but is more concerned with genealogies and the patriarchal origins of ritual or legal practices. Formal divisions such as the ten 'generations' of *Genesis and the covenants with Adam, Noah, Abraham and Moses are generally credited to P. The complexity of the legal and ritual structure of P is usually interpreted as a sign of a post-exilic date, especially when P (*e.g.* Ex. 25–31; 35–40; Lv.; the laws in Nu.) is compared with the simple ritualism of Jdg. and 1 Sa. As a literary document P cannot be compared with the earlier sources, because the penchant for laborious details (*e.g.* the genealogies and detailed descriptions of the tabernacle) tends to discourage literary creativity. The concern of the priestly movement for the holiness and transcendence of God reveals itself in P, where the entire legislation is viewed as a means of grace whereby God bridges the gap between himself and Israel.

c. Pentateuchal criticism after AD *1900*

Documentary analysis did not stop with Wellhausen's researches. Rudolf Smend, expanding a suggestion made in 1883 by Karl Budde, attempted to divide the Yahwistic document into J^1 and J^2 throughout the Hexateuch (*Die Erzählung des Hexateuch auf ihre Quellen untersucht*, 1912). What Smend had called J^1, Otto Eissfeldt identified as a Lay-source (L), because it contrasts directly with the Priestly document and emphasizes the nomadic ideal in opposition to the Canaanite mode of life. Julian Morgenstern's *Kenite document (K), purportedly dealing with Moses' biography and the relations between Israel and the Kenites (*HUCA* 4, 1927, pp. 1–138), R. H. Pfeiffer's S (South or Seir) document in Genesis, corresponding somewhat to Eissfeldt's L (*ZAW* 48, 1930, pp. 66–73), and Gerhard von Rad's division of the priestly document into P^A and P^B (*Die Priesterschrift im Hexateuch*, 1934) are further refinements of a documentary criticism which had reached its extreme in the detailed dissections of P in B. Baentsch's work on Leviticus (1900), where seven main sources of P are further modified by the discovery of one or more redactors. This atomizing tendency is represented in the works of C. A. Simpson (notably *The Early Traditions of Israel: a Critical Analysis of the Pre-Deuteronomic Narrative of the Hexateuch*, 1948).

d. Reactions to the Graf–Wellhausen theory

Conservatives, convinced that their view of inspiration and the whole structure of theology built on it were at stake, joined battle almost immediately with pentateuchal critics. In the van of this reaction were E. W. Hengstenberg (*Dissertations on the Genuineness of the Penta-*

teuch, 1847) and C. F. Keil. After the appearance of Wellhausen's monumental synthesis the battle was continued by W. H. Green (*The Higher Criticism of the Pentateuch*, 1895) and James Orr (*The Problem of the Old Testament*, 1906), whose careful scrutiny of the documentary analyses found them wanting in terms of both literary evidence and theological presuppositions. The pattern set by these scholars was continued in the researches of R. D. Wilson (*A Scientific Investigation of the Old Testament*, 1926, reprinted 1959), G. Ch. Aalders (*A Short Introduction to the Pentateuch*, 1949), O. T. Allis (*The Five Books of Moses*, 1943) and E. J. Young (*IOT*, 1949).

(i) *The use of the divine names.* Conservative attacks on the Wellhausenian theory have generally taken shape along the following lines. The use of the divine names as a criterion for separating documents has been questioned at four points: (1) The evidence of textual criticism, especially from the Pentateuch of the LXX, suggests that there was less uniformity and more variety in early manuscripts of the Pentateuch than in the *MT*, which has traditionally been used as the basis of documentary analysis (although J. Skinner's *The Divine Names in Genesis*, 1914, has weakened the force of this argument).

(2) R. D. Wilson's study of the divine names in the Qur'an (*PTR* 17, 1919, pp. 644–650) brought to light the fact that certain suras of the Qur'an prefer *Allah* (4; 9; 24; 33; 48, *etc.*), while others prefer *Rab* (18; 23; 25–26; 34, *etc.*), just as certain sections of Genesis use *Elohim* (*e.g.* Gn. 1:1–2:3; 6:9–22; 17:2ff., 20, *etc.*) and others *Yahweh* (*e.g.* Gn. 4; 7:1–5; 11:1–9; 15; 18:1–19:28, *etc.*), although there is no support among scholars for a documentary approach to Qur'anic studies based on the divine names.

(3) The use of *Yahweh Elohim* (Gn. 2:4–3:24; *cf.* also Ex. 9:30) presents a special problem for the Wellhausen theory, since it involves a combining of the names which are supposed to be clues to separate documents; the LXX contains many more instances of this combination (*e.g.* Gn. 4:6, 9; 5:29; 6:3, 5), while there is ample evidence of compound names for deities in Ugaritic, Egyp. and Gk. literature (*cf.* C. H. Gordon in *Christianity Today*, 23 Nov. 1959).

(4) It is likely that the interchange of Yahweh and Elohim in the Pentateuch reflects an attempt on the part of the author to stress the ideas associated with each name (*cf.* I. Engnell, *Gamla Testamentet*, 1, 1945, pp. 194ff.). These and similar problems pertaining to the divine names have long since caused documentary critics to minimize what was once the starting-point of the whole process of documentary analysis.

(ii) *Diction and style.* Differences in diction and style, an important link in the chain of evidence for the Wellhausen theory, have been called into question by a number of conservatives. Stress has been laid on the fact that the pentateuchal stories are too fragmentary to give an adequate sampling of an author's vocabulary and that insufficient attention has sometimes been given to the fact that different types of literature call for differing vocabularies. Words supposedly peculiar to one document are sometimes credited to a redactor when they occur in another source. This use of a redactor when the facts call in question critical theories seems a somewhat too convenient method of dealing with difficulties. As for matters of style, conservatives and others have frequently pointed out the subjectivity in such judgments and the very great difficulty involved in subjecting such opinions to scientific examination. What seems to be a graphic, vibrant narrative to one critic may seem dull or turgid to another. W. J. Martin has highlighted some of the difficulties encountered by literary critics in his *Stylistic Criteria and the Analysis of the Pentateuch*, 1955, although caution is imperative in the use of analogies from western literary criticism for the study of oriental literature.

(iii) *Double narratives.* The occurrence of double narratives (sometimes called doublets) has been considered key evidence for a diversity of sources. Aalders (*op. cit.*, pp. 43–53) and Allis (*op. cit.*, pp. 94–110, 118–123) have examined a number of these repetitions (*e.g.* Gn. 1:1–2:4a; 2:4b–25; 6:1–8, 9–13; 12:10–20; 20; 26:6–11) and have sought to show that their presence in the text need not be interpreted as evidence for multiplicity of sources. On the contrary, repetition within Heb. prose may be connected with the characteristically Heb. (and indeed Semitic) use of repetition for emphasis. Ideas are underscored in Heb. literature not by the logical connection with other ideas but by a creative kind of repetition which seeks to influence the reader's will. (*Cf.* J. Muilenburg, 'A Study in Hebrew Rhetoric: Repetition and Style' in *VT Supp* 1, 1953, pp. 97–111; J. Pedersen, *Israel*, 1–2, 1926, p. 123.) Liturgical use may also help to account for repetition in both narrative and legislative portions of the Pentateuch.

So far as Gn. is concerned, a conservative contribution was made by P. J. Wiseman in *New Discoveries in Babylonia about Genesis*, 1936; rev. ed., *Clues to Creation in Genesis*, 1977. He suggested that the *tôlēḏôt* passages (those beginning or ending with some such phrase as 'These are the generations . . .') mark the various sources available to Moses for compiling earlier narratives. This approach was popularized by J. Stafford Wright in *How Moses Compiled Genesis: A Suggestion*, 1946. For replies to the Wellhausenian theory of the development of the levitical system, see *Priests and Levites.

Conservatives have been quick to draw upon the conclusions of non-conservatives when these conclusions tended to question the validity of the documentary hypothesis. The sustained attack on the theories of Wellhausenians by B. D. Eerdmans is a case in point. Though denying the Mosaic authorship of the Pentateuch, Eerdmans staunchly defended the basic authenticity of the patriarchal narratives and affirmed his confidence in the antiquity of the ritual institutions of P. Further, T. Oestreicher and A. C. Welch endeavoured to tumble the documentary theory by removing the keystone—the identification of D with Josiah's book of the law. E. Robertson (*The Old Testament Problem*, 1950) regards Dt. as having been compiled under Samuel's influence as a law-book for 'all Israel', as having fallen into disuse when the disruption of the nation made its application impossible, and as having been opportunely rediscovered in Josiah's reign at a time when it was possible to treat 'all Israel' as a religious unit once more. The Decalogue and the Book of the Covenant, with which the Hebrews entered Canaan, were preserved in the early days of the settlement at various local sanctuaries, where they gathered around themselves bodies of divergent though related laws and traditions; the beginnings of national reunion in Samuel's day necessitated the compilation, on the basis of this material, of a law-book for the central administration. R. Brinker, a pupil of E. Robertson, elaborated certain aspects of this theory in *The Influence of Sanctuaries in Early Israel*, 1946. Using linguistic and stylistic criteria, U. Cassuto (*La Questione della Genesi*, 1934) argued for the unity of Gn., while F. Dornseiff (*ZAW* 52–53, 1934–5) defended the literary unity of the whole Pentateuch; *cf.* his *Antike und Alter Orient*, 1956.

From another angle A. R. Johnson warns us against what 'seems to be a real danger in OT study as a whole of misinterpreting what may be different but contemporary *strata* in terms of corresponding *stages* of thought, which can be arranged chronologically so as to fit into an over-simplified evolutionary scheme or similar theory of progressive revelation' (*The Vitality of the Individual in the Thought of Ancient Israel*, 1949, p. 3).

(iv) *Form criticism.* While not abandoning the documentary hypothesis, the pioneer form critics, H. Gunkel and H. Gressmann, laid stress both on the literary qualities and on the lengthy process of oral tradition which had shaped the various narratives into aesthetic masterpieces. This welcome relief from the coldly analytical approach of the documentary critics, who in their detailed dissection of the Pentateuch tended to neglect the power and beauty of the stories, paved the way for the researches of a group of Scandinavian scholars who have discarded the documentary approach in favour of an emphasis on oral tradition. Following the lead of J. Pedersen who in 1931 formally rejected the documentary theory (*ZAW* 49, 1931, pp. 161–181), I. Engnell (*Gamla Testamentet*, 1, 1945) affirmed that, far from being the result of the compilation of written documents, the Pentateuch is a combination of reliable oral traditions collected and shaped in two main traditionist circles: a 'P-circle' responsible for the Tetrateuch and a 'D-circle' which formulated Dt., Jos., Jdg., Sa. and Ki. The actual writing of the books is relegated to exilic or post-exilic times. Key factors in the development of this traditio-historical school are the advanced knowledge of Heb. psychology and the growing understanding of ancient oriental literature. According to Engnell, the devotees of the Wellhausenian approach tend to interpret the OT in terms of European literary methods and western logic. See Eduard Nielsen, *Oral Tradition*, 1954, for a concise presentation of the views of the Scandinavian School.

As H. Gunkel's preoccupation with the various literary units (identifiable by literary *form* within the Pentateuch) represented a kind of return to the *fragmentary* approach of Geddes, Vater and De Wette, so P. Volz (and to some extent W. Rudolph) called for a revival of a *supplementary* hypothesis by minimizing the importance of the Elohist, who is at the most, in Volz's view, a later editor of the great author of Gn., the Yahwist. In somewhat similar fashion G. von Rad (*The Problem of the Hexateuch and Other Essays*, E.T. 1966) has stressed the dominant role played by the Yahwist as both collector and author of the pentateuchal materials which took shape over a lengthy period of time and have a rich history of tradition behind them. The generally accepted dates for the documents are highly tentative, according to von Rad, and represent the final stages in compiling the materials.

The theological application of von Rad's theories of the Pentateuch is to be found in his *Old Testament Theology*, 1, E.T. 1962. His theory that the Pentateuch developed around Israelite creeds like Dt. 26:5ff. has recently been turned around with the suggestion that the creeds are not the source of the pentateuchal narrative but its summary (J. A. Soggin, *IOT*, E.T. 1976, p. 93).

M. Noth (*The Laws in the Pentateuch, and Other Essays*, E.T. 1966) has approximated some of the results of the Uppsala school of Engnell *et al.* without abandoning a documentary approach. Rather, he has paid close attention to the history of the oral traditions which lie behind the documents, while maintaining an approach to J, E and P which is quite conventional. Perhaps his divergence from the Wellhausenian tradition is best seen in his refusal to recognize a 'Hexateuch' and his removal of most of Dt. from the province of pentateuchal criticism.

In general, contemporary scholars are paying more attention to the forms of narrative, liturgical, contractual or legislative material than they are to the alleged sources of the documentary hypothesis, as recent introductions to the OT indicate. *Cf.* O. Kaiser, *IOT*, E.T. 1975, who lists the following chapter titles: Literary Types of Israelite Narrative, Literary Types of Israelite Law, The Growth of the Pentateuchal Narrative at the Pre-Literary Stage; also J. A. Soggin, *op. cit.* The precise relationship of form criticism to the more traditional source criticism is still under debate. What is clear is that much more attention must be paid to redaction criticism, the study of the import and thrust of the five individual books and the Pentateuch as a whole, whatever their process of composition may have been.

(v) *The evidence of archaeology.* The march of modern archaeology has contributed to the re-evaluation of the documentary hypothesis. The basic reliability of the historical narratives has been confirmed time and again, especially in the patriarchal period. (See H. H. Rowley, 'Recent Discovery and the Patriarchal Age' in *The Servant of the Lord*², 1965.) The evolutionary reconstruction of Israel's history and religion has been questioned more than once by outstanding archaeologists such as W. F. Albright (*e.g.From the Stone Age to Christianity*, 1957, pp. 88ff., 282) and C. H. Gordon (*e.g. Ugaritic Literature*, 1949, pp. 5–7; 'Higher Critics and Forbidden Fruit', *Christianity Today*, 23 Nov. 1959). A drastic re-appraisal of the documentary hypothesis from the standpoint of Israel's religion is found in the researches of Yehezkel Kaufmann, who affirms the antiquity of P. and its priority to D. Furthermore, he separates Gn. from the rest of the Pentateuch, maintaining that it is 'a stratum in itself whose material is on the whole most ancient' (*TheReligion of Israel*, 1960, p. 208).

e. The position today

The insights gained from these criticisms of the Graf–Wellhausen hypothesis, together with the continuing researches of its exponents, have resulted in considerable modification of the old theory. The simple evolutionary views of Israel's history and religion have been cast aside. The basic authenticity of the patriarchal stories is recognized by many scholars, since the light of archaeology has illuminated the setting of these stories. The Egyp. *milieu* of the Joseph cycle and the Exodus account has been established by archaeological, literary and linguistic considerations (*cf.* A. S. Yahuda, *The Language of the Pentateuch in its Relation to Egyptian*, 1931; C. H. Gordon, *The World of the Old Testament*, 1958, p. 139). The role of * Moses as the great lawgiver and the dominant figure in Israel's religion has been reaffirmed.

Though not discarded, the documentary theory has been modified by contemporary scholars. The development of each document is exceedingly complex and is generally considered to represent a whole 'school' rather than a single author. The growth of the various documents is not consecutive but parallel, since there are ancient elements found in each, as the use of pentateuchal elements by the prophets indicates (*cf.* Aalders, *op. cit.*, pp. 111–138). Minute dissections of verses and positive assignment of their parts to diverse sources have generally been abandoned. These modifications in the documentary hypothesis should be viewed by conservatives as a medical chart, not as an obituary. The Wellhausenian theory is still very much alive and remains a constant challenge to conservative scholarship, which has sometimes been content to take comfort in the reactions against the documentary hypothesis without producing a thorough introduction to the Pentateuch, which states positively the evidence for the basic unity of the law while taking into full consideration the indications of diversity on which the documentary theory is based. Our increased knowledge of Middle Eastern literature—thanks to discoveries in * Mari, * Nuzi, * Ugarit, Hatti, * Sumer and * Egypt—should be of measurable help in this task. Since the texts from * Ebla (Tell Mardikh) seem to be contemporary with the earlier chapters of biblical history, they are likely to illuminate both the literature of the Pentateuch and its cultural background.

Aalders' studies have broken fresh ground and point the way for further advance. Of particular interest are his recognition of post-Mosaic and non-Mosaic elements in the Pentateuch (*e.g.* Gn. 14:14; 36:31; Ex. 11:3; 16:35; Nu. 12:3; 21:14–15; 32:34ff.; Dt. 2:12; 34:1–12) and his awareness of the fact that neither Testament ascribes the entire work to Moses, although both attribute substantial parts of it to him. The great legal codes, for instance, are credited specifically to Moses (*e.g.* Ex. 20:2–23:33; 34:11–26; Dt. 5–26; *cf.* Dt. 31:9, 24), as is the Israelites' itinerary mentioned in Nu. 33:2. As far as the Gn. stories are concerned, Moses may or may not have been the one who compiled them from their written and oral forms. The evidences of post-Mosaic editing of the Pentateuch are found in the references cited above, and especially in the mention of such ancient documents as 'the Book of the Wars of the Lord' (Nu. 21:14). It is difficult to date the final redaction of the Pentateuch. Aalders' suggestion that it took place some time within the reigns of Saul and David is credible, although some further allowance should probably be made for the modernizing of vocabulary and style.

III. The religious message of the Pentateuch

'The Pentateuch must be defined as a document which gives Israel its understanding, its aetiology of life. Here, through narrative, poetry, prophecy, law, God's will concerning Israel's task in the world is revealed' (A. Bentzen, *IOT*², 1952, 2, p. 77). A record of revelation and response, the Pentateuch testifies to the saving acts of God who is sovereign Lord of history and nature. The central act of God in the Pentateuch (and indeed the OT) is the * Exodus from Egypt. Here God broke in upon the consciousness of the Israelites and revealed himself as the redeeming God. Insights gained from this revelation enabled them under Moses' leadership to re-evaluate the traditions of their ancestors and see in them the budding of God's dealings which had bloomed so brilliantly in the liberation from Egypt.

Having powerfully and openly proved himself as Lord in the Exodus, God led the Israelites into the realization that he was the Creator and Sustainer of the universe as well as the Ruler of history. The order is important: a knowledge of the *Redeemer* led to a knowledge of the *Creator*; an understanding of the God of *grace* prompted an understanding of the God of *nature*.The display of control over nature apparent in the plagues, the crossing of the sea, and the sustenance in the wilderness may well have influenced the Israelites to view God as Lord of nature as well as of history.

God's grace is revealed not only in his deliverance and guidance, but in the giving of the law and the initiation of the covenant. Israel's pledge of obedience, her oath of loyalty to God and his will is her response; but even her response is a gift of God's grace, for it is he who, though free from obligation, has fixed the terms of the covenant and provided the sacrificial system as a means of spanning the gap between himself and his people. God's grace demands a total recognition of his Lordship, a complete obedience to his will in every sphere of life. This demand is gracious because it involves what is good for Israel, what will help her to realize her true potential, and what she could not discover without divine revelation.

Whatever the origin of the Pentateuch, it stands now as a document possessing a rich inner unity. It is the record of God's revelation in history and his Lordship over history. It testifies both to Israel's response and to her failure to respond. It witnesses to God's holiness, which separates him from men, and his gracious love, which binds him to them on his terms. (* GENESIS, * EXODUS, * LEVITICUS, * NUMBERS, * DEUTERONOMY.)

BIBLIOGRAPHY. U. Cassuto, *The Documentary Hypothesis and the Composition of the Pentateuch*, E.T. 1961; A. T. Chapman, *An Introduction to the Pentateuch*, 1911; I. Engnell, *Critical Essays on the Old Testament*, 1970; H. F. Hahn, *The Old Testament in Modern Research*, 1956; K. Koch, *The Growth of the Biblical Tradition*, 1969; J. A. Motyer, *The Revelation of the Divine Name*, 1959; A. Noordtzy, 'The Old Testament Problem', *BS* 97, 1940, pp. 456–475; 98, 1940, pp. 99–120, 218–243; C. R. North, 'Pentateuchal Criticism', *OTMS*, pp. 48–83; M. Noth, *A History of Pentateuchal Traditions*, 1972; N. H. Ridderbos, 'Reversals of Old Testament Criticism', in *Revelation and the Bible*, ed. C. F. H. Henry, 1958; H. H. Rowley, 'Moses and the Decalogue', *BJRL* 34, 1951, pp. 81–118; *idem*, *The Biblical Doctrine of Election*, 1950; W. Rudolph, *Der 'Elohist' von Exodus bis Josua*, *BZAW* 68, 1938; R. de Vaux, *The*

Bible and the Ancient Near East, 1971; P. Volz and W. Rudolph, *Der Elohist als Erzähler: ein Irrweg der Pentateuchkritik?*, *BZAW* 63, 1933; G. E. Wright, *God Who Acts*, 1952; *idem*, *The Old Testament against its Environment*, 1950. D.A.H.

PENTECOST, FEAST OF. In Lv. 23:16 LXX reads *pentēkonta hēmeras* for the Heb. *ḥ^{a}miššîm yôm*, 'fifty days', referring to the number of days from the offering of the barley sheaf at the beginning of the Passover. On the 50th day was the Feast of Pentecost. Since the time elapsed was 7 weeks, it was called *ḥag̱ šāḇu'ôṯ*, 'feast of weeks' (Ex. 34:22; Dt. 16:10). It marks the completion of the barley harvest, which began when the sickle was first put to the grain (Dt. 16:9), and when the sheaf was waved 'the morrow after the sabbath' (Lv. 23:11). It is also called *ḥag̱ haqqāṣîr*, 'feast of harvest', and *yôm habbikkûrîm*, 'day of the first fruits' (Ex. 23:16; Nu. 28:26). The feast is not limited to the times of the Pentateuch, but its observance is indicated in the days of Solomon (2 Ch. 8:13), as the second of the three annual festivals (*cf.* Dt. 16:16).

The feast was proclaimed as a 'holy convocation' on which no servile work was to be done, and at which every male Israelite was required to appear at the sanctuary (Lv. 23:21). Two baked loaves of new, fine, leavened flour were brought out of the dwellings and waved by the priest before the Lord, together with the offerings of animal sacrifice for sin- and peace-offerings (Lv. 23:17–20). As a day of joy (Dt. 16:16) it is evident that on it the devout Israelite expressed gratitude for the blessings of the grain harvest and experienced heartfelt fear of the Lord (Je. 5:24). But it was the thanksgiving and fear of a redeemed people, for the service was not without sin- and peace-offerings, and was, moreover, a reminder of their deliverance from Egypt (Dt. 16:12) as God's covenant people (Lv. 23:22). The ground of acceptance of the offering presupposes the removal of sin and reconciliation with God.

In the intertestamental period and later, Pentecost was regarded as the anniversary of the law-giving at Sinai (Jubilees 1:1 with 6:17; TB, *Pesaḥim* 68b; Midrash, *Tanḥuma* 26c). The Sadducees celebrated it on the 50th day (inclusive reckoning) from the first Sunday after Passover (taking the 'sabbath' of Lv. 23:15 to be the weekly sabbath); their reckoning regulated the public observance so long as the Temple stood, and the church is therefore justified in commemorating the first Christian Pentecost on a Sunday (Whit Sunday). The Pharisees, however, interpreted the 'sabbath' of Lv. 23:15 as the Festival of Unleavened Bread (*cf.* Lv. 23:7), and their reckoning became normative in Judaism after AD 70, so that in the Jewish calendar Pentecost now falls on various days of the week.

In the NT there are three references to Pentecost: (1) Acts 2:1 (Gk. *tēn hēmeran tēs pentēkostēs*). On this day, after the resurrection and ascension of Christ (*c.* AD 30), the disciples were gathered in a house in Jerusalem, and were visited with signs from heaven. The Holy Spirit descended upon them, and new life, power and blessing was evident, which Peter explained was in fulfilment of the prophecy of Joel. (2) Acts 20:16. Paul was determined not to spend time in Asia and made speed to be in Jerusalem by the day of Pentecost (AD 57). (3) 1 Cor. 16:8. Paul purposed to stay at Ephesus until Pentecost (AD 54 or 55), because an effectual door was opened to him for his ministry.

BIBLIOGRAPHY. Mishnah, *Menaḥoṯ* 10. 3; Tosefta, *Menaḥoṯ* 10. 23, 528; TB, *Menaḥoṯ* 65a; L. Finkelstein, *The Pharisees*, 1946, pp. 115ff. D.F.

PENUEL. 'The face of God' was the name that Jacob gave to the place where he crossed the Jabbok on his way back to meet Esau. It is possible that it had been called Penuel before, perhaps after a peculiarly shaped rock, and that Jacob endorsed the name as a result of his experience with the angel. The blessing which he sought (Gn. 32:26) materialized in Esau's conciliatory attitude (*cf.* 33:10: 'Truly to see your face is like seeing the face of God').

That Penuel was the site of an important pass is shown by the fact that a tower was built there, which Gideon destroyed after defeating the Midianites (Jdg. 8:8ff.), and Jeroboam rebuilt the city there, presumably to defend the invader's route from the E to his new capital at Shechem. The exact site is unknown, but S. Merrill, *East of Jordan*, 1881, pp. 390–392, makes a good case for the ancient ruins 6 km E of Succoth on two hills called Tulul ed-Dahab. J.B.J.

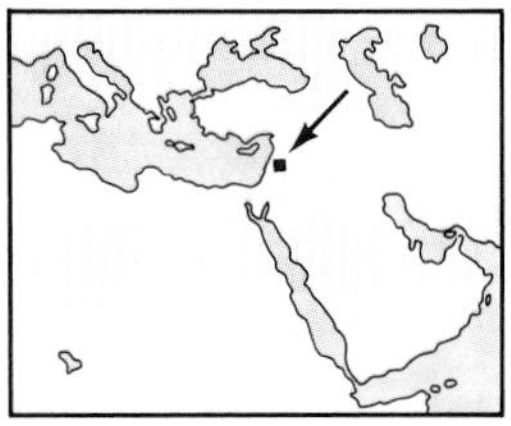

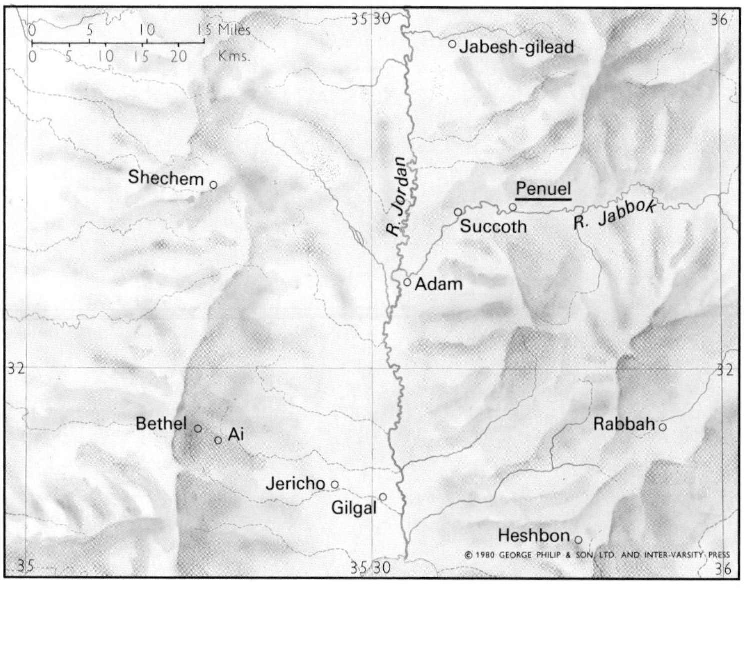

Penuel on the R. Jabbok.

PEOPLE. 1. Heb. *l^{e}'ôm*, occasionally sing., more frequently plur. *l^{e}'ummîm*, may mean: (*i*) a race or ethnic aggregate (Gn. 25:23, sing. and plur.); (*ii*) the sum total of the populace subject to a ruler, the same concept from a different viewpoint (Pr. 14:28, sing.); (*iii*) the totality or a large section of an ethnic community considered as the vehicle of judgment and feeling (Pr. 11:26, sing.); (*iv*) exceptionally, the Jewish people (Is. 51:4, sing.); (*v*) frequently, in the plur., the non-Jewish nations (*e.g.* Is. 55:4).

2. Heb. *gôy*, 'nation', 'people', came by association rather than etymology to mean specifically the

Gentiles; or, when applied to Israelites, to imply backsliding and religious unfaithfulness (Jdg. 2:20; Is. 1:4; *etc.*) The term is used in a vivid metaphor for a swarm of locusts in Joel 1:6. LXX regularly uses *ethnos* for *gôy*, yet NT sometimes uses *ethnos* for Israel, showing that these acquired associations cannot be pressed too rigidly.

3. With trifling exceptions (*cf.* Gn. 26:11, 'Philistines'; Ex. 9:15, 'Egyptians') Heb. *'am*, 'people', came to be applied fairly exclusively to Israel as the chosen race, but this meaning is acquired, not intrinsic. The LXX equivalent is *laos*. Further exceptions to Israelite reference are the metaphorical descriptions of ants and conies in community (Pr. 30:25f.). The unusual negative of Dt. 32:21, directly attached to the noun, denies to a flesh-and-blood people those spiritual characteristics which would justify their title (*cf.* 'Lo-ammi', Ho. 1:9, AV). The biblical phrase *'am hā'āreṣ* means in the earlier books the common people of the land, as distinct from the rulers and aristocracy. In the Ezra-Nehemiah period, the phrase sharpened to focus those Palestinians whose Judaism was mixed or suspect, with whom scrupulous Jews could not intermarry; *cf.* Ezr. 9:1–2, *etc.* In the rabbinic literature the term—now used in the sing. of an individual, in the plur. (*'ammê hā'āreṣ*) of a class—came to mean specifically all those who failed to observe the whole traditional law in all its details. A clear premonition of the rabbinic contempt for such persons is seen in Jn. 7:49.

4. The common NT equivalent to *'am* is *laos* or *dēmos*, as opposed to *ochlos*, which means merely a crowd. R.A.S.

PEOR. 1. A mountain somewhere to the N of the Dead Sea and opposite Jericho, described as looking towards the desert, but its location is not certainly identified. It was the last place from which Balaam blessed Israel (Nu. 23:28). See J. A. Jaussen-R. Savignac, *Mission en Arabie*, 1909, pp. 2, 650f.

2. The name of a deity, more fully Baal-peor, to which the Israelites were attracted (Nu. 25:3) and for the worship of which they were severely punished. Their punishment left a vivid impression and was recalled as a warning and example (Nu. 31:16; Dt. 4:3; Jos. 22:17). M.A.M.

PERAEA. A district in Transjordan, corresponding roughly to the *Gilead of the OT. It is never mentioned by name in the NT—that is left to Josephus—but is the district referred to several times (*e.g.* Mt. 19:1) as the land 'beyond Jordan'. The name Peraea came into use after the Exile, to denote an area E of the Jordan *c.* 16 km wide, stretching from the river Arnon in the S to some point between the Jabbok and the Yarmuk in the N. It comprised essentially the edge of the 1,000 m scarp overlooking the Jordan, with its towns, and was thus a highland region, with adequate (750 mm [30 in.] per annum) rainfall and tree cover in its higher parts. At intermediate elevations there were olives and vines, and cultivation tailed off E through the wheatfields and then the steppe pastures of lower lands. It was evidently an attractive region in OT times, for after seeing it and adjacent areas the tribes of Gad and Reuben (Nu. 32:1–5) lost interest in crossing Jordan with their cattle.

In the time of Christ Peraea was occupied by Jews and ruled by Herod Antipas, and by Jews it was regarded as possessing equality of status with Judaea and Galilee. As it adjoined both of these across the Jordan, it was possible by traversing its length to follow an all-Jewish route from Galilee to Judaea, thus by-passing the territory of the Samaritans. J.H.P.

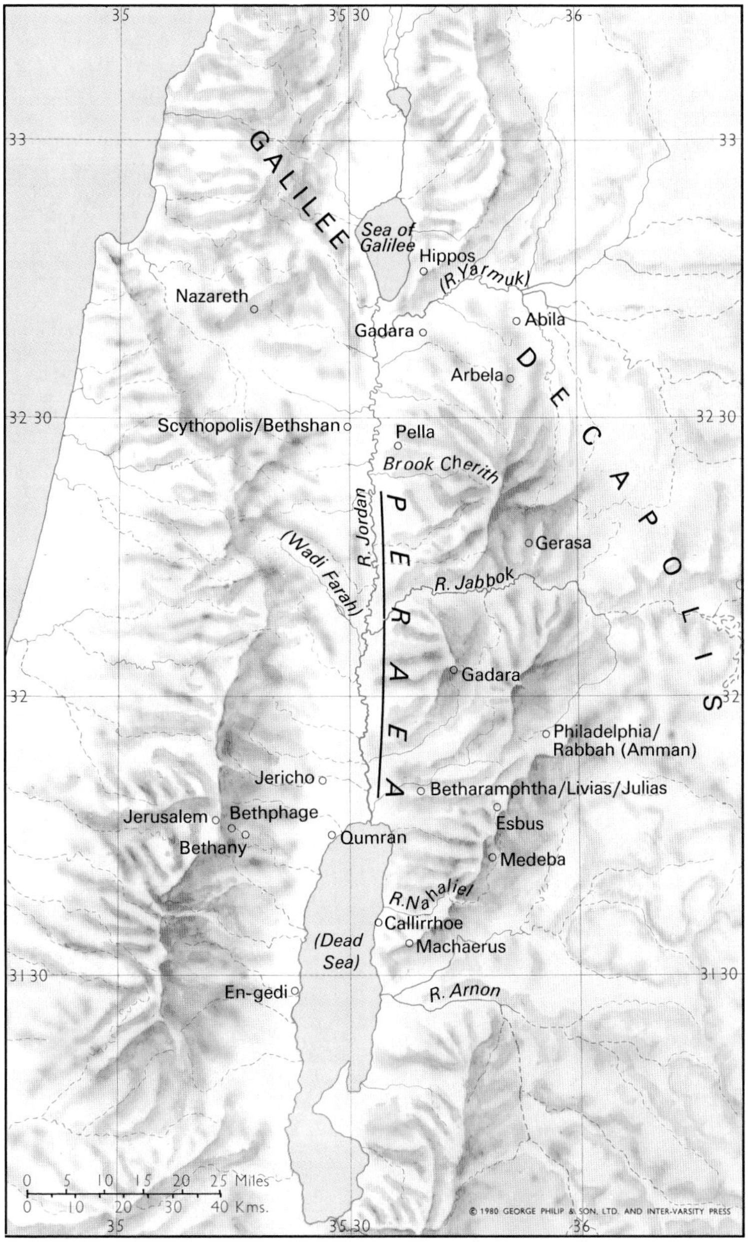

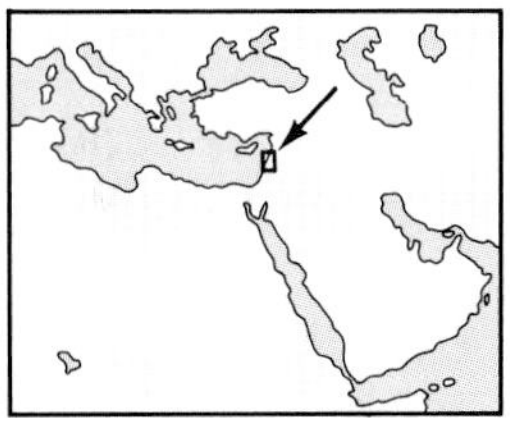

Peraea in Transjordan.

PERDITION (Gk. *apōleia*, 'loss', 'destruction'). A word employed in the NT, in the sense of 'destruction' and with special reference to the fate of the wicked and their loss of eternal life (Rev. 17:8, 11). (*HELL, *ESCHATOLOGY.)

In addition, the phrase 'son of perdition' occurs, a form of speech in which the Jews often expressed a man's destiny (*e.g.* 'sons of light', 'children of disobedience'; *cf.* Mt. 23:15; Lk. 10:6). It is applied to Judas Iscariot (Jn. 17:12) in a vivid sense which the Eng. does not fully convey as meaning literally 'not one perished but the son of perishing'. The term is used also by Paul to describe the 'man of lawlessness' (2 Thes. 2:3), for which see *Antichrist. The phrase 'sons of perdition' is found in *Jubilees* 10:3, with reference to those who perished in the Flood.

The Gk. word stands in direct antithesis to full and complete blessedness (*sōtēria*). J.D.D.

PERCUSSION INSTRUMENTS See Music, Part 2.

PEREZ, PEREZITES. Perez (Heb. *pereṣ*), one of the sons of Judah by Tamar his daughter-in-law (1 Ch. 2:4; 4:1), was so named because though his twin Zarah put out his hand first, Perez was the first delivered, and it was said that he had 'made a breach' (RSV) or 'broken forth' (AV) (*pāraṣ*; Gn. 38:29). He was the father of Hezron and Hamul (Gn. 46:12; Nu. 26:21; 1 Ch. 2:5), whose descendants were called Perezites (*parṣî*; Nu. 26:20; AV 'Pharzites'; see also Ne. 11:4, 6). Through him and Hezron passed the genealogy of the Messiah (1 Ch. 9:4; Ru. 4:18; Mt. 1:3; Lk. 3:33; *cf.* Ru. 4:12). The name occurs in LXX and NT as *Phares*, and this name is taken over unchanged into the AV NT. In the OT the AV gives 'Pharez' in all occurrences except 1 Ch. 27:3, and Ne. 11:4–6. In the later EVV the form Perez is used throughout. It may be compared with the Assyr. personal name *Parṣi* found in documents of the 8th century BC. See K. Tallqvist, *Assyrian Personal Names*, 1914, p. 180. T.C.M.

PERFECTION. The biblical idea of perfection is of a state of ideal wholeness or completion, in which any disabilities, shortcomings or defects that may have existed before have been eliminated or left behind.

In the OT, two Heb. roots express this idea: *šlm* and *tmm*. (For the literal sense of the adjective *šālēm*, see Dt. 25:15, RSV 'full', AV 'perfect'; 27:6, 'whole'; for that of *tāmîm*, see Lv. 3:9; 23:15.) In the NT the usual adjective (19 times) is *teleios* (noun *teleiotēs*, Col. 3:14; Heb. 6:1), which expresses the thought of having reached the appropriate or appointed *telos* ('end' in the sense of 'goal', 'purpose'). The corresponding verb, *teleioō* (16 times in this sense), means to bring into such a condition. In secular Greek *teleios* means also: (i) adult, full-grown, as opposed to immature and infantile, and (ii), in connection with mystery-cults, fully initiated. The former sense shines through in 1 Cor. 14:20; Eph. 4:13; Heb. 5:14; *cf.* 6:1; the latter in 1 Cor. 2:6 and perhaps Phil. 3:15; Col. 1:28. Two adjectives of similar meaning are: (i) *artios* (2 Tim. 3:17; AV 'perfect', RSV 'complete'), denoting ability and readiness to meet all demands made upon one, and (ii) *holoklēros* (Jas. 1:4, with *teleios*; 1 Thes. 5:23, RV 'entire', RSV 'sound'), for which Arndt gives 'whole, complete, undamaged, intact, blameless'. The NT also uses (7 times) the verb *katartizō*, translated 'perfect' in AV, meaning 'put in order', or 'bring to a fit state', by training, or supplying some lack, or correcting some fault.

Perfection is a relative term, meaning simply the attainment of a due end, or the enjoyment of an ideal state. What that end and state is varies in different cases. The Bible speaks of perfection in three distinct connections.

I. The perfection of God

Scripture speaks of God (Mt. 5:48), his 'work' (Dt. 32:4), his 'way' (2 Sa. 22:31 = Ps. 18:30), and his 'law' (Ps. 19:7; Jas. 1:25) as perfect. In each context some feature of his manifested moral glory is in view, and the thought is that what God

Perga, visited by Paul and Barnabas on their first missionary journey (Acts 13:13–14; 14:25). This colonnaded street was flanked by shops in Roman times. (RH)

says and does is wholly free from faults and worthy of all praise. In Mt. 5:48, Christ holds up the ideal conduct of the heavenly Father (particularly, in the context, his kindness to those who oppose him) as a pattern which his children must imitate.

II. The perfection of Christ

The writer to the Hebrews speaks of the incarnate Son of God as having been made 'perfect through sufferings' (Heb. 2:10). The reference here is not to any personal probation of Jesus as man, but to his being fitted by his experience of the power of temptation and the costliness of obedience for the high-priestly ministry to which God had called him (Heb. 5:7–10; *cf.* 7:28, RV). As high priest, having 'offered for all time a single sacrifice for sins' (Heb. 10:12), he became 'the source of eternal salvation to all who obey him' (Heb. 5:9), securing for them by his intercession constant access to God (Heb. 7:25; 10:19ff.) and giving them the constant sympathy and help that they need in their constant temptations (Heb. 4:14ff.). It was his own first-hand experience of temptation that fitted him to fulfil this latter ministry (Heb. 2:17f.; 5:2, 7ff.).

III. The perfection of man

This is spoken of with reference (*a*) to God's covenant relationship with man and (*b*) to his work of grace in man.

a. God's covenant relationship with man

The Bible speaks of *man's perfection in the covenant with God.* This is the perfection which the OT demands of God's people (Gn. 17:1; Dt. 18:13) and ascribes to individual saints (Noah, Gn. 6:9; Asa, 1 Ki. 15:14; Job, Jb. 1:1): loyal, sincere, whole-hearted obedience to the known will of their gracious God. It is faith at work, maintaining a right relationship with God by reverent worship and service. This perfection is essentially a matter of the heart (1 Ki. 8:61; 2 Ki. 20:3; 1 Ch. 29:9); outward conformity to God's commands is not enough if the heart is not perfect (2 Ch. 25:2). Perfection is regularly linked with uprightness, as its natural outward expression (Jb. 1:1, 8; 2:3; Ps. 37:37; Pr. 2:21). In Mt. 19:21 *teleios*, as well as expressing the negative thought, 'lacking nothing', would seem to carry the positive meaning, 'sincerely and truly in covenant with God'.

The Bible also speaks of *God's perfecting of his covenant relation with man.* This is the perfecting of men through Christ with which the writer to the Hebrews deals. 'The perfecting of men refers to their covenant condition. . . . To perfect . . . is to put the People into the true covenant relation of worshippers of the Lord, to bring them into His full fellowship' (A. B. Davidson, *Hebrews*, p. 208). God did this by replacing the old covenant, priesthood, tabernacle and sacrifices by something better. The 'old covenant' in Hebrews means the Mosaic system for establishing living fellowship between God and his people; but, says the writer, it could never 'perfect' them in this relationship, for it could not give full assurance of the remission of all sins (Heb. 7:11, 18; 9:9; 10:1–4). Under the new covenant, however, on the ground of Christ's single sacrifice of himself, believers receive God's assurance that he will remember their sins no more (10:11–18). Thus they are 'perfected for ever' (v. 14). This perfection of fellowship with God is something that OT saints did not know on earth (11:40)—though, through Christ, they enjoy it now, in the heavenly Jerusalem (12:23f.).

b. God's work of grace in man

The Bible speaks of *God's perfecting of his people in the image of Christ.* God means those who through faith enjoy fellowship with him to grow from spiritual infancy to a maturity (perfection) in which they will lack nothing of the full stature of Christ, in whose likeness they are being renewed (Col. 3:10). They are to grow till they are, in this sense, complete (*cf.* 1 Pet. 2:2; Heb. 5:14; 6:1; Gal. 3:14; Eph. 4:13; Col. 4:12). This thought has both a corporate and an individual aspect: the church corporately is to become 'a perfect man' (Eph. 4:13; *cf.* 2:15; Gal. 3:28), and the individual Christian will 'be perfect' (Phil. 3:12). In either case the conception is Christological and eschatological. The realm of perfection is 'in Christ' (Col. 1:28), and perfection of fellowship with Christ, and likeness to Christ, is a divine gift that will not be enjoyed till the day of his coming, the church's completing, and the Christian's resurrection (*cf.* Eph. 4:12–16; Phil. 3:10–14; Col. 3:4; 1 Jn. 3:2). Meanwhile, however, mature and vigorous Christians may be said to have attained a relative perfection in the realms of spiritual insight (Phil. 3:15, *cf.* v. 12), tempered Christian character (Jas. 1:4) and confident love towards God and men (1 Jn. 4:12, 17f.).

The Bible nowhere relates the idea of perfection directly to law, nor equates it directly with sinlessness. Absolute sinlessness is a goal which Christians must seek (*cf.* Mt. 5:48; 2 Cor. 7:1; Rom. 6:19) but which they do not as yet find (Jas. 3:2; 1 Jn. 1:8–2:2). No doubt when the Christian is perfected in glory he will be sinless, but to equate the biblical idea of perfection with sinlessness and then to argue that, because the Bible calls some men perfect, therefore sinlessness on earth must be a practical possibility, would be to darken counsel. The present perfection which, according to Scripture, some Christians attain is a matter, not of sinlessness, but of strong faith, joyful patience, and overflowing love. (*SANCTIFICATION.)

BIBLIOGRAPHY. Arndt; R. C. Trench, *New Testament Synonyms*[10], 1880, pp. 74–77; B. B. Warfield, *Perfectionism*, 1, 1931, pp. 113–301; R. N. Flew, *The Idea of Perfection in Christian Theology*, 1934, pp. 1–117; V. Taylor, *Forgiveness and Reconciliation*, 1941, ch. v; commentaries on Hebrews by A. B. Davidson, 1882, pp. 207–209, and B. F. Westcott[3], 1903, pp. 64–68; J. Wesley, *A Plain Account of Christian Perfection*, 1777. J.I.P.

PERGA. An ancient city of unknown foundation in *Pamphylia; well sited in an extensive valley, watered by the Cestrus. It was the religious capital of Pamphylia, like Ephesus, a 'cathedral city' of Artemis, whose temple stood on a nearby hill. Like most cities on that

Two wide colonnaded streets crossing at the centre of Roman Perga. (RH)

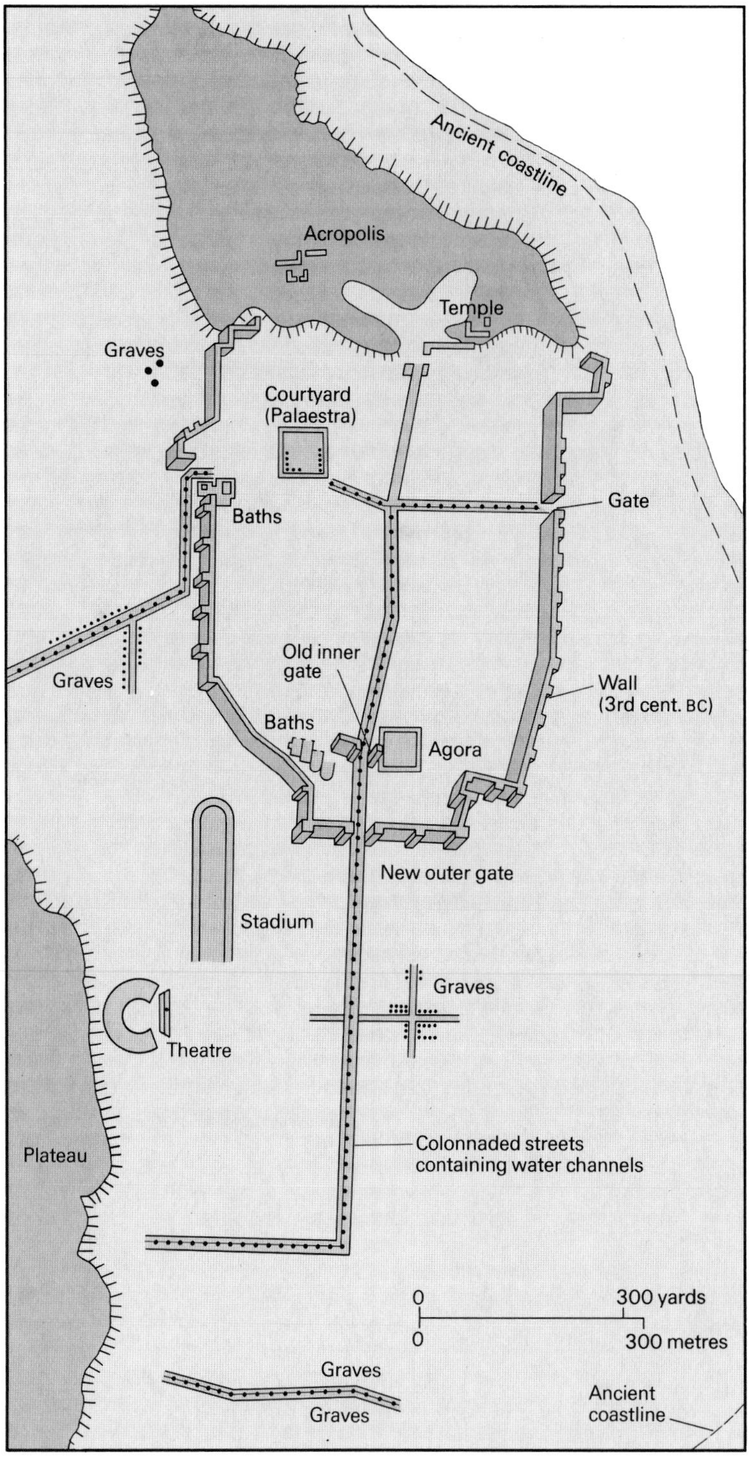

Plan of the site of Perga in Pamphylia.

pirate-ridden coast, Perga stands a little inland, and was served by a river-harbour. Attaleia, founded in the 2nd century BC, later served as Perga's port, but also absorbed her prosperity. Some ruins remain giving a pleasant impression of the ancient Perga, but Attaleia survives as an active port, the modern Adalia, one of the beauty-spots of Anatolia, so completely did Attalus' foundation overwhelm the more ancient towns. E.M.B.

PERGAMUM. A city of the Roman province of Asia, in the W of what is now Asiatic Turkey. It occupied a commanding position near the seaward end of the broad valley of the Caicus, and was probably the site of a settlement from a very early date. It became important only after 282 BC, when Philetaerus revolted against Lysimachus of Thrace and made it the capital of what became the Attalid kingdom, which in 133 BC was bequeathed by Attalus III to the Romans, who formed the province of *Asia from it. The first temple of the imperial cult was built in Pergamum (*c.* 29 BC) in honour of Rome and Augustus. The city thus boasted a religious primacy in the province, though *Ephesus became its main commercial centre.

Pergamum is listed third of the 'seven churches of Asia' (Rev. 1:11): the order suits its position in geographical sequence. This was the place 'where Satan's throne is' (Rev. 2:13). The phrase has been referred to the complex of pagan cults, of Zeus, Athena, Dionysus and Asclepius, established by the Attalid kings, that of Asclepius Soter (the 'saviour', 'healer') being of special importance. These cults are illustrative of the religious history of Pergamum, but the main allusion is probably to emperor worship. This was where the worship of the divine emperor had been made the touchstone of civic loyalty under Domitian. It marked a crisis for the church in Asia. Antipas (v. 13) is probably cited as a representative (perhaps the first) of those who were brought to judgment and execution here for their faith.

This letter is the primary source for the *Nicolaitans, who are emphatically equated with Balaam, and seem to be a party which advocated compromise under pagan pressures.

Here Christ possesses the real and ultimate authority, symbolized by the 'sharp two-edged sword' (v. 12), in the place where the Roman proconsul exercised the 'power of the sword' in judgment. The church is blamed for tolerating a party whose teaching would subvert it into idolatry and immorality like that of Balaam. But the 'conqueror' receives a pledge of Christ's inward relationship with him. The meaning of the 'white stone' (v. 17) is uncertain: it is properly a 'pebble' or *tessera* (tablet; Gk. *psēphos*). These had many uses, more than one of which may be apposite here. They represented acquittal, or served as a token or ticket of many kinds. The written name here is of the individual, and marks Christ's individual acceptance of the believer.

A small town (Bergama) still stands on the plain below the acropolis of the ancient city.

BIBLIOGRAPHY. W. M. Ramsay, *The Letters to the Seven Churches of Asia*, 1904, chs. 21–22; C. J. Hemer, *Buried History* 11, 1975, pp. 69–83; *idem*, *NIDNTT* 2, 1976, pp. 676–678.

M.J.S.R.
C.J.H.

PERIZZITES. These are mentioned: (1) among the occupants of Canaan generally (Gn. 15:20; Ex. 3:8; Dt. 7:1; 20:17; Jos. 3:10; 9:1; Jdg. 3:5; 1 Ki. 9:20; 2 Ch. 8:7; Ezr. 9:1; Ne. 9:8); (2) with the Jebusites, *etc.*, in the hills (Jos. 11:3); (3) with the Canaanites near Bethel (Gn. 13:7), near Shechem (Gn. 34:30), and in the Judaean hills (Jdg. 1:4f.); (4) with the Rephaim (Jos. 17:15). They were apparently hill-dwellers; this suits the interpretation of 'Perizzites', favoured by most commentators, as 'villagers' (from Heb. *p^erāzâ*, 'hamlet'. The fact that Gn. 10:15ff. does not name Perizzites among Canaan's 'sons' supports this possibility. See *POTT*, p. 101. J.P.U.L.

PERSECUTION. As encountered by Christians, this was nothing new. It was part of their Jewish heritage. The association of witness and suffering, begun as early as the second part of Isaiah, was crystallized in the Seleucid struggle. A theory of martyrdom rewarded by personal immortality grew up till it dominated the outlook of the Jews towards the Roman government (4 Macc. 17:8ff.). The possibility of death for Torah became accepted as a demand of Judaism. Thus

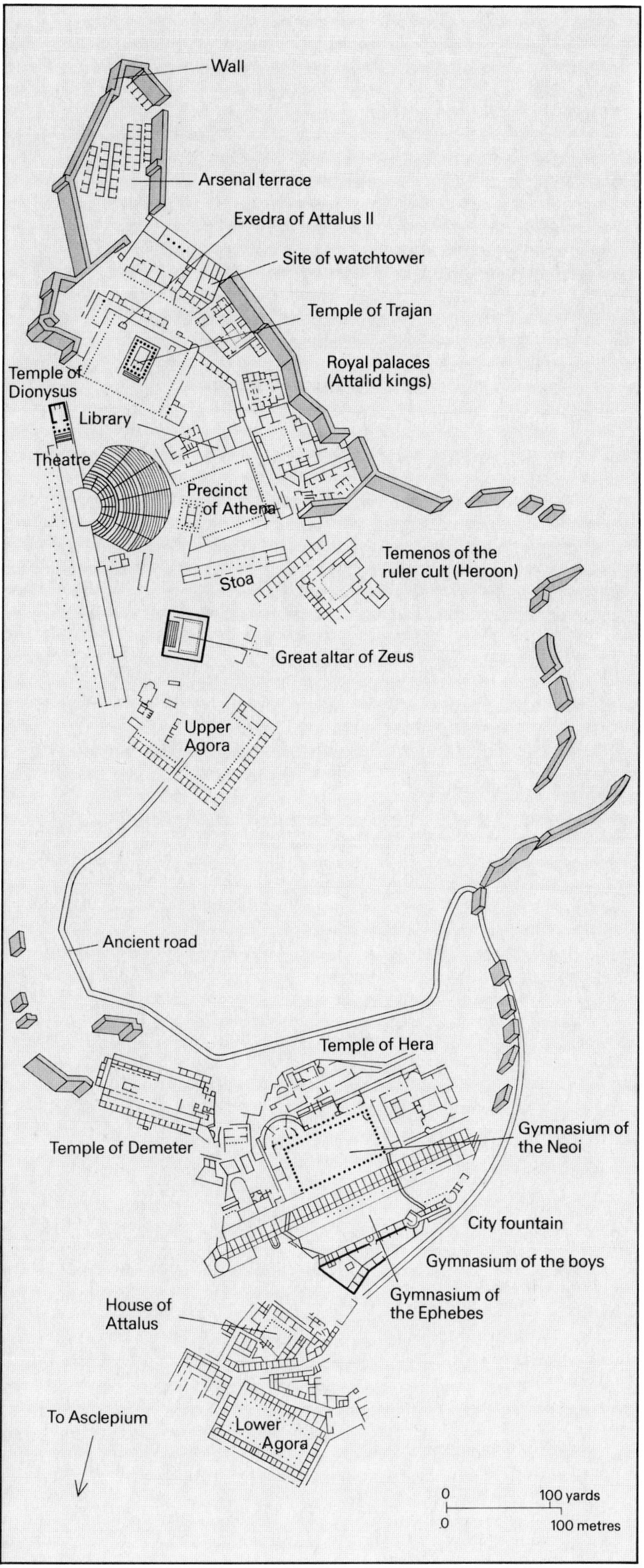

The site of Pergamum in Asia, showing temples of the imperial and other cults.

PERIDOT
See Jewels, Part 2.

PERIPHRASIS FOR GOD
See Heaven, Part 2.

The Temple of Athena at Pergamum. (PP)

the Jews were not averse to martyrdom; despite official Roman toleration of their religion, their cohesiveness, non-co-operation and uncanny financial success won them widespread hatred and spasmodic persecution, especially outside Palestine: pogroms were common in Alexandria. This legacy was taken over by the Christians. Their willingness to face suffering was intensified by the example of Jesus and by the association of persecution with the longed-for end of the age (Mk. 13:7–13). Even so, we must ask what aroused such animosity towards them among both the Jews and the Romans.

a. Opposition from the Jews

This gradually grew in intensity. The preaching of a crucified Messiah whose death was publicly blamed on the Jewish leaders was highly provocative. Even so, the people were favourable (Acts 2:46f.; 5:14) and the Pharisees moderate (Acts 5:34ff.; 23:6ff.), while opposition arose, naturally enough, among the Sadducees (Acts 4:1, 6; 5:17). Stephen's preaching of the transitoriness of the law (Acts 6:14) turned public opinion and brought about the first persecution in Jerusalem and elsewhere, *e.g.* Damascus. In AD 44 James was executed by Herod Agrippa, and throughout the Acts the Jews appear as Paul's most vehement enemies. This attitude could only have been made worse by the Apostolic Council which repudiated the need for circumcision, and it culminated in the excommunication of Christians at Jamnia, *c.* AD 80.

b. Opposition from the Romans

Rome's attitude underwent a marked change. At first, as we see in Acts, she gave Christians toleration and even encouragement. This soon gave way to fierce opposition. In Rome (Tacitus, *Ann.* 15. 44) such was their unpopularity by AD 64 that Nero could make them scapegoats for the fire. In Bithynia (Pliny, *Ep.* 10. 96–97) by *c.* AD 112 persistence in Christianity was a capital offence, though Trajan would not allow anonymous delation and he deprecated 'witch hunting'. Three explanations of this changed attitude are suggested:

(i) That Christians were prosecuted only for specific offences, such as cannibalism, incendiarism, incest, magic, illicit assembly and *majestas* (in their case, refusal to sacrifice to the *numen* of the emperor). There is, indeed, evidence that they were accused on all these counts, but 1 Pet. 2:12; 4:14–17; Pliny, *Ep.* 10. 97; and Suetonius, *Nero* 16, all make clear that at an early date the *nomen ipsum* of Christian, irrespective of the *cohaerentia flagitia* associated with it in the popular mind, was punishable.

(ii) That there was a general law throughout the empire, the *institutum Neronianum*, which proscribed Christianity. Tertullian makes this claim, and says that this was the only one of Nero's *acta* not rescinded later (*Ad. Nat.* 50. 7, see also *Apol.* 5), and the evidence of Suetonius, 1 Pet. and Rev. is patient of this interpretation. However, Christianity was probably not important enough to evoke such a general law, and if there was one it is hard to explain Pliny's ignorance of it, Trajan's failure to mention it, the property rights enjoyed by the church prior to the Decian persecution, and the remarkable lack of uniformity in its execution.

(iii) That persecution was at the discretion of the governor, who acted only in response to private accusation: there was no public prosecutor in Roman society. Whatever the formal charge, it is clear that by Pliny's time active membership of an organization believed to be criminal, and therefore, like the Bacchanals and the Druids, banned because in all three cult and *scelera* appeared indistinguishable, constituted an actionable offence, and *contumacia*, persistent refusal to recant, met with death. The competence of proconsuls and city prefects in *crimina extra ordinem* has been shown in recent years to have been very great. If a governor wished to take action against Christians he had the Neronian precedent to guide him and his coercive *imperium* to support him. Alternatively, it lay within his discretion, like Gallio (Acts 18:14–16), to refuse jurisdiction. If in doubt he could refer to the emperor, whose rescript would be binding on him as long as he remained in the province, though not necessarily upon his successors.

It is because the governors enjoyed such discretion that Tertullian addressed his Apology not to the emperor but to the governor: for it was in his hands that the remedy lay. This accounts for the spasmodic nature of persecution until the days of Decius. It depended so much on the policy of the governor and whether the extent of the unpopularity of Christians in the province was such as to drive private individuals to prosecute them. There is no satisfactory evidence (despite Orosius, 7. 7) for believing that there was any general action against Christians throughout the empire under Nero, though the sect seems to have become *illicita* in Rome itself (Suetonius, *Nero* 16). The actual evidence for a Domitianic persecution of the church is precarious despite the invective heaped on that emperor by the Fathers. A broad generalization in Dio (67. 14), concerning the death of Flavius Clemens, who was possibly, and Acilius Glabrio, who was probably, a Christian, and the banishment of Domitilla, is about all that can be summoned. But it is quite possible that Domitian, who minutely inspected and vigorously exacted the Jewish revenue (Suetonius, *Domit.* 12), discovered uncircumcised Christians sheltering under the religious privileges of the Jews and instituted against them a general persecution of which we have vivid traces in the Apocalypse, if this is to be dated under Domitian rather than Nero.

Persecution was therefore restricted by three factors: (i) that the Roman governors were reluctant to admit charges concerning private religious opinions (*superstitiones*) and tried to confine their attention to real offences; (ii) that accusations had to be made personally and publicly—and to bring a capital charge was both dangerous and difficult; (iii) that in each province only one man, the governor, could pass the death sentence.

These three factors combined to protect the majority of Christians long enough for the church to become firmly established throughout the empire.

BIBLIOGRAPHY. W. H. C. Frend, *Martyrdom and Persecution in the Early Church*, 1965; T. W. Manson, 'Martyrs and Martyrdom', *BJRL* 39, 1956–7, pp. 463ff.; H. B. Mattingley, *JTS* n.s. 9, 1958, pp. 26ff.; F. W. Clayton, *CQ* 41, 1947, pp. 83ff.; A. N. Sherwin-White, *JTS* n.s. 3, 1952, pp. 199ff.; H. Last, *JRS* 27, 1937, pp. 80ff.; E. M. Smallwood, *Classical Philology* 51, 1956, pp. 5–11; G. Ebel, R. Schippers, *NIDNTT* 2, pp. 805–809; A. Oepke, *TDNT* 2, pp. 229f.; H. Schlier, *TDNT* 3, pp. 139–148.

E.M.B.G.

PERSEVERANCE. The strictly biblical, as distinct from the later theological, significance of this term is indicated by the context of its sole occurrence in AV as a rendering of *proskarterēsis* in Eph. 6:18. The implication of steadfastness, patience, persistence is confirmed by the use of the verb *proskartereō*, to attend constantly, continue unswervingly, adhere firmly, hold fast to (*MM*, p. 548). It is used in Mk. 3:9 to describe a skiff quietly waiting to carry Jesus from the surging crowd, and in Acts 10:7 of the soldiers in Cornelius' bodyguard who were in uninterrupted attendance upon him. In its spiritual application it always has to do with continuance in the Christian way, particularly in relation to prayer (*cf.* Acts 1:14; 2:42, 46; 6:4; 8:13; Rom. 12:12; 13:6; Col. 4:2). RSV translates *hypomonē* as 'perseverance' in Heb. 12:1.

No doctrinal undertones attach to the term in the NT. It relates simply to the continual and patient dependence of the Christian upon Christ. Our Lord's parable of the importunate widow is the most relevant commentary (*cf.* Lk. 18:1–8). Christian perseverance is only a quality in the believer because initially it is a gift of God. It is by his power that those who trust in him are 'guarded through faith for a salvation ready to be revealed in the last time' (1 Pet. 1:5).

BIBLIOGRAPHY. I. H. Marshall, *Kept by the Power of God*, 1969; W. Mundle, *NIDNTT* 2, pp. 767f.

A.S.W.

PERSIA, PERSIANS. The Indo-European Persians, nomadic pastoralists from S Russia, probably entered the Iranian plateau late in the 2nd millennium BC. In 836 BC Shalmaneser III of Assyria received tribute from rulers of a Parsua near Lake Urmia. His successor found the land of Parsuash in the S where several tribes finally settled. This area, E of the Persian Gulf, is still called Farsistan. Persepolis and Parsagarda were the chief towns. Heb. *pāras*, 'Persia', refers to this land.

I. Persian and Jewish history

The early traditions of the Persian people are recorded in the sacred book, the Zend-Avesta. The earliest recorded kings ruled from Anshan, NW of Susa. The Achaemenes who was claimed as founder of the

A fine example of ancient Persian craftsmanship, this silver goose with eyes inlaid with gold was made by casting and tooling the metal. From the Oxus Treasure. Length c. 8·89 cm. 6th–5th cent. BC. (BM)

The Audience Hall (apadana) *of the palace built by Darius I at Persepolis, Iran, was approached by this monumental entrance. 522–486 BC.* (RS)

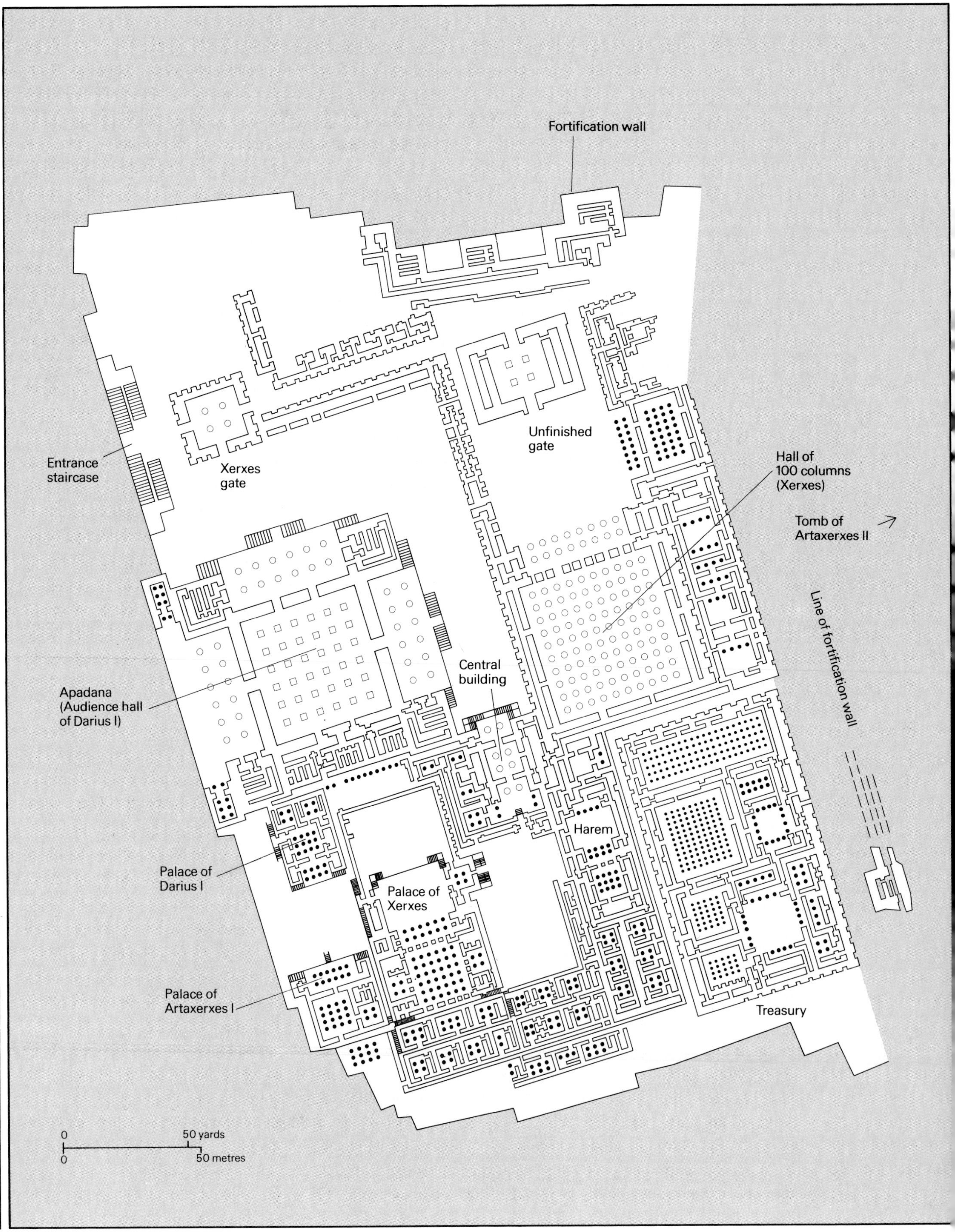
Fortification wall
Unfinished gate
Hall of 100 columns (Xerxes)
Tomb of Artaxerxes II
Entrance staircase
Xerxes gate
Line of fortification wall
Central building
Apadana (Audience hall of Darius I)
Harem
Palace of Darius I
Palace of Xerxes
Palace of Artaxerxes I
Treasury
0
50 yards
0
50 metres

A hollow golden fish, perhaps used as a flask or bottle. Part of the Oxus Treasure from Persia. Length c. 25·4 cm. 6th–5th cent. BC. (BM)

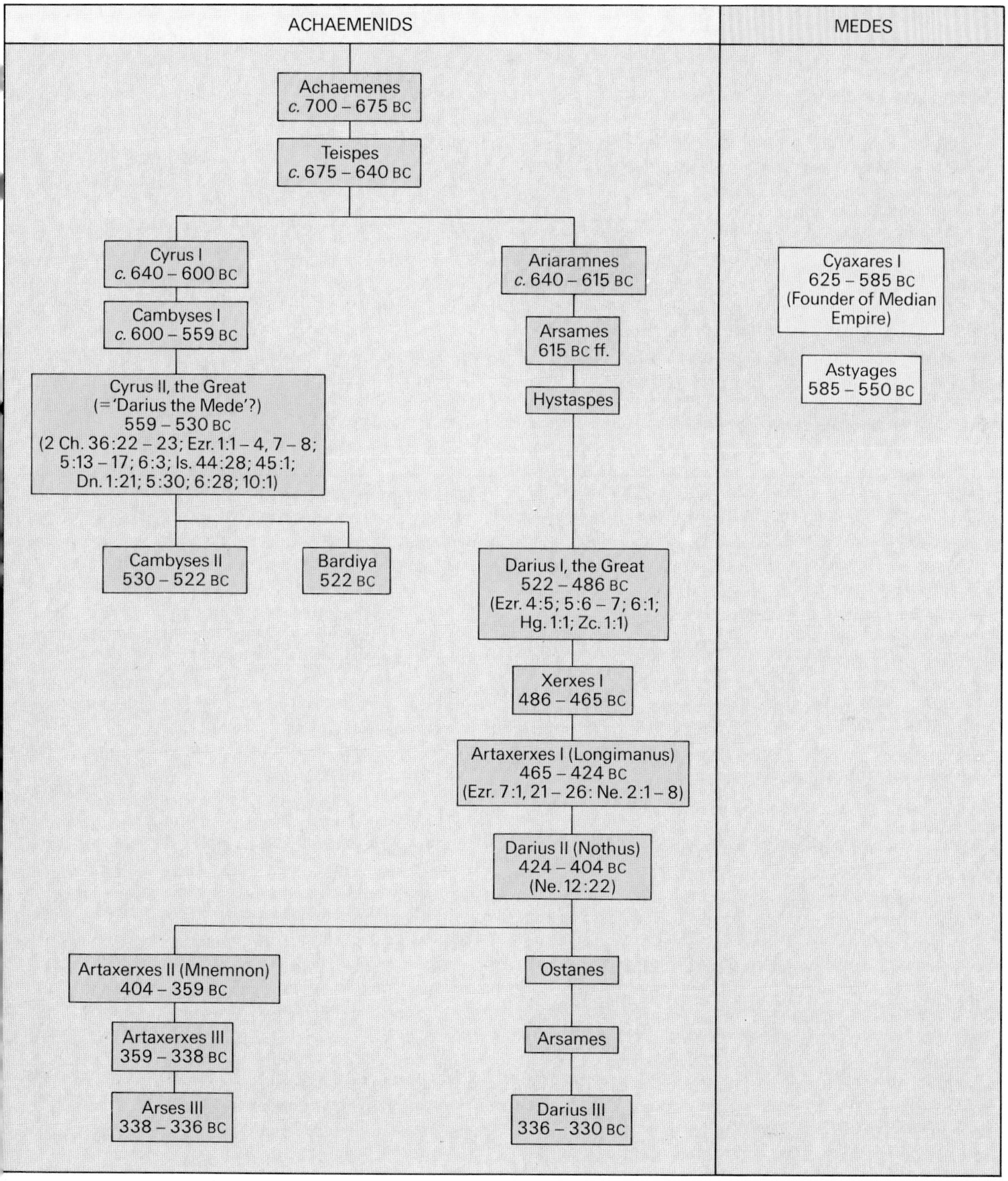

Persian rulers of the Achaemenid dynasty, with selected biblical references.

Opposite page: Plan of the principal Achaemenid royal buildings at Persepolis.

dynasty by later kings probably reigned *c*. 680 BC. His grandson, Cyrus I, opposed Ashurbanipal of Assyria, but later submitted. Cyrus II, grandson of Cyrus I, rebelled against his Median suzerain, Astyages, killing him and taking over his capital, *Ecbatana, in 550 BC. Thereafter Median language and customs had strong influence on the Persians. This success was followed by the subjugation of Anatolia and the conquest of Croesus of Lydia (547 BC). Cyrus then turned E to extend his realm into NW India. By 540 BC he was sufficiently strong to attack Babylonia. After several battles he entered Babylon in triumph on 29 October 539 BC, 17 days after the city had fallen to his army (Dn. 5:30f.; *CYRUS). The king soon returned to Susa, but his son Cambyses remained in Babylon to represent him in religious ceremonies. The whole empire was divided into large regions ruled by *satraps, chosen from Persian or Median nobles but with native officers under them (*cf*. Dn. 6). Various statues of gods which had been collected into Babylon by the last native king, Nabonidus (perhaps reflected in Is. 46:1f.), were returned to their own shrines. As there was no image of Yahweh to return to Jerusalem, Cyrus gave to back the Jews the precious vessels

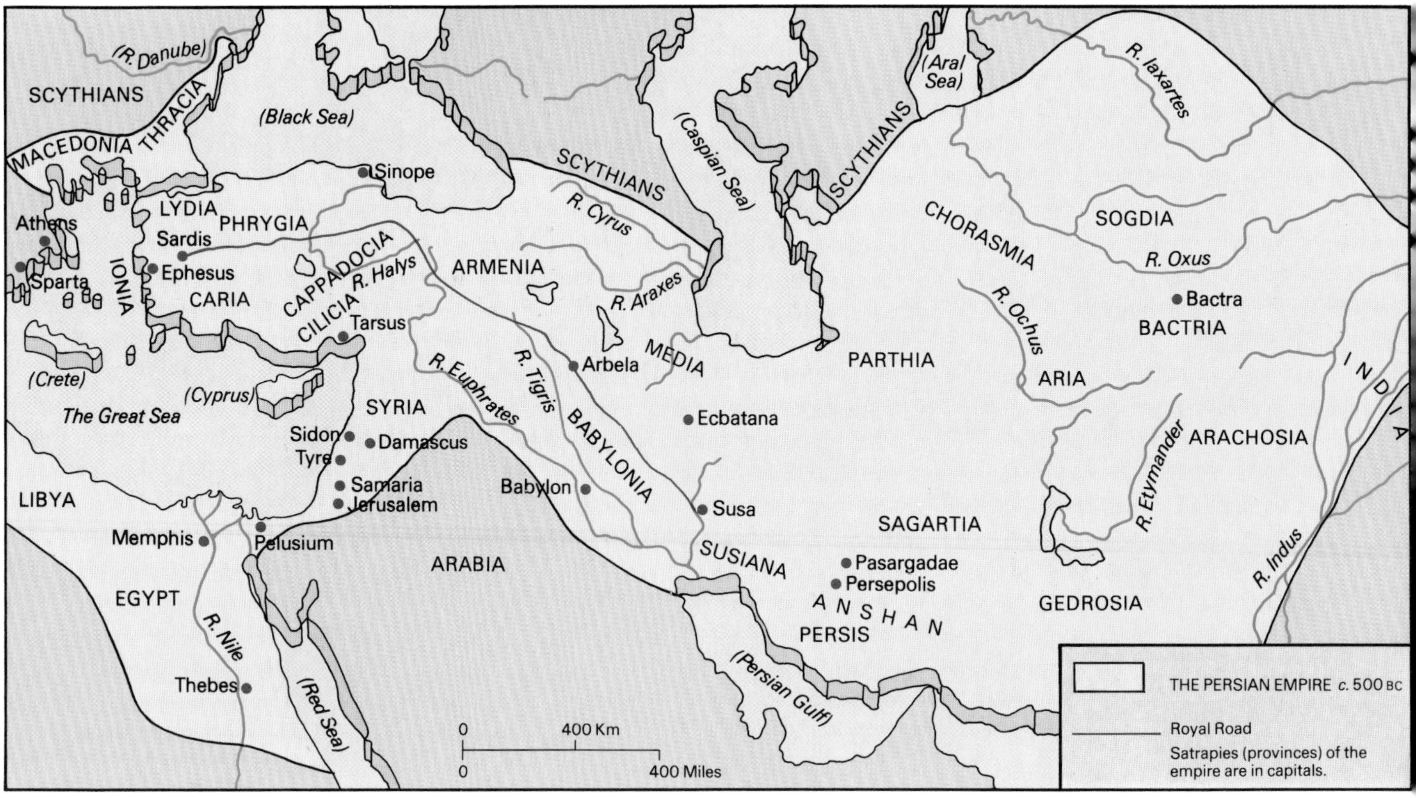

looted from the Temple by Nebuchadrezzar (Ezr. 1:7ff.; *cf. DOTT*, pp. 92–94). More important, he gave royal authorization for the rebuilding of the Temple to any Jew who wished to return to Judah (Ezr. 1:1–4). One Sheshbazzar was appointed governor (Ezr. 5:14). He was evidently a special officer responsible to the king. The governor of the province of 'Across the River' (the country W of the Euphrates) was clearly unaware of Cyrus' edict when in 520 BC he attempted to delay the work. His letter went to his superior, the satrap who had charge of Babylon and the W. No record was found among the archives kept at Babylon, but a memorandum was found at Ecbatana, where Cyrus had resided during his first regnal year. Darius I (522–486 BC) confirmed the decree and ordered his officials to help the Jews.

Darius and his successor Xerxes I (486–465 BC) expended considerable energy in an attempt to conquer the Greeks of the Peloponnese, almost the only area remaining outside the Persian empire in the known world, for Cambyses II (530–522 BC) had annexed Egypt in 525 BC. The defeat at Marathon (490 BC) by a small Gk. army was the only rebuff suffered by Darius. His reorganization of the satrapies, his system of military commanders, and his introduction of coinage, legal and postal systems lasted as long as the empire. These facilities coupled with the considerable degree of autonomy allowed to subject peoples contributed greatly to the stability of the empire and allowed such a small community as Judah to survive, Jewish officers acting as governors (*pḥh*) there.

Under Artaxerxes I (465–424 BC) Jewish affairs had official representation at court. * Ezra, it seems, was 'Secretary of State for Jewish Affairs' (Ezr. 7:12). He was accredited as special envoy to reorganize the Temple services at Jerusalem (458 BC). The eager Jews were led on by the encouragement they received to exceed the terms of Ezra's commission and rebuild the city wall. This was reported to the king by the governor of Samaria, who evidently had some responsibility for Judah. The royal reply (Ezr. 4:17–23) ordered the cessation of the work, for search of the records had shown that the city had revolted against earlier kings. Artaxerxes was faced with rebellion in Egypt (*c.* 460–454 BC), so he could not allow the construction of a fortress so near to that country. However, the royal cupbearer was a Jew, * Nehemiah, who was able to reverse the effects of this decree by having himself appointed * governor of Judah (Heb. *tiršāṯā'*, a Persian word, Ne. 8:9) with permission to rebuild the walls (445 BC). No record remains of relations between the Persian rulers and the Jews after this period. When the Persian empire was in the power of Alexander (331 BC) the Jews simply transferred their allegiance from one monarch to another.

II. Persian culture

The Indo-European Persian language was written in a cuneiform script composed of 51 simple syllabic signs (* WRITING) but this was restricted to imperial monuments almost exclusively. The imperial chancery used Aramaic language and characters for official communications (*e.g.* the letters in Ezra, *cf. DOTT*, pp. 256–269). Translations were made into local tongues (*cf.* Est. 3:12; 8:9).

The luxury of the Persian court as described in the book of * Esther is attested by objects found at several sites. A number of stone bas-reliefs depict the king and his courtiers and the tribute of the vanquished. Portraits of the different racial groups are especially fine examples of Persian stone carving. The Oxus treasure (now mostly in the British Museum) and other chance finds show the skill of goldsmiths and jewellers. Solid gold and silver bowls and vases illustrate the wealth of the kings. Gk. influences may be seen in some Persian works and Gk. craftsmen appear among lists of palace dependants.

III. Persian religion

The early Persians revered gods of nature, fertility and the heavens. The tribe of the Magi were nearly exclusively the priests. Some time after 1000 BC Zoroaster proclaimed a religion of lofty moral ideals based on the principle 'Do good, hate evil'. For him there was one god, Ahura-mazda, the Good, represented by purifying fire and water. Opposed to the good was a dark power of Evil. This creed was adopted by Darius I, but soon became lost among the more ancient cults. Zoroaster's doctrines survived and were spread abroad. Their influence has been traced in the writings of early Judaism (* DEAD SEA SCROLLS) and, by some scholars, in the NT.

BIBLIOGRAPHY. A. T. Olmstead, *History of the Persian Empire*, 1948; J. Bright, *A History of Israel*², 1972, pp. 409–414; R. N. Frye, *The Heritage of Persia*², 1975; E. Porada, *Ancient Iran*, 1965; M. Boyce, *A History of Zoroastrianism*, 1, 1975.

A.R.M.

PETER.

I. Early background

Peter's original name was apparently the Heb. Simeon (Acts 15:14; 2 Pet. 1:1): perhaps, like many Jews, he adopted also 'Simon', usual in the NT, as a Gk. name of similar sound. His father's name was Jonah (Mt. 16:17); he himself was married (Mk. 1:30), and in his missionary days his wife accompanied him (1 Cor. 9:5). The Fourth Gospel gives * Beth-saida, just inside Gaulanitis, and a largely Gk. city, as his place of origin (Jn. 1:44), but he had also a home in Capernaum in Galilee (Mk. 1:21ff.). Both places were at the lakeside, where he worked as a fisherman, and in both there would be abundant contact with Gentiles. (His brother's name is Gk.) Simon spoke Aramaic with a strong N-country accent (Mk. 14:70), and maintained the piety and outlook of his people (*cf.* Acts 10:14), though not trained in the law (Acts 4:13; literacy is not in question). It is likely that he was affected by John the Baptist's movement (*cf.* Acts 1:22): his brother Andrew was a disciple of John (Jn. 1:39f.).

II. Call

The Fourth Gospel describes a period of Christ's activity before the commencement of the Galilean ministry, and to this may be referred Peter's first introduction to him, by Andrew's agency (Jn. 1:41). This makes the response to the subsequent call by the lakeside (Mk. 1:16f.) more intelligible. The call to the intimate band of the Twelve followed (Mk. 3:16ff.).

It was as a disciple that Simon received his new title, the Aramaic *Kepha* ('Cephas'), 'rock' or 'stone' (1 Cor. 1:12; 15:5; Gal. 2:9), usually appearing in NT in the Gk. form *Petros*. According to Jn. 1:42, Jesus conferred this title (not known as a personal name previously) at their first encounter. John's usual designation is 'Simon Peter'. Mark calls him Simon up to 3:16, and Peter

Opposite page: Persian silver dish (viewed from beneath). From Erzincan, Armenia. Achaemenid period (5th cent. BC). (BM)

PERSONALITY, CORPORATE
See Servant of the Lord, Part 3.

PERVERSITY
See Wicked, Part 3.

Opposite page: The Persian Empire, 550–330 BC.

almost invariably thereafter. There is nothing in any case to suggest that the solemn words of Mt. 16:18 represented the first bestowal of the name.

III. Peter in the ministry of Jesus

Peter was one of the first disciples called; he always stands first in the lists of disciples; he was also one of the three who formed an inner circle round the Master (Mk. 5:37; 9:2; 14:33; *cf.* 13:3). His impulsive devotion is frequently portrayed (*cf.* Mt. 14:28; Mk. 14:29; Lk. 5:8; Jn. 21:7), and he acts as spokesman of the Twelve (Mt. 15:15; 18:21; Mk. 1:36f.; 8:29; 9:5; 10:28; 11:21; 14:29ff.; Lk. 5:5; 12:41). At the crisis near Caesarea Philippi he is the representative of the whole band: for the question is directed to them all (Mk. 8:27, 29), and all are included in the look that accompanies the subsequent reprimand (8:33).

On any satisfactory interpretation of Mk. 9:1 the transfiguration is intimately related to the apostolic confession which precedes it. The experience made a lasting impression on Peter: 1 Pet. 5:1; 2 Pet. 1:16ff. are most naturally interpreted of the transfiguration, and, for what they are worth, the *Apocalypse* and *Acts of Peter* (* NEW TESTAMENT APOCRYPHA) show that their authors associated the preaching of this subject with Peter.

In a measure, the disastrous boast of Mk. 14:29ff. is also representative of the disciples; and, as Peter's protestations of loyalty are the loudest, so his rejection of the Lord is the most explicit (Mk. 14:66ff.). He is, however, specially marked out by the message of the resurrection (Mk. 16:7), and personally receives a visitation of the risen Lord (Lk. 24:34; 1 Cor. 15:5).

IV. The commission of Peter

Mt. 16:18ff. is one of the most discussed passages of the NT. Rejection of the genuineness of the saying is arbitrary, and generally based on dogmatic assumptions (sometimes the assumption that Jesus never meant to found the church). Others have argued that the saying is genuine but displaced. Stauffer would see it as a resurrection commission, like Jn. 21:15; Cullmann would set it in a passion context, like Lk. 22:31f. Such reconstructions hardly do justice to the distinctiveness of Mt. 16:18ff. It is a benediction and a promise: the other passages are commands. We need not undervalue Mark's vivid account of the Caesarea Philippi incident, which concentrates attention on the disciples' failure to understand the nature of the Messiahship they have just confessed, to acknowledge that the 'rock' saying belongs to the occasion of the confession.

There is still no unanimity in interpreting the passage. The suggestion that 'rock' is simply a misunderstanding of a vocative 'Peter' in the underlying Aramaic (*SB*, 1, p. 732) is too facile: the passage has obviously something to do with the significance of Peter's name, which various Gospel sources show as having been solemnly bestowed by Jesus. From early times two main interpretations have been held, with many variants.

1. That the rock is substantially what Peter has said: either Peter's faith or the confession of the Messiahship of Jesus. This is a very early interpretation (*cf.* Origen, *in loc.*, 'Rock means every disciple of Christ'). It has the great merit of taking seriously the Matthean context, and emphasizing, as Mk. 8 does in a different way, the immense significance of the Caesarea

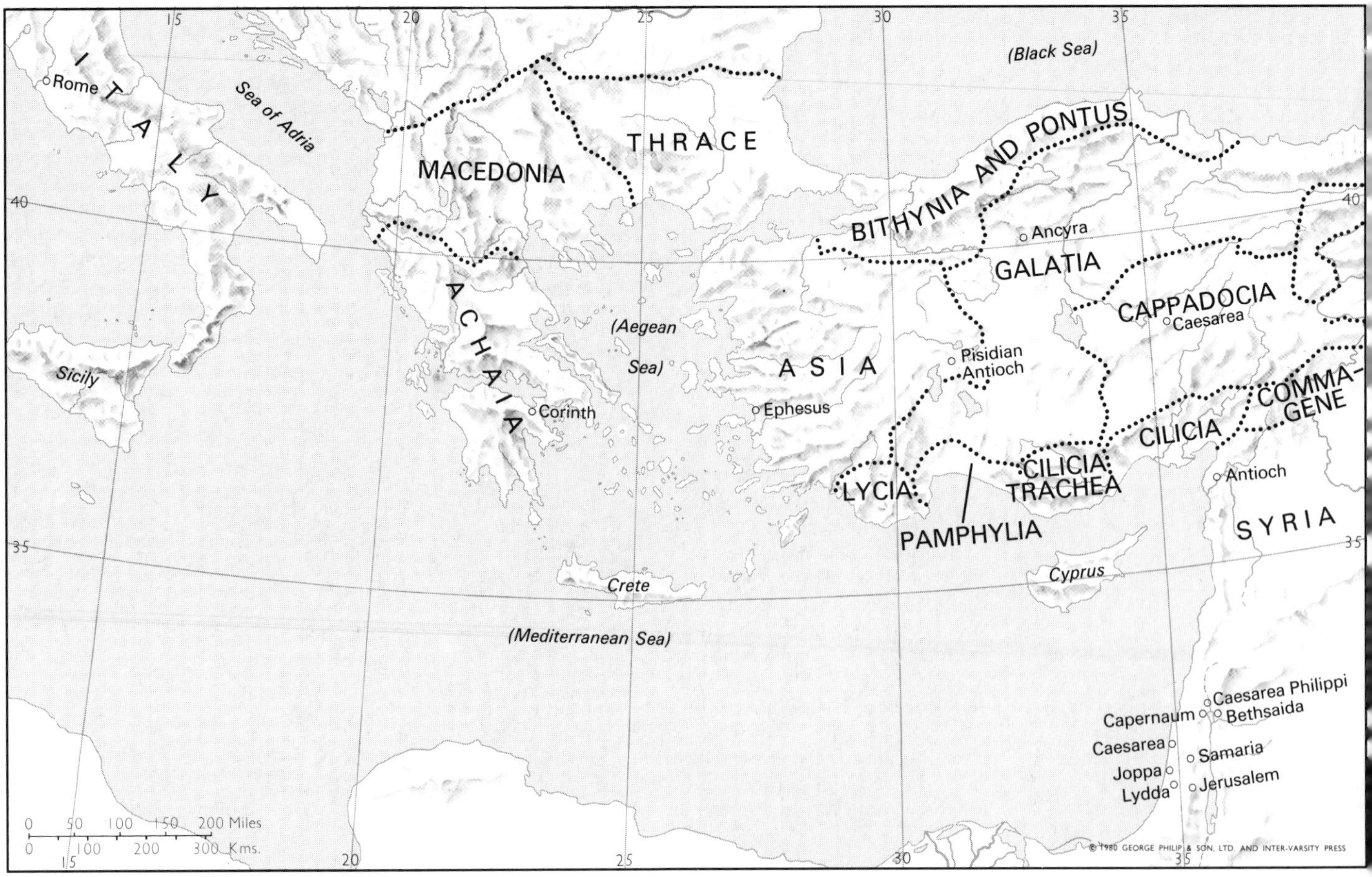

Map to illustrate the life of Peter.

Philippi confession. In historical perspective we should probably see the rock as, not simply faith in Christ, but the apostolic confession of Christ, spoken of elsewhere as the foundation of the church (*cf.* Eph. 2:20). The 'rock' saying touches the core of the apostolic function, and Peter, first among the *apostles, has a name which proclaims it. That his own faith and understanding are as yet anything but exemplary is irrelevant: the church is to be built on the confession of the apostles.

2. That the rock is Peter himself. This is found almost as early as the other, for Tertullian and the bishop, whether Roman or Carthaginian, against whom he thundered in *De Pudicitia*, assume this, though with different inferences. Its strength lies in the fact that Mt. 16:19 is in the singular, and must be addressed directly to Peter even if, like Origen, we go on to say that to have Peter's faith and virtues is to have Peter's keys. Comparison might also be made with the Midrash on Is. 51:1. When God looked on Abraham who was to appear, he said, 'Behold, I have found a rock on which I can build and base the world. Therefore he called Abraham a rock' (*SB*, 1, p. 733).

Many Protestant interpreters, including notably Cullmann, take the latter view; but it is perhaps significant that he cuts the saying from the Matthean setting. To read it where Matthew places it is surer than to treat it as an isolated logion.

It must be stressed, however, that the exegesis of this point has nothing to do with the claims for the primacy of the Roman Church or its bishop with which it has through historical circumstances become involved. Even if it could be shown that Roman bishops are in any meaningful sense the successors of Peter (which it cannot), the passage does not allow for the transfer of its provisions to any successors whatever. It refers to the foundation of the church, which in the nature of things cannot be repeated.

The words that follow about the keys of the kingdom should be contrasted with Mt. 23:13. The Pharisees, for all their missionary propaganda, shut up the kingdom: Peter, recognizing the Son who is over the house and who holds the keys (*cf.* Rev. 1:18; 3:7; 21:25), finds them delivered to him (*cf.* Is. 22:22) to open the kingdom. (*POWER OF THE KEYS.) The 'binding and loosing', a phrase for which there are illuminating rabbinic parallels, is here addressed to Peter, but elsewhere is assigned to all the apostles (*cf.* Mt. 18:18). 'The apostle would, in the coming Kingdom, be like a great scribe or Rabbi, who would deliver decisions on the basis, not of the Jewish law, but of the teaching of Jesus which "fulfilled" it' (A. H. McNeile, *in loc.*).

But that here and elsewhere a primacy among the apostles is ascribed to Peter is not in doubt. Lk. 22:31ff. shows the strategic position of Peter as seen by both the Lord and the devil and, in full knowledge of the approaching desertion, marks out his future pastoral function. The risen Lord reinforces this commission (Jn. 21:15ff.), and it is the Fourth Gospel, which demonstrates the peculiar relationship of the apostle John to Christ, that records it.

V. Peter in the apostolic church

The Acts shows the commission in exercise. Before Pentecost it is Peter who takes the lead in the community (Acts 1:15ff.); afterwards, he is the principal preacher (2:14ff.; 3:12ff.) the spokesman before the Jewish authorities (4:8ff.), the president in the administration of discipline (5:3ff.). Though the church as a whole made a deep impression on the community, it was to Peter in particular that supernatural powers were attributed (5:15). In Samaria, the church's first mission field, the same leadership is exercised (8:14ff.).

Significantly also, he is the first apostle to be associated with the Gentile mission, and that by unmistakably providential means (10:1ff.; *cf.* 15:7ff.). This immediately brings criticism upon him (11:2ff.); and not for the last time. Gal. 2:11ff. gives us a glimpse of Peter at Antioch, the first church with a significant ex-pagan element, sharing table-fellowship with the Gentile converts, and then meeting a barrage of Jewish-Christian opposition, in the face of which he withdraws. This defection was roundly denounced by Paul; but there is no hint of any theological difference between them, and Paul's complaint is rather the incompatibility of Peter's practice with his theory. The old theory (revived by S. G. F. Brandon, *The Fall of Jerusalem and the Christian Church*, 1951), of persistent rivalry between Paul and Peter, has little basis in the documents.

Despite this lapse, the Gentile mission had no truer friend than Peter. Paul's gospel and his had the same content, though a somewhat different expression: the Petrine speeches in Acts, Mark's Gospel and 1 Peter have the same theology of the cross, rooted in the concept of Christ as the suffering Servant. He was ready with the right hand of fellowship, recognizing his mission to Jews and Paul's to Gentiles as part of the same ministry (Gal. 2:7ff.); and at the Jerusalem Council is recorded as the first to urge the full acceptance of the Gentiles on faith alone (Acts 15:7ff.).

Peter's career after the death of Stephen is hard to trace. The references to him in Joppa, Caesarea and elsewhere suggest that he undertook missionary work in Palestine (James no doubt now assuming leadership in Jerusalem). He was imprisoned in Jerusalem, and on his miraculous escape he left for 'another place' (Acts 12:17). Attempts to identify this place are fruitless. We know that he went to Antioch (Gal. 2:11ff.); he may have gone to Corinth, though probably not for long (1 Cor. 1:12). He is closely associated with Christians in N Asia Minor (1 Pet. 1:1), and possibly the prohibition on Paul's entry into Bithynia (Acts 16:7) was due to the fact that Peter was at work there.

Peter's residence in Rome has been disputed, but on insufficient grounds. 1 Peter was almost certainly written from there (1 Pet. 5:13; *PETER, FIRST EPISTLE OF). That book shows signs of being written just before or during the Neronian persecution, and *1 Clement* 5 implies that, like Paul, he died in this outburst. Doubts cast on the interpretation of *1 Clement* (*cf.* M. Smith, *NTS* 9, 1960, pp. 86ff.) have little foundation. On the other hand, Cullmann's suggestion, based on the context in *1 Clement* and Paul's hints in Philippians of tensions in the church in Rome, that Peter, perhaps at Paul's request, came specifically to heal the breach, and that bitterness among Christians led to the death of both, is worth serious consideration. The story in the *Acts of Peter* of his martyrdom by crucifixion (*cf.* Jn. 21:18ff.) head downwards cannot be accepted as reliable, but this work (*NEW TESTAMENT APOCRYPHA) may preserve some valid traditions. Certainly these Acts, like other 2nd-century witnesses, emphasize the co-operation of the apostles in Rome.

Excavations in Rome have revealed an early cultus of Peter under St Peter's (*cf.* Eusebius, *EH* 2. 25): it is not safe to claim more for them. (*PETER, FIRST and SECOND EPISTLES OF.)

BIBLIOGRAPHY. F. J. Foakes Jackson, *Peter, Prince of Apostles*, 1927; E. Stauffer, *Zeitschrift für Kirchengeschichte* 62, 1944, pp. 1ff. (*cf. New Testament Theology*, 1955, pp. 30ff.); O. Cullmann, *Peter: Disciple—Apostle—Martyr*², 1962; *JEH* 7, 1956, pp. 238f. (on excavations); J. Toynbee and J. Ward Perkins, *The Shrine of St. Peter and the Vatican Excavations*, 1956; H. Chadwick, *JTS* n.s. 8, 1957, pp. 31ff.; O. Karrer, *Peter and the Church*, 1963; R. E. Brown, K. P. Donfried, J. Reumann (eds.), *Peter in the New Testament*, 1973.

A.F.W.

PETER, ACTS OF
See New Testament apocrypha, Part 2.

PETER, FIRST EPISTLE OF.
The letter is sent in the name of the apostle, to whose status and experience there is a modest allusion in 5:1. A certain function is ascribed to Silvanus (5:12)—almost certainly the *Silas of Acts. The address is the widest in the NT (1:1); to the Christians of five provinces (of which Bithynia and Pontus were for administrative purposes merged).

I. Outline of contents

a. Address and greeting (1:1–2)

Trinitarian in form and concerned with the work of salvation.

b. Thanksgiving (1:3–12)

In form a *berakhah*, or blessing of God, for the privileges of salvation (contrast Paul's thanksgivings), making reference to present suffering.

c. The implications of salvation (1:13–2:10)

God's purpose for his people: the nature of redemption and the call of the redeemed to fear God and love one another: the privileges of belonging to the people of God. The section includes the call to 'put off' the characteristics of the old life.

d. Christian relationships (2:11–3:12)

The appeal to good behaviour among the Gentiles: careful subjection to lawfully constituted authority; the duties of slaves, under good and bad masters, with the example of Christ; the duties for wives and husbands; the call to unity; love, gentleness and humility, swelling into Ps. 34.

e. Suffering and the will of God (3:13–22)

Preparedness to suffer injustice: Christ's suffering and its triumphant consequences.

f. Holy living (4:1–11)

Includes a call to watch: culminates in a benediction.

g. The fiery trial (4:12–19)

A sudden resumption of the theme of imminent suffering: its inherent blessing: the glory of suffering for the Name: the coming judgment.

h. Address to elders (5:1–4)

i. General address and benediction (5:5–11)

Including a renewal of the call to vigilance and to resistance to the evil one.

j. Personalia and greetings (5:12–14)

II. External attestation

The use of 1 Peter in the primitive church is at least as well attested as most other Epistles. Eusebius says that 'the ancient elders' made free use of it (*EH* 3. 3); some have found echoes of it in Clement of Rome (*c.* AD 96), and rather more in Ignatius, Hermas and Barnabas, belonging to different parts of the world, but all to the early 2nd century. Beyond question is its use by Polycarp (who may have been baptized as early as AD 69) and Papias, also of the sub-apostolic generation (Eusebius, *EH* 3. 39). It is reflected in the *Gospel of Truth*, which seems to use the books regarded as authoritative in Rome *c.* AD 140 (*NEW TESTAMENT APOCRYPHA). From the second half of the century onwards it seems universally known and read, at least in the Gk.-speaking church. There are fewer signs of it in Lat. writers. It is not mentioned—possibly by accident (*cf.* T. Zahn, *Geschichte des Neutestamentlichen Kanons*, 2. 1, 1890, pp. 105ff., 142)—in the Muratorian Fragment. By Eusebius' time, no question was raised about its authenticity, though other writings bearing Peter's name had long caused discussion (*EH* 3. 3).

Obviously the Epistle had considerable influence on the thought and expression of early Christians, and nothing suggests that it was ever attributed to anyone but Peter. Some who have on other grounds questioned its authenticity have been driven by its evident early attestation to the desperate conclusion that it must have circulated anonymously.

A date about AD 100–111 has often been urged for the passages about persecution. But this is tenable only if the traditional authorship is denied, and in any case is a dubious understanding of these passages (see section V, below). It is also worth remembering that Polycarp and Papias, both Asians, were, the one certainly, the other almost certainly, mature men at that time.

III. Place of writing

The letter conveys greetings from the church in 'Babylon' (5:13). Mesopotamian Babylon is unlikely: it is too much of a coincidence that Mark and Silvanus, old colleagues of Paul, should be there too. Still less can be said for Babylon on the Nile, a military depot. It is far more likely that, as in Rev. 14:8; 17:5, *etc.*, Babylon stands for Rome. The OT had compared it as a symbol of godless prosperity (*cf.* Is. 14); theories that it is a general allegory for 'the world' or a cryptogram for security purposes are needless. There are grounds for believing Peter worked in Rome, and the presence of Mark and Silvanus would be explained.

IV. Style and language

The Gk. of the Epistle is good and rhythmic, the style not pretentious but with a certain delicacy. Simple rhetorical devices are effectively used, but there are also some grammatical features best explained by Semitic influence. The quotations from and allusions to the OT almost invariably follow the LXX in a way which suggests thorough familiarity with it.

Some of these facts, reinforced by an exaggeration of the classical character of the Gk., have seemed at once to overthrow any claim to authorship by an Aramaic-speaking Galilean. A number of assumptions here, however, require testing. Gk. was widely understood and spoken, and was a vital cultural force, throughout 1st-century Palestine, and especially Galilee. Peter's own brother has a Gk. name, and Peter would doubtless be quite at home in the language. Further, the LXX was the 'Authorized Version' of most early Christians, and everyone connected with the Gentile mission would be familiar with it, and especially with the key passages most frequently in use.

These factors, however, would not themselves justify an easy assumption that Peter could write Gk. prose of the type of 1 Peter. But we must here ask, in what sense is the letter 'by' Silvanus (5:12)? Were he simply the messenger, one would expect the expression 'sent by' (*cf.* Acts 15:27). Contemporary literature attests that in the ancient world secretaries were often entrusted with considerable powers (*cf.* J. A. Eschlimann, *RB* 53, 1946, pp. 185ff.). Probably, therefore, 1 Pet. 5:12 indicates, and the diction and style evidence, the assistance of Silvanus in drafting the letter.

Silvanus, we learn from Acts, was a Jew, a Roman citizen, acceptable for the delicate task of explaining the resolutions of the Jerusalem Council (Acts 15:22ff.) and a devoted worker in the Gentile mission. He had been associated with Paul in the sending of 1 and 2 Thes. (1 Thes. 1:1; 2 Thes. 1:1). Selwyn has pointed to verbal parallels and connections of thought between those Epistles and 1 Peter (pp. 369ff., 439ff.) which, after due weight has been given to the criticisms of B. Rigaux (*Les Épîtres aux Thessaloniciens*, 1956, pp. 105ff.) and others, will repay careful study. An interesting light may be cast, for instance, on 1 Pet. 3:7 and 1 Thes. 4:3–5 if the one is read in the light of the other.

Those who deny the Petrine authorship usually write off the reference to Silvanus as part of the pseudepigraphic machinery. If, however, the hypothesis of a secretary introduces factors beyond proof it is also true that this method was used in antiquity, and must be allowed for.

V. The historical background

The principal data come from the references to persecution (1:6f.; 3:13–17; 4:12–19; 5:9). In the first two passages trials exist, unjust suffering is a possibility; in the second two a fierce ordeal is imminent: so much so that some have even urged that 4:12ff. comes from a later period. The vocabulary, however, is very similar: in each case *peirasmos*, 'trial', is used (1:6 and 4:12); persecution is a ground of rejoicing (1:6; 4:13); the same beatitude is applied (3:14; 4:14); the glory of suffering for doing good, or as a Christian, is proclaimed (3:17; 4:16); the undeserved suffering of Christians is linked with the will of God (3:17; 4:19); obedience to the civil power in things lawful and honest is enjoined (2:13ff.; 4:15), and the example of Christ's sufferings is set forth (1:11; 3:18; 4:13). The readers are also told that their fiery trial should be no surprise (4:12): and suffering they already know (*cf.* 1:6ff.). All this suggests that if the peril in 4:12ff. is new, it is in degree, not kind.

The antithesis in 4:12ff. between suffering for wrong committed and suffering for the name of Christ has attracted comparison with a letter from Pliny, appointed governor of Bithynia–Pontus in AD 110/111 to the usually liberal-minded emperor Trajan (Pliny, *Ep.* 10. 96).

Pliny, faced with vast numbers of Christians in his province, asks whether age, sex or recantation is to be allowed for in prescribing punishment: and, further, if the name of Christian (*nomen ipsum*) is sufficient reason for punishment, or only the crimes (putatively) congruent therewith (*flagitia cohaerentia*).

His own line of conduct had been to inquire whether people were Christians and to give them free pardon if they sacrificed to the emperor's genius; and, if they refused, to execute them for contumacy (*contumacia*). Some of those who sacrificed said they had ceased to be Christians 20 years back; but neither from them nor from two Christian girls (* DEACONESS), whom he tortured, could he find anything very reprehensible save a rather disgusting superstition. His vigorous action was having effect, and disused heathen rites were recommencing.

Trajan's reply (*Ep.* 10. 97) generally approves these actions but lays down that Christians are not to be sought out: if they are regularly accused and fail to recant they must suffer.

Pliny also says that Christians took an oath of abstention from crime (*cf.* 1 Pet. 4:15). And this all takes place in part of the area to which 1 Peter is addressed.

There is no evidence of widespread state-sponsored persecution in the provinces before this date: the savage pogroms of Nero and Domitian were directed at Roman Christians. Accordingly, many have seen in 1 Peter a tract designed for Pliny's time (*cf., e.g.,* J. Knox, *JBL* 72, 1953, pp. 187ff.).

To this thesis there are four strong objections.

1. 'The name' is used in 1 Peter in a primitive Christian, not a juristic Roman, sense. The 'name' of Jesus was immensely significant for Christians of the apostolic age, and in particular the accounts which we have of Peter's Jerusalem preaching (*cf.* Mk. 9:37, 41; 13:13; Lk. 21:12; Acts 2:21, 38; 3:6, 16; 4:12, 17f., 30; 5:28). Even in Jerusalem days persecution was for 'the name' (Acts 5:41; 9:16; *cf.* 9:4f.). The background of 'the name' in 1 Pet. 4 surely lies in these passages.

2. When Pliny talks of *flagitia cohaerentia* he is doubtless thinking of the common slander that Christians were guilty of cannibalism, incest and other horrors in their rites—he is looking for evidence. But the warnings in 1 Pet. 4:15f. have no such undertones: and 'a mischief-maker' does not denote a criminal offence at all.

3. The language of 1 Peter does not necessarily indicate legislative action. It is implied in 2:14; 3:15ff. that, in the ordinary administration of justice, Christians would have nothing to fear: though the same passages make clear that they might on occasions be subjected to flagrant injustice. In 3:15ff. the danger seems to be primarily from ill-disposed neighbours; in 4:14 reproach is specifically mentioned; and the readers' sufferings are the same as other Christians know elsewhere (5:9). Jewish jealousy, private spite, enraged commercial interests, mob violence and ill-judged actions by local magistrates could have dire effects (Acts *passim*; 2 Cor. 11:22ff.; 1 Thes. 2:14f.; 2 Tim. 3:11f.; Heb. 12:4ff.).

4. Pliny's jurisdiction extended over Bithynia–Pontus only: nothing suggests an enforcement of his policy in the other areas to which 1 Peter is addressed.

Pliny's action must have had its roots well in the past (*cf.* Ramsay, *CRE*, pp. 245ff.). Though not sure of the technicalities, he takes for granted that Christians must be punished for *something*: and even he does not execute for the *nomen ipsum* but for *contumacia*. Nor does Trajan give him a straight answer: it is still not clear whether Christianity is a crime or not. The law, kept deliberately vague, puts Christians at the mercy of gossips.

There is no need, however, to look to Vespasian's or Domitian's time: nothing in the *language* of 1 Peter requires a date later than the 60s. If a note of particular urgency appears at 4:12ff. the outbreak of the Neronian persecution would afford ample justification for this.

It seems certain that * Peter suffered in Rome under Nero, and 'Babylon' (5:13) almost certainly indicates that city. The E provinces tended to copy imperial actions on their own initiative. Rev. 2–3 suggests that this happened in Domitian's persecution in the 90s. From Rome, in the first rumblings of Nero's anti-Christian movement that became literally a fiery trial, Peter would have reason to predict an intensification of the suffering of his brethren in the East.

A suitable date for 1 Peter would thus be just before the outbreak of Nero's persecution: AD 63 or early 64; perhaps after Paul had died and left his colleagues Silvanus and Mark.

VI. The author's background

A rewarding study can be made of the connection between 1 Peter and the other parts of the NT with which Peter is associated: Mark's Gospel and the early speeches in Acts. It is not simply a matter of verbal links between 1 Pet. 2:20ff. and Mark's passion narrative (*cf.* Selwyn, p. 30). Mark, the Petrine speeches and 1 Peter all set forth Christ in terms of the suffering Servant of Isaiah 53; 1 Peter and Mk. both expound the Lord's death as a ransom (*cf.* Mk. 10:45 with 1 Pet. 1:18). Other NT writings, of course, are indebted to Is. 53, but it is remarkable that these three have this prophetic passage so deeply impressed that it may be regarded as their central thought about Christ. 1 Pet. 2, like Is. 53, describes both the Servant's conduct and sufferings and the significance of them. Much has been said of the call to the imitation of Christ in 1 Peter; but there is far more than a description of the passion and an appeal to imitation: the thought moves on to what is for ever inimitable, the redemption which only his suffering could effect.

The Petrine speeches in Acts share with 1 Peter the same sense of prophetic fulfilment (Acts 2:16ff.; 3:18; 1 Pet. 1:10ff., 20), the insistence on the cross as the foreordained action of God (Acts 2:23; 1 Pet. 1:20), the same connection of the resurrection and exaltation (Acts 2:32ff.; 1 Pet. 1:21); the call to repentance and faith-baptism (Acts 2:38, 40; 1 Pet. 3:20ff.); the certainty of Christ's judgment of the living and dead (Acts 10:42; 1 Pet. 4:5); joyous recognition of the Gentile mission and its blessings (Acts 10:9ff.; 11:17; 15:7ff.; 1 Pet. 1:1, 4–12; 2:3–10), expressed from a Jewish standpoint. It would take a Jew of Peter's views to speak of Gentile Christians as 'elect . . . sojourners of the Dispersion' (1:1, RV), and to describe them as entering Israel (2:9f.—note the modification of Hosea: the readers had *never been* God's people before). A Jew, too, could describe their background as 'what the Gentiles like to do' (4:3).

Again, in both 1 Peter and the Petrine speeches we are, as we have seen, in an atmosphere where the 'name' of Jesus means much (see **V**, above). Even details may be significant: the use of the oracle about the stone (Acts 4:10ff.; 1 Pet. 2:7) and the use of *xylon*, properly 'wood', for the cross (Acts 5:30; 10:39; 1 Pet. 2:24).

1 Peter contains an unusual number of apparent reminiscences of the Lord's words: generally not as formal quotations, but woven into the framework of the discourse (*e.g.* 1 Pet. 1:16 = Mt. 5:48; 1:17 = Mt. 22:16; 1:18 = Mk. 10:45; 1:22 = Jn. 15:12; 2:19 = Lk. 6:32 and Mt. 5:39; 3:9 = Mt. 5:39; 3:14 = Mt. 5:10; 4:11 = Mt. 5:16; 4:13 = Mt. 5:10ff.; 4:18 = Mt. 24:22; 5:3 = Mt. 20:25f.; 5:7 = Mt. 6:25ff.), and other passages take on a richer meaning if Peter were in fact the author. These connections are not exclusively from the Marcan tradition: but 1 Peter and Mk. alike display the theme of the suffering and the glory.

Some have sought the author's background in the Asian mystery cults (see R. Perdelwitz, *Die Mysterienreligionen und das Problem des 1 Petrusbriefes*, 1911, and *cf.* Beare) and found the letter too colourless in its treatment of the Lord's life for the work of one of the Twelve. The proponents of the mystery religion theory have, however, not made their case in a matter where dating is notoriously uncertain; and the parallels with the Galilean Gospel tradition are far more impressive. Eloquent is the judgment of Cullmann, who, while not discussing the authorship of 1 Peter, can be assured that it was written with knowledge of Peter's dominant theological themes (*Peter*, p. 68).

VII. 1 Peter and the rest of the New Testament

The theology of 1 Peter is essentially Pauline. This is not, as some think, an argument against authenticity: there is reason to hold that * Peter stood close to Paul in theology and none to think that he was an original theologian. Silvanus, too, had long worked with Paul. Moreover, though the agreement is close, the setting and expression of the theology in terms of the Servant is quite independent of Paul. It is worth remarking that K. Lake, drawn to a late date by the persecution passages, could say, 'The simplicity of the theology is marked, and affords an argument for an early date' (*EBr*[11], 21, p. 296) and that F. L. Cross can point to 'that remarkable co-presence of the end as future and yet as already here from which second century writings depart' (pp. 42f.).

More remarkable are the literary resemblances between 1 Peter and other NT writings, especially Rom., Eph., Heb. and Jas. Not all can be fortuitous: for instance, the unusual divergence from the LXX in the quotation in 1 Pet. 2:4–8 appears also in Rom. 9:32f. Problems of priority in literary relationships are always difficult and can rarely command certainty. C. L. Mitton claims to have proved the dependence of 1 Pet. on Eph. (*JTS* n.s. 1, 1950, pp. 67ff.)—the significance of this, if ascertained, will depend on the date given to Eph. Beare claims, with less demonstration, that the author of 1 Peter must have had access to the published Pauline Corpus (*The First Epistle of Peter*[3], p. 219).

A fruitful development in recent literary criticism has been the attention given to the common patterns of Christian teaching which appear in diverse NT writings (see P. Carrington, *The Primitive Christian Catechism*, 1946). A pattern of instruction for converts has been recovered, associated by many scholars, perhaps too categorically, with baptism. Jas. and 1 Peter, as well as Eph. and Col., reflect this pattern, which had among its components:

1. The call to put away sins and desires of the old pagan life (1 Pet. 2:1, 11).

2. The call to Christian humility, subjection and the subordination of self-interest—addressed to particular classes of society (1 Pet. 2:11–3:9—these are parentheses).

3. The call to watch and pray: twice in 1 Peter (1 Pet. 4:7; 5:8).

4. The call to resist the devil (1 Pet. 5:8f.).

Many of the strongest resemblances between 1 Peter and other Epistles occur in just these sections, and it seems probable that the explanation lies in the common forms of catechetical training, not in direct literary dependence.

Selwyn has gone further and seen other common patterns reflected in 1 Peter, more especially a body of teaching on persecution which declared it to be a ground of rejoicing, a test of character, a necessary visitation and a sign of the imminence of divine judgment and vindication: and which was anchored in the words of the Lord. Selwyn finds this same pattern in 1 and 2 Thes., also associated with Silvanus. In common with other writers, he sees various hymns and liturgical fragments (*e.g.* 1 Pet. 2:6–10; 3:18–22; and use of Ps. 34 in 3:10f.).

VIII. The nature and purpose of 1 Peter

1 Peter has long been treated as a sermon cast into epistolary form, dealing with baptism. This was given a new form by H. Preisker in 1951, who saw in the section 1:3–4:11 indications of a rite in progress and references to baptismal practice, and declared the work to be a baptismal liturgy with the rubrics omitted. Preisker's hypothesis was marred by stylistic hypercriticism, but this feature has been removed by F. L. Cross, who urges, with a wealth of illustration from patristic sources and especially from the *Apostolic Tradition* of Hippolytus, that 1 Peter is the president's part for an Easter baptismal eucharist: 1:3–12 is the president's opening solemn prayer; 1:13–21 his formal charge to the candidates. The baptism takes place at this point, and 1:22–25 gives the welcome to the newly baptized: passing to a discourse on the fundamentals of sacramental life (2:1–10), an address on Christian duties (2:11–4:6), and closing with admonitions and a doxology (4:7–11). It is a weakness of the theory that no explanation is given of 4:12ff.

This thesis rests on a vast amount of detailed study which cannot be discussed here. Many of the details have been called in question. (See the examination by T. C. G. Thornton, *JTS* n.s. 12, 1961, pp. 14ff.). A few general points, however, suggest the need for reserve.

First, baptism is far less prominent in the Epistle than the discussions of recent years suggest. There is only one explicit reference to it, and that is a parenthesis (3:21). Other allusions to baptism which some find are highly dubious: the 'born anew' (1:3; *cf.* 1:23) is already realized, and its result enjoyed: it cannot refer to an event to take place after 1:21. Its corresponding member in the catechetical form in Jas. 1:18 makes it clear that the begetting relates to the gospel, not baptism, and this is confirmed by 1:23, where the 'word of God' is defined as the enduring gospel preached to the readers. The repeated 'now' need not relate to a rite in progress; it is due rather to an exultant sense of the last times: and the 'now' in 3:21 in the context of baptism surely only points to a contrast with the ancient Flood.

Second, many of the allusions can be readily understood without the theory. The emphasis on Exodus typology is valuable, but this typology is not restricted to baptism. Van Unnik, for example, points to a rabbinic saying that proselytes entered Israel in the same way as Israel entered the covenant and infers that 1 Peter stresses the transition that the readers have made. They know God's election and covenant sprinkling (1:2ff.); they are now Israel (1:18f.); those who had never been God's people have become that people (2:10); the work of Christ is to bring us (*prosagein*) to God: and *prosagein* represents a technical term for becoming a proselyte.

On a reading like this, while conversion and the radical break with the old life are much to the fore, baptism in itself is not. The question of authorship is not, of course, directly affected by the formal nature of the work. Peter might preach a sermon and send it as a letter (though it is very hard to see a motive for converting a liturgical text into a letter). But 1 Peter as we have it *is* a letter, and on the sound critical principle of making sense of what we have, we must so read it. (*DESCENT INTO HADES; *PERSECUTION.)

BIBLIOGRAPHY. Commentaries by R. Leighton (d. 1684), *Practical Commentary upon 1 Peter*; F. J. A. Hort (posthumous, unfinished, Gk. text); E. G. Selwyn, 1946 (indispensable for Gk. text); H. Windisch–H. Preisker, 1951; F. W. Beare[3], 1970 (denies Petrine authorship; the 3rd ed. has an important supplement and bibliography); C. E. B. Cranfield[2], 1961; A. M. Stibbs and A. F. Walls, *TNTC*, 1959; K. H. Schelkle, *Die Petrusbriefe und der Judasbrief*[3], 1976; C. Spicq, *Les Épitres de Saint Pierre*, 1966; J. N. D. Kelly, *The Epistles of Peter and Jude*, 1969; E. Best, *1 Peter*, 1971; L. Goppelt, *Der Erste Petrusbrief*, 1978; F. L. Cross, *1 Peter: a Paschal Liturgy*[2], 1957; W. C. van Unnik, *ExpT* 68, 1956–7, pp. 79ff.; C. F. D. Moule, *NTS* 3, 1957, pp. 1ff.; R. H. Gundry, *NTS* 13, 1967, pp. 336–350; N. Hillyer, 'Rockstone Imagery in 1 Peter', *TynB* 22, 1971, pp. 58–81. A.F.W.

PETER, SECOND EPISTLE OF.

I. Outline of contents

After the salutation (1:1–2) the author speaks of the reliability of the Christian faith, attested as it is by growing personal experience (1:3–11), the testimony of eyewitnesses (1:12–18) and inspired ancient prophecy (1:19–21). Mention of true prophecy leads him on to condemn false prophecy (2:1–3:10). Current false teachers are the successors of the OT false prophets, and will incur the same judgment (2:1–9). Their depravity is shown by throwing off God's restraints in unbridled licence (2:10–18), which brings not liberty but bondage (2:19–22). Therefore judgment awaits them, despite their scepticism about the parousia. They should recall that a catastrophic end of the world had been foretold (3:1–4), and the certainty of this prophecy is substantiated by the Flood (3:5–7). The second coming is delayed because of the longsuffering of a God who is outside time (3:8–9), but, though delayed, it is none the less certain (3:10). It is the duty of the faithful not to be led away by the libertinism and scepticism of the false teachers, but to live an upright life in anticipation of Christ's return (3:11–end).

II. Occasion

The recipients are not defined, though their having 'a faith of equal standing *with ours*' (1:1) and their having escaped 'the corruption that is in the world' (1:4) suggests a predominantly Gentile audience. The writer has had a long and intimate acquaintance with them (1:12–13; 3:1) and writes to warn them against a false teaching both antinomian in practice

PETER IN ROME
See Rome, Part 3.

and radical in belief. The immorality (2:12ff.), insubordination to church leaders (2:10), scepticism (3:3), twisting of Scripture (they exploited in particular, no doubt, the Pauline doctrine of justification, 3:16), and greed of these false teachers (2:3, 15) evoke his most stringent denunciation. He writes to warn the church members of their moral and intellectual danger, to assure them of the basis for their belief, to explain their main problem—the parousia—and to encourage holy living and growth in grace. If the author was Peter the date would be around the mid-60s (he is anticipating death, 1:14). If not, the letter may have been written in the late 1st or early 2nd century. No mention is made of its provenance or destination: it may well have been written, like 1 Peter, from Rome to Asia Minor.

III. Authorship and date

The authorship of this Epistle is hotly contested on both external and internal grounds.

a. The external evidence

This is inconclusive. While no book in the Canon is so poorly attested in the Fathers, no book excluded from the Canon can claim comparable support. Origen, early in the 3rd century, is the first to cite it by name; he records the doubts which surrounded it, but himself accepts it. So does Jerome, while Eusebius is uncertain. After its inclusion in the Festal Letter of Athanasius in AD 367 and its ratification by the Council of Carthage in AD 397, its position in the Canon was unquestioned until the Reformation, when Luther accepted it, Erasmus rejected it and Calvin was dubious. Though not quoted by name until Origen, it was used much earlier; Clement of Alexandria had it in his Bible; Valentinus in the *Gospel of Truth*, Aristides in his *Apology* (AD 129) and Clement of Rome (*c.* AD 95) appear to allude to it. More probable still is its use by the author of the *Apocalypse of Peter*, whose existence is attested by the end of the 2nd century AD. For this reason many of the scholars who on other grounds reject the Epistle nevertheless regard its external attestation as sufficient.

b. The internal evidence

Many scholars are inclined to adjudge it a pseudepigraph, on the following grounds:

(i) *Its relationship with Jude.* There is an undeniable literary relationship between the two letters; which way it lies has not been fully established, although the majority today think 2 Peter borrowed from Jude. This, it is argued, would in itself rule out the possibility of apostolic authorship. No such conclusion is warranted. If, as is certain, Paul borrowed from a variety of sources, and if, as is possible, 1 Peter borrowed from James, it would not be surprising to find the same thing in 2 Peter. On the other hand, both 2 Peter and Jude may have incorporated a common document denouncing false teaching, just as Matthew and Luke appear to have drawn from 'Q' their common sayings-material. In neither case need the priority of Jude affect the authenticity of 2 Peter, whereas if Jude drew from 2 Peter (as Bigg and Zahn maintain), the apostolic authorship of the Epistle could hardly be denied.

(ii) *Its relationship with 1 Peter.* The marked difference of diction and style between the two letters led to the doubts of the early church about 2 Peter. Jerome thought that Peter used two different amanuenses (a possibility enhanced by the researches of E. G. Selwyn into the probable influence of Silvanus on 1 Peter), and this suggestion must be taken seriously, for despite the wide differences no book in the NT is so like 2 Peter as 1 Peter. They have been shown (by A. E. Simms, *The Expositor*, 5th series, 8, 1898, pp. 460ff.) to have

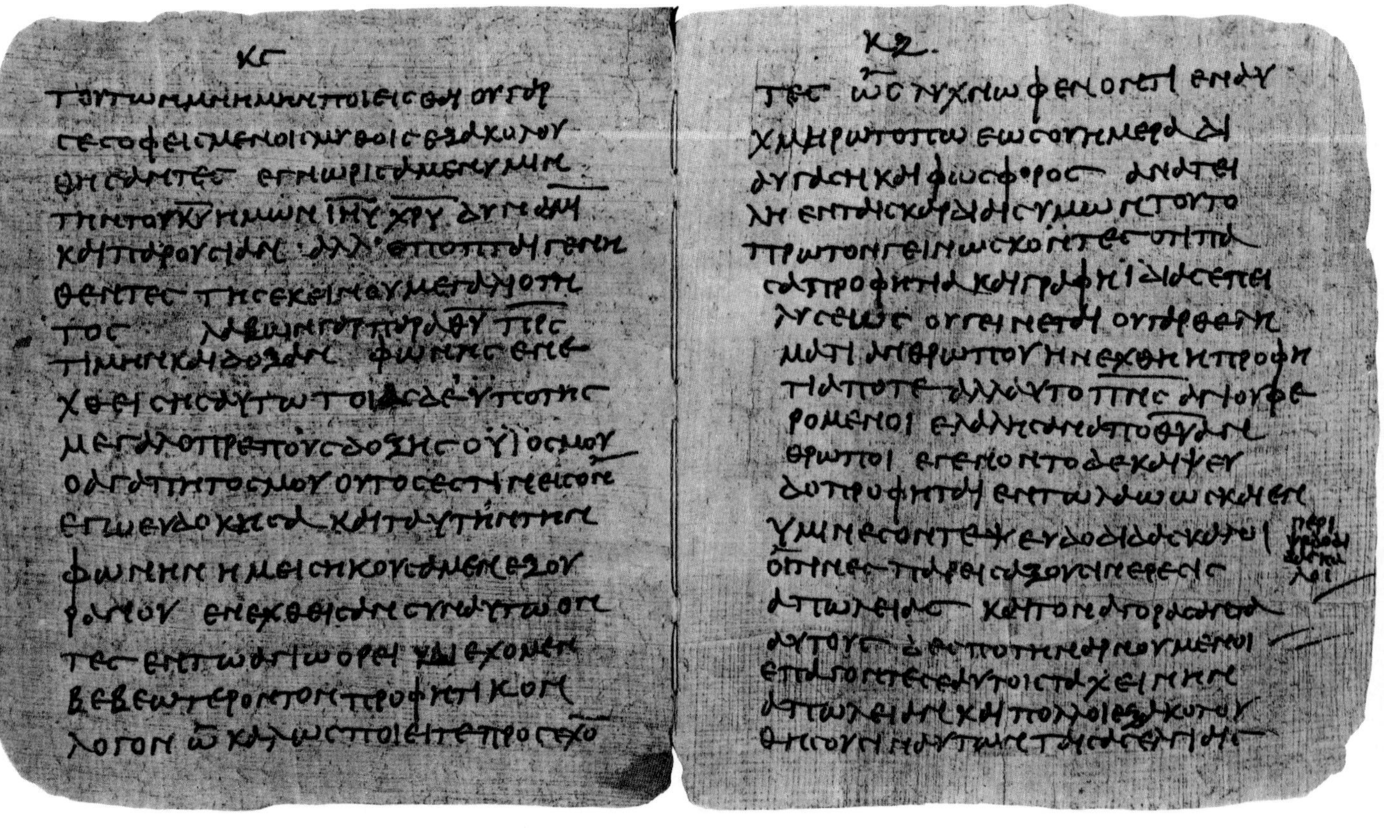

Part of the oldest known manuscript of the epistles of Peter (2 Pet. 1:16–2:2). c. AD 300. (BAV)

as close an affinity on a purely linguistic basis as 1 Timothy and Titus, where unity of authorship is universally admitted.

Modern writers concentrate less on the linguistic than on the doctrinal differences between the Epistles, and they are very different in this respect. The subject-matter of 1 Peter is hope, of 2 Peter knowledge. 1 Peter is written to Christians facing persecution, and therefore stresses the great events of the life of Christ for emulation and comfort; 2 Peter is written to Christians facing false doctrine and practice and therefore stresses the great hope of the return of Christ for warning and challenge. The best safeguard against the false teaching is full knowledge (*gnōsis*, *epignōsis*) of Christ, and it is this, accordingly, which is stressed in 2 Peter. The teaching of both letters is conditioned by the pastoral needs which evoked them. The differences can, in fact, easily be exaggerated; both letters draw attention to the warnings of the Flood, the small number saved, the longsuffering of God. Both emphasize prophecy, the inspiration of the OT, the solidarity of the old and the new Israel, and the value of eyewitness testimony. Both emphasize the primitive eschatological tension derived from the Christian's dual membership of this age and the age to come, with its consequences in holy living, in sharp contrast with the 2nd-century neglect of this doctrine. In short, the divergence of doctrinal emphasis in the two letters is great, but not impossible.

(iii) *Its anachronisms.* **1.** Such concepts as 'partakers of the divine nature' (1:4), escaping 'the corruption that is in the world' (1:4), and the repeated emphasis on knowledge and eyewitness (*epoptai*, 1:16, is a favourite word of the mystery-religions) suggest to some scholars a 2nd-century origin for the letter. There is no need to postulate so late a date, since the discovery of the Carian Inscription of AD 22 and parallel passages in Philo and Josephus show that this was the common cultural language of the day in the 1st century.

2. The destruction of the world by fire (3:7) was a common topic in the 2nd century, and may thus be an indication of a late date for 2 Peter. On the other hand, there is some reason to believe that the distinctly Christian belief in the destruction of the world by fire (as seen in Barnabas and Justin) may ultimately derive from this Epistle (see J. Chaine, *RB* 46, 1937, pp. 207ff.).

3. The phrase 'since the fathers fell asleep' (3:4) is held to favour a late date when the first Christian generation had almost disappeared. Even if these words did apply to the Christian 'fathers', it would not necessitate a late date. As early as 1 Thes. 4:15–17 or 1 Cor. 15:6, the state of those who had died before the parousia was a burning topic that had to be faced. However, here the context suggests that 'the fathers' refers to the OT fathers ('from the beginning of *creation*') as elsewhere in the NT (*e.g.* Heb. 1:1; Rom. 9:5).

4. The inclusion of Paul's letters among the 'other scriptures' favours the hypothesis of a late date, and suggests the formation of the Pauline Corpus of letters. If this is the case, to make Peter call Paul a 'beloved brother' was a stroke of genius in the *falsarius* unparalleled in the 2nd century, when divergencies between Peter and Paul were constantly exacerbated. No mention is made here of a corpus of letters, and the only real difficulty lies in one apostle's regarding the letters of another as Scripture. In view, however, of the apostolic assertion that the same Holy Spirit who inspired the OT writings was active in their own (1 Cor. 2:13), and the claims of Paul to have the mind of Christ (1 Cor. 2:16) and to lay down rules for all the churches (1 Cor. 7:17) which are equated with the commandment of Christ (1 Cor. 14:37) and rejection of which will bring rejection by God (1 Cor. 14:38), this possibility cannot be excluded.

IV. Conclusion

The evidence does not suffice to justify a dogmatic answer one way or the other to the question of authorship. There is nothing that forbids us to entertain the possibility of Petrine authorship, though many regard it as unlikely in view of the cumulative effect of the difficulties outlined above. However, no alternative solution is free from difficulty. The doctrine of the letter and the character of the false teaching do not readily fit into the 2nd-century scene. 2 Peter as a pseudepigraph has no satisfactory *raison d'être*; it adds nothing to our knowledge of Peter, has no unorthodox tendency, is no romance, makes no reference to burning 2nd-century problems, such as chiliasm, gnosticism or church leadership; in fact, it bears no resemblances to the undoubted pseudepigrapha of the Petrine circle. At all events, it is certain that the early church which deposed the author of the *Acts of Paul* for forgery (Tertullian, *de Baptismo* 17) and forbade the use of the *Gospel of Peter* because it was Petrine neither in authorship nor doctrine (Eus., *EH* 6. 12) thoroughly investigated 2 Peter's claims to authenticity. It passed the test before that same Council of Carthage which excluded from the Canon *Barnabas* and *Clement of Rome*, which had long been read in the churches. It cannot be shown that they were right; but it has still to be shown that they were wrong.

BIBLIOGRAPHY. Among those who reject the Petrine authorship are F. H. Chase, *HDB*, 3, 1900, pp. 796ff.; J. B. Mayor, *The Epistle of Jude and the Second Epistle of Peter*, 1907; C. E. B. Cranfield, *I and II Peter and Jude*, 1960; E. Käsemann, *ZTK* 49, 1952, pp. 272ff.; J. Moffatt, *INT*[3], 1918, pp. 358ff.; E. A. Abbott, *The Expositor* 2, 3, 1882, pp. 49ff., 139ff., 204ff.; C. Spicq, *Les Épitres de Saint Pierre*, 1966; J. N. D. Kelly, *The Epistles of Peter and of Jude*, 1969; K. H. Schelkle, *Die Petrusbriefe und der Judasbrief*[3], 1976. Those who accept the Epistle as Peter's include B. Weiss, *A Manual of Introduction to the New Testament*, 2, 1888, pp. 154ff.; T. Zahn, *INT*, 2, 1909, pp. 194ff.; J. Chaine, *Les Épîtres Catholiques*, 1939; C. Bigg, *St. Peter and St. Jude*, *ICC*, 1902; E. I. Robson, *Studies in 2 Peter*, 1915; E. M. B. Green, *2 Peter Reconsidered*, 1961; *idem*, *The Second Epistle General of Peter and the General Epistle of Jude*, *TNTC*, 1968. See also R. V. G. Tasker, *The Old Testament in the New Testament*[2], 1954, p. 129.

E.M.B.G.

PETHOR. A city of N Mesopotamia, S of Carchemish, mentioned in Nu. 22:5 as by the river (*i.e.* the Euphrates) and in Dt. 23:4 as in Mesopotamia, it was the home of Balaam. Thither Balak sent messengers to call him to curse Israel. Pethor in 'Amaw is the Pitru of Assyr. texts (*cf. ANET*, p. 278), described as on the river Sāgūr (modern Sājūr), near its junction with the Euphrates. On 'Amaw, see Albright, *BASOR* 118, 1950, pp. 15–16, n. 13, and for 'the eastern mountains (or hills)' note that in a

PETER'S HOUSE
See Capernaum, Part 1.

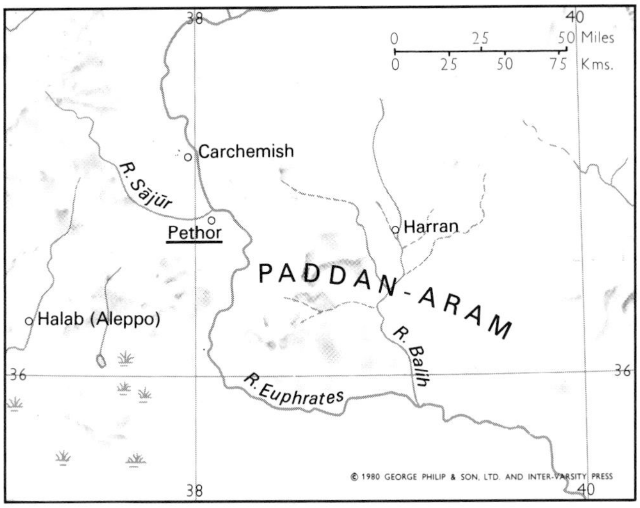

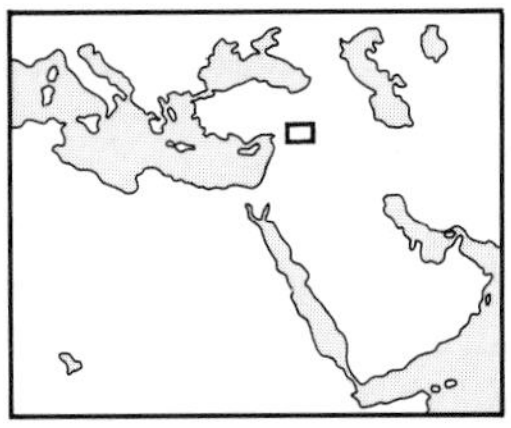

Pethor, home of Balaam.

15th-century BC Egyp. text, chariot-wood from 'Amaw is said to come from 'god's land (= the E) in the hill-country of Naharen'—*i.e.* hills overlooking 'Amaw on the Sājūr river flowing into the Euphrates on its W bank; this W extension of (Aram-) Naharaim is attested by both Heb. and Egyp. references.

R.A.H.G.

PHARAOH.

I. The term

The common title in Scripture for the kings of Egypt. It derives from Egyp. *pr-'',* 'great house'. This term was by origin simply a name for the royal palace and the Egyp. court, and is so used in the Old and Middle Kingdoms in the 3rd and first half of the 2nd millennium BC. But in the mid-18th Dynasty (*c.* 1450 BC) the term came to be applied to the person of the king himself, as a synonym for 'His Majesty'. The first examples of this usage apparently date from the reigns of Tuthmosis III(?) and IV, then under Amenophis IV/Akhenaten. From the 19th Dynasty onward, the simple term 'pharaoh' is constantly used in documents, just as it is particularly in Gn. and Ex. From the 22nd Dynasty onward (945 BC), the term 'pharaoh' could also be coupled with the king's name: thus, 'Pharaoh Sheshonq' occurs on a stele then, just like the slightly later OT references to Pharaoh Neco and Pharaoh Hophra. See Sir A. H. Gardiner, *Egyptian Grammar* [3], 1957, p. 75; J. Vergote, *Joseph en Égypte*, 1959, pp. 45–48, and the references cited.

II. Specific pharaohs

1. A contemporary of Abraham (Gn. 12:15–20). As Abraham lived *c.* 1900 BC, his pharaoh was most likely one of the several kings Amenemhat and Sesostris of the 12th Dynasty (*c.* 1991–1778 BC).

2. A contemporary of *Joseph (Gn. 37–50). Joseph lived *c.* 1700 BC; his pharaoh therefore would most likely be one of the Hyksos kings of the 15th Dynasty.

Figure of Pharaoh Tirhakah (Taharqa of Egypt) mentioned in Is. 37:9 and 2 Ki. 19:9. c. 690–664 BC. (RS)

3. The pharaoh(s) of the oppression. The number of individual rulers covered by the terms 'king of Egypt' and 'pharaoh' in Ex. 1–2 is a matter of interpretation—one, or two. In any case, he/they would directly precede the pharaoh of the Exodus.

4. The pharaoh of the Exodus (Ex. 5–12). If the Exodus occurred in the first half of the 13th century BC, as seems likeliest on the evidence available, the pharaoh of the Exodus and last oppressor would be Rameses II.

5. The father of Bithiah, wife of Mered of the tribe of Judah (1 Ch. 4:18). The date of Bithiah and so of her royal father is uncertain, and therefore he has not yet been identified.

6. The pharaoh who received the young prince Hadad of Edom as a refugee from David and Joab's devastation of the Edomites (1 Ki. 11:18–22), and married him off to his sister-in-law. The pharaoh in question would be late in the 21st Dynasty, *i.e.* Amenemope or Siamūn. The obscurities of 21st Dynasty chronology forbid any closer dating.

7. The pharaoh who reduced Gezer and bestowed it as dowry on that daughter of his whom he gave in marriage to Solomon (1 Ki. 9:16; *cf.* also 3:1; 7:8; 9:24; 11:1). Shishak's raid into Palestine in 925 BC, the 5th year of Rehoboam, was not later than his own 21st year, and he acceded *c.* 945 BC. Solomon died in 931/30 BC after a 40-year reign which began *c.* 970 BC; hence Shishak acceded in Solomon's 25th year. Therefore Solomon's Egyp. contemporaries for his first 25 years of reign would be the last two kings of the 21st Dynasty, Siamūn and Psusennes II. Of these two, Siamūn is perhaps the pharaoh who took Gezer and bestowed it with his daughter upon Solomon; a triumphal scene of his from Tanis (Zoan) may provide evidence for warlike activity of Siamūn in Philistia. On this period of Egypto-Israelite relations, *cf.* K. A. Kitchen, *Third Intermediate Period in Egypt*, 1972, pp. 273ff., 280ff.

8. *Shishak, who is Sheshonq I, founder of the 22nd (Libyan) Dynasty. **9.** *So, contemporary of Hoshea. **10.** *Tirhakah, of the 25th (Ethiopian) Dynasty. **11.** *Neco, second king of the 26th Dynasty, is the pharaoh of Je. 25:19. **12.** *Hophra, fourth king of the 26th Dynasty, is apparently the pharaoh of Je. 37:5, 7, 11; Ezk. 17:17; 29:2–3; and possibly of Je. 47:1. *Zerah was almost certainly *not* a pharaoh.

III. Other references

These are found mainly in the prophets. Is. 19:11 is part of a passage reflecting disruption in Egypt. Such internal fragmentation first became chronic early in Isaiah's time, in the late 22nd–24th Dynasties (*c.* 750–715 BC), and continued under the overlordship of the Ethiopian kings of the 25th Dynasty (*c.* 715–664 BC). Pride in the long and exalted continuity of pharaonic tradition in accordance with v. 11 was reflected in the deliberate archaisms fostered by the 25th and 26th Dynasty kings, who sought thus to recall the glories of earlier epochs. The deceptive outward repute of the Ethiopian kings and their actual inability to help Israel against Assyria's armies are epitomized in Is. 30:2–3. Shebitku ('Shabataka') was on the throne in 701 BC when the Assyrian Rabshakeh dismissed pharaoh as a 'broken reed' (Is. 36:6 = 2 Ki. 18:21). For 'Pharaoh's house in Tahpanhes' (Je. 43:9), *TAHPANHES.

Both Jeremiah (46:25–26) and Ezekiel (30:21–25; 31:2, 18; 32:31–32) from 587 BC onward prophesied that Egypt would be worsted by *Nebuchadrezzar II of Babylon. In 568 BC Nebuchadrezzar did actually war against Egypt, as indicated by a fragmentary Babylonian text, though the extent of his success against Ahmose II (Amasis) is still unknown because of the lack of relevant documents. Lastly, Ct. 1:9 merely reflects the great fame of the chariot-horses of the pharaohs of the New Kingdom (*c.* 1550–1070 BC) and later. (*EGYPT, History; *CHRONOLOGY OF THE OLD TESTAMENT.) K.A.K.

PHARISEES.

I. History

The work of *Ezra was continued by those who tried to master the text and teaching of the law in every detail—the scribes in the NT were their spiritual descendants—and the wider circle of those who meticulously tried to carry out their teaching. Early in the 2nd century BC we find them called ḥ^{a}sîḏîm, *i.e.* God's loyal ones (*HASIDAEANS).

The name Pharisee first appears in contexts of the early Hasmonaean priest-kings. The Ḥasidim had

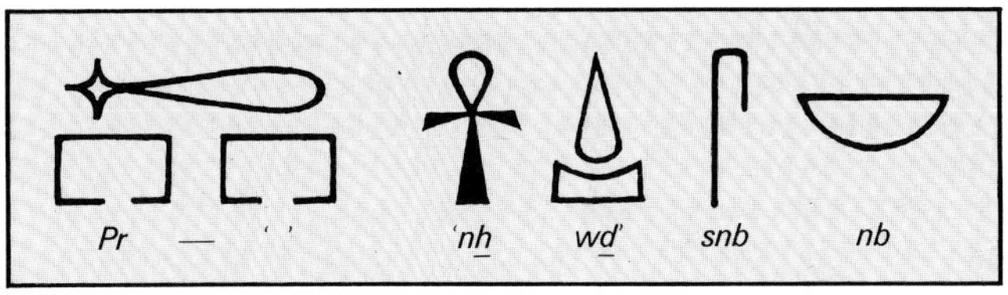

This address on a 14th-century BC letter reads: 'Pharaoh, life, prosperity, health, the Master.'

probably divided. The minority, basing itself on the illegitimacy of the high-priesthood and the abandonment of certain traditions, withdrew from public life, awaiting an eschatological intervention from God. The majority aimed at controlling the religion of the State. The traditional interpretation of Pharisees as 'the separated ones' is much more probable than T. W. Manson's suggestion of the nickname 'the Persians'. Their views on tithing (see below) made separation from the majority inescapable.

Under John Hyrcanus (134–104 BC) they had much influence and the support of the people (Jos., *Ant.* 13. 288–300), but when they broke with him he turned to the Sadducees. Pharisaic opposition under Alexander Jannaeus (103–76 BC) went so far that they even appealed for help to the Seleucid king, Demetrius III. Jannaeus triumphed and crucified some 800 of his leading opponents (Jos., *Ant.* 13. 380). On his deathbed, however, he advised his wife, Alexandra Salome, who succeeded him (76–67 BC), to put the government in the hand of the Pharisees, who from this time held a dominating position in the Sanhedrin.

They suffered heavily under Antipater and Herod (Jos., *BJ* 1. 647–655) and evidently learnt that spiritual ends could not be attained by political means, for after Herod's death we find some of them petitioning for direct Roman rule. For the same reason the majority of them opposed the revolt against Rome (AD 66–70). Hence Vespasian favoured Yohanan ben Zakkai, one of their leaders, and permitted him to establish a rabbinic school at Jamnia (Yavneh). By now the controversies between the party of the rigorist Shammai and of the more liberal Hillel had ended in compromise, the Sadducees had disappeared and the Zealots were discredited—after the defeat of Bar Kochba in AD 135 they too disappeared—and so the Pharisees became the unquestioned leaders of the Jews. By AD 200 Judaism and Pharisaic teaching had become synonymous.

PHARAOH-NECO
See Neco, Part 2.

PHARATHON
See Pirathon, Part 3.

PHARES, PHAREZ
See Perez, Part 3.

PHARZITES
See Perez, Part 3.

PHEBE
See Phoebe, Part 3.

II. Relation to other parties

The Pharisees were always a minority group. Under Herod they numbered something over 6,000 (Jos., *Ant.* 17. 42). The later bitterness of their relationship to the common people (*'am ha-'āreṣ*), shown by many Talmudic passages from the 2nd century AD, indicates that the rigour of their interpretation of the law had no intrinsic appeal. The apocalyptists had little influence except through the Zealots, and their appeal seems to have been mainly to a desperate proletariat. The Sadducees were drawn mainly from the richer landowners; Talmudic tradition distinguishes clearly between them and their allies, the house of Boëthus, the high-priestly clan. In their own way they were as rigorist as the Pharisees, only they applied the laws and their traditions irrespective of consequences—they were rich enough to bear them. The Pharisees were always mindful of the public interest. It is no coincidence that Shammai, the rigorist Pharisee, came of a rich, aristocratic family, while Hillel was a man of the people. The main attraction of the Pharisees for the people was that they came mostly from the lower middle and better artisan classes and, understanding the common man, did genuinely try to make the law bearable for him.

The differences stressed by Josephus (*BJ* 2. 162–166)—the Pharisees' belief in the immortality of the soul, which would be reincarnated (*i.e.* reanimate the resurrection body), and in the overruling of fate (*i.e.* God), and the Sadducees' disbelief in either (*cf.* Mt. 22:23; Acts 23:8)—were obviously secondary. Fundamentally the Sadducees considered that Temple worship was the centre and main purpose of the law. The Pharisees stressed individual fulfilment of all sides of the law, of which the cultus was only a part, as the reason for its existence. The outward differences showed their inner attitudes.

III. Teaching

Basic to the Pharisaic conception of religion was the belief that the Babylonian Exile was caused by Israel's failure to keep the Torah (the Mosaic law), and that its keeping was an individual as well as a national duty. But the Torah was not merely 'law' but also 'instruction', *i.e.* it consisted not merely of fixed commandments but was adaptable to changing conditions, and from it could be inferred God's will for situations not expressly mentioned. This adaptation or inference was the task of those who had made a special study of the Torah, and a majority decision was binding on all.

One of the earliest tasks of the scribes was to establish the contents of the written Torah (*tôrâ še-biḵtaḇ*). They determined that it contained 613 commandments, 248 positive, 365 negative. The next step was to 'make a hedge' about them, *i.e.* so to interpret and supplement them that there would be no possibility of breaking them by accident or ignorance. The best-known example is the frequently cited thirty-nine principal species of prohibited acts on the sabbath. There is, however, nothing unreasonable or illogical about them once we grant the literal prohibition of sabbath work. The commandments were further applied by analogy to situations not directly covered by the Torah. All these developments together with thirty-one customs of 'immemorial usage' formed the 'oral law' (*tôrâ še-bᵉ-'al peh*), the full development of which is later than the NT. Being convinced that they had the right interpretation of the Torah, they claimed that the 'tradition of the elders' (Mk. 7:3) came from Moses on Sinai.

Beyond an absolute insistence on the unity and holiness of God, the election of Israel and the absolute authority of the Torah for him, all the stress in the Pharisee's religion was ethical, not theological. Our Lord's condemnation of them (*HYPOCRITE) has to be interpreted in the light of the undoubted fact that they stood ethically higher than most of their contemporaries. The special Pharisaic stress on tithing and their refusal to buy food from or to eat in the homes of non-Pharisees, lest the food should not have been tithed, as was often the case, was due to the very heavy burden created by tithes superimposed on Hasmonaean, Herodian or Roman taxation. For the Pharisee full tithing was a mark of loyalty to God.

BIBLIOGRAPHY. G. F. Moore, *Judaism in the First Centuries of the Christian Era*, 3 vols., 1927, 1930; L. I. Finkelstein, *The Pharisees*², 1962; J. Jocz, *The Jewish People and Jesus Christ*, 1949; J. Parkes, *The Foundations of Judaism and Christianity*, 1960. H.L.E.

PHARPAR ('swift'). One of the two 'rivers of Damascus' of which Naaman boasted (2 Ki. 5:12). 64 km long, it is one of the tributaries of the *Abana or Barada, flows E from Hermon a little S of Damascus, and is today called the 'Awaj'. J.D.D.

PHILADELPHIA. A city in the Rom. province of Asia, in the W of what is now Asiatic Turkey. It was perhaps founded by Eumenes, king of Pergamum, in the 2nd century BC, and certainly named after his brother Attalus, whose loyalty had earned him the name Philadelphus. It was situated near the upper end of a broad valley leading down through Sardis to the sea near Smyrna; and it lay at the threshold of a very fertile tract of plateau country, from which much of its commercial prosperity derived. The area was subject to frequent earthquakes. A severe one in AD 17 destroyed the city; and as the shocks continued intermittently the people took to living outside the city (Strabo, *Geography* 12.8.18 [579]; 13.4.10 [628]). After an imperial bounty had helped it to recover, the city voluntarily assumed the new name of Neocaesarea. Later, under Vespasian, it took another imperial name, Flavia. The city was remarkable for the number of its temples and religious festivals. The site is now occupied by the town of Alaşehir.

The letter to 'the angel of the church in Philadelphia' (Rev. 3:7–13) probably alludes to some of the circumstances of the city. As Philadelphus was renowned for his loyalty to his brother, so the church, the true Philadelphia, inherits and fulfils his character by its steadfast loyalty to Christ (vv. 8, 10). As the city stands by the 'open door' of a region from which its wealth derives, so the church is given an 'open door' of opportunity to exploit (v. 8; *cf.* 2 Cor. 2:12). The symbols of the 'crown' and the 'temple' (vv. 11–12) point to a contrast with the games and religious festivals of the city. In contrast with the impermanence of life in a city prone to earthquakes, those who 'overcome' are promised the ultimate stability of being built into the temple of God. As at Smyrna, this church had met rejection from the Jews in the city (v. 9), but the conqueror shall enjoy final acceptance by the Lord whose name he had confessed (v. 8), signified again by the conferring on him of the divine names (v. 12), which recall the new names taken by the city from the divine emperors. Ignatius later visited the city on his way from Antioch to martyrdom in Rome, and sent a letter to the church there.

BIBLIOGRAPHY. W. M. Ramsay, *The Letters to the Seven Churches of Asia*, 1904, chs. 27–28; C. J. Hemer, *Buried History* 11, 1975, pp. 164–174. M.J.S.R.
C.J.H.

PHILEMON. The owner of the slave *Onesimus and almost certainly a resident of Colossae (*PHILEMON, EPISTLE TO, for other views). Though Paul had not himself visited Colossae (Col. 2:1), Philemon was apparently converted through him (Phm. 19) and had been a colleague (the normal meaning of 'fellow-worker', Phm. 1, RSV)—both, perhaps, in Ephesus,

Site of the city of Philadelphia with the remains of a Roman city wall. (SH)

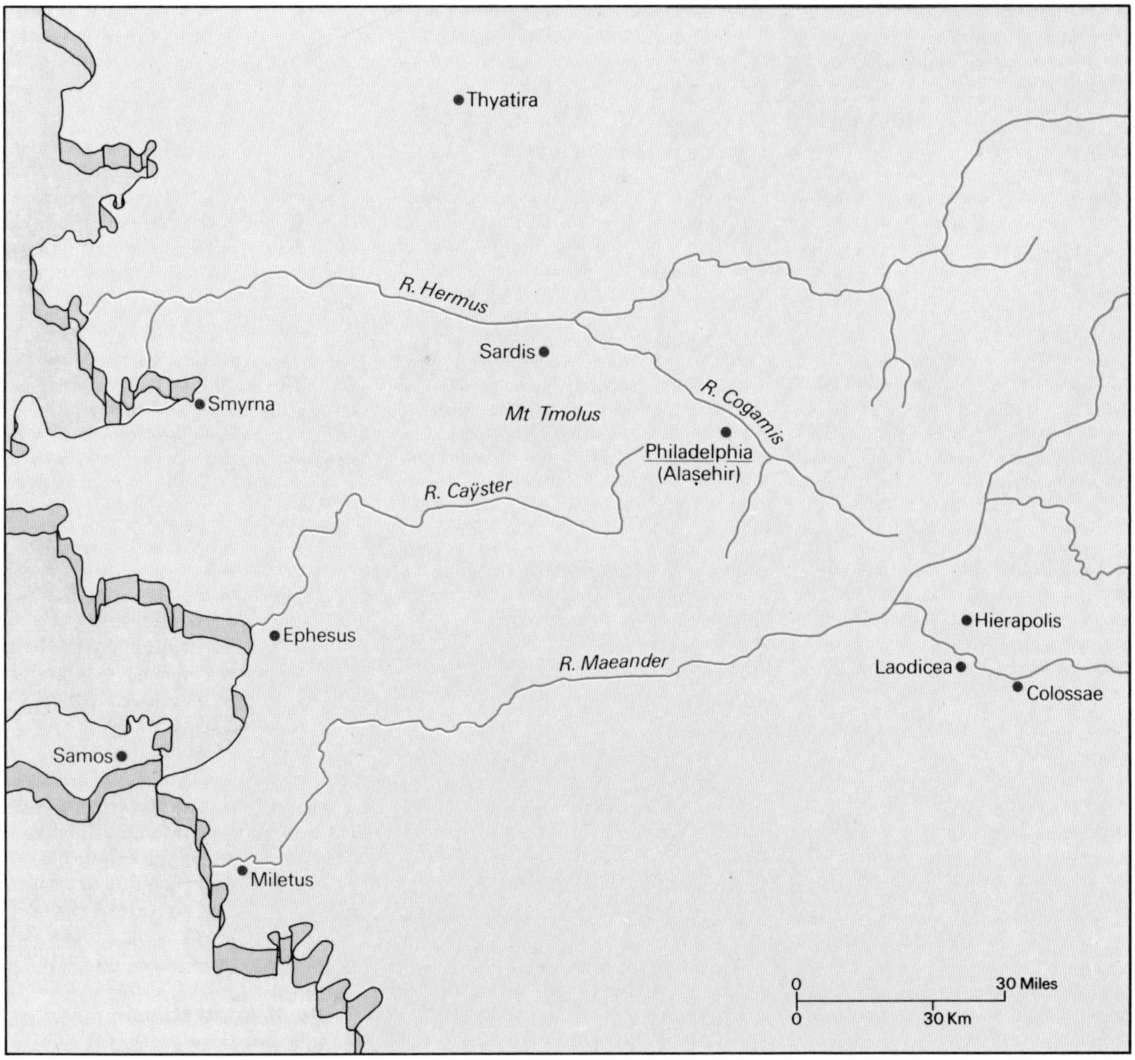

Philadelphia, one of the 'seven churches of Asia' (Rev. 1–3).

the provincial capital (*cf.* Acts 19:31). The argument of J. Knox (who applies Phm. 19 to Archippus), that Paul would regard the work of any of his associates as his own, is hardly borne out by Col. 1:7f., which he cites, nor is Phm. 5 ('*hear* of your love') incompatible with past acquaintance. A.F.W.

PHILEMON, EPISTLE TO.

I. Outline of contents

a. Address and greeting (vv. 1–3).

b. Thanksgiving: introducing themes, to be developed later, of love, fellowship (*koinōnia*; *cf. koinōnos*, 'partner' in v. 17) and refreshment (*cf.* v. 20) (vv. 4–7).

c. The request for Onesimus (vv. 8–21).

d. A request for hospitality (v. 22).

e. Greetings from Paul's friends (vv. 23–24).

f. Blessing (v. 25).

II. Significance

The earliest extant lists of the Pauline Corpus (Marcion's 'canon' and the Muratorian Fragment) contain Philemon, even though they omit the Pastoral Epistles. In the 4th century complaints appear not so much against its authenticity as of its alleged triviality (*cf.* Jerome, *Preface to Philemon*): most generations, however, have better valued the grace, tact, affection and delicacy of feeling which mark this little letter. Tertullian remarked that it was the only Epistle which Marcion left uncontaminated by 'editing' (*Adv. Marc.* 5. 21), and its authenticity has never been responsibly questioned. In recent years it has become a bastion of the theory of the Pauline Corpus associated with E. J. Goodspeed and John Knox (*PAUL, **III.** *d.* ii); gratitude for the fresh interest they have stimulated in Philemon, and the adoption of some of their suggestions, does not, however, demand acceptance of this highly dubious reconstruction.

III. Form

The personal and informal nature of Philemon (*cf.* Deissmann, *LAE*, pp. 234f., and *EPISTLE) may distract attention from its extremely careful composition and observance of literary forms (*cf.* Knox, pp. 18f.). It should also be noted that a house-church is in mind as well as the people named in the address (v. 2). Goodspeed and Knox over-emphasize the part the church is expected to play in swaying the slave-owner to 'do the Christian thing' (Goodspeed, p. 118): the second person singular is used throughout, even for the greetings: the only exceptions are in vv. 22 (the hoped-for visit) and 25 (the benediction). This affords a contrast with Ignatius' letter to Polycarp, which is addressed to an individual but with frequent passages in the second person plural which show that the church is being harangued. Philemon is addressed to the slave-owner, with his family and church presumably linked with him after the manner of Rom. 16:5; Col. 4:15.

Comparison has often been invited with Pliny's letter (*Ep.* 9. 21) on behalf of an errant but repentant freedman.

IV. Purpose and occasion

The core of the Epistle is an appeal by Paul on behalf of one Onesimus, a slave from Colossae (Col. 4:9) whose conduct had contrasted with his name ('useful'—a pun is involved in Phm. 10–11). It seems that Onesimus had robbed his master (18) and run away (15—not quite explicit). By some means unstated—perhaps his fellow-townsman Epaphras (Col. 4:12) was instrumental—he was brought into contact with the imprisoned Paul and radically converted. Not only so, but strong affection developed between Paul and his new 'son', in whom the veteran saw rich potential.

Under contemporary law, almost limitless vengeance could be wreaked on Onesimus by his owner: Graeco-Roman society was never free from the phobia of a servile war, and even an otherwise good master might think it his duty to society to make an example of the runaway. Frightful penalties also awaited those who harboured runaways (*cf.* P. Oxy. 1422). It is at this point that Paul interposes with his brother (7, 20), not commanding, but begging (8–9) that his owner will receive Onesimus as he would Paul himself (17), and solemnly undertaking all the slave's debts (18–19).

But probably Paul is asking more than mercy. Knox points out that *parakaleō* followed by *peri* (as in v. 10) usually means in late Gk. 'to ask *for*' rather than 'on behalf of'. Paul highly valued Onesimus; his departure caused him great sorrow; and but for the necessity of obtaining his owner's permission would have liked to keep him with him (11–14). The fullness of Paul's request would be that Onesimus might be released to Paul for Christian service. He would thenceforth stand in an unspeakably closer and more permanent relationship than the old domestic one (15–16). In any case, to Paul's ministry this correspondent owes his own conversion (19).

Paul is in prison (9–10): the occasion is the same as that indicated in Colossians, for Onesimus is to accompany Tychicus, the bearer of that letter (Col. 4:9). Paul's party in Phm. 23f. is the same as that in Col. 4:10–14, with the exception of Jesus Justus (unless this is a scribal omission; *cf.* E. Amling, *ZNW* 10, 1909–10, p. 261). The place of imprisonment will be decided mainly on grounds external to the letter: the real alternatives are Rome, in the first imprisonment (*c.* AD 62) or Ephesus about AD 55 (*PAUL; *CHRONOLOGY OF THE NEW TESTAMENT). Either city might have attracted Onesimus. Ephesus was near home, but large enough to be lost in; Rome was a haven for displaced persons of every kind. In either case there is some expectation of release and a journey to Philemon's area in the foreseeable future.

There are other links with Colossians. Col. 3:22ff. (*cf.* Eph. 6:5–9) could hardly have been written without Onesimus, and the possible effect on his career, in mind. Knox and Goodspeed have, however, little reason to associate the charge to Archippus and the 'Epistle from Laodicea' (Col. 4:16–17) with the Onesimus case. Knox himself has disposed of Goodspeed's suggestion that Onesimus' owner lived at Laodicea (pp. 40ff.), but his own suggestion that Philemon received the letter first as the (Laodicean) superintendent of the Lycus churches and that Archippus in Colossae was the slave-owner and principal addressee, fares no better. It requires an unnatural reading of the address, and a heavy burden on a few words (*e.g.* 'fellow worker' and 'fellow soldier' in vv. 1 and 2). Whether the epistle of Col. 4:16 was *Ephesians or some unknown letter is uncertain, but nothing suggests that it was Philemon. (*APPHIA; *ARCHIPPUS; *ONESIMUS; *PHILEMON.)

BIBLIOGRAPHY. Commentaries (with Colossians) on the Gk. text by J. B. Lightfoot[3], 1879; C. F. D. Moule, 1957; on the Eng. text by H. C. G. Moule, *CB*, 1893; J. Knox, *IB*, 1955; H. M. Carson, *TNTC*, 1960; R. P. Martin, *NCB*, 1974; E. J. Goodspeed, *INT*, 1937, pp. 109ff.; J. Knox, *Philemon among the Epistles of Paul*[2], 1959; F. F. Bruce, *BJRL* 48, 1965, pp. 81–97.

A.F.W.

PHILETUS. A teacher representative of those undermining the Christian doctrine of the resurrection (2 Tim. 2:17). (*HYMENAEUS.)

J.D.D.

PHILIP (Gk. *philippos*, 'horse-lover'). There are 4 characters of this name known to the NT writers.

1. A son of Herod the Great and Mariamne, the daughter of Simon the high priest. For a time he was next in succession to Antipater (Jos., *Ant.* 17. 53), but this arrangement was revoked by later wills, and he lived as a private citizen. A. H. M. Jones (*The Herods of Judaea*, 1938, p. 176n.) claims that his name was Herod, not Philip. (Jos., *Ant.* 18. 137, calls him Herod, but so many members of the *Herod family bore this name that an additional name was almost obligatory.) His wife *Herodias, the mother of Salome, left him in order to live with Herod Antipas, his half-brother (Mt. 14:3; Mk. 6:17; Lk. 3:19).

2. A son of Herod the Great by his fifth wife, Cleopatra of Jerusalem; Jos., *Ant.* 17. 21 states that he was brought up at Rome. By Augustus' settlement of Herod's will Philip was granted the tetrarchy of Gaulanitis, Trachonitis, Auranitis, Batanaea (Jos.), and Ituraea (Lk. 3:1). He ruled for 37 years until his death in the winter of AD 33/34, and differed from his kinsfolk in the moderation and justice of his rule (Jos., *Ant.* 18. 106). At his death the territory was incorporated into the province of Syria until AD 37, when the emperor Gaius Caligula granted it to Agrippa (the Herod of Acts 12:1, 19–23), son of Aristobulus and grandson of Herod and Mariamne. Philip rebuilt Panias (modern Banyas) as Caesarea Philippi (Mt. 16:13; Mk. 8:27) and Beth-saida Julias (Jos., *Ant.* 18. 28; *BJ* 2. 168), both names reflecting his pro-Roman sympathies. He was the first Jewish prince to impress the heads of Roman emperors on his coins. He married Salome, the daughter of *Herodias, and had no children (Jos., *Ant.* 18. 137).

3. Philip the apostle was called to follow Jesus on the day following the call of Andrew and Simon, and was instrumental in bringing Nathanael to follow him (Jn. 1:43–46). His home was *Beth-saida (Jn. 1:44): this was the Beth-saida of

Two of the members of Herod's family, according to the NT, were named Philip. Simplified family tree.

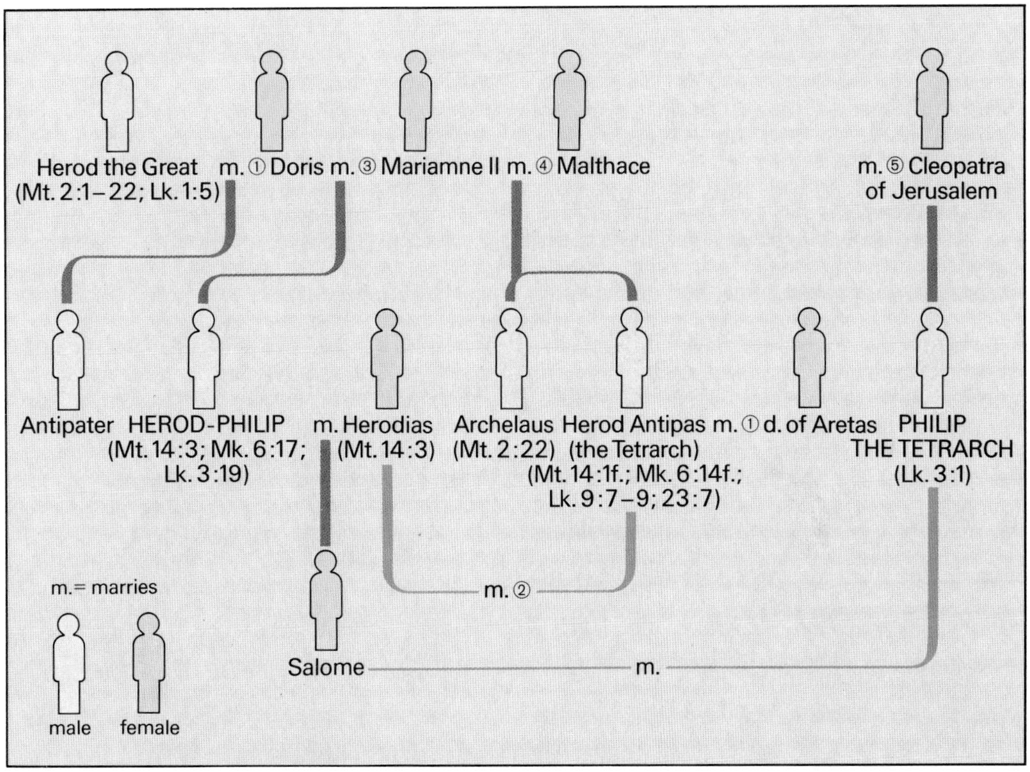

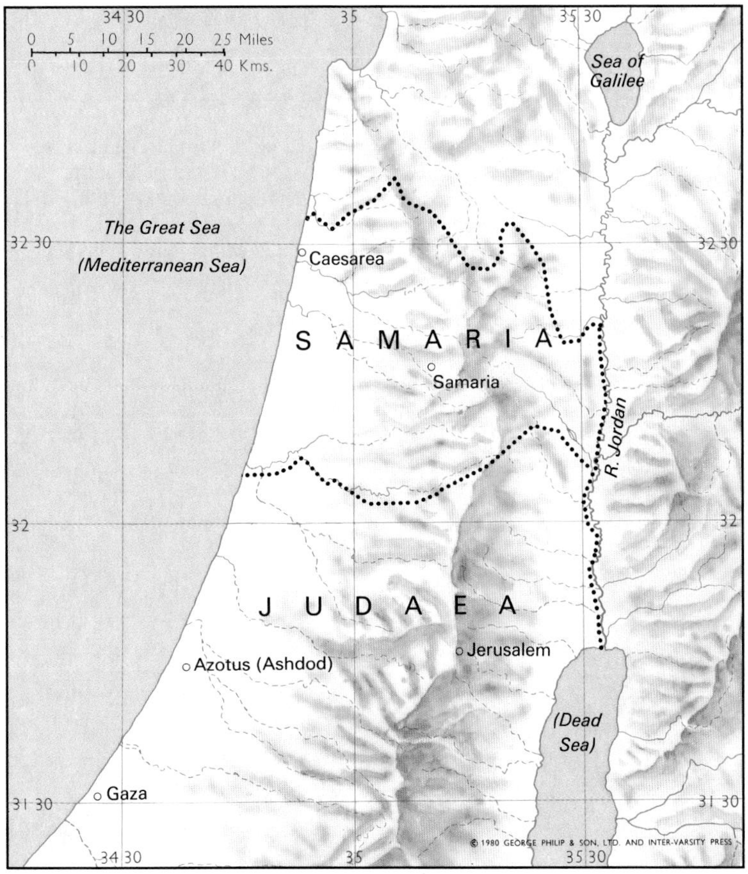

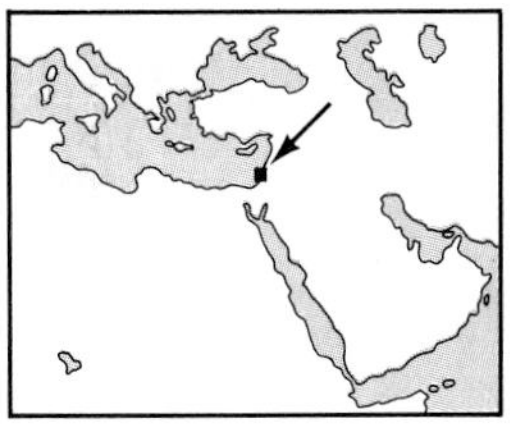

The area associated with Philip's ministry and meeting with the Ethiopian (Acts 8).

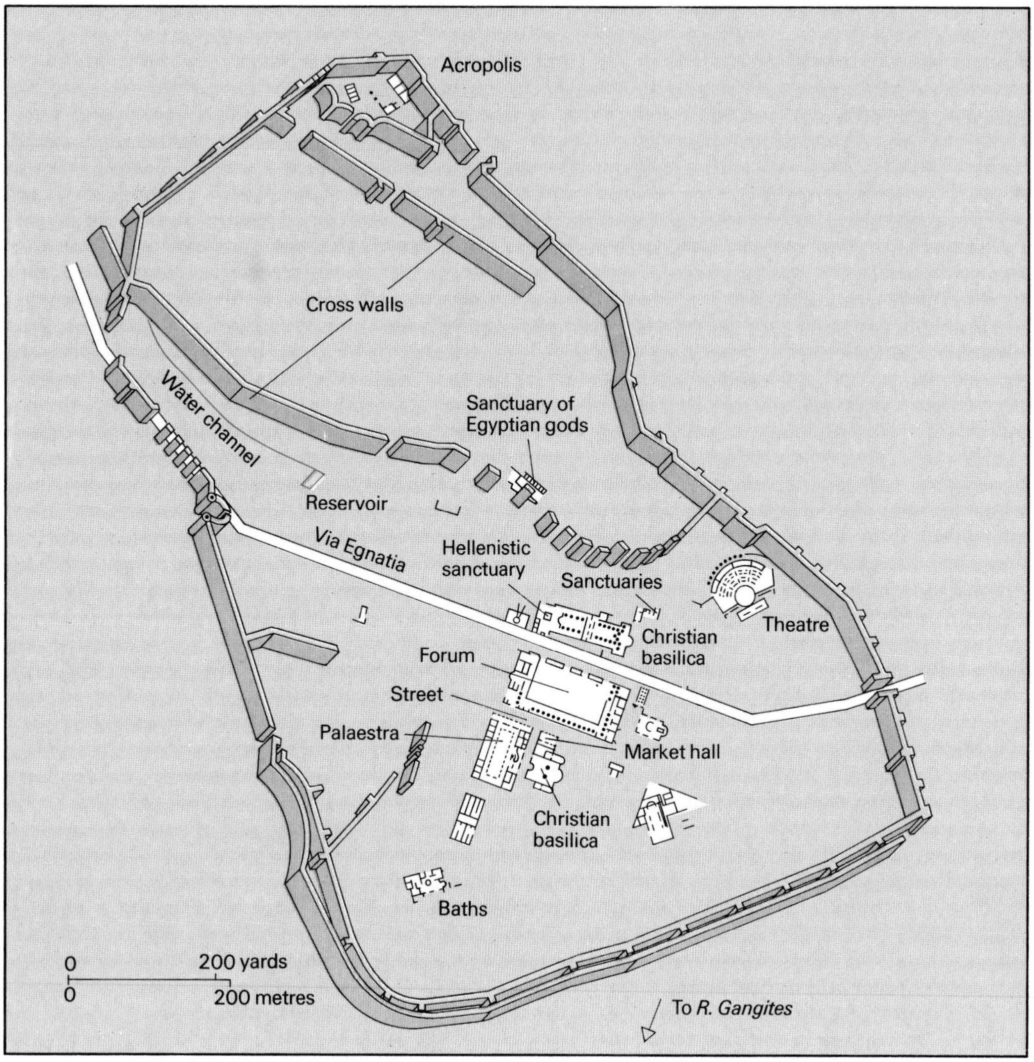

Plan of the site of Philippi, the 'leading city of the district of Macedonia' in Paul's day (Acts 16:12).

Galilee (Jn. 12:21), the home town of Andrew and Simon, and is thought to have been a fishing-village on the W shore of the lake. In the lists of the apostles in Mt. 10:3; Mk. 3:14; Lk. 6:14 he is placed fifth in order, with Bartholomew sixth: Acts 1:13 places him fifth, but puts Thomas in the sixth place. The only other references to him in the NT tell of his inability to suggest to Jesus how to supply the food for the 5,000 (Jn. 6:5), his bringing the Greeks to Jesus (Jn. 12:21f.), and his request of Jesus to see the Father (Jn. 14:8). Papias 2. 4 refers to him as one of the *presbyteroi* (see further below).

4. Philip was one of the 'Seven' who were chosen as officials (the first *'deacons') of the church at Jerusalem (Acts 6:5). On the persecution of the church following the martyrdom of Stephen he took the gospel to Samaria, where his ministry was much blessed (Acts 8:5–13), and subsequently he was sent S to the Jerusalem–Gaza road to lead the Ethiopian eunuch to Christ (Acts 8:26–38). After this incident he was 'Spirited' away to Azotus, the Philistine Ashdod, and from there conducted an itinerant ministry until he reached the port of Caesarea (Acts 8:39–40), where he appears to have settled (Acts 21:8). He was known as 'the evangelist', presumably to distinguish him from the apostle (**3**, above), and had four daughters who were prophetesses (Acts 21:9). Luke is here at great pains to distinguish the evangelist from the apostle. Eusebius twice (*EH* 3. 31; 5. 24) quotes Polycrates as referring to Philip, 'one of the twelve apostles', and his two aged virgin daughters as being buried at Hierapolis, while another daughter was buried at Ephesus. Perhaps this last was the one mentioned in 3. 30 (quoting Clement of Alexandria, who may use the plural here loosely) as having been given in marriage. Papias is also cited (*EH* 3. 39) as stating that 'the apostle Philip' and his daughters lived at Hierapolis and the daughters supplied him with information. A quotation from the *Dialogue of Gaius and Proclus* in Eus., *EH* 3. 31 that the tomb of Philip and his four prophesying daughters may be seen at Hierapolis, followed by a reference to Acts 21:8–9, shows that the historian had confused the apostle and

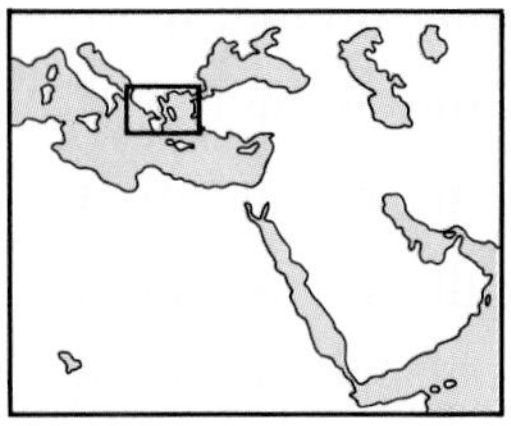

Philippi in Macedonia.

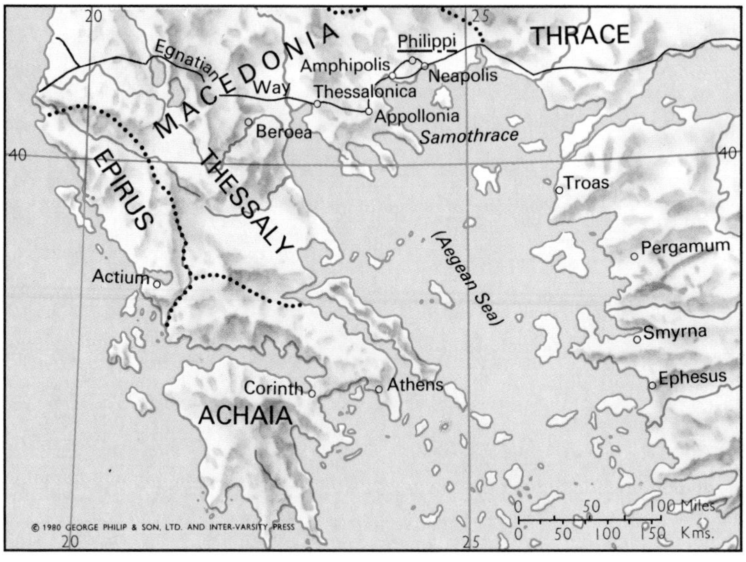

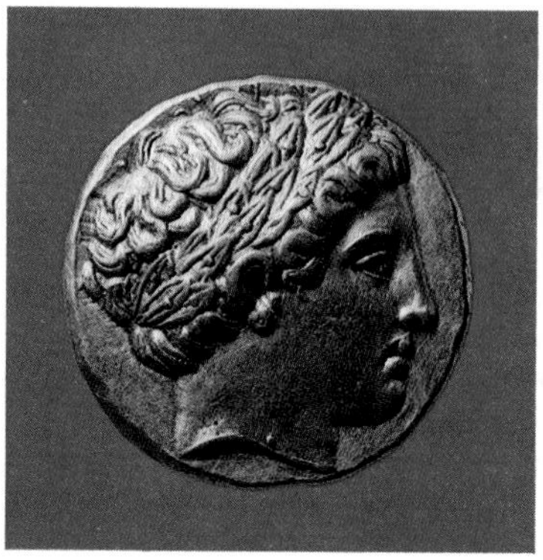

Bottom right:
Gold stater *of Philip of Macedon who gave the city of Philippi its name in 300* BC. *Diameter 21 mm.* (RG)

the evangelist. It would seem most likely that both the apostle and the evangelist had daughters, which would lead to their confusion. Lightfoot (*Colossians*, pp. 45ff.) is probably right in maintaining that it was the apostle who died in Hierapolis.

The papyrus finds at Nag Hammadi (*CHENOBOSKION) have revealed an apocryphal *Gospel according to Philip*: see R. McL. Wilson, *The Gospel of Philip*, 1962.

D.H.W.

PHILIPPI. In the course of his apostolic travels Paul received in a vision an invitation from a man of Macedonia who implored, 'Come over to Macedonia, and help us' (Acts 16:9). Interpreting this plea as a summons from God, Paul and his party sailed for Neapolis, the port of Philippi, 13 km S of the city and the terminus of the Egnatian Way, a military road which joined Rome and the East as a much valued line of communication.

The arrival at Philippi is marked in Acts 16:12 by a description of the city: 'the leading city of Macedonia and a Roman colony'. The stages by which the city attained the rank of this noble description may be traced.

The town derives its name from Philip of Macedon, who took it from the Thasians about 360 BC. He enlarged the settlement, and fortified it to defend his frontiers against the Thasians. At this time the gold-mining industry was developed, and gold coins were struck in the name of Philip and became commonly recognized. After the battle of Pydna in 168 BC it was annexed by the Romans; and when Macedonia was divided into four parts for administrative purposes Philippi was included in the first of the four districts. This fact supports a proposal of *prōtēs* in place of the TR's *prōtē* in Acts 16:12, suggested by F. Field and accepted by F. Blass, who explained it by this reference to the division of Macedonia into four districts by Aemilius Paullus in 167 BC (Livy, 45. 17–18, 29); *cf.* commentaries on Acts by H. Conzelmann and E. Haenchen, *ad loc.* On this emended reading the verse runs: 'a city of the first division of Macedonia'. If the text is not changed, Philippi's claim to be 'chief city of the district' can be accepted only in a general sense, as A. N. Sherwin-White observes (*Roman Society and Roman Law in the New Testament*, 1963, pp. 93ff.). The comment possibly reflects Luke's special interest in the city, which may have been his birth-place.

Ruins of the Roman Agora and a Byzantine church at Philippi in Macedonia. (PP)

In 42 BC the famous battle of Philippi was fought with Antony and Octavian ranged against Brutus and Cassius. After this date the town was enlarged, probably by the coming of colonists; the title *Colonia Iulia* is attested at this time. This prominence was enhanced further when, after the battle of Actium in 31 BC, in which Octavian defeated the forces of Antony and Cleopatra, the town 'received a settlement of Italian colonists who had favoured Antony and had been obliged to surrender their land to the veterans of Octavian' (Lake and Cadbury, p. 187). Octavian gave the town its notable title, *Col(onia) Iul(ia) Aug(usta) Philip(pensis)*, which has appeared on coins. Of all the privileges which this title conferred, the possession of the 'Italic right' (*ius Italicum*) was the most valuable. It meant that the colonists enjoyed the same rights and privileges as if their land were part of Italian soil.

The civic pride of the Philippians (who are given the equivalent of their Latin name *Philippenses* in Paul's letter, 4:15) is a feature of the Acts narrative, and reappears in allusions the apostle makes in the Epistle. See Acts 16:21; *cf.* 16:37. Official names are used (*duoviri* in 16:20, 22, and 'lictors' in 16:35). The Gk. word translated 'uncondemned' in 16:37 probably reflects the Latin *re incognita* or *indicta causa*, *i.e.* 'without examination'. In the letter to the Philippian church two passages, 1:27 and 3:20, speak of 'citizenship', a term which would have special appeal to the readers; and the virtues listed in 4:8 are those which the Roman mind would particularly appreciate.

After the apostle's first visit with his preaching, imprisonment and release, his further contact with the city is inferred from references in

Acts 20:1, 6; 1 Tim. 1:3.

BIBLIOGRAPHY. Historical details are supplied in *BC*, 1, 4, 1933, *ad loc.*; R. P. Martin, *Philippians*, *NCB*, 1976, Introduction, section 1, which describes the religious *milieu* of the city at the time of Paul's arrival there; while for archaeological information the work of P. Collart, *Philippes, ville de Macédoine*, 2 vols., containing plates and text, 1937, may be mentioned, along with W. A. McDonald, *BA* 3, 1940, pp. 18–24. R.P.M.

PHILIPPIANS, EPISTLE TO THE. The church at *Philippi was brought into being during the apostle's second missionary journey, recorded in Acts 16:12–40. Paul's letter to this Christian community has always been looked upon as a most personal and tender communication, although there is a noticeable change at the introduction to ch. 3.

I. Outline of contents

a. Address and greeting (1:1–2).

b. Paul's thanksgiving and confidence (1:3–7).

c. An apostolic prayer (1:8–11).

d. Paul's great ambition and joy (1:12–26).

e. Exhortation and example (1:27–2:18).

f. Future plans (2:19–30).

g. The great digression (3:1–21).

h. Encouragements, appreciations and greetings (4:1–23).

II. Date and provenance

From the record of Paul's life in the Acts of the Apostles we know of only three imprisonments (16:23–40; 21:32–23:30; 28:30), during one of which this letter was written (Phil. 1:7, 13–14, 16). It obviously cannot have been written during the first; and it seems at first sight that the choice is a simple one between his captivity at Caesarea and the 2 years' detention at Rome.

a. The Caesarean hypothesis

This view goes back to 1799, when it was propounded by H. E. G. Paulus. Rather surprising support came later from E. Lohmeyer in the Meyer commentary, and there have been several suggestive studies (see Martin, *Philippians*, *NCB*, 1976, pp. 45–48) in support of this setting of the letter. The suggestion of the letter's composition during the imprisonment at Caesarea contains some difficulties, which may be enumerated as follows:

1. The custody of Acts 23:35 does not suggest the imminent martyrdom which Lohmeyer takes as the controlling theme of the entire letter (*cf.* his analysis of the letter in these terms, pp. 5f.).

2. The size and type of the Christian community at the place of his captivity do not tally with what we know of the church at Caesarea (1:14ff.), as Moffatt indicates (*An Introduction to the Literature of the New Testament*, 1918, p. 169).

3. The apostle's outlook at the time of Acts 23–24 was bound up with a visit to Rome, but of this desire there is no hint in Philippians; rather he looks forward to a return visit to Philippi (2:24ff.).

b. The Roman hypothesis

The alternative proposal is that the letter was written and despatched during the apostle's Roman captivity; and this remains the traditional view, with many adherents. It has considerable evidence in its favour:

1. The allusions to the *praetorium* (1:13) and to 'Caesar's household' (4:22) correspond to the historical detail of the Roman detention, whatever the precise meaning of the terms may be.

2. The gravity of the charge and of the impending verdict (1:20ff.; 2:17; 3:11) suggests that Paul is on trial for his life in the highest judicial court, from which there can be no appeal. It is submitted that this piece of evidence shows that it cannot have been a provincial court whose judgment Paul awaits, for even if the verdict there were unfavourable, he would still have a 'trump card' (in C. H. Dodd's phrase) to play which would quash this local sentence and transfer his case to Rome. That he does not appear to have recourse to this is presumptive evidence that he has in fact so appealed, and that the appeal has brought him to the imperial city.

3. The church at Rome would correspond, in size and influence, to the references in 1:12ff., which point to a Christian fellowship of considerable importance.

4. The length of the imprisonment is sufficient, according to the proponents of this view, to allow for the journeys mentioned or implied by the letter. But this is a matter of debate.

5. There is indirect witness to the Roman provenance of the Epistle in the Marcionite prologue to the letter, which says, 'The apostle praises them from Rome in prison by Epaphroditus.'

There are, however, certain difficulties about this time-honoured view which have made scholars hesitate before accepting it. A. Deissmann was apparently the first to formulate these doubts, which we may state thus:

1. Deissmann drew attention to the fact that journeys to and from the place of captivity imply that the place cannot have been far from Philippi. It was argued that on the Roman hypothesis it is difficult to fit 'those enormous journeys', as he called them, into the 2 years mentioned as the duration of the Roman imprisonment.

2. Moreover, the situation reflected in the letter, with its foreboding of imminent martyrdom, hardly corresponds with the comparative freedom and relaxed atmosphere of Acts 28:30–31. If the letter came out of that detention it is clearly necessary to postulate an unfavourable development in the apostle's relations with the authorities which led to a change for the worse in his conditions and prospects.

3. A telling criticism of the traditional theory is the witness of 2:24, which expresses the hope that, if the apostle is set free, he intends to revisit the Philippians, and also to take up his missionary and pastoral work in their midst once again. This is an important *datum* from the internal evidence of the letter itself, for we know from Rom. 15:23–24, 28 that at that time he considered his missionary work in the E as completed, and was setting his face to the W, notably to Spain. If the letter emanates from Rome (*i.e.* if it is later than the writing of Rom. 15) it is necessary to believe that a new situation had arisen which led him to revise his plans. This possibility, indeed, is not unthinkable, as we know from his movements at Corinth; but it does show that the Roman view is not entirely free from weaknesses.

c. The Ephesian hypothesis

In place of the Roman dating it is proposed to place the letter in a putative Ephesian captivity. The evidence for this imprisonment is inferential and therefore lacking in complete cogency; but the scholars who support it find that the locating of the letter in this period of Paul's life eases the difficulties which the Roman theory encounters. For example, the intended re-visit to Philippi is then fulfilled in Acts 20:1–6, with Timothy's movements also tallying with the record of Acts. W. Michaelis, who has consistently championed the Ephesian origin, shows persuasively how, on this view, the movements mentioned both in Acts and in Philippians dovetail like the pieces of a jig-saw puzzle. The shorter distance between Philippi and Ephesus makes the journeys more within the bounds of likelihood, while there is inscriptional evidence that satisfies the requirement of 1:13 and 4:22. Ephesus was the centre of the imperial administration in Asia, and there would be a *praetorium* there.

The main difficulties which stand in the way of accepting this novel theory are:

1. Its speculative character. The Ephesian imprisonment cannot be proved from a direct source, although there is much indirect attestation of it, especially in 1 and 2 Cor.

2. The absence of any mention of a matter which (so it is argued) must have filled the apostle's mind at the time of this suggested dating, *viz.* the collection for the churches in Judaea.

3. Perhaps the strongest counter-objection is the failure to explain why it was that, if Paul were in jeopardy at Ephesus, he did not use his right as a Roman citizen and extricate himself by an appeal to the emperor to be tried in Rome. Of this possibility there is no mention in the letter.

Our conclusion, then, must be a disappointing one to those who expect a firm answer. The evidence, we feel, is finely balanced, and a final decision is not possible. The Roman dating may still be accepted with caution and one or two lingering doubts. The Ephesian hypothesis would have to be sufficiently strong to reverse the judgment of centuries, and this it fails to do, although it has many points in its favour; and were it more securely anchored in direct evidence it would command wider support. The tide of critical opinion is, however, running in favour of a dating in the Ephesian period (see Martin, *op. cit.*, pp. 36–57). (*PAUL.)

III. The unity of the letter

In the textual history the letter is known only as a complete whole; but there are many suggestions which contest its unity, mainly on the ground of an abrupt change in tone, style and content at the beginning of ch. 3. Explanations of this sudden change are given under the headings of 'Interpolation' and 'Interruption'.

a. Interpolation

On this view the reason for the abrupt change at 3:1b is that this verse introduces an interpolated fragment from another Pauline letter which has somehow become interwoven into the canonical Epistle. There is little agreement as to where the interpolation ends, whether 4:3 (so K. Lake), 4:1 (A. H. McNeile–C. S. C. Williams, F. W. Beare), or 3:19 (J. H. Michael). Beare envisages the letter as a composite document made up of three elements: a letter of thanks, acknowledging the Philippians' gift by Epaphroditus (4:10–20); an interpolated fragment which denounces the false teaching of the Jewish missionaries and the antinomianism of Gentile Christians (3:2–4:1), and may be directed to some church other than Philippi, as J. H. Michael earlier proposed; and the framework of the Epistle (1:1–3:1; 4:2–9, 21–23), regarded as being the last of Paul's extant letters and, in a sense, his farewell message to the church militant on earth. This analysis has several variations (see Martin, *op. cit.*, pp. 14–21 for details), but in the main the partition into three fragments is widely held. For a convincing defence of the letter's unity, see R. Jewett, *NovT* 12, 1970, pp. 40–53.

b. Interruption

The sudden change in style and outlook may more plausibly be accounted for by the interruption of the apostle as he dictated his letter, as Lightfoot suggested. See also E. Stange, 'Diktierpausen in den Paulusbriefen', in *ZNW* 18, 1917–18, pp. 115f.

On this interpretation, 3:1a is the intended conclusion of the letter. Paul is disturbed by stirring news which has just reached him, and quickly turns aside to dictate a vehement warning. 'The same things' is a prospective term, looking forward to the serious admonitions to watchfulness against the Judaizers which are to follow. See V. P. Furnish, *NTS* 10, 1963–4, pp. 80–88.

The integrity of the letter is, therefore, to be accepted, with a possible reservation only in the case of 2:5–11, which some regard as a pre-Pauline or post-Pauline composition, while F. W. Beare breaks new ground with the submission that this section owes its origin to an unknown Gentile writer who came under Pauline influence during the apostle's lifetime. Paul accepts his writing with his *imprimatur* by including it in his Epistle. There is a full discussion of the authorship and provenance of the Christological hymn in 2:5–11 in the writer's monograph; see below.

IV. The occasion and purpose of the letter

The most obvious reason why the letter came to be written is to be found in Paul's situation as a prisoner, and his desire to commend his colleagues Timothy and Epaphroditus to the church. Paul writes as though he wanted to prepare the way for the coming of these men, and particularly to disarm any criticism which might be raised against Epaphroditus (*cf.* 2:23ff.).

There is also the note of appreciation for the Philippians' gift, to which he alludes in several places (1:5; 4:10, 14ff.). This gift had evidently come through Epaphroditus, and Paul gratefully acknowledges both the gift and the presence of their messenger (2:25).

Epaphroditus had, it is clear, also brought news of the outbreak of various troubles at Philippi, especially the disturbing news of disunity within the ranks of the church members. This is clear from 2:2–4, 14; 4:2, where the disputants are named, and perhaps 1:27. Paul gently reproaches them for this, and recalls them to agreement in the Lord.

Another source of confusion in the fellowship seems to have been the existence and influence of a 'perfectionist' group within the church. There are grounds—known by inference from Paul's counter-arguments—for believing that the Philippians' confidence in being 'perfect' was based on a gnosticized eschatology that eliminated the future hope of the Christians and transferred it to a present experience. Paul's response in ch. 3 is directed to a rebuttal of this. (For details, see Martin, *op. cit.*, pp. 22–34.)

The Christian cause at Philippi seems to have been the object of persecution and attack from the outside world. There is definite allusion to the church's 'enemies' (1:28), and a description of the type

Philippians 4:2–12 in Greek on a page from a collection of Paul's letters copied on papyrus in the 3rd cent. AD. (CBL)

of society in which the church was called upon to live and bear witness to Christ is given (2:15). Hence the oft-repeated call to stand fast (1:27; 4:1). We may detect in a ministry of encouragement a further reason for the letter, although Lohmeyer's interpretation of the entire Epistle as a 'tract for martyrs' is somewhat extreme.

V. The value of the letter

Two outstanding features of the letter may be mentioned. First, the Philippian letter will always remain as a tribute to the apostle's attitude to his sufferings. By the grace of God he is able to rejoice under the most trying circumstances of his captivity and impending fate. His constant call to rejoicing (the word 'joy' and its cognate forms is found 16 times) is a distinguishing characteristic, as Bengel noted in his famous phrase: '*summa epistolae; gaudeo, gaudete*'. And the secret of that joy is fellowship with the Lord who is the centre of his life, whatever the future may hold (1:20–21).

Secondly, no introduction to the letter would be complete without a reference to the great passage in 2:5–11. Here we find the *locus classicus* of Paul's doctrine of the person of Christ and the nature and scope of Christian salvation, and for that reason the Philippian Epistle will ever remain in the forefront of Pauline studies so long as the great apostle's writings continue to engage the attention of Christian students.

Bibliography. Since the present writer's (*TNTC*, 1959) and F. W. Beare's (1959) commentaries appeared, there have been studies by K. Barth (E.T. 1962), K. Grayston (*CBC*, 1967) and J. L. Houlden, *Paul's Letters from Prison*, 1970. R. P. Martin's commentary (*NCB*, 1976) is the latest to be published. On ch. 2:5–11, R. P. Martin's *Carmen Christi*, 1967 seeks to survey scholarly opinion, while there is a popular exposition in *Broadman Bible Commentary*, vol. 11, 1971 (F. Stagg). R.P.M.

PHILISTIA
See Philistines, Part 3.

PHILISTINES, PHILISTIA.

I. Name

In the OT the name Philistine is written p^{e}lištî, usually with the article, and more commonly in its plural form p^{e}*lištîm* (rarely p^{e}*lištiyyîm*) generally without the article. The territory which they inhabited was known as 'the land of the Philistines' (*'ereṣ* p^{e}*lištîm*) or Philistia (p^{e}*lešeṯ*). It is from these that the modern name 'Palestine' derives. In the LXX the word is variously rendered *Phylistieim* (mainly in the Pentateuch, Joshua and Judges), *Hellēnas* (Is. 9:12 [11, Heb.]), and *allophylos*, *-oi*, 'stranger, foreigner' (but not in the Pentateuch or Joshua). It is probable that the name is to be identified with *prst* in the Egyp. texts (the hieroglyphic script using *r* for the *l* sound, which is not represented, in the writing of foreign names) and *palaštu* in the Assyr. cuneiform inscriptions.

II. In the Bible

a. Origin

The Philistines derived from Casluhim, the son of Mizraim (Egypt) the son of Ham (Gn. 10:14; 1 Ch. 1:12). When they later appeared and confronted the Israelites they came from *Caphtor (Am. 9:7).

b. In the time of the Patriarchs

Abraham and Isaac had dealings with a Philistine, Abimelech, the king of Gerar, and his general Phichol (Gn. 20–21; 26). In the time of the Monarchy the Philistines were almost proverbially aggressive, but Abimelech was a reasonable man. He had adopted many of the customs of the country, for he bore a Semitic name, and engaged with Isaac in a covenant.

c. At the time of the Exodus and the Judges

When the Israelites left Egypt the Philistines were extensively settled along the coastal strip between Egypt and Gaza, and they were obliged to detour inland to avoid 'the way of the land of the Philistines' (Ex. 13:17). The adjacent section of the Mediterranean was in fact referred to as the sea of the Philistines (Ex. 23:31). It is presumably the Philistines in this area who are referred to as Caphtorim in Dt. 2:23.

The Israelites did not encounter the Philistines in Canaan during the Conquest, but by the time Joshua was an old man they were established in the five cities of Gaza, Ashkelon, Ashdod, Ekron and Gath (Jos. 13:2–3). From this time for many generations these people were used by God to chastise the Israelites (Jdg. 3:2–3). Shamgar ben Anath repulsed them temporarily (Jdg. 3:31), but they constantly pressed inland from the coast plain, and the Israelites even adopted their gods (Jdg. 10:6–7). The great Israelite hero of the period of the Judges was Samson (Jdg. 13–16). In his time there were social links between Philistines and Israelites, for he married a Philistine wife, and later had relations with Delilah, who, if not a Philistine herself, was in close contact with them. The hill-country was not under Philistine control, and Samson took refuge there after his raids. When he was finally taken by them he was bound with bronze fetters (16:21) and forced to make sport for them while they watched from inside and on the roof of a pillared building (16:25–27).

d. In the reigns of Saul and David

It was probably largely due to the continuing pressure of the Philistines that the need for a strong military leader was felt in Israel. The ark was captured by the Philistines in a disastrous battle at Aphek and the shrine at Shiloh was destroyed (1 Sa. 4), and at this time they probably controlled Esdraelon, the coast plain, the Negeb, and much of the hill-country. They also controlled the distribution of iron, and thus prevented the Israelites from having useful weapons (1 Sa. 13:19–22). Saul was anointed king by Samuel, and after a victory over the Philistines at Michmash, drove them from the hill-country (1 Sa. 14). His erratic rule, however, allowed the Philistines to continue to assert themselves, as when they challenged Israel at Ephes-dammim, and David killed Goliath (1 Sa. 17–18). Saul turned against David, who became an outlaw and finally a feudatory vassal of Achish king of Gath (1 Sa. 27). He was not called upon to fight against Israel at the battle of Mt Gilboa when Saul and his sons were killed, and when he took over the kingship of Israel he must have remained on peaceful terms with Gath at least, and in fact maintained a personal Philistine bodyguard throughout his reign (*CHERETHITES). A final conflict had to come, however. David drove the Philistines out of the hill-country and struck a heavy blow in Philistia itself (2 Sa. 5:25), putting an end to the power of the Philistines as a serious menace.

e. During the divided Monarchy

The Philistines continued to cause trouble throughout the Monarchy. With the weakening of the kingdom at the death of David the Philistine cities (except for Gath, 2 Ch. 11:8) were independent and there was fighting on the frontier (1 Ki. 15:27; 16:15). Jehoshaphat received tribute from some of the Philistines (2 Ch. 17:11), but under Jehoram the border town of Libnah was lost to Israel (2 Ki. 8:22). They were still aggressive in the time of Ahaz (Is. 9:8–12), and the last time they are mentioned in the Bible is in the prophecy of Zechariah, after the return from the Exile.

III. Philistia

The area which took its name from the Philistines was that of the nucleus of their settlement. This centred on the five main Philistine cities of Gaza, Ashkelon, Ashdod, Ekron and Gath, and comprised the coastal strip S of Carmel, extending inland to the foothills of Judah. Other cities particularly associated with the Philistines in the Bible are *Bethshean and *Gerar. There is still uncertainty concerning the identification of the sites of some of the five principal Philistine cities (see under separate city names).

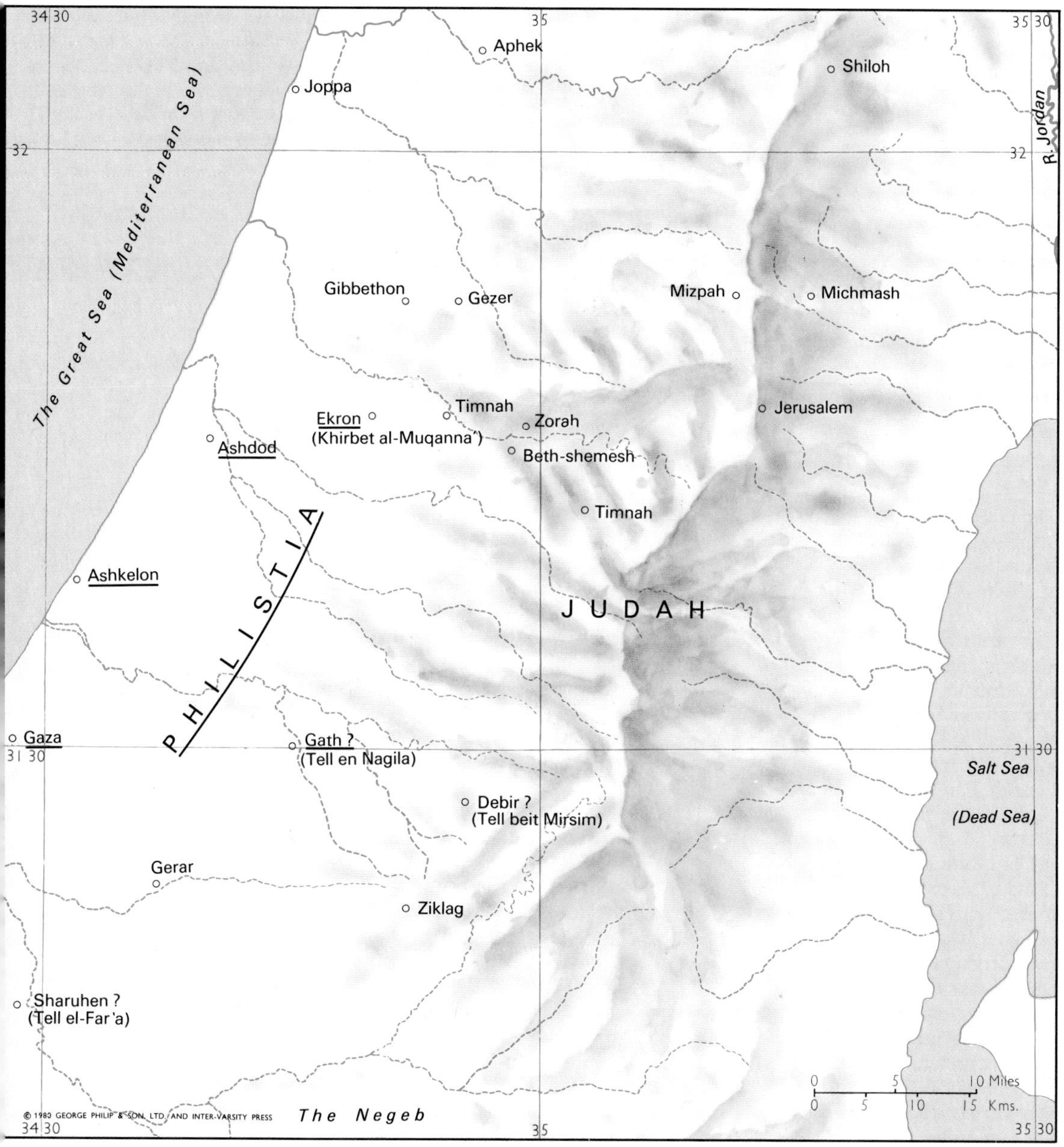

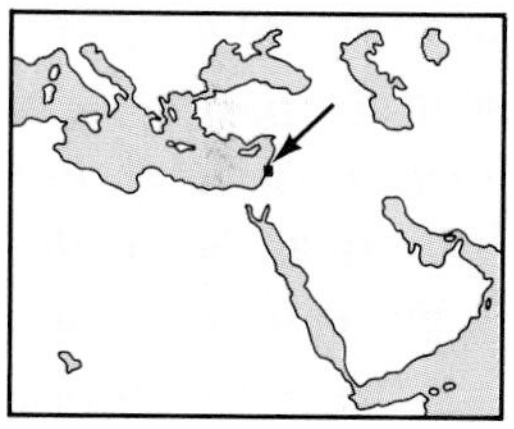

The cities of the Philistines and their neighbours.

Philistines (Sea People) with characteristic head-dress, shown among Egyptian prisoners. Relief from temple of Rameses III, Medinet Habu, Thebes. c. 1182–1151 BC. (PAC)

IV. In the inscriptions

The Philistines are first mentioned by name (*prst*) in the annals of Rameses III for his 5th (1185 BC) and subsequent years, inscribed in his temple to Ammon at Medinet Habu near Thebes. This describes his campaign against an invasion of Libyans and various other peoples generally known as the 'Sea Peoples', of whom the *prst* were one. Other members of the 'Sea Peoples' had already been mentioned in the inscriptions of Merenptah, Rameses II and in the 14th-century Amarna Letters (Lukku, Šerdanu, Danuna). The carved reliefs in the temple at Medinet Habu show the Sea Peoples arriving with their families and chattels by wagon and ship, and the *prst* and another group closely associated with them, the *ṯkr* (Tjekker), are depicted wearing head-dresses of feathers rising vertically from a horizontal band. A head wearing a similar head-dress is one of the pictographic signs on a clay disk found at Phaistos in Crete, and usually dated to the 17th century BC.

The Assyr. inscriptions mention Philistia as an area often in revolt. The first occurrence is in an inscription of Adad-nirari III (810–782 BC), where Philistia is mentioned among other tribute-paying states, including Israel. The Philistines are subsequently mentioned in the annals of Tiglath-pileser III, Sargon and Sennacherib, usually as defeated rebels.

In a group of cuneiform documents of the time of the Exile found at Babylon, the issue of rations to expatriates is recorded. Among these are mentioned men from Philistia.

V. Archaeology

a. Pottery

A type of pottery has been found in a number of sites centring on Philistia and from levels of the late 2nd millennium BC. Since this was the area and period of the Philistines, this pottery is usually attributed to them. In its decoration it shows marked affinities with that of the Aegean, and recent excavations at Enkomi and Sinda in Cyprus have brought to light locally-made pottery (*c*. 1225–1175 BC) which is classified as Mycenaean IIIC1b, deriving from Aegean originals, and most probably representing the forerunner of the Philistine pottery.

b. Clay coffins

Clay coffins, each with a face moulded in relief at the head end, have been discovered at *Beth-shean, Tell el-Far'a, Lachish and in Transjordan, which are probably to be connected with similar coffins found in Egypt, notably at Tell el-Yehudiyeh in the Delta. The date and distribution of these suggest that they may be attributed to the Philistines, a view supported by the fact that some of the faces are surmounted by a row of vertical strokes, perhaps indicating the feathered head-dress.

c. Weapons

The Egyp. reliefs show the *prst*,

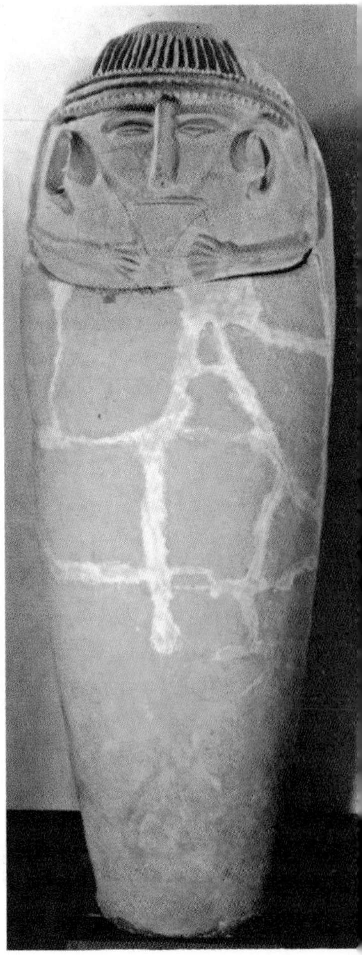

Anthropoid clay coffins, some, as here, with vertical strokes probably representing their characteristic feathered head-dress, have been attributed to the Philistines. From Bethshean. 12th cent. BC. (IM)

A Philistine (prst) *depicted on an Egyptian faience tile. c. 1195–1164 BC* (*Rameses III*). (OIUC)

with the Tjekker and Serdanu, as armed with lances, round shields, long broadswords and triangular daggers. They arrived in Palestine at the period of transition from the Bronze to Iron Age, so that the biblical statements that they bound Samson with fetters of bronze but, by the time of Saul, controlled the iron industry of the area are quite consistent.

VI. Culture

The Philistines, while retaining a few cultural features bespeaking their foreign origin, were largely assimilated to the Canaanite culture that surrounded them.

a. Government

The five Philistine cities were each ruled by a *seren* (Jos. 13:3; Jdg. 3:3; 16:5, 8, 18, 27, 30; 1 Sa. 5:8, 11; 6:4, 12, 16, 18; 7:7; 29:2, 6–7; 1 Ch. 12:19). The term is probably cognate with Luwian (Hieroglyphic Hittite) *tarwanas*, 'judge' or the like, and pre-Hellenic (probably Indo-European) Gk. *tyrannos*, 'absolute ruler'. The precise meaning of *seren* is uncertain, but 'ruler' (RSV) is a reasonable rendering.

b. Language

No Philistine inscriptions have been recovered, and the language is unknown, though some scholars have surmised that it may have derived from a possibly Indo-European, pre-Greek speech of the Aegean area. Certain words in the Bible may be Philistine loan-words. In addition to *seren*, the word for helmet, whose foreign origin is betrayed in the variant spellings *kôḇa'* and *qôḇa'*, is usually attributed to the Philistines. Another word which some scholars would label as Philistine is *'argāz*, 'box' (1 Sa. 6:8, 11, 15, AV 'coffer'). Other words have been designated as Philistine from time to time, but without general assent. Among the names, Achish (*'āḵîš*) is probably the same as *'kš*, which is listed as a *kftyw* (*CAPHTOR) name in an Egyp. inscription of about the 18th Dynasty and Goliath (*golyat*) is perhaps linked by its *-yat* termination with Luwian (Hieroglyphic Hittite) and Lydian names ending respectively in *-wattaš* and *-uattes*. Aside from these few words, it is clear that the Philistines adopted the Semitic tongue of the peoples they dispossessed.

c. Religion

Knowledge of the Philistine religion depends upon the Bible. The three gods mentioned, *Dagon, *Ashtoreth and *Baalzebub, were all Near Eastern, and it is perhaps to be assumed that they identified their own gods with those they found in Palestine, and accommodated their own religion to that already there. The excavator of Bethshean suggested that two temples found there might be those of Dagon and Ashtoreth, where Saul's trophies were hung, but no excavated temples may be certainly identified as Philistine. They offered sacrifices (Jdg. 16:23) and wore charms in battle (2 Sa. 5:21).

VII. Origin and role

The cumulative evidence leaves little doubt that the Philistines came immediately, though probably not ultimately, from the Aegean. Some scholars would equate the name with that of the *Pelasgoi*, the pre-Greek inhabitants of the Aegean, a view which is weighted by the occurrence of the name twice in Gk. literature, spelt with a *t* rather than a *g*. This view is still debated, and even granting it, the classical references to the *Pelasgoi* are too inconsistent to be helpful.

It seems that the Philistines were one of the Sea Peoples who, in the later 2nd millennium, moved out of the Aegean, probably as a result of the arrival of the Greeks, and migrated by land and sea, some

This figurine was found in the Philistine city of Ashdod. It represents a goddess and bed, and by its style reveals links with the Mycenaean world. Height 17 cm. 12th cent. BC. (IM)

via Crete and Cyprus, to the Near East, where they forced a foothold, first as mercenary troops of the pharaohs, the Hittite kings and the Canaanite rulers, and finally as settlers who were absorbed in the basic population. Though they retained their name for many centuries, the biblical Philistines, the Tjekker who occupied an adjacent coastal region, and doubtless others of the Sea Peoples, became for all practical purposes Canaanites.

VIII. Philistines in the patriarchal narratives

Since the Philistines are not named in extra-biblical inscriptions until the 12th century BC, and the archaeological remains associated with them do not appear before this time, many commentators reject references to them in the patriarchal period as anachronistic. Two considerations must be entertained, however. There is evidence of a major expansion of Aegean trade in the Middle Minoan II period (*c.* 1900–1700 BC; *CRETE) and objects of Aegean manufacture or influence have been found from this period at Ras Shamra in Syria, Hazor and perhaps Megiddo in Palestine, and Tôd, Harageh, Lahun and Abydos in Egypt. It is likely that a large part of this trade consisted in perishable goods such as textiles. A new type of spiral design which appears in Egypt and Asia (Mari) at this time may support this. Further evidence of contacts is afforded by a tablet from Mari (18th century) recording the sending of gifts by the king of Hazor to Kaptara (*CAPHTOR). Secondly, ethnic names in antiquity were not used with particular precision. The members of a mixed group such as the Sea Peoples were unlikely to be carefully distinguished by name, so that the absence of one name from the inscriptions may simply mean that the particular group was not sufficiently prominent to find special mention. The Sea Peoples, and their predecessors who traded with the Near East, arrived in waves, and dominant in a 12th-century wave were the Philistines, who consequently figured in the records. There is no reason why small groups of Philistines could not have been among the early Aegean traders, not prominent enough to be noticed by the larger states.

BIBLIOGRAPHY. R. A. S. Macalister, *The Philistines, Their History and Civilization*, 1914; W. F. Albright, *AASOR* 12, 1932, pp. 53–58; O. Eissfeldt in *RE*, 38, 1938, cols. 2390–2401; A. H. Gardiner, *Ancient Egyptian Onomastica*, Text, 1, pp. 200*–205*; T. Dothan, *Antiquity and Survival*, 2, 1957, pp. 151–164; G. E. Wright, *BA* 22, 1959, pp. 54–66; T. C. Mitchell in *AOTS*, pp. 404–427; K. A. Kitchen in *POTT*, pp. 53–78. T.C.M.

PHILO. Among the many bearers of the name Philo in antiquity, the most important for the student of the Bible is Philo of Alexandria, a member of a rich and influential Jewish family in that city in the 1st century. His brother Alexander was one of the richest men of his day, while his nephew Tiberius Alexander became in due time Procurator of Judaea and Prefect of Egypt, having apostatized from the Jewish faith.

Little is known of the life of Philo himself; neither his birth nor his death may be dated, the one sure date in his career being his membership in the embassy to Gaius (Caligula) in AD 39. From this it is evident that he was quite old at that time, and conjecturally we may place his dates as approximately 20 BC to AD 45. From his writings it may be deduced that, as a leader of the Jewish community, he spent much of his life in the duties of public service. His natural bent, however, was to the life of contemplation and the pursuit of philosophy, in which, as he asserts, he spent his youth (*Concerning the Special Laws*, 3. 1), perhaps in such a community as the Therapeutae, described by him in *Concerning the Contemplative Life*. Although he was obliged to leave this to take up his duties, he found opportunity to produce a body of writings on philosophical and theological topics.

His early work was on philosophical themes, in which he shows little originality, but provides valuable source material for the study of a little-known period of Hellenistic philosophy. His main work, however, was the production of expositions of the Pentateuch; he was motivated by the desire to demonstrate that the philosophical and religious quests of the Gentile world of the day found their true goal in the God of Abraham. Three large works remain, none of them complete nor in exact order, their several sections having been transmitted often as separate treatises in the MS tradition: *The Allegory of the Laws* (a commentary on Genesis); *Questions and Answers on Genesis and Exodus* (a shorter work of the same kind); and *The Exposition of the Laws* (a review of the history in the Pentateuch). By means of allegorical exegesis he is able to extract moral and mystical teaching from all parts of these books. His method of allegory is derived from that already applied to the Homeric books by philosophers. It may be analysed as: (i) 'cosmological' ('physiological' in his own terminology) in which allegory concerning the nature (*physis*) of things is perceived (*e.g.* the high priest and his vestments seen as the Logos and the universe, *Life of Moses*, 2. 117ff.), and (ii) 'ethical', in which reference to human psychology and moral struggle is seen (*e.g.* etymological interpretations of such figures as Isaac (= joy)). The basis of both the cosmology and psychology is the Stoic system, although it is evident that Pythagorean and Platonist are also laid under contribution in some details, a feature which probably reflects the eclecticism of the period.

Philo's greatest contribution to thought, according to recent students, is his use of philosophy in this way to provide a rationale of religion; he is in fact the 'first theologian', and philosophy is significant to him primarily as the handmaid of theology. The motivation of his work may be seen not simply in his missionary zeal, common to many Jews of that era, but also in the mystical experiences of the reality of his God of which he writes movingly in several places (*e.g. Special Laws*, *loc. cit.*). Central to his understanding both of the universe and of religious experience is the concept of the Logos, a term of Stoic origin which, in Philo, linked with such a concept as the Platonic World of Ideas, signifies the mode whereby the transcendent God creates and sustains the world, and further, reveals himself to his creatures. Moses is expounded as a type of the Logos by whom men are led to knowledge of God; the Patriarchs as instances of those who have freed themselves from the bondage of material things and are united with the divine Wisdom.

The definitive edition of the Gk. text of Philo is the six volumes by L. Cohn and P. Wendland, published 1896–1914, with a seventh volume of Indexes (1926–30) by

H. Leisegang. A number of works, extant only in Armenian, were edited by the Mechitarist J. B. Aucherian in 1822 and 1826; the version dates from the 5th century. There is also an Old Lat. version of Philo, of some value for the construction of his text. The most recent translation of Philo's extant works, both Gk. and Armenian, is that in the Loeb Classical Library by F. H. Colson, G. H. Whittaker and R. Marcus (10 vols. plus 2 supplementary vols., 1929–62).

As the best preserved and most extensive of Hellenistic Jewish writings, Philo's works are of value in illuminating the thought world of the NT. Certain of his OT citations bear upon the problem of the origin of the LXX (see P. Katz, *Philo's Bible*, 1950). Two writings at least of the NT may not be adequately understood without reference to his thought and method. The Epistle to the Hebrews in its treatment of the tabernacle and the figure of Melchizedek shows close affinity to his allegory, while its doctrine of the Son is related in several particulars to his Logos-teaching. The Gospel of John bears no resemblance to Philonic allegory (as has sometimes been asserted), but in the cosmology explicit in the Prologue and elsewhere implicit there is evidently close kinship to the Philonic allegory. This need not imply that these writers were directly dependent on Philo. A plausible explanation might be that they come from a like background of thought. Both possibilities have been pursued and demand still further investigation.

BIBLIOGRAPHY. H. Leisegang, article 'Philo' in *RE*; E. Bréhier, *Les Idées Philosophiques et Religieuses de Philon d'Alexandrie*, 1925; E. R. Goodenough, *An Introduction to Philo Judaeus*, 1939; *idem*, *By Light, Light*, 1935; R. Williamson, *Philo and the Epistle to the Hebrews*, 1970; and appropriate chapters in C. H. Dodd, *The Interpretation of the Fourth Gospel*, 1953, and C. Spicq, *L'Épitre aux Hébreux*, 1952. J.N.B.

PHINEHAS. A name of Egyp. origin, *P'-nḥsy*, 'the Nubian'; popular in Egypt during the New Kingdom (16th to 12th centuries BC). It is borne in the OT by three individuals.

1. Son of Eleazar, and grandson of Aaron (Ex. 6:25; 1 Ch. 6:4, 50; Ezr. 7:5), with priestly descendants (Ezr. 8:2). He slew an Israelite and the (pagan) Midianite woman he had taken, after Israel became involved in paganism at Shittim (Nu. 25; Ps. 106:30), and shared in the subsequent war against Midian (Nu. 31:6). Under Joshua, Phinehas helped settle the dispute with the Transjordanian tribes over their memorial altar (Jos. 22:9ff.). After burying his father in his own hill (Jos. 24:33) Phinehas was officiating priest early in the Judges' period (Jdg. 20:28; perhaps 1 Ch. 9:20).

2. Younger of the high priest Eli's two disreputable sons, late in the Judges' period (1 Sa. 1:3; *cf.* 2:12–17, 34). He was slain in the battle of Aphek when the Philistines captured the ark (1 Sa. 4). A grandson of this Phinehas was a priest in Saul's reign (1 Sa. 14:3).

3. The father of a priest Eleazar in Ezra's time (Ezr. 8:33). K.A.K.

PHOEBE (AV 'Phebe'). Lady Bountiful of Cenchreae (E port of Corinth, where hospitality would be important); *'deaconess' (AV 'servant') of the church and 'patroness' (AV 'succourer') of many, including Paul (Rom. 16:1–2; the terms are probably semi-technical). She apparently carried Paul's letter, and he asks worthy hospitality for her. E. J. Goodspeed (*HTR* 44, 1951, pp. 55ff.) holds that Rom. 16 is a separate letter to Ephesus to secure her a reception with those named. But would such oblique personal references be necessary?

The name (meaning 'radiant') is a surname of Artemis. A striking epitaph to 'The second Phoebe', a later deaconess, is cited in *MM* (*s.v. koimaomai*). See further M. D. Gibson, *ExpT* 23, 1911–12, p. 281. A.F.W.

PHOENICIA, PHOENICIANS. The territory on the E Mediterranean coast covering *c.* 240 km between the rivers Litani and Arvad (mod. Lebanon–S Latakia) and its inhabitants.

Phoenicia (AV Phenice) as such is named only in the NT as the place of refuge for Christians fleeing from persecution following the death of Stephen (Acts 11:19); through this land Paul and Silas journeyed on their way from Samaria to Antioch (Acts 15:3). Later Paul landed on the Phoenician coast near Tyre on his way to Jerusalem (Acts 21:2–3). In the time of Christ Phoenicia was referred to as 'the sea-coast and district of Tyre and Sidon' (Mt. 15:21; Lk. 6:17), and the inhabitants, including Greeks, were considered 'Syro-Phoenicians' (Mk. 7:26).

In OT times the territory occupied by the Phoenicians was called by the Hebrews 'Canaan' (Is. 23:11), 'Canaanite' (*i.e.* 'merchant') being probably the name applied by the inhabitants to themselves (Gn. 10:15). It was, however, the common practice in all periods to refer to Phoenicia by the name of its principal cities (*TYRE, *SIDON), since there was little political cohesion between them except for periods such as the reign of Hiram I. Other major settlements were Arvad, Simyra, Gebal/Byblos, Be(i)rut and Zarephath (*ZAREPTA).

I. History

The origin of the sea-faring Phoenicians is obscure, though according to Herodotus (1. 1; 7. 89) they arrived overland from the Persian Gulf area, via the Red Sea, and first founded Sidon. The earliest archaeological evidence of their presence may come from the 'proto-Phoenician' finds at Byblos (ancient Gubla or Gebal, Ezk. 27:9, modern Gebail) dated *c.* 3000 BC. This important site has been excavated since 1924 by the French under Montet and Dunand. Byblian ships are depicted on Egyp. reliefs of the time of Sahure in the 5th Dynasty (*c.* 2500 BC) and there can be no doubt that by the 18th century there was an extensive trade in timber and artistic commodities between Phoenicia and Egypt (*SHIPS). The Phoenicians by this time had settled in their first colonies along the coast at Joppa, Dor (Jdg. 1:27–31), Acre and Ugarit (Ras Shamra). They chose easily defensible natural harbours and gradually dominated the local population as at Ras Shamra (level IV).

For some centuries Phoenicia was under the economic and quasi-military control of the Egyptian 18th and 19th Dynasties, and Arvad was among the places claimed to have been captured by Tuthmosis III (*c.* 1485 BC). Nevertheless, the letters written by Rib-Addi of Byblos and Abi-milki of Tyre to Amenophis III at Amarna in Egypt show that, by *c.* 1400 BC, Ṣumur and Berut had disaffected and with Sidon, which appears to

PHILOSOPHER
See Epicureans, Part 1.

have maintained its independence, were blockading Phoenician cities (* AMARNA). When the 'sea-peoples' invaded the coast *c.* 1200 BC, Byblos, Arvad and Ugarit were destroyed and the Sidonians fled to Tyre, which now became the principal port, or, as Isaiah claims, the 'daughter of Sidon' (23:12).

By the time of David, Tyre was ruled by Hiram I son of Abi-Baal and his reign began a golden age. Phoenicia was allied commercially with David (2 Sa. 5:11; 1 Ki. 5:1) and Hiram by treaty supplied Solomon with wood, stone and craftsmen for the construction of the Temple and palace (1 Ki. 5:1–12; 2 Ch. 2:3–16), and ships and navigators to assist the Judaean fleet and to develop the port of Ezion-geber as a base for long voyages (1 Ki. 9:27). This aid resulted in territorial advantages, for Tyre was given twenty villages on her border in part payment (vv. 10–14). Phoenicia, herself long influenced by Egyp. art, motifs and methods, was now in a position to influence Heb. thought. Hiram was a conqueror and builder of several temples at Tyre, and a successful administrator who settled colonial revolts (W. F. Albright, in the *Leland Volume*, 1942, pp. 43f.). It was probably due to his initiative that by the 9th century Phoenician colonies were founded in Sardinia (Nova, Tharros), Cyprus (Kition) and Karatepe (N Taurus). Utica had been settled in the 12th century and Carthage, Sicily (Motya) and Tunisia by the 8th.

Hiram's successor, a high priest named Ethbaal, furthered the alliance with Israel by the marriage of his daughter Jezebel to Ahab (1 Ki. 16:31), with the consequence that the worship of the Phoenician Baals was increased (1 Ki. 18:19). Elijah fled for a while to Zarephath, which was part of the coast controlled by Sidon, and therefore at this time independent of Tyre (1 Ki. 17:9).

The Assyrian advances brought pressure on the Phoenician cities. Ashurnasirpal II (884–859 BC) counted among the tribute he received from Tyre, Sidon, Gebal and Arvad garments and dyed cloth, precious metals and carved ivory and wood. This tribute was renewed when Shalmaneser III besieged Damascus and marched to the Mediterranean coast at the Dog river in 841 BC. The act of submission to him and the gifts sent by Tyre and Sidon are pictured on the bronze gates set up in the Assyr. temple at Balawat (see *ANEP*, pp. 356–357). Adad-nirari III claimed Tyre and Sidon among his vassals in 803 BC (*DOTT*, p. 51). Hirammu of Tyre, Sibitti-Bi'ili of Gubla (Byblos) sent tribute to Tiglath-pileser III during his siege of Arpad (*c.* 741 BC) about the same time as Menahem of Israel submitted to him.

A few years later the Assyrian sent his *rab šaqe*-official (* RAB-SHAKEH) to collect taxes from Metenna of Tyre. Letters addressed to the Assyr. king show that Tyre and Sidon were under direct supervision of an Assyr. official, who forwarded the taxes, mostly paid in timber and goods, direct to Calah (*Iraq* 17, 1955, pp. 126–154). In 734 BC Tiglath-pileser captured the fortress of Kashpuna, which guarded the approaches to Tyre and Sidon, who were now allied in defence.

Sargon continued to raid the Phoenician coastlands, and Sennacherib (*c.* 701 BC) captured Ušše near Tyre and carried Phoenician prisoners off to Nineveh to build his new palace (as shown on reliefs) and to Opis to build the fleet planned to pursue the rebel * Merodach-baladan across the Persian Gulf. Nevertheless, the larger cities clung to their independence until Esarhaddon sacked Sidon and settled the survivors from it in a new town called 'Walled City of Esarhaddon' and in 15 adjacent villages. Other towns were placed under Ba'ali of Tyre, who was bound by treaty to Esarhaddon. This named Arvad, Acre, Dor, Gebal and Mt Lebanon and regulated trade and shipping. However, Ba'ali, incited by Tirhakah of

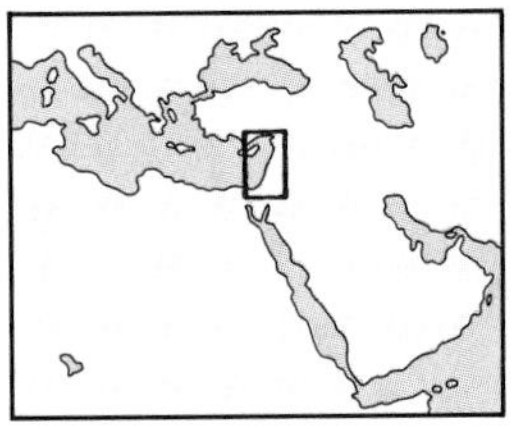

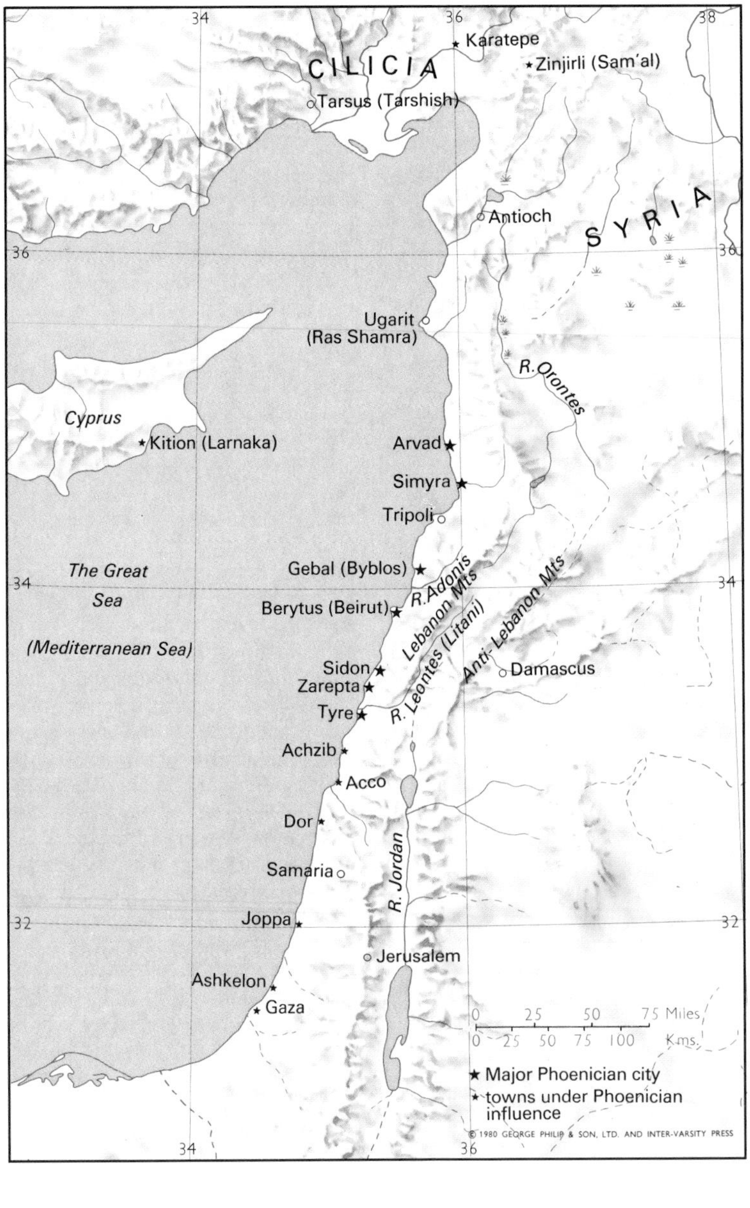

The major cities of Phoenicia.

A bronze bowl with decoration in relief, made in Phoenicia and taken to Nimrud, Assyria, as tribute. Diameter c. 22 cm. 8th cent. BC. (BM)

Egypt, revolted. Tyre was besieged and Phoenicia subordinated to a province. The rulers of the cities, including Milki-asapa of Gebal, and Matan-Ba'al of Arvad, were made to 'bear the corvée basket', that is, to act as labourers at the foundation of Esarhaddon's new palace at Calah, as Manasseh did in Babylon (2 Ch. 33:11).

Ashurbanipal continued the war against Phoenicia, containing Ba'ali by an attack in 665 BC prior to his advance on Egypt. He took Ba'ali's daughters as concubines and also received a heavy tribute. On the death of Ba'ali Azi-Ba'al was made king and Yakinlu appointed to rule Arvad.

With the decline of Assyria the cities regained their independence and traded with new ports opened in Egypt. Their Punic kinsfolk founded colonies in Algeria, Spain and Morocco in the 7th–5th centuries and by a naval victory over the Etruscans in 535 BC finally closed the W Mediterranean to the Phoenician traders.

Nebuchadrezzar II of Babylon in his advance towards Egypt besieged Tyre for 13 years *c.* 585–573 BC (Ezk. 26:1–29:1ff.), but, though Ithobaal was carried off prisoner to Babylon, the city retained a measure of autonomy, which it held throughout the Neo-Babylonian and Persian rule, trading with Egypt (Zp. 1:11) and supplying fish and other commodities to Jerusalem (Ne. 13:16) and in return probably receiving wood and homespun textiles (Pr. 31:24; *ARTS AND CRAFTS).

Alexander the Great captured the island city of Tyre by means of an artificially constructed causeway. The slaughter and destruction was heavy, but the city recovered and, like Sidon, was prosperous in Hellenistic and Roman times (*e.g.* Mt. 15:21).

II. Religion

The idolatrous religion of Phoenicia was condemned by Elijah (1 Ki. 18–19) and later Heb. prophets (Is. 65:11). The early period, seen in the Ras Shamra texts, reveals a polytheistic and natural mythology centred on Baal, also called Melek, 'king', the sun-god Saps, and Reshep (Mikkal) an underworld deity. Fertility cults honoured 'Anat (Astarte, Ashtart) and the popular blend of Semitic and Egyp. ideas resulted in the cult of Adonis and *Tammuz, in which the former was identified with Osiris. Other deities included Eshmun, the god of healing (Gk. Asklepios), and Melqart.

III. Art

The syncretistic tendencies of Phoenician religions are to be seen in the art which combines Semitic, Egyp. and Hurrian elements. This is due to the geographical location and the interchange of materials and influence which followed trade. The Phoenicians were primarily sea-traders and artists. They exported silk, linen and wool, dyed, woven and embroidered locally, hence the name Phoenicia may be derived from Gk. *phoinikoi*, 'red-purple folk' (the Akkadian *kinahhi/ kina'ain, i.e.* Canaan) (*ARTS AND CRAFTS; *POTT*, p. 34) and from their unbounded supplies in the hinterland of the Lebanon shipped wood and its products. The craftsmen worked stone (*e.g.* Ahiram sarcophagus *c.* 900 BC; *BASOR* 134, 1954, p. 9; *Syria* 11, 1930, pp. 180ff.), *ivory, and *glass, and though the Hebrews did not themselves allow images or the portrayal of the human figure (*ART), Phoenician silver and bronze coins are found inland in numbers from the 4th century BC onwards. The requirements of their trade led to the development of *writing (the so-called Phoenician, Byblian and Ugaritic alphabets), the *abacus* for counting, and *papyrus books. It is much to be regretted that the Phoenician literature, including the mythology of Sanchuniathon of Byblos and the history of Menander of Tyre, has survived only in a few quotations in later authors, for it was probably through their literature that much of the learning of the East reached Greece.

BIBLIOGRAPHY. D. B. Harden, *The Phoenicians*, 1962; S. Moscati, *The World of the Phoenicians*, 1968; D. R. Ap-Thomas, 'The Phoenicians', in *POTT*, pp. 259–286.

D.J.W.

PHOENIX. 1. A mythical bird, anciently thought to be born directly from its parent's corpse. Some early Christians (Tertullian, *De Resurr.* 13. 6; *cf. 1 Clement* 25), seeing an analogy of resurrection, warranted it by Ps. 92:12 (LXX 91:13), but *phoinix* there clearly means 'palm-tree'. Phoenix-and-palm was frequent in Christian art.

2. The harbour (AV 'Phenice') the nautical experts, despite Paul's entreaties, made for in winter (Acts 27:12). Data given by Strabo, Ptolemy and other writers seem to indicate the Cape Mouros area, where modern Loutro is the only safe harbour in S Crete (James

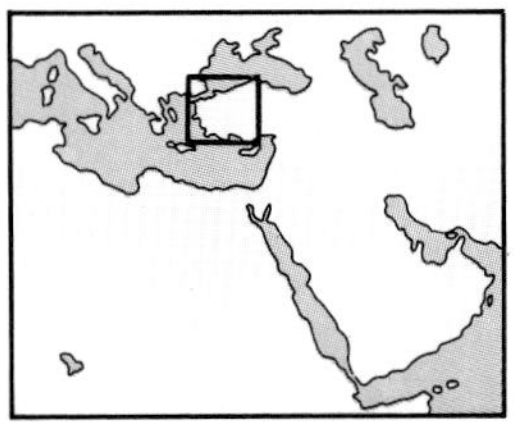

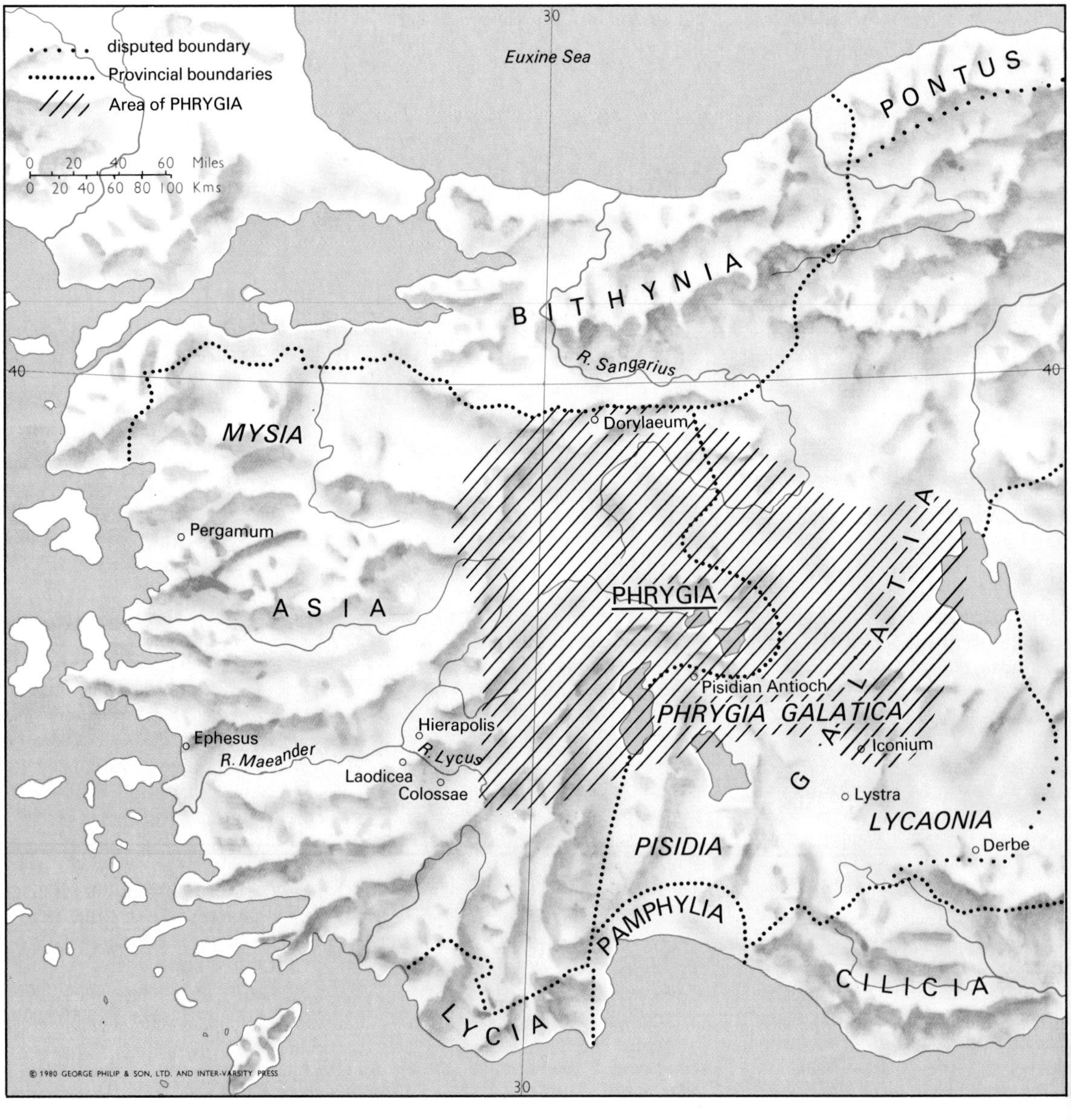

The territory of Phrygia.

Smith, *Voyage and Shipwreck of St. Paul*[4], 1880, p. 90n.). But Luke (AV) says Phoenix 'lieth toward the south-west and north-west (*sc.* 'winds')', *i.e.* faces W, while Loutro faces E. A narrow peninsula separates it from a W-facing bay, but one offering little shelter. Smith, urging the danger of W winter gales, suggested that Luke meant the direction *towards which* the winds blew, *i.e.* looking NE and SE (*cf.* RV, RSV); but this is unsubstantiated unless we assume some lost nautical idiom. Ramsay thought that Luke might have excusably misunderstood Paul's account of the discussion, but left open the possibility of a change in coastline (*cf. HDB*). Ogilvie's recent examination strongly suggests this occurred. The W bay was once better protected, and earthquake disturbance has apparently covered an inlet facing NW in classical times. A SW-facing inlet remains, and the disused W bay is still called Phinika. Ogilvie also found that locally the winter winds are N and E: in Acts 27 it was an ENE wind (* EURAQUILO) which caused the disaster.

BIBLIOGRAPHY. J. B. Lightfoot on *1 Clement* 25; J. Smith, *op. cit.*, pp. 87ff., 251ff.; R. M. Ogilvie, *JTS* n.s. 9, 1958, pp. 308ff. A.F.W.

PHRYGIA. A tract of land centred on the W watershed of the great Anatolian plateau, and reaching N into the valley of the upper Sangarius, SW down the valley of the Maeander, and SE across the plateau, perhaps as far as Iconium. The Phrygians formed the (legendary?) kingdom of Midas. They fell under direct Hellenic influence during the era of the Attalid kings of Pergamum, and in 116 BC most of Phrygia was incorporated by the Romans into their province of Asia. The E extremity (Phrygia Galatica) was included in the new province of Galatia in 25 BC. The Romans were deeply impressed by the ecstatic Phrygian cult of Cybele, and the national fanaticism apparently lies behind the defiant tombstones, presumably Montanist, of the 2nd century AD, which represent the earliest extant public manifesto of Christianity. There is no evidence of any indigenous Christian church in NT times, however. Such churches as fall technically within Phrygia (Laodicea, Hierapolis, Colossae, Pisidian Antioch and probably Iconium) were established in Gk. communities. It was most probably Jewish members of these Gk. states who visited Jerusalem (Acts 2:10). If Col. 2:1, as is just possible, is not taken to exclude a visit by Paul, it would be natural to assume that it is the first three of these cities, on the upper Maeander, that are referred to in Acts 16:6; 18:23. Failing that, we may resort to the view that 'the region of Phrygia and * Galatia' is a composite technical term for Phrygia Galatica and refers in particular to the churches at Iconium and Pisidian Antioch. Otherwise we cannot identify the disciples Paul left in 'Phrygia'.

BIBLIOGRAPHY. Strabo, 12; J. Friedrich, *RE*, 20, 1, pp. 781–891; W. M. Ramsay, *Cities and Bishoprics of Phrygia*, 1895–7; A. H. M. Jones, *Cities of the Eastern Roman Provinces*, 1937; D. Magie, *Roman Rule in Asia Minor*, 2 vols., 1950; W. M. Calder, *AS* 5, 1955, pp. 25–38. E.A.J.

PHYLACTERIES. The name is a transliteration of Gk. *phylaktērion*, meaning 'a means of protection' or * 'amulet'. Though some Jews have regarded them superstitiously, this attitude has always been marginal, so the Gk. name probably derives from heathen misinterpretation. The Jew speaks of *t*ᵉ*pillâ* (lit. 'prayer'), pl. *t*ᵉ*pillîn*. They represent the interpretation by the pious of Ex. 13:9, 16; Dt. 6:8; 11:18. Their present form became standardized by the early years of the 2nd century AD and consists of two hollow cubes made of the skin of clean animals. They vary between 1·25 cm and 4 cm a side. That for the head is divided into four equal compartments; that for the hand has no divisions. In them are placed the four passages Ex. 13:1–10; 13:11–16; Dt. 6:4–9; 11:13–21 written by hand on parchment (on four pieces for the head, on one for the hand). The phylacteries are attached to leather straps by which they are fastened to the left hand and the centre of the forehead by the men before morning prayers, whether in the home or the synagogue, except on the sabbath and high festivals. They are put on after the praying shawl (*ṭallîṯ*), that for the hand coming first. Both they and the straps are always coloured black. The phylactery for the head can be recognized by a three- and four-armed *šin* on its right and left sides.

In the * Qumran discoveries portions of phylacteries have been

PHUT
See Put, Part 3.

PHYGELUS
See Hermogenes, Part 2.

Man wearing prayer shawl with phylacteries. (SH)

found, which show they were not absolutely standardized before the destruction of the Temple. The main difference, however, was the inclusion of the Ten Commandments on the parchment in them. Their exclusion later, just like their exclusion from the daily services, was a reaction against the Jewish Christians.

Though Christian exegesis has always understood the abovementioned passages as metaphorical, our increasing knowledge of the ancient Near East would not rule out their possible literal intent (or for that matter of Dt. 6:9; 11:20, which the Jew fulfils by enclosing a parchment containing Dt. 6:4–9; 11:13–21 in a box called a *m^e^zûzâ* and affixing it to his door-post). All available evidence suggests, however, that they were a late innovation brought in by the *ḥ^a^sîḏîm* (*HASIDAEANS), being intended as a counterblast to increasing Hellenistic influence. There is no mention of them in the OT, and they seem always to have been unknown to the Samaritans. LXX clearly takes the passages on which the custom is based as metaphorical. The *Letter of Aristeas* mentions apparently only that for the arm and Philo that for the head.

Both the somewhat later Talmudic acknowledgment that they were not worn by the common people (*'am hā-'āreṣ*) and the failure of pagan writers to mention them indicate that in the time of Christ they were still worn only by a minority of the people. We may be sure that all Pharisees wore them, not merely during morning prayer but throughout the hours of daylight. Their later restriction to the time of prayer was due to their providing an all too easy mark of recognition of the Jew in times of persecution. We have no reason for thinking that they were worn either by Christ or his disciples. Even the condemnation in Mt. 23:5 suggests the temptation to the ultra-pious of stressing their adherence to a custom that was only slowly winning its way. Their use became universal before the end of the 2nd century AD.

The orthodox Jew interprets their use in a highly spiritual way. This is shown by the meditation to be used while putting them on, which is given early in the morning service in any standard Jewish Prayer Book.

BIBLIOGRAPHY. See the articles in *JewE*, *EJ*, 1971, and *SB*, 4, Excursus 11. H.L.E.

PICK
See Harrow, Part 2.

PIECES OF SILVER
See Money, Part 2.

PI-BESETH. Bubastis (Egyp. *Pr-B'stt*, 'mansion of the goddess Ubastet'), today Tell Basta, is situated on the Nile (Tanitic branch) SE of Zagazig. It is mentioned in Ezk. 30:17 with the more important city of Heliopolis (On or Aven). Of the main temple described by Herodotus (2. 138), little remains. Ubastet was a lioness or cat-goddess. Bubastis existed already in the time of Kheops and Khephren (4th Dynasty, *c.* 2600 BC) and Pepi I (6th Dynasty, *c.* 2400 BC). There are a few remains of the 18th Dynasty (14th century BC). The town was important under the Ramesside kings (19th Dynasty, 13th century BC) and gave its name to the 22nd Dynasty—that of Shishak, *c.* 945 BC—for whom it served as a residence like Tanis or Qantir.

BIBLIOGRAPHY. E. Naville, *Bubastis*, 1891, and *The Festival Hall of Osorkon II*, 1892; Labib Habachi, *Tell Basta*, 1957. C.D.W.

PIETY. AV used this word in 1 Tim. 5:4, of dutiful care for a widowed mother or grandmother (*cf.* the Lat. *pietas*, and the Eng. 'filial piety'). The verb is *eusebeō*, the regular Hellenistic word for performing acts of religious worship (so in Acts 17:23), which indicates that, to Paul, care for these widowed relatives was part of a Christian's religious duty. This is understandable in the light both of the fifth commandment and of the fact that hereby the Christian relieves the church of responsibility for supporting the widows concerned.

The corresponding noun, *eusebeia*, usually translated *'godliness' in EVV, appears 14 times in the Pastorals and 2 Peter (elsewhere only in Acts 3:12, where RSV renders 'piety') as a comprehensive term for the practice of Christian personal religion, the worship and service of God and the rendering of reverent obedience to his laws. In the plural the word denotes specific acts of piety (2 Pet. 3:11). Christian *eusebeia* springs from the divine gift of an inner principle of life and power (2 Pet. 1:3; 2 Tim. 3:5), which in its turn is bestowed with and through the sinner's believing response to the prior gift of saving truth (1 Tim. 3:16: the 'mystery'—revealed secret—from which 'godliness' springs is the gospel message of the incarnate and reigning Christ). It is characteristic of gospel truth that it is 'according to godliness' (1 Tim. 6:3; Tit. 1:1), *i.e.* godliness is the natural and necessary outcome of receiving it, so that ungodliness in those who profess it is presumptive evidence that they have not truly and heartily received it at all (*cf.* 2 Tim. 3:2–8; Tit. 1:16; 2 Pet. 2:19–22). All allegedly evangelical teaching should be tested by asking whether it makes for godliness—*i.e.* whether it enforces God's demands adequately, and whether it exhibits correctly the gift of renewal in Christ from which alone godliness can spring (2 Tim. 3:5–8).

The Bible views the piety that it inculcates from several complementary standpoints. The OT calls it 'the *fear of God', or 'the Lord' (over 30 times), thus showing that true piety is rooted in an attitude of reverence, submission and obedience towards God. The NT calls it 'obeying the gospel' or 'the truth' (Rom. 10:16; Gal. 5:7; 2 Thes. 1:8; 1 Pet. 1:22; *cf.* Rom. 6:16), thus characterizing piety as a response to revelation. From another standpoint, as the maintaining of a state of separation from the world and consecratedness to God, the NT calls it simply *'holiness' (*hagiasmos*, *hagiōsynē*: see 1 Thes. 4:3; Heb. 12:14; 2 Cor. 7:1; 1 Thes. 3:13; *etc.*). Christ taught that the 'work of God', the single comprehensive divine requirement in which all the individual 'works of God' are embraced, is faith in himself (Jn. 6:28f.); and Christian piety means simply living by this faith, and living it out. Accordingly, John characterizes the piety that God commands and accepts by singling out the two features that are most essential to it, and most distinctive of it—faith in Christ, and love to Christians (1 Jn. 3:22–24).

A full analysis of NT piety would include the practical expression of faith in a life of repentance, resisting temptation and mortifying sin; in habits of prayer, thanksgiving and reverent observance of the Lord's Supper; in the cultivation of hope, love, generosity, joy, self-control, patient endurance and contentment; in the quest for honesty, uprightness and the good of others in all human relations; in respect for divinely constituted authority in church, State, family and household. All these attitudes and practices are commanded by God, and glorify him.

BIBLIOGRAPHY. Arndt; *MM*; Richard Baxter, *A Christian Directory* (*Practical Works*), 1830, 1–5; 1838, 1); W. Mundle, W. Günther, *NIDNTT* 2, pp. 90–95; W. Foerster, *TDNT* 7, pp. 175–185.

J.I.P.

PIHAHIROTH. An unidentified place on the border of Egypt (Ex. 14:2, 9; Nu. 33:7–8). Of Egyptian equivalents proposed, the likeliest is either *Pi-Ḥrt*, 'House of the goddess *Ḥrt*' (*BASOR* 109, 1948, p. 16) or *P'-ḥr*, a canal near Ra'amses (*cf.* Caminos, *Late-Egyptian Miscellanies*, 1954, p. 74, two mentions).

C.D.W.
K.A.K.

PILATE. Pontius Pilatus was a Roman of the equestrian, or upper middle-class, order: his *praenomen* is not known, but his *nomen*, Pontius, suggests that he was of Samnite extraction and his *cognomen*, Pilatus, may have been handed down by military forbears. Little is known of his career before AD 26, but in that year (see P. L. Hedley in *JTS* 35, 1934, pp. 56–58) the emperor Tiberius appointed him to be the fifth *praefectus* (*hēgemōn*, Mt. 27:2, *etc.*; the same title is used of Felix in Acts 23 and Festus in Acts 26) of Judaea. Evidence of this title was discovered in 1961 on an inscription at Caesarea, and E. J. Vardaman (*JBL* 88, 1962, p. 70) suggests that this title was used in Pilate's earlier years, being replaced by *procurator* (the title used by Tacitus and Josephus) later. In accordance with a recent reversal in the policy of the Senate (in AD 21—Tacitus, *Annals* 3. 33–34) Pilate took his wife with him (Mt. 27:19). As procurator he had full control in the province, being in charge of the army of occupation (1 ala—*c.* 120 men—of cavalry, and 4 or 5 cohorts—*c.* 2,500–5,000 men—of infantry), which was stationed at Caesarea, with a detachment on garrison duty at Jerusalem in the fortress of Antonia. The procurator had full powers of life and death, and could reverse capital sentences passed by the Sanhedrin, which had to be submitted to him for ratification. He also appointed the high priests and controlled the Temple and its funds: the very vestments of the high priest were in his custody and were released only for festivals, when the procurator took up residence in Jerusalem and brought additional troops to patrol the city.

Even pagan historians mention Pilate only in connection with his authorization of the death of Jesus (Tacitus, *Annals* 15. 44): his only appearance on the stage of history is as procurator of Judaea.

Josephus relates (*Ant.* 18. 55; *BJ* 2. 169) that Pilate's first action on taking up his appointment was to antagonize the Jews by setting up the Roman standards, bearing images of the emperor, at Jerusalem: previous procurators had avoided using such standards in the holy city. Because of the determined resistance of their leaders in spite of threats of death, he yielded to their wishes after 6 days and removed the images back to Caesarea. Philo (*De Legatione ad Gaium* 299ff.) tells how Pilate dedicated a set of golden shields in his own residence at Jerusalem. These bore no image, only an inscription with the names of the procurator and the emperor, but representations were made to Tiberius, who sensibly ordered them to be set up in the temple of *Roma et Augustus* at Caesarea (*cf.* P. L. Maier, 'The Episode of the Golden Roman Shields at Jerusalem', *HTR* 62, 1969, pp. 109ff.).

Josephus (*Ant.* 18. 60; *BJ* 2. 175) and Eusebius (*EH* 2. 7) allege a further grievance of the Jews against Pilate, in that he used money from the Temple treasury to build an aqueduct to convey water to the city from a spring some 40 km away. Tens of thousands of Jews demonstrated against this project when Pilate came up to Jerusalem, presumably at the time of a festival, and he in return sent his troops in disguise against them, so that a large number were slain. It is generally considered that this riot was caused by the Galileans mentioned in Lk. 13:1–2 (whose blood Pilate had mingled with their sacrifices), and C. Noldius (*De Vita et Gestis Herodum*, 1660, 249) claimed that Herod's enmity against Pilate (Lk. 23:12) arose from the fact that Pilate had slain some of Herod's subjects. This explains Pilate's subsequent care (Lk. 23:6–7) to send Jesus to be tried before Herod. It is not known whether the tower at Siloam which collapsed (Lk. 13:4) was part of this aqueduct.

Pilate finally over-reached himself by the slaughter of a number of Samaritans who had assembled at Mt Gerizim in response to the call of a deceiver who had pro-

Bronze coin issued by Pilate, bearing a lituus *(augur's staff), as used in pagan religious ceremonies, and the name of Tiberius Caesar. AD 29–31.* (BM)

The names of Tiberius and Pilatus (Pilate) on a stone from the theatre at Caesarea. (MAIC)

■ **PIG**
See Animals, Part 1.

■ **PIGEON**
See Animals, Part 1.

mised to show them that Moses had hidden the sacred vessels there. In spite of the obvious falsehood of this claim (Moses had never crossed Jordan: some consider that there is a textual error, *Mōÿseōs* for *Ōseōs*, and Josephus is referring to the Samaritan tradition that Uzzi the high priest (1 Ch. 6:6) had hidden the ark and other sacred vessels in Mt Gerizim), a great multitude came armed to the mountain, and Pilate surrounded and routed them, capturing many and executing their ringleaders. A Samaritan delegation went with a protest to Vitellius, who was then governor of Syria, and he ordered Pilate to answer this accusation of the Jews before the emperor, ordering Marcellus to Judaea in Pilate's place (Jos., *Ant.* 18. 85–89). Pilate was on his journey to Rome when Tiberius died (AD 37). (*Cf.* E. M. Smallwood, 'The Date of the Dismissal of Pontius Pilate from Judaea', *JJS* 5, 1954, p. 12ff.) We know nothing of the outcome of the trial, but Eusebius (*EH* 2. 7) preserves a report of otherwise unknown Gk. annalists that Pilate was forced to commit suicide during the reign of Gaius (AD 37–41).

The above incidents are all related by Josephus or Philo. E. Stauffer (*Christ and the Caesars*, E.T. 1955, pp. 119f.) draws attention to a further instance of provocation of the Jews by Pilate. According to G. F. Hill (*Catalogue of the Greek Coins of Palestine*, 1914), the procurators minted small copper coins to meet local needs in Palestine. Normally these bore symbolic designs of natural features, such as trees and ears of corn, in deference to the second commandment. In AD 29–31 Pilate issued coins bearing imperial religious insignia, the *lituus*, or augur's staff, and the *patera*, or pagan libation bowl. Such issues ceased after AD 31, and the British Museum has a coin of Pilate on which his successor Felix appears to have overstamped the staff with a palmbranch, though Y. Meshorer (*Jewish Coins of the Second Temple Period*, 1967) states that Felix also produced coins with symbols of a provocative nature, such as Roman weapons, which underlined the Roman subjugation of Judaea.

Philo can find no good thing to say of Pilate: in *De Legatione ad Gaium* 301 he describes him as 'by nature rigid and stubbornly harsh' and 'of spiteful disposition and an exceeding wrathful man', and speaks of 'the bribes, the acts of pride, the acts of violence, the outrages, the cases of spiteful treatment, the constant murders without trial, the ceaseless and most grievous brutality' of which the Jews might accuse him. The verdict of the NT is that he was a weak man, ready to serve expediency rather than principle, whose authorization of the judicial murder of the Saviour was due less to a desire to please the Jewish authorities than to fear of imperial displeasure if Tiberius heard of further unrest in Judaea. This is made abundantly evident by his mockery of the Jews in the wording of the superscription (Jn. 19:19–22). It is most unfortunate that we do not know anything of his record apart from his government of the Jews, towards whom he would appear to have shown little understanding and even less liking.

For an interesting discussion of the significance of the inclusion of 'suffered under Pontius Pilate' in Christian creeds see S. Liberty, 'The Importance of Pontius Pilate

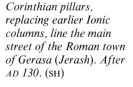

Corinthian pillars, replacing earlier Ionic columns, line the main street of the Roman town of Gerasa (Jerash). After AD 130. (SH)

in Creed and Gospel', *JTS* 45, 1944, pp. 38–56.

There are a number of *Acta Pilati* in existence: none of which is considered to be genuine.

BIBLIOGRAPHY. P. L. Maier, *Pontius Pilate*, 1968. D.H.W.

PILGRIMAGE. Sojourners in foreign lands may return home; sojourners in the flesh, with a foreshortened view of heavenly things, may enter the eternal realm by the portal of death. By established metaphor, the mortal life-span is called a pilgrimage, which simply means a sojourning. Biblical terminology is a little flexible.

The common Heb. phrase *'ereṣ m^e^gûrîm* means literally 'land of sojournings' (the latter term is grammatically rather than numerically plural, and should be singular in idomatic English). In the typical passages Gn. 17:8; 28:4; 36:7; 37:1; Ex. 6:4, LXX generally uses the verb *paroikeō* or a cognate; AV has 'land wherein thou art a stranger', or some variant; RV and RSV have, correctly if rather woodenly, 'land of sojournings', but the singular would be preferable. *Cf.* Ezk. 20:38; also Ps. 55:15; Jb. 18:19, where a cognate Heb. term means 'dwellings' or 'habitations', the singular being again preferable in English. The AV and RV text perceptively render the same word twice as 'pilgrimage' in Gn. 47:9—this may be upheld against RVmg. and RSV, because the meaning here is life's total span and experience. The LXX underlines this by using *zōē*, 'life'. There is a close parallel in Ps. 119:54, where 'the house of my pilgrimage' means simply 'my mortal body throughout its earthly existence'.

There are two technical terms for a resident alien—usually a Gentile dweller in Palestine—*gēr*, from the same Heb. root as *m^e^gûrîm*, and *tôšāḇ*. The first word usually implies a longer, the second a shorter, association, so that the difference is chiefly one of intensity. The coupling of the two lays a heavy emphasis on transitoriness. The second then follows climactically. The LXX translates the first term by *paroikos*, the second in its happier moments by *parepidēmos*. The four words may be found literally used in Gn. 22:4, *MT* and LXX. The metaphorical usages, stressing the brevity of life, are Ps. 39:12; 1 Ch. 29:15. The LXX spoils the sense in the second passage by substituting *katoikountes* for *parepidēmoi*, for the change of word would suggest settled dwelling, whereas the entire emphasis is the reverse. In both contexts 'pilgrim(s)' would afford a good translation.

The 'weary pilgrimage' of the oft-sung paraphrase has a similar ring about it, though strictly speaking it is a mistranslation. Jacob in his vow (Gn. 28:20) actually uses the word *dereḵ*, 'road' or 'way'. Metaphorically, this signifies manner of life, human or animal—even the behaviour of inanimate but propelled objects. (Pr. 30:19 aptly illustrates all three pictorial usages.) Jacob's reference is personal, practical, specific and contemporary. The 'weary pilgrimage', generalized in reference, is not strict translation, but good poetic licence, true to the spirit of the original prayer.

paroikos and *parepidēmos* or their cognates are used in the NT independently (1 Pet. 1:1, 17) and in OT quotation (Heb. 11:13; 1 Pet. 2:11). By NT times it is probably true to say that the *paroikos* not only resided longer in a place than the *parepidēmos*, but also that he was more fully incorporated into the civic life and fiscal obligations of his adopted community. The *eklektoi parepidēmoi* of 1 Pet. 1:1 are more than 'elect sojourners'. Their political status is strong metaphor for the fact that they are God's pilgrims, persons now in time and flesh, yet chosen for eternal life through Christ Jesus, therefore fundamentally different from the worldling. The *paroikia* of 1 Pet. 1:17 reverts by stylistic variation to the *gēr* emphasis, but still means essentially 'pilgrimage'. The *'strangers and pilgrims' of Heb. 11:13 AV, 'strangers and exiles' RSV, translates the Greek beautifully. There is a verbal echo of Ps. 39:12 and 1 Ch. 29:15, with perhaps a sidelong glance at Gn. 47:9. The phrase is more telling in view of the writer's 'idealist epistemology'—the Temple and all earthly things are but copies and shadows of heavenly things; the real world is the unseen one. *Cf.* 1 Pet. 2:11.

The concept of pilgrimage as a journey of religious volition or obligation to a sacred spot, such as Abraham's visit to Mt Moriah, is known from remote antiquity, though the Bible lacks a technical term for it. Any place held in veneration was liable to attract pilgrims, as even the earliest OT records show. Journeys to the statutory feasts at Jerusalem, where the Temple enjoyed exclusive prestige, were well established by NT times (*cf.* notably Lk. 2:41ff.). Each of them was a 'pilgrimage-festival' (Heb. *ḥaḡ*; *cf.* Arabic *ḥajj*). Before the Arab–Israeli partition of Jerusalem in 1948, and since the Six Days' War of 1967, Jews have regularly prayed at the Western Wall (formerly the Wailing Wall), which is all that remains of the Herodian Temple.

BIBLIOGRAPHY. D. J. Wiseman, *The Word of God for Abraham and To-day*, 1959; W. Grundmann, *TDNT* 2, pp. 64f.; O. Michel, *TDNT* 5, pp. 153–155; R. Meyer, K. L. and M. A. Schmidt, *TDNT* 5, pp. 841–853; H. Bietenhard, *NIDNTT* 1, pp. 690f.; *ibid.* 2, pp. 788f. R.A.S.

PILLAR.

a. Structural

Pillars of wood, stone or mud-brick were used from the earliest times to support the roofs of large rooms or to provide monumental decoration (as at Erech in S Mesopotamia; H. Frankfort, *Art and Architecture of the Ancient Orient*, 1954, pl. 2). From the latter part of the 2nd millennium onwards rectangular stone pillars or wooden posts on stone bases were used in larger Palestinian houses for carrying upper storeys or balconies on one or all sides of the central courtyard (*HOUSE). The evidence of Philistine sites suggests that the pillars held by Samson were of wood, set on stone bases (Jdg. 16:23–30; *cf.* R. A. S. Macalister, *Bible Sidelights from the Mound of Gezer*, 1906, pp. 135–138).

From the early Monarchy have survived several examples of official storehouses with rows of pillars (*cf.* the seven pillars of Wisdom's house, Pr. 9:1). At Megiddo these pillars also served as hitching-posts (see *ANEP*, nos. 741–742, and for official buildings, Z. Herzog in Y. Aharoni, *Beer-Sheba*, 1, 1973, pp. 23–30). Of finer quality are the carved capitals, imitating the top of a palm-tree (called proto-Aeolic or Ionic), found at several sites. While the majority were made for rectangular attached pillars (*e.g.* those from the palace at Samaria, *cf.* W. F. Albright, *Archaeology of Palestine*, 1960, p. 127, fig. 35), a few belonged to

PILATE, ACTS OF
See New Testament apocrypha, Part 2.

PILGRIM
See Foreigner, Part 1.

Memorial pillars (maṣṣēḇôt) *standing in a temple at Byblos. Tallest c. 2 m. c. 1900* BC. (ARM)

Carved proto-Aeolic (Ionic) pillar of a capital from a royal Judaean citadel at Ramat Raḥel (Beth-haccerem), near Jerusalem. c. 600 BC. (ZR)

free-standing columns. Solomon's Temple may have been enhanced with similar capitals, Heb. *timorâ*, 1 Ki. 6:29ff.; 7:36; *cf.* Ezk. 40:22ff.; 41:18ff.; 2 Ch. 3:5; see Y. Shiloh, *PEQ* 109, 1977, pp. 39–52. This simple design was elaborated, producing finally the complicated capitals at the Persian palaces of Persepolis and Susa (Est. 1:6, see R. Ghirshman, *Iran*, 1954, pl. 17b). Simple cylindrical pillars of this period have been found at Lachish (*PEQ* 69, 1937, p. 239) and possibly Bethel (*BASOR* 137, 1955, fig. 3).

During the Hellenistic and Roman periods pillars were widely employed as decorative features, *e.g.* lining the main streets of towns, as at Jerash (G. L. Harding, *Antiquities of Jordan*, 1959, pl. 10). The entrance to Solomon's Temple was flanked by two gigantic bronze pillars of uncertain significance (1 Ki. 7:15–22; see *JACHIN AND BOAZ). It was apparently by one of these that the king stood on ceremonial occasions (2 Ki. 11:14; 23:3; 2 Ch. 23:13; *cf.* the coronation of Abimelech, Jdg. 9:6, RV).

'Pillar' is also used to describe: Lot's wife smothered by salt (Gn. 19:26); the smoke and fire which protected the camp of Israel (Ex. 13:21); a palm-like column of smoke spreading at the top (Ct. 3:6; Joel 2:30, Heb. *tîmārâ*; *cf. timorâ*, above). The supporting function is used figuratively of: (i) the pillars of heaven and earth over which God alone has power (1 Sa. 2:8; Jb. 9:6; 26:11; Ps. 75:3); (ii) the legs of the beloved and the feet of an angel (Ct. 5:15; Rev. 10:1); (iii) the church as upholding the truth (1 Tim. 3:15); (iv) the position of James, Cephas and John in the church of Jerusalem (Gal. 2:9).

b. Monumental

Stones set up on end are found throughout the ancient world, often associated with a shrine or temple (*e.g.* an early Neolithic shrine at Jericho contained a niche in which was a stone cylinder, see *PEQ* 84, 1952, p. 72, pl. XIX. 1) or standing alone (the Celtic *menhir*). A consideration of all the OT passages in which such a pillar (Heb. *maṣṣēḇâ*, something erected) is mentioned shows that the basic significance was that of a memorial. Rachel's grave was thus marked (Gn. 35:20), and Absalom, being childless, set up a pillar, to which he gave his own name, as his own memorial (2 Sa. 18:18). The name conferred on the stone identified it with the bearer of that *name (*WORD). Important events were likewise commemorated. Jacob set up the stone he had used as a pillow, clearly a small slab, after the first theophany at Bethel and another stone after the second theophany. Libations were poured on both of these, marking them out from other stones. By naming the stones 'House of God' (Heb. *bêṯ'ēl*), Jacob recorded their significance to him (Gn. 28:18–22; 35:13–15). The covenants between Jacob and Laban and between Yahweh and Israel were also visibly indicated in this way (Gn. 31:45–54; Ex. 24:4; Jos. 24:26–27). So too were the crossing of the Jordan (Jos. 4:1–9) and the victory over the Philistines at Mizpah (1 Sa. 7:12, named 'stone of help', Heb. *'eḇen hā'ēzer*). This is the import of the victorious Christian who will be a pillar in the temple of God, bearing the names of God, the new Jerusalem and the Son of man's new name (Rev. 3:12).

In Canaanite religion the pillar had so far become identified with deity (particularly male deity) as to be an object of veneration. It was therefore forbidden to the Israelites, who were to destroy all they found (Ex. 23:24; Dt. 16:22; *cf.* *ASHERAH). Of the many standing stones found in and around Palestine (*e.g.* at Gezer, Lejjun, Byblos, Ras Shamra) the best examples are those at Hazor. An upright stone, with the top broken off, was found standing by the entrance to an important building in the Canaanite citadel, an offering before it (*BA* 22, 1959, p. 14, fig. 12). In the lower city lay a small shrine containing a row of several slabs about 45 cm high and many more stacked in a side room (*BA* 19, 1956, p. 10, fig. 7). These may well be ancestral monuments destroyed by the Israelites (*cf. ANEP*, nos. 630, 635). The practice continued in neighbouring countries and Isaiah foretold that the Egyptians would set up a pillar to Yahweh on their border when they turned to him (Is. 19:19). See C. F. Graesser, 'Standing Stones in Ancient Palestine', *BA* 35, 1972, pp. 34–63. A.R.M.

PINNACLE (Gk. *pterygion*, 'a little wing'; Vulg. *pinnaculum*; NEB 'highest ledge'). A part of the buildings of the Temple (Mt. 4:5; Lk. 4:9) mentioned in connection with the temptation of Jesus. Its precise location is uncertain, but two relevant factors should be noted. (i) Despite the AV's use of the indefinite article, we should follow other EVV in reading '*the* pinnacle of the temple' (*i.e.* suggesting that there was only one). (ii) The context calls for a position from which there was both a fearful drop and an impressive view of the surrounding countryside. These latter conditions are met if we locate the pinnacle in the SE corner of the Temple area, overlooking the Kidron Valley (*cf.* Jos., *Ant.* 15. 410f.). Different opinions have, however, been expressed. See, *e.g.*, *HHT*, 4, pp. 85–86. J.D.D.

PIRATHON. Fer'ata, 9 km WSW of Shechem, home of the Ephraimite judge Abdon ben Hillel (Jdg. 12:13, 15) and of David's captain Benaiah (2 Sa. 23:30; 1 Ch. 11:31; 27:14); probably not the Pharathon fortified by the Maccabees in Benjamin (1 Macc. 9:50), though the name Abdon is otherwise Benjaminite (Moore, *ICC*, Jdg. 12:13; Burney, *Judges*, *ad loc.*; the *Sellem* of the Greek is a corruption of 'Hillel'). The district was known as the Amalekite hills (*MT* and LXX B; LXX A, 'hill of Anak'); *cf.* Jdg. 5:14, though here also LXX A ('in the valley') disagrees. J.P.U.L.

PISGAH, ASHDOTH–PISGAH. Always accompanied by the definite article, Pisgah is associated with the ascent and either 'top' (head) or 'slope' (Ashdoth). From these facts it may be deduced that Pisgah is a common noun denoting a ridge crowning a mountain or hill. 'The Pisgah' would then be one or more of the ridges common on the Transjordan plateau. 'The slopes of Pisgah' (Ashdoth-pisgah) may refer to the entire edge of the Moabite plateau E of the Dead Sea (Dt. 3:17, AV; 4:49; Jos. 12:3; 13:20). These references relate to the territorial borders of the Amorites and later of the Reubenites.

Apart from the general plateau, Pisgah refers to a specific ridge or peak associated with Mt *Nebo. Nu. 21:20, a location on the route of the Israelites, and Nu. 23:14, one peak from which Balaam tried to curse God's people, are both close to the wilderness N and E of the Dead Sea (*JESHIMON), so also probably refer to the same ridge.

It was from 'the top of Pisgah, Mt Nebo' that Moses viewed the promised land before his death (Dt. 3:27; 34:1). This plateau headland is probably to be identified with Ras es Siyaghah, the second and slightly lower N ridge of Mt Nebo. As this ridge protrudes further W, it provides a wider and less obstructed view over the land, and so is more likely to be the place of Moses' vision.

BIBLIOGRAPHY. G. T. Manley, *EQ* 21, 1943, pp. 81–92. G.G.G.

PISIDIA. A highland area in Asia Minor bounded by Lycaonia to the E and N, Pamphylia to the S, and the province of Asia to the N and W. The district lay at the W end of the Taurus range, and was the home of lawless mountain tribes who defied the efforts of the Persians and their Hellenistic successors to subdue them. The Seleucids

PILLOW
See Cushion, Part 1.

PILOT
See Governor, Part 2.

PIM
See Weights and measures, Part 3.

PINE
See Trees (Cypress), Part 3.

PIONEER
See Prince, Part 3.

PIPE
See Music, Part 2.

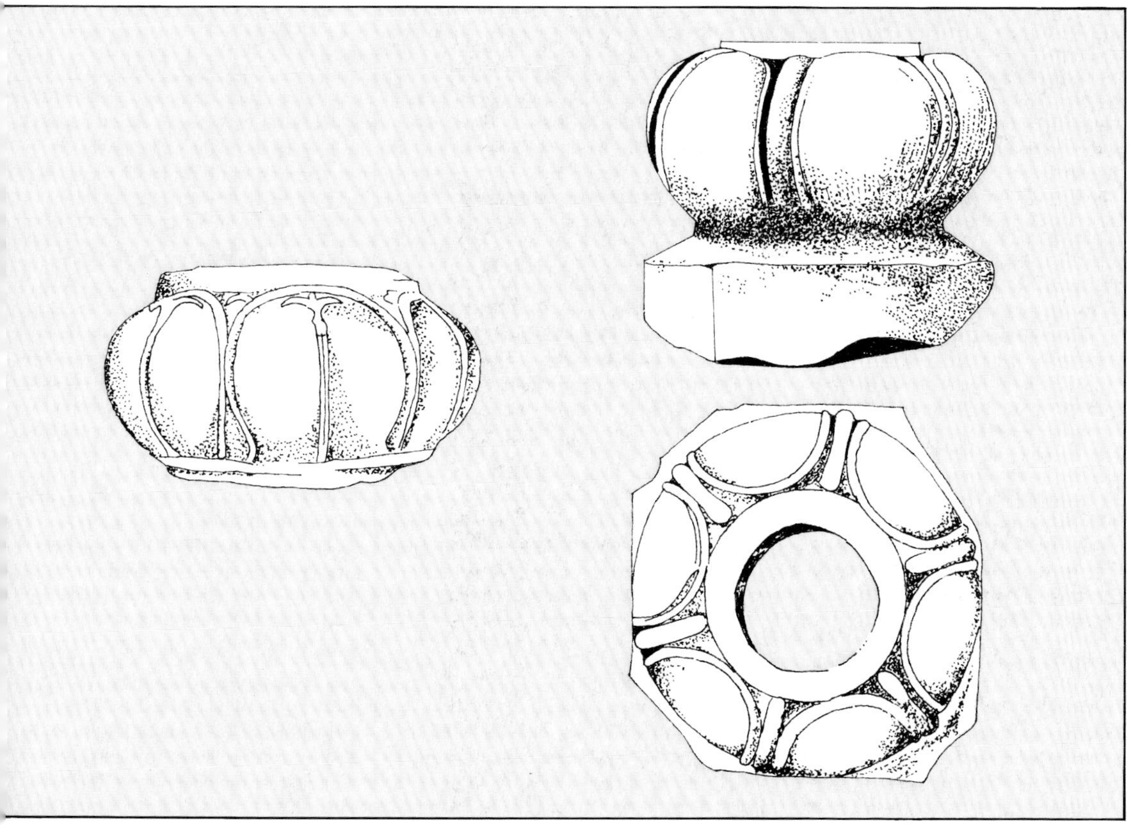

The use of pillars is demonstrated by these two stone pillar bases, excavated at Carchemish (left) and Dan (right). The pillars they supported may have been of wood.

founded Antioch (called 'the Pisidian' to distinguish it rather from the Phrygian Antioch on the Maeander than from the Seleucid capital of Syria) in order to control the Pisidian highlanders, and Amyntas with like aim founded a colony there about 25 BC, and linked the city with similar strong-points by a system of military roads. Paul's 'perils of robbers . . . perils in the wilderness' (2 Cor. 11:26) may have reference to this area, and it is a fair guess that, even in his day, the tradition of predatory independence was not yet dead among the mountaineers. Pisidia was part of the kingdom of Galatia assigned by Antony to Amyntas in 36 BC, and it was in warfare against the Pisidian hill tribes that Amyntas perished in 25 BC. Sulpicius Quirinius finally imposed some sort of order, and incorporated the region in the province of Galatia. The Roman Peace brought prosperity to the district and in the 2nd century several prosperous towns sprang up together with at least six strong churches. E.M.B.

PITCH
See Bitumen, Part 1.

PITY
See Compassion, Part 1.

PIT. Basically a deep hole, either natural or artificial, in the ground.

1. Heb. *bôr*, 'a deep hole', used to describe the place where Joseph was cast by his brethren (Gn. 37:20, 22, 24, *etc.*), a place to hide (1 Sa. 13:6), a place where lions lurked (2 Sa. 23:20; 1 Ch. 11:22), a place where prisoners were shut up (Is. 24:22; Zc. 9:11; *cf.* Je. 38:6), and where the rebel Ishmael cast the bodies of the men of Shechem, Shiloh and Samaria (Je. 41:7, 9).

The laws of Ex. 21:33–34 were directed to Israelites who opened up holes and left them uncovered (*cf.* Ec. 10:8, where the word is *gûmmāṣ*).

Metaphorically the word is used to describe the underworld, the place of departed spirits (Pss. 28:1; 30:3; 88:4, 6; 143:7; Pr. 1:12; Is. 14:15, 19; 38:18; Ezk. 26:20; 31:14, 16; 32:18, 24, *etc.*). A second metaphorical use describes the place from which God brings up his saints (Ps. 40:2; Is. 51:1).

2. Heb. *b*e*'ēr*, a well. The vale of Siddim was full of slime (bitumen) pits (Gn. 14:10). Used metaphorically, it is the pit of destruction (Pss. 55:23; 69:15). A harlot is described in Pr. 23:27 as a narrow pit.

3. Heb. *gēḇ* or *geḇe'*, a place where water is collected (Is. 30:14; Je. 14:3). **4.** Heb. *paḥaṯ*, 'a hole for trapping animals' (2 Sa. 17:9; 18:17; Is. 24:17–18; Je. 48:43–44). **5.** Heb. *š*e*'ôl*, Sheol, the underworld (Nu. 16:30, 33; Jb. 17:16). The same Heb. word is translated elsewhere in other ways. (*HELL.)

6. Three words from the Heb. root *šwḥ*: (i) *šûḥâ*, 'a pit in the desert' (Je. 2:6), a place where Jeremiah was trapped by wicked men (Je. 18:20, 22), and the mouth of a strange woman (Pr. 22:14). (ii) *šaḥaṯ*, a trap in the ground for wild animals (Ps. 35:7; Ezk. 19:4, 8), or, more usually, the underworld (Jb. 33:18, 24, 28, 30; Pss. 9:15; 30:9; 94:13; Is. 38:17; 51:14; Ezk. 28:8). (iii) *šîḥâ*, a trap (Pss. 57:6; 119:85; Je. 18:22).

7. Two words from the Heb. root *šḥh*. *š*e*ḥuṯ*, the pit which the wicked prepare for the righteous, into which they fall themselves (Pr. 28:10), and *š*e*ḥiṯ*, the lot of Zedekiah in 587 BC when he was taken in the pits of the enemy (La. 4:20).

8. In the NT the pit into which an ass falls is *bothynos* in Mt. 12:11 and *phrear* in Lk. 14:5. The bottomless pit of Rev. 9:1–2 is also *phrear*. (*ABYSS.)

Some idea of pits is to be obtained from archaeological discoveries. Quite regularly the cistern which served as a pit had a neck about the width of a man about 1 m in depth, and then opened out into a large bulbous cavity of varying size. Broken pottery and other remains in these pits are useful aids to dating the period when they were in use. (*POOL, *ARCHAEOLOGY.) The use of pits for trapping animals and men is also attested in extra-biblical texts. J.A.T.

PITHOM (Old Egyp. *Pr-itm*, 'mansion of the god Atum'). A city of Egypt where the Israelites were afflicted with heavy building burdens (Ex. 1:11). Most accept that it was situated in Wadi Tumilat, at Tell el-Maskhuta or Tell er-Retaba. Not far away from this place was the migdol of Tjeku, which may be the biblical Succoth (Ex. 12:37; 13:20; Nu. 33:5–6). In Papyrus Anastasi, V, 19. 5–20. 6 we read that the chief of the archers went to Tjeku to prevent slaves from running away, but he came too late. Somebody had seen them crossing the N wall of the migdol of Seti-Merenptah. A second report, in Papyr. Anas., V, 18. 6–19. 1, refers to Libyan mercenaries who tried to flee and were taken back to Tjeku. A third mention, in Papyr. Anas., VI, 5. 1, emanates from a civil servant who had finished passing Shasu-nomads from Edom, S of the Dead Sea, into Egypt, at the fort of Tjeku, towards the marshes of Pithom of Merenptah of Tjeku. (*ENCAMPMENT BY THE SEA.)

BIBLIOGRAPHY. E. Naville, *The Store-City of Pithom*, 1903; Montet, *Géographie de l'Égypte ancienne*, 1, 1957, pp. 214–219.
C.D.W.

PLAGUES OF EGYPT. In commissioning Moses to lead Israel out of Egypt, God had warned him that this would come about only through God's supreme power overcoming all the might of Pharaoh, whereby Egypt would be smitten with wonders or signs from God (*cf.* Ex. 3:19–20). After the sign of the rod that became a serpent and swallowed up those of the Egyptian magicians, which left Pharaoh unmoved, God's power was demonstrated to him and his people in a series of ten judgments. They were so applied as to portray clearly the reality and power of Israel's God, and thus by contrast the impotence of Egypt's gods. The first nine of these plagues bear a direct relation to natural phenomena in the Nile valley, but the tenth, the death of the first-born, belongs wholly to the realm of the supernatural.

These first nine plagues demonstrate the divine use of the created order to achieve his ends, and recent studies tend to confirm both the reality of what is described in Ex. 7–12 and the powers of accurate, first-hand observation of the narrator of this part of Exodus. The element of miracle in these plagues is usually bound up with their intensity, timing and duration. By far the most painstaking study of the plague phenomena is that by G. Hort in *ZAW* 69, 1957, pp. 84–103, and *ZAW* 70, 1958, pp. 48–59. While her treatment of the first nine seems excellent, her attempt to explain the tenth as 'firstfruits' instead of first-born is decidedly artificial and unlikely.

Hort has pointed out that the first nine plagues form a logical and connected sequence, beginning with an abnormally *high* Nile-inundation occurring in the usual months of July and August and the series of plagues ending about March (Heb. *Abib*). In Egypt too high an inundation of the Nile was just as disastrous as too low a flood.

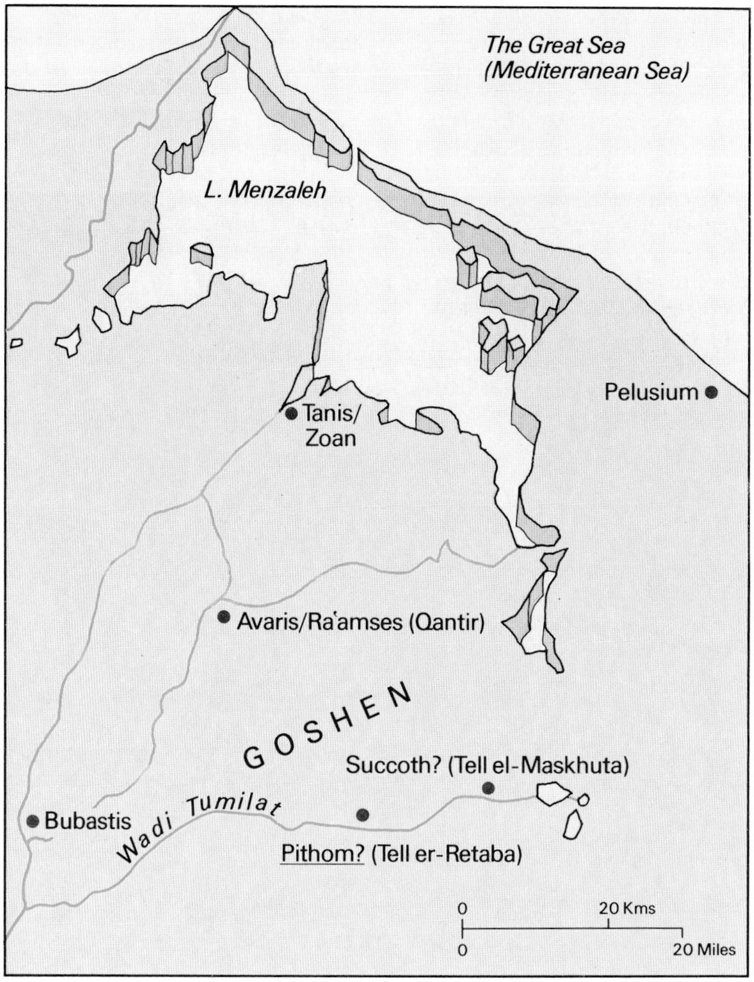

The suggested location of Pithom.

The first plague (Ex. 7:14–25)

Moses was commanded to stretch his rod over the Nile waters, that they should be 'turned to blood'; the fish in the river would die, the river stink, and its water be unpalatable; no immediate ending of these conditions is recorded. This would correspond with the conditions brought about by an unusually high Nile. The higher the Nile-flood, the more earth it carries in suspension, especially of the finely-divided 'red earth' from the basins of the Blue Nile and Atbara. And the more earth carried, the redder became the Nile waters. Such an excessive inundation could further bring down with it microcosms known as *flagellates* and associated bacteria: besides heightening the blood-red colour of the water, these would create conditions so unfavourable for the fish that they would die in large numbers as recorded. Their decomposition would foul the water and cause a stench. The rise of the Nile begins in July/August, reaches its maximum about September, and then falls again; this plague would therefore affect Egypt from July/August to October/November.

The second plague (Ex. 8:1–15)

Seven days later (7:25) Egypt was afflicted by swarms of frogs which, in accordance with God's promise, died *en masse* the following day and quickly decayed. That the frogs should swarm out of the river in August was most unusual. The numerous decomposing fish washed along the banks and backwaters of the Nile would pollute and infect the river-shore haunts of the frogs and the frogs themselves, which then came ashore in numbers, heading for the shelter of houses and fields. The sudden death and malodorous and rapid putrefaction of the frogs would indicate internal anthrax (from *Bacillus anthracis*) as the infection and cause.

The third plague (Ex. 8:16–19)

Hort suggests that this was an abnormal plague of mosquitoes (AV 'lice', RSV 'gnats'), whose already high rate of reproduction would be further encouraged by the specially-favourable breeding-conditions provided by an unusually high Nile.

The fourth plague (Ex. 8:20–32)

The particular 'fly' in question here was probably *Stomoxys calcitrans*. See below on the sixth plague, for which this insect is the likeliest agent.

The fifth plague (Ex. 9:1–7)

A 'very severe plague' upon all the Egyptians' cattle actually in the fields (not all livestock). A cattle pest that affected only the animals out in the fields might indicate that they had contracted anthrax from the infection carried into their fields by the frogs. If the Israelites' cattle were in their stalls they would not have been affected.

The sixth plague (Ex. 9:8–12)

The *boils 'breaking out in sores' were probably skin anthrax passed on by the bites of the carrier-fly *Stomoxys calcitrans*, which breeds in decaying vegetation and would have become a carrier of the disease from the infected haunts of the frogs and cattle. The boils may have affected particularly the hands and feet (Ex. 9:11: the magicians could not stand before Moses; *cf.* Dt. 28:27, 35), which would be a further clue in favour of the proposed identifications of the disease and its carrier, which would strike by about December/January.

The seventh plague (Ex. 9:13–35)

Heavy hail with thunder, lightning and rain. This ruined the barley and flax, but not the wheat and spelt, which were not yet grown up. This would fit early February. The concentration at this season of this sudden plague in Upper Egypt, but not in Goshen nearer the Mediterranean seaboard, fits the climatic phenomena of these areas.

The eighth plague (Ex. 10:1–20)

The heavy precipitation in Ethiopia and the Sudan which led to the extraordinarily high Nile would also provide favourable conditions for a dense plague of locusts by about March. These, following the usual route, would in due course be blown into N Egypt by the E wind; the 'west wind', *rûaḥ-yām*, is literally 'sea-wind'; *i.e.* really a N (or NW) wind, and this would blow the locusts right up the Nile valley. Hort would then emend 'Red Sea' (*yām sûp̄*) to 'South' (*yāmîn*), but this is not strictly necessary.

The ninth plague (Ex. 10:21–29)

The 'thick darkness' which could be felt. This was a *khamsin* dust-storm, but no ordinary one. The heavy inundation had brought down and deposited masses of 'red earth', now dried out as a fine dust over the land. The effect of this when whirled up by a *khamsin* wind would be to make the air extraordinarily thick and dark, blotting out the light of the sun. The 'three days' of Ex. 10:23 is the known length of a *khamsin*. The intensity of the *khamsin* may suggest that it was early in the season, and would thus come in March. If the Israelites were dwelling in the region of Wadi Tumilat, they would miss the worst effects of this plague.

The tenth plague (Ex. 11:1–12:36)

So far God had demonstrated his full control over the natural creation. He had caused his servant Moses to announce the successive plagues and brought them to pass in invincible sequence and growing severity when the pharaoh ever more persistently refused to acknowledge Israel's God in face of the clearest credentials of his authority and power. In this final plague came the most explicit sign of God's precise and full control: the death of the first-born only. Nor did it come without adequate warning (Ex. 4:23); the pharaoh had had every opportunity to acknowledge God and obey his behest, and so had to take the consequences of refusal.

Other aspects

In later days Joshua reminded Israel in Canaan of their mighty deliverance from Egypt through the plagues (Jos. 24:5). The Philistines also knew of them and feared their Author (1 Sa. 4:8). Later still, the psalmist sang of these awe-inspiring events (Ps. 78:43–51).

In Ex. 12:12 God speaks of executing judgments against all the gods of Egypt. In some measure he had already done so in the plagues, as Egypt's gods were much bound up with the forces of nature. Ha'pi, the Nile-god of inundation, had brought not prosperity but ruin; the frogs, symbol of Heqit, a goddess of fruitfulness, had brought only disease and wasting; the hail, rain and storm were the heralds of awesome events (as in the Pyramid Texts); and the light of the sun-god Rē' was blotted out, to mention but a few of the deities affected.

The account of the plagues is emphatically a literary unity: it is only the *total* details of the whole and unitary narrative that correspond so strikingly with observable physical phenomena. The mere fragments of plagues that would feature in supposed documentary sources (J, E, P, *etc.*) and the schematic uniformity of features postulated for these correspond to no known phenomena. Arbitrary

Elijah rested in the desert under a bush of the white-flowered broom (Retama raetam) *when fleeing from Jezebel* (*1 Ki. 19:4*). (FNH)

A castor-oil plant (Ricinus communis) *may have shaded Jonah while he kept watch over Nineveh* (*Jon. 4:6–11*). (FNH)

adaptation of such partial and stylized accounts into a new and conflated narrative that somehow then happens to correspond exactly to observable phenomena long past and in a distant land is surely beyond serious belief (so Hort). The plainer explanation and the unity of the narrative is to be preferred to a theory which involves unattested phenomena. K.A.K.

PLAIN, CITIES OF THE. The cities of the plain were, chiefly, Sodom, Gomorrah, Admah, Zeboiim and Bela or Zoar (Gn. 14:2). It has been held that these were located N of the Dead Sea, where the Jordan Valley broadens into the 'Circle' or 'Plain' of the Jordan (*cf.* Dt. 34:3), the evidence being 'that Abraham and Lot looked upon the cities from near Bethel (Gn. 13:10), that *Circle of Jordan* is not applicable to the S of the Dead Sea, that the presence of five cities there is impossible and that the expedition of the Four Kings (Gn. 14:7), as it swept N from Kadesh-barnea, attacked Hazazon-tamar, probably Engedi, *before* it reached the Vale of Siddim and encountered the king of Sodom and his allies' (G. A. Smith, *Historical Geography of the Holy Land*[25], 1931, pp. 505f.).

On the other hand the view that the cities lie buried beneath the shallow waters of the S tip of the Dead Sea (G. E. Wright, *Westminster Historical Atlas*, 1945, pp. 26, 65–66; *idem*, *Biblical Archaeology*, 1957, p. 50) can be maintained. First, Gn. 13:10 says that Lot saw, not the cities of the plain, but the 'Circle' of Jordan. He was attracted not by urban facilities but by good pasturage. Secondly, refusal to give the name 'Circle of Jordan' to, and denial of the possibility of five cities at, the S of the Dead Sea depends on present-day configuration, and disregards any alterations made by the overthrow. Thirdly, there is the identification of Hazazon-tamar with En-gedi. This depends on 2 Ch. 20:2, where the advancing Moabites and Ammonites are said to be 'in Hazazon-tamar (that is, En-gedi)'. The qualifying phrase ought not to be taken in this case as identifying the two places (as, *e.g.*, in Gn. 14:3), unless we make the absurd assumption that after the time of Jehoshaphat the name En-gedi replaced Hazazon-tamar, thus necessitating an explanation of the archaism. The qualification 'that is, En-gedi' must, therefore, state more precisely where the enemy was in the general district designated by the first place-name. This suits the usage in Gn. 14:7 where, in a chapter full of parenthetic explanations of archaic place-names, Hazazon-tamar is left unexplained. We may therefore picture the cities of the plain as sited in the now-flooded area which once formed the S extension of the Circle of the Jordan.

As Lot saw it, the Circle was supremely attractive from every material viewpoint (Gn. 13:10), but it was to become desolate. The efficient cause of this destruction of the cities was probably an earthquake, with an accompanying release and explosion of gaseous deposits. Biblically and fundamentally it was God's judgment, remembered again and again throughout the Bible (Dt. 29:23; Is. 1:9; Je. 49:18; La. 4:6; Am. 4:11; Lk. 17:29; 2 Pet. 2:6); and Sodom became synonymous with brazen sin (Is. 3:9; La. 4:6; Jude 7). Whereas Ezk. 16:49–51 lists the sins of Sodom as pride, prosperous complacency and 'abominations', Gn. 19:4–5 concentrates on sexual perversion, particularly homosexuality. Lot's vicious offer of his daughters (v. 8) indicates the life and demoralizing influence of Sodom.

The story of Sodom does not merely warn, but provides a theologically documented account of divine judgment implemented by 'natural' disaster. The history is faith's guarantee that the Judge of all the earth does right (Gn. 18:25). Being personally persuaded of its justice and necessity (Gn. 18:20–21), God acts; but in wrath he remembers mercy, and in judgment discrimination (Gn. 19:16, 29). (*Cf.* *ARCHAEOLOGY for bibliography.) J.A.M.

PLANTS. Any attempt to pronounce upon the nature and identity of the various biblical plants must avoid a number of pitfalls. One of these is the tacit assumption that they are identical with those designated by the same names in different parts of the world today. Another is the assumption that plants found in Palestine today were also native to that area in biblical times. In addition, different versions of Scripture frequently reflect wrong identifications and there is confusion of botanical nomenclature and the like by the translators. This is partly due to the fact that for the original writers present-day standards of accuracy in botanical matters were not pressing considerations, and, in addition, their terminology was by no means as comprehensive as that of the modern botanist. The AV, made at a time when little was known of the natural history of the Holy Land and before scientific classification had begun, contributed materially to the degree of confusion already existing regarding the identification of plants. The RSV and other modern versions correct obvious errors, but there remain differences of opinion as to the identity of some plant names, including that of *trees.

The following represent some wild biblical plants and those not included in single or composite entries.

Broom (Heb. *rōṯem* and variants; AV 'juniper'). A common Palestinian shrub (*Retama raetam*) of sandy places, 2–4 m high, with numerous white pea flowers in the spring. Elijah in despair sat under one (1 Ki. 19:4–5). Its roots produce excellent charcoal which was used for incendiary arrows (Ps. 120:4) and for warmth (Jb. 30:4), although some authors consider the latter verse refers to the parasitic plant *Cynomorium coccineum*, which grows upon broom roots and may be edible (*cf.* AV).

Castor-oil. The correct rendering of the Heb. *qîqāyôn* (Jon. 4:6) has been disputed by many scholars. Pliny and Herodotus assumed it to be the castor-oil plant (*Ricinus communis*, the *kroton* of the Greeks) and they are followed by many versions (RSVmg.). It is a rapidly-growing shrub which could have afforded shade to Jonah and is said to wither even after only slight handling, as Jonah's did. Others, starting from LXX (Gk. *kolokyntha*, but not the ground-trailing colocynth) suggest the bottle-gourd (*Cucurbita lagenaria*, Arab. *qar'ah*, AV 'gourd') which is more adequate botanically, since the biblical context requires a vine rather than a small tree like the castor-oil. The reference may therefore be to such a 'lodge' as sheltered watchers over cucumbers (see Is. 1:8), and which would also be subject to rapid withering, although there may not be a satisfactory natural explanation to an event that was clearly under the control of the Lord.

PLAIN OF MEONENIM
See Meonenim, oak of, Part 2.

PLAIN OF ONO
See Ono, Part 2.

PLAISTER
See Plaster, Part 3.

Crocus. In Is. 35:1 the Heb. *ḥᵃḇaṣṣeleṯ* means bulb, hence the RSV rendering 'crocus' (although strictly a corm). There are many species of *crocus* in Palestine flowering during the winter. The LXX rendered it as *krinon* ('lily'), AV 'rose', and NEB 'asphodel', which has root tubers. The polyanthus narcissus (*Narcissus tazetta*) would be an even better suggestion since it is a truly bulbous plant. Crocus may also be intended in the reference to the 'rose of Sharon', Ct. 2:1. See **Rose**, below.

Hyssop (Heb. *'ēzôḇ*; Gk. *hyssōpos*). Several distinct species of plant are evidently referred to by this name in the Bible, but there is considerable discussion as to their identity. It is certain, however, that the present-day herb known as hyssop (*Hyssopus officinalis*) was not one of them, since it is native to S Europe.

In the OT 'hyssop' was used in the Passover rites (Ex. 12:22) for the purification of lepers (Lv. 14:4, 6), for plague (Lv. 14:49–52) and at the red heifer sacrifice (Nu. 19:2–6; *cf.* Heb. 9:19). The purifying qualities of 'hyssop' are referred to in Ps. 51:7. This plant is generally considered to be the Syrian marjoram (*Origanum syriacum*) which is a fragrant grey-leaved wiry-stemmed perennial herb, 20–30 cm high, with white flowers in small heads, growing in dry rocky places. A different plant is considered to be mentioned in 1 Ki. 4:33, probably the caper (*Capparis spinosa*) which is commonly seen in walls of old buildings: it has very prickly woody stems and large whitish flowers.

In the NT the 'hyssop' employed at the crucifixion (Jn. 19:29, where NEB reads *hyssō*, 'on a javelin') was probably a reed or stick, but the reed-like cereal durra (*Sorghum vulgare*) has been considered the most likely suggestion.

Lily (Heb. *šôšān*, and variants; Gk. *krinon*). As with the 'rose' of the Bible there has been considerable speculation as to the botanical identity of the 'lily'. In common usage the word may be applied to several decorative plants. Most of the references in Ct. are thought to be to the hyacinth (*Hyacinthus orientalis*), a bulbous plant with blue flowers, although the lily-like lips of Ct. 5:13 may allude to the scarlet tulip (*Tulipa sharonensis*) or red poppy anemone (*Anemone coronaria*), myrrh resin also mentioned, being red. Although the white madonna lily (*Lilium candidum*) is wild in Palestine, it inhabits rocky places and it is unlikely to be the plant referred to in Ct. 6:2–3, as has been suggested. The 'lily' of Ho. 14:5 is by implication of a moist habitat likely to be the yellow flag (*Iris pseudacorus*), the 'fleur de lis' of the French.

The references to 'lily-work' on the columns of Solomon's Temple in 1 Ki. 7:19, 22, 26 and 2 Ch. 4:5 are probably to carved representations of the water-lily. The Egyptian lotus (the blue flowered *Nymphaea caerulea* and white *N. lotus*) exercised a wide influence over ancient Near Eastern art, as evidenced by the presence of the lotus motif in many Egyptian and Palestinian archaeological *objets d'art*.

The 'lilies of the field' (Mt. 6:28; Lk. 12:27) could refer to any of the spectacular and beautiful flowers of the Palestinian countryside. Many have been suggested, including the poppy anemone *Anemone coronaria* and the white daisy *Anthemis palaestina* or the crown marguerite *Chrysanthemum coronarium*.

Mallow (Heb. *mallûaḥ*, AV 'mallows', Jb. 30:4). The term implies 'saltiness', whether referring to the taste of the plant or to its habitat. The most likely species is the shrubby orache (*Atriplex halimus*), of salty places by the Dead Sea or Mediterranean. The mallow (*Malva rotundifolia*) may be used like spinach, but it is not salty to the taste and it is a common weed of waste but not saline places.

Mandrake (Heb. *dûḏā'îm*; *Mandragora officinarum*). A perennial herb of the nightshade family with a rosette of large leaves, mauve flowers during the winter and fragrant round yellow fruits in the spring (Ct. 7:13). It is reputed to have emetic, purgative and narcotic qualities. The forked, torso-like shape of the tap-root gave rise to many superstitions. Aphrodisiac properties have been ascribed to it since an early period, which explains the argument between Rachel and Leah (Gn. 30:14). It grows in fields and rough ground in Palestine and the Mediterranean region.

Mildew (Heb. *yērāqôn*, 'paleness', 'greenness'; *cf.* LXX *ikteros*, 'jaundice'). A common species of fungus (*Puccinia graminis*) which, in moist conditions, attacks the crops in Palestine. In biblical times it was regarded as God's punishment on the disobedient (Dt. 28:22; Am. 4:9; Hg. 2:17), and Solomon prayed for deliverance from it (1 Ki. 8:37; 2 Ch. 6:28). The Bible always mentions mildew in conjunction with the opposite conditions, 'blight' or 'blasting' (Heb. *šiddāpôn*, lit. 'scorching'), a drying up of plants by the hot sirocco or *ḥamsîn* wind from the S.

Mustard. Much controversy surrounds the identification of the plant (Gk. *sinapi*) whose seed was used by Christ as an illustration of something which develops rapidly from small beginnings, such as the kingdom of heaven (Mt. 13:31; Mk. 4:31; Lk. 13:19), or the faith of an individual (Mt. 17:20; Lk. 17:6). Some scholars consider that the black mustard (*Brassica nigra*) is indicated, since in NT times its seeds were cultivated for their oil as well as for culinary purposes. It can grow to a height of 5 m, although it is usually much smaller. One interpretation sees the 'mustard' as a monstrous plant foretelling the worldly expression of Christendom, with evil, as exemplified by the birds, in its branches.

Myrtle (Heb. *hᵃḏas*; *Myrtus communis*). A shrub of Palestinian hillsides, usually 2–3 m high, with fragrant evergreen leaves and scented white flowers used as perfumes. Scriptural references envisage the myrtle as symbolizing divine generosity. Isaiah foresaw the myrtle as replacing the brier in the wilderness (Is. 41:19; 55:13). Zechariah in a vision symbolizing peace saw a grove of myrtle trees (Zc. 1:8–11), while in Ne. 8:15 the Jews brought myrtle branches from Olivet to construct shelters at the Feast of Booths (Tabernacles) of Lv. 23:40; Dt. 16:16. The name Hadassah (Esther) was derived from the Heb. term.

Nettles. There is some uncertainty about the precise plants referred to in the above translation of the two Heb. words. **1.** *ḥārûl*, perhaps from the obsolete root *ḥāral*, 'to be sharp', 'to sting'. Found in Jb. 30:7 (LXX 'wild brushwood'); Pr. 24:31; Zp. 2:9; RVmg. in each case renders 'wild vetches' and NEB as 'scrub' or 'weeds'. **2.** *qimmôś* (Is. 34:13; Ho. 9:6). Probably the true nettle, of which the most common Palestine species is *Urtica pilulifera*, which occurs in waste places. (See also **Thistles**, below.)

Stems of the cereal durra (Sorghum vulgare) *may have been the 'hyssop' used at the crucifixion* (*Jn. 19:29*). (FNH)

Centre and Top left: The 'lilies of the field' (*Mt. 6:28; Lk. 12:27*) *may refer to the crown marguerite* (Chrysanthemum coronarium) *or to the white daisy* (Anthemis palaestina). (FNH)

An orache (Atriplex rosea), *one of the plants that could be the 'mallow' of Jb. 30:4.* (FNH)

Nuts. Two Heb. words are thus translated. **1.** *’^{e}ḡôz* (Arab. *gawz*), in Ct. 6:11 only, probably referring to the walnut (*Juglans regia*), an introduction from Persia. **2.** *boṭnîm* (Gn. 43:11 only) is usually considered to be the pistachio nut (*Pistachia vera*), the fruits of which must have been imported from further E where it grew before it was cultivated in the E Mediterranean area. However, the native terebinths (*P. atlantica* and *P. terebinthus* var. *palaestina*) also yield edible nuts of a small size. Some Jewish authors identify this Heb. word with the carob. (See **Pods**.)

Pods (Gk. *keratia*). A sweet dry fruit eaten by animals and by the poor. The prodigal son in his hunger would gladly have done so (Lk. 15:16, AV 'husks'). It is the seed-pod of the carob tree (*Ceratonia siliqua*), common in the Mediterranean region, where it is also called the locust bean and St John's bread from a tradition that they were the 'locusts' which John the Baptist ate, although these are more likely to have been the actual locust insect (*ANIMALS).

Reed. 1. Heb. *’āḥû* (Jb. 8:11, AV 'flag'; Gn. 41:2, 18, AV 'meadow'). This is a general word for water-

White mustard (Sinapis alba) *is similar to the black mustard* (Brassica nigra) *which is usually considered to be the plant referred to in the parable of the mustard seed* (*Mt.* *13:31–32*). (FNH)

Myrtle (Myrtus communis) *occurs in natural woodland in Palestine. Its leaves and flowers are fragrant. Jews use myrtle branches at the Feast of Booths* (*Tabernacles*). (FNH)

loving plants found in swamps and by river-banks—hence Bildad's rhetorical question ('Can the reed grow without water?').

2. Heb. *sûp̄*, 'reed' (Ex. 2:3, 5; Is. 19:6). Evidently specifically applied to the moisture-loving cat-tail or reed-mace (*Typha angustata*) still common around the Nile and its canals. The Red Sea (*yam sûp̄*) is literally the 'sea of Reeds' (*cf.* Egyp. *p'-ṯwf*).

3. Heb. *qāneh*; Gk. *kalamos*. Tall grasses growing in wet places (marshes, river-banks, *etc.*), often the haunts of large aquatic animals (*cf.* Jb. 40:21; Is. 19:6–7; 35:7). The Heb. and Gk. words are both quite general terms, although some think that the *Arundo donax* of Palestine and Egypt, growing to 3 m high or more, and the smaller common reed (*Phragmites communis*) are the plant usually intended. Israel under God's judgment is like a reed shaken in the water (1 Ki. 14:15); and in Christ's words, wind-blown reeds and richly dressed courtiers will not be found in a dry wilderness (Mt. 11:7–8; Lk. 7:24). If undue weight be rested on a reed-stalk it will break irregularly, and the snags will pierce the hand. Just so did Egypt fail Israel in the days of Isaiah (Is. 36:6; 2 Ki. 18:21), Jeremiah and Ezekiel (Ezk. 29:6–7). The 'bruised reed' could be symbolic of the weak whom the Messiah would not break off (Is. 42:3; Mt. 12:20).

Before the crucifixion, the sol-

Christ's crown of thorns (*Jn. 19:2*) *may have been made from the spiny burnet* (Poterium spinosum). (FNH)

diers gave Christ a reed as a mock sceptre, and then struck him with it (Mt. 27:29–30; Mk. 15:19). On the cross he was offered a spongeful of vinegar on the end of a reed (Mt. 27:48; Mk. 15:36; or 'hyssop', Jn. 19:29). A reed could serve as a measuring-rod, and gave its name to a measure of 6 cubits (Ezk. 40:3–8; 41:8 [the 6 cubits]; 42:16–19; Rev. 11:1; 21:15–16), as did the same term *qanu* in Mesopotamia. (*WEIGHTS AND MEASURES.)

Rose. The true rose, *e.g. Rosa phoenicia*, is uncommon in Palestine and the 'rose of Sharon' (Ct. 2:1) is unlikely to be this plant. *Anemone*, *Cistus*, *Narcissus*, *Tulipa* and *Crocus* have been mentioned as possibilities.

In the Apocrypha the 'rose' of Ecclus 1:8 bloomed in spring and may be either a tulip, narcissus or crocus. In Ecclus 24:14 and 39:13 the references are probably to oleander (*Nerium oleander*) which is a tall, pink-flowered shrub with poisonous leaves that inhabits rocky streams. The 'roses' of 2 Esdras 2:19 and 'rosebuds' of Wisdom 2:8 have been variously regarded as species of rock-rose (*Cistus*), rose (*Rosa*) or oleander.

Rush. The word rush should apply to species of *Juncus*, but the term is loosely applied to other water-loving plants (except marsh grasses, which are reeds), such as reed-mace also called cat-tail (*Typha*), and sedges such as papyrus (*Cyperus papyrus*) and corresponds to the Heb. *'agmōn* and *gōme'*. The former is a general word, 'rushes', 'reed'. For her unfaithfulness to God, Israel is stripped even of such ordinary basic raw materials as 'palm branch and reed' (Is. 9:14), while these, for all their utility, will not avail Egypt in her troubles (Is.

The wild corn poppy (Papaver rhoeas) *is one of the flowers of the Holy Land about which Jesus spoke* (*Mt. 6:28–29*). (FNH)

The mandrake (Mandragora officinarum) *has many superstitions ascribed to it. For this reason Rachel and Leah argued about the possession of some plants of it* (*Gn. 30:14ff.*). (FNH)

Bottom left: Pods of the carob tree (Ceratonia siliqua) *were fed to swine, as mentioned in the parable of the Prodigal Son* (*Lk. 15:16*). (FNH)

The giant reed (Arundo donax) *forms tall stands by water.* (FNH)

The flowering rush (Butomus umbellatus) has been suggested as the second water-plant mentioned in Jb. 8:11. (FNH)

difficulty identifying the thistles, thorns, briers, bramble and other prickly plants mentioned in Scripture, owing to the fact that over twenty different words are employed to describe such plants, of which there are many in the dry Palestinian countryside. These prickly *weeds fall into genera such as *Centaurea*, *Ononis*, *Silybum*, *Notobasis* and *Poterium*. In many instances the Heb. and Gk. words for them are as imprecise as Eng.

In general, thorns expressed the concept of fruitlessness or vexatious endeavour (Gn. 3:18; Nu. 33:55; Jos. 23:13). They were evidence of divine judgment on the ungodly (Na. 1:10), or of sheer misfortune (Ezk. 2:6). If allowed to grow unchecked in orchards or vineyards they made serious inroads on the productivity of the trees and vines (Pr. 24:31; Is. 5:6; Je. 12:13), but when kept in control and arranged in the form of hedges they served as effective barriers to wild animals (Ho. 2:6; Mt. 21:33).

19:15). Rushes could be woven into rope, or used as fuel (Jb. 41:2, 20). The head bowed in outward penitence is like the bent-over tip of the rush (Is. 58:5); here the papyrus plant is probably intended since it does not snap off but is easily bent by the wind and hangs down.

The term *gōme'* may signify the papyrus-plant (for which see *PAPYRI AND OSTRACA, I), or else reeds generally; either meaning suits the biblical references to *gōme'*, which is depicted growing in the marsh (Jb. 8:11), symbolizing swampy growth (Is. 35:7), used for papyrus skiffs in Egypt and Ethiopia (Is. 18:2) and Moses' basket of bulrushes (Ex. 2:3). Heb. *gōme'* is probably the same as Egyp. *gmy* and *ḳmy*, 'reeds', 'rushes', attested from the 13th century BC onwards, and *kam* in Coptic. (See R. A. Caminos, *Late-Egyptian Miscellanies*, 1954, pp. 167–168, 412; *cf.* W. Spiegelberg, *Koptische Etymologien*, 1920, pp. 4–6; T. O. Lambdin, *JAOS* 73, 1953, p. 149.)

Shrub (Heb. *'ar'ār*, Je. 17:6). The Heb. word, rendered 'shrub' in RSV (AV 'heath'), is considered by Jewish scholars to be the Phoenician juniper (*Juniperus phoenicea*). The tamarisk (*Tamarix* sp.) has also been suggested. A similar word *'ᵃrô'ēr* in Je. 48:6 appears as 'wild ass' in RSV and 'heath' in AV.

Thistles, Thorns. Botanists have

The curious parasitic plant (Cynomorium coccineum) which grows on the roots of some desert plants including broom. (FNH)

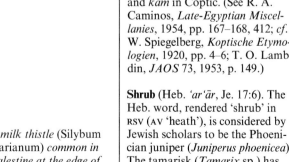

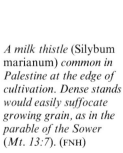

A milk thistle (Silybum marianum) common in Palestine at the edge of cultivation. Dense stands would easily suffocate growing grain, as in the parable of the Sower (Mt. 13:7). (FNH)

Thorns were popular quick-burning fuel in OT times, as among the modern bedouin Arabs (Ps. 58:9; Is. 9:18; 10:17). The destructive nature of thistles and thorns was expressed graphically in the Gospel parables (Mt. 13:7; Mk. 4:7; Lk. 8:7), as was their essential fruitlessness (Mt. 7:16). Thistles are herbaceous plants, whereas thorns are woody. In the parable of the sower (Mt. 13:7, *etc.*) the 'thorns' among which the grain fell were likely to have been the milk thistle (*Silybum marianum*) which infests field margins and grows rapidly.

Some of the biblical references to 'thorns' are to the holy bramble (*Rubus sanguineus*). Those of Pr. 15:19 and Ho. 2:6 may be the latter, while 'thorns of the wilderness' (Jdg. 8:7) may be an acacia, or *Ziziphus lotus*, and the 'briers' boxthorn (*Lycium* sp.), which is the 'bramble' of Jotham's parable (Jdg. 9:14). The crown of *thorns (Mt. 27:29; Mk. 15:17; Jn. 19:5) plaited for Jesus before his crucifixion would have been made of some locally available material. Although the 'Christ thorn' shrub (*Paliurus spina-christi*), which has long thorny branches, is not now found around Jerusalem, it is known to have grown near there in ancient times. However, some authors consider that the small spiny burnet (*Poterium spinosum*) or tree *Ziziphus spina-christi* was used; others have suggested the thorns of the *Phoenix dactylifera*, in mock imitation of the radiate crown (*cf.* H. St J. Hart, *JTS* n.s. 3, 1952, pp. 66ff.). (See also **Nettles**, above.)

Tumbleweed. Heb. *galgal* is rendered in EVV 'wheel', 'rolling thing', 'thistle down' and 'whirling dust' (Is. 17:13; Ps. 83:13, RSV 'tumble weed'). It implies one of the wind-distributed fruiting bodies of certain plants growing in open dry habitats. Such Palestinian plants are *Grundelia tournefortii* and *Cachrys goniocarpa*, as well as the hairy grains of some grasses that collect as rolling balls. *Anastatica hierochuntica* is not one of these, as has often been suggested, since it remains firmly anchored by its root even when dead.

Vine of Sodom. A variety of opinion exists regarding the nature of the allusions in the Song of Moses (Dt. 32:32). There is a distinct possibility that the expression may be figurative, describing the bitterness of Israel's enemies. If a real plant, one which conceals a powdery substance underneath an attractive rind is indicated. *Solanum sodomeum*, or *Calotropic procera*, with feathery seeds in an inflated fruit, has been suggested. More probably the phrase arose from association with the colocynth, a wild *gourd, *Citrullus colocynthis*, which trails on sandy ground near the Dead Sea and has bitter, light-weight fruits.

Weeds. Usually applied to wild plants of cultivated and waste ground. In the Bible represented as a scourge of useless, troublesome plants as indeed they were to the farmer. RSV renders several words as 'weeds', especially Gk. *zizania*, Arab. *zuwān*, which AV calls 'tares', and is probably more correctly considered (as in NEB) to be the darnel grass (*Lolium temulentum*). In the leafy stage this grass resembles wheat, but if the biblical counsel be followed and both are allowed to grow together till harvest (Mt. 13:30) the small ear is clearly distinguished, and usually to women and children falls the tedious manual task of separation. If the wheat grain is contaminated with the bitter darnel grains subsequent poisoning causes illness and vomiting. Sowing darnel in a field for purposes of revenge (*cf.* Mt. 13:25f.) was a crime under Roman legislation. The necessity for a law on the subject suggests that the action was not infrequent.

NEB renders other words as 'weeds' which appear in RSV as *nettles or *thorns.

The cockle (*Agrostemma githago*) was a curse of English wheat fields at the time the AV was being translated, but there is no evidence that it occurred in Palestine. Later translations are probably correct in rendering the Heb. *bo'šâ*, referred to by Job while defending his integrity (31:38–40), by some general term such as 'stinking weeds', AVmg.; 'noisome weeds', RVmg.; 'foul weeds', RSV; 'weeds', NEB. Evidently this weed was prickly and it has been identified with the oyster thistle (*Scolymus maculatus*) and the rest-harrow (*Ononis antiquorum*).

Wild vine, wild gourds (Heb. *paqqu'ōṯ*, 'bursters'). Mentioned in 2 Ki. 4:39 these gourds were the colocynth (*Citrullus colocynthis*). Like small melons in appearance, the fruits are a violent purge which may be dangerous. The colocynth trails along the ground in sandy places by the Dead Sea.

Wormwood (Heb. *la'ᵃnâ*, Gk. *apsinthos*). Many species of wormwood grow in Palestine, but the biblical references are either to *Artemisia herba-alba* or *A. judaica*. All species have a strong, bitter taste, leading to the use of the plant as a symbol of bitterness, sorrow and calamity (Pr. 5:4; La. 3:15, 19; Am. 5:7; 6:12 [AV 'hemlock']). Moses used it to show the perils of secret idolatry (Dt. 29:18, RSV 'bitter root'), as did Jeremiah in warning of the punishment awaiting disobedient Israel (Je. 9:15; 23:15).

BIBLIOGRAPHY. A. Alon, *The Natural History of the Land of the Bible*, 1969; A. Goor and M. Nurock, *Fruits of the Holy Land*, 1968; R. K. Harrison, 'The Biblical Problem of Hyssop', *EQ* 26, 1954, pp. 218–224; *idem*, 'The Mandrake and the Ancient World', *EQ* 28, 1956, pp. 87–92; *idem*, *Healing Herbs of the Bible*, 1966; F. N. Hepper, *Plants of Bible Lands*, in preparation; I. Löw, *Die Flora der Juden*, 1–4, 1924–34; H. N. and A. L. Moldenke, *Plants of the Bible*, 1952; W. Walker, *All the Plants of the Bible*, 1957; M. Zohary, *Plant-life of Palestine*, 1962; *Flora Palaestina*, 1966 onwards.

F.N.H. *et al.*

PLASTER. 1. The inner, and sometimes outer, walls of buildings were covered with a plaster commonly made of clay (Lv. 14:42–43; Heb. *ṭûaḥ*, 'to coat, overlay'; Arab. *ṭāḥa*). Such plaster is attested from prehistoric times (*JERICHO). A better plaster was made by heating crushed limestone or gypsum (Heb. *śîḏ*, 'to boil'). This enabled

Fragment of glazed enamel brick from Babylon showing the 'plaster' surface, perhaps that mentioned in Dn. 5:5. (DJW)

'Plaster', in the form of a coloured glaze later fired, was used on special wall surfaces. Here it is inscribed in archaizing cuneiform script. From reconstructed Ishtar Gate of Babylon in Berlin. c. 600 BC. (AMM)

PLEIADES
See Stars, Part 3.

PODS
See Plants, Part 3.

rough stones or brickwork to be covered with a fine surface which could be painted or inscribed, as was done on the altar at Ebal (Dt. 27:2, 4). (An example has been found at Deir 'Alla in the Jordan Valley.) It was used for basins, cisterns and walls. A glazed surface on brickwork was obtained by firing in a kiln (Is. 27:9; Heb. *gîr*). Such a 'plaister' (AV) was broken by the handwriting on the palace wall in Babylon (Dn. 5:5; Aram. *gîrâ*). (*GLASS.)

2. The 'plaister' used to cure Hezekiah (Is. 38:21, AV; Heb. *māraḥ*) was a poultice made of crushed figs. A similar medical term is used in the Ras Shamra texts and Egyp. Ebers Papyrus.

D.J.W.

PLOUGHMAN. In the OT there are three Heb. expressions which are rendered 'ploughman'.

1. *’ikkār*. The cognate Akkadian ideogram describes the *’ikkār* as 'man of the plough'. The exact social position and function of the *’ikkār* is uncertain, but the code of Hammurapi suggests that he was a hired agricultural foreman. The OT contrasts the shepherd with the *’ikkār* (Is. 61:5).

2. *yōḡēḇ* (2 Ki. 25:12; Je. 52:16). Consideration of the related Heb. *gûḇ* and Arab. *ğāba*, 'to bore', 'hollow out', may suggest that the *yōḡēḇ* was a spade labourer.

3. *’îš ’^{a}ḏāmâ* means literally 'man of soil', but a comparison of Gn. 9:20 and Zc. 13:5 shows that it refers indifferently to an arable or cattle farmer.

LXX and NT employ *geōrgos*, 'farmer, tenant farmer', throughout. God is pictured as the husbandman of the true vine (Jn. 15:1) and of the church (1 Cor. 3:9).

R.J.W.

POETRY.

I. In the Old Testament

Poetry, especially in the form of song or hymn, occupies an important place in Heb. literature. The Jews were evidently a music-loving people and famous for their songs. Hezekiah in 701 BC included in his tribute to Sennacherib male and female musicians (*i.e.* those who accompanied their songs with instruments; *DOTT*, p. 67), and the exiles in Babylon were pressed by their captors to sing one of their songs, of whose fame they must have heard (Ps. 137:3). Little of their secular poetry has remained, but references in the OT seem to indicate that it was of considerable volume. The 'Song of the Well' (Nu. 21:17–18) was probably a work-song used at the well or by well-diggers. Other occupations probably had special songs: reaping (Is. 9:3), and vintaging (Is. 16:10). Songs were also used on special occasions. Laban would have made use of songs at a farewell for Jacob (Gn. 31:27). No marriage feast would be complete without them (*cf.* Je. 7:34). Laments for the dead were often in poetic form. The elegies of David for Saul and Jonathan (2 Sa. 1:19–27), and for Abner (2 Sa. 3:33–34), are poetic compositions of the highest order. The short lament over Absalom has been called 'a masterpiece of rhythm' (2 Sa. 18:33). The Heb. language is very rhythmic so that this feature occurs in passages which are not strictly poetry, especially in speech. In the prophetic books, however, many oracles are given in poetic form as modern translations show. This is true, also, of Proverbs, Ecclesiastes, the Song of Songs and Job. Thus there is a vast amount of poetry in the OT.

Songs were nearly always accompanied by instrumental music (Ex. 15:20; 1 Ch. 25:6; Is. 23:16). In fact, instruments would appear to have existed for the sole purpose of accompanying song (Am. 6:5).

Among the terms used for poetic compositions are: *šîr*, 'song' (with or without an instrument); *mizmôr*, 'psalm' or 'hymn' (with instruments); *qînâ*, 'elegy' or 'lament'; *t^{e}hillâ*, 'hymn of praise'; *māšāl*, in addition to its more usual meaning of 'proverb', is a 'satirical song'.

The largest collection of Heb. songs is the book of Psalms, and it is here that we have the richest material for the study of poetic forms. Scholars disagree, however, as to the nature of Heb. poetry. Some hold that in a corpus of writings, such as the Psalms, covering many centuries no uniform system is to be expected. Others hold that, without a knowledge of the original pronunciation, it is impossible to recover the original forms. Some, again, think that the late introduction of vowel-signs may have brought with it many innovations in vocalization. Others raise the problem of the possibility of transcriptional errors. It would certainly be hazardous in the absence of any indication of vowel-patterns and stress-patterns to defend dogmatically any theory of the principles of Heb. prosody.

It is generally accepted that metre, as we understand it, is absent from Heb. poetry. There is nothing corresponding to the unit of metrical measure (the 'foot'), whether of vowel-quantity or of stress formation, so measured sequence between the 'accents' is hardly to be expected. There is wide agreement that Heb. poetry is 'accentual' in character and that the 'accent' or 'ictus' coincides with grammatical stress. As the number and disposition of unstressed syllables seem to play no essential part, they would be ignored in scanning. Variable rhythm, therefore, takes the place of definite metre. The absence of mechanical measure might seem to indicate a variety of free verse, but in Hebrew there is no deliberate admixture. It would be misleading, too, to compare it with logaoedic rhythm, a cross between the rhythm of prose and that of poetry, found on occasion in Gk. poetry, for it is true poetry. Perhaps as good a description as any would be the term 'sprung rhythm', coined by Gerard Manley Hopkins. Describing this rhythm, he said: 'It consists in scanning by accents or stresses alone, without any account of the number of syllables, so that a foot may be one strong syllable or it may be many light and one strong.'

To scan Heb. poetry, then, one should count merely the number of 'ictus units' or 'stress units', each one, irrespective of the number of syllables, providing only one 'beat'. Resultant groupings, corresponding very roughly to dimeter, trimeter, *etc.*, and combinations of these, could be made. In the nature of the case the procedure here is bound to be to a greater or lesser extent subjective. Nevertheless, there seem to be many instances of rhythmic patterns (*e.g.* in Ps. 29). It would, however, be unreasonable to expect rigid uniformity in poetry as subjective as Hebrew, and proposals to change the text to gain a regular pattern should be viewed sceptically.

One type of poem, the lament or dirge (*qînâ*), has, according to many scholars, a particular metre. The verse here consists of five anapaests with a caesura after the third. If this is so the choric use to which such a poem was put may well have dictated the form. In the case of other poems used in congregational singing, use may have been made of 'reciting notes'.

A common feature of Heb. poetry particularly in the Psalms is 'parallelism', as it was called by R. Lowth (*De sacra poesi Hebraeorum*, 1753). The simplest form is the restating in the second line of a couplet what has been expressed in the first. The relationship of the second line or 'stichos' of the couplet (distich) to the first may be synonymous, or synthetical, or antithetical, or climactic. Occasionally the stanza is a tristich, and then all three 'stichoi' may be involved in the parallelism.

An example of synonymous parallelism is 'Deliver me from my enemies, O God, protect me from those who rise up against me' (Ps. 59:1). Ps. 104 is full of parallelisms of this kind. In synthetic parallelism the second line amplifies or complements the first, *e.g.* 'O that I had wings like a dove! I would fly away and be at rest' (Ps. 55:6). In antithetical, the second line expresses a contrast to the first, *e.g.* 'The Lord knows the way of the righteous, but the way of the wicked will perish' (Ps. 1:6). In climactic parallelism there is a heightening of the effect in the second line (*cf.* Ps. 55:12–13). Less common forms, such as dimorphic parallelism, occur, *i.e.* one line followed by two different parallels (Ps. 45:1).

With the exception of rhyme, Hebrew makes full use of literary devices common to all poetry. Assonance is not absent. Simile and metaphor abound. Alliteration, usually as 'concealed', is enlisted. Anadiplosis and anaphora are used with telling effect (Jdg. 5:19, 27). The mnemonic help of the acrostic is invoked. The best-known example is that of Ps. 119, which is arranged in stanzas of 8 verses, and in which a letter of the Heb. alphabet is assigned to each stanza, and each verse begins with this letter.

Nowhere is the genius of Heb. poetry more apparent than in its imagery. It lays heaven and earth under tribute. It steals music from the morning stars, and light from the bridegroom who needs no virginal lamps. Its eternal summer fades not, and its snows are undefiled. It rules the raging of the sea, it drives on the clouds and rides on the wings of the wind. It makes the royal gold richer, the myrrh more fragrant and the frankincense sweeter. The offerings it takes from the shepherd suffer no death, and his flock is folded in evergreen pastures. The bread of its harvest will never waste, the oil from its press never fail and its wine is for ever new. So long as men can breathe, its eternal lines will form the litany of the praying heart. The strings it touches are the strings of the harp of God.

The rhythm of Heb. poetry is not the measured beat of the earth-locked body. It is the majestic rhythm of the soaring spirit, felt only by him who has the music of heaven in his soul. It rises above the metrical to a loftier plane and to a new dimension—the dimension of the spirit, where they who worship God worship him in spirit and in truth.

Its proper object is the Highest, the God of heaven and earth; its source and fount, the depths of the God-hungry heart. Its great theme is the personal encounter with the living God.

BIBLIOGRAPHY. R. Lowth, *De sacra poesi Hebraeorum*, 1753; E. Sievers, *Metrische Studien*, 1901–7; G. B. Gray, *The Forms of Hebrew Poetry*, 1915, reprinted 1972, with survey of more recent work, by D. N. Freedman; C. F. Burney, *The Poetry of our Lord*, 1925; F. F. Bruce, in *NBCR*, 1970, pp. 44f.; Articles by G. R. Driver, J. Muilenburg and T. H. Robinson in *VT Supp.* 1, 1953; H. Kosmala, 'Form and Structure in Ancient Hebrew Poetry', *VT* 14, 1964; W. F. Albright, 'Verse and Prose in Early Israelite Tradition', *Yahweh and the Gods of Canaan*, 1968, pp. 1–46; P. C. Craigie, 'The Poetry of Ugarit and Israel', *TynB* 22, 1971, pp. 3–31; P. W. Skehan (ed.), *Studies in Israelite Poetry and Wisdom*, 1971; F. M. Cross, D. N. Freedman, *Studies in Ancient Yahwistic Poetry*, 1975. W.J.M.

II. In the New Testament

a. Psalms

Three, perhaps four, typical Heb. hymns are preserved in Luke's Gospel: the **Magnificat* (Lk. 1:46–55), the **Benedictus* (Lk. 1:68–79), the **Nunc Dimittis* (Lk. 2:29–32) and the *Gloria* (Lk. 2:14). All of these passages are in the style and spirit of OT psalms, majestic in language, and constructed on the pattern of verbal parallelism proper to Heb. poetry.

b. Hymns

Early Christian hymns may have been poems of mixed tradition (Eph. 5:19), reflecting both the form of the Heb. psalm and that of the Gk. lyric. It has been suggested that numerous passages in the NT are direct and indirect quotations from this corpus of sacred poetry: *e.g.* Eph. 5:14 and 1 Tim. 3:16, where the Hebraic structure is especially striking. Perhaps Col. 1:13–20 and 2 Cor. 5:14–18 are of the same order.

c. Poetic language

This may be discussed under three heads:

(i) It is impossible decisively to distinguish between what may have been direct quotation of rhythmical and poetic utterance, and exalted prose couched in poetic language. In the warm, emotive style of Heb. writing it is always difficult to distinguish sharply poetry from prose, and in passages of deep emotion the NT often adopts such a style. Consider brief ascriptions of praise such as Jude 24–25, and Rev. 5:12–14; rhythmic constructions such as Jn. 14:27; Rom. 11:2, 33 and 1 Cor. 15:54–57; or parallelisms strong in their antitheses such as Jn. 3:20–21, or Rom. 2:6–10; and parallelism of chiastic form and pattern such as Phil. 3:3–10, and Jn. 10:14–15. All these passages, and many others, reveal the influence of the poetry of the OT on the language of the NT, both in form and colouring. Less in debt to Heb. speech, but still of the nature of poetry, are such lofty passages as Rom. 12; 1 Cor. 13 and Phil. 2.

(ii) Tropes and figures are part of the language and tradition of poetry, and have found some mention under *c* (i), above. Paronomasia and alliteration may, however, be separately considered. In several passages the Greek of the NT reveals an artificial assonance, accompanied sometimes by alliteration: *e.g.* Lk. 21:11 (*loimoi, limoi*); Rom. 1:29 (*phthonou, phonou*); Acts 17:25 (*zōēn, pnoēn*); Heb. 5:8 (*emathen, epathen*); Rom. 12:3 (*hyperphronein, phronein, sōphronein*). Mt. 16:18 (*Petros, petra*) and Phm. 10 and 20 (*Onēsimus, onaimēn*) involve puns. Acts 8:30 (*ginōskeis, anaginōskeis*) is probably accidental.

(iii) Mt. 24 and the parallel Synoptic passages, together with the whole of the Apocalypse, are couched in the traditional language of Heb. apocalyptic poetry or prophecy, a type of literature found in Daniel, Ezekiel and Zechariah. It is based on imagery of an allusive nature, and is sometimes designed for private interpretation. It is not unlike certain forms of modern poetry, first brought into fashion by G. M. Hopkins, and practised with some skill by T. S. Eliot. It follows that the 'poetic' interpretation is one legitimate approach to the Apocalypse, and certainly a rewarding one. It may also be remarked that some of the imagery of the book may lack interpretation because of the loss of the key to the allusion, once doubtless possessed.

d. Quotation

The NT is uncommonly full of quotation from the poetic literature of the OT. Parts of the Epistle to the Hebrews are composed almost entirely of such references. So are parts of the Epistle to the Romans. More elusive and less frequent are some direct quotations from Gk. literature. Acts 17:28, 'for we are indeed his offspring', is the former half of an hexameter by Aratus of Soli in Cilicia (315–240 BC). The same phrase occurs in a surviving fragment of Cleanthes, who was the head of the Stoic school from 263 to 232 BC. There is some evidence that the passage contains a more remote quotation from Epimenides, the half-legendary Cretan poet from whom Paul quotes a complete hexameter at Tit. 1:12. Then, in 1 Cor. 15:33 an iambic trimeter of Menander (342–291 BC), the Athenian comic poet, is quoted ('evil communications corrupt good manners'). Again, the Greek of Jas. 1:17 contains a pure hexameter. So do Acts 27:34b (omitting the conjunction *gar*, 'for'), Heb. 12:13 (reading the aorist imperative) and there is an iambic measure at Acts 23:5. It is impossible to say whether quotation is involved in these cases. Metrical writing can be accidental, *e.g.* 'Husbands love your wives and be not bitter against them.'

BIBLIOGRAPHY. C. F. Burney, *The Poetry of our Lord*, 1925; J. T. Sanders, *The New Testament Christological Hymns*, 1971.

E.M.B.

POISON. In Israelite thinking poison came either from plants, water or food, or from adders, vipers, serpents, *etc.* The commonest Heb. word for poison, *ḥēmâ*, basically means heat, and may derive from the burning sensation which followed the taking of poison or from the sting of a reptile.

There were poisonous *plants in

True hemlock (Conium maculatum) *was used to poison Socrates. It appears not to be referred to in the Bible (the 'hemlock' of Am. 6:12 being wormwood), although it does occur in Palestine.* (FNH)

A plaster-lined pool with access steps excavated at Masada, near the Dead Sea. 1st cent. AD. (JPK)

Palestine like hemlock (Ho. 10:4), and the poisonous gourd (2 Ki. 4:39), and, although the word is not used, the waters of Marah (Ex. 15:23) and Jericho (2 Ki. 2:19) were clearly regarded as poisonous (2 Ki. 2:21). (*GALL, *WORMWOOD.)

Several passages refer to the poison of reptiles, serpents (Dt. 32:24; Ps. 58:4), dragons (Dt. 32:33) and adders (Ps. 140:3). Zophar, in the story of Job, told how the wicked would suck the poison (*rō'š*) of asps (Jb. 20:16).

Metaphorically, the Almighty is said to send forth his arrows which give forth poison to distress one's spirit (Jb. 6:4). Again, the poison of the wicked is as the poison of serpents (Ps. 58:4), and the poison of adders is under their lips (Ps. 140:3). With this latter verse compare Rom. 3:13 (Gk. *ios*). Jas. 3:8 describes the tongue as full of poison (*ios*). J.A.T.

POLICE. A Roman magistrate was attended by a staff of lictors (the number depending on his rank) who carried bundles of rods (hence Gk. *rhabdouchoi*, 'rod-bearers', Acts 16:35) and axes symbolizing his capital powers. There being no regular police force, these lictors (AV 'serjeants') carried out police duties as well as escorting the magistrate. They occur at Philippi because it was a Roman colony. E.A.J.

PONTUS. The coastal strip of N Asia Minor, reaching from Bithynia in the W into the highlands of Armenia to the E. The region was politically a complex of Greek republics, temple estates and Iranian baronies in the interior. One of these houses established a kingdom whose greatest ruler, Mithridates, temporarily ejected the Romans from Asia Minor early in the 1st century BC. After his defeat the western part of Pontus was administered with Bithynia as a Roman province, the E part being left under a Greek dynasty. The Jews from Pontus (Acts 2:9; 18:2) presumably came from the Greek coastal states. We know nothing of the origin of Christianity there, but it was represented by the time of 1 Pet. 1:1.

BIBLIOGRAPHY. J. Keil, *CAH*, 11, pp. 575ff.; D. Magie, *Roman Rule in Asia Minor*, 2 vols., 1950. E.A.J.

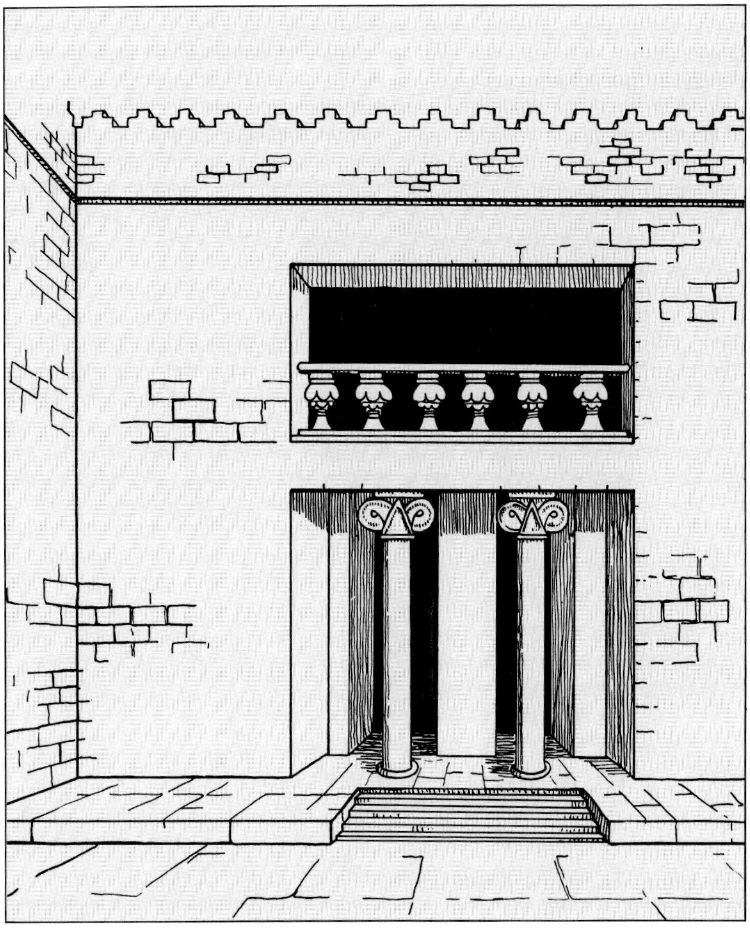

The entrance porch reconstructed here is based on the excavation of the palace of Yarimlim at Alalah, Syria. c. 1450 BC.

POLAR BEAR
See Animals, Part 1.

POLLUX
See Castor and Pollux, Part 1.

POOL OF SILOAM
See Siloam, Part 3.

POPULATION
See Number, Part 2.

POOL. During the summer, water which had collected in pools during the winter and spring formed an important source of supply. The ability to collect and keep water in artificial pools enabled the Israelites to settle uninhabited parts of Palestine (*CISTERN). Artificial pools were dug inside walled cities (the *MOABITE STONE records one) often fed through a tunnel leading from a spring outside, ensuring a supply in time of siege. Examples have been found at Gezer, *Hazor, Megiddo, Gibeon (*cf.* 2 Sa. 2:13) and elsewhere (see J. B. Pritchard, 'The Water System at Gibeon', *BA* 19, 1956, pp. 65–75). 'Hezekiah's tunnel' and the pool of *Siloam in Jerusalem are perhaps the best-known examples (Jn. 9:7, 11; Ne. 3:15). Lack of evidence precludes the certain location of the other pools named in Jerusalem (the lower and old pools, Is. 22:9, 11; the king's pool and the artificial pool, Ne. 2:14; 3:16; see also *SAMARIA, *BETHESDA.) A.R.M.

PORCH. Heb. *'ûlām, 'êlām* (*cf.* Assyr. *ellamu*, 'front') is used of the vestibule of Solomon's Temple (1 Ki. 6:3) and of the gateways of Ezekiel's Temple (Ezk. 40). Solomon's palace included a porch of pillars with a porch in front and another porch for the judgment throne (1 Ki. 7:6–7). These buildings may well be derived from the Syrian *bit hilāni*, a suite of rooms, consisting of a portico entered by a flight of steps and leading to an audience chamber, various other rooms and a stairway to an upper floor or roof. The unique Heb. *misdᵉrôn* (Jdg. 3:23, from root *sdr*, 'to set in order, arrange') is perhaps a portico of this nature in an upper storey, the word describing the row of pillars (see H. Frankfort, *Art and the Architecture of the Ancient Orient*, 1954, pp. 167–175, and the reconstruction in Sir Leonard Woolley's *A Forgotten Kingdom*, 1953, p. 113). Five porches (Gk. *stoa*) surrounded the pool of Bethesda to give shelter (Jn. 5:2). Peter denied his Lord in the entrance to the courtyard of the high priest's house (Mt. 26:71, *pylōn*; Mk. 14:68, *proaulion*). Solomon's Porch was a covered walk 30 cubits wide with two rows of pillars 25 cubits high

Porch of the palace of Kapara at Tell Halaf (Gozan). The architrave is supported by three stone figures, each 2·74 m high, standing on lion bases and topped by conical capitals. Reconstruction at Aleppo Museum. c. 8th cent. BC. (JDH)

along the E side of the Court of the Gentiles in Herod's Temple (Jn. 10:23; Acts 3:11; 5:12; Jos., *Ant.* 15. 380–425). (*TEMPLE.) A.R.M.

POTIPHAR. A high officer of Pharaoh, to whom the Midianites sold Joseph (Gn. 37:36; 39:1), and in whose household Joseph became chief steward (Gn. 39). His name is Egyptian, of the type *P'-di-X*, X being a deity. The simplest, but not wholly satisfactory, explanation of Potiphar is that it is an abbreviated variant of *Potiphera with loss of final *'ayin*. Two high officials at court with the same or similar names is not without parallel in Egyp. history. K.A.K.

POTIPHERA (Potipherah, AV). The 'priest of On', whose daughter, Asenath, Joseph received in marriage from Pharaoh (Gn. 41:45, 50; 46:20). He was possibly high priest of the sun-god Rē' in *On (Gk. Heliopolis). Potiphera (Heb. *pôṭîp̄era'*) is universally admitted to be Egyp. *P'-di-P'R'*, 'he whom P'Rē' (= sun-god) has given', on pattern *P'-di-X*, X being a deity. The exact form *P'-d'-P'R'* is inscriptionally attested only late (*c.* 1000–300 BC), but is merely a full Late-Egyptian form of this name-type which is known from the Empire period, especially the 19th Dynasty (13th century BC), the age of Moses. Potiphera/*P'-di-P'R'* may be simply a modernization in Moses' time of the older form *Didi-R'*, with the same meaning, of a name-pattern (*Didi-X*) which is particularly common in the Middle Kingdom and Hyksos periods, *i.e.* the patriarchal and Joseph's age (*c.* 2100–1600 BC). K.A.K.

POTTER, POTTERY. A reasonable explanation of the introduction of pottery is that a clay-lined basket was accidentally burnt, baking the lining and rendering it usable (see S. Cole, *The Neolithic Revolution*, 1959, p. 41). Pottery first appears in Neolithic times in the Near East. Until the invention of the potter's *wheel late in the 4th millennium BC, all pots were built up by hand, by the same methods which continue to be used for making large vessels in Palestine (G. M. Crowfoot, 'Pots

PORCUPINE
See Animals, Part 1.

PORPOISE
See Animals, Part 1.

PORTENT
See Miracle, Part 2.

POSSESSION
See Demon-possession, Part 1.

Potter's wheel. The upper stone pivoted in the recess cut in the lower stone. From Hazor. Basalt. Diameter c. 15 cm. Canaanite, c. 1500–1200 BC. (IM)

Ancient and Modern', *PEQ* 64, 1932, pp. 179–187). Examples of the professional potter's workshop discovered in Palestine (*e.g.* at Lachish [*PEQ* 70, 1938, p. 249, pl. XXV] and Khirbet Qumran [*RB* 63, 1956, p. 543, pl. XI]) show that the potter sat on the edge of a small pit in which stood the wheels (Heb. *'oḇnayim*), usually two stones, one pivoted upon the other, which he turned with his feet. Pebbles, shells, bone implements and broken shards were used to smooth and burnish the surface, to shape and to decorate. The power of the potter (Heb. *yôṣēr*; Gk. *kerameus*) over the clay (Heb. *ḥōmer*; Gk. *pēlos*) is used as a simile in Je. 18:1–12 and by Paul (Rom. 9:21). See R. H. Johnston, *BA* 37, 1974, pp. 86–106.

I. Ancient pottery

Simply because it is common, but fragile, pottery in large quantities lies strewn on every ancient tell (*cf.* Jb. 2:8). Careful observation of the

Early Bronze Age juglet (height c. 10 cm; from Bab edh Dhra) and flask (height c. 12 cm; from Beth-shemesh). (BM)

Middle Bronze Age wares from Hazor. Flat-base (height c. 12 cm) and pointed-base (height c. 18 cm) jugs. (BM)

Jug of Cypriot ware (height c. 24 cm) and flask of Mycenaean ware (height c. 16 cm). From Gezer. Late Bronze Age. (BM)

stratigraphical relationship of fragments found on one site enables a distinction to be made between the earliest pieces and the latest (usually those found at the bottom and the top of the mound respectively). Comparison with similar shards from other sites shows the contemporaneity or otherwise of the various levels (*ARCHAEOLOGY). Records of pottery finds from several sites in Palestine have enabled a sequence of forms to be drawn up which can be dated by other evidence. As a result, it is now possible to date pottery found on one site—and thus the site—by comparison with recognized dated forms. It is dangerous, however, to give a date more precisely than approximately 50 years either way solely on the evidence of pottery. Plotting the distribution of pottery types over a wide area can reveal trade routes and cultural boundaries.

The following brief description of some features of pottery found in Palestine should be read in conjunction with the chart. The superior figures refer to the numbers of the various objects included in it.

Opposite page: Chart showing the development of pottery in Palestine from Neolithic to Roman times.

Neolithic pots are of simple but diverse form, with burnishing and incised or painted decoration, perhaps imitating basket and leatherwork. The ware is mostly coarse, tempered with chopped straw. Some contact with Syria and Mesopotamia is suggested by the painted decoration of the next period (Chalcolithic). Definite rim-forms and ledge-handled jars now occur. Unique to it are cornet cups[4], and barrel-like vessels with a loop handle either end and a neck in the middle which are probably churns, imitating skin originals[2]. Use of kaolin in the Negeb seems to have given vessels made there a distinctive colour ('Cream Ware').

The Early Bronze Age may be divided into three phases on the basis of pottery types. Globular jars with criss-cross lines of reddish paint covering the whole body are typical of the earliest phase in S Palestine, while broad strokes of thick and thin paint appear in the N[9]. A grey-burnished ware may have imitated stone vessels[14]. Another typical form is the spouted jar ('teapot'). Ledge-handled jars, common at this time, were exported to Egypt. Several pieces of Early Bronze II ware have been found in Egyp. tombs of the 1st Dynasty. Especially noticeable are single-handled pitchers[8] and red-burnished dishes. Migrations from Anatolia *via* Syria brought a distinctive red- or black-burnished pottery with plastic decoration (Khirbet Kerak ware, Early Bronze III[10, 15]). This was used alongside local styles which are also found in Egyp. tombs of the Pyramid Age.

The different civilization of the Middle Bronze Age is apparent in the new pottery forms. Jars with short, narrow necks, and broad, flat bases are typical of the first phase, as are spouted pots[16] and combed decoration[23]. It may be that these forms were associated with the spread of the Amorites. Certainly the very fine pottery of the second phase can be linked with the movements which culminated in the Hyksos. General use of the wheel and careful burnishing produced wares that rivalled, but did not oust, expensive vessels of metal and stone. Jars and pitchers have small round or pointed bases[17, 21]. The lamp first came into use at this period[26]. Juglets of black ware with incised decoration filled with white paste found widely on sites of this period may be associated with the Hyksos[22].

Large vessels
Jugs and pitchers
Jars and pots
Flasks
Juglets
Cups
Bowls and plates
Lamps
Neolithic and Chalcolithic
1
2
3
4
5
6
Early Bronze Age
7
8
9
10
11
12
13
14
15
Middle Bronze Age
16
17
18
19
20
21
22
23
24
25
26
Late Bronze Age
27
28
29
30
31
32
33
34
35
36
37
38
Iron Age
39
40
41
42
43
44
45
46
47
48
49
50
51
Persian period
52
53
54
55
56
57
58
59
60
Hellenistic period
61
62
63
64
65
66
67
68
69
70
71
72
Roman period
73
74
75
76
77
78
79
80
81
82

II. Later styles

Towards the end of the Middle Bronze Age and during the first part of Late Bronze I, jugs and bowls with red and black geometric designs and animals appear[28]. This ware was exported to Cyprus and possibly to Cilicia. Mycenaean pottery[30] (F. H. Stubbings, *Mycenaean Pottery from the Levant*, 1951) was imported in large quantities in the second phase together with Cypriot wares (the metallic 'base-ring' and 'milk-bowl' types)[33, 37]. The 'pilgrim flask' is an innovation of this phase[31]. The break in culture between the Bronze and Iron Ages (*ARCHAEOLOGY) is clearly recognizable in the pottery. From the coastal plain, known to have been occupied by the Philistines, come large two-handled bowls and beer-jugs of cream ware, decorated with red and black geometric designs and stylized birds[36, 29]. This is a local imitation of the later forms of Mycenaean wares. Pottery from the highlands is, in some cases, a degenerate continuation of Late Bronze Age styles, but new forms of coarse ware and crude shape also appear. Heavy storage jars with short 'collar rims' and handles are reckoned typical of the Settlement period.

During the Monarchy there is a greater regularity of form and gradual improvement in ware. A tendency to angular shapes may be noticed[41]. Many dishes were burnished while turning on the wheel, but the finest are very thin and decorated with bands of red slip ('Samaria ware')[48]. Large storage jars[39] were often stamped on the handles with a royal seal bearing the name of one of four towns, possibly factories (Hebron, Ziph, Socoh and one unidentified, *mmšt*, *cf.* 1 Ch. 4:23; *DOTT*, p. 219). The mining communities of the Negeb used crude, hand-made pots.

Persian and Hellenistic pottery shows development of some forms (*e.g.* the amphora[52]) under Greek influence. Athenian black- and red-figured wares were imported. Narrow, elongated flasks were often placed in tombs at this time. A ribbed appearance is common on coarse pottery of the Roman period[74, 75]; most of the finer wares in use were imported (*e.g.* Italian and Gallic *terra sigillata*). The Nabataean centres in Transjordan produced very delicate buff dishes

A flask of the Late Bronze Age (II A) period, imitating imported Mycenaean pottery. From Hazor. 1400–1340 BC. (BM)

Iron Age juglet from Jerusalem (height c. 16 cm) and a decanter from Bethshemesh (height c. 20 cm). (BM)

Pottery bowl (Iron Age II) found at Hazor. 8th cent. BC. (BM)

with floral designs in red. Glazed ware (faience) was imported from Egypt in the Bronze Age but was never very common.

III. Hebrew names

It is not possible to identify the Heb. names for pottery vessels with certainty; these suggestions follow J. L. Kelso, *Ceramic Vocabulary of the Old Testament*, *BASOR* Supplementary Studies 5–6, 1948 (*cf. PEQ* 71, 1939, pp. 76–90). Heb. *'aggān*, a large bowl (*Cup); *'āsûḵ*, a large, spouted oil-jar (2 Ki. 4:2); *baqbûq*, the distinctive narrow-necked jug of the Iron II period (1 Ki. 14:3; Je.

Hellenistic juglet from Tell el-Far'ah. Height c. 20 cm. (BM)

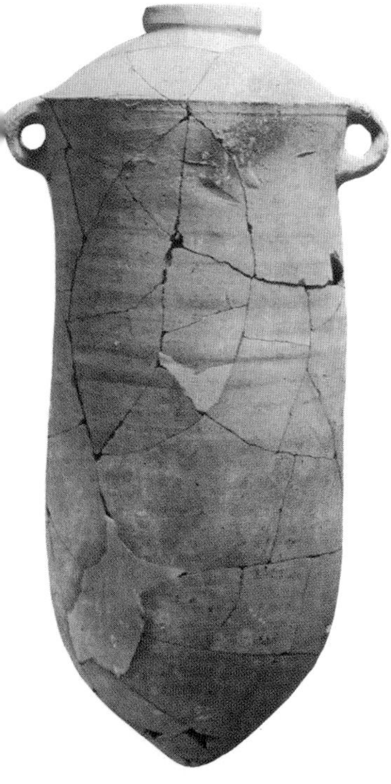

Bottom left: A typical storage-jar (Iron Age II) from Hazor. Height 68·58 cm. 8th cent. BC. (BM)

This method of moulding vessels on a potter's wheel has changed little since pottery was invented. Egypt. (SH)

POTTER'S FIELD
See Akeldama, Part 1.

POTTERY DECORATION
See Ornaments, Part 2.

POUND
See Weights and measures, Part 3.

19:1, 10); *gaḇîa'*, Je. 35:5, evidently a ewer, *cf.* *CUP; *dûḏ*, a spherical cooking-pot (1 Sa. 2:14; Jb. 41:20) (*BASKET); *kaḏ*, pitcher, probably both the large handled jar and the crock-like, hole-mouth jar (Gn. 24:14ff.; Jdg. 7:16ff.); *kôs* (*CUP); *kiyyôr*, a bowl of pottery (Zc. 12:6) or metal (Ex. 30:18; 1 Ki. 7:20; 1 Sa. 2:14; on 2 Ch. 6:13, see W. F. Albright, *Archaeology and the Religion of Israel*, 1956); *kîrayîm*, clay rings on which round-based jars stood (Lv. 11:35); *maḥ^{a}ḇaṯ*, a pottery or metal disc or griddle on which pancakes were baked (Lv. 2:5; Ezk. 4:3); *marḥešeṯ*, a cooking-pot (Lv. 2:7; 7:9); *maśrēṯ*, a cooking-pot or handled pan (2 Sa. 13:9); *miš'ereṯ*, kneading-trough; *nēḇel*, large wine jar (Is. 30:14; Je. 48:12; La. 4:2) (*BOTTLE); *sîr*, any large cooking-pot (2 Ki. 4:38; Jb. 41:31) (*FLESH-POTS); *cf.* *WASHBASIN; *sap̄*, a bowl (*CUP); *sēp̄el*, a large, valuable bowl (Jdg. 5:25; 6:38); *paḵ*, juglet (*BOX); *pārûr*, a pot with a handle for heating liquids (Jdg. 6:19); *ṣ^{e}lōḥîṯ*, a deep handle-less bowl (2 Ki. 2:20; 21:13); *ṣāmîḏ*, a shallow bowl serving as a lid (Nu. 19:15); *ṣappaḥaṯ*, a flask or juglet (1 Sa. 26:11ff.; 1 Ki. 17:12ff.; 19:6); *qallaḥaṯ*, a cooking-pot (1 Sa. 2:14; Mi. 3:3); Gk. *modios*, a vessel holding *c.* 9 litres (Mt. 5:15); *niptēr*, a wash-basin, defined as foot-wash-basin in papyrus Bodmer II (Jn. 13:5); *potērion* (*CUP); *tryblion*, a fairly large bowl (Mt. 26:23); *phialē*, a broad dish for holding unguents (Rev. 5:8).

BIBLIOGRAPHY. K. M. Kenyon, *Archaeology in the Holy Land*, 1960; W. F. Albright, *Archaeology of Palestine*, 1960; M. Burrows, *What Mean These Stones?*, 1941, pp. 159–171; R. B. K. Amiran, *Ancient Pottery of the Holy Land*, 1969; P. W. and N. Lapp, *Palestinian Ceramic Chronology, 200 B.C.–A.D. 70*, 1961. A.R.M.

POVERTY.

I. In the Old Testament

The impression is sometimes given that God prospered the righteous with material possessions (Ps. 112:1–3). While it is true that the benefits of industry and thrift to individuals and to the nation are clearly seen, and that God promises to bless those who keep his commandments (Dt. 28:1–14), there were numbers of poor people in Israel at every stage of the nation's history. Their poverty might have been caused through natural disasters leading to bad harvests, through enemy invasion, through oppression by powerful neighbours or through extortionate usury. There was an obligation on the wealthier members of the community to support their poorer brethren (Dt. 15:1–11). Those who were most likely to suffer poverty were the fatherless and the widows and the landless aliens (*gērîm*). They were often the victims of oppression (Je. 7:6; Am. 2:6–7a), but Yahweh was their vindicator (Dt. 10:17–19; Ps. 68:5–6). The law commanded that provision should be made for them (Dt. 24:19–22), and with them were numbered the Levites (Dt. 14:28–29) because they had no holding of land. A man could sell himself into slavery, but if he were a Hebrew he had to be treated differently from a foreigner (Lv. 25:39–46).

It was a problem to some of the psalmists to understand how in so many cases wealth had come into the wrong hands. On purely material grounds it might seem vain to serve Yahweh (Ps. 73:12–14), but in the end the wicked would come to destruction while the righteous enjoyed the richest possession—the knowledge of Yahweh himself (Ps. 73:16–28). But so often were the rich oppressors that 'the poor' became almost a synonym for 'the pious' (Ps. 14:5–6).

II. In the New Testament

There were heavy taxes of various kinds imposed on the Jews in NT times. Probably many were in severe economic straits, while others made considerable profits from collaborating with the Romans. The worldly-minded Sadducees were generally wealthy, as were the tax-collectors.

Jesus was the son of poor parents (Lk. 2:24), but there is no reason to suppose he lived in abject poverty. As the eldest son, he would probably have inherited something from Joseph, and it appears that he used to pay the Temple tax (Mt. 17:24). Some of his disciples were reasonably well-to-do (Mk. 1:20) and he had some fairly wealthy friends (Jn. 12:3). He and the Twelve, however, shared a common purse (Jn. 12:6). They were content to go without the comforts of home life (Lk. 9:58), and yet found occasion for giving to the poor (Jn. 13:29).

In the teaching of Jesus material possessions are not regarded as evil, but as dangerous. The poor are often shown to be happier than the rich, because it is easier for them to have an attitude of dependence upon God. It was to them that he came to preach the gospel (Lk. 4:18; 7:22). It is they who are the first to be blessed and to be assured of the possession of the kingdom of God (Lk. 6:20), if their poverty is the acknowledgment of spiritual bankruptcy (Mt. 5:3). A poor person's offering may be of much greater value than a rich man's (Mk. 12:41–44). The poor must be shown hospitality (Lk. 14:12–14), and given alms (Lk. 18:22), though charity was to be secondary to worship (Jn. 12:1–8).

The early church made an experiment in the communal holding of wealth (Acts 2:41–42; 4:32). This led at first to the elimination of poverty (Acts 4:34–35), but it has often been held that it was responsible for the later economic collapse of the church at Jerusalem. Much of the ministry of Paul was concerned with raising money in the Gentile churches to assist the poor Christians in Jerusalem (Rom. 15:25–29; Gal. 2:10). These churches were also taught to provide for their own poor members (Rom. 12:13, *etc.*). James is especially vehement against those who allowed distinctions of wealth in the Christian community (Jas. 2:1–7). The poor were called by God and their salvation brought glory to him (1 Cor. 1:26–31). The material wealth of the church of Laodicea was in sad contrast with her spiritual poverty (Rev. 3:17).

The most systematic exposition about poverty and wealth in the Epistles is found in 2 Cor. 8–9, where Paul sets the idea of Christian charity in the context of the gifts of God and especially that of his Son who, 'though he was rich, yet for your sake he became poor, so that by his poverty you might become rich'. In the light of that, running the risk of material poverty will lead to spiritual blessing, just as the apostles were poor but made many rich (2 Cor. 6:10). (*ALMS; *ORPHAN.)

BIBLIOGRAPHY. M. Hengel, *Property and Riches in the Early Church*, E.T. 1974. R.E.N.

POWER.

I. In the Old Testament

Various Heb. words are rendered 'power', the principal ones being *ḥayil*, *kōaḥ* and *'ōz*. True power, the ability to exercise authority effectively, belongs to God alone (Ps. 62:11). The power of God is shown in the creation (Ps. 148:5) and the sustaining of the world (Ps. 65:5–8). Some of his authority is delegated to mankind (Gn. 1:26–28; Pss. 8:5–8; 115:16), but God actively intervenes on many occasions, showing his power in miraculous deeds of deliverance. It was 'with mighty hand and outstretched arm' that he brought his people out of Egypt (Ex. 15:6; Dt. 5:15, *etc.*), and he demonstrated his power in giving them the promised land (Ps. 111:6).

II. In the New Testament

'Power' in EVV represents chiefly Gk. *dynamis* and *exousia*. *exousia* means derived or conferred 'authority', the warrant or right to do something (Mt. 21:23–27); from this it comes to denote concretely the bearer of authority on earth (Rom. 13:1–3), or in the spirit world (Col. 1:16). *dynamis* is ability (2 Cor. 8:3) or strength (Eph. 3:16), or it may mean a powerful act (Acts 2:22) or a powerful spirit (Rom. 8:38). Christ had all authority given him by his Father (Mt. 28:18) and he used it to forgive sins (Mt. 9:6) and to cast out evil spirits (Mt. 10:1). He gave authority to his disciples to become sons of God (Jn. 1:12) and to share in his work (Mk. 3:15).

Jesus came to his ministry in the power (*dynamis*) of the Spirit (Lk. 4:14), and his power was operative in healing miracles (Lk. 5:17) and he did many mighty works (Mt. 11:20). This was evidence of the power of the kingdom of God as a prelude to the new Exodus (Lk. 11:20; *cf.* Ex. 8:19). But the kingdom had not yet come in its full power. That would happen at Pentecost (Lk. 24:49; Acts 1:8; ?Mk. 9:1) and there would be the consummation at the parousia (Mt. 24:30, *etc.*).

In the Acts we see the power of the Spirit operative in the life of the church (4:7, 33; 6:8; *cf.* 10:38). Paul looks back to the resurrection as the chief evidence of God's power (Rom. 1:4; Eph. 1:19–20; Phil. 3:10) and sees the gospel as the means by which that power comes to work in men's lives (Rom. 1:16; 1 Cor. 1:18). (*AUTHORITY.)

BIBLIOGRAPHY. D. M. Lloyd-Jones, *Authority*, 1958; Cyril H. Powell, *The Biblical Concept of Power*, 1963; G. B. Caird, *Principalities and Powers*, 1956; A. Richardson, *An Introduction to the Theology of the New Testament*, 1958, pp. 62ff.; W. Grundmann in *TDNT* 2, pp. 284–317; 3, pp. 397–402; W. Foerster, *TDNT* 2, pp. 562–574; O. Betz in *NIDNTT* 2, pp. 601–611. R.E.N.

POWER OF THE KEYS. This is the phrase used to describe the authority given by our Lord to his disciples as described in Mt. 16:19; 18:18; Jn. 20:22–23. It is a power which may be said to operate in two ways. First, by preaching the gospel the kingdom of God is opened to believers and shut to the impenitent, and secondly, by discipline, serious offenders are excluded from the church until they repent, whereupon they are readmitted. In either case, forgiveness is mediated through the church, acting in the Spirit and through the Word.

'Since it is the doctrine of the gospel that opens heaven to us, it is beautifully expressed by the metaphorical appellation of "keys".' 'Binding and loosing are simply nothing other than the preaching and application of the gospel' (Luther). That keys and doctrine are so connected is seen from the fact that the delivery of a key was part of a scribe's ordination (Mt. 13:52; Lk. 11:52). Through the preaching of the gospel some men are reconciled to God by faith, others are more firmly bound by unbelief. The church, acting as Christ's representative (Lk. 10:16), pronounces absolution to the penitent. This is a real transaction only in so far as the church is filled with the Spirit of God, so that then it gives the actual judgment of God himself. * Binding and loosing mean not merely the authoritative announcement of the conditions of entrance into the kingdom; a stronger sense is necessary—determining which individuals have accepted the conditions.

This power was given in a special sense to Peter, for he, at Pentecost, opened the door of faith to the Jews, and later to the Gentiles and Samaritans. But it was given to all the apostles (Jn. 20:23) and to men of like faith and spirit ever since.

POWER, DIVINE See Spirit, Part 3.

PRAETOR
See Province, Part 3.

In the further exercise of the power of the keys, in ecclesiastical discipline, the thought is of administrative authority (Is. 22:22) with regard to the requirements of the household of faith. The use of censures, excommunication and absolution is committed to the church in every age, to be used under the guidance of the Spirit. 'Whoever, after committing a crime, humbly confesses his fault and entreats the church to forgive him, is absolved not only by men, but by God himself; and, on the other hand, whoever treats with ridicule the reproofs and threatenings of the church, if he is condemned by her, the decision which men have given will be ratified in heaven' (Calvin on 1 Cor. 5).

Since the Reformers it has been accepted that 'the power of the keys' represented this *duplex ministerium*, a real power of spiritual binding and loosing. But this judicial sense has been sharply challenged in favour of a legislative sense whereby 'loose' means 'permitted', and 'bind' means 'forbidden'. This is in agreement with rabbinic usage: the school of Shammai was said to *bind* when it declared that there was only one ground for divorce; the school of Hillel *loosed* when it allowed more laxity in this and other questions. For this use, see also Mt. 23:4; Rom. 7:2; 1 Cor. 7:27, 39. So Peter, in T. W. Manson's words, is to be 'God's vicegerent . . . The authority of Peter is an authority to declare what is right and wrong for the Christian community. His decisions will be confirmed by God' (*The Sayings of Jesus*, 1954, p. 205). But note that this special rabbinical application of the words was based on the juristic character of the rabbinic literature, and that it was originally used of the full power of the judge (*cf. TDNT* 3, p. 751). Even granting a late origin for Mt. 18:18, we are left with the question as to why a context of church discipline should early seem suitable for the words 'bind' and 'loose'. A. H. McNeile questions the authenticity of this passage altogether, but J. Jeremias has argued ingeniously for its trustworthiness (*TDNT* 3, pp. 752f.).

In any case, it is hardly right to make Peter, as this view does, a scribe in the kingdom of God. 'The apostle would, in the coming kingdom, be like a great scribe or Rabbi, who would deliver decisions on the basis . . . of the teaching of Jesus' (A. H. McNeile). But there is a great difference between the pronouncements of the apostles on ethical matters and the encyclopaedic casuistry of the scribes. Mt. 23:8 made it impossible for Peter to aspire to such a function. The principle of Christian ethics is to look after the big things (mercy, love, truth) and the little things will then look after themselves; not detailed prescribed legislation, but the guidance of the Spirit.

Bibliography. Calvin's Commentaries on the Matthaean passages and on 1 Cor. 5 present a fair representation of the views of all the Reformers. In addition to the modern writers cited, R. N. Flew discusses these questions in *Jesus and His Church*, 1938, pp. 131f. See also *DCG* (*s.v.* 'Absolution'); *ERE* (*s.v.* 'Discipline'); Calvin, *Institutes*, 4. 12; J. Jeremias, *TDNT* 3, pp. 744–753; D. Müller, C. Brown, *NIDNTT* 2, pp. 731–733. R.N.C.

PRAETORIUM. Originally the tent of the commander, or praetor, and, in consequence, the army headquarters (Livy, 7. 12; Caesar, *Bellum Civile* 1. 76). By extension the word came to mean the residence of a provincial governor (Mt. 27:27; Mk. 15:16; Jn. 18:28, 33; 19:9; Acts 23:35). If Paul was writing from Rome, Phil. 1:13 may refer to the emperor's residence on the Palatine. The word seems not to have been used for the permanent camp of the praetorian guards by the Porta Viminalis. It does, however, sometimes mean the forces of the praetorian guards (*CIL*, 5. 2837; 8. 9391), and, whether the letter was written at Ephesus or Rome, this gives good sense to Paul's phrase. Detachments of *praetoriani* were sent to the provinces, and in Rome they would have charge of prisoners in imperial custody.

E.M.B.

PRAISE. In the OT the words for praise mainly used are *hālal*, the root meaning of which is connected with making a noise; *yāḏâ*, which was originally associated with the bodily actions and gestures which accompany praising; and *zāmar*, which is associated with the playing or singing of music. In the NT *eucharistein* (lit. 'to give thanks') is the favourite word, implying on the part of the person who praises the attitude of one more intimate with the person praised than in the more formal *eulogein*, 'to bless'.

The whole of the Bible is punctuated with outbursts of praise. They rise spontaneously from the 'basic mood' of joy which marks the life of the people of God. God takes pleasure and delight in his works of creation (Gn. 1; Ps. 104:31; Pr. 8:30–31), and all creation, including the angels, expresses its joy in praise (Jb. 38:4–7; Rev. 4:6–11). Man also was created to rejoice in God's works (Ps. 90:14–16) and fulfils this purpose by accepting God's gifts (Ec. 8:15; 9:7; 11:9; Phil. 4:4, 8; *cf.* also W. Eichrodt, *Man in the Old Testament*, 1951, p. 35).

The coming of the kingdom of God into the midst of this world is marked by the restoration of joy and praise to the people of God and the whole creation (Is. 9:2; Ps. 96:11–13; Rev. 5:9–14; Lk. 2:13–14), a foretaste of which is already given in the ritual and worship of the Temple where praise arises from sheer joy in the redeeming presence of God (Dt. 27:7; Nu. 10:10; Lv. 23:40). The praise of God is rendered on earth for the works both of creation and redemption (Pss. 24; 136), this being an echo on earth of the praise of heaven (Rev. 4:11; 5:9–10). Praise, therefore, is a mark of the people of God (1 Pet. 2:9; Eph. 1:3–14; Phil. 1:11). It is the mark of the heathen that they refuse to render it (Rom. 1:21; Rev. 16:9). The act of praising implies the closest fellowship with the One who is being praised. 'Therefore praise not merely expresses but completes the enjoyment; it is its appointed consummation. . . . In commanding us to glorify Him, God is inviting us to enjoy Him' (C. S. Lewis, *Reflections on the Psalms*, 1958, p. 95).

Yet praise to God is frequently commanded from men as a duty and is obviously not meant to depend on mood or feeling or circumstances (*cf.* Jb. 1:21). To 'rejoice before the Lord' is part of the ordered ritual of the common life of his people (Dt. 12:7; 16:11–12), in which men encourage and exhort one another to praise. Though there are psalms which express the praise of the individual, it was always felt that praise could best be rendered within the congregation (Pss. 22:25; 34:3; 35:18), where praise not only gives honour and pleasure to God (Ps. 50:23) but also bears testimony to God's people (Ps. 51:12–15).

Elaborate arrangements were made for the conduct of praise in the Temple by the Levites. The Psalms were used in the liturgy and in sacred processions with 'glad shouts and songs' (Ps. 42:4). The singing was probably antiphonal, involving two choirs, or soloist and choir. Dancing, from earliest times a means of expressing praise (Ex. 15:20; 2 Sa. 6:14), was also used in the Temple to this end (Pss. 149:3; 150:4). Ps. 150 gives a list of musical instruments used in the praise. (*MUSIC AND MUSICAL INSTRUMENTS.)

The early Christians continued to express their gladness by attending worship in the Temple (Lk. 24:53; Acts 3:1). But their experience of new life in Christ was bound to express itself in new forms of praise (Mk. 2:22). Joy was the dominant mood of the Christian life, and though the formal worship and praise which it inspired is not explicitly described or prescribed, this was because it was so much taken for granted. As those who experienced and witnessed the healing and cleansing power of Jesus broke out spontaneously into praise (Lk. 18:43; Mk. 2:12), so also in the apostolic church there are frequent examples of such spontaneous outbursts, as men began to see and understand the power and goodness of God in Christ (Acts 2:46; 3:8; 11:18; 16:25; Eph. 1:1–14).

The Psalms were undoubtedly used to express the praise of the early church (Col. 3:16; *cf.* Mt. 26:30). There were also new Christian hymns (*cf.* Rev. 5:8–14), referred to in Col. 3:16; 1 Cor. 14:26. We have examples of such inspiration to new forms of praise in the *Magnificat, *Benedictus and *Nunc Dimittis (Lk. 1:46–55, 68–79; 2:29–32). Elsewhere in the text of the NT there are examples of the formal praise of the early church. It seems likely from its literary form and content that Phil. 2:6–11 was composed and used as a hymn of praise to Christ. Probably there are echoes of, or quotations from, early hymns in such passages as Eph. 5:14 and 1 Tim. 3:16. The doxologies in the book of Revelation (*cf.* Rev. 1:4–7; 5:9–14; 15:3–4) must have been used in public worship to express the praise of the congregation (*cf.* A. B. Macdonald, *Christian Worship in the Primitive Church*, 1934).

The close connection between praise and sacrifice should be noted. In the sacrificial ritual of the OT a place was found for the sacrifice of thanksgiving as well as of expiation (*cf.* Lv. 7:11–21). Gratitude was to be the fundamental motive behind the bringing of the first-fruits to the altar (Dt. 26:1–11). In the sincere offering of praise itself there is a sacrifice which pleases God (Heb. 13:15; Ho. 14:2; Ps. 119:108). In the priestly self-offering of Jesus this aspect of thanksgiving finds its place (Mk. 14:22–23, 26; Jn. 17:1–2; Mt. 11:25–26). The life of the Christian should, correspondingly, be a self-offering of gratitude (Rom. 12:1) in fulfilment of his royal priesthood (Rev. 1:5–6; 1 Pet. 2:9), and the fact that such a sacrificial self-offering can be made in a real way in the midst of suffering, links suffering and praise together in the Christian life (Phil. 2:17). Thanksgiving sanctifies not only suffering but all aspects of the life of the Christian (1 Tim. 4:4–5; 1 Cor. 10:30–31; 1 Thes. 5:16–18). Whatever else be the burden of prayer, it must include praise (Phil. 4:6).

BIBLIOGRAPHY. H. Ringgren, *The Faith of the Psalmists*, 1963; C. Westermann, *The Praise of God in the Psalms*, 1965; A. A. Anderson, *The Book of Psalms*, 1972, 1, pp. 31–36; H.-G. Link, *NIDNTT* 1, pp. 206–215; H. Schultz, H.-H. Esser, *NIDNTT* 3, pp. 816–820.

R.S.W.

PRAYER.

I. Introduction

In the Bible prayer is worship that includes all the attitudes of the human spirit in its approach to God. The Christian worships God when he adores, confesses, praises and supplicates him in prayer. This highest activity of which the human spirit is capable may also be thought of as communion with God, so long as due emphasis is laid upon divine initiative. A man prays because God has already touched his spirit. Prayer in the Bible is not a 'natural response' (see Jn. 4:24). 'That which is born of the flesh is flesh.' Consequently, the Lord does not 'hear' every prayer (Is. 1:15; 29:13). The biblical doctrine of prayer emphasizes the character of God, the necessity of a man's being in saving or covenant relation with him, and his entering fully into all the privileges and obligations of that relation with God.

II. In the Old Testament

Köhler (*Old Testament Theology*, 1957, p. 251, n. 153) finds 'about eighty-five original prayers in the OT. In addition there are about sixty whole psalms and fourteen parts of psalms which may be called prayers.'

a. The patriarchal period

In the patriarchal period prayer is calling upon the name of the Lord (Gn. 4:26; 12:8; 21:33); *i.e.* the sacred name is used in invocation or appeal. There is, consequently, an unmistakable directness and familiarity in prayer (Gn. 15:2ff.;

A divine intercessor, the Babylonian goddess Lama, raises both hands in prayer. Clay plaque from Ur, chapel of Hendursag. Height c. 13 cm. c. 2000 BC. (BM)

18:23ff.; 24:12–14, 26f.). Prayer is also closely connected with sacrifice (Gn. 13:4; 26:25; 28:20–22), although this association appears in later periods too. This offering of prayer in a context of sacrifice suggests a union of man's will with God's will, an abandonment and submission of the self to God. This is especially so in Jacob's conjoining prayer with a vow to the Lord. The vow, itself a prayer, promises service and faithfulness if the blessing sought is granted (Gn. 28:20ff.).

b. The pre-exilic period

1. In this period one of the main emphases in prayer is intercession; although this was also a factor in patriarchal times (Gn. 18:22ff.). Intercession was especially prominent in the prayers of Moses (Ex. 32:11–13, 31f.; 33:12–16; 34:9; Nu. 11:11–15; 14:13–19; 21:7; Dt. 9:18–21; 10:10). Dt. 30 is also largely a prayer of intercession, as are also the prayers of Aaron (Nu. 6:22–27), Samuel (1 Sa. 7:5–13; 12:19, 23), Solomon (1 Ki. 8:22–53), and Hezekiah (2 Ki. 19:14–19). The inference seems to be that intercession was confined to outstanding personalities who, by virtue of their position assigned to them by God as prophets, priests and kings, had peculiar power in prayer as mediators between God and men. But the Lord always remained free to execute his will; hence we hear of unsuccessful intercession (Gn. 18:17ff.; Ex. 32:30–35). In Am. 7:1–6 'the Lord repented' concerning a certain course of action in answer to the prophet's intercession, and in the next verses (7:7–8:2) Israel is to be led away captive after all. Jeremiah is even forbidden to intercede with God (Je. 7:16; 11:14; 14:11). On the other hand, success attended the intercession of Lot (Gn. 19:17–23), Abraham (Gn. 20:17), Moses (Ex. 9:27–33; Nu. 12:9ff.), and Job (Jb. 42:8, 10). It is the strongly personal relation with God in which those mediators stood that underlies these intercessory prayers.

2. It is surprising that among all the legal enactments of the Pentateuch there is nothing about prayer apart from Dt. 26:1–15. Even here it is formulae for worship rather than prayer that are being emphasized. In vv. 5–11 there is thanksgiving, and in vv. 13–14 there is a profession of past obedience, but only in v. 15 is there supplication. However, we are probably right in assuming that sacrifice would often be offered with prayer (Ps. 55:14), and where it was not it might be reproved (Ps. 50:7–15). On the other hand, the almost total absence of prayer in those parts of the Pentateuch where sacrifice is regulated suggests that sacrifice without prayer was fairly common.

3. Prayer must have been indispensable in the ministry of the prophets. The very reception of the revelatory Word from God involved the prophet in a prayerful relation with Yahweh. Indeed, it might well have been that prayer was essential to the prophet's receiving the Word (Is. 6:5ff.; 37:1–4; Je. 11:20–23; 12:1–6; 42:1ff.). The prophetic vision came to Daniel while he was at prayer (Dn. 9:20ff.). On occasion the Lord kept the prophet waiting for a considerable time in prayer (Hab. 2:1–3). We know from Jeremiah's writings that while prayer was the essential condition of, and reality in, the prophet's experience and ministry, it was often a tempestuous exercise of the spirit (18:19–23; 20:7–18), as well as a sweet fellowship with God (1:4ff.; 4:10; 10:23–25; 12:1–4; 14:7–9, 19–22; 15:15–18; 16:19; 17:12ff.).

4. In the Psalms there is a blending of pattern and spontaneity in prayer. Alongside the more formal 'sanctuary' prayers (*e.g.* 24:7–10; 100; 150) there are personal prayers for pardon (51), communion (63), protection (57), healing (6), vindication (109) and prayers that are full of praise (103). Sacrifice and prayer also blend in the psalms (54:6; 66:13ff.).

c. The exilic period

During the Exile the important factor in religion for the Jews was the emergence of the synagogue. The Jerusalem Temple was in ruins, and altar rites and sacrifices could not be performed in unclean Babylon. A Jew was now no longer one who had been born into the community, and was residing in it, but rather one who *chose* to be a Jew. The centre of the religious community was the synagogue, and among the accepted religious obligations such as circumcision, fasting and sabbath observance, prayer was important. This was inevitable because each little community in exile now depended upon the synagogue service where the Word was read and expounded, and prayers were offered. And after the return to Jerusalem, just as the Temple was not allowed to displace the synagogue, nor the priest the scribe, nor sacrifice the living Word, so ritual did not displace prayer. Both in Temple and synagogue, in priestly ritual and scribal exposition, the devout worshipper now sought the face of Yahweh, his personal presence (Pss. 100:2; 63:1ff.), and received his blessing in terms of the light of his countenance shining upon him (Ps. 80:3, 7, 19).

d. The post-exilic period

After the Exile there was undoubtedly a framework of devotion, but within it freedom was secured for the individual. This is exemplified in Ezra and Nehemiah, who, while insisting upon cult and law, and upon ritual and sacrifice and, therefore, upon the social aspects of worship, yet emphasized also the spiritual factor in devotion (Ezr. 7:27; 8:22f.; Ne. 2:4; 4:4, 9). Their prayers are also instructive (Ezr. 9:6–15; Ne. 1:5–11; 9:5–38; *cf.* also Dn. 9:4–19). We may also note here that concerning posture in prayer there were no fixed rules (Ps. 28:2; 1 Sa. 1:26; 1 Ki. 8:54; Ezr. 9:5; 1 Ki. 18:42; La. 3:41; Dn. 9:3 and v . 20 where we should read 'towards' instead of 'for'). So also in the matter of hours for prayer: prayer was effective at any time, as well as at the stated hours (Ps. 55:17; Dn. 6:10). In the post-exilic period, then, we find a blending of orderliness of Temple ritual, the simplicity of the synagogue meeting, and the spontaneity of personal devotion.

Prayer being what it is, it would be manifestly impossible to systematize it completely. Within the OT there are certainly patterns for prayer but no binding regulations governing either its contents or its ritual. Mechanical prayer, prayer hemmed in by coercive prescriptions, did not come until towards the close of the intertestamental period, as the Gospels make clear. Then, alas, both through Temple sacrifice in Jerusalem, and in the *diaspora* through the praise, prayer and exposition of the synagogue service, and through circumcision, sabbath observance, tithes, fasting and supererogatory deeds, worshippers in both Temple and synagogue sought to merit acceptance with God.

III. In the New Testament

There are certain clearly-defined areas where the NT teaching on prayer is set forth, but the fountain-head from which all its intruction in prayer flows is Christ's wn doctrine and practice.

. The Gospels

. As to Jesus' doctrine of prayer, his is set out principally in certain f his parables. In the parable of he friend who borrowed three oaves at midnight (Lk. 11:5–8) the ord inculcates importunity in rayer; and the ground on which he confidence in importunate rayer is built is the Father's gene- osity (Mt. 7:7–11). The parable of he unjust judge (Lk. 18:1–8) calls or tenacity in prayer, which in- ludes persistence as well as con- inuity. God's delays in answering rayer are due not to indifference ut to love that desires to develop nd deepen faith which is finally indicated. In the parable of the ax collector and the Pharisee (Lk. 8:10–14) Christ insists on humility nd penitence in prayer, and warns gainst a sense of self-superiority. elf-humiliation in prayer means cceptance with God, self- xaltation in prayer hides God's ace. Christ calls for charity in rayer in the parable of the unjust ervant (Mt. 18:21–35). It is prayer ffered by a forgiving spirit that God answers. Simplicity in prayer s taught in Mt. 6:5f.; 23:14; Mk. 2:38–40; Lk. 20:47. Prayer must be urged of all pretence. It should pring from simplicity of heart and notive, and express itself in sim- licity of speech and petition. The ord also urged intensity in prayer *cf.* Mk. 13:33; 14:38; Mt. 26:41). Here watchfulness and faith com- ine in sleepless vigilance. Again, n Mt. 18:19f. unity in prayer is em- hasized. If a group of Christians vho have the mind of Christ pray n the Holy Spirit their prayers will e effectual. But prayer must also e expectant (Mk. 11:24). Prayer hat is an experiment achieves little; rayer which is the sphere where aith operates in surrender to God's vill achieves much (Mk. 9:23).

2. On objectives in prayer Jesus ad singularly little to say. Doubt- ess he was content to let the Holy pirit prompt his disciples in rayer. What aims he referred to n prayer are to be found in Mk. :28f.; Mt. 5:44; 6:11, 13; 9:36ff.; k. 11:13.

3. As to method in prayer, the ord had two important things to each. First, prayer is now to be ffered to him, as it was offered to im when he was on earth (*e.g.* Mt. :2; 9:18). As he insisted on faith hen (Mk. 9:23), and tested sincerity (Mt. 9:27–31), and uncovered ignorance (Mt. 20:20–22) and sinful presumption (Mt. 14:27–31), in those who petitioned him, so he does today in the experience of those who offer prayer to him. Secondly, prayer is now also to be offered in the name of Christ (Jn. 14:13; 15:16; 16:23f.), through whom we have access to the Father. To pray in the name of Christ is to pray as Christ himself prayed, and to pray to the Father as the Son has made him known to us: and for Jesus the true focus in prayer was the Father's will. Here is the basic characteristic of Christian prayer: a new access to the Father which Christ secures for the Christian, and prayer in harmony with the Father's will because offered in Christ's name.

4. As to the Lord's practice of prayer, it is well known that he prayed in secret (Lk. 5:15f.; 6:12); in times of spiritual conflict (Jn. 12:20–28; Lk. 22:39–46); and on the cross (Mt. 27:46; Lk. 23:46). In his prayers he offered thanksgiving (Lk. 10:21; Jn. 6:11; 11:41; Mt. 26:27), sought guidance (Lk. 6:12ff.), interceded (Jn. 17:6–19, 20–26; Lk. 22:31–34; Mk. 10:16; Lk. 23:34) and communed with the Father (Lk. 9:28ff.). The burden of his high-priestly prayer in Jn. 17 is the unity of the church.

5. Since the *Lord's Prayer is treated more fully elsewhere, it will suffice to point out that after the invocation (Mt. 6:9b) there follow six petitions (9c–13b), of which the first three have reference to God's name, kingdom and will, and the last three to man's need of bread, forgiveness and victory: the Prayer then closes with a doxology (13c) which contains a threefold declaration concerning God's kingdom, power and glory. It is 'like this' that Christians are bidden to pray.

b. The Acts of the Apostles

The Acts is an excellent link between the Gospels and the Epistles, because in Acts the apostolic church puts into effect our Lord's teaching on prayer. The church was born in the atmosphere of prayer (1:4). In answer to prayer the Spirit

Man praying. Detail from the papyrus of the Book of the Dead of Hunefer. 19th Dynasty. 1300 BC. (RS)

was poured out upon her (1:4; 2:4). Prayer continued to be the church's native air (2:42; 6:4, 6). There remained in the church's thinking a close connection between prayer and the Spirit's presence and power (4:31). In times of crisis the church had recourse to prayer (4:23ff.; 12:5, 12). Throughout the Acts the church leaders emerge as men of prayer (9:40; 10:9; 16:25; 28:8) who urge the Christians to pray with them (20:28, 36; 21:5).

c. The Pauline Epistles

It is significant that immediately after Christ revealed himself to Paul on the Damascus road it is said of Paul, 'Behold, he is praying' (Acts 9:11). Probably for the first time Paul discovered what prayer really was, so profound was the change in his heart which conversion had effected. From that moment he was a man of prayer. In prayer the Lord spoke to him (Acts 22:17f.). Prayer was thanksgiving, intercession, the realization of God's presence (*cf.* 1 Thes. 1:2f.; Eph. 1:16ff.). He found that the Holy Spirit assisted him in prayer as he sought to know and do God's will (Rom. 8:14, 26). In his experience there was a close connection between prayer and the Christian's intelligence (1 Cor. 14:14–19). Prayer was absolutely essential for the Christian (Rom. 12:12). The Christian's armour (Eph. 6:13–17) included prayer which Paul describes as 'all prayer', to be offered at 'all seasons', with 'all perseverance', for 'all saints' (v. 18). And Paul practised what he preached (Rom. 1:9; Eph. 1:16; 1 Thes. 1:2); hence his insistence upon prayer when writing to his fellow-believers (Phil. 4:6; Col. 4:2).

In his Epistles Paul is constantly breaking out into prayer, and it is instructive to glance at some of his prayers because of their content.

1. In Rom. 1:8–12 he pours out his heart to God in thanksgiving (v. 8), insists upon serving Christ with his spirit (v. 9a), intercedes for his friends in Rome (v. 9b), expresses his desire to impart to them a spiritual gift (vv. 10f.), and declares that he too is depending upon them for spiritual uplift (v. 12).

2. In Eph. 1:15–19 Paul again thanks God for his converts (vv. 15f.), and prays that they may receive the Spirit through whom comes knowledge of God and illumination of heart (vv. 17–18a), in order that they may know the hope of God's calling, the wealth of God's inheritance, and the greatness of God's power which had been demonstrated in Christ's resurrection (vv. 18b–19).

3. Again, in Eph. 3:14–18 the apostle pleads with the Father (vv. 14f.) for his fellow-Christians that they might be increasingly conscious of God's power (v. 16), to the end that Christ might indwell them, and that they might be rooted in love (v. 17), that each together, being perfected, might be filled with the fullness of God (vv. 18f.). Both of these 'Ephesian' prayers are well summed up in Paul's threefold desire that Christians should receive knowledge and power issuing in the love of Christ, through which as individuals and a group they should achieve perfection.

4. In Col. 1:9ff. Paul again prays that the believers should know God's will through spiritual wisdom and understanding (v. 9), that practice might agree with profession (v. 10), that they might have power for their practice (v. 11), and be thankful for their immense privilege and position in the Lord Jesus (vv. 12f.).

But perhaps Paul's greatest contribution to our understanding of Christian prayer is in establishing its connection with the Holy Spirit. Prayer is in fact a gift of the Spirit (1 Cor. 14:14–16). The believer prays 'in the Spirit' (Eph. 6:18; Jude 20); hence prayer is a co-operation between God and the believer in that it is presented to the Father, in the name of the Son, through the inspiration of the indwelling Holy Spirit.

d. Hebrews, James and 1 John

The Epistle to the Hebrews makes a significant contribution to an understanding of Christian prayer. 4:14–16 shows why prayer is possible: it is possible because we have a great High Priest who is both human and divine, because he is now in the heavenly place and because of what he is now doing there. When we pray it is to receive mercy and find grace. The reference to the Lord's prayer life in 5:7–10 really teaches what prayer is: Christ's 'prayers' and 'supplications' were 'offered up' to God, and in this spiritual service he 'learned obedience' and therefore 'was heard'. In 10:19–25 the emphasis is upon corporate prayer, and the demands and motives which it involves. The place of prayer is described in 6:19.

The Epistle of James has three significant passages on prayer. Prayer in perplexity is dealt with in 1:5–8; correct motives in prayer are underlined in 4:1–3; and the significance of prayer in time of sickness is made clear in 5:13–18.

In his first Epistle, John points the way to boldness and efficacy in prayer (3:21f.), while in 5:14–16 he establishes the relation between prayer and the will of God, and shows that efficacy in prayer is especially relevant to intercession, but that situations do arise where prayer is powerless.

IV. Conclusion

The heart of the biblical doctrine of prayer is well expressed by B. F. Westcott: 'True prayer—the prayer that must be answered—is the personal recognition and acceptance of the divine will (Jn. 14:7; *cf.* Mk. 11:24). It follows that the hearing of prayer which teaches obedience is not so much the granting of a specific petition, which is assumed by the petitioner to be the way to the end desired, but the assurance that what is granted does most effectively lead to the end. Thus we are taught that Christ learned that every detail of His life and passion contributed to the accomplishment of the work which He came to fulfil, and so He was most perfectly "heard". In this sense He was "heard for his godly fear".'

BIBLIOGRAPHY. H. Trevor Hughes, *Prophetic Prayer*, 1947; F. Heiler, *Prayer*, 1932; J. G. S. S. Thomson, *The Praying Christ*, 1959; Ludwig Köhler, *Old Testament Theology*, 1957; Th. C. Vriezen, *An Outline of Old Testament Theology*, 1958; H. Schönweiss, C. Brown, G. T. D. Angel, *NIDNTT* 2, pp. 855–886; H. Greeven *et al.*, *TDNT* 2, pp. 40–41, 685–687, 775–808; 3, pp. 296–297; 5, pp. 773–799; 6, pp. 758–766; 8, pp. 244–245.

J.G.S.S.T.

PREACHING. In the NT, preaching is 'the public proclamation of Christianity to the non-Christian world' (C. H. Dodd, *The Apostolic Preaching and its Development*, 1944, p. 7). It is not religious discourse to a closed group of initiates, but open and public proclamation of God's redemptive activity in and through Jesus Christ. The current popular understanding of preaching as biblical exposition and exhortation has tended to obscure its basic meaning

I. The biblical terms

The choice of verbs in the Gk. NT for the activity of preaching points us back to its original meaning. The most characteristic (occurring over 60 times) is *kēryssō*, 'to proclaim as a herald'. In the ancient world the herald was a figure of considerable importance (*cf.* G. Friedrich, *TDNT* 3, pp. 697–714). A man of integrity and character, he was employed by the king or State to make all public proclamations. Preaching is heralding; the message proclaimed is the glad tidings of salvation. While *kēryssō* tells us something about the activity of preaching, *euangelizomai*, 'to bring good news' (from the primitive *eus*, 'good', and the verb *angellō*, 'to announce'), a common verb, used over 50 times in the NT, emphasizes the quality of the message itself. It is worthy of note that the RSV has not followed the AV in those places where it translates the verbs *diangellō*, *laleō*, *katangellō* and *dialegomai* by 'to preach'. This helps to bring into sharper focus the basic meaning of preaching.

It is not unusual to distinguish between preaching and teaching—between *kērygma* (public proclamation) and *didachē* (ethical instruction). An appeal is made to such verses as Matthew's summary of Jesus' Galilean ministry, 'He went about all Galilee, *teaching* . . . *preaching* . . . and *healing*' (Mt. 4:23), and Paul's words in Rom. 12:6–8 and 1 Cor. 12:28 on the gifts of the Spirit. While the two activities ideally conceived are distinct, both are based upon the same foundation. The *kērygma* proclaims what God has done: the *didachē* teaches the implications of this for Christian conduct.

While we have defined preaching within narrow limits in order to emphasize its essential NT meaning, this is not to suggest that it is without precedent in the OT. Certainly the Heb. prophets as they proclaimed the message of God under divine impulse were forerunners of the apostolic herald. Jonah was told to 'preach' (LXX *kēryssō*; Heb. *qârâ'*, 'to call out'), and even Noah is designated a 'preacher (*kēryx*) of righteousness' (2 Pet. 2:5). The LXX uses *kēryssō* more than 30 times, both in the secular sense of official proclamation for the king and the more religious sense of prophetic utterance (*cf.* Joel 1:14; Zc. 9:9; Is. 61:1).

II. New Testament features

Perhaps the most prominent feature in NT preaching is the sense of divine compulsion. In Mk. 1:38 it is reported that Jesus did not return to those who sought his healing power but pressed on to other towns *in order that he might preach there also*—'for that is why I came out'. Peter and John reply to the restrictions of the Sanhedrin with the declaration, 'We cannot but speak the things which we have seen and heard' (Acts 4:20). 'Woe to me if I do not preach the gospel', cries the apostle Paul (1 Cor. 9:16). This sense of compulsion is the *sine qua non* of true preaching. Preaching is not the relaxed recital of morally neutral truths: it is God himself breaking in and confronting man with a demand for decision. This sort of preaching meets with opposition. In 2 Cor. 11:23–28 Paul lists his sufferings for the sake of the gospel.

Another feature of apostolic preaching was its transparency of message and motive. Since preaching calls for faith, it is vitally important that its issues not be obscured with eloquent wisdom and lofty words (1 Cor. 1:17; 2:1–4). Paul refused to practise cunning or to tamper with God's Word, but sought to commend himself to every man's conscience by the open statement of the truth (2 Cor. 4:2). The radical upheaval within the heart and consciousness of man which is the new birth does not come about by the persuasive influence of rhetoric but by the straightforward presentation of the gospel in all its simplicity and power.

III. The essential nature of preaching

In the Gospels Jesus is characteristically portrayed as One who came 'heralding the kingdom of God'. In Lk. 4:16–21 Jesus interprets his ministry as the fulfilment of Isaiah's prophecy of a coming Servant-Messiah through whom the kingdom of God would at last be realized. This kingdom is best understood as God's 'kingly rule' or 'sovereign action'. Only secondarily does it refer to a realm or people within that realm. That God's eternal sovereignty was now invading the realm of evil powers and winning the decisive victory was the basic content of Jesus' *kērygma*.

When we move from the Synoptics into the rest of the NT we note a significant change in terminology. Instead of the 'kingdom of God' we find 'Christ' as the content of the preached message. This is variously expressed as 'Christ crucified' (1 Cor. 1:23), 'Christ . . . raised' (1 Cor. 15:12), 'the Son of God, Jesus Christ' (2 Cor. 1:19), or 'Christ Jesus as Lord' (2 Cor. 4:5). This change of emphasis is accounted for by the fact that Christ *is* the kingdom. The Jews anticipated the universal establishment of the sovereign reign of God, viz. his *kingdom*: the death and resurrection of Jesus Christ was the decisive act of God whereby his eternal sovereignty was realized in human history. With the advance of redemptive history the apostolic church could proclaim the kingdom in the more clear-cut terms of decision concerning the King. To preach Christ *is* to preach the kingdom.

One of the most important advances of NT scholarship in recent years has been C. H. Dodd's crystallization of the primitive *kērygma*. Following his approach (comparing the early speeches in Acts with the pre-Pauline credal fragments in Paul's Epistles) but interpreting the data with a slightly different emphasis, we find that the apostolic message was 'a proclamation of the death, resurrection and exaltation of Jesus that led to an evaluation of His person as both Lord and Christ, confronted man with the necessity of repentance, and promised the forgiveness of sins' (R. H. Mounce, *The Essential Nature of New Testament Preaching*, 1960, p. 84).

True preaching is best understood in terms of its relation to the wider theme of revelation. Revelation is essentially God's self-disclosure apprehended by the response of faith. Since Calvary is God's supreme self-revelation, the problem is, How can God reveal himself in the present through an act of the past? The answer is, through preaching—for preaching is the timeless link between God's redemptive act and man's apprehension of it. It is the medium through which God contemporizes his historic self-disclosure in Christ and offers man the opportunity to respond in faith.

BIBLIOGRAPHY. In addition to the books mentioned above, *cf.* C. K. Barrett, *Biblical Problems and Biblical Preaching*, 1964; E. P. Clowney, *Preaching and Biblical Theology*,

PRECEPT
See School, Part 3.

PRECIOUS STONES
See Jewels, Part 2.

1961; H. H. Farmer, *The Servant of the Word*, 1950; P. T. Forsyth, *Positive Preaching and the Modern Mind*, 1949; J. Knox, *The Integrity of Preaching*, 1957; J. S. Stewart, *Heralds of God*, 1946; J. R. W. Stott, *The Preacher's Portrait*, 1961. R.H.M.

PREDESTINATION.

I. Biblical vocabulary

The English 'predestinate' comes from Lat. *praedestino*, which the Vulgate uses to translate the Gk. *prohorizō*. RSV renders *prohorizō* as 'predestine' in Acts 4:28; Rom. 8:29–30; and 'destine' in Eph. 1:5, 12; though as 'decree' in 1 Cor. 2:7. RV has 'foreordain' in all six places.

prohorizō, which the NT uses only with God as subject, expresses the thought of appointing a situation for a person, or a person for a situation, in advance (*pro-*). The NT uses other *pro-* compounds in a similar sense: (1) *protassō*, 'arrange beforehand' (Acts 17:26); (2) *protithemai*, 'propose' (Eph. 1:9; of a human proposal, Rom. 1:13; *cf.* use of the cognate noun *prothesis*, 'purpose', 'plan', Rom. 8:28; 9:11; Eph. 1:11; 3:11; 2 Tim. 1:9); (3) *prohetoimazō*, 'prepare beforehand' (Rom. 9:23; Eph. 2:10); (4) *procheirizō*, 'appoint beforehand' (Acts 3:20; 22:14); (5) *procheirotoneō*, 'choose beforehand' (Acts 10:41). *problepō*, 'foresee', carries the thought of God's effective preordaining in Gal. 3:8; Heb. 11:40; as the context shows. So does *proginōskō*, 'foreknow' (Rom. 8:29; 11:2; 1 Pet. 1:20), and its cognate noun *prognōsis* (1 Pet. 1:2; Acts 2:23). The same sense is sometimes conveyed by the uncompounded verbs *tassō* (Acts 13:48; 22:10) and *horizō* (Lk. 22:22; Acts 2:23), the former implying a precise setting in order, the latter an exact marking out. This varied vocabulary well suggests the different facets of the idea expressed.

The NT formulates the thought of divine foreordination in another way, by telling us that what motivates and determines God's actions in his world, and among them the fortunes and destiny which he brings upon men, is his own will (nouns, *boulē*, Acts 2:23; 4:28; Eph. 1:11; Heb. 6:17; *boulēma*, Rom. 9:19; *thelēma*, Eph. 1:5, 9, 11; *thelēsis*, Heb. 2:4; verbs, *boulomai*, Heb. 6:17; Jas. 1:18; 2 Pet. 3:9; *thelō*, Rom. 9:18, 22; Col. 1:27), or his 'good pleasure' (noun, *eudokia*, Eph. 1:5, 9; Mt. 11:26; verb, *eudokeō*, Lk. 12:32; 1 Cor. 1:21; Gal. 1:15; Col. 1:19), *i.e.* his own deliberate, prior resolve. This is not, indeed, the only sense in which the NT speaks of the will of God. The Bible conceives of God's purpose for men as expressed both by his revealed commands to them and by his ordering of their circumstances. His 'will' in Scripture thus covers both his law and his plan; hence some of the above terms are also used with reference to particular divine demands (*e.g. boulē*, Lk. 7:30; *thelēma*, 1 Thes. 4:3; 5:18). But in the texts referred to above it is God's plan of events that is in view, and it is this that predestination concerns.

The OT lacks words for expressing the idea of predestination in an abstract and generalized form, but it often speaks of God purposing, ordaining or determining particular things, in contexts which call attention to the absolute priority and independence of his purposing in relation to the existence or occurrence of the thing purposed (*cf.* Ps. 139:16; Is. 14:24–27; 19:17; 46:10f.; Je. 49:20; Dn. 4:24f.).

The usage of the NT word-group is in favour of the traditional practice of defining predestination in terms of God's purpose regarding the circumstances and destinies of men. The wider aspects of his cosmic plan and government are most conveniently subsumed under the general head of *providence. To grasp the meaning of predestination as Scripture presents it, however, it must be set in its place in God's plan as a whole.

II. Biblical presentation

a. In the Old Testament

The OT presents God the Creator as personal, powerful and purposeful, and assures us that as his power is unlimited, so his purposes are certain of fulfilment (Ps. 33:10f.; Is. 14:27; 43:13; Jb. 9:12; 23:13; Dn. 4:35). He is Lord of every situation, ordering and directing everything towards the end for which he made it (Pr. 16:4), and determining every event, great or small, from the thoughts of kings (Pr. 21:1) and the premeditated words and deeds of all men (Pr. 16:1, 9) to the seemingly random fall of a lot (Pr. 16:33). Nothing that God sets before himself is too hard for him (Gn. 18:14; Je. 32:17); the idea that the organized opposition of man could in any way thwart him is simply absurd (Ps. 2:1–4). Isaiah's prophecy expands the thought of God's plan as the decisive factor in history more fully than does any other OT book. Isaiah stresses that God's purposes are everlasting, that Yahweh planned present and future happenings 'long ago', 'from the beginning' (*cf.* Is. 22:11; 37:26; 44:6–8; 46:10f.), and that, just because it is he, and no-one else, who orders all events (Is. 44:7), nothing can prevent the occurrence of the events that he has predicted (Is. 14:24–27; 44:24–45:25; *cf.* 1 Ki. 22:17–38; Ps. 33:10f.; Pr. 19:21; 21:30). Yahweh's ability to predict the seemingly incredible things that are going to happen proves his control of history, whereas the inability of the idols to foretell these things shows that they do not control it (Is. 44:6–8; 45:21; 48:12–14).

Sometimes Yahweh is pictured as reacting to developing situations in a way that might seem to imply that he had not anticipated them (*e.g.* when he repents, and reverses his prior action, Gn. 6:5; Je. 18:8, 10; 26:3, 13; Joel 2:13; Jon. 4:2). But in their biblical context it is clear that the purpose and point of these anthropomorphisms is simply to emphasize that Israel's God is really personal, and not to throw doubt on whether he really foreordains and controls human affairs.

That Yahweh governs human history teleologically, to bring about his own predestined purpose for human welfare, is made clear in the Bible story as early as the protevangelium (Gn. 3:15) and the promise to Abraham (Gn. 12:3). The theme develops through the wilderness promises of prosperity and protection in Canaan (*cf.* Dt. 28:1–14), and the prophetic pictures of the Messianic glory which would succeed God's work of judgment (Is. 9:1ff.; 11:1ff.; Je. 23:5ff.; Ezk. 34:20ff.; 37:21ff.; Ho. 3:4f., *etc.*); and it reaches its climax in Daniel's vision of God overruling the rise and fall of pagan world-empires in order to set up the rule of the Son of man (Dn. 7; *cf.* 2:31–45). A global eschatology of this order could not be seriously put forward save on the presupposition that God is the absolute Lord of history, foreseeing and foreordaining its whole course.

It is in terms of this view of God's relation to human history that the OT describes God's choice of Israel to be his covenant people, the object and instrument of his saving work. This choice was *unmerited* (Dt. 7:6f.; Ezk. 16:1ff.) and wholly gracious. It was *purposeful*; Israel was appointed a destiny, to be blessed and so to become a blessing to other nations (*cf.* Ps. 67; Is. 2:2–4; 11:9f.; 60; Zc. 8:20ff.; 14:16ff.). It was, however, for the time being *exclusive*; the selection of Israel meant the deliberate passing-by of the rest of the nations (Dt. 7:6; Ps. 147:19f.; Am. 3:2; *cf.* Rom. 9:4; Eph. 2:11f.). For more than a millennium God left them outside the covenant, objects only of his judgment for their national crimes (Am. 1:3–2:3) and for their malice against the chosen people (*cf.* Is. 13–19, *etc.*).

b. In the New Testament

The NT writers take for granted the OT faith that God is the sovereign Lord of events, and rules history for the fulfilling of his purposes. Their uniform insistence that Christ's ministry and the Christian dispensation represented the fulfilment of biblical prophecies, given centuries before (Mt. 1:22; 2:15, 23; 4:14; 8:17; 12:17ff.; Jn. 12:38ff.; 19:24, 28, 36; Acts 2:17ff.; 3:22ff.; 4:25ff.; 8:30ff.; 10:43; 13:27ff.; 15:15ff.; Gal. 3:8; Heb. 5:6; 8:8ff.; 1 Pet. 1:10ff., *etc.*), and that God's ultimate aim in inspiring the Heb. Scriptures was to instruct Christian believers (Rom. 15:4; 1 Cor. 10:11; 2 Tim. 3:15ff.), is proof enough of this. (Both convictions, be it noted, derive from our Lord himself: *cf.* Lk. 18:31ff.; 24:25ff., 44ff.; Jn. 5:39.) A new development, however, is that the idea of election, now applied, not to national Israel, but to Christian believers, is consistently individualized (*cf.* Ps. 65:4) and given a pre-temporal reference. The OT assimilates election to God's historical 'calling' (*cf.* Ne. 9:7), but the NT distinguishes the two things sharply, by representing election as God's act of predestinating sinners to salvation in Christ 'before the foundation of the world' (Eph. 1:4; *cf.* Mt. 25:34; 2 Tim. 1:9); an act correlative to his foreknowing Christ 'before the foundation of the world' (1 Pet. 1:20). The uniform NT conception is that all saving grace given to men in time (knowledge of the gospel, understanding of it and power to respond to it, preservation and final glory) flows from divine election in eternity.

Luke's language in the narrative of Acts bears striking witness to his belief, not merely that Christ was foreordained to die, rise and reign (Acts 2:23, 30f.; 3:20; 4:27f.), but that salvation is the fruit of prevenient grace (2:47; 11:18, 21–23; 14:27; 15:7ff.; 16:14; 18:27) given in accordance with divine foreordination (13:48; 18:10).

In John's Gospel Christ says that he has been sent to save a number of particular individuals whom his Father has 'given' him (Jn. 6:37ff.; 17:2, 6, 9, 24; 18:9). These are his 'sheep', his 'own' (10:14ff., 26ff.; 13:1). It was for them specifically that he prayed (17:20). He undertakes to 'draw' them to himself by his Spirit (12:32; *cf.* 6:44; 10:16, 27; 16:8ff.); to give them eternal life, in fellowship with himself and the Father (10:28; *cf.* 5:21; 6:40; 17:2; Mt. 11:27); to keep them, losing none (6:39; 10:28f.; *cf.* 17:11, 15; 18:9); to bring them to his glory (14:2f.; *cf.* 17:24), and to raise their bodies at the last day (6:39f.; *cf.* 5:28f.). The principle that those who enjoy salvation do so by reason of divine predestination is here made explicit.

The fullest elucidation of this principle is found in the writings of Paul. From all eternity, Paul declares, God has had a plan (*prothesis*) to save a church, though in earlier times it was not fully made known (Eph. 3:3–11). The aim of the plan is that men should be made God's adopted sons and be renewed in the image of Christ (Rom. 8:29), and that the church, the company of those so renewed, should grow to the fullness of Christ (Eph. 4:13). Believers may rejoice in the certainty that as part of his plan God predestinated them personally to share in this destiny (Rom. 8:28ff.; Eph. 1:3ff.; 2 Thes. 2:13; 2 Tim. 1:9; *cf.* 1 Pet. 1:1f.). The choice was wholly of grace (2 Tim. 1:9), having no regard to desert—being made, indeed, in defiance of foreseen ill-desert (*cf.* Jn. 15:19; Eph. 2:1ff.). Because God is sovereign, his predestinating choice guarantees salvation. From it flows an effectual 'calling', which elicits the response of faith which it commands (Rom. 8:28ff.; *cf.* 9:23f.; 1 Cor. 1:26ff.; Eph. 1:13; 2 Thes. 2:14); justification (Rom. 8:30); sanctification (1 Thes. 2:13); and glorification (Rom. 8:30, where the past tense implies certainty of accomplishment; 2 Thes. 2:14). Paul gives this teaching to Christians, persons who were themselves 'called', in order to assure them of their present security and final salvation, and to make them realize the extent of their debt to God's mercy. The 'elect' to whom, and of whom, he speaks in each Epistle are himself and/or the believers to whom he addresses it ('you', 'us').

It has been argued that God's foreknowledge is not foreordination, and that personal *election in the NT is grounded upon God's foresight that the persons chosen will respond to the gospel of themselves. The difficulties in this view seem to be: (1) this asserts in effect election according to works and desert, whereas Scripture asserts election to be of grace (Rom. 9:11; 2 Tim. 1:9), and grace excludes all regard to what a man does for himself (Rom. 4:4; 11:6; Eph. 2:8f.; Tit. 3:5); (2) if election is *unto* faith (2 Thes. 2:13) and good works (Eph. 2:10, AV) it cannot rest upon foresight of these things; (3) on this view, Paul ought to be pointing, not to God's election, but to the Christian's own faith, as the ground of his assurance of final salvation; (4) Scripture does appear to equate foreknowledge with foreordination (*cf.* Acts 2:23).

III. Election and reprobation

*'Reprobate' appears first in Je. 6:30 (*cf.* Is. 1:22), in a metaphor taken from metal refining. The thought is of something that, by reason of its corrupt condition, does not pass God's test, and which he therefore rejects. The metaphor reappears in the NT. It is used of the Gentile world (Rom. 1:28) and of professing Christians (1 Cor. 9:27; 2 Cor. 13:5f.; *cf.* 2 Tim. 3:8; Tit. 1:16). Christian theology since Augustine has, however, spoken of reprobation, not as God's rejection of particular sinners in history, but as that which (it is held) lies behind it—God's resolve, from all eternity, to pass them by, and not to give them his saving grace (*cf.* 1 Pet. 2:8; Jude 4). It has thus become common to define predestination as consisting of election and reprobation together.

It is disputed whether reprobation ought to be thus included in God's eternal *prothesis*. Some justify the inclusion by appeal to Rom. 9:17f., 21f.; 11:7f. It seems hard to deny, in face of 9:22, that the hardening and non-salvation of some, which in vv. 19–21 Paul proved to be within God's right, is actually part of his predestinating purpose; though it should be noticed that Paul is concerned to stress, not God's implacability towards the reprobate, but his long restraint of his wrath against persons who have become ripe for destruction (*cf.* 2:4). But to determine the exact scope of these verses in their context is not easy; see the commentaries.

BIBLIOGRAPHY. Arndt; B. B. Warfield, 'Predestination', and J. Denney, 'Reprobation', in *HDB*; Calvin, *Institutes*, 3. 21–24; *idem*, *Concerning the Eternal Predestination of God*, E.T. by J. K. S. Reid, 1960; E. Jacob, *Theology of the Old Testament*, E.T. 1958, pp. 183–207; G. C. Berkouwer, *Divine Election*, 1960; commentaries on Rom. 9–11, esp. W. Sanday and A. C. Headlam, *ICC*, 1902; P. Jacobs, H. Krienke, *NIDNTT* 1, pp. 692–697. J.I.P.

PREPARATION. The Gk. word *paraskeuē* is found in the NT with a twofold connotation. In its meaning of a definite day of preparation, it is used of the day preceding the weekly sabbath and the day which prepares for the annual Jewish Passover festival (*cf.* Jos., *Ant.* 16. 163), see Mt. 27:62; Mk. 15:42; Lk. 23:54; and especially Jn. 19, which mentions both types of preparation day. The reference in Jn. 19:14 is to *'ereḇ ha-pesaḥ*, *i.e.* the eve of the Passover (*cf. Pesaḥim* 10. 1 in the Mishnah). In Jn. 19:31, 42 there is no accompanying genitive, so the word must mean *'ereḇ šabbāṯ*, *i.e.* the day before the sabbath (as clearly in Mk. 15:42). This would be the 24 hours from 6 p.m. Thursday to 6 p.m. Friday. The second meaning is extended, in later Christian literature, to designate the sixth day of the week, *i.e.* Friday (*cf. Martyrdom of Polycarp* 7. 1; *Didache*, 8. 1); and this is the sense of *paraskeuē* in modern Greek.

For the controverted meaning of the phrase in Jn. 19:14, see J. Jeremias, *The Eucharistic Words of Jesus*, E.T.[2] 1966, pp. 80–82 (biblio.). R.P.M.

PRESBYTER, PRESBYTERY. These terms, in EVV usually rendered 'elder', 'eldership', *etc.*, are derived from the Gk. words *presbyteros*, *presbyterion* (as is also the contracted Eng. term 'priest'). The Heb. equivalent of *presbyteros* is *zāqēn*, and the Aram. equivalent is *śâb*, and all three words have the basic meaning 'old(er) man', in which sense *zāqēn* is used in Gn. 25:8; 1 Ki. 12:8; Ps. 148:12; Pr. 17:6; Je. 31:13, *etc.*, and *presbyteros* in Acts 2:17; 1 Tim. 5:1. This suggests that originally elders were men of advancing years; and that such still tended to be the case in NT times is indicated by 1 Pet. 5:1, 5; *Mishnah Aboth* 5. 21. *presbyteroi* can also mean 'men of old time', as in Mk. 7:3, 5; Heb. 11:2, and perhaps Rev. 4:4, 10, *etc.*, where the twenty-four elders may symbolize the authors of the books of the OT, which the Jews reckon as twenty-four in number (*CANON OF THE OT).

Throughout the Bible, seniority entitles people to respect (Lv. 19:32; 1 Tim. 5:1) and *age is thought of as bringing experience and therefore wisdom (1 Ki. 12:6–15; Pr. 4:1; 5:1). Consequently, the leading men of Israel, right through its OT history, are the elders of the nation (Ex. 3:16, 18; Lv. 4:15; Jdg. 21:16; 1 Sa. 4:3; 2 Sa. 3:17; 1 Ki. 8:1, 3; 2 Ki. 23:1; 1 Ch. 11:3; Ezr. 5:5, 9; Je. 26:17; Ezk. 8:1, *etc.*). Seventy of them are chosen to share the burden of ruling with Moses (Nu. 11:16–30), and the elders later do something similar for the king. Along with the priests, they are entrusted with the written Law, and charged to read it to the people (Dt. 31:9–13). When the people settle in the promised land, and are dispersed throughout its cities, the elders of the cities act as judges there (Dt. 19:12; 21:19f.; 22:15–18; Jos. 20:4; Ru. 4:2, 4, 9, 11; 1 Ki. 21:8, 11; 2 Ki. 10:1, 5), thus continuing the practice of having lay judges for lesser questions, which began in the wilderness (Ex. 18:13–26; Dt. 1:9–18). The appeal judges at Jerusalem, however, are partly lay, partly priestly (Dt. 17:8–13; 2 Ch. 19:8–11).

The lay judges of Ex. 18 and Dt. 1 are selected for their wisdom, piety and integrity. Similarly, the choice made among the elders in Nu. 11 probably reflects a recognition that age does not bring wisdom invariably. Indeed, a wise youth is better than a foolish old king (Ec. 4:13). This recognition continues in the intertestamental literature. Wisdom befits the aged, and elders ought to be wise (Ecclus. 6:34; 8:8f.; 25:3f.), but even the young are honoured if wise (Wisdom 8:10) and are treated as elders (Susanna 45, 50). Judges are men specially selected from among the elders (Susanna 5f., 41). The elders said to have been chosen from each tribe to translate the Pentateuch into Greek are marked not so much by age (*Letter of Aristeas* 122, 318) as by virtuous life and by knowledge and understanding of the Mosaic Law (32, 121f., 321). In conformity with Dt. 31, they include both laymen and priests (184, 310), but now with a large lay majority.

At Jerusalem also, the ancient link between elders and priests continues (La. 1:19; 4:16; 1 Macc. 7:33; 11:23) and is prominent in the NT (Mt. 21:23; 26:3, 47; 27:1, 3, 12, 20; 28:11f.; Acts 4:23; 23:14; 25:15). Out of it has now grown the Sanhedrin, which is the ruling council of the nation and its supreme court of justice, presided over by the high priest. The elders and chief priests are included among its seventy-one members (Mt. 27:1; Mk. 8:31; 14:53; 15:1; Lk. 22:66; Acts 4:5, 8, 23; 22:5), along with 'scribes' and 'rulers', terms which probably have very similar meanings to the other two. The elders also appear as rulers in the intertestamental literature, at Jerusalem and elsewhere (Judith 8:10f.; 1 Macc. 12:35).

For their duty of judging the people according to God's law, the priests and elders need a knowledge of God's law, and this is why the priests are given the further duty of teaching it (Lv. 10:10f.; Dt. 33:10; Mal. 2:6f.). In 1st-century Alexandria we still find the priests as well as the elders performing this duty, by expounding the Scriptures to the people in the synagogue on the sabbath (Philo, *Hypothetica* 7. 13), but in Palestine the task of teaching seems to have passed over almost entirely to the elders, who are called by this name in Lk. 7:3, in a Jerusalem synagogue inscription from before AD 70, and in the rabbinical literature, but in the NT are usually called 'scribes' (Scripture-experts), 'teachers of the law', 'lawyers' or 'rabbis'. They teach on occasion in the Temple (Lk. 2:46) but have their great centre of influence in the synagogue (Mt. 23:6; Mk. 1:21f.; Lk. 5:17; 6:6f.; 7:3–5). In the rabbinical literature, their primary duty is still to be judges, and this is why we read in the NT of excommunications from the synagogue (Jn. 9:22; 12:42; 16:2), and of punishments being inflicted in the synagogue (Mt. 23:34; Mk. 13:9; Acts 22:19; 26:11). The synagogue also has one or more 'synagogue-rulers', responsible for keeping order there (Lk. 13:14) and for choosing who should preach (Acts 13:15), read the lessons or lead the prayers; and an 'attendant' (Lk.

4:20). The non-biblical evidence suggests that these are local appointments attached to the synagogue building. The elder, on the other hand, is ordained by his teacher and thus has a wider scope for his ministry, though he usually settles and earns his living by a trade. He in turn ordains his own pupils, often with the co-operation of two other elders, and usually by the laying on of hands and thus a succession of teachers and judges, and a tradition of teaching and legal interpretation, is established and continued. Then, in the 2nd century AD, the right to ordain or authorize ordinations is concentrated in the national patriarch. *Cf.* esp. *Tosefta Sanhedrin* 1. 1; *Jerusalem Sanhedrin* 1. 2–4.

It is against this background that the Christian eldership is established, and the Jewish-Christian institution of eldership helps to unify the diversities of NT ministry, more than is often realized. Christ is the one great teacher or rabbi (Mt. 23:8). His disciples call themselves elders (1 Pet. 5:1; 2 Jn. 1; 3 Jn. 1). They pass on the teaching they have received and commit it to others, who are to commit it to others again (1 Cor. 11:23; 15:1, 3; 2 Thes. 2:15; 3:6; 2 Tim. 2:2). Those to whom it is committed are likewise called elders (Acts 14:23; Tit. 1:5). They are apparently appointed by the laying on of hands (Acts 6:6; *cf.* 11:30; 1 Tim. 4:14; 5:22; 2 Tim. 1:6). They must be ready to earn their own living if necessary (Acts 20:17, 33–35). They have the tasks of teaching (1 Tim. 5:17; Tit. 1:5, 9) and of acting as judges (Acts 15:2, 6, 22–29; 16:4). It is an open question whether a parallel is to be seen between the Jerusalem council or appeal court, consisting of apostles and elders, presided over by James the Lord's brother, and the Sanhedrin, consisting of chief priests and elders, presided over by the high priest. In addition to the tasks of teaching and judging, the task of ruling is re-emphasized in the Christian eldership, and given a pastoral rather than a political character (Acts 20:17, 28; 1 Tim. 5:17; Jas. 5:14; 1 Pet. 5:1–4; *cf.* Mt. 9:36–38; Eph. 4:11); hence the elder's other title of *bishop, and hence the disappearance of the separate office of 'synagogue-ruler' in Christianity, his task being partly absorbed by the elder, and partly, no doubt, by the owner of the house-church. The 'attendant', on the other hand, survives as the Christian deacon, though his office is still local to the extent that deacons appear in the NT only occasionally.

The Christian eldership is thus primarily an office of teaching, of adjudicating questions of right and wrong, and of providing pastoral oversight. Though elders are specially ordained, their office is not a priestly or a ceremonial one. The sacraments are under the supervision of the ordained ministry, but are not their personal prerogative. When the office of bishop becomes separated from that of elder in the 2nd century, the tasks of teaching, pastoral oversight and supervision of the sacraments are shared between the two offices; the task of acting as judge, in matters of excommunication and reconciliation, adheres primarily to the bishop; so too, for a time, does the assistance of the deacon; and so does the duty of ordination, the practice of having two others to co-operate in the bishop's own ordination, and the concept of a succession of teachers, each committing to his successor, through instruction and ordination, the message with which he has himself been entrusted. Elders, however, continue to have certain judicial duties, in the repelling of impenitent offenders from the Lord's table, and certain ordaining duties, in assisting with the ordination of other elders. (*CHURCH GOVERNMENT, *MINISTRY.)

BIBLIOGRAPHY. J. Newman, *Semikhah* (*Ordination*), 1950; E. Ferguson, *JTS* n.s. 26, 1975, pp. 1–12.

R.T.B.

PRESS, WINEFAT. A rectangular cavity hollowed out of rock or constructed artificially within which grapes were trampled underfoot, and from which the resultant juice drained into a lower receptacle. The term is applied to the whole apparatus. Its fullness was a sign of prosperity, while its emptiness represented famine.

It is used metaphorically in Is. 63:3 and in Joel 3:13, where the full press and overflowing vats indicate the greatness of the threatened carnage. It serves as a striking simile in La. 1:15, and in Rev. 14:18–20 forms part of the apocalyptic language following on the predicted fall of Babylon.

BIBLIOGRAPHY. M. Noth, *The Old Testament World*, 1966.

F.S.F.

PRESENCE
See Face, Part 1.

PRIDE. The emphasis placed on pride, and its converse humility, is a distinctive feature of biblical religion, unparalleled in other religious or ethical systems. Rebellious pride, which refuses to depend on God and be subject to him, but attributes to self the honour due to him, figures as the very root and essence of sin.

We may say with Aquinas that pride was first revealed when Lucifer attempted to set his throne on high in proud independence of God (Is. 14:12–14). The fallen devil (Lk.

An Egyptian wine-press was worked by treading grapes, which had been knocked off the vine tendrils, into juice. The extracted juice was drained off to be stored in amphorae. Copy of a wall-painting in the tomb of Nakht, Thebes. Original c. 1420 BC. (NDGD)

10:18) instilled the craving to be as gods into Adam and Eve (Gn. 3:5), with the result that man's entire nature was infected with pride through the Fall (*cf.* Rom. 1:21–23). The 'condemnation of the devil' is associated with pride in 1 Tim. 3:6 (*cf.* 'the snare of the devil' in 1 Tim. 3:7; 2 Tim. 2:26); pride was his undoing and remains the prime means by which he brings about the undoing of men and women. Hence we find a sustained condemnation of human arrogance throughout the OT, especially in the Psalms and Wisdom Literature. In Pr. 8:13 both *gē'â*, 'arrogance', and *ga'ᵃwâ*, 'insolence', are hateful to the divine wisdom: their manifestation in the form of national pride in Moab (Is. 16:6), Judah (Je. 13:9) and Israel (Ho. 5:5) are especially denounced by the prophets. The notorious 'pride which goes before a fall' is called *gā'ôn*, 'swelling excellence', in Pr. 16:18, and is rejected in favour of the lowly spirit. 'Haughtiness', *gōḇah*, appears as a root cause of atheism in Ps. 10:4. It is the downfall of Nebuchadrezzar in Dn. 4:30, 37. A milder word, *zāḏôn*, 'presumption', is applied to David's youthful enthusiasm in 1 Sa. 17:28, but in Ob. 3 even this is regarded as a deceitful evil. Further warnings against pride occur in the later Wisdom Literature, *e.g.* Ecclus. 10:6–26.

Greek teaching during the four last centuries BC was at variance with Judaism in regarding pride as a virtue and humility as despicable. Aristotle's 'great-souled man' had a profound regard for his own excellence; to underestimate it would have stamped him as mean-spirited. Similarly, the Stoic sage asserted his own moral independence and equality with Zeus. Insolence (*hybris*), however, is a deep source of moral evil in the Greek tragedy (*cf.*, *e.g.*, the *Antigone* of Sophocles).

The Christian ethic consciously rejected Greek thought in favour of the OT outlook. Humility was accorded supreme excellence when Christ pronounced himself 'gentle and lowly in heart' (Mt. 11:29). Conversely, pride (*hyperēphania*) was placed on a list of defiling vices proceeding from the evil heart of man (Mk. 7:22). In the Magnificat (Lk. 1:51f.) God is said to scatter the proud and exalt the meek. In both Jas. 4:6 and 1 Pet. 5:5, Pr. 3:34 is quoted to emphasize the contrast between the meek (*tapeinois*), whom God favours, and the proud (*hyperēphanois*), whom God resists. Paul couples the insolent (*hybristas*) and the boastful (*alazonas*) with the proud sinners in his sketch of depraved pagan society in Rom. 1:30; *cf.* 2 Tim. 3:2. Arrogant display or ostentation (*alazoneia*) are disparaged in Jas. 4:16 and 1 Jn. 2:16. Love, in 1 Cor. 13:4, is stated to be free from both the arrogance and the self-conceit which mar the heretical teachers of 1 Tim. 6:4.

Paul saw pride ('boasting' in knowledge of the law and in works/righteousness) as the characteristic spirit of Judaism and a direct cause of Jewish unbelief. He insisted that the gospel is designed to exclude boasting (Rom. 3:27) by teaching men that they are sinners, that self-righteousness is therefore out of the question, and that they must look to Christ for their righteousness and take it as a free gift by faith in him. Salvation is 'not because of works, lest any man should boast'; it is all of grace. No man, therefore, not even Abraham, may glory in the achievement of his own salvation (see Eph. 2:9; 1 Cor. 1:26–31; Rom. 4:1–2). The gospel message of righteousness through Christ sounds the death-knell of self-righteousness in religion; that is why it was a stumbling-block to the proud Jews (Rom. 9:30–10:4).

This NT emphasis made a deep impact on early and mediaeval ethics. Augustine, Aquinas and Dante all characterized pride as the ultimate sin, while Milton and Goethe dramatized it.

BIBLIOGRAPHY. *ERE*; Arndt; *MM*; R. Niebuhr, *The Nature and Destiny of Man*, 1944–5, ch. 7; E. Güting, C. Brown, *NIDNTT* 3, pp. 27–32; G. Bertram, *TDNT* 8, pp. 295–307, 525–529. D.H.T.

PRIESTS AND LEVITES. The relationship between the priests, who are the descendants of Aaron, and the Levites, the other members of Levi's tribe, is one of the thorny problems of OT religion. Any treatment of the Levites must deal with the biblical evidence, Julius Wellhausen's reconstruction of it and the numerous ways in which contemporary scholars have reacted to his evolutionary approach.

I. The biblical data

a. The Pentateuch

The Levites come into prominence in the Pentateuch in connection with Moses and Aaron (Ex. 2:1–10; 4:14; 6:16–27). After Aaron led the people into apostasy with the golden calf (Ex. 32:25ff.), the sons of Levi avenged the Lord's honour by punishing many of the miscreants. This display of fidelity to God may partially account for the signal responsibilities given the tribe in the pentateuchal legislation.

The role of the Levites as ministers in the tabernacle, clearly detailed in Numbers, is anticipated in Ex. 38:21, where they co-operate in the construction of the tabernacle under the supervision of Aaron's son, Ithamar. In the laws preparatory to the wilderness march, Levi was separated by God from the other tribes and placed in charge of the dismantling, carrying and erecting of the tabernacle (Nu. 1:47–54). The sons of Levi camped around the tabernacle and apparently served as buffers to protect their fellow-tribes from God's wrath, which threatened them if they unwittingly came in contact with the holy tent or its furnishings (Nu. 1:51, 53; 2:17).

Forbidden to serve as priests, a privilege reserved, on penalty of death, for Aaron's sons (Nu. 3:10), the Levites were dedicated to an auxiliary ministry for the priests, especially in regard to the manual labour of caring for the tabernacle (Nu. 3:5ff.). In addition, they performed an important service for the other tribes by substituting for each family's first-born, to whom God was entitled in view of the fact that he spared Israel's first-born at the Passover in Egypt (*cf.* Ex. 13:2ff., 13). As representatives of the tribes' first-born (Nu. 3:40ff.) the Levites were part of 'the far-reaching principle of *representation*' by which the concept of a people utterly dependent upon and totally surrendered to God was put across (*cf.* H. W. Robinson, *Inspiration and Revelation in the Old Testament*, 1953, pp. 219–221).

Each of the three families of Levi had specific duties. The sons of *Kohath* (numbering 2,750 in the age-group from 30 to 50 according to Nu. 4:36) were in charge of carrying the furniture after it had been carefully covered by the priests, who alone could touch it (Nu. 3:29–32; 4:1ff.). The Kohathites were supervised by Aaron's son, Eleazar. The sons of *Gershon* (2,630; Nu. 4:40) cared for the coverings, screens and hangings under the supervision of Aaron's son Ithamar (Nu. 3:21–26; 4:21ff.). *Merari's* sons (3,200; Nu. 4:44) had the task of carrying and erecting the frame of the tabernacle and its court (Nu. 3:35–37; 4:29ff.).

The representative function of the Levites is symbolized in the rituals of cleansing and dedication (Nu. 8:5ff.). For instance, both the fact that the Israelites (probably through their tribal leaders) laid hands on the Levites (8:10), acknowledging them as substitutes (*cf.* Lv. 4:24, *etc.*), and the fact that the priests offered the Levites as a wave-offering (probably by leading them to and then from the altar) from the people (8:11), suggest that the Levites were given by the Israelites to serve Aaron's sons in their stead. This is made explicit in 3:16ff., where Levi's sons are called *n^{e}ṯûnîm*, 'gifts'.

Their service began at 25 years of age and continued until the 50th year, when the Levite went into a kind of semi-retirement with limited duties (Nu. 8:24–26). There may have been a 5-year apprenticeship, because apparently the full responsibility of carrying the tabernacle and its furnishings fell on the shoulders of the men from 30 years to 50 (Nu. 4:3ff.). When David established a permanent site for the ark, the age was lowered to 20 years because there was no longer a need for mature Levites as porters (1 Ch. 23:24ff.).

The levitical responsibility of representing the people carried with it certain privileges. Although they had no inheritance in the land (*i.e.* no portion of it was appointed for their exclusive use: Nu. 18:23–24; Dt. 12:12ff.), the Levites were supported by the tithes of the people, while the priests received the parts of the offerings not consumed by sacrifice, the firstlings of flock and herd, and a tithe of the levitical tithes (Nu. 18:8ff., 21ff.; *cf.* Dt. 18:1–4). Occasionally both priests and Levites shared in the spoils of battle (*e.g.* Nu. 31:25ff.). In addition, the Levites had permission to reside in forty-eight cities set aside for their use (Nu. 35:1ff.; Jos. 21:1ff.). Surrounding each city an area of pasture-land was marked off for them. Six of the cities, three on each side of the Jordan, served as *cities of refuge.

The transition from the wilderness marches to settled life in Canaan (anticipated in Nu. 35 in the establishing of levitical cities) brought with it both an increased concern for the welfare of the Levites and an expansion of their duties in order to cope with the needs of the decentralized pattern of life. In Deuteronomy great stress is laid on the Israelites' responsibilities towards the sons of Levi, who were to share in the rejoicing of the tribes (12:12), in their tithes and certain offerings (12:18–19; 14:28–29), and in their chief festivals, especially Weeks and Tabernacles (16:11–14). The Levites dispersed throughout the land were to share equally both the ministry and the offerings with their brethren who resided at the central shrine (18:6–8).

Whereas Numbers characteristically calls the priests the *sons of Aaron* (*e.g.* 10:8), Deuteronomy frequently uses the expression 'the *Levitical priests*' (*e.g.* 18:1). Though some scholars (see below) have held that no distinction is made between priest and Levite in Deuteronomy, the fact that different portions are ascribed to priests in Dt. 18:3ff. and to Levites in 18:6ff. suggests that the distinction is maintained. The phrase 'the Levitical priests' (*e.g.* Dt. 17:9, 18; 18:1; 24:8; 27:9; *cf.* Jos. 3:3; 8:33) seems to mean 'the priests of the tribe of Levi'. To them the Deuteronomic code assigns numerous duties in addition to the care of the sanctuary: they serve as judges in cases involving difficult decisions (17:8–9), regulate the control of lepers (24:8), guard the book of the law (17:18) and assist Moses in the ceremony of covenant renewal (27:9).

Within the family of Kohath the office of high priest (Heb. *hakkōhēn*, 'the priest' [Ex. 31:10, *etc.*]; *hakkōhēn hammāšîaḥ*, 'the anointed priest' [Lv. 4:3, *etc.*]; *hakkōhēn haggāḏōl*, 'the high priest' [Lv. 21:10, *etc.*]) was exercised by the eldest representative of Eleazar's family, unless the sanctions of Lv. 21:16–23 were applicable. He was consecrated in the same manner as the other priests and shared in their routine duties. He alone wore the special vestments (Ex. 28; *BREASTPIECE OF THE HIGH PRIEST, *MITRE, *DRESS) and interpreted the oracles (*URIM AND THUMMIM). On the Day of *Atonement he represented the chosen people before Yahweh, sprinkling the blood of the sacrificial goat on the mercy-seat (*SACRIFICE AND OFFERING).

b. The Former Prophets

The priests play a more prominent role than the Levites in the book of Joshua, especially in the story of the crossing of Jordan and the conquest of Jericho. Sometimes called 'the priests the Levites' (*e.g.* Jos. 3:3; 8:33) and more often simply 'the priests' (*e.g.* Jos. 3:6ff.; 4:9ff.), they had the crucial task of bearing the ark of the Lord. The tabernacle, however, carried by the Levites is not mentioned (with the possible exception of 6:24) until it was pitched at Shiloh (18:1; 19:51) after the conquest of Canaan. Apparently the carrying of the ark was entrusted to the priests rather than the Kohathites (*cf.* Nu. 4:15) because of the supreme importance of these journeys: God, whose presence the ark symbolized, was marching forth conquering and to conquer. The Levites came into the forefront only when the time for dividing the land was at hand (*cf.* Jos. 14:3ff.). The distinction between priests and Levites is clearly maintained: the Levites remind Eleazar, the priest, and Joshua of Moses' command concerning levitical cities (Jos. 21:1–3); the Kohathites are divided into two groups—those who have descended from Aaron (*i.e.* the priests) and the rest (Jos. 21:4–5).

The general laxness of worship during the days between the conquest of Canaan and the establishment of the Monarchy is illustrated in the two levitical stories in Judges. Micah's Levite (Jdg. 17–18) is said to hail from Bethlehem and to be a member of the family of Judah (17:7). How was he both Levite and Judahite? The answer hangs on whether the Levite is to be identified with *Jonathan, the son of Gershom (18:30). If they are identical (as seems likely), then the Levite's relationship to Judah must be geographical, not genealogical, in spite of the phrase 'family of Judah' (17:7). If the two men are not identical, then the Levite may be an example of the possibility that men of other tribes could, in this period, join themselves to the priestly tribe. This may have been the case with *Samuel, an Ephraimite (*cf.* 1 Sa. 1:1; 1 Ch. 6:28). There is some evidence that the term *Levite* may have been a functional title meaning 'one pledged by vow' as well as a tribal designation (*cf.* W. F. Albright, *Archaeology and the Religion of Israel*[3], 1953, pp. 109, 204ff.); however, T. J. Meek (*Hebrew Origins*[3], 1960, pp. 121ff.) maintains that the Levites were originally a secular tribe who assumed a priestly function not only in Israel but perhaps in Arabia as well. The macabre story of the Levite and his concubine (Jdg. 19) is further testimony to the itinerations of the Levites and to the general laxness of the era. Lack of central authority curtailed the control which the central sanctuary at Shiloh should have enjoyed (Jdg. 18:31) and allowed numerous shrines to exist which paid little heed to the Mosaic regulations.

Levites appear only rarely in the rest of the Former Prophets, usually in connection with their role in carrying the ark (1 Sa. 6:15; 2 Sa. 15:24; 1 Ki. 8:4). When *Jeroboam I set up rival shrines at Dan and Bethel, he staffed them with non-levitical priests, probably in order to sever relationships with the Jerusalem Temple as completely as possible (1 Ki. 12:31; *cf.* 2 Ch. 11:13–14; 13:9–10). Royal control of the centre of worship in both kingdoms was an important feature of the Monarchy.

c. The Chronicles

The priestly perspective of the writer of the books of *Chronicles tends to accentuate the role of the Levites and fills in numerous details of their ministry which the authors of Kings have omitted. In the genealogies of 1 Ch. 6, which also describe the role of Aaron's sons (6:49–53) and the distribution of levitical cities (6:54–81), special attention is focused on the levitical singers, Heman, Asaph, Ethan and their sons, who were put in charge of the Temple music by David (6:31ff.; *cf.* 1 Ch. 15:16ff.). The list of Levites in 1 Ch. 9 bristles with problems. The similarities between it and Ne. 11 have led some (*e.g.* ASV, RSV) to treat it as the roll of Levites who returned to Jerusalem from the captivity (*cf.* 1 Ch. 9:1). Others (*e.g.* C. F. Keil) view it as a list of early inhabitants of Jerusalem. Both the carefully organized assignments of duty and the numbers of Levites involved (*cf.* the 212 gatekeepers of 1 Ch. 9:22 with the 93 of 1 Ch. 26:8–11) suggest a period subsequent to that of David. The close co-operation between Levites and sons of priests (*cf.* 1 Ch. 9:28ff.) and the fact that Levites cared for some of the holy vessels and helped to prepare the showbread may indicate that the rigid division of duties suggested in Nu. 4 and 18 broke down during the Monarchy, perhaps because the sons of Aaron were not numerous enough (the 1,760 in 1 Ch. 9:13 probably refers to the number of kinsmen, not to the number of heads of houses) to cope with the demands of their office. Therefore, in addition to their regular tasks as singers and musicians, gatekeepers, porters, *etc.*, the Levites had to help in the actual preparation of the sacrifices, as well as in the care of the courts and chambers, the cleansing of the holy things and the preparation of the showbread, the cereal offering, the unleavened bread, the baked offering, *etc.* (23:14).

David's orders in 1 Ch. 23 illustrate the two dominant factors which produced substantial changes in the levitical offices: the permanent location of the ark in Jerusalem, which automatically made obsolete all the regulations concerning the Levites' function as porters; and the centralization of responsibility for the official religion (as for all other affairs of life) in the king. The Heb. view of corporate personality saw the king as the great father of the nation whose essential character was derived from him. As David brought the central shrine to Jerusalem (1 Ch. 13:2ff.) and established the patterns of its function (1 Ch. 15:1ff.; 23:1ff.) in accordance with the principles of the Mosaic legislation, so Solomon built, dedicated and supervised the Temple and its cult according to his father's plan (1 Ch. 28:11–13, 21; 2 Ch. 5–8, note especially 8:15: 'And they did not turn aside from what the king had commanded the priests and Levites . . .').

Similarly, Jehoshaphat commissioned princes, Levites and priests to teach the law throughout Judah (2 Ch. 17:7ff.) and appointed certain Levites, priests and family heads as judges in Jerusalem (2 Ch. 19:8ff.) under the supervision of the chief priest. Joash (2 Ch. 24:5ff.), Hezekiah (2 Ch. 29:3ff.) and Josiah (2 Ch. 35:2ff.) supervised the priests and Levites and re-established them in their functions according to the Davidic pattern.

The relationship between the levitical office and the prophetic is a moot question. Were some Levites cult-prophets? No firm answer is possible, but there is some evidence that Levites sometimes exercised prophetic activity: Jahaziel, a Levite of the sons of Asaph, prophesied Jehoshaphat's victory over the Moabite–Ammonite coalition (2 Ch. 20:14ff.) and Jeduthun, the Levite, is called the king's *seer* (2 Ch. 35:15).

d. The Latter Prophets

Isaiah, Jeremiah and Ezekiel touch briefly upon the role of the Levites after the Exile. Is. 66:21 speaks of God's gathering of dispersed Israelites (or perhaps converted heathen) to serve him as priests and Levites. Jeremiah (33:17ff.) envisages a covenant with the levitical priests (or perhaps priests and Levites; *cf.* Syr. and Vulg.) which is as binding as God's covenant with David's family (*cf.* 2 Sa. 7). Ezekiel forces a sharp cleavage between the levitical priests, whom he calls the sons of Zadok (*e.g.* 40:46; 43:19), and the Levites. The former are deemed to have remained faithful to God (44:15; 48:11), while the latter went astray after idols and therefore could not approach the altar or handle the most sacred things (44:10–14). Actually Ezekiel's suggestion seems to be a return to the careful distinction between priest and Levite found in Numbers from the somewhat more lax view which prevailed during the Monarchy.

e. The post-exilic writings

Under Joshua and Zerubbabel 341 Levites returned (Ezr. 2:36ff.) with the 4,289 members of priestly families, and the 392 Temple servants (*n^e^ṯînîm*, *i.e.* 'given', 'appointed', who were apparently descendants of prisoners of war pressed into Temple service; *cf.* Jos. 9:23, 27; Ezr. 8:20). The difference between the large number of priests and the comparatively small number of Levites may be due to the fact that many Levites took on priestly status during the Exile. The other Levites responsible for menial tasks in the Temple seem to have been reluctant to return (Ezr. 8:15–20). The Levites played a prominent part at the laying of the foundation (Ezr. 3:8ff.) and at the dedication of the Temple (Ezr. 6:16ff.). Ezra, after recruiting Levites for his party (Ezr. 8:15ff.), instituted a reform to ban foreign marriages in which even priests and Levites had become involved (Ezr. 9:1ff.; 10:5ff.).

Similarly in Nehemiah, the Levites and priests engaged in their full range of duties. After repairing a section of the wall (Ne. 3:17), the Levites were busily occupied with instruction in the law (Ne. 8:7–9) and participation in the religious life of the nation (Ne. 11:3ff.; 12:27ff.). They were to receive tithes from the people and in turn to give a tithe of the tithes to

Aaron's sons (Ne. 10:37ff.; 12:47). The need for a central authority to enforce the levitical regulations was shown by the deterioration of the cult during Nehemiah's absence from Jerusalem: Tobiah, the Ammonite, was allowed to occupy the room in the Temple which should have served as a storeroom for the levitical tithes (Ne. 13:4ff.); deprived of their support, the Levites had forsaken the Temple and fled to their fields in order to sustain themselves (Ne. 13:10ff.).

It may have been during this period that the priests put personal gain above their covenanted responsibility to teach the law and accepted corrupt sacrifices (Mal. 1:6ff.; 2:4ff.). For Malachi, the purification of the sons of Levi was one of God's central eschatological missions (3:1–4).

The high priesthood remained in the family of Eleazar until the time of * Eli, a descendant of Ithamar. The conspiracy of * Abiathar led Solomon to depose him (1 Ki. 2:26f.). The office thus returned to the house of Eleazar in * Zadok and remained in that family until political intrigues resulted in the deposition of Onias III by the Seleucid king Antiochus Epiphanes (*c.* 174 BC). Thereafter it became the patronage of the ruling power.

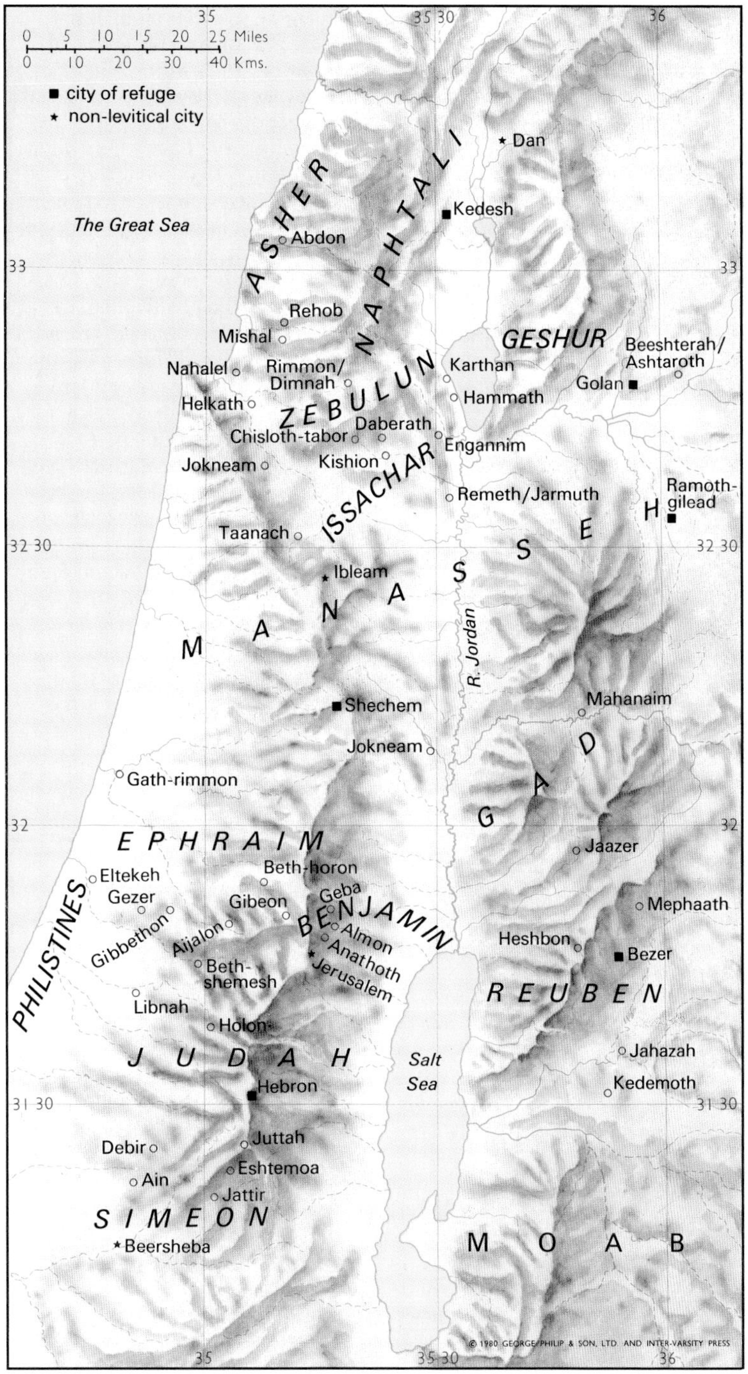

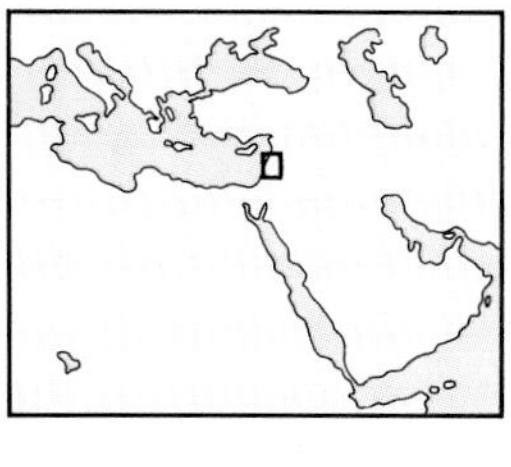

The cities allocated to the Levites.

II. Wellhausen's reconstruction

The development of the documentary hypothesis with its emphasis on the post-exilic date for the completion of the priestly code (* PENTATEUCH) brought with it a drastic re-evaluation of the development of Israel's religion. The classical form of this re-evaluation was stated by Julius Wellhausen (1844–1918) in his *Prolegomena to the History of Israel* (1878; E.T. 1885).

The crux of the relationship between priest and Levite for Wellhausen was Ezekiel's banning of Levites from priestly duties (44:6–16). From Ezekiel's statement Wellhausen drew two inferences: the separation of the holy from the profane was not part of the temple procedure, as the use of heathen temple servants (see above) indicates; Ezekiel reduced the Levites, who had hitherto performed priestly functions, to the status of temple-slaves. The sons of Zadok were exempt from Ezekiel's indictment because they served at the central sanctuary in Jerusalem and, unlike the Levites, had not defiled themselves by service at the high places throughout the land. When the sons of Zadok objected to relinquishing their exclusive control, Ezekiel devised 'moral' grounds for maintaining their exclusiveness, although actually the distinction between priests and Levites was accidental not moral (the priests *happened* to be at Jerusalem, the Levites at the high places). Wellhausen concluded that the priestly law of Numbers did not exist in Ezekiel's time.

Since the Aaronic priesthood is stressed only in the priestly code, it was viewed by Wellhausen as a fiction in order to give the priesthood an anchor in the Mosaic period. The genealogies in Chronicles are artificial attempts to link the sons of Zadok with Aaron and Eleazar.

Central in Wellhausen's reconstruction was the striking contrast between the 'elaborate machinery' of the wilderness cult and the decentralization of the period of the Judges, when worship played apparently only a minor role according to Jdg. 3–16. The latter period he took to be the authentic time of origin of Israelite worship, which began simply as various family heads offered their own sacrifices, and developed as certain families (*e.g.* Eli's at Shiloh) gained prominence at special sanctuaries. A startling example of the contrast between the complexity of the wilderness religion and the simplicity during the settlement was the fact that Samuel, an Ephraimite, slept nightly beside the ark (1 Sa. 3:3) in the place where, according to Lv. 16, only the high priest could enter annually.

When Solomon built the permanent shrine for the ark, the prominence of the Jerusalem priests (under Zadok, whom David had appointed) was assured. Like Judah, like Israel: Jeroboam's shrines were royal shrines and the priests were directly responsible to him (Am. 7:10ff.). In Judah the process of centralization reached its acme when Josiah's reform abolished the high places, reduced their priests to subsidiary status in the central sanctuary and set the stage for Ezekiel's crucial declaration.

Against this evolutionary schematization, Wellhausen set the various strata of the Pentateuch and found a remarkable degree of correspondence. In the laws of J (Ex. 20–23; 34) the priesthood is not mentioned, while the other parts of J mark Aaron (Ex. 4:14; 32:1ff.) and Moses (Ex. 33:7–11) as founders of the clergy. The mention of other priests (*e.g.* Ex. 19:22; 32:29) was disregarded by Wellhausen, who considered these passages as interpolations. It was in D (Dt. 16:18–18:22) that he saw the beginning of the use of the name *Levites* for the priests. The hereditary character of the priesthood began not with Aaron (who, according to Wellhausen, 'was not originally present in J, but owed his introduction to the redactor who combined J and E') but during the Monarchy with the sons of Zadok. Recognizing the basic authenticity of the inclusion of Levi in the tribal blessings of Gn. 49, Wellhausen believed that this tribe 'succumbed at an early date' and that the supposed tie between the official use of the term *Levite* and the tribe of Levi was artificial.

The priestly code (P) not only strengthened the hand of the clergy but introduced the basic division into the ranks of the clergy—the separation of priests (Aaron's sons) from Levites (the rest of the tribe). Therefore, while the Deuteronomist spoke of levitical priests (*i.e.* the priests the Levites) the priestly writers, especially the Chronicler, spoke of priests and Levites.

Another priestly innovation was the figure of the high priest, who loomed larger in Exodus, Leviticus and Numbers than anywhere else in the pre-exilic writings. Whereas in the historical books the king dominated the cult, in the priestly code it was the high priest, whose regal status, according to Wellhausen, could only reflect a period when the civil government of Judah was in the hands of foreigners and Israel was not so much a people as a church—the post-exilic period.

One need only consult such representative works as Max Loehr's *A History of Religion in the Old Testament*, 1936, *e.g.* pp. 136–137; W. O. E. Oesterley and T. H. Robinson's *Hebrew Religion*, 1930, *e.g.* p. 255; and R. H. Pfeiffer's *IOT*, 1948, *e.g.* pp. 556–557, to see the stubbornness with which Wellhausen's reconstruction has persisted.

III. Some reactions to Wellhausen's reconstruction

Among the conservatives who have set out to tumble Wellhausen's structure, three names are noteworthy: James Orr (*The Problem of the Old Testament*, 1906), O. T. Allis (*The Five Books of Moses*², 1949, pp. 185–196), G. Ch. Aalders (*A Short Introduction to the Pentateuch*, 1949, pp. 66–71).

Basic to Wellhausen's reconstruction is the assumption that the Levites who were invited in Dt. 18:6–7 to serve at the central shrine were the priests who had been disfranchised by the abolition of their high places during Josiah's reform. But solid evidence for this assumption is lacking. In fact, 2 Ki. 23:9 affirms the opposite: the priests of the high places did not come up to the altar of the Lord in Jerusalem. The critical view that priests and Levites are not clearly distinguished in Deuteronomy has been discussed above, where it was seen that a clear distinction was made between them in regard to the people's responsibility towards them (Dt. 18:3–5, 6–8). Nor can the view that the phrase 'the priests the Levites' (Dt. 17:9, 18; 18:1; 24:8; 27:9), not found elsewhere in the Pentateuch, argues for the identity of the two offices in Deuteronomy be maintained. The phrase serves merely to link the priests with their tribe. Confirmation for this seems to be found in 2 Ch. 23:18 and 30:27, where the 'Levitical priests' are distinguished from other Levites (30:25), gatekeepers, *etc.* (23:19).

Attention has frequently been directed by Wellhausen and others to the apparent discrepancy between the law of *tithes in Nu. 18:21ff. (*cf.* Lv. 27:30ff.), which earmarks the tithes for the Levites, and the counterpart in Dt. 14:22ff., which allows Israelites to eat of the tithes in a sacrificial meal while enjoining them to share it with the Levites. Judaism has traditionally reconciled these passages by calling the tithe of Deuteronomy 'a second tithe', *e.g.* in the Talmudic tractate *Ma'aśer Sheni.* This explanation may not be so acceptable as James Orr's (*op. cit.*, pp. 188–189): the laws of Deuteronomy, he held, apply to a time when the tithe-laws (and those relating to levitical cities) could not be fully enforced, since the conquest was not complete and there was no central agency to enforce them. In other words, Nu. 18:21ff. deals with Israel's ideal while Dt. 14:22ff. is an interim programme for the conquest and settlement.

Pivotal in Wellhausen's reconstruction is his interpretation of Ezekiel's denunciation of the Levites (44:4ff.), in which he finds the origin of the cleavage between priests (the sons of Zadok) and Levites (priests who had previously engaged in idolatry at the high places). But James Orr (*op. cit.*, pp. 315–319, 520) calls attention to the deplorable condition of the priesthood just prior to Ezekiel's time and points out that Ezekiel did not establish the law but rather re-established it by depriving Levites of privileges not rightly theirs, which they had usurped during the Monarchy and by demoting idolatrous priests to the already well-established lower rank of Levite. Furthermore, the ideal context of Ezekiel's pronouncement suggests that the degradation in view may never have been carried out, at least not literally. The tone of Ezekiel stands in contradiction to that of the priestly code in that the latter knows nothing of priestly degradation but stresses divine appointment. In addition, the priests in P are not Zadok's sons but Aaron's sons.

The office of high priest has been largely relegated to the post-exilic period by the Wellhausenian school. Though the title itself occurs only in 2 Ki. 12:10; 22:4, 8; 23:4 in pre-exilic writings (usually considered by documentary critics to be post-exilic interpolations), the existence of the office seems to be indicated by the title '*the* priest' (*e.g.* Ahimelech, 1 Sa. 21:2; Jehoiada, 2 Ki. 11:9–10, 15; Urijah, 2 Ki. 16:10ff.) and by the fact that a priesthood of any size at all involves an administrative chief, even if the king is the head of the cult. (*Cf.* J. Pedersen, *Israel*, 3–4, p. 189.)

In *The Religion of Israel*, 1960, Yehezkel Kaufmann examines a number of Wellhausen's key conclusions and finds them wanting. The high priest, for instance, far from being a royal figure reflecting the post-exilic religious leaders, faithfully mirrors the conditions of the military camp which is subject to the authority of Moses, not Aaron (*op. cit.*, pp. 184–187).

Kaufmann turns his attention to 'the one pillar of Wellhausen's structure that has not been shaken by later criticism'—the reconstruction of the relationship between priests and Levites. Noting the absence of evidence for the demotion of the rural priests, he then calls attention to a basic weakness in the documentary view: 'Nothing can make plausible a theory that the very priests who demoted their colleagues saw fit to endow them with the amplest clerical due, a theory the more improbable when the great number of priests and paucity of Levites at the Restoration (4,289 priests, Ezr. 2:36ff.; 341 Levites plus 392 temple servants, Ezr. 2:43ff.) is borne in mind' (p. 194).

Why did the priests preserve the story of the Levites' faithfulness during Aaron's defection (Ex. 32:26–29), while glossing over the idolatry, which, for Wellhausen, was responsible for their degradation, and according the Levites the honour of divine appointment rather than punishment? After affirming that the Levites are clearly a distinct class in the Exile, Kaufmann points out that they could not have developed as a distinct class in the brief period between Josiah's reform (to say nothing of Ezekiel's denunciation) and the return, and that on foreign soil.

Kaufmann's own reconstruction may not prove entirely satisfactory. He denies a hereditary connection between the sons of Aaron and the Levites, since he deems the Aaronids to be 'the ancient, pagan priesthood of Israel' (p. 197), and thus rejects the firm biblical tradition connecting Moses, Aaron and the Levites (*cf.* Ex. 4:14). In the golden calf incident the old secular tribe of Levi rallied with Moses against Aaron, but was forced to yield the privilege of altar service to the Aaronids (p. 198), while they themselves had to be content as *hierodules*. This raises the question as to how, apart from a connection with Moses, the Aaronids survived the catastrophe of the golden calf and continued as priests. Kaufmann's opinion that the Deuteronomic legislation was compiled during the latter part of the Monarchy and thus is considerably later than the priestly writings may be more of a return to an old critical position (*i.e.* that of Th. Noeldeke and others) than a fresh thrust at Wellhausen.

Rejecting the linear view of institutional evolution which was a main plank in Wellhausen's platform, W. F. Albright notes that Israel would be unique among her neighbours had she not enjoyed during the period of the Judges and afterwards a high priest, usually called (in accordance with Semitic practice) *the priest* (*Archaeology and the Religion of Israel*³, 1953, pp. 107–108). The lack of emphasis on the high-priestly office during the Monarchy represents a decline, while, after the Monarchy's collapse, the priesthood again rose to a position of prestige. Albright accepts the historicity of Aaron and finds no reason for not considering Zadok an Aaronid. Concluding that the Levite had first a functional (see above) and then a tribal significance, Albright points out that Levites may sometimes have been promoted to priests and that 'we are not justified either in throwing overboard the standard Israelite tradition regarding priests and Levites, or in considering these classes as hard and fast genealogical groups' (*op. cit.*, p. 110).

The assumption that the tabernacle in the wilderness was the idealization of the Temple and had no historical existence, so basic to Wellhausen's reconstruction, has now largely been abandoned (although *cf.* R. H. Pfeiffer's *Religion in the Old Testament*, 1961, pp. 77–78). Both arks and portable tent-shrines are attested among Israel's neighbours, as archaeology has revealed. Far from being figments of a later period, these, as John Bright notes, are 'heritages of Israel's primitive desert faith' (*A History of Israel*, 1960, pp. 146–147).

Obviously the last word has not been said on this puzzling problem of the relationship between priests and Levites. The data from the period of the conquest and settlement are meagre. It is hazardous to assume that the pentateuchal legislation, representing the ideal as it often does, was ever carried out literally. Even such stalwart kings as David, Jehoshaphat, Hezekiah and Josiah were not able to ensure complete conformity to the Mosaic pattern. But it is even more tenuous to hold that because laws were not enforced they did not exist. The combination of argumentation from silence, straight-line evolutionary reconstruction, and a resort to textual emendations and literary excisions when passages prove troublesome, has resulted more than once in interpretations of biblical history which have proved to be too facile to stand permanently in the face of the complexities of biblical data and Semitic culture. Wellhausen's ingenious reconstruction of the history of the Levites may prove to be a case in point.

BIBLIOGRAPHY. In addition to works cited above, R. Brinker, *The Influence of Sanctuaries in Early Israel*, 1946, pp. 65ff.; R. de Vaux, *Ancient Israel: Its Life and Institutions*, E.T. 1961; A. Cody, *A History of the Old Testament Priesthood*, 1969; M. Haran *et al.*, 'Priests and Priesthood', *EJ*, 13, 1970; H.-J. Kraus, *Worship in Israel*, E.T. 1966.

IV. Priesthood in the New Testament

a. Continuity with the Old Testament

With the single exception of the priest of Zeus, who wrongly seeks to venerate Paul and Barnabas in Lystra (Acts 14:13), references to priest and high priest in the Gospels and Acts assume an historical and religious continuity with the OT: no explanation is needed of the priest's function in the story of the good Samaritan (Lk. 10:31) or of the duties of the 'priest named Zechariah', father of John the Baptist (Lk. 1:5); Jesus recognized the lawful function of the priests in declaring lepers clean (Mt. 8:4; Mk. 1:44; Lk. 5:14; 17:14; see Lv. 14:3). Jesus also pitted the freer practice of some OT priests against the legalism of his opponents (Mt. 12:4–5). He had no basic quarrel with the prescribed functions of the Temple and priesthood.

b. Conflict with Judaism

The lion's share of references to

priests, especially high priests (or chief priests as RSV usually has them) are found, however, in contexts of conflict. Matthew depicts the high priests as actively involved in the gospel events from beginning (Mt. 2:4) to end (Mt. 28:11). Their opposition mounts as the claims and mission of Jesus become clear, *e.g.* in his challenge to the Sabbath legislation (Mt. 12:1–7; Mk. 2:23–27; Lk. 6:1–5) and in his parables that censured the religious leaders (Mt. 21:45–46). This conflict to the death was anticipated immediately after Peter's confession at Caesarea Philippi (Mt. 16:21; Mk. 8:31; Lk. 9:22), was intensified at the Palm Sunday reception and the subsequent Temple cleansing (Mt. 21:15, 23, 45–46; Mk. 11:27; Lk. 19:47–48; 20:1), and reached its bitter climax in the arrest and trial (Mt. 26–27). The Fourth Gospel also bears witness to the conflict (Jn. 7:32, 45; 11:47, where Pharisees are the partners in crime; 12:10, where the hostility focuses on Lazarus; 18:19, 22, 24, 35, where Caiaphas' role in Jesus' trial is stressed; *cf.* 19:15).

The chief priests (*archiereus*) rarely acted alone in their desire to crush Jesus' influence. Depending on the issue and circumstances, they were joined by other officials of the Sanhedrin (*archontes*, Lk. 23:13; 24:20), by scribes (*grammateis*, Mt. 2:4; 20:18; 21:15), by scribes and elders (*grammateis, presbyteroi*, Mt. 16:21; 27:41; Mk. 8:31; 11:27; 14:43, 53; Lk. 9:22), by elders (Mt. 21:23; 26:3). The singular 'high priest' usually refers to the president of the Sanhedrin (*e.g.* Caiaphas, Mt. 26:57; Jn. 18:13; Annas, Lk. 3:2; Jn. 18:24; Acts 4:6; Ananias, Acts 23:2; 24:1). The plural 'chief priests' describes members of the high-priestly families who serve in the Sanhedrin; ruling and former high priests together with members of the prominent priestly families (Acts 4:6). J. Jeremias has argued that 'chief priests' include Temple officers like treasurer and captain of police (*Jerusalem in the Time of Jesus*, E.T. 1969, pp. 160ff.).

The death and resurrection of Jesus did not quell the conflict, as Acts amply documents. The apostolic witness to the resurrection drew the Sadducees into the struggle alongside the chief priests and other Temple officials (Acts 4:1; 5:17). Priestly involvement in the story of Saul of Tarsus is noteworthy. The proposed persecution of Christians in Damascus apparently had the official sanction of the high priest (Acts 9:1–2, 14); the 'itinerant Jewish exorcists' who sought to duplicate Paul's miracles in Ephesus were described as 'seven sons of a Jewish high priest named Sceva' (Acts 19:13–14); like his Master, Paul stood trial before a high priest, Ananias, who also pressed charges against him before the Roman governors Felix and Festus (Acts 24:1ff.; 25:1–3). Almost nothing in the apostle's life illustrates so clearly the radical change wrought by his conversion than the dramatic reversal in his relationships to the priestly establishment: the beginning of his story found him riding with the hounds; the end, running with the foxes.

c. Consummation in Christ

At root this conflict sprang from the Christian conviction and the Jewish suspicion that Jesus' life, death, resurrection and ascension spelt the eclipse if not the destruction of the old priestly structures. Jesus' own teaching had placed him at the heart of a new sacerdotal structure: 'something greater than the temple is here' (Mt. 12:6); 'destroy this temple, and in three days I will raise it up' (Jn. 2:19); 'for the Son of man also came not to be served but to serve, and to give his life as a ransom for many' (Mk. 10:45).

Of the NT writers, it is the author of Hebrews who picks up these threads and weaves them into a many-coloured fabric. In its passion to prove that the Christian faith is superior to, indeed has replaced, the OT patterns of worship, Hebrews presses persistently its claim that Jesus has been appointed by God (5:5–10) to be the new, the true high priest who can finally deal with human sin. His priesthood, surpassing Aaron's (7:11) and reaching back to Melchizedek's (7:15–17), contains the perfection missing in the older sacrificial system (7:18): 1. It is based on God's own oath (7:20–22); 2. It is permanent because it is centred in the eternal Christ (7:23–25); 3. It partakes of the perfection of Christ who had no need to be purged of sin, as did the sons of Aaron (7:26–28); 4. It continues in the heavens where God himself has erected the true sanctuary of which Moses' tent was but 'a copy and shadow' (8:1–7); 5. It is the fulfilment of God's promise of a new covenant (8:8–13); 6. Its sacrifice needs no repeating but was rendered 'once for all' (7:27; 9:12); 7. Its offering was not 'the blood of bulls and goats', unable to take away sins, but 'the body of Jesus Christ', through which believers are sanctified (10:4, 10); 8. Its result is full and regular access to God for all Christians not just a priestly order (10:11–22); 9. Its promises and hopes are assured by the faithfulness of God and the assurance of Christ's second coming (9:28; 10:23); 10. Its full forgiveness provides the highest motivation for our works of love and righteousness (10:19–25); 11. Its effectiveness in the lives of God's people is guaranteed by Christ's constant intercession (7:25). Though Paul did not choose to make Christ's priesthood a dominant theme in his writings (probably because his ministry was largely to Gentiles, for whom a knowledge of their freedom from law and their new place in God's purpose was the pre-eminent need), we can be grateful that the rich insights of Hebrews are among God's gifts in the canon of Scripture. See G. E. Ladd, *A Theology of the New Testament*, 1974, pp. 578–584.

d. Commission of the church

As Christ's body and as his new Israel (*cf.* Ex. 19:6), the church is anointed to a priesthood in the world—a mediatorial service that declares the will of God to humankind and bears human needs before God's throne in prayer. Two related duties of this priesthood are mentioned by Peter: 1. 'to offer spiritual sacrifices acceptable to God through Jesus Christ' (1 Pet. 2:5), *i.e.* to worship God and do his loving will; 2. to 'declare the wonderful deeds of him who called you out of darkness into his marvellous light', *i.e.* to bear witness to his saving work in the world (1 Pet. 2:9).

Peter's 'royal priesthood' is echoed and amplified in Rev. where the beloved and forgiven church is called 'a kingdom, priests to his God and Father' (Rev. 1:6; *cf.* 5:10; 20:6). This royal role not only entails obedience to Christ 'the ruler of kings on earth' (Rev. 1:5) but also participation in his rule over others: 'and they shall reign on earth' (Rev. 5:10; *cf.* 20:6). Here the circle of conflict has taken a full turn: the people of Christ, afflicted by a priesthood that opposed their Master, will share in his victory as triumphant high priest and demonstrate his loving sovereignty in a hostile world.

The church's priesthood in the NT is corporate: no individual minister or leader is called 'priest'. The post-apostolic writings, however, move quickly in that direction: Clement (AD 95–96) describes Christian ministry in terms of high priest, priests and Levites (*1 Clem.* 40–44); the *Didache* (13:3) likens prophets to high priests. Tertullian (*On Baptism* 17) and Hippolytus (*Refutation of All Heresies*, preface) seemed to have pioneered the use of the titles 'priest' and 'high priest' for Christian ministers (*c.* AD 200).

BIBLIOGRAPHY. T. W. Manson, *Ministry and Priesthood: Christ's and Ours*, 1958; G. Schrenk, *TDNT* 3, pp. 247–251, 257–283; H. Seebas, *NIDNTT* 2, pp. 232–236; J. Baehr, *NIDNTT* 3, pp. 32–44. D.A.H.

PRINCE. A variety of Heb. words are translated 'prince', but are not always so rendered. 'Ruler', 'leader', 'captain', *etc.*, are also used. The frequency of the use of the word is an effect (still discernible in RSV) of the AV translators' so rendering, though not with entire consistency, the LXX *archōn*, which itself represents no less than 20 Heb. words, the most important being the word for 'head', *rō'š*.

The Heb. words fall into two categories. First, loan-words from other languages, usually referring to foreign dignitaries. For example, *xšaθrapavan*, 'satrap', and *fratama*, 'foremost', are Persian words transliterated in Dn. 3:2, *etc.* (Aram. *'aḥašdarpan*), 1:3 (Heb. plur. *partᵉmîm*). The *satrapies of the Persian empire were originally coextensive with the conquered kingdoms. But Darius reduced the number to twenty (Herodotus 3. 89–94). The power of the satrap was checked by certain officials responsible directly to the Great King, but otherwise approximated to that of a vassal king.

Secondly, words of indigenous origin representing the following salient ideas: (1) *śar*, 'exercising dominion', whether as supreme or subordinate to an overlord; (2) *nāgîḏ*, 'being in front', especially of military leader; (3) *nāśî'*, 'being exalted'; (4) *nāḏîḇ*, 'a volunteer', perhaps signifying a contrast with those whom a king might compel to fight on his behalf; (5) *qāṣîn*, 'a judge'.

Ezekiel often uses *nāśî'* of the Messiah: it corresponds with his conception of the true David (Ezk. 37:24–25). In Daniel, *śar* and *nāgîḏ* are used of him, corresponding to the military imagery with which the cosmic struggle is depicted. *śar* is also used of the guardian angels of countries, and particularly of Michael (Dn. 10:13, 21).

In the NT *archōn* is used of Satan, 'ruler of this world', and in the plural, of the Roman and Jewish authorities ('rulers'). It is once used of Christ (Rev. 1:5), 'ruler of the kings of the earth', but elsewhere where 'prince' is used in AV. The LXX *archēgos* (for Heb. *nāśî'* and *qāṣîn*) is used of Christ (*cf.* Acts 5:31), gathering from its Greek connections the additional idea of 'author' (Acts 3:15) and 'pioneer' (Heb. 2:10; 12:2). J.B.J.

PRISON.

I. In the Old Testament

The first mention of a prison in Scripture is that of *Joseph in Egypt (Gn. 39:20–23). For this the Hebrew text uses a special term *bêṯ-sōhar*; *sōhar* is usually compared with other Semitic words for 'round' or 'enclosure', and Joseph's prison is therefore commonly considered to be, or be in, a fortress. The comparison of Heb. *sōhar* with Egyp. *Ṯ'rw*, 'Silē' (mod. Qantara), is false, as this word is really *Ṯl* (J. Vergote, *Joseph en Égypte*, 1959, pp. 25–28). However, there is an Egyp. word *ṯ'rt*, occurring as early as *c.* 1900 BC as well as later, which means 'enclosed building', 'store', '(ship's) cabin', and this might just conceivably be connected with *sōhar*. Egyp. prisons served as forced-labour compounds, as 'lock-ups' and as places of remand for people like Joseph awaiting trial. The butler and baker were put in *mišmār*, detention, virtually house-arrest, in Joseph's prison (Gn. 40:2–3) until their case was decided. Joseph's brothers were likewise detained for 3 days (Gn. 42:17, 19). After capture by the Philistines, Samson was kept in prison, the 'house of the prisoners' (Jdg. 16:21, 25; lit. 'those bound'); a very similar term is used in Ec. 4:14.

In Judah the guardrooms of the palace guards served as a temporary prison for Jeremiah (32:2, 8, 12; 33:1; 37:21; 38:28; *cf.* also Ne. 3:25; 12:39). Both there and in a private residence, a cistern could be used as a dungeon, which would often be very unpleasant (Je. 37:16, 20; 38:6, 13) and dark (Is. 42:7), a symbol of bondage from which the Lord's servant should deliver his people (Acts 26:15–18; Lk. 1:79). Nor was Jeremiah the only prophet imprisoned for his faithfulness in declaring God's message: Asa of Judah put Hanani the seer into the stocks (2 Ch. 16:10), and Ahab had Micaiah put in prison on rations of bread and water (1 Ki. 22:27; 2 Ch. 18:26). Defeated kings were some-

PRINCIPLES, FIRST
See Elements, Part 1.

PRISCA, PRISCILLA
See Aquila, Part 1.

Prisoners, handcuffed together, are escorted by Assyrian guards, while another is executed. Relief from the palace of Sennacherib, Nineveh. c. 690 BC. (BM)

■ **PRISON GUARD**
See Officers, Part 2.

■ **PRISONER OF WAR**
See Slave, Part 3.

■ **PROCLAMATION**
See Preaching, Part 3.

times imprisoned by their conquerors: so Hoshea of Israel by the Assyrians (2 Ki. 17:4), Jehoiachin of Judah by Nebuchadrezzar (*cf.* Je. 24:1, 5; D. J. Wiseman, *Chronicles of Chaldaean Kings*, pp. 33–35, 73), and Zedekiah of Judah likewise (Je. 52:11). At Babylon Jehoiachin was but one of many noble captives and artisans detained under 'house-arrest' at the royal palace and environs. Ration-tablets for him, his five sons and many other foreigners were found at Babylon (*ANET*, 308b; *DOTT*, pp. 84–86; E. F. Weidner, *Mélanges R. Dussaud*, 2, 1939, pp. 923–935; Albright, *BA* 5, 1942, pp. 49–55). Eventually Evil-merodach granted him a greater measure of freedom (2 Ki. 25:27, 29; Je. 52:31, 33). Ezekiel (19:9) pictures Jehoiachin being brought to Babylon in a cage; for a much earlier Egyp. picture of a Semitic prince as a prisoner in a cage, see P. Montet, *L'Égypte et la Bible*, 1959, p. 73, fig. 12. K.A.K.

II. In the New Testament

Four Greek words are translated by 'prison' in the EVV. John the Baptist was imprisoned in a *desmōtērion*, a 'place of bonds'. This was at Herod's fortress at Machaerus in Peraea, E of the Dead Sea (Jos., *Ant.* 18. 119), where two dungeons have been discovered, one still showing traces of fetters. *phylakē*, a 'place of guarding', is the most general and frequently used term. It suggests a place where the prisoners were closely watched. The chief priests imprisoned the apostles (Acts 5:19) in what is also called a *tērēsis dēmosia*, a 'public place of watching' (*cf.* Acts 4:3).

When Herod put Peter in prison, probably in the fortress of Antonia, where Paul was later lodged (Acts 21:34; 23:30) and referred to here as an *oikēma*, 'house', the apostle was guarded continually by four soldiers, two chained to him and two outside the door (Acts 12:3–6). Beyond this there would appear to have been another guard and then the iron outer gate (Acts 12:10). At Philippi Paul was in custody in the town jail, under the charge of a keeper, where there was an inner, perhaps underground, chamber containing stocks (Acts 16:24). These would have several holes, allowing the legs to be forced wide apart to ensure greater security and greater pain. In Caesarea Paul was imprisoned (Acts 23:35) in Herod's castle, but when a prisoner at Rome he was allowed to stay in his own lodging, with a soldier always chained to him (Acts 28:16, 30). D.H.W.

PROCONSUL (Gk. *anthypatos*, AV 'deputy'). In the Roman empire as organized by Augustus this was the title of governors of provinces which were administered by the Senate because they did not require a standing army. Proconsuls mentioned in the NT are L. Sergius *Paullus, proconsul of Cyprus when Paul and Barnabas visited that island *c.* AD 47 (Acts 13:7), and L. Junius *Gallio, whose proconsulship of Achaia (AD 51–2) overlapped Paul's 18-month stay in Corinth (Acts 18:12). In Acts

Foreign prisoners, including a bearded Syrian, are tied together with ropes round their necks and bound at the elbows. Detail from the state chariot of Tutankhamun. Sheet-gold over gesso on a wooden base. c. 1340 BC. (MetNY)

Warriors are imprisoned in a net held by the god Ningirsu, patron of Lagash. Part of the 'Stele of the Vultures', the victory stele of Eannatum of Lagash. First half of 3rd millennium BC. (MC)

19:38 'proconsuls' may be a generalizing plural; the proconsul of Asia had recently been assassinated (October AD 54) and his successor had not yet arrived. F.F.B.

PROCURATOR. In Roman imperial administration the word indicated the financial officer of a province, but was also used as the title of the governor of a Roman province of the third class, such as Judaea (Gk. *epitropos*; but in the NT the procurator of Judaea is regularly described as the 'governor', Gk. *hēgemōn*). *Judaea was governed by imperial procurators or prefects from AD 6 to 41 and from 44 to 66. Three are mentioned in the NT: Pontius *Pilate, AD 26–36 (Mt. 27:2, *etc.*), Antonius *Felix, 52–59 (Acts 23:24ff.) and Porcius *Festus, 59–62 (Acts 24:27ff.). The procurators were generally drawn from the equestrian order (Felix, a freedman, was an exception). They had auxiliary troops at their disposal and were generally responsible for military and financial administration, but were subject to the superior authority of the imperial legate (propraetor) of Syria. Their seat of government was Caesarea. From the Pilate inscription found at Caesarea in 1961, where he is called 'prefect' of Judaea, it has been inferred that before AD 41 the governors of Judaea were officially called 'prefects', but Tacitus gives Pilate the title 'procurator' (*Ann.* 15. 44). F.F.B.

PROMISE. There is in the Heb. OT no special term for the concept or act of promising. Where our English translations say that someone promised something, the Hebrew simply states that someone said or spoke (*'āmar*, *dāḇar*) some word with future reference. In the NT the technical term, *epangelia*, appears—chiefly in Acts, Galatians, Romans and Hebrews.

A promise is a word that goes forth into unfilled time. It reaches ahead of its speaker and its recipient, to mark an appointment between them in the future. A promise may be an assurance of continuing or future action on behalf of someone: 'I will be with you', 'They that mourn shall be comforted', 'If we confess our sins, God will forgive us our sins.' It may be a solemn agreement of lasting, mutual (if unequal) relationship: as in the covenants. It may be the announcement of a future event: 'When you have brought the people from Egypt, you will serve God on this mountain.' The study of biblical promises must therefore take in far more than the actual occurrences of the word in the EVV. (See also *WORD, *PROPHECY, *COVENANT and *OATHS.) An oath often accompanied the word of promise (Ex. 6:8; Dt. 9:5; Heb. 6:13ff.).

That what he has spoken with his mouth he can and will perform with his hand is the biblical sign manual of God, for his word does not return void. Unlike men and heathen gods, he knows and commands the future (1 Ki. 8:15, 24; Is. 41:4, 26; 43:12, 19, *etc.*; Rom. 4:21; *cf.* Pascal, *Pensées*, 693). Through the historical books, a pattern of divine promise and historical fulfilment is traced (G. von Rad, *Studies in Deuteronomy*, 1953, pp. 74ff.), expressive of this truth.

The point of convergence of the OT promises (to Abraham, Moses, David and the Fathers through the prophets) is Jesus Christ. All the promises of God are confirmed in him, and through him affirmed by the church in the 'Amen' of its worship (2 Cor. 1:20). The OT quotations and allusions in the Gospel narratives indicate this fulfilment. The Magnificat and the Benedictus rejoice that God has kept his word. The promised Word has become flesh. The new covenant has been inaugurated—upon the 'better promises' prophesied by Jeremiah (Je. 31; Heb. 8:6–13). Jesus is its guarantee (Heb. 7:22), and the Holy Spirit of promise its first instalment (Eph. 1:13–14).

Awaiting the promise of Christ's coming again and of the new hea-

PROFIT
See Mammon, Part 2.

vens and a new earth (2 Pet. 3:4, 9, 13), the church sets forth on her missionary task with the assurance of his presence (Mt. 28:20) and with the news that 'the promise of the Father'—the Holy Spirit (after Joel 2:28)—is given to Jew and pagan in Jesus Christ, fulfilling the promise to Abraham of universal blessing through his posterity. The promise is correlated to faith and open to all who, by imitating Abraham's faith, become 'children of the promise' (Gal. 3; Rom. 4; 9). (*ESCHATOLOGY, *SCRIPTURE.)

BIBLIOGRAPHY. G. K. Chesterton, *A Defence of Rash Vows*, 1901; J. Jeremias, *Jesus' Promise to the Nations*, E.T. 1958; W. G. Kümmel, *Promise and Fulfilment*, E.T.² 1961; F. F. Bruce (ed.), *Promise and Fulfilment: Essays presented to S. H. Hooke*, 1963; J. Moltmann, *Theology of Hope*, E.T. 1967; J. Bright, *Covenant and Promise*, 1977; J. Schniewind and G. Friedrich, *epangellō, etc.*, *TDNT* 2, pp. 576–586; E. Hoffmann, *NIDNTT* 3, pp. 68–74. J.H.

PROMISED LAND. More interest in the theological issues of Israel and her land is now being developed. Several factors may explain this. First, the stress on Israel's faith as historical has been reinforced by existential thought, which emphasizes personal choice rather than the corporate character of cultural and geographical contexts. There is now somewhat of a reaction to this emphasis, with recognition of space as well as time, corporate as well as individual reality, needing to be interpreted within biblical theology. The OT emphasis on 'the land of Israel' is being rediscovered.

Secondly, the growing awareness both of symbolism and the use of metaphor is giving depth to the aridity of analysis and the flatness of quantification in much modern thought. Spatial relations are more than distance or other abstract values; they are personally meaningful and culturally perceived. Biblical motifs such as 'the promised land', 'Jerusalem', 'the wilderness', 'waste places', *etc.*, are now being recognized to have theological meaning at more than one level of thought. The contemporary spirit of the homelessness of man, of being alienated and lost, is generating interest in being 'in place', 'at home', in God's world. The human need of 'topophilia' is being recognized.

Thirdly, there is the ecological crisis which is bringing to our attention the needs of human stewardship of the earth. Does the biblical mandate for man to have dominion over the earth (Gn. 1:26–27) have any bearing on our existing environmental situation? The psalmist realized that 'man who is of the earth may strike terror' in it (Ps. 10:18). The creation mandate was given to man to 'till it and keep it' (Gn. 2:15). 'Take care that the land be able to support you, . . . that your days and the days of your children may be multiplied' (see Dt. 11:16–21). The prophets, especially Jeremiah, denounce Israel for failing to do her part in taking care of the land.

Fourthly, there is the emphasis that Israel is the historical and geographical reality of the promises of God, in covenant to Abraham and to the people of Yahweh. The land is expressive of the reality that God is King of the universe, the Creator, who made all things so that the land is his and his people also (Lv. 25:23; *cf.* Ps. 95:4–7). Yahweh is therefore 'holy', not to be confused with or rivalled by any other gods (Ex. 20:3; Ho. 2:4f.). He is no nature deity, but the Creator of heaven and earth. The land is also the inheritance of Israel, as a gift of God (Dt. 26:5–9), but it is a land which the Israelites cannot fully maintain or possess without the help of God (Jdg. 1:19; *cf.* Jos. 17). Promise and prohibition go together, under the covenant of God (Ex. 23:30–33).

Finally, there is the apocalyptic interest in the future of the land. To what extent is Zionism a biblical understanding of prophecy? W. Marxsen, in his geographical outline of Mark's Gospel, speaks of Mark writing a 'Galilean Gospel', where Galilee is the locale and motif of hiddenness, where Jesus worked, where Christ is working in eschatological reality, and where he will work in the coming *parousia*. H. Conzelmann, in his commentary on Luke, sees Luke's focus upon Jerusalem as the point of intersection between Judaism and Christianity, where the Way led to Jerusalem, and from which the gospel has gone out to all the earth. Both Gospel writers could therefore be reflecting a polemic against the Jewish claim of the priority of the land of Israel. Indeed, this had been anticipated by Jeremiah, who saw that the true Israel do not need the land of Israel, neither for their identity nor for their worship of Yahweh. The incarnation has fulfilled them both, and made more concrete the practical realities of living as God's people.

BIBLIOGRAPHY. W. Brueggemann, *The Land*, 1977; H. Conzelmann, *The Theology of St. Luke*, 1960; W. D. Davies, *The Gospel and the Land*, 1974; A. J. Heschel, *Israel*, 1967; R. H. Lightfoot, *Locality and Doctrine in the Gospel*, 1938; E. Lohmeyer, *Galiläa und Jerusalem*, 1936; W. Marxsen, *Mark the Evangelist*, 1969, pp. 54–116; *idem*, 'The Holy Land in Judaic Theology', in J. Neusner (ed.), *Understanding Jewish Theology*, 1973, pp. 73–90; R. de Vaux, *Ancient Israel*, 1961, pp. 74ff.; G. von Rad, *The Problem of the Hexateuch*, 1966, pp. 79–93; M. Weinfeld, *Deuteronomy and the Deuteronomic School*, 1972, pp. 313–316; G. H. Williams, *Wilderness and Paradise in Christian Thought*, 1962; L. Lambert, *The Uniqueness of Israel*, 1979. J.M.H.

PROPHECY, PROPHETS.

I. The prophetic office

a. The normative prophet

The first person whom the Bible calls a prophet (Heb. *nāḇî'*) was Abraham (Gn. 20:7; *cf.* Ps. 105:15), but OT prophecy received its normative form in the life and person of Moses, who constituted a standard of comparison for all future prophets (Dt. 18:15–19; 34:10; *MESSIAH). Every feature which characterized the true prophet of Yahweh in the classical tradition of OT prophecy was first found in Moses.

He received a specific and personal call from God. The initiative in making a prophet rests with God (Ex. 3:1–4:17; *cf.* Is. 6; Je. 1:4–19; Ezk. 1–3; Ho. 1:2; Am. 7:14–15; Jon. 1:1), and it is only the false prophet who dares to take the office upon himself (Je. 14:14; 23:21). The primary object and effect of the call was an introduction into God's presence, as the passages noted above show. This was the 'secret' or 'counsel' of the Lord (1 Ki. 22:19; Je. 23:22; Am. 3:7). The prophet stood before men, as a man who had been made to stand before God (1 Ki. 17:1; 18:15).

Opposite page: The approximate dates of the ministries of the OT prophets with their historical setting (see also *CHRONOLOGY OF THE OT).

Name of prophet	Approximate dates of ministry	Contemporary rulers of			Historical setting
		Judah	Israel	Babylon/Persia	
Joel	c. ?810–750 BC	Joash (=Jehoash), Amaziah, Uzziah (=Azariah)			2 Ki. 11:1–15:7
Amos	c. 760 BC	Uzziah (=Azariah)	Jeroboam II		2 Ki. 14:23; 15:7
Jonah	c. 760 BC		Jeroboam II		2 Ki. 14:23–29
Hosea	760–722 BC		Jeroboam II, Zechariah, Shallum, Menahem, Pekahiah, Pekah, Hoshea		2 Ki. 14:23–18:37
Micah	742–687 BC	Jotham, Ahaz, Hezekiah			2 Ki. 15:32–20:21; 2 Ch. 27:1–32:33; Is. 7:1–8:22; Je. 26:17–19
Isaiah	740–700 BC	Uzziah (=Azariah), Jotham, Ahaz, Hezekiah			2 Ki. 15:1–20:21; 2 Ch. 26:1–32:33
Nahum	somewhere between 664 and 612 BC	Josiah			2 Ki. 22:1–23:30; 2 Ch. 34:1–36:1; Zp. 2:13–15
Zephaniah	c. 640 BC onwards	Josiah			2 Ki. 22:1–23:34; 2 Ch. 34:1–36:4
Jeremiah	626–587 BC	Josiah, Jehoahaz, Jehoiakim, Jehoiachin, Zedekiah			2 Ki. 22:1–25:30; 2 Ch. 34:1–36:21
Habakkuk	c. 605 BC	Jehoiakim			2 Ki. 23:31–24:7
Daniel	605–535 BC	Jehoiakim, Jehoiachin, Zedekiah		Nebuchadrezzar, Belshazzar, Darius, Cyrus	2 Ki. 24:1–25:30; 2 Ch. 36:5–23
Ezekiel	593–570 BC			Nebuchadrezzar	2 Ki. 24:8–25:26; 2 Ch. 36:9–21
Obadiah	c. ?587 BC onwards			Nebuchadrezzar	2 Ki. 25; 2 Ch. 36:11–21
Haggai	520 BC			Darius	Ezr. 5:1–6:22
Zechariah	c. 520 BC onwards			Darius onwards	Ezr. 5:1–6:22
Malachi	c. 433 BC			Artaxerxes I	Ne. 13

Again, the prophetic awareness of history stemmed from Moses. When Isaiah makes his tremendous polemic against idolatry, one of his most potent contentions, that Yahweh alone is the Author of prophecy and that the idols are at best wise after the event (*e.g.* 45:20–22), stems directly from Moses and the Exodus. Yahweh sent Moses into Egypt possessed of the clues necessary to interpret the great events which were to follow. History became revelation because there was added to the historical situation a man prepared beforehand to say what it meant. Moses was not left to struggle for the meaning of events as or after they happened; he was forewarned of events and of their significance by the verbal communications of God. So it was with all the prophets. Alone of the nations of antiquity, Israel had a true awareness of history. They owed it to the prophets, and, under the Lord of history, the prophets owed it to Moses.

Likewise they owed to him their ethical and social concern. Even before his call Moses concerned himself with the social welfare of his people (Ex. 2:11ff.; *cf.* v. 17), and afterwards, as the prophetic lawgiver, he outlined the most humane and philanthropic code of the ancient world, concerned for the helpless (Dt. 24:19–22, *etc.*) and the enemy of the oppressor (*e.g.* Lv. 19:9ff.).

Many of the prophets were found confronting their kings and playing an active, statesman's part in national affairs. This was a function of the prophet which found its prototype in Moses, who legislated for the nation, and was even called 'king' (Dt. 33:5). It is interesting that the first two kings of Israel were also prophets, but this union of offices did not continue, and the Mosaic–theocratic rule was prolonged by the association of the anointed king and the anointed prophet.

We also see in Moses that combination of proclamation and prediction which is found in all the prophets. This will concern us in greater detail presently, as a feature of prophecy at large. We will pause only to show that Moses established the norm here also, namely, that in the interests of speaking to the present situation the prophet often undertakes to enlarge upon events yet to come. It is this interlocking of proclamation and prediction which distinguishes the true prophet from the mere prognosticator. Even when Moses uttered his great prophecy of the coming Prophet (Dt. 18:15ff.) he was dealing with the very pressing problems of the relation of the people of God to the practices and allurements of pagan cults.

Two other features characteristic of the prophets who were to succeed him are found in Moses. Many of the prophets used symbols in the delivery of their message (*e.g.* Je. 19:1ff.; Ezk. 4:1ff.). Moses used the uplifted hand (Ex. 17:8ff.) and the uplifted serpent (Nu. 21:8), not to mention the highly symbolic cultus which he mediated to the nation. And finally, the intercessory aspect of the prophetic task was also displayed in him. He was 'for the people to Godward' (Ex. 18:19, AV; Nu. 27:5) and on at least one notable occasion literally stood in the breach as a man of prayer (Ex. 32:30ff.; Dt. 9:18ff.; *cf.* 1 Ki. 13:6; 2 Ki. 19:4; Je. 7:16; 11:14).

b. The titles of the prophets

Two general descriptions appear to have been used for prophets: the first, 'man of God', describes how they appeared to their fellow-men. This title was first used of Moses (Dt. 33:1) and continued in use till the end of the Monarchy (*e.g.* 1 Sa. 2:27; 9:6; 1 Ki. 13:1, *etc.*). That it was intended to express the difference of character between the prophet and other men is made perfectly clear by the Shunammite: 'I perceive that this is a holy man of God . . .' (2 Ki. 4:9). The other general title was 'his, your or my servant'. It does not appear that any ever addressed the prophet as 'servant of God', but God often described the prophets as 'my servants' and consequently the other pronouns, 'his' and 'your', were also used (*e.g.* 2 Ki. 17:13, 23; 21:10; 24:2; Ezr. 9:11; Je. 7:25). Here the other relationship of the prophet, that towards God, is expressed, and this also was first a title of Moses (*e.g.* Jos. 1:1–2).

There are three Hebrew words used of the prophet: *nāḇî'*, *rō'eh* and *ḥōzeh*. The first of these is always translated 'prophet'; the second, which is, in form, an active participle of the verb 'to see', is translated 'seer'; the third, also an active participle of another verb 'to see', is unfortunately without distinctive English equivalent and is translated either 'prophet' (*e.g.* Is. 30:10) or 'seer' (*e.g.* 1 Ch. 29:29).

The derivation of *nāḇî'* has been the subject of long debate. The word can be traced to an Akkadian root, and the choice is between the prophet as one who is called, or one who calls, *i.e.* to men in the name of God. Either of these will admirably suit the nature of the prophet as found in the OT. The possibility that the prophet is one who calls to God, in prayer, has not been canvassed, but that too, and apparently from the start (Gn. 20:7), was a mark of a prophetic man.

Equally extensive discussion has centred on the relation of the three words *nāḇî'*, *rō'eh* and *ḥōzeh* to each other. Verses such as 1 Ch. 29:29, which appear to use the words with great discrimination (Gad is described in the Heb. as *ḥōzeh*), suggest that we ought to find a precise shade of meaning in each word. This, however, is not borne out by an examination of OT usage as a whole. The use of the words falls into two periods, marked out by 1 Sa. 9:9: first, there was the period when *nāḇî'* and *rō'eh* meant something different, the early period; then came the period, in which the author of 1 Sa. 9:9 lived, when *nāḇî'* had taken on the force of a synonym of *rō'eh*, with or without losing its own earlier meaning. The source document for the early period is 1 Sa. 9–10, and it certainly seems that we can decide the force of the two words as far as those chapters are concerned: the *nāḇî'* is a member of a group, given to corporate and infectious ecstasy (1 Sa. 10:5–6, 10–13; 19:20–24), whereas the *rō'eh* is solitary, and altogether a more important and impressive person. Out of a total of ten occurrences of the title, it is used six times of Samuel (1 Sa. 9:11, 18–19; 1 Ch. 9:22; 26:28; 29:29). He, therefore, demonstrates the *rō'eh par excellence*.

However, when we move to the later period indicated in 1 Sa. 9:9 it is impossible to be so precise. While it is noticeable that throughout Chronicles the *ḥōzeh* is always (except in 2 Ch. 29:30) mentioned in association with the king, the attractive suggestion that he was employed as a resident clairvoyant is not in accordance with the evidence. Even in Chronicles he often acts precisely as a *nāḇî'* would have done (*e.g.* 2 Ch. 19:2; 33:18), and the task most frequently attributed to him was that of court historian —a task equally found in the *nāḇî'* and the *rō'eh* (2 Ch. 9:29; 12:15; *cf.* 1 Ch. 29:29).

In general OT usage every shade of meaning in the verb *ḥāzâ* can be paralleled in the verb *rā'â*: both are used in connection with divination (Zc. 10:2; Ezk. 21:21), a connection which they share also with the *nāḇî'* (Mi. 3:11); both are used for the perception of the meaning of events (Ps. 46:8; Is. 5:12), and of the assessment of character (Ps. 11:4, 7; 1 Sa. 16:1); both are used of the vision of God (Ps. 27:4; Is. 6:5), and of prophetic activity (Is. 1:1; Ezk. 13:3); both are used of seeing vengeance carried out (Pss. 58:10; 54:7). In Is. 29:10 *nāḇî'* and *ḥōzeh* are parallel; in Is. 30:10, *rō'eh* and *ḥōzeh* are parallel; in Am. 7:12ff. Amaziah addresses Amos as *ḥōzeh*, urging him to prophesy (*nibbā'*) in Judah, and Amos replies that he is not a *nāḇî'*; in Ezk. 13:9 the reverse procedure is found: the noun *nāḇî'* is the subject of the verb *ḥāzâ*. These references could be prolonged extensively, and we conclude that the words are synonymous.

c. Foretelling and forthtelling

Too often in studies of the phenomenon of prophecy lip-service has been paid to the uniqueness of this movement in Israel, and at the same time it has been brought under judgment and criticism as though it were not unique, and as though the evidence could be explained on purely rationalistic grounds. We have only one mine of information about the OT prophet, however, and that is the OT itself, which must therefore be treated as a primary source document.

The prophet was first a man of the word of God. Even when he seemed to undertake other functions, such as the elaborate 'miming' of Ezekiel, it was subordinated to the interests of bringing the word of God to his fellow men. This word was not, so to speak, a mere passive opinion, as though God were anxious simply that men should be aware how he saw matters before they decided for themselves. It was rather the prophets' conviction that the proclamation of God's word radically changed the whole situation. For example, Is. 28–29 shows us a picture of a people struggling for a satisfactory solution to a pressing problem of political expediency, and, in the process, rejecting God's word; chs. 30 onwards reveal the situation which then transpires: the problem is no longer one of political balance of power as between Judah, Assyria and Egypt, but one of spiritual relationship between Judah, Assyria and Egypt, on the one hand, and the word of God, on the other. The word is an active ingredient added to the situation, which is henceforth impelled forward in terms of the word spoken (Is. 40:8; 55:11; see, *e.g.*, *CURSE).

Clearly, however, the prophets spoke to their situation primarily by means of warnings and encouragements concerning the future. Almost every prophet first appears as a foreteller, *e.g.* Am. 1:2. There are three grounds of this practice of foretelling: in the first place, it is clearly necessary, if people are to exercise due moral responsibility in the present, that they should be aware of the future. This at once lifts OT prediction out of the realm of mere prognostication and carnal curiosity. Calls to repentance (*e.g.* Is. 30:6–9) and calls to practical holiness (*e.g.* Is. 2:5) are equally based on a word concerning the future; the vision of wrath to come is made the basis of a present seeking of the mercy of God; the vision of bliss to come calls to a walking in the light now.

Secondly, prediction arises from the fact that the prophets speak in the name of the holy Ruler of history. We have already mentioned that the prophets' call was primarily to a knowledge of God. Out of this knowledge sprang the awareness of what he would do, as he guided history according to the unchangeable principles of his holy nature. This is to say, that, as prophets, they possessed all the basic information, for by Moses and the Exodus God had declared his name for ever (Ex. 3:15). They were 'in the know' (Am. 3:7).

Thirdly, prediction seems to belong to the very idea of the prophetic office. We may see this in Dt. 18:9ff.: Israel, entering the land of Canaan, is not only warned about the abominations of the Canaanite cults, such as infant sacrifice, but also about Canaanite religious practitioners, such as diviners. Certainly these men were concerned with what we call 'fortune-telling'; they offered to probe the future by one means or another. For Israel, instead of all these, there will be a prophet whom the Lord will raise up from among their brethren. This prophet, speaking in the name of the Lord, is to be judged by the accuracy of his forecasts (v. 22)—a clear proof that Israel expected prophetic prediction, and that it belonged to the notion of prophecy.

We may note here the extraordinarily detailed telepathic and clairvoyant gifts of the prophets. Elisha had the reputation of knowing what was said in secret afar off (2 Ki. 6:12) and gave evidence that it was not an inaccurate assessment of his powers. Ezekiel is justly famed for his detailed knowledge of Jerusalem at the time of his residence in Babylon (Ezk. 8–11). While it would be unrealistic to rule out direct communication between Ezekiel and Jerusalem, it is equally needless to try to evade this part of the biblical testimony. The prophets were men of remarkable psychic powers. It is, for example, unnecessary to question foreknowledge of personal names, such as is exemplified in 1 Ki. 13:2; Is. 44:28 (*cf.* Acts 9:12). Since there is no textual uncertainty at these points, the question is simply one of whether we accept the OT evidence as to what constitutes OT prophecy or not. The occurrence of such detailed prediction is perfectly 'at home' in the general picture of prophecy as the Bible reveals it. We should remember that it is illegitimate to pose the problem in terms of our knowledge of the lapse of time between prediction and fulfilment: 'How could the prophet know the name of someone not born till hundreds of years after his time?' There is nothing about 'hundreds of years' in the passages mentioned. This is our contribution to the question, because we know of the time-lapse. The real question is much simpler in statement: 'From what we know of the OT prophet, is there anything against his foreknowledge of personal names?' In the light of the OT, the negative reply may justly be made.

II. Prophetic inspiration and methods

a. Modes of inspiration

How did the prophet receive the message which he was commissioned to convey to his fellows? The answer given in the vast majority of cases is perfectly clear and yet tantalizingly vague: 'The word of the Lord came . . .', literally, the verb being the verb 'to be', 'the word of the Lord became actively present to . . .'. It is a statement of a direct, personal awareness. This is the basic experience of the prophet. It is stated for the first time in Ex. 7:1–2 (*cf.* 4:15–16). God is the author of the words which he conveys to the prophet, and through him to the people. It is this same experience which Jeremiah had when the Lord's hand touched his mouth (Je. 1:9), and this passage tells us as much as we are permitted to know: that in the context of personal fellowship which God has brought about the prophet receives a donation of words. Jeremiah later expressed this experience as 'standing in the counsel of the Lord' (23:22), whereby he was then able to make the people hear God's words. This, however, adds nothing in the way of psychological explanation.

Dreams and visions also had their place in the inspiration of the prophet. It is sometimes urged that Je. 23:28 teaches the invalidity of dreams as a method of ascertaining the word of the Lord. However, in the light of Nu. 12:6–7 and 1 Sa. 28:6, 15, which teach the validity of the dream, we see that Je. 23:28 is to be understood as 'a mere dream' or 'a dream of his own fancy'. Indeed, Jeremiah himself appears to have enjoyed the word of God through a dream (31:26). The experience of visions is best exemplified in the prophet Zechariah, but, like dreams, it adds nothing to our knowledge—or rather our ignorance—of the mechanics of inspiration. Exactly the same may be said of the cases where the word is perceived through a symbol (Je. 18; Am. 7:7ff.; 8:1–3). Inspiration is a miracle; we do not know in what way God makes the mind of a man aware of his word.

This raises the question of the activity of the Spirit of God in prophetic inspiration. There are 18 passages which associate prophetic inspiration with the activity of the Spirit: in Nu. 24:2 the reference is to Balaam; Nu. 11:29; 1 Sa. 10:6, 10; 19:20, 23 deal with the prophetic ecstasy; the plain assumption that prophecy arises from the Spirit of God is found in 1 Ki. 22:24; Joel 2:28–29; Ho. 9:7; Ne. 9:30; Zc. 7:12; a direct claim to the inspiration of the Spirit is made in Mi. 3:8; the Spirit's inspiration of the prophetic word is claimed by 1 Ch. 12:18; 2 Ch. 15:1; 20:14; 24:20; Ne. 9:20; and Ezk. 11:5. It is clear that this evidence is not evenly spread through the OT, and in particular that the pre-exilic prophets are sparsely represented. Indeed, Jeremiah does not mention the Spirit of God in any context whatever. This has been taken as showing a distinction between the 'man of the word' and the 'man of the Spirit' (see L. Koehler, *Old Testament Theology*, 1957; E. Jacob, *Theology of the Old Testament*, 1958; T. C. Vriezen, *An Outline of Old Testament Theology*, 1958), suggesting that the early prophets were anxious to dissociate themselves from the group inspiration of the so-called spirit-possessed men. This is not a necessary, nor even a probable, conclusion. For one thing, a straightforward identification of the earlier group-ecstatics with the later false prophets is not possible; and, for another, as E. Jacob points out, 'the word presupposes the spirit, the creative breath of life, and for the prophets there was such evidence of this that they thought it unnecessary to state it explicitly'.

b. Modes of communication

The prophets came before their contemporaries as men with a word to say. The spoken oracle is the form in which the word of God is expressed. Each prophet stamped the marks of his own personality and experience on this word: the oracles of Amos and Jeremiah are as unlike as are the personalities of the two prophets. There is, therefore, a double awareness in the books of the prophets: on the one hand, these words are the words which God gave to the prophet. God took this man to be his mouthpiece; they are the words of God. On the other hand, these words are the words of a certain man, spoken at a certain time, under certain circumstances. It is customary among modern writers (*e.g.* H. H. Rowley, *The Servant of the Lord*, 1952, p. 126) to draw the conclusion that the word thus became to an extent imperfect and fallible, because it was the word of imperfect and fallible men. We ought to be clear that such a conclusion must rest on grounds other than the testimony of the prophets themselves in so far as we have it in the books. This is not the place to discuss the relation between the words of inspired men and the words of the God who inspired them (*INSPIRATION), but it is the place to say that the books of the prophets may be searched without discovering any trace of suggestion that the prophets thought the word through them was in any way less than the word of God. We shall note presently that most of the prophets seemed totally unaware of the existence of voices other than, or contradictory to, their own. They possessed an overwhelming certainty concerning their words, such as is proper either to lunatics or to men who have stood in the counsel of God and received there what they are to say on earth.

Sometimes the prophets couched their oracles in the form of parable or allegory (*e.g.* Is. 5:1–7; 2 Sa. 12:1–7; and especially Ezk. 16 and 23), but the most dramatic presentation of their message was by means of the 'acted oracle'. If we start by thinking of the acted oracle as a 'visual aid' we will undoubtedly end with the wrong conception of its nature and function. Of course, it was a visual aid, but, in association with the Heb. notion of the efficacy of the word, it served to make the discharge of the word into the contemporary situation rather more powerful. This is best seen in the interview between King Joash and the dying Elisha (2 Ki. 13:14ff.). In v. 17 the arrow of the Lord's victory is shot against Syria. The prophet has introduced the king into a sphere of symbolic action. He now inquires how far the king has faith to embrace that word of promise: the king smites three times, and that is the extent to which the effective word of God will achieve accomplishment and not return void. Here we see very vividly the exact relation in which the symbol stood to the word, and in which both stood to the course of events. The word embodied in the symbol is exceedingly effective; it cannot fail to come to pass; it will accomplish exactly what the symbol declared. Thus, Isaiah walked naked and barefoot (Is. 20), Jeremiah smashed a potter's vessel in the place of potsherds (Je. 19), Ahijah tore his new coat into twelve pieces and gave Jeroboam ten (1 Ki. 11:29ff.), Ezekiel besieged a model city (Ezk. 4:1–3), dug through the house wall (12:1ff.), did not mourn for his dead wife (24:15ff.). We need to distinguish sharply between the acted oracle of the Israelite prophet and the sympathetic magic of the Canaanite cults. Essentially the latter is a movement from man to God: the performance of a certain action by man is an attempt to coerce Baal, or whatever god was in mind, to function correspondingly. The acted oracle was a movement from God to man: the word of God, the activity on which God had already decided, was thus declared and promoted on earth. In this, as in every other aspect of biblical religion, the initiative rests solely with God.

c. The books of the prophets

The question of the formation of the *Canon does not concern us here, but we cannot evade the question of the compilation of the writings of each prophet. It ought to be taken for granted that each of the prophetic books contains only a selection of the utterances of that prophet, but who did the selecting, editing and arranging? For example, the Judaean references in the book of Hosea are probably correctly seen as editorial work after the fall of Samaria, when the prophet's oracles were carried S. But who was the editor? Or, again, the series of questions and answers in Malachi are clearly a deliberate arrangement to convey a total message. Who arranged them? Or, on a larger scale, the book of Isaiah is manifestly a well-edited book; we have only to think of the way in which the series of six 'woes' (chs. 28–37) fall into two groups of three within which the first three respectively are exactly matched by the second three, or of the way chs. 38–39 have been taken out of chronological order so that they may become a historical preface to chs. 40–55. But who was the careful editor?

If we consult the books themselves we find three hints as to their written composition. First, that the prophets themselves wrote at least some of their oracles (*e.g.* Is. 30:8; Je. 29:1ff.; *cf.* 2 Ch. 21:12; Je. 29:25; *cf.* the use of the first person in Ho. 3:1–5); secondly, that in the case of Jeremiah, at least, a lengthy statement of his prophecies so far was made out with the help of a secretary (Je. 36), and that the command is both given and received without any sign that it was at all out of the way; and thirdly, that the prophets are sometimes associated with a group which was, presumably, the recipient of the teaching of the master-prophet, and may have been the repository of his oracles. Such a group is mentioned as 'my disciples' in Is. 8:16. These slender pieces of evidence suggest that the prophet himself was behind the recording of his words, whether by personal act, or by dictation, or by teaching. It could easily have been that the oracles of Isaiah took their present form as a manual of instruction for the prophet's disciples.

The name 'sons of the prophets' is used of these groups of disciples. It is actually found in the times of Elijah and Elisha, though Am. 7:14 shows that it survived as a technical term long after. We would gather from 2 Ki. 2:3, 5 that there were known groups of men settled here and there in the land under the general superintendence of the 'authorized' prophet. Elijah, in his effort to spare Elisha the strain of parting, appears to make a customary journey. Elisha in his turn had the management of the prophetic groups (2 Ki. 4:38; 6:1ff.), and availed himself of their services (2 Ki. 9:1). Clearly the members of these groups were men of prophetic gift (2 Ki. 2:3, 5), but whether they joined the group by divine call or attached themselves to the prophet, attracted by his teaching, or were called by him, we are not in a position to say.

There is no need to see in Am. 7:14 a slur on the prophetic groups, as though Amos were indignantly distinguishing himself from them. Amos could hardly be denying prophetic status to himself, seeing he is about to assert that the Lord commanded him to 'prophesy' (Heb. *hinnāḇē'*, to perform the part of a *nāḇî'*, 7:15). We may therefore take the words either as an indignant rhetorical question: 'Am I not a prophet, and a prophet's son? Indeed, I was a herdsman . . . and the Lord took me', or, preferably, 'I am no prophet . . . I am a herdsman, . . . and the Lord took me.' Amos is making no sinister accusation against the sons of the prophets as necessarily professional time-servers, but is alleging the authority of a spiritual call as against the accusation of lack of official status and authorization.

Very likely, at any rate, it is to such men, grouped round the great prophets, that we owe the safeguarding and transmission of their oracles, while at the same time it is going far beyond any information we possess regarding the groups of the 'sons of the prophets', their continuance and their work, to ascribe to them wholesale modifications, adaptations and additions to the inherited work of the 'master' prophet, as is becoming increasingly fashionable in specialist study.

III. True and false prophets

When Micaiah the son of Imlah and Zedekiah the son of Chenaanah confronted each other before King Ahab, the one warning of defeat and the other promising victory, and both appealing to the authority of the Lord (1 Ki. 22), how could they have been distinguished, the true from the false? When Jeremiah faced Hananiah, the former bowing under a yoke symbolizing servitude and the latter breaking the yoke symbolizing liberation (Je. 28), how could they have been distinguished? Or, a more extreme case, when the 'old prophet in Bethel' brought back the 'man of God' out of Judah with a lying message, and then rounded upon him with the true word of God (1 Ki. 13:18–22), was it possible to tell when he spoke with truth and when he spoke with deceit? The question of the discrimination of prophets is by no means academic but thoroughly practical and of the highest spiritual importance.

Certain external characteristics of a general kind have been alleged as distinguishing the true from the false. It has been urged that the prophetic ecstasy was the mark of the false prophet. We have already noted that group-ecstasy was the common mark of the *nāḇî'* in the time of Samuel (1 Sa. 9–10; *etc.*). This ecstasy was apparently spontaneous, or it could be induced, notably by music (1 Sa. 10:5; 2 Ki. 3:15) and by the ritual dance (1 Ki. 18:28). The ecstatic person apparently became very forgetful and quite insensible to pain (1 Sa. 19:24; 1 Ki. 18:28). It is easy, and indeed almost inevitable, that we should look with suspicion on a phenomenon such as this: it is so alien to our taste, and it is known as a feature of Baalism, and of Canaan in general. But these are not sufficient grounds for a plain identification between ecstatic and false. For one thing, there is no indication that the ecstasy was in any way frowned upon either by the people at large or by the best of their religious leaders. Samuel foretold with apparent approbation that Saul would join the ecstatic prophets and that this would signify his becoming a new man (1 Sa. 10:6). Also, the emissary of Elisha is called by Jehu's fellow captains 'this mad fellow' (2 Ki. 9:11), probably indicating that the ecstasy was still a feature of the prophetic group. Furthermore, Isaiah's Temple experience was certainly an ecstasy, and Ezekiel was without doubt an ecstatic.

Another suggested identification of false prophecy is professionalism: they were the paid servants of some king or other and it was to their interest to say what would please the king. But, again, this will hardly serve as a criterion. Samuel was clearly a professional prophet but was not a false prophet; Nathan was very likely a court official of David, but yet professionalism was by no means equivalent to sycophancy. Even Amos may have been professional, but Amaziah urges upon him that the living is better in Judah for a prophet like him (Am. 7:10ff.). Like the ecstatics, the court prophets are found in groups (1 Ki. 22), and no doubt their professional status could have been a corrupting influence, but to say that it was so is to run beyond the evidence. Jeremiah made no such accusation against Pashhur (Je. 20), though it would have been greatly to his advantage to have had a ready-made proof of his adversary's error.

There are three notable discussions of the whole question of false prophecy in the OT. The first is in Dt. 13 and 18. Dealing with the latter chapter first, it states a negative test: what does not come to pass was not spoken by the Lord. The wording here ought to be strictly observed; it is not a simple statement that fulfilment is the hall-mark of genuineness, for, as 13:1ff. indicates, a sign may be given and come to pass and yet the prophet be false. Inevitably, fulfilment was looked for as proof of genuine, godly utterance: Moses complained when what was spoken 'in the name' failed to have the desired effect (Ex. 5:23); Jeremiah saw in the visit of Hanamel a proof that the word was from the Lord (Je. 32:8). But Deuteronomy states only the negative, because that alone is safe and correct. What the Lord says will always find fulfilment, but sometimes the word of the false is fulfilled also, as a test for God's people.

Thus, we turn to Dt. 13, and the answer to the problem of discerning the false prophet: the test is a theological one, the revelation of God at the Exodus. The essence of the false prophet is that he calls the people 'after other gods, which you have not known' (v. 2), thus teaching 'rebellion against the Lord your God, who brought you out of the land of Egypt' (vv. 5, 10). Here we see the final feature of Moses, the normative prophet: he also fixed the theological norm by which all subsequent teaching could be judged. A prophet might allege that he spoke in the name of Yahweh, but if he did not acknowledge the authority of Moses and subscribe to the doctrines of the Exodus he was a false prophet.

This is substantially the answer, also, of Jeremiah. This sensitive prophet could not carry off the contest with the robust assurance which seemed so natural to Isaiah and Amos. The question of personal certainty was one which he could not evade, and yet he could not answer it except by the tautologous 'certainty is certainty'. We find him in the heat of the struggle in 23:9ff. It is clear from a reading of these verses that Jeremiah can find no external tests of the prophet: there is here no allegation of ecstasy or professionalism. Nor does he find the essence of the false prophet to consist in the acquisition of his oracles by dreams: that is, there is no test based upon prophetic technique. This, rather, is what Jeremiah alleges: the false prophet is a man of immoral life (vv. 10–14) and he places no barrier to immorality in others (v. 17); whereas the true prophet seeks to stem the tide of sin and to call people to holiness (v. 22). Again, the message of the false prophet is one of peace, without regard to the moral and spiritual conditions which are basic to peace (v. 17); whereas the true prophet has a message of judgment upon sin (v. 29).

We might interject here that Jeremiah ought not to be understood to say that the true prophet cannot have a message of peace. This is one of the most damaging notions that has ever entered the study of the prophets. There is a time when peace is the message of God; but it will always be in Exodus terms, that peace can come only when holiness is satisfied concerning sin. And this is exactly what Jeremiah is urging: the voice of the true prophet is always the voice of the law of God, once for all declared through Moses. Thus Jeremiah is bold to say that the false prophets are men of borrowed testimony, feigned authority and self-appointed ministry (vv. 30–32), whereas the true prophet has stood in the counsel of Yahweh and heard his voice, and has been sent by him (vv. 18, 21–22, 28, 32). Jeremiah's final position is in fact that 'certainty is certainty', but he is rescued from tautology by the positive revelation of God. He knows he is right because his experience is the Mosaic experience of standing before God (*cf.* Nu. 12:6–8; Dt. 34:10), and his message accords, as that of the false prophets does not, with the 'Exodus Quadrilateral' of Holiness (obedience), Peace, Sin, Judgment.

The answer of Ezekiel is substantially that of Jeremiah, and is found in Ezk. 12:21–14:11. Ezekiel tells us that there are prophets who are guided by their own wisdom and have no word from Yahweh (13:2–3). Thus they make people trust in lies and leave them without resource in the day of trial (13:4–7). The mark of these prophets is their message: it is one of peace and shallow optimism (13:10–16), and it is devoid of moral content, grieving the righteous and encouraging the wicked (v. 22). By contrast, there is a prophet who insists on piercing to the core of the matter, answering folk not according to their ostensible queries but according to their sinful hearts (14:4–5), for the word of Yahweh is always a word against sin (14:7–8). We see again that the true prophet is the Mosaic prophet. It is not just that in a vague sense he has a direct experience of God, but that he has been commissioned by the God of the Exodus to reiterate once again to Israel the moral requirements of the covenant.

IV. The prophets in the religion of Israel

a. Cultic prophets

Prophecy in a cultic setting is found in 2 Ch. 20:14. In a time of national anxiety King Jehoshaphat has led his people in public prayer in the court of the Lord's house. Immediately upon the conclusion of the prayer, a Levite, inspired by the Spirit of God, brings a word from the Lord promising victory. Here, then, is a Levite, that is, a cultic official, with a prophetic capacity. A further indication of the same happening may occur in some psalms (*e.g.* 60; 75; 82; *etc.*). In all these psalms there is a section in which a first person singular voice speaks: this is the oracular response, the prophet associated with the cult, bringing the contemporary utterance of God to his people. The suggestion made is that the guilds of levitical singers in the post-exilic period are the survival of groups of cultic prophets attached to the various sanctuaries in pre-exilic times. At every sanctuary, working alongside the priests, who had charge of the sacrificial aspect of the worship, there were prophets who declared the word of God publicly for the nation or privately for individual guidance.

The evidence for this practice, known, of course, in Canaanite circles, is largely inferential: we first meet a prophetic guild at the high place at Gibeah (1 Sa. 10:5); Samuel the prophet was an official at Shiloh (1 Sa. 3:19), and presided at a cultic meal at Ramah (1 Sa. 9:12ff.); the prophet Gad commanded David to erect the altar in Araunah's threshing-floor (2 Sa. 24:11, 18), and revealed God's will concerning the guilds of temple singers (2 Ch. 29:25); the prophet Nathan was consulted about the building of the Temple (2 Sa. 7:1ff.); Elijah staged a cultic scene at an ancient shrine (1 Ki. 18:30ff.); it was customary to visit the prophet on cultic occasions (2 Ki. 4:23); there are numerous references in which prophet and priest are coupled together in a way suggesting professional association (2 Ki. 23:2; Is. 28:7; Je. 2:26; 8:10; 13:13, *etc.*); there were prophetic quarters within the Temple (Je. 35:4).

It is difficult to see how any theory could be stable when it rests on such slight foundation. For example, the apparently strong connection established between prophet and Temple by the allocation of quarters, in Je. 35:4, is utterly negatived by the fact that the same verse speaks of chambers allocated to the princes. Again, the fact that prophets and guilds are found at cultic centres need mean nothing more than that they too were religious people! Amos was found at the sanctuary of Bethel (7:13), but this does not prove that he was paid to be there. David's consultation of his prophets tells us more about David's good sense than about his prophets' cultic associations. The theory of the cultic prophet remains a theory.

b. The prophets and the cultus

Even if the theory of the cultic prophet could be proved, it would still leave unsettled the relation of the canonical, or writing, prophet to the cultus. Their view of the cultus is somewhat of a crux of interpretation, and centres round six brief passages which are supposed by some to contain an outright condemnation of all cultic worship and a denial that it was ever the will of God (Am. 5:21–25; Ho. 6:6; Is. 1:11–15; 43:22–24; Mi. 6:6–8; Je. 7:21–23).

We may remark at once on the small number of verses involved. If the prophets were so opposed to the cultus, as some commentators have urged, it is extraordinary that their opposition was so rarely voiced, and then in such a manner as to leave it open to doubt whether they intended to condemn the cultus as such or the cultus as then abused. Furthermore, in other parts of their writings some of these prophets do not seem to take such a strong line about ceremonial and sacrifice. Isaiah, in his inaugural vision, certainly met with God and with peace of heart in a cultic setting. Are we to believe that he thought the cultus was worth nothing? Or again, Jeremiah, in ch. 7, the chapter from which the proof-text is drawn, does not condemn people for offering cultic worship (vv. 9–10) because Yahweh has forbidden it but because they couple it with moral indifference and iniquity; in v. 11 the Temple is 'this house, which is called by my name' and in v. 12, Shiloh is 'my place', which was destroyed, not to manifest divine rejection of the cultus but because of the iniquity of the worshippers. This all suggests, what detailed study of the verses will also indicate, that the anger of the prophets is directed against the cultus abused.

The heart of the exegetical problem in Am. 5:21–25 is in the last verse: 'Did you bring to me sacrifices and offerings the forty years in the wilderness . . . ?' In order to support the theory that Amos is a root-and-branch opponent of sacrifice, we must see him confidently expecting the answer 'No' to this question. But this is exactly what he could not have done. On any view of the origin of the Pentateuch, the traditions current in Amos' day would have spoken of sacrifice in the time of Moses, and of the Patriarchs before him. Vv. 21–23 tell of God's spurning of their current cultic practice. V. 24 tells us what is missing: a moral concern, a holy life. V. 25 is intended to enforce the truth that these things are not an 'either/or' but are the inseparable sides of religion according to the will of God. It should be stressed that the form of the question in the Hebrew does not suggest, let alone require, a negative answer, and if we translate v. 25 so as to bring out the emphasis of the prophet, we read: 'Was it sacrifices and offerings you brought to me in the wilderness forty years . . . ?' If they trace their religion back to its root in revelation, what do they find but a divine requirement of sacrifice in the context of a life obedient to the law of God? Because of their failure to follow this pattern (vv. 26f.) they will go into captivity. Mere *opus operatum* ritual is not worship of the God of the Bible.

According to Pr. 8:10, we are to 'Take my instruction instead of silver, and knowledge rather than choice gold.' Clearly this is a statement of priorities, not an exclusion of one thing in favour of the other. The importance of this verse is that its Hebrew is exactly parallel in construction to that of Ho. 6:6. In the light therefore of Hosea's failure to maintain an attitude of rejection towards the cultus throughout the rest of his prophecy, we may hold that he intends here a statement of priorities such as was given classical expression by Samuel: 'To obey is better than sacrifice' (1 Sa. 15:22).

The difficulty with the passage in Is. 1 is that it proves a great deal too much if it is taken simply as outright condemnation. Certainly vv. 11–12 appear to be a very strong attack on sacrifice, but no stronger than the attack upon the sabbath in v. 13, and upon prayer in v. 15. It cannot be that the prophet is utterly repudiating the sabbath and prayer. It must be that the final clause of v. 15, while referring directly to the earlier part of the verse, refers also to all the preceding condemnations. The prophet is simply urging that no religious activity avails in the context of a blatantly sinful life. This interpretation is proved to be correct by the initial verbs of v. 16, the first of which is constantly used throughout the levitical code for ceremonial purification, a very unlikely verb for the prophet to use if he considered all such things contrary to God's will; the second verb applies to moral purgation. The prophet's message is thus the Bible's message: the message of the joint requirement of the moral and ceremonial law.

We notice next Mi. 6:6–8. We have a somewhat analogous situation in the words of our Lord to the rich young ruler (Mk. 10:17ff.). By his exclusive reply in terms of the moral law does he intend to deny the divine authority of the ceremonial law of atoning sacrifice? In view of his constant regard for the Mosaic legislation (*e.g.* Mt. 8:4), not to mention his authentication of the terms of OT sacrifice by his teaching concerning his own death (Mk. 14:24), this is an unlikely interpretation of the words. Or again, we might ask if Lv. 18:5, presenting the moral law as a way of life, intends to invalidate the ceremonial law. Likewise, in the case of Micah, we must not understand him to reject whatever he does not specifically approve.

We have already noted certain background facts relative to the study of Je. 7:21–23. If Jeremiah, in the immediate context, seems, at the least, not to condemn sacrifice as *per se* unacceptable, may we so interpret 7:22? The difficulty is that, on the face of it, the words seem to require us to do so. However, closer examination of the Hebrew suggests that the difficulty belongs more to the English translation than to the original. The preposition which the English gives as 'concerning'—the vital word in the whole verse—is the Hebrew *'al-dib̲rê*, which can only mean 'concerning' by a weakening of its real significance 'because of' or 'for the sake of' (*cf.* Gn. 20:11; 43:18; Ps. 7, title; Je. 14:1; *etc.*). According to this, the verse says that Yahweh did not address Israel either 'because of' sacrifices: that is to say, the performance of sacrifice is not a means whereby pressure may be applied to God; nor did he address them 'for the sake of' sacrifices, for the living God stands in no need of anything man can supply. The nation has missed the divine priority by its concentration on the mere operation of a cult, for the cult is not a thing which exists on its own but rather for the sake of the spiritual needs of a people committed to obedience to the moral law of God.

We may allude finally to Is. 43:22ff., which is, in many ways, the most difficult verse of all. The emphasis in v. 22 requires the translation, 'Not me have you called . . .' On the supposition that this sets the tone of address throughout the verses, we are clearly within the same circle of possibilities: either, there is an indignant repudiation of the whole idea of divine authorization of sacrifice: 'whoever you may think you appeal to in your cultus, it is not to me, for I did not burden you with offerings'; or the accusation is that they abused the divine intention: 'in all your cultic labour you have not really called upon me, for it was never my plan that the cultus should turn you into slave-labour of ritual'. These alternatives of interpretation are so clear in the text that we may simply ask whether there are any other evidences whereby we might decide between them. The general consent of Scripture points to the second suggestion. Since there is no need to interpret the other crucial verses as an outright denial of sacrifice, we ought to reject that meaning here also. Moreover, within Isaiah, we have to reckon with 44:28, clearly approving the rebuilding of the Temple: for Isaiah to repudiate sacrifice and yet rejoice in the Temple would involve a complete contradiction in terms. There is also the inescapably sacrificial language of Is. 53.

c. The unity of Israel's religion

The religion of Israel began, as to its normative form, with the prophet-priest Moses, and it continued as a religion jointly of prophet and priest. This is declared in the covenant ceremony in Ex. 24:4–8. Yahweh has redeemed his people according to promise and they have acquiesced in the law he has imposed upon them as his redeemed people. Moses expressed the relationship symbolically: twelve pillars grouped round an altar (24:4). Here is the visual expression of the fulfilment of the covenant promise: 'I will take you for my people, and I will be your God' (Ex. 6:7). Notably, God is represented as an altar, for the holy God—the primary revelation of God to Moses (Ex. 3:5)—can dwell among sinners only by virtue of the atoning blood. Hence, the first thing Moses does with the blood is to sprinkle it upon the altar. As at the Passover, the initial movement of the blood is towards God in propitiation (Ex. 12:13).

The ceremony proceeds with the people's self-dedication to obedience to the law, and then the blood is sprinkled upon them. It is thus declared that while the people are brought to God by means of the blood of propitiation, the people themselves need the blood also in the context of their obligation to keep God's holy law. This, then, is the unity of prophet and priest: the former calls continually to obedience; the latter reminds constantly of the efficacy of the blood. If we drive them asunder the former becomes a moralist and the latter a ritualist; if we keep them together, as the religion of Israel does, and as the Bible does, we see the whole wonder of the God whom prophet and priest—and apostle too—proclaimed: a just God, and a Saviour, who will never relax his demand that his people walk in the light and be holy as he is holy, and who sets alongside that inflexible demand the blood which cleanses from all sin.

BIBLIOGRAPHY. H. H. Rowley, *The Servant of the Lord*, 1952, ch 3; *idem*, *The Unity of the Bible*, 1953, chs. 2, 4; *idem* (ed.), *Studies in Old Testament Prophecy*, 1950; *idem* (ed.), *The Old Testament and Modern Study*, 1951, chs. 5–6; H. W. Robinson, *Inspiration and Revelation in the Old Testament*, 1946, Parts 3 and 4; A. R. Johnson, *The Cultic Prophet in Ancient Israel*, 1944; A. B. Davidson, *Old Testament Prophecy*, 1904; C. Kuhl, *The Prophets of Israel*, 1960; E. J. Young, *My Servants the Prophets*, 1955; A. Lods, *The Prophets and the Rise of Judaism*, 1937; T. H. Robinson, *Prophecy and the Prophets in Ancient Israel*, 1923; J. Skinner, *Prophecy and Religion*, 1926; A. Guillaume, *Prophecy and Divination*, 1938; M. Noth, 'History and the Word of God in the Old Testament', *BJRL* 32, 1949–50, pp. 194ff.; O. T. Allis, *The Unity of Isaiah*, 1950, chs. 1–2; J. Lindblom, *Prophecy in Ancient Israel*, 1962; Y. Kaufmann, *The Religion of Israel*, 1961, Part 3; C. Westermann, *Basic Forms of Prophetic Speech*, 1967; R. E. Clements, *Prophecy and Covenant*, 1965; W. McKane, *Prophets and Wise Men*, 1965; C. H. Peisker, C. Brown, in *NIDNTT* 3, pp. 74–92; J. Bright, 'Jeremiah's Complaints—Liturgy or Expressions of Personal Distress?' in J. I. Durham and J. R. Porter (eds.), *Proclamation and Presence*, 1970, pp. 189ff.; H. H. Rowley, *From Moses to Qumran*, 1963, ch. 4.

J.A.M.

V. Prophecy in the New Testament

a. Continuity with the Old Testament

Prophecy and the prophets form the greatest line of continuity between the OT and NT. This is evident from the attitude of Christ and the apostles to OT prophecy, from the continuance of the phenomenon of prophecy both up to and after the ministry of Jesus, from the prophetic character of his own ministry, from the placing of the inspiration of NT apostles and prophets alongside that of OT prophets, and from the general outpouring of the Holy Spirit—the Spirit of prophecy—upon the church, leading to a continuing acceptance of prophets and prophesying in NT churches.

The OT prophetic line did not end with Malachi, but with John the Baptist, as our Lord expressly declares (Mt. 11:13). Prophetic utterances of John's father Zechariah, and of Anna, Simeon and Mary at the beginning of Luke's Gospel all bear witness to the continuance of prophetic inspiration (Lk. 1:46–55, 67–79; 2:26–38). The customary division into two 'Testaments' unfortunately obscures this marvellous unity of God's programme of revelation, but the line is continuous from Moses to John—and indeed beyond him, as we shall see.

Furthermore the NT stands in a relation of fulfilment to the actual message of the OT prophets. Time and again this is the burden of the NT: what God said of old he has now brought to pass (*e.g.* Mt. :22; 13:17; 26:56; Lk. 1:70; 18:31; Acts 3:21; 10:43, *etc.*). They all bore witness ultimately to Christ and his saving work (Lk. 24:25, 27, 44; Jn. 1:45; 5:39; 11:51). He came not to abolish the law and the prophets but to fulfil them (Mt. 5:17), and indeed based his understanding of his own mission and destiny principally upon their predictions.

The importance of this feature of the NT in authentication of the OT can scarcely be overemphasized. Though a persecuted minority (Mt. :12; 23:29–37; Lk. 6:23, *etc.*), the OT prophets are no mere idle speculative dreamers, but the most important voice coming to us from the ancient past, confirmed as proclaimers of eternal truth by the fulfilment of their greatest words in the greatest event of all time, the person and work of Jesus Christ. He himself points us back to them and their message as a permanent revelation of God, sufficient to lead to repentance and therefore to render culpable those who fail to listen to them (Lk. 16:29–31). They are authorized teachers of the Christian church, men whose words are still to be heeded as the word of God (*cf.* 2 Pet. 1:19–21).

. The greatest prophet and more

One of the commonest assessments of the person of Jesus of Nazareth by his contemporaries in Palestine was that he was a prophet from God, or a teacher from God, or both (Mt. 14:5; 21:11, 46; Lk. 7:16; Jn. 3:2; 4:19; 6:14; 7:40; 9:17, *etc.*). Their basic concept of a prophet was clearly based upon the OT prophetic ministry, and included declaring God's word, having supernormal knowledge, and evidencing the power of God (*cf.* Jn. 3:2; 4:19 *in loc.*; Mt. 26:68; Lk. 7:39).

Jesus accepted this title among others, and used it of himself (Mt. 13:57; Lk. 13:33), as well as accepting the title of teacher (Jn. 13:13), and even of scribe by implication (Mt. 13:51–52). The apostles came to realize that the ultimate fulfilment of Moses' prophecy (Dt. 18:15ff.) of the prophet like him whom God would raise up was found in Christ himself (Acts 3:22–26; 7:37; *MESSIAH). Only, in the case of Jesus we do not merely have a prophet, but the Son to whom the Spirit is not given by measure, in whose teaching ministry therefore the ministry of prophet and teacher are perfectly combined, and with whom the acme of prophetic revelation is reached (Mt. 21:33–43; Lk. 4:14–15; Jn. 3:34). However, more than the greatest prophet, we see in Jesus the one who sent the prophets (Mt. 23:34, 37), and one who not merely speaks the words of God, but is himself the Word made flesh (Jn. 1:1–14; Rev. 19:13; *LOGOS).

c. The Spirit of prophecy and the Christian church

Christ promised his disciples that after his ascension he would send them his Holy Spirit who would empower them to bear witness to him in the world, and would bear witness with them (Lk. 24:48–49; Jn. 14:26; 15:26–27; Acts 1:8). That this includes prophetic inspiration is clear from Mt. 10:19–20; Jn. 16:12–15, *etc.* The apostles and those who preached the gospel at the first did so in the power of the same 'Holy Spirit sent from heaven' who inspired the predictions of the OT prophets as they looked forward to the coming sufferings and glory of Christ (1 Pet. 1:10–12). Hence it is no surprise that when the Holy Spirit is poured out at Pentecost, the immediate result includes manifestations in speech (Acts 2:1–12), and Peter's explanation cites Joel 2:28–32, where a major result of the effusion of the Spirit on all flesh is that 'they shall prophesy', including not only prophetic words but also visions and dreams (Acts 2:18). Every Christian is potentially a prophet (thus realizing Moses' wish expressed in Nu. 11:29), for the Spirit given generally to the church for its testimony to Jesus is the Spirit of prophecy (1 Cor. 14:31; Rev. 19:10). Therefore Paul tells the Corinthian Christians, 'Earnestly desire the spiritual gifts, especially that you may prophesy' (1 Cor. 14:1).

When Christians initially received the power of the Holy Spirit, the commonest manifestations resulting at the time seem to have been speaking in another language (of praise and prayer) and prophesying (Acts 2:4, 17–18; 10:44–46; 19:6; 1 Cor. 1:5–7). It is not clear whether those who so spoke under the inspiration of the Spirit retained this faculty in all cases, or whether it was simply an initial confirmatory evidence of their reception of the Spirit, as in the case of the seventy elders, the nearest OT parallel in Nu. 11:25, where they prophesied only when the Spirit came upon them initially, 'but they did so no more'.

Jesus predicted that people would prophesy in his name (Mt. 7:22; though attention should be paid to his warning against reliance on this or any other work for one's spiritual standing), so prophecy is repeatedly mentioned as one of the gifts of the Holy Spirit with which Christ equips his members to function as his body in each place (Rom. 12:4–7; 1 Cor. 12:10–13; 1 Thes. 5:19–20; 1 Pet. 4:10–11; Rev. *passim*). This gift is differentiated both from tongues and interpretation and also from teaching. It differs from the former in being Spirit-inspired speech from God to man, whereas tongues and interpretations are addressed from man to God (Acts 2:11; 10:46; 1 Cor. 14:2–3); it differs from the latter (as in the OT) in being an utterance (frequently in the Lord's name) immediately inspired by direct revelation from the Holy Spirit, whereas teaching is mediated through patient study and exposition of truth already revealed. (Prophecy under the Spirit's inspiration will also often partly take the form, as in the OT, of a reiteration of truths already revealed in Scripture.)

The fullest guidance on the use of this gift in a church is given by Paul in 1 Cor. 14, along with instruction on the use of 'tongues'. From this and other references the following picture emerges. The exercise of this gift is in principle open to any Christian, under the sovereign distribution of the Spirit of Christ, including to women on occasion (vv. 5, 31; 11:5; 12:11; *cf.* Acts 21:9), although whether such feminine ministry was generally welcomed in the churches of the time is doubtful in view of 1 Cor. 14:33–36. Prophetic utterances are an intelligible word of revelation from God to the hearts and minds of those present, 'for their upbuilding and encouragement and consolation' (vv. 3–5, 26, 30–31). The reaction of the unbeliever to this prophetic ministry (vv. 24–25) shows that it could proclaim the whole message, of sin and judgment, as well as of grace and salvation.

'The spirits of prophets are subject to prophets' (v. 32), so that prophecy is neither to be abused by people succumbing to any supposedly uncontrollable ecstatic frenzy, nor to be exercised without the check of other members of the body, notably the elders and prophets weighing or discerning the accuracy and reliability of utterances purporting to issue from the Holy Spirit (vv. 29–33). It was doubtless just such abuses which led the apostle to write to another young church, 'Do not quench the Spirit, do not despise prophesying, but test everything; hold fast what is good' (1 Thes. 5:19–21)—a similar balance to that shown by him towards tongues in 1 Cor. 14:39–40.

Testing or weighing prophetic utterances is all the more necessary in view of the warnings of the NT (following the OT) against false prophets and false prophecy, by which Satan seeks to lead the unwary astray (Mt. 7:15; 24:11, 24; 2 Pet. 2:1; 1 Jn. 4:1ff.), and an example of which appears in Bar-Jesus at Paphos (Acts 13:5ff.). In the latter case occult sources are specified, although in other cases selfish human desires are blamed; but in either case the devil's anti-Christian cause is being served, as the symbolic figure of the false prophet serving the dragon in Rev. 13:11 and 19:20 makes plain. False prophets will on occasion work miracles (Mk. 13:22), but as in the OT (Dt. 13:1–5) are not to be given undiscerning credence merely on that account. The testing of any prophetic utterance will be in accordance with our Lord's warning, 'You will know them by their fruits' (Mt. 7:20 *in loc.*), and will include these criteria: *i.* their conformity to the teachings of Scripture, of Christ and of his apostles in both content and character (similar to OT, Dt. 18; but notice that a test of any man claiming spirituality or prophetic gifts is that 'he should acknowledge that what I am writing to you is a command of the Lord', 1 Cor. 14:37–38; 1 Jn. 4:6); *ii.* their over-all tendency and result or fruits (*e.g.*, do they glorify Christ and edify the church, as *per* Jn. 16:14 and 1 Cor. 14:3ff.?); *iii.* the consensus of the recognized prophets, and presumably elders and teachers, in that place weighing or discerning what is said (1 Cor. 14:29, 32); *iv.* the consistency of this utterance with other prophetic utterances in the body of Christ in that place (vv. 30–31); and *v.* the reverent confession of Jesus as the incarnate Lord by the Spirit speaking through the prophet (1 Cor. 12:2–3; 1 Jn. 4:1–3). In common with other spiritual gifts, Paul stresses that this gift is unprofitable and jarring in its exercise unless it proceeds from a loving heart and is ministered in a loving way in the church (1 Cor. 12:31–13:3).

Besides the possibility of any believer exercising this gift on occasions, there were also in the NT church those particularly recognized and set apart as 'prophets' for a more regular ministry of this nature. They are mentioned next after apostles in 1 Cor. 12:28–29 and Eph. 4:11, and they appear alongside teachers there and in the church at Syrian Antioch (Acts 13:1). Probably the best known in Acts is Agabus (11:28; 21:10–11), but others are also named (15:32), and the whole of the book of Revelation is an extended prophecy revealed to John (1:3; 10:11; 22:7, 10, 18–19). The ministry of prophets appears to have operated along with that of elders when Timothy was set apart for his ministry as an evangelist (1 Tim. 1:18; 4:14).

d. The character and form of New Testament prophecy

All the evidence from the examples of prophetic ministry in the NT shows that it was entirely of a piece with OT prophecy in its character and form. The ministries of John the Baptist, Agabus and the John who wrote the Apocalypse alike comprise the classic unity of prediction and proclamation, of foretelling and forth-telling, and the same is true of Zechariah, Simeon and others. Similarly they combined prediction of wrath to come or trouble in store and of coming grace (Lk. 3:7, 16ff.; Jn. 1:29ff.; Acts 11:28; Rev. 19–21). Equally we find prophecy and revelation by vision and occasionally by dream, as well as by the word of the Lord (Lk. 3:2; Rev. 1:10, 12, *etc.*; Acts 10:9–16; Mt. 1:20). The use of parable and symbol are well attested, including the acted oracle (Acts 21:11). It should be noted that in the last-named instance, Agabus' word was accepted by Paul as descriptively accurate, but not personally directive (vv. 12–14), although it agreed with the words he had received in other cities (Acts 20:23). However, both here and in 1 Tim. 4:14 and Acts 13:9ff. we see the power of the prophetic word still fully able to effect and convey that of which it speaks (*cf.* also Rev. 11:6).

e. Prophecy in the apostolic and later ages

It has often been assumed or argued that there can be no prophecy or prophets in the NT sense of the word in the church today, or in any other post-apostolic age, and many of those who use the term 'prophecy' to describe any current ministry have often diluted its meaning as equivalent to relevant preaching. But while evangelistic proclamation or a teaching ministry may on occasion approximate to prophecy, they are not the same. The biblical arguments for denying the possibility of prophets today (as summarized by J. R. W. Stott, in *Baptism and Fullness*, 1975, pp. 100–102) are twofold: first, besides being mentioned immediately after apostles in Eph. 4:11 and 1 Cor. 12:28, the two are bracketed together as constituting the foundation of the NT church in Eph. 2:20 and 3:5; and secondly, the formation of a completed or closed canon of the NT precludes the possibility of any fresh revelation of divine truth (Heb. 1:1–2). Others have sometimes sought to identify this completion of the NT canon with the time when prophecy will pass away according to 1 Cor. 13:8ff.; but this does violence to the context, which clearly shows that these gifts will pass away 'when the perfect comes', which is defined as when we 'see face to face' (*i.e.* beyond this life and age altogether). Nor will the Ephesian texts bear the weight thus placed on them, since the association of prophets with the founding of the church does not automatically rule out their ministry in its continuance. (There are

ther reasons for asserting the
niqueness of the original apos-
ɔlate, which do not apply equally
ɔ prophets.) Some would main-
ain that the prophets referred to
re OT prophets, but this is very
oubtful. The argument appears to
est in fact upon an equation of
rophecy with 'fresh revelation',
hat is, some material addition to
God's saving revelation of himself
ɔ mankind as a whole in Christ.
'ut there does not seem to be any
olid ground for making such an
evitable equation in either the OT
r NT. All may agree that there is
o new revelation to be expected
oncerning God in Christ, the way
f salvation, the principles of the
Christian life, *etc.* But there ap-
ears to be no good reason why the
ving God, who both speaks and
cts (in contrast to the dead idols),
annot use the gift of prophecy to
ive particular local guidance to a
hurch, nation or individual, or to
varn or encourage by way of pre-
iction as well as by reminders, in
ull accord with the written word of
cripture, by which all such utter-
nces must be tested. Certainly the
NT does not see it as the job of the
rophet to be a doctrinal innova-
or, but to deliver the word the
pirit gives him in line with the
ruth once for all delivered to the
aints (Jude 3), to challenge and
ncourage our faith.

Always in the NT the prophets
f both Testaments are regarded as
he pioneers of faith, who stand in
he front line in every age and reap
he full blast of the wind of perse-
ution stirred up in the world by
he devil against the people of God,
whether through Jewish or Gentile
pposition (Mt. 23:37; Lk. 11:47–
0; Acts 7:52; 1 Thes. 2:15; Rev.
1:3–8; 16:6; 18:20, 24). Sometimes
hey are bracketed with our Lord,
ometimes with the apostles and
ometimes with the saints, but the
reatment they receive as God's
pokesmen is typical of what all his
ervants and children who are faith-
ul in their testimony may expect in
fallen world, together with their
ictory, resurrection and
nheritance beyond it by God's
race (Mt. 5:10–12; Heb. 11:39–
2:2). For 'the testimony of Jesus is
he spirit of prophecy', and all his
eople are called to bear that testi-
ony faithfully in various ways by
he power of the same Spirit.

BIBLIOGRAPHY. H. A. Guy, *New
'estament Prophecy, its origin and
ignificance*, 1947; M. C. Harper,
'rophecy, 1964; A. Bittlinger, *Gifts and Graces*, 1967; *idem*, *Gifts and Ministries*, 1974; G. Friedrich, *TDNT* 6, pp. 828–861; J. Lindblom, *Gesichte und Offenbarungen*, 1968; E. E. Ellis, 'The Role of the Christian Prophet in Acts', in W. W. Gasque and R. P. Martin (eds.), *Apostolic History and the Gospel*, 1970; D. Hill, 'On the evidence for the creative rôle of Christian prophets', *NTS* 20, 1973–4, pp. 262–274; *idem*, *New Testament Prophecy*, 1979; J. D. G. Dunn, *Jesus and the Spirit*, 1975, pp. 170ff., 225ff.; U. B. Müller, *Prophetie und Predigt im Neuen Testament*, 1975; J. Panagopoulos (ed.), *Prophetic Vocation in the New Testament and Today* (*NovT Supp.* 45), 1977; C. H. Peisker, C. Brown, *NIDNTT* 3, pp. 74–92; F. F. Bruce, *The Time is Fulfilled*, 1978, pp. 97–114.

J.P.B.

PROPHETESS (Heb. *n^{e}ḇî'â*; Gk. *prophētis*). Throughout both Testaments 'prophetess' is used in as wide a sense of women as 'prophet' is of men.

Prophetesses specifically named are Miriam, sister of Moses, who led a choral dance in celebration of Israel's deliverance from Egypt (Ex. 15:20); Deborah, wife of Lappidoth, 'a mother in Israel' (Jdg. 5:7), who was consulted as an intertribal judge (Jdg. 4:4); Huldah, wife of the keeper of the royal wardrobe, who declared the divine will to Josiah after the discovery of the law-book (2 Ki. 22:14); Noadiah, who joined other prophets in attempting to intimidate Nehemiah (Ne. 6:14); and Anna, who praised God in the Temple at the appearance of the infant Jesus (Lk. 2:36ff.).

Isaiah's wife is called 'the prophetess' (Is. 8:3), perhaps because she was a prophet's wife. Philip's 4 unnamed daughters prophesied in Caesarea (Acts 21:9). In the early church, as Paul's Corinthian correspondence indicates, the gift of *prophecy was exercised by various Christians irrespective of sex (*cf.* 1 Cor. 11:4f.). This was in accordance with the prediction of Joel 2:28 ('your sons and your daughters shall prophesy'), fulfilled on the day of Pentecost (Acts 2:16ff.).

There were false prophetesses as well as false prophets in Israel (*cf.* Ezk. 13:17). In the NT unenviable notoriety is attained by 'the woman Jezebel, who calls herself a prophetess' (Rev. 2:20). M.B.

PROPITIATION. Propitiation properly signifies the removal of wrath by the offering of a gift. In the OT it is expressed by the verb *kipper* (*ATONEMENT). In the NT the *hilaskomai* word group is the important one. In modern times the whole idea of propitiation has been strongly criticized as savouring of unworthy ideas of God. Many suggest that the term 'propitiation' should be abandoned in favour of *expiation, and this is done, for example, in RSV.

The objection to propitiation arises largely from an objection to the whole idea of the wrath of God, which many exponents of this view relegate to the status of an archaism. They feel that modern men cannot hold such an idea. But the men of the OT had no such inhibitions. For them 'God is angry with the wicked every day' (Ps. 7:11, AV). They had no doubt that sin inevitably arouses the strongest reaction from God. God is not to be accused of moral flabbiness. He is vigorously opposed to evil in every shape and form. While he may be 'slow to anger' (Ne. 9:17, *etc.*), his anger is yet certain in the face of sin. We may even read 'The Lord is slow to anger, and abounding in steadfast love, forgiving iniquity and transgression, but he will by no means clear the guilty' (Nu. 14:18). Even in a passage dealing with the longsuffering of God his refusal to condone guilt finds mention. The thought that God is slow to anger is to men of the OT far from being a truism. It is something wonderful and surprising. It is awe-inspiring and totally unexpected.

But if they were sure of the wrath of God against all sin, they were equally sure that this wrath might be put away, usually by the offering of the appropriate sacrifice. This was ultimately due, not to any efficacy in the sacrifice, but to God himself. God says, 'I have given it for you upon the altar to make atonement for your souls' (Lv. 17:11). Pardon is not something wrung from an unwilling deity. It is the gracious gift of a God who is eager to forgive. So the psalmist can say, 'He, being compassionate, forgave their iniquity, and did not destroy them; he restrained his anger often, and did not stir up all his wrath' (Ps. 78:38). The averting of the wrath of God is not something which men bring about. It is due to none less than God himself, who 'turned his anger away' (AV).

PROPHECY, SPIRIT OF
See Prophecy, Part 3.

In the NT there are several passages where the expression 'the wrath of God' occurs, but the relevant evidence is not limited to these alone. Everywhere in the NT there is the thought that God is vigorously opposed to evil. The sinner is in no good case. He has put himself in the wrong with God. He can look for nothing other than the severity of the divine judgment. Whether we choose to call this 'the wrath of God' or not, it is there. And, while wrath is a term to which some objections may legitimately be raised, it is the biblical term and no satisfactory substitute has been suggested.

We see the force of the NT idea of propitiation from the occurrence of the term in Rom. 3:24f. We are 'justified freely by his grace through the redemption that is in Christ Jesus: whom God hath set forth to be a propitiation through faith in his blood' (AV). The force of Paul's argument up to this point is that all, Jew and Gentile alike, are under the condemnation of God. 'The wrath of God is revealed from heaven against all ungodliness and wickedness of men' (Rom. 1:18). Paul shows first that the Gentile world stands under God's condemnation and then that the Jewish world is in the same plight. It is against this background that he sees the work of Christ. Christ did not save men from nothing at all. He delivered them from a very real peril. The sentence of judgment had been passed against them. The wrath of God hung over them. Paul has strongly emphasized the wrath of God throughout these opening chapters, and therefore Christ's saving work must include deliverance from this wrath. This deliverance is described by the word 'propitiation'. There is nothing else to express this thought in the critical passage Rom. 3:21ff., which sets out the way in which God has dealt with this aspect of man's plight. *hilastērion* must be held here to signify something very like 'propitiation'. (See further *NTS* 2, 1955–6, pp. 33–43.)

In 1 Jn. 2:2 Jesus is described as 'the propitiation for our sins'. In the previous verse he is our 'advocate with the Father'. If we need an advocate with God, then our position is indeed a dangerous one. We are in dire peril. All this helps us to see that 'propitiation' is to be taken here in its usual sense. Jesus' activity for men is described as turning away the divine wrath. But the Bible view of propitiation does not depend on this or that specific passage. It is a reflection of the general import of its teaching. 'Propitiation' is a reminder that God is implacably opposed to everything that is evil, that his opposition may properly be described as 'wrath', and that this wrath is put away only by the atoning work of Christ.

BIBLIOGRAPHY. C. H. Dodd, *The Bible and the Greeks*, 1935; R. Nicole, *WTJ* 17, 1954–5, pp. 117–157; Leon Morris, *NTS* 2, 1955–6, pp. 33–43; *idem*, *The Apostolic Preaching of the Cross*², 1965; H.-G. Link, C. Brown, H. Vorländer, *NIDNTT* 3, pp. 145–176. L.M.

PROSELYTE. OT and Talmud bring proselytes ever more fully within covenant Judaism. The Heb. term *gēr* first meant a resident alien, not necessarily with religious affiliations—indeed the same word is used for dispersed Jews on foreign soil (Gn. 15:13; Ex. 23:9). Within the OT canon, or possibly later, it came to designate full proselytes. The term *tôšāḇ* has the same civil restriction as the earlier usage of *gēr*, but with a lesser implication of permanence. The LXX renders the common word *gēr* about a dozen times *paroikos*, 'neighbour'—a word which cannot mean religious proselyte—occasionally by some other term, and over 70 times by *prosēlytos*. There is both in Hebrew and in Greek an advance in significance of meaning, though we cannot always define precisely where one phase shades into another.

Several OT passages show a warmth of welcome to proselytes. Note the charity of Lv. 19:34 and parallels; the willingness to receive foreigners into religious fellowship, on condition of circumcision (Ex. 12:48), possibly even without this (Nu. 15:14–16); also the recognition of a single law for wrongdoers, whether Israelites or foreigners (Nu. 15:30). The alien is enjoined to observe the sabbath in Jewish company (Ex. 20:10, *etc.*). The most striking passages pass beyond mere legislation to the brotherhood of mankind. Nobly generous are the prayers of 1 Ki. 8:41–43, and the glowing potential universalism of Is. 2:2–4; 49:6; 56:3–8; Je. 3:17; Zp. 3:9. The short book of Ruth is the story of a particular woman proselyte whose memory later Judaism greatly honoured.

Political and geographical circumstances doubtless kept the number of proselytes relatively small in OT times. Such persons would normally be aliens resident in Palestine, voluntarily accepting circumcision, and with it the whole burden of the law. Yet Is. 19:18–25 and Zp. 2:11 breathe a vision singularly unfettered by racial tradition and prejudice. If certain strains of later Judaism were unwilling to receive proselytes, they possessed no valid OT excuse.

In the period of the Graeco-Roman Dispersion, proselytes became numerous. Jewish morality and monotheism appealed to earnest Gentiles, though many of them abhorred circumcision, sabbaths and abstention from pork. Certain converts went right through, submitting themselves to instruction, circumcision and baptism, thereafter offering sacrifice in the Temple. Others admired Judaism, yet remained unprepared to meet its requirements wholly. They worshipped and studied in the synagogue, but remained uncircumcised, rather like Christian adherents who never receive Holy Communion. Many scholars have dubbed these 'half-proselytes', and have debated as to whether they are to be identified with the 'God-fearers' of contemporary literature K. Lake's epigrammatic remark that 'fractional proselytes are impossible' pinpoints an element of truth, yet rather arbitrarily. There was an important and sizeable class of these uncircumcised sympathizers, as Philo, Josephus and others clearly testify.

In the rabbinic literature, the term *gēr* unquestionably means a full proselyte. A resident alien is a *gēr tôšāḇ* in the Mishnah; later, in mediaeval literature, a 'proselyte of the gate'. A convert through fear is contemptuously called a 'lion proselyte', in reference to 2 Ki. 17:25ff. In Midrash Rabbah on Numbers 8, in the extracts in R. Loewe and C. G. Montefiore, *A Rabbinic Anthology*, 1938, pp. 566–579, and in many other contexts, it is insisted that the privileges of the proselyte should be equal to, or greater than, those of the Jew by birth, that he should be the special object of human and of divine love.

Despite these noble sentiments, many rabbis abhorred the proselyte. The Babylonian Talmud insists in one context that such a person has a strong predisposition to sin, because of his evil background (*Baba Metzia* 59b), which suggests implicit denial of the potential of real conversion. In deprecating the admission of proselytes to Judaism, the same Talmud elsewhere likens them to a sore on the skin of Israel (*Yebamoth* 109b), an ugly sentiment, whatever its political context. The first-generation proselyte probably never attained real as distinct from theoretical equality with Jews of pure descent, though Scripture and the best rabbinic teachings ordained that he should. Exclusiveness, whether born of racial pride or of suffering, has disfigured Judaism throughout history, though the OT frequently rebukes this spirit, notably in the book of Jonah.

Proselytes were flowing more steadily into the Jewish fold by NT times, whatever the official reactions (*cf.* Acts 2:10; 6:5; 13:43). Diaspora Judaism was more hospitable to the honest Gentile enquirer than was the more narrow, legalistic and traditional cult of Palestine and Babylonia. The infant church was indeed largely recruited from the ranks of the uncircumcised sympathizers or God-fearers, the *theosebeis* or *sebomenoi*. To some who remained deterred by circumcision, the cross proved no stumbling-block. World history was trembling in the balance whilst Paul and his Judaistic colleagues argued over the circumcision controversy. Had the full Jewish levitical rites been required of all prospective Christians, as some extremists desired, conversions might have been sparse, and world history vastly different (*cf.* Acts 15).

There has been much controversy as to why Jesus should have used the words of Mt. 23:15, when the scribes and Pharisees were so notoriously indifferent to proselytization. The 'one' might refer to their meagre returns, or the verse might point to a particular historical incident, perhaps the seeking of some Roman convert in high places.

BIBLIOGRAPHY. *BC*, 5, 1933, pp. 74–96; *EJ*, 13, 1971, cols. 1182–1194; *JewE*, 10, pp. 220–224; K. G. Kuhn, in *TDNT* 6, pp. 727–744; Arndt, p. 722; R. A. Stewart, *Rabbinic Theology*, 1961, see Index; J. Becker, in *NIDNTT* 1, pp. 359–361. R.A.S.

PROSTITUTION. The OT speaks of both common prostitutes, *zōnôṯ*, and sacred prostitutes of both sexes, *qᵉḏēšôṯ* and *qᵉḏēšîm*, who were votaries of fertility cults. The NT term for a prostitute is *pornē* (*cf.* the word 'pornography').

Tamar is described as both a harlot (Gn. 38:15) and a cult prostitute (Gn. 38:21, RSVmg.). The two Heb. words are used as parallels in Ho. 4:14. Rahab the harlot (Jos. 2) hid the two spies in her home at Jericho. She was acclaimed for her faith (Heb. 11:31; Jas. 2:25) and became an ancestress of Christ (Mt. 1:5). The two mothers who claimed the same baby before Solomon were prostitutes (1 Ki. 3:16).

In the NT period prostitutes were among those who repented at the preaching of John the Baptist (Mt. 21:31–32).

In Dt. 23:17–18 the contemptuous phrase 'dog' evidently refers to a male cult prostitute. In Rehoboam's time the presence of such male prostitutes became widespread (1 Ki. 14:24). Asa, Jehoshaphat and Josiah attempted to root out this abomination (1 Ki. 15:12; 22:46; 2 Ki. 23:7).

Other passages which may contain possible allusions to sacred prostitution include Nu. 25:1–3; 1 Sa. 2:22; Je. 13:27; Ezk. 16; 23:37–41; Am. 2:7–8; 2 Macc. 6:4.

Numerous nude female figurines found throughout the Near East depict the goddesses who were venerated in sacred prostitution. Their votaries believed that they could stimulate the fertility of their crops by sympathetic magic when they engaged in intercourse.

We may assume that the worship of the major Canaanite goddesses —Ashera, Astarte, Anath—involved sacred prostitution, though there are no explicit texts which can prove this. In the Ugaritic texts of temple personnel we find the *qdšm*, who were probably male cult prostitutes. Explicit references to sacred prostitution in Syria and Phoenicia are found in the late texts of Lucian's *De Dea Syria* (2nd century AD). The prostitution of women in the service of Venus at Heliopolis (Baalbek) is attested as late as the 4th century AD.

There is good reason to believe that Phoenician influence was responsible for the importation of cultic prostitution as part of the Greek worship of Aphrodite by way of Cyprus and Cythera (*cf.* Homer's *Odyssey* 8. 288, 362).

Aphrodite was the goddess of Corinth and the patroness of prostitutes. Strabo 8. 6. 20 asserted that her temple on the Acrocorinthus had more than 1,000 hierodoules. When Paul warned the congregation at Corinth against immorality (1 Cor. 6:15–16), he was no doubt warning them in part against these cult prostitutes.

Prostitution is condemned as defiling our bodies which are the temples of the Holy Spirit (1 Cor. 6:18–20). Those who do not repent of such practices will be excluded from heaven (Rev. 21:8; 22:15).

The Scriptures often use the imagery of harlotry to depict the evil of idolatry and apostasy (Is. 57:3–5; Je. 2:23–25; Rev. 17:1ff.). Hosea was commanded to marry Gomer the harlot to illustrate Israel's infidelity (Ho. 1:2).

BIBLIOGRAPHY. M. Astour, *JBL* 85, 1966, pp. 185–196; E. Yamauchi, 'Cultic Prostitution', in H. Hoffner (ed.), *Orient and Occident*, 1973, pp. 213–222; J. Oswalt, *ZPEB*, 4, pp. 910–912; D. J. Wiseman, *THB* 14, 1964, pp. 8ff.; E. Fisher, *Biblical Theology Bulletin* 6, 1976, pp. 225–236. E.M.Y.

PROVERB. In RSV the word 'proverb' has a wider range of meanings than in normal English usage, due especially to the many meanings of *māšāl* (probably related to *mšl*, 'to be like', 'to be compared with', although some relate it to *mšl*, 'to rule'; hence a word spoken by a ruler). In addition to denoting 'a pithy saying, especially one condensing the wisdom of experience' (*cf.* 1 Sa. 10:12; 24:13; 1 Ki. 4:32; Pr. 1:1, 6; 10:1; 25:1; Ec. 12:9; Ezk. 12:22–23; 16:44; 18:2–3), 'proverb' may also serve as a synonym for 'byword' (*e.g.* Dt. 28:37; 1 Ki. 9:7; 2 Ch. 7:20; Ps. 69:11; Je. 24:9; Ezk. 14:8). The point seems to be that the sufferer becomes an object-lesson from which others may learn appropriate lessons. Similarly, 'proverb' may mean 'taunt-song' as in Is. 14:4ff., where the disastrous effects of the king of Babylon's presumptuous pride are paraded. In Hab. 2:6 (AV) 'proverb' translates *ḥîḏâ*, 'riddle', 'perplexing question'.

Two words are rendered 'proverb' in the NT: *parabolē* (Lk. 4:23) and *paroimia* (Jn. 16:25, 29, AV; 2 Pet. 2:22). In the Johannine passages *paroimia* apparently denotes a 'dark saying' or 'figure of speech in which . . . lofty ideas are concealed' (Arndt). The didactic role of proverbs in both Testaments should not be underestimated. Along with *parables, proverbs played a major part in the teaching

PROSPERITY OF THE WICKED
See Providence, Part 3.

PROTOGRAPH, BIBLICAL
See Biblical criticism, Part 1.

ministry of Christ (*e.g.* Mt. 6:21; Lk. 4:23; Jn. 12:24). (* WISDOM LITERATURE.)

BIBLIOGRAPHY. A. R. Johnson, 'Mashal' in *Wisdom in Israel and in the Ancient Near East*, ed. M. Noth and D. W. Thomas, 1955; W. McKane, *Proverbs*, 1970, pp. 10–33; R. B. Y. Scott, *Proverbs, Ecclesiastes, AB*, 1965, pp. 3–9; G. von Rad, *Wisdom in Israel*, 1972, pp. 24–34. D.A.H.

PROVERBS, BOOK OF. The Heb. title *mišlê*, 'proverbs of', is an abbreviation of *mišlê š^elōmōh*, 'the proverbs of Solomon' (1:1). The English name is derived from the Vulg. *Liber Proverbiorum*. A collection of collections, Proverbs is a guidebook for successful living. Without overtly stressing the great prophetic themes (*e.g.* the covenant), the proverbs show how Israel's distinctive faith affected her common life.

I. Outline of contents

a. The importance of wisdom (1:1–9:18)

Following an introductory statement of purpose (1:1–6), the writer instructs his son or pupil concerning the worth and nature of wisdom. In contrast to the proverbs of 10:1ff., each idea is discussed at some length in a didactic poem. These poetic essays are a highly polished development of the *māšāl* (* PROVERB, * WISDOM LITERATURE).

The author's aim is to paint the strongest possible contrast between the results of seeking wisdom and living a life of folly. He sets the stage for the several hundred specific proverbs which follow. Certain temptations loom large in the sage's mind: crimes of violence (1:10–19; 4:14–19); the binding of oneself by a rash pledge (6:1–5); sloth (6:6–11); duplicity (6:12–15); and especially sexual impurity (2:16–19; 5:3–20; 6:23–35; 7:4–27; 9:13–18). To the one who avoids these snares, * Wisdom offers happiness, long life, wealth and honour (3:13–18). The deeply religious nature of this section (*e.g.* 1:7; 3:5–12), its sensitive moral tone and its hortatory, didactic style are reminiscent of Deuteronomy.

Apparently the writer of these chapters is anonymous, since 1:1–6 probably refers to the entire book and 10:1 introduces a collection of proverbs which purport to be Solomonic. This section is customarily dated among the latest in the collection. Though its final editing may be relatively late (*c.* 600 BC), much of the material may be considerably earlier. W. F. Albright has drawn attention to the number of parallels in thought and structure between this section, especially chs. 8–9, and Ugaritic or Phoenician literature (*Wisdom in Israel*, pp. 7–9). He also suggests that 'it is entirely possible that aphorisms and even longer sections go back into the Bronze Age in substantially their present form' (p. 5). For the personification of Wisdom in 8:22ff., see * WISDOM.

b. The proverbs of Solomon (10:1–22:16)

This section is probably the oldest in the book, and there is a growing tendency among scholars to accept the accuracy of the tradition reflected in 1 Ki. 4:29ff.; Pr. 1:1; 10:1; 25:1 honouring * Solomon as the sage *par excellence*. His contacts with the court of Egypt, the far-reaching network of his empire and the combination of wealth and respite from war enabled him to devote himself to cultural pursuits on a scale denied his successors.

About 375 proverbs occur in this collection. Their structure is largely *antithetic* in chs. 10–15 and *synthetic* or *synonymous* in chs. 16–22. Most of the proverbs are unrelated; no system of grouping is discernible.

Though a religious note is by no means absent (*cf.* 15:3, 8–9, 11; 16:1–9, *etc.*), the bulk of the proverbs contain no specific reference to Israel's faith but are based on practical observations of everyday life. The extremely practical nature of the instruction which stresses the *profits* of wisdom has drawn the criticism of those who hold that pure religion should be disinterested. But how would a practical sage to whom God had not yet revealed the mystery of life after death make the issues clear without pointing out the blessings of the wise and the pitfalls of the fool?

c. The words of the wise (22:17–24:22)

The title is obscured in *MT* and EVV, being incorporated in 22:17. However, the obvious title 'These also are sayings of the wise' (24:23) suggests that 22:17–24:22 should be considered a separate collection. These maxims are more closely related and sustained in theme than those of the previous section. The topics are manifold: regard for the poor (22:22, 27), respect for the king (23:1–3; 24:21–22), discipline of children (23:13–14), temperance (23:19–21, 29–35), honour of parents (23:22–25), chastity (23:26–28), *etc.* Religious emphasis, though not dominant, is not lacking (*e.g.* 22:19, 23; 24:18, 21).

A formal relationship between the Egyp. proverbs of Amenemope and 22:17–23:11 is widely recognized. The debate centres in the question, Which influenced which? W. Baumgartner (*The Old Testament and Modern Study*, ed. by H. H. Rowley, 1951, p. 212) notes that 'the . . . theory that Amenemope is the original . . . has now been generally accepted'. This view, however, has now been challenged from within Egyptology itself, by É. Drioton, who has put up weighty reasons for a view that the Egyp. Amenemope is, in fact, merely a translation (sometimes too literal) from a Heb. original into Egyp.; this Heb. original would then be the 'words of the wise' from which Proverbs independently drew. See É. Drioton, *Mélanges André Robert*, 1957, pp. 254–280, and *Sacra Pagina*, 1, 1959, pp. 229–241. Against this, however, see R. J. Williams, *JEA* 47, 1961, pp. 100–106. The passage has been so refined by Israel's faith that, whatever its origin, it belongs to the OT revelation.

d. Additional sayings of the wise (24:23–34)

This brief collection exhibits the same irregularity of form as the one above. There are brief proverbs (*e.g.* v. 26) and extended maxims (*e.g.* vv. 30–34; *cf.* 6:6–11). The religious element is not prominent, but there is a keen sense of social responsibility (*e.g.* vv. 28–29). These two collections are apparently not Solomonic but are part of the legacy of Israel's sages, who created or collected and polished a vast body of wisdom sayings (*cf.* Ec. 12:9–11).

e. Additional proverbs of Solomon (25:1–29:27)

In content this section is not unlike 10:1–22:16 (*e.g.* 25:24 = 21:9; 26:13 = 22:13; 26:15 = 19:24, *etc.*). However, the proverbs here are less uniform in length; antithetic parallelism, the backbone of the earlier section, is less common, although chs. 28–29 contain numerous examples; comparison, rare in 10:1ff., occurs frequently (*e.g.* 25:3, 11–14, 18–20, *etc.*).

The statement in 25:1 has influ-

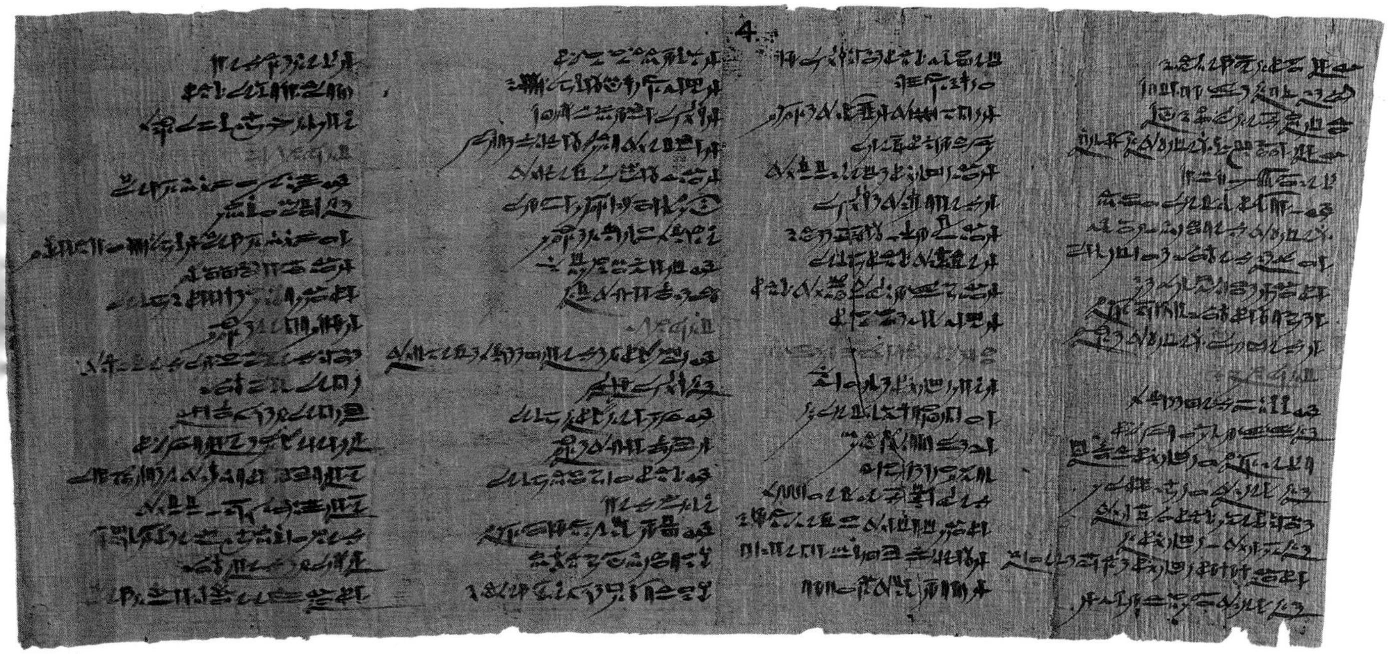

Egyptian papyrus scroll containing The Wisdom of Amenemope, *a book of proverbs and sayings similar to some in the biblical book of Proverbs. c. 950–650 BC.* (BM)

nced the Talmudic opinion (*Baba Bathra* 15a) that Hezekiah and his ompany wrote the Proverbs. The ole of Hezekiah's men in the editng of the book is not clear, but here is no reason to question the ccuracy of 25:1, which relates to he sayings in chs. 25–29. Hezeiah's interest in Israel's literature s attested in 2 Ch. 29:25–30, where e restores the Davidic order of vorship, including the singing of he psalms of David and Asaph. A. Bentzen suggests that these proerbs were preserved *orally* until Iezekiah's time, when they were ranscribed (*IOT*, 2, p. 173). . R. Driver (*An Introduction to the Literature of the Old Testament*, . 401) lists those proverbs which eflect a restiveness concerning the Monarchy (28:2, 12, 15f., 28; 29:2, , 16). In the selection of these roverbs, is there a reflection of the urbulence of the 8th century BC?

. The words of Agur (30:1–33)

Agur, his father Jakeh, Ithiel and Ucal (30:1) defy identification. See ITHIEL for an adjustment in the vord divisions which eliminates the ast two names completely. *Oracle* 30:1, RSVmg.) should probably be ead as a proper name * *Massa*.

The first few verses are difficult o interpret, but seem to be agnosic in tone. This agnosticism is nswered (5–6) with a statement bout the unchangeable word of God. Following a brief but moving rayer (7–9), the chapter concludes vith a series of extended proverbs escribing some commendable or ulpable quality. In many of these the number *four* is prominent. Several exhibit the x, x + 1 pattern well attested in the OT (*e.g.* Am. 1–2; Mi. 5:5) and common in Ugaritic (*cf.* C. H. Gordon, *Ugaritic Handbook*, 1947, pp. 34, 201).

*g. The words of * Lemuel* (31:1–9)

This king of * Massa is unknown. His mother's advice includes warnings against sexual excess and drunkenness and encouragement to judge even the poor with rectitude. The influence of Aramaic on this section is noteworthy (*e.g. bar*, 'son'; *mᵉlāḵîn*, 'kings').

h. In praise of a virtuous wife (31:10–31)

This well-wrought acrostic poem has no title, but is so different from the preceding section that it must be considered separately. Its stylized form suggests that it should be viewed among the latest sections of the book. The description of an industrious, conscientious and pious woman is a fitting conclusion to a book which discusses the practical out-workings of a God-directed life.

II. Date

Proverbs could not have been completed before Hezekiah's time (*c.* 715–686 BC). However, the acrostic poem (31:10–31) and the sayings of the Massaites (30:1–33; 31:1–9) may well have been added in the exilic or post-exilic period. A reasonable date for the final editing is the 5th century BC. The individual proverbs date in most cases from well before the Exile. W. F. Albright notes (*op. cit.*, p. 6) that the contents of Proverbs must, on literary grounds, be dated before the Aramaic sayings of Ahiqar (7th century BC).

III. Proverbs and the New Testament

Proverbs has left its stamp on the NT by several quotations (*e.g.* 3:7a = Rom. 12:16; 3:11–12 = Heb. 12:5–6; 3:34 = Jas. 4:6 and 1 Pet. 5:5b; 4:26 = Heb. 12:13a; 10:12 = Jas. 5:20 and 1 Pet. 4:8; 25:21–22 = Rom. 12:20; 26:11 = 2 Pet. 2:22) and allusions (*e.g.* 2:4 and Col. 2:3; 3:1–4 and Lk. 2:52; 12:7 and Mt. 7:24–27). As Christ fulfilled the Law and the Prophets (Mt. 5:17), so he fulfilled the wisdom writings by revealing the fullness of God's wisdom (Mt. 12:42; 1 Cor. 1:24, 30; Col. 2:3). If Proverbs is an extended commentary on the law of love, then it helps to pave the way for the One in whom true love became incarnate. See C. T. Fritsch, 'The Gospel in the Book of Proverbs', *Theology Today* 7, 1950, pp. 169–183.

BIBLIOGRAPHY. A. Cohen, *Proverbs*, 1945; C. T. Fritsch, *Proverbs*, *IB*; B. Gemser, *Sprüche Salomos*, 1937; W. O. E. Oesterley, *WC*, 1929; T. T. Perowne, *The Proverbs*, 1916; C. I. K. Story in *JBL* 64, 1945, pp. 319–337; D. W. Thomas, *Wisdom in Israel and in the Ancient Near East*, ed. M. Noth and D. W. Thomas, 1955, pp. 280–292; C. H. Toy, *ICC*, 1899; A. Barucq, *Le Livre des Proverbes*, 1964; D. Kidner, *Proverbs*, *TOTC*, 1964; W. McKane, *Proverbs*, 1970. D.A.H.

PROVIDENCE. No single word in biblical Hebrew or Greek expresses the idea of God's providence. *pronoia* is used for God's purposive foresight by Plato, Stoic writers, Philo, who wrote a book *On Providence* (*Peri pronoias*), Josephus, and the authors of Wisdom (*cf.* 14:3; 17:2) and 3, 4 Macc.; but in the NT *pronoia* occurs only twice (Acts 24:2; Rom. 13:14), both times denoting, not God's care and forethought, but man's. The cognate verb *pronoeō*, too, is used only of man (Rom. 12:17; 2 Cor. 8:21; 1 Tim. 5:8).

Providence is normally defined in Christian theology as the unceasing activity of the Creator whereby, in overflowing bounty and goodwill (Ps. 145:9 *cf.* Mt. 5:45–48), he upholds his creatures in ordered existence (Acts 17:28; Col. 1:17; Heb. 1:3), guides and governs all events, circumstances and free acts of angels and men (*cf.* Ps. 107; Jb. 1:12; 2:6; Gn. 45:5–8), and directs everything to its appointed goal, for his own glory (*cf.* Eph. 1:9–12). This view of God's relation to the world must be distinguished from: (*a*) *pantheism*, which absorbs the world into God; (*b*) *deism*, which cuts it off from him; (*c*) *dualism*, which divides control of it between God and another power; (*d*) *indeterminism*, which holds that it is under no control at all; (*e*) *determinism*, which posits a control of a kind that destroys man's moral responsibility; (*f*) the doctrine of *chance*, which denies the controlling power to be rational; and (*g*) the doctrine of *fate*, which denies it to be benevolent.

Providence is presented in Scripture as a function of divine sovereignty. God is King over all, doing just what he wills (Pss. 103:19; 135:6; Dn. 4:35; *cf.* Eph. 1:11). This conviction, robustly held, pervades the whole Bible. The main strands in it may be analysed as follows.

a. Providence and the natural order

God rules all natural forces (Ps. 147:8f.), all wild animals (Jb. 38–41), and all happenings in the world, great and small, from thunderstorms (Jb. 37; Ps. 29) and plagues (Ex.7:3–11:10; 12:29ff.; Joel 2:25) to the death of a sparrow (Mt. 10:29) or the fall of a lot (Pr. 16:33). Physical life, in men and animals, is his to give and to take away (Gn. 2:17; 1 Sa. 1:27; 2 Sa. 12:19; Jb. 1:21; Pss. 102:23; 104:29–30; 127:3; Ezk. 24:16ff.; Dn. 5:23, *etc.*); so are health and sickness (Dt. 7:15; 28:27, 60), prosperity and adversity ('evil', Am. 3:6; *cf.* Is. 45:7), *etc.*

Since the regularity of the natural order is thought of as depending directly upon the divine will (*cf.* Gn. 8:22), the Bible finds no difficulty in the idea of an occasional miraculous irregularity; God does what he wills in his world, and nothing is too hard for him (*cf.* Gn. 18:14).

God's providential government of the created order proclaims his wisdom, power, glory and goodness (Pss. 8:1, RV; 19:1–6; Acts 14:17; Rom. 1:19f.). The man who in face of this revelation does not acknowledge God is without excuse (Rom. 1:20).

The Bible presents God's constant fulfilling of his kindly purposes in nature both as matter for praise in itself (*cf.* Pss. 104; 147) and as a guarantee that he is lord of human history, and will fulfil his gracious promises in that realm also (*cf.* Je. 31:35ff.; 33:19–26).

b. Providence and world history

Since the Fall, God has been executing a plan of redemption. This plan pivots upon Christ's first coming and culminates in his return. Its goal is the creation of a world-wide church in which Jew and non-Jew share God's grace on equal terms (Eph. 3:3–11), and through this the reintegration of the disordered cosmos (Rom. 8:19ff.), under the rule of Christ at his second coming (Eph. 1:9–12; Phil. 2:9ff.; Col. 1:20; 1 Cor. 15:24ff.). Through Christ's present reign and future triumph, the OT prophecies of God's Messianic kingdom (*cf.* Is. 11:1–9; Dn. 2:44; 7:13–27) are fulfilled. The unifying theme of the Bible is God's exercise of his kingship in setting up this kingdom. No foe can thwart him; he laughs at opposition to his plan (Ps. 2:4), and uses it to his own ends (*cf.* Acts 4:25–28, quoting Ps. 2:1f.). The climax of history will be the overthrow of those who fight against God and his kingdom, as the book of Revelation shows (Rev. 19, *etc.*).

Paul analyses the steps in God's plan in terms of the Jew–Gentile and law–grace relationships in Gal. 3; Rom. 9–11; *cf.* Eph. 2:12–3:11.

c. Providence and personal circumstances

God told Israel as a nation that he would prosper them while they were faithful but bring disaster on them if they sinned (Lv. 26:14ff.; Dt. 28:15ff.). The attempt to understand the fortunes of individual Israelites in the light of this principle raised problems. Why does God allow the wicked to prosper, even when they are victimizing the just? And why is disaster so often the lot of the godly?

The first question is always answered by affirming that the wicked prosper only for a moment; God will soon visit them and take vengeance (Pss. 37 *passim*; 50:16–21; 73:17ff.), though for the present he may forbear, in order to give them further opportunity for repentance (Rom. 2:4f.; 2 Pet. 3:9; Rev. 2:21). The NT identifies the day of God's visitation with the final judgment (*cf.* Rom. 2:3ff.; 12:19; Jas. 5:1–8).

The second question is tackled in several ways. It is asserted: (i) that the righteous will be vindicated when the day of visitation for the wicked comes (Ps. 37; Mal. 3:13–4:3); (ii) that meanwhile suffering is valuable as a God-given discipline (Pr. 3:11f.; Ps. 119:67, 71); (iii) that suffering, faithfully borne, even if not understood, glorifies God and leads to blessing in the end (Jb. 1–2; 42); (iv) that communion with God is the supreme good, and to those who enjoy it outward impoverishments are of no ultimate importance (Ps. 73:14, 23ff.; Hab. 3:17f.).

In the NT the fact that believers suffer ill-treatment and adverse circumstances is no longer a problem, since it is recognized that fellowship in Christ's sufferings is fundamental to the Christian vocation (*cf.* Mt. 10:24f.; Jn. 15:18ff.; 16:33; Acts 9:16; 14:22; Phil. 3:10ff.; 1 Pet. 4:12–19). This recognition, in conjunction with the OT principles mentioned above, completely disposed of the 'problem of suffering' for the first Christians. Knowing something of their glorious hope (1 Pet. 1:3ff.), and of the strengthening and sustaining power of Christ (2 Cor. 1:3ff.; 12:9f.), they could contentedly face all situations (Phil. 4:11) and rejoice in all troubles (Rom. 8:35ff.), confident that through adversity their loving Father was disciplining them in sanctity (Heb. 12:5–11), developing their Christian character (Jas. 1:2ff.; 1 Pet. 5:10; *cf.* Rom. 5:2ff.), proving the reality of their faith (1 Pet. 1:7), and so ripening them for glory (1 Pet. 4:13). In all things God works for the spiritual wel-are of his people (Rom. 8:28); and ıe supplies them with whatever naterial things they need through- ut their earthly pilgrimage (Mt. :25–33; Phil. 4:19).

Belief in providence determines nany of the basic attitudes of bib- cal piety. The knowledge that God determines their circumstances eaches the faithful to wait on him n humility and patience for vindi- ation and deliverance (Pss. 37; 0:13ff.; Jas. 5:7ff.; 1 Pet. 5:6f.). It orbids them to grow despondent r despairing (Pss. 42–43), and rings them courage and hope when harassed (Pss. 60; 62). It in- pires all prayers for help, and raise for every good thing that s enjoyed.

. Providence and human freedom

God rules the hearts and actions of ll men (*cf.* Pr. 21:1; Ezr. 6:22), ften for purposes of his own which they do not suspect (*cf.* Gn. 5:5–8; 50:20; Is. 10:5ff.; 44:28– 5:4; Jn. 11:49ff.; Acts 13:27ff.). God's control is absolute in the ense that men do only that which e has ordained that they should o; yet they are truly free agents, in he sense that their decisions are their own, and they are morally responsible for them (*cf.* Dt. 30:15ff.). A distinction, however, must be drawn between God's allowing (or 'giving up') sinners to practise the evil that they have preferred (Ps. 81:12f.; Acts 14:16; Rom. 1:24–28), and his gracious work of prompting his people to will and do what he commands (Phil. 2:13); for in the former case, according to the biblical rule of judgment, the blame for the evil done belongs entirely to the sinner (*cf.* Lk. 22:22; Acts 2:23; 3:13–19), whereas in the latter case the praise for the good done must be given to God (*cf.* 1 Cor. 15:10).

BIBLIOGRAPHY. Arndt; A. E. Garvie, in *HDB*; A. H. Strong, *Systematic Theology*[12], 1949, pp. 419–443; L. Berkhof, *Systematic Theology*[4], 1949, pp. 165–178; Calvin, *Institutes*, 1. 16–18; K. Barth, *Church Dogmatics*, 3. iii, E.T. 1960, pp. 3–288; A. S. Peake, *The Problem of Suffering in the Old Testament*, 1904; O. Cullmann, *Christ and Time*, E.T. 1951; G. C. Berkouwer, *The Providence of God*, 1952; P. Jacobs, H. Krienke, *NIDNTT* 1, pp. 692–697; J. Behm, *TDNT* 4, pp. 1009–1017. J.I.P.

PROVINCE. Originally the word denoted a sphere of duty or administration. The *praetor urbanus*, *e.g.*, held an *urbana provincia*, and this was defined as the administration of justice within the city (Livy, 6. 42; 31. 6). Tacitus speaks of the suppression of a slave revolt at Brundisium in AD 24 by a quaestor 'whose province was the hill-country pastures', *calles* (*Annals* 4. 27). The reading is confirmed by Suetonius (*Iul.* 19), who speaks of 'provinces' covering the supervision of 'woods and pasture-lands'. The reference shows that, long after the term developed territorial and geographical significance, it retained its ancient meaning. The intermediate use is seen in the employment of the term of a military command. 'To Sicinius,' says Livy, 'the Volsci were assigned as his province, to Aquilius the Hernici' (2. 40). That is, the task of pacification in these two Italian tribal areas was allotted respectively to these two consuls. It was an easy step from, *e.g.*, Spain as a military command to Spain as a conquered territory and defined area of administration. In this

The Roman provinces in AD 14.

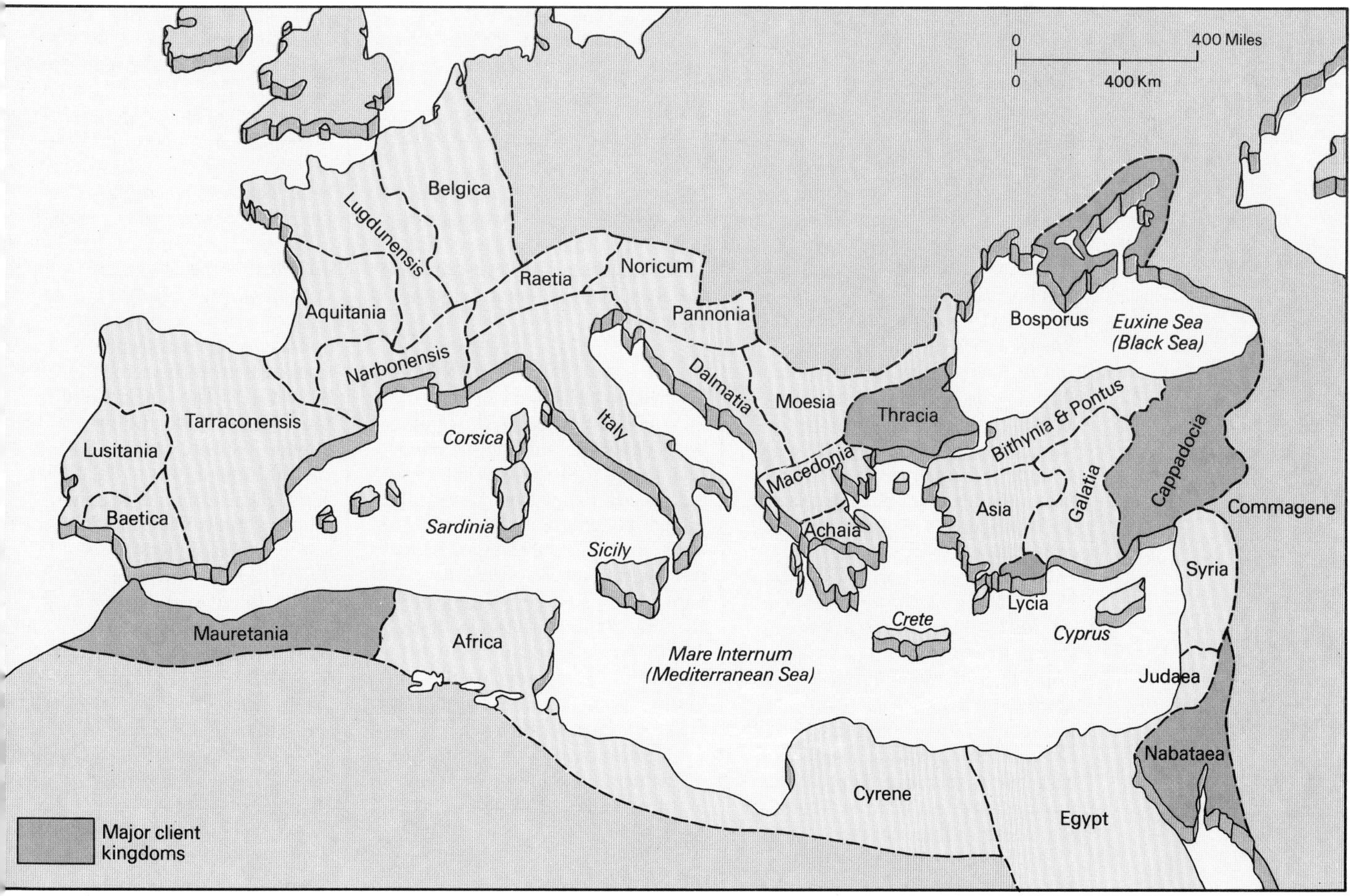

later, commoner and wider sense of the word, there were no provinces until Rome extended her conquests beyond the Italian peninsula. Sicily was the first country to be made thus into 'a Roman province' (Cicero, *In Verr*. 2. 2). This was in 241 BC. Sardinia followed in 235 BC. In 121 BC Rome annexed a piece of territory in S Gaul between the Alps and the Cévennes to secure communications with Spain, and this area, Gallia Narbonensis, became known as 'the Province' above all others, and its inhabitants *provinciales*. (Hence Provence today.) Similarly the rest of the provinces were acquired piecemeal, the list being closed by the annexation of Britain by Claudius and Dacia by Trajan.

The earliest provinces were administered by magistrates elected for the purpose. *E.g.*, two additional praetors were elected from 227 BC for Sicily and Sardinia, and two more 20 years later, to govern the two Spanish provinces. The scheme was then discontinued for over a century, Macedonia (148 BC), Achaia and Africa (146 BC) and Asia (133 BC), *e.g.*, being ruled by *magistrates already in office, their *imperium* being extended for the purpose. The term **proconsul* signified a consul whose *imperium* was thus 'prorogued' after his year of office, for the purpose of a provincial governorship. A proconsulship could, however, be held without preceding tenure of the consulship. This was the case with Pompey in 77, 66 and 65 BC.

Under the principate the provinces were divided into senatorial and imperial. The former were governed by ex-consuls and expraetors with the title of **proconsul*, normally in yearly tenure; the latter were administered by legates of the emperor (*legati Augusti pro praetore*), men of senatorial rank or selected equestrian officials. Tenure of office was at the emperor's pleasure. Imperial provinces were usually those involving legionary garrisons. Transference from one list to another was not uncommon. Tacitus mentions the transfer of Achaea and Macedonia from the senate to the emperor in AD 15 (*leuari proconsulari imperio tradique Caesari . . .*) (*Ann*. 1. 76). Cyprus is a similar example. Annexed in 57 BC, it was incorporated in Cilicia in 55 BC and made an imperial province in 27 BC. In 22 BC Augustus transferred it and Gallia Narbonensis to the senate in exchange for Dalmatia. Hence there was a proconsul in command, as Luke, with his usual accuracy, indicates (Acts 13:7). (*ROMAN EMPIRE.)

BIBLIOGRAPHY. T. Mommsen, *The Provinces of the Roman Empire from Caesar to Diocletian*, 1909; G. H. Stevenson, *Roman Provincial Administration*, 1939. E.M.B.

PRUNING HOOK
See Hook, Part 2.

PSALMS, BOOK OF.

I. The importance of the Psalter

It would be difficult to overestimate the significance, for Jew and Gentile, of the book of Psalms. Here are mirrored the ideals of religious piety and communion with God, of sorrow for sin and the search for perfection, of walking in darkness, unafraid, by the lamp of faith; of obedience to the law of God, delight in the worship of God, fellowship with the friends of God, reverence for the Word of God; of humility under the chastening rod, trust when evil triumphs and wickedness prospers, serenity in the midst of storm.

The Hebrew poets were inspired to take these spiritual insights and experiences and make them the themes of their songs. But it should be remembered that 'the Psalms are poems, and poems intended to be sung, not doctrinal treatises, nor even sermons' (C. S. Lewis, *Reflections on the Psalms*, 1958, p. 2)—hence the Hebrew title of the Psalms, *tᵉhillîm*, 'songs of praise'—also that they were giving expression to the religion of Israel to which the psalmists were heirs, not merely to their personal religious experiences.

II. The formation of the Psalter

It has been customary to describe the book of Psalms as 'the hymn-book of the second Temple', and such it undoubtedly was. The title is misleading, however, if it is interpreted to mean that all the psalms were written in the exilic or post-exilic periods. It is important to notice that this type of literature is not only confined to the Psalter in the OT but is found in many different periods in Hebrew history. It is found among the Hebrews as early as the Exodus period (Ex. 15), and another example comes from a time subsequent to, but relatively close to, the invasion of Canaan under Joshua (Jdg. 5). Hannah's psalm (1 Sa. 2:1–10) comes at the close of the Judges period.

The pre-exilic prophetic literature also contains examples of psalm composition (*cf.*, *e.g.*, Ho. 6:1–3; Is. 2:2–4; 38:10–20; Je. 14:7–9; Hab. 3:1ff., *etc*.). And from the post-exilic period come such passages as Ezr. 9:5–15 and Ne. 9:6–39, which are strongly reminiscent of many of the psalms. Clearly, then, the Psalter is not an isolated literary phenomenon. Indeed, the same type of *poetry is found among the Babylonians and the citizens of Ugarit as the Ras Shamra tablets testify. The OT Psalter is a collection of poems which are typical of a literary form which the Hebrews, in common with other cultures, used from at least the Exodus right up until the post-exilic or second Temple period. And, of course, if one reckons with the non-canonical psalms it is clear that this literary form persisted among the Jews until quite a long way into the Christian era.

a. Authorship

No fewer than 73 psalms are attributed to David. Other authors named in the titles are Asaph (50; 73–83), the sons of Korah (42–49; 84–85; 87–88), Solomon (72; 127), and Heman (88), Ethan (89), both Ezrahites, and Moses (90), who have one psalm each attributed to them. Davidic authorship of many of the psalms has often been denied principally on the ground that David the psalmist of popular belief bears no resemblance to David the warrior of the books of Samuel and Kings. It can also be argued that the ascription *lᵉdāwiḏ* ('of David') need not be a note of authorship, but only a rubric appointing certain psalms to be used in a royal ritual for the 'David' (the Davidic king) of the time. We do know, however, that David was a musician (1 Sa. 16:14ff.) and a poet (2 Sa. 1:17ff.; 3:33f.). The attempts of some scholars to disprove the Davidic authorship assigned to 2 Sa. 22:1ff.; 23:1–7, and to excise the words 'like David' from Am. 6:5 (where the tradition of David and his music and songs is referred to 300 years after his death) have the air of special pleading. Moreover the NT not only accepts but bases arguments upon Davidic authorship of this material. On this, see also section **IV**, below.

This hymn-book of the second Temple contains very ancient material. This is not at all surprisng when it is recalled that the Ras Shamra tablets show that, when Israel invaded Canaan, the type of poetry represented in the Psalms was already a long-established tradition among the inhabitants of Ugarit. The Song of Moses, then, in Ex. 15, and the Song of Deborah (Jdg. 5), were neither isolated nor unprecedented examples of Semitic poetry. The Mosaic and Solomonic authorships referred to in the titles of three psalms suggest that the ancient religion of the tabernacle and the first Temple would require its sacred music. Religion in the days of Amos (5:21–23) and Isaiah (30:29), during the Exile (Ps. 137:1ff.) and the period following the return, and the building of the second Temple, would also require its solemn chants. But it is the prominence of the king in the Psalter (see section **IV**) which has done most to convince recent scholars that the classical period of psalm composition was the Monarchy, i.e. from David to the beginning of the Exile.

. *Organization*

The OT Psalter as we now have it consists of five books. This division goes back to the LXX version, which was begun as early as the 3rd century BC. Every section is easily recognizable because a doxology closes each book. These doxologies are short except the one that ends Book V; there an entire psalm is given over to the closing doxology. The five divisions of the Psalter are as follows: Book I, Pss. 1–41; Book II, Pss. 42–72; Book III, Pss. 73–89; Book IV, Pss. 90–106; Book V, Pss. 107–150. Many have seen in this fivefold division an attempt to imitate the division of the Torah into five books, the Pentateuch. (See N. H. Snaith, *Hymns of the Temple*, 1951, pp. 18–20, where the significance of this is discussed.)

Various features suggest that there were separate collections of psalms in use before the final compilation. *E.g.* certain psalms, in whole or in part (notably Pss. 14 and 53; Ps. 40:13–17 and Ps. 70; Pss. 57:7–11 plus 60:6–13 to make Ps. 108), occur in more than one part of the Psalter. Further, a large group (42–83) speaks predominantly of 'God' rather than 'the LORD', whereas other blocks (1–41; 84–89; 90–150) have the opposite preference, even in psalms attributed to some of the authors of the former group (42–83). Again, Ps. 72:20 evidently marks the close of a particular set of Davidic psalms, but not of David's whole output, as the rest of the Psalter demonstrates.

It seems likely, as various scholars have suggested, that the penultimate stage in compiling the Psalter was the gathering of groups of psalms into three main psalters, perhaps used at different centres or periods, as follows: *a.* the Davidic Pss. 3–41 or 2–41, which prefer the divine name Yahweh (the LORD); *b.* the Korahite, Asaphite and Davidic Pss. 42–83 (the 'Elohistic psalter'), where the term *'ᵉlōhîm* (God) predominates (to which group was added an appendix, 84–89, in which 'Yahweh' prevails); *c.* a collection of mostly anonymous psalms, 90–150 (with 'Yahweh' again), containing certain clusters marked by particular themes or uses (*e.g.* God's kingship, 93–100; the 'Egyptian Hallel', 113–118, traditionally associated with the Passover; the Songs of Ascents, 120–134; the closing Hallelujah psalms, 146–150). Finally, on this view, to match the books of Moses the three collections were further divided to make five, and Ps. 1 (or 1 and 2) placed at the beginning to introduce the whole.

III. Technical terms in the Psalter

The title of the book in Hebrew is *tᵉhillîm*, 'Songs of Praise', or 'Praises'. In English the title *Psalter* comes from LXX A *Psaltērion*, while *The Psalms* comes from LXX B *Psalmoi* or the Vulg. *Liber Psalmorum*. In addition to the title given to the book, the majority of individual psalms have separate headings. Since, however, many of the technical terms in the titles and elsewhere were already obscure to the Jewish translators of the LXX (3rd to 2nd centuries BC), any comments must be tentative.

1. *Technical designations of psalms.* The most frequent term is *mizmôr*, 'a psalm', a word which suggests the use of an instrumental accompaniment. 'A song' (*šîr*) is a more general term, not confined to worship. In the Psalter it is often coupled with *mizmôr* (*e.g.* 48, title), and there are 15 consecutive 'Songs of Ascents' (120–134), probably pilgrim songs or else processional songs for the festivals. Thirteen psalms have the heading *maśkîl*, which would seem to mean 'making wise or skilful'. The psalms in question (32; 42; 44–45; 52–55; 74; 78; 88–89; 142) reflect extremely chastening experiences—with one striking exception (45). The title may, however, refer not to the content or context of the psalm but to its literary style. We have to confess ignorance. Six psalms are called *miḵtām*, which LXX interprets as 'an inscription', and AV mg. (hardly less improbably) as 'a golden psalm' (from *keṯem*, 'gold'). Mowinckel, however, draws attention to Akkad. *katamu*, to cover, and infers a psalm for atonement, since he classifies all these psalms (16; 56–60) as laments. But the 'cover' which they seek is not atonement but defence, and the most likely meaning is 'a plea for protection'; almost, in our terms, 'an SOS'. Other titles are 'a prayer' (17; 86; 90; 102; 142), 'a praise' or 'doxology' (145) and 'a shiggaion' (*šiggāyôn*, Ps. 7; *cf.* Hab. 3:1, plur.). This last term is not clear to us; it has been linked with *šgh*, to wander or reel, and (Mowinckel) with Akkad. *šegu*, to howl or lament. But both Ps. 7 and Hab. 3, while they face desperate situations, react to them with notable faith and hope.

2. *Musical directions.* Many directions which appear to be of this kind occur in conjunction with the heading *lamᵉnaṣṣēaḥ*, 'to (or 'of') the choirmaster' (*cf.* RSV of Pss. 4ff., *etc.*), which may indicate a special collection of psalms (there are 55, scattered through all five books) more elaborately performed than the rest. But that is a guess, and various other meanings have been suggested for this Heb. term derived from a root meaning to excel, endure or shine: *e.g.* LXX has 'to the end'; Mowinckel, 'to dispose Yahweh to mercy' (making his face shine)—to mention only two.

*Musical instruments prescribed in the titles include *nᵉgînôṯ* (strings) and *nᵉḥîlôṯ* ('flutes', RSV), and the pitch of instruments or voices may perhaps be indicated by *'ᵃlāmôṯ* (Ps. 46), 'trebles'(?)—lit. 'girls'—and *šᵉmînîṯ* (Pss. 6 and 12), 'an octave below'(?)—lit. 'eighth'—on the admittedly enigmatic basis of 1 Ch. 15:20f.

Some terms, usually coupled with the preposition *'al* (RSV 'according to'), have been interpreted as either liturgical directions (see 3, below) or tune-names. The chief examples are *a.* Gittith (*gittîṯ*, 8; 81; 84), a word derived from Gath or from the wine or olive press; *b.* Muth-labben (*'al-mûṯ labbēn*, 9), 'death of the son' (but revocalized as *'ᵃlāmôṯ lāḇīn*, as L. Delekat suggests, it could perhaps be construed

Scroll of psalms or hymns of thanksgiving, showing the abiding influence of the biblical psalms in the many quotations made. Qumran. 1st cent. AD. (ELS)

as 'trebles for clarity'); *c.* 'The Hind of the Dawn' (*'ayyeleṯ ha-šaḥar*, 22); but LXX has 'the help at dawn' (*cf.* *'^{e}yālûṯî*, 'my help', in v. 19 (20, Heb.), as B. D. Eerdmans points out). See, however, 3, below. *d.* 'Lilies' (*šōšannîm*, 45; 69; 80), 'Lily of testimony or covenant' (*šûšan 'ēḏûṯ*, 60); but instead of 'lilies', LXX has 'those who make changes' (*šeššōnîm*?). *e.* 'The Dove on Far-off Terebinths', or, 'The Silent Dove of Far-off Places' (*yônaṯ 'ēlem r^{e}ḥōqîm*, 56): is this, however, a concluding note to Ps. 55, in view of 55:6f. (7f., Heb.)? On a cultic interpretation, see 3, below. *f.* 'Do Not Destroy' (*'al-tašḥēṯ*, 57–59; 75) is a phrase from the vineyards in Is. 65:8, and conceivably the name of a vintage-song and its tune. But the same words occur more significantly in Dt. 9:26, which may underlie both Is. 65:8b and this title. *g.* 'Mahalath' (*maḥ^{a}laṯ*, 53; 88) appears to be derived from *ḥlh*, either 'be ill' or 'propitiate'. It could be 'a catchword in a song, giving the name to a tune' (*BDB*), and the additional word *l^{e}'annôṯ* in the title of Ps. 88 could mean either 'to sing antiphonally' (*cf.* Vulg.) or 'to afflict or humble'. But see the next paragraph, against the notion of tune-names.

3. *Liturgical directions.* The preposition *'al* (RSV 'according to'), which introduces most of the terms in the above paragraph, means basically 'on'. Mowinckel therefore relates the above titles, *a.* to *g.*, to cultic acts, 'over' which the psalms would be sung. So, *e.g.*, *e.* would refer to a ritual such as that of Lv. 14:5–7, where one bird was sacrificed and one released to fly away, and *g.* would indicate a ritual for the sick. Likewise *'al-y^{e}ḏûṯûn* (62; 77; *cf.* 39) would refer not to the singer Jeduthun (2 Ch. 5:12) but to an act of confession over which the psalms were to be sung. Mowinckel's suggestions are speculative; but so, admittedly, are most others. Perhaps his most dubious example is the title of Ps. 22, taken to refer to the sacrifice of a hart, a non-sacrificial animal (Dt. 12:15, *etc.*).

Selah (*selâ*) occurs 71 times, and is still obscure to us. Since it often seems to mark a division in a psalm, it may be an instruction to the worshippers to 'lift up' (*sll*) their voices or instruments in a refrain or interlude.

Higgaion (*higgāyôn*, 9:16 [17, Heb.]). like Selah, evidently calls for music. It is a term in Ps. 92:3 (4, Heb.) for the sound of a stringed instrument.

IV. The liturgical approach to the Psalter

A landmark in the modern study of the Psalter was the work of H. Gunkel in the early decades of this century. To him it was all-important to start by distinguishing the different classes (*Gattungen*) of psalms by attending to *a.* the worship-situations from which they had sprung ('some definite divine service', rather than some event in the history of the nation or the writer); *b.* the thoughts and moods which different psalms were found to have in common; and *c.* the recurrent features of style, form and imagery which served these various ends. He found the following main types: Hymns of Praise, Personal Thanksgivings, Communal Laments and Personal Laments. In addition there were smaller categories such as Entrance Liturgies, Blessings and Cursings, Wisdom Psalms, Royal Psalms; and there were also mixed types. His classification has been widely adopted, and his insistence on the importance of such an approach seldom questioned.

While Gunkel regarded most of the canonical psalms as literary descendants of Israel's original psalmody, S. Mowinckel saw them as products of the living cultus. He set himself to reconstruct the rites and festivals of Israel from the clues which he confidently detected there, independently of any confirmation from the Pentateuch. His early psalm studies, in the 1920s, made much of a postulated festival of Yahweh's accession as King, supposedly celebrated at the New Year somewhat after the fashion of the Babylonian *akitu* festival, leaving its traces in about 40 of the psalms and in the development of OT eschatology. This lead was quickly followed, sometimes to excess, by other scholars, notably the so-called Myth and Ritual School of British and Scandinavian scholars in the 1930s, who drew heavily upon comparative religion to construct in detail a cultic drama of divine combat and nuptials and the fixing of destinies, which accounted for many of the cries of anguish or triumph in the Psalter and most of its allusions to seas and springs, enemies and monsters, defeat and victory, and the attributes and activities of the king.

Not all scholars, however, who acknowledge a debt to Mowinckel have agreed in detail with him or (still less) with those who carried his methods to extremes. Mowinckel himself makes less of the Accession motif in his later writings than in his early studies, and other scholars who emphasize the influence of the new year festival on the Psalter would see its main aspect as covenant-renewal (A. Weiser) or the reaffirming of God's choice of Zion and the house of David (H. J. Kraus). But the legacy of Gunkel and Mowinckel remains, in the preoccupation of most commentators with the task of assigning each psalm to its proper class, and in the viewing of almost all the material as ecclesiastical.

This is distinct from the view, with which there can be no quarrel, that the psalms were collected and used for worship, and in many cases written expressly for such use. Instead, it assumes that even those psalms which profess to have sprung from episodes in the life of David (*e.g.* the bulk of Pss. 51–60), or which are attested as his writings by the NT (*e.g.* Pss. 16; 69; 109–110), arose on the contrary out of the cult-drama or were anonymously composed as set pieces for worship situations that might arise for the individual, the Davidic king or the congregation. Thus Ps. 51, despite the introductory statement which is part of the Hebrew text, is allegedly not David's prayer after his sin with Bath-sheba, and Ps. 110, despite our Lord's account of it, is not allowed to be the work of (as he himself put it in Mk. 12:36) 'David himself, inspired by the Holy Spirit'. Within this dominant school of thought, however, there are varieties of opinion as to the right classification of individual psalms, and there is more confidence in saying who did not write the psalms than in deciding who did.

The attempt to place the psalms within their setting, we suggest, should be governed by the evidence in each separate case. This will include the internal characteristics to which Gunkel and his successors have drawn attention, but it will be controlled by the statements, where there are such, in the titles and other scriptures. It will also bear in mind the fact that a psalmist could speak (as Peter pointed out in Acts 2:30f.) as 'a prophet', aware of God's promises and foreseeing what was far beyond his own horizon.

V. The theology of the Psalter

1. The marrow of the religious life of the psalmists was undoubtedly their *knowledge of God.* They never tire of singing his majesty in creation. In all his works in the heavens, the earth and the sea he has made himself known as the all-powerful, the all-knowing, the everywhere-present God. He is also the God of all history who guides everything towards the final goal which he has purposed to fulfil. But this Ruler of the world, this King of kings, is also Lawgiver and Judge, the Vindicator of all who are oppressed and their Saviour. He is therefore merciful and faithful, just and righteous, the Holy One whom men and angels adore. But the God of the psalmists is also, and uniquely, the God of Israel. The God who revealed himself to Abraham, Isaac and Jacob, who through Moses delivered Israel from Egypt, entered into covenant with them and gave them the promised land, is the God of Israel still, the Lord and Defender of the chosen people.

With such a high conception of God it is not surprising that the psalmists found their chief delight and privilege in prayer to God. There is a directness, a spontaneity and an immediacy in the prayers of the psalmists that convince us of the reality of prayer for them. They believe in his providence, trust in his presence, rejoice in his righteousness, rest in his faithfulness, confide in his nearness. In their prayers they praise, petition and commune with their God, and find refuge from sickness, want, pestilence and slander, and humble themselves under his mighty hand. In the progressive life of the community their behaviour is marked by fidelity to God, reverent obedience to the law, kindness to the oppressed and joy in the worship of God's people.

2. Set against such a background of faith and obedience *the imprecatory psalms* (see especially 35:1–8; 59; 69; 109) may be felt to constitute a moral difficulty. Similar prayers for vengeance are found in Jeremiah 11:18ff.; 15:15ff.; 18:19ff.; 20:11ff. The underlying idea in these passages in the Psalter, where curses and revengeful punishments are invoked upon the enemy, is expressed in 139:21f., 'Do I not hate them that hate thee, O Lord? . . . I count them my enemies.' That is to say, the psalmists are motivated by zeal for the Holy One of Israel who must exercise retribution in the present moral order in the world. Behind the imprecations is a recognition of a divine moral governance in the world, a belief that right and wrong are meaningful for God, and that therefore judgment must operate in the moral world order as well as grace. It was natural, then, for men living under the dispensation of the law to pray for the destruction of *God's* enemies through judgment, although Christians now living in the dispensation of grace pray for all men that they may be saved, while still believing in the reality of a here-and-now judgment as well as judgment that is a future event.

It should be remembered too that while the psalmists were aware of the tensions between righteousness and unrighteousness, between the people of God and the enemies of God, they had as yet no conception of judgment in an eschatological sense, nor had they any doctrine of a future state in which the ungodly would be punished and the godly rewarded. Therefore if righteousness is to be vindicated it has to be vindicated now, if wickedness is to be punished it has to be punished now. For when the righteous man prayed for the destruction of wickedness he did not distinguish in his mind between the ungodly and his ungodliness. The destruction of the one without the other was unthinkable to the pious Hebrew. It was even difficult if not impossible for some psalmists to distinguish between the ungodly man and his family. All that belonged to the wicked man was involved with him in his wickedness. The Christian therefore must have these things in mind when he reads these imprecatory psalms. He must not empty them of all significance. They are at least a powerful reminder of the reality of judgment in this moral world, and they testify to a burning zeal for the cause of righteousness which flamed in the hearts of some of the psalmists, and to their refusal to condone sin.

3. Has the Psalter a theology of a *future life*? The answer here is, No. There is a hope but no assured belief concerning the future. There is no *certain* reference to resurrection in the Psalter. Flashes of revelation or insight concerning the future life there may be, but there is no doctrine, no such article of religious faith. The germ of such a hope may be found in Pss. 16–17; 49; 73, but simply a hope it remains. Nowhere does a psalmist attain to an assured belief in resurrection.

4. The *Messianic psalms*. One of the most important factors in the national survival of Israel has been the Messianic hope. This hope centres on the return of the age of David whose reign in the past marked the golden age in Israel's history; and it is against this background that the Messianic hope in the Psalter should be viewed. The picture of the Messiah that emerges from the Psalter is a twofold one.

First, since Messiah is to be a scion of the Davidic dynasty, he is to be the *King* of the Messianic age. The Psalter envisages a divine Messianic King against whom nations will rebel in vain (Ps. 2). The Messianic age is depicted in Ps. 72, while in Ps. 2 the kingdom is described as a universal kingdom which belongs to God but over which Messiah rules in association with the Lord. In Ps. 110 Messiah is King, Priest and Victor who sits in glory at God's right hand. Ps. 45 speaks of eternal dominion, while Ps. 72 emphasizes the universality of Messiah's rule.

But secondly, the Psalter also prepares men's minds for a suffering Messiah. Is. 53 has its counterpart in the Psalter. The anointed Son of Yahweh, the Priest-King whose throne will stand for ever and whose reign of peace and righteousness will cause all nations to be blessed in him, is to submit himself to dreadful suffering (Pss. 22; 69, *etc.*). However, not until Christ interpreted the Psalter to the apostles were these and similar psalms considered to be Messianic (Lk. 24:27–46). Only as the Lord enlightened the disciples' minds did the church understand the meaning of these passages in the Psalter and make it the hymn-book and the prayer-book of the church.

VI. The Christian and the Psalter

Apart from the inherent religious and devotional qualities of the psalms two factors have compelled the Christian church to make the Psalter her prayer-book.

1. There is the fact that the Psalter occupied such a large place in the life and teaching of our Lord. It was the prayer-book which he would use in the synagogue service, and his hymn-book in the Temple festival. He used it in his teaching, met temptation with it, sang the Hallel from it after the Last Supper, quoted it from the cross and died with it on his lips.

2. Moreover, from earliest times the Psalter has been both the hymn-book and the prayer-book of the Christian church. Some of her great hymns of praise are modelled on the psalms (Lk. 1:46ff., 68ff.; 2:29ff.). The Psalter was the inspiration of the apostles in persecution (Acts 4:25f.), it was embedded in their message (Acts 2:25ff.; 13:33), it was used to set forth their profoundest beliefs concerning the Lord (Heb. 1:6, 10–13; 2:6–8; 5:6; 10:5–7). In all ages the church has found in the Psalter 'a Bible in miniature' (Luther), or 'the Bible within the Bible'. And while this 'Bible in miniature' originated in the Jewish church, and is intimately related to the OT, yet, because it is illuminated by the light that breaks from the Gospels, the Christian church claims it and uses it too in all her access to God whom she evermore worships and adores.

BIBLIOGRAPHY. *Commentaries*: A. F. Kirkpatrick, 1901; A. Weiser, 1962; J. H. Eaton, 1967; M. J. Dahood, 1966–70; A. A. Anderson, 1972; D. Kidner, 1975. *Other Studies*: H. Gunkel, *The Psalms* (E.T. 1967, Facet Books); B. D. Eerdmans, *The Hebrew Book of Psalms*, 1947; N. H. Snaith, *Hymns of the Temple*, 1951; S. Mowinckel, *The Psalms in Israel's Worship*, 1962; H. Ringgren, *The Faith of the Psalmists*, 1963; C. Westermann, *The Praise of God in the Psalms*, 1966; D. J. A. Clines, *TynB* 18, 1967, pp. 103–126; *TynB* 20, 1969, pp. 105–125; B. S. Childs, *JSS* 16, 1971, pp. 137–150.

J.G.S.S.T.
F.D.K.

PSEUDEPIGRAPHA. The term is used to describe those Jewish writings which were excluded from the OT Canon and which find no place in the Apocrypha. For the purpose of this article the term will also exclude the sectarian documents of the Qumran library (*DEAD SEA SCROLLS). Unlike the Apocrypha, which were included in the Greek Scriptures, these pseudepigrapha never approached canonical status. They nevertheless played an important role during the intertestamental period and are valuable for the light they shed on the Jewish background of the NT. While not all the writings included in this group are pseudepigraphic in the strict sense of writings published under assumed names (*PSEUDONYMITY), the majority of them are and the name is therefore generally appropriate. It will be convenient to divide them roughly between Palestinian and Jewish–Hellenistic groups, as their place of origin strongly affected their form and purpose. Because of a dominant thread which runs through the majority of these writings they have aptly been described as the literature of the apocalyptic movement.

I. The Palestinian group

The Palestinian group contains three different literary types, poetry, legend and apocalypse, the *Psalms of Solomon* almost certainly belongs to the second half of the 1st century BC and is an example of the anti-Sadducean polemic of the Pharisees at that period. In the majority of these 18 psalms, which are modelled on the Davidic Psalms, there is no reference to the Messiah (*Ps. Sol.* 17 is the main exception), but much about the Messianic kingdom. The overthrow of the Hasmonean dynasty by the Roman Pompey is regarded as a divine act, although Pompey himself is condemned for his profanation of the Temple. There were other psalm collections during the intertestamental period, an example of which is the *Psalms of Joshua* found in the Qumran library.

There were many books which were legendary expansions of biblical history, based mainly on the law, although including some legends about the prophets. Among the earliest of these is the *Testaments of the Twelve Patriarchs*, based on Gn. 49. Each of Jacob's sons gives his instructions to his descendants and much of this teaching is of a high moral order. They are represented as reviewing their own failings to serve as a warning to others, but two of the patriarchs, Joseph and Issachar, are able to commend their own virtues. The original work was a Pharisaic production written towards the end of the 2nd century BC, but this was later expanded by additions. The library at Qumran contained certain parts of an earlier recension of the *Testaments* of Levi and Naphtali, in Aramaic and Hebrew, but does not appear to have possessed the whole. This new evidence has confirmed Charles' opinion that the *Testaments* contained some late Jewish and Christian additions. Some have supposed that the final editing was completed by a Christian, *c.* AD 200. There are in these writings some similarities to the teachings of Jesus, as, for example, exhortations to humility, brotherly love and almsgiving. These parts represent some of the best moral injunctions of pre-Christian Judaism.

Another book based on Genesis is the *Book of Jubilees*, so styled from its system of dating. The author advocated a 364-day year in order to assist the Jews to keep the feasts on the proper day. This is typical of his legalistic approach. The whole book, in fact, purports to be a revelation to Moses on Mt Sinai and is clearly intended to uphold the eternal validity of the law. The Pharisaic author was intent on combating the encroachments of Hellenism during the latter part of the 2nd century BC. In the course of the revelations there are many legendary accretions to the biblical history, as for example the attribution to Satan and not to God of the suggestion that Abraham should sacrifice Isaac (17:16; 18:9, 12). The author insisted on the strict observance of Jewish rites, particularly circumcision and sabbath observance (15:33f.; 2:25–31; 50:6–13). The book was well known at Qumran and possesses many points of contact with the Damascus Document.

In a similar vein to the *Testaments of the Twelve Patriarchs* is the *Testament of Job*, in which Job delivers to the children of his second wife a parting address. He is represented as reviewing his past life, and the book concludes with an account of the special ability granted to his three daughters to sing heavenly songs while his soul is transported by chariot to heaven. The book appears to have been the work of an author belonging to one of the stricter Jewish sects (possibly the *ḥasidim*) and may be dated possibly about 100 BC.

Several legendary works of a similar character, but which at least in their extant texts appear to have been subjected to Christian influence, must be included among this group of writings. The *Life of Adam and Eve*, which exists only in a Latin text, although it runs parallel in parts to the *Apocalypse of Moses* (in Greek), is an imaginative reconstruction of the history subsequent to the Fall, and in the course of it Adam has a vision in which he sees a picture of the developments of Jewish history to post-exilic times. It can confidently be dated before AD 70, since it supposes that Herod's Temple is still standing (29:6f.).

The *Martyrdom of Isaiah* is a partly Jewish and partly Christian book, extant only in Ethiopic. It tells how Isaiah came to be 'sawn asunder' (*cf.* Heb. 11:37) with a wood saw (1–5). A *Vision of Isaiah*, which has been interpolated into the original work, is clearly a Christian addition because it records the devil's indignation over Isaiah's foretelling of redemption through Christ and mentions Christian history up to the time of the Neronian persecutions (3:13–4:18). The part of the book known as the *Ascension of Isaiah* is also Jewish-Christian, for Isaiah is not only told by God of the coming of Jesus but witnesses the birth, death and resurrection of the Coming One. It is thought that the Jewish part may date from the 2nd century BC, but no trace of it has so far been found at Qumran.

In addition to these there was some pre-Christian pseudo-Jeremianic and pseudo-Danielic literature which has only recently come to light from the Qumran library and which has not been sufficiently investigated at the time of writing for an account of it to be included in this survey. But a previously extant work known as the *Paralipomena of Jeremiah the Prophet*, which shows marked Christian influences, may well look back to some earlier Jeremianic cycle. It is aimed particularly against mixed marriages.

By far the most important group of Jewish pseudepigrapha is the apocalypses, among which the *Book of Enoch* takes pride of place. It is a composite work, of which the various parts were composed at different times during the last two centuries BC. The oldest sections belong to the Maccabean period, according to Rowley and Torrey, although Charles had earlier maintained a pre-Maccabean date. There are five main divisions in the book as it now exists. The first describes a vision given to Enoch of future judgment, especially of the fallen angels. The second, known as *The Similitudes of Enoch*, consists of three parables dealing mainly with the theme of judgment upon the world, but with assurances to the righteous through the Messianic hope. The third is an astronomical book. The fourth consists of two visions, one about the flood and the other recounting the history of the world down to the Messianic age. The fifth is a miscellaneous collection of exhortations and other material, of which the most notable is an *Apocalypse of Weeks* which divides world-history into 10 weeks, the last 3 being apocalyptic. This book is of great importance for studies in the intertestamental period and furnishes valuable data for pre-Christian Jewish theology. It is also of interest in being cited in the NT Epistle of Jude. The *Apocalypse of Weeks* has been thought to be connected with the Qumran sect, but because there is no trace of the *Similitudes* at Qumran it is possible that this part should be dated in the Christian era (*cf.* J. C. Hindley).

There was another book which circulated under the name of Enoch, commonly known as the *Book of the Secrets of Enoch* or *2 Enoch*. It is also sometimes described as the *Slavonic Enoch* because it is extant only in some Slavonic MSS. Unlike *1 Enoch* it comes from a Hellenistic background and parts of the work are believed to belong to the Christian period. Since it was cited in the later parts of the *Testaments of the Twelve Patriarchs*, at least a section of *2 Enoch* must have preceded those parts. The whole is generally dated during the 1st century AD. It consists of an account of Enoch's journey through the seven heavens, together with certain revelations given to Enoch about creation and the history of mankind and includes Enoch's admonitions to his children. Much of the ethical instruction is noble in character and is reminiscent of the type of teaching in Ecclesiasticus.

The *Assumption of Moses* may have consisted of two distinct works known as the *Testament*, and *Assumption, of Moses* respectively (according to Charles, but Pfeiffer is reserved about this). In any case no MS is extant which gives the dispute over the body of Moses, which formed the basis of the *Assumption* (it is alluded to in the Epistle of Jude), but in the *Testament* Moses gives to Joshua an apocalyptic review of Israel's history from the occupation of Canaan until the end of time. There is a marked absence of any Messianic hope in the book. Because of close parallels with the Qumran War Scroll and the Damascus Document, it has recently been concluded that the author was probably an Essene.

Another work belonging to the Christian period is the *Apocalypse of Ezra* (or *2* [or *4*] *Esdras*). In this book various visions are ascribed to Ezra in Babylon which deal with the problem of Israel's sufferings and bring the issue down to the author's own day (*i.e.* to the period after AD 70 when the problem became acute). The sense of hopelessness pervading the account is finally relieved only by the vague belief in a coming golden age. The book is a sincere but unsuccessful attempt to solve a pressing problem. It is generally dated towards the end of the 1st century AD.

About the same time appeared the *Apocalypse of Baruch* (or *Syriac Baruch*), which has many similarities of thought with the last-mentioned book. It is in fact regarded by some scholars as an imitation of the more brilliant *2 Esdras*. Through the pessimism resulting from the overthrow of the city of Jerusalem there is faint hope until the Messianic reign of peace begins. The present is unrelieved despair, typified by very dark waters, but the coming of Messiah, represented by lightning, brings consolation.

II. The Jewish–Hellenistic group

Among the more notable Jewish–Hellenistic pseudepigrapha are propaganda works (the *Letter of Aristeas* and parts of the *Sibylline Oracles*), legendary history (*3 Maccabees*), philosophy (*4 Maccabees*) and apocalyptic (part of the *Slavonic Enoch* already mentioned and part of the *Greek Baruch*; *APOCRYPHA).

The *Letter of Aristeas* purports to come from the time of the production of the LXX said to have been proposed by Ptolemy II, Philadelphus, of Egypt (285–245 BC). The narrative itself is legendary and was written in fact by a Jew (*c.* 100 BC) who wished to commend the Jewish law and religion to his Hellenistic contemporaries. It is an apology for Judaism against its Gentile detractors.

About 140 BC an Alexandrian Jew produced some *Sibylline Oracles* in imitation of the ancient Greek oracles attributed to the Sibyl, a pagan prophetess held in high regard not only by contemporary Greeks but also among many Jews and even Christians at a later period. Numerous additions were subsequently made to these oracles. Of the twelve extant books the majority appear to be Christian in origin, but books 3–5 are generally regarded as Jewish. These are specifically devoted to propaganda and consist particularly of judgments on Gentile nations. In book 3 occurs a review of Israelitish history from Solomon's time down to Antiochus Epiphanes and his successors, but the Jews are to benefit by the coming Messiah. There is a special appeal to Greece to cease its pagan worship, and this strong apologetic purpose is further seen in the claim that the Sibyl is in reality a descendant of Noah.

3 Maccabees, like *2 Maccabees*, is a legendary embellishment designed for the glorification of the Jews in Egypt under Ptolemy Physcon. *4 Maccabees* is a philosophical homily in which a Hellenistic Jewish author, of a definitely legalistic persuasion, discourses on the main theme of the control of the passions by reason, and in this he betrays his Stoic leanings. But his real admiration is nevertheless for the Mosaic law, and he seeks unsuccessfully to achieve a synthesis between the two.

As a whole this pseudepigraphic literature throws interesting light on the preparation period for the gospel. It belongs to times when prophetic declarations had ceased and when there was an increasing reverence for the law. They were times of perplexity, and apocalyptic emerged to attempt to reconcile the prophetic promises with the disastrous course of current history and to project the fulfilment of these promises into an age yet to come. These books had wide circulation among the Jews, and many of the NT writers may have known them.

The literary device used seems strange to modern ideas, but the great preponderance of pseudonymous ascriptions in these books is evidence of its contemporary effectiveness. It may have been adopted by reason both of security and of the need to ensure the maximum authority for the writings (*PSEUDONYMITY).

There are many theological differences and developments in this literature as compared with the earlier prophetical period. The future age differs essentially from the present. It has a supernatural origin and will displace the present age, which is conceived of as under the domination of evil influences. This doctrine of the two ages is characteristic of the intertestamental period and finds some echoes in NT thought. It is significant that owing to this apocalyptic approach to future history the Messianic hope was not as dominant during this period as it had been earlier. The clearest picture is in the *Book of Enoch*, where the Messianic conception has become more transcendental, parallel with the increasing transcendentalism of the conception of God. The Son of man as a heavenly pre-existent Being is conceived as sharing with God in judgment. Another striking feature of this literature is the receding interest in pure nationalism and in the development of individualism, on the one hand, and universalism, on the other. But perhaps the greatest service rendered by the literature was its antidote to the increasing legalism of Judaism, particularly among the Pharisees, in spite of the fact that this legalism is not entirely lacking from many of these books. (*APOCALYPTIC; *APOCRYPHA.)

BIBLIOGRAPHY. R. H. Charles (ed.), *The Apocrypha and Pseudepigrapha in English*, 1913; A.-M. Denis, *Introduction aux Pseudepigraphes Grecs d'Ancien Testament*, 1970; J. C. Hindley, 'Towards a date for the Similitudes of Enoch', *NTS* 14, 1967–8, pp. 551–565; R. H. Pfeiffer, *History of New Testament Times with an Introduction to the Apocrypha*, 1949; L. Rost, *Judaism outside the Hebrew Canon* (E.T., D. E. Green), 1976; H. H. Rowley, *The Relevance of*

Apocalyptic, 1944; D. S. Russell, *The Method and Message of Jewish Apocalyptic*, 1964; E. P. Sanders, *Paul and Palestinian Judaism*, 1977, pp. 346–418; E. Schürer, *HJP*², 1, 1973. D.G.

PSEUDONYMITY. Pseudonymity is the practice of attributing literary works to assumed names, a device widely used in the ancient world. Numerous examples are known from the Graeco-Roman world, but in studying the Christian attitude towards such a device the Jewish pseudepigrapha are very much more significant (*PSEUDEPIGRAPHA, I). The former were not, as the latter were, expressions of a religious approach, and because of the wide differences in content between secular and religious writings the Jewish writings naturally form a closer parallel with the numerous Christian pseudepigrapha circulating during the first 3 centuries AD.

There is no doubt that these writings enjoyed considerable popularity, and for this reason demand some explanation of their character and method. It is difficult for modern minds accustomed to the literary condemnation of plagiarism (the use of another's material) to appreciate this ancient practice of using another's name. But it is often assumed that the ancient approach was essentially different from the modern and implied nothing reprehensible. Undoubtedly many of the authors who resorted to this practice were men of sincerity, and herein lies the problem. Are there any ascertainable principles which throw any light on the apparent contradiction?

I. The Greek approach

There are many causes which are thought to account for the abundance of pseudonymous writings among the Greeks. There was a tendency to ascribe anonymous works to some well-known author of works of the same kind, for instance, epics to Homer or Virgil. Many writings by scholars were attributed to their masters, from whom they had learnt their wisdom, as, for example, among the followers of Plato. Moreover, rhetorical exercises were frequently attributed to famous persons (*cf.* the forgery known as the *Epistle of Phalaris*). A more deliberate type of forgery prevalent in the Greek world was the practice of publishing MSS under the names of popular authors as a method of selling them. A later motive was the desire to produce documents in support of certain doctrines by attributing them to some ancient and honoured teacher (*e.g.* among the Neopythagoreans, and in a Christian context the Clementine literature and the works attributed to Dionysius the Areopagite).

II. The Jewish approach

This seems to have inherited little directly from Greek practices, since the majority of the pseudonymous writings were the products of Palestinian Judaism. The widespread Greek secular usage may have had some small impact, although the *Letter of Aristeas* and the *Slavonic Enoch* are almost the only clear instances of the practice even among the Hellenistic Jews (*PSEUDEPIGRAPHA, II). The main causes for pseudonymity must clearly be sought elsewhere. Undoubtedly the most significant factor was the rigidity of the law and the cessation of prophecy. An authoritative message for the contemporary Jews of the 2 centuries before Christ could be established, it was thought, only by attributing such a message to some hero of the past whose authority was unquestioned. This accounts for the prominence of the patriarchal names among the pseudepigrapha. Indeed, all the assumed authors except Aristeas are mentioned either in the Law or the Prophets. This illustrates clearly the fundamental difference between Greek and Jewish pseudonymous practice. The latter possessed what the former lacked, an authoritative body of writings which formed the basis of their religious beliefs, and their pseudonymous productions were therefore extensions of canonical material (the nearest Greek parallel is the *Sibylline Oracles*). It is this phenomenon which raises problems for Jewish pseudonymity which were almost entirely absent from the Greek world. The Jewish authors were religious men, and it is not easy to see how they could resort to a literary method which to us seems morally questionable. There are a number of possible explanations.

The false ascription may have been occasioned by the use of materials traditionally handed down in association with some famous name. Some scholars, for instance, have virtually maintained this viewpoint when suggesting that Jude cites not the *Book of Enoch* but an earlier oral ascription believed to have been a true saying of Enoch which was later incorporated into the pseudonymous book (*cf.* Jude 14). But unfortunately data for verifying this procedure are practically non-existent. Another suggestion arises from the nature of apocalyptic. This mode of thought frequently made use of symbolic figures of speech, which the readers were clearly not expected to take literally, and the same tacit assumption may have been made over the pseudonym. Sometimes the device may have been used in self-defence when the author was not anxious to parade his identity for fear of arousing the suspicions of the tyrannical occupying power. In this case the readers would readily appreciate the reason for the pseudonym and would absolve the writer from any moral censure. Yet in few cases is this explanation clearly applicable. It is possible that the Jews paid little attention to literary property and were far more concerned with contents than authorship, and if this were generally so it might explain the readiness with which the writings circulated.

III. The Christian approach

There is no doubt that the prevalence of pseudonymous early Christian writings owed more to Jewish than to Greek influences. By the 2nd century AD a canon of Christian writings had come into existence which, although lacking formal codification (except in the case of Marcion), was nevertheless real and authoritative. There were pseudonymous counterparts to all 4 types of NT literature—Gospels, Acts, Epistles and Apocalypses. The majority of these sprang from heretical sources, and in these cases the use of the pseudonymous device is transparent. Esoteric doctrines outside the theology of orthodoxy sought support by the theory that secret teachings had been handed down to the initiates of a particular sect but had been hidden from others. The production of pseudonymous apostolic writings was thus made easy. Since the interval separating the assumed author from the real author was not as great as in the majority of Jewish writings of this character, it did not stretch the credulity of the readers too much to be told that some new

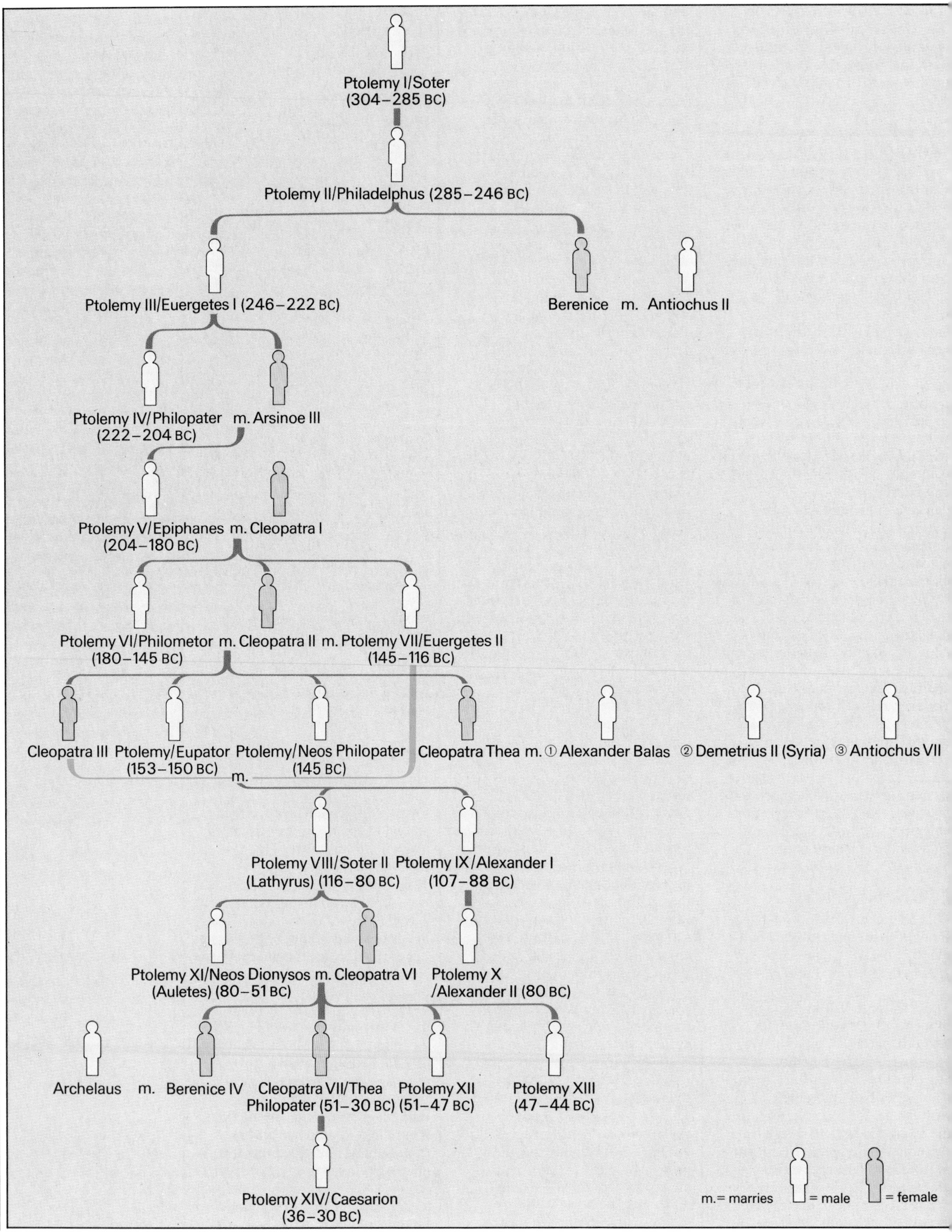
Ptolemy I/Soter
(304–285 BC)
Ptolemy II/Philadelphus (285–246 BC)
Ptolemy III/Euergetes I (246–222 BC)
Berenice m. Antiochus II
Ptolemy IV/Philopater m. Arsinoe III
(222–204 BC)
Ptolemy V/Epiphanes m. Cleopatra I
(204–180 BC)
Ptolemy VI/Philometor m. Cleopatra II m. Ptolemy VII/Euergetes II
(180–145 BC)
(145–116 BC)
Cleopatra III
Ptolemy/Eupator
(153–150 BC)
m.
Ptolemy/Neos Philopater
(145 BC)
Cleopatra Thea m. ① Alexander Balas ② Demetrius II (Syria) ③ Antiochus VII
Ptolemy VIII/Soter II
(Lathyrus) (116–80 BC)
Ptolemy IX/Alexander I
(107–88 BC)
Ptolemy XI/Neos Dionysos m. Cleopatra VI
(Auletes) (80–51 BC)
Ptolemy X
/Alexander II (80 BC)
Archelaus m. Berenice IV
Cleopatra VII/Thea
Philopater (51–30 BC)
Ptolemy XII
(51–47 BC)
Ptolemy XIII
(47–44 BC)
Ptolemy XIV/Caesarion
(36–30 BC)
m.= marries
= male
= female

writing was in fact an apostolic production, assuming that they were ignorant of its true source.

In spite of the fact that pseudonymity was a widespread practice, it must not be assumed that it would have been regarded as a harmless literary device among the orthodox Christians. What external evidence there is suggests rather that the church took a firm stand against the practice (*e.g.* the Muratorian Canon, Serapion, Tertullian). Tertullian in fact records the unfrocking of the Asian presbyter who confessed to writing the *Acts of Paul* out of his love for Paul, which does not suggest it was an acknowledged practice to produce such literature. For this reason the assumption by some scholars that certain NT books are really pseudonymous raises an acute psychological and moral problem, which few of the supporters of these hypotheses are willing to admit. There is a presumption against NT canonical pseudepigrapha which can be nullified only by overwhelming and conclusive evidence to the contrary, and even here each case must be judged entirely on its own merits.

On the question of pseudonymity in OT literature, see *DANIEL, BOOK OF; *DEUTERONOMY; *ECCLESIASTES; *PENTATEUCH.

BIBLIOGRAPHY. R. H. Charles, *Religious Development between the Old and New Testaments*, 1914; D. Guthrie, 'Epistolary Pseudepigraphy', *New Testament Introduction*, 1970, pp. 671–684; J. Moffatt, *An Introduction to the Literature of the New Testament*[2], 1912, pp. 40ff.; H. J. Rose, 'Pseudepigraphic Literature', *Oxford Classical Dictionary*, 1949; R. D. Shaw, *The Pauline Epistles*[4], 1913, pp. 477ff.; A. Sint, *Pseudonymität im Altertum: ihre Formen und Gründe*, 1960; and especially F. Torm, *Die Psychologie der Pseudonymität im Hinblick auf die Literatur des Urchristentums*, 1932.

D.G.

PTOLEMAIS.

I. In the Old Testament

The name given in the late 3rd or early 2nd century BC by Ptolemy I or II of Egypt to the seaport of Accho, on the N point of the Bay of Acre (named from Accho), about 13 km N of Carmel headland which faces it across the bay. Accho was the only natural harbour on the coast S of Phoenicia in OT times, and various routes connected it with Galilee and its lake, the Jordan valley and beyond. The only reference to Accho in the OT is in Jdg. 1:31, where it is assigned to Asher, but the tribe failed to capture it, and it probably remained Phoenician throughout the OT period. Some would emend Ummah in Jos. 19:30 to read Accho (*e.g. GTT*, p. 139), though this is but a conjecture.

Accho is more frequently mentioned in non-biblical texts. A prince of Accho (Egyp. *'ky*) is apparently already mentioned in the Egyp. Execration Texts of the 18th century BC (G. Posener, *Princes et Pays d'Asie et de Nubie*, 1940, p. 87, E49; *ANET*, p. 329, n. 9). Accho later appears in topographical lists of the 15th and 13th centuries BC, in the Amarna tablets of the 14th century BC (*e.g. ANET*, pp. 484–485, 487), and in an Egyp. satirical letter of *c.* 1240 BC (*ANET*, p. 477b). In later days Sennacherib of Assyria mentions Accho as part of the realm of Tyre and Sidon on his Palestinian campaign of 701 BC (*ANET*, p. 287b), and Ashurbanipal attacked it in the 7th century BC (*ANET*, p. 300b). On the relation of Accho to Asher and Galilee inland, see D. Baly, *Geography of the Bible*[2], 1974, pp. 121–124.

K.A.K.

II. In the New Testament

During the intertestamental period the name Accho was changed to Ptolemais, presumably in honour of Ptolemy Philadelphus (285–246 BC). Under this name it played an important role in the Jews' struggle for freedom under the Maccabees (*cf.* 1 Macc. 5:15; 12:45–48), but is only once noticed in the NT (Acts 21:7). Paul, sailing from Tyre to Caesarea towards the end of his missionary journey, put in at Ptolemais, and while his ship lay at anchor in the harbour he spent a day with the Christians of the place. This was probably not the only time he passed through the city, since he came along the Phoenician coast several times.

In Paul's day Ptolemais was a *colonia*, the emperor Claudius having settled a group of veterans there. After the Roman period it assumed its original name 'Akka and has maintained it to the present day. During the Crusades Ptolemais rose to importance under the Gallicized name Acre or St Jean d'Acre. Today it is overshadowed by the prominence of the city of Haifa, which lies directly across the bay.

W.W.W.

Ptolemais (formerly Accho; cf. Jdg. 1:31) was a Roman colonia *in the days of Paul. This aqueduct dates from about this time.* (MEPhA)

PTOLEMY.

The name borne by the 14 kings of the purely Macedonian Greek dynasty that ruled Egypt *c.* 323 to 30 BC.

I. The early Ptolemies

After the death of Alexander the Great at Babylon in 323 BC one of his marshals, Ptolemy son of Lagus, had himself appointed as satrap of Egypt, recognizing the nominal reigns of Alexander's half-brother Philip Arrhidaeus and infant son Alexander the younger, as did the great conqueror's other marshals in Babylon, Syria, Asia Minor and Greece. But in 310 BC the boy Alexander had been murdered, and each marshal tried unsuccessfully to take the whole empire from his rivals, so that it was carved up between them. Ptolemy therefore took the title king of Egypt in 304 BC, reigning till 285. Under him, his son Ptolemy II Philadelphus (285–246 BC), and his grandson Ptolemy III Euergetes I (246–222 BC), Egypt became once more a power in the Near East, no longer as a pharaonic but as a

Opposite page: Simplified family tree of the Ptolemies, the Hellenistic rulers of Egypt.

Hellenistic monarchy. Ptolemy IV Philopator (222–204 BC) was a dissolute ruler, echoes of whose Syrian wars occur in 3 Macc. 1:1–5.

Like the Ptolemaic kings themselves, all their chief ministers, all the upper ranks of the vast, centralized bureaucracy now instituted to govern Egypt, the main armed forces, the official language of administration—all were Greek. Egypt was the king's personal estate and run on strictly business lines to extract the maximum profit for the crown. *Alexandria was the capital, famous for its buildings, institutions ('Museum', Library, Serapeum, *etc.*), and its exports of grain, papyrus, perfumes, glass, *etc.* There was early a large community of Greek-speaking Jews in Alexandria; in the 3rd century BC the law was rendered into Greek for their use, and the rest of the OT followed, and thus was born the Septuagint version (*TEXTS AND VERSIONS).

The Ptolemies endeavoured to retain the loyalty of the native population of Egypt by gifts of money, lands and new temple buildings to the great, traditional Egyptian priesthoods. Large new temples arose (*e.g.* at Edfu, Dendera, Kom Ombo) in the old pharaonic style, but the 'pharaohs'

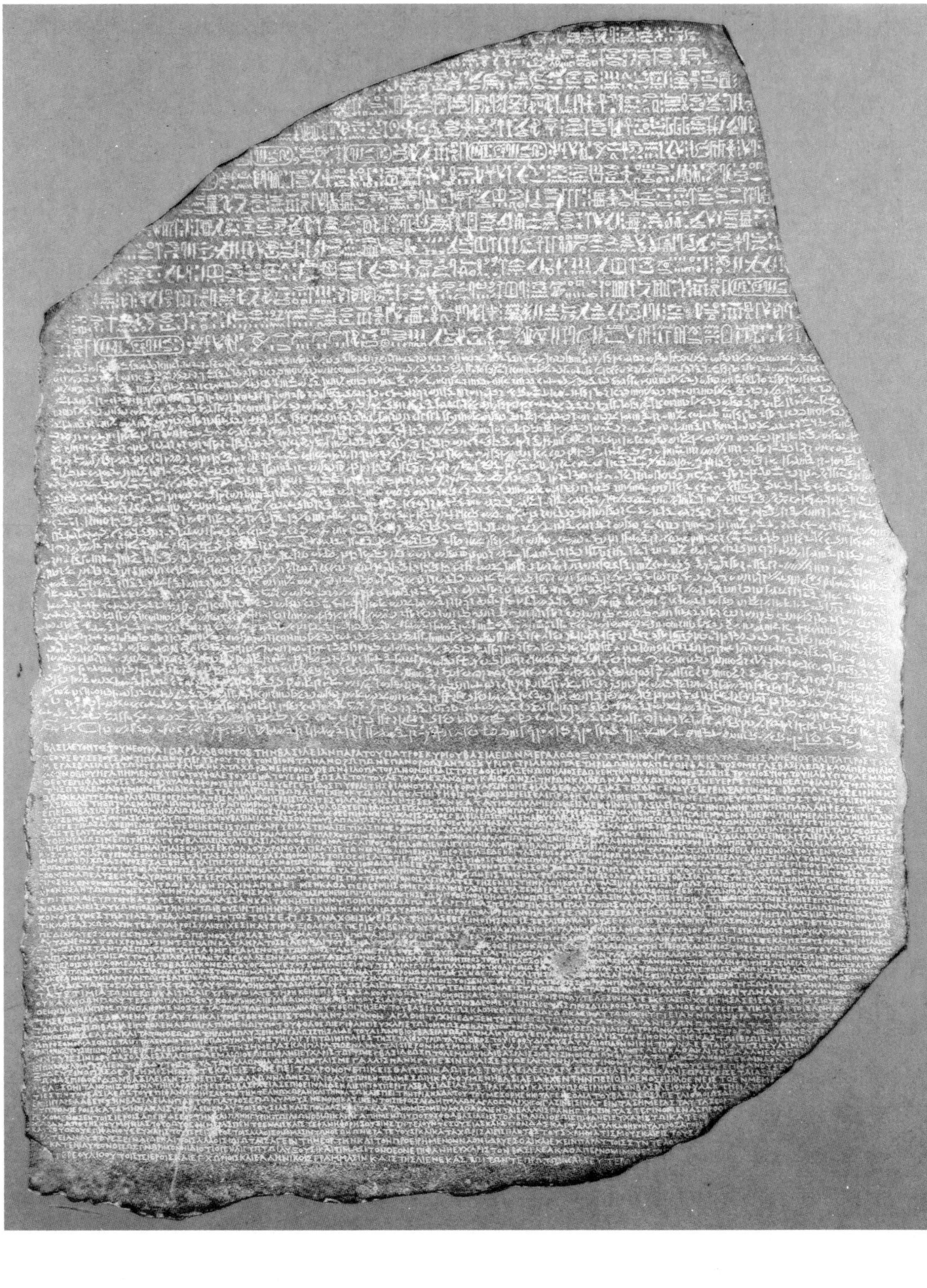

A decree commemorating the coronation of Ptolemy V (Epiphanes) inscribed on the Rosetta stone in Egyptian hieroglyphic and demotic, and Greek scripts. Rashid, Egypt. Black basalt. Height 1. 14 m. 195 BC. (BM)

Ptolemy III (Euergetes I) and his successors built this temple of Horus at Edfu, Upper Egypt. The great pylon gateway leads into the main hall of the temple. Gateway 1st cent. BC. (KAK)

sculptured on their walls bear in hieroglyphs the names of the Ptolemies.

The long hieroglyphic texts in these temples were written in a specially intricate way by the nationalistic priests so that no foreigners should penetrate their secret traditions; they contain a vast deposit of information on Egyptian religion and mythology, much of it handed down from, and valuable for the study of, pharaonic Egypt.

At first, Palestine—including the Jewish community—and *Coele-Syria formed part of the Ptolemaic kingdom along with Cyprus and Cyrenaica. But after a series of battles in 202–198 BC Antiochus III of Syria finally drove the forces of young Ptolemy V Epiphanes (204–180 BC) out of Syria–Palestine; this area, with its Jewish inhabitants, thus passed under Syrian (Seleucid) rule.

The Rosetta Stone is a decree of Ptolemy V, *c.* 196 BC, inscribed in both Egyptian (hieroglyphs and demotic) and Greek; its discovery in 1799 provided the key for the decipherment of the Egyptian hieroglyphs and the founding of modern Egyptology (*WRITING).

II. The later Ptolemies

The change from an Egyptian to a Syrian overlord was to have drastic consequences for the Jews some 30 years later, under *Antiochus IV. Down to this period, some of the clashes between the kingdoms of Egypt and Syria (of the 'South' and 'North') are foreshadowed in

Bottom left: Tetradrachm *of Ptolemy VI Philometor (180–145 BC). Diameter 32 mm.* (RG)

The court and temple of Horus behind the great façade built by the Ptolemaic Dynasty at Edfu. 3rd–1st cent. BC. (KAK)

Dn. 11:4ff. (*DANIEL, BOOK OF). Under Ptolemy VI Philometor (180–145 BC) dynastic strife first divided the royal family; his ruthless brother Ptolemy VII Euergetes II was for a time joint king and eventually succeeded him. Ptolemy VI favoured the Jews in Egypt and permitted the son of the dispossessed high priest, Onias III of Jerusalem, to establish a rival temple in Egypt at Leontopolis, about 16½ km N of Heliopolis. Ptolemy VI's activities in Syria are mentioned in 1 Macc. 10:51–57; 11:1–18; those of Ptolemy VII (145–116 BC) in 1 Macc. 1:18 and 15:16 (links with Rome). Other, non-royal, Ptolemies who are named in the Apocrypha are a general of Antiochus IV Epiphanes (1 Macc. 3:38; 2 Macc. 4:45; 6:8; 8:8; and perhaps 10:12) and a son-in-law of Simon Maccabaeus who murdered Simon and two brothers-in-law at Dok near Jericho in 135 BC (1 Macc. 16:11ff.).

Under the later Ptolemies the Egyptian state steadily declined. Native revolts were more frequent; the kings and their ruthless queens (Cleopatras and Berenices) were dissolute (family murders being common), while the power of Rome grew apace. Last of the line were the brilliant but unscrupulous Cleopatra VII and her son by Julius Caesar, Ptolemy XIV Caesarion. She captivated both Caesar and Antony, but made no impression on Octavian (Augustus), and so committed suicide to avoid the humiliation of appearing in a Roman triumphal procession. So Egypt passed under the heel of Rome in 30 BC.

BIBLIOGRAPHY. E. Bevan, *A History of Egypt under the Ptolemaic Dynasty*, 1927; see also *CAH*, 7, 1928; and for the religious background, Sir H. I. Bell, *Cults and Creeds in Graeco-Roman Egypt*, 1953. For the numbering and reigns of the Ptolemies, *cf.* T. C. Skeat, *The Reigns of the Ptolemies*, 1954; also A. E. Samuel, *Ptolemaic Chronology*, 1962. K.A.K.

PUAH
See Tola, Part 3.

PUBLICAN
See Tax-collector, Part 3.

PUL
See Tiglath-pileser, Part 3.

PULSE
See Vegetables, Part 3.

PUPIL
See School, Part 3.

PUBLIUS. *Poplios* is the Greek version of the Latin name, probably *praenomen*, of the 'chief man of the island' of Malta in Acts 28:7. The title 'chief man' appears to be correct local usage (*IG*, 14. 601; *CIL*, 10. 7495), and may refer either to a native officer or to the chief Roman official. In the latter case the use of *praenomen* alone may perhaps be explained as the familiar usage of the local inhabitants.

BIBLIOGRAPHY. W. M. Ramsay, *SPT*, p. 343; *BC*, 4, *in loc.*; Arndt. J.H.H.

PUDENS. A Roman Christian who joined *Claudia and others in greeting Timothy (2 Tim. 4:21). Martial (4. 13) salutes Aulus Pudens and his bride Claudia, and another Pudens ('modest') and Claudia are linked in an inscription (*CIL*, 6. 15066): but identification with Timothy's friends is improbable. Tradition called Pudens a senator, locating his house-church at the church of S Pudentiana (*cf. Liber Pontificalis*, ed. Duchesne, 1, pp. 132f.); for excavations, *cf.* R. Lanciani, *Pagan and Christian Rome*, 1895, pp. 110ff. A.F.W.

PURIM. A Jewish festival celebrated during the 13–15th days of the month Adar. On this occasion the book of Esther is read, and traditionally the congregation in the synagogue shouts and boos whenever the name of Haman is mentioned. The book of Esther gives the origin of the festival. In the reign of Ahasuerus, probably Xerxes (486–465 BC) but possibly Artaxerxes II (404–359 BC), *Haman, the vizier, determined to massacre all the Jews. Since he was a superstitious man, he cast lots to find an auspicious day. The word *pûr*, which in Est. 3:7; 9:24, 26, is said to mean 'lot', is not a Hebrew word, but is almost certainly the Assyrian *puru*, which means a pebble, or small stone, which would be used for casting lots.

The earliest reference to the festival outside the OT is 2 Macc. 15:36, where a decree is made in 161 BC to celebrate annually the defeat of Nicanor by Judas Maccabaeus on 'the thirteenth day of the twelfth month, which is called Adar in the Syrian language—the day before Mordecai's day'. If 2 Maccabees is dated somewhere in the middle of the 1st century BC, this shows that by 50 BC Purim was celebrated on the 14th of Adar. The parallel passage in 1 Macc. 7:49 speaks of the institution of what was later called Nicanor's Day on the 13th of Adar, but makes no reference to Purim on the 14th. No conclusions can be drawn from this silence.

Josephus, at the end of the 1st century AD, says that Nicanor's Day was kept on Adar 13 (*Ant.* 12. 412) and Purim on Adar 14 and 15 (*Ant.* 11. 295). Curiously enough, Josephus does not use the term *Purim*, but says that the Jews call the 2 days *phroureas* (other readings are *phrouraias*, *phroureous*, *phrouraios*). This Gk. word seems to be based on the verb *phroureō*, meaning 'guard', 'protect'.

Nicanor's Day was not observed after the 7th century AD, but Adar 13 was gradually made part of Purim. As opposed to Adar 14 and 15, which were days of celebration, Adar 13 was a day of fasting.

Suggestions (*e.g.* J. C. Rylaarsdam, *IB*, 3, pp. 968f.) that the festival is a Jewish adaptation of a myth of a struggle between Babylonian or Persian deities have little to commend them. It is unlikely that for a supremely national celebration the Jews would have adapted a drama of pagan polytheism.

BIBLIOGRAPHY. J. H. Greenstone, *Jewish Feasts and Fasts*, 1946; B. M. Edidin, *Jewish Holidays and Festivals*, 1940. J.S.W.

PURITY. The original biblical significance was ceremonial. It was to be obtained by certain ablutions and purifications which were enjoined upon the worshipper in the performance of his religious duties. Purifications were common to many other religions, but there they were merely ceremonial and had no ethical significance. In the case of Israel most of the ceremonial purifications had both sanitary and ethical significance. Though Gn. 35:2 and Ex. 19:14 indicated that the general idea did not originate with the Mosaic law, it is clear that only with the giving of the ceremonial law under Moses were these regulations codified and detailed. In the teaching of the prophets the significance largely passed from the merely ceremonial to the ethical. In the NT the teaching of Christ and the descent of the Spirit lifted the meaning of purity into the moral and spiritual sphere.

In the general sense common to the NT, and to the devotional literature of the OT, purity indicates a state of heart where there is complete devotion to God. As unadulterated water is said to be pure, and gold without alloy is pure gold, so the pure heart is the undivided heart where there is no conflict of loyalties, no cleavage of interests, no mixture of motives, no hypocrisy and no insecurity. It is wholeheartedness God-wards. This is probably the sense in which our Lord used it in the Beatitudes (Mt. 5:8). The reward of the undivided heart is the vision of God. No vision of God can come to the heart that is unclean because it is out of harmony with the nature and character of God. In the further teaching of Christ (see Mk. 7:14–28) he transfers the state of defilement, and so of purity, entirely from the outer to the inner man. Purity in this sense may be said to be a state of heart reserved completely for God and freed from all worldly distractions.

In the specialized sense purity came to mean freedom from sensual pollution, particularly in the sexual life, though the NT does not teach that sexual activity is polluting in itself and, indeed, makes it clear that rightly ordered sexual behaviour is not (*cf.* Heb. 13:4). Nevertheless, the NT teaches the sanctity of the body as the temple of the Holy Spirit (*cf.* 1 Cor. 6:19f.) and inculcates the duty of self-restraint and self-denial even to the extent of personal loss. Purity is thus the spirit of renunciation and of the obedience which brings every thought and feeling and action into subjection to Christ. It begins within and extends outwards to the entire life, cleansing all the centres of living and controlling all the movements of body and spirit.

BIBLIOGRAPHY. H. Baltensweiler *et al.*, *NIDNTT* 3, pp. 100–108; F. Hauck, *TDNT* 1, pp. 122f.; R. Meyer, F. Hauck, *TDNT* 3, pp. 413–431. R.A.F.

PUT, PHUT. 1. Third son of Ham (Gn. 10:6; 1 Ch. 1:8). **2.** Warriors alongside * Lubim, Egyptians and Ethiopians unable to save No-Amon (Thebes) from Assyria (Na. 3:9). Elsewhere the word is found only in Je. 46:9; Ezk. 30:5 (as Egyp. allies), in Ezk. 38:5 (in Gog's armies; AV 'Libya[ns]') and in Ezk. 27:10 (warriors of Tyre). Put is certainly African, but its location is disputed. Claiming that Lubim (Libyans) and Put are distinct in Na. 3:9, some wish to equate Put with *Pw*(*n*)*t* (E Sudan?) of Egyp. texts. But Old Persian *putiya* and Bab. *puṭa* (= Heb. *pûṭ*) become *T' Ṯmḥw*, 'Libya', in Egyp. thus making Put Libya (G. Posener, *La Première Domination Perse en Égypte*, 1936, pp. 186–187). Lubim and Put in Na. 3:9 are like Lubim and * Sukkiim in 2 Ch. 12:3. Also, Tyre would employ Libyan rather than Somali auxiliaries. *pûṭ* may derive from Egyp. *pḏty*, 'foreign bowman', or similar; especially as the Libyans were archers (W. Hölscher, *Libyer und Ägypter*, 1937, pp. 38–39). K.A.K.

PUTEOLI. Mod. Pozzuoli, near Naples, a Samian colony from Cumae founded in the 6th century BC. Puteoli probably fell into Roman hands with Capua in 338 BC, and rapidly be ame an important arsenal and trading port. Livy mentions a garrison of 6,000 during the Hannibalian invasion (24. 13), and the embarkation of large reinforcements for Spain (26. 17). Rome's E traffic, notably the Egyp. grain, passed through Puteoli. Seneca describes the arrival of the Alexandrian corn-fleet (Ep. 77), and Paul arrived on an Alexandrian freighter (Acts 28:13). The recently discovered chapel in Herculaneum probably marks the home of some who met Paul at nearby Puteoli. The Via Domitiana linked Puteoli with the Via Appia. E.M.B.

PYTHON. This is the Greek name given to the mythological serpent or dragon which lived at Pytho beneath Mt Parnassus, and guarded the Delphic oracle. Apollo slew it, but the name was then applied to anyone who prophesied under the inspiration of Apollo. Such persons generally spoke with the mouth closed, uttering words quite beyond their own control, and so were also known as *engastrimythoi* or ventriloquists (Plutarch, *De Defectu Oraculorum*, 9, p. 414E).

Acts 16:16 records how Paul met and subsequently exorcized a young woman with such a spirit of * divination at Philippi: it is significant that Luke uses a word with pagan connections, *manteuomenē*, not elsewhere employed in the NT, to describe her oracular speech, obviously inspired by a demonic power. D.H.W.

QUARRY. 1. Heb. *šᵉḇārîm*, a place from which stone is dug. In Jos. 7: 5 'Shebarim' is better understood as 'quarries' (so RVmg.) in describing the place to which the Israelites fled after their abortive attack on Ai. Stone was quarried

PURSE
See Bag, Part 1.

PUT OFF FLESH
See Circumcision, Part 1.

PYGARG
See Animals, Part 1.

PYRAMIDS
See Memphis, Part 2.

QESITAH
See Weights and measures, Part 3.

Remains of the Flavian amphitheatre at Puteoli (modern Puzzuoli). After AD 69. (RS)

The so-called Solomon's stables beneath Jerusalem were probably ancient quarries. (MEPhA)

QUART
See Weights and measures, Part 3.

QUARTZ
See Jewels, Part 2.

QUEEN OF THE SOUTH
See Sheba, queen of, Part 3.

QUERN
See Mill, Part 2.

QUINCE
See Trees (Apple), Part 3.

through the centuries in Palestine. Good limestone lies close to the surface in most places and is broken out of its bed by cracking the stone along lines of cleavage. The so-called stables of Solomon in Jerusalem near to the Temple area are almost certainly ancient quarries. (*MINING.)

2. The word *p^{e}sîlîm* refers to a carved stone, and should be so translated in Jdg. 3:19, 26 (as in Dt. 7:5; Ps. 78:58; Is. 10:10; Mi. 5:13), rather than AV 'quarries'. J.A.T.

QUARTUS. The Latin name, meaning 'fourth', of a Christian at Corinth whose greetings Paul conveys (Rom. 16:23). He is called 'the brother'. This may mean either 'brother of Erastus', mentioned with him (several Corinthian Christians have Latin names); or 'our brother', *i.e.* our 'fellow-Christian', the title balancing the appellations of the others in vv. 21–23; or 'your brother', *i.e.* 'fellow-Roman Christian' (*cf.* 1 Cor. 1:1; *SOSTHENES). If Tertius and he were not separated by two other names, one might conjecture that they were third and fourth sons in the same family. Later, menologies allocated him to the Seventy (*Acta Sanctorum*, Nov. 1, p. 585). A.F.W.

QUEEN (Heb. *malkâ*, Gk. *basilissa*). The word 'queen' is not widely used in the Bible. It is used to describe women from countries outside Palestine who were reigning monarchs in their own right. Examples of this are the queen of *Sheba (1 Ki. 10:1; *cf.* Mt. 12:42; Lk. 11:31), and *Candace, queen of *Ethiopia (Acts 8:27).

In this same sense the word is used once in Israelite history with reference to Athaliah, who usurped the throne of Judah and reigned for 6 years (2 Ki. 11:3). In post-biblical Jewish history Salome Alexandra, widow of Alexander Jannaeus, succeeded her husband as queen regnant for 9 years (76–67 BC).

As consort the wife of the reigning monarch did not as a rule concern herself with affairs of state. Among the most noteworthy exceptions to this are Bathsheba (1 Ki. 1:15–31) and Jezebel (1 Ki. 21). The most important woman in the royal household, in Israel and Judah as in neighbouring lands, was the queen-mother. She was pre-eminent among the ladies of the court, and sat at the monarch's right hand (Bathsheba, 1 Ki. 2:19), crowned (Nehushta, Je. 13:18). In the history of Judah the queen-mothers were always named. A king might have many wives, but he had only one mother, and he was under obligation to honour her (Ex. 20:12). That her position was more than an honorary one is evident from the record of Maacah, who was queen-mother not only during the reign of her son Abijam but also during the reign of her grandson Asa, until the latter deposed her for idolatry (1 Ki. 15:2, 10, 13; 2 Ch. 15:16). The Chaldean queen of Dn. 5:10 was probably the queen-mother; the same may be true of the Persian queen of Ne. 2:6. M.B.

QUEEN OF HEAVEN. Cakes, possibly in the shape of figurines or crescent moons, were made for the *m^{e}leket* of the heavens by the inhabitants of Jerusalem (Je. 7:18) and incense burnt as to a deity (Je. 44:17–19, 25). The unusual word is rendered as 'queen' (*malkat*), and may be Phoen., a title of Astarte, Assyr. Ishtar. It may refer to *Ashtaroth or to the Canaanite Anat (so Egyp. 19th century *BETHSHEAN); *cf.* the female personal name (*Ham*)*mōleket* (1 Ch. 7:18). Alternatively, this may be a rare writing of *m^{e}le'ket*, 'heavenly handiwork' (*i.e.* stars), also denoting an idolatrous practice. D.J.W.

QUICKSANDS. (Gk. *syrtis*, 'a sandbank', RSV 'Syrtis', Acts 27:17). The ship in which Paul was travelling found it necessary to take precautions against being driven on to the Greater Syrtis, quicksands W of Cyrene on the N African coast. Now called the Gulf of Sidra, its treacherous sands and waters were greatly feared by sailors. J.D.D.

QUIRINIUS (Lk. 2:2, RV, RSV, NEB; AV 'Cyrenius' corresponds closely to Gk. *Kyrēnios*). Publius Sulpicius Quirinius was consul at Rome in 12 BC, and not long afterwards conducted a campaign against the unruly Homanadensians of central Asia Minor. In 3 BC he became proconsul of Asia; in AD 3–4 he was adviser to the imperial heir-apparent, Gaius Caesar, during the latter's Armenian expedition; from AD 6 to 9 he was imperial legate (*legatus pro praetore*) of Syria-Cilicia. This appears to have concluded his public career; thereafter he lived at Rome, where he died in AD 21. At the beginning of his governorship of Syria–Cilicia he organized the census in Judaea when that territory became a Roman province on the deposition of Archelaus (*HEROD, **2**). This census, recorded by Josephus (*Ant.* 18. 1–3, 26), is that referred to in Acts 5:37. From the *Lapis Venetus* (*CIL*, 3. 6687) we gather that it was not only in Judaea that a census was held under Quirinius' auspices; this inscription records the career of an officer who served under Quirinius during his legateship of Syria–Cilicia and held a census on his behalf in the Syrian city of Apamea. The *census of Lk. 2:1ff., however, must be at least 9 years earlier.

The statement in Lk. 2:2 about this earlier census has for the most part been understood in two alternative ways: 'This was the first registration of its kind; it took place when Quirinius was governor of Syria' (NEB), or 'This was the first registration carried out while Quirinius was governor of Syria' (NEBmg.). The possibility that Quirinius may have been governor of Syria on an earlier occasion (*CHRONOLOGY OF THE NT) has found confirmation in the eyes of a number of scholars (especially W. M. Ramsay) from the testimony of the *Lapis Tiburtinus* (*CIL*, 14. 3613). This inscription, recording the career of a distinguished Roman officer, is unfortunately mutilated, so that the officer's name is missing, but from the details that survive he could very well be Quirinius. It contains a statement that when he became imperial legate of Syria he entered upon that office 'for the second time' (Lat. *iterum*). The question is: did he become imperial legate of Syria for the second time, or did he simply receive an imperial legateship for the second time, having governed another province in that capacity on the earlier occasion?

The wording is ambiguous. Ramsay held that he was appointed an additional legate of Syria between 10 and 7 BC, for the purpose of conducting the Homanadensian war, while the civil administration of the province was in the hands of other governors, including Sentius Saturninus (8–6 BC), under whom, according to Tertullian (*Adv. Marc.* 4. 19), the census of Lk. 2:1ff. was held. A strong case, however, has been made out (especially by R. Syme) for the view that Quirinius's earlier legateship was not over Syria but over Galatia, where the Homanadensians would have been on his doorstep. It has been suggested that 'Saturninus', which Tertullian appears to have read in his copy of Lk. 2:2, was the original reading rather than 'Quirinius' (so B. S. Easton, *The Gospel according to St Luke*, 1926, p. 20; J. W. Jack, 'The Census of Quirinius', *ExpT*

The 'Queen of heaven' was probably a title of Ishtar (Astarte), the goddess of war and love, shown here on an Assyrian cylinder-seal and its impression. Height c. 5 cm. 8th–7th cent. BC. (BM)

The queen or consort of Ashurbanipal, king of Assyria (668–627 BC) drinking from a bowl at a royal or ritual banquet. Nineveh. (RS)

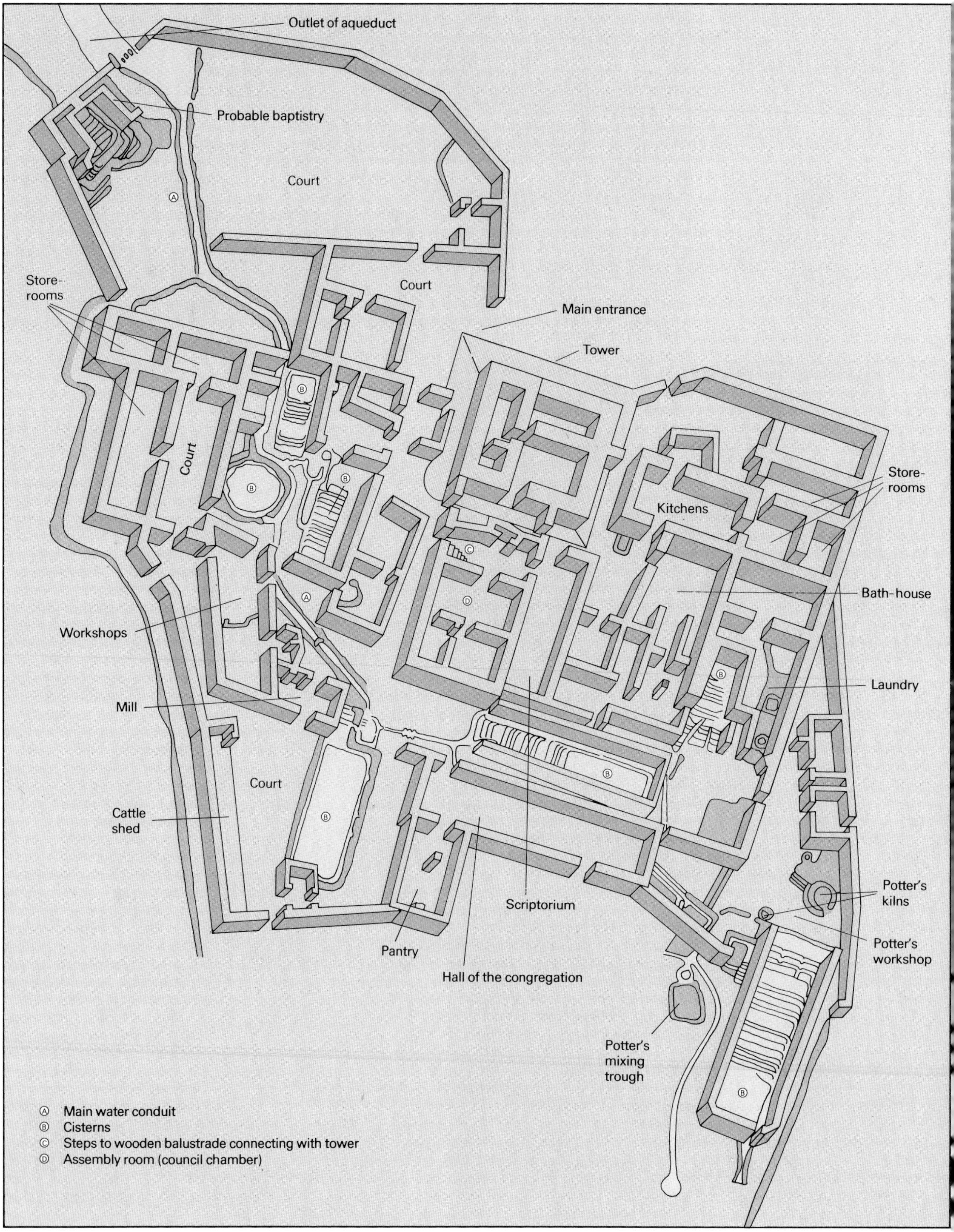

Outlet of aqueduct
Probable baptistry
Court
Court
Store-rooms
Main entrance
Tower
Court
Store-rooms
Kitchens
Bath-house
Workshops
Laundry
Mill
Court
Cattle shed
Potter's kilns
Potter's workshop
Scriptorium
Pantry
Hall of the congregation
Potter's mixing trough
Ⓐ Main water conduit
Ⓑ Cisterns
Ⓒ Steps to wooden balustrade connecting with tower
Ⓓ Assembly room (council chamber)

40, 1928–9, pp. 496ff.); another possibility is that the verse should be rendered: 'This enrolment was earlier than that held when Quirinius was governor of Syria' (so M. J. Lagrange, *RB* n.s. 8, 1911, pp. 60ff.; F. M. Heichelheim in T. Frank (ed.), *An Economic History of Ancient Rome*, 4, 1938, pp. 160ff.; N. Turner, *Grammatical Insights into the NT*, 1965, pp. 23f.).

BIBLIOGRAPHY. W. M. Ramsay, *Was Christ Born in Bethlehem?*, 1905; L. R. Taylor, 'Quirinius and the Census of Judaea', *American Journal of Philology* 54, 1933, pp. 120ff.; R. Syme, 'Galatia and Pamphylia under Augustus', *Klio* 27, 1934, pp. 122ff.; and other literature listed in *TCERK*, 1, 1955, p. 222 (*s.v.* 'Census'). F.F.B.

General view of the Qumran area showing caves in which various 'Dead Sea scrolls' were found. (MEPhA)

QUMRAN, the name of a wadi and of an ancient ruin in its vicinity, NW of the Dead Sea. The derivation of the name is uncertain; attempts (*e.g.* by F. de Saulcy) to connect it with Gomorrah are unacceptable. The name was recorded by a number of travellers who passed that way, but was practically unknown until the MS discoveries in neighbouring caves, in 1947 and the following years, put it on the map (*DEAD SEA SCROLLS). The excavations carried out at Khirbet Qumran ('ruin of Qumran') between 1951 and 1955 are generally regarded as demonstrating that this complex of buildings formed the headquarters of the community to which the Qumran MSS belonged. A cemetery lying between Khirbet Qumran and the Dead Sea (investigated by C. S. Clermont-Ganneau in 1873) was probably the burying-ground of the community; over 1,000 burials have been identified here, the bodies lying N and S, with the head to the S.

The site was evidently occupied in the period of the Judaean Monarchy, to which period a circular cistern is assigned (*cf.* 2 Ch. 26:10; *SALT, CITY OF). The most interesting phases of occupation, however, are those generally associated with the 'people of the scrolls'. Phase Ia (*c.* 130–110 BC) was marked by the clearing of the old circular cistern and the construction of two new rectangular cisterns, together with a few rooms and a potter's kiln. This was followed by Phase Ib, marked by a thoroughgoing reconstruction of the headquarters on an elaborate scale, evidently to meet the requirements of a greatly enlarged community. This phase came to an end *c.* 40 BC, perhaps because of the Parthian invasion. During the temporary absence of the community the buildings were seriously damaged by the earthquake of 31 BC (mentioned in Josephus, *Ant.* 15. 121f.). The site lay derelict until *c.* 4 BC, when the damaged buildings were repaired and strengthened. This marks the beginning of Phase II, during which the place evidently served the same purpose as it had done during Phase Ib. Among the installations which can be clearly identified are assembly rooms, scriptorium, kitchen, laundry, pottery factory (the best-preserved one thus far known from ancient Palestine), flour mills,

Buildings at Khirbet Qumran believed to have been occupied by an Essene community. 2nd cent. BC–1st cent. AD. (RS)

QUIVER

See Armour, Part 1.

Opposite page: Plan of the settlement excavated at Qumran. 1st cent. BC–1st cent. AD.

storage bins, ovens, smelting furnaces, metal workshops and an elaborate system of cisterns, into which water was led by an aqueduct fed from rock-hewn cisterns in the hills to the NW.

The phases of occupation are fairly clearly indicated by the coin record, several hundreds of contemporary coins having been found in the course of the excavations. This record suggests that Phase II came to an end *c.* AD 68. Evidence of another kind shows that the end of Phase II was violent; the walls were demolished, a layer of black ash covered the site and a quantity of arrow-heads added their silent testimony to the general picture. It is tempting to connect these events with mopping-up operations in that region at the time of the Roman occupation of Jericho in the summer of AD 68. Whether the Qumran community had remained in possession up to that time, or an insurgent garrison had taken over such well-built headquarters, remains uncertain.

A few rooms were built over the ruins and manned for some years by a Roman garrison (Phase III).

Since the excavation of Khirbet Qumran it has been widely identified with the * Essene settlement referred to by Pliny the Elder (*NH* 5. 17) as lying above En-gedi.

BIBLIOGRAPHY. Literature listed under * DEAD SEA SCROLLS and * ESSENES; with H. Bardtke, *Die Handschriftenfunde am Toten Meer*, 2 vols., 1953, 1958; J. van der Ploeg, *The Excavations at Qumran*, 1958; R. de Vaux, *Archaeology and the Dead Sea Scrolls*, 1973; E. M. Laperrousaz, *Qoumrân: l'établissement essénien des bords de la Mer Morte*, 1976.

F.F.B.

QUOTATIONS (IN THE NEW TESTAMENT). There are some 250 express citations of OT in NT. If indirect or partial quotations and allusions are added, the total exceeds 1,000. The book of Rev., *e.g.*, has no quotations, but is virtually interlaced with allusions to OT texts. The importance of the OT, which is indicated by this usage, is further defined by the introductory formulas: to say 'the Scripture says' is equivalent to saying 'God says' (*e.g.* Mt. 19:4); 'that it might be fulfilled' (*e.g.* Mt. 2:15) points to the essential connection between the message of God in the old covenant and in the new (*cf.* Ellis, *Prophecy*, pp. 148ff., 165–169; *idem*, Paul, pp. 22–25).

Some citations are taken from an OT Targum (Rom. 12:19) or from the Heb. text itself (Rom. 11:35; 1 Cor. 3:19). However, as one would expect in a Gk. document written for Gk. readers, the large majority of quotations are derived from the LXX, but with varying degrees of exactness. (Although textually dated, Turpie's manual is still helpful for classification and comparison of the Gk. and Heb. texts.) The inaccuracies which occur show the lack of concern (more than memory lapse) of the biblical writers for verbal exactness: it is the meaning rather than the words in themselves that are important.

In a considerable number of cases variant renderings are deliberately chosen, *ad hoc* or from other known versions, in order to bring out the 'fulfilment' as seen by the NT writer (*e.g.* 1 Cor. 15:54f.). In this process, known from its use at Qumran as *midrash pesher*, the commentary is merged into the quotation to give it a present-time, eschatological application. K. Stendahl has shown the affinity of this hermeneutical method in Mt. with the practices of the Qumran community; it is also present elsewhere in the NT (see Ellis, *Prophecy*). Interpretative renderings may not have originated with the NT writer himself. Rendel Harris suggested that behind some NT quotations lay a pre-canonical 'testimony book', a collection of selected, combined (*e.g.* Mk. 1:2f.), and interpreted OT passages, worked out in the early Christian community for apologetic purposes. While C. H. Dodd has suggested some modifications to this theory, the presence of *testimonia* in the Dead Sea Scrolls shows that the practice was not unknown and substantiates, in some measure, Harris's conjecture. It also appears

Colossal granite head of Rameses II, from Luxor. Height of bust c. 2·36 m. 13th cent. BC. (BM)

probable that some of these paraphrases originated in the teachings of primitive Christian prophets (Ellis, *Paul*, pp. 107–112; *idem, Prophecy*, pp. 130–138, 182–187, 224–229). Thus the problem of textual variation points beyond itself to the larger question of interpretation and application of OT by NT.

Often OT passages are applied quite at variance with the original historical meaning. Hosea's reference to the Exodus of Israel is 'fulfilled' in the baby Jesus' return from Egypt (Mt. 2:15). A number of passages having historical reference to Israel are referred by the NT to the church (*e.g.* Rom. 8:36; Eph. 4:8). A passage referring to Solomon, king of Israel, is applied both to Jesus Christ (Heb. 1:5) and to the church (2 Cor. 6:18). The rationale for this usage seems to lie (1) in a typological correspondence between OT *Heilsgeschichte* and the 'new age' fulfilment in Jesus Christ; (2) in the Semitic idea of corporate solidarity in which the king of Israel and Israel, Christ (Israel's true king) and the 'body of Christ', stand in realistic relationship to one another; and (3) in the conviction that the church is the true Israel and, therefore, the heir to the promises and the object of the prophecies. While the subject-matter of NT quotations covers virtually all doctrinal issues, the emphasis throughout is on the Messiah and Messianic-age fulfilments. Sometimes the application of the quotations is dependent upon the wider context of the OT (*e.g.* Acts 8:49f.); such 'pointer' quotations also may have been designed to call the reader's attention to a wider theme or topic (Dodd, p. 126).

A number of quotations occur in expository patterns similar, in varying degree, to those found in Philo (*cf.* Borgen), Qumran and the rabbinic literature (*cf.* Ellis, *Prophecy*, pp. 147–236). One such pattern opens with an OT quotation (or summary) followed by commentary, sometimes including a parable and/or supporting citations, and ends with a final quotation (Mt. 21:33–46; 1 Cor. 1:18–31; Gal. 4:21–5:1; Heb. 10:5–39; 2 Pet. 3:5–13; *cf.* Acts 13:17–41). It may be that some *testimonia* represent excerpts from such expositions. Quotations other than from the OT also appear. Eph. 5:14 (*cf.* 1 Cor. 15:45b; 1 Tim. 5:18b) may be an excerpt from an early Christian hymn or oracle; Jude 14 is taken from the pseudepigraphical book of *Enoch*; and Acts 17:28 is a quotation from a pagan writer.

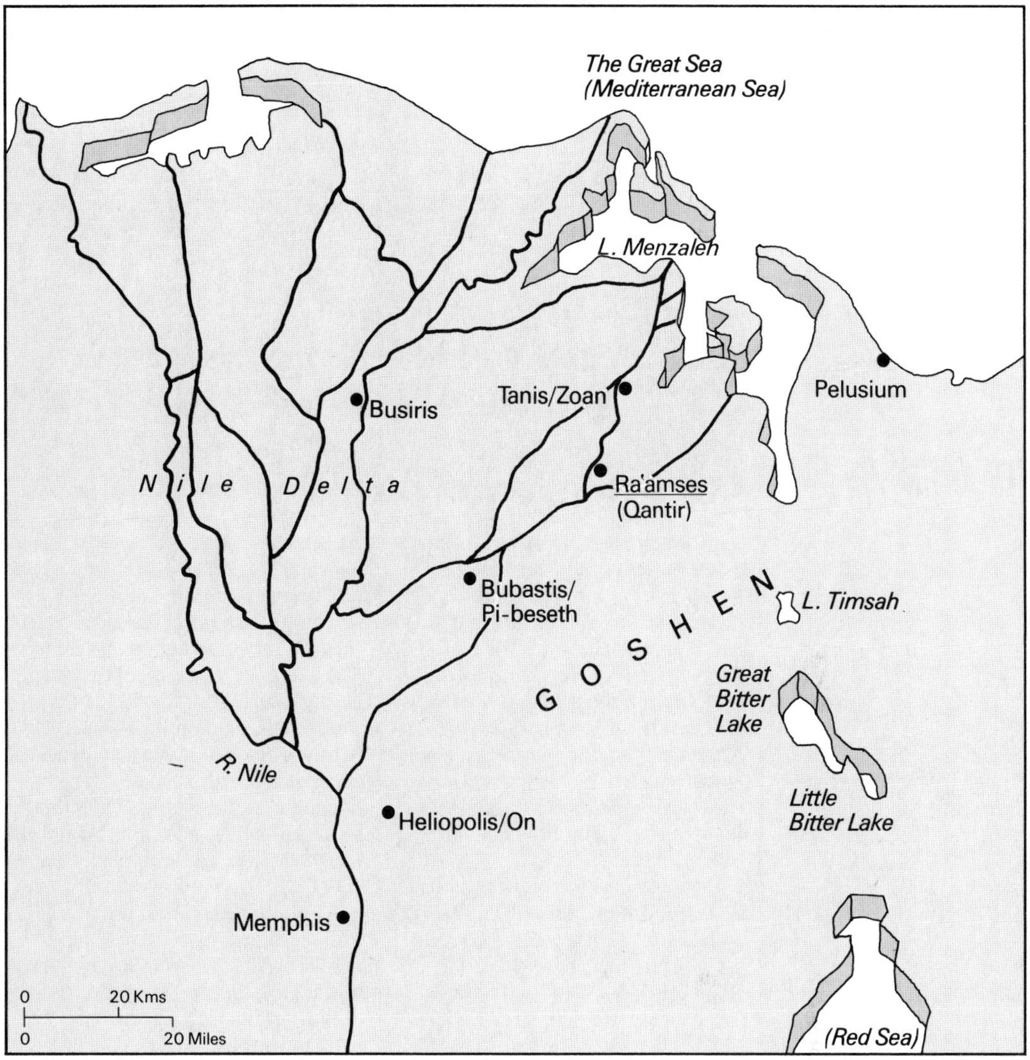

BIBLIOGRAPHY. D. L. Baker, *Two Testaments, One Bible*, 1976; R. Bloch, 'Midrash', in *Approaches to Ancient Judaism*, ed. W. S. Green, 1978; P. Borgen, *Bread from Heaven*, 1965; C. H. Dodd, *According to the Scriptures*, 1953; E. E. Ellis, *Paul's Use of the Old Testament*, 1957; *idem, Prophecy and Hermeneutic*, 1978; *idem*, in *The Jewish People in the First Century*, ed. M. de Jonge, 2, ii, 1979; R. T. France, *Jesus and the Old Testament*, 1971; L. Goppelt, *TYPOS*², 1969 (E.T. 1979); J. R. Harris, *Testimonies*, 2 vols., 1916, 1920; L. Hartman, *Prophecy Interpreted*, 1966; B. Lindars, *New Testament Apologetic*, 1961; R. L. Longenecker, *Biblical Exegesis in the Apostolic Period*, 1975; H. M. Shires, *Finding the Old Testament in the New*, 1974; K. Stendahl, *The School of St Matthew*², 1969; D. M. Turpie, *The Old Testament in the New*, 1868. E.E.E.

RAAMAH (Heb. *ra'mâ, ra'mā*, 'trembling'). A 'son' of Cush (Gn. 10:7; 1 Ch. 1:9). The tribe of Raamah has not been identified, but inscriptions found in Sheba suggest a location N of Marib in Yemen. With Sheba, Raamah sold spices, precious stones and gold to Tyre (Ezk. 27:22). A.R.M.

RA'AMSES, RAMESES (Egyp. *Pr-R'mssw*, Pi-Ramessē, 'Domain of Ramesses'). A city of Egypt mentioned with Pithom, where the Hebrews were afflicted with heavy burdens (Ex. 1:11; 12:37; Nu. 33:3). This was the famous E-Delta residence of Ramesses II (*c.* 1290–1224 BC). The kings of the 18th Dynasty did no building here. Scholars once located Pi-Ramessē at Pelusium, then at Tanis (*ZOAN), following Montet's excavations there. But all

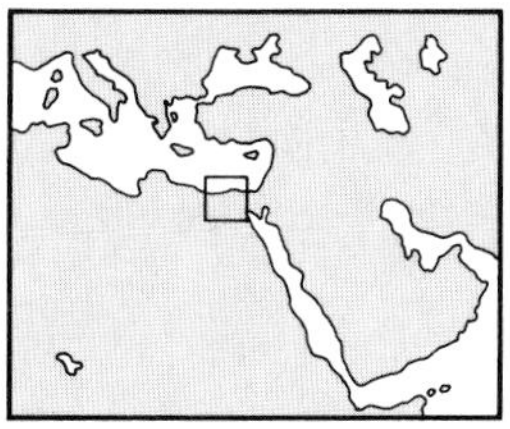

Ra'amses (Qantir) in Goshen.

Cartouche with hieroglyph naming Rameses II. Relief from the Temple of Amun at Karnak. c. 1290–1224 BC. (WM)

RABBIT
See Animals, Part 1.

the Ramesside stonework at Tanis is re-used material from elsewhere. Remains of a palace, a glaze-factory and of houses of princes and high officials (with trace of a temple) at and near Qantir, 30 km S of Tanis, almost certainly mark the real site of Ra'amses/Pi-Ramessē. The Exodus began from Ra'amses (Ex. 12:37) (*ENCAMPMENT BY THE SEA). Centuries before, Jacob had settled in the district (Gn. 47:11).

BIBLIOGRAPHY. A. H. Gardiner, *JEA* 5, 1918, pp. 127–138, 179–200, 242–271; P. Montet, *RB* 39, 1930, pp. 5–28; L. Habachi, *ASAE* 52, 1954, pp. 443–562; J. van Seters, *The Hyksos*, 1966, pp. 127–151; M. Bietak, *Tell el-Dab'a*, 2, 1975, especially pp. 179–221, pl. 44f.

C.D.W.
K.A.K.

RABBAH. 1. A town with associated villages in the hill country of Judah (Jos. 15:60), possibly Rubute of the Amarna Letters and Tuthmosis III, which lay in the region of Gezer.

2. The capital of Ammon, now Amman, capital of Jordan, 35 km E of the river Jordan. Its full name occurs in Dt. 3:11; 2 Sa. 12:26; 17:27; Je. 49:2; Ezk. 21:20 as 'Rabbah of the Ammonites' (*rabbat b^{e}nê ammôn*), and is shortened to Rabbah (*rabbâ*) in 2 Sa. 11:11; 12:27; Je. 49:3, *etc.* The name evidently means 'Main-town' (LXX has *akra*, 'citadel', at Dt. 3:11). The iron coffin of Og, king of Bashan, rested there (Dt. 3:11; AV 'iron bedstead').

Ammonite power grew simultaneously with Israelite, so that David faced a rival in Hanun, son of Nahash. After defeating Hanun's Aramaean allies and the Ammonite army, David and Joab were able to overrun Ammon, Joab besieging Rabbah, but leaving David the honour of taking the citadel. The inhabitants were put to forced labour (2 Sa. 10; 12:26–31; 1 Ch. 19:20). After Solomon's death, Ammon reasserted her independence and troubled Israel. The prophets spoke against Rabbah as representing the people of Ammon (Je. 49:2–3; Ezk. 21:20; 25:5; Am. 1:14).

Rabbah, rebuilt and renamed Philadelphia by Ptolemy Philadelphus (285–246 BC), became one of the cities of the Decapolis and an important trading centre.

Considerable archaeological remains exist in the vicinity of Amman today. At the airport a building of the 13th century BC (Late Bronze Age) has been unearthed. It was used as a depository for cremated human remains, many of them of young children, perhaps sacrificed to *Molech. On the citadel itself are extensive ruins of the mediaeval, Byzantine, Roman and Hellenistic cities, and among them sculptures and inscriptions of the 8th and 7th centuries BC have been found. Traces of a Late Bronze Age fortification have also been noticed.

BIBLIOGRAPHY. F. M. Abel, *Géographie de la Palestine*, 2, 1933, pp. 423–425; G. L. Harding, *Antiquities of Jordan*, 1967, pp. 61–70; J. B. Hennessy, *PEQ* 98, 1966, pp. 155–162; C. M. Bennett, *Levant* 10, 1978, pp. 1–9.

J.A.T.
A.R.M.

RABBI, RABBONI. Heb. *rab̲* meant 'great', and came to be used for a person in a respected position; *rabbi*, 'my great one', was used as a reverential form of address. By the end of the 2nd century BC the word *rab̲* was used for a teacher, and *rabbi* as the respectful address, 'my teacher'. Later the suffix lost its possessive significance, and the word 'rabbi' came to be used as the title of the authorized teachers of the Law; in modern Judaism it is used for those who are ordained to this work. By NT times the word had not come to be restricted to the official usage. It was certainly a title of honour, applied once to John the Baptist and twelve times to our Lord. In Mt. 23:7f., in contrast to the scribes' delight in being called 'rabbi', the disciples are told not to be so called—'for you have one teacher', Jesus said to them, 'and you are all brethren'. The Heb. word is transliterated into Gk.

Rabbah (modern Amman, Jordan) was the capital of the kingdom of Ammon. This figure probably represents an Ammonite king. Limestone. Height c. 45 cm. 9th–8th cent. BC. (DAA)

Top left:
Part of the citadel wall at Rabbah (Amman) as excavated, showing a join between the citadel and the city wall. Middle Bronze Age IIC. c. 1600 BC. (AN)

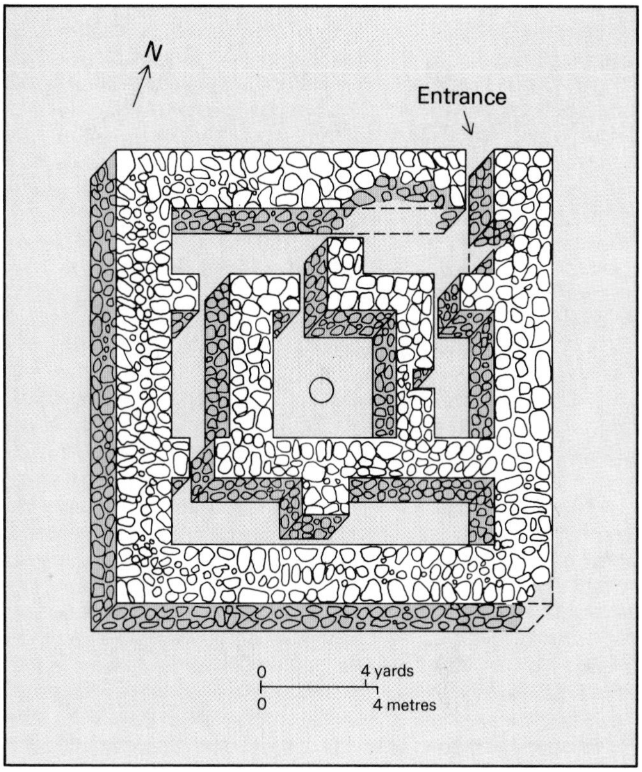

Plan of a Late Bronze Age temple excavated at Rabbah (Amman, Jordan), near the modern airport. c. 1250 BC.

as *rhabbi* or *rhabbei* and in this passage quoted, and also in Jn. 1:38 and 20:16, it is made clear that the Heb. word was equivalent in meaning to the Gk. *didaskalos*.

'Rabboni' (*rhabbouni*) is a heightened form of 'rabbi' used to address our Lord in Mk. 10:51 and Jn. 20:16.

BIBLIOGRAPHY. G. H. Dalman, *The Words of Jesus*, 1902, pp. 331–340; E. Lohse, on *rhabbi, rhabbouni, TDNT* 6, pp. 961–965; H. L. Ellison, *NIDNTT* 3, pp. 115f.

F.F.

RABMAG. The official position of the Bab. *Nergal-sharezer at the time of the sack of Jerusalem in 587 BC (Je. 39:3, 13). It has been compared with *rabu emga*, 'noble and wise', a royal title claimed by Neriglissar, and with *rab maḫḫu*, 'chief of the *maḫḫu* (administrative rather than religious) officials'. It is probably, however, the Heb. form of *rab mu(n)gi*, the title of an Assyr. and Bab. court official, though its precise meaning is unknown.

D.J.W.

RABSARIS. The title, 'chief official', of the following: **1.** One of the three Assyrians sent by Sennacherib to parley with Hezekiah at Jerusalem (2 Ki. 18:17; *cf.* Is. 36:3, where it is omitted). **2.** The Bab. Nabushazban who removed Jeremiah from prison and handed him over to Gedaliah (Je. 39:13). **3.** *Sarsechim, one of three Babylonians who sat as judges in the gate of Jerusalem after its capture in 587 BC (Je. 39:3).

The office of 'chief of the court eunuchs' (Bab. *rab ša rēši*) was held by a high-ranking palace dignitary (*cf.* Dn. 1:7). It is common in Assyr. texts and is attested in an Aram. docket from Nineveh (*rbsrs*, B.M. 81–2–4, 147). On this official see J. V. Kinnier Wilson, *The Nimrud Wine Lists*, 1972, pp. 47f. An Assyr. eponym, whose usual title of *šaknu* of the land of Marqasu, is glossed in an Aram. contract as *rbsrs, i.e. rab ša rēši* (*JAOS* 87, 1967, p. 523).

D.J.W.

RABSHAKEH. The title of the Assyr. official who, with the *Tartan and *Rabsaris, was sent by Sennacherib, king of Assyria, from Lachish to demand the surrender of Jerusalem by Hezekiah (2 Ki. 18:17, 19, 26–28, 37; 19:4–8; Is. 36:2, 4, 11–13, 22; 37:4, 8). He acted as spokesman for the delegation, addressing the citizens in the Judaean dialect. Hezekiah's representatives asked him to speak in Aram. to avoid disclosing his mission. He refused and, at the failure of his task, returned to Lachish. The office (*rab̲šāqē*) ranked below that of the army commander (*TARTAN), after whom it is listed. The Assyr. *rab* ('chief') *šāqē* was once thought to be 'chief cupbearer' (Heb. *mašqeh*), but is now known to be connected with *šaqû*, 'to be high'. The Assyr. *rab šāqē* is listed among the senior officials who governed provinces (*cf.* *RABSARIS).

D.J.W.

RACA. This is probably an Aram. word *rêqā'* or *rêqâ*, which means 'scoundrel' or 'fool'. Since the discovery in a papyrus of Gk. *rhachas* (of which *rhacha* may be a vocative) used in a bad sense (*Antiochon ton rhachan*), some scholars have suggested that the word is Gk. Raca is, however, to be derived from Aram. and Heb. Heb. *rêqîm* is used in the OT for good-for-nothings. In Jdg. 11:3 the 'worthless fellows' who associated themselves with Jephthah are called *rêqîm*; in 2 Sa. 6:20 Michal despised David because he uncovered himself as one of the *rêqîm* (RSV 'vulgar fellows'). The word is also used in Zadokite Documents (10:18), where it is combined with *nāb̲āl* (*cf.* Mt. 5:22, Gk. *mōre* for Heb. *nāb̲āl*) as an adjective to 'word'. Raca is abundantly used in rabbinical literature (*cf. SB*, 1, pp. 278–279) in the sense of 'fool'.

The word *raca* is present in Mt. 5:22 in the Sermon on the Mount. Jesus gave a new spirit to the well-known law of homicide. It is not actually a question of killing, but also of disposition. People are not allowed to call their brother names in their resentment. In spirit this is as great a transgression as real murder.

F.C.F.

RACHEL (Heb. *rāḥēl*, 'ewe'; LXX *Rachēl*). An Aramaean woman, known primarily as the second and favourite wife of Jacob, her first cousin. The daughter of Laban, and mother of Jacob's two youngest sons, Joseph and Benjamin, Rachel was endowed with great beauty (Gn. 29:17). Jacob appar-

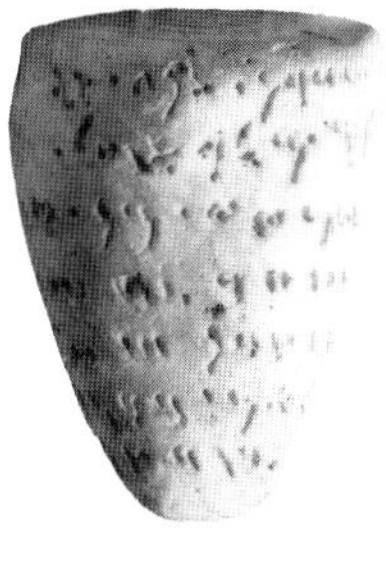

The Rab-Saris (Aramaic rbsrs*), the 'chief of the eunuchs', is named on this docket recording interest for a grain loan. Nineveh. 682* BC. (BM)

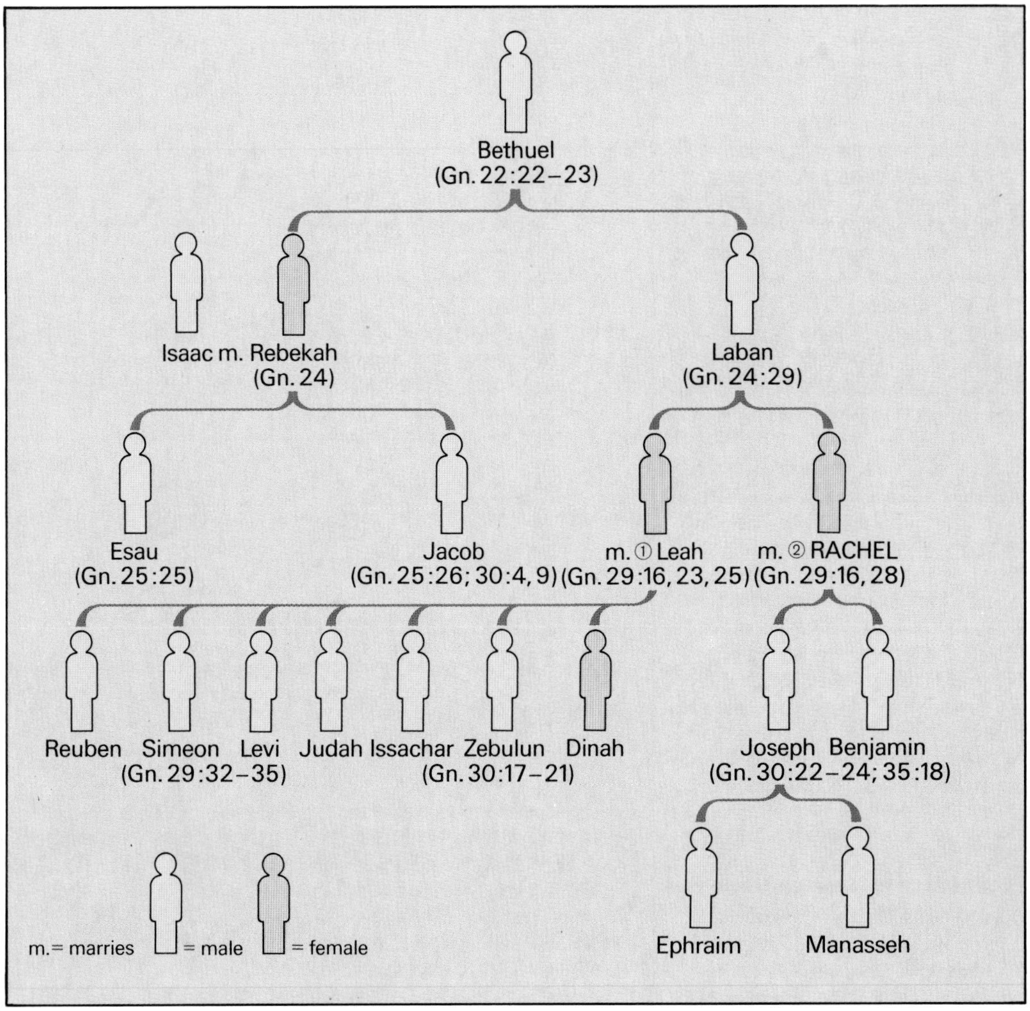

Rachel's lineage.

▬ RACHAB

See Rahab, Part 3.

ently fell in love with her at first sight, and his affection remained undiminished until the day of her death. She was also capable of devious behaviour, however (Gn. 31:19, 34–35), and lacked the single-minded devotion to God which Jacob had learnt through his experiences at Bethel and Peniel. She probably did not put away her pagan gods until shortly before she died. Rachel was the ancestress of three tribes, Benjamin, Ephraim and Manasseh, and she and her sister Leah were honoured by later generations as those 'who together built up the house of Israel' (Ru. 4:11).

(*a*) *Marriage* (Gn. 29:6–30). Jacob had been sent by Isaac and Rebekah to find a wife among his mother's relatives in Paddan-aram (28:1–2; *FAMILY). He met Rachel in the region of Harran as she was shepherding her father's flocks, and he at once helped her to water the animals by rolling the stone from the well's mouth. Laban welcomed him into his household where he lived for 20 years. Jacob's love for Rachel is one of the Bible's outstanding examples of human love—7 years 'seemed to him but a few days because of the love he had for her' (29:20). As a result of Laban's trickery in making Leah Jacob's first wife, presumably accomplished by the veiling of the bride, Jacob served another 7 years for Rachel, but his love did not waver.

Some details of Rachel's marriage can be paralleled outside the OT. Serving for a wife in lieu of payment is known from a 15th century BC document from *Nuzi (JEN 661), though the circumstances were very different. Laban's gift of the slave-girl Bilhah as part of Rachel's dowry was a practice also known at Nuzi, though more examples are known in earlier Old Babylonian texts. By contrast, the custom to which Laban appealed of marrying the elder daughter before the younger is so far unique—it was either a local Aramaean practice, or perhaps invented by Laban, though one cannot be certain. The suggestion that Jacob's marriages to Leah and Rachel involved his adoption by Laban on the basis of Nuzi custom, is better explained in other ways (*ADOPTION, *NUZI).

(*b*) *Children* (29:31; 30:1–8, 14–15, 22–24). Rachel's early years of marriage were barren, and, inspired by envy of Leah's fertility, she gave her slave-girl Bilhah to Jacob to bear children for her. Infertility was a well-known problem in the ancient Near East, and the husband would often take a second wife or a concubine because of it. Sometimes, however, the wife provided her husband with her own slave-girl to protect her own position, as with Rachel, Leah, Sarah, and extrabiblical examples from *Alalaḫ, *Nuzi, *Babylon (Laws of Hammurapi) and elsewhere. The slave-girl gained in status as a secondary wife (Bilhah is designated *'iššâ*, 'wife', 30:4; *cf.* Nuzi *ana aššūti*, 'as a wife', HSS 5. 67), and the resultant offspring could become heirs if adopted or legitimated by the husband and wife. The Nuzi text just mentioned also indicates that the chief wife could exercise authority over such children. Thus Bilhah's two boys Dan and Naphtali were reckoned to Rachel (lit. 'I may be built up through her'—30:3), and by naming them Rachel signified her authority over them. Subsequently Rachel bore Joseph, Jacob's favourite son, though whether Reuben's mandrakes, plants with supposed aphrodisiac qualities, had any effect is not clear (30:14–15). The birth of Rachel's second son Benjamin brought about her death (35:18–19).

(*c*) *Return to Palestine* (30:25–26; 31:4–55). Influenced by the hostility of Rachel's brothers, and a revelation from God, Jacob decided to return home after Joseph was born. Rachel and Leah readily concurred, since Laban had used up the money set aside for their dowry (31:15—an identical phrase, *kaspa akālu* 'to consume the money', was used several times at Nuzi in very similar circumstances). Without any inheritance from their father, the girls were regarded by him as 'foreigners'. It is frequently suggested that Rachel's theft of her father's household gods or *teraphim (*t*^{e}*rāpîm*) was an attempt to regain an inheritance for herself and Jacob, but the fact that they were stolen rules out this interpretation. Perhaps Rachel sought for protection on the long journey, or simply wanted to deprive her father of his valued possessions. Jacob, however, who was unaware of his wife's action, regarded the offence as worthy of death, though the threat was never carried out. Rachel continued as Jacob's favourite wife after the incident (33:2, 7), and the *t^erāpîm* were probably among the images later disposed of because their existence was a hindrance to the worship of God (35:2–4). On the same journey, Laban and Jacob agreed a covenant by which Jacob undertook not to maltreat his wives nor to marry any other. Both these conditions are found in marriage contracts from various periods in the ancient Near East.

(*d*) *Death* (35:16–20). Rachel died between Bethel and Bethlehem when her second son Benjamin was born. Jacob's continuing love for her is evidenced by the memorial pillar (*maṣṣēḇâ*) he set up over her grave, and its location was still known in Saul's day, when it was described as being on the border of Benjamin at Ṣelṣaḥ (*ZELZAH, 1 Sa. 10:2). The site is unknown today, though Je. 31:15 (*cf.* Mt. 2:18) suggests it may have been near Ramah, *c.* 8 km N of Jerusalem. However, Rachel's memory was also preserved at Bethlehem in the time of Ruth (Ru. 4:11), probably because it was near her burial-place.

BIBLIOGRAPHY. C. H. Gordon, *BA* 3, 1940, pp. 1–12; M. J. Selman, *TynB* 27, 1976, pp. 114–136; *ANET*, pp. 219f. M.J.S.

RAHAB (Heb. *rāḥāḇ*, possibly connected with root *rḥb*, 'broad'). A harlot who lived in a house which formed part of the town wall of Late Bronze Age Jericho. Joshua's two spies lodged with her. When they were pursued she hid them under drying stalks of flax on the roof. The pursuers were sent off on a false trail and then Rahab made terms with her lodgers. She knew that Jericho must fall to the servants of Yahweh and so she asked for protection for herself and her family. The spies escaped from a window, with her help. When Jericho was destroyed the family was saved and Rahab joined up with the Israelites (Jos. 2:6, 17, 22–25).

In the NT the writer to the Hebrews includes her among ancient examples of faith in God (Heb. 11:31), and she is quoted as one who was justified by her works in Jas. 2:25. She is almost certainly to be identified with Rahab (AV 'Rachab'), the wife of Salmon and mother of Boaz, ancestor of David, who is included in our Lord's genealogy in Mt. 1:5.

BIBLIOGRAPHY. D. J. Wiseman, 'Rahab of Jericho', *THB* 14, 1964, pp. 8ff. M.B.

RAHAB (Heb. *rahaḇ*, lit. 'pride', 'arrogance'), the female monster of chaos (*cf.* Bab. Tiamat), closely associated with *Leviathan. The curbing of the forces of chaos (pre-eminently the unruly sea) at the creation is poetically described in terms of God's smiting Rahab (*cf.* Jb. 26:12, and more generally Jb. 9:13; 38:8–11). But this imagery in the OT is usually transferred from the creation story to the narrative of the redemption of Israel from Egypt, when God again showed his mastery over the sea and other forces opposed to his will; it is the Exodus that is indicated by references to the smiting of Rahab in Ps. 89:10; Is. 51:9 (*cf.* Ps. 74:12ff., where the sense is the same, although Rahab is not expressly mentioned). From this usage Rahab comes to be employed quite generally as a poetic synonym for Egypt, as in Ps. 87:4 ('Among those who know me I mention Rahab and Babylon') and Is. 30:7 ('Rahab who sits still'); and her dragon-associate becomes a figure of Pharaoh (*cf.* Ezk. 29:3). F.F.B.

RAIN. The importance and character of rainfall is emphasized in the OT by the use of several words. The general term is *māṭār*, combined sometimes with *gešem*, a violent downpour (1 Ki. 18:41; Ezr. 10:9, 13), to suggest torrential rains (Zc. 10:1; Jb. 37:6); *zerem*, a rainstorm (Is. 25:4; 28:2; 32:2; Hab. 3:10; Jb. 24:8), is sometimes accompanied by hail (Is. 28:2; 30:30). In contrast are the *r^eḇîḇîm*, 'showers' (Dt. 32:2; Ps. 65:10; Je. 3:3; 14:22; Mi. 5:7), and *r^esîsîm*, a 'rain-mist' (Ct. 5:2). Seasonal rainfall, *yôreh* and *môreh*, 'former rains', and *malqôš*, 'the latter rains', are a reference to the onset and termination of the rainy season (Dt. 11:14; Jb. 29:23; Ho. 6:3; Joel 2:23; Zc. 10:1f.; Jas. 5:7).

Frequently the term *māṭār* indicates that this source of blessing to man comes from God himself, from the heavens. The Baalim were early associated with the springs, wells and streams, but Yahweh was the rain-giver (Je. 14:22), for can 'any among the false gods of the nations . . . bring rain?' This challenge was vindicated by Elijah before the priests of Baal (1 Ki. 18:17–40). Heaven is thus invoked for rainfall (Ps. 72:6), and its blessings are compared with the mechanical devices of the Egyp. *shaduf* for lifting river water from the Nile (Dt. 11:11). Heb. *šeṭep̄*, 'torrential rain', 'flood-water' (Ps. 32:6; Pr. 27:4; Dn. 9:26; 11:22; Na. 1:3), is used in the plural in Jb. 38:25 to denote irrigation channels (normally *peleḡ*, as in Pss. 1:3; 119:136; Pr. 5:16; 21:1; Is. 30:25; 32:2; La. 3:48), as though a heavy downpour were likened to a channel of water poured from the reservoir of heaven (*cf.* 'the *peleḡ* of God', Ps. 65:9; also Gn. 7:11, where the *'^arubbôṯ* or 'sluices' of the sky are opened). Gentle rain or rain-mist (*ṭal*) is associated with beneficent gifts (Dt. 33:13). It is the first of blessings promised to Jacob's land (Gn. 27:28) and to Israel (Dt. 28:12). The descent of rain is likened to the blessings of the kingdom (Ps. 72:6–7). In contrast, the presence of clouds and wind without rain is likened to a man who 'boasts of a gift he does not give' (Pr. 25:14). (*DEW.)

The rainfall of Palestine is so closely identified with the cool season that the Arab. *šitā'* refers to both winter and rain. There is the same significance in Ct. 2:11, 'For, lo, the winter is past, the rain is over and gone.' Equally the summer season is suggestive of the hot, dry period, *e.g.* 'My strength was dried up as by the heat of summer' (Ps. 32:4). During the preliminary period of mid-Sept. to mid-Oct. the moist sea air encountering the very hot dry air from the land surface causes thunderstorms and the irregular distribution of rainfall. This is vividly described in Am. 4:7, 'I would send rain upon one city, and send no rain upon another city: one field would be rained upon, and the field on which it did not rain withered.' The onset of the effective rains usually begins in mid- or late Oct., but may be delayed until even Jan. These 'former rains', so earnestly longed for, cause a fall in temperature so that convectional currents are eliminated and the damp atmosphere produces a brilliance in the sky, described by Elihu: 'And now men cannot look on the light when it is bright in the skies, when the wind has passed and cleared them' (Jb. 37:21). The cool, rainy season is the pastoral

RACHEL TRIBES
See Tribes of Israel, Part 3.

RAFTS
See Ships and boats, Part 3.

RAGUEL
See Hobab, Part 2.

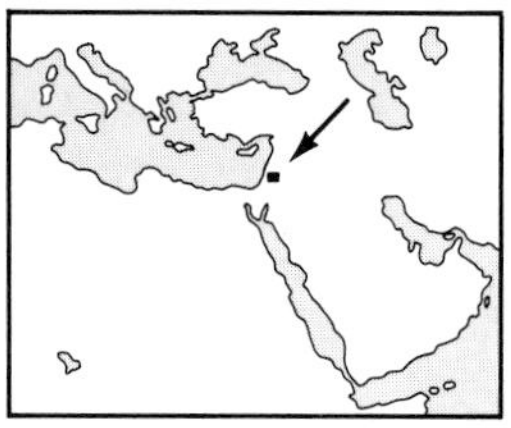

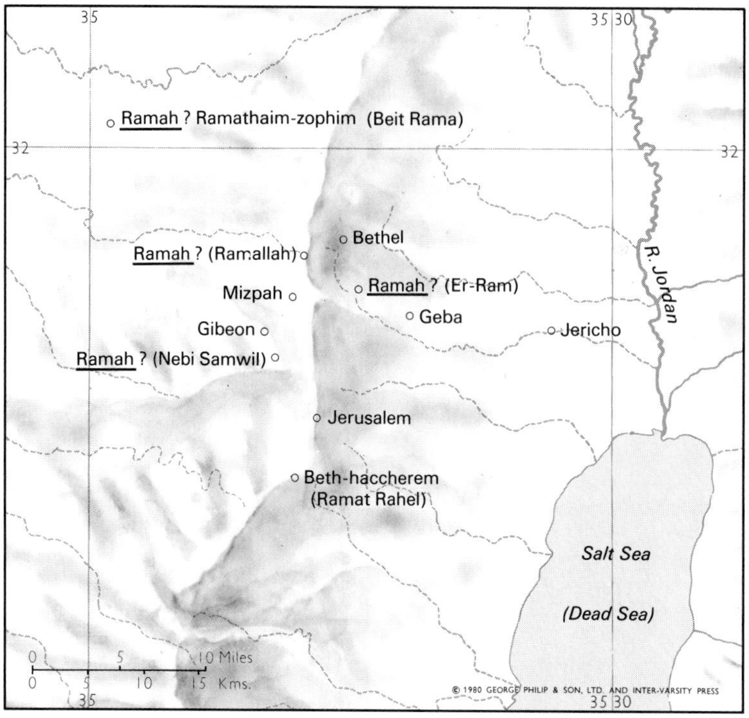

Possible locations for biblical Ramah.

setting to the joys described by the psalmist (Ps. 65:12–13). Between April and early May, the 'latter rains' describe the last showers at the close of the rainy season (Am. 4:7).

Modern scholars agree that no climatic change has occurred within historic times. See J. W. Gregory, 'The Habitable Globe: Palestine and the Stability of Climate in Modern Times', *Geog. Journ.* 76, 1947, pp. 487ff.; W. C. Lowdermilk, *Palestine, Land of Promise*, 1944, pp. 82ff.; A. Reifenberg, *The Struggle between the Desert and the Sown*, 1956, pp. 20–24; N. Shalem, 'La Stabilité du Climat en Palestine', *Proc. Desert Research*, UNESCO, 1953, pp. 153–175. This does not mean that there have not been minor fluctuations in climate, but they have not been great enough to influence civilizations materially. Prolonged droughts such as those recorded in 1 Ki. 17:7; Je. 17:8; Joel 1:10–12, 17–20, indicate their disastrous effects, especially when there is no dew to compensate the lack of rainfall (2 Sa. 1:21; 1 Ki. 17:1; Hag. 1:10). (*Cloud; *Dew; *Palestine.)

J.M.H.

RAINBOW. There is no special word for rainbow in Heb. The ordinary word for war-bow (Heb. *qešeṯ*) is used. The NT word is *iris*. In Gn. 9:13, 15, God's war-bow, *qešeṯ*, is said to be put in the clouds as the sign of his covenant with Noah, and was his pledge that never again would he destroy all flesh by a flood.

The meaning seems to be that what was ordinarily an instrument of war, and a symbol of vengeance, became a symbol of peace and mercy by virtue of its now being set in the clouds. Against the black storm clouds God's war-bow is transformed into a rainbow by the sunlight of his mercy and grace. God is at peace with his covenant people.

So also in Ezk. 1:28 the rainbow of mercy appears around the throne of divine glory and judgment. In Rev. 4:3; 10:1, John has a vision similar to Ezekiel's.

J.G.S.S.T.

RAINBOW LIZARD
See Animals, Part 1.

RAISINS
See Vine, Part 3.

RAMATH-LEHI
See Lehi, Part 2.

RAMESES
See Ra'amses, Part 3.

RAMOTH
See Jarmuth, Part 2.

RAMAH. The Heb. name *rāmâ*, from the root *rûm*, 'to be high', was used of several places, all of them on elevated sites.

1. Ramah of Benjamin, near Bethel, in the area of Gibeon and Beeroth (Jos. 18:25), was a resting-place on the road N. Here the Levite and his concubine planned to stay (Jdg. 19:13). Deborah the prophetess lived close by (Jdg. 4:5). When Asa of Judah and Baasha of Israel were at war, Baasha built a fort here, but when the Syrians attacked Israel Asa destroyed it and built Geba and Mizpah with the materials (1 Ki. 15:17, 21–22; 2 Ch. 16:1, 5–6).

Here Nebuzaradan gathered the exiles after the fall of Jerusalem and released Jeremiah (Je. 40:1). The town was reoccupied after the return from Babylon (Ezr. 2:26; Ne. 11:33).

Ramah features in the messages of some of the prophets (Ho. 5:8; Is. 10:29; Je. 31:15). It is probably to be identified with Er-Ram, 8 km N of Jerusalem, or Ramat Rahel (Beth Haccherem), near the traditional tomb of Rachel (Je. 31:15; 1 Sa. 10:2; Mt. 2:18; Jos., *Ant.* 8. 303).

2. The birthplace and subsequent home of Samuel, also called Ramathaim-zophim (1 Sa. 1:19; 2:11), from which he went on circuit annually (1 Sa. 7:17). Here Saul first met him (1 Sa. 9:6, 10), and here the elders of Israel came to demand a king (1 Sa. 8:4ff.). After his dispute with Saul Samuel came here (1 Sa. 15:34ff.). David found refuge in Ramah and later fled to Nob (1 Sa. 19:18; 20:1).

There are four sites proposed for Ramah today: Ramallah, 13 km N of Jerusalem; Beit Rama, 19 km NW of Bethel; Er-Ram, the Ramah of Benjamin; and Nebi Samwil. There still remains some uncertainty.

The word is also used as the name for **3.** a town on the boundary of Asher (Jos. 19:29); **4.** a walled town of Naphtali (Jos. 19:36); **5.** a town of Simeon (Jos. 19:8; 1 Sa. 30:27); and **6.** an abbreviation for Ramoth-gilead (*cf.* 2 Ki. 8:28–29 and 2 Ch. 22:5–6).

See F. M. Abel, *Géographie de la Palestine*, 2, 1933, p. 427; D. Baly, *Geography of the Bible*², 1974.

J.A.T.

RAMOTH-GILEAD. A walled city in the territory of Gad, E of the Jordan, which featured frequently in Israel's wars with Syria. It was one of the *cities of refuge (Dt. 4:43; Jos. 20:8) and was assigned to the Merarite Levites (Jos. 21:38; 1 Ch. 6:80). It has been identified with Mizpeh, Mizpeh of Gilead (Jdg. 11:29) and Ramath-mizpeh ('height of Mizpeh', Jos. 13:26). Modern equivalents suggested are Huṣn-'Ajlûn and Remtheh, but the suggestion of Nelson Glueck (*BASOR* 92, 1943) that it is Tell-Rāmîth has strong claims.

It was probably the home of Jephthah (Jdg. 11:34). Ben-geber, one of Solomon's twelve administrators, lived here (1 Ki. 4:13). According to Josephus (*Ant.* 8. 399), the city was taken by Omri

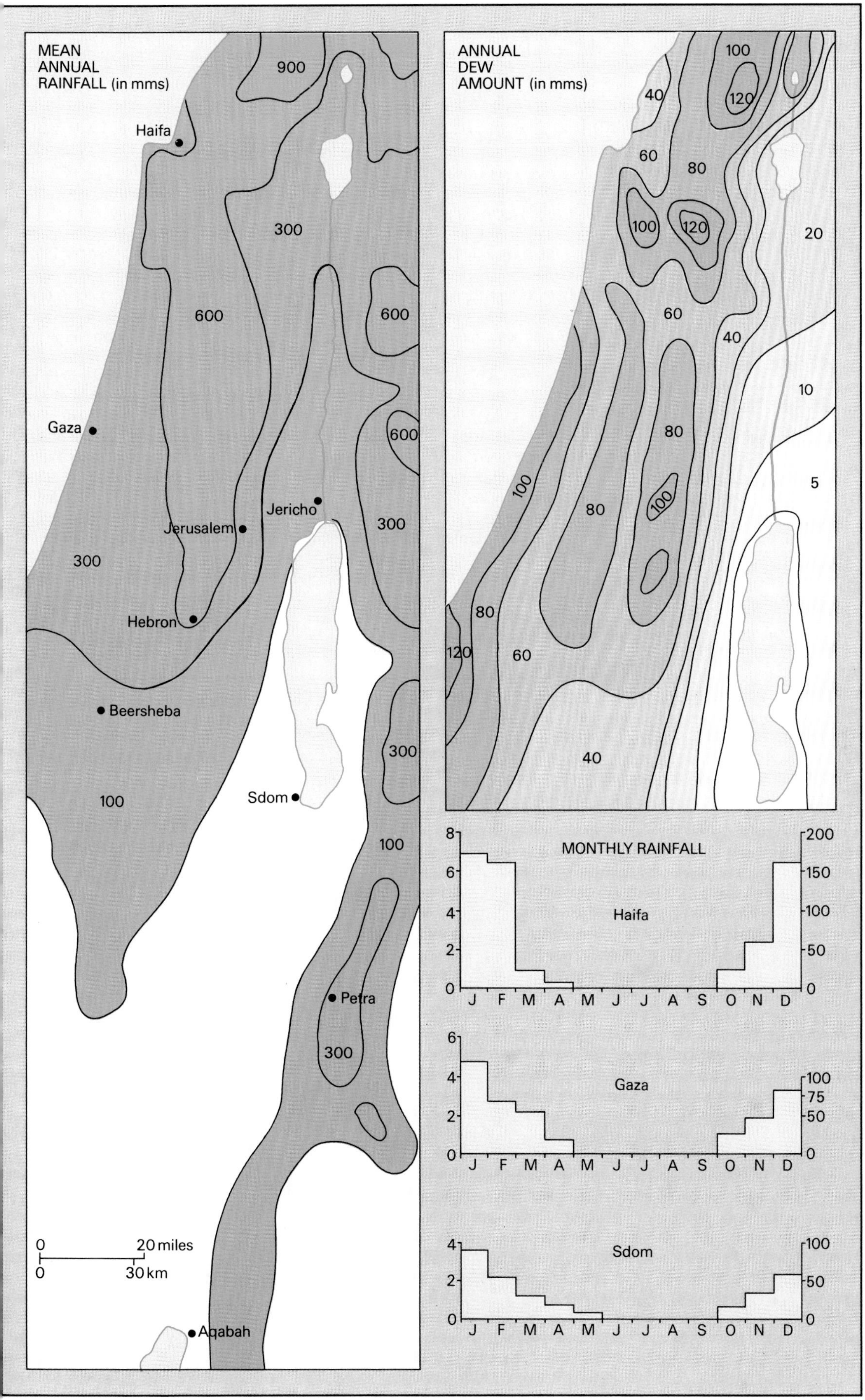

Left:
Palestine: mean annual rainfall.

Right:
Palestine: annual dew amount.

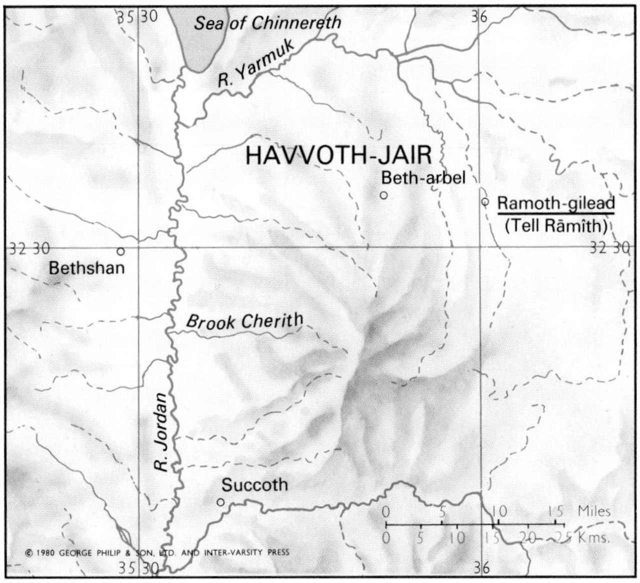

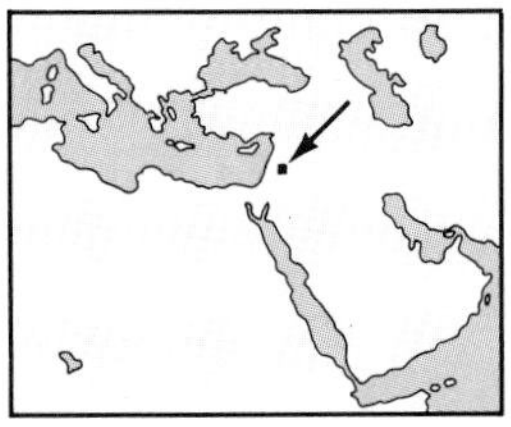

The position of Ramoth-gilead, one of the levitical cities of refuge.

from Ben-hadad I. The town changed hands between Israel and the Syrians several times. Even after Ahab had defeated the Syrians (1 Ki. 20), it remained in their hands and Ahab enlisted the help of Jehoshaphat of Judah to retake it (1 Ki. 22:3–4). He was wounded and died (1 Ki. 22:1–40; 2 Ch. 18). His son Joram took up the attack but was likewise wounded (2 Ki. 8:28ff.). During his absence from the camp at Ramoth-gilead, Jehu the army captain was anointed at Elisha's instigation (2 Ki. 9:1f.; 2 Ch. 22:7). Jehu later murdered all the seed royal, but Josephus says that the city was taken before Jehu departed (*Ant.* 9. 105).

BIBLIOGRAPHY. N. Glueck, 'Ramoth Gilead', *BASOR* 92, 1943, pp. 10ff.; F. M. Abel, *Géographie de la Palestine*, 2, 1933, pp. 430–431; H. Tadmor, 'The Southern Border of Aram', *IEJ* 12, 1962, pp. 114–122; D. Baly, *Geography of the Bible*², 1974. J.A.T.

RAS SHAMRA
See Ugarit, Part 3.

RAVEN
See Animals, Part 1.

READING OF THE LAW
See Synagogue, Part 3.

REAPING
See Agriculture, Part 1.

REASON
See Stoics, Part 3.

REBIRTH
See Regeneration, Part 3.

REBEKAH, REBECCA (Heb. *ribqâ*, *cf.* Arab. 'a looped cord for tying young animals' from *rabaqa*, 'to tie fast'; Gk. *rhebekka*). The wife of Isaac, daughter of Bethuel, Abraham's nephew (Gn. 22:23). The account of the choice of Rebekah as Isaac's wife (Gn. 24) strongly emphasizes the guidance and overruling providence of God. Abraham sent his chief steward, not named but probably Eliezer, to his home-country to seek a wife for his son. After prayer, the steward was led directly to Rebekah. Bethuel and her brother, Laban, having heard all the circumstances, agreed to the marriage.

She was barren for the first 20 years of her marriage. Isaac entreated God, and she bore twin sons, Esau and Jacob, receiving from Yahweh before the birth an oracle in which their divergent destinies were foretold (Gn. 25:20–26). The beginning of tragedy is foreshadowed in Gn. 25:28, where we read of the favouritism of Isaac and Rebekah for different sons, which made inevitable the destruction of family unity.

Reminiscent of Abraham and Sarah was the incident during Isaac's sojourn in Gerar, when he deceived Abimelech and the Philistines by pretending that Rebekah was his sister (Gn. 26:1–11; *cf.* Gn. 20). Both Isaac and Rebekah were grieved at Esau's marriages to women of an alien race, the Hittites (Gn. 26:34f.).

In the deed of treachery whereby Jacob supplanted Esau in obtaining the blessing from his aged father, Rebekah took the initiative and planned the deception (Gn. 27:5–17). When this was successful, fearing that Esau would kill Jacob, she sent him away to his uncle Laban in Paddan-aram, justifying the action to Isaac by suggesting that Jacob ought to seek a wife of their own people (Gn. 27:42–28:5).

The only remaining episodes recorded concerning Rebekah are the death of her nurse, Deborah (Gn. 35:8), and her burial with Isaac in the family grave in the cave at Machpelah (Gn. 49:31).

In the NT, the sole reference to Rebekah is in Rom. 9:10, where RSV follows the Vulg. spelling 'Rebecca' (NEB 'Rebekah'). Paul refers to the oracle she received before the birth of Esau and Jacob as illustrating God's election of grace.

Rebekah was a woman of strong will and ambition, devoted at first to her husband, but later transferring some at least of that devotion to her younger son, with disastrous results for the family unity, though the sequel shows that in the overruling of God even this was enlisted to the furtherance of the divine purpose.

BIBLIOGRAPHY. G. von Rad, *Genesis*, 1961; W. Vischer, *The Witness of the Old Testament to Christ*, 1949, pp. 145–151. J.G.G.N.

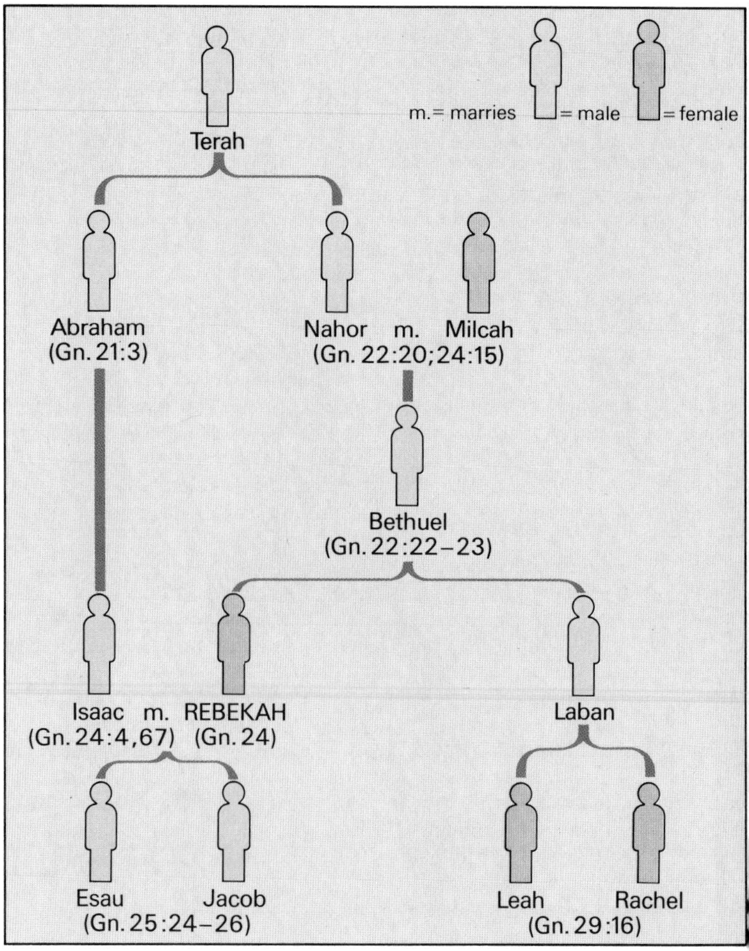

The family of Rebekah.

RECHABITES. Jehonadab (or Jonadab), the son of Rechab, and the man who gave to the name 'Rechabite' its special connotation, appears first in 2 Ki. 10:15–31. Jehu son of Nimshi was in the midst of his savage ascent to the throne of Israel (*c.* 840 BC) when he chanced to meet Jehonadab 'coming to meet him' (v. 15). By thus deliberately and whole-heartedly associating himself with the militant Yahwism of Jehu and the atrocious massacre of the worshippers of Baal, Jehonadab shows himself to be an extremist with more zeal for Yahweh than discrimination. This same unrealistic extremism is found in the regulations he imposed on his family; but at the same time it says much for his force of character that his descendants were still obedient to him over 200 years later, as Je. 35 shows (*c.* 600 BC). In response to Jeremiah's offer of wine (vv. 5–10), they describe their distinctive life. They eschew all the marks of a settled, agricultural civilization—a house, the regular sowing of crops, the vine which demanded years of unbroken attention if it was to bear fruit—and follow the nomad life as in the wilderness period when Israel walked faithfully with God (*e.g.* Je. 2:1–3). To preserve the outward marks of this pure following of God, and not as a 'temperance order', the Rechabites obeyed their ancestor's regulations, and it was their obedience which won divine approval (Je. 35:18–19). J.A.M.

RECONCILIATION. There are four important NT passages which treat of the work of Christ under the figure of reconciliation, namely, Rom. 5:10f.; 2 Cor. 5:18ff.; Eph. 2:11ff.; Col. 1:19ff. The important Gk. words are the noun *katallagē* and the verbs *katallassō* and *apokatallassō*. Reconciliation properly applies not to good relations in general but to the doing away of an enmity, the bridging over of a quarrel. It implies that the parties being reconciled were formerly hostile to one another. The Bible tells us bluntly that sinners are 'enemies' of God (Rom. 5:10; Col. 1:21; Jas. 4:4). We should not minimize the seriousness of these and similar passages. An enemy is not someone who comes a little short of being a friend. He is in the other camp. He is altogether opposed. The NT pictures God in vigorous opposition to everything that is evil.

Now the way to overcome enmity is to take away the cause of the quarrel. We may apologize for the hasty word, we may pay the money that is due, we may make what reparation or restitution is appropriate. But in every case the way to reconciliation lies through an effective grappling with the root cause of the enmity. Christ died to put away our sin. In this way he dealt with the enmity between man and God. He put it out of the way. He made the way wide open for men to come back to God. It is this which is described by the term 'reconciliation'.

It is interesting to notice that no NT passage speaks of Christ as reconciling God to man. Always the stress is on man's being reconciled. This in the nature of the case is very important. It is man's sin which has caused the enmity. It is man's sin that has had to be dealt with. Man may very well be called on in the words of 2 Cor. 5:20 to be 'reconciled to God'. Some students go on from this to suggest that Christ's reconciling activities are concerned only with man. But it is difficult to harmonize this with the general NT position. That which set up the barrier was the demand of God's holiness for uprightness in man. Man, left to himself, is content to let bygones be bygones. He is not particularly worried by his sin. Certainly he feels no hostility to God on account of his sin. The barrier arises because God demands holiness in man. Therefore when the process of reconciliation has been effected it is impossible to say it is completely man-ward, and not God-ward in any sense. There must be a change from God's side if all that is involved in such expressions as 'the wrath of God' is no longer exercised towards man.

This does not mean a change in God's love. The Bible is very clear that God's love to man never varies no matter what man may do. Indeed, the whole atoning work of Christ stems from God's great love. It was 'while we were yet sinners' that 'Christ died for us' (Rom. 5:8). This truth must be zealously guarded. But at the same time we must not allow ourselves to slip into the position of maintaining that reconciliation is a purely subjective process. Reconciliation in some sense was effected outside man before anything happened within man. Paul can speak of Christ 'through whom we have now received our reconciliation' (Rom. 5:11). A reconciliation that can be 'received' must be proffered (and thus in some sense accomplished) before men received it. In other words, we must think of reconciliation as having effects both Godward and man-ward.

BIBLIOGRAPHY. Arndt; J. Denney, *The Christian Doctrine of Reconciliation*, 1917; L. Morris, *The Apostolic Preaching of the Cross*[3], 1965; H.-G. Link, C. Brown, H. Vorländer, *NIDNTT* 3, pp. 145–176; F. Büchsel, *TDNT* 1, pp. 254–258.
L.M.

REDEEMER, REDEMPTION. Redemption means deliverance from some evil by payment of a price. It is more than simple deliverance. Thus prisoners of war might be released on payment of a price which was called a 'ransom' (Gk. *lytron*). The word-group based on *lytron* was formed specifically to convey this idea of release on payment of ransom. In this circle of ideas Christ's death may be regarded as 'a ransom for many' (Mk. 10:45).

Again, slaves might be released by a process of ransom. In the fictitious purchase by a god the slave would pay the price of his freedom into the temple treasury. Then he would go through the solemn formality of being sold to the god 'for freedom'. Technically he was still the slave of the god, and some pious obligations might accordingly be laid upon him. But as far as men were concerned he was thenceforth free. Alternatively, the slave might simply pay his master the price. The characteristic thing about either form of release is the payment of the ransom price (*lytron*). 'Redemption' is the name given to the process.

Among the Hebrews we may discern a different situation, well illustrated in Ex. 21:28–30. If a man had a dangerous ox he must keep it under restraint. If it got out and gored someone so that he died the law was plain, 'the ox shall be stoned, and its owner also shall be put to death'. But this is not a case of wilful murder. There is no malice aforethought. Thus, it is provided that a ransom (Heb. *kōp̄er*) might be 'laid on him'. He could pay a sum of money and thus redeem his forfeited life.

Other usages of redemption in antiquity provide for the redemption of property, *etc.*, but the three

RECLINE See Meals, Part 2.

RED CORD See Line, Part 2.

RED DEER See Animals, Part 1.

The modern Red Sea and its northern reaches at the time of the Exodus (inset).

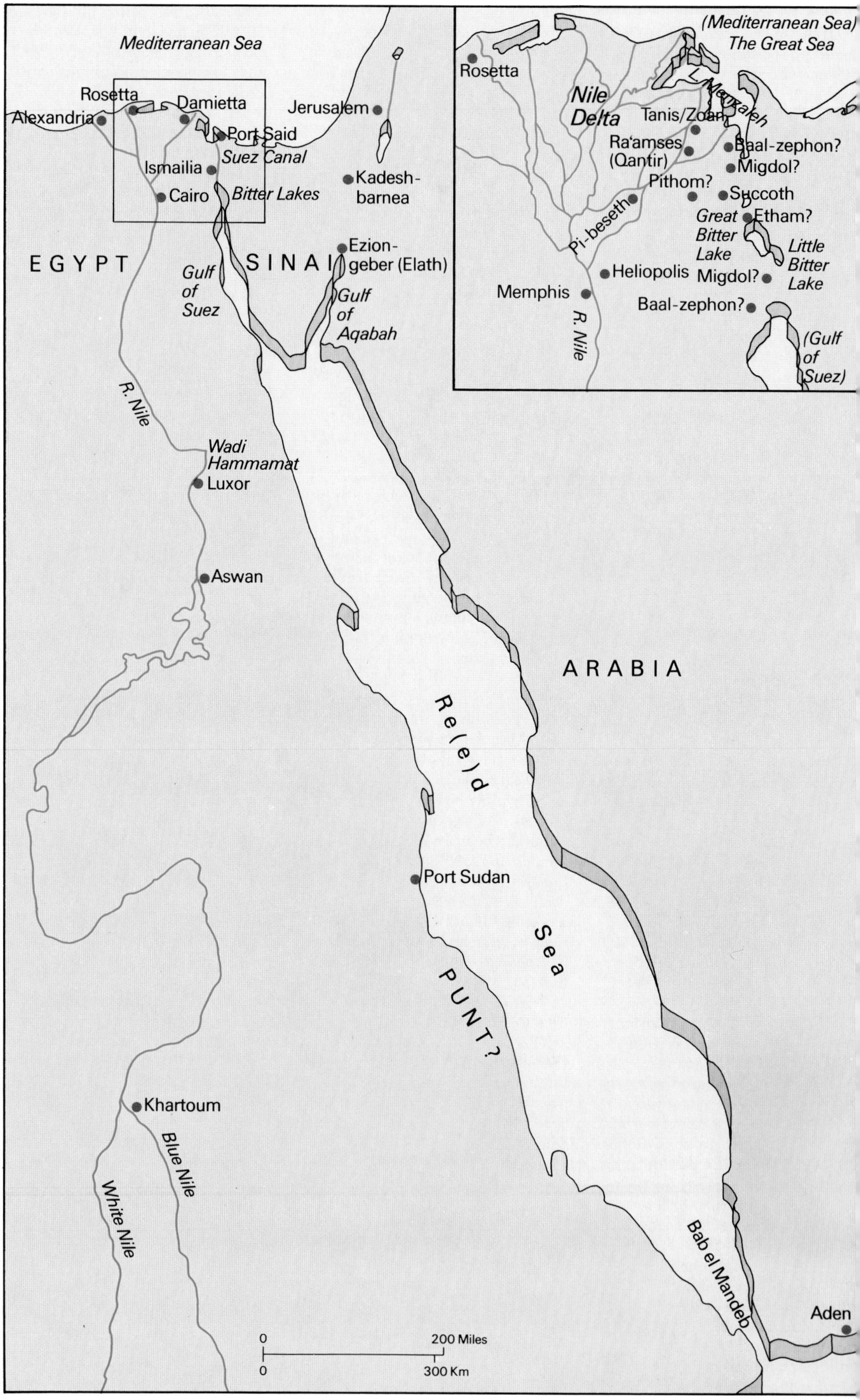

we have noticed are the most important. Common to them all is the idea of freedom secured by payment of a price. Outside the Bible the usage is practically unvarying. A few metaphorical passages occur, but these serve only to make clear the basic meaning of the word. The payment of a price for deliverance is the basic and characteristic thing.

It is this which makes the concept so useful for the early Christians. Jesus had taught them that 'everyone who commits sin is a slave to sin' (Jn. 8:34). In line with this, Paul can think of himself as 'carnal, sold under sin' (Rom. 7:14), sold as under a cruel slavemaster. He reminds the Romans that in earlier days they had been 'slaves of sin' (Rom. 6:17). From another point of view men were under sentence of death on account of their sin. 'For the wages of sin is death' (Rom. 6:23). Sinners are slaves. Sinners are doomed to death. Either way the ancient world would have regarded the situation as crying out for redemption. Failing redemption, the slavery would continue, the sentence of death be carried out. The cross of Christ is seen against this background. It is the price paid to release the slaves, to let the condemned go free.

What gives the metaphor force is the constant presence of the price-paying idea. But it is precisely this that is disputed by some who think that redemption is no more than another way of of saying 'deliverance'. The big reason for thinking this is that there are some OT passages where Yahweh is said to have redeemed his people (Ex. 6:6; Ps. 77:14f., *etc*.), and it is unthinkable that he should pay a price to anyone. But too much is being deduced. The metaphor has not been robbed of its point (*cf*. the saying 'he sold his life dearly'). Sometimes in the OT Yahweh is thought of as being so powerful that all the might of the nations is but a puny thing before him. But redemption is not used in such passages. Where redemption occurs there is the thought of effort. Yahweh redeems 'with a stretched out arm'. He makes known his strength. Because he loves his people he redeems them at cost to himself. His effort is regarded as the 'price'. This is the whole point of using the redemption terminology.

The characteristic NT word for redemption is *apolytrōsis*, a comparatively rare word elsewhere. It is found ten times in the NT but apparently there are only eight occurrences in all the rest of Gk. literature. This may express the conviction of the early Christians that the redemption wrought in Christ was unique. It does not mean, as some have thought, that they understand redemption simply as 'deliverance'. For that they use such a word as *rhyomai*, 'rescue'. *apolytrōsis* means deliverance on payment of a price, and that price is the atoning death of the Saviour. When we read of 'redemption through his blood' (Eph. 1:7), the blood of Christ is clearly being regarded as the price of redemption. It is not otherwise with Rom. 3:24f., 'Being justified freely by his grace through the redemption that is in Christ Jesus: whom God hath set forth to be a propitiation through faith in his blood' (AV). Here Paul is using three metaphors, those of the law court, and of the sacrifices, and of manumission. Our concern is with the last. Paul envisages a process of freeing, but by the payment of a price, the blood of Christ. Redemption is linked with Christ's death also in Heb. 9:15. Sometimes, again, we have the mention of price, but not redemption, as in references to being 'bought with a price' (1 Cor. 6:19f.; 7:22f.). The basic idea is the same. Christ bought men at the price of his blood. In Gal. 3:13 the price of redemption is given thus: 'having become a curse for us'. Christ redeemed us by taking our place, by bearing our curse. This points us to the definitely substitutionary idea in redemption, an idea which sometimes receives stress, as in Mk. 10:45 ('a ransom for many').

Redemption not only looks back to Calvary, but forward to the freedom in which the redeemed stand. 'You were bought with a price,' Paul can say, 'so glorify God in your body' (1 Cor. 6:20). Precisely because they have been redeemed at such a cost believers must be God's men. They must show in their lives that they are no longer caught up in the bondage from which they have been released and are exhorted to 'stand fast therefore in the liberty wherewith Christ hath made us free' (Gal. 5:1, AV).

BIBLIOGRAPHY. *LAE*, pp. 318ff.; L. Morris, *The Apostolic Preaching of the Cross*[3], 1965, ch. 1; B. B. Warfield, *The Person and Work of Christ*, ed. S. G. Craig, 1950, ch. 9; O. Procksch, F. Büchsel, in *TDNT* 4, pp. 328–356; C. Brown *et al*., in *NIDNTT* 3, pp. 177–223. L.M.

RED SEA. In modern geography, the sea that divides NE Africa from Arabia and extends some 1,900 km from the straits of Bab el-Mandeb near Aden N to the S tip of the Sinai peninsula. For nearly another 300 km, the Gulfs of Suez and Aqabah continue the sea N on the W and E sides of the Sinai peninsula respectively. In classical antiquity the name Red Sea (*erythra thalassa*) included also the Arabian and Indian Seas to the NW coast of India. In the OT the term *yam sûp̄*, 'sea of reeds' (and/or 'weed'), is used to cover: (*a*) the Bitter Lakes region in the Egyptian Delta N of Suez along the line of the present Suez Canal; and (*b*) the Gulfs of Suez and Aqabah and possibly the Red Sea proper beyond these.

I. The Bitter Lakes region

In general terms, the Israelites were led from Egypt on the way of the wilderness and the *yam sûp̄* (Ex. 13:18). Ex. 14 and 15 are more specific: on leaving Succoth (Tell el-Maskhuta) and Etham, Israel were to turn back and camp before Pihahiroth, between Migdol and the 'sea', before Baal-zephon (Ex. 14:1–2, 9; *cf*. *ENCAMPMENT BY THE SEA). It was this 'sea', near all these places, that God drove back and divided by a 'strong east wind' for Israel to cross dryshod, and then brought back upon the pursuing Egyptians (Ex. 14:16, 21–31; 15:1, 4, 19, 21). From the 'sea of reeds', *yam sûp̄*, Israel went into the wilderness of Shur (Ex. 15:22; Nu. 33:8) and then on towards Sinai. Various points suggest that this famous crossing, the Exodus in the narrow sense, took place in the Bitter Lakes region, roughly between Qantara (48 km S of Port Said) and just N of Suez. First, geographically, the wilderness of Shur, which Israel entered directly from crossing the *yam sûp̄* (Ex. 15:22), is opposite this very area (*SHUR). Secondly, geophysically, the reedy waters of the Bitter Lakes and Lake Menzaleh can be affected by strong E winds precisely in the way described in Ex. 14:21 and experienced on a small scale by Aly Shafei Bey in 1945–6 (*Bulletin de la Société Royale de Géographie d'Égypte* 21, August 1946, pp. 231ff.; *cf*. also *JTVI* 28, 1894–5, pp. 267–280). Thirdly, philologically, the Heb. word *sûp̄* is generally admitted to be a loan-word from Egyp. *ṯwf(y)*, 'papyrus', and *p'-ṯwf*, a location, 'the papyrus-marshes'

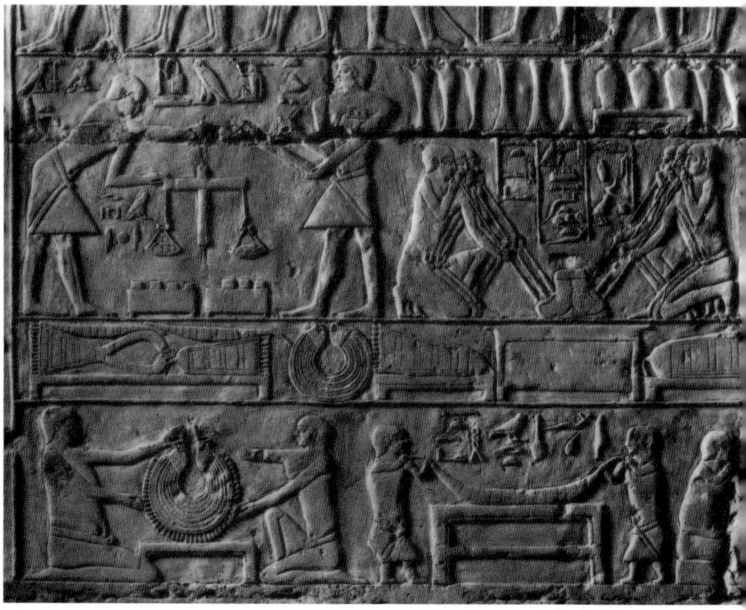

Egyptian goldsmiths at work weighing and recording, refining and melting for casting, and finishing the moulded objects. Limestone relief from the tomb of Mereruka, Saqqara (Memphis). Height c. 52 cm. c. 2350 BC. (OIUC)

REED
See Weights and measures, Part 3.

REED INSTRUMENTS
See Music, Part 2.

REFLECTION
See Mirror, Part 2.

REFUGE, CITIES OF
See Cities of refuge, Part 1.

par excellence in the NE part of the Delta between Tanis (Zoan), Qantir and the present line of the Suez Canal N of Ismailia, on the former Pelusiac arm of the Nile. For details and references, see A. H. Gardiner, *Ancient Egyptian Onomastica*, 2, 1947, pp. 201*–202*; R. A. Caminos, *Late-Egyptian Miscellanies*, 1954, p. 79; Erman and Grapow, *Wörterbuch d. Aegypt. Sprache*, 5, 1931, p. 359: 6–10. Ps. 78:12, 43, puts the great events preceding the Exodus in the 'field of Zoan', *i.e.* in the NE Delta.

II. The Gulfs of Suez and Aqabah

Turning S from Shur *via* Etham, Marah and Elim, the Israelites pitched by the *yam sûp̄* and then went on to Sin and Dophkah (Nu. 33:10–11). This would appear to refer to the Gulf of Suez. Whether Ex. 10:19 during the plagues refers to the Lakes region, the Gulf of Suez or the Red Sea proper is not certain; see *Plagues of Egypt (eighth plague) and G. Hort, *ZAW* 70, 1958, pp. 51–52. The *yam sûp̄* of Ex. 23:31 is ambiguous, but perhaps it is the Gulf of Aqabah.

Various references clearly show that the term *yam sûp̄* applied to the Gulf of Aqabah. After their first halt at Kadesh-barnea (*KADESH), the Israelites were ordered into the wilderness by the way to the *yam sûp̄* (Nu. 14:25; Dt. 1:40; 2:1), *i.e.* by the Arabah towards the Gulf of Aqabah as suggested by the physical circumstances in which the earth swallowed Korah and his company (*WILDERNESS OF WANDERING; G. Hort, *Australian Biblical Review* 7, 1959, pp. 19–26). After a second sojourn at Kadesh, Israel went by the way of the *yam sûp̄* to go round Edom (Nu. 21:4; Jdg. 11:16), again with reference to the Gulf of Aqabah. Solomon's seaport of Ezion-geber or *Elath on this gulf is placed on the *yam sûp̄* by 1 Ki. 9:26; Teman in Edom is associated with it (Je. 49:21).

That the term *yam sûp̄* should have a wider use for the two N arms of the Red Sea as well as the more restricted application to the line of reedy lakes from Suez N to Lake Menzaleh and the Mediterranean is not specially remarkable or unparalleled. About 1470 BC, for example, Egyp. texts of a single epoch can use the name *Wadj-wer*, 'Great Green (Sea)', of both the Mediterranean and Red Seas (Erman-Grapow, *op. cit.*, 1, p. 269: 13–14, references), and *Ta-neter*, 'God's Land', of both Punt (E Sudan?) in particular and E lands generally (*ibid.*, 5, p. 225: 1–4, references). K.A.K.

REFINER, REFINING. The Heb. root *ṣrp* expresses the melting, testing, and refining of metals, especially precious metals such as gold and silver. This same terminology was also used of God testing men and of God's tried and tested word. A less-common term for refining or purifying was *zqq*. In the ancient world crude metal was customarily remelted to remove impurities and to make metal castings (tools, weapons, images, *etc.*). The metal was heated in pottery crucibles (Pr. 17:3; 27:21) in ovens or hearths, bellows often being used to provide a draught to create greater heat.

The Heb. term *ṣōrēp̄* for refiner, metal-worker, is often rendered as goldsmith in EVV. In the days of the Judges Micah's mother had a silver image cast (Jdg. 17:4), while much later Isaiah (40:19; 41:7; 46:6) and Jeremiah (10:8–9; 51:17) graphically describe the futile manufacture of metal and metal-plated idols. David provided refined gold and silver for the future Temple at Jerusalem (1 Ch. 28:18; 29:4); various metal-smiths shared in the repair of Jerusalem's walls under Nehemiah (Ne. 3:8, 31–32).

God, like a master-refiner seeking the pure metal, is often said to try or test (*ṣrp*) men's hearts. *Cf.* Jdg. 7:4 (Gideon's men); Pss. 17:3b; 26:2b; 66:10; 105:19; Is. 48:10; Je. 9:7; Zc. 13:9; Mal. 3:2–3. See also the graphic pictures in Ps. 12:6 and Pr. 30:5 of God's Word. For the latter concept, *cf.* also 2 Sa. 22:31 (= Ps. 18:30); Ps. 119:140. Pure metal was used for casting (*cf.* Pr. 25:4). God sought to purify his people from sin as the removal of dross and alloy (Is. 1:25), but in simile even a fire heated with the bellows was sometimes not enough to do this (Je. 6:29–30). Trials are sometimes used to refine men, and the wise refine (purify) themselves (Dn. 11:35; 12:10). Wine is once so referred to (Is. 25:6). (*ARTS AND CRAFTS.)

BIBLIOGRAPHY. For Egyp. scenes of such metal-working, actual moulds and crucibles, see *ANEP*, p. 40, figs. 133–136; Singer, Holmyard and Hall, *A History of Technology*, 1, 1954, p. 578, fig. 383 (use of bellows). In general, see *ibid.*, pp. 577–584; R. J. Forbes, *Studies in Ancient Technology*, 6, 1958, pp. 70–73, 81–85; 8, 1964, pp. 133ff., 170ff., 239ff.; 9, 1964, pp. 67ff.; A. Lucas, *Ancient Egyptian Materials and Industries*, 1962, ch. 11.
K.A.K.

REGENERATION. The Gk. noun *palingenesia* occurs only twice in the NT (Mt. 19:28, RSV 'new world', AV 'regeneration'; Tit. 3:5, 'regeneration'). In the Mt. passage it is used eschatologically to refer to the restoration of all things, reminding us that the renewal of the individual is part of a wider and cosmic renewal. In Tit. the word is used with an individual reference.

Elsewhere various words are used to express the change which the Holy Spirit effects. *gennaō* (with *nōthen*, Jn. 3:3, 7), meaning 'to eget' or 'give birth to', is used in n. 1:13; 3:3–8; 1 Jn. 2:29; 3:9; 4:7; :1, 4, 18. In 1 Pet. 1:3, 23 the word *nagennaō*—'to beget again' or 'to ring again to birth'—is found. hese words are used to describe ne initial act of renewal. The vords *anakainōsis* (Rom. 12:2; it. 3:5) with the verb *anakainoō* 2 Cor. 4:16; Col. 3:10) denote a naking anew or renewing. The eferences will indicate that the use f these two words is not limited to he initial renewal but extends to he resultant process. We may note vith reference to the result of the ew birth such terms as *kainē ktisis*, a new creation' (2 Cor. 5:17; Gal. :15), and *kainos anthrōpos*, 'a new nan' (Eph. 2:15; 4:24). Twice we ave the term *synzōopoieō*, 'to nake alive with' (Eph. 2:5; Col. :13), which hints at a change, not nly as dramatic as birth, but as ramatic as resurrection. *apokyeō* Jas. 1:18) denotes to bear or bring orth.

Surveying these terms, we notice hat they all indicate a drastic and ramatic change which may be ikened to birth, rebirth, re-creation r even resurrection. Several of the erms in their context indicate that his change has permanent and far-eaching effects in its subject.

. Old Testament presentation

The idea of regeneration is more rominent in the NT than in the OT. Many OT passages have the oncept of national renewal. This hought is present in the statements oncerning the new covenant and he law being written in the heart r the giving of a new heart (Je. 24:7; 31:31f.; 32:38f.; Ezk. 11:19; 36:25–27, and the 'valley of dry ones' passage, 37:1–14).

Although it is the nation that is n view in these scriptures, a nation an be renewed only when the indi-viduals within it are changed. Thus, n the very idea of national renewal ve find the concept of 'new hearts' eing given to individuals. Other assages deal more directly with he individual (*cf.* Is. 57:15). We otice especially Ps. 51, where David's prayer is expressed in v. 10. Considering the serious view of sin and its effects expressed in his Psalm, it is hardly surprising to ind more than a hint of the need or individual renewal.

II. New Testament presentation

This doctrine must be considered in he context of man in sin (Jn. 3:6; Eph. 2:1–3, 5). The effects of sin on human nature are considered to be so serious that, without the new birth, the sinner cannot see, let alone enter into, the kingdom of God (Jn. 3:3, 5; *cf.* 1 Cor. 2:6–16).

The initiative in regeneration is ascribed to God (Jn. 1:13); it is from above (Jn. 3:3, 7) and of the Spirit (Jn. 3:5, 8). The same idea occurs in Eph. 2:4–5; 1 Jn. 2:29; 4:7; *etc.* This divine act is decisive and once for all. Aorists are used in Jn. 1:13; 3:3, 5, 7. The use of per-fects indicates that this single, ini-tial act carries with it far-reaching effects, as in 1 Jn. 2:29; 3:9; 4:7; 5:1, 4, 18. The abiding results given in these passages are doing righteous-ness, not committing sin, loving one another, believing that Jesus is the Christ, and overcoming the world. These results indicate that in spiritual matters man is not altogether passive. He is passive in the new birth; God acts on him. But the result of such an act is far-reaching activity; he actively repents, believes in Christ, and henceforth walks in newness of life.

Jn. 3:8 serves to warn us that there is much in this subject that is inscrutable. Yet we must inquire what actually happens to the indi-vidual in the new birth. It would be safe to say that there is no change in the personality itself; the person is the same. But now he is differ-ently controlled. Before the new birth sin controlled the man and made him a rebel against God; now the Spirit controls him and directs him towards God. The regenerate man walks after the Spirit, lives in the Spirit, is led by the Spirit, and is commanded to be filled with the Spirit (Rom. 8:4, 9, 14; Eph. 5:18). He is not perfect; he has to grow and progress (1 Pet. 2:2), but in every department of his personality he is directed towards God.

We may define regeneration as a drastic act on fallen human nature by the Holy Spirit, leading to a change in the person's whole out-look. He can now be described as a new man who seeks, finds and fol-lows God in Christ.

III. The means of regeneration

In 1 Pet. 3:21 baptism is closely connected with entry into a state of salvation, and in Tit. 3:5 we have the reference to the washing of regeneration. 1 Pet. 1:23 and Jas. 1:18 mention the Word of God as a means of new birth. Many, from such scriptures, contend that these are the necessary channels by which regeneration comes to us. With 1 Cor. 2:7–16 in mind, we must question whether the Word of God is a means of regeneration in this way. Here we are clearly taught that the natural man is in such a state that he cannot receive the things of the Spirit of God. A divine inter-vention which makes the natural man receptive to God's Word must be antecedent to hearing the Word in a saving manner. When this has occurred the Word of God brings the new life into expression. It is clear that the new birth of 1 Pet. 1:23; Jas. 1:18 is conceived more comprehensively than in John. John distinguishes between regener-ation and the faith which results from it (*e.g.* Jn. 1:12–13; 1 Jn. 5:1); Peter and James, by including the reference to the Word as the means, show that they have in mind the whole process whereby God brings men to conscious faith in Christ.

We can also think of the issue in terms of conception and birth. The Holy Spirit plants or begets new life by a direct action on the soul. It is subsequently brought to the birth (*apokyeō*, Jas. 1:18) by the word. *gennaō* (1 Pet. 1:23) can have the meaning of birth as well as beget-ting.

There are further biblical objec-tions to the idea that baptism itself conveys regenerating grace. To look at baptism in this *ex opere operato* manner is contrary to other scriptures, especially the prophetic protest against the abuse of priestly rites, and Paul's strictures on Jewish views concerning circum-cision (*cf.* Rom. 2:28f.; 4:9–12). We actually have incidents of con-version without baptism (Acts 10:44–48; 16:14–15). The latter case is especially interesting, for the opening of Lydia's heart is specific-ally mentioned before baptism. If it be argued that things are different concerning Christians of subsequent generations, Paul's attitude to similar views with regard to circumcision ought to settle the issue. Regenerating grace comes direct by the Spirit to lost sinners. The Word of God brings it into expression in faith and repent-ance. *Baptism bears witness to the spiritual union with Christ in death and resurrection through which new *life is conveyed, but does not convey it automatically where *faith is not present.

BIBLIOGRAPHY. Articles on Re-generation by J. V. Bartlet (*HDB*), J. Denney (*DCG*), A. Ringwald *et*

■ **REGISTER**
See Genealogy, Part 1.

al., *NIDNTT* 1, pp. 176–188. Most works on systematic theology deal with this subject—especially note Hodge (vol. 3, pp. 1–40) and Berkhof (pp. 465–479); T. Boston, *Human Nature in its Fourfold State*, 1720, pp. 131–168; B. Citron, *The New Birth*, 1951. M.R.G.

REHOB (Heb. *r^{e}ḥōḇ*, 'open place, market-place [of town or village]', a name occuring in the Bible as a personal and as a place-name).

1. The most N city observed by Joshua's spies in Canaan (Nu. 13:21). It was an Aramaean centre which supplied the Ammonites with troops in the time of David (2 Sa. 10:6–8). The name is written 'Beth-rehob' in 2 Sa. 10:6 and in Jdg. 18:28, which latter passage suggests that it was situated near the source of the Jordan, though the precise location is unknown.

2. A city in Canaan which fell to the lot of Asher (Jos. 19:28, 30) and was declared a levitical city (Jos. 21:31; 1 Ch. 6:75), though it was among the cities not taken at the time of the Conquest (Jdg. 1:31). The suggested identification with Tell eṣ-Ṣârem S of Bethshean is unsubstantiated.

3. The father of Hadadezer, the king of Zobah in the time of David (2 Sa. 8:3, 12). Compare Ruḫubi, the name of the father of Ba'sa, the Ammonite ally of Ahab at the battle of Qarqar in 854 BC (Shalmaneser III, Kurḫ Stele 2. 95).

4. One of the Levites who sealed the covenant in the time of Nehemiah (Ne. 10:11).

(* REHOBOTH; * REHOBOTH-IR.)

BIBLIOGRAPHY. W. F. Albright, *BASOR* 83, 1941, p. 33; J. Garstang, *Joshua–Judges*, 1931, pp. 73–74, 241; H. Tadmor, *Scripta Hierosolymitana* 8, 1961, p. 245. T.C.M.

REHOBOAM (Heb. *r^{e}ḥaḇ'ām*, 'expansion of the people'). The son of * Solomon and Naamah who, upon his father's death, became the last king of a united Israel and the first of the S kingdom of Judah.

The chronology of Rehoboam's reign is disputed. Assuming a 17-year reign (1 Ki. 14:21; 2 Ch. 12:13) the dating would be *c.* 931–913 BC (* CHRONOLOGY OF THE OT), but some have truncated the reign to *c.* 922–915 BC (W. F. Albright, *BASOR* 100, 1945, pp. 16–22).

The oppressive measures needed by Solomon to ensure the funds for his public and royal expenditures led to a confrontation between Rehoboam and the N kingdom.

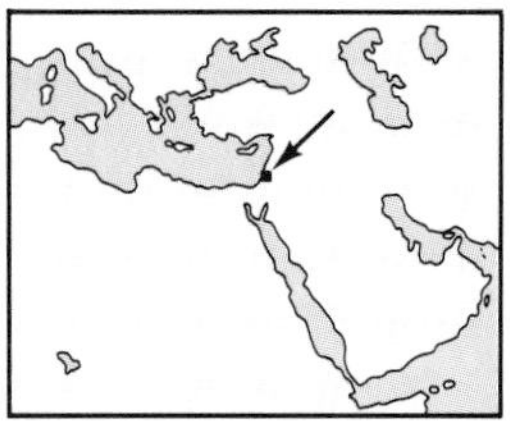

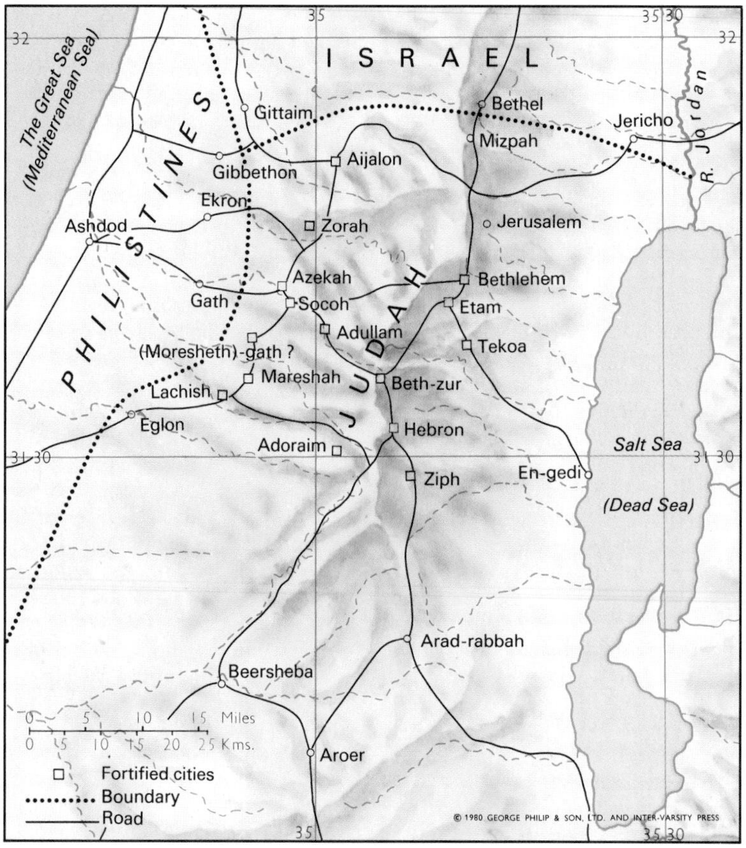

Judah at the time of Rehoboam (c. 931–913 BC).

His arrogance led him to accept ill-considered advice to increase this burden, which Israel would not accept. When Rehoboam sent his *corvée*-officer to the N, he was stoned, and * Jeroboam was made king over the ten tribes of Israel (1 Ki. 12:1–20; 2 Ch. 10). When Rehoboam mustered troops to quell the revolt, Shemaiah, a prophet, forestalled him (1 Ki. 12:21–24).

Judah built fortified towns (2 Ch. 11:5–12), probably against incursions by the Philistines (*cf.* 1 Ki. 15:27; 16:15) and Egypt. Rehoboam was also in conflict with Israel (14:30), from which the priests and Levites had fled, in reaction to the pagan practices there (2 Ch. 11:13–17). The Egyp. king, * Shishak (Shoshenq), came against Palestine *c.* 926 BC and plundered it from end to end (*LOB*, pp. 283–290; fully studied by K. A. Kitchen, *The Third Intermediate Period in Egypt*, 1972, pp. 432–447), pillaging Jerusalem (1 Ki. 14:25–27).

Pagan cultic practices appeared in Judah (1 Ki. 14:22–24), possibly influenced by the presence of foreign women in important positions, such as the king's mother, Naamah (1 Ki. 14:21, 31), and his favourite wife, Maacah (15:13; *cf.* W. F. Albright, *Archaeology and the Religion of Israel*, 1968, pp. 152f.). When Shemaiah the prophet pointed out that the invasion by Egypt was divine punishment for this apostasy, Rehoboam repented (2 Ch. 12:5–8, 12).

When he died, Rehoboam was buried in Jerusalem, 'with his fathers' (1 Ki. 14:31; 2 Ch. 12:16). His name is mentioned in the genealogy of Jesus (Mt. 1:7). D.W.B.

REHOBOTH (Heb. *r^{e}ḥōḇôṯ*, 'broad places, room'; LXX *eurychōria*). **1.** A well dug by Isaac near Gerar (Gn. 26:22), so named because no quarrel ensued with the herdsmen of Gerar. **2.** A city 'by the river' (Gn. 36:37), probably beside the Wadi el-Hesā, which divides Moab from Edom. 'The River' is normally the Euphrates (see RSV), but the context here forbids it. J.W.C.

REHOBOTH-IR (Heb. *r^{e}ḥōḇōṯ 'îr*). One of four cities built by As(s)hur (RSV * NIMROD) in Assyria (Gn. 10:11–12). Of these Nineveh and Calah are well known, but no Assyr. equivalent is known for this place. Since the large and ancient city of Aššur (80 km S of Nineveh) would be expected in the context, some consider this name an interpretation from the Sum. *AŠ.UR* (*AŠ* = Assyr. *rebātu*; *UR* = Assyr. *ālu*; Heb. *'îr*). A suburb of Nineveh (*rebit Ninua*) is mentioned in Assyr. texts (Esarhaddon), and this may have been founded at the same time. The phrase 'open-places of the city' may here be a description of Nineveh itself. The LXX read as a proper name (*Rhoōbōth*). See G. Dossin, *Le Muséon* 47, 1934, pp. 108ff.; W. F. Albright, *Recent Discoveries in Bible Lands*, 1955, p. 71.

D.J.W.

REHUM. A name borne by several men in post-exilic times, including Rehum the 'commander' (RSV), or 'high commissioner' (NEB), who joined in writing the letter of complaint in Ezr. 4:8. His title *b^{e}'ēl ṭ^{e}'ēm* means 'lord of judgment' (or 'report'), and may refer either to administration or to communication (A. H. Sayce suggested 'postmaster').

J.S.W.

REI. Occurs in 1 Ki. 1:8 only. EVV render it as a personal name, thus linking Rei with the group of Solomon's supporters. J. Taylor (*HDB*, *ad loc.*) suggests that he was an officer of the royal guard. Josephus (*Ant.* 7. 346) translates 'the friend of David' instead of 'and Rei, and the mighty men which belonged to David', but this indicates that he was probably following a shorter Heb. text, and the longer form is difficult to account for if it is not original. Suggested conjectural emendations and identification with other persons of the Davidic period are unconvincing.

G.W.G.

RELIGION. The word 'religion' came into Eng. from the Vulg., where *religio* is in a 13th-century paraphrase of Jas. 1:26f. In Acts 26:5 it denotes Judaism (*cf.* Gal. 1:13f.). Here and in the Apocrypha, *thrēskeia* refers to the outward expression of belief, not the content, as when we contrast the Christian religion with Buddhism. RSV uses the word, however, in something approaching this sense in 1 Tim. 3:16, to translate Gk. *eusebeia* (AV 'godliness'), and in 2 Tim. 3:5, where again our instinct would be to use the word 'Christianity'. Because of the association of *thrēskeia* with Judaism, James's use is probably ironical. The things which he calls the elements of '*thrēskeia* that is pure and undefiled' would not in the view of his opponents, who restricted it to ritual, have counted as *thrēskeia* at all.

Hesitance today in using the word 'religion' either of the content of the Christian faith or of its expression in worship and service, is due to the conviction that Christianity is not simply one among many religions, but differs from all others in that its content is divinely revealed and its outward expression by believers is not an attempt to secure salvation but a thank-offering for it.

J.B.J.

REPENTANCE. In the OT two words are regularly translated 'repent' or some near equivalent—*nāḥam* ('be sorry, change one's mind') and *šûḇ* (in the sense, 'turn back, return').

nāḥam is used infrequently of man (Ex. 13:17; Jb. 42:6; Je. 8:6; 31:19), but regularly of God, where it is often said that God 'repents of evil' proposed or initiated. This vigorous speech arises out of Israel's understanding of God's attitude to men in terms of personal relationship. The language of course did not imply anything fickle or arbitrary on God's side, but simply that the *relation* was a changing one. In particular, when man removes himself by his self-will from God's direction and care he finds that the God-willed consequence of his evil is more evil (Gn. 6:6f.; 1 Sa. 15:11, 35; 2 Sa. 24:16; Je. 18:10). But whoever repents, even at the eleventh hour, whoever turns (again) to God, finds a God of mercy and love, not of judgment (Je. 18:8; 26:3, 13, 19; Jon. 3:9f.; the importance of the intercessor who is willing to stand before God on behalf of his people is emphasized in Ex. 32:12–14 and Am. 7:3, 6). So even though God's firmness of judgment against *sin is in no doubt (Nu. 23:19; 1 Sa. 15:29; Ps. 110:4; Je. 4:28; Ezk. 24:14; Zc. 8:14), he has shown himself more often as a gracious God, faithful to his people even when they are faithless—a God, in other words, 'who repents of evil' (Ex. 32:14; Dt. 32:36; Jdg. 2:18; 1 Ch. 21:15; Pss. 106:45; 135:14; Je. 42:10; Joel 2:13f.; Jon. 4:2).

The call for repentance on the part of man is a call for him to return (*šûḇ*) to his creaturely (and covenant) dependence on God. Such calls are particularly frequent in the pre-exilic prophets. Am. 4:6–11 makes it clear that the evil that God intends as a consequence of Israel's sin is not malicious or vindictive, but rather is intended to bring Israel to repentance. He who commits evil finds further evil willed by God. But he who repents of his evil finds a God who repents of *his* evil. One of the most eloquent pleas for repentance comes in Ho. 6:1–3 and 14:1–2—a plea alternating with hope and despair (3:5; 5:4; 7:10), with 11:1–11 particularly poignant. Equally moving are the hopes of Isaiah expressed in the name of his son, Shearjashub ('a remnant shall return', 7:3; see also 10:21f.; 30:15; *cf.* 19:22) and the pleadings of Jeremiah (3:1–4:4; 8:4–7; 14:1–22; 15:15–21), both mingled with foreboding and despair (Is. 6:10; 9:13; Je. 13:23).

Other powerful expressions are Dt. 30:1–10; 1 Ki. 8:33–40, 46–53; 2 Ch. 7:14; Is. 55:6–7; Ezk. 18:21–24, 30–32; 33:11–16; Joel 2:12–14. See also particularly 1 Sa. 7:3; 2 Ki. 17:13; 2 Ch. 15:4; 30:6–9; Ne. 1:9; Ps. 78:34; Ezk. 14:6; Dn. 9:3; Zc. 1:3f.; Mal. 3:7. The classic example of national repentance was that led by Josiah (2 Ki. 22–23; 2 Ch. 34–35).

In the NT the words translated 'repent' are *metanoeō* and *metamelomai*. In Gk. they usually mean 'to change one's mind', and so also 'to regret, feel remorse' (*i.e.* over the view previously held). This note of remorse is present in the parable of the tax collector (Lk. 18:13), probably in Mt. 21:29, 32; 27:3 and Lk. 17:4 ('I am sorry'), and most explicitly in 2 Cor. 7:8–10. But the NT usage is much more influenced by the OT *šûḇ*; that is, repentance not just as a feeling sorry, or changing one's mind, but as a turning round, a complete alteration of the basic motivation and direction of one's life. This is why the best translation for *metanoeō* is often 'to convert', that is, 'to turn round' (*CONVERSION). It also helps to explain why John the Baptist demanded *baptism as an expression of this repentance, not just for obvious 'sinners', but for 'righteous' Jews as well—baptism as a decisive act of turning from the old way of life and a throwing oneself on the mercy of the Coming One (Mt. 3:2, 11; Mk. 1:4; Lk. 3:3, 8; Acts 13:24; 19:4).

Jesus' call for repentance re-

REINS
See Kidneys, Part 2.

REJECT
See Reprobate, Part 3.

RELEASE
See Liberty, Part 2.

RELIEFS
See Art, Part 1.

REMARRIAGE
See Marriage, Part 2.

REMETH
See Jarmuth, Part 2.

RENAMING
See Name, Part 2.

RENEWAL
See Regeneration, Part 3.

REPA
See Rephan, Part 3.

ceives little explicit mention in Mk. (1:15; *cf.* 6:12) and Mt. (4:17; 11:20f.; 12:41), but is emphasized by Lk. (5:32; 10:13; 11:32; 13:3, 5; 15:7, 10; 16:30; 17:3f.; *cf.* 24:47). Other sayings and incidents in all three Gospels, however, express very clearly the character of the repentance which Jesus' whole ministry demanded. Its radical nature, as a complete turning round and return, is emphasized by the parable of the Prodigal Son (Lk. 15:11–24). Its unconditional character appears from the parable of the Pharisee and tax collector—repentance means acknowledging that one has no possible claim upon God, and submitting oneself without excuse or attempted justification to God's mercy (Lk. 18:13). The 'turn round' in previous values and life-style is highlighted by the encounter with the rich young man (Mk. 10:17–22) and Zacchaeus (Lk. 19:8). Above all, Mt. 18:3 makes it clear that to convert is to become like a child, that is, to acknowledge one's immaturity before God, one's inability to live life apart from God, to accept one's total dependence on God.

The call for repentance (and promise of forgiveness) features regularly in Luke's record of the preaching of the first Christians (Acts 2:38; 3:19; 8:22; 17:30; 20:21; 26:20). Here *metanoeō* is complemented by *epistrephō* ('to turn round, return'—Acts 3:19; 9:35; 11:21; 14:15; 15:19; 26:18, 20; 28:27), where *metanoeō* means more a turning away (from sin) and *epistrephō* a turning to (God) (see particularly Acts 3:19; 26:20), though each by itself can embrace both senses (as in Acts 11:18; 1 Thes. 1:9).

It is clear from Acts 5:31 and 11:18 that no difficulty was felt in describing repentance both as God's gift and as man's responsibility. At the same time Is. 6:9–10 is cited several times as an explanation of men's failure to convert (Mt. 13:14f.; Mk. 4:12; Jn. 12:40; Acts 28:26f.).

The writer to the Hebrews also indicates the importance of initial repentance (6:1), but whereas he questions the possibility of a second repentance (6:4–6; 12:17), others are even more emphatic in their belief that *Christians* can and need to repent (2 Cor. 7:9f.; 12:21; Jas. 5:19f.; 1 Jn. 1:5–2:2; Rev. 2:5, 16, 21f.; 3:3, 19).

There are only a few other references to repentance in the NT (Rom. 2:4; 2 Tim. 2:25; 2 Pet. 3:9; Rev. 9:20f.; 16:9, 11). We should not assume that talk of repentance and *forgiveness invariably featured in the earliest preaching. In particular Paul rarely uses either concept, and they do not occur at all in the Gospel and Epistles of John, whereas both strongly emphasize that the Christian life starts from the positive commitment of *faith.

BIBLIOGRAPHY. G. Bertram, *epistrephō*, *TDNT* 7, pp. 722–729; G. Bornkamm, *Jesus of Nazareth*, 1960, pp. 82–84; J. Jeremias, *New Testament Theology*, 1: *The Proclamation of Jesus*, 1971, pp. 152–158; O. Michel, *metamelomai*, *TDNT* 4, pp. 626–629; J. P. Ramseyer, in J. J. von Allmen (ed.), *Vocabulary of the Bible*, 1958, pp. 357–359; A. Richardson, *An Introduction to the Theology of the New Testament*, 1958, pp. 31–34; E. Würthein and J. Behm, *metanoeō*, *TDNT* 4, pp. 975–1008; F. Laubach, J. Goetzmann, *NIDNTT* 1, pp. 353–359.

J.D.G.D.

REPHAIM (Heb. *rᵉpāʾîm*). One of the pre-Israelite peoples of Palestine mentioned, together with the Zuzim and Emim, in the time of Abraham as having been defeated by Chedorlaomer (Gn. 14:5). They are also listed among the inhabitants of the land God promised to Abraham's seed (Gn. 15:20). At the time of the conquest the Rephaim seem to have inhabited a wide area, but were known by different local names. In Moab the Moabites, who succeeded them there, called them *Emim (Dt. 2:11), and likewise in Ammon, where they preceded the Ammonites, they were known as *Zamzummim (Dt. 2:20–21).

They were a formidable people, being compared in stature with the Anakim (*ANAK) (Dt. 2:21), and LXX renders the name by *gigas*, 'giant' in Gn. 14:5; Jos. 12:4; 13:12, and 1 Ch. 11:15; 14:9; 20:4, a rendering adopted by AV in Dt. 2:11, 20; 3:11, 13; Jos. 12:4; 13:12; 15:8; 17:15; 18:16; 1 Ch. 20:4. (LXX translates it *Titanes* in 2 Sa. 5:18, 22.)

It may be that the forms *rāpāʾ* and *rāpâ* (2 Sa. 21:16, 18, 20, 22; 1 Ch. 20:6, 8), which are rendered 'giant' in EVV (LXX *gigas* in 2 Sa. 21:22; 1 Ch. 20:6), are variant forms of the name *rᵉpāʾîm*, but the context of these occurrences, in connection with a Philistine, is perhaps better suited by the meaning *'giant'. The name is unknown in an ethnic sense outside the Bible.

In Ps. 88:11 (v. 10, RSV); Pr. 2:18; 9:18; 21:16; Jb. 26:5; Is. 14:9; 26:14, 19, the word *rᵉpāʾîm* occurs in the sense of 'ghosts of the dead', and it is suggested by some that the name Rephaim was applied by the Israelites to the early inhabitants of the land as persons long since dead. The word occurs in Ugaritic (*rpùm*), perhaps referring to a class of minor gods or a sacred guild, though the meaning is uncertain, and in Phoenician tomb inscriptions (*rpʾm*) in the sense of 'ghost'.

BIBLIOGRAPHY. J. Gray, 'The Rephaim', *PEQ* 81, 1949, pp. 127–139, and 84, 1952, pp. 39–41; H. W. F. Saggs, *FT* 90, 1958, pp. 170–172.

T.C.M.

REPHAN (AV **REMPHAN**). The name of a god identified or connected with the planet Saturn, quoted in Acts 7:43 from the LXX of Am. 5:26. The LXX reading, *Rhaiphan* (cod. B, A; *Rhemphan* 239), is thought by some to be a mistaken transliteration of the *MT* reading, *kiyyûn* (RSV *KAIWAN, AV Chiun), by others to be a deliberate substitution of *Repa*, a name of Seb, the Egyp. god of the planet Saturn.

D.W.G.

REPHIDIM. The last stopping-place of the Israelites on the Exodus from Egypt, before they reached Mt Sinai (Ex. 17:1; 19:2; Nu. 33:14–15). Here the Israelites under Joshua fought against Amalek, and the successful outcome of the battle depended on Moses' holding up his hands, which he did with the support of Aaron and Hur (Ex. 17:8–16). After the battle, Jethro, Moses' father-in-law, persuaded Moses to give up judging the people entirely by himself, and to appoint deputies for this purpose (Ex. 18). The site of Rephidim is uncertain, the usual suggestion being the Wadi Refayid in SW Sinai.

BIBLIOGRAPHY. B. Rothenberg, *God's Wilderness*, 1961, pp. 143, 168.

T.C.M.

REPROBATE. It is convenient to retain the AV term as a heading under which to include words used in RSV (unfit, refuse, dross, disqualified) to translate Heb. and Gk. equivalents which present the idea of divine investigation leading to rejection because of an ineradicable sin. OT prophets compare the sin of Israel to impurity in metal (Is. 1:22; Je. 6:30; Ezk. 22:19–20). In Je. 6:30, 'Refuse silver they are called, for the Lord has rejected them', the Heb. verb *mā'as* is rendered 'reprobate' in AV (AVmg., RSV, RV 'refuse'), *i.e.* 'tested and rejected by Yahweh because of ineradicable sin'. In Is. 1:22 LXX renders Heb. *sîgîm* by the adjective *adokimos*, which occurs eight times in the NT with the meaning 'rejected after a searching test'.

In Rom. 1:28, the Gk. puns *dokimazein* with *adokimos*, and may be rendered 'since they did not see fit to retain God in their mind he handed them over to an unfit mind', where 'unfit' (AV 'reprobate', AVmg. 'a mind void of judgment') means 'unfit to pass judgment', in the active or passive sense, because of wickedness, *etc.* (vv. 29–30).

In 1 Cor. 9:27 Paul concludes 'an exhortation to self-denial and exertion' (Hodge), given in athletic metaphors, by attributing his personal bodily discipline to fear of disqualification, 'lest I . . . be disqualified (*adokimos*)'. But from what? Salvation or ministerial reward? The context favours reward (*cf.* 3:10–15) and stresses the need of ceaseless vigilance against sin (*cf.* 10:12). The remaining occurrences of *adokimos* are in 2 Cor. 13:5–7, where the test proposed is 'whether you are holding to your faith', and the context implies that faith has empirical proofs, lacking which the Corinthians are failures, and even Paul himself would be a failure, since he would be unable to demonstrate his apostolic authority; in 2 Tim. 3:8 and in Tit. 1:16, where *adokimos* means 'proved to be morally worthless'; and in Heb. 6:8, where 'barren' (*adokimos*) soil illustrates the situation of hardened backsliders. None of these occurrences necessarily implies judicial abandonment to *perdition, yet all are consonant with such a doctrine: in each case the rejection follows demonstrable faults; in some God, in others man, makes the test. The human verdict anticipates the divine.

BIBLIOGRAPHY. Arndt (*s.v. adokimos*); J. Denney in *HDB* for full bibliography; E. K. Simpson, *Words Worth Weighing in the Greek New Testament*, 1946, pp. 17f.; H. Haarbeck, *NIDNTT* 3, pp. 808–810. M.R.W.F.

RESEN (Gk. *Dasen*). The city located between Nineveh and Calah founded by *Nimrod or Ashur (so AV) and with them part of a great populated area (Gn. 10:12). *rēš-êni* ('fountain-head') designated a number of places in Assyria. The sites of this name on the Ḫabur and Khosr Rivers (NE of Nineveh) do not, however, easily fit the geographical situation given in Gn. 10. The proposed equation with Selamiyeh (3 km N of Calah) is based on the false identification of this place with Larissa (Xenophon, *Anabasis* 3. 4), now known to be the Gk. name for Calah itself. A possible site for Resen is the early ruins of Hamam Ali with its adjacent sulphur springs on the right bank of the river Tigris about 13 km S of Nineveh. D.J.W.

REST. The non-theological sense of 'rest' is prominent in the Bible. *E.g.* the Lord rests from activity (Gn. 2:2f.); the sabbath is to be a day of rest (Ex. 31:15); the land of promise was to have rest every 7th year (Lv. 25:4f.); and the Temple was the Lord's resting-place among his people (Ps. 132:8, 14).

In its theological sense 'rest' is even more prominent in the Bible. Israel was promised rest by the Lord in the land of Canaan (Dt. 3:20), and to this rest the exiles would return from Babylon (Je. 46:27). Rest and felicity were to be David's great gifts to Israel (1 Ch. 22:7–10). Alas, this great ideal of rest remained unfulfilled in Israel's experience (Heb. 3:7–4:10) because of unbelief and disobedience (Ps. 95:8–11).

However, although rest in the OT remains in the sphere of promise, in the NT there is fulfilment. Christians, by faith in Christ, have entered into rest (Heb. 12:22–24). He is their peace. To all who come to him he gives rest, rest that is relief, release and satisfaction to the soul (Mt. 11:28–30).

But 'rest' in Scripture has also an eschatological content. 'There remains a sabbath rest' for the Christian as for Israel (Heb. 4:9). The celestial city and the heavenly country (Heb. 11:10, 16) are still in the future. Today there is the task (1 Cor. 3:9), the good fight of faith (Eph. 6:10–20), the pilgrimage (Heb. 11:13–16). And even the rest to which death is the prelude (Rev. 14:13) is not fullness of rest (Rev. 6:9–11). But those who have entered into the rest of faith, by casting anchor within the veil where Christ has gone, know that the final state of rest is secure. J.G.S.S.T.

RESTORATION. The Gk. noun *apokatastasis* is found only in Acts 3:21, while the corresponding verb is used three times in the sense of a final restoration.

The idea goes back to the great prophets of the OT. They foresaw the Exile, but they also prophesied that God would restore his people to their own land (Je. 27:22; Dn. 9:25, *etc.*). When this took place conditions in Judah were far from ideal, and thus men looked and longed for a further restoration, a restoration of prosperity and bliss.

In time this came to be associated with the Messiah. The Jews as a whole understood this restoration in terms of material prosperity, but Jesus saw it in the work of John the Baptist, who fulfilled the prophecy of Mal. 4:5 (Mt. 17:11; Mk. 9:12). Here, as elsewhere, he reinterpreted the Messianic category which had become distorted among the Jews.

In the full sense the restoration is yet future. Though they had Jesus' interpretation of the prophecy of Malachi, the disciples could ask on the eve of the ascension, 'Lord, will you at this time restore the kingdom to Israel?' (Acts 1:6). Jesus' answer discourages them from speculation about matters which do not concern them, but it does not deny that there will be a restoration. The fullest reference comes in Acts 3:19ff. Here Peter looks for 'times of refreshing' which he associates with the return of the Lord Jesus Christ (v. 20), who is in heaven 'until the time for establishing (*i.e.* restoration) all that God spoke . . .'. From one point of view the restoration awaits the return of the Lord, and Peter sees this as a subject of prophecy from the very first. It is legitimate to infer that the restoration points to some such state as that of prefallen man, though there is no biblical passage which says this in so many words. Some have reasoned from the expression 'time for establishing all that God spoke' to the thought of universal salvation. This is more than the expression will bear. That question must be determined by the teaching of Scripture as a whole.

BIBLIOGRAPHY. H.-G. Link, *NIDNTT* 3, pp. 146–148. L.M.

REPRODUCTION
See Seed, Part 3.

REPTILE
See Animals, Part 1.

RESURRECTION. The most startling characteristic of the first Christian preaching is its emphasis on the resurrection. The first preachers were sure that Christ had risen, and sure, in consequence, that believers would in due course rise also. This set them off from all the other teachers of the ancient world. There are resurrections elsewhere, but none of them is like that of Christ. They are mostly mythological tales connected with the change of the season and the annual miracle of spring. The Gospels tell of an individual who truly died but overcame death by rising again. And if it is true that Christ's resurrection bears no resemblance to anything in paganism it is also true that the attitude of believers to their own resurrection, the corollary of their Lord's, is radically different from anything in the heathen world. Nothing is more characteristic of even the best thought of the day than its hopelessness in the face of death. Clearly the resurrection is of the very first importance for the Christian faith.

The Christian idea of resurrection is to be distinguished from both Greek and Jewish ideas. The Greeks thought of the body as a hindrance to true life and they looked for the time when the soul would be free from its shackles. They conceived of life after death in terms of the immortality of the soul, but they firmly rejected all ideas of resurrection (*cf.* the mockery of Paul's preaching in Acts 17:32). The Jews were firmly persuaded of the values of the body, and thought these would not be lost. They thus looked for the body to be raised. But they thought it would be exactly the same body (*Apocalypse of Baruch* 1:2). The Christians thought of the body as being raised, but also transformed so as to be a suitable vehicle for the very different life of the age to come (1 Cor. 15:42ff.). The Christian idea is thus distinctive.

I. Resurrection in the Old Testament

There is little about resurrection in the OT. That is not to say that it is not there. It is. But it is not prominent. The men of the OT were very practical men, concentrating on the task of living out the present life in the service of God, and they had little time to spare for speculation about the next. Moreover, it must not be forgotten that they lived on the other side of Christ's resurrection, and it is this which gives the doctrine its basis. Sometimes they used the idea of resurrection to express the national hope of the rebirth of the nation (*e.g.* Ezk. 37). The plainest statement on the resurrection of the individual is undoubtedly that in Dn. 12:2, 'many of those who sleep in the dust of the earth shall awake, some to everlasting life, and some to shame and everlasting contempt'. This clearly envisages a resurrection both of the righteous and of the wicked, and it sees also eternal consequences of men's actions. There are other passages which look for resurrection, chiefly some in the Psalms (*e.g.* Pss. 16:10f.; 49:14f.). The precise meaning of Job's great affirmation (Jb. 19:25–27) is disputed, but it is difficult to think that there is no thought of resurrection here. Sometimes the prophets also give utterance to this thought (*e.g.* Is. 26:19). But on the whole the OT says little about it. This may, perhaps, be due to the fact that some doctrine of resurrection was found among such peoples as the Egyptians and Babylonians. At a time when syncretism was a grave danger this would have discouraged the Hebrews from taking too great an interest in it.

During the period between the two Testaments, when that danger was not so pressing, the idea is more prominent. No uniformity was reached, and even in NT times the Sadducees still denied that there was a resurrection. But by then most Jews accepted some idea of resurrection. Usually they thought that these same bodies would be brought back to life just as they were.

II. The resurrection of Christ

On three occasions Christ brought back people from the dead (the daughter of Jairus, the son of the widow of Nain, and Lazarus). These, however, are not to be thought of as resurrection so much as resuscitation. There is no indication that any of these people did other than come back to the life that they had left. And Paul tells us explicitly that Christ is 'the first fruits of those who have fallen asleep' (1 Cor. 15:20). But these miracles show us Christ as the master of death. This comes out again in the fact that he prophesied that he would rise 3 days after he was crucified (Mk. 8:31; 9:31; 10:34, *etc.*). This point is important. It shows Christ as supremely the master of the situation. And it also means that the resurrection is of the very first importance, for the veracity of our Lord is involved.

The Gospels tell us that Jesus was crucified, that he died and that on the third day the tomb in which he had been placed was found to be empty. Angels told certain women that he had risen from the dead. Over a period of some weeks Jesus appeared to his followers from time to time. Paul lists some of these appearances but he does not explicitly mention the empty tomb and some scholars accordingly suggest that it was absent from the earliest tradition. But it may be fairly countered that Paul implies that the tomb was empty. What else does he mean by saying that Jesus 'was buried, that he was raised on the third day . . .' (1 Cor. 15:4)? The express mention of burial is pointless if he does not have the empty tomb in mind. And it is referred to in all four Gospels. It must be accepted as part of the authentic Christian tradition. Some have suggested that the disciples went to the wrong tomb, where a young man in white said, 'He is not here', meaning 'He is in another tomb'. But in the first place this is pure speculation, and in the second it raises all sorts of questions. It is impossible to hold that the right tomb was completely forgotten by all, friend and foe alike. When the first preaching laid such stress on the resurrection we can be sure that the authorities would have spared no effort in the attempt to find the body.

But if the tomb was empty it would seem that there are only three possibilities: that friends took the body away, that foes took the body away, or that Jesus rose. The first hypothesis is more than difficult to maintain. All our evidence goes to show that there was no thought of resurrection in the minds of the disciples, and that they were men without hope on the evening of the first Good Friday. They were dispirited, beaten men, hiding away for fear of the Jews. Moreover, Matthew tells us that a guard was set over the tomb, so that they could not have stolen the body even had they wanted to do so. But the crowning improbability is that they would have suffered for preaching the resurrection as Acts tells us they did. Some were imprisoned, and James was executed. Men do not suffer such penalties for upholding what they know to be a lie. It must also be borne in mind that when the Christian sect was troublesome enough for the authorities to persecute it, the chief priests would have been very ready to have paid for information as to the stealing of the body, and the case of Judas is sufficient to show that a traitor could be found in the ranks. All in all, it is impossible to hold that Christians stole away the body of Christ.

It is just as difficult to maintain that his foes removed the body. Why should they? There seems no conceivable motive. To have done so would have been to start the very rumours of a resurrection that the evidence shows they were so anxious to prevent. Moreover, the guard over the tomb would have been just as big an obstacle to them as to the friends of the Lord. But the absolutely decisive objection is their failure to produce the body when the first preaching began. Peter and his allies put great emphasis on the resurrection of their Lord. Clearly it had gripped their imagination. In this situation, had their enemies produced the body of Jesus, the Christian church must have dissolved in a gale of laughter. The silence of the Jews is just as significant as the speech of the Christians. The failure of the enemies of Jesus to produce the body is conclusive evidence that they could not do so.

Since it seems impossible to hold either that friends or foes removed the body, and since the tomb was empty, it seems that we are shut up to the hypothesis of the resurrection. This is confirmed also by the resurrection appearances. Altogether there are ten different appearances recorded in our five accounts (the four Gospels and 1 Cor. 15). These accounts are not easy to harmonize (though this is not impossible, as is often asserted; the attempt made in the *Scofield Reference Bible*, for example, may or may not be the right one, but it certainly shows that harmonization is possible). The difficulties show only that the accounts are independent. There is no stereotyped repetition of an official story. And there is impressive agreement on the main facts. There is great variety in the witnesses. Sometimes one or two saw the Lord, sometimes a larger number, as the eleven apostles, once as many as 500 disciples. Men as well as women are included in the number. Mostly the appearances were to believers, but possibly that to James was to one who had not believed up till that point. Specially important is Paul. He was not credulous, but an educated man who was bitterly hostile to the Christians. And he is emphatic that he saw Jesus after he had risen from the dead. Indeed, so sure was he of this that he based the whole of the rest of his life on the certainty. Canon Kennett puts this point trenchantly. He speaks of Paul as having been converted within 5 years of the crucifixion and says, 'within a very few years of the time of the crucifixion of Jesus, the evidence for the resurrection of Jesus was in the mind of at least one man of education absolutely irrefutable' (*Interpreter* 5, 1908–9, p. 267).

We should not overlook the transformation of the disciples in all this. As noted before, they were beaten and dispirited men at the crucifixion, but they were ready to go to prison and even to die for the sake of Jesus shortly afterwards. Why the change? Men do not run such risks unless they are very sure of themselves. The disciples were completely convinced. We should perhaps add that their certainty is reflected in their worship. They were Jews, and Jews have a tenacity in clinging to their religious customs. Yet these men observed the Lord's day, a weekly memorial of the resurrection, instead of the sabbath. On that Lord's day they celebrated the holy communion, which was not a commemoration of a dead Christ, but a thankful remembrance of the blessings conveyed by a living and triumphant Lord. Their other sacrament, baptism, was a reminder that believers were buried with Christ and raised with him (Col. 2:12). The resurrection gave significance to all that they did.

Sometimes it is said that Christ did not really die, but swooned. Then in the coolness of the tomb he revived. This raises all sorts of questions. How did he get out of the tomb? What happened to him? Why do we hear no more? When did he die? Questions multiply and the answers do not appear. Some have thought the disciples to have been the victims of hallucination. But the resurrection appearances cannot be so explained. Hallucinations come to those who are in some sense looking for them, and there is no evidence of this among the disciples. Once started they tend to continue, whereas these stop abruptly. Hallucinations are individual affairs, whereas in this case we have as many as 500 people at once seeing the Lord. There seems no point in exchanging a miracle on the physical level for one on the psychological level, which is what this view demands.

But many scholars today deny outright the possibility of a physical resurrection. They may lay it down that 'the bones of Jesus rest in the soil of Palestine'. They may say that Jesus rose into the *kerygma*; the disciples came to see that he had survived through death and that they could thus preach that he was alive. Or they may locate the change in the disciples. These men had known Jesus to live in true freedom and now they entered that experience for themselves. This meant that they came to see that Jesus was not dead but a living influence. There are two big difficulties in the way of all such views. The first is that this is not what the sources say. As plain as words can do it they say that Jesus died, was buried, and rose to life again. The second is the moral difficulty. There is no question but that the disciples believed that Jesus had risen. It was this that gave them their drive and it was this that formed the theme of their preaching. If Jesus was in fact dead then God has built the church on a delusion, an unthinkable conclusion. Moreover, such views ignore the empty tomb. This is a stubborn fact. Perhaps it is worth adding that these views are quite modern (though occasionally there have been forerunners, *cf.* 2 Tim. 2:17f.). They form no part of historic Christianity, and if they are correct nearly all Christians have at all times been in serious error concerning a cardinal doctrine of the faith.

III. The resurrection of believers

Not only did Jesus rise, but one day all men too will rise. Jesus refuted the scepticism of the Sadducees on this point with an interesting argument from Scripture (Mt. 22:31–32). The general NT position is that the resurrection of Christ carries with it the resurrection of believers. Jesus said, 'I am the resurrection and the life; he who believes in me, though he die, yet shall he live' (Jn. 11:25). Several times he spoke of raising believers up at the last day (Jn. 6:39–40, 44, 54). The Sadducees were grieved because the apostles were 'proclaiming in Jesus the resurrection from the dead' (Acts 4:2). Paul tells us that 'as by a man came death, by a man came also the resurrection of the dead. For as in Adam all die, so also in Christ shall all be made alive' (1 Cor. 15:21f.; *cf.* 1 Thes. 4:14). Likewise Peter says, 'we have been born anew to a living hope through the resurrection of Jesus Christ from the dead' (1 Pet. 1:3). It is plain enough that the NT writers did not think of Christ's resurrection as an isolated phenomenon. It was a great divine act, and one fraught with consequences for men. Because God raised Christ he set his seal on the atoning work wrought out on the cross. He demonstrated his divine power in the face of sin and death, and at the same time his will to save men. Thus, the resurrection of believers follows immediately from that of their Saviour. So characteristic of them is resurrection that Jesus could speak of them as 'sons of God, being sons of the resurrection' (Lk. 20:36).

This does not mean that all who rise rise to blessing. Jesus speaks of 'the resurrection of life' but also of 'the resurrection of judgment' (Jn. 5:29). The plain NT teaching is that *all* will rise, but that those who have rejected Christ will find the resurrection a serious matter indeed. For believers the fact that their resurrection is connected with that of the Lord transforms the situation. In the light of his atoning work for them they face resurrection with calmness and joy.

Of the nature of the resurrection body Scripture says little. Paul can speak of it as 'a spiritual body' (1 Cor. 15:44), which appears to mean a body which meets the needs of the spirit. He expressly differentiates it from the 'physical body' which we now have, and we infer that a 'body' answering to the needs of the spirit is in some respect different from that which we now know. The spiritual body has the qualities of incorruptibility, glory, and power (1 Cor. 15:42f.). Our Lord has taught us that there will be no marriage after the resurrection, and thus no sexual function (Mk. 12:25).

Perhaps we can gain some help by thinking of the resurrection body of Christ, for John tells us that 'we shall be like him' (1 Jn. 3:2), and Paul that 'our lowly body is to be 'like his glorious body' (Phil. 3:21). Our Lord's risen body appears to have been in some sense like the natural body and in some sense different. Thus on some occasions he was recognized immediately (Mt. 28:9; Jn. 20:19f.), but on others he was not (notably the walk to Emmaus, Lk. 24:16; *cf.* Jn. 21). He appeared suddenly in the midst of the disciples, who were gathered with the doors shut (Jn. 20:19), while contrariwise he disappeared from the sight of the two at Emmaus (Lk. 24:31). He spoke of having 'flesh and bones' (Lk. 24:39). On occasion he ate food (Lk. 24:41–43), though we cannot hold that physical food is a necessity for life beyond death (*cf.* 1 Cor 6:13). It would seem that the risen Lord could conform to the limitations of this physical life or not as he chose, and this may indicate tha when we rise we shall have a simila power.

IV. Doctrinal implications of the resurrection

The Christological significance of the resurrection is considerable. The fact that Jesus prophesied that he would rise from the dead on the third day has important implications for his Person. One who coul do this is greater than the sons of men. Paul clearly regards the resurrection of Christ as of cardina importance. 'If Christ has not been raised,' he says, 'then our preaching is in vain, and your faith is in vain. . . . If Christ has not been raised, your faith is futile and you are still in your sins' (1 Cor. 15:14, 17). The point is that Christianity i a gospel, it is good news about how God sent his Son to be our Saviour But if Christ did not really rise, then we have no assurance that ou salvation has been accomplished. The reality of the resurrection of Christ is thus of deep significance. The resurrection of believers is also important. Paul's view is that if the dead do not rise we may as well adopt the motto 'Let us eat and drink, for tomorrow we die' (1 Cor 15:32). Believers are not men for whom this life is all. Their hope lies elsewhere (1 Cor. 15:19). This gives them perspective and makes for depth in living.

The resurrection of Christ is connected with our salvation, as when Paul says that 'Jesus our Lord was put to death for our trespasses and

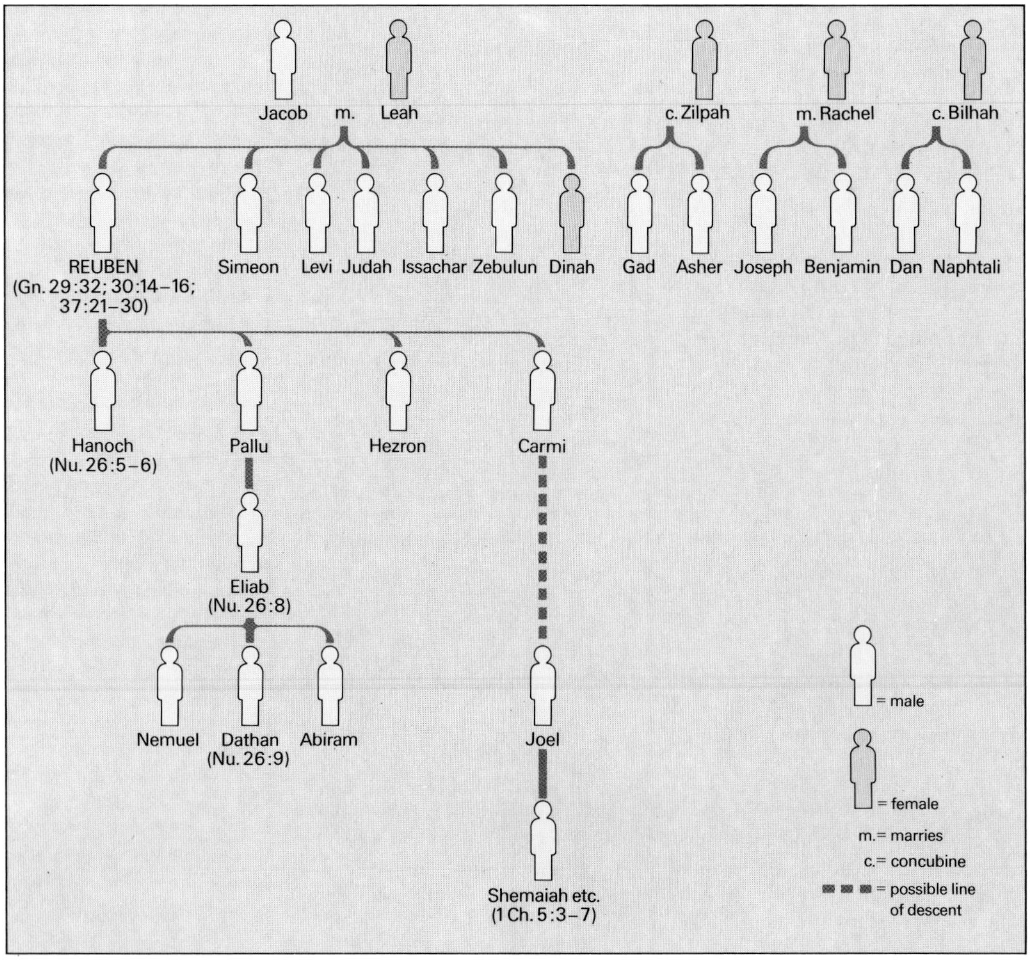

The family and descendants of Reuben.

aised for our justification' (Rom. ':25; *cf.* 8:33f.). There is no need ere to go into the precise signifi- ance of the two uses of 'for'. That s a task for the commentaries. We ontent ourselves with noting that he resurrection of Christ is con- ected with the central act whereby ve are saved. Salvation is not omething that takes place apart rom the resurrection.

Nor does it stop there. Paul peaks of his desire to know Christ and the power of his resurrection' Phil. 3:10), and he exhorts the Colossians, 'If then you have been aised with Christ, seek the things hat are above . . .' (Col. 3:1). He as already reminded them that hey were buried with Christ in aptism, and in the same sacrament vere raised with him (Col. 2:12). In ther words, the apostle sees the ame power that brought Christ ack from the dead as operative vithin those who are Christ's. The esurrection is ongoing.

BIBLIOGRAPHY. W. Milligan, *The Resurrection of our Lord*², 1883; . Orr, *The Resurrection of Jesus*, 909; W. J. Sparrow-Simpson, *The Resurrection and Modern Thought*, 911; P. Gardner-Smith, *The Nar- atives of the Resurrection*, 1926; K. Barth, *The Resurrection of the Dead*, E.T. 1933; A. M. Ramsey, *The Resurrection of Christ*, 1946; G. Vos in *PTR* 27, 1929, pp. 1–35, 93–226; N. Clark, *Interpreting the Resurrection*, 1967; W. Marxsen, *The Resurrection of Jesus of Naza- eth*, 1970; L. Coenen, C. Brown in *NIDNTT* 3, pp. 257–309. L.M.

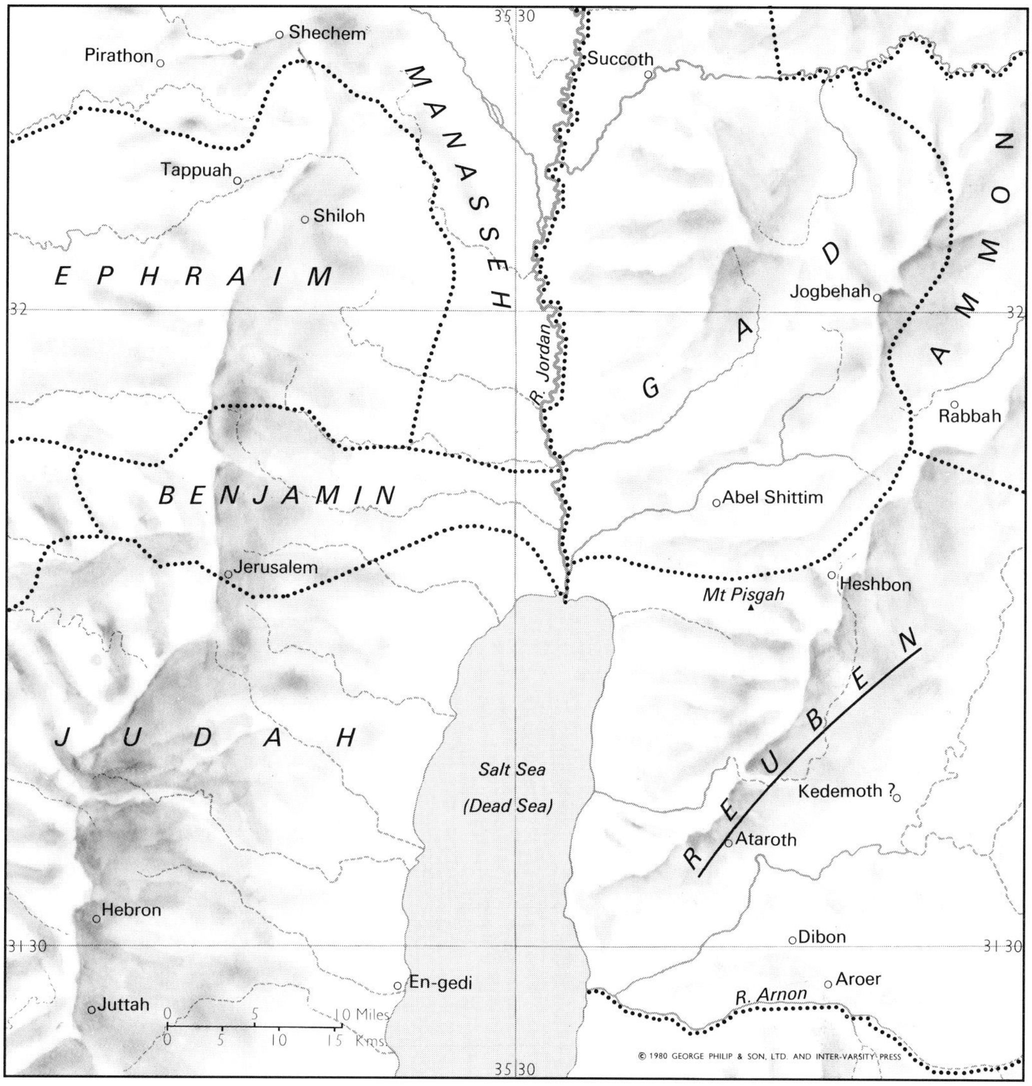

REUBEN (*MT* r^e*'ûḇēn*; LXX *Rou- ēn*; Pesh. *Roubîl*; Jos. *Roubēlos*; Arab. *Ra'ûbîn*; Lat. *Rubin*).

. The first-born of Jacob by Leah Gn. 29:32), whose choice of name connected with the phrase, 'the Lord *has looked upon my affliction*' Heb. *rā'â . . .* b^e*'onyî*). That this meaning was attached to the name s clear from the other names in this ection: 'Simeon (Heard) . . . the Lord has *heard*', 'Levi (Attached) . . my husband . . . will be *ttached*', 'Judah (Praise) . . . I will *raise* the Lord', 'Dan (Judge) . . . God has *judged* me', *etc.* Attempts ave been made to give the desired meaning, 'He has looked upon my ffliction', to the Heb. consonants or 'Reuben', which in our present ext appears to mean, 'Behold a on'. Possibly the vocalization of he name is at fault.

Reuben had some admirable qualities in his character; unfor- tunately, they were offset by his incestuous act with Bilhah, his father's concubine (Gn. 35:22). It was Reuben who advised his brothers not to kill Joseph, and returned to the pit to release him (Gn. 37:21, 29). Later he accused them of bringing calamity upon themselves, when they were held in the Egyp. court as suspected spies (Gn. 42:22). Again, it was Reuben who offered his own two sons as sufficient guarantee for the safety of Benjamin (Gn. 42:37).

In the blessing of the sons of Jacob, Reuben is recognized legally as the first-born, although in actual fact the double-portion which went with the birthright (Dt. 21:17) was symbolically be- queathed to Joseph, through his two sons, Ephraim and Manasseh. However, after a eulogy of Reuben, no doubt sincerely meant, there is added a significant and prophetic utterance by the Patriarch: 'Un- stable as water, you shall not have pre-eminence . . .' (Gn. 49:4). This legal recognition as first-born is upheld in 1 Ch. 5:1, where we are told that the birthright belonged to Joseph *de facto* but not *de jure*, for 'he [Joseph] is not to be enrolled in the genealogy according to the birthright' (*cf.* Gesenius, *Heb. Gram.*²⁸, p. 349, § 114k). So it is that in Gn. 46:8; Ex. 6:14; Nu. 26:5, Reuben retains his status as first- born. Reuben had four sons before the descent into Egypt.

2. The tribe of Reuben was in- volved in the rebellion in the wilder- ness (Nu. 16:1). The tribe was linked with Gad and occupied ter- ritory E of Jordan. In the N it was contiguous with Gad, in the S it was bounded by the Arnon. The tribe's pursuits would be mainly pastoral, but those to the W of Jordan were mainly agricultural. This may have led to a separation of interests, for Reuben took no part in repelling the attack of Sisera

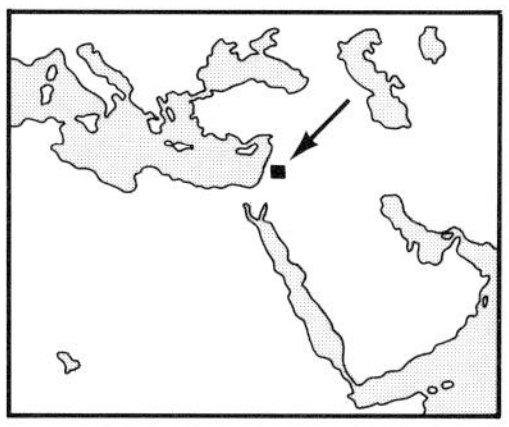

The territory allotted to the tribe of Reuben.

(Jdg. 5:15f.). In the time of Saul they united with Gad and Manasseh in an attack on the Hagarites, apparently a nomad people (1 Ch. 5:10, 19f.).

Though there is mention of Gad on the Moabite Stone, there is none of Reuben, and thus it appears that at that time, *c.* 830 BC, they had lost their importance as warriors. However, they were never forgotten by their brethren; a place is reserved for the tribe of Reuben in Ezekiel's reconstructed Israel (Ezk. 48:7, 31), and they are numbered among the 144,000, sealed out of every tribe of the children of Israel, in the Apocalypse of John (Rev. 7:5). R.J.A.S.

REUEL (Heb. *r^{e}'û'ēl*, Gk. *raguel*; the name appears to mean 'friend of God').

1. A son of Esau (Gn. 36:4, 10, 17; 1 Ch. 1:35). **2.** A Midianite priest, also called *Jethro, who received Moses when he fled from Egypt, and gave him his daughter Zipporah (Ex. 2:18; Nu. 10:29). **3.** Father of Eliasaph of Gad, a commander under Moses (Nu. 1:14; 2:14; 7:42, 47; 10:20). **4.** A Benjaminite chief living at Jerusalem under Solomon (1 Ch. 9:8). J.P.U.L.

REVELATION.

I. The idea of revelation

The Eng. word 'reveal', from Lat. *revelo*, is the regular rendering of the Heb. *gālâ* and the Gk. *apokalyptō* (noun, *apokalypsis*), which corresponds to *gālâ* in the LXX and NT. *gālâ*, *apokalyptō* and *revelo* all express the same idea—that of unveiling something hidden, so that it may be seen and known for what it is. Accordingly, when the Bible speaks of revelation, the thought intended is of God the Creator actively disclosing to men his power and glory, his nature and character, his will, ways and plans—in short, himself—in order that men may know him. The revelation vocabulary in both Testaments is a wide one, covering the ideas of making obscure things clear, bringing hidden things to light, showing signs, speaking words and causing the persons addressed to see, hear, perceive, understand and know. None of the OT words is a specifically theological term—each one has its profane usage—but in the NT *apokalyptō* and *apokalypsis* are used only in theological contexts, and the ordinary profane use of them does not appear, even where one might have expected it (*cf.* 2 Cor. 3:13ff.); which suggests that for the NT writers both terms possessed quasi-technical status.

Other NT words expressing the idea of revelation are *phaneroō*, 'manifest, make clear'; *epiphainō*, 'show forth' (noun, *epiphaineia*, 'manifestation'); *deiknuō*, 'show'; *exēgeomai*, 'unfold, explain, by narration', *cf.* Jn. 1:18; *chrēmatizō*, 'instruct, admonish, warn' (used in secular Gk. of divine oracles, *cf.* Arndt, *MM*, *s.v.*; noun, *chrēmatismos*, 'answer of God', Rom. 11:4).

From the standpoint of its contents, divine revelation is both indicative and imperative, and in each respect normative. God's disclosures are always made in the context of a demand for trust in, and obedience to, what is revealed—a response, that is, which is wholly determined and controlled by the contents of the revelation itself. In other words, God's revelation comes to man, not as information without obligation, but as a mandatory rule of faith and conduct. Man's life must be governed, not by private whims and fancies, nor by guesses as to divine things unrevealed, but by reverent belief of as much as God has told him, leading to conscientious compliance with as many imperatives as the revelation proves to contain (Dt. 29:29).

Revelation has two focal points: (1) God's purposes; (2) God's person.

1. On the one hand, God tells men about himself—who he is, what he has done, is doing and will do, and what he requires them to do. Thus he took Noah, Abraham and Moses into his confidence, telling them what he had planned and what their part in his plan was to be (Gn. 6:13–21; 12:1ff.; 15:13–21; 17:15–21; 18:17ff.; Ex. 3:7–22). Again, he declared to Israel the laws and promises of his covenant (Ex. 20–23, *etc.*; Dt. 4:13f.; 28, *etc.*; Pss. 78:5ff.; 147:19). He disclosed his purposes to the prophets (Am. 3:7). Christ told his disciples 'all that I have heard from my Father' (Jn. 15:15), and promised them the Holy Spirit to complete his work of instructing them (Jn. 16:12ff.). God revealed to Paul the 'mystery' of his eternal purpose in Christ (Eph. 1:9ff.; 3:3–11). Christ revealed to John 'what must soon take place' (Rev. 1:1). From this standpoint, as God's own precise disclosure of his saving purpose and work, Paul calls the gospel 'the truth', in contrast with error and falsehood (2 Thes. 2:11–13; 2 Tim. 2:18; *etc.*). Hence the use of the phrase 'revealed truth' in Christian theology to denote what God has told men about himself.

2. On the other hand, when God sends men his word, he also confronts them with himself. The Bible does not think of revelation as a mere broadcasting of information, divinely guaranteed, but as God's personal coming to individuals to make himself known to them (*cf.* Gn. 35:7; Ex. 6:3; Nu. 12:6–8; Gal. 1:15f.). This is the lesson to be learnt from the theophanies of the OT (*cf.* Ex. 3:2ff.; 19:11–20; Ezk. 1; *etc.*), and from the part played by the enigmatic 'angel (messenger) of Yahweh', who is so evidently a manifestation of Yahweh himself (*cf.* Gn. 16:10; Ex. 3:2ff.; Jdg. 13:9–23): the lesson, namely, that God is not only the author and subject of his messages to men but he is also his own messenger. When a man meets God's word, however casual and accidental the meeting may seem to be, God meets that man, addressing the word to him personally and calling for a personal response to himself as its Author.

Speaking generally, the older Protestant theologians analysed revelation in terms entirely of God's communicating truths about himself. They knew, of course, that God ordered biblical history and that he now enlightens men to accept the biblical message, but they dealt with the former under the heading of providence and the latter under the heading of illumination, and did not formally relate their concept of revelation to either The focal centre of their doctrine of revelation was the Bible; they viewed Holy Scripture as revealed truth in writing, and revelation as the divine activity that led to its production. They correlated revelation with inspiration, defining the former as God's communication to the biblical writers of otherwise inaccessible truth about himself, and the latter as his enabling them to write it all down truly, according to his will. (This formulation evidently has its roots in the book of Daniel: *cf.* Dn. 2:19, 22, 28ff., 47; 7:1; 10:1; 12:4.)

Many modern theologians, reacting against this view under pressure of a supposed need to abandon the notion of Scripture as revealed truth, speak of revelation wholly in terms of God's directing biblical history and making individuals aware of his presence, activity and claims. The focal centre of the doctrine of revelation is thus shifted to the redemptive history which the Bible records. With this commonly goes the assertion that there is, properly speaking, no such thing as communicated truth ('propositional revelation') from God; revelation is essentially non-verbal in character. But this is to say in effect that the biblical idea of God *speaking* (the commonest and most fundamental revelatory act which Scripture ascribes to him) is only a misleading metaphor; which seems implausible. On these grounds, it is further held that the Bible is not, properly speaking, revelation, but a human response to revelation. This, however, seems unbiblical, since the NT uniformly quotes OT statements—prophetic, poetic, legal, historical, factual and admonitory—as authoritative utterances of God (*cf.* Mt. 19:4f.; Acts 4:25f.; Heb. 1:5ff.; 3:7ff.; *etc.*). The biblical view is that God reveals himself by both deeds and words: first by ordering redemptive history, then by inspiring a written explanatory record of that history to make later generations 'wise unto salvation' (*cf.* 2 Tim. 3:15ff.; 1 Cor. 10:11; Rom. 15:4), and finally by enlightening men in every age to discern the significance and acknowledge the authority of the revelation thus given and recorded (*cf.* Mt. 16:17; 2 Cor. 4:6). Thus, the positive emphases in the two sets of ideas contrasted above are complementary rather than contradictory; both must be combined in order to cover the full range of the biblical concept of revelation.

II. The necessity of revelation

The Bible assumes throughout that God must first disclose himself before men can know him. The Aristotelian idea of an inactive God whom man can discover by following out an argument is quite unbiblical. A revelatory initiative is needed, first, because *God is transcendent.* He is so far from man in his mode of being that man cannot see him (Jn. 1:18; 1 Tim. 6:16; *cf.* Ex. 33:20), nor find him out by searching (*cf.* Jb. 11:7; 23:3–9), nor read his thoughts by shrewd guesswork (Is. 55:8f.). Even if man had not sinned, therefore, he could not have known God without revelation. In fact, we read of God speaking to unfallen Adam in Eden (Gn. 2:16). Now, however, there is a second reason why man's knowledge of God must depend on God's revelatory initiative. *Man is sinful.* His powers of perception in the realm of divine things have been so dulled by Satan (2 Cor. 4:4) and sin (*cf.* 1 Cor. 2:14), and his mind is so prepossessed by his own fancied 'wisdom', which runs contrary to the true knowledge of God (Rom. 1:21ff.; 1 Cor. 1:21), that it is beyond his natural powers to apprehend God, however presented to him. In fact, according to Paul, God presents himself constantly to every man through his works of creation and providence (Rom. 1:19ff.; Acts 14:17; *cf.* Ps. 19:1ff.), and the spontaneous operations of natural conscience (Rom. 2:12–15; *cf.* 1:32); yet he is not recognized or known. The pressure of this continual self-disclosure on God's part produces idolatry, as the fallen mind in its perversity seeks to quench the light by turning it into darkness (Rom. 1:23ff.; *cf.* Jn. 1:5), but it does not lead to knowledge of God, or to godliness of life. God's 'general revelation' (as it is usually called) of his eternity, power and glory (Rom. 1:20; *cf.* Ps. 19:1), his kindness to men (Acts 14:17), his moral law (Rom. 2:12ff.), his demand for worship and obedience (Rom. 1:21) and his wrath against sin (Rom. 1:18, 32), thus serve only to render men 'without excuse' for their 'ungodliness and wickedness' (Rom. 1:18–20).

This shows that fallen man's need of revelation goes beyond Adam's in two respects. First, he needs a revelation of God as a redeemer and restorer, one who shows mercy to sinners. God's revelation through creation and conscience speaks of law and judgment (Rom. 2:14f.; 1:32), but not of forgiveness. Second, supposing that God grants such a revelation (the Bible is one long proclamation that he does), fallen man still needs spiritual enlightenment before he can grasp it; otherwise he will pervert it, as he has perverted natural revelation. The Jews had a revelation of mercy in the OT, which pointed them to Christ, but on most of their hearts there was a veil which kept them from understanding it (2 Cor. 3:14ff.), and so they fell victim to a legalistic misconception of it (Rom. 9:31–10:4). Even Paul, who calls attention to these facts, had himself known the Christian gospel before his conversion—and tried to stamp it out; not till 'it pleased God . . . to reveal his Son in me'—*in*, by inward enlightenment—did Paul recognize it as the word of God. The need of divine enlightening to reveal to individuals the reality, authority and meaning of revelation objectively given, and to conform their lives to it, is occasionally indicated in the OT (Ps. 119:12, 27, *etc.*; Je. 31:33f.); in the NT it is stressed most by Paul and in the recorded teaching of Christ (Mt. 11:25; 13:11–17; Jn. 3:3ff.; 6:44f., 63ff.; 8:43–47; 10:26ff.; *cf.* 12:37ff.).

III. The content of revelation

a. Old Testament

The foundation and framework of Israel's religious outlook was the covenant which God announced between himself and Abraham's seed (Gn. 17:1ff.). A *covenant is a defined relationship of promise and obligation binding two parties together. This covenant was a royal imposition whereby God pledged himself to Abraham's clan as *their* God, thus authorizing them to invoke him as *our* God and *my* God.

The fact that God made known his name (Yahweh) to Israel (Ex. 3:11–15; 6:2ff.; on the exegesis, *cf.* J. A. Motyer, *The Revelation of the Divine Name*, 1960) was a witness to this relationship. The 'name' stands for all that a person is, and for God to tell the Israelites his name was a sign that, such as he was, in all his power and glory, he was pledging himself to them for their welfare. The goal of his relationship with Israel was the perfecting of the relationship itself: that is, that God should bless Abraham's seed with the fullness of his gifts, and that Abraham's seed should perfectly bless God by a perfect worship and obedience. Hence God continued to reveal himself to the covenant community by his words of law and promise, and by his redemptive deeds as Lord of history for the realizing of this covenant eschatology.

God made the royal character of his covenant more explicit at Sinai, where, having dramatically shown his saving power in the Exodus from Egypt, he was formally acknowledged as Israel's Sovereign (Ex. 19:3–8; Dt. 33:4f.), and through the mouth of Moses, the archetypal prophet (*cf.* Dt. 18:15), promulgated the laws of the covenant, making it clear that enjoyment of covenant blessing was conditional upon obedience to them (Ex. 19:5; *cf.* Lv. 26:3ff.; Dt. 28). These laws were committed to writing, the Decalogue in the first instance by God himself (Ex. 24:12; 31:18; 32:15f.), the whole code eventually by Moses, as, in effect, God's amanuensis (Ex. 34:27f.; Dt. 31:9ff., 24ff.; *cf.* Ex. 24:7). It is noteworthy that God through Hosea later spoke of the entire work of writing the law as his own work, though tradition was unanimous that Moses did it (Ho. 8:12); here are some of the roots of the idea of biblical *inspiration. The law, once written, was regarded as a definitive and permanently valid disclosure of God's will for his people's life, and the priests were made permanently responsible for teaching it (Dt. 31:9ff.; *cf.* Ne. 8:1ff.; Hg. 2:11f.; Mal. 2:7f.).

God forbade Israelites to practise sorcery and divination for day-to-day guidance, as the Canaanites did (Dt. 18:9ff.); they were to seek guidance from him only (Is. 8:19). He promised them a succession of prophets, men in whose mouths he would put his own words (Dt. 18:18; *cf.* Je. 1:9; 5:14; Ezk. 2:7–3:11; Nu. 22:35, 38; 23:5), to give his people such periodic direction as they needed (Dt. 18:15ff.). Prophets in Israel fulfilled a vital ministry. The great prophets, at Yahweh's bidding, spoke God's words and interpreted his mind to kings and to the nation; they expounded and applied his law, pleading for repentance and threatening judgment in his name, and they declared what he would do, both in judgment and also in fulfilling the covenant eschatology by bringing in his kingdom after the judgment was over. And prophets may also have had a place in the cult as seers, men who could give answers from God to individuals who asked particular questions about guidance and the future (*cf.* 1 Sa. 9:6ff.; 28:6–20; 1 Ki. 22:5ff.; see A. R. Johnson, *The Cultic Prophet in Ancient Israel*, 1944). A further means of guidance in pre-exilic Israel was the sacred lot, *Urim and Thummim, manipulated by the priests (Dt. 33:8ff.; *cf.* 1 Sa. 14:36–42; 28:6). Divine guidance for life of a more general sort was supplied also by the maxims of the 'wise men', whose wisdom was held to be from God (*cf.* Pr. 1:20; 8).

In addition to these arrangements for verbal or quasi-verbal communication from God, Israel knew certain theophanic and experimental manifestations which betokened the nearness of God: the *'glory' (*cf.* Ex. 16:10; 40:34; Nu. 16:19; 1 Ki. 8:10f.; Ezk. 1, *etc.*); the thunderstorm (Pss. 18:6–15; 29); the sight of his 'face' and the joyful awareness of his 'presence' to which faithful worshippers aspired (Pss. 11:7; 16:11; 17:15; 51:11f.).

The chief emphases in the OT revelation of God are upon:
(*a*) God's uniqueness, as the Maker and Ruler of all things;
(*b*) his *holiness, *i.e.* the conjunction of awesome characteristics which set him apart from men—majesty and greatness and strength, on the one hand, and purity and love of righteousness and hatred of wrongdoing, on the other;
(*c*) his covenant faithfulness and patience and mercy, and his loyalty to his own gracious purposes towards the covenant people.

b. New Testament

In the NT Christ and the apostles are organs of new revelation, corresponding to Moses and the prophets in the OT. The fulfilment of OT covenant eschatology is found in the kingdom of Christ and the Christian hope of glory. The one God of the OT is revealed as Triune, by the coming first of Christ and then of the Spirit, and the disclosing of the divine redemptive purpose as one in which all three Persons of the Godhead work together (*cf.* Eph. 1:3–14; Rom. 8). Two events which will bring God's plan of human history to its climax are spoken of as acts of revelation still to come (the appearing of antichrist, 2 Thes. 2:3, 6, 8, and of Christ, 1 Cor. 1:7; 2 Thes. 1:7–10; 1 Pet. 1:7, 13). The NT claims that the revelation of the OT has been augmented along two chief lines.

(i) *The revelation of God in Christ.* The NT proclaims that 'God . . . in these last days . . . has spoken to us by a Son' (Heb. 1:1f.). This is God's crowning and final revelation, his last word to man. By his words and works, and by the over-all character of his life and ministry, Jesus Christ perfectly revealed God (Jn. 1:18; 14:7–11). His personal life was a perfect revelation of the character of God; for the Son is the image of God (2 Cor. 4:4; Col. 1:15; Heb. 1:3), his *logos* ('word', regarded as expressing his mind, Jn. 1:1ff.), in whom, as incarnate, all the divine fullness dwelt (Col. 1:19; 2:9). Equally, his Messianic work revealed perfectly the saving purposes of God; for Christ is the wisdom of God (1 Cor 1:24), through whom, as Mediator (1 Tim. 2:5), all God's saving purposes are worked out and all the wisdom that man needs for his salvation may be found (Col. 2:3; 1 Cor. 1:30; 2:6f.). The revelation of the Father by the Son, whom the Jews condemned as an impostor and blasphemer for declaring his Sonship, is a major theme of John's Gospel.

(ii) *The revelation of God's plan through Christ.* Paul declares that the 'mystery' (secret) of God's 'good pleasure' for the saving of the church and the restoring of the cosmos through Christ is now revealed, after having been kept hidden up to the time of the incarnation (Rom. 16:25f.; 1 Cor. 2:7–10; Eph. 1:9ff.; 3:3–11; Col. 1:19ff.). He shows how this revelation abolishes the old wall of partition between Jew and Gentile (Rom. 3:29ff.; 9–11; Gal. 2:15–3:29; Eph. 2:11–3:6); similarly, the writer to the Hebrews shows how it abolishes the old priestly and sacrificial Jewish cultus (Heb. 7–10).

IV. The nature of revelation

It is clear from the foregoing that the Bible conceives of revelation as primarily and fundamentally verbal communication—God's *tôrâ* ('teaching, instruction, law'), or *d^e^ḇārîm* ('words'), in the OT, and his *logos* or *rhēma*, 'word, utterance', in the NT. The thought of God as revealed in his actions is secondary, and depends for its validity on the presupposition of verbal revelation. For men can 'know that he is Yahweh' from seeing his works in history only if he speaks to make it clear that they are his works, and to explain what they mean. Equally, men could never have guessed or deduced who and what Jesus of Nazareth was, apart from God's statements about him in the OT, and Jesus' own self-testimony (*cf.* Jn. 5:37–39; 8:13–18). (*INSPIRATION, *PROPHECY.)

BIBLIOGRAPHY. Arndt; A. Oepke, *TDNT* 3, pp. 563–592; C. F. D. Moule, *IDB*, 4, pp. 54–58; B. B. Warfield, *The Inspiration and Authority of the Bible*, 1951; H. H. Rowley, *The Faith of Israel*, 1956; L. Köhler, *Old Testament Theology* E.T. 1953; H. W. Robinson, *Inspiration and Revelation in the Old Testament*, 1946; E. F. Scott, *Revelation in the New Testament*,

1935; J. Orr, *Revelation and Inspiration*, 1910; B. Ramm, *Special Revelation and the Word of God*, 1961; G. C. Berkouwer, *General Revelation*, 1955. J.I.P.

REVELATION, BOOK OF. The last book of the Bible is, for most Christians, one of the least read and most difficult. A few passages from it are well known and well loved (*e.g.* 7:9–17); but for the most part modern readers find the book unintelligible. This is largely because it abounds in symbolism of a type that we do not use and to which we no longer possess the key. Yet this kind of imagery was readily comprehensible to the men of the day. Indeed, this partly accounts for our difficulties. The author could assume that his readers would detect his allusions, and therefore he felt no need to make explanations.

Revelation is classed with the literature known as *apocalyptic. It is the only book of this type in the NT, though there are apocalyptic passages in other books (*e.g.* Mt. 24), and the OT visions of Daniel belong to the same class. Characteristic of apocalyptic is the thought that God is sovereign, and that ultimately he will intervene in catastrophic fashion to bring to pass his good and perfect will. He is opposed by powerful and varied forces of evil, and these are usually referred to symbolically as beasts, horns, *etc.* There are visions; angels speak; there is the clash of mighty forces; and ultimately the persecuted saints are vindicated. Much of this is conventional (which is why the first readers of Revelation would have understood it quite easily), but in the hands of many enthusiasts it led to turgid and grotesque phantasies. Biblical apocalyptic is much more restrained.

Another difference between Revelation and the usual run of apocalyptic is that the author's name is given, whereas apocalypses were usually pseudonymous. The writers took names from the great ones of the past and ascribed their works to them. For our present purpose it is important to notice that in this book the Holy Spirit has made use of a recognized literary form, but that the book is not simply a conventional apocalypse. It has features of its own, and is a genuine prophecy, as the first three verses indicate.

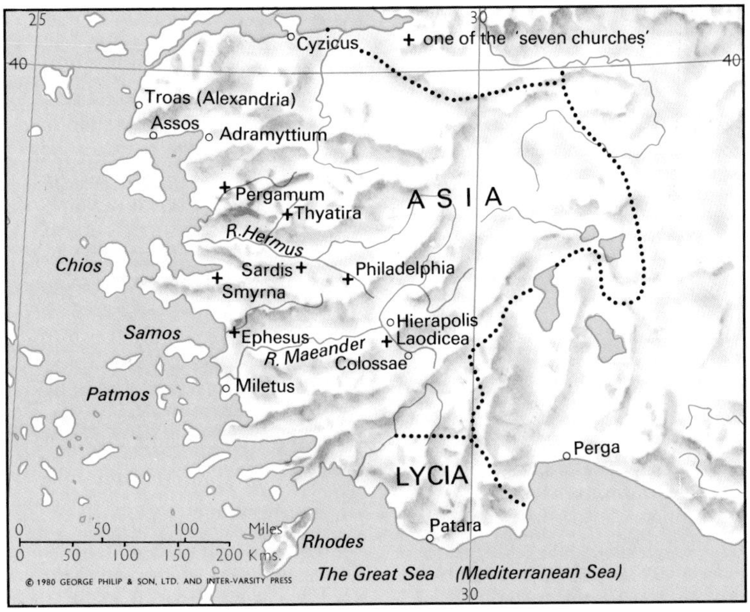

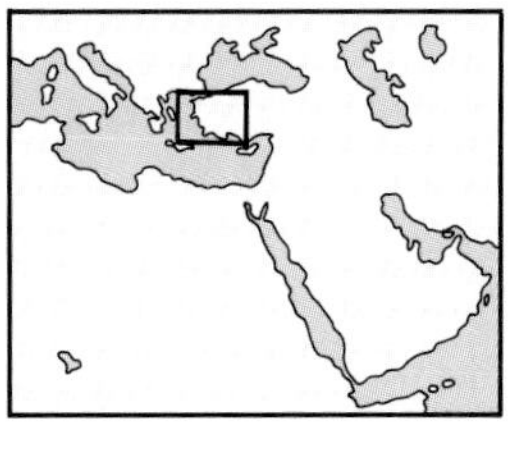

The 'seven churches of Asia' of Rev. 1–3 and the island of Patmos where John received the revelation.

I. Outline of contents

The book begins with a vision of the risen Lord, who gives messages to seven churches, those in Ephesus, Smyrna, Pergamum, Thyatira, Sardis, Philadelphia and Laodicea, a group of cities in the Roman province of Asia (1:1–3:22). The messages rebuke these churches where they have failed and encourage them on the path of Christian service. Then come visions of God and of the Lamb (4:1–5:14), after which we read of the 7 seals. As each seal is opened there is a vision recorded (6:1–17; 8:1). This leads on to the 7 trumpets, with a vision recorded after each trumpet is sounded (8:2–9:21; 11:15–19). Between the 6th and 7th seals there is an interlude (7:1–17), and another between the 6th and 7th trumpets (10:1–11:14). John then records various wonders in heaven, a woman bringing forth a man child, and opposed by Satan (12:1–17), beasts opposing themselves to God (13:1–18), the Lamb on Mount Zion and his followers (14:1–20). Next the 7 last plagues are recounted. John sees 7 angels with bowls, and as each pours out his bowl upon the earth one of the plagues follows (15:1–16:21). Further judgments are then denounced on the scarlet woman and on Babylon (17:1–19:21), and the book concludes with visions of the millennium, of the new heavens and the new earth (20:1–22:21).

It is uncertain how much of the book duplicates other sections. The recurrence of the number 7 makes it fairly clear that some, at least, of the series are described in more than one way. What is certain is that the book envisages terrific opposition to God and the people of God, but that in the end God will triumph over every evil thing.

Greek papyrus of the book of Revelation (12:12–13:1). 3rd cent. AD. (CBL)

II. Authorship and date

The author tells us that his name was John, and he describes himself as God's 'servant' (Rev. 1:1), as one of the 'prophets' (Rev. 22:9) and as 'your brother' (Rev. 1:9). Tradition has affirmed this John to be identical with John the apostle, and further, that he was the author of the Fourth Gospel and of the three Johannine Epistles. The view that the author was John the apostle goes back to Justin Martyr (*c.* AD 140), and is supported by Irenaeus and many others. The principal objection is the style of Revelation. The Greek is in many respects unlike that of the other Johannine writings. It is so unusual and sometimes shows such scant respect for the rules of Gk. grammar that it is felt that it cannot come from the same pen as do the Gospel and the Epistles. (Charles speaks of it as 'unlike any Greek that was ever penned by mortal man'.) The question is too intricate to be discussed fully here. Suffice to say that, whereas most scholars today deny the apostolic authorship, there are some who find it best to think of all five Johannine writings as from one author, and that author the apostle John (*e.g.* E. Stauffer).

The book was obviously written at a time when the church was undergoing persecution and difficulty. During the possible time for the composition of the book the two most important periods when this was so were during the reigns of Nero and of Domitian. The principal argument for the former date is Rev. 17:9f., 'This calls for a mind with wisdom: the seven heads are seven mountains on which the woman is seated; they are also seven kings, five of whom have fallen, one is, the other has not yet come.' If this refers to the emperors of Rome, then Nero was the fifth, and the writing would date from shortly after his reign. This is strengthened by the prophecy that 'the beast that was and is not, it is an eighth but it belongs to the seven' (Rev. 17:11). This appears to refer to the 'Nero *redivivus*' myth, the idea that Nero, though dead, would appear once more on this earth. Support is adduced from Rev. 13:18, which gives 'the number of the beast' as 666. Numbers were written in the 1st century, not with our convenient notation, but with letters of the alphabet. Each letter had a numerical value. By taking the numerical values of the letters making up 'Nero Caesar' in Hebrew we get 666. But it is difficult to see why it should be in Hebrew (when the book is in Greek), and anyway to get the desired result a variant spelling has to be adopted.

The later date is attested by a number of ancient authors, such as Irenaeus and Eusebius, who state categorically that the book was written in the time of Domitian. This is supported by certain indications of a general type within the book, though not by specific allusions to identifiable events. Thus the book speaks of certain groups of Christians as complacent and declining in spirituality. In Nero's reign the church was still very young and vigorous. By the time of Domitian there is much more possibility of development and of degeneration. Most scholars today are agreed that the later date is to be preferred.

III. Interpretation

How are we to understand all this? Four chief ways of looking at the book have emerged in the Christian church.

a. The preterist view

This takes the book to describe past events. It sees all the visions as arising out of conditions in the Roman empire of the 1st century AD. The seer was appalled at the possibilities for evil inherent in the Roman empire and he used symbolic imagery to protest against it, and to record his conviction that God would intervene to bring about what pleased him. In general, liberal scholars endorse this point of view. It enables them to understand the book without finding much place for predictive prophecy, and at the same time to see in Revelation a much-needed assertion of the truth of God's moral government of the world. Such a view roots the book in the circumstances of the writer's own day, which is surely right. But it overlooks the fact that the book calls itself a 'prophecy' (Rev. 1:3), and that some at any rate of its predictions refer to what is still future (*e.g.* chs. 21–22).

b. The historicist view

This regards the book as setting forth in one grand sweep a panoramic view of history from the 1st century to the second coming of Christ. The writer's own day is mentioned, and so is the final time, but there is no indication of a break anywhere. Therefore, upholders of such views reason, the book must be held to give a continuous story of the whole period. Such views were held by most of the Reformers, who identified papal Rome with the beast. But the difficulties seem insuperable, and it is significant that, while stoutly maintaining that all history is here set forth, historicists have not been able to agree among themselves as to the precise episodes in history which the various visions symbolize. In 1,900 years at least the main outlines should have emerged with clarity. It is also difficult to see why the outline of history should confine itself to W Europe, especially since in earlier days at least much of the expansion of Christianity was in E lands.

c. The futurist view

This maintains that from ch. 4 onwards Revelation deals with events at the end-time. The book is not concerned with the prophet's own day, nor with later historical events, but with those happenings that will take place in connection with the second coming of the Lord. This view takes seriously the predictive element in the book (Rev. 1:19; 4:1). And it has in its favour the fact that Revelation undeniably leads up to the final establishment of the rule of God, so that some of the book must refer to the last days. The principal objection is that this view tends to remove the book entirely from its historical setting. It is not easy to see what meaning it would have had for its first readers if this is the way it is to be understood.

d. The idealist or the poetic view

This insists that the main thrust of the book is concerned with inspiring persecuted and suffering Christians to endure to the end. To bring about this aim the writer has employed symbolic language, not meaning it to be taken for anything other than a series of imaginative descriptions of the triumph of God. Such views can be linked with other views, and are often found, for example, in combination with preterist ideas. The difficulty is that the seer does claim to be prophesying of later days.

None of the views has proved completely satisfying, and it is probable that a true view would combine elements from more than one of them. The outstanding merit of preterist views is that they give the book meaning for the men of the day in which it was written, and, whatever else we may say of the book, this insight must be retained. Historicist views similarly see the book as giving light on the church throughout its history, and this cannot be surrendered. Futurist views take with the greatest seriousness the language of the book about the end-time. The book does emphasize the ultimate triumph of God and the events associated with it. Nor can the idealist view be abandoned, for the book does bring before us a stirring challenge to live for God in days when the opposition is fierce. Moreover, the Christian must always welcome the assurance that God's triumph is sure.

BIBLIOGRAPHY. Commentaries by H. B. Swete, 1906; R. H. Charles, *ICC*, 1920; M. Kiddle, *MNT*, 1940; A. Farrer, 1964; L. Morris, *TNTC*, 1969; G. E. Ladd, 1972; G. R. Beasley-Murray, 1974; N. B. Stonehouse, *The Apocalypse in the Ancient Church*, 1929; W. M. Ramsay, *Letters to the Seven Churches in Asia*, 1909; W. Hendriksen, *More than Conquerors*, 1962; M. Wilcock, *I saw heaven opened*, 1975; M. C. Tenney, *Interpreting Revelation*, 1957; D. T. Niles, *As Seeing the Invisible*, 1962. The literature is enormous; most of the books here listed have extensive bibliographies. L.M.

REWARD. Thirteen Heb. roots, of which *śāḵār* and *šōḥaḏ* are the chief, lie behind OT expressions of 'reward'. In Gk. the verb *apodidōmi* and noun *misthos* are used. All convey the meaning of payment, hire or wages, and there are instances of 'reward' as pay for honest work done (1 Tim. 5:18) and dishonest gain, *i.e.* bribe (Mi. 3:11).

1. Any reward depends for its significance upon the character of its bestower, and God's rewards, with which the biblical writers are chiefly concerned, both as blessings and as punishments, are manifestations of his justice, *i.e.* of himself (*e.g.* Ps. 58:11) and inseparable from the covenant (Dt. 7:10) to which his commands are annexed. Thus the second commandment relates the penalty of disobedience to the jealousy of God, and the reward of obedience to his mercy (Ex. 20:5). Dt. 28 explains Israel's well-being in terms of submission to the covenant, a theme developed by the later prophets (*e.g.* Is. 65:6–7; 66:6). That obedience to God will bring visible temporal rewards is rightly expected throughout the Bible, but two false conclusions were also drawn from such teaching as Dt. 28, namely (i) that righteousness is automatically rewarded materially, and (ii) that suffering is a certain sign of sin (Job; Pss. 37; 73, all reflect the tension created by these false deductions, and Ec. 8:14 marks an extreme cynicism). Yet it must be noted that in the OT God himself and his salvation are already known to be the supreme reward (Is. 62:10–12; Ps. 63:3), rather than his gifts.

2. Jesus promised rewards to his disciples (Mk. 9:41; 10:29; Mt. 5:3–12), so coupled with self-denial and suffering for the gospel's sake as to prevent a mercenary attitude. He slew the Pharisaic notion of meritorious service (Lk. 17:10) and discouraged desire for human reward (Mt. 6:1), since the Father is the disciple's best reward. Jesus shows that reward is inseparable from himself and from God, and the apostles laboured to establish the complete dependence of man's obedience and faith upon mercy and grace (Rom. 4:4; 6:23). Work, and therefore reward, is certainly looked for, but simply as an index of living faith (Jas. 2:14–16; Jn. 6:28), not as a basis of claim upon God. The reward of salvation in Christ begins in time (2 Cor. 5:5) and its fulfilment is looked for after *judgment (final rewards and punishments) when the covenant people enter into full enjoyment of the vision of God which is their enduring reward (Rev. 21:3).

BIBLIOGRAPHY. Arndt (*s.v. misthos*); J.-J. von Allmen, *Vocabulary of the Bible*, 1958 (*s.v.* 'reward'); *TWBR* (*s.v.* 'reward'); K. E. Kirk, *The Vision of God* (abridged version), 1934, pp. 69–76; P. C. Böttger *et al.*, *NIDNTT* 3, pp. 134–145. M.R.W.F.

REZEPH. A town destroyed by the Assyrians and named in a letter to Hezekiah sent by Sennacherib as a warning to Jerusalem of the fate of those cities who resisted their demands for surrender (2 Ki. 19:12 = Is. 37:12). The details of any revolt or sack of Assyr. Raṣappa are not known, though Assyr. texts mention the town and name several governors in the years 839–673 BC. This important caravan-centre on the route from the Euphrates to Hamath was identified by Ptolemy (5. 16; Gk. *Rhēsapha*) and is the modern *Reṣāfa*, about 200 km ENE of Hama, Syria. D.J.W.

REZIN. The king of *Damascus who, in alliance with *Pekah of Samaria, threatened *Ahaz of Judah (2 Ki. 15:37; 16:5). Their aim was probably to form an anti-Assyrian front, but in fact they drove Ahaz into alliance with Assyria, despite Isaiah's advice that Rezin was not to be feared (Is. 7:1, 8; 8:6). *Tiglath-pileser III listed Rezin as tributary about 738 BC, but captured Damascus and killed him in 732 BC (2 Ki. 16:9). See M. Weippert, *ZDPV* 89, 1973, pp. 26–53 (pp. 46f. for form of the name). A.R.M.

REZON. The son of Eliadah, who fled with a band of followers when David attacked Hadadezer of Zobah (1 Ki. 11:23–24). He occupied Damascus and became its ruler, opposing Israel during the reign of Solomon in alliance with Hadad of Edom (v. 25). He later 'reigned over Syria', and is thus thought to have outlived the united Hebrew monarchy and to be identified with Hezion, father of Tab-Rimmon and grandfather of *Ben-hadad I, the king of *Damascus, with whom Asa of Judah made an alliance (1 Ki. 15:18). If this is correct, Rezon was the founder of the dynasty of *Aram who opposed Israel. Rezon (and Rezin) may be a title meaning 'prince' (*cf.* Pr. 14:28).

BIBLIOGRAPHY. M. F. Unger, *Israel and the Aramaeans of Damascus*, 1957. D.J.W.

RHEGIUM. The modern Reggio di Calabria, a port-city on the Italian shore of the Strait of Messina, in S Italy. An old Gk. colony, Rhegium owed its importance under the Roman empire to its position in relation to the navigation of the Strait and the Italian W coast. With the whirlpool of Charybdis and the rock of Scylla endangering navigation through the Strait, it was important to attempt the passage only with the most favourable sailing wind, and shipping moving N would wait at Rhegium for a S wind. This was done by the master of the ship which was taking Paul to Rome (Acts 28:13). J.H.P.

RHODA (Gk. *rhodē*, 'rose'). A slave-girl in the house of John Mark's mother who announced Peter's arrival (Acts 12:13ff.) after the angel had released him from prison. See *BRD*, pp. 209ff. J.D.D.

REVENGE
See Avenger of blood, Part 1.

REVERENTIAL AWE
See Fear, Part 1.

REVILE
See Blasphemy, Part 1.

REVISED STANDARD VERSION
See English versions of the Bible, Part 1.

REVISED VERSION
See English versions of the Bible, Part 1.

RHAIPHAN
See Rephan, Part 3.

RHEMPHAM
See Rephan, Part 3.

Kamiros, on the W coast, was the second city of ancient Rhodes. The excavated remains include Hellenistic houses, a temple and stoa of the 3rd cent. BC. (RH)

RIE, RYE
See Grain, Part 2.

RHODES. The large island extending towards Crete from the SW extremity of Asia Minor, and thus lying across the main sea route between the Aegean and the Phoenician ports. It was partitioned among three Gk. states, of Dorian stock, early federated and sharing a common capital at the NE point of the island. It was this city, also called Rhodes, that Paul touched at on his last journey to Palestine (Acts 21:1). After Alexander's conquests, and the establishment of the Macedonian kingdoms and many Hellenized states throughout the E periphery of the Mediterranean, Rhodes grew to be the leading Gk. republic, outstripping those of the old homeland. This was not only because she was now the natural clearing-house for the greatly increased E–W traffic, but because her position gave her an effective diplomatic leverage against the pressures of the rival kingdoms who disputed the hegemony of the strategic Aegean islands. As the champion of the old autonomy principle, she took the lead in calling for Roman intervention to protect it. Rhodes fell from favour with the Romans, however, who deliberately advanced Delos to destroy her ascendancy. By Paul's time her importance was gone, except as a resort of mellow distinction in learning and leisure.

BIBLIOGRAPHY. M. Rostovtzeff, *CAH*, 8, pp. 619–642. E.A.J.

RIBLAH, RIBLATH. 1. A place in the district of Hamath, on the river Orontes in Syria, on the right bank of which are ruins near a modern village, Ribleh, 56 km NE of Baalbek and S of Hama. The site is easily defended and commands the main route from Egypt to the Euphrates as well as the neighbouring forests and valleys, from which ample supplies of food or fuel are obtained. For such reasons Riblah was chosen by Neco II as the Egyp. headquarters, following his defeat of Josiah at Megiddo and the sack of Qadesh in 609 BC. Here he deposed Jehoahaz, imposed tribute on Judah and appointed Jehoiakim its king (2 Ki. 23:31–35). When Nebuchadrezzar II defeated the Egyptians at Carchemish and Hamath in 605 BC he likewise chose Riblah as his military base for the subjugation of Palestine. From it he directed operations against Jerusalem in 589–587 BC, and here was brought the rebel Zedekiah to be blinded after watching the death of his sons (2 Ki. 25:6, 20–21; Je. 39:5–7; 52:9–27). The AV Diblath (RV 'Diblah') of Ezk. 6:14 may be the same place (see RSV), since an otherwise unknown situation is unlikely in the context.

2. Riblath at the NE corner of the ideal boundary of Israel (Nu. 34:11) might be the same place as **1**, though the border is generally considered to lie farther S (*cf.* Ezk. 47:15–18). The suggestion commonly adopted, that this is to be read 'to Harbel' (LXX), modern Harmel in the Beqa', helps little in evaluating the border, since this place lies only 13 km SW of Riblah **1** itself. D.J.W.

RIGHTEOUSNESS (Heb. *ṣeḏeq*, *ṣᵉḏāqâ*; Gk. LXX and NT, *dikaiosynē*). The Heb. *ṣeḏeq* probably derives from an Arab. root meaning 'straightness', leading to the notion of an action which conforms to a norm. There is, however, a considerable richness in the biblical understanding of this term and it is difficult to render either the Heb. or Gk. words concerned by a simple Eng. equivalent. One basic ingredient in the OT idea of righteousness is relationship, both between God and man (Ps. 50:6; Je. 9:24) and between man and man (Dt. 24:13; Je. 22:3).

Referred to relations between men, righteous action is action which conforms to the requirements of the relationship and in a more general sense promotes the well-being and peace of the community (1 Sa. 24:17; Pr. 14:34). It is therefore linked in a forensic sense with *justice though even then the idea is less that of conformity to some formal legal norm as the strongly ethical notion of action which is to be legally upheld because it is productive of communal well-being (Dt. 1:16; Am. 5:7). In the prophetic period righteousness comes to include the idea of helping the poor and needy (Dn. 4:27; Am. 5:12, 24), and hence almsgiving (Mt. 6:1f.).

When we move from relations between men to those between God and men (though this distinction is arguably somewhat formal since the thought of God was probably never completely absent whenever the Hebrew used the word *ṣeḏeq*) righteousness implies a correct relationship to the will of God which was particularly expressed and interpreted by Israel's covenant with God. Righteous action is hence action which flows out of God's gracious election of Israel and accords with the law of the covenant (Dt. 6:25; Ezk. 18:5–9). God himself is righteous (2 Ch. 12:6; Ps. 7:9), and hence may be relied upon to act in accordance

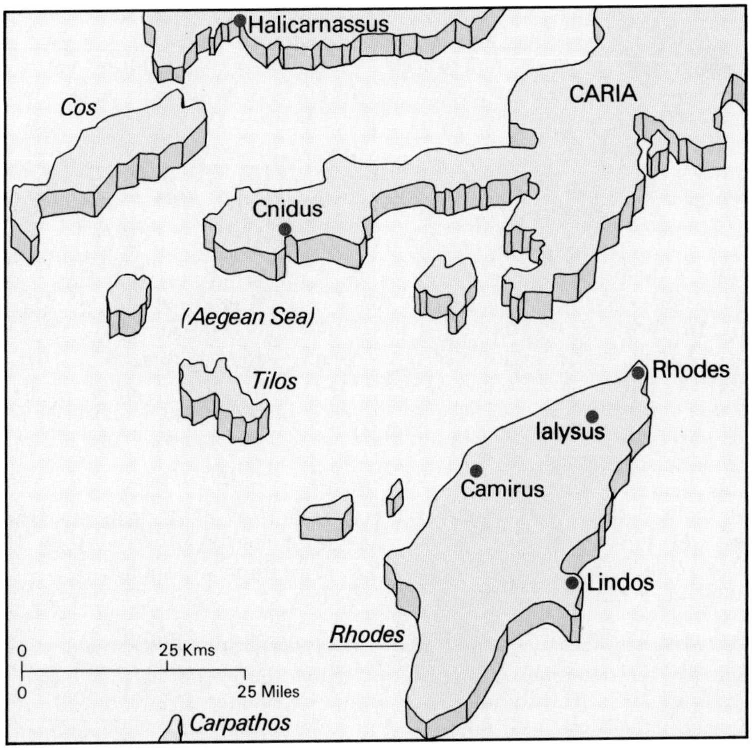

The island of Rhodes, showing major towns.

with the terms of his relationship with Israel. God is therefore a righteous judge who acts for his people (Ps. 9:4; Je. 11:20), and upon whose righteousness his people depend for deliverance and vindication (Ps. 31:1; Je. 11:20).

Thus emerges the conflation of the notions of righteousness and salvation. God is 'a righteous God and (therefore) a Saviour' (Is. 45:21; *cf.* Ps. 36:6; Is. 61:10). For the OT God is Creator and therefore he is the ground and guarantor of the moral order. His righteousness is hence intimately related to other more general moral attributes such as his holiness. The Creator, however, is also the Redeemer, and his righteousness is interpreted by his redemptive activity. Further, Israel's experience of God's righteous deliverance in the past led her to an expectation of a future act of salvation. The coming Messianic ruler is seen as the special recipient and instrument of the divine righteousness (Ps. 72:1f.; Is. 11:3–5; 32:1–20; Je. 23:5). The 'Righteous One' was a Messianic title (Is. 53:11; *cf.* Acts 3:14; 7:52; 22:14).

The NT uses righteousness in the sense of conformity to the demands and obligations of the will of God, the so-called 'righteousness of the law' (Gal. 3:21; Phil. 3:6, 9; *cf.* Tit. 3:5). Human attainment of righteousness is at points relatively positively viewed (Lk. 1:6; 2:25; Mt. 5:20), but in the end this attainment in all men falls far short of a true conformity to the divine will (Rom. 3:9–20; Lk. 18:9–14; Jn. 8:7). In contrast to this human unrighteousness stands the righteousness of God (Rom. 1:17) which in consistency with OT understanding conveys the thought of God's active succour of man in the miracle of his grace.

This righteousness is proclaimed by Jesus as a gift to those who are granted the kingdom of God (Mt. 5:6). By faith in Jesus Christ and his work of atonement man, unrighteous sinner though he is, receives God's righteousness, *i.e.* he is given a true relationship with God which involves the forgiveness of all sin and a new moral standing with God in union with Christ 'the Righteous One' (Rom. 3:21–31; 4:1–25; 10:3; 1 Cor. 1:30; 2 Cor. 5:21; Phil. 3:9). By dealing with all the consequences of man's sin and unrighteousness (both Godward and manward) in the cross, God at once maintains the moral order in which alone he can have fellowship with man *and* in grace delivers the needy (Rom. 3:26).

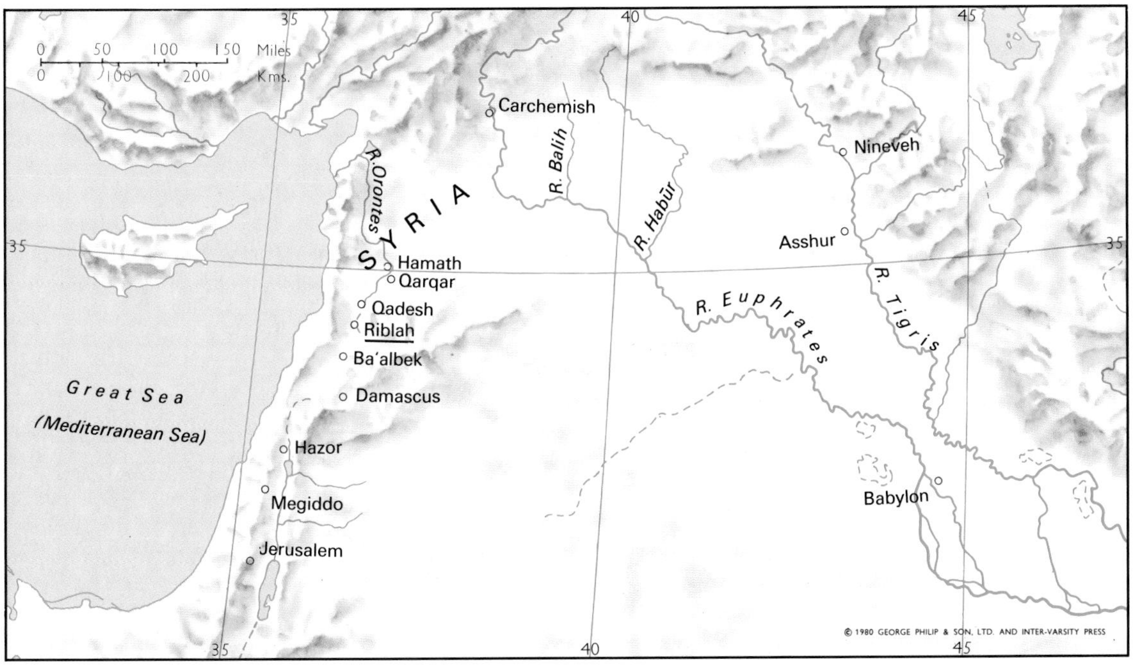

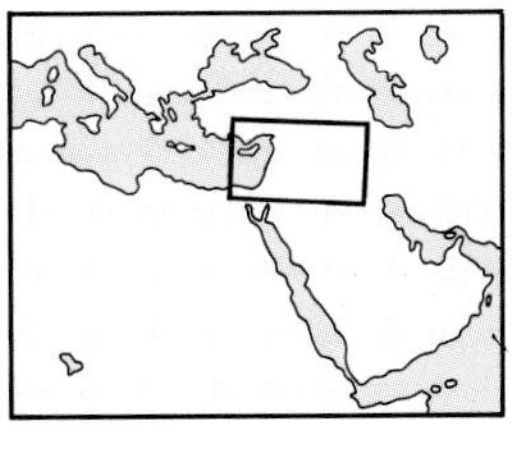

Riblah on the R. Orontes.

The gift of God's righteousness involves entry into the new realm of divine salvation, the gift of eternal life under the reign of God (Rom. 6:12–23; 2 Cor. 6:7, 14; Phil. 1:11; Eph. 4:24). Hence the extrinsic righteousness imputed through the cross finds inevitable expression in the intrinsic righteousness of a life which in a new way conforms to the will of God, even though the ultimate realization of this conformity must await the consummation of the kingdom (1 Jn. 3:2; Phil. 3:12–14; 1 Cor. 13:12f.; 2 Pet. 3:11–13). (*JUSTIFICATION.)

BIBLIOGRAPHY. G. Schrenk, in *TDNT* 2, pp. 192–210; N. Snaith, *Distinctive Ideas of the Old Testament*, 1944; J. Denney, *Romans* in *EGT*, 1; *idem*, *The Death of Christ*, reprinted 1951; A. Nygren, *Commentary on Romans*, E.T. 1952; G. Rupp, *The Righteousness of God*, 1953; H. Seebass, C. Brown, in *NIDNTT* 3, pp. 352–377.

B.A.M.

RIGHT HAND
See Hand, Part 2.

RITUAL CLEANSING
See Clean, Part 1.

RIMMON. 1. 'Thunderer', a title of the storm-god Hadad (*cf.* *HADAD-RIMMON) worshipped in Damascus. Grateful for his cure from leprosy by Elisha, the Syrian army commander Naaman requested two mule-loads of earth from Israel. He proposed to erect an altar on this soil in Rimmon's temple so that he might worship Israel's God on his own ground (2 Ki. 5:17–18). The temple was probably on the site in Damascus occupied by the Roman temple of Zeus, whose emblem, like Rimmon's, was a thunderbolt. The famous Umayyad mosque now stands there. See J. C. Greenfield, *IEJ* 26, 1976, pp. 195–198.

2. A Benjaminite from Beeroth, father of Baanah and Rechab, who assassinated Ishbosheth (2 Sa. 4:2, 9). This personal name, like the similar place-names, if not an abbreviation of a form including the divine element Rimmon, is probably to be derived from the Heb. *rimmôn*, 'pomegranate'. See following article. D.J.W.

RIMMON (Heb. *rimmôn*, 'pomegranate'). **1.** En(Ain)-Rimmon was a place in the Negeb near Edom assigned to Simeon (Jos. 19:7; 1 Ch. 4:32) but incorporated into the Beersheba district (Jos. 15:32). Zechariah envisaged it as the S part of the high plateau seen from Jerusalem (14:10). It was settled by returning exiles (Ne. 11:29), and usually identified with Khirbet er-Ramamim *c.* 16 km NNE of Beersheba. Some identify this with the Rimmon-perez between Hazeroth and Moseroth where the Israelites encamped (Nu. 33:19–20).

2. A village in Zebulun (Jos. 19:13), possibly mod. Rummaneh 10 km NNE of Nazareth (the Crusader Romaneh). AV 'Remmon-methoar' is to be translated 'Rimmon as it bends towards . . .', as in RSV. A Levitical city (1 Ch. 6:77), Dimnah (Jos. 21:35), read by some VSS as Remmon, may be the site; it was captured by the Assyrians *en route* to Jerusalem (so Is. 10:27, RSV).

3. A rocky cliff with caves near Gibeah, to which the Benjaminites escaped (Jdg. 20:45–47); perhaps modern Rammon, 8 km E of Bethel. D.J.W.

RIVER. Hebrew has a good many different words often rendered 'river', although this is not always an accurate translation of the original term.

The Heb. word *naḥal* is common, meaning a wadi or torrent-valley; in summer a dry river-bed or ravine, but a raging torrent in the rainy season. The Jabbok was

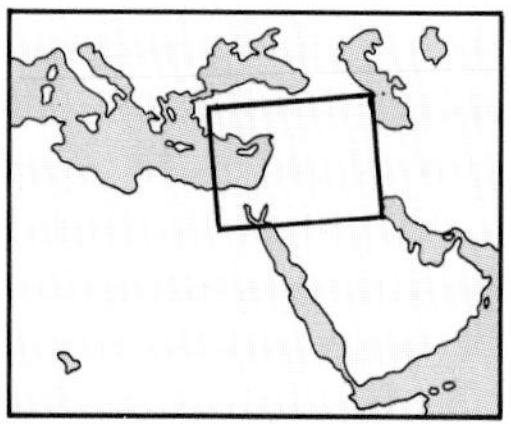

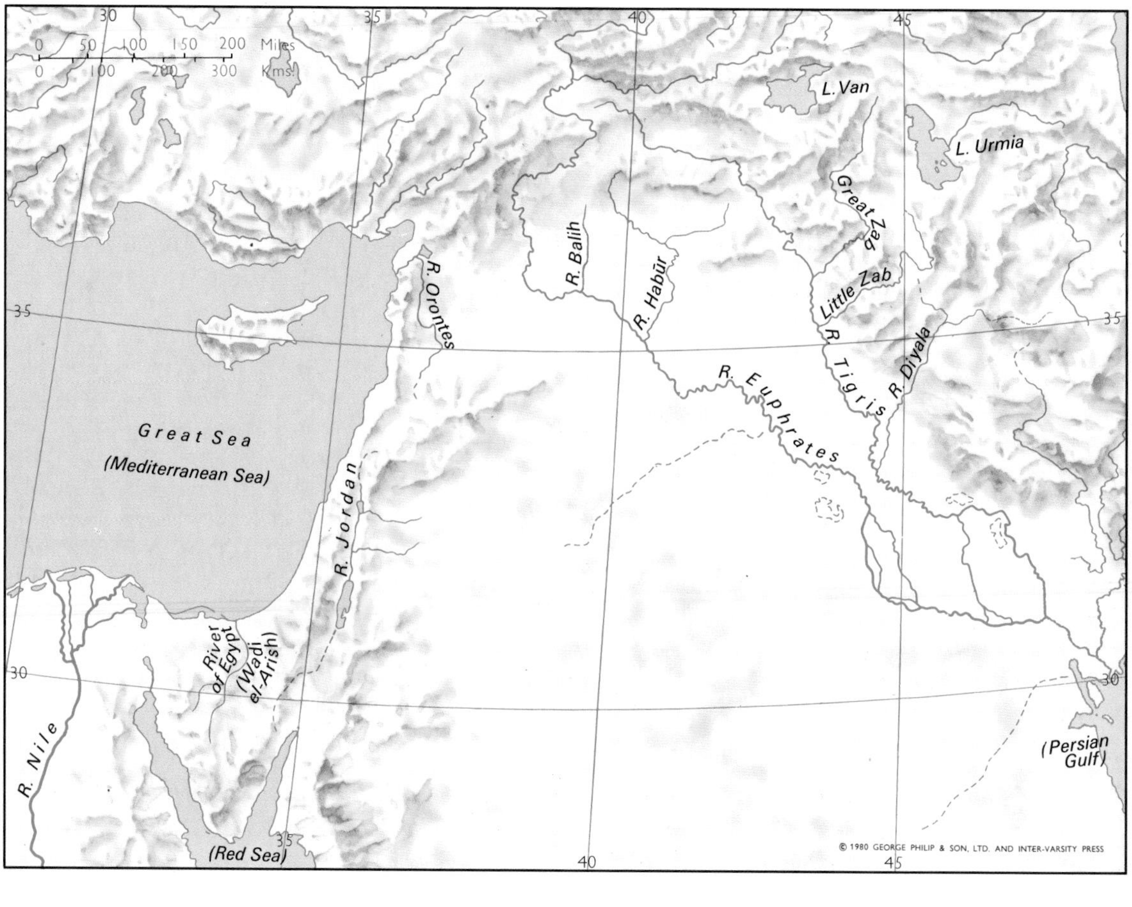

The larger rivers of Bible lands.

A wadi (dried-up bed of a river) in the Negeb desert filled with winter rain. (RS)

such a wadi (Dt. 2:37), as were all the streams mentioned in the Elijah stories. Because these river-beds could suddenly become raging torrents, they often symbolize the pride of nations (Is. 66:12), the strength of the invader (Je. 47:2), and the power of the foe (Ps. 124:4). In his vision it was a *naḥal* that Ezekiel saw issuing from the Temple (47:5–12).

The second term, *nāhār*, is the regular word for 'river' in Heb. It is used of particular rivers: *e.g.* the rivers of Eden (Gn. 2:10, 13–14), the Euphrates (Dt. 1:7), and the rivers of Ethiopia (Is. 18:1), Damascus (2 Ki. 5:12), *etc.* In Ex. 7:19; Ps. 137:1, the word should almost certainly be rendered 'canals'. The waters from the rock struck by Moses formed a *nāhār* (Ps. 105:41).

The word used most frequently of the Nile is *y^{e}'ôr*. The term is also found in Coptic, and was probably an Egyp. loan-word (*BDB*): see, *e.g.*, Gn. 41:1; Ex. 1:22. It is used by Jeremiah (46:7f.) as a similitude of Egyp. invasion.

Other Heb. terms for 'river' are *peleḡ*, irrigating canals (Pss. 1:3; 65:9); *'ăp̄iq*, channel or river-bed (Ps. 42:1; Is. 8:7; and *yûḇāl* or *'ûḇāl*, a stream or watercourse (Is. 30:25; Dn. 8:2–3, 6). In the NT the word for 'river' is *potamos*. It is used of the Euphrates (Rev. 16:12) and the Jordan (Mk. 1:5); of the river issuing from God's throne (Rev. 22:1f.); and of the Holy Spirit under the figure of living water (Jn. 7:38f.).

J.G.S.S.T.

RIZPAH (Heb. *riṣpâ*, 'a hot stone', 'a live coal'). A daughter of a certain Aiah, and a concubine of Saul. On Saul's death, Abner, no doubt wishing to gain some advantage, and following the custom of those who occupied a throne after a king's death, took Rizpah himself (2 Sa. 3:7). When rebuked by Ishbosheth, he reminded the king's son that he had stayed to support him rather than desert to David, and Ishbosheth was silenced (2 Sa. 3:8–11).

Rizpah gave two sons to Saul, Mephibosheth and Armoni (2 Sa. 21:8). In later years King David learnt that a severe famine in the land was a judgment on the people for the bloody deeds of Saul among the Gibeonites (2 Sa. 21:1). When he learnt that the Gibeonites required the death of seven of Saul's sons as an atonement, he surrendered the two sons of Rizpah along with the sons of Michal (2 Sa. 21:1ff.). All were hanged and left unburied, and the grief-stricken Rizpah watched over the bodies for several months. This devotion led David to undertake the proper burial of the bones of Jonathan and Saul along with those of the men who had been hanged. J.A.T.

ROCK. In the OT rock (Heb. *sela'*; *ṣûr*) symbolizes the security and defence of a steep and inaccessible refuge (*cf.* Is. 32:2; 33:16). Similarly, it is used of an immovable foundation (*cf.* Ps. 40:2): to remove 'the rock' is equivalent to shaking the world (*cf.* Jb. 18:4). In an interplay of these symbols it is not surprising to find God spoken of as a rock who gives security and safety to his people (*cf.* 2 Sa. 22:32). In Is. 8:14 *ṣûr* is used of the Messianic stone rejected by the Jewish 'temple builders'. Together with Ps. 118:22 and Is. 28:16 it becomes important for NT typology: Jesus Christ, the rejected 'rock of offence', becomes the *cornerstone of God's true Temple, the Christian *ekklēsia* (Rom. 9:33; 1 Pet. 2:6ff.; *cf.* Ellis, *Paul*, pp. 88ff.). In Paul the typology is extended to the identification of Christ with the rock whose nourishing water followed the Israelites in the wilderness (1 Cor. 10:1ff.; *cf.* Ellis, *Prophecy*, pp. 209–212). The relation (and probable identification) of *Peter with the rock in Mt. 16:18 is the subject of continuing discussion (*cf.* Cullmann, pp. 155–212).

BIBLIOGRAPHY. 'Cornerstone', *Baker's Dictionary of Theology*, 1959; O. Cullmann, *Peter: Disciple, Apostle, Martyr*, 1953; E. E. Ellis, *Paul's Use of the Old Testament*, 1957; *idem.*, *Prophecy and Hermeneutic*, 1977; O. Cullmann, in *TDNT* 6, pp. 95–112; W. Mundle *et al.*, in *NIDNTT* 3, pp. 381–394.

E.E.E.

ROD (STAFF). A word with a variety of meanings. **1.** A stem, branch (Gn. 30:37; Je. 1:11). **2.** A support carried by travellers (Gn. 32:10; Mk. 6:8), shepherds (Ex. 4:2; Ps. 23:4, 'staff'), old men (Zc. 8:4; Heb. 11:21) and men of rank (Gn. 38:18); figurative in 2 Ki. 18:21; Is. 3:1; Ezk. 29:6. Passing under a rod or staff was a shepherd's way of counting his sheep (Lv. 27:32; *cf.* Ezk. 20:37). **3.** An instrument of punishment (Pr. *passim*; 1 Cor.

ROCK-BADGER
See Animals, Part 1.

ROCK CRYSTAL
See Jewels, Part 2.

ROCK DOVE
See Animals, Part 1.

ROCK GECKO
See Animals, Part 1.

ROCK PARTRIDGE
See Animals, Part 1.

ROCK RABBIT
See Animals, Part 1.

The rod or staff, the symbol of judgment by the Assyrian king (Is. 10:5), is here held by King Ashurnasirpal II of Assyria. Height of figure 90 cm. Nimrud stele. c. 876 BC. (DJW)

4:21). **4.** A club carried by soldiers (1 Sa. 14:27; 2 Sa. 23:21) and shepherds (1 Sa. 17:40; *cf.* Ps. 23:4, where rod and staff respectively are used figuratively of divine protection and guidance; *cf.* Mi. 7:14). **5.** A symbol of authority, both human (Jdg. 5:14), *e.g.* a sceptre (Gn. 49:10; Je. 48:17), and divine, like Moses' rod (Ex. 4:20) and Aaron's which confirmed the levitical priesthood (Nu. 17; Heb. 9:4). **6.** A pole upon which ring-shaped loaves were hung. Breaking it is figurative of famine (Lv. 26:26; Ps. 105:16; Ezk. 4:16; 5:16; 14:13). Alternatively it may be simply a symbol for bread as a staple means of supporting life. **7.** A magician's or diviner's wand (Ex. 7:12; Ho. 4:12). **8.** A threshing-stick (Is. 28:27). **9.** A measuring stick (Rev. 11:1; 21:15f.; *cf.* Ezk. 40:3).

In Ezk. 7:10 probably *MT hammaṭṭeh*, 'rod' (RSVmg.), has been rightly revocalized as *hammuṭṭeh*, 'injustice'.

BIBLIOGRAPHY. *BDB*; Arndt, *s.v.*; L. Koehler, *Lexicon in Veteris Testamenti Libros*, 1953. L.C.A.

ROEDEER
See Animals, Part 1.

ROMAN CITIZENSHIP
See Tarsus, Part 3.

ROMAN EMPIRE. The term in its modern usage is neither biblical nor even classical, and does not do justice to the delicacy and complexity of Roman methods of controlling the peoples of the Mediterranean. The word *imperium* signified primarily the sovereign authority entrusted by the Roman people to its elected magistrates by special act (the *lex curiata*). The *imperium* was always complete, embracing every form of executive power, religious, military, judicial, legislative and electoral. Its exercise was confined by the collegiality of the magistracies, and also by the customary or legal restriction of its operation to a particular *provincia*, or sphere of duty. With the extension of Rom. interests abroad, the province became more and more often a geographical one, until the systematic use of the magisterial *imperium* for controlling an 'empire' made possible the use of the term to describe a geographical and administrative entity. In NT times, however, the system was still far from being as complete or rigid as this implies.

I. The nature of Roman imperialism

The creation of a Rom. *province, generally speaking, neither suspended existing governments nor added to the Rom. state. The 'governor' (there was no such generic term, the appropriate magisterial title being used) worked in association with friendly powers in the area to preserve Rome's military security, and if there was no actual warfare his work was mainly diplomatic. He was more like the regional commander of one of the modern treaty organizations which serve the interests of a major power than the colonial governor with his monarchical authority. The solidarity of the 'empire' was a product of the sheer preponderance of Roman might rather than of direct centralized administration. It embraced many hundreds of satellite states, each linked bilaterally with Rome, and each enjoying its individually negotiated rights and privileges. While the Romans obviously had it in their power to cut their way clean through the web of pacts and traditions, this suited neither their inclination nor their interest, and we find them even struggling to persuade dispirited allies to enjoy their subordinate liberties. At the same time there was going on a process of piecemeal assimilation through individual and community grants of Rom. citizenship which bought out the loyalty of local notabilities in favour of the patronal power.

Marble bust of Augustus Caesar, the Roman emperor at the time of the birth of Christ. Height 53·3 cm. c. 29 BC–AD 14. (BM)

II. Growth of the provincial system

The art of diplomatic imperialism as explained above was developed during Rome's early dealings with her neighbours in Italy. Its genius has been variously located in the principles of the fetial priesthood, which enforced a strict respect for boundaries and allowed no other grounds for war, in the generous reciprocity of early Rom. treaties, and in the Rom. ideals of patronage, which required strict loyalty from friends and clients in return for protection. For whatever reason, Rome soon acquired the leadership of the league of Latin cities, and then over several centuries, under the impact of the sporadic Gallic and German invasions, and the struggles with overseas powers such as the Carthaginians and certain of the Hellenistic monarchs, built up treaty relations with all of the Italian states S of the Po valley. Yet it was not until 89 BC that these peoples were offered Rom. citizenship and thus became municipalities of the republic. Meanwhile a similar process was taking place throughout the Mediterranean. At the end of the first Punic War Sicily was made a province (241 BC), and the Carthaginian threat led to further such steps in Sardinia and Corsica (231 BC), Hither and Further Spain (197 BC), and finally to the creation of a province of Africa itself after the destruction of Carthage in 146 BC. By contrast the Romans at first hesitated to impose themselves on the Hellenistic states of the E, until after the repeated failure of free negotiation provinces were created for Macedonia (148 BC) and Achaia (146 BC). In spite of a certain amount of violence, such as the destruction of both Carthage and Corinth in 146 BC, the advantages of the Rom. provincial system soon became recognized abroad, as is made clear by the passing of three states to Rome by their rulers' bequest, leading to the provinces of Asia (133 BC), Bithynia and Cyrene (74 BC). The Romans had been busy tidying up on their own account, and the threat to communications caused by piracy had by this time led to the creation of provinces for Narbonese Gaul, Illyricum and Cilicia.

The careerism of Rom. generals now began to play a prominent part. Pompey added Pontus to Bithynia and created the major new province of Syria as a result of his Mithridatic command of 66 BC, and in the next decade Caesar opened up the whole of Gaul, leaving the Romans established on the Rhine from the Alps to the North Sea. The last of the great Hellenistic states, Egypt, became a province after Augustus' defeat of Antony and Cleopatra in 31 BC. From this time onwards the policy was one of consolidation rather than expansion. Augustus pushed the frontier up to the Danube, creating the provinces of Raetia, Noricum, Pannonia and Moesia. In the next generation local dynasties were succeeded by Rom. governors in a number of areas. Galatia (25 BC) was followed by Cappadocia, Judaea, Britain, Mauretania and Thrace (AD 46).

The NT thus stands at the point where the series of provinces has been completed and the whole Mediterranean has for the first time been provided with a uniform supervisory authority. At the same time the pre-existing governments still flourished in many cases, though with little prospect of future progress. The process of direct incorporation into the Rom. republic went ahead until Caracalla in AD 212 extended citizenship to all free residents of the Mediterranean. From this time onwards the provinces are imperial territories in the modern sense.

III. The administration of the provinces

Until the 1st century BC the provinces had fallen to the Rom. magistrates either for their year of office itself or for the immediately subsequent year, when they continued to exercise the *imperium* as pro-magistrate. For all the high sense of responsibility of the Rom. aristocrat, and his life-long training in politics and law, it was inevitable that his province was governed with a single eye to his next step in the capital. The first standing court at Rome was established for the trial of provincial governors for extortion. So long as the competition for office remained unrestrained, the creation of 3-, 5- and 10-year commands only worsened the position. They became the basis for outright attempts at military usurpation. The satellite states were left in a hopeless plight. They had been accustomed to protect their interests against capricious governors by seeking the patronage of powerful houses in the senate, and justice was done in the long run. Now during the 20 years of civil war that followed the crossing of the Rubicon (49 BC) they were compelled to take sides and risk their wealth and liberty in an unpredictable conflict. Three times the great resources of the East were mustered for an invasion of Italy itself, but in each case the invasion was abortive. It then fell to the victor, Augustus, during 45 years of unchallenged power to restore the damage. He first accepted a province for himself embracing most of the regions where a major garrison was still needed, notably Gaul, Spain, Syria and Egypt. This grant was renewed periodically until the end of his life, and the custom was maintained in favour of his successors. Regional commanders were appointed by his delegation, and thus a professional class of administrators was established, and consistent long-term planning was possible for the first time.

The remaining provinces were still allotted to those engaged in the regular magisterial career, but the possibilities of using the position improperly were ruled out by the overwhelming strength of the Caesars, and inexperience tended to defer to them in any case, so that the Caesarian standard of administration was widely maintained.

If it came to the worst a mal-administered province could be transferred to the Caesarian allotment, as happened in the case of Bithynia in Pliny's day.

Three of the main responsibilities of the governors are well illustrated in the NT. The first was military security and public order. Fear of Rom. intervention on this ground led to the betrayal of Jesus (Jn. 11:48–50), and Paul was arrested by the Romans on the assumption that he was an agitator (Acts 21:31–38). The governments at Thessalonica (Acts 17:6–9) and at Ephesus (Acts 19:40) demonstrate the paralysis that had crept in through fear of intervention. On the other hand, among the Phoenician states (Acts 12:20) and at Lystra (Acts 14:19) there are violent proceedings with no sign of Rom. control. The second major concern was with the revenues. The Caesars straightened out the taxation system and placed it on an equitable census basis (Lk. 2:1). Jesus (Lk. 20:22–25) and Paul (Rom. 13:6–7) both defended Rom. rights in this matter. The third and most onerous of their duties was jurisdiction. Both by reference from the local authorities (Acts 19:38) and by appeal against them (Acts 25:9–10) litigation was concentrated around the Rom. tribunals. Long delays ensued as the cost and complexity of procedure mounted up. Hard-pressed governors struggled to force the onus back on to local shoulders (Lk. 23:7; Acts 18:15). Christians, however, freely joined in the chorus of praise for Rom. justice (Acts 24:10; Rom. 13:4).

IV. The Roman empire in New Testament thought

While the intricate relations of governors, dynasts and republics are everywhere apparent in the NT and familiar to its writers, the truly imperial atmosphere of the Caesarian ascendancy pervades it all. Caesar's decree summons Joseph to Bethlehem (Lk. 2:4). He is the antithesis of God in Jesus' dictum (Lk. 20:25). His distant envoy seals Jesus' death warrant (Jn. 19:12). Caesar commands the perjured loyalty of the Jews (Jn. 19:15), the spurious allegiance of the Greeks (Acts 17:7), the fond confidence of the apostle (Acts 25:11). He is the 'emperor' to whom Christian obedience is due (1 Pet. 2:13). Yet his very exaltation was fatal to Christian loyalty. There was more than a grain of truth in the repeated insinuation (Jn. 19:12; Acts 17:7; 25:8). In the last resort the Christians will defy him. It was the hands of 'lawless' men that crucified Jesus (Acts 2:23). The vaunted justice is to be spurned by the saints (1 Cor. 6:1). When Caesar retaliated (Rev. 17:6) the blasphemy of his claims revealed his doom at the hand of the Lord of lords and King of kings (Rev. 17:14).

Thus, while Rom. imperial peace opened the way for the gospel, Rom. imperial arrogance flung down a mortal challenge.

BIBLIOGRAPHY. *CAH*, 9–11; G. H. Stevenson, *Roman Provincial Administration*, 1949; A. N. Sherwin-White, *Roman Society and Roman Law in the New Testament*, 1963; F. E. Adcock, *Roman Political Ideas and Practice*, 1959; F. Millar, *The Roman Empire and its Neighbours*, 1967; H. Mattingly, *Roman Imperial Civilization*, 1957; J. P. V. D. Balsdon, *Rome: the Story of an Empire*, 1970; E. A. Judge, *The Social Pattern of the Christian Groups in the First Century*, 1960.

E.A.J.

ROMANS, EPISTLE TO THE.

I. Outline of contents

a. Introduction (1:1–15)

The apostle gives a long greeting followed by his reasons for his desire to visit the Roman church.

b. Doctrinal exposition (1:16–8:39)

The major theme is the righteousness of God.

(i) Both Gentiles and Jews are equally guilty in face of God's righteousness (1:18–3:20). This is in spite of the many privileges of the Jews.

(ii) God has nevertheless dealt with this situation. He has provided a propitiatory sacrifice in Christ (3:21–26). Since the benefits of this are appropriated by faith, the way is open for both Jews and Gentiles (3:27–31). The example of Abraham shows justification to be by faith and not works (4:1–25). Many blessings attend the believer's justification (5:1–11). As sin is universal through Adam, so life comes through Christ (5:12–21).

(iii) Righteousness must have an application to life. This is achieved through union with Christ, for as the believer has died with him so he now lives in him (6:1–14). This new life involves a new type of service, for the believer, although freed from the law, has become a slave of God (6:15–7:6). Law is no help towards sanctification, since it produces inner conflict (7:7–25). But life in the Spirit brings victory to the believer, for sin is robbed of its power and a new status of sonship replaces the bondage of sin (8:1–17). The believer has great hope for the future, which is shared even by the material creation (8:18–25). The present life is strengthened by the Spirit's intercession and by the security provided by God's love (8:26–39).

c. The problem of Israel (9:1–11:36)

The theme of God's righteousness is now treated historically in answer to its apparent conflict with the rejection of Israel.

(i) God's actions are sovereign and just. No creature has the right to question the Creator's decisions (9:1–29).

(ii) Israel's rejection is not arbitrary but due to their own fault, for they have had ample opportunity to repent (9:30–10:21).

(iii) Nevertheless Israel may hope for restoration. God has always preserved a remnant (11:1–6). Israel's own failing has led to the inclusion of the Gentiles (11:7–12). The Gentiles will be the means of Israel's restoration (the olive-tree analogy) (11:13–24). The final state of Israel is in the hands of God in whom is inscrutable wisdom (11:25–36).

d. Practical exhortations (12:1–15:13)

(i) Duties resulting from dedicated lives of a personal and general character (12:1–21).

(ii) Duties affecting society as a whole, such as the duty of civic obedience, neighbourliness and sober conduct (13:1–14).

(iii) The need for toleration among Christians. This is worked out in relation to the special problem of foods (14:1–15:13).

e. Conclusion (15:14–16:27)

(i) The writer states his motive in writing (15:14–21).

(ii) His future plans are then mentioned (15:22–29).

(iii) He asks for prayer support for his Jerusalem visit (15:30–33).

(iv) Many Christians are greeted by name (16:1–16).

(v) Warnings are given about false teachers (16:17–19).

(vi) Further personal greetings, a benediction and doxology close the Epistle (16:20–27).

II. The Christian church at Rome

In the world of Paul's day the name of Rome meant much and was not without its strong fascination for the apostle himself, since he expresses a strong desire to preach the gospel there. As a missionary strategist he recognized the immense importance of the Christian church at the centre of the empire, and this may well have influenced the form of the Epistle which he addressed to it. Of the origin of this important church we know little, and it is perhaps useless to conjecture. It may have been founded by converts from the day of Pentecost who returned to their Roman homes rejoicing in their new-found faith, but, although some Romans are mentioned in Acts 2, there is no indication whether any of these were converted to Christianity on that day. But travel between Rome and her provinces was relatively easy in those days, and many Christians must have been among the travellers along the imperial highways. All that is certainly known is that by the time Paul writes to them the church was not only established but of considerable proportions. If the expulsion of Jews from Rome under the emperor Claudius had anything to do with the Christian church, as seems most probable from the reference to 'Chrestus' in the report of Suetonius, it is evident that it was of sufficient dimensions for such drastic action to be taken. And certainly under the Neronian persecutions not many years after this Epistle was written the Christians numbered a considerable multitude.

The question of Peter's connection with Rome cannot be answered with any conciseness, although any claims that Peter was founder of the church there may at once be dismissed. The apostle was still in Jerusalem at the time of the edict of Claudius, and the church must have been started many years before this. Moreover, Paul makes no mention of Peter in this Epistle, which would be hard to explain if Peter were in fact the head of the church at Rome at this time, as well as being directly opposed to his statement in 15:20. Nevertheless, tradition strongly supports the view that Peter and Paul both suffered martyrdom in Rome, since so early a witness as Clement of Rome attests to this.

There has been some discussion regarding the composition of the Roman church, but it would seem most probable that it consisted of both Gentiles and Jews, with the former in the majority. Such a

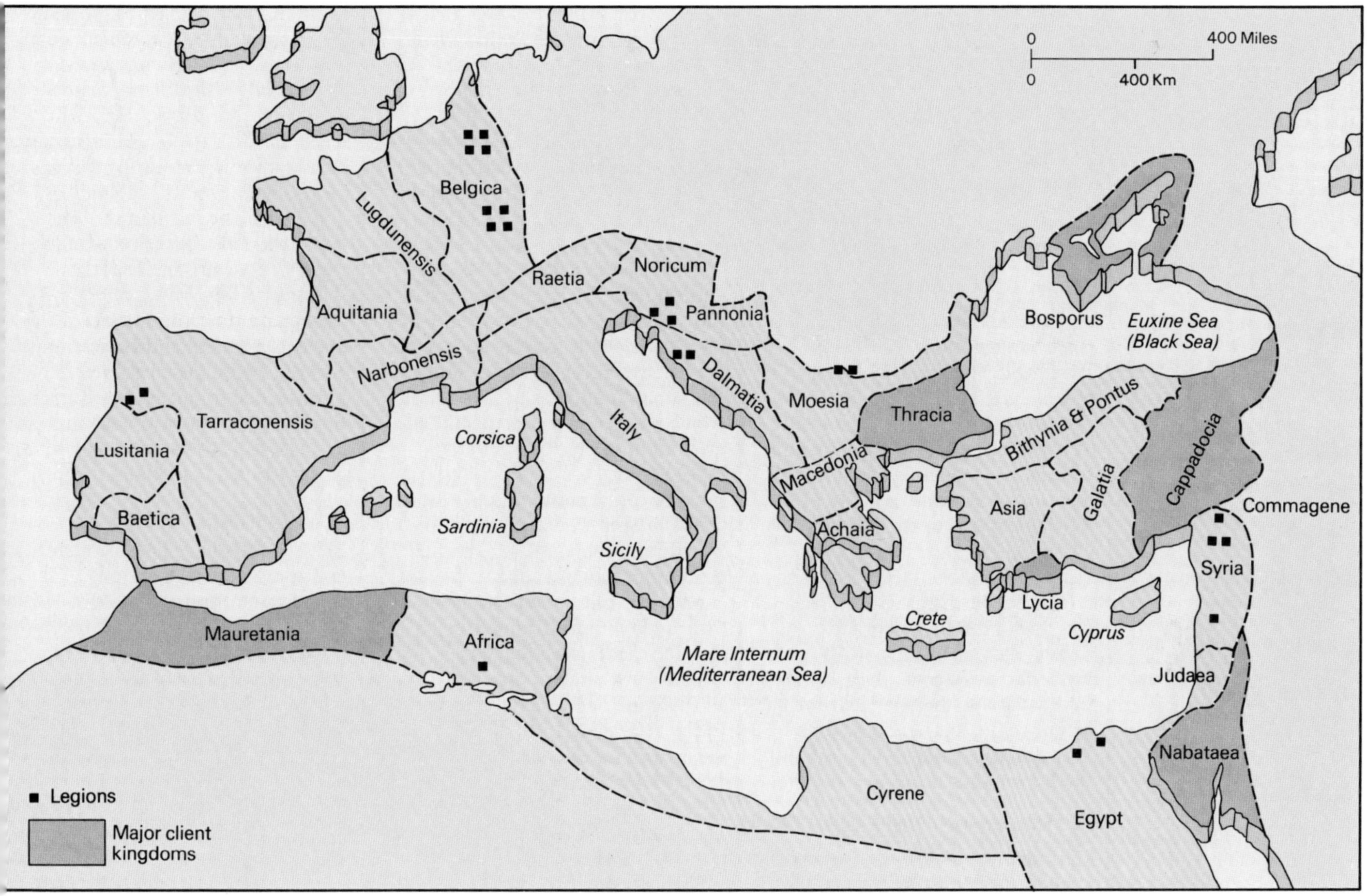

The Roman Empire in AD 14. The gradual extension of direct Roman rule in the E led to a somewhat changed provincial organization, especially in Asia Minor, by the time of Paul.

composition is to be expected in a cosmopolitan city with a strong Jewish colony, and is supported by an analysis of the Epistle itself. In some parts of his argument Paul seems to be addressing Jews, as, for instance, when he appeals to Abraham as 'our father' (4:1) and his direct address to a Jewish questioner in ch. 2; in other parts he turns his thought exclusively towards Gentiles (*cf.* 1:5ff.; 11:13, 28–31). It is an interesting question from what source the Christian tradition within this church had been mainly derived, but there is little indication that it had been derived from the narrower Jewish–Christian stream and it is most natural to suppose that these Christians maintained an outlook similar to that of Paul himself. There is no evidence of the tension of the Jewish–Gentile controversy so apparent in the Galatian Epistle.

III. Date and place of writing

Such indications as are given in this Epistle about Paul's present location all point to the period of his stay in Greece at the close of his third missionary journey (Acts 20:2). His face is now definitely turned towards the W, for he plans not only soon to visit Rome but to proceed with further missionary work in Spain (Rom. 15:24, 28). His E travels are therefore at an end, and this would well fit his situation in Acts 20. Moreover, he is there on his way to Jerusalem, and in Rom. 15:25 he says that his present plans are to go to Jerusalem with the contributions which many churches have made for the support of poverty-stricken Christians there. No doubt can exist, therefore, that the apostle writes this letter just before the final part of his third journey.

In confirmation of this conclusion there are certain indications in ch. 16 which point to Corinth as

Two pages from a Greek papyrus of Paul's letter to the Romans (10:12–11:2). 3rd cent. AD. (CBL)

the place of despatch, although not all scholars are prepared to appeal to this chapter in support, since some believe it was sent to Ephesus and not Rome (see below). But leaving this aside, it is significant that *Phoebe is commended, and she was a deaconess of the church at Cenchrea, one of the two ports of Corinth. There is also a passing reference to a certain *Gaius who was Paul's host at the time of writing, and it is possible that he is the Christian mentioned in 1 Cor. 1:14. Possibly the *Erastus referred to in Rom. 16:23 is the Erastus mentioned in 2 Tim. 4:20 as being left at Corinth, but this is by no means certain. More significant is the mention of Timothy and Sopater (Sosipater) (Rom. 16:21), both of whom accompanied Paul on his visit to Jerusalem (Acts 20:4).

The Epistle may therefore be dated with relative accuracy, although the problems of NT *chronology in general and Pauline chronology in particular forbid any absolute dating. Some time between AD 57 and 59 would fit all the known data.

IV. The purpose of the Epistle

Certain immediate circumstances suggest themselves as the occasion which prompted the production of this Epistle. Paul's intention to do further missionary work in Spain caused him to appeal to the Christians at Rome to support him in this venture (*cf.* Rom. 15:24). As he contemplates his visit to the Roman church he realizes that he may have a spiritual gift to impart to them and that he as well as they may be mutually encouraged (1:11–12).

The apostle may have heard of some practical difficulties which the Christians were experiencing, and he intends to correct in the ethical part of his letter (especially in ch. 14) any wrong emphases. There is an allusion to false teachers in 16:17–19, where the Christians are told to avoid them, but this cannot be considered as part of the primary purpose of the letter, since it is appended almost as an afterthought. Clearly an anti-heretical purpose does not dominate the Epistle.

But the incidental purposes so far considered do not account for the theological form of the main part of the letter. What prompted the apostle to give such a prolonged theological exposition? He scarcely needed to have done this in order (on his approaching visit) to encourage interest in his western missionary plans. He must obviously have had some other dominating purpose. The first eleven chapters after the introductory portion (1:1–15) read more like a treatise than a letter, and it is important to consider the reason for this.

The view that Paul wished to deposit with the Roman church a full statement of his doctrinal position has much to commend it. Here are enshrined for posterity some of the noblest concepts of Christianity which have rightly been accorded an honoured place in Christian theology. But a clear distinction must be made between the basic use that Christians have made of this Epistle and the purpose for which Paul originally intended it. It cannot be maintained that he envisaged laying the foundations of Pauline theology in this way. Moreover, there are some aspects of this theology which find no part in the argument of this Epistle, such as eschatology and the doctrine of the church. It is not possible, therefore, to regard this Epistle as a full statement of Paul's doctrine. Nevertheless, it provides a well-reasoned presentation of some of his most dominant concepts, and it may well be that it was Paul's intention to inform the Roman church of these so that when he visited them the Christians would be intelligently acquainted with his teaching.

It is most probable that the apostle is deeply conscious that he has now reached the turning-point of his missionary career and his mind dwells upon some of the major concepts which have formed part of his continuing teaching work. In this case the inclusion of his matured reflections in a letter addressed to Rome may have been no more than an accident of circumstances in that at the time his face was turned Romeward. But it seems better to attach some importance to Paul's own esteem for the strategic importance of this church and to suppose that consciousness of this played some part in the character of his letter.

A more precise problem relating to the dogmatic purpose of the letter is the relative importance of the section dealing with the Jews' position (chs. 9–11). Some of the earlier critical scholars (*i.e.* of the Tübingen school) regarded this portion as the kernel of the letter, in which case the purpose was supposed to be an endeavour to reconcile opposing Jewish and Gentile elements. But this theory is now wholly discounted. It is more in harmony with the facts to maintain that this section naturally follows on the earlier, more theological, debate. The problem in these chapters is the difficulty of reconciling the righteousness of God, the theme of the earlier chapters, with the apparent non-fulfilment of the ancient promises in the rejection of Israel. This theme must have been a burning one for all Jewish Christians, and would have been relevant in an address to any church with a group of such Christians.

V. The integrity of the Epistle

Few scholars have had the temerity to question the authenticity of this Epistle, and the arguments of those who have done so are now recognized as wholly unfounded and subjective. But there are many scholars who question the concluding chapter, not on grounds disputing Pauline authorship but on the grounds that it does not belong to this Epistle. This opinion is based on several considerations: the large number of personal greetings which are supposed to be improbable to a church which Paul had never visited; the fact that three people, Aquila, Priscilla and Epaenetus, had connections with Asia rather than Rome (although the first two originally came from Rome); the commendation of Phoebe, which is considered less appropriate when addressed to a church where Paul was unknown; the unexpectedness of the allusions to the false teachings in vv. 17–19; and the suitability of 15:33 as an ending to the Epistle. But these considerations are not conclusive and can be otherwise explained. It was not Paul's practice to single out individuals in churches where he was known, and in view of travel facilities it is not surprising that he knew many at Rome or that some last heard of in Asia were then at Rome. Since Paul was well enough known at Rome to write them an Epistle, the commendation of Phoebe presents no difficulty, while the warnings regarding false teachers may have been abruptly introduced either because Paul's notice had just been drawn to them or else because he purposely left the matter to the end so as not to emphasize it disproportionately. The ending 15:33 may be possible as an ending, but is unparalleled in Paul's other Epistles. On the internal evidence from the Epistle there would seem to be insufficient grounds for regarding the chapter as originally detached and as sent to a quite different destination, either Ephesus or anywhere else.

Something must be said about the textual evidence for the ending of this Epistle, although this is not the place for a full discussion. It is sufficient to mention that there are different streams of textual evidence for the position of the benediction and the doxology, and some variations in the reference to Rome in 1:7, 15. There are even some indications that in some quarters the Epistle circulated without its two concluding chapters. This seems to have been particularly associated with Marcion. It is by no means easy to find a theory which accounts for all the variations in the textual evidence, and many different hypotheses have been proposed, some regarding chs. 1–14 as original, some 1–15, and others 1–16. It is probable that the Epistle is original as it now stands, but that Marcion shortened it. In that case his text would have been responsible for the various textual traditions.

VI. The leading themes of the Epistle

a. The righteousness of God

At the commencement of the doctrinal part of the Epistle Paul introduces the theme of God's righteousness, which he claims is now revealed to the believer (1:17). To understand the development of Paul's argument as a whole it is necessary to consider in what ways he uses the concept of * righteousness (*dikaiosynē*). Sanday and Headlam, in their excellent article on the righteousness of God (*A Critical and Exegetical Commentary on the Epistle to the Romans*, 1895, pp. 34–39), point out four different aspects of the manifestation of divine righteousness in this Epistle. The first is fidelity; for the promises of God must be fulfilled to accord with the divine nature (3:3–4). The second is wrath, a particular aspect of righteousness in its abhorrence of all sin, and not as is sometimes supposed a quality opposed to righteousness (*cf.* 1:17f.; 2:5). Righteousness and wrath are, in fact, indivisible, and it is a false exegesis which can treat of God's righteousness without allowing for the operation of God's wrath. The third is the manifestation of righteousness in the death of Christ, of which the classic statement is found in 3:25f. More will be said of this later, but for the present purpose it is necessary to note that in some way God's gift of Christ as a propitiatory sacrifice manifests his righteousness. It is not considered arbitrary or capricious, but is preeminently right and just. Only so could it reveal righteousness. The fourth aspect is the linking of righteousness with faith. It may be said to be characteristic of Pauline theology that the righteousness of God which has been manifested can also be appropriated by faith. God's righteousness is therefore considered as being active as well as passive, and in its active role it declares as righteous those who by nature are at enmity with God (see 5:10). This is the meaning of justification; not that men are actually made righteous but that they are accounted as righteous. The whole Epistle is in reality an exposition of this theme, and it has become basic not only to Pauline theology but to the subsequent Reformed theology which draws so much from it.

b. The goodness of God

In case anyone should think that Paul's conception of God was mainly influenced by God's righteousness irrespective of his other attributes, it is well to be reminded that in this Epistle Paul has much to say about the loving character of God. The mere fact that God's righteousness is conceived of as active in man's salvation points to a motive of love linked with holiness. But Paul specifically draws attention to God's kindness and forbearance and patience (2:4). He points out that the supreme manifestation of God's love is in the amazing fact that Christ died for us while we were still sinners (5:8). And the classic statement of the enduring quality of that love is found in 8:35ff., where Paul can think of nothing, either circumstantial or spiritual, which could possibly separate us from God's love.

When dealing with the problem of the rejection of Israel, Paul makes much of God's mercy and flatly refuses to acknowledge the possibility of his injustice (9:15). He quotes approvingly the statement of Isaiah that all day long God had stretched out his hands to the disobedient people of Israel (10:21). Even when the apostle is obliged to speak of the severity of God, he at once reminds his readers of God's kindness to those who continue to abide in him (11:22). It is the great prerogative of God to have mercy (11:32). Even in the practical part of the Epistle, Paul frequently thinks of the gracious character of God. His will is good, acceptable and perfect (12:2). He receives both the weak and the strong, and this is cited as a reason why the one should not judge the other. He is called the God of steadfastness and encouragement (*tēs hypomonēs kai tēs paraklēseōs*, 15:5), and this forms the basis of an exhortation to develop similar qualities in ourselves. Similarly, because God is a God of hope (15:13), Christians by the power of the Spirit are to abound in hope. Throughout the Epistle, in fact, Paul's thought is dominated by his conception of God. But one other aspect demands a brief comment on its own.

c. The sovereignty of God

It is mainly in chs. 9–11 that God's sovereignty comes into focus. Here Paul is discussing the destiny of Israel and its relationship to the destiny of the Gentiles. The theme at once raises the problem of the justice of God, and Paul sets out his view of God's choice. He illustrates his point by reference to both patriarchal and Mosaic times. To any who still dispute the sovereign choice of God through Israel's past history, he uses the illustration of the potter and the clay (9:19ff.) and shows that the power of God is always mixed with mercy. His sovereign purposes are seen not only in the inclusion of the Gentiles, but also in the promise of Israel's restoration. Throughout this discussion Paul is at pains to affirm the sovereignty of God even if it leads to problems. It is the conviction that God's ways must be right which leads the apostle to the majestic doxology in 11:33–36.

d. The grace of God

No account can be given of God's grace until full appreciation has been made of man's sin, and this is well illustrated in this Epistle. The first three chapters are designed to show man's failure to attain to God's righteousness. Not only does Paul give a startling inventory of Gentile sins (ch. 1) but he points out Israel's culpability in spite of their privileges. As his argument develops, Paul lays stress on the sinful nature of man under the terminology of flesh (*sarx*), by which he means moral rather than physical sinfulness. When speaking of Christ Paul is careful to differentiate his flesh, which was only in the likeness of sinful flesh, and man's flesh. It is clear that Christ had to become man to redeem man, for that is basic to Paul's doctrine of the two *Adams (5:12ff.). In his description of his own struggles with sin (ch. 7) Paul has an acute sense of the power of sin. It is almost a personal enemy which does its utmost to destroy the soul. It takes advantage of the flesh. It brings all the members into bondage to its principles, which Paul calls the law of sin (7:23). It reduces man to the utmost wretchedness, from which only God through Christ can deliver.

This leads to a consideration of the saving activity of God in Christ. There has been much discussion over the significance of the word *hilastērion* (propitiatory) in 3:25, and this is not the place to discuss its meaning. But it is important to remember that the most significant aspect of Paul's statement is that God took the initiative. This is in line with Paul's whole approach to the processes of redemption in this Epistle. The work of Christ on the cross is seen as an objective sacrifice provided by God on the basis of which sins may be remitted.

Paul deals in ch. 6 with the operation of God's grace and shows that the superabundance of that grace must never be regarded as an occasion to commit greater sin. This is impossible because of the believer's close union with Christ, a doctrine which has an important place in Paul's thought. The illustration of baptism is used to show the character of the transformation which has been effected. Sin no longer has dominion because we are now under grace (6:14). Nevertheless, grace has made us slaves of God, so that a new obligation has replaced the old (6:20f.).

e. The law of God

That the apostle had a high regard for the Jewish law is made clear by his statement that the commandment is holy, just and good (7:12). He also recognizes the useful function of the law in manifesting the character of sin (7:7). Yet he is convinced by bitter experience that the law is completely ineffective as a means of salvation, not because of any inherent deficiencies in the law, for man's better self delights in the law (7:22), but because of man's own deficiencies.

Yet as he considers the law of God, the apostle at once perceives that for the Christian this comprises more than the mere letter of the Mosaic law. It involves what he calls the law of the Spirit (8:2), and his doctrine of the Holy Spirit, especially in his work of sanctification (in ch. 8), ought not to be divorced from its close connection with the law of God. Under the new covenant the commandments were to be written on the heart, and this is effected only through the indwelling Spirit. He introduces a new way of looking at God's requirements, for these become the laws of a Father under an entirely new relationship.

The Spirit of God is set over against the flesh (8:4f.), gives life in place of death (8:11), bears witness

Plan of the city of Rome in AD 64, the year of Nero's massacre of the Christians.

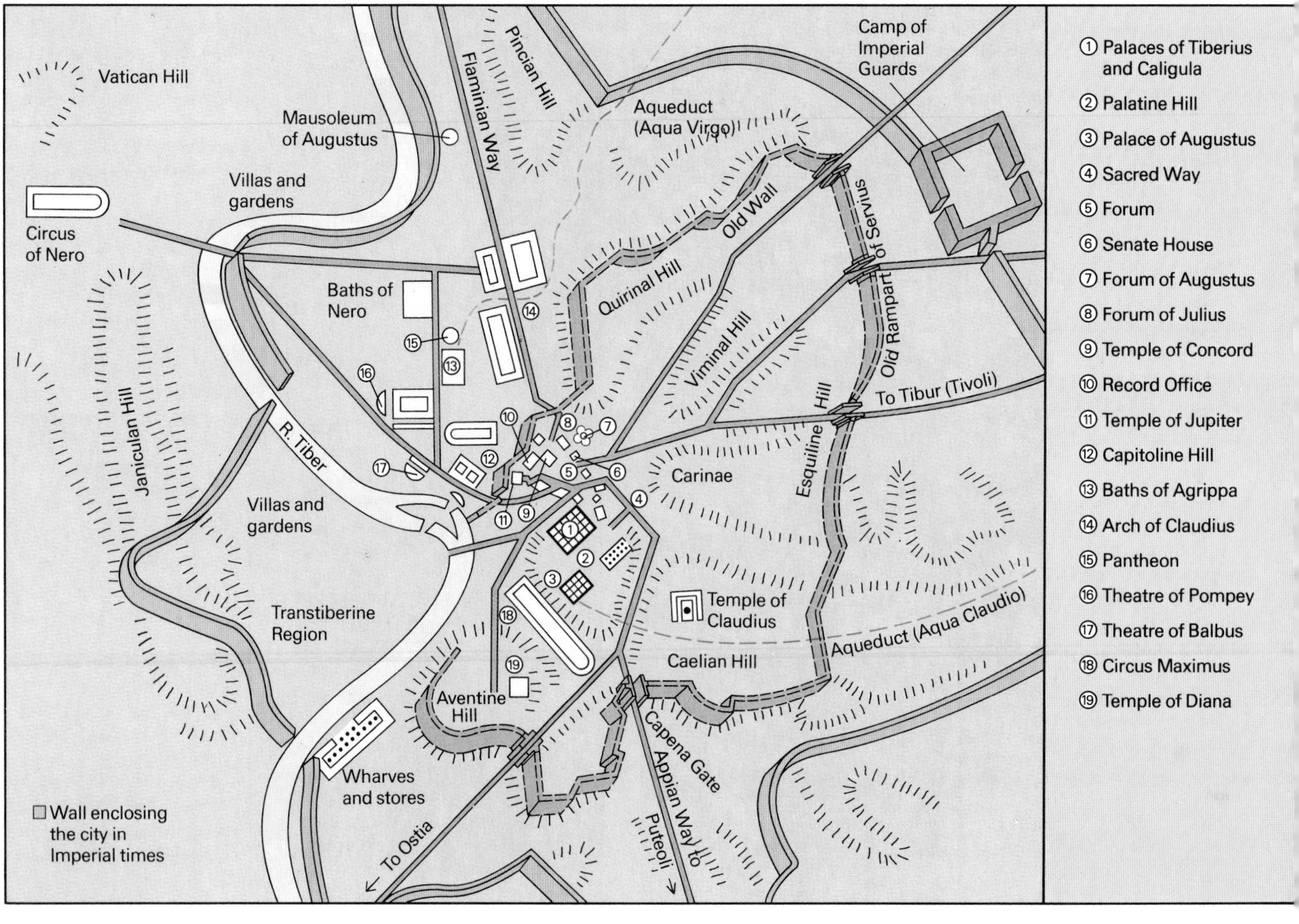

Part of the Colosseum at Rome. Built by Vespasian and completed by Titus, it was used as a place of persecution of some Christians. (VI)

o the Christian's sonship (8:14f.) nd intercedes for them in accord-nce with God's will (8:26f.). Chris-ian life is, therefore, not a matter f submission to a legal code, but a ife controlled by the Spirit on the asis of a new law which involves uch qualities as righteousness, eace, joy, hope and love (*cf.* 5:3f.; 2:11; 14:17; 15:13, 30).

BIBLIOGRAPHY. Commentaries by . Haldane, 1874, reprinted 1958; . Hodge, 1886, reprinted 1951; I. C. G. Moule, *EB*, 1893; J. Den-ey, *EGT*, 1900; W. Sanday and . C. Headlam, *ICC*, 1902; . H. Dodd, *MNT*, 1932; K. Barth, .T. 1933; O. Michel, *KEK*[12], 1963; . K. Barrett, 1957; J. Murray, *VLC*, 1960, 1965; F. F. Bruce, *TNTC*, 1963; F. J. Leenhardt, 1957; 1. Black, 1973; C. E. B. Cranfield, *CC*, 1, 1975; T. W. Manson, St. Paul's Letter to the Romans—and Others', *BJRL* 31, 1947–8, pp. 224ff.; D. Guthrie, *New Testament Introduction*, 1970, pp. 393ff.

D.G.

ROME. Founded traditionally in 753 BC on its seven hills (the bluffs formed where the Latin plain falls away into the Tiber bed at the first easy crossing up from the mouth), Rome, as the excavations have shown, was in origin a meeting-place and a melting-pot, rather than the home of a pre-existing people. The process of accretion, stimulated at an early stage by the strategic requirements of the Etruscan states to the N and S, acquired its own momentum, and by a liberal policy of enfranchisement unique in antiquity Rome attracted to herself men and ideas from all over the Mediterranean, until nearly 1,000 years from her beginning she had incorporated every other civilized community from Britain to Arabia. Rome was cosmopolitan and all the world was Roman. Yet this very comprehensiveness destroyed the uniqueness of the city, and the strategic centrality that had dictated her growth was lost with the opening up of the Danube and the Rhine, leaving Rome in the Middle Ages little more than a provincial city of Italy.

In NT times Rome was in the full flush of her growth. Multi-storey tenement blocks housed a proletariat of over a million, drawn from every quarter. The aristocracy, becoming just as international through the domestic favours of the Caesars, lavished the profits of three continents on suburban villas and country estates. The Caesars themselves had furnished the heart of the city with an array of public buildings perhaps never equalled in any capital. The same concentration of wealth provided the overcrowded masses with generous economic subsidies and entertainment. It also attracted literary and artistic talent from foreign parts. As the seat of the senate and of the Caesarian administration Rome maintained diplomatic contact with every other state in the Mediterranean, and the traffic in foodstuffs and luxury goods fortified the links.

I. Rome in New Testament thought

The Acts of the Apostles has often been supposed to be an apostolic odyssey set between Jerusalem and Rome as the symbols of Jew and Gentile. The opposite pole to Jerusalem is, however, given as the 'end of the earth' (Acts 1:8), and, while the narrative certainly concludes at Rome, no great emphasis is laid on that. Attention is concentrated on the legal struggle between Paul and his Jewish opponents, and the journey to Rome serves as the resolution of this, culminating in Paul's denunciation of the Jews there and the unhindered preaching to the Gentiles. The theme of the book seems to be the release of the gospel from its Jewish matrix, and Rome provides a clear-cut terminal point in this process.

In Revelation, however, Rome acquires a positively sinister significance. 'The great city, which has dominion over the kings of the earth' (Rev. 17:18), seated upon seven mountains (v. 9), and upon 'the waters' which are 'peoples and multitudes and nations and tongues' (v. 15), is unmistakably the imperial capital. The seer, writing in Asia Minor, the greatest centre of luxury trade in antiquity, discloses the feelings of those who suffered through the consortium with Rome. He scorns the famous compromise with 'the kings of the earth' who 'were wanton with her' (Rev. 18:9), and catalogues the sumptuous traffic (vv. 12–13) of the 'merchants of the earth' who have 'grown rich with the wealth of her wantonness' (v. 3). He stigmatizes the artistic brilliance of the city (v. 22). How widespread such hatred was we do not know. In this case the reason is plain. Rome has already drunk the 'blood of the martyrs of Jesus' (Rev. 17:6).

II. The origin of Christianity at Rome

So far as the NT goes, it is not clear how the circle of Christians was established in Rome, nor even whether they constituted a church in the regular way. There is no unequivocal reference to any meeting or activity of the church as such, let alone to bishops or sacraments. The church of Rome simply fails to appear in our documents. Let it be said at once that this need not mean that it was not yet formed. It may merely be the case that it was not intimately connected with Paul, with whom most of our information is concerned.

Paul's first known link with Rome was when he met *Aquila and Priscilla at Corinth (Acts 18:2). They had left the city as a result of Claudius' expulsion of the Jews. Since it is not stated that they were already Christians, the question must be left open. Suetonius says (*Claudius*, 25) that the trouble in Rome was caused by a certain Chrestus. Since this could be a variant of Christus, it has often been argued that Christianity had already reached Rome. Suetonius, however, knew about Christianity, and, even if he did make a mistake, agitation over Christus could be caused by any Jewish Messianic movement, and not necessarily by Christianity alone. There is no hint in the Epistle to the Romans that there had been any conflict between Jews and Christians at Rome, and when Paul himself reached Rome the Jewish leaders professed personal ignorance of the sect (Acts 28:22). This not only makes it unlikely that there had been a clash, but sharpens the question of the nature of the Christian organization at Rome, since we know that by this stage there was a considerable community there.

Some few years after meeting Aquila and Priscilla, Paul decided that he 'must also see Rome' (Acts 19:21). When he wrote the Epistle shortly afterwards his plan was to visit his friends in the city on the way to Spain (Rom. 15:24). A considerable circle of these is named (ch. 16), they had been there 'many years' (Rom. 15:23), and were well known in Christian circles abroad (Rom. 1:8). Paul's reference to his not building 'on another man's foundation' (Rom. 15:20) does not necessarily refer to the situation in Rome; it need only mean that this was the reason why his work abroad had been so lengthy (Rom. 15:22–23); indeed, the authority he assumes in the Epistle leaves little room for an alternative leader. The most natural assumption, on the internal evidence, is that Paul is writing to a group of persons who have collected in Rome over the years after having had some contact with him in the various churches of his foundation. A number of them are described as his 'kinsmen', others have worked with him in the past. He introduces a new arrival to them (Rom. 16:1). Although some bear Roman names, we must assume that they are recently enfranchised foreigners, or at least that the majority of them are not Romans, since Paul's references to the government allude to its capital and taxation powers over non-Romans in particular (Rom. 13:4, 7). Although some are Jews, the group seems to have a life of its own apart from the Jewish community (ch. 12). The reference in at least five cases to household units (Rom. 16:5, 10–11, 14–15) suggests that this may have been the basis of their association.

When Paul finally reached Rome several years later, he had been met on the way by 'the brethren' (Acts 28:15). They do not appear again, however, either in connection with Paul's dealings with the Jewish authorities or, so far as the brief notice goes, during his 2 years' imprisonment. The seven letters that are supposed to belong to this period do sometimes contain greetings from 'the brethren', though they are mainly concerned with personal messages. The reference to rival preachers (Phil. 1:15) is the nearest we come to any positive NT evidence for a non-Pauline contribution to Roman Christianity. On the other hand, the assumption of a church organized independently of Paul might explain the amorphous character of Roman Christianity in his writings.

III. Was Peter ever in Rome?

In the late 2nd century AD the tradition appears that Peter had worked in Rome and died there as a martyr, and in the 4th century the claim that he was first bishop of the Roman church appears. These traditions were never disputed in antiquity and are not inconsistent with NT evidence. On the other hand, nothing in the NT positively supports them. Most students assume that 'Babylon' (1 Pet. 5:13) is a cryptic designation for Rome, but, although there are parallels for this in apocalyptic literature, it is difficult to see what the need for secrecy was in a letter, nor who was likely to be deceived in this case when the meaning was supposed to be plain to so wide a circle of readers. The so-called *First Epistle of Clement*, written when the memory of the apostles was still preserved by living members of the church at Rome, refers to both Peter and Paul in terms which imply that they both died martyrs' deaths there. The tantalizing fact that this is not positively asserted may, of course, simply mean that it was taken for granted. From about a century later comes the information that there were 'trophies' of Peter on the Vatican hill and of Paul on the road to Ostia. On the assumption that these were tombs, the two churches bearing the apostolic names were erected over them at later times. The Vatican excavations have revealed a monument which could well be the 2nd-century 'trophy' of Peter. It is associated with a burial-ground that was used in the late 1st century.

We still lack any positive trace of Peter in Rome, however. The excavations strengthen the literary tradition, of course, and in default of further evidence we must allow the distinct possibility that Peter died in Rome. That he founded the church there and ruled it for any length of time has much feebler support in tradition, and faces the almost insuperable obstacle of the silence of Paul's Epistles.

The tradition of the martyrdom of the apostles is supplied with a lurid occasion by the massacre of AD 64 (*NERO). The account by

Tacitus (*Annals* 15. 44) and the shorter notice by Suetonius (*Nero* 16) supply us with several surprising points about the Christian community at Rome. Its numbers are described as very large. Its connection with Jesus is clearly understood, and yet it is distinguished from Judaism. It is an object of popular fear and disgust for reasons which are not explained, apart from a reference to 'hatred of the human race'. Thus Nero's mad atrocities merely highlight the revulsion with which the Christians were received in the metropolis of the world.

BIBLIOGRAPHY. See under *ROMAN EMPIRE. J. P. V. D. Balsdon, *Life and Leisure in Ancient Rome*, 1974; O. Cullmann, *Peter: Disciple, Apostle, Martyr*, 1962.

E.A.J.

ROSH. 1. In the RV this word occurs in the title of Gog who is described as 'prince of Rosh' (Ezk. 38:2–3; 39:1). AV, RVmg. and RSV interpret as a title itself, 'chief', 'prince'. However, the name of a N people or country such as Meshech and Tubal is more probable. Gesenius suggested Russia, but this name is not attested in the area, and a very distant people named thus early is unlikely in the context. Most follow Delitzsch in identifying Rosh with Assyr. *Rašu* on the NW border of Elam (*i.e.* in Media).

2. The name of the seventh son of Benjamin (Gn. 46:21). LXX makes him son of Bela, grandson of Benjamin; but *cf.* lists in Nu. 26:38f.; 1 Ch. 8:1–5.

D.J.W.

RUFUS ('red'). A name of Italic rather than Latin origin, found twice in the NT (Mk. 15:21; Rom. 16:13), probably referring to the same man. In Mk. 15:21 Simon of Cyrene is identified for the benefit of a later generation as the father of Alexander and Rufus, brothers who were presumably known in Rome when Mark's Gospel was published there. The Roman Rufus who is greeted by Paul (on the assumption that Rom. 16 was sent to Rome) can hardly have been a different man. Paul describes him as a choice Christian. His mother had shown herself a mother to Paul (perhaps in Antioch, if we may further identify Simon of Cyrene with Simeon of Acts 13:1).

F.F.B.

RUHAMAH (Heb. *ruḥāmâ*, 'pitied'). A symbolic name of Israel (Ho. 2:1, AV; *cf.* Rom. 9:25–26; 1 Pet. 2:10) used to indicate the return of God's mercy. A play on words is involved, for the second child of Gomer, wife of *Hosea, was called Lo-ruhamah ('unpitied'), denoting a time when God had turned his back on Israel because of her apostasy.

J.D.D.

RUMAH. Mentioned in 2 Ki. 23:36 only. Josephus, in a parallel account, calls it 'Abouma', and probably means 'Arumah', a place mentioned in Jdg. 9:41, in the vicinity of Shechem. But the name Rumah is quite possible; the name and site are probably preserved in Khirbet al-Rumah, some 35 km inland from Mt Carmel.

D.F.P.

RUNNER. Urgent messages were sent in antiquity by a swift runner (Heb. *rāṣ*), often a member of the royal bodyguard or 'out-runners' (2 Sa. 15:1). So the late term 'runner' or royal messenger (Je. 51:31) was used for those who carried letters between cities (2 Ch. 30:6, 10), usually on fast horses (Est. 8:10, 14). Thus the term 'post' (AV) was synonymous with speed (Jb. 9:25). Throughout the Persian empire, as in earlier Babylonian times, regular posts were established between provincial capitals (G. R. Driver, *Aramaic Documents of the Fifth Century BC*, 1956, pp. 10–12).

D.J.W.

RUTH (Heb. *rûṯ*, perhaps contracted from *reʿûṯ*, 'female companion'). Ruth is the heroine of the book which bears her name (see next article). She was a Moabitess who lived in the time of the Judges.

In her own land Ruth had married Mahlon (Ru. 4:10), the elder son of Elimelech and Naomi, Israelites from Bethlehem-judah who came to Moab during a famine. Naomi was widowed and then her two sons died without heirs. She determined to return to her native country, whereupon Ruth announced that she intended to accompany her, adopting both

RUBY
See Jewels, Part 2.

RUDDER
See Ships and boats, Part 3.

RUDIMENTS
See Elements, Part 1.

RUE
See Herbs, Part 2.

RULE OF LIFE
See Walk, Part 3.

RULERS OF THE CITY
See Authorities, city, Part 1.

RUMINANTS
See Animals, Part 1.

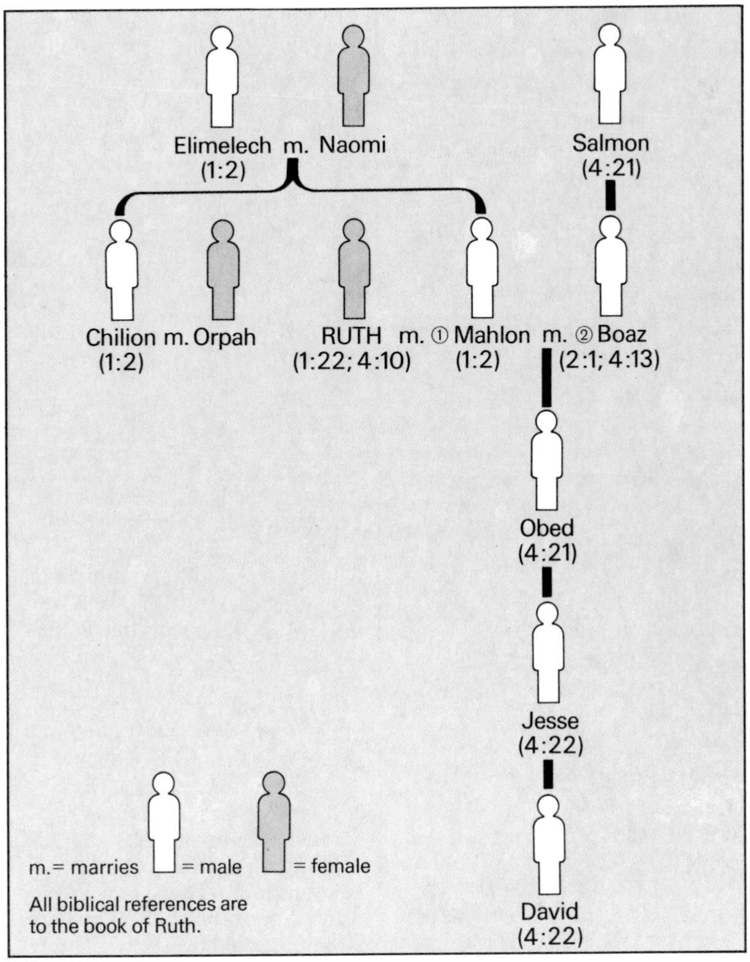

The family of Ruth.

her nation and her God. Only by death would they be separated (Ru. 1:17).

During the barley harvest in Bethlehem Ruth went to glean in the fields of Boaz, a wealthy relative of Elimelech. Boaz noticed her and gave her his protection in acknowledgment of her loyalty to Naomi. She was invited to eat with the reapers, and was favoured throughout the barley harvest and the wheat harvest.

When all was harvested and the threshing had begun, acting on Naomi's instructions Ruth went to the threshing-floor at night and claimed Boaz's protection by appealing to his chivalry. He sent her back home as soon as it was light, with a present of six measures of barley, and the undertaking that, if her near kinsman was not prepared to marry her under the levirate marriage law, he would act as her kinsman-redeemer (*cf.* Lv. 25:25, 47–49).

With ten elders of the city as witnesses, he appealed to Naomi's kinsman to redeem a plot of land which had belonged to Elimelech, and which was a sacred trust that must not pass out of the family (*cf.* Lv. 25:23). To this he added the obligation of levirate marriage to Ruth (Ru. 4:5). The kinsman could not afford this and renounced his right in favour of Boaz.

Ruth was married to Boaz, and their first child Obed was given to Naomi to continue the names of Elimelech, Mahlon and Chilion. He was the grandfather of David (1 Ch. 2:12; Mt. 1:5). M.B.

*Part of a leather scroll including the book of Ruth (2:13–19) found at Qumran (*MS *2Q16). Height of letters c. 3 mm. Mid 1st cent.* AD. (RM)

RUTH, BOOK OF. In the Heb. Bible Ruth is one of the five *Megilloth* or 'rolls', included in the 'Writings', the third division of the Canon. It is read annually by the Jews at the Feast of Weeks. In the LXX, Vulg., and most modern versions it comes immediately after Judges; Josephus (*Contra Apionem* 1. 8) apparently reckons it to be an appendix to Judges and does not count it separately in enumerating the total number of books in the Canon.

For the plot of the book, see *RUTH.

I. Outline of contents

a. Naomi, widowed and bereft of her sons, returns from Moab to her native Bethlehem with her Moabite daughter-in-law Ruth (1:1–22).

b. Ruth gleans in the field of Naomi's wealthy kinsman Boaz (2:1–23).

c. Ruth appeals to Boaz to perform the part of a kinsman-redeemer (3:1–18).

d. Ruth is married to Boaz and gives birth to Obed (4:1–17).

e. Genealogy from Perez to David (4:18–22).

II. Authorship, date and purpose

The book of Ruth is fraught with difficulties for the critic, because, like Job, it contains no clue to its authorship. Tradition alone ascribes this idyllic pastoral to the last of the Judges, the prophet-priest Samuel.

The setting is that of the period of the Judges (Ru. 1:1), but its writing belongs to a later date. This is indicated when the author explains former customs (Ru. 4:1–12). A very wide range of dating is offered for its actual composition, ranging from early pre-exilic times to a late post-exilic date.

The classical style and language do point to an early date, as does the attitude to foreign marriages, for under the Deuteronomic law a Moabite could not enter the congregation (Dt. 23:3). The late dating is based on the antiquarian interest displayed in the book, and on its supposed connection with the reforms of Ezra and Nehemiah. One school of thought sees evidence of both early and late work in the book, supposing that the genealogy of David (Ru. 4:18–22) and the explanations of early customs belong to a much later date than the book itself.

Many suggestions as to the purpose of the book have been put forward, among them the following. It was intended to supply a family tree for the greatest of the kings of Hebrew history, David, because this was omitted from the books of Samuel. It was a political pamphlet, an anti-separatist tract, written to counteract the stringency of Ezra and Nehemiah on the subject of mixed marriages. It was a humanitarian plea on behalf of the childless widow so that the next of kin would assume responsibility for her. It was designed to depict an overruling providence. It was to present a case for racial tolerance. Perhaps there was no ulterior motive at all, but it was a tale that had to be told. It certainly presents a most pleasing contrast with the narratives at the end of Judges, which belong to the same general period (Jdg. 17–21).

BIBLIOGRAPHY. H. H. Rowley, 'The Marriage of Ruth', *HTR* 40, 1947, pp. 77ff., reprinted in *The Servant of the Lord and other Old Testament Essays*, 1952, pp. 161ff.; E. Robertson, 'The Plot of the Book of Ruth', *BJRL* 32, 1949–50, pp. 207ff.; A. E. Cundall and L. Morris, *Judges and Ruth*, *TOTC*, 1968. M.B.

RYE
See Grain, Part 2.

SABAEANS
See Sheba, Part 3.

SABBATH (Heb. *šabbāṯ*, from the root *šāḇaṯ*, 'to cease', 'to desist'). In the Bible the principle is laid down that one day in 7 is to be observed as a day holy to God. From the reason given for keeping the sabbath day in the Ten Commandments we learn that the example for the sabbath rest had been set by God himself in the creation. The sabbath therefore is a creation ordinance (Ex. 20:8–11).

In the account of creation the actual word 'sabbath' is not found, but the root from which the word is derived does occur (Gn. 2:2). The work of creation had occupied 6 days; on the 7th God rested (lit. 'ceased') from his labour. Thus there appears the distinction between the 6 days of labour and the one day of rest. This is true, even if the 6 days of labour be construed as periods of time longer than 24 hours. The language is anthropomorphic, for God is not a weary workman in need of rest. Nevertheless, the pattern is here set for man to follow. Ex. 20:11 states that God 'rested' (Heb. *wayyānaḥ*) on the 7th day, and Ex. 31:17 says that he ceased from his work and 'was refreshed' (*wayyinnāpaš*). The language is purposely strong so that man may learn the necessity of regarding the sabbath as a day on which he himself is to rest from his daily labours.

It has been held in contradistinction to what has been stated above that the institution of the sabbath derived from Babylonia. It is true that the Babylonian word *šabbatum* is related to the corresponding Hebrew word, but the force of the words is quite different. For one thing the Babylonians had a 5-day week. Examination of contract tablets reveals that the days designated *šabbatum* were not days of cessation from labour. Contracts from Mari (Tel el-Harîrî) show that work was performed, sometimes over a period of several days, without any interruption every 7th day. The Bible clearly attributes the origin of the sabbath to the divine example.

The fourth commandment enjoins observance of the sabbath. In Genesis there is no mention of the sabbath apart from the creation account. There is, however, mention of periods of 7 days (*cf.* Gn. 7:4, 10; 8:10, 12; 29:27ff.). We may also note in the narrative in Job that the seven sons celebrated a feast each on his day, and this was followed by the prayers and sacrifices of Job for the benefit of his children (Jb. 1:4–5). This was not a single round, but was regularly practised. It may be that here is an intimation of worship on the 1st day of the cycle. At least the principle that one day in 7 is holy to the Lord appears to be recognized here.

In Ex. 16:21–30 explicit mention is made of the sabbath in connection with the giving of manna. The sabbath is here represented as a gift of God (v. 29), to be for the rest and benefit of the people (v. 30). It was not necessary to work on the sabbath (*i.e.* to gather manna), for a double portion had been provided on the 6th day.

The sabbath was therefore known to Israel, and the injunction to remember it was one that would be understood. In the Decalogue it is made clear that the sabbath belongs to the Lord. It is therefore primarily his day, and the basic reason for observing it is that it is a day which belongs to him. It is a day that he has blessed and that he has set apart for observance. This is not contradicted by the Decalogue given in Dt. 5:12ff. In this latter passage the people are commanded to keep the sabbath in the manner in which the Lord has already commanded them (the reference is to Ex. 20:8–11), and the fact that the sabbath belongs to the Lord is again stated (v. 14). An additional reason, however, is given for the observance of the command. This reason is merely additional; it does not conflict with those already given. Israel is commanded to observe the sabbath day, in order 'that your manservant and your maidservant may rest as well as you'. Here is a humanitarian emphasis; but here also is emphasis upon the fact that the sabbath was made for man. Israel had been a slave in Egypt and had been delivered; so Israel must show the mercy of the sabbath towards those in her own midst who were slaves.

Throughout the remainder of the Pentateuch the sabbath legislation is found. It is interesting to note that there is a reference to the sabbath in each of the four last books of the Pentateuch. Genesis presents the divine rest; the remaining books emphasize the sabbatical legislation. This shows the importance of the institution. Sabbath legislation, it may be said, is integral and essential to the basic law of the OT and the Pentateuch (*cf.* Ex. 31:13–16; 34:21; 35:2ff.; Lv. 19:3, 30; 23:3, 38).

In this connection the significance of the sabbatical legislation appears in the severe punishment that is meted out upon a sabbath-breaker. A man had been gathering sticks upon the sabbath day. For this act a special revelation from God decreed that he should be put to death (*cf.* J. Weingreen, *From Bible to Mishna*, 1976, pp. 83ff.) This man had denied the basic principle of the sabbath, namely, that the day belonged to the Lord, and therefore was to be observed only as the Lord had commanded (*cf.* Nu. 15:32–36).

Upon the Pentateuchal legislation the prophets build; their utterances are in accordance with what had been revealed in the Pentateuch. The 'sabbaths' are often linked together with the 'new moons' (2 Ki. 4:23; Am. 8:5; Ho. 2:11; Is. 1:13; Ezk. 46:3). When prophets like Hosea (2:11) pronounced divine judgment on new moons, sabbaths and other appointed feasts, they were not condemning the sabbath as such; they were condemning a misuse of the sabbath and of the other Mosaic institutions.

On the other hand, the prophets do point out the blessings that will follow from a proper observance of the sabbath. There were those who polluted the sabbath and did evil on that day (Is. 56:2–4), and it was necessary to turn from such things. In a classic passage (Is. 58:13) Isaiah sets forth the blessings that will come from a true observance of the day. It is not a day in which man is to do what pleases him, but rather one on which he is to do the will of God. God, not man, must determine how the sabbath is to be observed. Recognizing that the day is holy to the Lord will bring the true enjoyment of the promises.

During the Persian period emphasis was again laid upon observance of the sabbath day. The pre-exilic ban on engaging in commercial transactions on the sabbath (Am. 8:5) or carrying burdens on that day (Je. 17:21f.) was reinforced by Nehemiah (Ne. 10:31; 13:15–22). During the period between the Testaments, however, a change gradually crept in with respect to the understanding of the purpose of the sabbath. In the synagogues the law was studied on the sabbath. Gradually oral tradition made its growth among the Jews, and attention was paid to the minutiae of observance. Two tractates of the Mishnah, *Shabbath* and *'Erubin*, are devoted to a consideration of how the sabbath was to be observed in detail. It was against this burdening of the commands of God with human tradition that our Lord inveighed. His remarks were not directed against the institution of the sabbath as such and not against the OT teaching. But he did oppose the Pharisees who had made the Word of God of none effect with their tradition. Christ identified himself as the Lord of the sabbath (Mk. 2:28). In so speaking, he was not depreciating the importance and significance of the sabbath nor in any way contravening the OT legislation. He was simply pointing out the true significance of the sabbath with respect to man and indicating his right to speak, inasmuch as he himself was the Lord of the sabbath.

As Lord of the sabbath, Jesus went to the synagogue on the sabbath day, as was his custom (Lk. 4:16). His observance of the sabbath was in accord with the OT prescription to regard the day as holy to the Lord.

In his disagreement with the Pharisees (Mt. 12:1–14; Mk. 2:23–28; Lk. 6:1–11) our Lord pointed out to the Jews their complete misunderstanding of the OT commands. They had sought to make the observance of the sabbath more rigorous than God had commanded. It was not wrong to eat on the sabbath, even if the food must be obtained by plucking corn from the ears. Nor was it wrong to do good on the sabbath day. To heal was a work of mercy, and the Lord of the sabbath is merciful (*cf.* also Jn. 5:1–18; Lk. 13:10–17; 14:1–6).

On the first day of the week the Lord rose from the dead, and therefore it early and increasingly became the day above all others—'the * Lord's day' (Rev. 1:10)—on which Christians met for worship (*cf.* Acts 20:7; also *Didache* 14. 1; Justin, *First Apology* 67. 3).

Bibliography. J. Orr, *The Sabbath Scripturally and Practically Considered*, 1886; N. H. Snaith, *The Jewish New Year Festival*, 1947; J. Murray, *Principles of Conduct*, 1957, pp. 30–35; W. Rordorff, *Sunday*, 1968; F. N. Lee, *The Covenantal Sabbath*, 1972; R. T. Beckwith and W. Stott, *This is the Day*, 1978; W. Stott, *NIDNTT* 3, pp. 405–415; A. Lamaire, *RB* 80, 1973, pp. 161–185; S. Bacchiocchi, *From Sabbath to Sunday: An Historical Investigation of the Rise of Sunday Observance in Early Christianity*, 1977.

E.J.Y.
F.F.B.

SABBATH DAY'S JOURNEY
See Weights and measures, Part 3.

SACKBUT
See Music, Part 2.

SABBATICAL YEAR. This term refers to the provision made concerning the land. Lv. 25:2 has *w^{e}šāḇ^{e}ṯâh ā'āreṣ šabbāṯ*, 'the land shall keep a sabbath'. It is also called 'sabbath of solemn rest' and 'year of solemn rest' (Lv. 25:4–5). After 6 years of sowing, pruning and gathering, the land lay fallow for one year. The unattended growth of the field was for the poor to glean and what remained was for the beasts (Ex. 23:11; Dt. 15:2–18). To quiet fears of privation the Israelites were assured by the Lord that the 6th year would provide enough for 3 years (Lv. 25:20f.). From the time of its institution this year of rest was observed in Israel (Ne. 10:31; 1 Macc. 6:49, 53; *cf.* Jos., *Ant.* 12. 378; 14. 206). Lv. 26:34–43; 2 Ch. 36:21; Je. 34:14–22 refer to God's anger concerning the violation of this ordinance.

The culmination of the sabbatical years was reached each 50th year. This was a jubilee (Heb. *yôḇēl*, 'ram', thence 'trumpet' [ram's horn] by which the year was heralded). The sanctions of the sabbatical year were enforced. In addition, property reverted to its original owners, debts were remitted, and Hebrews who had been enslaved for debt were released. It was a time of thanksgiving and an occasion for the exercise of faith that God would provide food (Lv. 25:8, *etc.*).

The significance of rest for the land every 7th year does not lie merely in principles of soil chemistry. Neither does it follow the Canaanite pattern of a 7-year cycle without a harvest followed by 7 years of plenty. In the text the land lies fallow for one year. (See C. H. Gordon, *Ugaritic Literature*, 1949, pp. 5f.) The underlying reason for this arrangement lies in the disclosure that the 7th year of rest is a sabbath of rest both for the land and for the Lord (Lv. 25:2, 4). There is evident here a relation to the * sabbath institution which is grounded in God's creative activity. In accord with this disclosure other elements may be observed, namely, that man is not the sole owner of the soil and he does not hold property in perpetuity but possesses it in trust under God (Lv. 25:23). The Israelite was also to remember he possessed nothing by inherent right, for he was a slave in Egypt (Dt. 15:15). Generosity is motivated by gratitude. D.F.

SABTA, SABTAH. The third son of Cush (Gn. 10:7, *saḇtâ*; 1 Ch. 1:9, *saḇtā'*) whose name also applied to his descendants. From the fact that among the other descendants of * Cush there are names later associated with S Arabia, it is probable that Sabta refers to a tribe in this area.

Bibliography. J. A. Montgomery, *Arabia and the Bible*, 1934, p. 42. T.C.M.

SABTECA. The fifth son of Cush (Gn. 10:7 = 1 Ch. 1:9) whose name also referred to his descendants. The other descendants of Cush include names later associated with S Arabian tribes, indicating that the descendants of Sabteca probably later lived in this area. The name is otherwise unknown.

T.C.M.

SACKCLOTH. A coarse cloth (Heb. *śaq*, Gk. *sakkos*, from which the Eng. word is derived), usually made of goats' hair (*Siphra* 53b) and black in colour (Rev. 6:12). The same Heb. word sometimes means 'sack' (*e.g.* Gn. 42:27), which was evidently made of this material.

Sackcloth was worn as a sign of mourning for the dead (Gn. 37:34; 2 Sa. 3:31; Joel 1:8; Judith 8:5), or of mourning for personal or national disaster (Jb. 16:15; La. 2:10; Est. 4:1; 1 Macc. 2:14), or of penitence for sins (1 Ki. 21:27; Ne. 9:1; Jon. 3:5; Mt. 11:21), or of special prayer for deliverance (2 Ki. 19:1–2; Dn. 9:3; Judith 4:10; Baruch 4:20; 1 Macc. 3:47).

The form of the symbolic sackcloth was often a band or kilt tied around the waist (1 Ki. 20:31–32; Is. 3:24; 20:2; 2 Macc. 10:25). It was usually worn next to the skin (2 Ki. 6:30; Jb. 16:15; 2 Macc. 3:19), and was sometimes kept on all night (1 Ki. 21:27; Joel 1:13). In one case it replaces a robe, presumably over other clothes (Jon. 3:6). Sometimes the sackcloth was spread out to lie on (2 Sa. 21:10; Is. 58:5), or spread out before the altar or on the altar (Judith 4:11).

Palestinian shepherds wore sackcloth because it was cheap and durable (TB, *Shabbath* 64a). Prophets sometimes wore it as a symbol of the repentance which they preached (Is. 20:2; Rev. 11:3). According to Jon. 3:8 and Judith 4:10 even animals were clothed in sackcloth as a sign of national supplication. Wearing sackcloth for mourning and penitence was practised not only in Israel but also in Damascus (1 Ki. 20:31), Moab (Is. 15:3), Ammon (Je. 49:3), Tyre (Ezk. 27:31) and Nineveh (Jon. 3:5).

Clothing with sackcloth is used figuratively of the darkening of the heavenly bodies in Is. 50:3.

Bibliography. G. Dalman, *Arbeit und Sitte*, 5, 1939, pp. 18, 165, 176, 202; H. F. Lutz, *Textiles and Costumes among the Peoples of the Ancient Near East*, 1923, pp. 25–26, 176–177; P. Heinisch, 'Die Trauergebräuche bei den Israeliten', *Biblische Zeitfragen* 13, 1931, 7–8, pp. 16–17. J.T.

SACRAMENTS. The word 'sacrament' (Lat. *sacramentum*) in its technical theological sense, when used to describe certain rites of the Christian faith, belongs to the period of the elaboration of doctrine much later than the NT. The Vulgate in some places thus renders Gk. *mystērion* (Eph. 5:32; Col. 1:27; 1 Tim. 3:16; Rev. 1:20; 17:7), which was, however, more commonly rendered *mysterium* (* Mystery). In early ecclesiastical usage *sacra-*

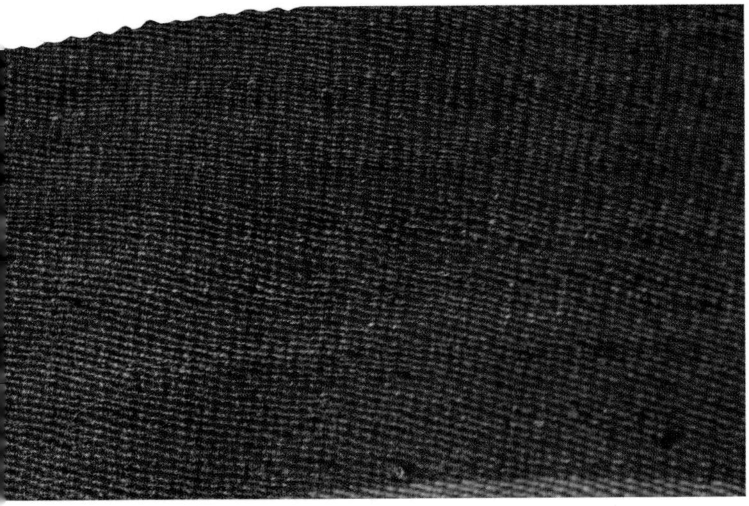

Sackcloth usually denotes a black and cheap coarse cloth woven from goats' hair. (RS)

mentum was used in a wide sense of any ritual observance or sacred thing.

In everyday usage the word had been applied in two ways: (1) as a pledge or security deposited in public keeping by the parties in a lawsuit and forfeited to a sacred purpose; (2) as the oath taken by a Roman soldier to the emperor, and thence to any oath. These ideas later combined to produce the concept of a sacred rite which was a pledge or token, the receipt of which involved an oath of loyalty, and this led in time to the limitation of the word 'sacrament' to the two major rites of divine institution, Baptism and the Lord's Supper. The wider use continued for many centuries. Hugo of St Victor (12th century) can speak of as many as thirty sacraments, but Peter Lombard in the same period estimated seven as the number. The latter estimation is officially accepted by the Roman Church.

The common definition of a sacrament accepted by the Reformed and Roman Churches is that of an outward and visible sign, ordained by Christ, setting forth and pledging an inward and spiritual blessing. The definition owes much to the teaching and language of Augustine, who wrote of the visible form which bore some likeness to the thing invisible. When to this 'element', or visible form, the word of Christ's institution was added, a sacrament was made, so that the sacrament could be spoken of as 'the visible word' (see Augustine, *Tracts on the Gospel of John* 80; *Epistles* 98; *Contra Faustum* 19. 16; *Sermons* 272).

Does the NT teach the obligation of sacramental rites on all Christians? What spiritual benefit is there in their reception, and how is it conveyed?

The obligation to continue sacramental rites depends on: (1) their institution by Christ; (2) his express command for their continuance; (3) their essential use as symbols of divine acts integral to the gospel revelation. There are only two rites obligatory in these ways on all Christians. There is no scriptural warrant for giving the other so-called sacramental rites (*i.e.* Confirmation, Orders, Matrimony, Penance, Extreme Unction) the same status as *Baptism and the *Lord's Supper, which from the beginning are together associated with the proclamation of the gospel and the life of the church (Acts 2:41–42; *cf.* 1 Cor. 10:1–4). They are linked with circumcision and the Passover, the obligatory rites of the OT (Col. 2:11; 1 Cor. 5:7; 11:26). The Christian life is associated in its beginning and in its continuance with sacramental observance (Acts 2:38; 1 Cor. 11:26). Some of the deepest lessons of holiness and perfection are implicit in what Scripture says regarding the Christian's sacramental obligations (Rom. 6:1–3; 1 Cor. 12:13; Eph. 4:5). References to the sacraments may underlie many passages where there is no explicit mention of them (*e.g.* Jn. 3; 6; 19:34; Heb. 10:22). The risen Lord's great commission to the disciples to go to all nations with the gospel specifically commands the administration of Baptism and clearly implies observance of the Lord's Supper (Mt. 28:19–20). Christ promises to be with his servants until the end of time. The work to which he has called them, including the observance of the sacraments, will not be completed before then. Paul also has no doubt that the Lord's Supper is to be continued, as a showing forth of the death of Christ, till he comes again (1 Cor. 11:26). It is true that Matthew and Mark do not record the command 'this do in remembrance of me', but the evidence of the practice of the early church (Acts 2:42; 20:7; 1 Cor. 10:16; 11:26) more than compensates for this.

The efficacy of the sacraments depends on the institution and command of Christ. The elements in themselves have no power; it is their faithful use that matters. For through them men are brought into communion with Christ in his death and resurrection (Rom. 6:3; 1 Cor. 10:16). Forgiveness (Acts 2:38), cleansing (Acts 22:16; *cf.* Eph. 5:26) and spiritual quickening (Col. 2:12) are associated with baptism. Participation in the body and blood of Christ is realized through Holy Communion (1 Cor. 10:16; 11:27). Baptism and the cup are linked together in the teaching of our Lord when he speaks of his death, and in the mind of the church when it remembers its solemn obligations (Mk. 10:38–39; 1 Cor. 10:1–5).

The sacraments are covenant rites: 'This cup is the new covenant' (Lk. 22:20; 1 Cor. 11:25). We are baptized 'into the name' (Mt. 28:19, RV). The new covenant was initiated by the sacrifice of the death of Christ (*cf.* Ex. 24:8; Je. 31:31–32). Its blessings are conveyed by God through his word and promise in the gospel and its sacraments. There is clear evidence that many in apostolic days received blessing through the administration of the sacraments accompanied by the preaching of the word (Acts 2:38ff.). It was the gospel word or promise accompanying administration which gave meaning and efficacy to the rite. Those who had received only John's baptism were baptized again 'in the name of the Lord Jesus' (Acts 19:1–7). It is apparent also that some received the sacraments without spiritual benefit (Acts 8:12, 21; 1 Cor. 11:27; 10:5–12). In the case of Cornelius and his household (Acts 10:44–48) we have an example of some who received the gifts which baptism seals, before they received the sacrament. Nevertheless, they still received the sacrament as bestowing benefit and as an obligation.

In the NT there is no conflict suggested between the use of sacraments and spirituality. When they are rightly received the sacraments do convey blessings to the believer. But these blessings are not confined to the use of the sacraments, nor when they are conveyed through the sacraments does their bestowal conflict in any way with the strong, scriptural emphasis on faith and godliness. The sacraments, when administered in accordance with the principles laid down in Scripture, recall us continually to the great ground of our salvation, Christ in his death and resurrection, and remind us of the obligations we have to walk worthily of the calling wherewith we are called.

BIBLIOGRAPHY. O. C. Quick, *The Christian Sacraments*, 1932; G. Bornkamm in *TDNT* 4, pp. 826f.; J. Jeremias, *The Eucharistic Words of Jesus*, 1955; W. F. Flemington, *The New Testament Doctrine of Baptism*, 1957; A. M. Stibbs, *Sacrament, Sacrifice and Eucharist*, 1961; G. R. Beasley-Murray, *Baptism in the New Testament*, 1962; J. I. Packer (ed.), *Eucharistic Sacrifice*, 1962; D. Cairns, *In Remembrance of Me*, 1967. R.J.C.

SACRED PROSTITUTION
See Prostitution, Part 3.

SACRIFICE AND OFFERING.

I. In the Old Testament

a. Terms

The OT has no general word for 'sacrifice', except the rather sparsely used *qorbān*, 'that which is brought near' (*qrb*), which is practically confined to the levitical literature. (AV renders this term 'Corban' in the single NT reference of Mk. 7:11.) *'iššeh* may also serve this purpose in the laws, but it is debated whether it should not be limited to 'fire-offerings' (*'ēš*) (but *cf.* Lv. 24:9). The other frequently used words describe particular kinds of sacrifice, and are derived either from the mode of sacrifice, as *zeḇaḥ* (sacrifice), 'that which is slain' (*zāḇaḥ*), and *'ôlâ* (burnt-offering), 'that which goes up', or from its purpose, as *'āšām* (guilt-offering), 'for guilt' (*'āšām*), and *ḥaṭṭā'ṯ* (sin-offering), 'for sin' (*ḥaṭṭā'ṯ*). These may be distinguished in part by the disposal of the victim, whether wholly burnt (*'ôlâ*, Lv. 1), or eaten by priests and worshippers together (*zeḇaḥ*, Lv. 3), or eaten by the priests alone (*ḥaṭṭā'ṯ* and *'āšām*, Lv. 4–5). For the distinction of *'ôlâ* and *zeḇaḥ*, see Dt. 12:27 (*cf.* Je. 7:21, where the prophet ironically suggests an obliteration of the distinction).

Also included under *qorbān* were the non-blood offerings 'offering, oblation', the cereal-offering (*minḥâ*, Lv. 2), the firstfruits (*rē'šîṯ*, *bikkûrîm*), the sheaf of 16 Nisan, the dough of the Feast of Weeks, and the tithes.

b. Theories of the beginnings

Sacrifice was not confined to Israel among the nations of antiquity (*cf.* Jdg. 16:23; 1 Sa. 6:4; 2 Ki. 3:27; 5:17), and many parallels from surrounding nations have been adduced in explanation of Israelite sacrifice. W. R. Smith ('Sacrifice', *EBr*[9], 21, 1886, pp. 132–138; *The Religion of the Semites*, 1889) constructed, from the pre-Islamic nomadic Arabs, a hypothetical 'Semite', to whom the sacrificial meal was the earliest form, and the communion of the worshippers and the deity the controlling idea. The Pan-Babylonian movement (H. Winckler, A. Jeremias, from *c.* 1900 onwards) looked to the higher civilization of Mesopotamia, and to the developed ritual of propitiatory sacrifice practised there.

R. Dussaud preferred a Canaanite background, and found parallels first in the Carthaginian sacrificial tariffs (*Le sacrifice en Israel et chez les Phéniciens*, 1914; *Les origines cananéennes du sacrifice israélite*, 1921), and later in the Ras Shamra texts (*Les découvertes de Ras Shamra et l'Ancien Testament*, 1937). Here the materials of ancient Ugarit (*c.* 1400 BC) indicated a developed ritual of sacrifices bearing names similar to those of the OT. The *šrp* was a burnt-offering, the *dbḥ*, a slain-offering for a meal, the *šlm*, possibly a propitiatory sacrifice, and the *'aṯm*, the equivalent of the Heb. *'āšām*. (These were not Dussaud's identifications.) The myth and ritual school (S. H. Hooke, *The Origins of Early Semitic Ritual*, 1938; I. Engnell, *Studies in Divine Kingship in the Ancient Near East*, 1943) stressed this sedentary background and laid weight on the substitutionary role of the suffering king in the cult.

This was not convincing to A. Alt, who had earlier claimed (*Der Gott der Väter*, 1929, now in *Essays on OT History and Religion*, 1966, pp. 1–77) that the real antecedents of Israelite faith were to be sought rather among the nomad Patriarchs, who had practised a form of religion centring in the god of the head of the clan (the 'God of Abraham', the 'God of Isaac', the 'God of Jacob'). V. Maag ('Der Hirte Israels', *Schweizerische Theologische Umschau* 28, 1958, pp. 2–28) took this further by noticing the dominance of the shepherd metaphor in the descriptions of this God, and from a background of the migrant shepherd cultures of the Asiatic steppes, suggested that their sacrifice was the fellowship meal in which the god took over the responsibility of the shed blood which would otherwise have exacted vengeance (*cf.* A. E. Jensen, 'Über das Töten als kulturgeschichtliche Erscheinung', *Paideuma* 4, 1950, pp. 23–38; H. Baumann, 'Nyama, die Rachemacht', *ibid.*, pp. 191–230). Israelite religion, as it appears in the OT, is a syncretism in which the nomadic *zeḇaḥ* sacrifice exists alongside of gift sacrifices of the *'ôlâ* type, which come in from the sedentary Canaanite side (V. Maag, *VT* 6, 1956, pp. 10–18).

Such a view finds place for both the sedentary and nomadic aspects, but becomes subjective when applied to particular OT narratives. The OT depicts early Israel less as nomadic than as a people in process of sedentarization. The Patriarchs already have the larger bovines and engage in some agriculture, and it may well be that a closer parallel to Hebrew sacrifice may be found among a tribe such as the African Nuer, whose sacrifice, as described by E. Evans-Pritchard (*Nuer Religion*, 1956) involved the offering of an ox in substitution for sin. The Wellhausen school, which traced an evolution from a joyous sacrificial meal in the earlier time to sin-offerings and guilt-offerings only in the post-exilic period (J. Wellhausen, *Prolegomena to the History of Israel*, 1885; W. R. Smith, *op. cit.*), regarded the connection of sacrifice with sin as the latest element. But this is no longer probable (*cf.* the writer's *Penitence and Sacrifice in Early Israel*, 1963), as the following historical sketch will show.

c. The development in the history

1. *Patriarchal.* It is significant that the first sacrifices mentioned in Gn. were not *zᵉḇāḥîm* meals, but the gift-offerings of Cain and Abel (*minḥâ*, Gn. 4:3–4), and the burnt-offering of Noah (*'ôlâ*, Gn. 8:20; we have here the first reference to an altar). Patriarchal altars are often described (*e.g.* Gn. 12:6–8), but unfortunately details as to the type of sacrifice are lacking. Maag thinks of the *zeḇaḥ* communion

meal, but T. C. Vriezen (*An Outline of Old Testament Theology*, 1958, p. 26) thinks the *'ôlâ* more typical. Gn. 22 gives some support to the latter position. Isaac knows that Abraham is in the habit of offering *'ôlâ* and that a lamb is the likely victim (v. 7). Sacrificial meals do, however, seal covenants (Gn. 31:54, first use of *zeḇaḥ*), but not all covenants are of this type. Gn. 15:9–11 is best understood as a purificatory ritual like that of the Hittite text translated by O. Masson (*RHR* 137, 1950, pp. 5–25; *cf.* O. R. Gurney, *The Hittites*, 1952, p. 151).

As to the motives of sacrifice in this period, honouring of God and thanksgiving for his goodness were prominent, but more solemn thoughts cannot be ruled out. Noah's offering is to be seen, not simply as a thank-offering for deliverance, but as an expiation or atonement. When Jacob goes to Egypt (Gn. 46:1), he pauses to seek God's will, and offers sacrifices (*zeḇaḥ*), which were possibly expiatory (*cf.* I. Rost, *VTSupp* 7, 1960, p. 354; *ZDPV* 66, 1943, pp. 205–216). In Egypt Israel is called to a solemn sacrifice in the wilderness (Ex. 5:3, *zeḇaḥ*), which required animal victims (Ex. 10:25–26) and was distinguished from any offered by the Egyptians (Ex. 8:26).

2. *Tribal.* The establishment of Israel as a tribal organization, which Noth thinks of as coming into being only on the soil of Palestine in the time of the Judges (*cf. The History of Israel*, 1958), is taken back by strong biblical tradition to the time of Moses. Chief among tribal occasions were the three festivals, at which sacrifice was to be offered: 'none shall appear before me empty-handed' (Ex. 23:15). The sacrifices we know best were those of the *Passover and the *covenant. The Passover combined the elements of sacrifice as an apotropaic and sacrifice as a communion meal. Secure in the knowledge that the blood had been shed to ward off evil, the members of each family could sit down to joyful fellowship (Ex. 12; Jos. 5:5–12). Similar elements probably entered into the covenant sacrifice and its renewals (Ex. 24:1–8; Dt. 27:1ff.; Jos. 8:30ff.; 24; *cf.* Ps. 50:5). The blood-sprinkling purified the covenant and the eating of the meal marked its consummation.

In addition, many other sacrifices both national and local were offered. Typical of national sacrifices were those in times of disaster or war (Jdg. 20:26; 21:4; 1 Sa. 7:9), when penitence seems to have been the main note (*cf.* Jdg. 2:1–5). Dedications and new beginnings were marked by sacrifice (Jdg. 6:28; Ex. 32:6; 1 Sa. 6:14; 11:15; 2 Sa. 6:17), as were individual occasions of celebration (1 Sa. 1:3), intercession (Nu. 23:1ff.), and perhaps hospitality (Ex. 18:12).

3. *Monarchic.* The building of the Temple by Solomon provided opportunity for initiatory (1 Ki. 8:62ff.) and regular sacrifices (1 Ki. 9:25), but as the sources are books of 'kings' they speak rather of royal participation (*cf.* 2 Ki. 16:10ff.) than of that of the people. That the everyday cult was in progress, however, is attested by such a verse as 2 Ki. 12:16, and by the frequent mention of sacrifice in the prophets and psalms. The many favourable references in the latter show that the condemnations of the former are not to be taken in an absolute sense, as if prophet and priest were opposed. The prophets object less to the cult itself than to the magic-working ideas borrowed from the fertility cults (Am. 4:4–5; Is. 1:11–16), and to such innovations as idolatry and child sacrifice introduced by apostatizing rulers (Je. 19:4; Ezk. 16:21).

An Isaiah can receive his call in the Temple (Is. 6), and a Jeremiah or an Ezekiel can find a place for a purified cult in the future (Je. 17:26; Ezk. 40–48). This is also the predominant feeling of the psalmists, who constantly speak of their sacrifices of thanksgiving in payment of their vows (*e.g.* Ps. 66:13–15). Expressions of penitence and the joy of forgiveness are also present (Pss. 32; 51) and, although sacrifice is not often mentioned in these contexts, it is probably to be assumed from the fact that forgiveness is experienced in the Temple (Ps. 65:1–5). While there is no need to make all such references post-exilic, the prophets' complaint that penitence did not often enough accompany sacrifice in the late kingdom period should also be borne in mind.

4. *Post-exilic.* The disaster of the Exile is usually seen as resulting in a deeper sense of sin, and no doubt this is true (*cf.* 2 Ki. 17:7ff.; Ne. 9), but not in the sense of Wellhausen that only then could the expiatory note of Lv. 1–7 and Lv. 16 have entered Israelite religion. References to sacrifice in the non-levitical writings before and after the Exile, although usually too fragmentary to decide the issue, give little support to such an evolution. Joy, as well as penitence, continues to characterize sacrifice (Ezr. 6:16–18; Ne. 8:9ff.). Temple and cult are valued (Hg. 1–2; Joel 2:14, and especially Chronicles), but only as they are the vehicles of sincere worship (Mal. 1:6ff.; 3:3ff.). Apocalyptic and Wisdom literature take the cult for granted (Dn. 9:21, 27; Ec. 5:4; 9:2) and also continue the

Sacrificial animals carried in a procession. Basalt relief from Carchemish. Height 1 m. 9th–8th cent. BC. (BM)

prophetic moral emphasis (Ec. 5:1; Pr. 15:8).

d. The regulations of the laws

Laws for sacrifice are scattered through all the codes (Ex. 20:24ff.; 34:25ff.; Lv. 17; 19:5ff.; Nu. 15; Dt. 12, *etc.*), but the sacrificial 'torah' *par excellence* is Lv. 1–7. Chs. 1–5 deal in turn with the burnt-offering (*'ôlâ*), cereal-offering (*minḥâ*), peace-offering (*zeḇaḥ*), sin-offering (*ḥaṭṭā'ṯ*) and guilt-offering (*'āšām*), while chs. 6–7 give additional regulations for all five—6:8–13 (burnt); 6:14–18 (cereal); 6:24–30 (sin); 7:1–10 (guilt); 7:11ff. (peace). From these and other references the following synthetic account is compiled.

1. *The materials.* The sacrificial victim had to be taken from the clean animals and birds (Gn. 8:20), and could be bullock, goat, sheep, dove or pigeon (*cf.* Gn. 15:9), but not camel or ass (Ex. 13:13) (*CLEAN AND UNCLEAN). These provisions are not to be traced to the idea of sacrifice as 'food for the gods' (*viz.* that the gods ate what man ate)—as might be suggested by Lv. 3:11; 21:6; Ezk. 44:7—for fish (Lv. 11:9) and wild animals (Dt. 12:22) could be eaten but not sacrificed. The principle seems rather to have been that of property (*cf.* 2 Sa. 24:24), the wild animals being regarded as in some sense already God's (Ps. 50:9ff.; *cf.* Is. 40:16), while the domestic animals had become man's by his labours (Gn. 22:13 is only apparently an exception), and were in a kind of 'biotic rapport' with him. This was even more clearly the case with the non-blood offerings, which had been produced by 'the sweat of his brow' (cereals, flour, oil, wine, *etc.*), and were also staple articles of the kitchen. Property unlawfully acquired was not acceptable (Dt. 23:18).

The principle of 'the best for God' was observed throughout—as to sex, males being preferred to females (Lv. 1:3; but *cf.* Lv. 3:1; Gn. 15:9; 1 Sa. 6:14; 16:2); as to age, maturity being especially valuable (1 Sa. 1:24); as to physical perfection, 'without blemish' being constantly emphasized (Lv. 1:3; 3:1; Dt. 15:21; 17:1; 22:17–25; *cf.* Mal. 1:6ff., but note the exception for free-will offerings Lv. 22:23); and in some cases as to colour, red being chosen (Nu. 19:2), perhaps as representing blood (*cf.* prehistoric cave paintings of animals). The difference between Israel and her neighbours is clearly seen in the rejection of the extension of this principle to what might be thought its logical climax in the human first-born. The child sacrifice, which was present in the late kingdom (2 Ki. 21:6), and the human sacrifices occasionally reported of earlier times (Jdg. 11:29ff.), were from outside influences, and were condemned by prophet (Je. 7:31ff.), precept (Lv. 20:4) and example (Gn. 22). Ex. 22:29b is clearly to be interpreted by Ex. 34:19–20 and Ex. 13:12–16. The principle of substitution is present, not only in this replacing of the human first-born by an animal victim but in the provision given to the poor to offer the cheaper doves for a sin-offering (Lv. 5:7) and, if even this was too much, a cereal-offering (Lv. 5:11). The words 'such as he can afford' (Lv. 14:22, *etc.*) are very significant here.

Libations of oil (Gn. 28:18), wine (Gn. 35:14) and water (?1 Sa. 7:6) seem to have had a place in the cult, but only the wine-offerings are referred to in the basic laws (Nu. 28:7, *etc.*). The prohibition of leaven and honey (with some exceptions), and possibly also of milk, is probably to be put down to their liability to putrefaction. For the opposite reason salt was probably added to the sacrifices, because of its well-known preservative qualities (mentioned only in Lv. 2:13 and Ezk. 43:24, but *cf.* Mk. 9:49). *Incense (*l^eḇônâ, q^eṭōreṯ*) played a considerable role, both as an independent offering (Ex. 30:7, *cf.* the instructions for its making in vv. 34–38) and as an accompaniment of the cereal-offering (Lv. 2). Many scholars, doubting its early use on the ground that it was neither edible nor home-grown property (Je. 6:20), think *q^eṭōreṯ* in the historical books describes the burning of the fat (*qṭr*) rather than incense, but this is not certain. (See N. H. Snaith, *IB*, 3, 1954, p. 40, and J. A. Montgomery, *ICC*, *Kings*, 1952, p. 104, also *VT* 10, 1960, pp. 113–129.)

2. *The occasions.* The regulations cover both national and individual offerings, and daily and festival occasions. The first public sacrifices with good attestation are the seasonal ones, the Feast of Unleavened Bread, Firstfruits or Weeks and Ingathering or *Tabernacles (Ex. 23:14–17; 34:18–23; Dt. 16). With the first the *Passover was early connected (Jos. 5:10–12), and with the last, in all probability, covenant renewal ceremonies (*cf.* Ex. 24; Dt. 31:10ff.; Jos. 24) and possibly new year and atoning rites (*cf.* Lv. 23:27ff.) (*PENTECOST.) A full tariff of sacrifices for these, and for additional observances, monthly (new moon), weekly (sabbath) and daily (morning and evening), is found in Nu. 28–29, and may be set out in tabular form (see the chart on p. 1363).

The date of the beginning of the twice-daily burnt-offering is controverted, and certainty is difficult to arrive at, because of the ambiguous nature of *minḥâ* for both cereal- and burnt-offerings. (See the chart at the top of p. 1364.) *'ôlâ* and *minḥâ* are also referred to without time notes in 1 Sa. 3:14; Je. 14:12; and Ps. 20:3, and continual *'ōlôṯ* and *minḥôṯ* in Ezr. 3:3ff. and Ne. 10:33.

Sacrifices of a more private nature were the Passover, for which the unit was the family (Ex. 12; *cf.* 1 Sa. 20:6, but this was a new moon, not a full moon), and individual sacrifices, such as those in fulfilment of a vow (1 Sa. 1:3, *cf.* v. 21; 2 Sa. 15:7ff.), or in confirmation of a treaty (Gn. 31:54), veneration of God (Jdg. 13:19), personal dedication (1 Ki. 3:4), consecration (1 Sa. 16:3) or expiation (2 Sa. 24:17ff.). Whether the extending of hospitality to a guest was always regarded as a sacrificial occasion is not clear (Gn. 18; Nu. 22:40; 1 Sa. 28:24 may not have involved altar rites, but *cf.* 1 Sa. 9). Additional occasions mentioned in the laws are the cleansing of the leper (Lv. 14), purification after child-birth (Lv. 12), the consecration of a priest (Lv. 8–9) or a Levite (Nu. 8), and the release of a Nazirite from his vows (Nu. 6). Less frequent sacrifices were those of sanctuary dedication (2 Sa. 6:13; 1 Ki. 8:5ff.; Ezk. 43:18ff.; Ezr. 3:2ff.), royal coronations (1 Sa. 11:15; 1 Ki. 1:9), and days of national penitence (Jdg. 20:26; 1 Sa. 7) or preparation for battle (1 Sa. 13:8ff.; Ps. 20).

Among seasonal offerings brought annually in recognition of God's share in productivity were firstlings and firstfruits (Ex. 13; 23:19; Dt. 15:19ff.; 18:4; 26; Nu. 18; *cf.* Gn. 4:3–4; 1 Sa. 10:3; 2 Ki. 4:42), *tithes, and the offerings of the first sheaf (Lv. 23:9ff.) and the first dough (Nu. 15:18–21; Ezk. 44:30; *cf.* Lv. 23:15ff.). Their purpose was probably not to consecrate the rest of the crop, but to deconsecrate it. All was God's until the first portion had been offered and accepted in lieu of the whole.

Only then was the restriction on the human use of the remainder removed (Lv. 23:14, *cf.* 19:23–25). Even the portion brought was usually presented only in token at the altar, and afterwards taken away for the use of the priests or for a sacrificial meal. This was also the final fate of the weekly *showbread.

3. *The ritual.* The major altar sacrifices of Lv. 1–5 are described in a framework of a stereotyped ritual comprising six acts, of which three belong to the worshipper and three to the priest. They may be illustrated from the *'ôlâ* and the *zebaḥ* (*cf.* R. Rendtorff, *Die Gesetze in der Priesterschrift*, 1954). (See the chart on p. 1365.) The provisions for the sin-offering, several times repeated for various classes (Lv. 4:1–12, 13–21, 22–26, 27–31), follow the same scheme, except in minor details. The burnt-offering of a bird (Lv. 1:14–17) and the cereal-offering (Lv. 2) of necessity present greater variations, but are not entirely dissimilar. A similar formula for the guilt-offering is not given (*cf.*, however, 7:1–7), but it may be understood as coming under the law of the sin-offering (Lv. 7:7).

(i) The worshipper brings near (*hiqrîḇ*) his offering (also *hēḇî'*, *'āśâh*). The place of the sacrifice is the tabernacle forecourt on the N side of the altar (for burnt-, sin- and guilt-offerings, but not for the more numerous peace-offerings), although in earlier times it may have been the door of the tabernacle (Lv. 17:4), or local sanctuary (1 Sa. 2:12ff.), or a rough altar of stone or earth (Ex. 20:24ff.) or a rock (1 Sa. 6:14) or pillar (Gn. 28:18). Killing *on* the altar, although implied by Gn. 22:9 and Ex. 20:24 (Ps. 118:27 is corrupt), is not normal in the cult.

(ii) He lays (*sāmaḵ*) his hands, or in the biblical period more probably one hand (*cf.* Nu. 27:18), upon the victim, and possibly confesses his sin. This latter is mentioned, however, only in connection with the scapegoat, where the blood was not shed (Lv. 16:21) and with some sin-offerings (Lv. 5:5) and guilt-offerings (Nu. 5:7) (*cf.*, however, Dt. 26:3; Jos. 7:19–20), so that the *s^emîḵâ* cannot certainly be claimed as a transferring of sin. On the other hand, it seems inadequate to regard it simply as an identification by the owner of his property, for such an identification is not made with the non-blood sacrifices, where it would have been equally appropriate. Representation, if not transference, seems to be clearly involved (*cf.* the use of the same word for the commissioning of Joshua (Nu. 27:18) and the Levites (Nu. 8:10) and the stoning of a blasphemer (Lv. 24:13f.)). See P. Volz, *ZAW* 21, 1901, pp. 93–100, and for an opposite view J. C. Matthes, *ibid.* 23, 1903, pp. 97–119.

(iii) The slaughtering (*šāḥaṭ*) is performed by the worshipper, except for the national offerings (Lv. 16:11; 2 Ch. 29:24). In the non-levitical literature the verb *zāḇaḥ* is used, but this may have referred to the subsequent cutting up of the sacrifice, and the laying of the parts on the altar (*mizbēaḥ*, not *mišḥaṭ*) (so K. Galling, *Der Altar*, 1925, pp. 56ff.). For this, however, *ntḥ* is normally used (1 Ki. 18:23; Lv. 1:6), and *zāḇaḥ* describes rather the *z^eḇāḥîm* sacrifices, except for a few passages (Ex. 20:24; 1 Ki. 3:4; *cf.* 2 Ki. 10:18ff.) where it occurs with *'ōlôṯ*. These are perhaps to be put down to a loose use of the verb, which in the cognate languages can even be used of vegetable offerings, and in the *Piēl* in Heb. seems to be used quite generally for the whole round of the (usually apostate) cult. It is not certain, then, that every use of *zeḇaḥ* was sacrificial, or that meat could be eaten only on occasions of sacrifice, although this was often the case in antiquity (*cf.* the problem of the idol-meat at Corinth) (see N. H. Snaith, *VT* 25, 1975, pp. 242–246).

(iv) The manipulation (*zāraq*) of the blood is in the hands of the priest, who collects it in a basin and dashes it against the NE and SW corners of the altar in such a way that all four sides are spattered. This takes place with the animal burnt-offerings (Lv. 1), peace-offerings (Lv. 3) and guilt-offerings (Lv. 7:2), but not with the burnt-offering of birds (Lv. 1:15), where the quantity of blood was insufficient, and so was drained out on the side of the altar. The sin-offering (Lv. 4) uses a different set of verbs, *hizzâ* ('sprinkle') or *nāṯan* ('put') according to whether the offering is of primary or secondary rank (see below). The remainder of the blood is then poured out (*šāp̄aḵ*) at the base of the altar. The blood rite is referred to in the historical books only in 2 Ki. 16:15 (but *cf.* 1 Sa. 14:31–35; Ex. 24:6–8). (See Th. C. Vriezen, *OTS* 7, 1950, pp. 201–235; D. J. McCarthy, *JBL* 88, 1969, pp. 166–176; 92, 1973, pp. 205–210; N. H. Snaith, *ExpT* 82, 1970–71, pp. 23f.)

(v) Some burning (*hiqṭîr*) took place with all the sacrifices. Not only the blood but also the fat belonged to God, and this was first burnt (Gn. 4:4; 1 Sa. 2:16). This was not the fat in general, but specifically the fat of the kidneys, liver and intestines. From the peace-, sin- and guilt-offerings only this was burnt, from the cereal-offerings a portion called the *'azkārâ* was separated off and burnt, but the burnt-offering was wholly burnt except for the skin, which became the perquisite of the priests (Lv. 7:8). A different kind of burning (*śārap̄*) away from the altar was the fate of the primary rank sin-offerings. In this burning the skin was also included.

(vi) The remaining portions of the sacrifice were eaten (*'āḵal*) in a sacrificial meal, either by the priests and worshippers together (peace-offering), or by the priests and their families, or by the priests alone. Priestly food was classified as either holy or most holy. The former included the peace-offerings (Lv. 10:14; 22:10ff.) and firstfruits and tithes (Nu. 18:13), and could be eaten by the priest's family in any clean place, but the latter included the sin-offerings (Lv. 6:26), guilt-offerings (Lv. 7:6), cereal-offerings (Lv. 6:16), and showbread (Lv. 24:9), and could be eaten only by the priests themselves, and within the Temple precincts. The people's sacrificial meal from the peace-offering was the popular accompaniment of local worship in early times (1 Sa. 1; 9), but with the centralization of the cult in Jerusalem (*cf.* Dt. 12) tended to recede before the formal aspects of worship. As late as Ezk. 46:21–24, however, provision continued to be made for it.

4. *The kinds.* (i) *'ôlâ.* The burnt-offering seems to have a better claim to be regarded as the typical Hebrew sacrifice than the *zeḇaḥ* favoured by the Wellhausen school. It is present from the beginning (?Gn. 4; 8:20; 22:2; Ex. 10:25; 18:12; Jdg. 6:26; 13:16), early became a regular rite (1 Ki. 9:25; *cf.* 1 Ki. 10:5), was never omitted on great occasions (1 Ki. 3:4; Jos. 8:31), and retained its dominant role to the latest times (Ezk. 43:18; Ezr. 3:2–4) (see R. Rendtorff, *Studien zur Geschichte des Opfers im alten Israel*, 1967). Whatever may be said for Robertson Smith's view of a primary peace-offering, from

Opposite page: Equipment for sacrifice, and perhaps the dawn ritual, in front of a stepped temple-tower (ziggurat), *includes altars and libation bowls. Bronze model from Susa, Iran. Length 60 cm, width 40 cm. 12th cent.* BC. (MC)

Opposite page: Chart of the occasions laid down for public sacrifice and offerings (*Nu. 28–29*).

which the burnt-offering later developed, as far as the OT is concerned it is from the *'ôlâ* that the *minḥâ*, *'āšām*, *ḥaṭṭā'ṯ* and even *šᵉlāmîm* seem to have arisen. The *kālîl* referred to five times (1 Sa. 7:9; Ps. 51:19; Dt. 33:10; *cf.* Dt. 13:16 and Lv. 6:22–23) is also another name for the *'ôlâ*, although apparently differing somewhat in the Carthage and Marseilles tariffs.

While there is truth in Rost's view that the incidence of the *'ôlâ* is confined to Greece and the region 'bordered by the Taurus in the N, the Mediterranean in the W and the desert in the E and S' ('Erwägungen zum israelitischen Brandopfer', *Von Ugarit nach Qumran* (Eissfeldt Festschrift), 1958, pp. 177–183), it does not follow that its origins in Israel are in human sacrifice (2 Ki. 3:27) or rites of aversion of the Greek kind. Its undoubted gift character is apparent from the sublimation of the elements into a form in which they can be transported to God (Jdg. 6:21; 13:20; *cf.* Dt. 33:10), but this does not say anything about the purpose of the gift, which may have been of homage and thanksgiving, or to expiate sin. The latter note is present in Jb. 1:5; 42:8 and many early passages, and is given as the reason for the sacrifice in Lv. 1:4 (*cf.* the Ugaritic Text 9:7, where the burnt-offering (*šrp*) is connected to forgiveness of soul (*slḥ npš*)). When the sin-offering came to take precedence as the first of the series of sacrifices (Mishnah, *Zebahim* 10. 2) it tended to take over this function, but this was not originally the case (*cf.* Nu. 28–29, and *cf.* Nu. 6:14 with 6:11).

(ii) *minḥâ* ('meal-offering', AV 'meat-offering', RSV 'cereal-offering'. It is somewhat confusing that this term is used in three different ways in the OT: 34 times it simply means 'present' or 'tribute' (*cf.* Jdg. 3:15; 1 Ki. 4:21—the root is probably *mānaḥ*, 'to give', *cf.* the peculiar form of the plural in the *MT* of Ps. 20:3), 97 times in the levitical literature it is the cereal-offering (*e.g.* in Lv. 2), and an indeterminate number of the remaining instances also have this meaning (*e.g.* Is. 43:23; 66:20), but in the others it refers to sacrifice generally (1 Sa. 2:29; 26:19, and probably in Malachi), and to animal sacrifice in particular (1 Sa. 2:12–17; Gn. 4:3–4; but see N. H. Snaith, *VT* 7, 1957, pp. 314–316). S. R. Driver rightly defines *minḥâ* as not merely expressing the neutral idea of gift, but as denoting 'a present made to secure or retain good-will' (*HDB*, 3, 1900, p. 587; *cf.* Gn. 33:10), and this propitiatory sense is to the fore also in such sacrificial references as 1 Sa. 3:10–14; 26:19.

In these references the *minḥâ* is an independent sacrifice, whereas in the laws it is the accompaniment of burnt-offerings and peace-offerings (Nu. 15:1–16), except in Nu. 5:15, 25; Lv. 5:11–13; 6:19–23. According to Lv. 2, it is to consist of either flour (2:1–3), baked cakes (2:4–10) or raw grain (2:14–16), together with oil and frankincense (*lᵉḇônâ*). With this '*minḥâ* of the forecourt' may be compared what J. H. Kurtz called the '*minḥâ* of the holy place' —the altar of incense, the showbread on the table and the oil in the lamp (*The Sacrificial Worship of the Old Testament*, 1865). Other ingredients might be salt (Lv. 2:13) and wine (Lv. 23:13). None of these offerings was eaten by the worshippers (but ?Lv. 7:11–18). They went to the priests, but only after a 'memorial portion' (Lv. 2:2) had been burnt on the altar. This RSV translation implies a derivation of *'azkārâ* from *zāḵar*, but G. R. Driver has suggested the meaning 'token', a part for the whole (*JSS* 1, 1956, pp. 97–105), and this would be yet another instance of the principle of substitution in the sacrifices.

(iii) *zeḇaḥ* and *šᵉlāmîm*. Again there is a variety of usage, in which *zeḇaḥ* and *šᵉlāmîm* are sometimes interchangeable (Lv. 7:11–21; 2 Ki. 16:13, 15), sometimes distinguished (Jos. 22:27; *f.* Ex. 24:5; 1 Sa. 11:15), sometimes independent (2 Sa. 6:17–18; Ex. 32:6), and sometimes combined into a compound expression *zeḇaḥ šᵉlāmîm* or *ziḇᵉḥê šᵉlāmîm* (so usually in the levitical law). It is doubtful if all these uses are to be understood as referring simply to the *zeḇaḥ* sacrificial meal. *šᵉlāmîm*, when used alone, was possibly not a meal at all (*cf.*, however, 2 Sa. 6:19), but a solemn expiatory offering akin to the *'ôlâ* (so R. Rendtorff, *Studien zur Geschichte des Opfers*), and in conjunction with other sacrifices may still have retained this meaning. A *šlm* of a propitiatory kind seems to have been known at Ugarit (D. M. L. Urie, 'Sacrifice among the West Semites', *PEQ* 81, 1949, pp. 75–77) and is reflected in such passages as Jdg. 20:26; 1 Sa. 13:9; 2 Sa. 24:25. It is in no way inconsistent that a joyous meal followed, if the joy was the joy of forgiveness, for the *zeḇaḥ* covenant meal also usually marked a reconciliation after estrangement (Gn. 31:54; *cf.* S. I. Curtiss, 'The Semitic Sacrifice of Reconciliation', *The Expositor*, 6th series, 6, 1902, pp. 454–462).

Either of the proposed derivations of *šelem*—from *šālôm*, 'peace', so 'to make peace' (*cf.* G. Fohrer, 'to make complete' so 'concluding offering'; *TDNT* 7, pp. 1022–1023) or from *šillēm*, 'compensate', so 'to pay off, expiate' (*cf.* B. A. Levine, 'a tribute, a present, a gift of greeting', *In the Presence of the Lord*, 1974)—would be in keeping and preferable to the reduction of the peace-offering to what were in fact only segments 'vow-offering' or 'thank-offering'. These two, together with the freewill-offering, made up three classes within the peace-offering proper, and the regulations governing them (Lv. 7:11ff.) are a supplement to those of Lv. 3. All three were thank-offerings, but the vow-offering, which discharged an earlier promise at the time of its accomplishment, was no longer optional, while the others were. Possibly it was for this reason that the vow reverted to the stricter regulation of a victim without blemish (Lv. 22:19; *cf.* Mal. 1:14, where it is added that it should be a male), while this requirement was relaxed for the freewill-offering (Lv. 22:23). Lv. 7 also adds the rules for the sacrificial meal, which had been missing in Lv. 3—*viz.* that the thank-offering was to be eaten the same day, and the vow and free-will-offering not later than the next. The priests' portions are defined (Lv. 7:32ff.) as the 'wave' breast and the 'heave' shoulder (thigh). G. R. Driver (*op. cit.*) suggests some such meaning as 'contribution' for the terms 'wave' (*tᵉnûp̄â*) and 'heave' (*tᵉrûmâ*), and this seems better than the older suggestion of horizontal and vertical motions at the altar, which are scarcely appropriate when rams, he-goats and Levites are the objects of the actions (Nu. 8:11). (See W. B. Stevenson, 'Hebrew *'Olah* and *Zebach* Sacrifices', *Festschrift Alfred Bertholet*, 1950, pp. 488–497; *cf.* J. Milgrom, 'The Alleged Wave-Offering in Israel and in the Ancient Near East', *IEJ* 22, 1972, pp. 33–38.)

(iv) *'āšām and ḥaṭṭā'ṯ*. The names of these offerings, guilt-offering (trespass-offering) and sin-offering, are the names of the offences for which they are to atone, *'āšām* ('guilt') and *ḥaṭṭā't* ('sin'). In a cultic context these terms refer, not so much to moral offences, as to those which are ceremonially defiling, although the moral aspect is by no means ruled out. Of the former kind are the sin-offerings of the leper (Lv. 14; *cf.* Mk. 1:44) and the mother after childbirth (Lv. 12; *cf.* Lk. 2:24), and of the latter, those of deception and misappropriation in Lv. 6:1–7, and passion in Lv. 19:20–22. These examples can have been but little more than random specimens to illustrate the laws, and should not be regarded as giving a full account of sacrifice for sin in these laws, much less in the cult as a whole. In the history, for example, these sacrifices scarcely

Animals to be offered		Bullocks	Rams	Lambs	Goats
Occasions for offerings	Daily (morning and evening)			□□	
	Additional offerings on the Sabbath			□□	
	New moons	□□	□	□□□□□□□	□
Annual festivals	Unleavened Bread (daily offering)	□□	□	□□□□□□□	□
	Total for 7 days	■□□□□	□□□□□□□	■■■■□□□□□□□□□	□□□□□□□
	Weeks (Firstfruits)	□□	□	□□□□□□□	□
	1st day of 7th month	□	□	□□□□□□□	□
	Day of Atonement	□	□	□□□□□□□	□
	Tabernacles 1st day	■□□□	□□	■□□□□	□
	2nd day	■□□	□□	■□□□□	□
	3rd day	■□	□□	■□□□□	□
	4th day	■	□□	■□□□□	□
	5th day	□□□□□□□□□	□□	■□□□□	□
	6th day	□□□□□□□□	□□	■□□□□	□
	7th day	□□□□□□□	□□	■□□□□	□
	8th day	□	□	□□□□□□□	□
	Total for 8 days	■■■■■■■□	■□□□□□	■■■■■■■■■■□□□□□	□□□□□□□□

Key
■ 10 animals
□ 1 animal

Numbers of animals to be offered at the public sacrifices, daily, weekly and at festivals.
The two lambs on the Sabbath are additional to the usual daily 2.
The total for seven days refers to the seven days of the Festival of Unleavened Bread (*i.e.* 2 bullocks per day for 7 days=14).
Similarly, the total for eight days refers to the eight days of the Feast of Tabernacles (*e.g.* 1 goat per day for 8 days=8 goats).

The main references to the twice-daily offerings, the ʿôlâ *and the* minḥâ.

Offerings	Morning		Evening	
Bible references	*ʿôlâ* (burnt-offering)	*minḥâ* (cereal-offering)	*ʿôlâ* (burnt-offering)	*minḥâ* (cereal-offering)
Ex. 29: 38-42	☐	☐	☐	☐
Nu. 28: 3-8	☐	☐	☐	☐
1 Ki. 18: 29				☐
2 Ki. 3: 20		☐		
2 Ki. 16: 15	☐			☐
Ezk. 46:13-14	☐	☐		

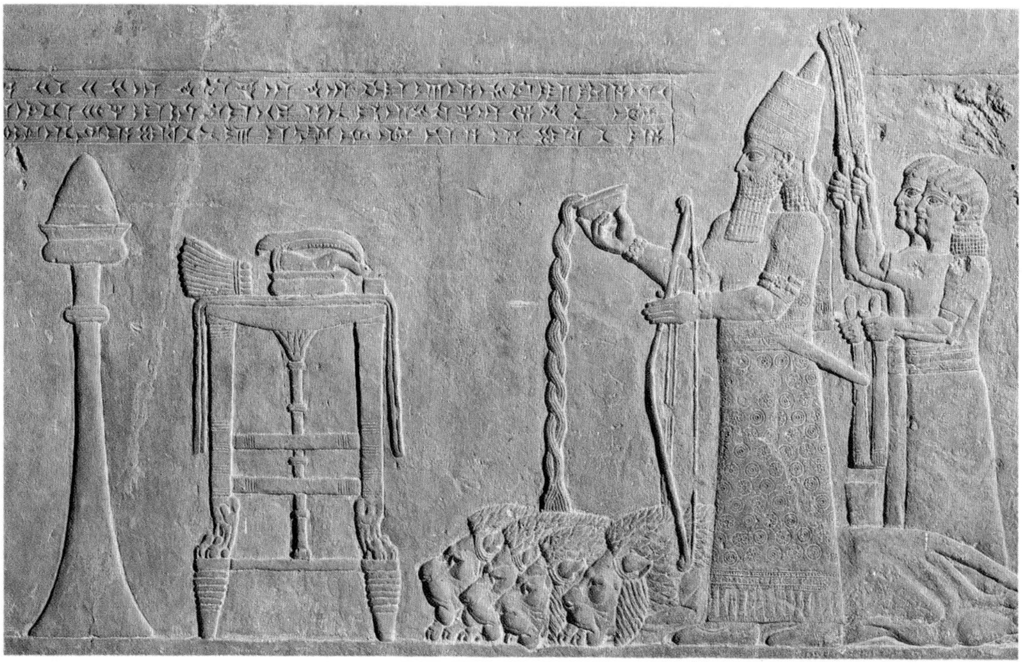

Following a successful lion-hunt, sacrifices were offered by Ashurbanipal, king of Assyria. He pours a libation over dead lions, before an altar heaped with offerings, and an incense-stand. Relief from the North palace at Nineveh. c. 640 BC. (BM)

figure at all. They are not mentioned in Deuteronomy (*cf.* Dt. 12), and are probably not to be understood in Ho. 4:8. But this is to be put down less to their post-exilic origin as Wellhausen argued—for they are well known to Ezekiel (*cf.* 40:39; 42:13) and may be hinted at in Ps. 40:6; 2 Ki. 12:16; 1 Sa. 6:3 (unless these are only monetary)—than to their individual nature (this might explain the silence concerning the *ʾāšām*, which was not a festival sacrifice), and the fragmentary character of the records. They are equally silent for the post-exilic period (*ʾāšām* is mentioned, doubtfully, only in Ezr. 10:19 and *ḥaṭṭāʾṯ* in Ne. 10:33 and what appears a formula of the Chronicler in Ezr. 6:17; 8:35; 2 Ch. 29:21ff.).

Equally obscure is the relation between the two offerings (*e.g.* they are used synonymously in Lv. 5:6). All that can certainly be said is that sins against the neighbour are more prominent in the *ʾāšām* and those against God in the *ḥaṭṭāʾṯ*. The *ʾāšām* therefore requires a monetary compensation in addition to the sacrifice. The value of the misappropriation plus a fifth is to be repaid to the wronged neighbour (Lv. 6:5) or, if he or his representative is not available, to the priest (Nu. 5:8). The sacrificial victim in the guilt-offering, usually a ram, also became the priest's, and after the regular blood and fat ritual could be eaten by the priests as 'most holy' (Lv. 7:1–7). The same provision applies (Lv. 6:24–29) to the sin-offerings of the ruler (Lv. 4:22–26) and the common man (Lv. 4:27–31), but in these cases the blood is put on the horns of the altar.

The sin-offerings of the high priest (Lv. 4:1–12) and the whole community (Lv. 4:13–21) follow a still more solemn ritual, in which the blood is sprinkled (*hizzâ*, not *zāraq*) before the veil of the sanctuary, and the bodies of the victims are not eaten but burnt (*śārap̄*, not *hiqṭîr*) outside the camp (Lv. 6:30; *cf.* Heb. 13:11). In addition to these four classes provisions are made for substitute offerings from the poor (Lv. 5:7–13). Chs. 4 and 5 thus contain a graduated scale of victims: bull (high priest and congregation, but *cf.* Nu. 15:24; Lv. 9:15; 16:5), he-goat (ruler), she-goat or lamb (common man), turtle-doves or pigeons (poor), flour (very poor). The following principles may be remarked: everyone must bring some sin-offering, no-one may eat of his own sin-offering, and the more propitiatory the rite the nearer the blood must come to God. On the Day of Atonement the veil itself was penetrated and the blood sprinkled on the ark. (See D. Schötz, *Schuld- und Sündopfer im Alten Testament*, 1930; L. Morris, ' *ʾAsham*', *EQ* 30, 1958, pp. 196–210; J. Milgrom, *VT* 21, 1971, pp. 237–239; D. Kellerman, *TDOT* 1, pp. 429–437.)

5. *The meaning*. The oft-stated purpose of the sacrifices in Lv. is 'to atone' (*kipper*, Lv. 1:4, *etc.*). This verb may be explained in one of three ways: 'to cover', from the Arab. *kafara*; 'to wipe away', from the Akkad. *kuppuru*; 'to ransom by a substitute', from the Heb. noun *kōp̄er*. Although the second is favoured by most modern writers, it is the third which seems most in keeping with the theory of sacrifice given in Lv. 17:11, AV, 'the life of the flesh is in the blood . . . it is the blood that maketh an atonement for the soul' (but *cf.* RSV and J. Milgrom, *JBL* 90, 1971, pp. 149–156), and with the principle at work in many of the practices encountered above: the choice of offering material in 'biotic rapport'; their designation by the laying on of the hand; the burning of a token such as the fat or the *ʾazkārâ*; the offering of a

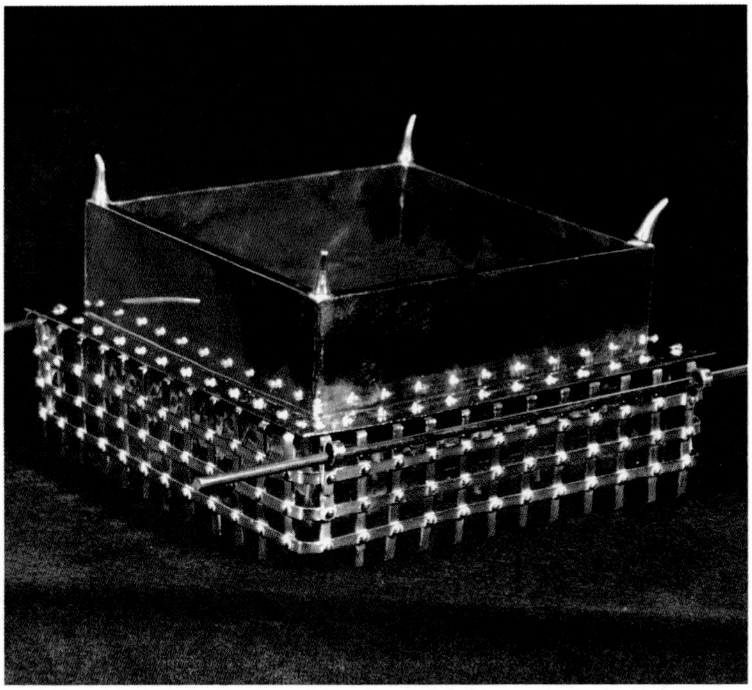

Reconstruction of the sacrificial altar made of acacia wood and bronze which stood in the tabernacle court (Ex. 27:1–8). (JCL)

first portion and the redemption of the first-born (*cf.* S. H. Hooke, 'The Theory and Practice of Substitution', *VT* 2, 1952, pp. 1–17, and for an opposite view A. Metzinger's articles, *Bib* 21, 1940). To these might be added the ritual of the heifer in Dt. 21 and the scapegoat in Lv. 16, which, although not blood sacrifices, reflect ideas which must *a fortiori* have been true of blood sacrifices. It was in this light that Lv. 16 was understood in the Jewish tradition (*e.g.* Mishnah, *Yoma* 6. 4, 'bear our sins and be gone').

Such passages are a warning against confining the atonement to a single act, as if it were the death alone, or the presentation of the blood, or the disposal of the victim, which atoned. The death was important—the live goat is only half of the ritual in Lv. 16 (*cf.* v. 15 with 14:4–7; 5:7–11). The blood manipulation was also important—in 2 Ch. 29:24 it seems to make atonement subsequent to the killing. The final disposal of the victim by fire or eating or to Azazel also had its place—in Lv. 10:16–20 the priestly eating of the sin-offering is more than just declaratory. The view that the death of the victim was only to release the life that was in the blood, and that the atonement consisted only of the latter, is as one-sided as that which sees the death as a quantitative penal satisfaction. To the latter view it has been objected that the sins for which sacrifice was offered were not those meriting death, that sin-offerings did not always require death (*cf.* Lv. 5:11–13), and that the killing could not have been central or it would have been in the hands of the priest, not the layman. These objections tell only against extreme forms of the substitution theory, not against the principle of substitution itself.

The real advantage of the substitution theory is that it retains the categories of personal relationships, where other views tend to descend to sub-personal dynamistic categories, in which the blood itself is thought of as effecting mystic union or revitalizing in a semi-magical way (*cf.* the theories of H. Hubert and M. Mauss, *Sacrifice: Its Nature and Function*, 1964; A. Loisy, *RHLR* n.s. 1, 1910, pp. 1–30, and *Essai historique sur le sacrifice*, 1920; S. G. Gayford, *Sacrifice and Priesthood*, 1924; A. Bertholet, *JBL* 49, 1930, pp. 218–233, and *Der Sinn des kultis-*

Order of acts	1	2	3	4	5	6
Hebrew terms	*hiqrîḇ*	*sāmaḵ*	*šāḥaṭ*	*zāraq*	*hiqṭîr*	*'āḵal*
'ôlâ (burnt-offering) Leviticus 1: 1-17						
Bull	Lv. 1: 3	Lv. 1: 4	Lv. 1: 5a	Lv. 1: 5b	Lv. 1: 9b	–
Sheep or goat	Lv. 1: 10b	–	Lv. 1: 11a	Lv. 1: 11b	Lv. 1: 13b	–
zeḇaḥ (peace-offering) Leviticus 3: 1-17						
Bull	Lv. 3: 1b	Lv. 3: 2a	Lv. 3: 2a	Lv. 3: 2b	Lv. 3: 5	–
Lamb	Lv. 3: 6b	Lv. 3: 8a	Lv. 3: 8a	Lv. 3: 8b	Lv. 3: 11	–
Goat	Lv. 3: 12b	Lv. 3: 13a	Lv. 3: 13a	Lv. 3: 13b	Lv. 3: 16	–

The ritual procedures laid down for sacrifices of burnt- and peace-offerings (Lv. 1 and 3).

chen Opfers, 1942; E. O. James, *The Origins of Sacrifice*, 1933).

A weightier objection to the substitution theory is that which finds difficulty in the description of the sin-offering after the sacrifice as 'most holy', and as fit for priestly food. If a transfer of sin had taken place, would it not be unclean and fit only for destructive burning (*śārap̄*)? This was in fact the case with the primary rank sin-offerings. In the other cases the priestly eating is perhaps to be similarly interpreted, as if the power of superior 'holiness' in the priests through their anointing absorbed the uncleanness of the offering (*cf.* Lv. 10:16–20 and the article 'Sin-Eating', *ERE*, 11, 1920, pp. 572–576 (Hartland)). That we are dealing here with categories of 'holiness', which are not ours, is evident from the instruction to break the earthen vessels in which the sin-offering has been boiled (Lv. 6:28; *cf.* *CLEAN AND UNCLEAN). Alternatively, the death of the victim could be understood as neutralizing the infection of sin, so that the fat and blood could come unimpeded to the altar as an offering to God.

Whether other views of sacrifice such as 'homage' and 'communion' are possible alongside that outlined here, as favoured by most scholars (A. Wendel, *Das Opfer in der altisraelitischen Religion*, 1927; W. O. E. Oesterley, *Sacrifices in Ancient Israel*, 1937; H. H. Rowley, *The Meaning of Sacrifice*, 1950), or whether certain types of sacrifice express one of these aspects more than another (*e.g.* burnt-offering, homage, and peace-offering, communion) is best left an open question. But in the laws at least the burnt-offering, the cereal-offering and even the peace-offering (but only rarely; *cf.* Ex. 29:33; Ezk. 45:15), as well as the sin- and guilt-offerings, are said to atone. And what is true of the laws seems to be true also of the history.

The question as to whether the offering was both an expiation (*i.e.* of sins) and a propitiation (*i.e.* of wrath) or only an expiation is also difficult to answer. *kipper* undoubtedly means propitiation in some instances (Nu. 16:41–50; Ex. 32:30), and this is supported by the use of the expression *rēaḥ nîḥōaḥ*, 'sweet-smelling savour', throughout the laws (*cf.* also Gn. 8:21, and LXX of Dt. 33:10). *rēaḥ nîḥōaḥ* may, however, have a weakened sense (G. B. Gray, *Sacrifice in the Old Testament*, 1925, pp. 77–81, points out that it is used where we should hardly expect it, with cereal and *zeḇaḥ* offerings, but not where we do expect it with sin- and guilt-offerings), and this is even more evidently the case with *kipper* when it is used in connection with such material things as the tabernacle furniture (Ex. 29:37; Ezk. 43:20; 45:19), and must be rendered simply 'cleanse'.

Of importance to the discussion here is the recognition that God himself gave the ritual to sinful man (Lv. 17:11, 'the blood . . . I have given it for you upon the altar to make atonement for your souls'). The sacrifices are to be seen as operating within the sphere of the covenant and covenanting grace. They were not 'man's expedient for his own redemption' as L. Köhler (*Old Testament Theology*, 1957) suggests, but were 'the fruit of grace, not its root' (A. C. Knudson, *The Religious Teaching of the Old Testament*, 1918, p. 295). The question as to whether within this context propitiation has a place is similar to the NT one, and will depend on the view taken of sin, and law and the nature of God (*ATONEMENT; also L. Morris, *The Apostolic Preaching of the Cross*, 1955).

It remains to be said that within the OT itself there is much to suggest that its system was not a final one. No sacrifices availed, for example, for breach of covenant (*cf.* Ex. 32:30ff.)—it is in this light that the prophetic rejection of sacrifice is to be understood—or for sins of a 'high hand' that put man outside the covenant (Nu. 15:30), though perhaps idolatry and apostasy would be illustrations here. While not accepting the view, on the one hand, that the efficacy of sacrifice was limited to inadvertent sins, which were no real sins at all, or, on the other, that prophets and pious psalmists saw no value in sacrifice whatsoever, it remains true that the cult was liable to abuse, when the inward tie between worshipper and means of worship was loosed, and prophetic religion became necessary to emphasize the priority of a personal relation to God. It is no accident, however, that when priestly and prophetic religion meet in the figure of the Servant of the Lord in Is. 53 the highest point of OT religion is reached, as all that is valuable in cult is taken up into a person, who both makes a sacrificial atonement (*hizzâ*, 'lamb', 'guilt-offering') and calls for the love and personal allegiance of the human heart.

BIBLIOGRAPHY. The works referred to throughout the article: articles on sacrifice in *EB*, *HDB*, *HDB* (one vol.), *ERE*, *ISBE*, *IDB*, *ZPEB*; S. I. Curtiss, *Primitive Semitic Religion Today*, 1902; articles in *The Expositor*, 6th series, 1902–5; R. de Vaux, *Les Sacrifices de l'Ancien Testament*, 1964; F. C. N. Hicks, *The Fulness of Sacrifice*[3], 1946; F. D. Kidner, *Sacrifice in the Old Testament*, 1952; R. K. Yerkes, *Sacrifice in Greek and Roman Religions and Early Judaism*, 1952; H. Ringgren, *Sacrifice in the Bible*, 1962, and *Israelite Religion*, 1965; R. de Vaux, *Studies in Old Testament Sacrifice*, 1964, and *Ancient Israel*[2], 1965; G. Fohrer, *History of Israelite Religion*, 1973; B. A. Levine, *In the Presence of the Lord*, 1974; F. M. Young, *Sacrifice and the Death of Christ*, 1975. R.J.T.

II. In the New Testament

The Greek words used are *thysia*, *dōron*, *prosphora* and their cognates, and *anapherō*, translated 'sacrifice, gift, offering, offer' (*thysia* in Mk. 12:33 probably means 'meal-offering'); *holokautōma*, 'whole burnt offering'; *thymiama*, 'incense'; *spendō*, 'pour out as a drink-offering'. All were adopted, with the other terms given below, from LXX.

a. Old Testament sacrifices in the New

The OT sacrifices (see **I**, above) were still being offered during practically the whole period of the composition of the NT, and it is not surprising, therefore, that even their literal significance comes in for some illuminating comment. Important maxims are to be found in Mt. 5:23–24; 12:3–5 and parallels, 17:24–27; 23:16–20; 1 Cor. 9:13–14. It is noteworthy that our Lord has sacrifice offered for him or offers it himself at his presentation in the Temple, at his last Passover, and presumably on those other occasions when he went up to Jerusalem for the feasts. The practice of the apostles in Acts removes all ground from the opinion that after the sacrifice of Christ the worship of the Jewish Temple is to be regarded as an abomination to God. We find them frequenting the Temple, and Paul himself goes up to Jerusalem for Pentecost, and on that occasion offers the sacrifices (which included sin-offerings) for the interruption of vows (Acts 21; *cf.* Nu. 6:10–12). However, in principle these sacrifices were now unnecessary, for the old covenant was now indeed 'old' and 'ready to vanish away' (Heb. 8:13), so that when the Romans destroyed the Temple even the non-Christian Jews ceased to offer the sacrifices.

The Epistle to the Hebrews contains the fullest treatment of the OT sacrifices. The teaching of this writer has its positive side (11:4), but his great concern is to point out their inadequacy except as types. The fact that they cannot gain for men entrance into the Holy of holies proves that they cannot free the conscience from guilt, but are simply carnal ordinances, imposed until a time of reformation (9:6–10). Their inadequacy to atone is shown also by the fact that mere animals are offered (10:4), and by the very fact of their repetition (10:1–2). They are not so much remedies for sin as reminders of it (10:3).

b. 'Spiritual sacrifices'

'Spiritual sacrifices' (1 Pet. 2:5; *cf.* Jn. 4:23–24; Rom. 12:1; Phil. 3:3) are the NT substitute for carnal ordinances, and appear frequently (Rom. 12:1; 15:16–17; Phil. 2:17; 4:18; 2 Tim. 4:6; Heb. 13:15–16; Rev. 5:8; 6:9; 8:3–4). Even in the OT, however, the psalmists and prophets sometimes use the language of sacrifice metaphorically (*e.g.* Pss. 50:13–14; 51:16–17; Is. 66:20), and the usage is continued in the intertestamental literature (Ecclus. 35:1–3; *Testament of Levi* 3. 6; *Manual of Discipline* 8–9; Philo, *De Somniis* 2. 183). The attempt of F. C. N. Hicks (*The Fulness of Sacrifice*³, 1946) to refer such passages to literal sacrifices must be reckoned on the whole a failure. The sacrifices mentioned in these passages are not always immaterial, and sometimes involve death: the sense in which they are 'spiritual' is that they belong properly to the age of the Holy Spirit (Jn. 4:23–24; Rom. 15:16). But sometimes they are immaterial, and they never have a prescribed ritual. It appears, in fact, that every act of the Spirit-filled man can be reckoned as a spiritual sacrifice, and the sense in which it is a sacrifice is that it is devoted to God and is acceptable to God. It does not, of course, atone. The antitype of atoning sacrifice is to be sought not here but in the sacrifice of Christ, without which spiritual sacrifices would not be acceptable (Heb. 13:15; 1 Pet. 2:5).

c. The sacrifice of Christ

The sacrifice of Christ is one of the chief themes of the NT. His saving work is sometimes spoken of in ethical, sometimes in penal, but often also in sacrificial terms. He is spoken of as the slain lamb of God, whose precious blood takes away the sin of the world (Jn. 1:29, 36; 1 Pet. 1:18–19; Rev. 5:6–10; 13:8)—a lamb being an animal used in various sacrifices. More specifically, he is spoken of as the true Passover lamb (*pascha*, 1 Cor. 5:6–8), as a sin-offering (*peri hamartias*, Rom. 8:3, *cf.* LXX Lv. 5:6–7, 11; 9:2–3; Ps. 40:6, *etc.*), and in Heb. 9–10 as the fulfilment of the covenant sacrifices of Ex. 24, the red heifer of Nu. 19, and the Day of Atonement offerings. The NT constantly identifies our Lord with the suffering Servant of Is. 52–53, who is a guilt-offering (Is. 53–10), and with the Messiah (Christ) of Dn. 9, who is to atone for iniquity (v. 24). The NT uses the terms 'propitiate' and 'ransom' (*PROPITIATION, *REDEEMER) of Christ in a sacrificial sense, and the idea of being cleansed by his blood (1 Jn. 1:7; Heb. *passim*) is sacrificial (*ATONEMENT, **III.** *b*; *SANCTIFICATION).

The doctrine is most fully worked out in the Epistle to the Hebrews. The writer stresses the importance, in Christ's sacrifice, of his death (2:9, 14; 9:15–17, 22, 25–28; 13:12, 20), and the fact that his sacrifice is over (1:3; 7:27; 9:12, 25–28; 10:10, 12–14, 18), but his other statements have led some Anglo-Catholics (*e.g.* S. C. Gayford, *Sacrifice and Priesthood*, 1924) and the Presbyterian W. Milligan (*The Ascension and Heavenly Priesthood of our Lord*, 1892) to suppose, on the contrary, that the death is not the important element in Christ's sacrifice, and that his sacrifice goes on for ever. It is quite true that the Epistle confines Christ's priesthood and sanctuary to heaven (8:1–5; 9:11, 24), but it emphatically does not confine his sacrifice there. It states indeed that he offered there (8:3), but 'offer' is a word used equally of the donor who brings and kills a sacrifice outside the sanctuary and of the priest who presents it, either there on the altar or within. The reference here is doubtless to the sprinkling or 'offering' of blood in the Holy of holies on the Day of Atonement by the high priest (9:7, 21–26), a typical action fulfilled by Christ. All that was costly in the sacrifice—the part of the donor and the victim—took place at the cross: there remained only the priestly part—the presentation to God by an acceptable mediator—and this Christ performed by entering into his Father's presence at the ascension, since when his sprinkled blood has remained there (12:24). There is no call to think of any *literal* presentation of himself or of his blood at the ascension: it is enough that he entered as the Priest of the sacrifice slain once for all at the cross, was immediately welcomed, and sat down in glory. His everlasting priestly intercession in heaven (7:24f.; *cf.* Ps. 99:6; Joel 2:17) is not some further activity, but is all part of his 'now appearing in the presence of God on our behalf' (9:24). On the basis of his finished work on the cross, and with his sufferings now all past, his simple appearance in God's presence on our behalf is both continual intercession for us and continual *'expiation' or *'propitiation' for our sins (2:10, 17f.; note present tense in the Gk.). See also *PRIESTS AND LEVITES.

It is a mistake to view Christ's sacrifice as being any more a literal sacrifice than the spiritual sacrifices are. Both transcend their OT types, and neither is ritual. The contention of Owen and others that Christ's sacrifice was a real sacrifice was directed against the Socinian view that Christ's death does not fulfil what the OT sacrifices set out to do, and failed to do—the view which denied that Christ's death makes propitiation. But apart from the slaying (and this is not performed, as in OT ritual, by the donor), everything in his sacrifice is spiritualized. For the body of an animal we have the body of God's Son (Heb. 10:5, 10). For spotlessness, we have sinlessness (Heb. 9:14; 1 Pet. 1:19). For a sweet smell, we have true acceptableness (Eph. 5:2). For the sprinkling of our bodies with blood, we have forgiveness (Heb. 9:13–14, 19–22). For symbolical atonement, we have real atonement (Heb. 10:1–10).

d. Sacrifice and the Lord's Supper

Sacrifice and the *Lord's Supper are indissolubly connected—not indeed in the way that Romanists, Non-jurors and Tractarians have wished to connect them, by making the eucharist an act of oblation, but as complementary to each other. To give 'do' and 'remem-

SACRILEGE, DESOLATING
See Desolating sacrilege, Part 1.

SADDLE
See Chariot, Part 1.

SAFFRON
See Herbs, Part 2.

SAINTS
See Holiness, Part 2.

brance' (Lk. 22:19; 1 Cor. 11:24–25) a technical sacrificial sense is merely an afterthought of those who have already accepted the eucharistic sacrifice on non-scriptural grounds. The same is true of the attempt to exclude a future meaning from the participles 'given' and 'shed' (Mt. 26:28; Mk. 14:24; Lk. 22:19–20). And to correlate the eucharist with the eternal sacrifice of Christ in heaven is impossible if the eternal sacrifice is disproved. But to regard the eucharist as a *feast* upon Christ's sacrifice is demanded by the argument of 1 Cor. 10:14–22, in which it is made to correspond with Jewish and Gentile sacrificial meals; by the allusion to Ex. 24:8 in Mt. 26:28 and Mk. 14:24; and by the traditional interpretation of Heb. 13:10. Since the sacrifice of Christ is in so many points to be spiritualized, the language about the feast on his sacrifice is doubtless to be spiritualized also, but it is not to be bereft of its meaning. The meaning of the sacrificial meal was not so much the appropriation of atonement as the fellowship with God which it effected, and this was betokened by a feast with God upon the victim. Whether in enjoying this fellowship with God we also truly partake of Christ or of his body and blood is the central point of controversy about the sacrament. But since Jn. 6 teaches that those who believe on Christ when they see him or hear his words do feed on him, on his body and blood, through the Spirit, there does not seem to be any reason for doubting that what happens through his words also happens through the tokens of bread and wine which he instituted, though in an equally spiritual manner.

BIBLIOGRAPHY. Commentaries on the Epistle to the Hebrews; V. Taylor, *Jesus and His Sacrifice*, 1943; B. B. Warfield, *The Person and Work of Christ*, 1950, pp. 391–426; N. Dimock, *The Doctrine of the Death of Christ*, 1903; A. Cave, *The Scriptural Doctrine of Sacrifice and Atonement*, 1890; G. Vos, *The Teaching of the Epistle to the Hebrews* (ed. and rewritten by J. G. Vos), 1956; T. S. L. Vogan, *The True Doctrine of the Eucharist*, 1871; H.-G. Link *et al.*, *NIDNTT* 3, pp. 415–438. R.T.B.

SADDUCEES. Our sources are all hostile and inadequate for an accurate picture. They are: (1) Josephus, *BJ* 2. 119, 164–166; *Ant.* 13. 171–173, 293–298; 18. 11, 16–17; 20. 199; *Vit.* 10–11; (2) the Mishnah, *'Erubin* 6. 2, *Ḥagigah* 2. 4, *Makkoth* 1. 6, *Parah* 3. 3, 7, *Niddah* 4. 2, *Yadaim* 4. 6–8; (3) the NT, Mt. 3:7; 16:1–12; 22:23–34; Mk. 12:18–27; Lk. 20:27–38; Acts 4:1–2; 5:17; 23:6–8.

The name and origins of the party are alike disputed. The name has been derived from Zadok, either Solomon's contemporary whose descendants were regarded as the pure priestly line (*cf.* Ezk. 44:15f.; 48:11) or a hypothetical founder or early leader of the party (the statement in *Aboth of Rabbi Nathan* 5 that Antigonos of Socoh had two disciples, Zadok and Boëthus, who lapsed into heresy, has probably little historical basis). But the ruling Hasmonaean high-priestly family was not Zadokite (1 Macc. 2:1; 14:29), and the double 'd' in both the Heb. and Gk. forms of the name is difficult to account for if it is derived from Zadok. T. W. Manson suggests a derivation from the Gk. *syndikoi*, 'fiscal controllers' (the double 'd' being accounted for by the assimilation of the 'n'). The connection with the word *ṣaddîq*, 'righteous', may have been a later assonance.

There are four theories of the origin of the Sadducees. M. H. Segal, following Wellhausen, thought that they were mainly a political party, derived ultimately from the Judaean Hellenists. G. H. Box, following Geiger, thought that they were a religious party, and that some of the scribes in the Gospels were Sadducee scribes. L. Finkelstein thought that they were originally a rural aristocratic body, as opposed to the urban Pharisees. T. W. Manson thought that they were originally state officials (*cf.* above).

In manner the Sadducees were rather boorish, being rude to their peers as to aliens, and counting it a virtue to dispute with their teachers. They had no following among the populace, but were restricted to the well-to-do. They were more severe in judgment than other Jews. Many, but not all, priests were Sadducees; nearly all Sadducees, however, appear to have been priests, especially of the most powerful priestly families. Under the early Hasmonaeans some Sadducees held office in the *gerousia* ('senate' or Sanhedrin). John Hyrcanus, taking offence at the request of Eleazar, member of a Pharisaic deputation, that he resign the high-priesthood, transferred his allegiance from the Pharisees to the Sadducees. The Sadducees enjoyed the favour of the Hasmonaean rulers until the reign of Salome Alexandra (76–67 BC), who preferred the Pharisees. Under the Herods and Romans the Sadducees predominated in the Sanhedrin. The party died out with the destruction of the Temple in AD 70. Josephus says that, even when in power, the Sadducees were compelled for fear of the people to concur with the Pharisees.

In religion the Sadducees are marked for their conservatism. They denied the permanent validity of any but the written laws of the Pentateuch. They rejected the later doctrines of the soul and its after-life, the resurrection, rewards and retributions, angels and demons. They believed that there was no fate, men having a free choice of good and evil, prosperity and adversity being the outcome of their own course of action.

BIBLIOGRAPHY. *HJP*[2], 2, pp. 404–414; M. H. Segal, *Expositor* 8th series, 13, 1917, pp. 81ff.; G. H. Box, *Expositor* 15, 1918, pp. 19ff., 401ff., and 16, 1918, pp. 55ff.; L. Finkelstein, *HTR* 22, 1929, pp. 185ff.; T. W. Manson, *BJRL* 22, 1938, pp. 144ff.; J. Z. Lauterbach, in *Studies in Jewish Literature in honour of Prof. K. Köhler*, 1913, pp. 180–190; J. W. Lightley, *Jewish Sects and Parties in the Time of Jesus*, 1923, pp. 5–178; J. Klausner, *Jesus of Nazareth*, tr. H. Danby, 1925, pp. 219–221 for ritual and legal differences from the Pharisees. See also L. Finkelstein, *The Pharisees*, 1938; J. J. Scott, *NIDNTT* 3, pp. 439–441. A.G.

SAKKUTH, SIKKUTH, SICCUTH. *MT sikkûṯ* is translated 'tabernacle' (as though it were equivalent to *sukkaṯ*) in Am. 5:26, AV—a verse which refers to Israel's adoption of Assyrian gods. In this verse the unvocalized consonants are *skkt mlkkm*, which are better translated, 'Sakkuth your king', than by AV and LXX, 'the tabernacle of your Moloch'. The consonants *skkt* were vocalized to read *sikkûṯ*, 'tabernacle', probably by using the vowels of *šiqqûṣ*, 'an abominable thing'. However, the verse makes good sense if we read Sakkuth instead of 'tabernacle'. Sakkuth was the name of the god of war, and of sun and light, Adar-malek or Saturn (*cf.* 2 Ki. 17:31, Adrammelech), otherwise known as

Ninurta (SAG.KUT). Kaimanu or Kaiwanu are alternative names for the planet. Hence Am. 5:26 should be translated, as in RSV, 'You shall take up Sakkuth your king, and Kaiwan your star-god, your images, which you made for yourselves . . .' (Others, however, like NEB, regard this astral interpretation as improbable, and follow LXX in seeing in *Sikkuth* a reference to tent-shrines, while translating *Kaiwan* as 'pedestal(s)'—an interpretation attested as early as the *Zadokite Work* of the 1st century BC.) (* REMPHAN.) J.A.T.

Colonnade enclosing a palaestra *(courtyard), part of the gymnasium at Salamis, Cyprus. Early 2nd cent. AD.* (PP)

SALAMIS. A town on the E coast of the central plain of * Cyprus, not to be confused with the famous island off the coast of Attica. It rivalled in importance Paphos, the Roman capital of the whole island, and eventually superseded it. The harbour which made Salamis a great commercial centre is now completely silted up. In the 1st century AD the Jewish community there was large enough to have more than one synagogue (Acts 13:5). Destroyed by earthquakes,

SALAMIEL
See Shemuel, Part 3.

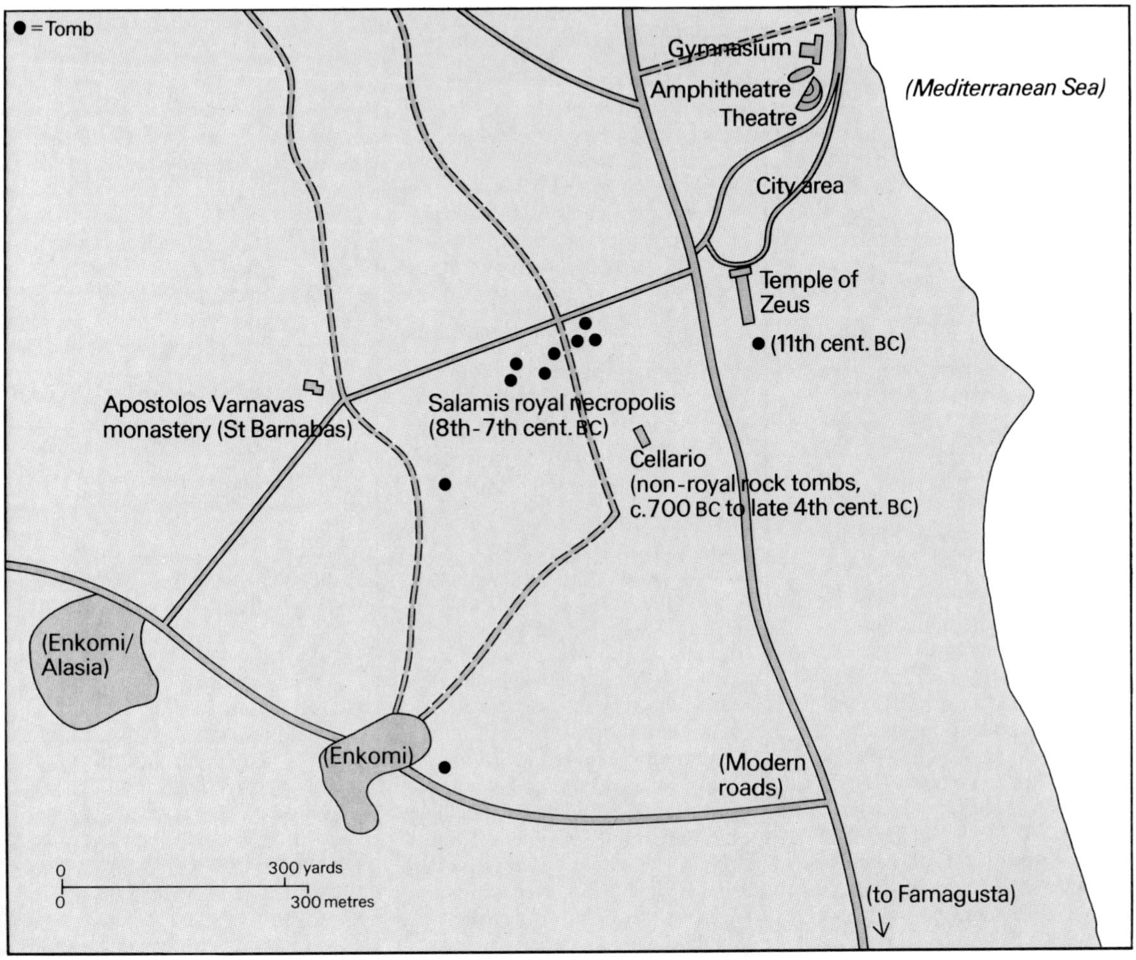

The location of ancient sites at Salamis, Cyprus.

the town was rebuilt in the 4th century AD as Constantia. Its ruins are 5 km from Famagusta. K.L.McK.

SALECAH, SALCAH. A place in the extreme E of *Bashan (Dt. 3:10; Jos. 12:5; 13:11). Though Bashan fell to the lot of Manasseh, the area occupied by Gad included Salecah (1 Ch. 5:11). It probably was within the area conquered by David, but after Solomon's time it lay outside Israelite territory. The site is possibly the modern Ṣalḫad (Nabataean *ṣlḥd*) on a S spur of the Hauran, though this identification is not universally accepted. See *LOB*, p. 383. T.C.M.

SALEM. The place where Melchizedek ruled (Gn. 14:18; Heb. 7:1, 8) near the valley of Shaveh (Gn. 14:17; explained as 'the King's Valley'). It is mentioned in parallel with Zion (Ps. 76:2). Following Jos. (*Ant*. 1. 180), it is usually identified with the ancient site of *Jerusalem, the city of Salem, *Uru-salem, uru-salimmu* of the cuneiform and Egyptian inscriptions. This would suit the route probably taken by Abraham on his return from Damascus to Hebron when he encountered Melchizedek. Those who assume his return down the Jordan valley look for a more E location such as *Salim. The Samaritans link Salem with *Shalem, a city of Shechem (Gn. 33:18, AV), E of Nablus, but this may be due to their ancient rivalry with Judah, where a 'Valley of Salem' is known as late as Maccabean times (Judith 4:4). In Je. 41:5 the LXX (B) reads Salem for Shiloh.

The name *šālēm* (Gk. *Salem*) means 'safe, at peace', though Jerusalem has been interpreted as 'Salem founded' implying a divine name Salem. For the early occurrence of this name form, *cf. šillēm* (Gn. 46:24; Nu. 26:49). D.J.W.

SALIM. An apparently well-known place (Gk. *Saleim*) near Aenon on the river Jordan where John baptized (Jn. 3:23). Of the many identifications proposed, the Salim (Salumias) or Tell Abu Sus about 12 km S of Beisan (*Beth-shan-Scythopolis) is the most likely. The ruins of Tell Ridgha or Tell Sheikh Selim, as it is also called after the local shrine, lie near several springs which might have been called Aenon (Arab. *'ain*, 'spring'). This site would be under the control of Scythopolis. Salim is mentioned by Eusebius, and marked on the 6th century AD Medaba map. The Salim E of Nablus with which the Samaritans identify the *Salem of Gn. 14:18 lies in the heart of Samaria. The land of Salim (RSV 'Shaalim') is a region in hilly Ephraim, possibly between Aijalon and Ramah (1 Sa. 9:4). *Cf.* W. F. Albright, *The Archaeology of Palestine*, 1960, p. 247; *idem*, in *The Background of the New Testament and its Eschatology* (ed. W. D. Davies and D. Daube), 1956, p. 159. (*SHAALBIM.) D.J.W.

SALMON, SALMA. 1. Of Judah's line (Mt. 1:4–5; Lk. 3:32). The son of Nahshon, and father of Boaz the husband of Ruth and the great-grandfather of David the son of Jesse (Ru. 4:20; 1 Ch. 2:11). According to Mt. 1:5 he married Rahab (of Jericho). **2.** Also of Judah's line. A son of Caleb (not to be confused with Caleb, son of Jephunneh), and father of the Bethlehemites, Netophathites and other groups associated with the Kenites (1 Ch. 2:51–54). C.H.D.

SALMONE. A promontory at the extreme E end of Crete, now known as Cape Sidero. On his way to Rome Paul's ship was prevented by a NW wind from proceeding from off Cnidus along the N coast of Crete, and, tacking past Salmone, sheltered in the lee of the island (Acts 27:7). K.L.McK.

SALOME (Heb. *šālôm*, 'peace', with Gk. suffix). **1.** According to Mk. 15:40 and 16:1, of three women who saw the crucifixion and went to the tomb on Easter morning two were called Mary and one Salome. Mt. 27:56 names two women called Mary, and the mother of the sons of Zebedee, who is probably to be identified with Salome. Jn. 19:25 refers to two women called Mary, plus the mother of Jesus and his mother's sister, who stood near the cross. If his mother's sister is identified with Salome, then James and John, the sons of Zebedee, would be cousins of Jesus. It is equally possible, however, that John has made a different selection of names out of the 'many other women' who, according to Mk. 15:41, were present at the crucifixion.

2. The daughter of Herodias, by her first husband Herod Philip (Josephus, *Ant*. 18. 136f.). Though not named in the Gospel accounts, she is usually identified with the girl who danced before Herod (Mk. 6:22; Mt. 14:6). She married her father's half-brother Philip the tetrarch. D.R.H.

SALT. Whereas the Phoenicians obtained quantities of salt from the Mediterranean by evaporation in salt-pans, the Hebrews had access to an unlimited supply on the shores of the Dead Sea (Zp. 2:9) and in the hill of Salt (Jebel Usdum), a 15-square-mile (4,000 hectares) elevation at the SW corner of the Dead Sea. This area was traditionally associated with the fate of Lot's wife (Gn. 19:26).

Such salt was of the rock or fossil variety, and, because of impurities and the occurrence of chemical changes, the outer layer was generally lacking in flavour. The reference in Mt. 5:13 is to this latter, much of which was discarded as worthless. Salt was valued as a preservative and for seasoning food (Mt. 5:13; Mk. 9:50; Col. 4:6). It was often used among Oriental peoples for ratifying agreements, so that salt became the symbol of fidelity and constancy. In the levitical cereal-offerings (Lv. 2:13) salt was used as a preservative to typify the eternal nature of the 'covenant of salt' existing between God and Israel (Nu. 18:19; 2 Ch. 13:5).

The effect of salt on vegetation was to render the land infertile (Dt. 29:23). Thus the 'parched places of the wilderness' (Je. 17:6) were synonymous with a barren salt land (Jb. 39:6). Abimelech followed an ancient custom in sowing ruined Shechem with salt (Jdg. 9:45) as a token of perpetual desolation. Elisha used salt to sweeten the brackish waters of the Jericho spring (2 Ki. 2:19–22). New-born infants were normally rubbed with salt prior to swaddling (Ezk. 16:4). Under Antiochus Epiphanes Syria imposed a tax upon salt, which was paid to Rome.

BIBLIOGRAPHY. E. P. Deatrick and F. C. Fensham, *BA* 25, 1962, pp. 41–49; N. Hillyer, *NIDNTT* 3, pp. 443–449. R.K.H.

SALT, CITY OF (Heb. *'îr hammelaḥ*). In Jos. 15:62 one of the frontier posts of the tribal territory

The shore of the Dead Sea, showing deposits of salt. (RS)

of Judah 'in the wilderness', S of Middin, Secacah and Nibshan (now identifiable, on the basis of excavations, with the Buqei'a Iron Age II settlements at Khirbet Abū Ṭabaq, Khirbet es-Samrah and Khirbet el-Maqāri), and N of En-gedi. Its identification with Khirbet Qumran, first suggested by M. Noth (*Josua*, 1938, p. 72; *ZDPV* 71, 1955, pp. 111ff.), has been confirmed by the discovery of an Iron Age II fortress beneath the *Qumran community settlement (*cf.* F. M. Cross Jr., J. T. Milik, *BASOR* 142, 1956, pp. 5ff.; R. de Vaux, *Archaeology and the Dead Sea Scrolls*, 1973, pp. 91ff. F.F.B.

SALT, VALLEY OF. Saline encrustations in steppe and desert lands are common. Some are of climatic origin; in other cases the climate has preserved geological salinity in the rocks. It is not possible to identify one topographic location from the biblical references. David and his lieutenant Abishai had memorable victories over the Edomites in the Valley of Salt (2 Sa. 8:13; 1 Ch. 18:12). Later Amaziah had a similar victory (2 Ki. 14:7; 2 Ch. 25:11). Traditionally the site has been accepted as the plain SSW of the Dead Sea, opposite the oasis of the Zered delta, where a plain 10–13 km long is overlooked by the salt range of Jebel Usdum, 8 km long and 200 m high. This plain passes imperceptibly into the glistening lowland of the Sebkha to the SE, a soft, impassable waste of salt marsh, where an army could well be routed in confusion. But, equally well, the site could be Wadi el-Milh (salt), E of Beersheba, also overlooked by a rocky hill, Tel el-Milh. All that the more precise reference of 2 Ch. 25:11 suggests is that the plain was overlooked by a rocky hill, somewhere between Judah and Edom, presumably in the Arabah.

J.M.H.

SALVATION (Heb. *yēšaʿ*; Gk. *sōtēria*).

I. In the Old Testament

The principal Heb. term translated 'salvation' is *yēšaʿ* and its cognates. Its basic meaning is 'bring into a spacious environment' (*cf.* Pss. 18:36; 66:12), but it carries from the beginning the metaphorical sense of 'freedom from limitation' and the means to that; *i.e.* deliverance from factors which constrain and confine. It can be referred to deliverance from disease (Is. 38:20; *cf.* v. 9), from trouble (Je. 30:7) or enemies (2 Sa. 3:18; Ps. 44:7). In the vast majority of references God is the author of salvation. Thus God saves his flock (Ezk. 34:22); he rescues his people (Ho. 1:7) and he alone can save them (Ho. 13:10–14); there is no other saviour besides him (Is. 43:11). He saved the fathers from Egypt (Ps. 106:7–10) and their sons from Babylon (Je. 30:10). He is the refuge and saviour of his people (2 Sa. 22:3). He saves the poor and needy when they have no other helper (Ps. 34:6; Jb. 5:15). The word of Moses, 'stand firm, and see the salvation of the Lord' (Ex. 14:13), is of the essence of the OT idea. Thus to know God at all is to know him as a saving God (Ho. 13:4) so that the words 'God' and 'Saviour' are virtually identical terms in the OT. The great normative instance of God's saving deliverance was the exodus (Ex. 12:40–14:31). The redemption from Egyptian bondage through the intervention of God at the Red Sea was determinative of all Israel's subsequent reflection on God's nature and activity. The exodus was the mould into which all the subsequent interpretation of the drama of Israel's history was poured. It was sung in worship (Ps. 66:1–7), retold in story (Dt. 6:20–24), re-enacted in ritual (Ex. 13:3–16). Thus the notion of salvation emerged from the exodus indelibly stamped with the dimension of God's mighty acts of deliverance in history.

This profoundly significant element laid the basis in turn for a further major OT contribution to the idea of salvation, *viz.* eschatology. Israel's experience of God as saviour in the past projected her faith forward in anticipation of his full and final salvation in the future. Precisely because Yahweh has shown himself to be the Lord of all, creator and ruler of the whole earth, and because he is a righteous and faithful God, he will one day effect his total victory over his foes and save his people from all their ills (Is. 43:11–21; Dt. 9:4–6;

SALTPETRE See Nitre, Part 2.

SALUTATION See Greeting, Part 2.

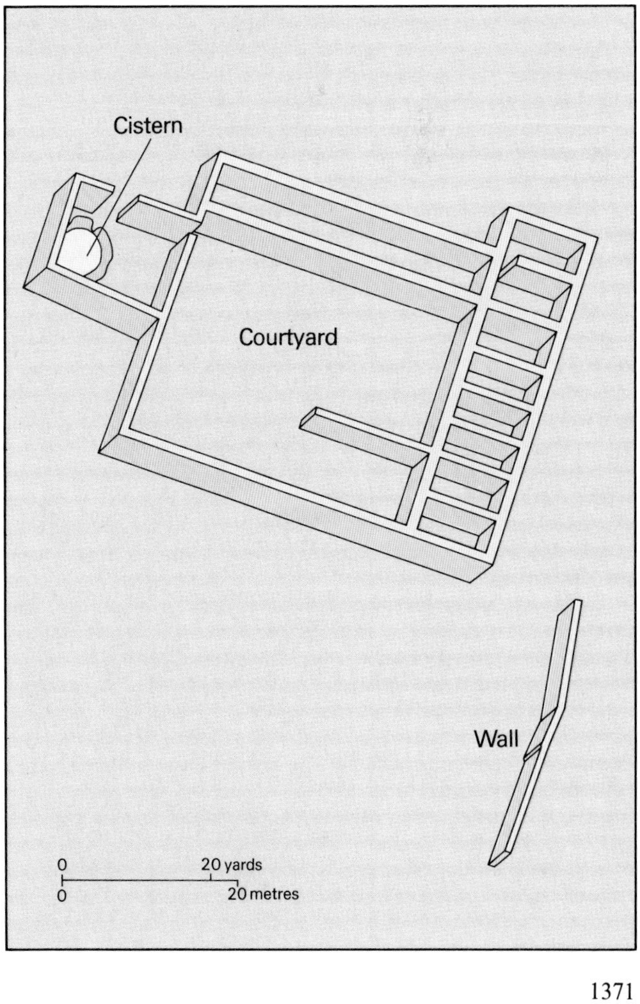

The identification of the OT 'City of Salt' with Khirbet Qumran was supported by the discovery of an Iron Age II (8th–7th cent. BC) fortress there.

Ezk. 36:22–23). In the earlier period this hope of salvation centres more upon immediate historic intervention for the vindication of Israel (*cf.* Gn. 49; Dt. 33; Nu. 23f.). In the prophetic period it finds expression in terms of a 'Day of Yahweh' in which judgment would combine with deliverance (Is. 24:19f.; 25:6–8; Joel 2:1f., 28–32; Am. 5:18f.; 9:11f.). The experience of the Exile gave concrete imagery and a concrete setting for the expression of this hope as a new exodus (Is. 43:14–16; 48:20f.; 51:9f.; *cf.* Je. 31:31–34; Ezk. 37:21–28; Zc. 8:7–13); but the disappointing and limited results of the restoration projected the hope forward again and transmuted it into what has been termed the *transcendental-eschatological* (Is. 64:1f.; 65:17f.; 66:22), the hope of the *'olām habba'*, the new world at the end of the present age in which God's sovereign rule and righteous character would be manifested among all the nations.

Reference should also be made to other related terms which the LXX renders by *sotēria*; in particular the root *g'l* 'to redeem', to recover property which had fallen into alien hands, to 'purchase back', often by payment. The person effecting this redemption, or salvation, is the *gō'ēl*, the 'kinsman-redeemer' (*cf.* Lv. 25:26, 32; Ru. 4:4, 6). God is the great *gō'ēl* of Israel (Ex. 6:6; Ps. 77:14f.). This usage is synonymous with *yēša'* in the latter part of Isaiah (Is. 41:14; 44:6; 47:4). They appear as parallel terms in Is. 43:1–2; 60:16; 63:9 (*cf. TDNT* 7, pp. 977–978).

Finally we note that the saving activity of God in the OT is expanded and deepened in terms of a particular instrument of this salvation, the Messiah-Servant. Salvation implies an agent, or saviour, though not necessarily one other than Yahweh himself. In general while Yahweh may employ particular human agents, or saviours, at particular historical junctures (Gn. 45:7; Jdg. 3:9,15; 2 Ki. 13:5; Ne. 9:27), he alone is the saviour of his people (Is. 43:11; 45:21; Ho. 13:4). This general assertion however requires qualification in the context of the development of the hope of salvation in the OT where in the Servant Songs we encounter a personal embodiment of Yahweh's moral salvation, even though the Servant is never directly referred to as saviour. Corporate imagery is clearly present here but the personification of the Servant's ministry is clear in the text, and in the light of NT fulfilment needs no further defence. In the song, Is. 49:1–6, he is to be the instrument of God's universal salvation (v. 6; *cf.* too v. 8). The final song, 52:13–53:12, does not contain the term but the idea of salvation is everywhere present in terms of a deliverance from sin and its consequences. Thus the OT leads us finally to the understanding that God delivers his people through his saviour-Messiah.

II. In the New Testament

In the NT we begin with the general observation that the 'religious' usage of a moral/spiritual deliverance becomes almost wholly dominant as far as the idea of salvation is concerned. Non-religious usage is virtually confined to saving from acute danger to life (Acts 27:20, 31; Mk. 15:30; Heb. 5:7).

a. The Synoptic Gospels

The word salvation is mentioned by Jesus only once (Lk. 19:9), where it may refer either to himself as the embodiment of salvation imparting pardon to Zacchaeus, or to that which is evidenced by the transformed conduct of the publican. Our Lord, however, used 'save' and kindred terms to indicate first what he came to do (by implication, Mk. 3:4; and by direct statement, Lk. 4:18; Mt. 18:11; Lk. 9:56; Mt. 20:28), and secondly, what is demanded of man (Mk. 8:35; Lk. 7:50; 8:12; 13:24; Mt. 10:22). Lk. 18:26, and context, shows that salvation calls for a contrite heart, childlike, receptive helplessness, and the renunciation of all for Christ—conditions it is impossible for man unaided to fulfil.

The testimony of others to our Lord's saving activity is both indirect (Mk. 15:31) and direct (Mt. 8:17). There is also the witness of his own name (Mt. 1:21, 23). All these varied usages suggest that salvation was present in the person and ministry of Christ and especially in his death.

b. The Fourth Gospel

This double truth is underlined in the Fourth Gospel, in which each chapter suggests different aspects of salvation. Thus in 1:12f. men are born as sons of God by trusting in Christ; in 2:5 the situation is remedied by doing 'whatever he tells you'; in 3:5 new birth from the Spirit is essential for entering the kingdom, but 3:14, 17 make it clear that this new life is not possible apart from trust in the death of Christ, without which men are already under condemnation (3:18); in 4:22 salvation is of the Jews—by revelation historically channelled through God's people—and is a gift inwardly transforming and equipping men for worship.

In 5:14 the one made whole must sin no more lest a worse thing come; in 5:39 the Scriptures testify of life (= salvation) in the Son, to whom life and judgment are committed; in 5:24 believers have already passed from death to life; in 6:35 Jesus declares himself the bread of life, to whom alone men should go (6:68) for the quickening words of eternal life; in 7:39 water is the symbol of the saving life of the Spirit who was to come after Jesus had been glorified.

In 8:12 the Evangelist shows the safety of the guidance of light and in vv. 32, 36 the liberty through truth in the Son; in 9:25, 37, 39 salvation is spiritual sight; in 10:10 entrance into the safety and abundant life of the fold and of the Father is through Christ; in 11:25f. resurrection-life belongs to the believer; in 11:50 (*cf.* 18:14) the saving purpose of his death is unwittingly described; in 12:32 Christ, lifted up in death, draws men to him; in 13:10 his initial washing signifies salvation ('clean all over'); in 14:6 he is the true and living way to the Father's abode; in 15:5 abiding in him, the Vine, is the secret of life's resources; in 16:7–15 for his sake the Spirit will deal with the obstacles to salvation and prepare for its realization; in 17:2–3, 12 he keeps safely those who have knowledge of the true God and of himself; in 19:30 salvation is accomplished; in 20:21–23 the words of peace and pardon accompany his gift of the Spirit; in 21:15–18 his healing love reinstils love in his follower and reinstates him for service.

c. The Acts

Acts traces the proclamation (*cf.* 16:17) of salvation in its impact first upon the crowds which are exhorted to be saved 'from this crooked generation' (2:40) by repentance (itself a gift and part of salvation, 11:18), remission of sins, and receiving the Holy Spirit; then upon a sick individual, ignorant of his true need, who is healed by the name of Jesus, the only name whereby we must be saved; and thirdly, upon the household of him who asked 'What must I do to be saved?' (16:30ff.).

d. The Pauline Epistles

Paul claims that the Scriptures 'are able to instruct you for salvation through faith in Christ Jesus' (2 Tim. 3:15ff.) and provide the ingredients essential for the enjoyment of a full-orbed salvation. Enlarging and applying the OT concept of the righteousness of God, which itself had adumbrations of the saving righteousness of the NT, Paul shows how there is no salvation by means of the law, since it could only indicate the presence and excite the reactionary activity of sin and stop men's mouths in their guilt before God (Rom. 3:19; Gal. 2:16). Salvation is provided as the free gift of the righteous God acting in grace towards the undeserving sinner who, by the gift of faith, trusts in the righteousness of Christ who has redeemed him by his death and justified him by his resurrection. God, for Christ's sake, justifies the unmeriting sinner (*i.e.* reckons to him the perfect righteousness of Christ and regards him as if he had not sinned), forgives his sin, reconciles him to himself in and through Christ 'making peace by the blood of his cross' (2 Cor. 5:18; Rom. 5:11; Col. 1:20), adopts him into his family (Gal. 4:5f.; Eph. 1:13; 2 Cor. 1:22), giving him the seal, earnest, and firstfruits of his Spirit in his heart, and so making him a new creation. By the same Spirit the subsequent resources of salvation enable him to walk in newness of life, mortifying the deeds of the body increasingly (Rom. 8:13) until ultimately he is conformed to Christ (Rom. 8:29) and his salvation is consummated in glory (Phil. 3:21).

e. The Epistle to the Hebrews

The 'great' salvation of the Epistle to the Hebrews transcends the OT foreshadowings of salvation. The NT salvation is described in the language of sacrifice; the oft-repeated offerings of the OT ritual that dealt mainly with unwitting sins and provided only a superficial salvation are replaced by the one sacrifice of Christ, himself both saving Priest and Offering (Heb. 9:26; 10:12). The outpouring of his life-blood in death effects atonement, so that henceforth man with a cleansed conscience can enter the presence of God in terms of the new covenant ratified by God through his Mediator (Heb. 9:15; 12:24). Hebrews, which lays such stress on Christ's dealing with sin by his suffering and death to provide eternal salvation, anticipates his second appearing, not then to deal with sin, but to consummate his people's salvation and, presumably, their attendant glory (9:28).

f. The Epistle of James

James teaches that salvation is not by 'faith' only but also by 'works' (2:24). His concern is to disillusion anyone who relies for his salvation on a mere intellectual acknowledgment of the existence of God without a change in heart resulting in works of righteousness. He does not discount true faith, but urges that its presence be shown by a conduct that in turn indicates the saving energies of true religion at work through the ingrafted Word of God. He is as concerned as any to bring back the sinner from the error of his way and save his soul from death (5:20).

g. 1 and 2 Peter

1 Peter strikes a similar note to Hebrews about the costly salvation (1:19) which was searched for and foretold by the prophets but is now a present reality to those who, like straying sheep, have returned to the Shepherd of their souls (2:24f.). Its future aspect is known by those who 'are guarded . . . for a salvation ready to be revealed' (1 Pet. 1:5).

In 2 Peter salvation involves escaping the corruption that is in the world through lust by being partakers of the divine nature (1:4). In the context of sin the believer yearns for the new heavens and the new earth wherein dwells righteousness, but recognizes that the postponement of the parousia is due to the longsuffering of his Lord, which is itself an aspect of salvation (3:13, 15).

h. 1, 2 and 3 John

For 1 John the sacrificial language of Hebrews is congenial. Christ is our salvation by being the propitiation for our sins, as the outcome of God's love. It is God in his love in Christ's outpoured life-blood who covers our sins and cleanses us. As in the Fourth Gospel, salvation is conceived in terms of being born of God, knowing God, possessing eternal life in Christ, living in the light and truth of God, dwelling in God and knowing his dwelling in us through love by his Spirit (3:9; 4:6, 13; 5:11). 3 John has a significant prayer for general prosperity and bodily health (natural well-being) to accompany prosperity of soul (v. 2).

i. The Epistle of Jude

Jude 3, in referring to the 'common salvation', has in mind something akin to the 'common faith' of Tit. 1:4, and allies it to the 'faith' (*cf.* Eph. 4:5) for which believers are to contend. This salvation comprises the saving truths, privileges, demands and experiences common to the variety of his readers. In vv. 22f. he would urgently present this salvation to various groups in doubt, danger and degradation.

j. The Revelation

Revelation reiterates the theme (of 1 Jn.) of salvation as liberation or cleansing from sin by virtue of the blood of Christ and its constitution of believers as royal priests (1:5f.). In a manner reminiscent of the psalmist, the seer, in adoration, ascribes salvation in its comprehensiveness to God (7:10). The closing chapters of the book depict salvation in terms of the leaves of the tree of life which are for the healing of the nations, to which tree, as to the city of salvation, admission is given only to those whose names are written in the book of life.

III. Relation to other views of salvation

a. The Essenes

Considerable attention has been given in the years since the discovery of the *Dead Sea Scrolls (1947 onwards) to this monastic movement within Judaism, and various attempts made to evaluate its contribution to NT origins. As far as the doctrine of salvation is concerned the Qumran Essenes shared the biblical sense of man's inherent sinfulness apart from God, and one notable passage (1QS 11. 9f.; *cf.* also the *Hymn of Thanksgiving*) approaches very near to the NT doctrine of salvation as acquittal by the action of God's righteousness, salvation through utter reliance upon the grace and mercy of God. This however is not altogether surprising bearing in mind the debt of the Qumran covenanters to the psalter and the great OT prophets. It would be wrong to over-stress the points of correspondence; at other points the parallel with NT teaching is much more tenuous. The universalism of the

Christian gospel is totally lacking; salvation is certainly *not* for the common mass of sinners. The Qumran understanding of the Suffering Servant of Is. 53 is disputed, but the prophecy appears to have been seen as fulfilled in the inner council (*sôḏ*) of the community. Nor can one entirely evade the simple fact that there is not one unambiguous reference to the Essenes in the entire NT.

b. Gnosticism

The precise dating of gnostic teaching is disputed, and the attempt to demonstrate a Christian dependence upon gnostic ideas is today a distinctly uncertain enterprise. There is however evidence in the NT (*cf.* 1 and 2 Cor.; Col.; 1 and 2 Tim; Tit.; 1 Jn.; Rev.) that the early church had to distinguish its salvation teaching from views which were embodied in later gnostic doctrines. In essence the gnostic claimed salvation by an immediate knowledge of God. This knowledge was intellectual as against moral, and esoteric in its being confined to the élite circle of initiates. Gnosticism also taught a dualism of soul and body, only the former being significant for salvation; and a hierarchy of spiritual and angelic intermediaries between God and man. Salvation was the escape from the domination of alien astrological forces and human passions by coming to 'know' in response to a 'call' from the divine world expressed in the so-called 'gnostic-redeemer myth', the story of the heavenly man who came down from the world of celestial light to 'save' 'fallen' men by the impartation of this secret knowledge.

As has already been implied, the attempt to locate such a view in the pre-Christian period and hence to see it as lying behind NT notions of salvation falls a long way short of demonstration. The evidence is far more compatible with the view that in the syncretistic religious atmosphere of the time certain latent gnostic tendencies were in the 2nd and 3rd centuries wedded to Christian salvation motifs to produce the doctrines of the gnostic sects which we have outlined above and of which we hear from writers such as Irenaeus in the post NT period. Against incipient forms of such notions of salvation the biblical writers stress the universal scope of God's offer of salvation, its essentially moral nature, the true humanity and the true deity of the mediator, and the focus of salvation in the historic acts of God in the birth, life, death and resurrection of Jesus Christ (*cf.* NT sections cited above).

c. The mystery religions

Another point at which the NT writers had to distinguish their doctrine of salvation from current ideas was in relation to the mystery cults. This 1st-century phenomenon was a combination of Hellenistic and oriental elements which had their origin in ancient fertility rites. They claimed to offer 'salvation' from fate, and a life beyond the grave free from the unsatisfactory and oppressive conditions of the present. Salvation was attained by the meticulous performance of certain cultic rituals. Language similar to the NT occurs at points. The initiates could be referred to as 'born again to eternal life'. Cult deities such as Dionysius attained the title 'Lord and Saviour'. Links with Christian theology have been alleged, particularly at the sacramental level, since sacred lustrations and the idea of uniting with the gods in a solemn meal were known. At even a cursory examination, however, the differences from the early Christian message and the life of the early Christian communities are stark and obvious. Salvation in the mysteries was essentially non-moral. The 'saved' worshipper was not expected to be a better man than his pagan neighbour, nor in most cases was he. The rational element was minimal; there were no great central saving acts, and so no great common theological affirmations.

The alleged parallels to the Christian (Pauline) baptismal and eucharistic teaching have also been shown to be almost certainly without foundation; the evidence rather pointing to the apostle's debt to biblical salvation-history centred in God's mighty deed of redemption in Jesus Christ.

d. The imperial cult

The age-long mirage of salvation through political power and organization was reflected in the 1st century in the imperial cult. The myth of a God-King who was the saviour and benefactor of his people appears widely in various forms in the ancient world particularly in the orient. In Rome the impetus for the official cult stems from the career of Augustus who after Actium in 31 BC established the *Pax Romana*, the golden age of peace after decades of bloodshed. He was commonly addressed as *sōtēr*, 'Saviour of the world', and through his relationship to Julius Caesar, 'the Son of God'. Even in Augustus' case however some caution needs to be exercised since it has been shown that the title *sōtēr* was certainly not confined to the emperor, nor was the title always invested with the full oriental implications. The successive emperors of the 1st century showed a varying degree of enthusiasm for the claims made on their behalf in the official cult. Caligula, Nero and Domitian certainly took their divine status seriously and this may account to some extent for some of the appearances of the title referred to Jesus Christ and the Father in the NT (*cf.* 1 Tim. 1:1; 4:10; Tit. 1:3; 3:4; 1 Jn. 4:14; Jude 25; Rev. 7:10; 12:10; 19:1).

e. Summary

In general, while there are clear parallels in language, the case for the dependence of Christian salvation teaching upon any or all of these contemporary movements has certainly not been made. In attempting to communicate the gospel to their contemporaries the NT preachers and writers certainly were not unprepared to translate the message, including its salvation language, into 1st-century thought-patterns, but the true origin and justification of their salvation language lies outside that world, in the salvation-history tradition of the OT as focused and fulfilled in the person and mission of Jesus Christ.

IV. Biblical salvation: Summary

1. Salvation is historical. The OT view of salvation as effected through historic, divine intervention is fully honoured in the NT. As against Gnosticism, man is not saved by wisdom; as against Judaism, man is not saved by moral and religious merit; as against the Hellenistic mystery cults, man is not saved by a technique of religious practice; as against Rome, salvation is not to be equated with political order or liberty. Man is saved by God's action in history in the person of Jesus Christ (Rom. 4:25; 5:10; 2 Cor. 4:10f.; Phil. 2:6f.; 1 Tim. 1:15; 1 Jn. 4:9–10, 14). While the birth, life and ministry of Jesus are not unimportant, the stress falls upon his death and resurrection (1 Cor. 15:5f.); we are saved by the

blood of his cross (Acts 20:28; Rom. 3:25; 5:9; Eph. 1:7; Col. 1:20; Heb. 9:12; 12:24; 13:12; 1 Jn. 1:7; Rev. 1:5; 5:9). As this message is proclaimed and men hear and come to respond in faith God's salvation is brought to them (Rom. 10:8, 14f.; 1 Cor. 1: 18–25; 15:11; 1 Thes. 1:4f.).

2. Salvation is moral and spiritual. Salvation relates to a deliverance from sin and its consequences and hence from guilt (Rom. 5:1; Heb. 10:22), from the law and its curse (Gal. 3:13; Col. 2:14), from death (1 Pet. 1:3–5; 1 Cor. 15:51–56), from judgment (Rom. 5:9; Heb. 9:28), also from fear (Heb. 2:15; 2 Tim. 1:7, 9f.) and bondage (Tit. 2:11–3: 6; Gal. 5:1f.). It is important to indicate the negative implications of this, *i.e.* what Christian salvation does *not* include. Salvation does not imply material prosperity or worldly success (Acts 3:6; 2 Cor. 6:10), nor does it promise physical health and well-being. One must be careful not to overstate this particular negative, as clearly remarkable healings did and do take place and 'healing' is a gift of the Spirit to the church (Acts 3:9; 9:34; 20:9f.; 1 Cor. 12:28). But healing is not invariable, and hence is in no sense a 'right' of the saved man (1 Tim. 5:23; 2 Tim. 4:20; Phil. 2:25f.; 2 Cor. 12:7–9). Further, salvation does not include deliverance from physical hardship and danger (1 Cor. 4:9–13; 2 Cor. 11:23–28), nor even, perhaps, seemingly tragic events (Mt. 5:45?). It does not mean being absolved from social injustice and ill-treatment (1 Cor. 7:20–24; 1 Pet. 2:18–25).

3. Salvation is eschatological. There is a danger of stating the meaning of salvation too negatively. Here we recall the recognition above of the paucity of references to salvation from the lips of Jesus. His central category was the kingdom of God, the manifestation of God's sovereign rule. In Rev. 12:20 however salvation and the kingdom are virtually equated. For the author of the Apocalypse as for Jesus salvation is equivalent to life under the reign of God, or, as in the witness of the Fourth Gospel, eternal life. Salvation therefore gathers up all the contents of the gospel. It includes deliverance from sin and all its consequences, and positively, the bestowal of all spiritual blessings in Christ (Eph. 1:3), the gift of the Holy Spirit and the life of blessedness in the future age. This future perspective is crucial (Rom. 8:24; 13:11; 1 Cor. 5:5; Phil. 3:20; Heb. 1:14; 9:28; 1 Pet. 1:5, 9). All that is known of salvation now is but a preliminary and foretaste of the fullness of salvation which awaits the fullness of the kingdom at the parousia of the Lord.

(*ATONEMENT; *ELECTION; *FORGIVENESS; *JUSTIFICATION; *SANCTIFICATION; *SIN; *GRACE; *RECONCILIATION.)

BIBLIOGRAPHY. W. Foerster, G. Fohrer, in *TDNT* 7, pp. 965–1003; M. Green, *The Meaning of Salvation*, 1965; G. C. Berkouwer, *Faith and Justification*, E.T. 1954; *idem, Faith and Sanctification*, E.T. 1952; M. Black (ed.), *The Scrolls and Christianity*, 1969; E. Yamauchi, *Pre-Christian Gnosticism*, 1973; G. Wagner, *Pauline Baptism and the Pagan Mysteries*, E.T. 1967; J. R. W. Stott, *Christian Mission in the Modern World*, 1975, ch. 5; *Let the Earth Hear His Voice*, 1975; *NIDNTT* 3, *s.v.* 'Reconciliation', 'Redemption'.

G.W.
B.A.M.

SAMARIA. The name of the N Israelite capital and of the territory surrounding it.

I. History

After reigning 6 years at Tirzah, Omri built a new capital for the N kingdom on a hill 11 km NW of Shechem commanding the main trade routes through the Esdraelon plain. He purchased the site for two talents of silver and named it after its owner Shemer (1 Ki. 16:24). The place is otherwise unknown unless it is to be identified with Shamir, the home of Tola (Jdg. 10:1; F. M. Abel, *Géographie de la Palestine*, 2, p. 444). The hill, which is *c.* 100 m high and commands a view over the plain, was impregnable except by siege (2 Ki. 6:24), and the name (*šōmᵉrôn*) may be connected with the Heb. 'watch-post'.

Omri allowed the Syrians of Damascus to set up bazaars (AV 'streets') in his new city (1 Ki. 20:34). For 6 years he worked on the construction of Samaria, and this was continued by Ahab, who built a house decorated or panelled with ivory (1 Ki. 22:39). In a temple for Baal of Sidon (Melqart), the deity whose worship Jezebel encouraged (1 Ki. 18:22), Ahab set up a pillar (*'ăšērâ*) near the altar which Jehoram later removed (2 Ki. 3:2). Other shrines and build-

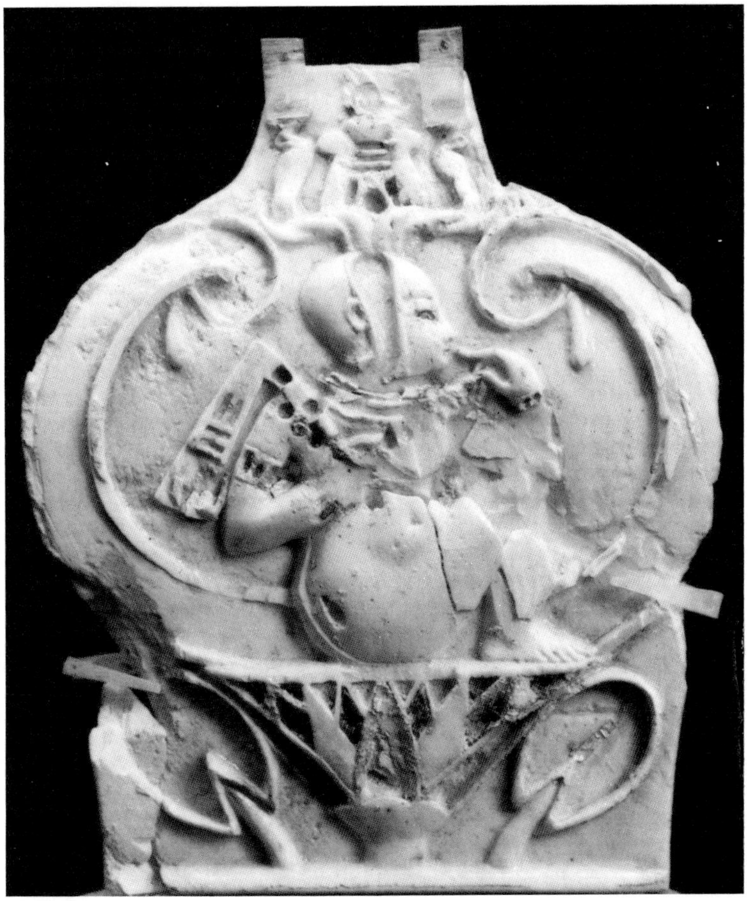

Ivory in Egyptian style depicting the infant god Horus seated on a lotus flower. Originally inlaid with coloured glass and covered with gold foil. From the palace at Samaria. 9th cent. BC. (IM)

Opposite page: The Israelite citadel enclosure at Samaria, built by Omri and Ahab.

Plan of the site of Samaria and Sebaste.

ings used by the idolatrous priests must have been in use from this time until the reform undertaken by Jehu (2 Ki. 10:19). Samaria itself was long considered by the prophets a centre of idolatry (Is. 8:4; 9:9; Je. 23:13; Ezk. 23:4; Ho. 7:1; Mi. 1:6).

Ben-hadad II of Syria besieged Samaria, at first unsuccessfully (1 Ki. 20:1–21), but later the Syrians reduced it to dire famine (2 Ki. 6:25). It was relieved only by the panic and sudden withdrawal of the besiegers, which was discovered and reported by the lepers (2 Ki. 7). Ahab was buried in the city, as were a number of Israelite kings who made it their residence (1 Ki. 22: 37; 2 Ki. 13:9, 13; 14:16). His descendants were slain there (2 Ki. 10:1), including Ahaziah, who hid in vain in the crowded city (2 Ch. 22:9). Samaria was again besieged in the time of Elisha and miraculously delivered (2 Ki. 6:8ff.).

*Menahem preserved the city from attack by paying tribute to *Tiglath-pileser III (2 Ki. 15:17–20). His son *Pekah, however, drew the Assyrian army back again by his attack on Judah, then a vassal-ally of Assyria. The city, called *Samerina* or *Bit-Ḫumri* ('House of Omri') in the Assyrian Annals, was besieged by Shalmaneser V of Assyria in 725–722 BC. 2 Ki. records that he captured the city, agreeing with the Babylonian Chronicle, but evidently his death intervened before it was finally secured for Assyria. The citizens, incited by Iau-bi'di of Hamath, refused to pay the tax imposed on them, and in the following year (721 BC) Sargon II, the new king of Assyria, initiated a scheme of mass deportation for the whole area. According to his annals, Sargon carried off 27,270 or 27,290 captives, and the effect was to terminate the existence of the N kingdom of Israel as a homogeneous and independent state. The exiles were despatched to places in Syria, Assyria and Babylonia and replaced by colonists from other disturbed parts of the Assyrian empire (2 Ki. 17:24). The resultant failure to cultivate the outlying districts led to an increase in the incursions of lions (v. 25). Some Israelites, called *Samaritans (v. 29), still inhabited part of the city and continued to worship at Jerusalem (Je. 41:5). The town, according to a cuneiform inscription (*HES*, 247) and to other records, was under an Assyrian governor and both Esarhaddon (Ezr. 4:2) and Ashurbanipal (Ezr. 4:9–10) brought in additional peoples from Babylonia and Elam. The contention between Samaria and Judah, of earlier origin, gradually increased in intensity, though Samaria itself declined in importance.

The discovery of papyri from Samaria in a cave of the Wadi ed-Dâliyeh 14 km N of Jericho seems to confirm the reports of ancient historians that Samaria was initially favourable to Alexander who captured the city in 331 BC. However, while Alexander was in Egypt they murdered his prefect over Syria. On his return, Alexander destroyed Samaria, massacred the city's leaders in the cave to which they had fled and resettled the area with Macedonians. Information contained in the papyri enables a list of Samaritan governors to be constructed, beginning with Sanballat I *c.* 445 BC.

Samaria was besieged by John Hyrcanus, and the surrounding countryside was devastated *c.* 111–107 BC. Pompey and Gabinius began to rebuild (Jos., *Ant.* 14. 75), but it was left to Herod to embellish the city, which he renamed Sebaste (Augusta) in honour of his emperor. In it he housed 6,000 veterans, including Greeks. On his death, Samaria became part of the territory of Archelaus and later a Roman colony under Septimus Severus. Despite the mutual antagonism between Judah and Samaria, Jesus Christ took the shorter route through Samaria to Galilee (Lk. 17:11), resting at Sychar near Shechem, a Samaritan city (Jn. 4:4). Philip preached in Samaria, but perhaps the district rather than the city is intended, since the definite article is absent in Acts 8:5.

II. Archaeology

The site was occupied in the Early Bronze Age, then deserted until the Iron Age. Sixteen levels of occupation were recognized by the Harvard (1908–10) and, later, joint Harvard–Hebrew University–British School of Archaeology in Jerusalem expeditions (1931–5). Further excavations were made by the Department of Antiquities of Jordan in 1965 and the British School of Archaeology in Jerusalem in 1968. The site is difficult to work because of the dense and continuous habitation, with constant rebuilding. Of the periods of occupation unearthed, seven have been assigned to the Israelites: Levels I–II = Omri–Ahab (28 years). The inner (1·5 m thick) and outer (6 m thick) fortification wall, completed by the latter king, enclosed the summit. A main gateway seems to have had a columned entrance court. The palace, which was later adapted by Jeroboam II, had a wide court in which lay a reservoir or pool (10 by 5m), probably the one in which Ahab's bloodstained chariot was washed down (1 Ki. 22:38). In an adjacent storeroom more than 200 plaques or fragments of ivories were discovered. These show Phoenician and pseudo-Egyptian styles and influences and may well have been inlays for furniture in Ahab's ivory house (1 Ki. 22:39) (*IVORY). Sixty-five ostraca, inscribed in Old Hebrew, noted the capacity and original owners of the wine-jars, with the date of their contents (*DOTT*, pp. 204–208; *WRITING). These are probably to be assigned to the reign of Jeroboam II.

Level III marks the period of Jehu with adaptations of earlier buildings. Then, after an interval, come levels IV–VI, the Israelite period covering Jeroboam and the 8th century BC. The city was repaired in the last decades before its fall to the Assyrians in 722 BC, which is marked by the destruction level VII.

The remains of the Hellenistic buildings are well preserved, with a round tower standing nineteen courses of stone high, a fortress, the city wall (near the West Gate), coins, stamped jar-handles and Greek pottery remaining.

The Roman city of Herod is notable for the great temple dedicated to Augustus, built over the Israelite palaces. Other remains include the enclosure wall, and West Gate, with three round towers, a 820-m long colonnaded street bordered by porticos and shops, the temple of Isis rededicated to Kore, a basilica (68 by 32 m), divided into three naves by Corinthian columns, a forum, a stadium and an aqueduct. Many of the visible ruins are probably to be dated to later restorers, especially Septimus Severus (AD 193–211).

BIBLIOGRAPHY. A. Parrot, *Samaria*, 1958; J. W. Crowfoot, K. Kenyon, *etc.*, *Samaria*, 1, *The Buildings at Samaria*, 1943; 2, *Early Ivories at Samaria*, 1938; 3, *The Objects from Samaria*, 1957; *BA* 26, 1963, pp. 110–121; J. B. Hennessy, 'Excavations at Samaria–

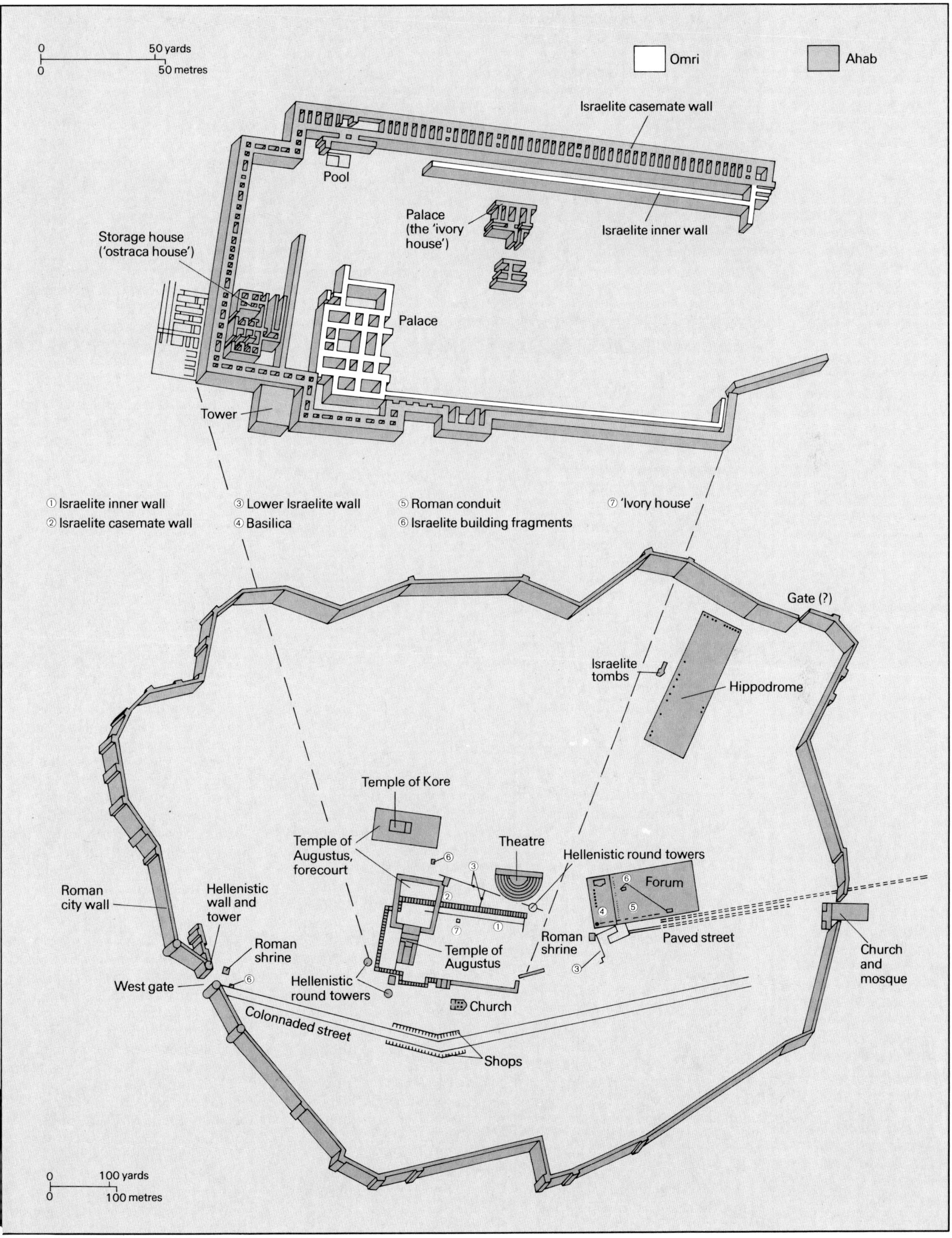
0 50 yards
0 50 metres
Omri
Ahab
Israelite casemate wall
Pool
Palace
(the 'ivory
house')
Israelite inner wall
Storage house
('ostraca house')
Palace
Tower
① Israelite inner wall
② Israelite casemate wall
③ Lower Israelite wall
④ Basilica
⑤ Roman conduit
⑥ Israelite building fragments
⑦ 'Ivory house'
Gate (?)
Israelite
tombs
Hippodrome
Temple of Kore
Temple of
Augustus,
forecourt
Theatre
Hellenistic round towers
Forum
Roman
city wall
Hellenistic
wall and
tower
Roman
shrine
Paved street
Roman
shrine
Temple of
Augustus
Church
and
mosque
West gate
Hellenistic
round towers
Church
Colonnaded street
Shops
0 100 yards
0 100 metres

Ivory furniture decoration in local style showing a lion grappling with a bull. Found at Samaria. Height 4·2 cm, length 11·4 cm. 9th cent. BC. (IM)

SAMARIA WARE
See Potter, Part 3.

Sebaste 1968', *Levant* 2, 1970, pp. 1–21; P. W. and N. L. Lapp, *Discoveries in the Wâdī ed-Dâliyeh*, *AASOR* 41, 1974. D.J.W.

SAMARITANS. In EVV of the OT, Samaritans are mentioned only in 2 Ki. 17:29, a passage which describes the syncretistic religion of those peoples whom the king of Assyria transported to the N kingdom of Israel to replace the exiled native population after the fall of Samaria (722/721 BC).

Several reasons argue strongly against the identification, favoured by Josephus and many others since, of this group with the Samaritans as they are more widely known from the NT (Mt. 10:5; Lk. 9:52; 10:33; 17:16; Jn. 4:9, 39–40; 8:48; Acts 8:25), some of whose descendants survive to the present day in two small communities at Nablus and Holon: (*i*) the word used (*haššōmrōnîm*) seems merely to mean 'inhabitants of (the city or province of) Samaria (*šōmrôn*)', and this fits the context of 2 Ki. 17 best; (*ii*) there is no evidence that the later Samaritans inhabited Samaria. The earliest certain references to them, by contrast, all point clearly to their residence at Shechem (Ecclus. 50:26; 2 Macc. 5:22f.; 6:2; *cf.* Jn. 4:5f., 20), whilst one of Josephus' sources refers to them as 'Shechemites' (*cf. Ant.* 11. 340–347; 12. 10); (*iii*) nothing whatever that is known of later Samaritan religion and practice suggests the pagan influence of 2 Ki. 17 or Ezr. 4.

The origins of the Samaritans of the NT as a distinctive group should probably not be sought before the start of the Hellenistic period (end of the 4th century BC), when Shechem was rebuilt after a long period of desolation. The enemies of the Jewish community in the earlier Persian period mentioned in Ezr. and Ne. would then be some of the inhabitants of the N province whose opposition to the rebuilding of Jerusalem was mainly stirred by political motives. That some adhered to the Israelite faith (Ezr. 4:2) is not surprising, since the OT itself acknowledges that not all the inhabitants of the old N kingdom were exiled in 721 BC (2 Ch. 30) and some of the newcomers could well have assimilated to those who remained.

It is not known precisely what factors led to the resettlement of Shechem and the consequent crystallization of the Samaritan community. An attractive suggestion is that following the complete Hellenization of Samaria after the conquests of Alexander the Great, a group of religious purists (possibly joined by some priests whose marriage to women of the N made their continued residence in Jerusalem impracticable) decided to make a fresh start where they could practise their religion unmolested. The find of over 200 skeletons (together with papyri which originated in Samaria) in a remote cave in Wadi ed-Dâliyeh, about 14 km N of Jericho, suggests that other refugees may not have been so fortunate.

Be that as it may, once the community had taken on a distinctive identity, and a temple had been built on Mt Gerizim (both Josephus, *Ant.* 11. 321ff., for all the other difficulties of his narrative at this point, and archaeological remains, if correctly identified, agree on a date in the Hellenistic period), it was inevitable that attitudes between the Jews of Jerusalem and the Samaritans should have begun to harden. Whilst it may be misleading to speak of a particular schism, it is clear that Ben-Sira (*c.* 180 BC) regarded the Samaritans as a quite separate group (Ecclus. 50:26), and this would have been accentuated by their capitulation in the period of the Maccabean revolt, when their temple was dedicated to Zeus Xenios. Perhaps, however, the breach was made final when, *c.* 128 BC, John Hyrcanus extended the Hasmonaean dominance of the area by capturing Shechem and destroying the Gerizim temple.

This by no means marked the end of the friction, however. From the scanty sources available, we learn that between AD 6 and 9 some Samaritans scattered bones in the Jerusalem Temple during a certain Passover. In AD 52 Samaritans massacred a group of Galilean pilgrims at En-gannim, though in the consequent dispute before Claudius, which followed a Jewish reprisal raid, the decision was given in favour of the Jews. Furthermore, the Samaritans suffered at the hands of the Roman rulers: in AD 36 a Samaritan fanatic assembled a crowd on Mt Gerizim, promising to reveal the sacred vessels thought to have been hidden there by Moses, and many of them were massacred by Pilate. A year after the start of the Jewish War (AD 66–70), a group of Samaritans switched allegiance to join the revolt, only to be slaughtered on Mt Gerizim by Vettulenus Cerealis.

Since the main theological writings of the Samaritans (*e.g. Memar Marqah*, the Samaritan liturgy known as the *Defter*, and a number of Chronicles) come from only the

The round towers of the West Gate at Samaria were built, on earlier foundations, by Herod. 40–4 BC. (MEPhA)

4th century AD, and often much later, it is almost impossible to reconstruct in detail their beliefs in the NT period. For this reason, attempts to find a *distinctively* Samaritan background to (*e.g.*) Jn., Acts 7 or Heb. should be treated with the greatest caution.

Only the five books of the Pentateuch in their Samaritan recension (2nd century BC) were regarded as canonical, and this is reflected in their creed, whose elements must date back to early times: belief in one God, in Moses the prophet, in the law, in Mt Gerizim as the place appointed by God for sacrifice (which is made the tenth commandment in the SP), in the day of judgment and recompense, and in the return of Moses as *Taheb* (the 'restorer' or 'returning one').

The attitude of the Jewish Mishnah and Talmud towards the Samaritans, as of Josephus, is ambiguous. This may reflect a favourable attitude which recognized an essential affinity of both race and religion with the Samaritans, but which was subsequently heavily overlaid with later polemic, encouraged by the developing antagonism and based on 2 Ki. 17 and Ezr. 4.

It is thus noteworthy that the NT is almost consistently favourable towards them (see refs. above), and that the Samaritans are portrayed as responding enthusiastically both to Jesus himself and to the preaching of the early Christian church.

BIBLIOGRAPHY. For details of editions of Samaritan texts and

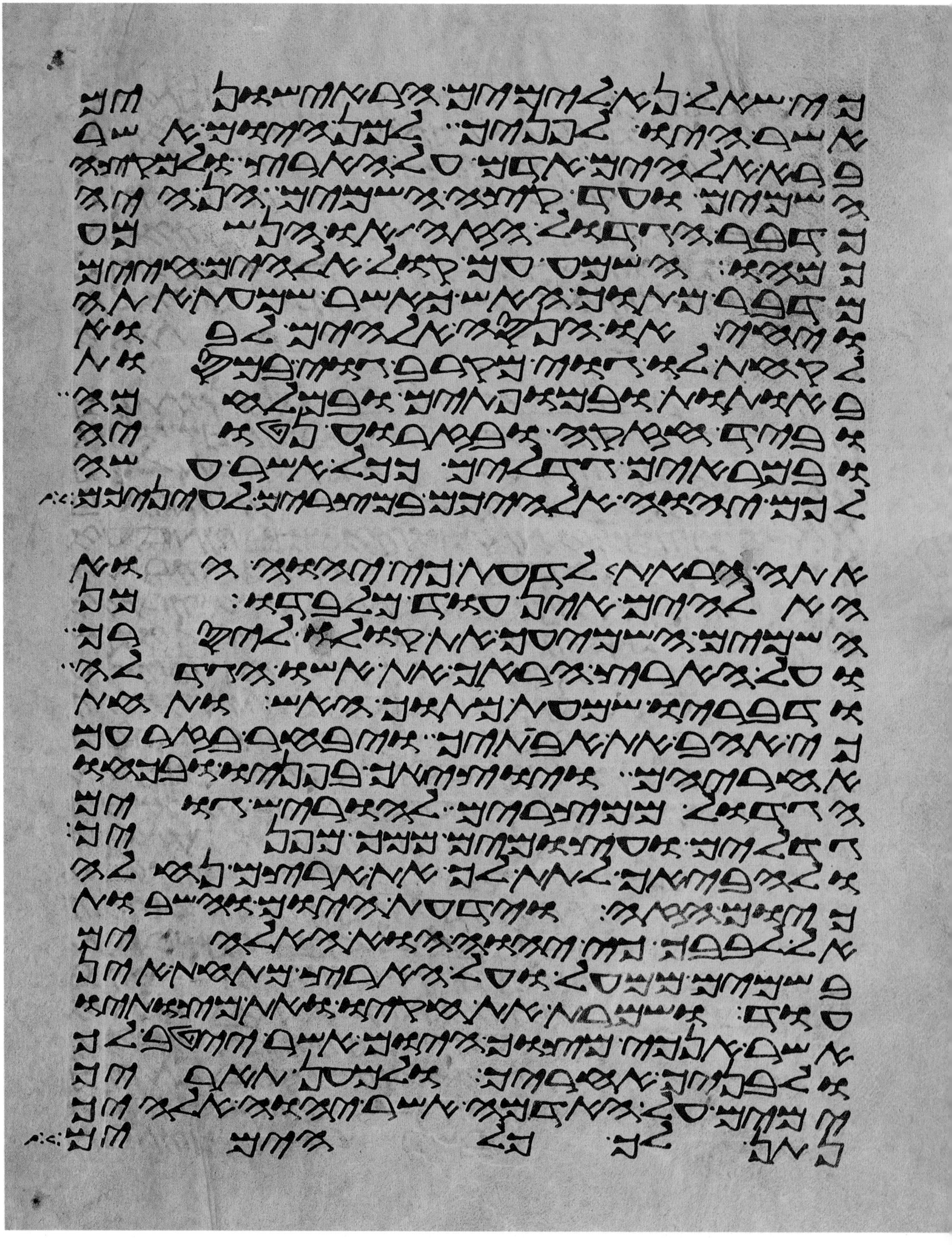

some other bibliography, *cf.* J. Macdonald, *The Theology of the Samaritans*, 1964. Still of value is J. A. Montgomery, *The Samaritans*, 1907, repr. 1968. More recent studies include: G. E. Wright, *Shechem*, 1965, ch. 10; J. D. Purvis, *The Samaritan Pentateuch and the Origin of the Samaritan Sect*, 1968; R. J. Bull, *BA* 31, 1968, pp. 58–72; H. G. Kippenberg, *Garizim und Synagoge*, 1971; C. H. H. Scobie, *NTS* 19, 1972–3, pp. 390–414; R. Bergmeier, *Journal for the Study of Judaism* 5, 1974, pp. 121–153; J. D. Purvis, *NovT* 17, 1975, pp. 161–198; R. J. Coggins, *Samaritans and Jews*, 1975; K. Haacker, *NIDNTT* 3, pp. 449–467. H.G.M.W.

SAMGAR-NEBO (Heb. *samgar-nᵉḇô*; Gk. many variants, *e.g. Samagoth, Eissamagath*). Je. 39:3 lists officers of Nebuchadrezzar who sat in the middle gate of Jerusalem after its capture in 587 BC: 'Nergal-sharezer, Samgar-nebo, Sarsechim the Rabsaris, Nergal-sharezer the Rabmag'. Since a list of Nebuchadrezzar's courtiers includes a Nergal-shar-uṣur with the title Sinmagir (*ANET*, p. 308), it is thought that the text is confused and should read 'Nergal-sharezer the Simmagir'. The following Nebo would then belong with * Sarsechim as the name of the * Rabsaris, perhaps corrupted from Nebushazban as in v. 13. All this remains conjecture. A.R.M.

SAMOS. One of the larger islands in the Aegean Sea, off the coast of Asia Minor SW of Ephesus. An Ionian settlement, it had been an important maritime state. Under the Romans it was part of the province of Asia until Augustus made it a free state in 17 BC. On his way back to Judaea from his third missionary journey Paul sailed between Samos and the mainland (Acts 20:15). K.L.McK.

SAMOTHRACE (modern Samothraki). A small mountainous island in the N of the Aegean off the coast of Thrace, with a town of the same name on the N side. One of its peaks rises above 1,700 m, forming a conspicuous landmark. Sailing NW from Troas on his way to Neapolis, Paul must have had a favourable wind to reach Samothrace in one day and Neapolis in one more (Acts 16:11; *cf.* 20:6).

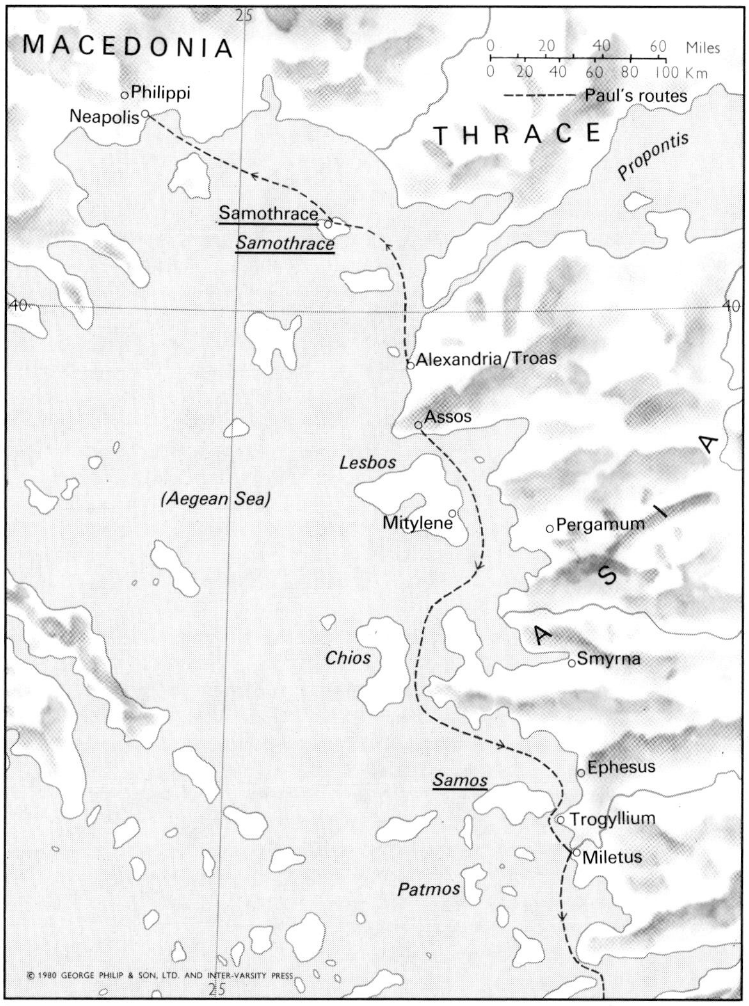

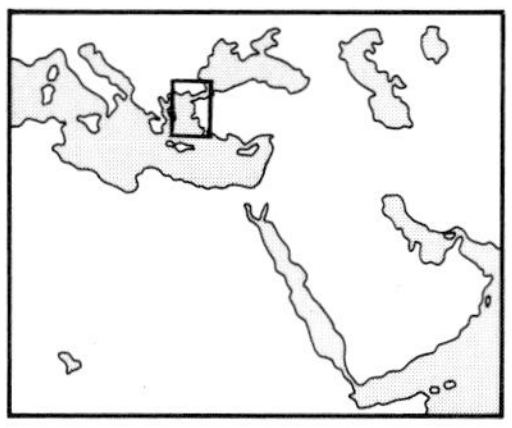

The islands of Samos and Samothrace, both visited by Paul (Acts 20:15; 16:11).

Opposite page: Samaritan Pentateuch (here Dt. 4:32–40). AD 1362–3. (BL)

The island of Samos, with mainland Turkey in the distance across a narrow strait. Paul may have called here on his way to Miletus (Acts 20:15). (RS)

Plan of the main town on the island of Samothrace.

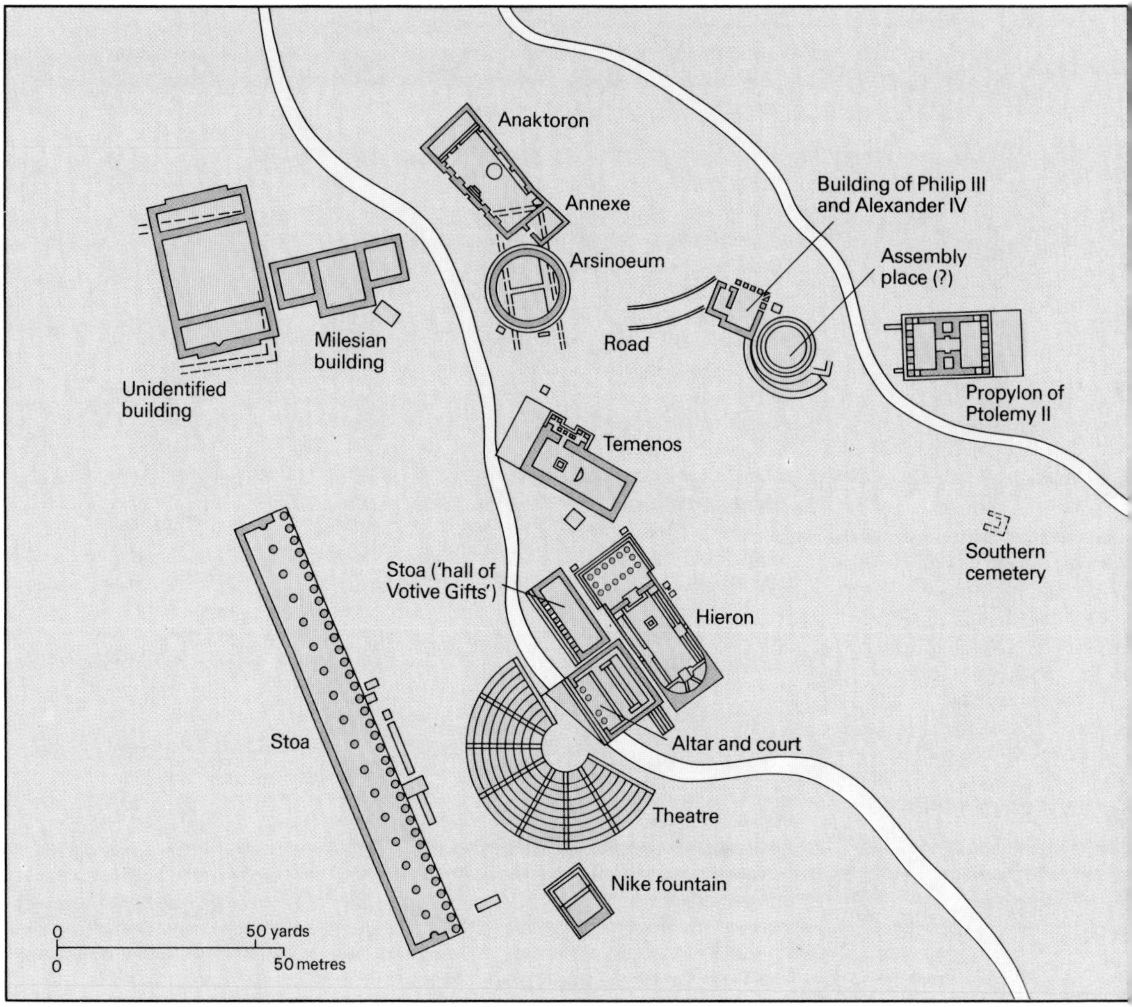

Samothrace was renowned as a centre of the mystery cult of the Kabeiroi, ancient fertility deities who were supposed to protect those in danger, especially at sea.

K.L.McK.

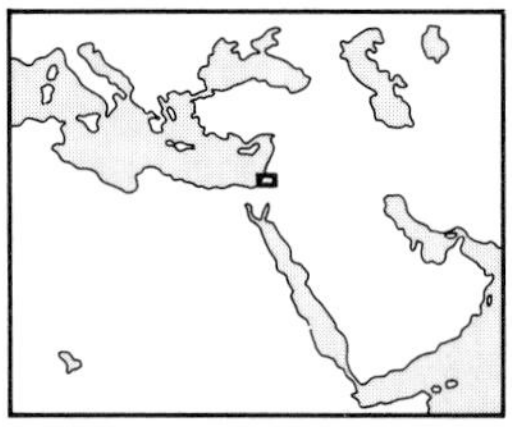

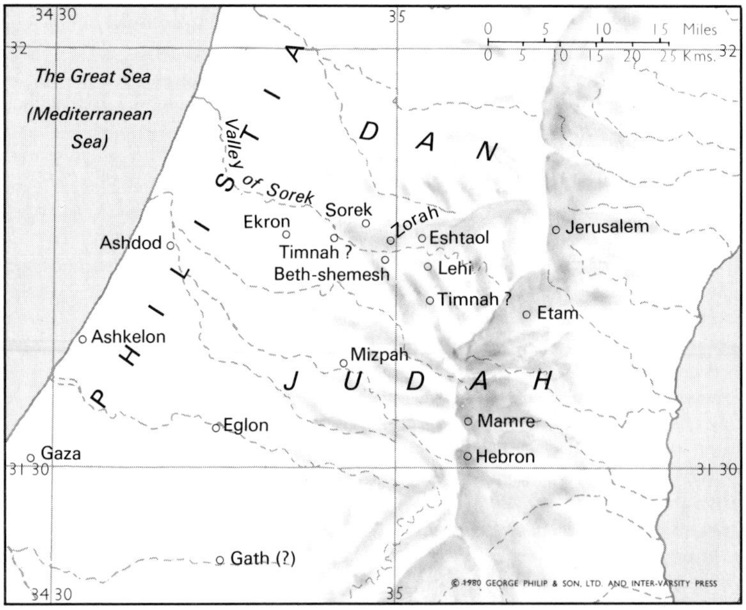

Places connected with the life of Samson.

SAMSON. Greater attention is given to Samson than to any other of Israel's judges before Samuel (Jdg. 13–16). His name, *šimšôn* (Jdg. 13:24), derives from Heb. *šemeš*, 'sun', which has led some scholars to suggest a connection with a sun-mythology, Samson's exploits being equated with the 'twelve labours' of Gilgamesh or Hercules. The proximity of Beth-shemesh to Samson's birth-place, Zorah, the fact that one of his feats of strength took place 'at the time of wheat harvest' (Jdg. 15:1), *i.e.* approaching mid-summer, and his death between the pillars of a Philistine temple, possibly symbolic of sunset, are used in support of this view. But the essential historicity of the biblical record can hardly be doubted. Samson's birth and death are carefully documented and there is a close connection with an actual historical situation. Names like Samson are found in Ugaritic texts of the 14th and 15th centuries BC and most likely a common Canaanite name like this was widely used by Israel also.

I. Historical background

The Samson narratives provide an invaluable background to the earlier part of the Philistine oppression. The Philistines settled on the coastal plain *c.* 1200 BC, a generation after the Conquest, and once established they attempted to expand into the Israelite hill-country. Shamgar's exploit probably gave temporary relief (Jdg. 3:31), but a combination of Philistine and Amorite pressure (Jdg. 1:34) forced part of Samson's tribe, the Danites, to migrate N (Jdg. 18). The Danite remnant which remained, with Judah, bore increasingly the brunt of Philistine pressure. At this stage Philistine rule was not onerous, Judah accepting it without demur (Jdg. 15:11). It was established by infiltration rather than by force, and promised obvious economic advantages to the subject peoples. The insidious nature of this domination was a major threat to Israel's continued independence. Samson's activities were significant in this light. Nowhere had he armed support from his compatriots but his one-man campaign highlighted the danger and brought the conflict into the open. Even so, Israel eventually overcame the Philistines only with the greatest difficulty. Samson may be dated in the period of open Philistine aggression, *c.* 1070 BC, contemporary with Jephthah, who dealt with the Ammonite menace (*cf.* Jdg. 10:7) and *c.* 20 years before Israel's double defeat at Aphek (1 Sa. 4:1–11).

II. Personal history

a. Samson was the son of Manoah, whose wife, like Sarah, Hannah and Elizabeth, was barren. His birth, like those of Isaac and John the Baptist, was announced by an angel (Jdg. 13:3). He was to be a Nazirite (Heb. *nāzîr*, 'separated' or 'consecrated') from birth. Usually the Nazirite vow was voluntarily taken for a limited period (Nu. 6:1–21). Of the stipulations required by the Nazirite vow, Samson took only one seriously, that concerning his hair. He was often in contact with corpses (*e.g.* 14:8f.) and it is unlikely that he abstained from strong drink.

Samson's parents lived at Zorah, on the border between Dan and Judah, in the Shephelah *c.* 22 km W of Jerusalem.

b. Samson's first love (14:1–15:8). Seeing a Philistine woman in Timnah, 6 km SW of Zorah, he demanded that his unwilling parents arrange a marriage. Understandably they were aggrieved that he should seek a wife outside the covenant-community. At the wedding feast he used a riddle to test the thirty young men, who appear more as protection against Samson than as guests (14:11). They put pressure upon Samson's bride to extract the answer, whereupon an enraged Samson slew thirty Philistines at Ashkelon to pay his debt and then departed (14:13–19). To escape disgrace his bride was given to his 'best man' (14:20). The type of marriage indicated did not involve permanent cohabitation, but when Samson arrived back in the early summer with the present customary in such a relationship (15:1) he was refused entrance. He took his revenge by catching 300 'foxes', probably jackals, which unlike foxes are not solitary and are more easily caught, tying fire-brands to their tails and releasing them (15:2–5). At harvest-time the loss would be considerable. The Philistines, in their turn, took an equally vicious revenge upon the Timnite and his family (15:6). In a further escalation of violence Samson retaliated by slaughtering the offending Philistines (15:7f.).

c. The attempt to capture Samson at Lehi (15:9–20). Seeking refuge at the rock of Etam, Samson was taken into custody by 3,000 men of Judah, resentful that he had disturbed their peaceful situation under the Philistines (15:9–13). His abnormal strength enabled him to break free and attack the surprised Philistines with a jawbone of an ass, a formidable weapon in the hands of a determined man (15:14–17). Samson was weakened with thirst after this spectacular success and God provided miraculously for his need (15:18f.). V. 20, with its formal statement of Samson's judgeship, probably marked the end of one account of his life.

d. His downfall and death (16:1–31). Samson's uncontrolled sexual urge, involving foreign prostitutes, eventually proved his undoing. A warning of his vulnerability in such circumstances was given at Gaza, but his unique strength enabled him to escape (16:1–3). Gaza, the southernmost of the five Philistine cities, was 60 km from Hebron, but the narrative may indicate that Samson lifted the city-gates to a hill in the general direction of Hebron.

After this Samson became infatuated with Delilah, whose home in the valley of Sorek lay just below Zorah (16:4). She collaborated with the Philistines and with heartless tenacity extracted from Samson the secret of his strength (16:5–20). Blinded and humiliated, 'eyeless in Gaza', he was paraded as the butt at a festival (16:21–27). For the first time a religious act on Samson's part is noted, and in answer to his prayer, coupled with the fact that the Philistines had carelessly allowed his hair to grow again, Samson was able to demolish a probably over-stressed temple, killing both himself and more Philistines than he had slain during his life (16:28–31). As the Philistines formed a ruling class superimposed upon native population, the effect of this decimation would be considerable.

e. Moral problems raised by the Samson narratives. Most of the judges had moral and religious shortcomings, but these are greatly accentuated in the case of Samson, whose sensuality, irresponsibility and lack of true religious concern are apparent. Yet he is included in the catalogue of heroes of faith (Heb. 11:32). Especially perplexing is the relationship of his enduement with the Spirit of God to his character. A clue to the significance of chs. 13–16 is the absence of the religiously motivated comment which abounds elsewhere in the book of Judges, as though the editor deems further comment unnecessary, the narratives themselves testifying openly to the prevailing low standards. We should distinguish between the level of appreciation of the average contemporary Israelite, who would thoroughly approve of the hated Philistines' discomfiture, and that of the godly men who finally collected Israel's traditions; they would be well aware of Samson's blemishes. Nor must we read back the clear NT connection between Spirit-endowment and holiness—a charismatic anointing in the OT period did not necessarily produce purity of life. God could still make use of a person apart from the quality of his life. Amongst his unlikely instruments were Balaam (Nu. 22–24), Nebuchadrezzar (Je. 25:9; 27:6; 43:10) and Cyrus (Is. 44:28; 45:1–4). We may question his use of an agent like Samson, and be embarrassed by the details, but God is sovereign, and he used Samson, in the 'Dark Ages' of the Judges' period, to fulfil a lone but vital role.

BIBLIOGRAPHY. F. F. Bruce, 'Judges', *NBCR*, 1970, pp. 269–272; R. G. Boling, *Judges*, *AB*, 1975, pp. 217–253; A. E. Cundall

Map to illustrate the life of Samuel.

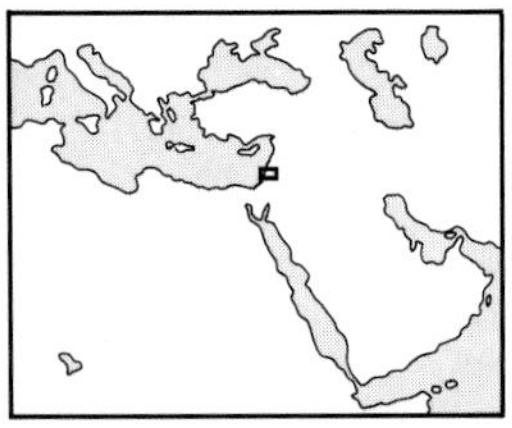

and L. Morris, *Judges and Ruth*, *TOTC*, 1968, pp. 153–181; J. Gray, *Joshua, Judges and Ruth*, *CB*, 1967, pp. 342–362; J. D. Martin, *The Book of Judges*, *CBC*, 1975, pp. 153–181; J. C. Moyer, 'Samson', *ZPEB*, 5, pp. 249–252. A.E.C.

SAMUEL (Heb. *šᵉmûʾēl*, '(?)name of God'). **1.** A Simeonite leader (Nu. 34:20), in NEB; most EVV have *Shemuel. **2.** Grandson of Issachar (1 Ch. 7:2), in NEB; most EVV have *Shemuel. **3.** The prophet, contemporary with Saul and David, whose career is related in 1 Sa., and who has given his name to the two books of Samuel. Acts 3:24 views him as the first of the prophets, Acts 13:20 as the last of the judges.

I. Career

Samuel was born into an Ephraimite family of Ramah (though of levitical stock, according to 1 Ch. 6:33f.). His parents were Elkanah and Hannah; the latter had previously been barren, and she dedicated Samuel before his birth as a *Nazirite. After his weaning, therefore, he was brought up in the Shiloh temple by Eli (1 Sa. 1). While still a boy, he experienced the prophetic call, and in due course 'was established as a prophet of the Lord' (1 Sa. 3).

A major Philistine victory was accompanied by the capture of the ark of the covenant, the death of Eli and the transfer of the priesthood from *Shiloh (1 Sa. 4); Samuel's movements are not recorded. He subsequently mustered the Israelite troops at Mizpah and won a victory over the Philistines (*EBENEZER). He now fulfilled the role of judge in Israel, with a circuit in Bethel, Gilgal, Mizpah and Ramah (1 Sa. 7).

In his old age, his leadership was challenged by the tribal elders who clamoured for a king. Samuel at first resisted this pressure but received divine guidance to agree to it (1 Sa. 8). He then met *Saul and was told by God to anoint him; and in a complex of events Samuel presided over the institution of the Israelite monarchy, though not without issuing stern warnings to king and people alike (1 Sa. 9–12).

Before long, a breach occurred between Samuel and Saul, when the latter took it upon himself to offer sacrifice before battle (1 Sa. 13). This breach became absolute when Saul later broke a solemn oath in sparing the life of the Amalekite king Agag. Samuel himself killed Agag, and then retired to Ramah. He explicitly rejected Saul, and never had any further dealings with him (1 Sa. 15). His final act was to anoint David, privately, to be next king of Israel (1 Sa. 16). He died in Ramah and was buried there (1 Sa. 25:1). Even afterwards a desperate Saul tried to ascertain God's will through him (1 Sa. 28).

II. Critical evaluation

Recent critical assessments of Samuel tend to be negative. The minimal view would see him as a mere local seer, quite unknown to Saul, on the basis of 1 Sa. 9:6, 18. Few scholars, however, would deny that he not only superintended the institution of the Monarchy but also later broke with Saul and repudiated him. Saul's subsequent insecurity strongly supports the biblical picture of Samuel as a man of power and influence.

The chief arguments against historicity are (i) the 'legendary' character of some of the stories (*e.g.* the infancy narrative), (ii) the fact that Samuel is depicted in such a diversity of roles (prophet, judge, war-leader, national leader and perhaps priest), and (iii) the problem of aligning these various roles with the supposed literary sources or unwritten traditions underlying 1 Sa. In the absence of extra-biblical data about Samuel, the first of these arguments admits of no objective criteria. The third problem, moreover, offers no secure basis for judgment in view of the fact that there is so little certainty about the sources utilized in the *books of Samuel. The second problem is therefore the main issue. Two points may be made about the roles Samuel is said to have filled. First, while it may be admitted that different literary strata may have emphasized or highlighted different roles, it is nevertheless true that the latter were not so disparate as might appear: the book of Judges shows that the offices of war-leader, national leader and judge (in the judicial sense) could be combined in ancient Israel; and there is evidence from inside and outside Israel that *prophecy at times embraced sacrificial roles, and that prophets at times appointed and repudiated kings. Secondly, Samuel lived in a period of crisis and transition, and in the absence of any other figurehead, the Israelite tribes may well have looked to him to fill an exceptional role. Basically, he combines the offices of judge and prophet; Deborah offers a minor analogy (*cf.* Jdg. 4:4).

BIBLIOGRAPHY. A. Weiser, *Samuel: seine geschichtliche Ausgabe und religiöse Bedeutung* (*FRLANT* 81), 1962; J. L. McKenzie, 'The Four Samuels', *Biblical Research* 7, 1962, pp. 3–18. See also standard histories of Israel and standard commentaries. D.F.P.

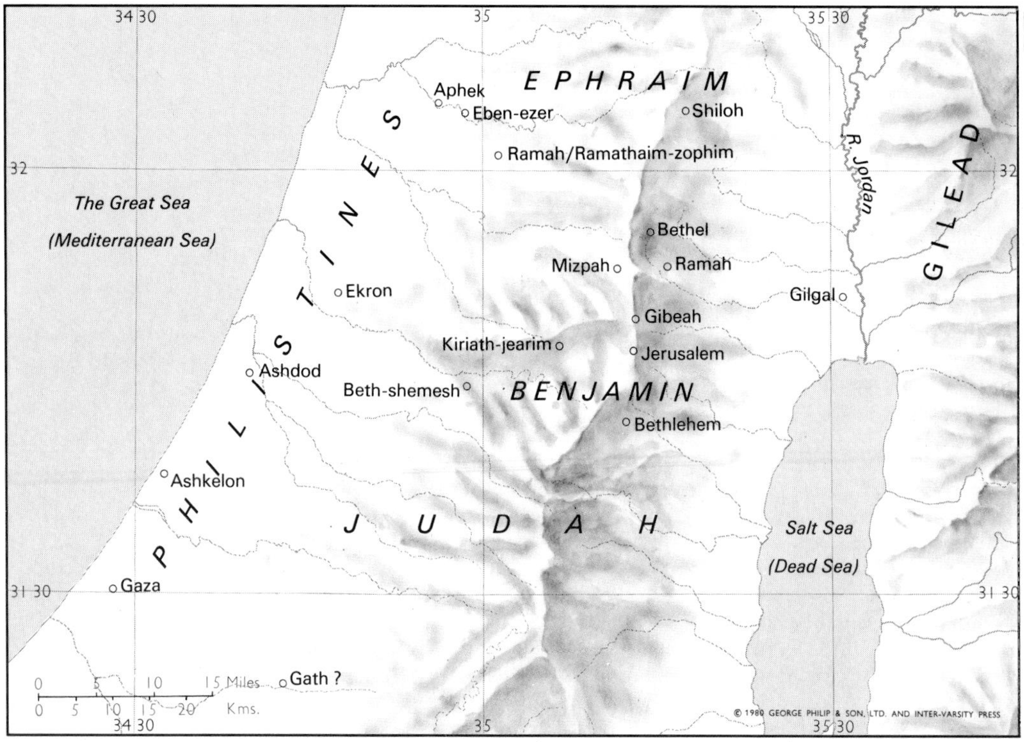

SAMUEL, BOOKS OF. The two books of Samuel were originally one; not until the 15th century were they ever divided in the Heb. Bible. The division into two books goes back to the LXX. The English title 'Samuel' is the same as the Heb.; the LXX linked the four books of Samuel and *Kings together as 1–4 'Reigns' (or 'Kingdoms'), while the Vulg. calls them 1–4 'Kings' (*cf.* the titles of these books in AV). In the Heb. Bible Samuel stands third in the 'Former Prophets', *i.e.* the four-volume history Joshua–Judges–Samuel–Kings. Many modern scholars consider that these four were from the beginning a single, connected history (styled 'the Deuteronomic History'). It is at least true that Samuel provides the transition from the era of the judges to the period of the Monarchy, and that the divisions between the books seem to be arbitrary at some points.

The title 'Samuel' is not altogether appropriate; the prophet Samuel is only the first of the three major figures whose lives are recorded in these books; the other two are Saul and David. Samuel's death is recorded in 1 Sa. 25:1; he cannot then have been the author, in spite of the tradition in TB Baba Bathra 14*b*). 'The Chronicles of Samuel the seer' (1 Ch. 29:29) may be a source document of the books of Samuel; the books of Samuel themselves cannot be meant.

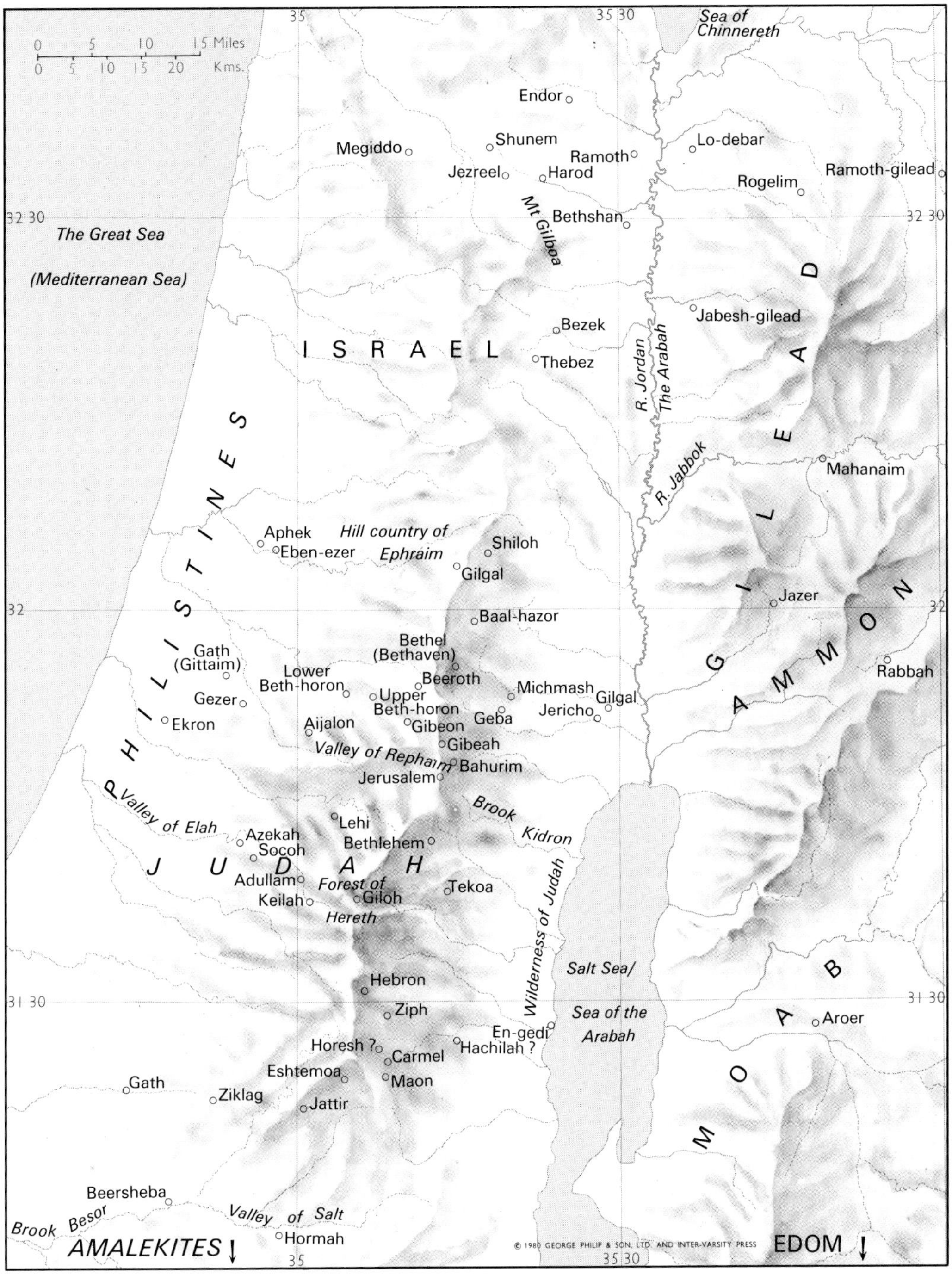

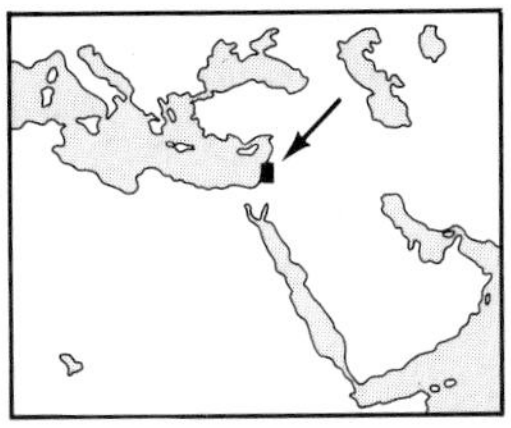

Israel and Judah at the time of Samuel.

I. Outline of contents

The books of Samuel span a period of roughly a century, *c.* 1050–950 BC. There are six main sections:

a. Samuel's early years (1 Sa. 1:1–7:14)

(i) Samuel and Eli (1:1–3:21)
(ii) War with the Philistines (4:1–7:14)

b. Samuel and Saul (7:15–15:35)

(i) Saul becomes king (7:15–12:25)
(ii) War with the Philistines (13:1–14:52)
(iii) The defeat of Amalek (15:1–35)

c. Saul and David (16:1–31:13)

(i) David reaches the royal court (16:1–17:58)
(ii) David and Jonathan (18:1–20:42)
(iii) David as a fugitive (21:1–26:25)
(iv) David in Philistine territory (27:1–30:31)
(v) Defeat and death of Saul and Jonathan (31:1–13)

d. The early years of David's reign (2 Sa. 1:1–8:18)

(i) David's reaction to the news of Saul's death (1:1–27)
(ii) David and Ish-bosheth (2:1–4:12)
(iii) David defeats the Philistines (5:1–25)
(iv) David, the ark and the house of God (6:1–7:29)
(v) Further victories (8:1–18)

e. King David and his court (9:1–20:26)

(i) David and Mephibosheth (9:1–13)
(ii) Warfare with Ammon and its consequences (10:1–12:21)
(iii) David and his eldest sons (13:1–18:33)
(iv) David's return and Sheba's revolt (19:1–20:26)

f. Appendix (21:1–24:25)

(i) Famine and warfare (21:1–22)
(ii) Two psalms of David (22:1–23:7)

(iii) His mighty men (23:8–39)
(iv) Census and plague (24:1–25)

II. Sources and composition

There can be no doubt at all that the writer of the books of Samuel made use of some earlier documents, though it is impossible to know how many. No single individual lived right through the eras of Samuel, Saul and David; and statements incorporating the phrase 'to this day' (*e.g.* 1 Sa. 27:6) suggest a further lapse of time before the author's own date. Attempts have therefore been made to isolate the sources from which the author took his material; and a number of quite different schemes have resulted.

Some scholars (notably K. Budde and O. Eissfeldt) have argued that documentary strata underlying the *Pentateuch are also visible in Samuel. Few contemporary scholars would agree. The present trend is to consider Samuel an amalgam of individual narratives, brought together by stages (see, *e.g.*, Weiser, Fohrer). The chief interest centres in the attempt to isolate the earlier units or documents. A. R. S. Kennedy long ago proposed (*CB*, 1904) that five basic documents had been utilized by the author of Samuel: a history of Samuel's early years, a history of the ark of the covenant, a history of the Monarchy favourable to it, a history of the Monarchy hostile to it and a court history of David. British scholarship has tended to follow this hypothesis (*e.g.* Anderson, Rowley); the strongest case can be made for the second and fifth of Kennedy's documents. There is wide agreement that a history of the ark underlies 1 Sa. 4:1–7:1, and many scholars have also agreed that 2 Sa. 9–20, with 1 Ki. 1f., constitute a distinct unit (usually known as 'The Succession Narrative'), though some recent studies have challenged this view (Delekat, Würthwein). The Succession Narrative is usually considered to have been composed by, or at least to derive from, an eyewitness. Absent from this section are 'doublets', a feature characteristic of the rest of Samuel; many scholars have stressed the significance of such 'duplicate narratives' in arguing for a variety of (conflicting) sources. This argument has been overpressed (see D. F. Payne, 'Duplicate Accounts', in *NBCR*, pp. 284f.), but on the other hand it may be admitted that such doublets tend to suggest separate sources: historicity is, or should be, a different issue from source criticism. Thus 1 Sa. 16:14–23 tells how Saul first met David as a musician; 1 Sa. 17:55–58 may well derive from a separate source, in which the challenge from Goliath provided the circumstances for David's first coming to the attention of the king. If so, the compiler of the book has drawn on both earlier sources, and made his own clear decision as to which was the earlier event; the 'duplication' denies the historicity of neither story.

Both the number and the nature of the sources of Samuel remain unclear and disputed, then. The author himself undoubtedly made his own contribution, as references to his own day (1 Sa. 27:6) and explanatory remarks (1 Sa. 9:9) make clear. By general consent, however, his activity was very discreet; apart from such minor touches, it is only in 1 Sa. 7, 12 and 2 Sa. 7 that his hand is generally thought to be clearly visible. It is noteworthy that the clear editorial structures and formulae of *Judges and *Kings are absent from Samuel; this fact, among others, argues for a distinct origin for Samuel and militates against the hypothesis of a unified Deuteronomic history, Joshua–Kings. It may be, nevertheless, that a final redaction, of limited extent, took place when Samuel and Kings were brought together, in the exilic period or soon afterwards.

III. Purpose

In covering the era of the transition from a loose tribal constitution under the judges to a monarchy, the books of Samuel necessarily offer a view on the value of the monarchy; but different passages give rather differing impressions. 1 Sa. 8 offers a biting critique of kingship, and in 1 Sa. 12:19 the people acknowledge that they had done evil in seeking a king; but in 1 Sa. 10:24–27; 11:14f. a positive view is taken. Recent studies have found a similar tension within the Succession Narrative, some passages being favourable to David and Solomon, while others are distinctly critical of them. These differing viewpoints have often been used as a criterion, as regards sources and historicity; but as Bright and others have argued, the tension is certainly an original one, on any credible historical reconstruction, and the value of the criteria is dubious. In any case, since he incorporated material tending in both directions, it is unlikely that the final author was either pro-monarchic or anti-monarchic. Rather his attitude was typically prophetic, seeing the monarchy as a constitution which had been ordained by God, but taking a detached and objective view of each individual monarch. J. A. Soggin is right to emphasize that the primary interests of the author are election and rejection.

It is important not to overlook the biographical motive. There was a genuine interest in the careers and achievements of leading Israelites. It was the biblical writers' conviction that God had involved himself in history, and that he governed its whole course, which gave the historical books of the OT their theological quality and content. Theologically-coloured history is none the less history.

IV. Text

There are numerous problems in the Heb. text (*MT*) of Samuel, and commentaries and translations often turn to the LXX (especially LXX^B and LXX^L) for help. The LXX MSS not only elucidate many verses where the Heb. is obscure or problematic but also offer variant readings where the Heb. makes good sense. The most notable variation is in 1 Sa. 17f., where LXX^B is much shorter than *MT* (17:12–31 and 17:55–18:5 are entirely absent). (See D. F. Payne, *NBCR*, p. 318.) Two other sources of evidence are parallel passages in Chronicles, and fragmentary copies of Samuel found at Qumran. The Qumranic material tends to support LXX where it differs from *MT*, and recent EVV, especially NEB, have made considerable use of its evidence. It is widely held that the evidence suggests not so much that the Heb. text of Samuel was poorly preserved as that there existed different recensions of the book.

BIBLIOGRAPHY. L. Rost, *Die Überlieferung von der Thronnachfolge Davids*, 1926; R. A. Carlson, *David, the Chosen King*, 1964; R. N Whybray, *The Succession Narrative*, 1968; G. Wallis, *Geschichte und Überlieferung*, 1968, pp. 45–66. Commentaries by H. W. Hertzberg, *OTL*, E.T. 1960; W. McKane, *TBC* 1963; J. Mauchline, *NCB*, 1971; H. J. Stoebe, *KAT*, 1973. See also standard introductions to the OT, especially those of A. Weiser, O. Eissfeldt, R. K. Harrison and J. A. Soggin. D.F.P.

SANBALLAT. The name is Babylonian, *Sinuballiṭ*, *i.e.* 'Sin (the moon-god) has given life'. In Ne. 2:10, 19; 13:28 he is called the Horonite, probably denoting that he came from Beth-horon, about 30 km NW of Jerusalem (*cf.* Jos. 10:10, *etc.*). He was one of the chief opponents of Nehemiah. The Elephantine Papyri show that in 407 BC he was governor of Samaria. If when Nehemiah came in 445 BC he was either governor or hoping to be governor, he doubtless wanted to have control of Judaea also. The Elephantine Papyri speak of his two sons, Delaiah and Shelemiah, and these names may show that Sanballat was a worshipper of Yahweh. This means that he was descended either from an Israelite family which had not gone into captivity in 721 BC or from one of the peoples whom the Assyrian kings had imported into Palestine. In either case his religion was probably syncretistic (2 Ki. 17:33), though he put Yahweh first, and so won sympathy even from the high priest's family, into which his daughter married (Ne. 13:28). Josephus (*Ant.* 11. 302) makes Sanballat responsible for the building of the Samaritan temple, which he dates under Darius III (336–331 BC). If the story is true, Josephus has confused the date; unless he is referring to a second governor with the same name. (There was at least one further Sanballat, if not two, among the governors of Samaria under the Persian empire.)

BIBLIOGRAPHY. H. H. Rowley, 'Sanballat and the Samaritan Temple', *BJRL* 38, 1955–6, pp. 166ff., reprinted in *Men of God*, 1965, pp. 246ff.; F. M. Cross, 'Discovery of Samaria Papyri', *BA* 26, 1963, pp. 110ff. J.S.W.

SANCTIFICATION, SANCTIFY. This noun and verb, derived from Lat. *sanctus*, 'holy', and *facere*, 'to make', translate Heb. *qdš* and Gk. *hagiasmos, hagiazō*.

The basic sense of the Heb. root *qdš* is variously given as (1) 'set apart', (2) 'brightness'. The former could underlie references to holiness or sanctification in terms of position, status, relationship, where the words are translated 'cut off', 'separated', 'set apart for exclusive use', 'dedicated' or 'consecrated', 'regarded as sacred or holy in contrast to common, profane or secular'. The latter could underlie those usages which relate to condition, state or process, leading on in the NT to the thought of an inward transformation gradually taking place, resulting in purity, moral rectitude, and holy, spiritual thoughts expressing themselves in an outward life of goodness and godliness. In this connection it should be noted that, while the verb 'sanctify' is used in the AV of the OT, the noun 'holiness' is used rather than 'sanctification'.

Sanballat, governor of Samaria, and his sons Delaiah and Shelemiah, are mentioned in this Aramaic papyrus found at Elephantine. It is a copy of a letter written by the local chief priest Yedoniah to the Persian viceroy of Judaea, asking for orders to be given to commence rebuilding the Elephantine temple. 408 BC. (SMB)

I. In the Old Testament

The two sets of meanings outlined above may be roughly designated the priestly and the prophetic, but they are not mutually exclusive. The primary reference of both is Godward.

a. God is depicted as holy in majesty, mysterious in his numinous otherness, loftily removed from man, sin and earth (*cf.* Ex. 3:5; Is. 6:3ff.).

The people are exhorted to regard the Lord of hosts as holy (Is. 8:13), and God says he will sanctify himself and be sanctified in or by them, *i.e.* recognized in his sovereign claims (similarly he will be glorified, *i.e.* his sublimity will be acknowledged through his people's attitude and relationship to him).

Any thing or person sanctified is recognized as set apart by God as well as by man (*e.g.* sabbath, Gn. 2:3; altar, Ex. 29:37; tabernacle, Ex. 29:44; garments, Lv. 8:30; fast, Joel 1:14; house, Lv. 27:14; field, Lv. 27:17; people, Ex. 19:14; congregation, Joel 2:16; priests, Ex. 28:41). This does not necessarily involve an inward change. The ceremonial ritual of the law made provision for the infringements of which the people of God, who were set apart by God to belong exclusively to him to be used as his instruments, were guilty.

b. While these were primarily external and ritual instances of sanctification, they were sometimes accompanied by the deeper, inward reality. God's exhortation, 'Be holy, for I am holy', required a moral and spiritual response from the people, a reflection of his moral excellences of righteousness, purity, hatred of moral evil, loving concern for the welfare of others in obedience to his will; for the Holy One of Israel was actively engaged for the good of his people (Ex. 19:4) as well as being separated from evil. His holiness was both transcendent and immanent (Dt. 4:7; Ps. 73:28), and theirs was to be correspondingly characterized. The prophets were alert to the dangers of a merely outward sanctification, and so they exhorted the people to reverence the Lord; they even went so far as to disparage the external, 'holy' observances when they were not accompanied by practical holiness (Is. 1:4, 11; 8:13). The children of Israel were derogating from the holiness of God by their unholy lives among the nations. They were failing to observe the law of holiness (Lv. 17–26) which combined admirably both the moral and ritual aspects.

II. In the New Testament

There are six references to sanctification (*hagiasmos*) and another four instances in which the same word is translated 'holiness' in RSV. Five other Gk. terms are translated 'holiness' (*hagiotēs, hagiōsynē, eusebeia, hosiotēs, hieroprepēs*). As in the OT, we find a twofold usage of sanctification, but there are significant differences. The two synoptic usages of the verb 'sanctify' are ceremonial or ritual. Our Lord speaks of the Temple that sanctifies the gold and the altar that sanctifies the gift (Mt. 23:17, 19). Here the primary meaning is consecration; the gold and gift are dedicated, set apart, and reckoned as especially sacred and valuable by their relation to the already holy Temple and altar. In a parallel use of this concept, but one more exalted and more directly spiritual since it has to do with the personal realm, Christ sanctifies or consecrates himself for his sacrificial work, the Father sanctifies him, and he bids his followers 'hallow' (regard with sacred reverence, devote a unique position to) the Father (Jn. 10:36; 17:19; Mt. 6:9). A further extension of the thought comes in Christ's sanctifying of the people with his own blood (Heb. 13:12) and possibly in Jn. 17:17 the Father's sanctifying of the believers through the word of truth.

Concerning the latter and kindred texts the word 'possibly' is used advisedly because the idea of 'sanctification' seems here to widen its meaning in the direction of a moral and spiritual change. The Epistle to the Hebrews forms a bridge between the external and internal meanings of sanctification. Christ by his sacrifice sanctifies his brethren not only in the sense of setting them apart but also in that of equipping them for the worship and service of God. This he does by making propitiation for their sins (Heb. 2:17) and cleansing their consciences from dead works (Heb. 9:13ff.). This sanctification, however, is not conceived of primarily as a process but as an accomplished fact, for 'by a single offering he has perfected for all time those who are sanctified' (Heb. 10:10, 14). At the same time the exhortation to grow in sanctification is not absent (*cf.* Heb. 12:14, where holiness is more of a state than a status).

While 'sanctification' in Hebrews is somewhat akin to 'justification' in such Epistles as Romans and Galatians, the distinction between the usages of 'sanctification' in these writings must not be overdrawn. Paul uses the term in two senses also. In some cases he regards it as a status conferred upon believers who are in Christ for sanctification as for justification. The derived word 'saint' refers primarily to their status in Christ ('sanctified in Christ Jesus', 1 Cor. 1:2; *cf.* 1 Pet. 1:2). A vicarious sanctification is the privilege of the non-Christian partner and children when one parent is a believer; this again is status-sanctification (1 Cor. 7:14).

The second meaning of sanctification in Paul concerns the moral and spiritual transformation of the justified believer who is regenerated, given new life, by God. The will of God is our sanctification (1 Thes. 4:3), and to be sanctified wholly is to be conformed to the image of Christ and so to realize in experience what it is to be in the image of God. Christ is the content and norm of the sanctified life: it is his risen life that is reproduced in the believer as he grows in grace and reflects the glory of his Lord. In this progressive experience of liberation from the letter of the law, man's spirit is set free by the Lord the Spirit (2 Cor. 3:17–18). The Holy Spirit is the operator in man's sanctification, but he works through the word of truth and the prayer of faith, and through the fellowship of believers (Eph. 5:26) as they test themselves in the light of the ideal of the love of the Spirit and the indispensability of holiness (Heb. 12:14). Faith, itself produced by the Spirit, lays hold of the sanctifying resources.

As justification implies deliverance from the penalty of sin, so sanctification implies deliverance from the pollutions, privations and potency of sin. As to the intensity and extensiveness and steps of this latter deliverance, however, there is much discussion. The prayer that God will sanctify the believers wholly so that their whole spirit, soul and body be preserved blameless unto the coming of Christ is followed by the assertion that 'He who calls you is faithful, and he will do it' (1 Thes. 5:23–24). This raises three important questions.

a. Will God do it all at once?

Does sanctification by faith mean that complete sanctification is received as a gift in the same manner as justification, so that the believer is instantaneously made holy and enters once for all into actual, practical holiness as a state? Some urge that in a crisis-experience, subsequent to conversion, the old man is crucified once for all, and the root of sin extracted or the principle of sin eradicated. Some go further and stress the need for the reception and the exercise of the gifts of the Spirit (notably the gift of tongues) as evidence of such a work of the Spirit. Others consider that NT teaching is definitely opposed to this view and that the very existence of the Epistles with their reasoned statements of doctrine, arguments, appeals and exhortations, contradicts it. See also below

b. Will God do it all within the believer's lifetime?

Among both those who emphasize the crisis-character of the experience of sanctification and those who see it rather as a process are some who claim for themselves very high attainments of sanctified living. Underlining such injunctions as 'You, therefore, must be perfect' (Mt. 5:48) and not interpreting 'perfection' here as meaning 'maturity', they maintain that perfect love is achievable in this life. High claims in the direction of 'sinless perfection', however, usually minimize both the description of sin and the standard of moral living required. Sin is defined as 'the voluntary transgression of a known law' (Wesley) rather than as 'any want of conformity unto, or transgression of, the law of God' (*Westminster Shorter Catechism*), the latter being a definition which covers our sinful state and sins of omission as well as sins openly and deliberately committed. Others, agreeing that unbroken holiness and unblemished perfection may not be possible, claim that it is possible nevertheless to have the perfect possession of the perfect motive of love.

A minimizing of the standard occurs in C. G. Finney's claim that the Bible 'expressly limits obligation by ability'. 'The very language ɔf the law', he writes, 'is such as to evel its claims to the capacity of he subject however great or small hat subject may be. "Thou shalt ove the Lord thy God with all thy ıeart, with all thy soul, with all thy nind, and with all thy strength." Here then it is plain, that all the aw demands, is the exercise of whatever strength we have, in the ervice of God. Now as entire sanc-ification consists in perfect obedi-ence to the law of God, and as the aw requires nothing more than he right use of whatever strength we have, it is, of course, forever ettled, that a state of entire sancti-ication is attainable in this life, on he ground of natural ability' *Systematic Theology*, 1851, p. 407). This is based on a lamentable mis-understanding of Dt. 6:5.

·. Will God do it all without the believer's activity?

Those who minimize sin and the tandard of holiness God requires re in danger of placing undue tress on human enterprise in sanc-ification. There is, however, an ɔpposite extreme which lays the entire onus of sanctification on God. He is expected to produce a aint instantaneously, or gradually o infuse a Christian with grace or he Spirit. This is to reduce man to a mere robot with no moral fibre and thus virtually to produce an mmoral sanctification—which is a contradiction in terms. Those who re concerned for the intrinsic char-acter of human spirit deny such mpersonal operations of the Holy Spirit. They are also dubious of the claims that the Spirit works directly ıpon the unconscious, rather than hrough the conscious processes of man's mind.

The believer is to have no illu-sions about the intensity of the truggle with sin (Rom. 7–8; Gal. 5), but should realize also that anctification does not occur in nstalments merely by his own en-deavours to counteract his own evil endencies. There is a progression ɔf moral accomplishment but there s also a mysterious, sanctifying work within him. Moreover, it is not merely a synergism whereby the Spirit and the believer each con-tribute something. The action is attributable both to the Spirit and o the believer in the paradox of grace. God the Spirit works hrough the faithful recognition of he law of truth and the believer's esponse of love, and the net result s spiritual maturity expressed in the fulfilling of the law of love to one's neighbour. The consum-mation of sanctification to the believer who, by gracious faith in the work of Christ, by the Spirit 'purifies himself' (1 Jn. 3:3), is indicated by the assurance: 'we know that, when he appears, we shall be like him; for we shall see him as he is' (1 Jn. 3:2). (*SPIRIT, HOLY; *SALVATION.)

BIBLIOGRAPHY. W. Marshall, *The Gospel Mystery of Sanctification*, 1692, reprinted 1955; J. Wesley, *A Plain Account of Christian Perfection*, reprinted 1952; C. Hodge, *Systematic Theology*, 3, 1871–3; J. C. Ryle, *Holiness*, reprinted 1952; B. B. Warfield, *Perfectionism*, 2 vols., 1931; R. E. D. Clark, *Conscious and Unconscious Sin*, 1934; N. H. Snaith, *The Distinctive Ideas of the Old Testament*, 1944; D. M. Lloyd-Jones, *Christ our Sanctification*, 1948; G. C. Berkouwer, *Faith and Sanctification*, 1952; W. E. Sangster, *The Path to Perfection*, 1957; J. Murray, 'Definitive Sanctification', *CTJ* 2, 1967, p. 5; K. F. W. Prior, *The Way of Holiness*, 1967. G.W.

SANCTUARY. The Heb. words *miqdāš*, and its correlative *qōḏeš*, define a place set apart for the worship of God or gods. Whereas the Bible uses these words almost entirely of the place where Yahweh was worshipped, a study of cognate languages such as Canaanite shows that the same terms were used for the worship of the earlier inhabitants of Palestine. Excavation has revealed a wide variety of sanctuaries extending back to the 4th millennium BC. The most complete range of these at present known was excavated at Megiddo. A considerable variety of cult images and tools is now available for study.

Israel's earliest sanctuary was the movable tent known as the *tabernacle where the ark containing the tables of the covenant was housed (Ex. 25:8, *etc.*). Detailed descriptions of the various parts of this structure occur in Ex. 25–31 and 36–40, and the elaborate ritual associated with it is detailed in Leviticus.

With the settlement of Israel in the land, David planned, and Solomon completed, a permanent place of worship (1 Ch. 22:19; 28:10, *etc.*).

Apostasy during the days of the kings brought foreign cult-practices into the Temple. Ezekiel and Zephaniah reproached God's people for defiling his sanctuary (Ezk. 5:11; 23:39; 28:18, *etc.*; Zp. 3:4).

Israel's early sanctuaries were set up in the places where God appeared to his people or 'caused his name to dwell'. Finally Jerusalem became the official centre of worship. (*HIGH PLACE; *TEMPLE.)

In NT the 'sanctuary' (Gk. *naos*)

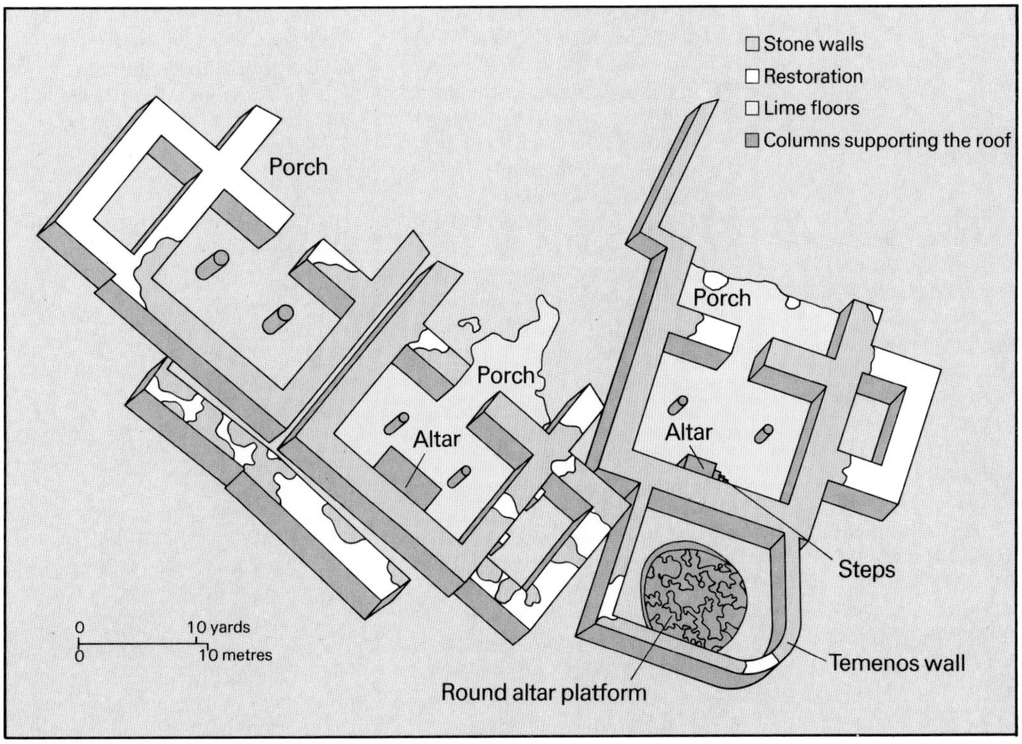

The circular altar in the Canaanite sanctuary at Megiddo dates from c. 2600–2300 BC. The three adjacent temples were built in the 21st to 19th cent. BC.

is the holy house, the dwelling-place of God, whether literal (*e.g.* Mk. 14:58; 15:38; Jn. 2:19) or figurative (*e.g.* 1 Cor. 3:16f.; 6:19), as distinct from 'temple' (*hieron*), the whole sacred enclosure (*e.g.* Mk. 11:11, 15; Lk. 2:27, 46; Jn. 2:14).

J.A.T.

The dais on which once stood a statue of the god, with an altar base before it in the temple of Nabû (Bēl). Babylon. c. 590 BC. (DJW)

SAND (Heb. *ḥôl*; Gk. *ammos*). The Heb. word derives from the verb *ḥûl* ('to whirl, dance'), doubtless a reference to the ease with which the light particles of silex, mica, felspar, *etc.*, are lifted and whirled by the wind. Sand is found extensively along the Mediterranean shores of S Palestine and Egypt, and in desert regions, thus providing a striking symbol of countless multitude (*e.g.* Gn. 22:17; Is. 10:22; Rev. 20:8). It is used also to convey an idea of weight (Jb. 6:3), longevity (Jb. 29:18) and instability (Mt. 7:26). A somewhat obscure allusion (Dt. 33:19) speaks of 'the hidden treasures of the sand'; perhaps a source of prosperity would be found in the seas (fishing, maritime commerce) and on the shores (shellfish; dye, from shellfish; glass, from sand; *cf.* Jos., *BJ* 2. 190; Pliny, *NH* 5. 17; 36. 65). The promise probably applies only to Zebulun, the tribe associated with the sea in the last words of Jacob (Gn. 49:13–15).

J.D.D.

SANDAL
See Dress, Part 1.

SAND LIZARD
See Animals, Part 1.

SANHEDRIN, the transcription used in the Talmud for Gk. *synedrion* (from which Heb. *sanhedrîn* is a loan-word). Both before and at the time of Christ, it was the name of the highest tribunal of the Jews which met in Jerusalem and also for various lesser tribunals. In EVV the term is often translated 'council'. There are parallels in classical writings to similar courts in Greece and Rome. Josephus used the word for the council that governed the five districts into which the Roman Gabinius, proconsul of Syria 57–55 BC, divided Judaea (*Ant.* 14. 90; *BJ* 1.170). Josephus first uses it of the Jews when referring to the summoning of the young Herod before it for alleged misdemeanours (*Ant.* 14. 163–184). In the NT the term refers either to the supreme Jewish court (Mt. 26:59; Mk. 14:55; Lk. 22:66; Jn. 11:47; Acts 4:15; 5:21ff.; 6:12ff.; 22:30; 23:1ff.; 24:20) or simply to any court of justice (Mt. 5:22). In a few cases other words are substituted for *synedrion*, *e.g.* *presbyterion*, 'body of elders' (Lk. 22:66; Acts 22:5), and *gerousia*, 'senate' (Acts 5:21).

I. History

The history of the Sanhedrin is not clear at all points. Traditionally it originated with the seventy elders who assisted Moses (Nu. 11:16–24). Ezra is supposed to have reorganized this body after the Exile. The Persians gave authority to the Jews in local affairs (Ezr. 7:25–26; 10:14), and it is possible that the elders of Ezr. 5:5, 9; 6:7, 14; 10:8, and the rulers of Ne. 2:16; 4:14, 19; 5:7; 7:5, made up a body which resembled the later Sanhedrin. Later, the Greeks permitted a body known as the *gerousia* ('senate') which was made up of elders and represented the nation (Jos., *Ant.* 12. 142; 1 Macc. 12:3, 6; 14:20). In the days of the Seleucids this *gerousia* had dealings with such rulers as Antiochus the Great in 208 BC and with Antiochus V (Jos., *Ant.* 12. 128), and was then apparently composed of elders drawn from the aristocracy (1 Macc. 12:6; 2 Macc. 1:10; 4:44; 11:27). In the days of the Maccabean revolt it was this council that united with Jonathan, the high priest and leader of the people, to make an alliance with Sparta (1 Macc. 12:5ff.), and it was they who advised him about building fortresses in Judaea (1 Macc. 12:35; *cf.* 13:36; 14:20, 28, 47). It would appear that the high priest presided over this body.

Under the Romans, except for a short period under Gabinius, this body had wide powers. The term used for the district councils was subsequently adopted for the more powerful *gerousia* at Jerusalem, and by the close of the 1st century BC this council was known as the *synedrion*, though other terms such as *gerousia* and *boulē* ('council') were also used at times. It was Julius Caesar who reversed the plan of Gabinius and extended the power of the Sanhedrin once again over all Judaea, although during the reign of *Herod (37–4 BC) its powers were severely curtailed. Under the procurators (AD 6–66) the powers of the Sanhedrin were extensive, the internal government of the country being in its hands (Jos., *Ant.* 20. 200), and it was recognized even among the *diaspora* (Acts 9:2; 22:5; 26:12) in some ways From the days of Archelaus, son of *Herod the Great, its direct powers were, however, limited to Judaea, since it had no power over Jesus while he was in Galilee. In Judaea there were, of course, the local authorities who tried cases locally but reported certain cases to the central authority. The councils (*synedria*) of Mt. 5:22; 10:17; Mk. 13:9, and the *boulai* of Jos., *Ant.* 4. 214, *etc.* were local courts of at least seven elders, and in large towns up to twenty-three elders.

After AD 70 the Sanhedrin was abolished and replaced by the Beth Din (Court of Judgment) which is said to have met at Jabneh (AD 68–80), Usah (80–116), Shafran (140–163), Sepphoris (163–193) and Tiberias (193–220). Though regarded in the Talmud as continuous with the Sanhedrin, it was essentially different, being composed of scribes whose decisions had only moral and religious authority.

II. Constitution and composition

The constitution of the Sanhedrin was modified during the years. Originally composed basically of the predominantly Sadducean priestly aristocracy, its membership hanged from the days of Queen Alexandra (76–67 BC) when Pharisees were included, as well as *scribes. The method of appointment is not clear, but the aristocratic origin of the body suggests direct appointment of members of ancient families, to which were added secular rulers. Under Herod, who favoured the Pharisees and desired to restrict the *Sadducees and the influence of the old nobility, the Sadducean element became less prominent, and the Pharisaic element, which had been growing in strength since the days of Queen Alexandra, became more influential. In NT times the Great Sanhedrin in Jerusalem comprised the high priests (*i.e.* the acting high priest and those who had been high priest), members of the privileged families from which the high priests were taken, the elders (tribal and family heads of the people and the priesthood), and the scribes, *i.e.* the legal experts. The whole comprised both Sadducees and Pharisees (Mt. 26:3, 57, 59; Mk. 14:53; 15:1; Lk. 22:66; Acts 4:1, 5ff.; 5:17, 21, 34; 22:30; 23:6). The members were councillors (*bouleutēs*, Mk. 15:43; Lk. 23:50), as, for example, Joseph of Arimathaea.

According to Josephus and the NT, the high priest at the time was president (Jos., *Ant.* 4. 224; 20. 224ff.; Mt. 26:57; Acts 5:17ff.; 7:1; 9:1ff.; 22:5; 24:1). Thus, Caiaphas was president at the trial of Jesus, and Ananias at the trial of Paul (Acts 23:2). It would seem that in earlier times the high priest had supreme authority, but this was curbed somewhat later. The appointment was no longer hereditary, but political, and ex-high priests with their close associates (such as the captain of the Temple) made up the 'rulers' (Jn. 7:26; Acts 4:5–8, *etc.*).

III. Extent of jurisdiction

The jurisdiction was wide at the time of Christ. It exercised not only civil jurisdiction according to Jewish law but also criminal jurisdiction in some degree. It had administrative authority and could order arrests by its own officers of justice (Mt. 26:47; Mk. 14:43; Acts 4:1ff.; 5:17ff.; 9:2). It was empowered to judge cases which did not involve capital punishment (Acts 4–5). Capital cases required the confirmation of the Roman procurator (Jn. 18:31), though the procurator's judgment was normally in accordance with the demands of the Sanhedrin, which in Jewish law had the power of life and death (Jos., *Ant.* 14. 168; Mt. 26:66). In the special case where a Gentile passed the barrier which divided the inner court of the Temple from that of the Gentiles the Sanhedrin was granted the power of death by Roman administrators (Acts 21:28ff.); and this concession may have extended to other offences against the Temple by deed or, as with Stephen (Acts 6:13f.), by word. The only case of capital sentence in connection with the Sanhedrin in the NT is that of our Lord, but the execution was carried out by the judgment of the Roman governor. The case of Stephen has some features of an illegal mob act.

A study of the NT will give a cross-section of the kinds of matters that came before the Sanhedrin. Thus, Jesus was charged with blasphemy (Mt. 26:57ff.; Jn. 19:7), Peter and John were charged with teaching the people false doctrine (Acts 4), Paul with transgressing the Mosaic law (Acts 22–24). These, of course, were religious matters. But at times the collection of revenue was the responsibility of the Sanhedrin, as in the time of Florus (Jos., *BJ* 2. 406). There was, however, always a theoretical check on the powers of the Sanhedrin, for the Romans reserved the right to interfere in any area whatever, if necessary independently of the Jewish court. Paul's arrest in Acts 23 is a case in point. It is probably best to regard the Sanhedrin as having two main areas of responsibility, political (administrative and judicial) and religious. It is not always clear how these two were carried out, and some writers have even suggested two different bodies, each known as the Sanhedrin. This is probably not necessary, but is suggested because of our lack of clear knowledge of procedures.

IV. Procedure

There were correct times and places for meeting, according to the tradition preserved in the Mishnaic tractate *Sanhedrin.* Local courts met on the 2nd and 5th days of the week, and the Sanhedrin in Jerusalem at definite (though unknown to us) times. They did not meet on festival days and on sabbaths.

There were proper procedures. The Sanhedrin sat in a semicircle and had two clerks of court, one to record votes of acquittal and the other votes of condemnation. Disciples attended the courts and sat in front. Prisoners attended dressed in humble fashion. In capital cases the arguments for acquittal were presented, then those for conviction. If one spoke for acquittal he could not reverse his opinion, but if he spoke for condemnation he could later change his vote. Students could speak in favour of acquittal but not for condemnation. Acquittal might be declared on the day of the trial, but condemnation must wait till the day following. In voting, members stood, beginning with the youngest. For acquittal a simple majority sufficed, for condemnation a two-thirds majority was required. If 12 of the 23 judges necessary for a quorum voted for acquittal, and 11 for conviction, the prisoner was discharged. If 12 voted for conviction, and 11 against, the number of judges had to be increased by 2, and this was repeated up to a total of 71, or until an acquittal was achieved. The benefit of the doubt was allowed to persons where the case was as doubtful as this. Indeed, always, the benefit lay with the accused (Mishnah, *Sanhedrin* 5. 5).

In this regard, the legality of the trial of Jesus has been discussed by many writers, and it is fairly clear that there are elements about it which point in the direction of a miscarriage of justice.

Bibliography. E. Schürer, *HJP*, 1901, 2, i, pp. 163–195; J. Z. Lauterbach, *JewE*, 11, 1905, pp. 41–44; I. Abrahams, *ERE*, 2, 1920, pp. 184–185; H. Danby, *The Mishnah*, E.T. 1933, tractate *Sanhedrin*, pp. 382–400; *idem*, 'The Trial of Jesus', *JTS* 21, 1919–20, pp. 51–76; J. Blinzler, *The Trial of Jesus*, 1959; P. Winter, *On the Trial of Jesus*, 1961.

J.A.T.

SAPPHIRA (Gk. *sappheira*, transliteration of Aram. *šappîrâ*, fem. sing., 'beautiful'). In Acts 5:1ff. wife of *Ananias, a member of the primitive Jerusalem church. The name, in Greek and Aramaic, was found on an ossuary in Jerusalem in 1923, but J. Klausner's theory (*From Jesus to Paul*, 1944, pp. 289f.) that the Sapphira of Acts is intended requires confirmation.

F.F.B.

SARAH, SARAI (Heb. *śārâ*, 'princess'). The principal wife of Abram, and also his half-sister on his father

SAPHIR
See Shaphir, Part 3.

SAPPHIRE
See Jewels, Part 2.

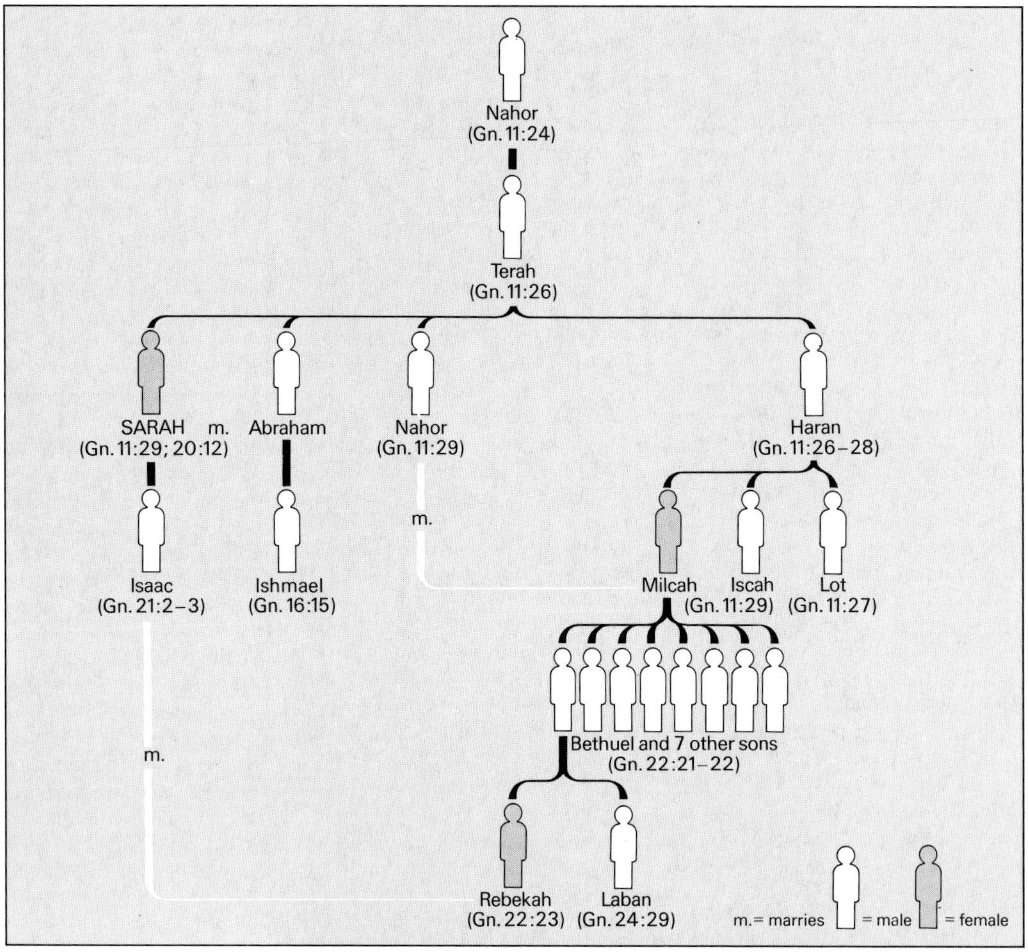

The family of Sarah.

Terah's side (Gn. 20:12). She went with him from Ur of the Chaldees, through Harran, to the land of Canaan. Famine caused them to turn aside to Egypt, and, as Abram feared that her outstanding beauty might endanger his life, Sarai posed as his sister. Pharaoh was attracted by her and took her into his harem. Then he suspected the truth, and husband and wife were sent away (Gn.12).

She posed as Abraham's sister on a second occasion, at the court of Abimelech, king of Gerar, in accordance with her husband's instructions: 'This is the kindness you must do me; at every place to which we come, say of me, He is my brother' (Gn. 20:13)—words which suggest a settled policy. This incident further increased Abraham's wealth, for gifts were given him as compensation to an injured husband (Gn. 20:14).

Her barrenness was a continual reproach to Sarai, and she gave her handmaiden, the Egyptian *Hagar, to her husband as his concubine. Hagar's pregnancy aroused her jealousy, and she ill-treated her to such an extent that Hagar ran away for a time. On her return Ishmael was born (Gn.16).

At the age of 90, Sarai's name was changed to Sarah, and her hus-

Site of the citadel of Sardis overlooking the valley of the Hermus. (SH)

band's from Abram to Abraham. Yahweh blessed her and said she would bear a son, and become the mother of nations' (Gn.17).

When Abraham was granted a theophany, Sarah was asked to make cakes for the divine visitors. She overheard the prophecy about her son, and laughed; then, afraid, she denied her derision in face of the words, 'Is anything too hard for the Lord?' (Gn. 18:14). On the birth of Isaac, Sarah's reproach was removed. She was so incensed by Ishmael's scorn at the feast to celebrate Isaac's weaning that she asked for Hagar and her son to be cast out (Gn. 21).

Aged 127, she died in *Kiriath-arba and was buried in the cave of the field of Machpelah (Gn. 23:1ff.) (*HEBRON).

Sarah is named in Is. 51: 2 as an example of trust in Yahweh. In the NT Paul mentions both Abraham and Sarah among those whose faith was counted for righteousness (Rom. 4:19), and he writes of Sarah as the mother of the children of promise (Rom. 9:9). The writer of the Epistle to the Hebrews includes Sarah in the list of the faithful (11:11). She is named also as an example of a wife's proper regard for her husband (1 Pet. 3:6).

M.B.

SARDIS. A city in the Roman province of Asia, in the W of what is now Asiatic Turkey. It was the capital of the ancient kingdom of Lydia, the greatest of the foreign powers encountered by the Greeks during their early colonization of Asia Minor. Its early prosperity, especially under Croesus, became a byword for wealth; its riches are said to have derived in part from the gold won from the Pactolus, a stream which flowed through the city. The original city was an almost impregnable fortress-citadel, towering above the broad valley of the Hermus, and nearly surrounded by precipitous cliffs of treacherously loose rock. Its position as the centre of Lydian supremacy under Croesus was ended abruptly when the Persian king Cyrus besieged the city and took the citadel (546 BC), apparently by scaling the cliffs and entering by a weakly defended point under cover of darkness. The same tactics again led to the fall of the city in 214 BC, when it was captured by Antiochus the Great. Though it lay on an important trade route down the Hermus valley, it never regained under Roman rule the spectacular prominence it had had in earlier centuries. In AD 26 its claim for the honour of building an imperial temple was rejected in favour of its rival Smyrna. There is now only a small village (Sart) near the site of the ancient city.

The letter to 'the angel of the church in Sardis' (Rev. 3:1–6) suggests that the early Christian community there was imbued with the same spirit as the city, resting on its past reputation and without any present achievement, and failing, as the city had twice failed, to learn from its past and be vigilant. The

SARDINE See Jewels, Part 2.

Plan of the site of Sardis, showing the main areas worked during recent excavations.

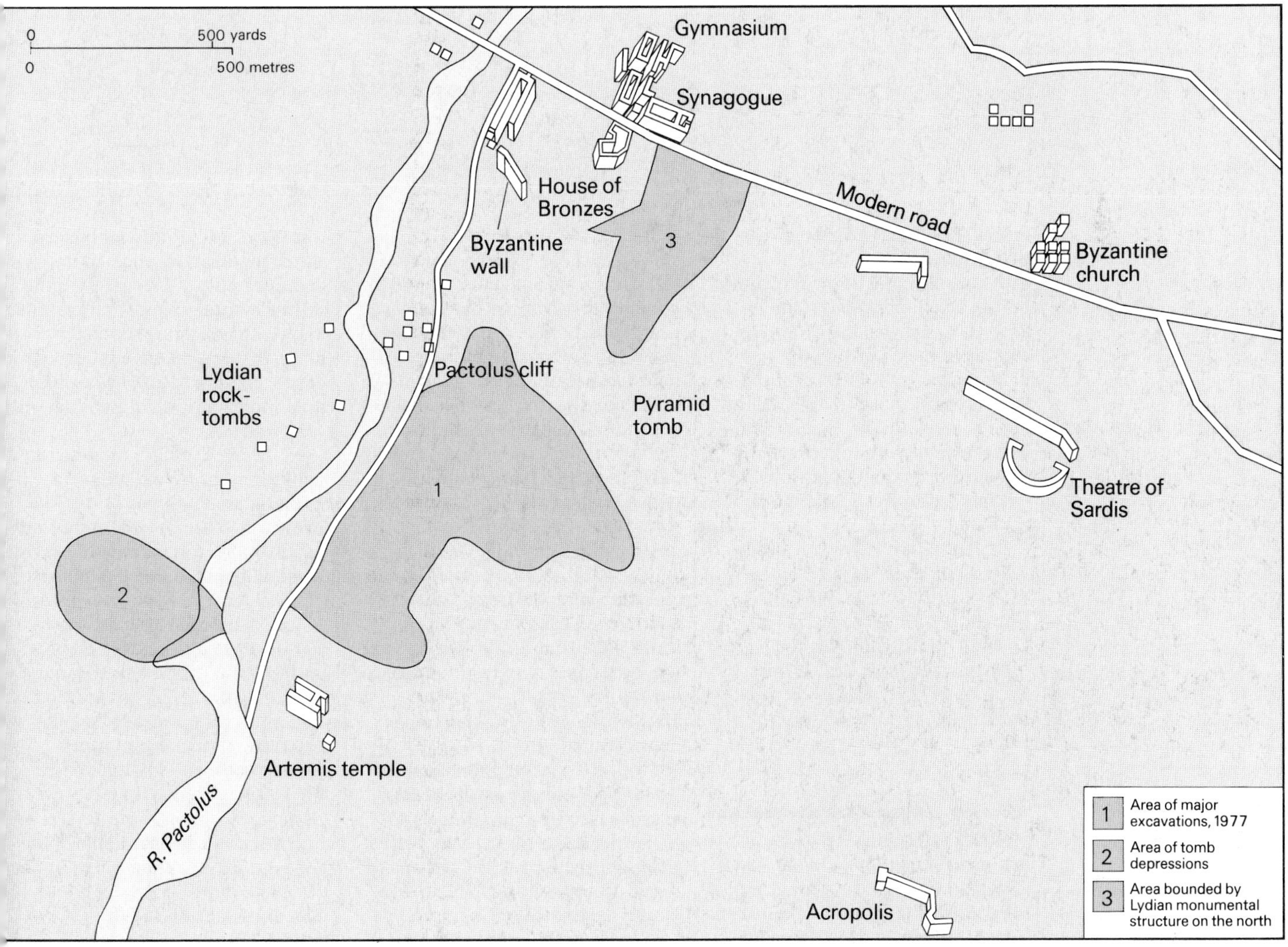

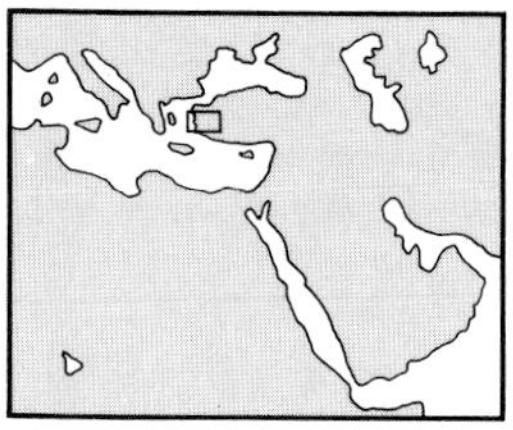

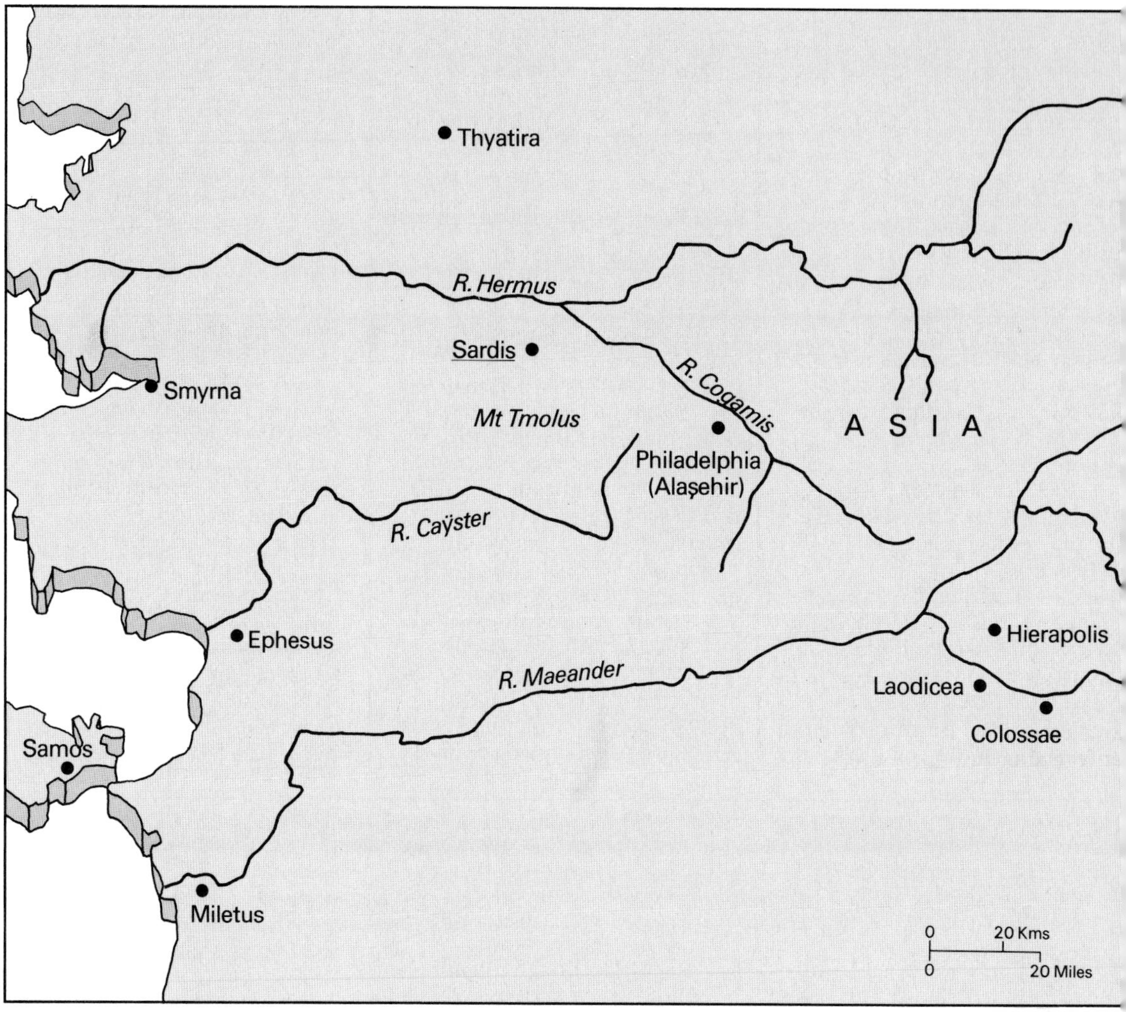

Sardis, one of the 'seven churches of Asia' (Rev. 1–3).

SARDIUS
See Jewels, Part 2.

SARDONYX
See Jewels, Part 2.

SAREPTA
See Zarephath, Part 3.

symbol of 'white garments' was rich in meaning in a city noted for its luxury clothing trade: the faithful few who are vigilant shall be arrayed to share in the triumphal coming of their Lord.

Important current excavations have brought much to light, including a superb late synagogue. Sardis had evidently been for centuries a principal centre of the Jewish Diaspora, and was probably the Sepharad of Ob. 20.

BIBLIOGRAPHY. W. M. Ramsay, *The Letters to the Seven Churches of Asia*, 1904, chs. 25, 26; D. G. Mitten, *BA* 29, 1966, pp. 38–68; G. M. A. Hanfmann, regular reports in *BASOR*; C. J. Hemer, *NTS* 19, 1972–3, pp. 94–97; *idem*, *Buried History* 11, 1975, pp. 119–135.

E.M.B.G.
C.J.H.

SARGON. Sargon (Heb. *sargōn*; LXX *Arna*; Assyr. *Šarru-ūkîn*, '[the god] has established the king[ship]') ruled Assyria 722–705 BC. His reign is known in much detail from inscriptions at his palace at Khorsabad built in 717–707 BC, and from historical texts and letters found at Nineveh and Nimrud. Although he is named only once in the OT (Is. 20:1), his campaigns in Syro-Palestine are of importance in understanding the historical background of the prophecies of Isaiah.

Sargon claimed the capture of Samaria, which had been besieged by his predecessor Shalmaneser V for 3 years (2 Ki. 17:5–6) until his death on 20 December 722 BC or 18 January 721 BC. It is probable that Sargon completed this operation and hurried back to Assyria to claim the throne. Although he bore the same royal name as the heroic Sargon I of Agade (*c.* 2350 BC; *ACCAD; *NIMROD), there is evidence that he was the legal successor to the throne and not a usurper.

During the first months of his reign he faced a major domestic crisis which was settled only by the grant of privileges to the citizens of Assur. In the spring of 720 BC he moved S against the Chaldean Marduk-apla-iddina II (*MERODACH-BALADAN), who had seized the Babylonian throne. An indecisive battle at Der arrested the advance of the supporting Elamites and Arabian tribes, but disturbances in the W rendered it expedient for Sargon to leave Marduk-apla-iddina as king in Babylon (721–710 BC).

In the W, Yaubi'di of Hamath led Damascus, Arpad, Simirra, Samaria, and possibly Hatarikka, in an anti-Assyrian coalition. Late in 720 BC Sargon marched to defeat these allies in a battle near Qarqar, N Syria, and, reducing the participating cities once more to vassalage, he moved to destroy Raphia and thus cut off the rebel Hanun of Gaza from an Egyptian force, under its commander, which was defeated. This interpretation follows the identification of *So or Sib'e (2 Ki. 17:4) as a Hebrew rendering of the term for leader (*re'e*) and not as the proper name of an unidentified Egyptian king (*JNES* 19, 1960, pp. 49–53) or of a king of Sais (*s'w* = So; *BASOR* 171, 1963, pp. 64–67).

During these operations Isaiah varned Judah of the inadvisability of participating, or of trusting, in Egyptian help, illustrating his mesage by the fate of Carchemish, Iamath, Arpad, Samaria and Damascus (Is. 10:9). On his return rom the Egyptian border Sargon leported a large part of the popuation of Samaria, which he began o rebuild as the capital of a new Assyrian province of Samaria. The process of repopulating the city vith foreigners took several years and appears to have continued in he reign of Esarhaddon (Ezr. 4:2).

In 716 BC Sargon sent his army ommander (*turtan*; the *'tartan') o war against the Arabs in Sinai. This led to the reception of tribute rom the pharaoh Shilkanni (Osorcon IV) of Egypt and from Samsi, queen of the Arabs. Despite these Assyrian successes, the people of Ashdod displaced their Assyrian-dominated ruler, Ahimetu, by a usurper Iadna (or Iamani) who initiated yet another Syro-Palestinian league against Assyria, doubtless relying on Egyptian help. In 712 BC the same *turtan* was sent to conquer Ashdod (Is. 20:1), which was reduced to the status of an Assyrian province. Since Azaqa ('Azeqah or Tell es-Zakariye) on the Judaean border near Lachish surrendered in this campaign, it will be seen how narrowly independent Judah escaped a further invasion. Iamani fled to Nubia for refuge, only to be extradited to Nineveh by the ruler Shabaka.

On other fronts Sargon fought many battles, defeating the Mannaeans and Rusas of Urarṭu in 719–714 BC, and incorporating the defeated Carchemish as a provincial centre. In 710 and 707 BC, following raids into Media to neutralize the hill tribes, Sargon once more advanced against Merodach-baladan, who fled to Elam. Sargon's latter years were spent in suppressing rebellions in Kummukh and Tabal (where he was killed in action). He was succeeded by his son Sennacherib on 12 Ab, 705 BC. That he was 'not buried in his house' was later attributed to his sin in adopting a pro-Babylonian policy following his 'taking the hands of the god Bel (Marduk)' as king there in 709 BC.

BIBLIOGRAPHY. H. Tadmor, 'The Campaigns of Sargon II of Assur', *JCS* 12, 1958, pp. 22–40, 77–100;

Head of Sargon II, king of Assyria, 721–705 BC. Khorsabad. Height 89 cm.

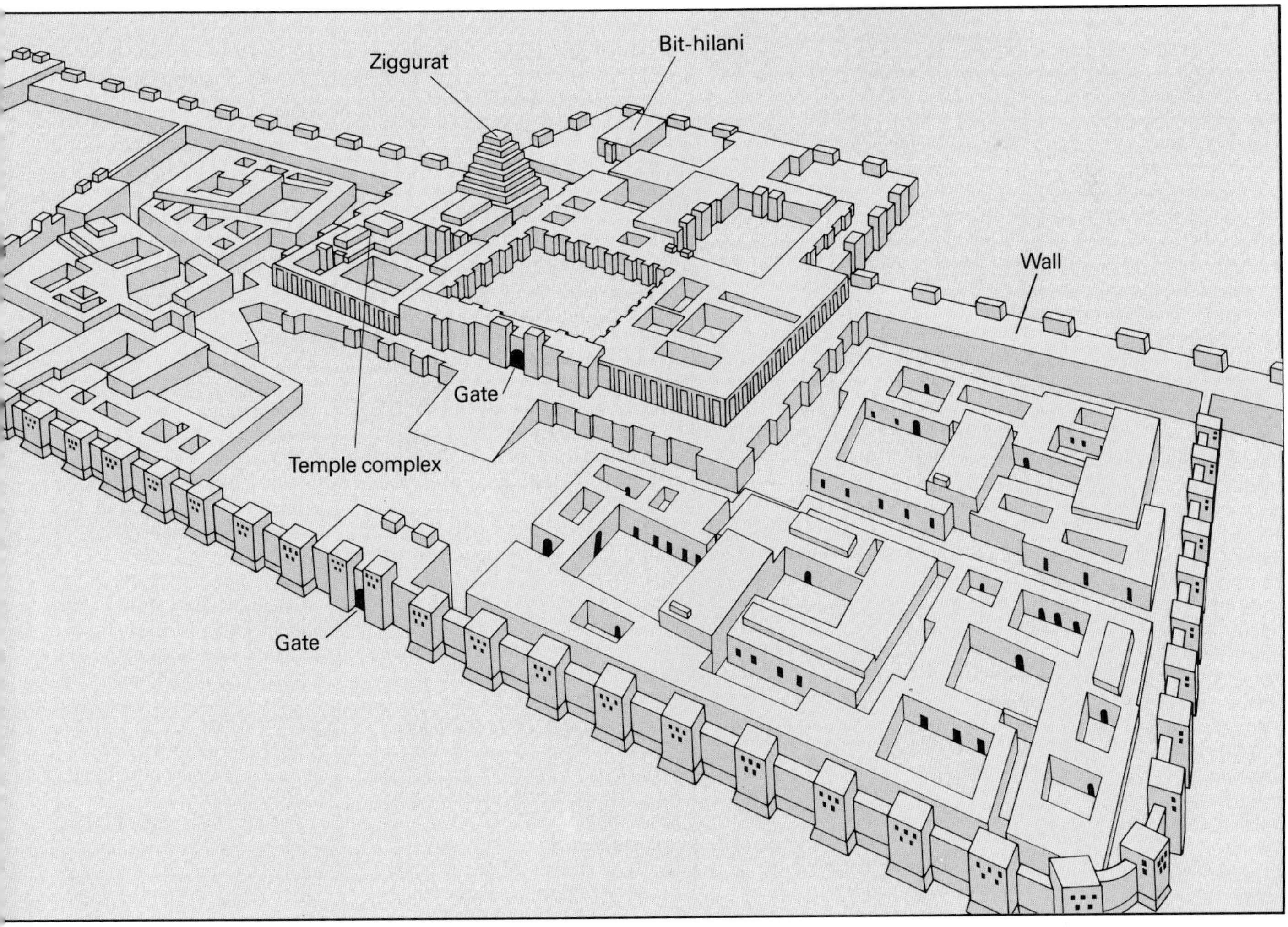

A reconstruction of the palace complex built by Sargon II at Khorsabad (Dūr Sharrūkin). 8th cent. BC.

H. W. F. Saggs, in *Iraq* 17, 1955, pp. 146–149; 37, 1975, pp. 11–20; D. J. Wiseman, *DOTT*, pp. 58–63.

D.J.W.

SARID. A town on the S boundary of Zebulun (Jos. 19:10, 12). Some ancient MSS of LXX read *Sedoud*, and this has given rise to the common identification with Tell Shadud, 8 km SE of Nazareth (*LOB*, p. 106). The weight of textual evidence, however, favours the *MT* Sarid of unknown location.

W.O.

SARSECHIM. The name of a Babylonian official present in Jerusalem after the capture of the city in 587 BC (Je. 39:3). The name is as yet unidentified. It has been proposed to identify him with Nebushazban the *Rabsaris (Je. 39:13). This would require taking Nebo from the preceding *Samgar-nebo to read Nebo-sar-sechim as a corruption of Nabū-šezibanni (*n^{e}ḇô-šazibôn*?). Or *śar-s^{e}kîm* could be a title, 'chief of the . . .'

D.J.W.

SATAN. The name of the prince of evil, Heb. *śāṭān*, Gk. *Satanas*, means basically 'adversary' (the word is so rendered, *e.g.*, in Nu. 22:22). In the first two chapters of Job we read of 'the Satan' as presenting himself before God among 'the sons of God'. It is sometimes said that in such passages Satan is not thought of as especially evil, but as simply one among the heavenly hosts. Admittedly we have not yet the fully developed doctrine, but the activities of 'the Satan' are certainly inimical to Job. The OT references to Satan are few, but he is consistently engaged in activities against the best interests of men. He moves David to number the people (1 Ch. 21:1). He stands at the right hand of Joshua the high priest 'to accuse him', thus drawing down the Lord's rebuke (Zc. 3:1f.). The psalmist thinks it a calamity to have Satan stand at one's right hand (Ps. 109:6, AV, but *cf.* RV 'an adversary', RSV 'an accuser'). John tells us that 'the devil sinned from the beginning' (1 Jn. 3:8), and the OT references to him bear this out.

Most of our information, however, comes from the NT, where the supremely evil being is referred to as Satan or as 'the devil' (*ho diabolos*) indifferently, with Beelzebub (or Beelzeboul, or Beezeboul) also employed on occasion (Mt. 10:25; 12:24, 27). Other expressions, such as 'the ruler of this world' (Jn. 14:30) or 'the prince of the power of the air' (Eph. 2:2), also occur. He is always depicted as hostile to God, and as working to overthrow the purposes of God. Matthew and Luke tell us that at the beginning of his ministry Jesus had a severe time of testing when Satan tempted him to go about his work in the wrong spirit (Mt. 4; Lk. 4; see also Mk. 1:13). When this period was completed the devil left him 'until an opportune time', which implies that the contest was later resumed. This is clear also from the statement that he 'in every respect has been tempted as we are' (Heb. 4:15). This conflict is not incidental. The express purpose of the coming of Jesus into the world was 'to destroy the works of the devil' (1 Jn. 3:8; *cf.* Heb. 2:14). Everywhere the NT sees a great conflict between the forces of God and of good, on the one hand, and those of evil led by Satan, on the other. This is not the conception of one writer or another, but is common ground.

There is no doubting the severity of the conflict. Peter stresses the ferocious opposition by saying that the devil 'prowls around like a roaring lion, seeking some one to devour' (1 Pet. 5:8). Paul thinks rather of the cunning employed by the evil one. 'Satan disguises himself as an angel of light' (2 Cor. 11:14), so that it is small wonder if his minions appear in an attractive guise. The Ephesians are exhorted to put on 'the whole armour of God, that you may be able to stand against the wiles of the devil' (Eph. 6:11), and there are references to 'the snare of the devil' (1 Tim. 3:7; 2 Tim. 2:26). The effect of such passages is to emphasize that Christians (and even archangels, Jude 9) are engaged in a conflict that is both relentlessly and cunningly waged. They are not in a position to retire from the conflict. Nor can they simply assume that evil will always be obviously evil. There is need for the exercise of discrimination as well as stout-heartedness. But determined opposition will always succeed. Peter urges his readers to resist the devil 'firm in your faith' (1 Pet. 5:9), and James says, 'Resist the devil and he will flee from you' (Jas. 4:7). Paul exhorts 'give no opportunity to the devil' (Eph. 4:27), and the implication of putting on the whole armour of God is that thereby the believer will be able to resist anything the evil one does (Eph. 6:11, 13). Paul puts his trust in the faithfulness of God. 'God is faithful, and he will not let you be tempted beyond your strength, but with the temptation will also provide the way of escape' (1 Cor. 10:13). He is well aware of the resourcefulness of Satan, and that he is always seeking to 'gain the advantage over us'. But he can add 'we are not ignorant of his designs' (or, as F. J. Rae translates, 'I am up to his tricks') (2 Cor. 2:11).

Satan is continually opposed to the gospel, as we see throughout the Lord's ministry. He worked through Jesus' followers, as when Peter rejected the thought of the cross and was met with the rebuke 'Get behind me, Satan' (Mt. 16:23). Satan had further designs on Peter, but the Lord prayed for him (Lk. 22:31f.). He worked also in the enemies of Jesus, for Jesus could speak of those who opposed him as being 'of your father the devil' (Jn. 8:44). All this comes to a climax in the passion. The work of Judas is ascribed to the activity of the evil one. Satan 'entered into' Judas (Lk. 22:3; Jn. 13:27). He 'put it into the heart of Judas Iscariot, Simon's son, to betray him' (Jn. 13:2). With the cross in prospect Jesus can say 'the ruler of this world is coming' (Jn. 14:30).

Satan continues to tempt men (1 Cor. 7:5). We read of him at work in a professed believer, Ananias ('why has Satan filled your heart . . . ?', Acts 5:3), and in an avowed opponent of the Christian way, Elymas ('You son of the devil', Acts 13:10). The general principle is given in 1 Jn. 3:8, 'He who commits sin is of the devil'. Men may so give themselves over to Satan that they in effect belong to him. They become his 'children' (1 Jn. 3:10). Thus we read of 'a synagogue of Satan' (Rev. 2:9; 3:9), and of men who dwell 'where Satan's throne is' (Rev. 2:13). Satan hinders the work of missionaries (1 Thes. 2:18). He takes away the good seed sown in the hearts of men (Mk. 4:15). He sows 'the sons of the evil one' in the field that is the world (Mt. 13:38f.). His activity may produce physical effects (Lk. 13:16). Always he is pictured as resourceful and active.

But the NT is sure of his limitations and defeat. His power is derivative (Lk. 4:6). He can exercise his activity only within the limits that God lays down (Jb. 1:12; 2:6; 1 Cor

10:13; Rev. 20:2, 7). He may even be used to set forward the cause of right (1 Cor. 5:5; *cf.* 2 Cor. 12:7). Jesus saw a preliminary victory in the mission of the Seventy (Lk. 10:18). Our Lord thought of 'eternal fire' as 'prepared for the devil and his angels' (Mt. 25:41), and John sees this come to pass (Rev. 20:10). We have already noticed that the conflict with Satan comes to a head in the passion. There Jesus speaks of him as 'cast out' (Jn. 12:31), and as 'judged' (Jn. 16:11). The victory is explicitly alluded to in Heb. 2:14; 1 Jn. 3:8. The work of preachers is to turn men 'from the power of Satan unto God' (Acts 26:18). Paul can say confidently, 'the God of peace will soon crush Satan under your feet' (Rom. 16:20).

The witness of the NT then is clear. Satan is a malignant reality, always hostile to God and to God's people. But he has already been defeated in Christ's life and death and resurrection, and this defeat will become obvious and complete in the end of the age.

(*ANTICHRIST; *DEMON; *DEMON-POSSESSION; *EVIL SPIRITS.)

BIBLIOGRAPHY. F. J. Rae, *ExpT* 66, 1954–5, pp. 212–215; J. M. Ross, *ExpT* 66, 1954–5, pp. 58–61; W. O. E. Oesterley in *DCG*; E. Langton, *Essentials of Demonology*, 1949; W. Robinson, *The Devil and God*, 1945; H. Bietenhard, C. Brown, in *NIDNTT* 3, pp. 468–473. L.M.

SATRAP (Heb. *'ᵃḥašdarpān*; Aram. *'ᵃḥašadrpān*; Akkad. *aḫšad(a)-rapannu*; from Old Persian *ḫšaṯapāvan*, 'protector of the kingdom', originally *Median *khshathrapā*). Provincial governor under the Persians (Ezr. 8:36; Est. 3:12; Dn. 3:2; 6:1, *etc.*). The provincial system in the ancient Near East had been in use since the 3rd millennium BC (*e.g.* at *Ur and under *Assyria and *Babylonia). The system was adopted by the Persians. Possibly under *Darius I the empire was divided into twenty satrapies, each comprising smaller units (Herodotus 3. 89–95). Syro-Palestine was part of the satrapy 'Beyond the River' (Ne. 3:7).

BIBLIOGRAPHY. A. F. Rainey, *AJBA* 1, 1969, pp. 51–78. D.W.B.

SATYR (*śā'îr*, 'hairy one', 'he-goat'). The Heb. plural (*śᵉ'îrîm*) is rendered 'satyrs' in Lv. 17:7 and 2 Ch. 11:15 (AV 'devils', RV 'he-goats'). A similar meaning may be intended in 2 Ki. 23:8 if Heb. *šᵉ'ārîm* ('gates'), which seems meaningless in the context, be regarded as a slip for *śᵉ'îrîm*. The precise nature of these 'hairy ones' is obscure. They may have been he-goats in the ordinary sense, or gods having the appearance of goats. Sacrifices were made to them in high places, with special priests performing the ritual.

From goat to demon in Semitic belief was an easy transition (*cf.*

SATCHEL
See Ornaments, Part 2.

SATURNINUS
See Quirinius, Part 3.

SATURN
See Sakkuth, Part 3.

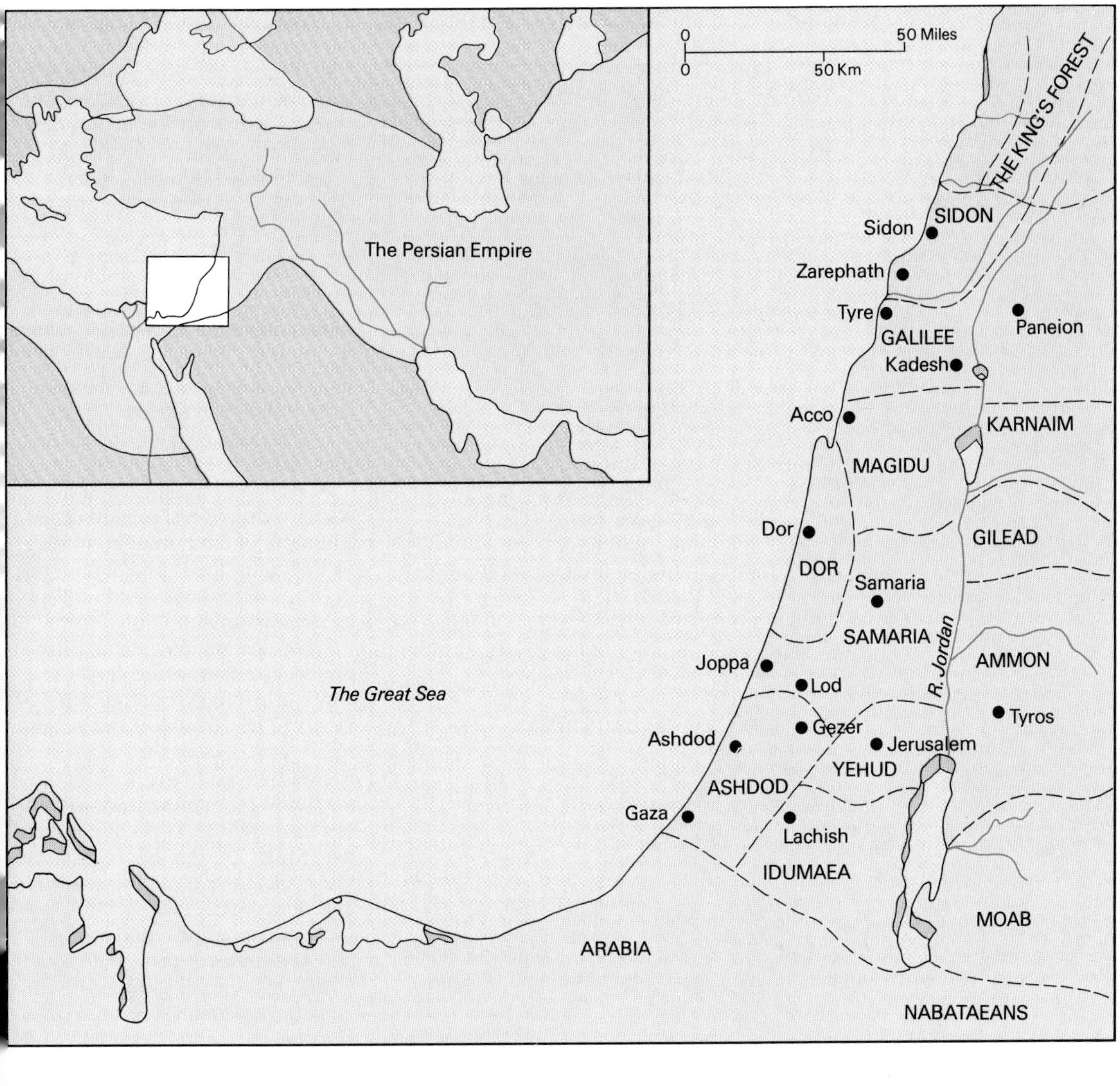

The southern part of the Fifth Satrapy ('the province Beyond the River', Ezr. 4:10; Ne. 3:7) and its place in the Persian Empire. (For the location of the other satrapies see the map on page 1198.)

A composite genie, part human and part animal, possibly a satyr, depicted on the wall of the palace of Ashurbanipal at Nineveh. c. 640 BC. (BM)

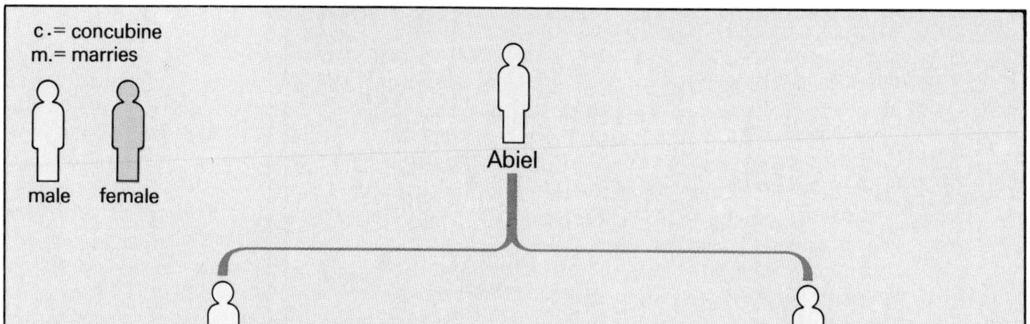

Saul's family.

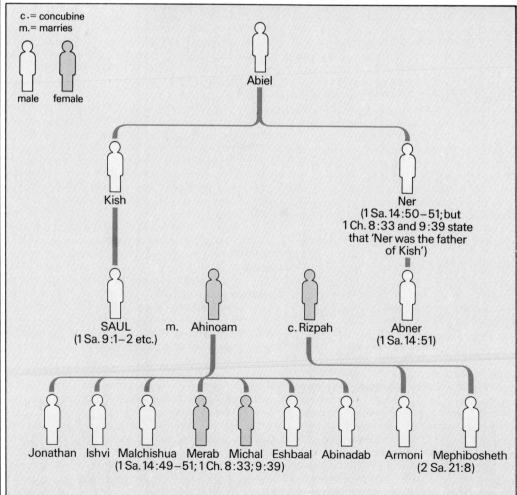

*SCAPEGOAT). Satyrs, apparently demonic creatures, danced on the ruins of Babylon (Is. 13:21), and figured also in the picture of the desolation of Edom (Is. 34:14).

BIBLIOGRAPHY. Oesterley and Robinson, *Hebrew Religion*, 1930, pp. 13, 64ff.; *EBi* (*s.v.* 'satyr').

J.D.D.

SAUL (Heb. *šā'ûl*, 'asked', *i.e.* of God.) **1.** King of ancient Edom, from Rehoboth (Gn. 36:37). **2.** A son of Simeon (Gn. 46:10; Ex. 6:15; Nu. 26:13).

3. First king of Israel, son of Kish, of the tribe of Benjamin. The story of Saul occupies most of 1 Sa. (chs. 9–31) and depicts one of the most pathetic of all God's chosen servants.

Head and shoulders above his brethren, a man whose personal courage matched his physique, kingly to his friends and generous to his foes, Saul was the man chosen by God to institute the monarchy, to represent within himself the royal rule of Yahweh over his people. Yet three times over he was declared to have disqualified himself from the task to which he had been appointed, and even in that appointment there was a hint of the character of the man whom God, in his sovereignty, chose to be king.

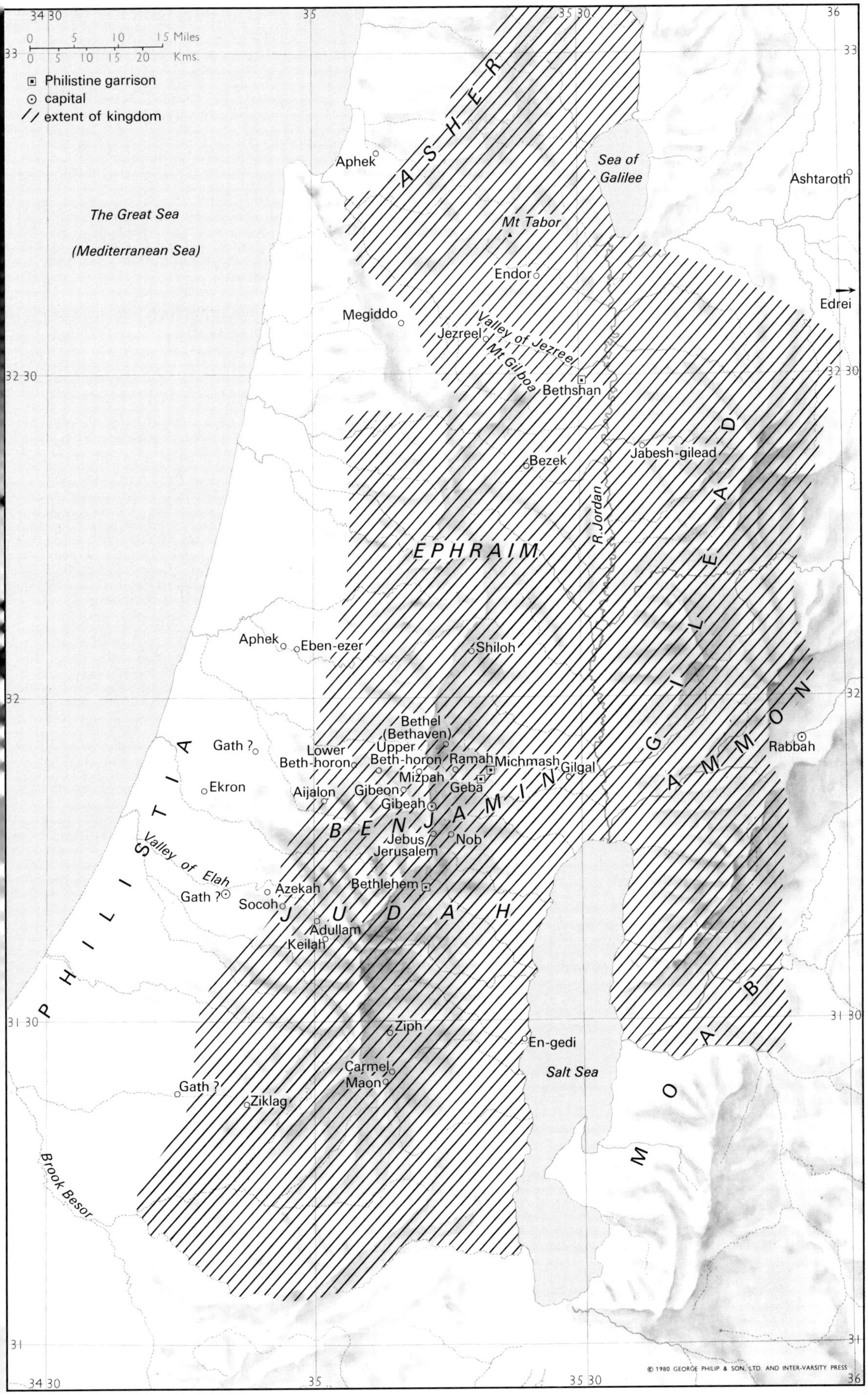

0 5 10 15 Miles
0 5 10 15 20 Kms.
Philistine garrison
capital
extent of kingdom
The Great Sea
(Mediterranean Sea)
ASHER
Aphek
Sea of Galilee
Ashtaroth
Mt Tabor
Endor
Edrei
Megiddo
Jezreel
Valley of Jezreel
Mt Gilboa
Bethshan
GILEAD
Jabesh-gilead
Bezek
R. Jordan
EPHRAIM
Aphek
Eben-ezer
Shiloh
AMMON
Rabbah
PHILISTIA
Gath ?
Lower Beth-horon
Upper Beth-horon
Bethel (Bethaven)
Ramah
Michmash
Gilgal
Ekron
Aijalon
Mizpah
Gibeon
Geba
Gibeah
BENJAMIN
Jebus Jerusalem
Nob
Valley of Elah
Azekah
Gath ?
Socoh
Bethlehem
JUDAH
Adullam
Keilah
MOAB
Ziph
En-gedi
Carmel
Maon
Salt Sea
Gath ?
Ziklag
Brook Besor
© 1980 GEORGE PHILIP & SON, LTD. AND INTER-VARSITY PRESS

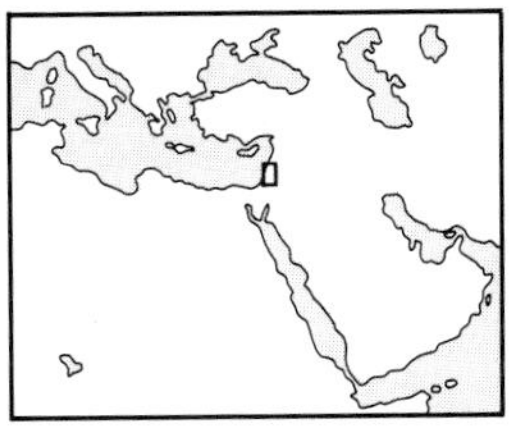

The extent of Saul's kingdom.

SAVE
See Salvation, Part 3.

SCARABS
See Art, Part 1.

SCARLET
See Colours, Part 1.

Under the pressure of the Philistine suzerainty, the Israelites came to think that only a visible warrior-leader could bring about their deliverance. Rejecting the spiritual leadership of Yahweh, mediated through the prophetic ministry of Samuel, they demanded a king (1 Sa. 8). After warning them of the evils of such government—a warning which they did not heed—Samuel was instructed by God to grant the people's wish, and was guided to choose Saul, whom he anointed secretly in the land of Zuph (1 Sa. 10:1), confirming the appointment later by a public ceremony at Mizpeh (10:17–25). Almost immediately Saul had the opportunity of showing his mettle. Nahash the Ammonite besieged Jabesh-gilead and offered cruel terms of surrender to its inhabitants, who sent for help to Saul, who was on the other side of the Jordan. Saul summoned the people by means of an object-lesson typical of his race and age, and with the army thus raised won a great victory (11:1–11). It is an evidence of his finer instincts that he refused at this time to acquiesce in the desire of his followers to punish those who had been unwilling to pay him homage (10:27; 11:12–13).

Following this, a religious ceremony at Gilgal confirmed the appointment of Saul as king, which had obviously received divine approval in the defeat of the Ammonites. With a parting exhortation to the people to be assiduous in their obedience to God, which was accompanied by a miraculous sign, Samuel left the new king to the government of his nation. On three occasions only, one of them posthumously, was the old prophet to emerge from the background. Each time it was to remonstrate with Saul for disobeying the terms of his appointment, terms involving utter obedience to the slightest command of God. The first occasion was when Saul, through impatience, arrogated to himself the priestly office, offering sacrifice at Gilgal (13:7–10). For this sacrilege his rejection from kingship was prophesied by Samuel, and Saul received the first hint that there was already, in the mind of God, the 'man after his heart' whom the Lord had selected to replace him.

The second occasion was when Saul's disobedience brought forth the prophet's well-known dictum that 'to obey is better than sacrifice, and to hearken than the fat of rams' (15:22). Again Saul's rejection from rule over Israel is declared and symbolically shown, and Samuel severs all contact with the fallen monarch. It is from the grave that Samuel emerges to rebuke Saul for the third and last time, and, whatever problems are raised by the story of the medium of Endor (ch. 28), it is clear that God permitted this supernatural interview with the unhappy king in order to fill Saul's cup of iniquity and to foretell his imminent doom.

For the long conflict between Saul and David, see *DAVID, which deals with other aspects of Saul's character. It is significant that when the public anointing of David was made in Bethlehem, Samuel rejected Eliab, David's most manly brother, and was warned against assuming that natural and spiritual power necessarily went together (16:7).

Saul is an object-lesson in the essential difference between the carnal and the spiritual man, as his NT namesake was to distinguish the two (1 Cor. 3, *etc*.). Living in a day when the Holy Spirit came upon men for a special time and purpose, rather than indwelling the children of God permanently, Saul was peculiarly susceptible to moodiness and uncertainty within himself (*HEALTH). Yet his disobedience is presented by the authors of 1 Sa. and 1 Ch. as inexcusable, for he had access to the Word of God, as it was then ministered to him through Samuel.

His downfall was the more tragic because he was a public and representative figure among the people of God.

4. The Jewish name of the apostle *Paul (Acts 13:9).

BIBLIOGRAPHY. J. C. Gregory, 'The Life and Character of Saul', *ExpT* 19, 1907–8, pp. 510–513; A. C. Welch, *Kings and Prophets of Israel*, 1952, pp. 63–79; E. Robertson, *The Old Testament Problem*, 1946, pp. 105–136; J. Bright, *A History of Israel*², 1972, pp. 180–190.

T.H.J.

SAVOUR. With one exception (Joel 2:20) the word is used in AV of a sweet or acceptable smell. It is characteristic of sacrifice; and in this connection it is used pointedly of the effect of the Christian's life on his fellows (2 Cor. 2:15–16; RSV 'aroma', 'fragrance'). In Eph. 5:2 it is used of the sacrifice of Christ (RSV 'fragrant offering').

Two other references, referring to a loss of savour (Mt. 5:13; Lk. 14:34), connect this with insipidity or foolishness.

Common to all is the implicit association of cost, or distinctiveness, or strength with savour. Something is missing from God's people or the worship of God when there is no 'savour'.

In Mt. 16:23; Mk. 8:33, AV 'savour' renders Gk. *phronein*, 'to set the mind on' (RSV 'be on the side of').

C.H.D.

SCAPEGOAT. The word Azazel (Heb. *ʿᵃzāʾzēl*) occurs only in the description of the Day of Atonement (Lv. 16:8, 10 (twice), 26). There are four possible interpretations. **1.** The word denotes the 'scapegoat' and is to be explained as 'the goat (*ʿēz*) that goes away (from *ʾāzal*)'. **2.** It is used as an infinitive, 'in order to remove'; *cf*. Arab. *ʿazala*, 'to remove' **3.** It means a desolate region (*cf*. Lv. 16:22) or 'precipice' (G. R. Driver; *cf*. NEB). **4.** It is the name of a demon haunting that region, derived from *ʿāzaz* 'to be strong' and *ʾēl* 'God'.

Most scholars prefer the last possibility, as in v. 8 the name appears in parallelism to the name of the Lord. As a fallen angel Azazel is often mentioned in *Enoch* (6:6 onwards), but probably the author got his conception from Lv. 16. The meaning of the ritual must be that sin in a symbolical way was removed from human society and brought to the region of death (*cf*. Mi. 7:19). It is not implied that a sacrifice was presented to the demon (*cf*. Lv. 17:7).

BIBLIOGRAPHY. W. H. Gispen, 'Azazel', in *Orientalia Neerlandica*, 1948, pp. 156–161; G. R. Driver, *JSS* 1, 1956, pp. 97f.

A. van S.

SCEPTRE (Heb. *šēḇeṭ*, *šarᵉḇîṭ*; Gk. *rhabdos*). A staff or *rod, often very ornate, borne as a symbol of personal sovereignty or authority, normally by kings, but the same word is used of the rod of office of others (Gn. 38:18; Lv. 27:32; Ps. 23:4; Mi. 7:14; Is. 28:27). The term *šarᵉḇîṭ* (Akkad. *šabittu*) is used only of the sceptre of Persian rulers (Est. 4:11; 5:2; 8:4).

The term *šēḇeṭ* is used for the sceptre of the rulers of Egypt (Zc. 10:11), the Aramaean state of Bit Adini (Am. 1:5), Ashkelon (Am. 1:8), Babylon (Is. 14:5) and of the rulers of Israel (Ezk. 19:11, 14).

In Gn. 49:10 and Nu. 24:17 the term refers to Israel's future rulers. Both of these passages came to have Messianic significance. The same word occurs in Ps. 45:6, a verse which was used in the NT to describe Christ as Son (Heb. 1:8), the sceptre of whose kingdom is a sceptre of righteousness.

The reed placed in our Lord's hand (Mt. 27:29) was a symbol of sovereignty used in mockery. J.A.T.

SCEVA. Actual or putative father of a group of seven magical practioners who, endeavouring to imitate Paul in Ephesus, used a spell with the name of Jesus for exorcism, were repudiated by the demon and set upon by the demoniac: an incident which deeply impressed Jew and Gentile alike (Acts 19:13ff.). The story was doubtless valued as a demonstration that the 'name' was no magical formula with automatic effect.

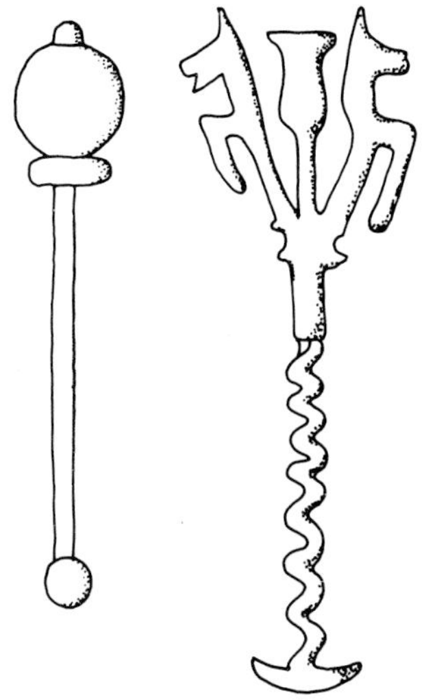

Left, *a royal mace;* right, *an elaborate sceptre held by the goddess Ishtar.*

Sceva is described as a 'Jewish high priest'. Though this could denote a member of the senior priestly families, it is probably here a self-adopted title for advertisement—rather as a modern conjuror styles himself 'Professor'. 'The Sons of the High Priest Sceva' may have been the collective designation for this 'firm' of itinerant mountebanks (*cf.* v. 13); a Jewish high priest would, in the eyes of superstitious pagans, be an impressive source of esoteric knowledge. B. A. Mastin, however, argues that, as befitted priests, they were genuine, if unsuccessful, exorcists.

The MSS show many variants in detail.

BIBLIOGRAPHY. K. Lake and H. J. Cadbury, *BC*, 1. 4, pp. 241–243; B. A. Mastin, *JTS* n.s. 27, 1976, pp. 405–412. A.F.W.

SCHISM
See Heresy, Part 2.

SCHOOL.

I. In the Old Testament

From the earliest times in the ancient Near East schools were used for regular instruction in reading and writing. Among the Hebrews Moses, trained in Egypt (Acts 7:22), was commanded to teach the people the law (Dt. 4:10) and statutes (Lv. 10:11). This was done by repetition and example (Dt. 11:19), public reading (Dt. 31:10–13), and the use of specially composed songs (v. 19). Parents were responsible for their children's education (Gn. 18:19; Dt. 6:7).

With the establishment of local sanctuaries and the Temple, young men were doubtless taught by the prophets (1 Sa. 10:11–13; 2 Ki. 4:1), and among other instruction read-

The young Rameses II carries the royal sceptres of Egypt, the crook and flail, symbols of authority. Height 1·41 m. c. 1290–1270 BC. (BM)

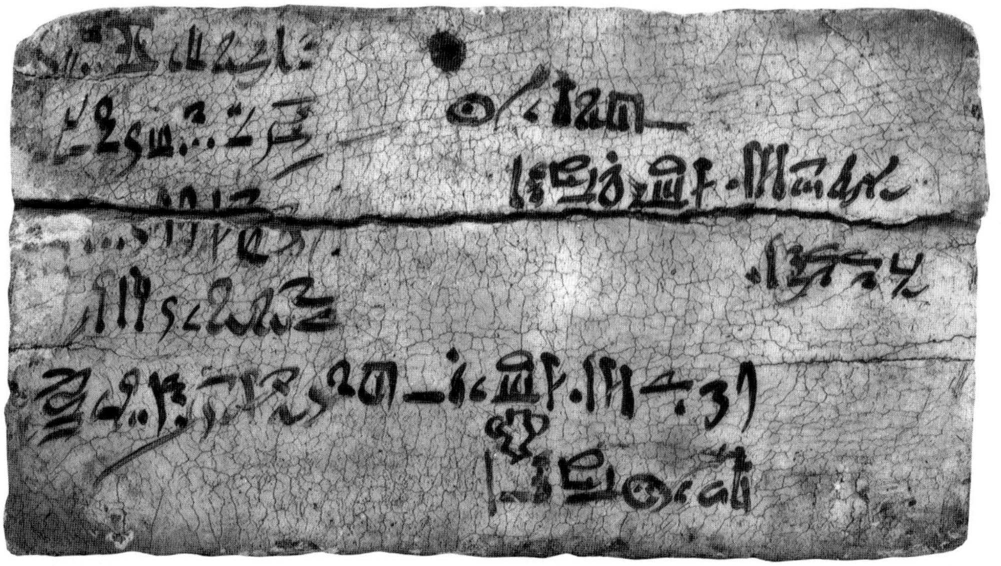

Egyptian writing-board with student's exercise in hieratic script which includes a list of names of people of the land of Keftiu. Length c. 25 cm. c. 1450 BC. (BM)

ing and writing was given (Jdg. 8:14; Is. 10:19). The alphabet was learned by repetition (Is. 28:10, 'precept upon precept . . .' being literally 'ṣ after ṣ, *q* after *q* . . .'), but most subjects were imparted orally by question and answer (Mal. 2:12, AV 'master and scholar', lit. 'he who rouses and he who answers', may, however, refer to watchmen).

The pupils (*limmûḏîm*, AV 'disciples') were taught by the prophets (Is. 8:16; 50:4; 54:13), as were kings (*e.g.* 2 Sa. 12:1–7). There are no direct references in the OT to special school buildings, but the introduction *c.* 75 BC in Judah by Simon ben-Sheṭaḥ of compulsory elementary education for boys aged 6–16 indicates the prior existence of such schools from the time of the second Temple. 1 Ch. 25:8 refers to scholars (*talmîḏ*) at the time of the first Temple.

*Education played a significant part in the cultural influence of Mesopotamia from the 3rd millennium, and its school texts and curriculum appear to have been copied in Anatolia, Syria (*UGARIT, *MARI) and Palestine itself (*MEGIDDO). For Mesopotamian education and the part played by the scribe, see S. N. Kramer, *The Sumerians*, 1963, pp. 229–248; and for the Egyptian, R. J. Williams, *JAOS* 92, 1972, pp. 214–222.

D.J.W.

II. In the New Testament

There is no trace in the NT of schools for Hebrew children. It seems that the home was the place of elementary instruction. The synagogue was the centre of religious instruction with teaching in the hands of the scribes (Mt. 7:29; Lk. 4:16–32; Acts 19:9). The word 'school' occurs in only one NT context (Acts 19:9, AV; RSV, 'hall'). There is nothing to indicate whether 'the school of Tyrannus' was devoted to elementary teaching (6–14 years) or to the advanced subjects of the Greek curriculum, philosophy, literature and rhetoric (14–18 years). A 'Western' addition to Acts 19:9 runs: 'from the fifth to the tenth hour'. Tyrannus' accommodation was available for hire from 11 a.m. onwards. Instruction began at dawn simultaneously with the obligations of Paul's own calling (Acts 18:3). He used the afternoon for teaching in the hired school-house. (*EDUCATION.)

E.M.B.

SCHOOLMASTER. AV thus renders the Greek *paidagōgos* in Gal. 3:24–25 (RSV 'custodian'; RV reads 'tutor', as also in 1 Cor. 4:15). There is no satisfactory rendering, for the word has passed into a derivative of quite dissimilar meaning, and the office it signified passed with the social conditions which devised it. The Greek and Roman pedagogue was a trusted male attendant, commonly a slave, who had the general supervision of the boy and saw him safely to and from school. This is the point of Paul's metaphor.

E.M.B.

SCOURGING, SCOURGE. The Eng. translation of several Heb. and Gk. words. **1.** Heb. *biqqōreṯ*, translated in Lv. 19:20, AV as 'she shall be scourged'; or (AVmg.), 'there shall be a scourging'. The Heb. term, however, expresses the idea of investigation, conveyed by RSV, 'an inquiry shall be held'.

2. Heb. *šôṭ* (Jb. 5:21; Is. 10:26, *etc.*), *šōṭēṭ* (Jos. 23:13), 'a scourge', but generally used in a metaphorical sense.

3. Gk. *mastigoō* (Mt. 10:17; Jn. 19:1, *etc.*), *mastizō* (Acts 22:25), 'to whip', 'to scourge'; *phragelloō*, derived from Lat. *flagello* (Mt. 27:26; Mk. 15:15). The scourging in Mt. 27:26; Mk. 15:15, was a preliminary stage in the execution of the sentence to *crucifixion; that proposed in Lk. 23:16, 22 (*paideuō*) and carried out in Jn. 19:1 preceded the death-sentence and may have been intended as a milder penalty.

J.D.D.
F.F.B.

SCRIBE. In ancient Israel, following the spread of the alphabet, the scribes' monopoly of writing was broken, but theirs remained an important profession. The words for 'scribe' in Heb. (*sôpēr*, from *sāpar*, 'to count, tell'; Pi'el, 'to recount'), Canaanite (*spr*) and Akkad. (*šapāru*, 'to send', 'write') cover the main duties of this highly skilled trade. Many scribes were employed by the public as secretaries to transcribe necessary legal contracts (Je. 32:12), write letters, or keep accounts or records, usually from dictation (Je. 36:26). Others, known as 'the king's scribes' (2 Ch. 24:11), were employed in public administration and were attached to the royal household, where the Chief Scribe acted as 'Secretary of State' and ranked before the Chronicler (*mazkîr*), who kept the state records (2 Sa. 8:16; 1 Ki. 4:3). As a high official the Chief Scribe was one of the royal advisers (1 Ch. 27:32). Thus Shebna the scribe, who later rose to be 'over the household' (*i.e.* Prime Minister), was sent by Hezekiah with the Prime Minister and elders to parley with the Assyrians besieging Jerusalem (2 Ki. 18:18; 19:2; Is. 36:3). Some scribes were especially employed for military duties, which included the compilation of a list of those called out for war (Jdg. 5:14) or of the booty won, their senior official being designated 'principal scribe of the host' (2 Ki. 25:19; Je. 52:25). Although other scribes were allotted to tasks in the Temple involving the collection of revenues (2 Ki. 12:10), the scribal profession was, until the Exile, separate from the priesthood, who had their own

An Egyptian scribe using a palette squats in front of a low desk. Relief from the mastaba of Mereruka, Saqqara. 6th Dynasty. c. 2345–2181 BC. (PAC)

literate officials. Senior scribes had their own rooms in the palace (Je. 36:12–21) or Temple (Je. 36:10).

Shaphan the scribe was given the newly discovered scroll of the law to read before the king (2 Ki. 22:8), but it was only in the post-exilic period that the scribes assumed the role of copyists, preservers and interpreters of the law (Ezr. 7:6). *Ezra was both priest and scribe (7:11) and may well have acted as adviser on Jewish affairs to the Babylonian court, in the same way as did the specialist scribes of Assyria and Babylonia. By the 2nd century BC the majority of scribes were priests (1 Macc. 7:12) and were the prototypes of the religious *scribes of the NT day.

Athenian vase-painting showing a seated youth studying the alphabet. c. 440 BC. (BM)

The scribe, as a person of education and means, was able to wear fine garments with a pen-case or 'inkhorn' hanging from his girdle (Ezk. 9:2). His equipment included reed-pens (Je. 8:8); a small knife for erasures and cutting papyrus (Je. 36:23), and, in some cases, styli for *writing in the cuneiform script. The profession was often followed by whole families (1 Ch. 2:55), and several sons are named as following their fathers in office.

BIBLIOGRAPHY. A. S. Diamond, *The Earliest Hebrew Scribes*, 1960; B. M. Metzger, 'When did Scribes begin to use Writing Desks?', *Akten der XI internationalen Byzantinisten-Kongress*, 1960, pp. 356ff.

D.J.W.

SCRIBES (Heb. *sōp̄ᵉrîm*; Gk. *grammateis*, *nomikoi* (lawyers) and *nomodidaskaloi* (teachers of the law)). Scribes were experts in the study of the law of Moses (*Torah*). At first this occupation belonged to the priests. Ezra was priest and scribe (Ne. 8:9); the offices were not necessarily separate. The chief acti-

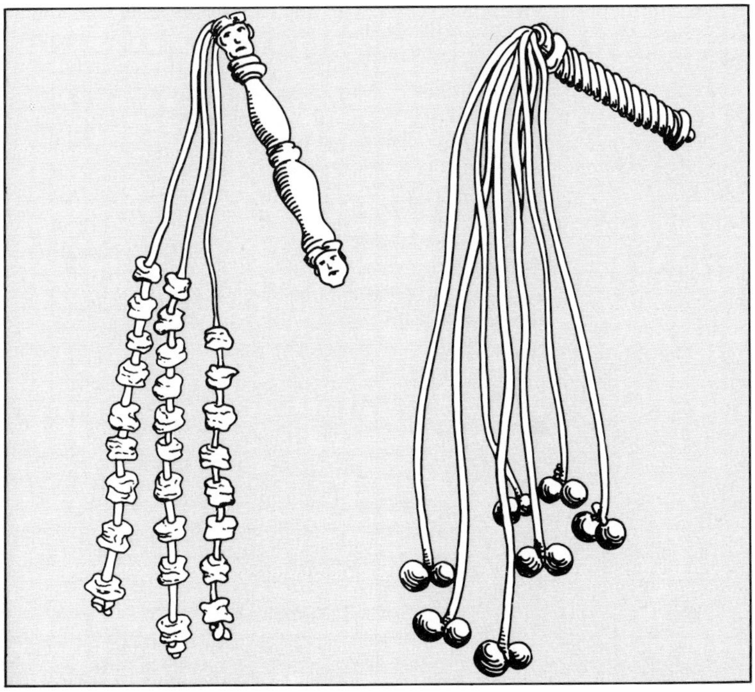

Roman scourges, barbed with pieces of bone and lumps of lead.

Egyptian scribes recording the grain harvest. Wall-painting from the tomb of Menna, Thebes. Height c. 38 cm. c. 1420 BC. (DJW)

SCRIP

See Bag, Part 1.

vity of the scribe was undistracted study (Ecclus. 38:24). The rise of the scribes may be dated after the Babylonian Exile. 1 Ch. 2:55 would suggest that the scribes were banded together into families and guilds. They were probably not a distinct political party in the time of Ben-Sira (beginning of the 2nd century BC), but became one by the repressive measures of Antiochus Epiphanes. Scribes were found in Rome in the later imperial period, and in Babylonia in the 5th and 6th centuries AD. Not until about AD 70 are there detailed facts concerning individual scribes. They were mainly influential in Judaea up to AD 70, but they were to be found in Galilee (Lk. 5:17) and among the Dispersion.

The scribes were the originators of the synagogue service. Some of them sat as members of the Sanhedrin (Mt. 16:21; 26:3). After AD 70 the importance of the scribes was enhanced. They preserved in written form the oral law and faithfully handed down the Heb. Scriptures. They expected of their pupils a reverence beyond that given to parents (*Aboth* 4. 12).

The function of the scribes was threefold.

1. They preserved the law. They were the professional students of the law and its defenders, especially in the Hellenistic period, when the priesthood had become corrupt. They transmitted unwritten legal decisions which had come into existence in their efforts to apply the Mosaic law to daily life. They claimed this oral law was more important than the written law (Mk. 7:5ff.). By their efforts religion was liable to be reduced to heartless formalism.

2. They gathered around them many pupils to instruct them in the law. The pupils were expected to retain the material taught and to transmit it without variation. They lectured in the Temple (Lk. 2:46; Jn. 18:20). Their teaching was supposed to be free of charge (so Rabbi Zadok, Hillel and others), but they were probably paid (Mt. 10:10; 1 Cor. 9:3–18, for Paul's statement of his right), and even took advantage of their honoured status (Mk. 12:40; Lk. 20:47).

3. They were referred to as 'lawyers' and 'teachers of the law', because they were entrusted with the administration of the law as judges in the Sanhedrin (*cf.* Mt. 22:35; Mk. 14:43, 53; Lk. 22:66; Acts 4:5; Jos., *Ant.* 18. 16f.). 'Lawyer' and 'scribe' are synonymous, and thus the two words are never joined in the NT. For their services in the Sanhedrin they were not paid. They were therefore obliged to earn their living by other means if they had no private wealth.

The OT Apocrypha and Pseudepigrapha are sources for the origin of the scribal party. The books of Ezra, Nehemiah, Daniel, Chronicles and Esther also indicate something of the beginnings of the movement, whereas Josephus and the NT speak of this group in a more advanced stage of development. There is no mention of the scribes in the Fourth Gospel. They belonged mainly to the party of the Pharisees, but as a body were distinct from them. On the matter of the resurrection they sided with Paul against the Sadducees (Acts 23:9). They clashed with Christ, for he taught with authority (Mt. 7:28–29), and he condemned external formalism which they fostered. They persecuted Peter and John (Acts 4:5), and had a part in Stephen's martyrdom (Acts 6:12). However, although the majority opposed Christ (Mt. 21:15), some believed (Mt. 8:19).

BIBLIOGRAPHY. G. F. Moore, *Judaism*, 1, 1927, pp. 37–47; G. H. Box in *EBr*, 1948 edn.; J. D. Prince in *EBi*; D. Eaton in *HDB*; E. Schürer, *HJP*, 2, 1978; W. Robertson Smith, *The Old Testament in the Jewish Church*, 1892, pp. 42–72 (with bibliography on p. 42); A. Finkel, *The Pharisees and the Teacher of Nazareth*², 1974; J. W. Bowker, *Jesus and the Pharisees*, 1973; N. Hillyer, *NIDNTT* 3, pp. 477–482; J. Jeremias, *TDNT* 1, pp. 740–742; *idem*, *Jerusalem in the Time of Jesus*, 1969, ch. 10; *EJ* (*s.v.* 'Scribes'). C.L.F.

SCRIPTURE, SCRIPTURES.

I. Vocabulary

Two Gk. words are translated 'Scripture(s)' in EVV. *gramma*, originally 'an alphabetical character', is used in NT for 'document' (Lk. 16:6; Acts 28:21), in a special sense by Paul for the law (Rom. 2:27, 29; 7:6; 2 Cor. 3:6) and in the plural for the 'writings' of Moses (Jn. 5:47); for 'learning', sacred or profane (Jn. 7:15; Acts 26:24), and only once in the phrase *ta hiera grammata*, 'the holy scriptures' (2 Tim. 3:15). *graphē*, on the other hand, which in secular Gk. meant simply 'a writing' (though sometimes an authoritative writing in particular), is in the NT appropriated to 'the Scriptures' in a technical sense some 50 times, in most cases unmistakably the OT. Associated with *graphē* is the formula *gegraptai*, 'it is written', occurring some 60 times in the NT, and found in Greek usage for legal pronouncements (*cf.* A. Deissmann, *Bible Studies*², 1909, pp. 112ff.). Analogous forms occur in the Mishnah, but the rabbis more often used formulae like 'It is said . . .'. The term 'the Scripture' (*ha-kāṯûḇ*) is also employed. (See B. M. Metzger, *JBL* 70, 1951, pp. 297ff., for quotation formulae in rabbinic and NT documents.)

II. Significance

gegraptai meant 'It stands written in the Scriptures', and all Christians or Hellenistic Jews recognized that these comprised (Lk. 24:44) 'the law, . . . the prophets, and . . . the psalms' (*i.e.* the *Keṯuḇim*, or Writings; *CANON OF THE OLD TESTAMENT). Though the AV, RSV translation of 2 Tim. 3:16 ('every [all] scripture is inspired . . .') is probably preferable to that of RV, NEB, no contemporary would doubt the extent of 'every inspired scripture'. It was what Christians called the OT, in which the gospel was rooted, of which Christ was the fulfilment, which was through faith in Christ able to lead a man to salvation, and was used in the primitive church for all the purposes outlined in 2 Tim. 3:15–17.

The question arises, however, at what date and in what sense Christians began to use the term 'Scriptures' for *Christian* writings. It has sometimes been suggested that 'according to the scriptures' in 1 Cor. 15:3f. refers to Christian testimony books or early Gospels, since no OT passage specifies the resurrection on the third day. This is unacceptable: Paul means the OT, as the groundwork of Christian preaching (*GOSPEL), and probably relates simply the fact of resurrection, not its occurrence on the third day, to prophecy (*cf.* B. M. Metzger, *JTS* n.s. 8, 1957, pp. 118ff.). Still less acceptable is Selwyn's suggestion that the anarthrous *en graphēi* in 1 Pet. 2:6 means 'in writing' (*e.g.* in a hymn), for the passage quoted is from the OT. Nevertheless, there were undoubtedly collections of authoritative sayings of the Lord in the apostolic church (*cf.* O. Cullmann, *SJT* 3, 1950, pp. 180ff.; *TRADITION), and 1 Tim. 5:18 seems to represent a quotation from such a collection, linked with an OT citation, the two together being described as 'scripture'. Again, Paul in 1 Cor. 2:9 cites by *gegraptai* a passage which, unless it is an extremely free rendering of Is. 64:4; is unidentifiable. It occurs in various forms elsewhere in early literature, however, and now as Logion 17 of the *Gospel of Thomas* (*NEW TESTAMENT APOCRYPHA).It is perhaps worth considering whether Paul is quoting a saying of the Lord not recorded in our Gospels (as in Acts 20:35) and citing it as he would 'scripture'.

If indeed the tradition of the Lord's words was so early called 'Scripture' it would be an easy step so to describe apostolic letters read in church; and, despite many dogmatic statements to the contrary, there would be no reason why this should not have occurred in apostolic times, as 2 Pet. 3:16, as usually translated, represents: though perhaps we should translate 'they wrest the Scriptures *as well*' (*cf.* C. Bigg, *St. Peter and St. Jude*², *ICC*, 1901, *in loc.*).

We have, however, reached a dark place in NT history, though one where we may hope for future light. (*BIBLE; *CANON; *INSPIRATION.)

BIBLIOGRAPHY. G. Schrenk, *TDNT* 1, pp. 742–773; B. B. Warfield, *DCG* (= *Inspiration and Authority of the Bible*, 1948, pp. 229–241); C. H. Dodd, *According to the Scriptures*, 1952; E. E. Ellis, *Paul's Use of the Old Testament*, 1957. A.F.W.

SCYTHIANS. A tribe of horse-riding nomads and warriors from W Siberia inhabiting the Black Sea–Caspian area from about 2000 BC. In the late 8th century BC they moved into N Persia and Urarṭu, driving the Cimmerians westward (*GOMER). Their initial advances SW were checked by Sargon II of Assyria (722–705 BC), but according to Herodotus (1. 116; 4. 1) the Scythians dominated Asia for 28 years through a number of military ventures. They assisted Assyria against the Medes, relieving Nineveh *c.* 630 BC, though later they attacked Harran and raided Palestine, to be stopped from raiding Egypt only when Psammetichus I bought them off. Some scholars consider this event to account for a prophecy of Jeremiah (ch. 47; *IEJ* 1, 1950, pp. 154–159) and Zephaniah, but there are few references to the Scythians (Askuzai, Ummanmanda) in contemporary texts. Scholars vary in fixing the time of Scythian incursion into Syria–Palestine, but *c.* 645–617 BC (L. Piotrowicz) seems likely. They do not appear to have been a strong group (I. M. Diakonoff). Some are believed to have settled at Bethshean, called Scythopolis (so Jdg. 1:27, LXX).

The Scythians under Scylurus established their capital at Neapolis, in the Crimea, in 110 BC, their control of the steppes making them an intermediary in trade from Russia, especially in grain and slaves. The latter were called by the Pontic Greeks 'Scythians', though these were often their prisoners rather than their fellow nomadic freemen. Paul may use 'Scythian' in the latter sense (Col. 3:11).

BIBLIOGRAPHY. T. Talbot Rice, *The Scythians*, 1957; R. P. Vaggione, *JBL* 92, 1973, pp. 523–550. D.J.W.

SEA (Heb. *yām*; Gk. *thalassa* and *pelagos*: this latter term, meaning 'open sea', occurs only once, Acts 27:5).

The predominating sea in the OT is, of course, the Mediterranean. Indeed, the word *yām* also means 'west', 'westward', *i.e.* 'seaward', from the geographical position of the Mediterranean with reference to Palestine. The Mediterranean is termed 'the Great Sea' (Jos. 1:4), 'the western sea' (Dt. 11:24), and 'the sea of the Philistines' (Ex. 23:31).

Other seas mentioned in the OT are the Red Sea, lit. 'sea of reeds' (Ex. 13:18); the Dead Sea, lit. 'sea of salt' (Gn. 14:3); the Sea of Galilee, lit. 'sea of *kinnereṯ*' (Nu. 34:11). The word *yām* was also used of a particularly broad river, such as the

SCULPTURE
See Art, Part 1.

SCYTHOPOLIS
See Salim, Part 3.

A Scythian horseman depicted on a painted wall-hanging from Pazirik (S Russia). 5th cent. BC. (WM)

Euphrates (Je. 51:35f.) and the Nile (Na. 3:8). It is used with reference to the great basin in the Temple court (1 Ki. 7:23).

As one would expect, the NT *thalassa* is used with reference to the same seas as are mentioned in the OT.

The Hebrews betrayed little interest in, or enthusiasm for, the sea. Probably their fear of the ocean stemmed from the ancient Semitic belief that the deep personified the power that fought against the deity. But for Israel the Lord was its Creator (Gn. 1:9f.), and therefore its Controller (Ps. 104:7–9; Acts 4:24). He compels it to contribute to man's good (Gn. 49:25; Dt. 33:13) and to utter his praise (Ps. 148:7). In the figurative language of Isaiah (17:12) and Jeremiah (6:23) the sea is completely under God's command. Many of the manifestations of the Lord's miraculous power were against the sea (Ex. 14–15; Ps. 77:16; Jon. 1–2). So also Christ's walking on the sea and stilling the storm (Mt. 14:25–33; *cf.* G. Bornkamm, 'The Stilling of the

Cylinder-seal with impression, showing a goddess in a shrine flanked by worshippers. From Palestine. Height 10 mm. c. 1600 BC. (ARM)

Neo-Assyrian cylinder-seal and impression. Jasper. Height 38 mm. 7th cent. BC. (BM)

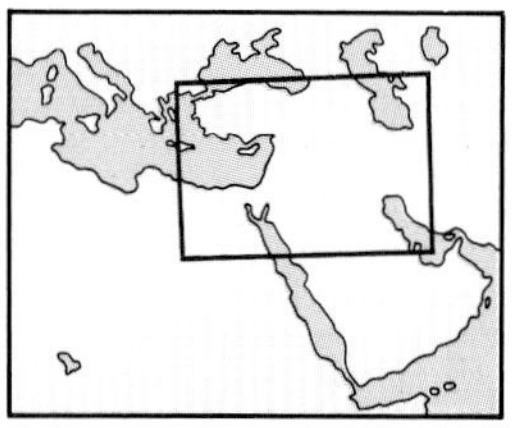

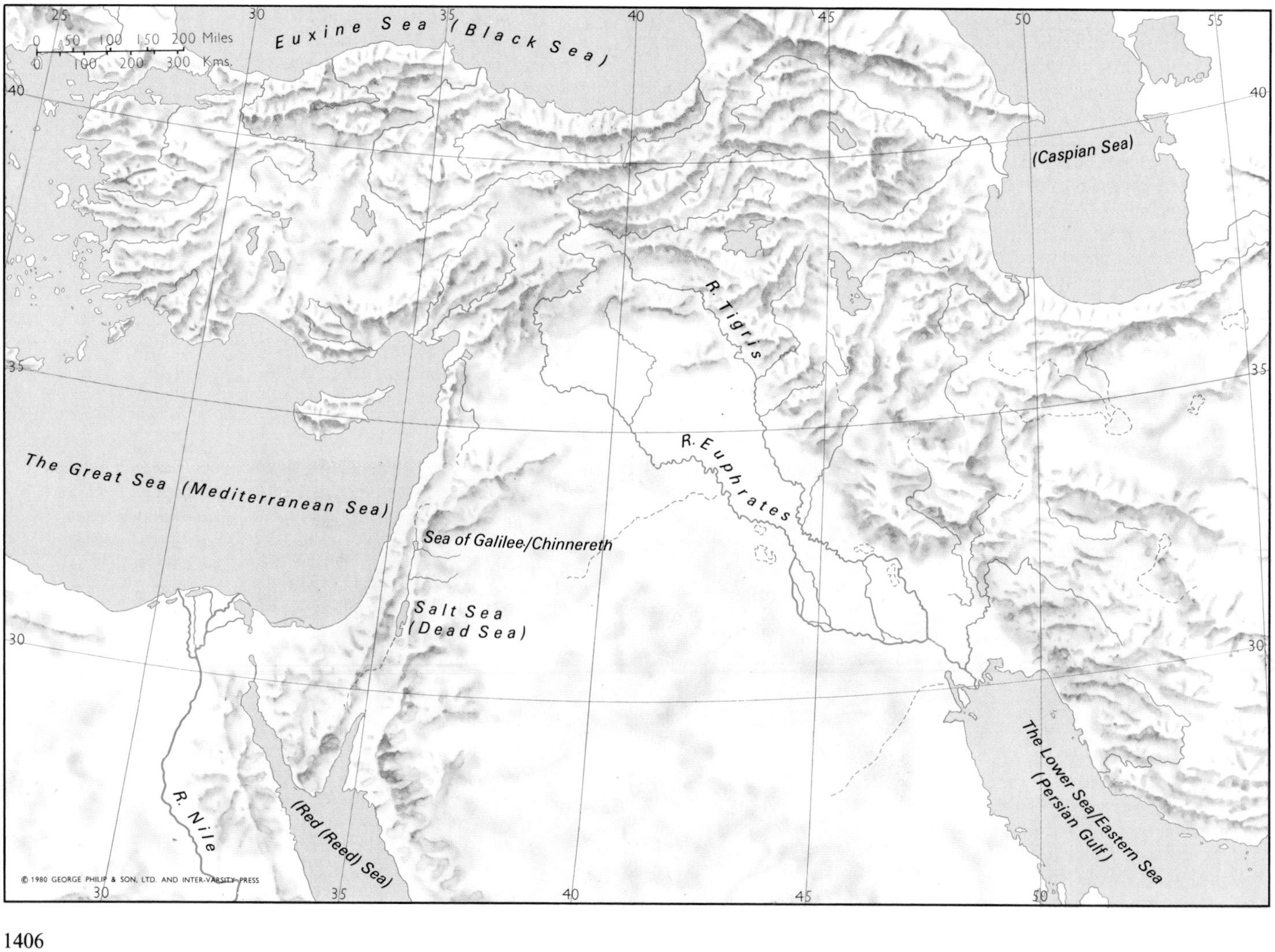

The 'seas' of the Bible lands.

Storm in Matthew', in G. Bornkamm, G. Barth and H. J. Held, *Tradition and Interpretation in Matthew*, 1963, pp. 52ff.). God's final triumph will witness the disappearance of the sea in the world to come (Rev. 21:1). J.G.S.S.T.

SEA OF GLASS. Twice John saw in heaven 'as it were a sea of glass' (*hōs thalassa hyalinē*), 'before the throne' of God 'like crystal' (Rev. 4:6) and later 'mingled with fire' (Rev. 15:2). The picture of a sea in heaven may be traced through the apocalyptic literature (*e.g. Testament of Levi* 2:7; *2 Enoch* 3:3) back to 'the waters which were above the firmament' of Gn. 1:7; Pss. 104:3; 148:4. The likeness to crystal stands in contrast with the semi-opacity of most ancient *glass and speaks of the holy purity of heaven; the mingling with fire suggests the wrath of God (*cf.* Gn. 7:11; *1 Enoch* 54:7–8). Beside or on the sea stand the victors over the beast: their song (Rev. 15:3) recalls that of the Israelites beside the Red Sea (Ex. 15:1ff.). M.H.C.

Late Assyrian cylinder-seal and impression showing a priest before an Assyrian king. Green jasper. Height 35 mm. Early 4th cent. BC. (BM)

Fine Achaemenid cylinder-seal and impression. Chalcedony. Height 5 cm. 5th cent. BC. (BM)

Cylinder-seals were rolled on damp clay, as illustrated here with a Babylonian example of c. 1750 BC. (DJW)

SEAL, SEALING.

I. In the Old Testament

In the Near East, from which many thousands of individual seals have been recovered, engraved seals were common in ancient times, the Hebrews using a general term which did not specify the form of the seal itself (*ḥōṯām*; Egyp. *ḥtm*). The varied uses of such seals were much the same as in modern times.

a. Uses

(i) As a mark of authenticity and authority. Thus pharaoh handed a seal to Joseph his deputy (Gn. 41:42) and Ahasuerus sealed royal edicts (Est. 3:10; 8:8–10). The action describes the passing of the master's word to his disciples (Is. 8:16) and Yahweh granting authority to Zerubbabel (Hg. 2:23; *cf.* Je. 22:24). For a non-biblical example of delegated seals on a covenant, see *Iraq* 21, 1958.

(ii) To witness a document. The seal was impressed on the clay or wax (*WRITING). Thus, his friends witnessed Jeremiah's deed of purchase (Je. 32:11–14) and Nehemiah and his contemporaries attested the covenant (Ne. 9:38; 10:1) and Daniel a prophecy (Dn. 9:24).

(iii) To secure by affixing a seal. Thus, a clay document within its envelope or other receptacle, or a scroll tied by a cord to which was attached a lump of clay bearing a seal impression, could be examined and read only when the seal had been broken by an authorized person (*cf.* Rev. 5:1f.). A sealed prophecy (Dn. 12:9) or book (Is. 29:11) was thus a symbol for something as yet unrevealed.

To prevent unauthorized entry doors would be sealed by a cord or clay, with the sealing stretched across the gap between the door and its lock. This was done to the lions' den at Babylon (Dn. 6:17; Bel and the Dragon 14) and to tombs (Herodotus, 2. 121; *cf.* Mt. 27:66). A crocodile's close-knit scales were likened to a sealed item (Jb. 41:15).

Metaphorically the seal stood for what is securely held, as are the sins of man before God (Dt. 32:34; Jb. 14:17), who alone has the authority to open and to seal (Jb. 33:16). He sets his seal as a token of completion (Ezk. 28:12). The metaphor in Ct. 4:12 is probably of chastity.

b. Form

With the invention of writing in the 4th millennium BC seals were used in large numbers. The cylinder-seal was the most common and was rolled on clay, though stamp seals are also found in contemporary use. In Palestine, under both Mesopotamian (often through Syrian and Phoenician) and Egyptian influences, cylinder-seals and

SEA GULL
See Animals, Part 1.

SEAH
See Weights and measures, Part 3.

Egyptian scarab seals and their impressions. From Gezer, Palestine. Length 2 cm and 3 cm. c. 1710–1570 BC. (BM)

Winged human-headed bull and a bird on a typical Achaemenid-period conical seal with impression. Diameter 25 mm. 5th–4th cent. BC. (BM)

scarabs were in use in the Canaanite period. The latter predominated for use on wax or clay lumps appended to papyrus. With the Monarchy, stamp seals, 'button', conoid or scaraboid prevail.

The seal was pierced so that it could be worn on a cord round the neck (Gn. 38:18; Je. 22:24; Ct. 8:6) or on a pin, traces of which sometimes remain, for attachment to the dress. The scaraboid seals or seal stones were set in a ring to be worn on the hand or arm (Est. 3:12).

c. Materials

Poor persons could purchase roughly engraved seals made of local terracotta, bitumen, limestone, frit or wood. The majority of seals, however, were specially engraved by a skilled seal-cutter who used copper gravers, a cutting wheel, and sometimes a small bow-drill, perhaps the 'pen of iron; with a point of diamond' (Je. 17:1; *ARTS AND CRAFTS), to work the hard semi-precious stones (*ART). In Palestine, as elsewhere, carnelian, chalcedony, agate, jasper, rock crystal and haematite were imported and frequently used. Imported Egyptian scarabs were of glazed steatite and, later, glazed composition.

Engraved stones (Ex. 28:11–23; 39:8) were used as insets in the high priest's breast ornament. The fine stones and workmanship led to these seal stones or signet-rings (Heb. *ṭabba'aṯ*; Akkad. *ṭimbu'u*) being used as ornaments (Is. 3:21), votive offerings, or for sacred purposes (Ex. 35:22; Nu. 31:50), like the group of seals in the Canaanite shrine at Hazor, or as *amulets. The Heb. *ṭabba'aṯ* is used also of rings in general (Ex. 25:12).

d. Designs

Before the Monarchy cylinder-seals followed the Phoenician or Syrian style, showing patterns, well-filled designs, rows of men or designs characteristic of the different fashions prevailing at various periods in Mesopotamia. The later Palestinian seals, usually oval, bear representations of lions (see *IBA*, fig. 52), winged human-headed lions or sphinxes (cherubim), griffins or the winged uraeus-snake. Egyptian motifs, with the lotus flower, the *ankh*-symbol of life or the Horus-child, frequently occur. Scenes of worship, seated deities and animals and birds seem to show that this art did not offend Hebrew religious feeling. After the 7th century BC, however, the majority of seals bear only a two-line inscription.

e. Inscriptions

More than 200 Hebrew seals have been recovered, inscribed with their owners' names. The name may stand alone, or be followed by the father's name or by a title. Several belonged to royal retainers, described as 'servant of the king'. The finest of them is the jasper seal 'Of Shema, servant of Jeroboam' (*i.e.* Jeroboam II), found in excavations at Megiddo. Another shows a cock, with an inscription reading 'Of Jaazaniah, servant of the king', and may indicate as owner the Jaazaniah of 2 Ki. 25:23, or a contemporary of the same name (Je. 35:3; 40:8; *cf.* Ezk. 11:1). The seals were impressed into lumps of clay, and some of these

Jar-handle bearing a stamp-seal impression of a flying scroll and a Hebrew inscription lmlk (*'of the king'*) mmšt (*an unidentified place-name*). *Lachish. Late 7th cent.* BC. (BM)

have been recovered, carrying on the back the marks of the papyrus documents they once secured. One such sealing, termed *bulla*, had been stamped by the seal 'Of Gedaliah who is over the household'. It was found at Lachish, and may have belonged to the governor of Judah (2 Ki. 25:22–25; for the title *cf.* 2 Ki. 18:18, and *SHEBNA). One impression is particularly important because its date is certain. The seal was inscribed 'Of Jehozerah, son of Hilkiah, servant of Hezekiah' (*IEJ* 24, 1974, pp. 27–29), Hezekiah being the king of Judah, and Hilkiah his steward's father (2 Ki. 18:18, *etc.*). Several men are entitled 'son of the king', although it is not clear whether these were members of the royal family or of the larger palace community. Also uncertain is the identity of the master on the seal inscribed 'Of Eliakim, retainer (*na'ar*) of Yawkin'. Yawkin may have been *Jehoiachin, king of Judah, but the masters on other seals so inscribed were not all kings. Some seals certainly belonged to women, *e.g.* the seal of one Hannah (*ḥnh*; *PEQ* 108, 1976, pp. 59–61), or 'Of Abigail, wife of Asaiah'.

The value of these seals lies in the range of Hebrew personal names they reveal, not all known from the OT (*e.g.* Gamariah, Halasiah). The titles they reveal widen our knowledge of the administration. The large number of seals, many bearing no design apart from the names, implies a widespread ability to read in the relatively small state of Judah, whence most of the seals come.

Clay bulla with Hebrew seal impression: 'Belonging to Hananiah son of Gedaliah'. The papyrus impression is shown on the reverse. Palestine. 11 mm × 9 mm. Late 7th–early 6th cent. BC. (BM)

Hebrew scaraboid seal and impression: 'Nehemiah son of Micaiah'. Crystal. Length 15 mm. 7th–6th cent. BC. (BM)

Important historical information is supplied by a collection of clay sealings and some stamps on jar-handles, apparently carrying the names of three post-exilic governors of Judah (Elnathan, Yehoezer, Ahzai) each styled *peḥa*, to be placed after Zerubbabel, and before Ezra. These names are otherwise unknown. (See N. Avigad, *Bullae and Seals from a Post-Exilic Judaean Archive*, 1976.)

f. Stamped jar-handles

Excavations in Palestine have produced about 1,000 jar-handles bearing seal impressions. Some appear to be royal pottery marks (*cf.* 1 Ch. 4:23) giving the place of manufacture. The impressions are usually of four-winged scarabeus or a flying scroll with 'Of the king' (*lammelek̲*) above, and (below) a place, *e.g.* Hebron, Ziph, Socoh and *mmšt*. Others bear personal names (perhaps of the potter), *e.g.* Shebnaiah, Azariah, Yopiah. Such stamped jar-handles have been found in quantity at Megiddo, Lachish and Gibeon. A group of fiscal stamp impressions inscribed in Aramaic *yhd* (Judah) dated 400–200 BC are of special interest (*MONEY; *BASOR* 147, Oct. 1957, pp. 37–39; 148, Dec. 1957, pp. 28–30; *IEJ* 7, 1957, pp. 146–153).

BIBLIOGRAPHY. (1) Palestinian seals: A. Rowe, *Catalogue of Egyptian Scarabs in the Palestine Archaeological Museum*, 1936;

Bottom right: Handle from pottery storage-jar stamped by a seal showing a five-pointed star, inscribed yršlm (*'Jerusalem'*) *between the points. This dates from the time when Jerusalem was the centre of an administrative district under Persian rule (the time of Ezra and Nehemiah). Ophel, Jerusalem. 5th–4th cent.* BC. (BM)

B. Parker, 'Cylinder Seals of Palestine', *Iraq* 11, 1949; J. Nougayrol, *Cylindres sceaux et empreintes . . . trouvés en Palestine au cours des fouilles régulières*, 1939; A. Reifenberg, *Ancient Hebrew Seals*, 1950; D. Diringer, in *DOTT*, pp. 218–226. (2) For other Near Eastern seals: H. Frankfort, *Cylinder Seals*, 1939; D. J. Wiseman, *Cylinder Seals of Western Asia*, 1958. D.J.W.
A.R.M.

II. In the New Testament

a. Literal use

The verb *sphragizō* (noun *sphragis*) is occasionally used in the NT in a literal sense, *e.g.* of the sealing of the tomb of Christ after his burial (Mt. 27:66 *cf. Ev. Petr.* 8:33), the sealing of Satan in the abyss (Rev. 20:3) and the sealing of the apocalyptic roll against unauthorized scrutiny (Rev. 5:1–8:1, *passim*). The practice of 'sealing' mentioned in this latter context would have been as familiar to Jews as to Romans (*cf.* Rev. 22:10, where the *logoi* are not 'sealed' because 'the time is at hand', and they are to be imminently used; contrast Dn. 12:4, 9).

b. Figurative use

(i) In Rom. 15:28 Paul refers to his intention of delivering a contribution (*koinōnia*) of the Gentiles to the saints in Jerusalem, and so of having 'sealed' (*sphragisamenos*) their offering. This may possibly imply a guarantee of his honesty ('under my own seal', NEB), but it will in any case denote Paul's *approval* of the Gentile action (so Theodore of Mopsuestia; *cf.* Jn. 3:33, where *esphragisen* is used of man's 'approval' of the truth of God, and Jn. 6:27, where precisely the same form of the verb is used with reference to God's attestation of the Christ).

(ii) An unusual use of the word *sphragis*, which carries still the sense of 'authentication', occurs in 1 Cor. 9:2, when Paul describes his converts in the church at Corinth as the 'seal' affixed by Christ to his work; the vindication, indeed, of his apostolate.

(iii) In the discussion of Abraham's exemplary faith in Rom. 4, Paul mentions the *sēmeion* of circumcision as the confirming 'seal' (v. 11; NEB 'hallmark') of a righteousness which existed, by faith, before the rite itself was instituted. This use of the term 'seal' compares with that in the Apocalypse (Rev. 7:2–8; 9:4), where the servants of God are described as being 'sealed' with 'the seal of the living God' (7:2f.; *cf.* Ezk. 9:4; Rev. 14:1), as a safeguard as well as a mark of possession, A. G. Hebert suggests (*TWBR*, p. 222) that these passages 'readily fall into a baptismal context'.

III. Sealing by the Spirit

One important NT image associates *sphragis* with *pneuma*. The Pauline characterization of the Christian inheritance in Eph. 1, for example, proceeds against a background filled with Christian hope. In v. 13, accordingly, the Ephesian Christians are described as 'sealed with the promised Holy Spirit'; they have received in time, that is to say, an earnest of what they will become in eternity. Once more this use of 'sealing' includes the concept of 'possession' (*cf.* 2 Tim. 2:19; Gal. 6:17). Similarly, mention of the Holy Spirit in Eph. 4:30, during a piece of practical exhortation to Christ-like behaviour, is followed by the qualifying phrase, 'in whom (*en hō*) you were sealed for the day of redemption'; while in 2 Cor. 1:21f. believers are described as 'anointed' by God, who has 'put his seal' upon them, and given them the Holy Spirit as an eternal guarantee. We have to consider the nature of this 'seal', as well as the moment and results of the 'sealing'.

a. The nature of the seal. Considerable discussion has taken place on this point. R. E. O. White, for example (*The Biblical Doctrine of Initiation*, 1960, p. 203 and n.), takes the aorists of *sphragizō* in Eph. 1:13; 4:30; 2 Cor. 1:22 to refer to the gift of the Spirit, acting as a 'divine seal upon baptism'. He discovers in support of this suggestion a 'regular' NT use of the aorist tense in connection with the reception of the Spirit by the believer in baptism. W. F. Flemington, on the other hand (*The New Testament Doctrine of Baptism*, 1953, pp. 66f.), proposes baptism itself as the seal, and relates this to the word *sphragis* used in connection with the Jewish rite of circumcision. (So also O. Cullmann, *Baptism in the New Testament*, 1950, p. 46.)

Clearly the Heb. background to the theology of baptism, and to the notion of 'seal' itself, cannot be discounted; and Gregory Dix has indicated the extent to which the early Fathers were indebted to their Jewish antecedents in this respect (*Th* 51, 1948, pp. 7–12). At the same time, as Dix points out, it is not necessarily the NT which justifies any later connection made between 'baptism' and 'seal'; even the *Didachē* does not call water baptism a 'sealing', or connect the sacrament in any way with the gift of the Holy Spirit.

b. The moment of sealing. These considerations will suggest the doubt that also exists about the precise moment of the believer's 'sealing'. If we are right to associate the gift of the Holy Spirit with baptism (which is a frequent but not altogether regular pattern in the NT, *cf.* Acts 8:36ff.; 10:44), we may consider that this 'sealing' by the Spirit takes place at baptism, or more precisely, perhaps, at the moment of commitment that finds its focus and expression in the sacrament of baptism. So, *e.g.*. G. W. H. Lampe (*The Seal of the Spirit*, 1951) has carefully examined the origin and meaning of the cognate NT terms *sphragis* and *chrisma*, associated with the 'chrism' of Christ himself in whom the Spirit of God was actively present, and shown that (in Pauline language) incorporation into the body of Christ is effected by baptism (rather than by any equivalent of 'confirmation', incidentally), and 'sealed' by the gift of the Holy Spirit (pp. 6, 61f.; for a summary of the arguments involved, and their proponents, see further White, *op. cit.*, pp. 352ff.).

c. The results of sealing. It has become clear from 1st-century papyri that the language of 'sealing' came to acquire in the E the extended and important meaning, particularly in legal circles, of giving validity to documents, guaranteeing the genuineness of articles and so on. (The possible parallels that exist between *sphragizō* and initiation into Gk. mystery cults are less likely to be significant.) It is easy as a result to see how the word *sphragis* and its cognates fit naturally into NT contexts which presuppose the theology of the covenant, and denote, in terms of the gift of the Holy Spirit, authentication as well as ownership. We have already discovered these to be aspects of the meaning of the term in other NT passages.

The occurrence of similar ideas in other contexts may be noticed in this connection. The 'mark' of initiation administered by John the Baptist, *e.g.*, was an entirely eschatological rite (Lk. 3:3ff.; note the reaction of the people to John's identity in v. 15); and in line with

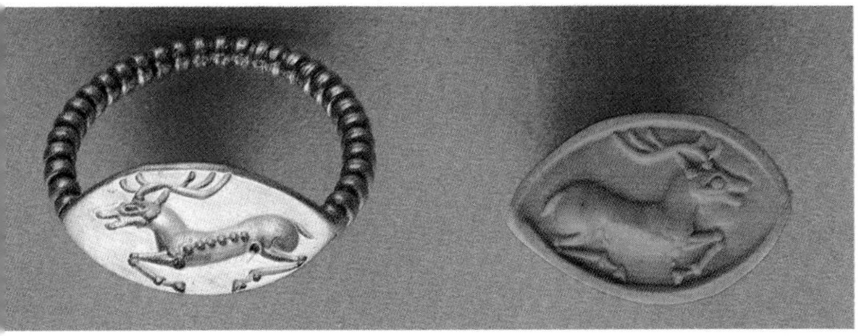

An engraved ring-seal in gold. Other signet-rings had a seal-stone inset. From Persia. 5th–4th cent. BC. (BM)

ıormative Jewish apocalyptic his ɔaptism signified an 'earmarking' 'or salvation in view of coming udgment comparable to certain ɔarts of the *Psalms of Solomon* *e.g.* 15:6f., 8; *cf.* 2 Esdras 6:5), and ɔf the NT itself (2 Tim. 2:19; and *:f.* the thought of 'sealing for secur-ty' already noticed in Rev. 7:2ff., *ɜtc.*; see White, *op. cit.* p. 88).

In the NT uses of the term 'seal' we have considered, the ideas of ɔwnership, authentication and security predominate. The three Pauline passages reviewed (Eph. 1:13; 4:30; 2 Cor. 1:22) together ndicate that the *arrabōn* of the Holy Spirit given to the believer, ncorporated *en Christō* by bap-ism through faith, is a 'token and ɔledge of final redemption' (Lampe, *op. cit.* p. 61). In this way the gift ɔf the Spirit is equivalent to 'put-ing on' Christ, sharing his *chrisma*, and becoming members of his ɔody, the true Israel of God (*ibid.*; *:f.* 1 Cor. 12:13). The gift of the Holy Spirit, in fact, confirms the covenant in which believers are sealed' as God's own.

BIBLIOGRAPHY. The standard English work on this subject (NT) s G. W. H. Lampe, *The Seal of the Spirit*, 1951 (esp. Part 1). For the history of the idea see also G. Dix, *Th* 51, 1948, pp. 7–12. For a fuller liscussion of the relevant texts see he major works on baptism in the NT, notably O. Cullmann, *Baptism n the New Testament*, 1950; W. F. Flemington, *The New Testa-ment Doctrine of Baptism*, 1953; P.-Ch. Marcel, *The Biblical Doctrine of Infant Baptism*, 1953; R. E. O. White, *The Biblical Doctrine of Initiation*, 1960; R. Schnackenburg, *Baptism in the Thought of St. Paul*, 1964; J. D. G. Dunn, *Baptism in the Holy Spirit*, 1970; R. Schippers, *NIDNTT* 3, pp. 497–501. S.S.S.

SEBA. 1. Son of Cush, classed under Ham (Gn. 10:7; 1 Ch. 1:9). **2.** Land and people in S Arabia, apparently closely related to the land and people of *Sheba; in fact *s^{e}ḇā'* (Seba) and *š^{e}ḇā'* (Sheba) are commonly held to be simply the Old Arab. and Heb. forms of the one name of a people, *i.e.* the well-known kingdom of Sheba. In a psalm (72:10) dedicated to Solomon, he is promised gifts from 'the kings of Sheba and (or: "yea") Seba'. In Isaiah's prophecies, Israel's ransom would take the wealth of Egypt, Ethiopia (Cush) and Seba (Is. 43:3), and the tall Sabaeans were to acknowledge Israel's God (Is. 45:14), first fulfilled in the wide spread of Judaism and first impact of Christianity there during the first 5 centuries AD. The close association of Seba/Sheba with Africa (Egypt and Cush) may just possibly reflect connections across the Red Sea between S Arabia and Africa from the 10th century BC onwards; for slender indications of this, see W. F. Albright, *BASOR* 128, 1952, p. 45 with nn. 26–27. Strabo (16. 4. 8–10) names a town Sabai and harbour Saba on the W or Red Sea coast of Arabia. K.A.K.

SECACAH (Heb. *s^{e}ḵāḵâh*). A settlement in NE Judah (Jos. 15:61); probably Khirbet es-Samrah, the largest (68 m by 40 m) of three fortified sites in el-Buqei 'a, controlling irrigation works which made it possible to settle in this area; first occupied in the 9th century BC, doubtless to secure the frontier (Cross and Milik, *BASOR* 142, 1956, pp. 5–17). J.P.U.L.

SECU (RSV), **SECHU** (AV). The Heb. name, perhaps meaning 'outlook', of a place near Ramah, which Saul visited when seeking David and Samuel (1 Sa. 19:22). A possible but uncertain identification is Khirbet Shuweikeh, 5 km N of el-Râm (biblical Ramah). Some MSS of LXX read the unknown town Sephi, which represents, according to some scholars, Heb. *š^{e}pî*, 'bare hill'; and the Pesh. similarly renders *sûpâ*, 'the end'; but other Gk. MSS and the Vulg. support the Massoretic Hebrew.

BIBLIOGRAPHY. F. M. Abel, *Géographie de la Palestine*, 2, 1938, p. 453; C. R. Conder and H. H. Kitchener, *The Survey of Western Palestine*, 3, 1883, p. 52. J.T.

SECUNDUS. A Thessalonian Christian accompanying Paul (Acts 20:4), probably as a delegate, with Aristarchus, of his church, to bring the collection for Jerusalem (*cf.* 1 Cor. 16:1ff.). Agreement on the precise significance of Acts 20:4 is incomplete, but Secundus seems included among those who awaited Paul at Troas. Zahn (*INT*, 1, 1909, p. 213) conjectured that Secundus was another name of the Macedonian Gaius (mentioned with Aristarchus in Acts 19:29), distinguished here from his companion *Gaius of Derbe.

The name is Latin, and attested in Thessalonian inscriptions. A.F.W.

SEED. The fertilized and mature ovule of a flowering plant which enables the species to perpetuate itself. Seed-bearing plants are of great antiquity (Gn. 1:11).

The progeny of the species *Homo sapiens* was also regarded as 'seed' (Gn. 3:15; 13:15). Thus the seed of Abraham constituted Isaac and his descendants (Gn. 21:12; 28:14). The relationship between God and his people provided a perpetual establishment for the seed of Israel (Ps. 89:4), who would be ruled over by a descendant of the house of David (Acts 2:30), interpreted by the early Christians in terms of Christ the Messiah (2 Tim. 2:8).

The idea of the seed as the unit of reproduction of plant life found expression in several of Christ's parables. The spiritual significance of the seed varied with the differing circumstances under which the parables were narrated. In that of the seeds and the sower (Mt. 13:3–23; Lk. 8:5–15), the seed was interpreted in Matthew as the 'word of the kingdom', while in Mark (4:3–20) and Luke it was the 'word of God'. In the parable of the seed and the tares (Mt. 13:24–30), the 'good seed' represented the children of the kingdom, while in the parable of the mustard seed (Mt. 13:31–32; Mk. 4:30–32) the seed represented the kingdom of heaven.

SEALSKIN
See Animals, Part 1.

SEA MONSTER
See Animals, Part 1.

SEA OF ARABAH
See Dead Sea, Part 1.

SEA OF GALILEE
See Chinnereth, Part 1.

SEA OF REEDS
See Red Sea, Part 3.

SEA OF TIBERIAS
See Chinnereth, Part 1.

SEBAM
See Sibmah, Part 3.

SEBAT
See Calendar, Part 1.

SECOND DEATH
See Death, Part 1.

SECRET
See Mystery, Part 2.

SECRET ARTS
See Magic, Part 2.

SECURITY
See Seal, Part 3.

SEDAN
See Trees (Cedar), Part 3.

SEDUCER
See Magic, Part 2.

In Mk. 4:26–29 the mystery surrounding the development of the divine kingdom was likened to that connected with the germination and growth of a seed.

The Pauline doctrine of the resurrection body (1 Cor. 15:35ff.) reflected the thought of Christ concerning the necessity of wheat-grains dying before they could produce abundantly (Jn. 12:24). The resurrection body of the believer will be significantly different in kind and degree from that laid to rest in the grave, bearing a relationship to it similar to that existing between an acorn and the mature oak. R.K.H.

SEED-TIME
See Calendar, Part 1.

SEETHING A KID
See Milk, Part 2.

SEINE
See Nets, Part 2.

SELEMIAH
See Shallum, Part 3.

SEIR. 1. The word *śē'îr* defines a mountain (Gn. 14:6; Ezk. 35:15), a land (Gn. 32:3; 36:21; Nu. 24:18) and a people (Ezk. 25:8) in the general area of old Edom. Esau went to live there (Gn. 32:3), and his descendants overcame the original inhabitants, the Horites (Gn. 14:6; 36:20; Dt. 2:12; Jos. 24:4). The Simeonites later destroyed some Amalekites who took refuge there (1 Ch. 4:42–43).

2. A landmark on the boundary of Judah (Jos. 15:10). J.A.T.

SELA. Etymologically the Heb. word *(has-)sela'* means '(the) rock' or 'cliff' and may be used of any rocky place. The name occurs several times in the Bible.

1. A fortress city of Moab, conquered by Amaziah king of Judah and renamed Joktheel (2 Ki. 14:7; 2 Ch. 25:12). Obadiah, in condemning Edom, refers to those who dwelt in the clefts of the rock (Sela, Ob. 3). Is. 42:11 may refer to the same place. For centuries the site has been identified with a rocky outcrop behind Petra, an identification which goes back to the LXX, Josephus and Eusebius. The massive rocky plateau Umm el-Biyara towers 300 m above the level of Petra (the Gk. translation of Sela), and 1,130 m above sea level. It was investigated by Nelson Glueck in 1933 and W. H. Morton in 1955. Part of an Iron Age Edomite settlement there was excavated by Mrs C. M. Bennett in 1960–5, and the houses found belong to the 7th century BC, but may have replaced older ones. The site was taken by the *Nabataeans *c.* 300 BC and they converted the great valley to the N, some 1,370 m long and 225–450 m across, quite enclosed by mountain walls, into the amazing rock-cut city of Petra—the 'rose-red city half as old as time'.

More recently it has been claimed that another Iron Age site, *es-Sela'*, 4 km NW of Bozra (Buseira) suits the biblical and post-biblical evidence better. This site was overlooked because of the impressive and continuous support for Petra. (See A. F. Rainey, *IDBS*, p. 100.)

2. An unidentified site, on the border of the Amorites in the time of the Judges (Jdg. 1:36), apparently within Judah. **3.** Isaiah, referring to the coming judgment of Moab, spoke of fugitive Moabites sending tribute to Judah from distant Sela (Is. 16:1). The site is unidentified.

BIBLIOGRAPHY. On Umm el-Biyara, see N. Glueck, *AASOR* 14, 1933–4, pp. 77f.; W. H. Morton, *BA* 19, 1956, pp. 26f.; *RB* 71, 1964, pp. 250–253; C. M. Bennett, *RB* 73, 1966, pp. 372–403. On the identity of Sela, see J. Starcky, *DBS*, 1966, cols. 886–900. J.A.T.

SELAH. An isolated word occurring 71 times in the Psalms and three times in Habakkuk (3:3, 9, 13, 'the minor Psalter'). Since all of these, except Pss. 41 and 81, name the kind of melody or psalmody in the title, it is generally agreed that Selah must be a musical or liturgical sign, though its precise import is not known. The following are the main suggestions:

1. A term in *music or a musical direction to the singers and/or orchestra to 'lift up', *i.e.* to sing or play *forte* or *crescendo*. Thus LXX has *diapsalma* in each instance, perhaps a musical rather than a doxological interlude.

2. A liturgical mark (*sālal*, 'to lift up'; *cf.* Akkad. *sullu*, 'prayer'), perhaps to lift up the voice or the hands in prayer. It may have come into use, possibly in the exilic period, in connection with psalms used in public worship to denote those places at which the priest should pronounce a benediction. Some take it to mean 'to lift up' the eyes, for the purpose of repeating the verse, thus the equivalent of '*da capo*'. Others would derive it from an Aramaic root *sl*, 'to bow', and so interpret it as directing the worshipper at this point to prostrate himself.

3. The Targ. Aquila and Vulg. render Selah by phrases implying an ejaculation 'for ever', and make it a cry of worship like 'Amen' and 'Hallelujah' (Ps. 46:3) at the close of the liturgy or at specified points within it (Ps. 3:2, 4, *etc.*). D.J.W.

SELEUCIA. 1. The former port of Antioch in Syria (1 Macc. 11:8) which lay 8 km N of the mouth of the Orontes river and 25 km away from Antioch. Seleucia (*Seleukeia*) was founded by Seleucus Nicator in 301 BC, 11 years after he had established the Seleucid kingdom. The

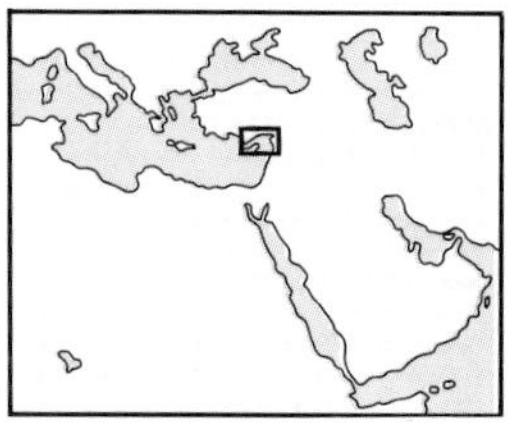

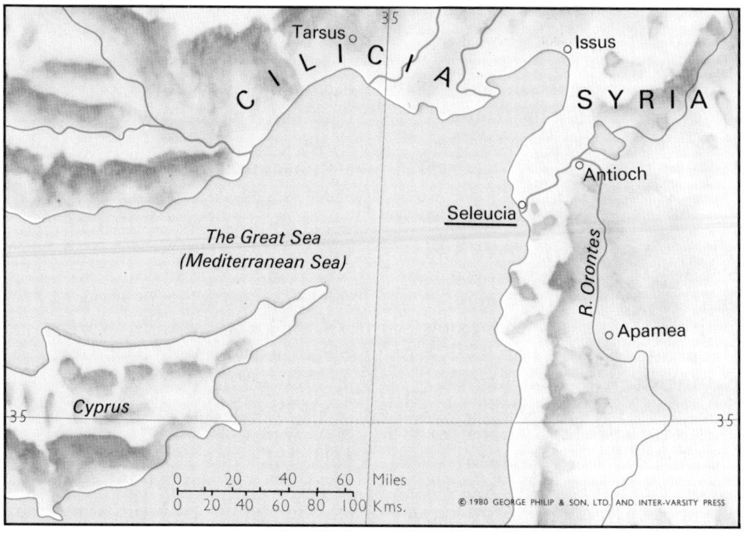

Seleucia was a seaport near the mouth of the R. Orontes in Syria.

Bottom right: Tetradrachm *with the head of Seleucus Nicator who founded the city of Seleucia in 301 BC. Diameter 30 mm.* (RG)

:ity lay at the foot of Mt Rhosus, o the N, and was itself in the NE :orner of a beautiful fertile plain still noted for its beauty. It was ortified on the S and W and surounded by walls, but, although egarded as impregnable, it was aken by the Ptolemy Euergetes 1 Macc. 11:8) in the Ptolemaic–eleucid wars and remained in the ands of the Ptolemies till 219 BC, when Antiochus the Great recaptured it. He greatly beautified it, and, although it was lost again for a short time to Ptolemy Philometor n 146 BC, Seleucia was soon reaken. The Romans under Pompey nade it a free city in 64 BC, and rom then on it flourished until it began to decay fairly early in the Christian era. It is known in the Bible only in Acts 13:4, as the port of embarkation of Paul and Barnabas after they had been commisioned by the church in Antioch. From Seleucia they set sail for Cyprus on their first missionary ourney. It is probably the port nferred in Acts 14:26; 15:30, 39, hough it is not named.

Seleucia today is an extensive uin, subject to archaeological investigation by a number of expediions since 1937. The city area can be traced, and evidence of buildngs, gates, walls, the amphitheatre, he inner harbour and the great water conduit built by Constantius n AD 338 in solid rock to carry off he mountain torrent from the city are all to be seen. The channel which connected the inner harbour o the sea has, however, long since been silted up.

2. A city in Gaulanitis SE of Lake Huleh captured by Alexander Yannai during his campaign in Transjordan in the 1st century AD. Josephus records that Agrippa II persuaded the people of the trongly fortified town to surrender o the Romans.

3. A city on the Tigris S of Baghdad founded by Seleucus I (312–280 BC) and occupied by Greeks and Syrians. It became a home for Jews in the 1st century of the Christian era. Animosity against them ed to the slaughter of 50,000; the survivors fled to Nisibis and other owns. This site has been partially excavated by the Italians. J.A.T.

SELEUCUS. One of Alexander's esser generals, who took control of he far E satrapies after his death and became a leading advocate of partition. After the battle of Ipsus in 301 BC he founded the port of *Seleucia (in Pieria) (Acts 13:4) to serve his new W capital of Antioch, and the Seleucid domains were later extended over most of Asia Minor. The dynasty, many of whose kings bore the names of Seleucus or Antiochus, ruled from Syria for *c.* 250 years, until suspended by the Romans. The vast and heterogeneous population called for a policy of active hellenization if their power was to be established. This and the fact that Palestine was the disputed frontier with the Ptolemies of Egypt caused trouble for the Jews. The Maccabaean revolt, with its legacy of petty kingdoms and principalities, and the religious sects of Jesus' time, was the result of the Seleucid attempt to secure Palestine.

BIBLIOGRAPHY. E. R. Bevan, *The House of Seleucus*, 1902; V. Tcherikover, *Hellenistic Civilization and the Jews*, 1959. E.A.J.

SELF-CONTROL (AV 'temperance') translates the Gk. *enkrateia*, which occurs in three NT verses. The corresponding adjective *enkratēs* and verb *enkrateuomai* are used both positively and negatively. Another word translated 'temperate', *nēphalios*, sometimes carries a restricted reference to drinking, such as is often read into the modern word 'temperance'.

The verb *enkrateuomai* is first used in the LXX in Gn. 43:31 to describe Joseph's control of his affectionate impulses towards his brothers. It refers also to the false self-restraint of Saul in 1 Sa. 13:12, and of Haman in Est. 5:10. According to Josephus, the Essenes exercised 'invariable sobriety' (*BJ* 2. 133), and some of them rejected marriage as incompatible with continence. The Greeks held temperance to be a cardinal virtue.

A very significant use of *enkrateia* is found in Acts 24:25. Since an adulteress sat beside Felix while Paul discussed self-control, its bearing on unchastity is easily apparent, and the verse compares naturally with 1 Cor. 7:9. This restricted reference to chastity often features in later literature. The Encratites enjoined complete abstinence from marriage; and some Christian clergy today may not marry. This distorted interpretation is called demonic in 1 Tim. 4:2–3, and the qualification 'self-controlled' (*enkratēs*) is applied to the married bishop in Tit. 1:8 (*cf.* 1 Pet. 3:2).

The association of *enkrateia* with righteousness in Acts 24:25 is parallel to other contexts where it is listed in catalogues of graces. In Gal. 5:22–23 it is the last of nine virtues, and seems to be opposed to drunkenness and carousing in the corresponding list of vices. In 2 Pet. 1:6 it forms a midway stage in a distinct moral progress of the believer, which commences in faith and culminates in love. (The form of the passage recalls expositions of Stoic moral *prokopē*.) The related words *nēphalios* and *sōphrōn* (sober-minded) appear in a list of virtues demanded of older Christian men in Tit. 2:2, 12.

The precise reference of *nēphalios*, 'temperate', is to drunkenness, and the word is actually opposed to 'drunkard' in 1 Tim. 3:2–3. It can broaden out, however, to include other forms of self-control, as in Tit. 2:2 and 1 Tim. 3:11. This extended application should be recollected when rendering the verb *nēphō*, which in RSV is translated 'to be sober', but which usually means 'to be vigilant' in contexts like 1 Thes. 5:6 and 1 Pet. 1:13; 4:7; 5:8. In 1 Cor. 9:25 the widest possible reference is given to *enkrateuomai* when the Christian athlete is said to exercise self-control in all things.

In the NT self-control is essentially a 'fruit of the Spirit' (Gal. 5:22–23). A deliberate antithesis between spiritual life and carnal drunkenness is introduced into several passages describing prophetic inspiration (*e.g.* Acts 2:15–17 and Eph. 5:18). Believers who 'drink of the Spirit' (1 Cor. 12:13) are thought by the world to be 'drunk'; and indeed so they are, not with wine, but with zeal for the Christian warfare. This passion to be good soldiers of Christ expresses itself not in excess but in sober discipline; it is the true imitation of a Master, whose life, as Bernard says, was the 'mirror of temperance'.

BIBLIOGRAPHY. R. L. Ottley in *ERE* (*s.v.* 'Temperance'); Arndt; H. Rashdall, *Theory of Good and Evil*, 1907; H. Baltensweiler, *NIDNTT* 1, pp. 494–497.

D.H.T.

SENAAH. In the list of exiles who returned with Zerubbabel there are 3,630 (Ezr. 2:35) or 3,930 (Ne. 7:38) belonging to the town of Senaah. In Ne. 3:3 the name of the town occurs again with the definite article. Since in both passages

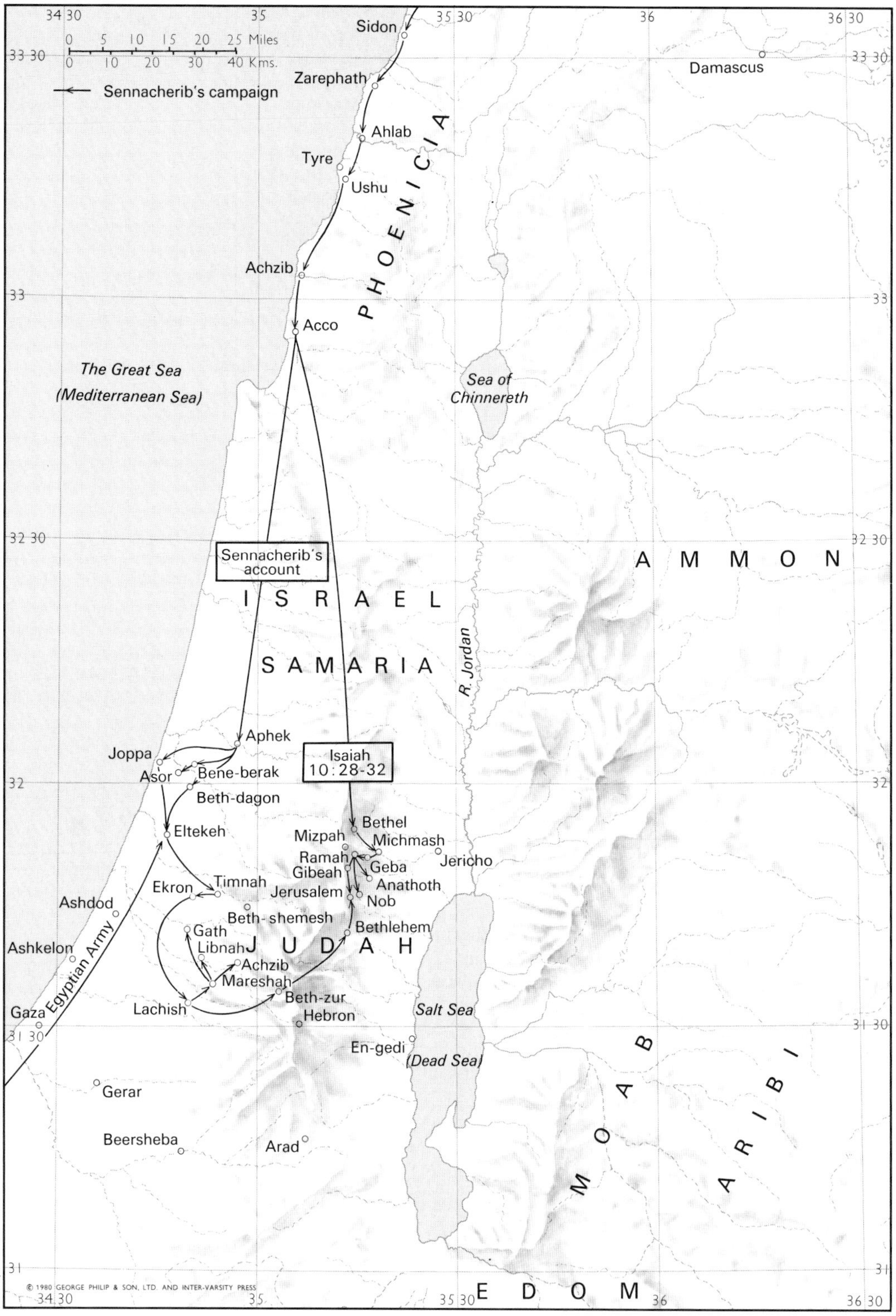

The campaign of Sennacherib in relation to the territory of Hezekiah in 701 BC.

Jericho is mentioned in close proximity, Senaah may have been near Jericho. J.S.W.

SENATE, SENATOR. 1. The AV translation in Ps. 105:22 (Heb. *z^e qēnîm*; LXX *presbyteroi*), where RSV has *'elders'. **2.** Gk. *gerousia*, 'assembly of elders', Acts 5:21 (*SANHEDRIN). J.D.D.

SENEH ('pointed rock') and **BOZEZ** ('slippery'?) were two rocks between which Jonathan and his armour-bearer entered the garrison of the Philistines (1 Sa. 14:4ff.). (*MICHMASH.) No precise identification of the location of these two rocky crags has been made, but see *GTT*, p. 317. J.D.D.

SENIR. According to Dt. 3:9, the Amorite name for Mt Hermon (*ś^e nîr*; AV Shenir); but in Ct. 4:8 and 1 Ch. 5:23, apparently one of the peaks in the ridge, the name being loosely applied to the whole. Manasseh expanded N to Senir (1 Ch. 5:23), and the slopes supplied fir (*TREES) for Tyrian ships, Lebanon yielding cedars (Ezk. 27:5). Shalmaneser III names Senir (*sa-ni-ru*) as a stronghold of Hazael (*ANET*, p. 280). A.R.M.

SENNACHERIB. Sennacherib (Heb. *sanḥērîb* [but possibly pronounced *śnḥrîb* as in Aram. papyri; *JSS* 21, 1976, p. 9]; Assyr. *Sin-aḫḫē-eriba*, 'Sin [moon-god] has increased the brothers') ruled Assyria 705–681 BC. When his father, whom he had served as governor of the N frontier, was assassinated, Sennacherib first marched to Babylonia, where Marduk-apla-iddina II (*MERODACH-BALADAN) was in revolt. He had ousted a local nominee Marduk-zakir-šum in 703 BC and was rallying support against Assyria. It was probably about this time that Merodach-baladan sent envoys to Hezekiah of Judah (2 Ki. 20:12–19; Is. 39). Late in 702 BC Sennacherib defeated the Chaldean and his Elamite and Arab allies in battles at Cutha and Kish. He was then welcomed in Babylon, where he set Bel-ibni on the throne. The Assyrians ravaged Bît-Yakin and returned to Nineveh with many prisoners, Merodach-baladan himself having escaped to Elam.

Sennacherib had little difficulty in controlling his N frontier, an area well known to him while crown prince. After a series of raids against the hill peoples in the E he moved against the W, where an anti-Assyrian coalition, backed by Egypt, was gaining power. The leader, Hezekiah of Judah, had seized Padi, the pro-Assyrian ruler of Ekron (2 Ki. 18:8), strengthened the fortifications and improved the water supplies at Jerusalem by building the *Siloam tunnel (2 Ki. 20:20), and called for help from Egypt (Is. 30:1–4).

Sennacherib's third campaign in Hezekiah's 14th year (701 BC) was directed against this coalition. He first marched down the Phoenician coast, capturing Great and Little Sidon, Zarephath, Mahalliba (*AHLAB), Ushu, Akzib and Acco, but not attempting to lay siege to Tyre. He replaced Luli (Elulaeus),

King Sennacherib of Assyria in his royal chariot, wearing his crown. Relief from the palace at Nineveh. c. 690 BC. (BM)

ing of Sidon, who fled and died in xile, by Ethba'al (Tuba'al). The ings of Sidon, Arvad, Byblos, Beth-ammon, Moab and Edom ubmitted, but Ashkelon refused nd, with its neighbouring towns, ncluding Beth-Dagon and Joppa, vas despoiled. Sennacherib claims o have marched to Eltekeh, where e defeated an Egyptian army. He hen slew the nobles of Ekron for anding over Padi to Hezekiah, nd sent detachments to destroy orty-six walled towns and many illages in Judah, from which he ook 200,150 people and much poil. He himself took part in the iege and capture of *Lachish, nd is depicted on his palace reliefs eviewing the spoil. From here he ent officers to demand the surren-er of Jerusalem (2 Ch. 32:9).

Sennacherib's own account of his campaign claims tribute from Iezekiah (Annals) and describes ow he besieged 'Hezekiah the Jew . . I shut him up like a caged bird vithin his royal capital, Jerusalem. put watch-posts closely round the ity and turned back to his fate nyone who came out of the city ate' (Taylor Prism, BM). Heze-iah paid the Assyrians tribute 2 Ki. 18:13–16; Is. 36:1f.) which vas later sent to Nineveh (Taylor Prism, dated 691 BC) and freed Padi, to whom some of the former udaean territories were now given.

Sennacherib's account makes no mention of any conclusion of the siege (*cf.* 2 Ki. 19:32–34) or of the defeat of the Assyrian army by the hand of the Lord, perhaps by a plague (v. 35) described by Herodotus (2. 141) as 'a multitude of field mice which by night devoured all the quivers and bows of the enemy, and all the straps by which they held their shields . . . next morning they commenced their fight and great numbers fell as they had no arms with which to defend themselves'.

The majority of scholars hold that the mention of the approach of the Egyptian forces under *Tirhakah (2 Ki. 19:9; Is. 37:9) is an anachronism (but see K. A. Kitchen, *Third Intermediate Period in Egypt*, 1972). Moreover, they consider 2 Ki. 19:37 implies that the death of Sennacherib occurred soon after his return to Nineveh. They therefore postulate a second, and unsuccessful, Assyrian campaign against Jerusalem, perhaps following the attack on the Arabs 689–686 BC. Neither the extant Assyrian annals nor Babylonian chronicles mention such a campaign, and vv. 36f. do not necessarily state the length of time between Sennacherib's return from Palestine and his death in 681 BC, and this must have been some years on any interpretation. Thus the theory of a single campaign in 701 BC can still reasonably be held.

In 700 BC the Assyrians once more marched to Babylonia, where Bel-ibni had rebelled. Sennacherib placed his own son, Aššur-nadin-šum, on the throne, and he held sway until captured by the Elamites. In the series of campaigns which followed, Sennacherib fought the Elamites, and in 694 mounted a naval expedition across the Persian Gulf directed against those who had harboured Merodach-baladan. Erech was captured and, finally, Babylon sacked in 689 BC. On other frontiers Sennacherib invaded Cilicia and captured Tarsus, as well as raiding the Arabs S and E of Damascus.

At home Sennacherib was aided by his energetic W Semitic wife, Naqi'a-Zakutu, in the reconstruction of Nineveh, where he built a 'palace without a rival', an armoury, new city walls and gates. By providing a new source of water-supply from the river Gomel (Bavian), led by an aqueduct (Jerwan) down to a dam (Ajeila) E of the metropolis, he was able to irrigate parks and large tracts of land as well as to improve the natural defences of Nineveh formed by the rivers Tigris and Khosr.

He also built extensively at Assur and Kakzi and introduced many technological advances.

Sennacherib was assassinated by his sons while worshipping in the temple of Nisroch (2 Ki. 19:37). The flight of the sons, possibly *Adrammelech and *Sharezer, may be reflected in an account of the disturbances following his death in December 681 BC given by his younger son Esarhaddon, who had been elected crown prince in 687 BC, and now succeeded to the throne (v. 37). There is little support for the theory that Esarhaddon was the unnamed 'son' mentioned as assassin by the Babylonian Chronicle, or that the death took place in Babylon.

BIBLIOGRAPHY. D. D. Luckenbill, *The Annals of Sennacherib*, 1924; D. J. Wiseman in *DOTT*, pp. 64–73.

D.J.W.

SEPARATION
See Holiness, Part 2.

SEPHAR. The name of a 'mountain of the east' (*har haq-qeḏem*), mentioned in the Table of *Nations in defining the boundary of the territory of the sons of Joktan (Gn. 10:30). Judging from the names of other sons of Joktan, a mountain or promontory in S Arabia seems likely, and the coastal town of Ẓafār in the E Hadramaut has

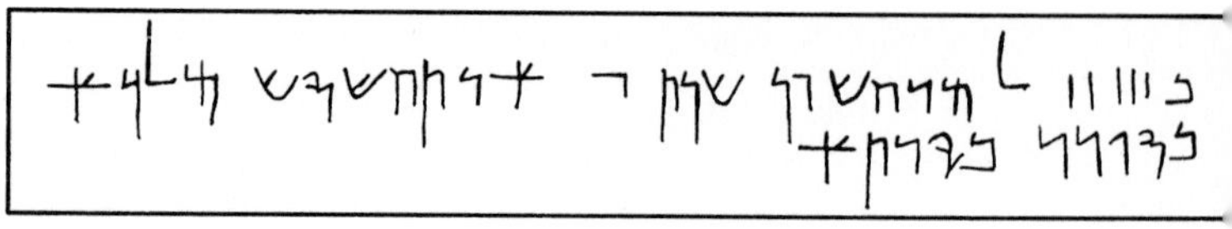

The opening words of an Aramaic tombstone from Sardis, containing the place-name in its ancient form sfrd *(Sepharad). Dated by Artaxerxes of Persia, perhaps Artaxerxes II or III, i.e. 394 or 348* BC. *The text reads: 'On the fifth of (the month) Marcheswan, tenth year of Artaxerxes, in the citadel Sardis . . .'* (ARM)

been suggested. In view, however, of the lack of precision in the Bible statement, and the discrepancy in the sibilants, there can be no certainty.

See J. A. Montgomery, *Arabia and the Bible*, 1934, p. 41. T.C.M.

SEPHARAD. The place in which captives from Jerusalem were exiled (Ob. 20). The location is as yet unidentified. Of many conjectures, the most plausible identifies the place as Sardis, capital of Lydia in Asia Minor. Known in Persian times as Sfard, it is written in Aramaic with the same consonants as in Obadiah. It may be the Saparda named in the Assyrian Annals of Sargon and Esarhaddon as a country allied to the Medes. The Targum of Jonathan interpreted it as Spain, hence the term Sephardim for Spanish Jews. A location in Anatolia is favoured by the Vulgate (*in Bosphoro*). See *JNES* 22, 1963, pp. 128–132. D.J.W.

SEPTUAGINT
See Texts and versions, Part 3.

SEPULCHRE
See Burial and mourning, Part 1.

SEPHARVAIM. A city captured by the Assyrians (2 Ki. 17:24, 31; 18:34; 19:13; Is. 36:19; 37:13). The context implies that it lies in Syria or adjacent territory and this is supported by the name of its deities (*ADRAMMELECH; *ANAMMELECH). The place is unidentified, though Halévy's suggestion that it is the same as the later Sibraim near Damascus (Ezk. 47:16) is possible. It cannot be the same as the Šab/mara'in of the Babylonian Chronicle, as this is Samaria. The usual interpretation of Sepharvaim as the twin cities of Sippar (of Šamaš and Anunitum) in Babylonia is unsupportable (though Sippar-amnanim is mentioned in texts), as Sippar had no independent king (*cf.* 2 Ki. 19:13). D.J.W.

SEPULCHRE OF THE KINGS, SEPULCHRE OF DAVID. The Bible indicates that the kings of Israel were buried in a special area near Jerusalem. Expressions like 'tombs of the kings of Israel' (2 Ch. 28:27), 'sepulchres of David' (Ne. 3:16), 'tombs of the sons of David' (2 Ch. 32:33), refer specifically to the royal tombs of the Judaean kings of David's line in the city of David. These tombs were close to the King's Garden and the pool of Shelah (1 Ki. 2:10; 2 Ch. 21:20; Ne. 3:15–16). Thus when Nehemiah was building the wall of Jerusalem

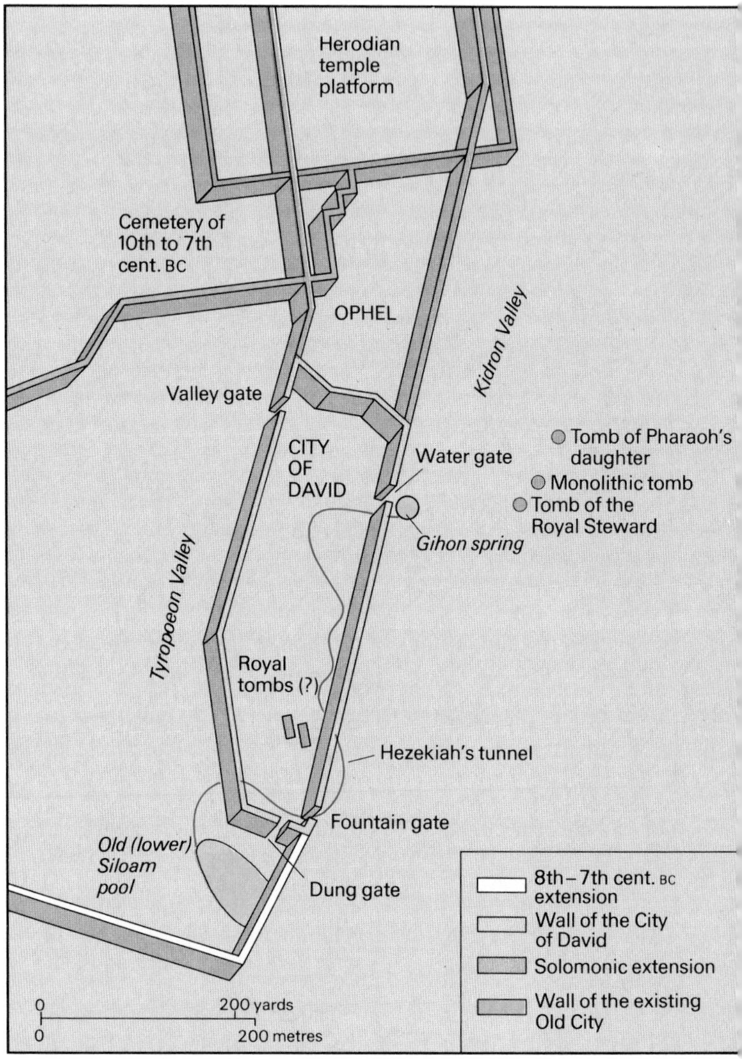

Plan showing the probable location of the 'Sepulchres of the Kings' within the city of David, and the positions of other tombs dating from Solomon to the fall of Judah.

one of his parties worked 'over against the sepulchres of David', not far from the 'pool of Shelah (Shiloah)' (Ne. 3:15–16).

Most of the kings from David to Hezekiah were buried in the city of David, though some kings had their own private sepulchres, *e.g.* Asa (2 Ch. 16:14), and possibly Hezekiah (2 Ch. 32:33), Manasseh (2 Ki. 21:18), Amon (2 Ki. 21:26) and Josiah (2 Ki. 23:30; 2 Ch. 35:24). Several kings died outside the bounds of Palestine: Jehoahaz in Egypt, Jehoiachin and Zedekiah in Babylon. Possibly Jehoiakim was not buried at all (Je. 22:19), and Jehoram, Joash, Uzziah and Ahaz were not admitted to the royal sepulchre (2 Ch. 21:20; 24:25; 26:23; 28:27).

The location of the tombs in the city of David was still referred to after the Exile. Josephus reported that they were plundered by the Hasmonean king John Hyrcanus and also by Herod (*Ant.* 13. 249; 16. 179).

In the NT the sepulchre of David was still remembered (Acts 2:29) and Josephus (*BJ*, 5. 147) spoke of the third wall passing by the sepulchred caverns of the kings. An inscribed tablet found by E. Sukenik states that the bones of King Uzziah had been removed to the top of the Mount of Olives.

The exact site of the tombs of the kings is not known today. Monuments in the Kedron Valley are late, both architecture and epigraphy pointing to the time of Herod the Great.

The term 'City of David' in the

vicinity of which these tombs lay does not denote the entire city of Jerusalem but merely the citadel of the stronghold of Zion. Evidence points to the spur which juts S between the Tyropoean and Kedron valleys, later known as Ophel, as the location of the City of David. It overlooks the gardens and pools of Siloam. In this general area long horizontal tunnels have been found in the rock and these may have been the burial-place of the kings of David's line. But the site was desecrated and destroyed, possibly at the time of the Bar Kokhba revolt (AD 135), and thereafter the exact location forgotten.

Various other sites have been proposed over the centuries. A popular tradition reaching back for 1,000 years places the tomb of David on the W hill at the place now called Mt Zion. The tradition was accepted by Jewish, Muslim and Christian traditions, and Benjamin of Tudela (*c.* AD 1173) reported the miraculous discovery of David's Tomb on Mt Zion during the repair of a church on the site. Pilgrimages are still made to the site, but there is little to commend its authenticity.

The so-called Tombs of the Kings of Judah some distance to the N of the modern wall mark the tomb of Helen, queen of Adiabene, a district in Upper Mesopotamia referred to by Josephus (*Ant.* 20. 17, 35).

BIBLIOGRAPHY. S. Krauss, 'The Sepulchres of the Davidic Dynasty', *PEQ* 1947, pp. 102–112; S. Yeivin, 'The Sepulchres of the Kings of the House of David', *JNES* 7, 1948, pp. 30–45.

J.A.T.

SERAIAH (Heb. *śᵉrāyâ, śᵉrāyāhû*, 'Yahweh has prevailed'). **1.** David's scribe (2 Sa. 8:17, RSV 'secretary'), called also 'Sheva' (2 Sa. 20:25), 'Shisha' (1 Ki. 4:3), and *'Shavsha' (1 Ch. 18:16).

2. Son of Azariah and a chief priest in the time of Zedekiah. He was put to death by the king of Babylon at Riblah (2 Ki. 25:18 = Je. 52:24). **3.** A son of Tanhumeth the Netophathite, and a captain who was among those whom Gedaliah, governor of Judaea, advised to submit to the Chaldeans (2 Ki. 25:23 = Je. 40:8). **4.** A son of Kenaz (1 Ch. 4:13–14). **5.** A Simeonite, son of Asiel (1 Ch. 4:35). **6.** A priest who returned with Zerubbabel to Jerusalem (Ezr. 2:2; Ne. 12:1, 12). **7.** One who sealed the covenant (Ne. 10:2), perhaps the same as **6** above. **8.** A priest, son of Hilkiah (Ne. 11:11) and 'ruler of the house of God' in post-exilic Jerusalem. **9.** One of the officers of King Jehoiakim, ordered by him to arrest Baruch and Jeremiah (Je. 36:26). **10.** A prince of Judah who accompanied King Zedekiah to Babylon in the 4th year of his reign. Seraiah carried Jeremiah's prophecy against Babylon (Je. 51:59, 61). Some would associate him with **3** above.

J.D.D.

SERAPHIM. The only mention of these celestial beings in Scripture is in the early vision of Isaiah (Is. 6). The seraphim (incorrectly rendered in AV as 'seraphims') were associated with *cherubim and ophanim in the task of guarding the divine throne. The heavenly beings seen by Isaiah were human in form, but had six wings, a pair to shield their faces, another to conceal their feet and a third for flight. These seraphim were stationed above the throne of God, and appear to have led in divine worship. One chanted a refrain which Isaiah recorded: 'Holy, holy, holy is the Lord of hosts; the whole earth is full of his glory.'

So vigorous was this act of worship that the thresholds of the divine Temple shook, and the holy place was filled with smoke. The prophet lay in self-abasement before God and confessed his iniquity. Then one of the seraphim flew to him with a burning coal taken from the altar, and in an act of purification announced to Isaiah that his sin had been forgiven and his guilt removed.

It would appear that for Isaiah the seraphim were angelic beings responsible for certain functions of guardianship and worship. How-, ever, they appear to have been distinct moral creatures, not just projections of the imagination or personifications of animals. Their moral qualities were employed exclusively in the service of God, and their position was such that they were privileged to exercise an atoning ministry while at the same time extolling the ethical and moral character of God.

The origin and meaning of the Heb. term are uncertain. The *śārāp̄* of Nu. 21:6; Dt. 8:15 was a venomous serpent which bit the Israelites in the desert, while Is. 14:29; 30:6 referred to a reptile popular in folklore (see D. J. Wiseman, *TynB* 23, 1972, pp. 108–110). If the noun be derived from Heb. *śārap̄* 'to burn up', the seraphim may be agents of purification by fire, as Is. 6. indicates. A meaning 'bright, shining ones' cannot be taken from *śārap̄*.

A sculpture found at Tell Halaf (*GOZAN) depicts a creature with a human body, two wings at the shoulders and four below the waist (*ANEP*, no. 655). It is dated about 800 BC. For other ancient representations, see *CHERUBIM.

BIBLIOGRAPHY. J. Strachan in *HDB*; H. S. Nash in *SHERK* (*s.v.* 'angel'); J. de Savignac, *VT* 22, 1972, pp. 320–325; H. Heppe, *Reformed Dogmatics*, E.T. 1950, pp. 210ff.

R.K.H.
A.R.M.

SERMON ON THE MOUNT. The Sermon on the Mount is the title commonly given to the teachings of Jesus recorded in Mt. 5–7. Whether the name can be properly used for the somewhat parallel portion in Luke (6:20–49) depends upon one's interpretation of the literary relationship between the two. The latter is often called the Sermon on the Plain because it is said to have been delivered on 'a level place' (Lk. 6:17) rather than 'on the mountain' (Mt. 5:1). But both expressions probably denote the same place approached from two different directions (see W. M. Christie, *Palestine Calling*, 1939, pp. 35f.).

Canon Liddon, in his Bampton Lectures, refers to the Sermon as 'that original draught of essential Christianity'. If this be interpreted to mean that the Sermon on the Mount is Christianity's message to the pagan world, we must counter with the reminder that it is manifestly *didachē* (teaching), not *kerygma* (proclamation). By no stretch of the imagination can it be considered 'good news' to one depending upon fulfilment of its demands for entrance into the kingdom. (Imagine a man outside of Christ, without the empowering aid of the Holy Spirit, trying to exceed the righteousness of the scribes and Pharisees.) It is rather a character sketch of those who have already entered the kingdom and a description of the quality of ethical life which is now expected of them. In this sense, it is true, it is 'essential Christianity'.

I. Composition

In times past it was taken for

SERED
See Zebulun, Part 3.

SERGIUS PAULUS
See Paulus, Sergius, Part 3.

SERJEANTS
See Police, Part 3.

granted that the Sermon on the Mount was a single discourse delivered by Jesus on a specific occasion. Certainly this is what appears to be the case as it is reported in Matthew. The disciples sat down (v. 1), Jesus opened his mouth and taught them (v. 2), and when it was over the crowds were astonished at his teaching (7:28). However, most scholars are of the opinion that the Sermon is really a compilation of sayings of the Lord—'a kind of epitome of all the sermons that Jesus ever preached' (W. Barclay, *The Gospel of Matthew*, 1, p. 79). It is argued that: (1) There is far too much concentrated material here for one sermon. The disciples, not noted for acute spiritual perception, could never have assimilated such a wealth of ethical teaching. (2) The wide range of topics (description of kingdom blessedness, counsel on divorce, admonition concerning anxiety) is inconsistent with the unity of a single discourse. (3) The abruptness with which certain sections emerge in the Sermon (*e.g.* the teaching on prayer in Mt. 6:1–11) is very noticeable. (4) Thirty-four verses occur in other, and often more suitable, contexts throughout Luke (*e.g.* the Lord's Prayer in Luke is introduced by a request from his disciples that he teach them to pray, Lk. 11:1; the saying about the narrow gate comes in response to the question, 'Will those who are saved be few?' Lk. 13:23), and it is more likely that Matthew transposed sayings of Jesus into the Sermon than that Luke found them there and then scattered them throughout his Gospel. (5) It is characteristic of Matthew to gather together teaching material under certain headings and insert them into the narrative of Jesus' life (*cf.* B. W. Bacon, *Studies in Matthew*, 1930, pp. 269–325), and that the Sermon on the Mount is therefore simply the first of these didactic sections. (Others deal with the themes of discipleship (9:35–10:42), the kingdom of heaven (13), true greatness (18) and the end of the age (24–25).)

These considerations, however, do not force one to view the entire Sermon as an arbitrary composition. The historical setting in Mt. 4:23–5:1 leads us to expect an important discourse delivered on a specific occasion. Within the Sermon itself are various sequences which appear to be 'sermonettes' of Jesus and not topical collections of separate *logia*. A comparison with Luke's Sermon shows enough points of similarity (both begin with Beatitudes, close with the parable of the builders, and the intervening Lucan material—on loving one's enemies (6:27–36) and judging (6:37–42)—follows in the same sequence in Matthew) to suggest that behind both accounts there was a common source. Before either Evangelist wrote there was in all probability a primitive framework which corresponded to an actual discourse delivered on a definite occasion. Such questions as whether the Sermon as it occurs in Matthew is closer to the original than the Lucan version, or whether Matthew followed a framework supplied by an earlier source, are still matters of scholarly debate. For our purpose it is enough to conclude that Matthew took a primitive sermon source and expanded it for his particular purpose by the introduction of relevant material.

II. Language of the Sermon

In the last generation Aramaic scholarship has taught us much about 'The Poetry of Our Lord'—to borrow the title of C. F. Burney's book (1925). Even in translation we can recognize the various types of parallelism, which are the distinguishing feature of Semitic poetry. Mt. 7:6, for example, is a fine illustration of 'synonymous' parallelism:

> 'Do not give dogs what is holy;
> and do not throw your pearls
> before swine.'

It appears that the Lord's Prayer is a poem of two stanzas, each of which has three lines of four beats apiece (*cf.* Burney, pp. 112f.). The practical value of recognizing poetry where it occurs is that we are not so likely to interpret the text with such an inflexible literalism as we might employ in interpreting prose. How tragic if someone should (and history records that some have done so) literally 'pluck out his eye' or 'cut off his hand' in an attempt to do away with the passion of lust. A. M. Hunter notes that 'proverbs indeed are principles stated in extremes'. We must always avoid interpreting paradox with a crude literalism, but rather seek the principle that underlies the proverb (*Design for Life*, pp. 19–20).

In this connection let us consider the quality of absoluteness in Jesus' moral imperatives. Verses like Mt. 5:48, 'You, therefore, must be perfect, as your heavenly Father is perfect', have long troubled men. Part of the answer lies in the fact that these are not 'new laws' but broad principles set forth in terms of action. They fall into the category of prophetic injunction, which was always deeper and demanded more than the mere letter of the law. And they were ethics of the new age, designed for those who partook of a new power (*cf.* A. N. Wilder, 'The Sermon on the Mount', *IB*, 7, 1951, p. 163).

III. Circumstances

Both Matthew and Luke place the Sermon in the first year of Jesus' public ministry; Matthew a little earlier than Luke, who locates it immediately after the choosing of the Twelve and implies that it should be understood as somewhat of an 'ordination sermon'. In either case, it came in that period before the religious teachers could muster their opposition, and yet late enough for Jesus' fame to have spread through the land. The first months of his Galilean ministry were spent in synagogue preaching, but soon the enthusiasm of his crowds necessitated some sort of outdoor preaching. A corresponding change can be seen in the character of his message. The early proclamation, 'Repent: for the kingdom of heaven is at hand' (Mt. 4:17), has given way to exposition on the nature of the kingdom for those who seriously desired to learn.

Since the Sermon falls within the Galilean ministry of Jesus, it is natural to assume that the scene of the Sermon would be one of the foothills which surrounded the N plain. As Jesus entered Capernaum soon after (Mt. 8:5), it was perhaps located in that general area. A Latin tradition, dating from the 13th century, names a two-peaked hill, Karn Hattin, which lies a bit farther to the S, but only guides and tourists seem to take this identification with any degree of seriousness.

The Sermon is addressed primarily to disciples. This is the apparent meaning of both Mt. 5:1–2 and Lk. 6:20. Luke's use of the second person in the Beatitudes, in sayings like 'You are the salt of the earth' (Mt. 5:13), and the exalted ethic of the Sermon as a whole, can only mean that it was designed for those who had deserted paganism for life in the kingdom. Yet at the close of each account (Mt. 7:28–29; Lk. 7:1

ve learn of the presence of others. The solution seems to be that the rowd was there and heard Jesus as ie taught, but that the discourse tself was directed primarily to the ircle of disciples. Occasional utterinces, such as the 'woes' of Lk. 5:24–26, unless rhetorical devices, seem to be 'asides' to some who night be listening in and who ieeded such admonition.

V. Analysis

Regardless of whether one sees the Sermon as the summary of an ictual discourse or as a mosaic of ethical sayings arranged by Mathew, there is little doubt that Mt. 5–7 has a real unity marked by the ogical development of a basic heme. This theme is presented in he Beatitudes and can be expressed is 'the quality and conduct of life n the kingdom'. The following is a lescriptive analysis of the content of the Sermon.

. The blessedness of those in the ingdom, 5:3–16

(i) The Beatitudes (5:3–10).

(ii) An expansion of the final Beatitude and a digression to show he role of the disciple in an unbelieving world (5:11–16).

. The relationship of the message of Jesus to the old order, 5:17–48

(i) The thesis stated (5:17). Jesus' message 'fulfils' the law by penetrating behind the letter and clarifying its underlying principle, thus bringing it to its ideal completion.

(ii) The thesis enlarged (5:18–20).

(iii) The thesis illustrated (5:21–48).

1. In the command not to kill, anger is the culpable element (5:21–26).

2. Adultery is the fruit of an evil heart nourished on impure desire (5:27–32).

3. Kingdom righteousness demands an honesty so transparent that oaths are unnecessary (5:33–37).

4. *Lex talionis* must give way to a spirit of non-retaliation (5:38–42).

5. Love is universal in application (5:43–48).

. Practical instructions for kingdom onduct, 6:1–7:12

(i) Guard against false piety (6:1–8).

1. In almsgiving (6:1–4).

2. In prayer (6:5–15).

3. In fasting (6:16–18).

(ii) Dispel anxiety with simple rust (6:19–34).

(iii) Live in love (7:1–12).

d. Challenge to dedicated living, 7:13–29

(i) The way is narrow (7:13–14).

(ii) A good tree bears good fruit (7:15–20).

(iii) The kingdom is for those who hear and *do* (7:21–27).

V. Interpretation

The Sermon on the Mount has had a long and varied history of interpretation. For Augustine, who wrote a treatise on the Sermon while still a bishop at Hippo (AD 393–396), it was the 'perfect rule or pattern of Christian life'—a new law in contrast with the old. Monastic orders interpreted it as a 'counsel of perfection' designed not for the populace but for the chosen few. The Reformers held it to be the 'uncompromising expression of divine righteousness directed towards all'. Tolstoy, the Russian novelist and (in later life) social reformer, resolved it into five commandments (suppression of all anger, chastity, no oaths, non-resistance, unreserved love of enemies), which if literally obeyed would do away with the existing evils and usher in a Utopian kingdom. Weiss and Schweitzer held that the demands were too radical for all times, and thus declared them 'interim ethics' for the early Christians, who believed that the end of all things was at hand. Still others, making great allowance for figurative language, understood the Sermon as the expression of a noble way of thinking—teaching which dealt with what man should *be* rather than with what he should *do*.

Thus the 20th-century interpreter is presented with a bewildering number of 'keys' with which to unlock the essential meaning of the Sermon on the Mount. With Kittel he can take the demands as purposely exaggerated so as to drive man to a sense of failure (and hence to repent and believe), or with Windisch he can differentiate between historical and theological exegesis and defend the practicability of the demands. With Dibelius he can interpret the great moral imperatives as the absolute ethic of the inbreaking kingdom, or with the Dispensationalists he can relegate the entire sermon to a future millennial reign of Christ.

How, then, shall we interpret the Sermon? The following will at least give us our guide-lines: *a.* Although couched in poetry and symbol, the Sermon still demands a quality of ethical conduct which is breathtaking in its dimensions. *b.* Jesus is not laying down a new code of legal regulations but stating great ethical principles and how they affect the lives of those within the kingdom. 'It would be a great point gained if people would only consider that it was a Sermon, and was *preached*, not an *act* which was passed' (J. Denney). *c.* The Sermon is not a programme for the direct improvement of the world, but is directed to those who have denied the world in order to enter the kingdom. *d.* It is neither an impractical ideal nor a fully attainable possibility. In the words of S. M. Gilmour, it is 'the ethic of that transcendental order which broke into history in Jesus Christ, has built itself into history in the church, but whose full realization lies beyond history when God will be "all in all" ' (*Journal of Religion* 21, 1941, p. 263).

BIBLIOGRAPHY. In addition to the extensive literature cited in other Bible dictionaries (see, *e.g.*, Votaw's article in *HDB*, extra vol., pp. 1–45), see H. K. McArthur, *Understanding the Sermon on the Mount*, 1960; J. W. Bowman and R. W. Tapp, *The Gospel from the Mount*, 1957; W. D. Davies, *The Setting of the Sermon on the Mount*, 1964; M. Dibelius, *The Sermon on the Mount*, 1940; A. M. Hunter, *Design for Life*,1953; D. M. Lloyd-Jones, *Studies in the Sermon on the Mount*², 1976; A. N. Wilder's article in *IB*, 7, 1951, pp. 155–164; H. Windisch, *The Meaning of the Sermon on the Mount*, 1951 (translation of revised edition of *Der Sinn der Bergpredigt*, 1929); D. Bonhoeffer, *The Cost of Discipleship*, 1948; C. F. H. Henry, *Christian Personal Ethics*, 1957, pp. 278–326; J. Jeremias, *Die Bergpredigt*⁷, 1970; J. R. W. Stott, *Christian Counter-Culture*, 1978.

R.H.M.

SERPENT.

I. General.

Serpents or snakes (*ANIMALS) are reptiles that have head, body and tail but no limbs, and move over the ground on their belly, so that with their flickering tongue they are often described as licking or eating the dust (Gn. 3:14; *cf.* Is. 65:25; Mi. 7:17; and implicitly, Pr. 30:19). In simile, compare the nations creeping like snakes, to acknowledge

Egyptian kings were protected by a goddess whose emblem, the cobra, they wore on their crowns. Shown here are Akhenaton and Nefertiti engraved on a piece of limestone. El-Amarna. Height 15·7 cm. 1380–1362 BC. (BrM)

Israel's God (Mi. 7:17) and Egypt's flight from battle like a hissing snake down its bolt-hole (Je. 46:22, in contrast to the Egyptian concept of the sacred uraeus-snake on a pharaoh's brow leading him to victory). The ability of various snakes to inject deadly poison into a wound when they bite or strike (Gn. 49:17; Ec. 10:8, 11; implicitly, Mt. 7:10; Lk. 11:11) enters into many biblical similes. Subjects of such similes include the harmfulness of the wicked (Dt. 32:33 (rebellious Hebrews); Pss. 58:4; 140:3) or of overmuch wine (Pr. 23:32), the Day of the Lord (Am. 5:19), and in metaphor foreign oppressors (Is. 14:29). Like war, famine, *etc.*, snake-bite could feature among divine judgments and punishments (Nu. 21:4–6; Je. 8:17; Am. 9:3), and deliverance from this harm could be granted to God's servants (Mk. 16:18; Lk. 10:19; *cf.* Acts 28:3–6). Some snakes could be charmed (Ec. 10:11), others were considered 'deaf' to the charmer's techniques (Ps. 58:4–5; Je. 8:17). Snake-charmers may possibly be represented on Egyptian scarab-amulets (P. Montet, *L'Égypte et la Bible*, 1959, pp. 90–94, fig. 17). On snake-charming in Egypt, ancient and modern, *cf.* L. Keimer, *Histoires de Serpents dans l'Égypte Ancienne et Moderne*, 1947, and for Mesopotamia, see N. L. Corkill, 'Snake Specialists in Iraq', *Iraq* 6, 1939, pp. 45–52.

Besides the general word *nāḥāš*, 'snake, serpent', and *śārāp̄*, 'burning' (see **II**, below), Heb. possesses several other words for serpents. The old word *pe̱ṯen* (Dt. 32:33; Jb. 20:14, 16; Pss. 58:4; 91:13; Is. 11:8; AV 'adder, asp') occurs as *bṯn* in the Ugaritic texts of the 14th century BC. This is often considered to be the Egyptian cobra (Arab. *naja haje*; and the related *naja nigricollis*, M. A. Murray, *JEA* 34, 1948, pp. 117–118), and is the 'asp' of classical writers. The cobra gave rise to two Egyptian hieroglyphs. This venomous beast gave point to passages like Dt. 32:33 and Jb. 20:14, 16. The word *'ep̄'eh* (Jb. 20:16; Is. 30:6; 59:5; AV 'viper') is identical with Arab. *afa'â*, and like that word appears to be a further general term for serpents and sometimes more specifically for vipers (*cf.* L. Keimer, *Études d'Égyptologie*, 7, 1945, pp. 38–39, 48–49). In Gn. 49:17 (AV 'adder'), Heb. *šᵉp̄îp̄ôn* is often thought to represent the *cerastes* vipers: either or both the 'horned viper', *Cerastes cornutus*, and the hornless *Vipera cerastes*. In Egypt and Palestine these have been familiar from ancient times, and in Egypt became the hieroglyph for 'f', from the onomatopoeic words *fy, fyt*, 'cerastes-viper' (Keimer, *Études d'Égyptologie* 7, 1945; P. E. Newberry, *JEA* 34, 1948, p. 118). The identification of *'aḵšûḇ* in Ps. 140:3 is uncertain; in Rom. 3:13 it is rendered by Gk. *aspis*, 'asp'. The word *ṣip̄'ônî* is rendered by AV as 'adder' in Pr. 23:32, and, like *ṣep̄a'* in Is. 14:29, as 'cockatrice' in Is. 11:8; 59:5; Je. 8:17; these words certainly denote snakes of some kind. The animal that fastened on Paul's hand in Acts 28:3 is often considered to be the common viper of the Mediterranean region; the same Greek word (*echidna*) is used in the powerful metaphors of Mt. 3:7; 12:34; 23:33; Lk. 3:7.

II. Specific

a. The first serpent in Scripture is the subtle creature of Gn. 3, used by Satan to alienate man from God (Rom. 16:20; 2 Cor. 11:3), controlled by the devil like the demons in men and swine in NT days. For its part, the serpent was put under a curse that it would never rise above its (already customary) creeping posture (Gn. 3:14). The serpent thus remained a biblical symbol of deceit (Mt. 23:33), and the arch-deceiver himself is 'that old serpent' (Rev. 12:9, 14–15; 20:2); Christians should match the serpent in his fabled wisdom if in no other respect (Mt. 10:16).

b. A sign performed by Moses before Israel (Ex. 4:2–5, 28–30) and by Moses and Aaron before pharaoh (Ex. 7:8–12) was to cast down his rod so that it became a serpent and take it up again as a rod, having on the latter occasion swallowed up the serpent-rods of the

A snake, the Egyptian cobra, is the hieroglyph for Udjo, patron goddess of Lower Egypt. Relief from the kiosk of Sesostris I, Karnak. Height of snake c. 8 cm. c. 1950 BC. (PAC)

Egyptian magicians (* MAGIC AND SORCERY, **2. II.** *c*).

c. In the wilderness rebellious Israel was once punished by the onset of 'fiery serpents' (*nāḥāš śārāp*), whose venom was fatal (Nu. 21:4–9; *cf*. Dt. 8:15). When Israel sought deliverance God commanded Moses to set up a bronze figure of a serpent on a pole, that those bitten might look to it, trusting in God's healing power, and live (* SERPENT, BRONZE). The term *śārāp*, 'burning', or 'fiery', may refer to the effect of the venom or poison of the snakes concerned; it recurs in Is. 14:29 and 30:6 (where 'flying' might refer to the speed with which such reptiles may strike, as though 'winged'—so, modern Arab usage; for this and other explanations, see Keimer, *Histoires de Serpents*, p. 10, n. 2; D. J. Wiseman, *TynB* 23, 1972, pp. 108–110.

d. Some Hebrew references to 'serpents' apply rather to other fearful creatures, or are metaphorical of certain great military powers in the biblical world. Thus, the 'serpent' of Am. 9:3 is probably some large denizen of the deep rather than a snake. In Is. 27:1 the sword to be raised against 'Leviathan the fleeing (or, swift) serpent, Leviathan the twisting (or, winding) serpent, and . . . the dragon that is in the sea' (*cf*. RSV) most probably expressed coming judgment upon Assyria (land of the swift Tigris), Babylonia (of the winding Euphrates) and Egypt (*tannîn*, 'dragon, monster', as in Ezk. 29:3; 32:2) respectively. Isaiah may here be announcing God's judgment on these pagan lands in terms of the ancient Canaanite myth of Baal's destruction of Lôtan or Leviathan and the many Mesopotamian tales of slaying dragons and serpents

Serpents surround a female figure on this silver and bronze cult-standard from Hazor. 12·5 cm × 7 cm. Canaanite. c. 1400–1200 BC. (IM)

Serpents decorate this pottery stand used in a Canaanite temple. Bethshean. 11th cent. BC. (UMUP)

A bronze serpent, perhaps part of a votive offering. From Susa. (Similar examples are known from Palestinian sites.) Length 30 cm. 12th cent. BC. (MC)

(Labbu, Zu, *etc.*), not to mention the Egyptian overthrowing of 'Apep, condemning them under their own popular imagery. In Jb. 26:13 the identity of the 'fleeing serpent' as associated with the sky is uncertain. Since the serpent can stand for Satan (*cf. a*, above, and Rev. 12:7–10, 14–15; 20:2) one may possibly compare here his alternative (?) designation of fallen Day Star (AV 'Lucifer'), to whom the king of Babylon is likened in Is. 14:12, 15; *cf.* Jude 6 and 2 Pet. 2:4.

In no case does any of these passages, biblical or non-biblical, refer to a creation-struggle of deity and monster, as all the serpent-slaying in them is done within an already created world. Furthermore, the Babylonian Ti'amat, whose death at Marduk's hands *is* associated with creation, was *not* a serpent or dragon, and therefore gives no support for assuming a struggle of deity and serpent/dragon at creation either (*cf.* A. Heidel, *The Babylonian Genesis*, 1951, pp. 83–88, 102–114). (* DRAGON; * LEVIATHAN; * RAHAB.)

In Canaanite, Mesopotamian, Anatolian and Egyptian mythology and cults, serpent deities are known, and serpents in various contexts are symbols of protection (Egyptian uraeus), of evil (*e.g.* Egyptian 'Apep or Apopis), of fecundity (Egypto-Canaanite goddesses of sex; *ANEP*, figs. 471–474), or of continuing life (symbolized by repeated shedding of its skin, *cf.* A. Heidel, *The Gilgamesh Epic and Old Testament Parallels*, 1949, p. 92, n. 212). For Canaanite altar-stands with serpents modelled on them, see *ANEP*, figs. 585, 590. In the texts from Ugarit note the prescribed sacrifice of 'a head of small cattle (for) 'Anat-Lôtan' (C. H. Gordon, *Ugaritic Literature*, 1949, pp. 114, 107, n. 1) and an incantation against snakes (C. Virolleaud, in *Ugaritica* 5, 1968, pp. 564ff., No. 7; M. Astour, *JNES* 27, 1968, pp. 13–36; A. F. Rainey, *JAOS* 94, 1974, pp. 189f., 194; M. Dietrich *et al.*, *UF* 7, 1975, pp. 121–125. K.A.K.

SERPENT, BRONZE. On the borders of Edom, rebellious Israel suffered deadly snakebite as a punishment and begged Moses to intercede with God for them, to save them from the serpents. God then commanded Moses to make a bronze figure of a serpent and set it up on a pole, so that anyone bitten by a serpent need only look at the bronze serpent-figure and he would live (Nu. 21:4–9; 1 Cor. 10:9, 11). By this means God granted the people deliverance and enforced the lesson of dependence upon himself both for that deliverance and as a general principle. Centuries later, during his purge of idolatrous objects and customs, King Hezekiah of Judah destroyed the bronze serpent because the people had turned it into an idol, burning incense to it (2 Ki. 18:4). The following phrase *wayyiqrā' lô n^eḥuštān* may mean either 'he (= Hezekiah) called it Nehushtan' (*i.e.* 'only a bit of bronze'), or 'it was called Nehushtan' (*i.e.* by the people from of old). In either case it is a pun on the phrase *n^eḥaš-n^eḥošeṯ*, 'serpent of bronze', two very similar-sounding words in Heb. The significance of serpents in surrounding paganism made Hezekiah's action especially imperative (*cf.* * SERPENT, end of section **II.** *d*; see also H. H. Rowley, 'Zadok and Nehushtan', *JBL* 58, 1939, pp. 113ff.). A bronze serpent was found at Gezer (see R. A. S. Macalister, *The Excavation of Gezer*, 2, 1912, pp. 398–399 and fig.; or I. Benzinger, *Hebräische Archäologie*[3], 1927, p. 327, fig. 418), a serpent standard at Hazor, and a gilded copper snake from a shrine at Timna (B. Rothenberg, *Timna, Valley of the Biblical Copper Mines*, 1972, pp. 152, 183–184, pls. XIX–XX).

When speaking of his coming crucifixion, Jesus Christ used the incident of the serpent, which was lifted up that man might look in faith and live, in order to illustrate the significance of that impending event. Those who put faith in him, uplifted on the cross for their sins, would have life eternal (Jn. 3:14). K.A.K.

SERPENT'S STONE ('Stone of Zoheleth', AV) (*'eḇen hazzōḥeleṯ*). A stone near En-rogel, to the SE of Jerusalem, the scene of the slaughtering of animals by Adonijah (1 Ki. 1:9). The meaning of *zōḥeleṯ* is uncertain, but it is usually connected with *zāḥal*, 'to withdraw, crawl away'. From this, some would interpret the phrase as 'the stone of slipping' and connect it with a steep and slippery rock slope, called by the Arabs *zaḥweileh*, or some neighbouring surface, near Siloam. The translation 'serpent's stone' may be linked with a possible identification of * En-rogel with the Jackal's Well (Ne. 2:13).

BIBLIOGRAPHY. J. Simons, *Jerusalem in the Old Testament*, 1952, pp. 160–162. T.C.M.

SERVANT OF THE LORD.

I. In the Old Testament

a. The 'Servant Songs'

B. Duhm's commentary on Isaiah (1892) distinguished four passages which have since been regarded as the 'Servant Songs': Is. 42:1–4; 49:1–6; 50:4–9; 52:13–53:12. Some scholars (*e.g.* S. Mowinckel) have gone so far as to assign these passages to a separate author and period from the surrounding text. Modern scholarship is generally agreed, however, that they are an integral part of Isaiah 40ff., with many echoes in neighbouring passages. The term 'servant' (*'eḇeḏ*) occurs as frequently outside Duhm's selected passages as within them (*e.g.* Is. 41:8f.; 43:10; 44:1f., 21; 45:4; 48:20), with reference to the nation of Israel. It is also used in the OT for individuals in a close relationship with God, such as the Patriarchs, prophets and kings, and particularly Moses and David (*e.g.* Gn. 26:24; Ex. 14:31; Dt. 34:5; 2 Sa. 7:5; Is. 20:3; Am. 3:7). But in the 'Servant Songs' a distinctive conception of 'servanthood' comes into sharper focus, so that without divorcing these passages from their context most scholars continue to speak of a 'Servant figure' as a distinct element in the prophet's message; and the most distinctive element in this figure is that of obedient, undeserved suffering, leading to death, as the means of taking away the sin of his people and 'making many to be accounted righteous'.

For a fuller treatment of the character and mission of the Servant in the context of the message of Is. 40ff., see *Messiah, **I.** *b*. 1.

b. The identity of the Servant

The following are the main lines of interpretation suggested.

1. *Collective*. The explicit description of Israel as God's 'servant' both in the 'Servant Songs' (Is. 49:3) and in the surrounding text leads many to regard the Songs as a description of the prophet's ideal for Israel, identifying the Servant either as the nation as a whole or, more probably, a pious remnant within the nation, with a mission to Israel (49:5f.), involving suffering to redeem the whole nation (53:4–6, 8, 11f.).

2. *Individual*. The language about the Servant is often strongly individual, describing the birth, suffering, death and eventual triumph of what is apparently a person rather than a group. Various historical identifications have been proposed, such as Moses, Jeremiah, Cyrus, Zerubbabel or the prophet himself. But the traditional interpretation, Jewish and Christian, is that the Servant is an ideal individual figure of the future, God's agent in redeeming his people, *i.e.* the *Messiah. In later Palestinian Judaism this was the dominant interpretation (Hellenistic Judaism was apparently more favourable to a collective interpretation), so that the *Targum of Jonathan on Is. 53, while clearly embarrassed by the idea of Messianic suffering to the extent of drastically reconstructing the text to eliminate this implication, still explicitly identifies the Servant as the Messiah (see text in Zimmerli and Jeremias, *The Servant of God*[2], pp. 69–71; and for other early Jewish interpretations, *ibid*., pp. 37–79).

3. *Cultic*. Some Scandinavian scholars find the background to the Servant in the Babylonian myth of the dying and rising god *Tammuz and its associated liturgy. The Servant would then be a mythological concept rather than a historically identifiable figure or group. The existence of such myth and ritual in Israel is, however, highly debatable.

4. *'Corporate personality'*. Interpretations **1** and **2** above reflect important characteristics of the texts: both collective and individual aspects are clearly present in the Servant figure. Most scholars today tend, therefore, to look for an exegesis similar to H. W. Robinson's concept of 'corporate personality', *i.e.* the recognition that in the OT an individual (*e.g.* king or father) may represent and embody the group of which he is the head, so that he both *is* that group and yet can also be placed over against it as its leader. So the Servant *is* Israel (49:3), he sums up in himself all that Israel represents, and yet he is an individual with a mission *to* Israel (49:5f.) and his experiences on their behalf are the object of the nation's interest (53:1–6). The close juxtaposition of 49:3 and 49:5f. shows that these two aspects of the Servant are inseparable. The individual character of the Servant is most clearly expressed in 52:13–53:12, so that in this passage 'what began as a personification (has) become a person' (Rowley), and here all the emphasis is on the vicarious nature of his suffering as a substitute for his people. But this role is only possible because he *is* Israel, as its representative head.

II. In the New Testament

Some recent scholarship (esp. M. D. Hooker; also C. K. Barrett, C. F. D. Moule) has argued that the Servant figure was a minor element in the NT understanding of Jesus' redemptive work, and that the OT ground for his role of suffering and rejection was found rather in the 'son of man' of Dn. 7. It is pointed out that relatively few formal quotations from Servant passages occur in the NT, and that several of these quotations are of parts of the Songs which do not speak explicitly of suffering, or at least of redemptive suffering.

It is not legitimate, however, to restrict consideration to formal quotations, as allusive references are if anything even more impressive evidence of the influence of the Servant figure, and even where the words alluded to are not directly concerned with redemptive suffering, it is hard to believe that these passages could be referred to with no thought of their most distinctive theme and of its relevance to the mission of Jesus. Above all, it is indisputable that Is. 53 is by far the clearest indication of Messianic suffering in the OT, so that even if no explicit allusions to the Servant occurred, it would be very likely that this was the main source (together with certain psalms and parts of Zc. 9–13) of the repeated conviction that the Messiah *must* suffer, because 'it is written' of him. No such role of Messianic suffering is explicit in Dn. 7, nor did contemporary Jewish exegesis find it there.

In fact the explicit evidence of the influence of the Servant figure (esp. Is. 53, where the redemptive element is emphatic) is far from negligible.

a. In the teaching of Jesus

Is. 53:12 is explicitly quoted in Lk. 22:37. There are further clear allusions to Is. 53:10–12 in Mk. 10:45 and 14:24. Mk. 9:12 probably echoes Is. 53:3, and other possible allusions have been found in Mt. 3:15 (*cf.* Is. 53:11), Lk. 11:22 (*cf.* Is. 53:12; not a very likely allusion) and in the use of *paradidosthai* ('be delivered') in Mk. 9:31; 10:33; 14:21 (*cf.* Is. 53:12). In addition the voice at Jesus' baptism (Mk. 1:11), outlining his mission in terms of Is. 42:1, must have influenced Jesus' thinking.

Note the concentration in these allusions on Is. 53, and particularly on vv. 10–12 where the redemptive role of the Servant is most explicit. In Mk. 10:45 and 14:24 in particular the vicarious and redemptive character of Jesus' death is stressed, in terms drawn from Is. 53.

b. In the rest of the New Testament

The actual title 'servant' (*pais*) is confined to Peter's speech in Acts 3:13, 26 and the prayer of the church in Acts 4:27, 30, but the influence of the Servant figure is clear also in 1 Pet. 2:21–25; 3:18, suggesting that it featured prominently in Peter's understanding of Jesus' mission. Paul's explanations of Christ's redemptive work often contain ideas, and sometimes verbal allusions, which suggest that he too saw Jesus' work foreshadowed in Is. 53. (See *e.g.* Phil. 2:6–11; Rom. 4:25; 5:19; 8:3f., 32–34; 1 Cor. 15:3; 2 Cor. 5:21.) The use of 'lamb of God' by John (1:29, 36) also probably shows the influence of Is. 53:7. Heb. 9:28, 'to bear the sins of many', echoes Is. 53:12.

There are also a number of formal quotations from Servant

passages, with reference to Jesus and the gospel, *viz.* Mt. 8:17; 12:18–21; Jn. 12:38; Acts 8:32f.; Rom. 10:16; 15:21. None of these is with specific reference to Jesus' redemptive work, and some focus on other aspects of his mission, but all testify further to the early church's conviction that the Servant figure, and particularly Is. 53, was a divinely ordained pattern for the Messianic mission of Jesus.

BIBLIOGRAPHY. For the whole article: W. Zimmerli and J. Jeremias, *The Servant of God*², 1965 (= *TDNT* 5, pp. 654–717).

For section **I**: H. W. Robinson, *The Cross of the Servant*, 1926, reprinted in *The Cross in the Old Testament*, 1955, pp. 55–114; I. Engnell, *BJRL* 31, 1948, pp. 54–93; C. R. North, *The Suffering Servant in Deutero-Isaiah*, 1948; J. Lindblom, *The Servant Songs in Deutero-Isaiah*, 1951; H. H. Rowley, *The Servant of the Lord*, 1952, pp. 1–88; S. Mowinckel, *He That Cometh*, 1956, pp. 187–257; H. Ringgren, *The Messiah in the Old Testament*, 1956, pp. 39–53.

For section **II**: J. L. Price, *Int* 12, 1958, pp. 28–38; C. K. Barrett in A. J. B. Higgins (ed.), *New Testament Essays in memory of T. W. Manson*, 1959, pp. 1–18; O. Cullmann, *The Christology of the New Testament*, 1959, pp. 51–82; M. D. Hooker, *Jesus and the Servant*, 1959; B. Lindars, *New Testament Apologetic*, 1961, pp. 77–88; C. F. D. Moule, *The Phenomenon of the New Testament*, 1967, pp. 82–99; R. T. France, *TynB* 19, 1968, pp. 26–52, and *Jesus and the Old Testament*, 1971, pp. 110–132; J. Jeremias, *New Testament Theology*, 1, 1971, pp. 286–299. R.T.F.

SETH. 1. The third son of Adam and Eve, born after the murder of Abel, and called Seth (*šēṯ*) because, Eve said, 'God has appointed (*šāṯ*) me another seed instead of Abel' (Gn. 4:25). It was through Seth that the genealogy of Noah passed (Gn. 5:3–4; 1 Ch. 1:1; Lk. 3:38). His son Enosh was born when he was 105 years old (*MT* and SP; LXX reads 205) and he lived to the great age of 912 years (*MT*, SP and LXX agree; Gn. 4:26; 5:6–8). The individual in the Sumerian King List, Alalgar, who corresponds to Seth is credited with a reign of 36,000 years.

2. An unknown individual whose name is rendered Sheth (Nu. 24:17, AV and RSV; RV gives 'tumult'), the ancestor of a people mentioned by Balaam as enemies of Israel.

T.C.M.

SEVEN WORDS, THE. The 'seven words' are so reckoned by bringing the data of all four Gospels together and identifying the 'loud cry' of Mk. 15:37 with one of the articulate utterances quoted by another Evangelist.

The first of the words spoken by our Lord from the cross (Lk. 23:34) reveals a love that is utterly unexpected and utterly undeserved. He prayed for the Roman soldiers and even, as Peter suggests (Acts 3:17), for the religious guides of the nation. (This saying is omitted by some ancient witnesses to the text, but the omission is probably due to an editor who considered that the events of AD 70 showed that God had not forgiven the Jewish authorities who accused Jesus before Pilate, as though the prayer had them in view.)

The second word was spoken to the penitent brigand (Lk. 23:43), who, beyond the cross, saw the crown and the coming glory, and who said, 'Jesus, remember me when you come in your kingly power' (v. 42). To him Jesus said in effect, 'Not far down the ages, but before the sun sets, you will be with me in the bliss of Paradise'.

The third word (Jn. 19:25–27), comprising sayings addressed both to the mother of Jesus and to the beloved disciple, proves that we have in Jesus the supreme example of a 'heart at leisure from itself, to soothe and sympathize'. Though suffering severe physical pain and enduring far more awful agony of soul, he thought of his mother and made provision for her future. The sword was piercing her heart (Lk. 2:35), but the tender words of her Son must have brought to her deep comfort and healing.

The first three words were spoken during the bright morning hours before noon. The fourth awe-inspiring word (Mt. 27:46; Mk. 15:34) was probably spoken by Jesus as the mysterious, supernatural 3 hours' darkness was lifting (*ELOI, ELOI, LAMA SABACHTHANI).

The fifth word (Jn. 19:28) followed close upon the fourth. It is the only word that speaks of physical suffering. Jesus had refused a drugged drink (Mk. 15:23), but he accepted another kind of drink, in order to moisten his parched throat and lips, so that, with a loud voice, he might make the declaration contained in the sixth word. The Evangelist notes the fulfilment of Ps. 69:21b.

That word (Jn. 19:30) consists of one comprehensive Gk. verb, *tetelestai*, 'It is finished'. It is the cry, not of a vanquished victim but of a Victor, who has finished the work he had to do, has fulfilled all the OT prophecies and types, and has once for all offered the one final sacrifice for sin (Heb. 10:12).

In the final word (Lk. 23:46) Jesus quoted Ps. 31:5, traditionally the pious Jew's evening prayer. The redeemed are so really brothers of the Redeemer (Heb. 2:11–13) that, in the moment of dying, they can use the same language, as they commend their souls into the hands of the Father—his Father, and their Father in him.

BIBLIOGRAPHY. V. Taylor, *Jesus and His Sacrifice*, 1937, pp. 157ff., 197ff.; R. G. Turnbull, *The Seven Words from the Cross*, 1956. A.R. F.F.B.

SEVENEH. The RV, ASV rendering of the *MT sᵉwēnēh* (Egyp. *Swn*, 'place of barter', 'market', Coptic *Suan*, Arab. *'Aswân*) in Ezk. 29:10; 30:6, where AV, RSV retain the classical form, *Syene. Located on the first cataract of the Nile, Syene (modern 'Aswân) marked the boundary between Egypt and Ethiopia. 'From Migdol ('tower' in AV, RV) to Syene' means 'the length of Egypt from N to S'. *MT sᵉwēnēh* should be read *sᵉwēnâ* or *sᵉwānâ*, the *â* signifying direction: 'to Syene'. A border fortress and a base for expeditions up the Nile, a terminus for river traffic and a source of red granite for Egyp. monuments (syenite), Syene was of special importance to the Jews because of its proximity to the island of Elephantine, which housed a colony of Jews who sought refuge in Egypt after Jerusalem fell (587 BC). The Qumran MS of Is. suggests that 'Syenites' should replace *sînîm* (Is. 49:12); LXX reads *Syene* for *Sin* in Ezk. 30:16.

BIBLIOGRAPHY. E. G. Kraeling, 'New Light on the Elephantine Colony', *BA* 15, 1952, pp. 50–68.

D.A.H.

SHAALBIM. A village inhabited by Amorites near Mt Heres and Aijalon when they withstood the Danites. Later the Amorites were ubjugated by the house of Joseph Jdg. 1:35). With Makaz, Beth-hemesh and Elon-beth-Hanan, ;haalbim formed part of Solo-non's second administrative listrict (1 Ki. 4:9). It is almost cer-ainly the same as Shaalabbin, in-luded with Aijalon in the list of)an's territory (Jos. 19:42), and ;haalbon, the house of Eliahba, ›ne of David's warriors (2 Sa. :3:32; 1 Ch. 11:33). Because of the imilar area covered it has been sug-;ested that Shaalbim of Jdg. 1:35; Ki. 4:9 may also be the same lace. The position of modern ;elbīṭ, 5 km NW of Aijalon and 3 km N of Beth-shemesh, suits all hese contexts well, though the ame is philologically different. ;haalbim, *etc.*, may mean 'haunt of oxes'. D.J.W.

;HAARAIM (Heb. *ša'ᵃraim*). **1.** On he line of the Philistine flight from \zekah, before the parting of the ways to Gath and Ekron (1 Sa. 7:52). This is compatible with Jos. 5:36. See *GTT*, p. 318. **2.** In 1 Ch. :31, for *Sharuhen. J.P.U.L.

;HADOW (Heb. *ṣēl*, 'shadow', shade', 'defence'; Gk. *skia*, 'a hade', 'a shadow'; both words vith derivative forms). The repre-entation made by any solid body nterposing between the sun or light nd another body. As a shadow is onstantly varying till at last, per-aps suddenly, it ceases to be, so re our days unsubstantial and leeting, our death sudden (1 Ch. 9:15; Jb. 14:2; 17:7). Darkness and loominess are associated with sha-lows, and thus with 'the shadow of leath' (Jb. 3:5; 16:16; 24:17; Ps. 3:4), though this common inter-retation of Heb. *ṣalmûṯ* is strictly naccurate and should be rendered deep darkness', as usually in RSV.

As a man can find welcome relief n the shade from the scorching eat (*cf.* Jon. 4:5–6), so the rule and helter of the Almighty are called a hadow (La. 4:20; Ezk. 31:6; Ps. 1:1; Is. 25:4; *cf.* Ct. 2:3). The ser-ant's eagerly anticipated time for topping work is called the 'sha-low' (Jb. 7:2). In contrast to the igns of approaching desolation and uin, the 'shadows of evening' (Je. :4), the day of everlasting glory is vhen 'the shadows flee' (Ct. 2:17).

The ancient ceremonies are called 'shadow of the good things to ome' (Heb. 10:1; *cf.* Col. 2:17). 'he unchangeableness of God is contrasted with the 'play of passing shadows' (Jas. 1:17, NEB). In Heb. 9:5 AV 'shadowing' (RSV 'over-shadowing') comes from *kata-skiazō*, 'to (cause a) shadow' or 'to shade fully' (*cf.* Heb. *ṣālal*). J.D.D.

SHALEM. A word treated by AV as the name of a place near Shechem, which was visited by Jacob (Gn. 33:18). RV ('in peace') and RSV ('safely'), however, prefer to take it in an adverbial sense, from the verb

An unfinished obelisk cut from the red granite (syenite) quarries at Seveneh (Aswan). New Kingdom. 15th–13th cent. BC. (MH)

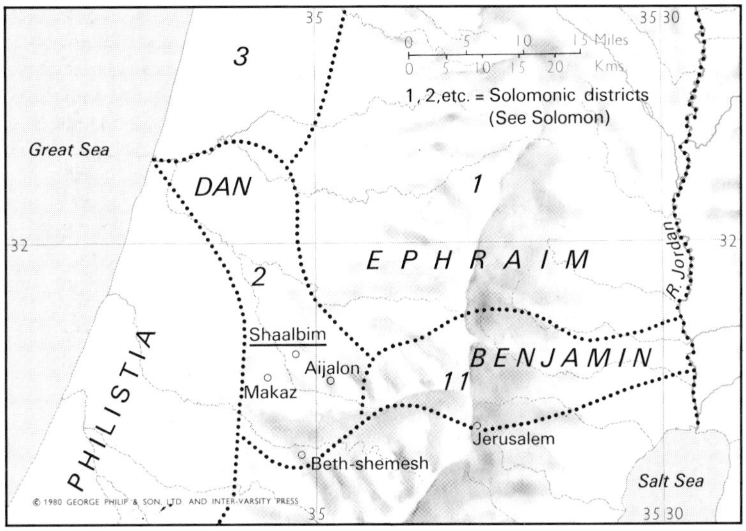

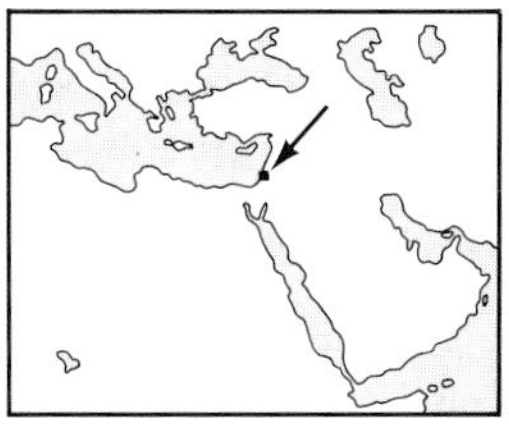

Shaalbim, an Amorite village in the territory of Dan.

SHADRACH See Hananiah, Part 2.

Inscribed statue of Shalmaneser III, king of Assyria. Nimrud. Height 1·03 m. 839/8 BC. (MELM)

SHAMBLES
See Meat market, Part 2.

šālēm, 'to be complete, sound', and this appears to make better sense. The word *šālēm*, identical in form, does occur as a place-name in connection with Melchizedek, but is given as *Salem in EVV. T.C.M.

SHALISHAH. The district reached by Saul after passing through the hills of Ephraim and before reaching the land of Shaalim, or *Salim, in pursuit of his father's lost asses (1 Sa. 9:4). The place seems to have had its own deity or shrine, Baal-shalishah (2 Ki. 4:42). Since the places in conjunction with which Shalishah is cited are of uncertain location, its own situation is not known. Conder proposed the ruins of Khirbet Kefr Thilth, 30 km NE of Jaffa. D.J.W.

SHALLUM (Heb. *šallûm*, *šallum*). **1.** A Jerahmeelite through the line of an ancestress who married an Egyp. slave (1 Ch. 2:40–41; *cf.* vv. 34–35). **2.** A descendant of Korah who served under David as chief gatekeeper at the King's Gate in the sanctuary (1 Ch. 9:17–19; Ezr. 2:42). Apparently this was an inherited position of some importance (*cf.* Ezr. 2:42; Ne. 7:45). Possibly a short form of Meshelemiah (1 Ch. 26:1; 9:21) and of Selemiah (26:14). **3.** Son of Jabesh and 16th king of the N kingdom of Israel (*c.* 745 BC). By assassinating *Zechariah, son of *Jeroboam II, he brought an end to the dynasty of *Jehu (2 Ki. 15:10), thus fulfilling prophecy (10:30; *cf.* 15:12). He was killed in turn in Samaria by *Menahem after a reign of only 1 month (15:13–15). **4.** The husband of *Huldah, the prophetess who was 'keeper of the wardrobe' (2 Ki. 22:14; 2 Ch. 34:22). **5.** Son of *Josiah (1 Ch. 3:15; Je. 22:11) and 18th king of Judah (*c.* 609 BC) whose throne-name was *Jehoahaz. He was deposed after a 3-month reign (2 Ki. 23:31). **6.** An Aaronide predecessor of *Ezra (Ezr. 7:2; *cf.* 1 Ch. 6:12–13). Possibly an abbreviated form of Meshullam (1 Ch. 9:11; Ne. 11:11; 12:13).

The various forms of this name are based on the same root in different nominal patterns. D.W.B.

SHALMAN. The person who sacked Beth-arbel (Ho. 10:14). This action was sufficiently well known to serve as a warning to Israel. It is generally assumed that this could be a reference to *Shalmaneser V, the Assyr. king who besieged Samaria in 725–723 BC. In this event Arbel might be Arbela, W of Galilee (1 Macc. 9:2). But against this, Shalmaneser's name is elsewhere written fully and the Galilee area fell to Tiglath-pileser III in 734–732 BC. Thus Shalman may refer to Salamanu, king of Moab, mentioned in the annals of *Tiglath-pileser. Identification remains uncertain. D.J.W.

SHALMANESER (Heb. *šalman'eser*; Gk. *Salmennasar*; Assyr. *Šulmanu-ašaridu*, 'the god Šulman is chief'). The Heb. may have been read *šlmn'sr* (*JSS* 21, 1976, p. 8).

Shalmaneser was the name borne by several rulers of *Assyria. The king of Assyria to whom Hoshea of Israel became subject (2 Ki. 17:3) was Shalmaneser V (727–722 BC), son of Tiglath-pileser III. When Hoshea failed to pay tribute in his 7th regnal year Shalmaneser began a 3-year siege of the Israelite capital *Samaria. There are no annals of this king extant, but the Assyr. Eponym List records the siege and the Bab. Chronicle says that Shalmaneser 'broke (the resistance of) the city of Shamara'in'. It is likely that the 'king of Assyria' to whom the city fell (2 Ki. 17:6) was this same Shalmaneser, though the final capture of the city is claimed by his successor Sargon II in 722/1 BC. It is possible that Sargon usurped the throne during the siege and continued the campaign (*DOTT*, pp. 58–63).

Shalmaneser III, king of Assyria 859–824 BC, frequently raided the W, and the first recorded Assyr. contact with the Israelites is found in his Annals. In 853 BC he fought a coalition of Syrian kings under Irhuleni of Hamath and Hadadezer of Damascus at Qarqar. Among their allies was 'Ahab the Israelite', who, according to the Assyrians, provided 2,000 chariots and 10,000 men as his contribution. The Assyr. advance was temporary and Shalmaneser did not return for 3 years (1 Ki. 16:29; 20:20; 22:1).

In his account of operations against Syria in 841 BC, Shalmaneser III claims to have defeated Hazael of Damascus (see 1 Ki. 19:15). He did not, however, capture the city and moved *via* the Hauran to the Lebanon, where he received tribute from 'Jehu, son of Omri', an event not mentioned in the OT portrayed on the Black Obelisk from Nimrud (*CALAH).

BIBLIOGRAPHY. *CAH*^{3}, 3, 1978.
D.J.W.

SHAME. The Eng. word and its cognates appear about 190 times in OT and 46 times in NT. These occurrences are translations of original forms representing at least 10 different Heb. and 7 different Gk. roots and a considerably larger number of other words.

Two main meanings can be distinguished: descriptions of states of ıind, and descriptions of physical ɛates. The states of mind may be ɬassified into three broad categories: first, those where an individual is or might be the object of contempt, derision or humiliation; ɛcond, those where he feels bashfulness or shyness; third, those where he feels respect or awe. The physical states involve a degree of xposure or nudity, or the words re used as euphemisms for the ɛxual organs.

The most frequent usage by far ıvolves the ideas connected with contempt, derision and humiliation. hame follows when the law of God is disregarded or forgotten Ho. 4:6–7). God sends it upon the nemies of his people (Ps. 132:18). t is the result of sin and is removed ı the day of liberty and restoration Is. 61:7). It appears at times to be

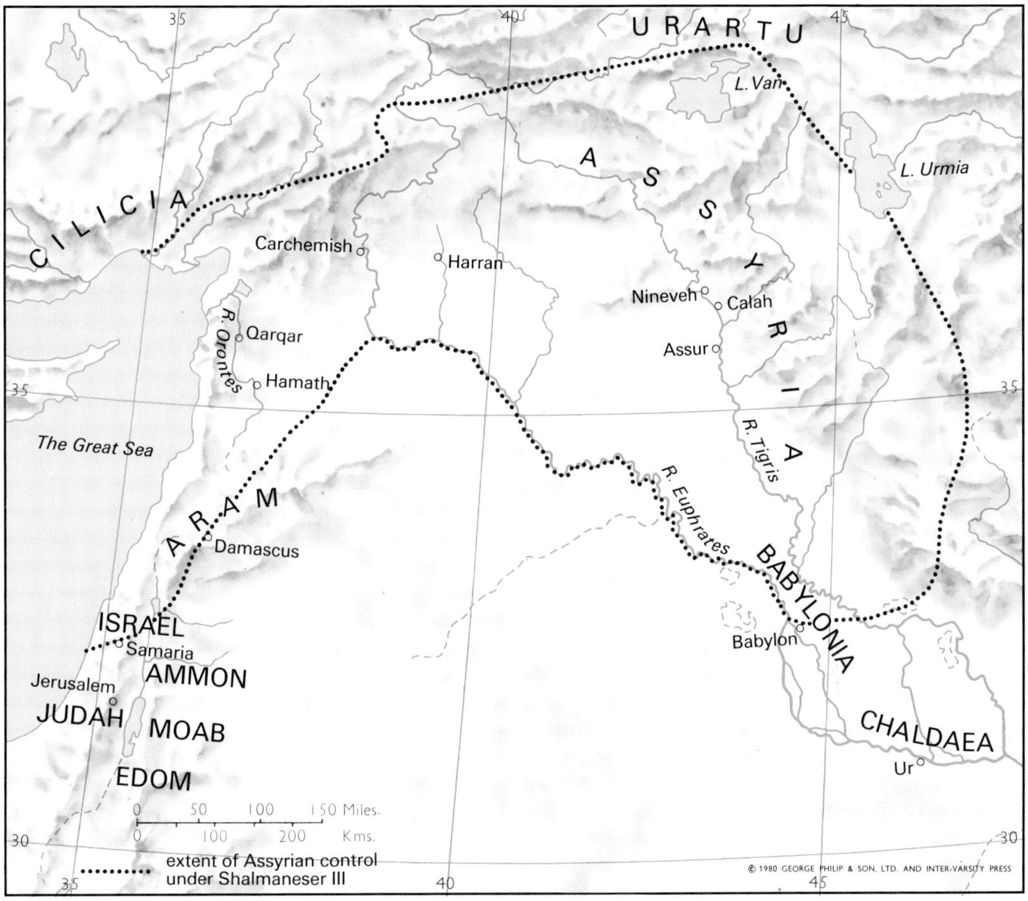

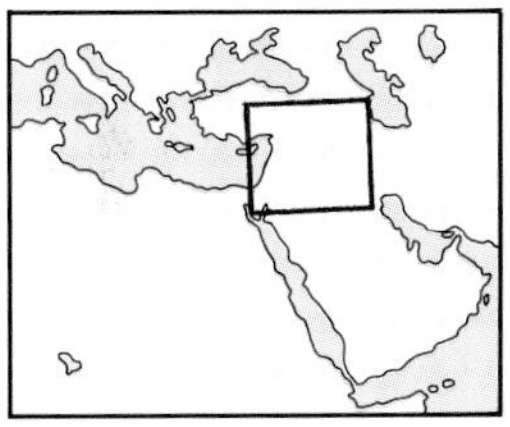

The lands dominated by Shalmaneser III of Assyria.

a punishment (Ps. 44:7, 9, 15). In contrast, it is also sometimes a positive preventive manifestation of the grace of God (Ezk. 43:10). It may induce positive action (Jdg. 3:25). False shame at that which is not shameful, *viz.* allegiance to Christ, is to be avoided (Mk. 8:38). There is also a figurative use of the term, as in Is. 24:23 and in Jude 13.

The usage representing shyness or bashfulness is not as important, since it occurs infrequently. A clear example is the statement concerning the man and his wife before the fall in Gn. 2:25. The usage which represents awe or respect is also rare. An OT instance is Ezr. 9:6; and there is the apostolic injunction of 1 Tim. 2:9. In the former instance the common Heb. root *bôš*, which appears on over 90 other occasions in the OT text in the Qal stem alone, is used; whereas 1 Tim. 2:9 is the only passage where *aidōs* occurs in the NT.

The uses of the words with a physical reference are concerned with nakedness. These occurrences are not frequent.

The biblical concept of shame is basically that of the mental state of humiliation due to sin, and to departure from the law of God, which brings obloquy and rejection by both God and man. The development of the concept is most extensive in the prophets and in the Pauline Epistles. The references to matters connected with sex are illustrative or figurative, and do not indicate that there is any more basic connection between shame and sexual functions than between shame and other functions which may occasion embarrassment by sinful use.

BIBLIOGRAPHY. R. Bultmann, *TDNT* 1, pp. 189–191; H.-G. Link, E. Tiedtke, *NIDNTT* 3, pp. 561–564. P.W.

SHAMGAR (Heb. *šamgar*, probably from Hurrian *šimiqari*). A personal name repeatedly attested in Nuzian texts (*cf.* R. H. Pfeiffer and E. A. Speiser, *AASOR* 16, 1936, p. 161), called 'the son of Anath' (Jdg. 3:31; 5:6), *i.e.* a native of Beth-anath (presumably a S Beth-anath; *cf.* Jos. 15:59). His killing of 600 Philistines must belong to the earliest period of Philistine settlement in Canaan, since the reference to him in the Song of Deborah (Jdg. 5:6) indicates that he flourished before the battle of Kishon (*c.* 1125

'Jehu son of Omri' kneels before Shalmaneser III, king of Assyria. Black obelisk, Nimrud. Height 2·02 m. 841 BC. (BM)

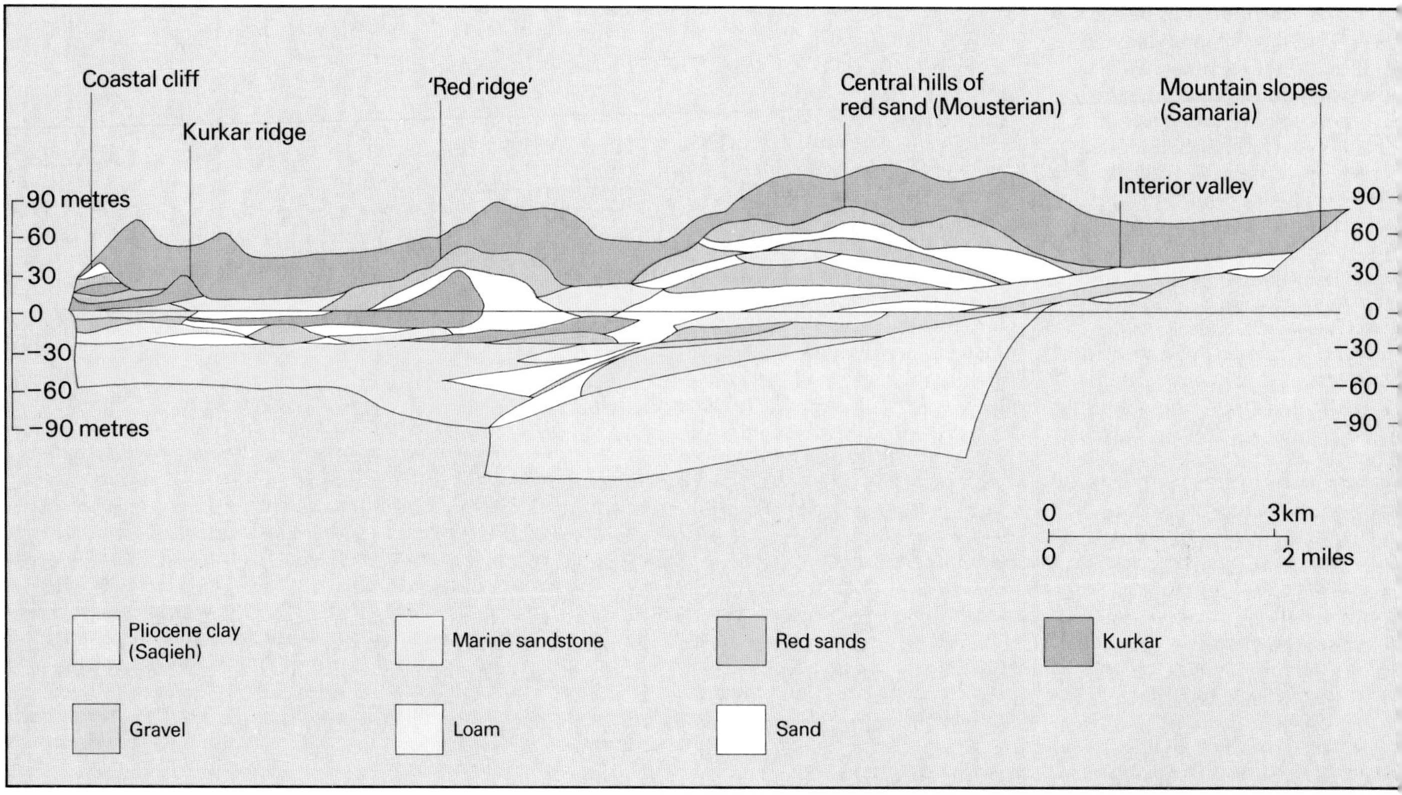

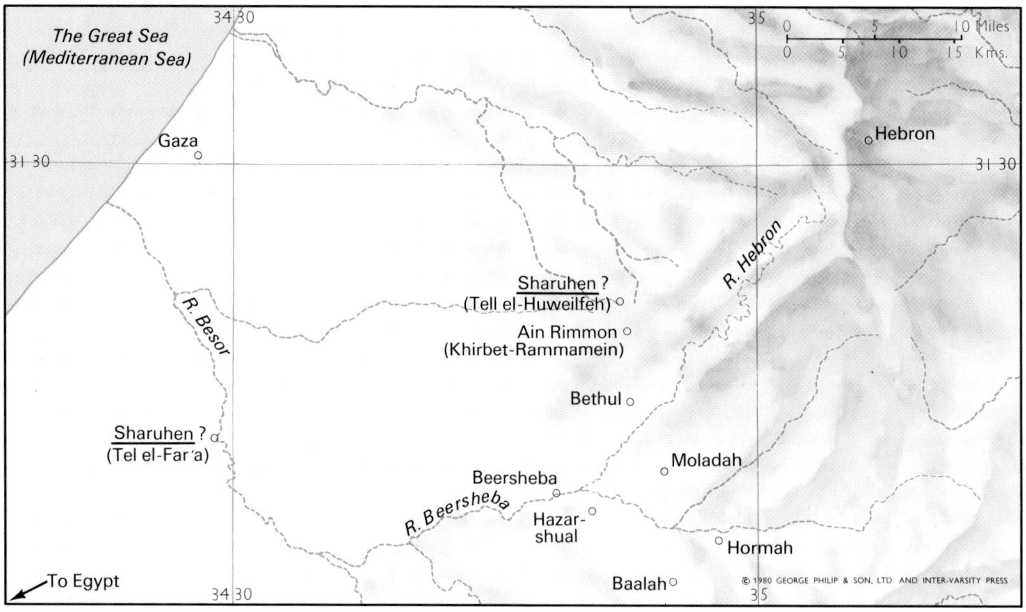

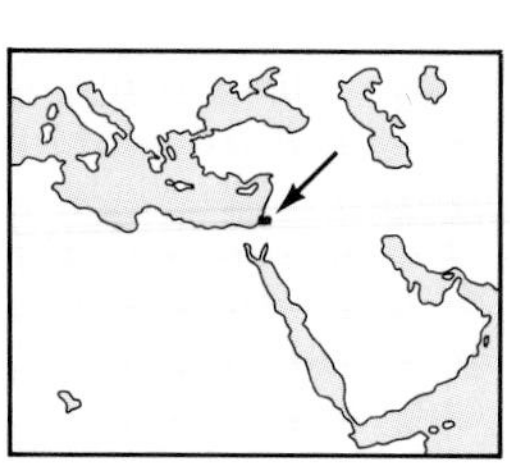

Proposed locations of Sharuhen.

BC). The ox-goad (Heb. *malmāḏ*) with which he wrought such havoc would have a metal tip which was sharpened as required (*GOAD). He is not described as a judge of Israel—indeed, he may well have been a Canaanite—but his exploit afforded the neighbouring Israelites some relief. Some LXX and other recensions repeat Jdg. 3:31 at the end of ch. 16, in a more 'Philistine' context. J. Garstang's surmise that Shamgar is identical with Ben-anath, a Syrian sea-captain and son-in-law of Rameses II (*c.* 1260 BC) is not convincing (*Joshua–Judges*, 1931, pp. 63f., 284ff.); still less so is Sir C. Marston's suggestion that 'The Ox-goad' was the name of his ship (*The Bible is True*, 1934, pp. 247ff.).

BIBLIOGRAPHY. G. F. Moore, 'Shamgar and Sisera', *JAOS* 9, 1898, pp. 159f.; F. C. Fensham, *JNES* 20, 1961, pp. 197–198; B. Maisler, 'Shamgar ben Anath', *PEQ* 66, 1934, pp. 192ff.; E. Danelius, *JNES* 22, 1963, pp. 191–193. F.F.B.

SHAMMAH. 1. A tribal chieftain (Heb. *'allûp̄*) of Edom, descended from Esau (Gn. 36:17). **2.** A brother of King David, and son of Jesse (1 Sa. 16:9). Variant forms of the name are Shammua, Shimea, Shimeah, Shimeam and Shimei. **3.** One of the outstanding three of David's warriors (2 Sa. 23:11), described as a Hararite. The Shammah of 2 Sa. 23:30 is almost certainly the same man, but there are textual problems; *cf.* NEB. **4.** Another of David's warriors, a Harodite (2 Sa. 23:25). 1 Ch. 11:27 renders his name as Shammoth (a plural form of the name), and the Shamhuth of 1 Ch. 27:8 may well be the same man. D.F.P.

SHAPHAN. 1. The son of Azaliah who was state secretary (AV 'scribe') to Josiah. Hilkiah reported to him the discovery of the book of the law in the Temple (2 Ki. 22:3; 2 Ch. 34:8–24). He read from this book before Josiah who sent him to the prophetess Huldah. Shaphan was father of at least three sons. (i) Ahikam who assisted the prophet Jeremiah (2 Ki. 22:12; 2 Ch. 34:20; Je. 26:24); (ii) Elasah who, with another man, was entrusted by Jeremiah with a letter to the exiles in Babylonia (Je. 29:3); (iii) Gemariah who tried to prevent

Jehoiakim from burning the scroll containing Jeremiah's prophecies (Je. 36:10–12, 25). Shaphan had as grandsons Micaiah (Je. 36:11, 13) and Gedaliah, the governor of Judah after the Babylonian invasions of 589–587 BC, who helped Jeremiah (Je. 39:14).

2. The father of Jaazaniah, seen sacrificing to idols in Ezekiel's vision (Ezk. 8:11).

Even if the name is to be connected with Heb. *šāpān*, 'rock-badger', there is no evidence that it betokens totem worship (as G. B. Gray, *Hebrew Proper Names*, 1896, p. 103). D.J.W.

SHAPHIR (AV Saphir). A town in the Philistine plain against which Micah prophesied (Mi. 1:11). The exact site is uncertain, but may be one of the three hut settlements es-Sūāfir near Ashdod. The identification of Shaphir with Shamir (Jos. 15:48; Jdg. 10:1–2) is tenuous. R.J.W.

SHAREZER. 1. A brother of Adrammelech who with him murdered their father Sennacherib in 681 BC (2 Ki. 19:37; Is. 37:38). His name is known only from this reference and is probably an abbreviation from the Assyr.–Bab. *šar-uṣur*, 'He has protected the king', normally prefixed by the name of a deity. By reference to *Nergilus* in the account by Abydenus of the same event Nergal-sharezer has been proposed. Johns considered the name a corruption of Šar-eṭir-Aššur, the known name of a son of Sennacherib. Alternatively, a Nabū-šar-uṣur, governor of Marqasi and eponym for the year 682 BC, may be in mind.

2. A contemporary of Zechariah who inquired concerning the propriety of continuing the fast celebrating the anniversary of the destruction of the Temple (Zc. 7:2). Because the text is difficult (see RVmg.) it has been suggested that 'the people of Bethel' may imply that the full name was the common Belshazzar (Bab. Bel-šar-uṣur) or Bethel-sharezer. D.J.W.

SHARON (Heb. *šārôn*; 'Saron', Acts 9:35, AV) means a level place or plain. It comprises the largest of the coastal plains in N Palestine. Lying between the extensive marshes of the lower Crocodile river (Nahr ez-Zerka) and the valley of Aijalon and Joppa in the S, it runs some 80 km N–S and is 15 km wide. Its features have been largely determined by the Pleistocene shorelines and deposits. Inland from the belt of recent sand-dunes which divert and choke some of the coastal rivers, rises a zone of Mousterian red sands to *c.* 60 m, forming in the N a continuous belt of some 30 km. Formerly, this zone was thickly forested with oaks, probably *Quercus infectoria*, and today this is one of the richest agricultural districts of Israel, planted with citrus groves. Inland from the belt of Mousterian sands, the streams have partially excavated a longitudinal trough along the foothills of an earlier Pleistocene shoreline. The river valleys, especially in the N of this trough, tended to be marshy until modern drainage developments. In the past, only in the S border of Sharon was the land more favourable for settlement, and it is clear that most of Sharon was never colonized by the Israelites (but Tell Qasile, N of Joppa, was founded *c.* 1200 BC). In the N, Socoh, a district centre under Solomon (1 Ki. 4:10), and Gilgal, seat of the petty kings defeated by Joshua (Jos. 12:23), lay in the Samaritan foothills E of the plain.

References to Lod and Ono in the S, which were both fortified outposts (1 Ch. 8:12; Ezr. 2:33; Ne. 7:37), and 'the valley of the craftsmen' separating them (Ne. 11:35; *cf.* 1 Sa. 13:19–20) appear to indicate they were settled by the returning exiles.

The 'majesty' of Sharon (Is. 35:2), like the 'jungle' of Jordan (Je. 12:5; 49:19), would suggest the dense vegetation cover rather than the fertility which Sharon has subsequently proved to possess in its Pleistocene sands, now under orange groves. For settlement it has long remained a 'desert' (Is. 33:9), and was used only for pasturage (1 Ch. 5:16; Is. 65:10). It was here that Shitrai supervised King David's flocks (1 Ch. 27:29). The 'rose of Sharon' (Ct. 2:1–3) suggests the flowers (*PLANTS) of the dense undergrowth. Four red flowers still follow each other in quick succession, an anemone (*Anemone coronaria*), a buttercup (*Ranunculus asiaticus*), a tulip (*Tulipa montana*) and a poppy (*Papaver sp.*).

BIBLIOGRAPHY. D. Baly, *The Geography of the Bible*, 1957, pp. 133–137. J.M.H.

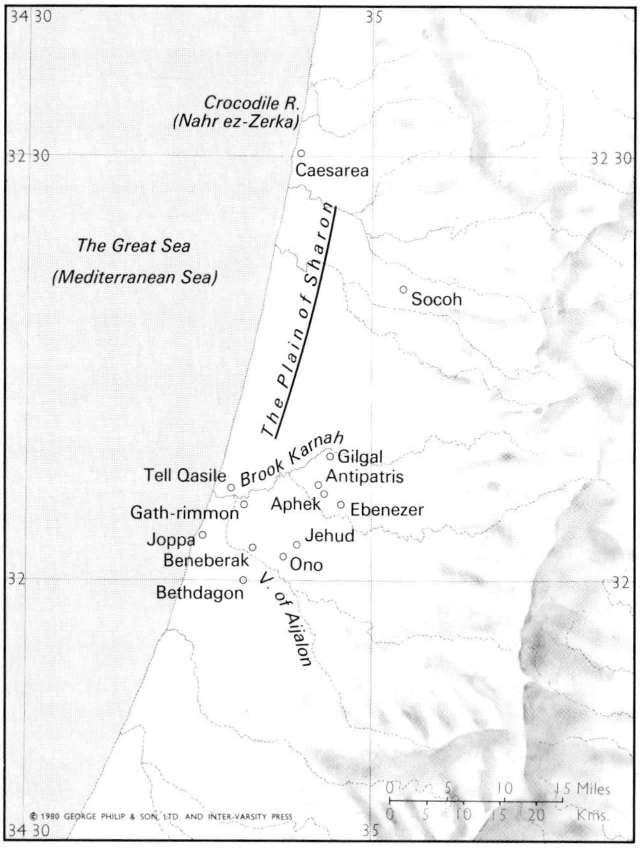

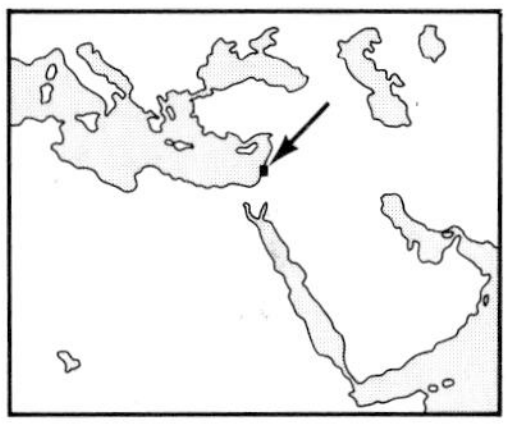

The plain of Sharon.

Opposite page:
Top:
Geological profile of the Sharon plain.

SHARUHEN. A Simeonite settlement (Jos. 19:6). Egyp. sources mention *Šrḥn*, a Hyksos fortress which resisted Ahmose for 3 years *c.* 1550 BC, barring his way to further conquests; usually identified with Tell el-Far'a, 24 km S of Gaza (Albright, *BASOR* 33, 1929, p. 7). Petrie's brief excavation revealed a strong Philistine occupation. The Joshua context also suits Tell el-Huweilfeh, ½ km N of Khirbet Rammamein (Ain Rimmon?), proposed earlier by Albright, *JPOS* 4, 1924, p. 135. See also Alt, *JPOS* 15, 1935, pp. 311ff. *Cf.* also refs. in E. K. Vogel, *Bibliography of Holy Land Sites*, 1974, p. 84. J.P.U.L.

SHAUL (Heb. *šā'ûl*, 'asked for'). In Heb., the same as *'Saul'. **1.** A king of Edom (1 Ch. 1:48–49; *cf.* Gn. 36:37–38), belonging to Rehoboth. **2.** A son of Simeon by a Canaanitess (Gn. 46:10), from whom the Shaulites took their name (Nu. 26:13). **3.** A son of Kohath (1 Ch. 6:24), called 'Joel' in 1 Ch. 6:36. G.W.G.

SHAVEH, VALLEY OF. A valley near Salem (Gn. 14:17f.), also known as 'the King's Valley',

SHAMHUTH
See Shammah, Part 3.

SHAMIR
See Shaphir, Part 3.

SHAMMOTH
See Shammah, Part 3.

SHAVEH-KIRIATHAIM
See Kiriathaim, Part 2.

where Absalom raised his memorial pillar (2 Sa. 18:18). If Salem is Jerusalem, the site may be at the top of the Valley of Hinnom. But an ancient Jewish tradition reads *ś-r-h*, another word meaning 'king', for *š-w-h* ('Shaveh'). (This involves only one slight consonantal change.) D.F.P.

SHAVSHA. The name of a secretary of state under David (2 Sa. 8:17, where he is called Seraiah). He is called Shisha in 1 Ki. 4:3, Shavsha in 1 Ch. 18:16, and Sheva in 2 Sa. 20:25. Following de Vaux, Grollenberg (*Atlas of the Bible*) suggests that the form which must underlie these names indicates that the official was an Egyptian. His eldest son's name, Elihoreph, could mean 'my god is the Nile (god)', or in its LXX form Elihaph, 'my god is Apis'. If so, then the Egyp. father gave his son a hybrid name, the first element being Heb. but the second expressing his allegiance to the religion of his Egyp. ancestors. This would further suggest that David brought in Egyptians to fill offices in his kingdom, organizing it at least in part on Egyp. models. But both of these names (and their bearers) may in fact be Semitic; if so, the evidence for Egyp. influence in the organization of David's kingdom is then much less.

T. N. D. Mettinger (*Solomonic State Officials*, 1971, pp. 25–30), largely following A. Cody (*RB* 72, 1965, pp. 381–393), explains Shavsha as a misunderstood corruption of the Egyp. title *sh-š'*, 'secretary' ('scribe of letters'); while possible, the assumed phonetic changes are highly dubious.

BIBLIOGRAPHY. *RB* 48, 1939, pp. 398–400; H. Ranke, *Ägyptische Personennamen*, 1935, 2, p. 318, No. 9; *KB*, p. 958 (*s.v.* 'Shavsha'); C. H. Gordon, *Ugaritic Textbook*, 3, 1965, p. 507, Vocabulary No. 2767; C. Virolleaud, *Palais Royal d'Ugarit*, 2, 1957, no. 82:7 *šśy*.

R.A.H.G.
K.A.K.

SHAWL
See Ornaments, Part 2.

SHEATH
See Armour, Part 1.

SHEBAH
See Shibah, Part 3.

SHEBAM
See Sibmah, Part 3.

SHEBAT
See Calendar, Part 1.

SHEAR-JASHUB. A symbolical name ('a remnant will return') given to one of Isaiah's sons to express the truth that out of the judgment God would save a remnant (*e.g.* Is. 1:9). When Isaiah went to Ahaz, Shear-jashub accompanied him as a reminder that the nation, even at that dark time, would not completely perish (Is. 7:3). E.J.Y.

SHEBA. 1. A city (Heb. *šeḇa'*) in the territory allotted to Simeon in S Palestine near Beersheba and Moladah (Jos. 19:2; *MT* at 1 Ch. 4:28 omits it in the parallel list, but LXX has 'Sama'). LXX reads 'Samaa' in MS B (*cf.* Jos. 15:26) and 'Sabee' in MS A. S. Cohen (*IDB*, 4, p. 311) suggests that Sheba ('seven') was named for the seven lambs with which Abraham made covenant with Abimelech (Gn. 21:28–29) and may have been the older part of Beersheba.

2. A Benjaminite (*šeḇa'*) who revolted unsuccessfully against David after Absalom's death (2 Sa. 20:1–2, 6–7, 10, 21–22). **3.** A leader (*šeḇa'*) of the tribe of Gad (1 Ch. 5:13). **4.** A descendant (*š^eḇâ'*) of Cush through Raamah (Gn. 10:7; 1 Ch. 1:9); brother of *Dedan. **5.** A descendant (*š^eḇâ'*) of Shem through Joktan (Gn. 10:28; 1 Ch. 1:22). **6.** Son of Jokshan (*š^eḇā'*) and grandson of Abraham and Keturah (Gn. 25:3; 1 Ch. 1:32); brother of Dedan.

7. The land (*š^eḇā'*) whose queen (*SHEBA, QUEEN OF) visited Solomon (1 Ki. 10:1ff.; 2 Ch. 9:1ff.) was in all probability the home of the Sabaeans in SW Arabia. J. A. Montgomery (*ICC*, *Kings*, 1951, pp. 215f.) contends that the Sabaeans were still in N Arabia in the 10th century BC although they controlled the trade routes from S Arabia. On the other hand, J. Bright (*History of Israel*², 1972, p. 211), while recognizing that the Sabaeans were originally camel nomads, affirms, with greater probability, that by Solomon's time they had settled in the E area of what is modern Yemen. So also G. W. Van Beek, *IDB*, 4, p. 145.

The relationship between the Sabaeans and the three Shebas mentioned in Gn. is by no means clear. They may be distinct tribes, but the similarities among the groupings are striking: Raamah's sons (Gn. 10:7, Hamites, bear the same names as Abraham's grandsons—Sheba and Dedan (25:3); both Cush, the Hamite (10:7), and Joktan, the Semite, have descendants named Sheba and Havilah (10:28–29). The Table of *Nations in Gn. 10 may reflect both the Semitic origin of the Sabaeans and also the fact that they settled in close proximity to Hamitic groups, *i.e.* Egyptians and Ethiopians. Indeed, classical Abyssinian culture testifies to a blending of Hamitic and Semitic elements, and the role that S Arabians who crossed the Bab al-Mandab as traders and colonists played in shaping this culture is impressive.

It is as traders or raiders (Jb. 1:15, although E. Dhorme, *Job*, E.T. 1967, p. xxv, identifies Sheba here with an area near Tema and Dedan, oases substantially N of the Sabaean homeland) that the OT most frequently speaks of the people of Sheba. Gold (1 Ki. 10:2; Ps. 72:15; Is. 60:6), frankincense (Is. 60:6; Je. 6:20), spices and jewels (1 Ki. 10:2; Ezk. 27:22) were brought to N markets in their caravans (Jb. 6:19). Commercial opportunists, they were not above engaging in slave trade according to Joel 3:8 (where less preferably LXX reads 'into captivity' for 'to the Sabaeans'). This extensive trading activity apparently led the Sabaeans to found colonies at various oases in N Arabia. These served as caravan bases and probably gave the colonists a degree of control over the N area. Testimony to intercourse between Sheba and Canaan is found in a S Arabian clay stamp (*c.* 9th century BC) unearthed at Bethel (*BASOR* 151, 1958, pp. 9–16).

The most prominent of the Arab states (which included Hadramaut, Ma'īn and Qatabān) during the first half of the 1st millennium BC, Sheba was ruled by *mukarribs*, priest-kings, who supervised both the political affairs and the polytheistic worship of the sun, moon and star gods. Explorations by the University of Louvain with H. St J. Philby (1951–2) and the American Foundation for the Study of Man (1950–3) found some outstanding examples of Sabaean art and architecture, especially the temple of the moon-god at Mārib, the capital, which dates from the 7th century BC, and the sluices, hewn through solid rock at the dam in Mārib (*c.* 6th century BC).

BIBLIOGRAPHY. R. L. Bowen, Jr., and F. P. Albright, *Archaeological Discoveries in South Arabia*, 1958; *GTT*; S. Moscati, *Ancient Semitic Civilizations*, 1957, pp. 181–194; G. Ryckmans, *Les religions arabes préislamiques*², 1951; J. Ryckmans, *L'institution monarchique en Arabie méridionale avant l'Islam*, 1951; G. W. Van Beek in *BA* 15, 1952, pp. 2–18; *ibid.*, 'South Arabian History and Archaeology', in G. E. Wright (ed.), *The Bible and the Near East*, 1961; A. K. Irvine in *POTT*, pp. 299ff.

D.A.H.

SHEBA, QUEEN OF. An unnamed Sabaean (*SHEBA) monarch who journeyed to Jerusalem to test Solomon's wisdom (1 Ki. 10:1–10, 13; 2 Ch. 9:1–9, 12). A major purpose of her costly (1 Ki. 10:10) yet successful (1 Ki. 10:13) visit may have been to negotiate a trade-agreement with Solomon, whose control of the trade routes jeopardized the income which the Sabaeans were accustomed to receive from the caravans which crossed their territory—an income on which Sheba (or better Saba) was dependent despite considerable achievement in agriculture due to favourable rainfall and an effective irrigation system. The spices, gold and precious stones with which she sought Solomon's favour (1 Ki. 10:3, 10) would have been typical of the luxurious cargoes of these caravans, which linked the resources of E Africa, India and S Arabia to the markets of Damascus and Gaza by way of oases like Mecca, Medina and Tema.

Both Assyr. and S Arab. inscriptions testify to the presence of queens in Arabia as early as the 8th century BC. (See N. Abbott, 'Pre-Islamic Arab Queens', *AJSL* 58, 1941, pp. 1–22.) The widespread domestication of the camel 2 centuries or so before Solomon's time made the Queen of Sheba's trip of about 2,000 km feasible (1 Ki. 10:2).

Her willingness to make this arduous journey is contrasted by Christ with the Jews' complacency in Mt. 12:42, where she is called 'Queen of the South', a title which reflects a Semitic construction like *malkaṯ sᵉḇā'* or *malkaṯ yāmîn*, Queen of Sheba or Yemen.

This queen is enshrined in Ethiopian legends, particularly the *Kebra Nagast* ('Glory of the Kings'), as the queen of Ethiopia who bore by Solomon the first king of Ethiopia. This legend reflects the close tie which existed in antiquity between S Arabia and E Africa, which Josephus also notes when he calls this ruler 'Queen of Egypt and Ethiopia' (*Ant.* 8. 165–175; *cf.* also Gregory of Nyssa, *Homilies on the Song of Songs* 7). Arabian legends remember her as Bilqis.

BIBLIOGRAPHY. Samuel Abramsky, *EJ*, 15, pp. 96–111; J. Gray, *I and II Kings*², 1970, pp. 258–262; James B. Pritchard (ed.), *Solomon and Sheba*, 1974.
D.A.H.

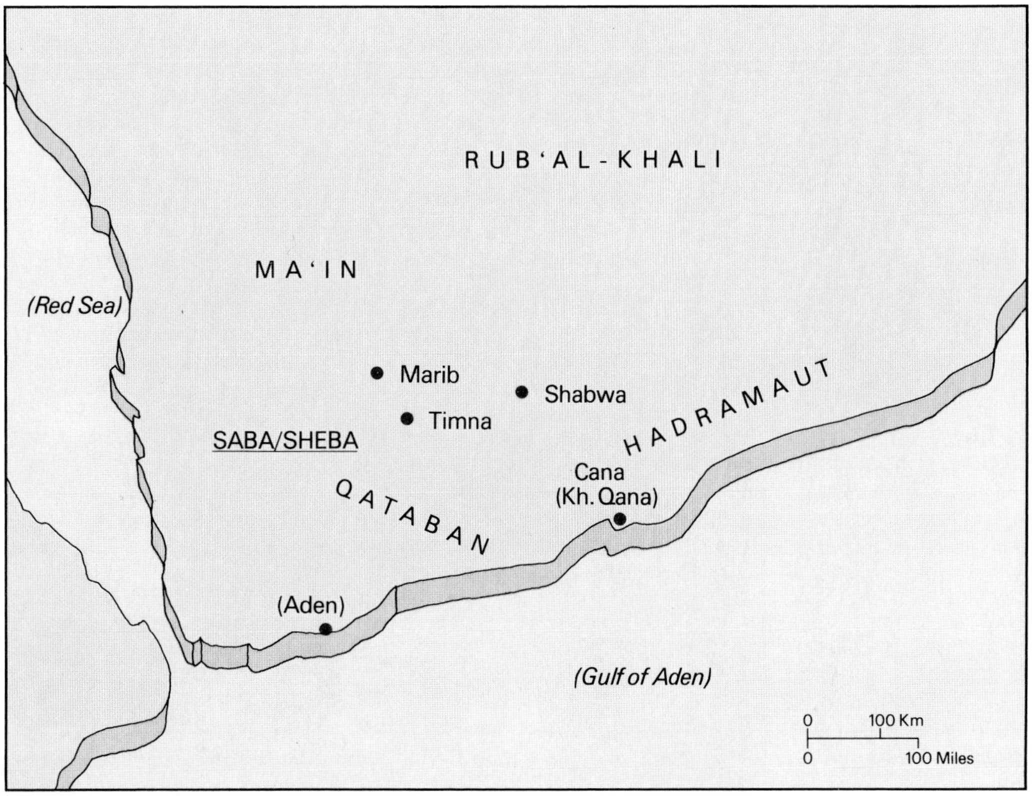

The land of Sheba.

SHEBNA. A high official under Hezekiah, variously designated minister ('which is over the house', Is. 22:15), secretary (*sōp̄ēr*, 'scribe', 2 Ki. 18:18; 19:2; Is. 36:3), and state official (*sōḵēn*, 'treasurer', Is. 22:15). A man of wealth, he was rebuked by Isaiah for preparing a conspicuously monumental rock-hewn tomb and his downfall predicted (Is. 22:15–19). Part of the inscribed lintel from such a tomb has been recovered (N. Avigad, *IEJ* 3, 1953, pp. 137–152; D. J. Wiseman, *IBA*, 1958, p. 59). The full name of Shebna may be Shebanyah(u), a name which occurs in

This early Hebrew inscription formed the lintel of the tomb of one [ ]-yahu, a royal steward ('he who is over the house'), at Siloam, Jerusalem. This may well be the tomb of Shebna, accused by Isaiah of carving a sumptuous grave for himself in the rock (Is. 22:15–16). Length 2·2 m. 7th cent. BC. (BM)

contemporary inscriptions and on Heb. seals (*IEJ* 18, 1968, pp. 166–167), and which may be compared with that later borne by levitical priests (Ne. 9:4–5; 10:10; 1 Ch. 15:24). D.J.W.

SHECHEM. 1. The son of Hamor, the Hivite, prince of Shechem (Gn. 34; Jos. 24:32; Jdg. 9:28) who defiled Jacob's daughter Dinah. **2.** A descendant of Joseph's son Manasseh (Nu. 26:31), founder of a family (Jos. 17:2). **3.** Son of Shemidah, of the tribe of Manasseh (1 Ch. 7:19).

4. An important town in central Palestine with a long history and many historical associations. Normally it appears in the Bible as Shechem (*šᵉḵem*), but also once as Sichem (Gn. 12:6, AV) and twice as Sychem (Acts 7:16, AV). It was situated in the hill country of Ephraim (Jos. 20:7), in the neighbourhood of Mt Gerizim (Jdg. 9:7). The original site is today represented by Tell Balaṭa, which lies at the E end of the valley running between Mt Ebal on the N and Mt Gerizim on the S, about 50 km N of Jerusalem and 9 km SE of Samaria.

The excavated East Gate at Shechem (Tell Balata). c. 1650–1550 BC. (MEPhA)

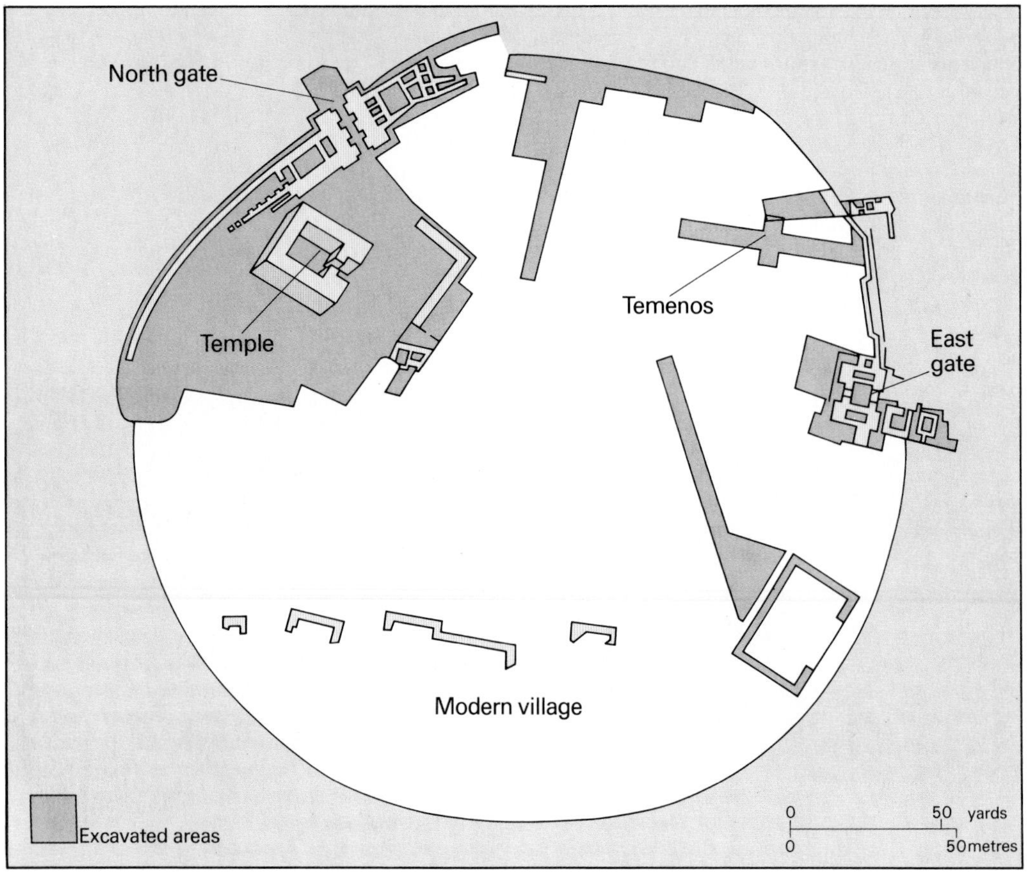

Plan of the site of Shechem, showing the areas of excavations.

Shechem (Sichem) is the first Palestinian site mentioned in Gn. Abram encamped there at the 'oak of Moreh' (Gn. 12:6). The 'Canaanite was then in the land', but the Lord revealed himself to Abram and renewed his covenant promise. Abram thereupon built an altar to the Lord (Gn. 12:7).

Abram's grandson, Jacob, on his return from Harran, came to Shalem, a city of Shechem, and pitched his tent (Gn. 33:18–19) on a parcel of ground which he bought from Hamor, the Hivite prince of the region (Gn. 33:18–19; 34:2). When Shechem, the son of Hamor, defiled Dinah, Simeon and Levi killed the men of the region (Gn. 34:25–26), and the other sons of Jacob pillaged the town (vv. 27–29), though Jacob condemned the action (Gn. 34:30; 49:5–7).

Here Jacob buried the 'strange gods' under the oak (Gn. 35:1–4) and raised an altar to El-elohe-Israel ('God, the God of Israel', Gn. 33:20; *GOD, NAMES OF). Joseph later sought his brothers near the rich pasture-lands round Shechem (Gn. 37:12ff.).

In the 15th century BC the town fell into the hands of the Habiru, as we learn from the Tell el-Amarna letters (*ANET*, pp. 477, 485–487, 489–490). The name probably occurs earlier in Egyp. records dating back to the 19th–18th centuries BC (*ANET*, pp. 230, 329).

After the Israelite conquest of Palestine Joshua called for a renewal of the covenant at Shechem. Various features of the typical covenant pattern well known in the East, 1500–700 BC, may be identified in Jos. 8:30–35 (*SACRIFICE AND OFFERING, **I.** *c.* 2). Before his death, Joshua gathered the elders again to Shechem, reiterated the covenant, and received the oath of allegiance to God, the King (Jos. 24). Many modern scholars see in these assemblies a strong suggestion of an amphictyonic league centred at Shechem (*cf.* M. Noth, *The History of Israel*, 1958).

The boundary between Ephraim and Manasseh passed near the town (Jos. 17:7), which was one of the cities of refuge, and a levitical city assigned to the Kohathite Levites (Jos. 20:7; 21:21; 1 Ch. 6:67). The town lay in Ephraim (1 Ch. 7:28). Here the Israelites buried the bones of Joseph which they had brought from Egypt (Gn. 50:25; Jos. 24:32).

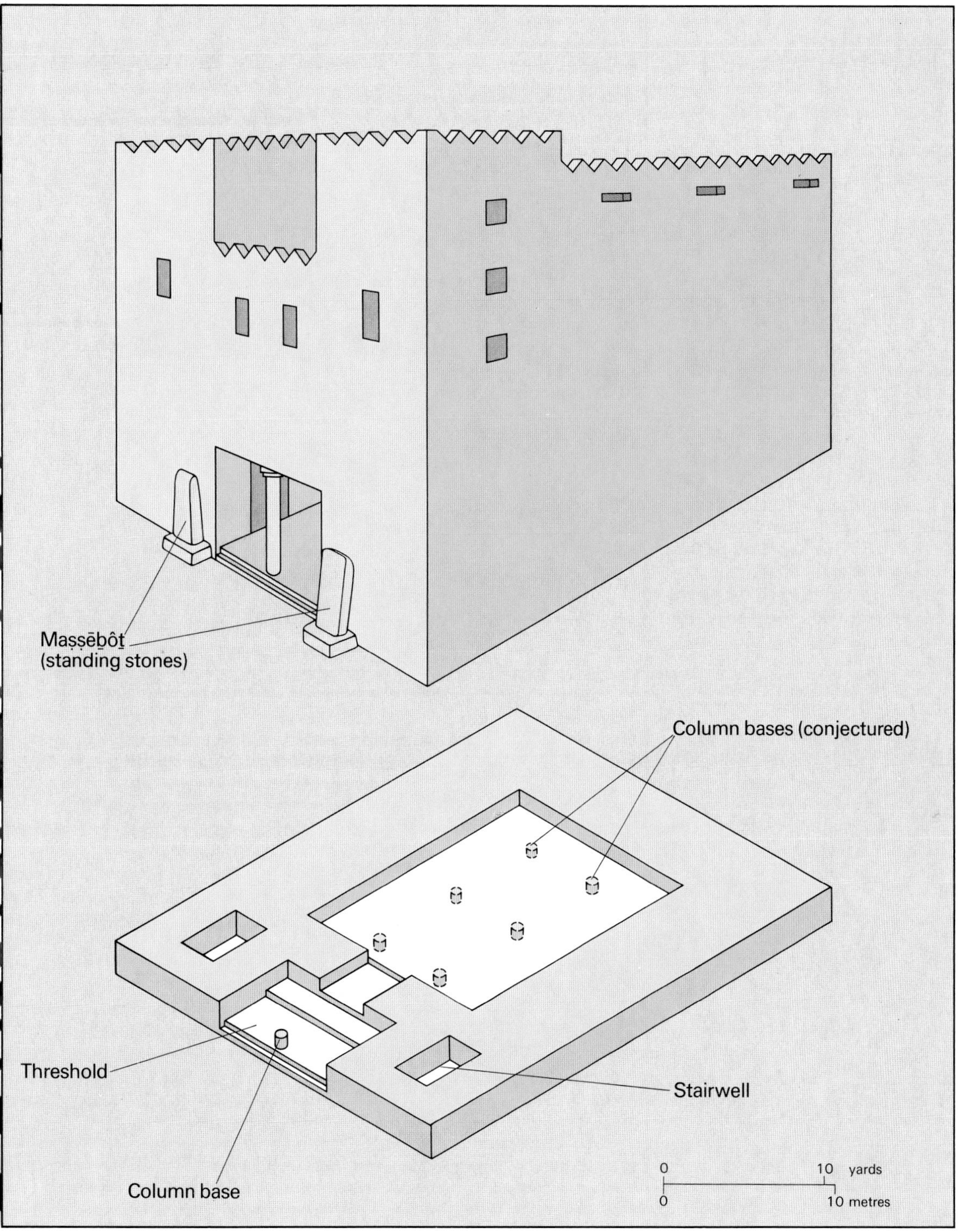

Plan and suggested reconstruction of the early phase of the fortress-temple (migdol) *excavated at Shechem. The standing stones may not have been erected until the later phase of the building. 17th cent. BC.*

In the time of the judges, Shechem was still a centre of Canaanite worship and the temple of Baal-berith ('the lord of the covenant') features in the story of Gideon's son Abimelech (Jdg. 9:4), whose mother was a Shechemite woman. Abimelech persuaded the men of the city to make him king (Jdg. 9:6; *cf.* 8:22–23). He proceeded to slay the royal seed, but Jotham, one son who escaped the bloody purge, spoke a parable about the trees as he stood on Mt Gerizim (Jdg. 9:8–15), appealing to the citizens of Shechem to forsake Abimelech. This they did after 3 years (vv. 22–23), but Abimelech destroyed Shechem (v. 45) and then attacked the stronghold of the temple of Baal-berith and burnt it over the heads of those who sought refuge there (vv. 46–49).

After Solomon's death the assembly of Israel rejected Rehoboam at Shechem and made Jeroboam king (1 Ki. 12:1–19; 2 Ch. 10:1–11). Jeroboam restored the town and made it his capital for a time (1 Ki. 12:25), but later moved the capital to Penuel, and then to Tirzah. The town declined in importance thereafter, but continued in existence long after the fall of Samaria in 722 BC, for men from Shechem came with offerings to Jerusalem as late as 586 BC (Je. 41:5).

In post-exilic times Shechem became the chief city of the Samaritans (Ecclus. 50:26; Jos., *Ant.* 11. 340), who built a temple here. In 128 BC John Hyrcanus captured the town (Jos., *Ant.* 13. 255). In the time of the first Jewish revolt Vespasian camped near Shechem, and after the war the town was rebuilt and named Flavia Neapolis in honour of the emperor Flavius Vespasianus (hence the modern Nablus).

Important excavations conducted at Tell Balaṭa by C. Watzinger (1907–9), E. Sellin and his colleagues (between 1913 and 1934) and by G. E. Wright (1956–66) have revealed the story of this site from the mid-4th millennium BC down to *c.* 100 BC when the Hellenistic city came to an end. Although there was a sizeable Chalcolithic village during the 4th millennium BC, the city of the historical period arose *c.* 1800 BC in the Middle Bronze Age and reached the height of its prosperity during the Hyksos period (*c.* 1700–1550 BC). During these years several courtyard temples and city walls were built. About 1600 BC a massive stone wall was erected, earlier walls covered over and a fortress temple built on the filling, which was to remain with some changes till *c.* 1100 BC and may well represent in its later stages the temple of Baal-berith (Jdg. 9:4) known to the early Israelites. The town remained important until the 9th–8th centuries BC when it began to deteriorate. Masses of fallen brick and burnt debris attest the destruction of the city by the Assyrians in 724–721 BC. For 4 centuries the town reverted to a village until it gained new life, probably as a Samaritan centre, between *c.* 325 and *c.* 108 BC. There is a continuous coin record for this period. The town ceased to exist after its destruction by John Hyrcanus *c.* 108 BC.

The question of whether Shechem is the same as the *Sychar of Jn. 4:5 has not been solved. There are only a few traces of Roman occupation at Tell Balaṭa. Sychar may have lain in the same general vicinity.

BIBLIOGRAPHY. E. F. Campbell, Jr., and J. F. Ross, 'The Excavation of Shechem and the Biblical Tradition', *BA* 26, 1963, pp. 2–26; E. Nielsen, *Shechem, A Traditio-Historical Investigation*, 1955; E. Sellin, *ZDPV*, 1926, 1927, 1928; E. Sellin and H. Steckeweh, *ZDPV*, 1941; G. E. Wright, *Shechem, The Biography of a Biblical City*, 1965; 'Shechem', in *AOTS*, pp. 355–370.

J.A.T.

SHEEP-POOL
See Bethesda, Part 1.

SHEERAH (RSV), **SHERAH** (AV). The Heb. name, meaning 'a female relative', of a daughter of Ephraim, or of the daughter or sister of his son, Beriah (1 Ch. 7:24). She built or rebuilt three towns in the territory assigned to Ephraim, Lower and Upper Beth-horon and Uzzen-sheerah. This is the only example in the Bible of a woman builder of towns. Codex Vaticanus of the LXX takes this name as a common noun, 'those remaining', and the Pesh. translates the name as a verb, 'she was left', but other Gk. MSS and the Vulg. support the interpretation as a proper name.

J.T.

SHEET. 1. Heb. *sāḏîn*, RSV 'linen garments' (Jdg. 14:12–13). See reference to 'shirt' in *Dress. **2.** Gk. *othonē*, 'a piece of linen', 'a linen sheet', used in describing Peter's vision at Joppa (Acts 10:11; 11:5).

J.D.D.

SHEKINAH. The Shekinah (Heb. *šᵉḵînâ*), the radiance, glory or presence of God dwelling in the

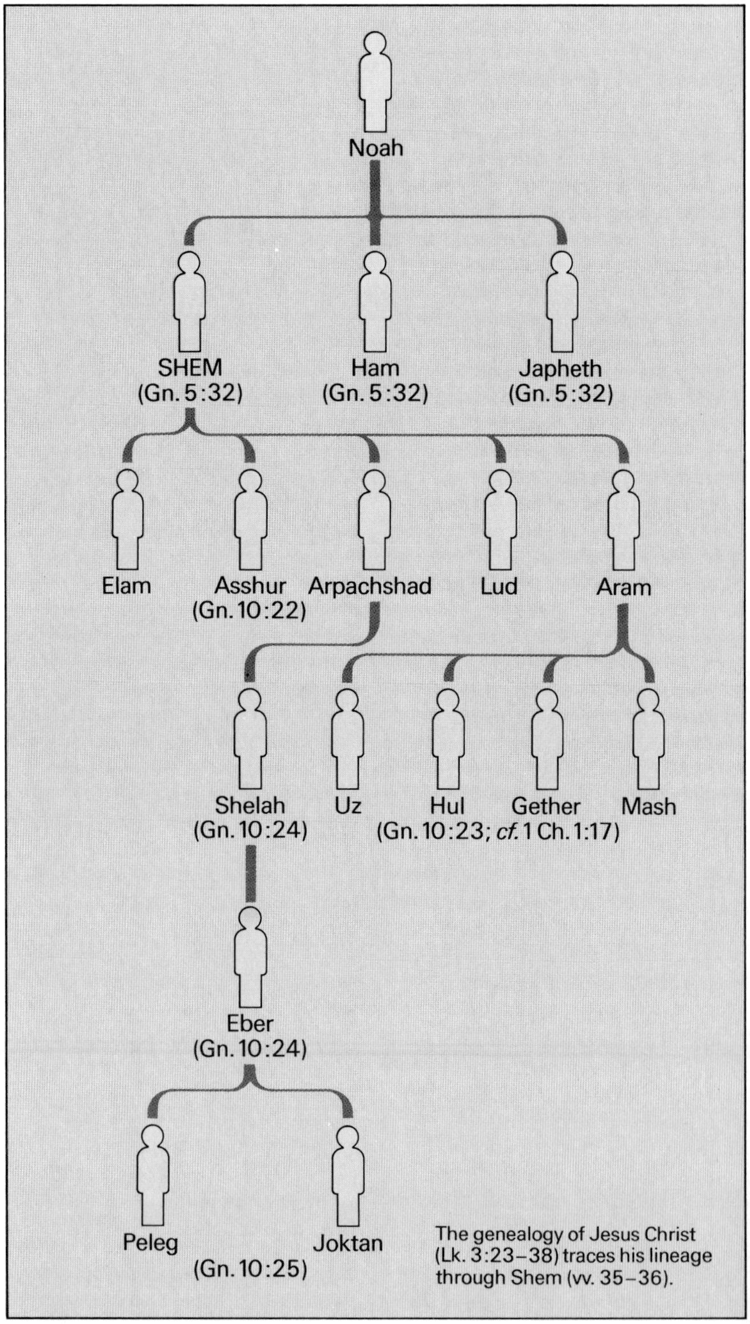

The genealogy of Shem.

midst of his people, is used by Targumist and Rabbi to signify God himself, for legal Judaism dislikes ascribing form or emotion to deity. Nevertheless the God conceived in purified human terms inspired the noblest prophetic utterances, whereas the legalist God became cold, abstract, aloof. The Shekinah, nearest Jewish equivalent to the Holy Spirit, became, with other OT ideas or derivatives (Word, Wisdom, Spirit, *etc.*) a bridge between man's corporeality and God's transcendence. The term is post-biblical, but the concept saturates both Testaments. It underlies the teaching that God dwells in his sanctuary (Ex. 25:8, *etc.*), or among his people (Ex. 29:45f., *etc.*). These and cognate passages use the root verb *šāḵan*, 'to dwell', from which Shekinah is derived.

The glory of God (*kāḇôḏ* in the Heb. Bible, *doxa* in LXX and NT) is another name for the Shekinah. The Heb. and Gk. words may be applied to the glory of mere human beings, such as Jacob (Gn. 31:1, AV) or Solomon (Mt. 6:29), but it is clear enough when they refer to God. Thunder, lightning and cloud may be the outward concomitants of God's glory (Ex. 19:16; 24:15ff.; Pss. 29; 97; Ezk. 1:4); or it may be specially associated with the tent of meeting (Ex. 40:34–38) or with the Temple (Ezk. 43:2, 4); but it is manifest also in creation (Ps. 19), and possesses elements more numinous and mysterious than any of these (Ex. 33:18–23). In fact, the glory of God regularly becomes more glorious when it is deliberately divorced from Temple or mercy-seat.

In the NT as in the OT, glory may be predicated of God (Lk. 2:9; Acts 7:55; 2 Cor. 3:18) or ascribed to him (Lk. 2:14; Rom. 11:36; Phil. 4:20; Rev. 7:12, *etc.*). The attribution of this glory is mentioned as a human duty, whether fulfilled (Rom. 4:20) or unfulfilled (Acts 12:23; Rev. 16:9). The glory is present in a special way in the heavenly temple (Rev. 15:8) and in the heavenly city (Rev. 21:23).

The NT freely ascribes comparable glory to Christ as divine, before as well as after the dividing-point of Easter. The Synoptics are slightly reticent about associating this glory with the earthly Jesus, except in reference to the parousia (Mk. 8:38; 10:37; 13:26; also parallels), or in reference to Christ transfigured (Lk. 9:32). John ascribes this glory much more freely (*cf.* 1:14; 2:11; 11:4); nevertheless he distinguishes a fuller or final revelation as subsequent to the earthly ministry (7:39; 12:16, *etc.*). This seeming fluctuation is not unnatural—the view of the earthly Jesus and the heavenly Christ would sometimes become foreshortened after the Passion. The cognate verb *doxazō* frequently replaces the noun (Jn. 12; 17, *etc.*). The resemblance between the Heb. word and Gk. *skēnē*, *etc.*, may suggest the *shekinah* motif in Jn. 1:14 (*eskēnōsen*, 'dwelt') and Rev. 21:3 (*skēnē*, 'dwelling').

Other passages are worthy of special attention—*cf.* 1 Tim. 3:16; Tit. 2:13; Heb. 1:3; 13:21; Jas. 2:1; 1 Pet. 1:11, 21; 4:13; 5:1; Rev. 5:12f.

BIBLIOGRAPHY. See *HDB* (*s.v.* 'Shekinah'); *JewE* (*s.v.* 'Anthropomorphism', 'Shekinah'); *EJ*, 14, 1971 (*s.v.* 'Shekhinah'); G. Kittel, G. von Rad, in *TDNT* 2, pp. 237–251; R. A. Stewart, *Rabbinic Theology*, 1961, pp. 40–42.

R.A.S.

SHELAH. 1. Son of Arpachshad of the family of Shem, and father of Eber (Gn. 10:24; 11:12–15; 1 Ch. 1:18, 24; Lk. 3:35). **2.** Youngest son of Judah by Shua (Gn. 38:5; 46:12; 1 Ch. 2:3; 4:21), promised by Judah to his daughter-in-law Tamar after Er and Onan had died (Gn. 38:11, 14, 26). Father of the Shelanites (Nu. 26:20). The Syr. gives 'Shelanite' for 'Shilonite' in Ne. 11:5 (*cf.* 1 Ch. 9:5). **3.** In Ne. 3:15 (RSV) the name of the pool better known as Siloam. AV gives 'Siloah'.

J.G.G.N.

SHEM. The eldest son of Noah (Gn. 5:32; 6:10; 1 Ch. 1:4), and the ancestor of many descendants (Gn. 10). He was one of the eight people to escape the Flood in the ark (Gn. 7:13), and after it, when Noah was drunk, he and Japheth covered their father's nakedness (Gn. 9:18, 23, 26–27). Two years after the Flood, when Shem was 100 years old, he became father of Arpachshad (Gn. 11:10), through whom passed the line of descent to the Messiah (Lk. 3:36), and it may be in reference to this fact that Noah made his prophetic statement (Gn. 9:26). Since among the descendants of Shem listed in Gn. 10:21–31 a number are identified with peoples who are known to have spoken related languages in antiquity, the term 'Semitic' has been applied for convenience to this group by modern philologists. This is a modern use of the term, however, and does not imply that all the descendants of Shem spoke Semitic languages. It is stated that Shem lived for 500 years after the birth of Arpachshad (Gn. 11:11), giving him a life of 600 years. All the major versions agree on these figures. An early theory (Poebel) has been recently revived (Kramer), to the effect that the name *šem* is derived, through various phonetic changes, from *šumer*, written *ki.en.gi* by the Sumerians, the Akkadian name of this people who formed an important element in the early population of Mesopotamia. This theory has not been widely accepted.

BIBLIOGRAPHY. S. N. Kramer, *Analecta Biblica* 12, 1959, pp. 203–204; *The Sumerians*, 1963, pp. 297–299.

T.C.M.

SHEMUEL (Heb. *šᵉmû'ēl*, '(?) name of God'; *cf.* Samuel).

1. The son of Ammihud, leader of the tribe of Simeon, appointed to assist in the division of Canaan (Nu. 34:20). In Nu. 1:6; 2:12; 7:36, 41; 10:19 the leader of the tribe is called Shelumiel, the son of Zurishaddai, and the LXX gives the name Salamiēl in all these instances.

2. A grandson of Issachar (1 Ch. 7:2).

R.A.H.G.

SHEOL. This word is used in the OT for the place of the dead. The derivation of the Heb. word *šᵉ'ôl* is uncertain. Two main theories have been proposed.

a. Some have suggested that it comes from a weakened form of the root *š'l*, from which derive the words for a hollow hand (Is. 40:12) and a hollow way (between vineyards, Nu. 22:24). In post-biblical Heb. *ša'al* means the 'deep' of the sea. If this derivation is correct, the original sense will be the hollow, or more probably deep, place.

b. More scholars now hold the view that it is derived from the root *š'l* meaning 'ask' or 'enquire'. In this case it may have been originally the place of enquiry, where oracles could be obtained. The root *š'l* is frequently used in the OT of consulting oracles, but the idea is certainly not a leading one in the conception of Sheol. There is a connection of *thought* with this root in the personification of Sheol as a gaping, craving monster (Is. 5:14;

SHELUMIEL
See Shemuel, Part 3.

SHEMAIAH
See Nehelam, Part 2.

SHENAZZAR
See Sheshbazzar, Part 3.

SHENIR
See Senir, Part 3.

cf. Hab. 2:5, *etc.*). Delitzsch (Commentary on Is. 5:14) thought that an equivalent Assyr. word had been found in *šualu*, but Jensen and others have disputed the existence of this word (*cf. Transactions of the Society of Biblical Archaeology* 8, 1885, p. 269).

The meaning of Sheol moves between the ideas of the grave, the underworld and the state of death. Throughout the ancient Near East, as elsewhere, the dead were pictured as existing in a subterranean realm known in Bab. as *aralu* and in Ugaritic as *'ereṣ*, 'earth'. But whereas these were ruled by their own gods, Yahweh was the ruler of Sheol.

Sheol was below the surface of the earth (Ezk. 31:15, 17; Ps. 86:13), a place of dust (Jb. 17:16), darkness (Jb. 10:21), silence (Ps. 94:17) and forgetfulness (Ps. 88:12). Sometimes the distinctions of earthly life are pictured as continuing in Sheol (Is. 14:9; Ezk. 32:27), but always it is a place of weakness and joylessness.

In some passages Sheol has a punitive aspect (*e.g.* Ps. 49:13–14) and premature committal to Sheol is a form of judgment. The OT sees earthly life as the arena for the service of Yahweh; it is there that his word can be received, his sacrifices offered, his interventions experienced. Therefore in a real sense to be in Sheol is to be cut off from his hand (Ps. 88:3–5). However, Yahweh is both present in Sheol (Ps. 139:8) and able to deliver from it (Ps. 16:10).

Some have seen in words such as *'ᵃḇaddôn*, 'destruction' (Jb. 31:12; 26:6; 28:22; Ps. 88:11; Pr. 15:11; 27:20), *šaḥaṯ*, 'pit' and perhaps sometimes also 'corruption' (E. F. Sutcliffe, *The Old Testament and the Future Life*, 1946, pp. 39f.; Jb. 33:24; Ps. 16:10; Ezk. 28:8, *etc.*) and *bôr*, 'pit' (Ps. 30:3; Ezk. 31:14), a place of punishment within Sheol. But no passage where they occur necessitates this interpretation, and the idea is not explicitly formulated in the OT. These words are better regarded as synonyms of Sheol, with which they all sometimes occur in parallelism.

In the later Jewish literature we meet with divisions within Sheol for the wicked and the righteous, in which each experiences a foretaste of his final destiny (*Enoch* 22:1–14). This idea appears to underlie the imagery of the parable of the rich man and Lazarus in Lk. 16:19–31. The Gk. *hadēs* used in this passage represents the underworld, or realm of the dead, in the classics. In the LXX it almost always translates *šᵉ'ôl*, and in the NT the Pesh. renders it by *šᵉyûl*. It is therefore the NT equivalent of Sheol. It is used in connection with the death of Christ in Acts 2:27, 31, which quotes Ps. 16:10. In Mt. 16:18 Christ says that the gates of Hades (*cf.* Is. 38:10; Pss. 9:13; 107:18) shall not prevail against his church. As the gates of a city are essential to its power, the meaning here is probably the power of death. The phrase 'brought down to Hades' in Mt. 11:23 is best understood metaphorically of the depths of shame. In Rev., Christ holds the keys of Death and Hades (1:18). Their power (6:8) is broken and they are banished to the lake of fire (20:13–14).

BIBLIOGRAPHY. R. H. Charles, *A Critical History of the Doctrine of a Future Life*, 1913; A. Heidel, *The Gilgamesh Epic and OT Parallels*, 1946, pp. 137–223; N. J. Tromp, *Primitive Conceptions of Death and the Nether World in the OT*, 1969; H. Bietenhard, in *NIDNTT* 2, pp. 205–210. D.K.I.

SHEPHELAH (Heb. *šᵉpēlâ*), a geographical term for the low hill tract between the coastal plain of *Palestine and the high central ranges. The term is used only in the AV of 1 Macc. 12:38, which elsewhere translates as 'vale', 'valley' or (low) 'plain(s)', although the district is frequently referred to in the OT. The RV rendering 'lowland' (sometimes also in RSV) would give a truer picture if used in the plural form, to indicate its rolling relief of both hills and valleys. But its root-meaning ('to humble' or 'make low') suggests more accurately a district of relatively low relief at the foot of the central mountains. In RSV 'Shephelah' occurs in 1 Ki. 10:27; 1 Ch. 27:28; 2 Ch. 1:15; 9:27; 26:10; 28:18; Je. 17:26; 32:44; 33:13; Ob. 1:19. Passages such as 2 Ch. 26:10 and 28:18 clearly distinguish it from the coastal plain. The location of the 'Shephelah' of Jos. 11:2, 16 is distinct. There it refers to the hills around the town of Carmel (v. 2). 'Israelite Shephelah' in v. 16, according to G. A. Smith, may mean the land between Carmel and Samaria, a structural continuation of the true Shephelah farther S.

BIBLIOGRAPHY. D. Baly, *The Geography of the Bible*, 1957, pp. 142–147; *LOB*. J.M.H.

SHEPHERD. Biblical shepherds may be literal or metaphorical: those in charge of sheep; those also, divine or mortal, in charge of men. Similar praise or censure may be applied to both types. The Heb. term for shepherd is the participial *rō'eh*, the Gk. *poimēn*. Care exercised over fellow-mortals may be political or spiritual. Homer and other secular writers frequently called kings and governors shepherds (*Iliad* 1. 263; 2. 243, *etc.*), a usage reflected, in deeper metaphors, in Ezk. 34.

The literal shepherd pursued, and still pursues, an exacting calling, one as old as Abel (Gn. 4:2). He must find grass and water in a dry and stony land (Ps. 23:2), protect his charges from weather and from fiercer creatures (*cf.* Am. 3:12), and retrieve any strayed animal (Ezk. 34:8; Mt. 18:12, *etc.*). When his duties carried him far from human haunts, a bag held his immediate necessities (1 Sa. 17:40, 49), and a tent might be his dwelling (Ct. 1:8). He might use dogs to assist him, like his modern counterpart (Jb. 30:1). When shepherds and flocks take up their more permanent abode in any city, this is a mark of depopulation and disaster through divine judgment (Je. 6:3; 33:12; Zp. 2:13–15). The shepherd on duty was liable to make restitution for any sheep lost (Gn. 31:39), unless he could effectively plead circumstances beyond his foresight or control (Ex. 22:10–13). Ideally the shepherd should be strong, devoted and selfless, as many of them were. But ruffians were sometimes found in an honourable profession (Ex. 2:17, 19), and some shepherds inevitably failed in their duty (Zc. 11, *passim*; Na. 3:18; Is. 56:11, *etc.*).

Such is the honour of the calling that the OT frequently delineates God as the Shepherd of Israel (Gn. 49:24; Pss. 23:1; 80:1), tender in his solicitude (Is. 40:11), yet able to scatter the flock in wrath, or gather it again in forgiveness (Je. 31:10). Sometimes the note is predominantly one of judgment, when human shepherd and sheep alike stand condemned and punished (Je. 50:6; 51:23; Zc. 13:7; and Gospel applications). These unfaithful shepherds may well tremble to stand before the Lord (Je. 49:19; 50:44). Sometimes there is a note of compassion when the sheep are deserted by those responsible for them (Nu. 27:17; 1 Ki. 22:17; Mk.

6:34, *etc.*). Two shepherds mentioned with special approval are Moses (Is. 63:11) and, surprisingly enough, that heathen executor of God's purposes, Cyrus (Is. 44:28). Scripture earnestly stresses the serious responsibility of human leaders to those who follow them. One of the most solemn chapters in the OT is the denunciation of the faithless shepherds in Ezk. 34 (*cf.* Je. 23:1–4, and even more sternly Je. 25:32–38). These, for their belly's sake, have fed themselves and not their sheep; they have killed and scattered their charges for their own profit; they have grievously neglected their proper pastoral care; therefore God will re-gather the sheep and judge the shepherds. He will in fact appoint one shepherd (Ezk. 34:23). This is critically interpreted as signifying the union of the N and S kingdoms, but it portrays much better the expected Christ.

In the NT it is Christ's mission to be Shepherd, even Chief Shepherd (Heb. 13:20 and 1 Pet. 2:25; also 1 Pet. 5:4). This is worked out in detail in Jn. 10, which merits detailed comparison with Ezk. 34. John's main points are: the iniquity of those who 'creep, and intrude and climb into the fold'; the using of the door as a mark of the true shepherd; the familiarity of the sheep with the voice of their appointed leader (modern shepherds in the E use precisely the same methods); the teachings regarding the Person of Christ, who is likened to the door (E shepherds frequently slept right across the 'door' or opening in the fold wall); likened to the good shepherd, but contrasted with the worthless hireling. John stresses also the relationship of Christ, his followers and God; the bringing into the 'one flock' of the 'other sheep' (v. 16); and the rejection of those who are not the true sheep of Christ. (*Cf.* Milton, *Lycidas*, esp. lines 113–131.)

BIBLIOGRAPHY. E. Beyreuther, in *NIDNTT* 3, pp. 564–569; F. F. Bruce, 'The Shepherd King', in *This is That*, 1968, pp. 100–114; J. Jeremias, in *TDNT* 6, pp. 485–502. R.A.S.

SHESHACH. Probably an artificial word (Je. 25:26; 51:41, AV, RSV mg.), formed by the device known as Athbash. The Eng. equivalent would be to replace *a* by *z*, *b* by *y*, *c* by *x*, *etc.* The Heb. consonants *š-š-k*, then, really represent *b-b-l*,

A shepherd leads sheep and goats from a pen. A typical scene represented on early Ancient Near Eastern seals. Babylonia. Height 3·6 cm. c. 2300 BC. (BM)

i.e. bāḇel, 'Babylon'. The vowels have no value. The device is here word-play, not cipher, since Je. 51:41 later mentions Babylon explicitly. Possibly, however, Sheshach was a genuine name for Babylon. D.F.P.

SHESHBAZZAR. The person made governor (Heb. *nāśî*, 'prince') of Judah by Cyrus (Ezr. 1:8), to whom the temple vessels captured by Nebuchadrezzar II were entrusted for return to Jerusalem (Ezr. 5:14–15). His name may represent the Bab. *Šaššu-aba-uṣur* ('May Šaššu/Shamash protect the father'). His role and identity have been much discussed, some taking this as another, perhaps court, name for *Zerubbabel, others that he was the Bab. official leader of the returning party of Jewish exiles. He may well be the person entitled *Tirshatha in Ezr. 2:63; Ne. 7:65, 70. An identity with Shenazzar (Gk. *Sanesar*; *cf.* 1 Esdr. 2:11), an uncle of Zerubbabel (1 Ch. 3:8) is unlikely (P.-R. Berger, *ZAW* 83, 1971, pp. 98–100). D.J.W.

SHIBAH. The name of a well dug by Isaac's servants and named Shibah (Heb. *šiḇ'â*), or Shebah (Gn. 26:33, AV), because of a covenant with Abimelech. The word itself means 'seven' or 'oath'. Already, before Isaac's time, Abraham had encountered trouble with Abimelech king of Gerar and had finally entered into a covenant (Gn. 21:22–34). Seven ewe lambs were presented to Abimelech as a witness to the fact, and Abraham preserved the memory of this covenant by calling the place Beersheba ('well of seven', 'well of an oath'). Isaac revived the old name, using the feminine form *šiḇ'â* of the word *šeḇā'*. J.A.T.

SHIBBOLETH. A test-word by which the Gileadites under Jephthah detected the defeated Ephraimites who tried to escape across the Jordan after the battle (Jdg. 12:5–6). Since in the Ephraim local Semitic dialect initial *sh* became *s*, their true identity was disclosed when they pronounced *šibbōleṯ* as *sibbōleṯ*. Both words mean 'a stream in flood' (*cf.* Ps. 69:2; Is. 27:12), though the former is also apt to be confused with *šibbōleṯ*, 'an ear of corn'. Those Ephraimites who were thus discovered were slain immediately (v. 6). In modern usage the word stands for the catchword or mark of a sect or party, often used disparagingly. D.J.W.

SHIHOR-LIBNATH. A small river forming part of the S boundary of the tribe of Asher (Jos. 19:26). Probably the modern Nahr ez-Zerqa, which runs S of Mt Carmel (*EGYPT, RIVER OF). See *GTT*, p. 190, n. 78; L. H. Grollenberg, *Atlas of the Bible*, 1957, pp. 58–59. Aharoni (*LOB*, pp. 237–238) argued for the *Kishon. T.C.M.

SHILOH. According to Jdg. 21:19, Shiloh is situated 'north of Bethel, on the east of the highway that goes up from Bethel to Shechem, and south of Lebonah'. This identifies it as the modern Seilūn, a ruined site on a hill about 14 km N of Bethel (Beitīn) and 5 km SE of el-Lubbān. The site was excavated by Danish expeditions in 1926–9 and 1932, and evidence was found of Middle Bronze occupation (*c.* 2100–1600 BC); but then there was a lull until about 1200 BC when a further period of activity extended until about 1050 BC. About this

SHERAH
See Sheerah, Part 3.

SHETH
See Seth, Part 3.

SHEWBREAD
See Showbread, Part 3.

SHIELD
See Armour, Part 1.

SHIHOR
See Egypt, river of, Part 1.

Ruins of the site of biblical Shiloh. (RS)

time parts of the city may have been destroyed, presumably by the Philistines. No sign was found of an early Israelite temple from this period of occupation.

According to the biblical record, it was at Shiloh that the tent of meeting was set up in the early days of the Conquest (Jos. 18:1), and it was the principal sanctuary of the Israelites during the time of the Judges (Jdg. 18:31). It was the site of a local annual festival of dancing in the vineyards, perhaps at the Feast of Ingathering (Ex. 23:16), which once provided the men of Benjamin with an opportunity to seize the maidens for wives (Jdg. 21:19ff.), and this festival probably developed into the annual pilgrimage in which Samuel's parents were later to take part (1 Sa. 1:3). By the time of Eli and his sons the sanctuary had become a well-established structure for centralized worship, and the tent of Joshua had been replaced by a temple (*hêḵāl*) with door and door-posts (1 Sa. 1:9). Although Scripture does not refer directly to its destruction, it is possible from archaeological evidence that this did take place and this would fit in well with the references to Shiloh as an example of God's judgment upon his people's wickedness (Ps. 78:60; Je. 7:12, 14; 26:6, 9). On the other hand, Ahijah the Shilonite is mentioned in 1 Ki. 11:29; 14:2, and other inhabitants of Shiloh in Je. 41:5. Some limited habitation must have continued after 1050 BC, but the priesthood transferred to Nob (1 Sa. 22:11; *cf.* 14:3) and Shiloh ceased to be a religious centre.

A reference of peculiar difficulty comes in Gn. 49:10, 'the sceptre shall not depart from Judah, nor the ruler's staff from between his feet, until Shiloh come' (RV). The Heb. *'aḏ kî-yāḇō' šîlōh* can be rendered in several ways. (i) As RV, taking Shiloh as a Messianic title. (ii) As RVmg. 'till he come to Shiloh', with the subject as Judah and the fulfilment in the assembling of Israel to Shiloh in Jos. 18:1, when the tribe of Judah nobly relinquished the pre-eminence it had formerly enjoyed. (iii) By emending *šîlōh* to *šellōh* and translating with the LXX 'until that which is his shall come', *i.e.* 'the things reserved for him', a vaguely Messianic hope. (iv) By emending *šîlōh* to *šay lô*, as in NEB, 'so long as tribute is paid to him'. (v) Following a variant reading in LXX, 'until he comes to whom it belongs' (RSV), whatever 'it' may be (Onkelos says it is the kingdom).

The last of these was generally favoured by the Fathers, while the first does not seem to have been put forward seriously until the 16th century except in one doubtful passage in the Talmud. Against (i) is its uniqueness: nowhere else is Shiloh used as a title for the Messiah and the NT does not recognize it as a prophecy. If it were taken as a title it would have to mean something like 'the peace-giver', but this is not very natural linguistically. (ii) is plausible, but it scarcely fits in with what we know of the subsequent history of Judah; nor is it usual for a patriarchal blessing to have such a time-limit. A variant to get round that objection is the translation 'as long as people come to Shiloh', *i.e.* 'for ever', but it strains the Heb. (iii), (iv) and (v)

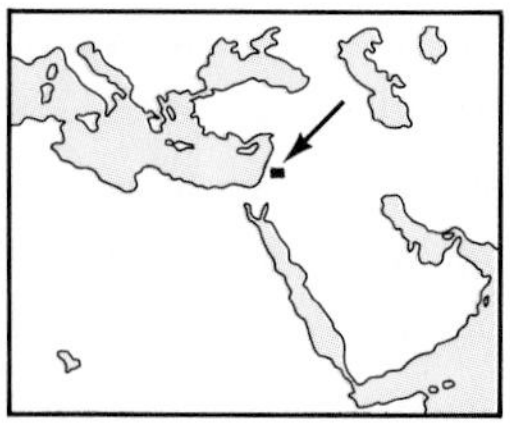

The location of Shiloh.

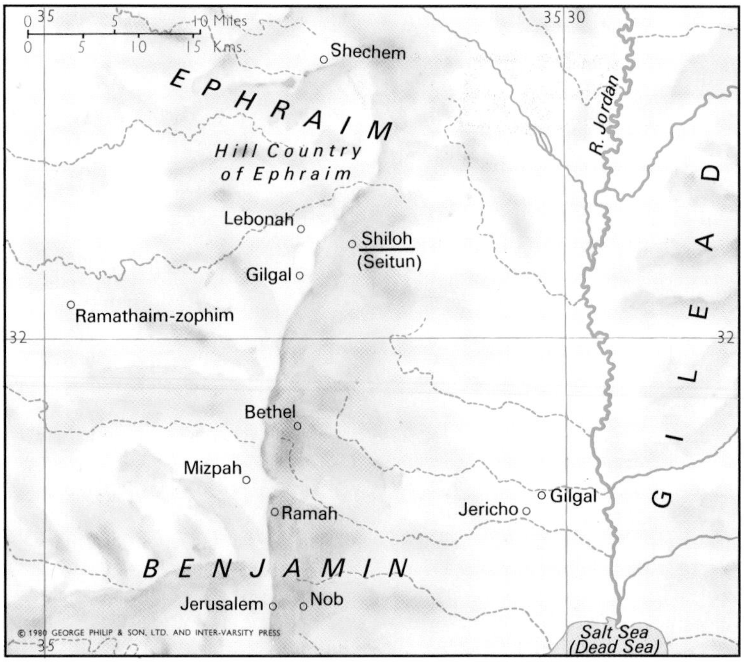

involve a minor emendation, and the renderings leave much to the imagination, but Ezk. 21:27 (v. 32 in Heb.) shows that a similar construction can stand; indeed, Ezk. 21:27 is probably a deliberate echo and interpretation of Gn. 49:10. The use of *še-* for the relative particle is, however, normally regarded as late (but *cf.* Jdg. 5:7).

For reviews of the possible interpretations, see especially the commentaries of J. Skinner and E. A. Speiser; an interesting theory by J. Lindblom is found in *VT Supp.* 1 (= Congress Volume, 1953), pp. 78–87. For archaeological information, see W. F. Albright in *BASOR* 9, 1923, pp. 10f.; H. Kjaer in *PEQ* 63, 1931, pp. 71–88; M.-L. Buhl and S. Holm-Nielsen, *Shiloh . . . : The Pre-Hellenistic Remains*, 1969.

J.B.Tr.

SHIMEATH. In 2 Ki. 12:21 an Ammonitess, the mother of Jozacar (called Zabad in 2 Ch. 24:26), one of the murderers of Joash. J.D.D.

SHIMEI (Heb. *šim'î*, perhaps abridged from *šᵉma'yāhû*, 'Yahweh has heard'). The OT records 19 men named Shimei. The first of note was a grandson of Levi (Nu. 3:21), and his family (the Shimeites) had part of the responsibility for maintaining the tent of meeting as their sacred charge (Nu. 3:25–26).

The best-known is Shimei the son of Gera, a Benjaminite and a kinsman of Saul, who cursed David for being a man of blood (2 Sa. 16:5ff.). The reference appears to be twofold: *a.* to David's conciliation of the Gibeonites (2 Sa. 21:1–10) by delivering to them seven of Saul's sons and grandsons to be hanged for Saul's slaughter of the Gibeonites (v. 1); *b.* to Absalom's rebellion, which would bring an end to David's reign, a just recompense for the blood of Saul's house which had been shed before the union of Judah and Israel; in fact David had not been responsible for the killings (2 Sa. 3:6–27; 4:8–11). David seems to have accepted this meekly, believing that Shimei spoke an admonition from the Lord (2 Sa. 16:11–12), as if acknowledging that at all events he was the occasion of the deaths. Later in life, however, David concluded that Shimei had sown dissension, and was not therefore a guiltless man (1 Ki. 2:8–9). Solomon showed clemency to Shimei, giving him a place in Jerusalem; but, to take revenge on Shimei for his bitterness towards David, had him slain, after 3 years, on the (wrong) grounds of his suspected complicity with the Philistines of Gath (1 Ki. 2:36–46).

C.H.D.

SHIMRON-MERON. A Canaanite city whose king was allied with Hazor (Jos. 11:1, simply 'Shimron') and so defeated by Joshua in his Galilean war (Jos. 12:20); probably identical with Shimron in the territory assigned to Zebulun, in the Bethlehem district (Jos. 19:15). If so, it is possibly the present Tell es-Semuniyeh, about 5 km SSE of Bethlehem, but this is disputed (see A. F. Rainey, *Tel Aviv*, 3.2, 1976, pp. 57–69). *Merom in 'Waters of Merom' is quite distinct from Shimron-meron. Whether Shimron should be identified with the *Šmw'nw/Šm'n* of the Egyp. lists of the 18th and 15th centuries BC (the Šamḫuna of the El-Amarna letters) through the LXX form *Symoōn* is highly doubtful.

K.A.K.

SHINAR. The land in which were situated the great cities of Babylon, Erech and Akkad (Gn. 10:10). It lay in a plain to which early migrants came to found the city and tower of Babel (Gn. 11:2) and was a place of exile for the Jews (Is. 11:11; Dn. 1:2). The LXX interprets it as 'Babylonia' (Is. 11:11) or the 'land of Babylon' (Zc. 5:11), and this accords with the location implied in Gn. 10:10. (*ACCAD or Agade, which gave its name to N Babylonia.) Heb. *šin'ār* represents *šanhar* of cuneiform texts from the Hittite and Syrian scribal schools of the 2nd millennium BC, and was certainly a name for Babylonia, perhaps a Hurrian form of Sumer. This equation is proved by several texts (see H. G. Güterbock, *JCS* 18, 1964, p. 3), ruling out older ideas. D.J.W.

SHIPS AND BOATS. As both Egypt and Mesopotamia were divided by rivers and canals, the development of water-borne transport was necessary for successful trade and communication. Rafts constructed from bundles of reeds were in use from a very early period and appear as an early pictographic sign on a clay tablet from *c.* 3500 BC. The raft has remained a popular craft in the marshes of S Mesopotamia. A clay model of a boat found at Eridu from *c.* 3500 BC is very similar to the round coracle (*quffa*) made from wood and hide depicted in Assyr. relief sculpture of *c.* 870 BC and which remain in use on the river Euphrates. Rafts of skins, inflated or stuffed with straw, are another ancient craft with a long and continuous history. Official transport in Sumer, however, was undertaken in vessels with high swinging stems and sterns which were propelled by paddles or poles or maybe on occasions towed from the bank. A model of this type of craft was found in a tomb

SHILONITE
See Shiloh, Part 3.

SHIMEAH, SHIMEAM
See Shammah, Part 3.

Silver model boat from the Royal Cemetery at Ur. The arched band may have supported an awning. Thwarts for the rowers and leaf-blade paddles were found in place. Length 64 cm, height of peak 20 cm, width 8 cm. c. 2500 BC. (SAOB)

Ships with horse-headed prows and high sterns transport or tow large logs of wood. Relief from the palace of Sargon II at Khorsabad. 721–705 BC. (MC)

A raft made of logs of wood being used to transport another raft of reeds and an animal skin, perhaps themselves the constituent parts of another common form of river transport (kelek). *Relief from the palace of Sennacherib, Nineveh. c. 690 BC.* (BM)

at Fara from *c.* 3000 BC, enabling a reliable reconstruction of the hull shape which also appears on Sumerian cylinder seals and in Egyp. carvings of the same period. During the 3rd millennium, overseas trade developed from Mesopotamia through the Persian Gulf and into the N Indian Ocean. Very little is known about the vessels which facilitated this enterprise, although one text from *c.* 2000 BC mentions a craft weighing 300 *gur* (28,400 kg or 28 tonnes).

In Egypt the earliest wooden boats were replicas of reed craft, and although hull shape developed to suit timber, decorative motifs such as lotus bud ends common on reed vessels continue. In addition to the many portrayals of ships in tomb decoration, the understanding of Egyp. vessels has been greatly aided by the discovery of actual boats. The oldest was found adjacent to the pyramid of Cheops at Giza (*c.* 2600 BC) and is 43·4 m long; two others, about 10 m in length, were found at Dahshur and belong to the 12th Dynasty (1991–1786 BC). The absence of good timber in Egypt necessitated its importation from Lebanon and so seagoing ships were developed. The presence of Egyp. vessels along the coast of Palestine gives force to Moses' warning that Israel may return to Egypt by ship (Dt. 28:68) especially as Asiatic slaves are depicted being transported to Egypt in ships as early as in the reign of

Model of a Philistine warship, reconstructed on the basis of a relief in the funerary temple of Rameses III at Medinet Habu. c. 1195–1164 BC. (NMMH)

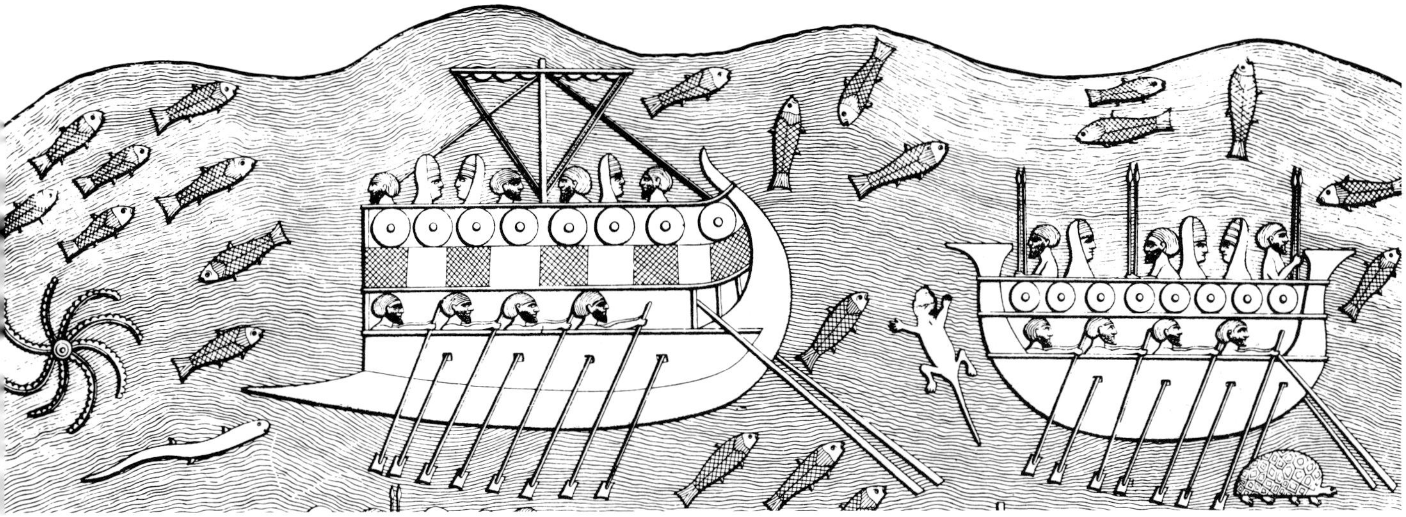

Phoenician warships escaping from Sidon. From a relief in the palace of Sennacherib, Nineveh. c. 690 BC.

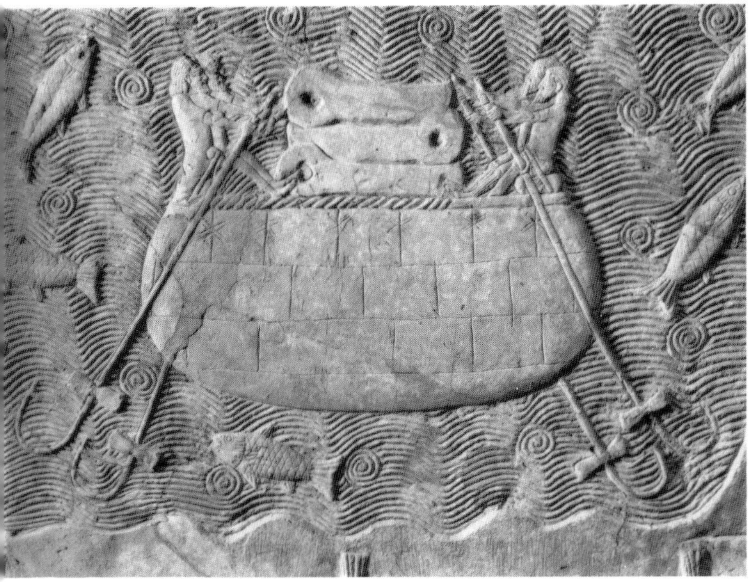

A circular Assyrian coracle (quffa) rowed by four oarsmen, used to carry a heavy load. Similar boats were used on the R. Tigris and R. Euphrates until early in this century. Relief from the palace of Sennacherib, Nineveh. c. 690 BC. (BM)

A Phoenician trading vessel carved on the end of a stone sarcophagus from Tyre. 2nd–1st cent. BC. (RS)

Sahuré, *c.* 2500 BC. Expeditions were also made on the Red Sea in ships of about 30 m length and powered by sail and oars. A distinctive feature of early Egyp. seagoing ships is the rope truss which passed around each end of the vessel and over forked sticks above the deck where it was tensioned like a tourniquet. This device was required to compensate for the absence of a keel by keeping the craft rigid when encountering waves.

I. In the Old Testament

While the Hebrews were not a seafaring people, their geographic situation made it impossible for them not to have contact with seamen and their ships. The tribes of Zebulun, Issachar, Dan and Asher had at some time seaside territories (Gn. 49:13; Dt. 33:19; Jdg. 5:17) and Israel's neighbours, the *Phoenicians and *Philistines, were leading maritime powers. The ship, however, remained a source of wonder for the Hebrews (Pr. 30:19) and a safe passage was considered a demonstration of God's goodness and power (Ps. 107:23–30). A ship's motion was reminiscent of the drunkard (Pr. 23:34) and its swift transit like the passing of life (Jb. 9:26).

The general Heb. word for ship, *'^{o}niyyâ*, refers most commonly to seagoing merchant vessels (*e.g.* Pr. 31:14) which are often described as 'ships of Tarshish' (1 Ki. 22:48f.). Whether or not *Tarshish is to be identified with a geographical location such as Tartessus in S Spain or Tarsus in Cilicia or is thought to mean something like 'ore-carrier', the ship so described is a Phoenician long-range merchantman. Barnett (*Antiquity* 32, 1958, p. 226) believes that the Phoenician trans-

A reed boat, of a form which survives as the modern tarada, *being paddled through the marshlands of S Iraq, c. 710* BC. *Relief from the palace of Sennacherib, Nineveh. c. 690* BC. (MH)

port vessels with round bows depicted on relief sculptures of Sennacherib (*c.* 700 BC) are 'ships of Tarshish'. These boats are powered by double banks of oars; and while it is true that the merchant galley remained a valuable craft in the Mediterranean, plagued by calms all summer, the absence of sail makes this identification questionable. Phoenician shipping developed during the 2nd millennium BC and is known to us from Egyp. tomb paintings and from texts. The paintings reveal that, unlike contemporary Egyp. ships, Canaanite (early Phoenician) vessels were built with a keel and had a fence-like structure along the deck, which some believe acted as a lee cloth, while others believe that it barricaded the cargo. A document from Ras Shamra, *c.* 1200 BC, refers to one of these merchantmen as having a cargo of 457,000 kg (450 tonnes) with no indication that it was at all unusual. Such a large vessel had to rely on sail power and could be rowed only for brief periods in an emergency.

The ship that Jonah embarked on at Joppa is called a *s^{e}pînâ* (Jon. 1:5), which may indicate that it was a large vessel with a deck, possibly similar to a Gk. merchantman painted on a cup of *c.* 550 BC. It was manned by sailors, Heb. *mallāḥîm* (Jon. 1:5) and captained by one called *raḇ haḥōḇēl* (Jon. 1:6), the 'chief pilot'.

Smaller vessels were used by the Phoenicians for short-range cargo assignments. These vessels were paddled and were distinctive because of their high stem and stern posts, one of which bore the carved head of a horse and so they were naturally called *hippos* by the Greeks. An Assyr. relief sculpture, *c.* 710 BC, depicts these vessels in a logging operation which was no doubt similar to that undertaken by King Hiram of Tyre for Solomon (1 Ki. 5:9).

Another Heb. word for ship, *ṣî*, would appear to apply specifically to warships. This vessel is mentioned with a 'galley with oars', *'^{o}nî šayiṭ* (Is. 33:21), where it is stated that no such ship will approach Jerusalem when the city is at peace. These warships had streamlined hulls being built for speed and with a ram at the front. In order to shorten the vessel and increase its manoeuvrability without losing speed, the oarsmen, *šāṭîm* (Ezk. 27:8), were double-banked on each side. The Greeks were particularly skilful at fighting in these vessels, which may be referred to as the feared 'ships of Kittim' (Dn. 11:30; *cf.* Nu. 24:24). Because of their speed warships were particularly suited for delivering urgent messages over water (Ezk. 30:9; Thucydides 3. 49. 3).

BIBLIOGRAPHY. G. Bass, *A History of Seafaring*, 1972; B. Landström, *The Ship*, 1971; L. Casson, *Ships and Seamanship in the Ancient World*, 1971. C.J.D.

II. In the New Testament

a. On the Sea of Galilee

The Galilean boats were used mainly for *fishing (*e.g.* Mt. 4:21f.; Mk. 1:19f.; Jn. 21:3ff.), but also generally for communications across the lake (*e.g.* Mt. 8:23ff.; 9:1; 14:13ff.; Mk. 8:10ff.). Our Lord sometimes preached from a boat so that his voice might not be restricted by the crowd's pressing too close (Mk. 4:1; Lk. 5:2f.).

These vessels were not large: one could accommodate Jesus and his disciples (*e.g.* Mk. 8:10), but an unusually large catch of fish enclosed by a single net was enough to overload two of them (Lk. 5:7). While they were no doubt fitted with sails, they were regularly equipped with oars to enable them to progress in calm weather and in the heavy storms which occasionally sweep across the lake (Mk. 6:48; Jn. 6:19).

b. On the Mediterranean

The main characteristics of Mediterranean ships had changed little over several centuries. Warships ('long ships', their length being eight or ten times their width) were regularly propelled by oars and rarely went far from the coast. Merchant ships ('round ships', their length being three or four times their width) relied on sails, but might carry some oars for emergencies. They also generally remained reasonably close to land, but under favourable conditions would cross the open sea (*PATARA). Most

Papyrus skiffs used by Egyptian noblemen for hunting in papyrus swamps. Copy (on modern papyrus) of a wall-painting from Thebes. Length 33 cm. New Kingdom. (FNH)

eagoing ships were of between 70 ɩnd 300 tonnes, but Pliny mentions ɩne of apparently 1,300 tonnes.

Most of Paul's missionary 'oyages were probably undertaken ɩ small coastal vessels, but on his ourney to Rome he sailed in two of he great grain ships plying between Egypt and Italy, which might easily arry a complement of 276 crew ɩnd passengers (Acts 27:37). About he same period Josephus travelled in a ship carrying 600 (*Vita* 15). Lucian (*Navigium* 1ff.) gives a description of a large grain ship of AD 150; and in recent years underwater archaeologists have examined a number of ancient wrecks. Thus we can get some idea of Paul's 'Twin Brothers' (* CASTOR AND POLLUX). Such a ship would have a central mast with long yard-arms carrying a large square mainsail and possibly a small topsail, and a small foremast sloping forward almost like a bowsprit, with a foresail (Gk. *artemōn*) which might be used to give the ship steerage way when it was not desired to take full advantage of the wind (Acts 27:40), and to head the ship round and check drifting in a storm (in Acts 27:17 'lowered the gear' may mean 'set the foresail' or 'let out a sea-anchor' or 'let down the mast-top gear'). By bracing the sails these

The ceremonial barge of the Egyptian nobleman, Huy, viceroy of Nubia. Copy by N. de G. Davies of a wall-painting in the tomb of Huy, Thebes. c. 1360 BC. (MH)

Wooden model of a boat pulled by 14 oarsmen. The pilot stands in the bows beside the owner (wrapped in cloak), and the boat is steered by a large oar in the stern. From Egypt. c. 1800 BC. (BM)

ships could sail within about 7 points of the wind.

The bows were swept up to a carved or painted figure to represent the name of the ship (Acts 28:11), and on the stern, which was also raised, generally into a gooseneck shape, was a statue of the patron deity of the vessel's home port. Two large oars in the stern served as rudders, either operated separately or rotated together by means of tiller bars or ropes attached to a central piece of gear. These could be lashed in position in bad weather (*cf.* Acts 27:40).

Some anchors were wholly of iron, but most had a wooden stock with lead or stone arms. They might weigh more than 600 kg, and had small marker-buoys attached. There would be three or more on board, and when anchoring off a beach one or two of them would be let down from the bows, mooring cables from the stern being attached to the shore. For manoeuvring or riding out a gale, however, anchors might be let out from the stern (Acts 27:29). A sounding-lead was used to check the depth when near shallows (Acts 27:28), and might be greased to bring up samples of the bottom.

A dinghy was towed astern in good weather, but hoisted on board in a storm (Acts 27:16f.) to prevent its being swamped or smashed. This was for use in harbour rather than as a lifeboat: if the ship was wrecked, survivors had to rely on spars. Paul had been shipwrecked three times before his journey to Rome (2 Cor. 11:25).

The risks of any voyage were great, but so were the profits if it was successful (*cf.* Rev. 18:19). The owner often commanded his ship, perhaps with the assistance of a professional steersman or navigator; but in doubtful situations

Wooden model of an Egyptian ship, with restored sail and rigging. The crew are shown working the halyards, and the presence of a mummy near the stern (partly obscured) indicates that the boat was one used for the symbolical funerary journey undertaken by the dead. From Meir. c. 1800 BC (12th Dynasty). (BM)

the passengers might share in making decisions (Acts 27:9–12: the centurion was responsible for his party, not for the ship). There might be as many as three decks on a large merchantman, and some luxuriously fitted cabins, but most passengers camped on deck or in the hold.

Ships were normally dismasted and laid up to avoid the winter storms from mid-November to mid-February (Acts 20:3, 6; 28:11; 1 Cor. 16:6ff.; 2 Tim. 4:21; Tit. 3:12), and periods of about a month before and after this season were considered dangerous (Acts 27:9). The main difficulty seems to have been the obscuring of the sky by storm clouds, thus making navigation by the sun and stars impossible. Delays due to weather were common. According to Josephus (*BJ* 2. 203) one letter from the emperor Gaius in Rome to Petronius in Judaea took 3 months to get there (* SAMOTHRACE).

There is some doubt about the meaning of 'undergirding the ship' in Acts 27:17. The traditional, and most likely, view is frapping, that is, passing ropes under the ship, from side to side, to hold its timbers firm; but some explain it as the use of a hogging truss (unlikely in a large ship with decks to strengthen it), or horizontal cables round the hull.

c. Figurative use

Nautical metaphors are rare in the NT. In Heb. 6:19 hope is called 'an anchor of the soul'; and Jas. 3:4–5 compares the tongue with a ship's rudder.

BIBLIOGRAPHY. L. Casson, *Ships and Seamanship in the Ancient World*, 1971; J. Smith, *The Voyage and Shipwreck of St. Paul*[4], 1880; C. Torr, *Ancient Ships*[2], 1964; K. L. McKay, *Proceedings of the Classical Association* 61, 1964, pp. 25f.; H. J. Cadbury in *BC*, 5, pp. 345ff. K.L.McK.

Sailing boat depicted on a mosaic at Ostia Antica, Italy. 1st cent. AD. (RS)

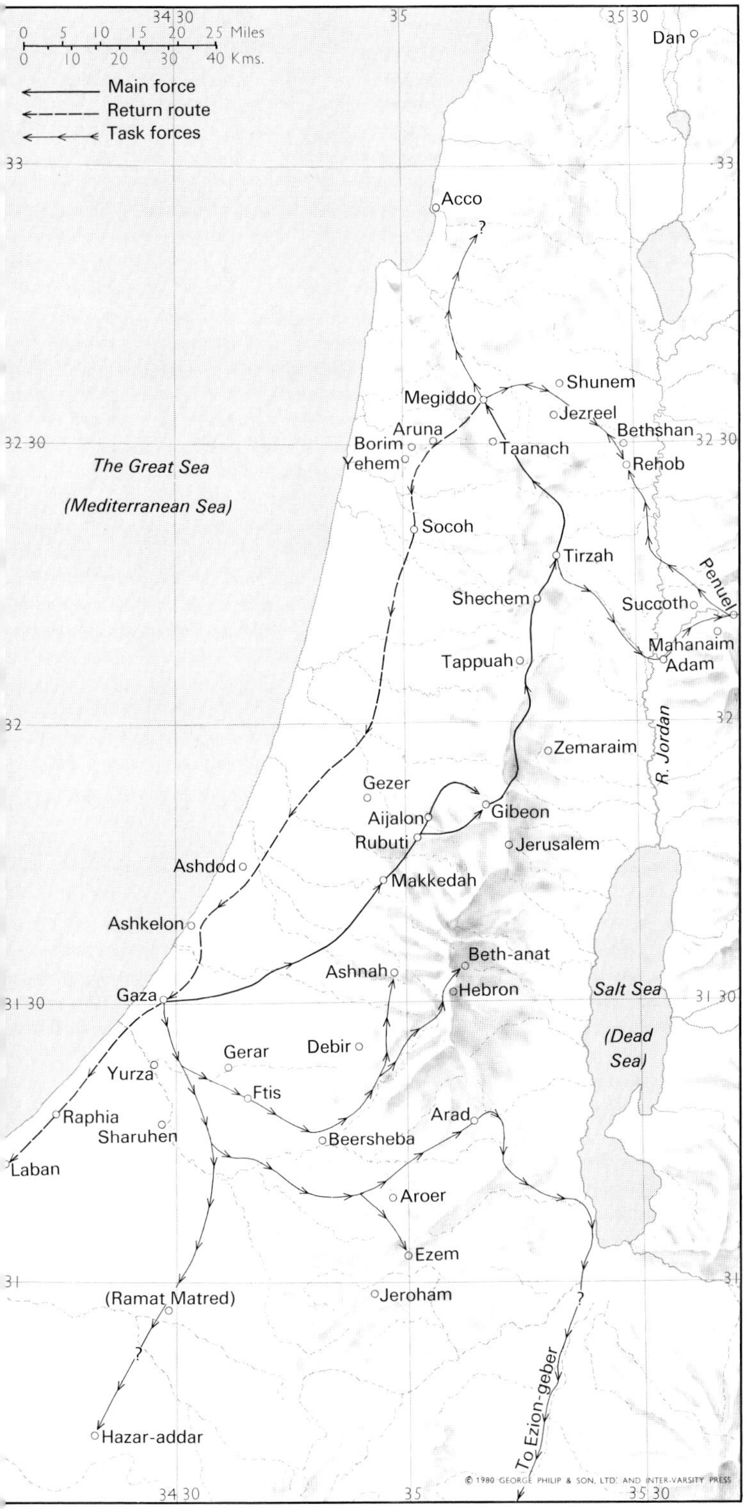

Shishak's Palestinian campaign.

SHISHAK. Libyan prince who founded Egypt's 22nd Dynasty as the Pharaoh Sheshonq I. He reigned for 21 years, *c.* 945–924 BC. He harboured Jeroboam as a fugitive from Solomon, after Ahijah's prophecy of Jeroboam's future kingship (1 Ki. 11:29–40). Late in his reign, Shishak invaded Palestine in the 5th year of Rehoboam, 925 BC. He subdued Judah, taking the

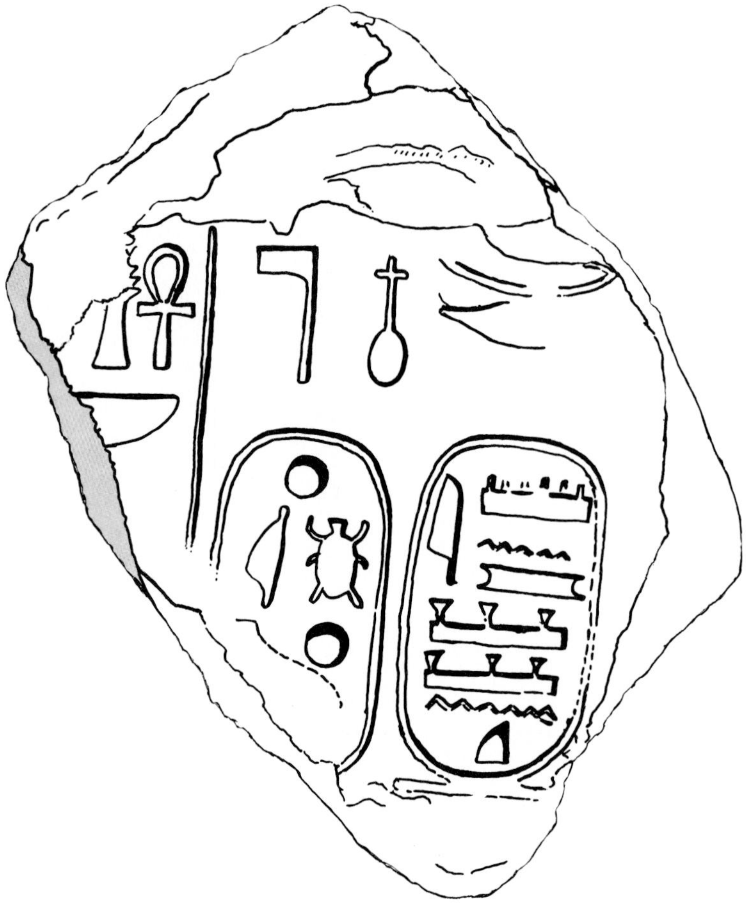

The name of Pharaoh Shishak is shown in Egyptian hieroglyphs on this fragment of a triumphal inscription found at Megiddo. c. 926 BC. (YY)

■ **SHITTAH**
See Trees (Acacia), Part 3.

Shishak (Sheshonq I) of Egypt, with raised hands (right: unfinished relief) before the god Amun, celebrates the conquest of Judah and Israel in c. 925 BC. The captured cities are named in cartouches.(PAC)

treasures of Jerusalem as tribute (1 Ki. 14:25–26; 2 Ch. 12:2–12), and also asserted his dominion over Israel, as is evidenced by a broken stele of his from Megiddo. At the temple of Amūn in Thebes, Shishak left a triumphal relief-scene, naming many Palestinian towns; see *ANEP*, p. 118, fig. 349, p. 290. See also * LIBYA, * SUKKIIM. For Shishak's invasion, see K. A. Kitchen, *The Third Intermediate Period in Egypt*, 1972, pp. 292–302, 432–447. K.A.K.

SHITTIM. 1. One of the names given to the final Israelite encampment before they crossed the Jordan, opposite Jericho (Nu. 25:1; Jos. 2:1; 3:1; *cf.* Mi. 6:5). Nu. 33:49 uses a longer form of the name, Abel-shittim ('the brook(?) of the acacias', since *šiṭṭîm* means 'acacias'), for one extremity of the camp. Josephus mentions a city of his time called Abila, which was 60 stades from the Jordan in this general area (*Ant.* 5. 4), which appears to represent the element 'Abel' of this name. Abila was probably located at Tell el-Hammam (Glueck, Aharoni), though other scholars have preferred Tell el-Kefrein, which lies a little to the NW. See *IDB*, 4, p. 339.

2. The 'valley of Shittim/acacias' in Joel 3:18, which is to be watered by a stream flowing from the Temple (*cf.* Ezk. 47:1–12), cannot be the same place, because a location for it W of the Jordan is required. It is most likely to be either a general term for the wadis of the Judaean wilderness or a name for the lower part of the Kidron valley, which leads into the Dead Sea from the W (rather than referring to the Wadi es-Sanṭ).

BIBLIOGRAPHY. H. W. Wolff, *Joel and Amos* (Hermeneia), on Joel 4:18 (3:18). For Shittim wood see * TREES (Acacia). G.I.D.

SHOA. Ezekiel (23:23) prophesies that this people, together with other dwellers in Mesopotamia, will attack Jerusalem. Shoa has been identified with the people called *Sutu* or *Su* in Akkadian sources, though some now question this identification. According to the Amarna letters, they were Semitic nomads living in the Syrian desert in the 14th century BC. Later they migrated to the area E of Baghdad, and Assyr. records often mention them with the *Qutu*, called Koa in Ezk. 23:23, as warring against Assyria. Some scholars (*e.g.* O. Procksch) take the word usually translated 'crying' (RSV 'shouting') in Is. 22:5 to be the name Shoa.

BIBLIOGRAPHY. F. Delitzsch, *Wo lag das Paradies?*, 1881, pp. 233–237; G. A. Cooke in *ICC*, 1936, on Ezk. 23:23; R. T. O'Callaghan, *Aram Naharaim, Analecta Orientalia* 26, 1948, pp. 88, 92–98, 101. J.T.

SHOBACH. The Aramaean general in command of the forces of Hadadezer, king of Aram, at the time of the war with Ammon (2 Sa. 10:16–18). He is not mentioned in the earlier operations at Rabbah when Joab and Abishai routed the Syrian army (vv. 10–14), but this could be due to the presence of the king himself in command. It is therefore assumed that he held office after the event and is named (*šôbak*; Gk. *sōbak*; *cf.* *šôpak*, 1 Ch. 19:16–18) as the leader of the combined forces from Syria and E of the Euphrates in the battle at Helam, E of Jordan. Shobach was fatally wounded and the Aramaeans routed by David. D.J.W.

SHOBAL. 1. The second son of Seir, an Edomite (Gn. 36:20), father of a clan (v. 23) and a Horite leader (v. 29 = 1 Ch. 1:38, 40). **2.** A son of Caleb and 'father' (founder) of Kiriath-jearim (1 Ch. 2:50, 52), also a Judaean (1 Ch. 4:1–2). It is probable that **1** and **2** are related persons. D.J.W.

SHOBI (2 Sa. 17:27–29). An Ammonite, a prince of Rabbah, whose father Nahash (perhaps the son of the Nahash referred to in 1 Sa. 11:1) had shown kindness to David (2 Sa. 10:2; 1 Ch. 19:2), apparently when he was a fugitive.

When David came to the height of his power he, in his turn, showed kindness to the house of Nahash. This kindness was appreciated by Shobi, so that when David was retreating to Mahanaim before Absalom, Shobi was one of those who provided rest and refreshment for David's company. C.H.D.

SHOVEL (Heb. *yāʿ*). Bronze shovels were made for clearing ashes from off the altar of burnt-offering (Ex. 27:3) and later by Hiram for Solomon's Temple (1 Ki. 7:40, 45). Some Canaanite shovels have been discovered, *e.g.* at Megiddo (*BA* 4, 1941, p. 29 and fig. 9).

Heb. *rahat* is mentioned in Is. 30:24; it was probably wooden. (*FAN, *AGRICULTURE.) A.R.M.

SHOWBREAD. Heb. *leḥem happānîm*, lit. 'bread of the face', *i.e.* bread set before the face or presence of God (Ex. 25:30; 35:13; 39:36, *etc.*) or *leḥem hamma ʿareḵeṯ*, lit. 'bread of ordering' (1 Ch. 9:32, *etc.*). After Moses had received divine instructions concerning the making of a table, dishes, spoons, covers and bowls for the holy place of the tabernacle, he was directed to place 'showbread' on the table. This arrangement was never to cease (Ex. 25:30). The showbread consisted of twelve baked cakes, made of fine flour, each containing two-tenths of an ephah (*WEIGHTS AND MEASURES). These were set in two rows, six to a row (*maʿareḵeṯ*, Lv. 24:6). Upon each row (lit. 'the row', Lv. 24:7) of cakes frankincense was placed 'as a memorial' (*leʾazkārâ*) and was offered by fire to the Lord (Lv. 24:7). It was the duty of the priest each sabbath day to place fresh or hot bread on the table (1 Sa. 21:6). The old cakes then became the perquisite of Aaron and his sons who ate them in the holy place because they were 'most holy' (Lv. 24:5–9). It was these loaves that David requested of Ahimelech, the priest, for himself and his men (1 Sa. 21:1–6; *cf.* Mt. 12:4; Mk. 2:26; Lk. 6:4).

The position of the table upon which the showbread was placed was in the holy place on the N side of the tabernacle opposite the lampstand (Ex. 26:35). The table was made of acacia wood overlaid with gold and bordered with a golden crown. It had a ring at each corner for the rods by which it was carried (Ex. 25:23–28). According to the original commandment it never failed to appear in the appointed place of God's worship (2 Ch. 4:19; 13:11). The Kohathites had charge of the showbread (1 Ch. 9:32).

The passages referred to do not themselves indicate the significance of the showbread, but it is possible to infer from these data that God is man's provider and sustainer, and that man lives constantly in the presence of God. This truth makes it obligatory for man to offer his life to God (Rom. 12:1). D.F.

SHUA. 1. Shua (Heb. *šûʿā'*) the daughter of Heber of the tribe of Asher (1 Ch. 7:32). **2.** Shua (*šûaʿ*) a Canaanite of Adullam whose daughter, Bathshua (1 Ch. 2:3), Judah took to wife (Gn. 38:2, 12). **3.** Shuah (*šûaḥ*) a son of Abraham by his wife Keturah (Gn. 25:2; 1 Ch. 1:32). **4.** Shuhah (*šûḥâ*) a descendant of Judah and brother of Chelub father of Mehir (1 Ch. 4:11). T.C.M.

SHUAL, LAND OF. A district in Benjamin mentioned as lying in the path of a company of plundering Philistines, as they moved from Michmash to Ophrah (1 Sa. 13:17). Unknown outside the Bible, but probably near Michmash. Shual ('fox') is identified by some with Shaalim where Saul searched for lost donkeys (1 Sa. 9:4). T.C.M.

SHULAMMITE. A feminine noun (*šûlammîṯ*) applied to the heroine in Ct. 6:13, 'Shulammite' has been a formidable problem to scholars. Some (*e.g.* Koehler's *Lexicon*) have connected it with an unknown town, Shulam; some (*e.g.* *ISBE*) classify it as a variant of Shunammite (below); others (*e.g.* L. Waterman and H. Torczyner) identify the Shulammite with *Abishag, the Shunammite. E. J. Goodspeed (*AJSL* 50, 1934, pp. 102ff.) and H. H. Rowley (*AJSL* 56, 1939, pp. 84–91) deny any connection with Shunem but view the word as a feminine counterpart of Solomon, 'the Solomoness'. Attempts have been made to derive the names Solomon and Shulammite from the god Shelem. See H. H. Rowley, *The Servant of the Lord*, 1952, p. 223. D.A.H.

SHOPHAR
See Atonement, Day of, Part 1.

SHRUB
See Plants, Part 3.

SHUNAMMITE
See Shunem, Part 3.

A bronze incense shovel, found at Ashkelon. Length 30 cm. 2nd–3rd cent. AD. (MC)

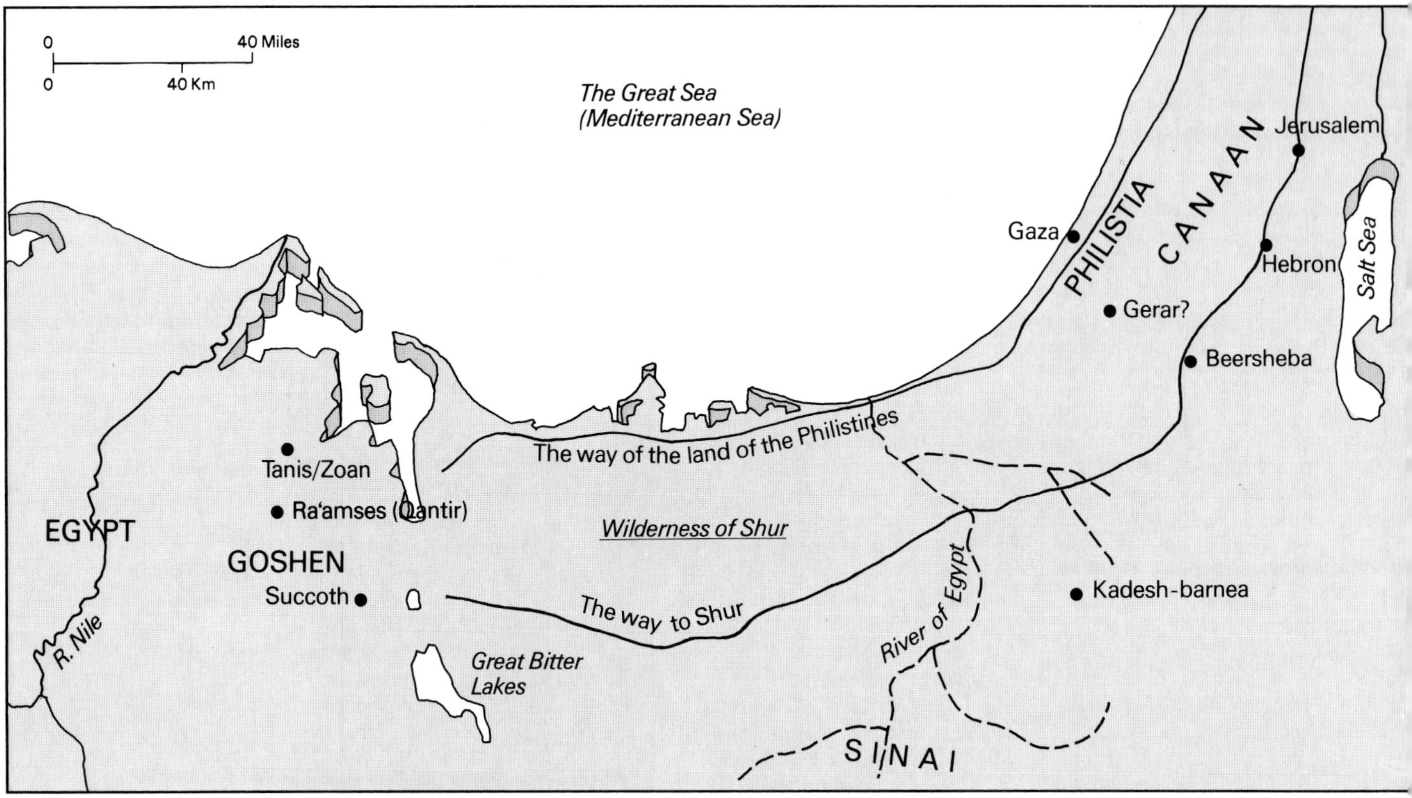

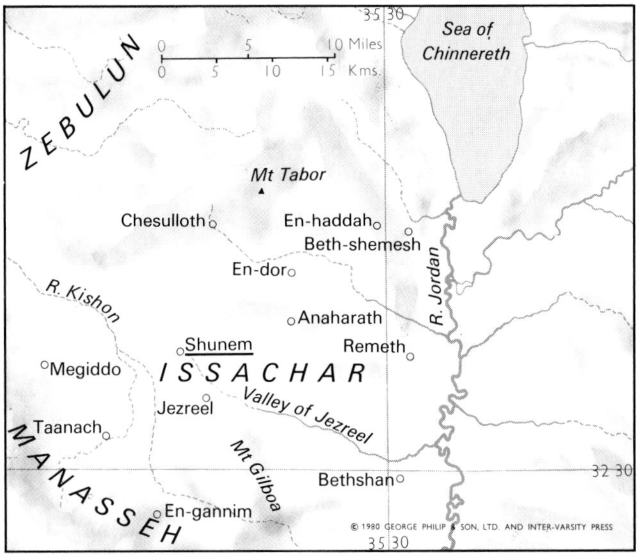

Shunem in the territory of Issachar.

Top: The location of the 'wilderness of Shur'.

SHUPPIM
See Manasseh, Part 2.

SHUSHAN
See Susa, Part 3.

SHUTTLE
See Spinning, Part 3.

SHUNEM, SHUNAMMITE. A town (probably modern Solem) in the territory of Issachar near Jezreel (Jos. 19:18), Shunem (*šûnēm*) was the site of the Philistine camp before the battle of Gilboa (1 Sa. 28:4).

Elisha sojourned in Shunem frequently in the home of a generous woman (called the Shunammite, a feminine adjective derived from Shunem) whose son, born according to Elisha's prediction, was miraculously raised up by the prophet after being smitten with sun-stroke (2 Ki. 4:8ff.). It is this woman whose property was restored at Gehazi's behest after she had temporarily abandoned it to seek relief from famine in Philistia (2 Ki. 8:1–6). From Shunem also David's men brought the beautiful *Abishag to comfort their aged king (1 Ki. 1:3, 15). Adonijah's request for her hand in marriage cost him his life (1 Ki. 2:17, 21–22). (*SHULAMMITE.) D.A.H.

SHUR. A wilderness-region in the NW part of the Sinai isthmus, S of the Mediterranean coastline and the 'way of the land of the Philistines', between the present line of the Suez Canal on its W and the 'River of *Egypt' (Wadi el-'Arish) on its E. Abraham and Sarah's handmaid Hagar fled to a well past Kadesh on the way to Shur (Gn. 16:7).

For a time Abraham 'dwelt between Kadesh and Shur' and then sojourned at Gerar (Gn. 20:1); Ishmael's descendants ranged over an area that reached as far as 'Shur, which is opposite [*i.e.* E of] Egypt' (Gn. 25:18). After passing through the sea (*RED SEA), Israel entered the wilderness of Shur before going S into Sinai (Ex. 15:22). Shur lay on the direct route to Egypt from S Palestine (1 Sa. 15:7 and, most explicitly, 27:8). K.A.K.

SIBMAH. A town wrested from Sihon king of the Amorites and allotted by Moses to the tribe of Reuben (*śibmâ*, Jos. 13:19, 21). It is identical with Sebam ('Shebam', AV); possibly its name was changed when it was rebuilt (Nu. 32:3, 38). By the time of Isaiah and Jeremiah, who bewailed its devastation, it had reverted to the Moabites (Is. 16:8–9; Je. 48:32). Originally a land for cattle (Nu. 32:4), it became famous for its vines and summer fruit. Jerome (*Comm. in Is.* 5) placed it about 500 paces from Heshbon: Khirbet Qurn el-Qibsh, 5 km WSW, is a feasible site. J.W.C.

SIDDIM, VALLEY OF (Heb. *siddîm*, perhaps derived from Hittite *siyantas*, 'salt'). In Gn. 14:3, 10 a valley identified with the 'Salt Sea' and described as 'full of bitumen pits'. Here the kings of the Jordan pentapolis were defeated by Chedorlaomer and his allies from the E. It was probably a fertile, well-watered region S of the Lisan peninsula, later submerged by the S extension of the Dead Sea through earthquake action and consequent faulting of the rock-formation. From the bituminous products of the Dead Sea (still in evidence) the Greeks called it *Asphaltitis*.

BIBLIOGRAPHY. J. P. Harland,

Sodom and Gomorrah', *BA* 5, 942, pp. 17ff.; 6, 1943, pp. 41ff.

F.F.B.

SIDON (Heb. *ṣîḏôn, ṣîḏōn*). A major walled city and port in ancient *Phoenicia (now located on the coast of Lebanon). Sidon (AV also 'Zidon'; modern Saida) had twin harbours and was divided into Greater Sidon (Jos. 11:8) and Lesser Sidon.

According to tradition, Sidon was the first Phoenician city to be founded and became a principal Canaanite stronghold (Gn. 10:19; 1 Ch. 1:13). For some centuries the harbour was subordinate to the Egyptian 18th–19th Dynasties. With declining Egyptian military control the city ruler Zimri-ada committed defection *c.* 1390 BC (so *Amarna tablets). It is possible that the attempt to include Dor in Sidonian territory led to war with the Philistines, who *c.* 1150 BC plundered Sidon, whose inhabitants fled to Tyre. The city was, however, strong enough to oppose Israel (Jdg. 10:12), and during a period of active colonization apparently made an unsuccessful attempt to settle at Laish in the Upper Jordan (Jdg. 18:7, 27). Opposition to Phoenician expansion came also from the Assyrians, who under *Tiglath-pileser I, *c.* 1110 BC, began to exact tribute from the ports, including Sidon. Ashurnasirpal II (*c.* 880 BC) claimed the city as a vassal, and in 841 BC *Shalmaneser III marched to the Dog river to receive the tribute of Tyre, Sidon and Israel (*JEHU), and depicted this on the temple gates at Balawat (now in BM). The Assyrian demands increased and the Sidonians rebelled. Tiglath-pileser III captured Tyre and perhaps Sidon in 739–738 (H. Tadmor, *Scripta Hierosolymitana* 8, 1961, p. 269, makes Zc. 9:2 refer to this time). When Sennacherib marched, in an attack foretold by Isaiah (23:2–12), Luli fled and died in exile and was replaced by Ethba'al (Tuba'lu) when Great and Little Sidon had been captured.

On Sennacherib's death Sidon once more revolted and Esarhaddon invaded Sidon, killed the ruler Abdi-milkutti, sacked the port and moved its inhabitants to Kar-Esarhaddon, and brought prisoners from Elam and Babylonia to replace the depleted population.

Sidon recovered its independence with the decline of the Assyrians, only to be besieged again and captured by Nebuchadrezzar *c.* 587 BC as foretold by Jeremiah (25:22;

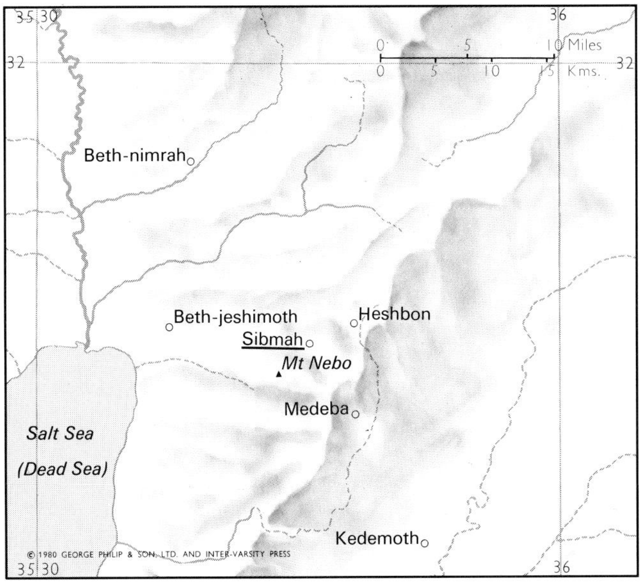

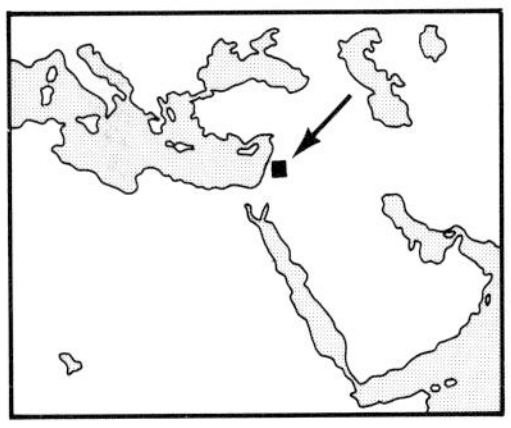

The Reubenite town of Sibmah.

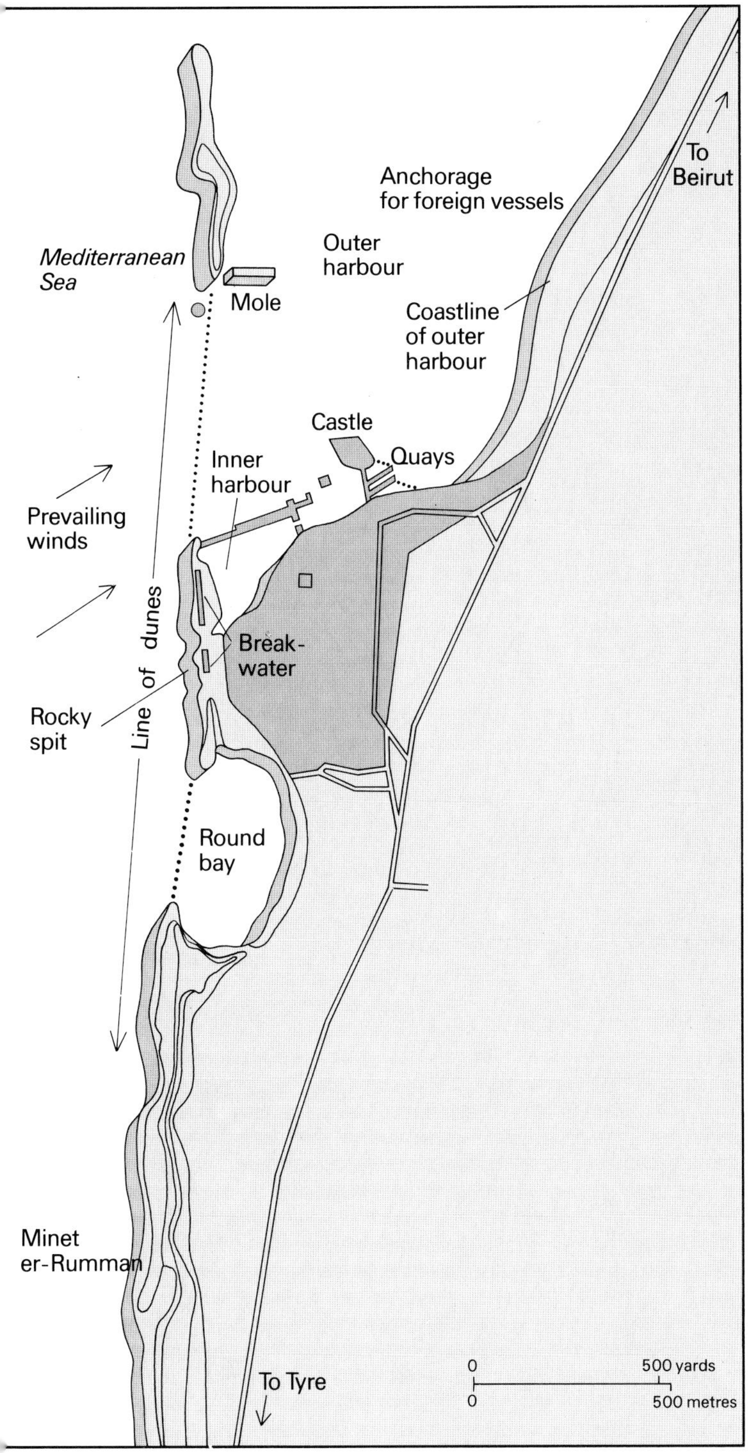

Plan of the port of Sidon, showing the position of its harbours in relation to the prevailing winds.

SICCUTH See Sakkuth, Part 3.

SICHEM See Shechem, Part 3.

SICKLE See Agriculture, Part 1.

SIDE See Thigh, Part 3.

Opposite page: This silver double shekel demonstrates Persian control of Sidon. It shows the Great King of Persia in his chariot. Diameter 29 mm. c. 400–350 BC. (BM)

Opposite page: This double shekel from Sidon shows a galley before the city walls. Diameter 29 mm. 4th cent. BC. (PAC)

27:3; 47:4). Under the Persians it provided the majority of the Persian fleet (*cf.* Zc. 9:2). About 350 BC, under Tabnit II (Tannes), Sidon led the rebellion of Phoenicia and Cyprus against Artaxerxes III (Ochus). The city was betrayed and 40,000 perished, the survivors burning the city and fleet. The fortifications were never rebuilt. The city under Strato II yielded to Alexander the Great without opposition and helped his siege of Tyre.

Under Antiochus III Sidon was a prosperous part of the kingdom of Ptolemy and later passed to the Seleucids and then to the Romans, who granted it local autonomy. Through all its history the principal temple was that of Eshmun, the god of healing. It is thus significant that it was in the region of Sidon that Christ healed the Syro-Phoenician woman's daughter (Mk. 7:24–31; *cf.* Mt. 11:21). Many Sidonians listened to his teaching (Mk. 3:8; Lk. 6:17; 10:13–14). Herod Agrippa I received a delegation from Sidon at Caesarea (Acts 12:20) and Paul visited friends in the city on his way to Rome (Acts 27:3). The inhabitants of Sidon, which was renowned as a centre of philosophical learning, were mainly Greek (*cf.* Mk. 7:26). Many coins bear inscriptions of Sidonian rulers, and among the discoveries in the area are remains from the Middle Bronze Age onwards, the inscribed sarcophagus of Eshmunazar (*c.* 300 BC) and buildings in the port area of NT times (A. Poidebard and J. Lauffray, *Sidon*, 1951). For Phoenician inscriptions from Sidon, see G. A. Cooke, *North Semitic Inscriptions*, 1903, pp. 26–43, 401–403. D.J.W.

SIEGE, SIEGECRAFT
See Fortification and siegecraft, Part 1.

SIGN. In the OT the Heb. word *'ōṯ* is used with several shades of meaning.

1. A visible mark or object intended to convey a clear message, *e.g.* the sun and moon (Gn. 1:14), the mark of Cain (Gn. 4:15), tribal standards (Nu. 2:2).

2. An assurance or reminder, *e.g.* rainbow (Gn. 9:12), to Rahab (Jos. 2:12), stones from the Jordan (Jos. 4:6).

3. Omens named by prophets as pledges of their predictions, *e.g.* the death of Eli's sons (1 Sa. 2:34); Saul's prophetic ecstasy (1 Sa. 10:6f.); the young woman with child (Is. 7:10–14); various symbolic acts (as in Is. 20:3; Ezk. 4:1–3).

4. Works of God. When the word 'sign' is used in the plural together with 'wonders' (*mōpēṯ*) the events are understood to be the works of God, or attestations of his active presence among his people. This is seen in the account of the Exodus, where the plagues are described as signs (Ex. 4:28; 7:3; 8:23). The Exodus itself, with the deaths of the Egyptian first-born, the crossing of the Red Sea and the destruction of the Egyptian army, provides the supreme example of such signs and wonders (Dt. 4:34; 6:22; 7:19). This conviction is found throughout the OT (*e.g.* Nu. 14:11; Jos. 24:17; Ps. 78:43; Je. 32:21; Ne. 9:10), and Israel was assured that when God revealed himself again it would be with 'signs and wonders' to herald his coming (Joel 2:30).

Similarly in the NT Gk. *sēmeion* can mean simply some act or object conveying a recognizable meaning (Mt. 26:48; Lk. 2:12; Rom. 4:11; 2 Thes. 3:17). In 1 Cor. 14:22 tongues are 'a sign for unbelievers', since Is. 28:11f. shows that utterance in an unknown language is a sign of God's judgment on unbelief. Signs in heaven are quite frequently mentioned as indications of the last days (Mt. 24:30; Lk. 21:11, 25; Acts 2:19; Rev. 12:1, 3; 15:1). In Mk. 13 the tribulations accompanying the fall of Jerusalem and the end of the age are not a sign (Mk. 13:4; Mt. 24:3; Lk. 21:7) which enables a calculation of the end (Mk. 13:32), but an assurance to those caught up in the tribulation that the end cannot be long delayed.

So too 'signs and wonders' (miraculous healings, exorcisms, *etc.*) are regarded as proofs of God's powerful activity in the missionary work of the churches (Rom. 15:19; Heb. 2:4). Acts in particular gives a special prominence to such miracles ('wonders and signs', Acts 2:22, 43; 4:30; 5:12; 6:8; 7:36; 14:3; 15:12; see also 4:16, 22; 8:6, 13). Elsewhere however the NT writers (and Jesus) are a good deal more cautious in their talk of signs. Jesus responds critically to the Pharisees' request for signs (Mk. 8:11f.; Mt. 12:38f.; 16:1–4; Lk. 11:16, 29; so with Herod, 23:8f.), and warns against 'false Christs and false prophets' who 'show signs and wonders' (Mk. 13:22; Mt. 24:24). In similar vein Paul warns against the 'pretended signs and wonders' of 'the lawless one' (2 Thes. 2:9) and the seer of Rev. against the signs of the beast, the false prophet and the demonic spirits (Rev. 13:13f.; 16:14; 19:20). Paul is equally critical of the Jews' demand for signs (1 Cor. 1:22); and although he can point to 'signs and wonders' in his own ministry (2 Cor. 12:12), the context of his 'boasting' shows that he values such acts much less highly than the 'false apostles' at Corinth (2 Cor. 10–13).

The Fourth Gospel uses *sēmeion* more often (17 times) than any other NT writing, almost always in reference to Jesus' miracles. John is particularly concerned to demonstrate the true relation between 'sign' (significant action) and faith. Thus he is critical of a faith based on miracles as such—faith in Jesus (merely) as a miracle worker is defective faith, the shallow applause of the fickle crowd (Jn. 2:23–3:2; 4:48; 6:2, 14, 30; 7:31; 9:16; 12:18). The real significance of the miracles of Jesus is that they point forward to Jesus' death, resurrection and ascension, to the transformation brought by the new age of the Spirit, and thus lead to a faith in Jesus the (crucified) Christ, the (risen) Son of God (2:11; 6:26; 12:37; 20:30f.).

The problem with any sign is that it is ambiguous. It can be interpreted in different ways. The message it holds for faith can be seen only by faith. So, *e.g.*, 'the sign of the prophet Jonah' (Mt. 12:39f.) means nothing to those who do not believe in the resurrection (*cf.* Jn. 2:18f.; Lk. 2:34; 16:31). Consequently a faith based or nurtured exclusively on signs, rather than on the reality to which they point, is immature and at grave risk. Mature faith rejoices in what signs it perceives, but does not depend on them. (*MIRACLE; *POWER; *SYMBOL; *WONDER.)

BIBLIOGRAPHY. K. H. Rengstorf, *TDNT* 7, pp. 200–261; A. Richardson, *IDB*, 4, pp. 346–347; O. Hofius, C. Brown, *NIDNTT* 2, pp. 626–635.
J.D.G.D.

SIHON. An Amorite king (13th century BC), whose capital was *Heshbon. According to Nu. 21:26–30 and Je. 48:45, Sihon conquered the Moabites and took their territory as far S as the river Arnon. His vassals included five Midianite princes (Jos. 13:21). His domain included the area from the Arnon on the S to the Jabbok on the N, and from the Jordan on the W to the desert on the E (Nu. 21:24; Jdg. 11:22), and Jos. 12:3

and 13:27 seem to extend his control N of the Jabbok to the Sea of Chinnereth. Moses sent an embassy to Sihon asking permission for the Israelites to pass through his kingdom (Nu. 21:21–22; Dt. 2:26–28). When Sihon refused, the Israelites defeated and killed him at Jahaz and occupied his territory (Nu. 21:21–32). This area was assigned to the tribes of Reuben and Gad (Nu. 32:33–38; Jos. 13:10). The victory over Sihon is often recalled in the subsequent history of Israel (Dt. 31:4, by Moses; Jos. 2:10, by Rahab; Jos. 9:10, by the Gibeonites; Jdg. 11:19–21, by Jephthah; Ne. 9:22, by Levites in a prayer of confession; and Pss. 135:11; 136:19). The name Jebel Šîḥân for the mountain S of Ḏîbân (biblical Dibon) preserves in Arabic form the name of this king in the area which he once ruled. TB *Niddah* 61a records a tradition not found in the Bible that Sihon was the brother of King Og (also an Amorite), and a son of Ahijah, son of the legendary fallen angel Shamhazai.

Bibliography. G. A. Smith, *The Historical Geography of the Holy Land*[25], 1931, pp. 588–591, 691–693; A. Musil, *Arabia Petraea*, 1. *Moab*, 1907, pp. 375–376; M. Noth, *ZAW* 58, 1940, pp. 161–189.

J.T.

SILAS. A leading member of the church at Jerusalem who also had prophetic gifts (Acts 15:22, 32). Silas may be a Semitic name, possibly *šᵉʾîlā*, the Aram. form of Saul. There is little doubt that he is to be identified with 'Silvanus' (2 Cor. 1:19; 1 Thes. 1:1; 2 Thes. 1:1; 1 Pet. 5:12), which is probably the Latinized form of 'Silas', though it may be a separate *cognomen* chosen for its similarity.

In Acts Silas was sent by the church at Jerusalem to welcome into fellowship the Gentiles converted through the church of Antioch (Acts 15:22–35). When Paul and Barnabas quarrelled about John Mark, Barnabas went off with Mark and Paul took Silas as his companion on his second missionary journey (15:36–41). The fact of his Roman citizenship (16:37–39) may have been one of the reasons for the choice, and his membership of the Jerusalem church would have been helpful to Paul. His role seems to have been to replace Mark rather than Barnabas. Nowhere is he referred to in a general way as an 'apostle' (contrast Barnabas in Acts 14:14) and his position seems to be subordinate. Mark was the 'minister' (*hypēretēs*) of the apostles before (13:5), and that may indicate that he had some function similar to the synagogue attendants (Lk. 4:20) in looking after the Scriptures and possibly catechetical scrolls later developed into his Gospel. If the function of Silas was similar we can more readily see how he could have the literary role assigned to Silvanus in the Epistles. He accompanied Paul through Syria, Asia Minor, Macedonia and Thessalonica. When Paul left for Athens Silas stayed at Beroea and then joined Paul at Corinth (Acts 16–18). Paul mentions his work there in 2 Cor. 1:19. He was associated with Paul in the letters written from Corinth (1 Thes. 1:1; 2 Thes. 1:1) and is not named again until the reference to him in 1 Peter.

Peter says that he is writing *dia Silouanou* (1 Pet. 5:12). This implies a literary function with probably a good amount of freedom. This could account for some of the resemblances in wording between 1 Peter, 1 and 2 Thessalonians, and the apostolic decree of Acts 15. See E. G. Selwyn, *The First Epistle of St. Peter*, 1946, pp. 9–17.

R.E.N.

SILK. The RSV rendering of two biblical words. **1.** Heb. *mešî* (Ezk. 16:10, 13), perhaps 'silken thread', but the sense is obscure. Since the Heb. word seems to be an Egyp.

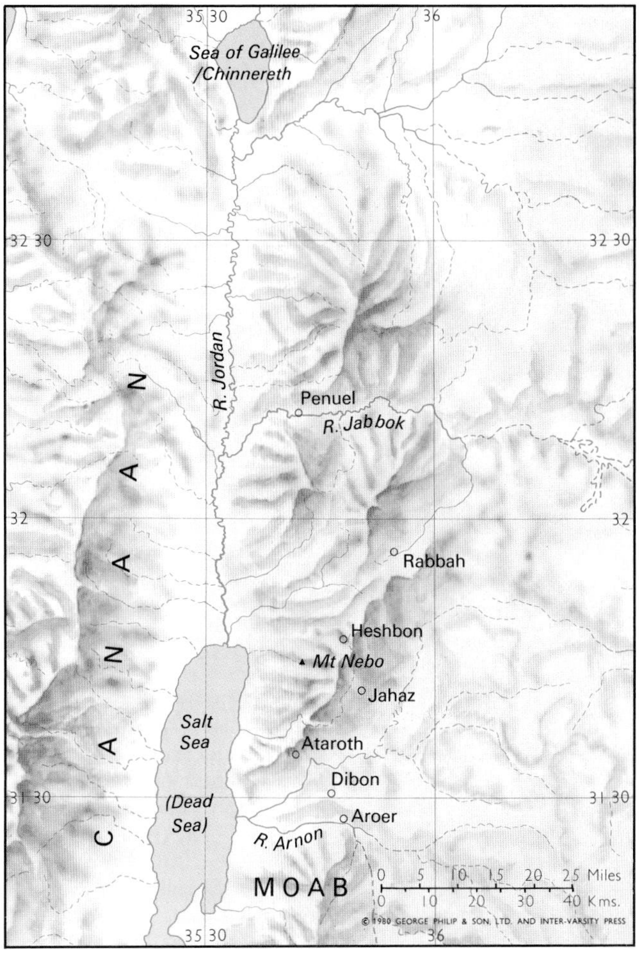

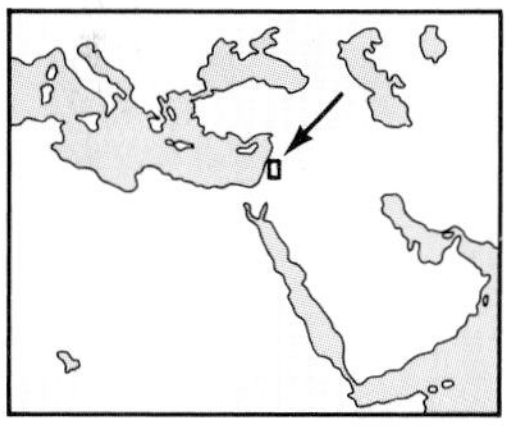

The area ruled from Heshbon by Sihon the Amorite in the 13th cent. BC.

loan-word (usually meaning linen in Egyp.) and silk was not introduced into Egypt until the Roman period, some doubt is cast on the identification. LXX has *trichaptos*, 'woven hair'; variants occur in other versions. **2.** Gk. *sērikon* (Rev. 18:12) 'silk', 'silken', listed among the precious wares sold in the markets of Babylon.

AV also renders as silk the Heb. *šēš* (Pr. 31:22 and mg. of Gn. 41:42 and Ex. 25:4) which other versions consider to be fine *linen.

True silk is obtained from the cocoon of a Chinese moth fed on the leaves of white mulberry (*Morus alba*). Silk thread was a precious article of trade obtained direct from China, since the rearing of these moths did not take place in the W until the Middle Ages. There is, however, another species of silk moth indigenous to the E Mediterranean that feeds on cypress and oak. It has been generally overlooked that from it in ancient times an industry arose in Cos and Sidon producing transparent silk that may have been intended in the biblical references.

J.D.D.
F.N.H.

SIKKUTH
See Sakkuth, Part 3.

The 'pool of Siloam' and the mouth of Hezekiah's tunnel. (SH)

SILOAH
See Shelah, Part 3.

SILOAM. One of the principal sources of water supply to Jerusalem was the intermittent pool of Gihon ('Virgin's Fountain') below the Fountain Gate (Ne. 3:15) and ESE of the city. This fed water along an open canal, which flowed slowly along the SE slopes, called *šilôaḥ* ('Sender'; LXX *Silōam*, Is. 8:6). It followed the line of the later 'second aqueduct' (Wilson) which fell only 5 cm in 300 m, discharging into the Lower or Old Pool (mod. *Birket el-Ḥamra*) at the end of the central valley between the walls of the SE and SW hills. It thus ran below 'the wall of the Pool of Shelah' (Ne. 3:15) and watered the 'king's garden' on the adjacent slopes.

This Old Pool was probably the 'Pool of Siloam' in use in NT times for sick persons and others to wash (Jn. 9:7–11). The 'Tower of Siloam' which fell and killed 18 persons—a disaster well known in our Lord's day (Lk. 13:4)—was probably sited on the Ophel ridge above the pool which, according to Josephus (*BJ* 5. 145), was near the bend of the old wall below Ophlas (Ophel). According to the Talmud (*Sukkoth* 4. 9), water was drawn from Siloam's pool in a golden vessel to be carried in procession to the Temple on the Feast of Tabernacles. Though there are traces of a Herodian bath and open reservoir (about 18 m by 5 m, originally 22 m square with steps on the W side), there can be no certainty that this was the actual pool in question. It has been suggested that the part of the city round the Upper Pool (*'Ain Silwān*) 100 m above was called 'Siloam', the Lower being the King's Pool (Ne. 2:14) or Lower Gihon.

When Hezekiah was faced with the threat of invasion by the Assyrian army under Sennacherib he 'stopped all the springs', that is, all the rivulets and subsidiary canals leading down into the Kedron 'brook that flowed through the land' (2 Ch. 32:4). Traces of canals blocked at about this time were found by the Parker Mission. The king then diverted the upper Gihon waters through a 'conduit' or tunnel into an upper cistern or pool (the normal method of storing water) on the W side of the city of David (2 Ki. 20:20). Ben Sira tells how 'Hezekiah fortified his city and brought water into the midst of it; he tunnelled the sheer rock with iron and built pools for water' (Ecclus. 48:17–19). Hezekiah clearly defended the new source of supply with a rampart (2 Ch. 32:30). The digging of the reservoir may be referred to by Isaiah (22:11).

In 1880 bathers in the upper pool (also called *birket silwān*) found about 5 m inside the tunnel a cursive Heb. inscription, now in Istanbul (*WRITING), which reads: '. . . was being dug out. It was cut in the following manner . . . axes, each man towards his fellow, and while there were still 3 cubits to be cut through, the voice of one man calling to the other was heard, showing that he was deviating to the right. When the tunnel was driven

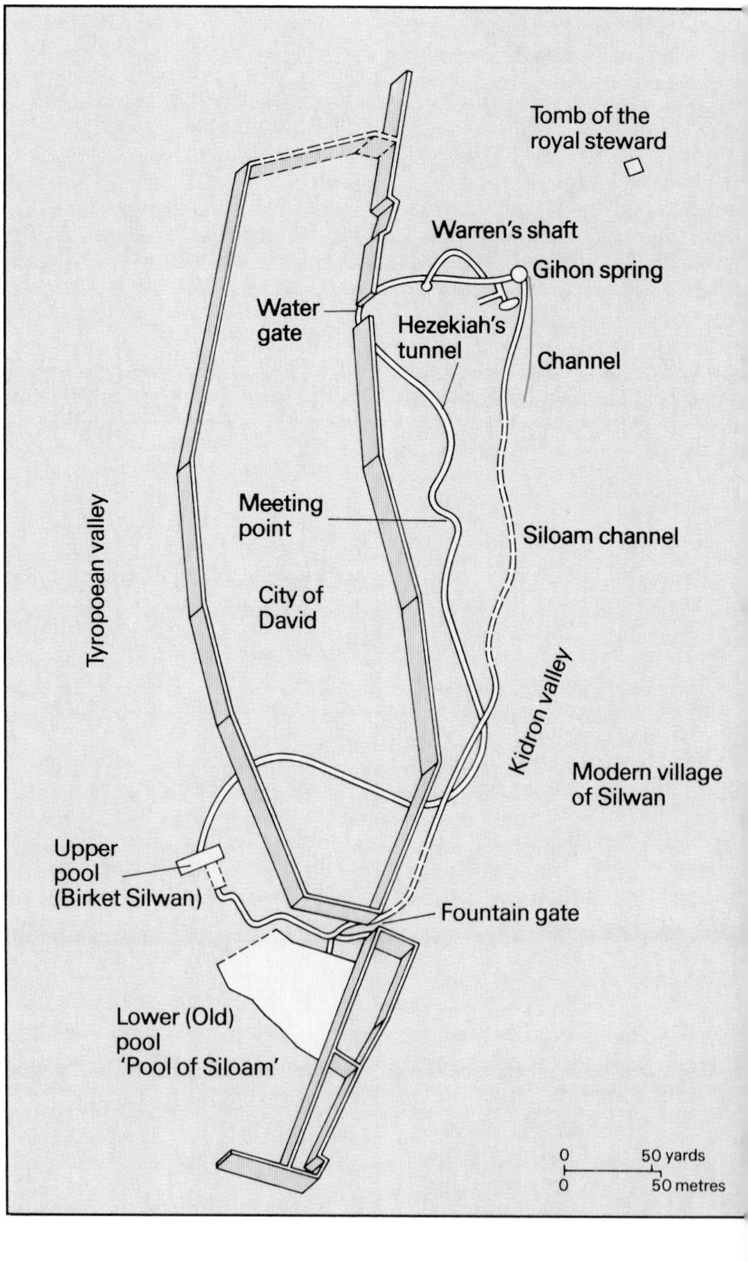

Plan of the Siloam area, including the pools and the channels which carried the water into the city of Jerusalem.

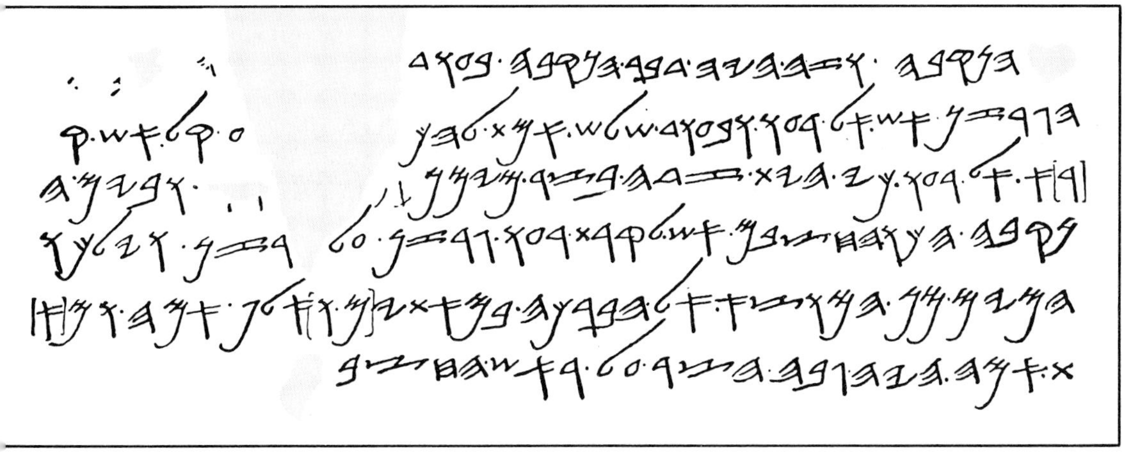

Facsimile of the inscription found in the Siloam tunnel describing how the miners excavating the water conduit from each end finally met. The archaic Hebrew script supports a date in Hezekiah's reign. Jerusalem. Length 75 cm. c. 710 BC. (GHG)

hrough, the excavators met man o man, axe to axe, and the water lowed for 1,200 cubits from the pring to the reservoir. The height of the rock above the heads of he excavators was 100 cubits' D. J. Wiseman, *IBA*, pp. 61–64).

When this remarkable Judaean engineering feat was excavated the marks of the picks and deviations o effect a junction midway were raced. The tunnel traverses 540 m (or 643 m, Ussishkin), twisting to avoid constructions or rock faults or to follow a fissure, to cover a direct line of 332 m. It is about 2 m high and in parts only 50 cm wide. Modern buildings prevent any archaeological check that the upper pool is the 'reservoir' (b^e*rēḵâ*) of Hezekiah or that from this the waters overflowed direct to the lower pool. The pool was probably underground at first, the rock roof collapsing or being quarried away later.

Hezekiah's tunnel begins from an earlier tunnel which channelled water from the spring of Gihon to the bottom of a shaft which rises to join an inclined tunnel which led to a point inside the Jebusite city. This shaft and tunnel system was built by the Jebusites to provide a secure water-supply and is possibly the 'gutter' or 'water shaft' (*ṣinnôr*) that David's men climbed to capture the city (2 Sa. 5:8).

Below the modern village of Siloam (Silwān, first mentioned in 1697) on the E escarpment opposite the hill of Ophel are a number of rock-cut tombs. These were prepared for the burial of 'Pharaoh's Daughter' and for ministers and nobles of the kingdom of Judah. One of these bore a Heb. inscription, the epitaph of a royal steward, probably the *Shebna who was rebuked by Isaiah (22:15–16). See *IBA*, p. 59; *IEJ* 3, 1953, pp. 137–152; K. M. Kenyon, *Digging Up Jerusalem*, 1974, pp. 153–159.

BIBLIOGRAPHY. J. Simons, *Jerusalem in the Old Testament*, 1952;

The tunnel, c. 534 m long, cut beneath Jerusalem to carry water to the pool of Siloam, in the time of Hezekiah. (HW) (MEPhA)

D. Ussishkin, 'The Original Length of the Siloam Tunnel', *Levant* 8, 1976, pp. 82–95; J. Wilkinson, 'The Pool of Siloam', *Levant* 10, 1978, pp.116–125. D.J.W.

SIMEON. 1. The second son of Jacob by Leah (Gn. 29:33). Heb. *šim'ôn* was derived from *šāma'* ('to hear'), and its significance is given in Gn. 29:33. Simeon took part with Levi in the massacre of the men of Shechem for dishonouring their sister Dinah (Gn. 34). He also played a prominent part in the affair of Joseph and his brothers, being given as a hostage so that they should return with Benjamin. Simeon may have been chosen by Joseph because he played a leading part in selling him to Egypt, or it may be because he was second to Reuben, who had acted more responsibly than the others (Gn. 37:21–22; 42:22). In the blessing of Jacob, Simeon and Levi were rebuked for their violent nature, and they were to be divided and scattered (Gn. 49:5–7). The sons of Simeon were Jemuel, Jamin, Ohad, Jachin, Zohar and Shaul, the son of a Canaanite woman (Gn. 46:10; Ex. 6:15).

2. The tribe of Simeon. The number of the tribe is given as 59,300 in Nu. 1:22–23 and 22,200 'families' in Nu. 26:14. They were to camp next to Reuben (Nu. 2:12–13). The tribe of Simeon was among those to be set on Mt Gerizim and blessed (Dt. 27:12), but it was not named (along with Issachar) in the blessing of Moses in Dt. 33. In the Promised Land it was given a portion at the S extremity and it came almost to be absorbed into the territory of Judah (Jos. 19:1–9). The towns of the area were reckoned to belong to Judah in Jos. 15:26–32, 42 and elsewhere. Judah and Simeon joined forces at the beginning of the conquest of Canaan (Jdg. 1:3, 17), but Judah was clearly the more powerful tribe. The sons of Simeon, despite keeping a genealogical record, did not multiply as fast as Judah (1 Ch. 4:24–33). They did, however, win a victory over the Amalekites under Hezekiah (1 Ch. 4:41–43), and they provided more men for David than did Judah (1 Ch. 12:24–25). The Chronicler seems to imply that Simeon belonged to the N kingdom, but numbers of Simeonites joined Asa in restoring the worship of Yahweh (2 Ch. 15:9). The tribe is not mentioned after the Exile, and the only other reference to it is among those sealed in Rev. 7:7, where it comes seventh in the list.

3. An ancestor of Jesus (Lk. 3:30).

4. A man in Jerusalem who was righteous and devout and who was looking for 'the consolation of Israel' (Lk. 2:25–35). He is not to be identified with Rabbi Simon ben Hillel. He was one of the remnant who were longing for the coming of the Messiah, and had received a direct revelation that he would not die before seeing the Messiah with his own eyes. When the presentation of Jesus was about to take place he was guided by the Spirit to come into the Temple. On seeing Jesus he uttered the hymn of praise now known as the *Nunc Dimittis. He saw that the Messiah would vindicate Israel in the eyes of the Gentiles. Simeon went on to speak to the astonished Mary of the role of Christ within Israel. He was to be like a stone causing some to fall and some to rise. He was to be a sign which would not be heeded but spoken against (34). Her own suffering as she watched his life and death was to be acute and he was to reveal the inmost thoughts of men (35). Having given his testimony to the Christ, Simeon fades silently from the picture.

5. A disciple at Antioch, with prophetic and teaching gifts, who was one of those who ordained Barnabas and Saul for their first missionary journey (Acts 13:1–2). He was surnamed Niger, which suggests that he was an African, but he has not been proved to be the same person as Simon of Cyrene (Lk. 23:26, *etc.*). Here RV and RSV read 'Symeon', which is the more normal rendering of the Gk. but not of the Heb.

6. The archaic version of the name of Simon Peter used by James in his speech to the Council of Jerusalem (Acts 15:14). RV and RSV render 'Symeon'. Some good MSS read *Symeon* also in 2 Pet. 1:1 (*cf.* RVmg., NEB). R.E.N.

SILVANUS
See Silas, Part 3.

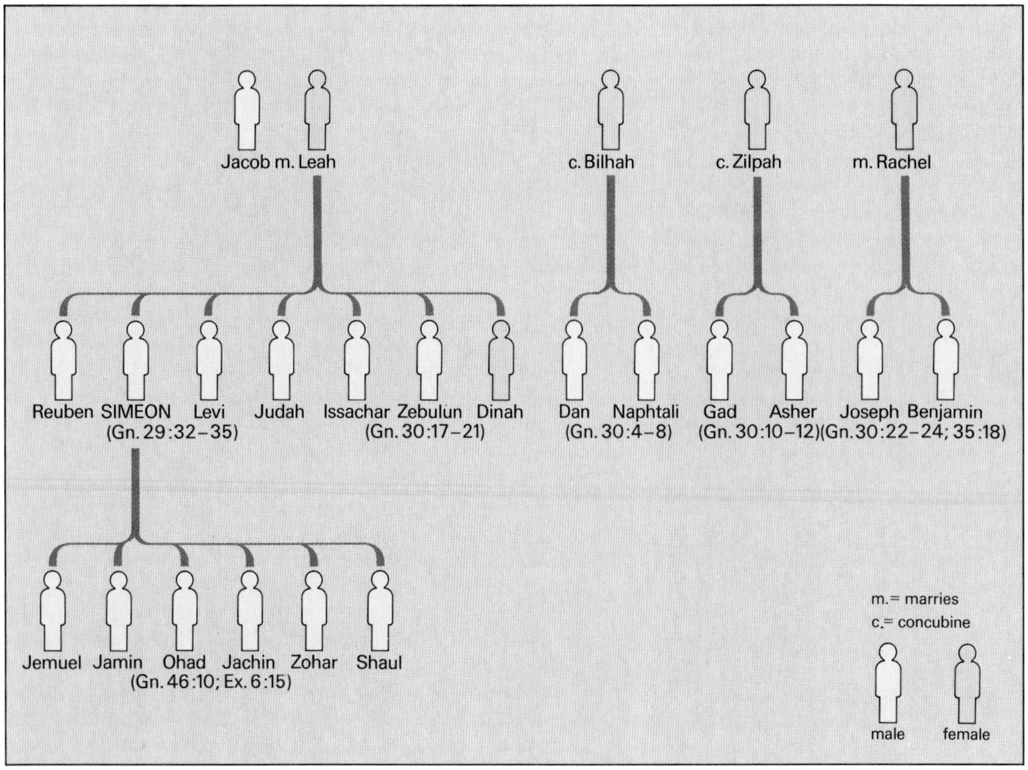

The family of Simeon.

SIMON. A later form of the OT name of Simeon (see Acts 15:14, where James uses the older form; also 2 Pet. 1:1, RVmg., NEB).

1. The chief disciple and apostle of Jesus, who was the son of Jonas (or John) and the brother of Andrew. Jesus gave him the name of *Peter.

2. The 'Canaanite' (Mt. 10:4; Mk. 3:18, AV). 'Canaanite' here cannot mean an inhabitant of Canaan, nor can it represent one who dwells at Cana. Rather it should be rendered *Cananaean (RV, RSV), an adherent of the party later known as the *Zealots and rendered so by Luke (Lk. 6:15; Acts 1:13). Whether Simon was a zealot in the political sense or the religious sense is a matter of some debate. **3.** One of the brothers of our Lord (Mt. 13:55; Mk. 6:3). **4.** A leper in Bethany in whose house the head of Jesus was anointed with oil (Mt. 26:6; Mk. 14:3), probably related to * Martha, * Mary and * Lazarus (see J. N. Sanders, 'Those whom Jesus loved', *NTS* 1, 1954–5, pp. 29–41). **5.** A man of Cyrene who was compelled to carry the cross of Jesus (Mk. 15:21), possibly the Simeon of Acts 13:1 (* RUFUS). **6.** A Pharisee in whose house the feet of Jesus were washed with tears and anointed (Lk. 7:40). Some scholars equate this Simon with **4** above and regard the stories as doublets; but they are strikingly different in their details (* MARY). **7.** Simon Iscariot, the father of * Judas Iscariot (Jn. 6:71; 12:4; 13:2). **8.** * Simon Magus. **9.** A tanner at Joppa in whose house Peter lodged (Acts 9:43). F.S.F.

SIMON MAGUS. In the NT we meet Simon in 'the city of Samaria' (Sebaste?— Acts 8:9–24), where he has 'swept the Samaritans off their feet with his magical arts' (NEB, v. 9). Luke does not suggest that Simon was himself a Samaritan. In essence a Levantine mountebank, Simon cultivated the legend that he was a divine emanation—'that Power of God which is called the Great Power'. The concept and the title were pagan enough (*cf.* for analogies, Ramsay, *BRD*, p. 117; Deissmann, *Bible Studies*², 1909, p. 336 n.), but the Samaritans would by 'God' intend 'Yahweh', and Simon must have acclimatized himself to his religious surroundings. He already represents, then, a significant syncretism of magical, Hellenistic and erratic Jewish elements.

In the mass movement attending Philip's preaching Simon professed conversion and was baptized. Luke uses his regular expression 'believed', and there is no reason to doubt Simon's sincerity thus far. The sequel, however, shows that his basic attitudes were still those of the magician. So impressed was he with the visible manifestations of the Holy Spirit following the apostles' laying on of hands, that he applied to them, as to higher proficients in the same trade, for the formula at an appropriate price. Peter's crushing rebuke evidently terrified him, for he begged the apostles' intercession to avert the threatened peril. Simon was obsessed with the idea of *power*: throughout he conceived of it as residing in the apostles as super-magicians.

Here, rather abruptly, Luke leaves Simon; but a tangle of traditions about his later career survive in primitive Christian literature. If they include incongruities and legends there is no need, with E. de Faye, to discount the patristic descriptions, or to deny a connection between the Simon of Acts and the Simonian sect. Even Lucian's rascally oracle-monger Alexander discoursed on the errors of Epicurus: and there is nothing incredible in Simon, with striking ability and personality, and real psychic powers, and perhaps some education, combining the charlatan and the heresiarch.

Justin (*Apology* 26, *cf.* 56, and *Trypho* 120), himself from Samaria, says that Simon was born in the village of Gitta; that his companion Helen, a former prostitute, was widely regarded as his first divine 'idea', while he himself was acclaimed by multitudes in Samaria and Rome as a divinity. Indeed, Roman adulation had erected a statue inscribed *Simoni Deo Sancto*, 'to Simon the Holy God'. (This statue may actually have been erected to the Sabine deity Semo Sancus, but the Simonians, who worshipped at statues, perhaps saw opportunities in this one.)

Irenaeus (*Adv. Haer.* 1. 16, Harvey), Hippolytus (*Philos.* 6. 7ff.) and Epiphanius (*Panarion.* 21. 2ff.) describe Simonian doctrine, the two latter employing publications which they allege, perhaps erroneously in Hippolytus' case, to emanate from the sect of Simon. He seems to have developed his old theme of 'the Great Power of God' into a Trinitarian scheme: Simon appeared to the Samaritans as the Father, to the Jews as the Son (he only *seemed* to suffer) and to the world at large as the Holy Spirit. He had a Redemption myth in which he rescued Helen ('the lost sheep') from the bondage of successive transmigrations in various female bodies; and he preached salvation by grace, requiring faith in Helen and himself, but allowing unrestrained liberty in morals afterwards. But Simon also borrowed heavily from Gk. paganism and Gk. philosophy, and some concepts appear which recur in more sophisticated Christian * Gnosticism. Irenaeus and the others regard him as the first major heretic, the initiator of a long chain of interrelated errors. The modern association of Gnostic origins with heretical forms of Judaism may suggest that their instinct was not far wrong.

Literature such as the Clementine romance and the *Acts of Peter* has many imaginative stories of encounters between Simon and Peter in Rome. (The once-popular idea that in the Clementines Simon is a cipher for Paul need no longer be taken seriously.) According to Hippolytus, his final exhibition misfired. He was buried alive, pro-

The territory of Simeon.

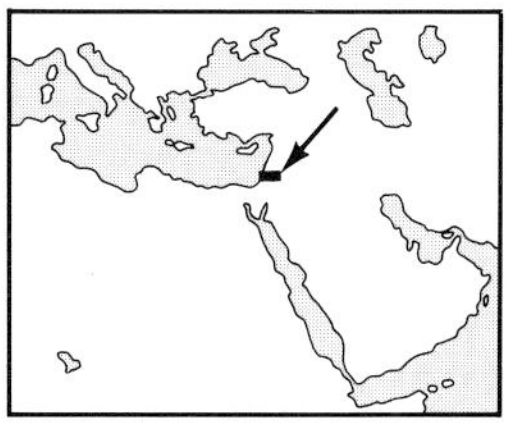

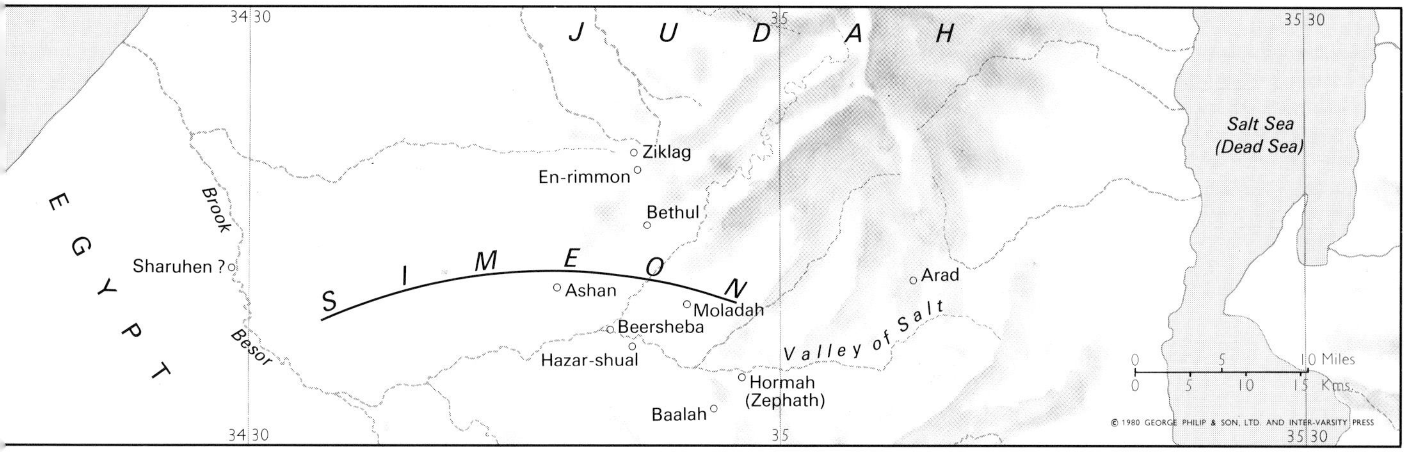

mising to reappear in 3 days; but he did not, for, in Hippolytus' laconic phrase, 'he was not the Christ'.

BIBLIOGRAPHY. R. P. Casey in *BC*, 5, 1933, pp. 151ff.; E. de Faye, *Gnostiques et Gnosticisme*², 1925, pp. 413ff.; R. M. Grant, *Gnosticism and Early Christianity*, 1960, pp. 70–96; A. A. T. Ehrhardt, *The Framework of the New Testament Stories*, 1964, pp. 161–164; J. W. Drane, 'Simon the Samaritan and the Lucan Concept of Salvation History', *EQ* 47, 1975, pp. 131–137.

A.F.W.

SIN. The Egyp. *sinw*, *swn*, 'fortress', is connected later with Egyp. *sin*, 'clay, mud', hence its Gk. name Pelusium, 'mud-city'. A fortress-city, it is now Tell Farama, on the seashore about 32 km SE of Port Said; an Egyp. key defence-post against invasion from the E through Palestine. Emendation in Ezk. 30:15–16 to Seven(eh) (= Aswan) is unnecessary. On the name Sin, see Gardiner, *JEA* 5, 1918, pp. 253–254. K.A.K.

SIN.

I. Terminology

As might be expected of a book whose dominant theme is human sin and God's gracious salvation from it, the Bible uses a wide variety of terms in both OT and NT to express the idea of sin.

There are four main Heb. roots. *ḥṭ'* is the most common and with its derivatives conveys the underlying idea of missing the mark, or deviating from the goal (*cf.* Jdg. 20:16 for non-moral usage). The vast proportion of its occurrences refer to moral and religious deviation, whether in respect of man (Gn. 20:9), or God (La. 5:7). The noun *ḥaṭṭā'ṯ* is frequently used as a technical term for a sin-offering (Lv. 4, *passim*). This root does not address the inner motivation of wrong action but concentrates more on its formal aspect as deviation from the moral norm, usually the law or will of God (Ex. 20:20; Ho. 13:2; *etc.*). *pš'* refers to action in breach of relationship, 'rebellion', 'revolution'. It occurs in a non-theological sense, *e.g.*, with reference to Israel's secession from the house of David (1 Ki. 12:19). Used of sin it is perhaps the profoundest OT term reflecting as it does the insight that sin is rebellion against God, the defiance of his holy lordship and rule (Is. 1:28; 1 Ki. 8:50; *etc.*). *'wh* conveys a literal meaning of deliberate perversion or 'twisting' (Is. 24:1; La. 3:9). Used in relation to sin it reflects the thought of sin as deliberate wrongdoing, 'committing iniquity' (Dn. 9:5; 2 Sa. 24:17). It occurs in religious contexts particularly in a noun form *'āwôn* which stresses the idea of the guilt which arises from deliberate wrongdoing (Gn. 44:16; Je. 2:22). It can also refer to the punishment which is consequent upon the sin (Gn. 4:13; Is. 53:11). *šāḡâh* has as its basic idea straying away from the correct path (Ezk. 34:6). It is indicative of sin as arising from ignorance, 'erring', 'creaturely going astray' (1 Sa. 26:21; Jb. 6:24). It often appears in the cultic context as sin against unrecognized ritual regulations (Lv. 4:2). Reference should also be made to *rāša'*, to be wicked, to act wickedly (2 Sa. 22:22; Ne. 9:33); and *'āmal*, mischief done to others (Pr. 24:2; Hab. 1:13).

The principal NT term is *hamartia* (and cognates), which is equivalent to *ḥṭ'*. In classical Gk. it is used for missing a target or taking a wrong road. It is the general NT term for sin as concrete wrongdoing, the violation of God's law (Jn. 8:46; Jas. 1:15; 1 Jn. 1:8). In Rom. 5–8 Paul personifies the term as a ruling principle in human life (*cf.* 5:12; 6:12, 14; 7:17, 20; 8:2). *paraptōma* occurs in classical contexts for an error in measurement or a blunder. The NT gives it a stronger moral connotation as misdeed or trespass (*cf.* 'dead through . . .', Eph. 2:1; Mt. 6:14f.). *parabasis* is a similarly derived term with similar meaning, 'transgression', 'going beyond the norm' (Rom. 4:15; Heb. 2:2). *asebeia* is perhaps the profoundest NT term and commonly translates *pš'* in the LXX. It implies active ungodliness or impiety (Rom. 1:18; 2 Tim. 2:16). Another term is *anomia*, lawlessness, a contempt for law (Mt. 7:23; 2 Cor. 6:14). *kakia* and *ponēria* are general terms expressing moral and spiritual depravity (Acts 8:22; Rom. 1:29; Lk. 11:39; Eph. 6:12). The last of these references indicates the association of the latter term with Satan, the evil one, *ho ponēros* (Mt. 13:19; 1 Jn. 3:12). *adikia* is the main classical term for wrong done to one's neighbour. It is translated variously as 'injustice' (Rom. 9:14), 'unrighteousness' (Lk. 18:6), 'falsehood' (Jn. 7:18), 'wickedness' (Rom. 2:8), 'iniquity' (2 Tim. 2:19). 1 Jn. equates it with *hamartia* (1 Jn. 3:4; 5:17). Also occurring are *enochos*, a legal term meaning 'guilty' (Mk. 3:29; 1 Cor. 11:27), and *opheilēma*, 'debt' (Mt. 6:12).

The definition of sin, however, is not to be derived simply from the terms used in Scripture to denote it. The most characteristic feature of sin in all its aspects is that it is directed against God (*cf.* Ps. 51:4; Rom. 8:7). Any conception of sin which does not have in the forefront the contradiction which it offers to God is a deviation from the biblical representation. The common notion that sin is selfishness betrays a false assessment of its nature and gravity. Essentially, sin is directed against God, and this perspective alone accounts for the diversity of its form and activities. It is a violation of that which God's glory demands and is, therefore, in its essence the contradiction of God.

II. Origin

Sin was present in the universe before the Fall of Adam and Eve (Gn. 3:1f.; *cf.* Jn. 8:44; 2 Pet. 2:4; 1 Jn. 3:8; Jude 6). The Bible however does not deal directly with the origin of evil in the universe, being concerned rather with sin and its origin in human life (1 Tim. 2:14; Jas. 1:13f.). The real thrust of the demonic temptation in the account of the Fall in Gn. 3 lies in its subtle suggestion of man's aspiring to equality with his maker ('you will be like God . . .', 3:5). Satan's attack was directed against the integrity, veracity and loving provision of God, and consisted in an enticement to wicked and blasphemous rebellion against man's proper Lord. In this act man snatched at equality with God (*cf.* Phil. 2:6), attempted to assert his independence of God, and hence to call in question the very nature and ordering of existence whereby he lived as creature in utter dependence upon the grace and provision of his creator. 'Man's sin lies in his pretension to be God' (Niebuhr). In this act, further, man blasphemously withheld the worship and adoring love which is ever his proper response to God's majesty and grace, and instead paid homage to the enemy of God and to his own foul ambitions.

Thus the origin of sin according to Gn. 3 ought not to be sought so much in an overt action (2:17 with 3:6) but in an inward, God-denying aspiration of which the act of disobedience was the immediate expression. As to the problem of how Adam and Eve could have been subject to temptation had they not previously known sin, Scripture does not enter into extended discussion. However, in the person of Jesus Christ it witnesses to a Man who, though without sin, was subject to temptation 'in every respect as we are' (Heb. 4:15; *cf.* Mt. 4:3f.; Heb. 2:17f.; 5:7f.; 1 Pet. 1:19; 2:22f.). The ultimate origin of *evil is part of the 'mystery of lawlessness' (2 Thes. 2:7), but an arguable reason for Scripture's relative silence is that a 'rational explanation' of the origin of sin would have the inevitable result of directing attention away from the Scripture's primary concern, the confession of *my personal guilt* (*cf.* G. C. Berkouwer, *Sin*, 1971, ch. 1). In the end, sin, by the nature of the case, cannot be 'known' objectively; 'sin posits itself' (S. Kierkegaard).

III. Consequences

The sin of Adam and Eve was not an isolated event. The consequences for them, for posterity and for the world are immediately apparent.

a. Man's attitude to God

The changed attitude to God on the part of Adam indicates the revolution that took place in their minds. They 'hid themselves from the presence of the Lord God' (Gn. 3:8; *cf.* v. 7). Made for the presence and fellowship of God, they now dreaded encounter with him (*cf.* Jn. 3:20). *Shame and fear were now the dominant emotions (*cf.* Gn. 2:25; 3:7, 10), indicating the disruption that had taken place.

b. God's attitude to man

Not only was there a change in man's attitude to God, but also in God's attitude to man. Reproof, condemnation, curse, expulsion from the garden are all indicative of this. Sin is one-sided, but its consequences are not. Sin elicits God's wrath and displeasure, and necessarily so, because it is the contradiction of what he is. For God to be complacent towards sin is an impossibility, since it would be for God to cease to take himself seriously. He cannot deny himself.

c. Consequences for the human race

The unfolding history of man furnishes a catalogue of vices (Gn. 4:8, 19, 23f.; 6:2–3, 5). The sequel of abounding iniquity results in the virtual destruction of mankind (Gn. 6:7, 13; 7:21–24). The Fall had abiding effect not only upon Adam and Eve but upon all who descended from them; there is racial solidarity in sin and evil.

d. Consequences for creation

The effects of the Fall extend to the physical cosmos. 'Cursed is the ground because of you' (Gn. 3:17; *cf.* Rom. 8:20). Man is the crown of creation, made in God's image and, therefore, God's vicegerent (Gn. 1:26). The catastrophe of man's Fall brought the catastrophe of curse upon that over which he was given dominion. Sin was an event in the realm of the human spirit, but it has its repercussions in the whole of creation.

e. The appearance of death

*Death is the epitome of sin's penalty. This was the warning attached to the prohibition of Eden (Gn. 2:17), and it is the direct expression of God's curse upon man the sinner (Gn. 3:19). Death in the phenomenal realm consists in the separation of the integral elements of man's being. This dissolution exemplifies the principle of death, namely, separation, and it comes to its most extreme expression in separation from God (Gn. 3:23f.). Because of sin death is invested with a fear and terror for man (Lk. 12:5; Heb. 2:15).

IV. Imputation

The first sin of Adam had unique significance for the whole human race (Rom. 5:12, 14–19; 1 Cor. 15:22). Here there is sustained emphasis upon the one trespass of the one man as that by which sin, condemnation and death came upon all mankind. The sin is identified as 'the transgression of Adam', 'the trespass of the one', 'one trespass', 'the disobedience of the one', and there can be no doubt that the first trespass of Adam is intended. Hence the clause 'because all men sinned' in Rom. 5:12 refers to the sin of all in the sin of Adam. It cannot refer to the actual sins of all men, far less to the hereditary depravity with which all are afflicted, for in v. 12 the clause in question clearly says why 'death spread to all men', and in the succeeding verses the 'one man's trespass' (v. 17) is stated to be the reason for the universal reign of death. If the same sin were not intended, Paul would be affirming two different things with reference to the same subject in the same context. The only explanation of the two forms of statement is that all sinned in the sin of Adam. The same inference is to be drawn from 1 Cor. 15:22, 'in Adam all die'. If all die in Adam, it is because all sinned in Adam.

According to Scripture the kind of solidarity with Adam which explains the participation of all in Adam's sin is the kind of solidarity which Christ sustains to those united to him. The parallel in Rom. 5:12–19; 1 Cor. 15:22, 45–49 between Adam and Christ indicates the same type of relationship in both cases, and we have no need to posit anything more ultimate in the case of Adam and the race than we find in the case of Christ and his people. In the latter it is representative headship, and this is all that is necessary to ground the solidarity of all in the sin of Adam. To say that the sin of Adam is imputed to all is but to say that all were involved in his sin by reason of his representative headship.

While the imputation of Adam's sin was immediate according to the evidence of the relevant passages, the judgment of condemnation passed upon Adam, and hence upon all men in him, is in Scripture seen as confirmed in its justice and propriety by every man's subsequent moral experience. Thus Rom. 3:23 'all have sinned' is amply proved by reference to the specific, overt sins of Jews and Gentiles (Rom. 1:18–3:8) before Paul makes any reference whatever to imputation in Adam. In similar vein Scripture universally relates man's ultimate judgment before God to his 'works' which fall short of God's standards (*cf.* Mt. 7:21–27; 13:41; 25:31–46; Lk. 3:9; Rom. 2:5–10; Rev. 20:11–14).

Rejection of this doctrine betrays not only failure to accept the witness of the relevant passages but also failure to appreciate the close relation which exists between the principle which governs our relation to Adam and the governing principle of God's operation in salvation. The parallel between Adam as the first man and Christ as the last Adam shows that the accomplishment of salvation in Christ is based on the same operating principle as that by which we have become sinners and the heirs of death. The history of mankind is finally subsumed under two complexes, sin–condemnation–death and righteousness–justification–life.

The former arises from our union with Adam, the latter from union with Christ. These are the two orbits within which we live and move. God's government of men is directed in terms of these relationships. If we do not reckon with Adam we are thereby excluded from a proper understanding of Christ. All who die die in Adam; all who are made alive are made alive in Christ.

V. Depravity

Sin never consists merely in a voluntary act of transgression. Every volition proceeds from something that is more deep-seated than the volition itself. A sinful act is the expression of a sinful heart (*cf.* Mk. 7:20–23; Pr. 4:23; 23:7). Sin must always include, therefore, the perversity of heart, mind, disposition and will. This was true, as we saw above, in the case of the first sin, and it applies to all sin. The imputation to posterity of the sin of Adam must, therefore, carry with it involvement in the perversity apart from which Adam's sin would be meaningless and its imputation an impossible abstraction. Paul states that 'by one man's disobedience many were made sinners' (Rom. 5:19). The depravity which sin entails and with which all men come into the world is for this reason a direct implicate of our solidarity with Adam in his sin. We come to be as individuals by natural generation, and as individuals we never exist apart from the sin of Adam reckoned as ours. Therefore the psalmist wrote, 'Behold, I was brought forth in iniquity, and in sin did my mother conceive me' (Ps. 51:5) and our Lord said, 'That which is born of the flesh is flesh' (Jn. 3:6).

The witness of Scripture to the pervasiveness of this depravity is explicit. Gn. 6:5; 8:21 provides a closed case. The latter reference makes it clear that this indictment was not restricted to the period before the judgment of the Flood. There is no evading the force of this testimony from the early pages of divine revelation, and later assessments are to the same effect (*cf.* Je. 17:9–10; Rom. 3:10–18). From whatever angle man is viewed, there is the absence of that which is well-pleasing to God. Considered more positively, all have turned aside from God's way and become corrupted. In Rom. 8:5–7 Paul refers to the mind of the flesh, and flesh, when used ethically as here, means human nature directed and governed by sin (*cf.* Jn. 3:6). Further, according to Rom. 8:7, 'The mind that is set on the flesh is hostile to God'. No stronger condemnatory judgment could be arrived at, for it means that the thinking of the natural man is conditioned and governed by enmity directed against God. Nothing less than a judgment of total depravity is the clear implication of these passages, *i.e.* there is no area or aspect of human life which is absolved from the sombre effects of man's fallenness, and hence no area which might serve as a possible ground for man's justification of himself in the face of God and his law.

Depravity however is not registered in actual transgression to an equal extent in all. There are multiple restraining factors. God does not give over all men to uncleanness, to a base mind, and to improper conduct (Rom. 1:24, 28). Total depravity (total, that is, in the sense that it touches everything) is not incompatible with the exercise of the natural virtues and the promotion of civil righteousness. Unregenerate men are still endowed with conscience, and the work of the law is written upon their hearts so that in measure and at points they fulfil its requirement (Rom. 2:14f.). The doctrine of depravity, however, means that these works, though formally in accord with what God commands, are not good and well-pleasing to God in terms of the full and ultimate criteria by which his judgment is determined, the criteria of love to God as the animating motive, the law of God as the directing principle, and the glory of God as the controlling purpose (Rom. 8:7; 1 Cor. 2:14; *cf.* Mt. 6:2, 5, 16; Mk. 7:6–7; Rom. 13:4; 1 Cor. 10:31; 13:3; Tit. 1:15; 3:5; Heb. 11:4, 6).

VI. Inability

Inability is concerned with the incapacity arising from the nature of depravity. If depravity is total, *i.e.* affecting every aspect and area of man's being, then inability for what is good and well-pleasing to God is likewise comprehensive in its reference.

We are not able to change our character or act differently from it. In the matter of understanding, the natural man cannot know the things of the Spirit of God because they are spiritually discerned (1 Cor. 2:14). In respect of obedience to the law of God he is not only not subject to the law of God but he cannot be (Rom. 8:7). They who are in the flesh cannot please God (Rom. 8:8). A corrupt tree cannot bring forth good fruit (Mt. 7:18). The impossibility in each case is undeniable. It is our Lord who affirms that even faith in him is impossible apart from the gift and drawing of the Father (Jn. 6:44f., 65). This witness on his part is to the same effect as his insistence that apart from the supernatural birth of water and the Spirit no-one can have intelligent appreciation of, or entrance into, the kingdom of God (Jn. 3:3, 5f., 8; *cf.* Jn. 1:13; 1 Jn. 2:29; 3:9; 4:7; 5:1, 4, 18).

The necessity of so radical and momentous a transformation and re-creation as regeneration is proof of the whole witness of Scripture to the bondage of sin and the hopelessness of our sinful condition. This bondage implies that it is a psychological, moral and spiritual impossibility for the natural man to receive the things of the Spirit, to love God and do what is well-pleasing to him, or to believe in Christ to the salvation of his soul. It is this enslavement which is the premise of the gospel, and the glory of the gospel lies precisely in the fact that it provides release from the bondage and slavery of sin. It is the gospel of grace and power for the helpless.

VII. Liability

Since sin is against God, he cannot be complacent towards it or indifferent with respect to it. He reacts inevitably against it. This reaction is specifically his wrath. The frequency with which Scripture mentions the wrath of God compels us to take account of its reality and meaning.

Various terms are used in the OT. In Heb., *'ap̄* in the sense of 'anger', and intensified in the form *h^a^rôn 'ap̄* to express the 'fierceness of God's anger' is very common (*cf.* Ex. 4:14; 32:12; Nu. 11:10; 22:22; Jos. 7:1; Jb. 42:7; Ps. 21:9; Is. 10:5; Na. 1:6; Zp. 2:2); *ḥēmâ* is likewise frequent (*cf.* Dt. 29:23; Pss. 6:1; 79:6; 90:7; Je. 7:20; Na. 1:20); *'eḇrâ* (*cf.* Ps. 78:49; Is. 9:19; 10:6; Ezk. 7:19; Ho. 5:10) and *qeṣep̄* (*cf.* Dt. 29:28; Ps. 38:1; Je. 32:37; 50:13; Zc. 1:2) are used with sufficient frequency to be worthy of mention; *za'am* is also characteristic and expresses the thought of indignation (*cf.* Pss. 38:3; 69:24; 78:49; Is. 10:5; Ezk. 22:31; Na. 1:6). It is apparent that the OT is permeated with references to the wrath of God. Often more than one of these terms appear together in order to strengthen and confirm the thought expressed. There is intensity in the terms themselves and in the constructions in which they occur to convey the notions of displeasure, fiery indignation and holy vengeance.

The Gk. terms are *orgē* and *thymos*, the former frequently predicated of God in the NT (*cf.* Jn. 3:36; Rom. 1:18; 2:5, 8; 3:5; 5:9; 9:22; Eph. 2:3; 5:6; 1 Thes. 1:10; Heb. 3:11; Rev. 6:17), and the latter less frequently (*cf.* Rom. 2:8; Rev. 14:10, 19; 16:1, 19; 19:15; see *zēlos* in Heb. 10:27).

The *wrath of God is therefore a reality, and the language and teaching of Scripture are calculated to impress upon us the severity by which it is characterized. There are three observations which particularly require mention. First, the wrath of God must not be interpreted in terms of the fitful passion so commonly associated with anger in us. It is the deliberate, resolute displeasure which the contradiction of his holiness demands. Secondly, it is not to be construed as vindictiveness but as holy indignation; nothing of the nature of malice attaches to it. It is not malignant hatred but righteous detestation. Thirdly, we may not reduce the wrath of God to his will to punish. Wrath is a positive outgoing of dissatisfaction as sure as that which is pleasing to God involves complacency. We must not eliminate from God what we term emotion. The wrath of God finds its parallel in the human heart, exemplified in a perfect manner in Jesus (*cf.* Mk. 3:5; 10:14).

The epitome of sin's liability is, therefore, the holy wrath of God. Since sin is never impersonal, but exists in, and is committed by, persons, the wrath of God consists in the displeasure to which we are subjected; we are the objects. The penal inflictions which we suffer are the expressions of God's wrath. The sense of guilt and torment of conscience are the reflections in our consciousness of the displeasure of God. The essence of final perdition will consist in the infliction of God's indignation (*cf.* Is. 30:33; 66:24; Dn. 12:2; Mk. 9:43, 45, 48).

VIII. The conquest of sin

Despite the sombreness of the theme, the Bible never completely loses a note of hope and optimism when dealing with sin; for the heart of the Bible is its witness to God's mighty offensive against sin in his historical purpose of redemption centred in Jesus Christ, the last Adam, his eternal Son, the Saviour of sinners. Through the whole work of Christ, his miraculous birth, his life of perfect obedience, supremely his death on the cross and resurrection from the dead, his ascension to the right hand of the Father, his reign in history and his glorious return, sin has been overcome. Its rebellious, usurping authority has been vanquished, its absurd claims exposed, its foul machinations unmasked and overthrown, the baleful effects of the Fall in Adam counteracted and undone, and God's honour vindicated, his holiness satisfied and his glory extended.

In Christ, God has conquered sin; such are the great glad tidings of the Bible. Already this conquest is demonstrated in the people of God, who by faith in Christ and his finished work are already delivered from the guilt and judgment of sin, and are already experiencing, to a degree, the conquest of sin's power through their union with Christ. This process will be culminated at the end of the age when Christ will return in glory, the saints will be fully sanctified, sin banished from God's good creation and a new heaven and earth brought into being in which righteousness will dwell. (*Cf.* Gn. 3:15; Is. 52:13–53:12; Je. 31:31–34; Mt. 1:21; Mk. 2:5; 10:45; Lk. 2:11; 11:14–22; Jn. 1:29; 3:16f.; Acts 2:38; 13:38f.; Rom. *passim*; 1 Cor. 15:3f., 22f.; Eph. 1:3–14; 2:1–10; Col. 2:11–15; Heb. 8:1–10:25; 1 Pet. 1:18–21; 2 Pet. 3:11–13; 1 Jn. 1:6–2:2; Rev. 20:7–14; 21:22–22:5.)

BIBLIOGRAPHY. J. Muller, *The Christian Doctrine of Sin*, 1877; J. Orr, *Sin as a Problem of Today*, 1910; F. R. Tennant, *The Concept of Sin*, 1912; C. Ryder Smith, *The Bible Doctrine of Sin*, 1953; E. Brunner, *Man in Revolt*, 1939; R. Niebuhr, *The Nature and Destiny of Man*, 1941 and 1943; J. Murray, *The Imputation of Adam's Sin*, 1959; G. C. Berkouwer, *Sin*, 1971; W. Günther, W. Bauder, *NIDNTT* 3, pp. 573–587; *TDNT* 1, pp. 149–163, 267–339; 3, pp. 167–172; 5, pp. 161–166, 447–448, 736–744; 6, pp. 170–172, 883–884; 7, pp. 339–358.

B.A.M.

SIN, WILDERNESS OF. A wilderness through which the Israelites passed between Elim and Mt Sinai (Ex. 16:1; 17:1; Nu. 33:11–12). It is usually identified with Debbet er-Ramleh, a sandy tract below Jebel et-Tih in the SW of the Sinai pen-

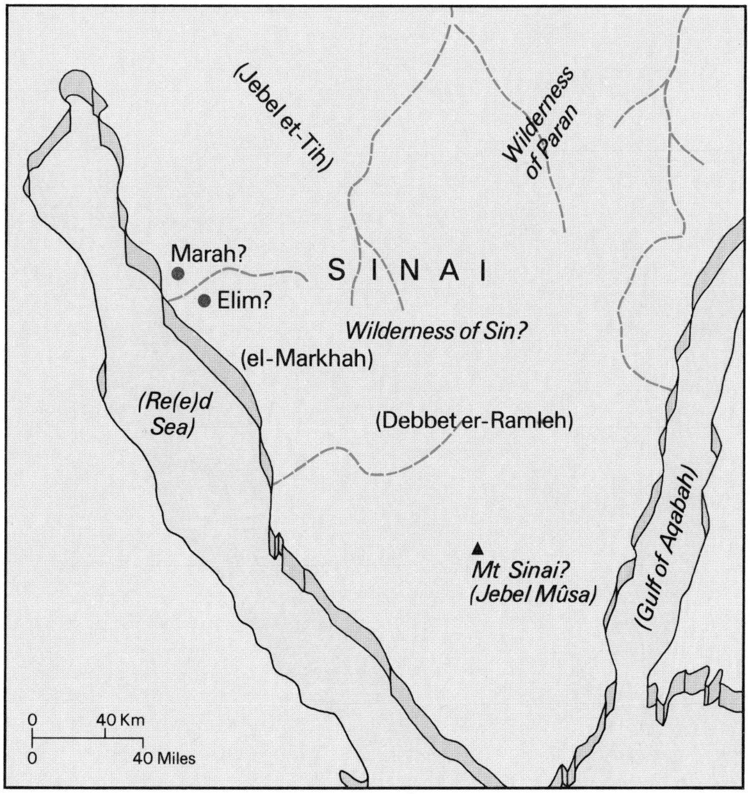

The probable location of 'the wilderness of Sin' in the Sinai peninsula.

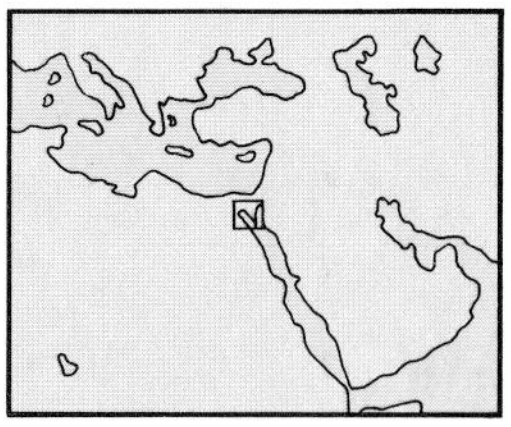

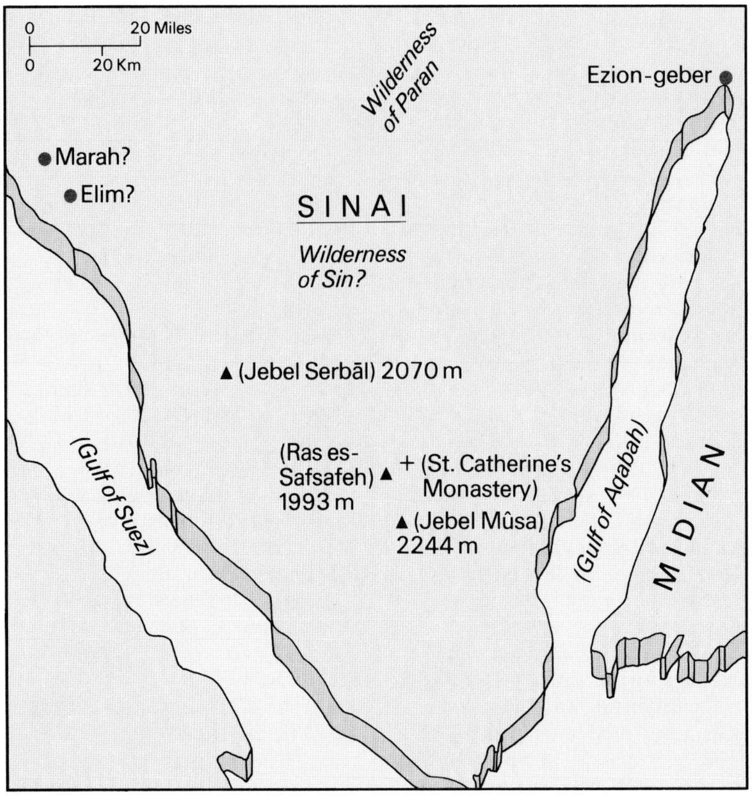

The Sinai peninsula.

The granite summit of Jebel Mûsa, the most probable location of Mt Sinai. (RS)

insula; but another suggested location is on the coastal plain of el-Markhah. As its position depends on the fixing of Mt *Sinai, which is uncertain, it is impossible to determine the exact site. J.M.H.

SINAI, MOUNT.

I. Situation

The location of this mountain is uncertain. The following mountains are regarded by various scholars as Mt Sinai: Jebel Mûsa, Ras eṣ-ṣafṣafeh, Jebel Serbāl and a mountain near al-Hrob. The tradition in favour of Jebel Serbāl can be traced back as far as Eusebius; the tradition in favour of Jebel Mûsa only as far as Justinian. The situation of Jebel Serbāl, *e.g.* the fact that there is no wilderness at its foot, makes it improbable as the mountain of the covenant. The once widely accepted view of A. Musil that the volcanic mountain near al-Hrob is to be identified with Mt Sinai is no longer popular with scholars, because it makes the reconstruction of the route of the Exodus impossible and it reads too much into Ex. 19. Modern attempts to identify Sinai with volcanic mountains E of the Gulf of Aqaba are so uncertain that not much can be derived from them. This leaves two possibilities: Jebel Mûsa and Ras eṣ-ṣafṣafeh. These two mountains are situated on a short ridge of granite of about 4 km stretching from NW to SE. Ras eṣ-ṣafṣafeh (1,993 m) is situated at the N edge and Jebel Mûsa (2,244 m) at the S one. Tradition and most of the modern scholars accept Jebel Mûsa as Mt Sinai. There is, none the less, a strong preference among certain scholars for Ras eṣ-ṣafṣafeh as the mountain of the covenant because of the considerable plain at its foot which would have been spacious enough for the large body of Israelites (*cf.* Ex. 20:18: 'they stood afar off'). However, tradition in favour of Jebel Mûsa is so ancient (about 1,500 years) and the granite formations so imposing that it is quite probably Mt Sinai. Furthermore, a few stations *en route* to the mountain point to the same conclusion.

II. In the Old Testament

Mt Sinai is also called Horeb in the OT. Travelling past Marah and Elim, the Israelites reached Sinai in the 3rd month after their departure from Egypt (Ex. 19:1), and camped at its foot on a plain from which the top was visible (Ex. 19:16, 18, 20). The Lord revealed himself to Moses on this mountain and gave the Ten Commandments and other laws. The covenant made here between God and the people played a major role in binding the tribes together and moulding them into one nation serving one God. Although the authenticity of this account is rejected by certain modern schools, it is clear from Jdg. 5:5 that the Sinai tradition is an ancient part of Israelite belief. The prominent role of Mt Sinai in the OT and the strong tradition attached to it provide ample evidence in support of the historicity of the account (* EXODUS).

At the foot of Jebel Mûsa is the monastery of St Catherine. It was here that Tischendorf discovered the famous 4th-century uncial MS of the Greek Bible called Codex Sinaiticus. The library of St Catherine has ancient MSS in Gk., Arabic, Ethiopic and Syriac (many of which have recently been made generally available on microfilm).

BIBLIOGRAPHY. B. Rothenberg, *God's Wilderness*, 1961; W. Beyerlin, *Origins and History of the Oldest Sinaitic Traditions*, 1965; B. Zuber, *Vier Studien zu den Ursprüngen Israels*, 1976, pp. 16–49.

F.C.F.

III. In the New Testament

1. During his last speech before martyrdom, Stephen twice mentions Mt Sinai in a reference to the theophany to Moses at the burning bush (Acts 7:30, 38; in Ex. 3:1ff. the synonym Horeb is used). Stephen reminds his accusers that even a Gentile place like Sinai in NW Arabia became holy ground because God was pleased to reveal himself there; he was not limited by Jewish geography.

2. In Gal. 4:21–31 Paul uses an allegory to identify Israel first with the slave-wife Hagar (Gn. 16:15; 21:2, 9) and then with Mt Sinai 'in Arabia' (*i.e.* appropriately in a barren wilderness area). Hagar and Sinai are symbolic respectively of being outside the covenant of promise and of bondage to the law of Moses. Together they are taken as representing 'the present Jerusalem', *i.e.* Judaism, which is slavery (to the Law and its intolerable burden of Pharisaic additions as well as to the Romans). By contrast 'the Jerusalem above' is 'free' (freeborn) and 'our mother', the mother of all who are Christians, *i.e.* 'children of promise, as Isaac was'.

3. In Heb. 12:19–29, although not named directly, Mt Sinai, symbolizing the old covenant, is contrasted with Mt Zion, symbolizing the offer of the gospel under the new covenant. The awesome terrors of Sinai at the giving of the Law are described in terms of Ex. 19:16–19; 20:18–21; Dt. 4:11f.; and the reader is warned that rejecting the gospel and its privileges incurs a far more dreadful judgment even than that which followed disobedience to the Law.

BIBLIOGRAPHY. C. Brown, *NIDNTT* 3, pp. 1013–1015; E. Löhse, *TDNT* 7, pp. 282–287.

N.H.

SINEW. Heb. *gîḏ*, the sinew viewed as that which bound the bones together (Ezk. 37:6; Jb. 10:11).

The custom mentioned in Gn. 32:32 is obscure. C. A. Simpson in *IB* quotes Robertson Smith as explaining it from the idea that the thigh was sacred as the seat of life, and Wellhausen as calling attention to a trace of it in ancient Arabia. The application of the custom involves the removing of the sinew in the thigh-joint before the flesh is cooked.

The term is not found in the NT.

B.O.B.

SION. A synonym for, or part of, Mt Hermon (Dt. 4:48, AV; *cf.* RSV mg.). It is probably another form of 'Sirion' (Dt. 3:9); indeed, Pesh. reads 'Sirion' here, as also do RSV, NEB. A different word from 'Zion'.

J.D.D.

SIRAH, CISTERN OF (AV 'well of Sirah'). The place from which Joab secretly recalled Abner, former captain of Saul's armies, following his visit to David to discuss the surrender of Israel. Unknown to David, Joab slew Abner (2 Sa. 3:26). Probably modern Ain Sarah, 2½ km NW of Hebron.

J.A.T.

SIRION (Heb. *śiryōn*). The Canaanite name for Mt * Hermon as used in the Bible by the Sidonians (Dt. 3:9; *cf.* Ps. 29:6) and found in the form *šryn* in the Ugaritic texts. See C. H. Gordon, *Ugaritic Textbook*, 1965, p. 495. (* SION.)

T.C.M.

SISERA (*sîseᵉrā'*, a non-Semitic, possibly Illyrian name).

1. The commander of * Jabin's army (Jdg. 4:2f.) and possibly the petty king of Harosheth-ha-goiim (Haroseth of the nations), tentatively identified with Tell el-'Amr, 19 km NW of Megiddo, a strategic location for the deployment of Jabin's 900 chariots. His dominant military role in the battle against Deborah and Barak explains his prominence in the biblical record when compared with his overlord, Jabin (who is not mentioned at all in Jdg. 5). After his crushing defeat at Mt Tabor and subsequent flight, he was treacherously slain by * Jael (Jdg. 4:15–21; 5:24–27). See A. E. Cundall, *Judges and Ruth*, *TOTC*, 1968, pp. 81–100.

2. The family-name of a class of Temple servants of foreign origin

SINITES See Syene, Part 3.

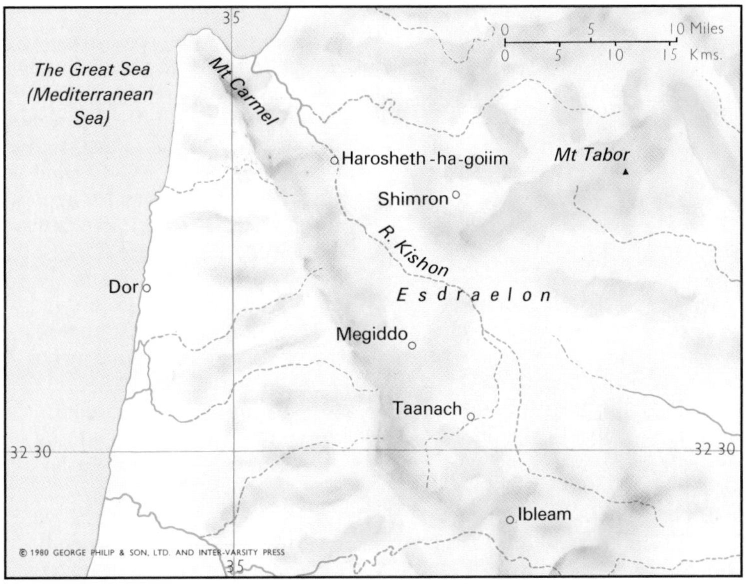

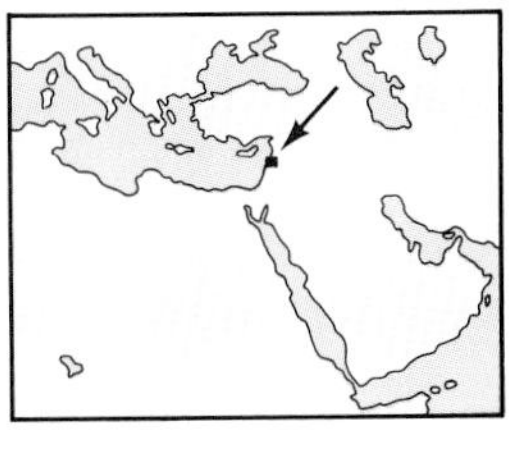

The area covered in the campaign of Sisera.

SIVAN
See Calendar, Part 1.

SIX
See Number, Part 2.

SKILL
See Wisdom, Part 3.

SKIN
See Vessels, Part 3.

SKINK
See Animals, Part 1.

SLANDER
See Talebearing, Part 3.

who returned with Zerubbabel from Exile in 537 BC (Ezr. 2:53; Ne. 7:55). A.E.C.

SITNAH (Heb. *śiṭnâ*, 'hatred', 'contention'). A name given to a well which Isaac's servants dug in Gerar (Gn. 26:21) and which was seized by the servants of Abimelech. For general location, see *GERAR. J.D.D.

SKIRT. The translation of three Heb. words. **1.** *kānāp̄*, 'wing', 'extremity', is the usual term (Ru. 3:9; 1 Sa. 24:4; *etc.*). **2.** *šûl* (Je. 13:22, 26; La. 1:9; Na. 3:5) means 'hem', and is so rendered elsewhere in AV. **3.** *peh* (Ps. 133:2, AV) is the common word for 'mouth', and the context is clearer if we follow RSV, which in the verse concerned renders the Heb. as 'collar'. J.D.D.

SLAVE, SLAVERY.

I. In the Old Testament

a. Introduction

Under the influence of Roman law, a slave is usually considered to be a person (male or female) owned by another, without rights, and—like any other form of personal property—to be used and disposed of in whatever way the owner may wish. In the ancient biblical East, however, slaves could and did acquire various rights before the law or by custom, and these included ownership (even of other slaves) and the power to conduct business while they were yet under their masters' control. Slavery is attested from the earliest times throughout the ancient Near East, and owed its existence and perpetuation primarily to economic factors.

b. Sources of slaves

(i) *By capture.* Captives, especially prisoners of war, were commonly reduced to slavery (Gn. 14:21, claimed by the king of Sodom; Nu. 31:9; Dt. 20:14; 21:10ff.; Jdg. 5:30; 1 Sa. 4:9 (*cf.* RSV); 2 Ki. 5:2; 2 Ch. 28:8, 10ff.), a custom that goes back as far as written documents themselves, to roughly 3000 BC and probably further (references in I. Mendelsohn, *Slavery in the Ancient Near East*, 1949, pp. 1–3).

(ii) *By purchase.* Slaves could readily be bought from other owners or general merchants (*cf.* Gn. 17:12–13, 27; Ec. 2:7). The law allowed Hebrews to buy foreign slaves from foreigners at home or abroad (Lv. 25:44f.). In antiquity, slaves were sold among all kinds of other merchandise and from country to country. Thus, the Midianites and Ishmaelites sold *Joseph to an Egyptian high official (Gn. 37:36; 39:1), and Phoenician Tyre imported slaves and bronzeware from Asia Minor (Ezk. 27:13) and sold Jews to the Ionians, thereby incurring a threat of like treatment of her own nationals (Joel 3:4–8). For evidence of the large numbers of Semitic slaves that reached Egypt in Joseph's general period, probably mainly by trade, see references in *Joseph or in Bibliography below. For Babylonian merchant-enterprise in slave-trading abroad in places such as Tyre, see Mendelsohn, *op. cit.*, pp. 3–5.

(iii) *By birth.* Children 'born in the house' of slave-parents became 'house-born slaves'; such are mentioned in Scripture from patriarchal times onward (Gn. 15:3; 17:12–13, 27; Ec. 2:7; Je. 2:14), and equally early in Mesopotamian documents (Mendelsohn, pp. 57–58).

(iv) *As restitution.* If a convicted thief could not make restitution and pay his fines and damages, funds towards this could be raised by selling him as a slave (Ex. 22:3; *cf.* a similar provision in Hammurapi's Code, §§ 53–54: *ANET*, p. 168).

(v) *By default on debts.* Debtors who went bankrupt were often forced to sell their children as slaves, or their children would be confiscated as slaves by the creditor (2 Ki. 4:1; Ne. 5:5, 8). The insolvent debtor himself, as well as his wife and family, commonly became the slave of his creditor and gave him his labour for 3 years to work off the debt and then go free, in Hammurapi's Code (§ 117: *DOTT*, p. 30, or *ANET*, pp. 170–171). This seems to be the background to the Mosaic law in Ex. 21:2–6 (and 7–11), and in Dt. 15:12–18, where a Hebrew slave must work 6 years, explicitly a 'double' period of time (Dt. 15:18) compared with Hammurapi's 3 years (*cf.* Mendelsohn, pp. 32–33), but on release he was to be granted stock to start up on his own again (see also *d.* (i) 1, below). Insolvency was a major cause of reduction to slave status in the biblical East (Mendelsohn, pp. 23, 26–29).

(vi) *Self-sale.* Selling oneself voluntarily into slavery, *i.e.* dependence on another, to escape poverty, was widely known (Mendelsohn, pp. 14–19, for data). Lv. 25:39–43, 47ff., recognized this, but provided for redemption at (or with foreign owners, even before) Jubilee year.

(vii) *Abduction.* To steal a person, and to reduce a kidnapped person to slavery, was an offence punishable by death in the laws of both Hammurapi (§ 14: *DOTT*, p. 30; *ANET*, p. 166) and Moses (Ex. 21:16; Dt. 24:7). The brothers of *Joseph were guilty of essentially such an offence (Gn. 37:27–28 with 45:4), and might well be 'dismayed' and need reassurance not to be 'distressed' (Gn. 45:3, 5, and *cf.* Gn. 50:15).

c. Price of slaves

The price of slaves naturally varied somewhat according to circumstances and the sex, age and condition of slaves, but the average price of slaves gradually rose like that of other commodities during the course of history; the female of child-bearing age being always more valuable than the male slave. In the late 3rd millennium BC in Mesopotamia (Akkad and 3rd Ur Dynasties) the average price of a slave was 10–15 shekels of silver (references in Mendelsohn, pp. 117–155). About 1700 BC Joseph was sold to the Ishmaelites for 20 shekels of silver (Gn. 37:28), precisely the current price for the patriarchal period, where ⅓ of a mina is 20 shekels (§§ 116, 214, 252: *DOTT*, p. 35; *ANET*, pp. 170, 175–176, in (*e.g.*) Hammurapi's Code, *c.* 1750 BC), in contemporary Old Babylonian tablets (*cf.* Mendelsohn, *loc. cit.*), and at Mari (G. Boyer, *Archives Royales de Mari*, 8, 1958, p. 23, No. 10, lines 1–4). By about the 15th century BC the average price was 30 shekels at Nuzi (B. L. Eichler, *Indenture at Nuzi*, 1973, pp. 16–18, 87), and could be 20, 30 or 40 shekels at Ugarit in N Syria (Mendelsohn, pp. 118–155; J. Nougayrol, *Palais Royal d'Ugarit*, 3, 1955, p. 228: 2 with refs., p. 23 n. 1) in the 14th/13th centuries BC, comparing well with the contemporary price of 30 shekels reflected in Ex. 21:32. In later days the average price for a male slave rose steadily under the Assyrian, Babylonian and Persian empires, to about 50–60 shekels, 50 shekels and 90–120 shekels respectively (Mendelsohn, pp. 117–118, 155). For 50 shekels in Assyrian times, *cf.* 2 Ki. 15:20, where the Israelite notables under Menahem had to pay their value as slaves, presumably as ransom to avoid deportation to Assyria (D. J. Wiseman, *Iraq* 15, 1953, p. 135, and *JTVI* 87, 1955, p. 28). The successive and identical rises in average price for slaves in both the biblical and external records strongly suggest that the former are based directly on accurate traditions from the specific periods in question, *i.e.* the early and late 2nd millennium and early 1st millennium BC, and are not at these points the elaboration of later traditionists or of over-statistical priestly redactors.

d. Privately owned slaves in Israel

(i) *Hebrew slaves.* 1. The law sought (like Hammurapi's Code 5 centuries earlier) to avoid the risk of wholesale population-drift into slavery and serfdom under economic pressure on small farmers, by limiting the length of service that insolvent debtors (see *b.* (v), above) had to give to 6 years, their release to be accompanied by the provision of sufficient assets to make a new start (Ex. 21:2–6; Dt. 15:12–18). A man already married when thus enslaved took his wife with him at release, but if he was formerly single and was given a wife by his master, that wife and any children remained the master's. Hence, those who wished to stay in service and keep their family could do so permanently (Ex. 21:6; Dt. 15:16f.); at Jubilee he would be released in any case (Lv. 25:40) in connection with the restoration of inheritance then (Lv. 25:28), even if he chose to stay on with his master permanently. Insolvent debtors in temporary enslavement similar to that of Ex. 21:2ff. are probably the subject of Ex. 21:26–27, the permanent loss of a member cancelling the debt and so bringing immediate release from the creditor/master (Mendelsohn, *op. cit.*, pp. 87–88). In Jeremiah's day the king and the wealthy flagrantly abused the law of 7th-year release by freeing their slaves only to seize them again, and were duly condemned for this very sharp practice (Je. 34:8–17).

2. A Hebrew who voluntarily sold himself into slavery to escape from poverty was to serve his master until Jubilee year, when he would go free (Lv. 25:39–43) and receive back his inheritance (Lv. 25:28). But if his master was a foreigner he had the option of purchasing his freedom or being redeemed by a relative at any time before Jubilee (Lv. 25:47–55).

3. Female slaves were the subject of further specific law and custom. That a chief wife's servant-maids might bear children to their master for the childless wife is attested both in the patriarchal narrative (Gn. 16) and in cuneiform documents, *e.g.* from Ur (Wiseman, *JTVI* 88, 1956, p. 124). Under the law, if a Hebrew girl was sold as a slave (Ex. 21:7–11) her marital status was carefully safeguarded: she might marry her master (and be redeemed if rejected), or his son, or become a properly maintained concubine, but would go free if the master failed to implement whichever of the three possibilities he had agreed to. In Mesopotamia such contracts were usually harsher, often having no safeguards whatever (*cf.* Mendelsohn, pp. 10ff., 87).

(ii) *Foreign slaves.* 1. Unlike Hebrew slaves, these could be enslaved permanently and handed on with other family property (Lv. 25:44–46). However, they were included in the commonwealth of Israel on patriarchal precedent (circumcision, Gn. 17:10–14, 27) and shared in festivals (Ex. 12:44, Passover; Dt. 16:11, 14) and sabbath-rest (Ex. 20:10; 23:12).

2. A woman captured in war could be taken as full wife by a Hebrew, and would thereby cease to have slave status; thus, if she was subsequently divorced she went free and did not become a slave (Dt. 21:10–14).

(iii) *General conditions.* 1. The treatment accorded to slaves depended directly on the personality of their masters. It could be a relationship of trust (*cf.* Gn. 24: 39:1–6) and affection (Dt. 15:16), but discipline might be harsh, even fatal (*cf.* Ex. 21:21), though to kill a slave outright carried a penalty (Ex. 21:20), doubtless death (Lv. 24:17, 22). It is just possible that Hebrew slaves, like some Babylonians, sometimes carried an outward token of their servitude (Mendelsohn, p. 49), though this remains uncertain. In some circumstances slaves could claim justice (Jb. 31:13) or go to law (Mendelsohn, pp. 65, 70, 72), but—like the Egyptian spared by David—could be abandoned by callous masters when ill (1 Sa. 30:13). In patriarchal times a childless master could adopt a house-slave and make him his heir, as is recorded of Abraham and Eliezer before the births of Ishmael and Isaac (Gn. 15:3), and of various people in cuneiform documents (Ur, *cf.* Wiseman, *JTVI* 88, 1956, p. 124).

2. Throughout ancient history, the available documents bear witness to the large numbers of people who tried to escape from slavery by running away, and those who in any way aided and abetted them could expect punishment, especially in early times (Mendelsohn, pp. 58ff.). However, slaves that fled from one country to another came under a different category. States sometimes had mutual extradition clauses in their treaties; this may explain how Shimei so easily recovered two runaway slaves of his from King Achish of Gath in Philistia (1 Ki. 2:39–40; *cf.* Wiseman, *op. cit.*, p. 123). However, some states also at times decreed that if any nationals of theirs enslaved abroad returned to their homeland they would be set free and not be extradited. This was stipulated by Hammurapi of Babylon (Code, § 280: *DOTT*, p. 35; *ANET*, p. 177; *cf.* Mendelsohn, pp. 63–64, 75, 77–78), and is probably the meaning of Dt. 23:15f. (Mendelsohn, pp. 63–64).

(iv) *Manumission.* In the Heb. laws an enslaved debtor was to be released after 6 years (Ex. 21:2; Dt. 15:12, 18), or as compensation for injury (Ex. 21:26–27), and a girl could be redeemed or set free if repudiated, or if conditions of service were not honoured (Ex. 21:8, 11; see *d.* (i) 3 above). A Hebrew who sold himself into slavery was to be freed at Jubilee, or could be redeemed by purchase at any time from a foreign master (Lv. 25:39–43, 47–55; *d.* (i) 2 above). On Dt. 23:15f., see preceding section. A female captive could become a freedwoman by marriage (Dt. 21:10–14).

In 1 Ch. 2:34f., a Hebrew Sheshan had no sons, and so married his daughter to his Egyptian slave Jarha in order to continue his family line; it is most probable that Jarha would be made free in these circumstances (Mendelsohn, p. 57), and likewise Eliezer of Damascus (Gn. 15:3), if he had not been replaced as heir to Abraham by Ishmael and then Isaac.

In Heb. the term which denotes that a person is 'free', not (or no longer) a slave (*e.g.* Ex. 21:2, 5, 26–27; Dt. 15:12–13, 18; Jb. 3:19; Je. 34:9–11, 14, 16; *etc.*), is *ḥopšî*, which has a long history in the ancient East, occurring as *ḫupšu* in cuneiform texts from the 18th to the 7th centuries BC, and usually referring to freedmen who are small landholders, tenant farmers or hired labourers. When a Hebrew was freed this is the class he would be in. He would become a small landholder if he regained his inheritance (as at Jubilee) or a tenant or labourer on land held by others. On manumission in the ancient East, see Mendelsohn, pp. 74–91; on *ḥopšî*, see Bibliography below.

e. State and Temple slavery

(i) *State slavery in Israel.* This was practised on a restricted scale. David caused the conquered Ammonites to do forced labour (2 Sa. 12:31), and Solomon conscripted the surviving descendants of the peoples of Canaan into his *mas-'ōḇēḏ*, permanent state labour-levy, but not true Israelites (see 1 Ki. 9:15, 21–22; burden-bearers and quarriers, v. 15 and 2 Ch. 2:18). The Israelites served on temporary corvée (*mas*) in Lebanon only, by rota (1 Ki. 5:13f.). There is no contradiction between 1 Ki. 5 and 9 on the corvées; *cf.* M. Haran, *VT* 11, 1961, pp. 162–164, following and partly correcting Mendelsohn, pp. 96–98. *Cf.* A. F. Rainey, *IEJ* 20, 1970, pp. 191–202. The famous coppermines near Ezion-geber (*ELATH) were most likely worked with Canaanite and Ammonite/Edomite slave-labour (N. Glueck, *BASOR* 79, 1940, pp. 4–5; Mendelsohn, p. 95; Haran, *op. cit.*, p. 162). Such use of war-captives was common throughout the Near East, and in other countries outside Israel their less fortunate nationals and ordinary slaves could sometimes be taken over by the state (Mendelsohn, pp. 92–99).

(ii) *Temple slaves in Israel.* After the war with Midian, Moses levied from the warriors and Israel at large 1 in 500 and 1 in 50 respectively of their spoils in persons and goods, for service with the high priest and Levites at the tabernacle, obviously as menials (Nu. 31:28, 30, 47). Then there were added to these the Gibeonites spared by Joshua, who became 'hewers of wood and drawers of water' for the house and altar of the Lord (Jos. 9:3–27), *i.e.* menials for the tabernacle and its personnel. Also, David and his officers had dedicated foreigners (Nethinim) for similar service with the Levites who served the Temple, some of their descendants returning from captivity with Ezra (8:20); to these were added 'Solomon's servants' (Ezr. 2:58). Ezekiel (44:6–9) possibly warned against allowing these uncircumcised menials to usurp a place in the worship of a Temple that was not theirs. Under Nehemiah (3:26, 31) some of these lived in Jerusalem and helped repair its walls.

f. Conclusion: general trends

Generally, a more humane spirit breathes through the OT laws and customs on slavery, as illustrated by the repeated injunctions in God's name not to rule over a brother Israelite harshly (*e.g.* Lv. 25:43, 46, 53, 55; Dt. 15:14f.). Even when Heb. law and custom on slaves shares in the common heritage of the ancient Semitic world, there is this unique care in God's name for these people who by status were not people, something absent from the law codes of Babylon or Assyria. It should, moreover, be remembered that, by and large, the economy of the ancient Near East was never one substantially or mainly based on slave-labour as in 'classical' and later Greece or above all in imperial Rome (*cf.* Mendelsohn, pp. 111–112, 116:117, 121; I. J. Gelb, *Festschrift for S. N. Kramer*, 1976, pp. 195–207, on statistics and comparisons; limited numbers and economic opportunities of Neo-Babylonian slaves, *cf.* F. I. Andersen (summary of Dandamayer), *Buried History* 11, 1975, pp. 191–194). And Job (31:13–15) heralds the concept of the equality of all men, of whatever station, before their creator God.

BIBLIOGRAPHY. A fundamental work which makes frequent reference to the OT data is I. Mendelsohn, *Slavery in the Ancient Near East*, 1949, following up earlier studies, and supplemented by *IEJ* 5, 1955, pp. 65–72. The biblical data are summarized and evaluated by A. G. Barrois, *Manuel d'Archéologie Biblique*, 2, 1953, pp. 38, 114, 211–215, and by R. de Vaux, *Ancient Israel: its Life and Institutions*, 1961, pp. 80–90, 525). On Temple slaves in Israel, see M. Haran, *VT* 11, 1961, pp. 159–169. On *ḥopšî*, 'free(dman)', see Mendelsohn, *BASOR* 83, 1941, pp. 36–39, and *ibid.*, 139, 1955, pp. 9–11; E. R. Lacheman, *ibid.*, 86, 1942, pp. 36–37; D. J. Wiseman, *The Alalakh Tablets*, 1953, p. 10. For the Egyp. data on slavery, see the monograph by A. M. Bakir, *Slavery in Pharaonic Egypt*, 1952, supplemented for Joseph's period by W. C. Hayes, *A Papyrus of the Late Middle Kingdom in the Brooklyn Museum*, 1955, pp. 92–94, 98–99, 133–134, and especially G. Posener, *Syria* 34, 1957, pp. 147, 150–161. K.A.K.

II. In the New Testament

a. Systems of slavery in NT times

Jewish slavery, to judge by the Talmud, remained governed as always by the tight national unity of the people. There was a sharp distinction between Jewish and Gentile slaves. The former were subject to the sabbath-year manumission, and the onus fell upon Jewish communities everywhere to ransom their nationals held in slavery to Gentiles. Thus no fundamental division into bond and free was recognized. At the same time the whole people might be thought of as the servants of Yahweh.

By contrast, Greek slavery was justified in classical theory by the assumption of a natural order of slaves. Since only the citizen class were, strictly speaking, human, slaves were merely chattels. While this idea was carried into practice only in the rare cases where common sense and humanity broke down, the fact remains that throughout classical antiquity the institution of slavery was simply taken for granted, even by those who worked for its amelioration.

There was a very great diversity at different times and places in the extent and uses of slavery. Modern sentiment is dominated by the horrors of the mass agricultural slavery in Italy and Sicily during the 2 centuries between the Punic wars and Augustus, which were dramatized by a series of heroic slave-revolts. This was a by-product of the rapid Roman conquest of the Mediterranean, the main source of the glut of slaves being war prisoners. In NT times, however, there was very little warfare, and in any case the slave ranches were a peculiarly Roman method of farming. In Egypt, for instance, there was practically no agricultural slavery, the land being worked by a free peasantry under bureaucratic supervision. In Asia Minor and Syria there were great temple estates whose tenant farmers were in a kind of serfdom. In Palestine, to judge by the parables of Jesus, slaves were employed on country estates more in administrative positions, the labour being recruited on a casual basis.

Domestic and public slavery were the most widespread forms. In the former case the slaves were purchased and employed as an index of wealth. Where only one or two were owned, they worked beside their master at the same occupations. At Athens they were indistinguishable in the streets from free men, and the familiarity of slaves towards their owners was a stock theme of comedy. At Rome the great houses employed scores of slaves for sheer luxury. Their work was highly specialized and often largely effortless. In the case of public slaves, their status conferred a good deal of independence and respect. They performed all sorts of duties in the absence of a civil service, including even police services in some cases. Professions such as medicine or education were commonly filled by slaves.

The main sources of slavery were: (1) birth, depending on the law of the particular state concerning the various degrees of servile parentage; (2) the widespread practice of exposing unwanted children, who were then available for the use of anyone who cared to rear them; (3) the sale of one's own children into slavery; (4) voluntary slavery as a solution to problems such as debt; (5) penal slavery; (6) kidnapping and piracy; (7) the traffic across the Roman frontiers. Not all these sources were open in one place at any one time: there was a great deal of variation in local law and sentiment. The degree of slavery also varied greatly, and is impossible to calculate. It may have reached one-third of the population in Rome and the great metropolitan cities of the east. In areas where there was a peasant economy, however, it was reduced to a small fraction of that.

Manumission could be readily arranged at any time if owners wished. In Rome it was most commonly performed by testament, and limits had to be placed on the generosity of owners to prevent the too rapid dilution of the citizen body with persons of foreign extraction. In Gk. states 2 common forms were a type of self-purchase, in which the legal incompetence of the slave was overcome by the ownership technically passing to a god, and manumission in return for a contract of services which simply meant that the slave continued in the same employment though legally free.

The condition of slavery was everywhere being steadily mitigated in NT times. Although slaves had no legal personality, owners recognized that they worked better the more their condition approximated to freedom, and the owning of property and contracting of marriages were normally allowed. Cruelty was condemned by the growing sentiment of common humanity, and in some cases legally controlled; in Egypt, for instance, the death of a slave was subject to a coroner's inquest. While in Gk. states emancipated slaves became resident aliens of their former master's city, at Rome they automatically became citizens on manumission. Thus the vast flow of slaves into Italy, especially during the last 2 centuries before Christ, had the effect of internationalizing the Roman republic, anticipating the government's own policy of steadily broadening membership.

b. The NT attitude to slavery

The twelve disciples of Jesus apparently had no part in the system of slavery. They included neither slaves nor owners. The institution figures frequently in the parables, however (*e.g.* Mt. 21:34; 22:3), because the regal and baronial households to which it belonged afforded a nice analogy for the kingdom of God. Jesus repeatedly spoke of the relation of the disciples to himself as that of servants to their lord (*e.g.* Mt. 10:24; Jn. 13:16). At the same time he stressed the inadequacy of this figure. The disciples were emancipated, as it were, and admitted to higher privileges of intimacy (Jn. 15:15). Or again, to their acute embarrassment, Jesus himself adopted the servile role (Jn. 13:4–17), with the object of encouraging them to mutual service.

Outside Palestine, however, where the churches were often established on a household basis, the membership included both masters and servants. Slavery was one of the human divisions that became meaningless in the new community in Christ (1 Cor. 7:22; Gal. 3:28). This apparently led to a desire for emancipation (1 Cor. 7:20) and perhaps even to the active encouragement of it by some (1 Tim. 6:3–5). Paul was not opposed to manumission if the opportunity was offered (1 Cor. 7:21), but studiously refrained from

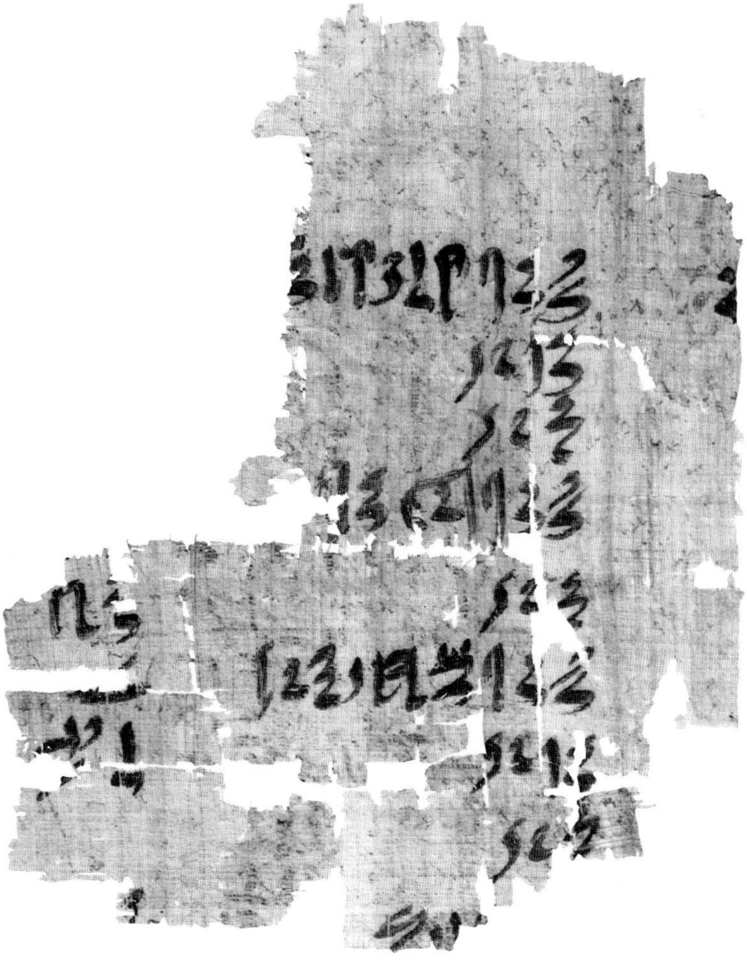

Part of a papyrus listing slaves, including Semites, in Egypt about the time of Joseph. c.1750 BC. (BrM)

SLIME
See Bitumen, Part 1.

SLING
See Armour, Part 1.

SLOTH
See Sleep, Part 3.

SLOW-WORM
See Animals, Part 1.

SMARAGDOS
See Jewels, Part 2.

SMELL
See Nose, Part 2.

SMELTING
See Mining, Part 2.

SMITH
See Arts and crafts, Part 1.

SMOKE
See Nose, Part 2.

SNAIL
See Animals, Part 1.

Smyrna, one of the 'seven churches of Asia' (Rev. 1–3).

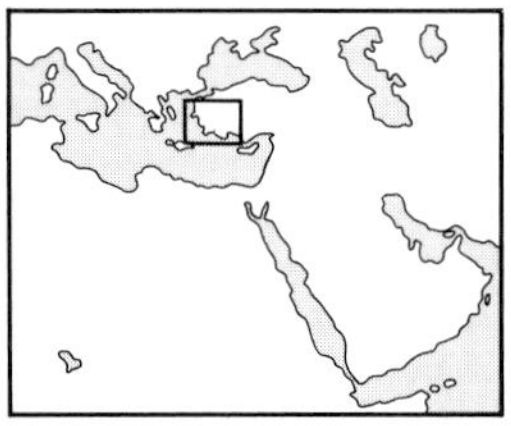

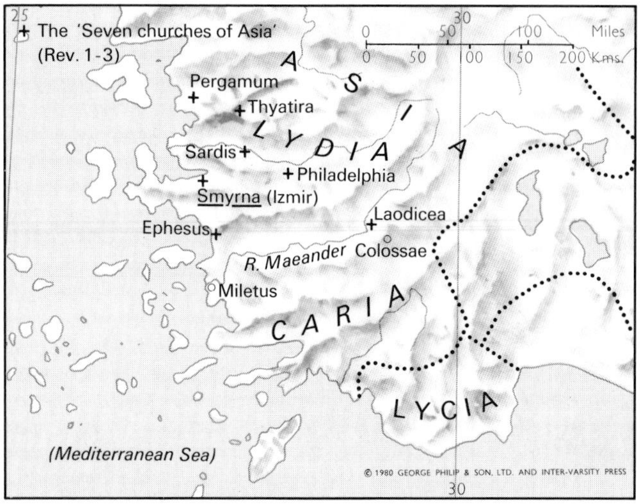

putting pressure on owners, even where personal sentiment might have led him to do so (Phm. 8, 14). Not only was there the practical reason of not laying the churches open to criticism (1 Tim. 6:1f.), but the point of principle that all human stations are allotted by God (1 Cor. 7:20). Slaves should therefore aim to please God by their service (Eph. 6:5–8; Col. 3:22). The fraternal bond with a believing master should be an added reason for serving him well (1 Tim. 6:2). A master, on the other hand, might well let the fraternal sentiment prevail (Phm. 16), and certainly must treat his slaves with restraint (Eph. 6:9) and strict equity (Col. 4:1).

The fact that household slavery, which is the only kind referred to in the NT, was generally governed by feelings of goodwill and affection, is implied by its figurative use in the 'household of God' (Eph. 2:19). The apostles are regularly God's stewards (1 Cor. 4:1; Tit. 1:7; 1 Pet. 4:10) and even plain servants (Rom. 1:1; Phil. 1:1). The legal character of 'the yoke of slavery' (Gal. 5:1) was not forgotten, however, and the idea of manumission and adoption into the family itself was a proud conclusion to this train of thought (Rom. 8:15–17; Gal. 4:5–7). Thus, whether in practice or by analogy, the apostles clearly branded the institution as part of the order that was passing away. In the last resort the fraternity of the sons of God would see all its members free of their bonds.

BIBLIOGRAPHY. W. W. Buckland, *The Roman Law of Slavery*, 1908; R. H. Barrow, *Slavery in the Roman Empire*, 1928; W. L. Westermann, *The Slave Systems of Greek and Roman Antiquity*, 1955 (with full bibliography); M. I. Finley (ed.), *Slavery in Classical Antiquity: Views and Controversies*, 1960; J. Jeremias, *Jerusalem in the Time of Jesus*, 1969, pp. 314, 334–337; J. Vogt, *Ancient Slavery and the Ideal of Man*, 1974; S. S. Bartchy, *Mallon Chresai: First-Century Slavery and the Interpretation of 1 Cor. 7:21*, 1973. E.A.J.

SLEEP. The OT uses several words for 'sleep', the NT has fewer; but no particular significance attaches to them. They signify sleep in the sense of physical rest and recuperation.

As might be expected, 'sleep' is used in a figurative sense in both Testaments. In Pr. 19:15, *etc.*, it describes mental torpor, and in Pr. 24:33 it refers to physical sloth and laziness. Paul uses the figure to describe the state of spiritual torpor of the non-Christians (Eph. 5:14), which unmans them and renders them unprepared for Christ's second advent (Mt. 25:22). By contrast, the Christian has awakened from this spiritual torpor, but he is challenged to remain awake (1 Thes. 5:4–8; Rom. 13:11f.; Mt. 25:13; 26:41).

Sleep is also a synonym for physical death (Jb. 14:12; Jn. 11:11–14; 1 Cor. 15:18). This signifies that death, like sleep, is neither a permanent state, nor does it 'destroy the identity of the sleeper' (Lk. 24:39f.), in spite of the change to be effected at the resurrection (1 Cor. 15:13ff.).

'Deep sleep', *tardēmâ*, was supernaturally induced (Gn. 2:21; 1 Sa. 26:12), and was equivalent almost to a *'trance' (Gn. 15:12), in which visions were granted (Jb. 4:13; Dn. 8:18). Its NT equivalent is *hypnos* (Acts 20:9). But visions also came in the course of 'ordinary ' sleep (Gn. 28:10ff.; 1 Sa. 3:2ff.). See also *DREAM; L. Coenen, *NIDNTT* 1, pp. 441–443. J.G.S.S.T.

SLEIGHT. AV rendering (RSV 'cunning') of Gk. *kybeia*, 'dice-playing', Eph. 4:14 (*cf. kybeuō*, 'to deceive', in Epictetus 2. 19; 3. 21). NEB approaches the Greek differently from AV and RSV, and renders the last part of the verse 'dupes of crafty rogues and their deceitful schemes'. Paul is warning against instability and against those whose slick dealings present a plausible mixture of truth and error. J.D.D.

SMYRNA. A city in the Roman province of Asia, on the Aegean shore of what is now Asiatic Turkey. There was a Gk. colony near by from very early times, but it was captured and destroyed by the Lydians about the end of the 7th century BC and virtually ceased to exist until it was refounded on its present site by Lysimachus in the early 3rd century BC. It grew to be one of the most prosperous cities in Asia Minor. It was the natural port for the ancient trade route through the Hermus valley, and its immediate hinterland was very fertile. Smyrna was a faithful ally of Rome long before the Roman power became supreme in the E Mediterranean. Under the empire it was famous for its beauty and for the magnificence of its public buildings. It is now Izmir, the second largest city in Asiatic Turkey.

The gospel probably reached Smyrna at an early date, presumably from Ephesus (Acts 19:10). The 'angel of the church in Smyrna' is the recipient of the second (Rev. 2:8–11) of the letters to the 'seven churches . . . in Asia'. As in other commercial cities, the church encountered opposition from the Jews (Rev. 2:9; *cf.* 3:9). The description of the Christ as the one who was dead and lived again (v. 8) may allude to the resurgence of the city to new prosperity after a long period in obscurity. The 'crown' (v. 10) was rich in associations at Smyrna. It may suggest the victor's wreath at the games, or current forms of eulogy which used the image of the beauty and glory of the city and its buildings. *Cf.* also Jas. 1:12. The call to faithfulness (v. 10) is a call to the church to fulfil in the deepest way the historic reputation of the city. It was exemplified in the courage with which the aged bishop Polycarp refused to recant; he was martyred there *c.* AD 155 or later. (See W. M. Ramsay, *The Letters to the Seven Churches of Asia*, 1904, chs. 19–20; C. J. Cadoux, *Ancient Smyrna*, 1938; C. J. Hemer, *Buried History* 11, 1975, pp. 56–67.) E.M.B.G. C.J.H.

SNARE. Mechanical device, often with a bait, for catching birds or animals. AV uses 'snare' for 7 Heb. and 2 Gk. words, but RSV translates more accurately by other terms in Jb. 18:8, 10; La. 3:47; 1 Cor. 7:35. Heb. *paḥ* (*cf.* Egyp. *pḥ'*) is translated

Smyrna (modern Izmir, Turkey) in the Roman province of Asia. The aqueducts were built in the Roman period to carry water to the city, and remained in use for several centuries. (PP)

A clap-net snare is here being used to trap wildfowl. The signal to close the net is given by the man hidden behind a papyrus thicket. Copy of a wall-painting in the tomb of Nakht, Thebes. Original c. 1420 BC. (NDGD)

'snare' 22 times in RSV; literally it is used of bird traps only (see Ps. 124:7; Pr. 7:23; Ec. 9:12; Am. 3:5). The last passage mentions two kinds of traps used by fowlers, one which pins the bird to the ground and one with a noose which catches the bird around the neck and springs up. In the majority of cases *paḥ* is used figuratively, for example in Jos. 23:13; Jb. 22:10; Ps. 119:110. AV translates *paḥ* by 'gin' in Jb. 18:9; Is. 8:14. Heb. *môqēš*, perhaps meaning 'striker', is translated 'snare' in RSV 22 times, literally only in Jb. 40:24, which implies that a snare cannot take the behemoth or hippopotamus. Examples of the figurative use of *môqēš* are: Ex. 10:7; 23:33; 2 Sa. 22:6; Ps. 64:5; Pr. 20:25; 22:25; Is. 8:14. AV translates *môqēš* by 'gin' in Pss. 140:5; 141:9; Am. 3:5. Other Heb. words translated 'snare' in a figurative sense are: *māṣôḏ*, 'means of hunting' (Ec. 7:26) and the related *m*ᵉ*ṣûḏâ* (Ezk. 12:13; 17:20).

In the Apocrypha 'snare' (Gk. *pagis*) is used in reference to a gazelle (Ecclus. 27:20) and also figuratively (Ecclus. 9:3, 13; 27:26, 29).

In the NT Gk. *pagis* is translated 'snare' in a literal sense only in Lk. 21:34, which compares the suddenness of the Lord's coming to the springing of a trap. The figurative uses of *pagis* are Rom. 11:9; 1 Tim. 3:7; 6:9; 2 Tim. 2:26.

In Egypt today the following kinds of snares, some with ancient counterparts, are used: a clap-net, a clap-board over a hole, a clap-box, a springing noose, a trap with two jaws which close on the neck of the victim, and a cage with a sliding or springing door.

BIBLIOGRAPHY. G. Dalman, *Arbeit und Sitte* 6, 1939, pp. 321–340; G. Gerleman, *Contributions to the Old Testament Terminology of the Chase*, 1946; G. R. Driver, 'Reflections on Recent Articles, 2. Heb. *môqēš*, "striker" ', *JBL* 73, 1954, pp. 131–136.

J.T.

SNOW (Heb. *šeleḡ*). The few references to it indicate its rarity in Palestine, where it is scarcely ever found S of Hebron and is unknown along the sea coast and Jordan valley. Only twice is a snowfall recorded (in 2 Sa. 23:20 [= 1 Ch. 11:22] and in 1 Macc. 13:22). But the snow cover of Lebanon, 'the white mountain', is proverbial (Je. 18:14), and lower down in the Hauran it is not infrequent (Ps. 68:14). Elsewhere it is a rare feature, as the biblical incident of Benaiah would suggest (2 Sa. 23:20).

Snow as a symbol is variously employed. It is God-given and controlled (Jb. 38:22), one of the wonders of God's power (Jb. 37:6; Ps. 147:16), and given for fertility (Is. 55:10f.) and to accomplish moral ends (Jb. 38:22–23). It expresses whiteness (Ex. 4:6; Nu. 12:10; 2 Ki. 5:27; La. 4:7; Dn. 7:9), and therefore moral purity (Dn. 7:9; Mk. 9:3; Mt. 28:3; Rev. 1:14). It describes the complete acceptance of the penitent sinner (Ps. 51:7; Is. 1:18).

J.M.H.

SNUFFERS. For trimming and adjusting the wicks of the lamps in the tabernacle and Temple two, clearly distinct (see 1 Ki. 7:49–50; 2 Ch. 4:21–22), instruments were used: **1.** *m*ᵉ*zamm*ᵉ*rôṯ*, translated 'snuffers' (1 Ki. 7:50; 2 Ki. 12:13 [14]; 25:14; 2 Ch. 4:22; Je. 52:18), probably a kind of scissors.

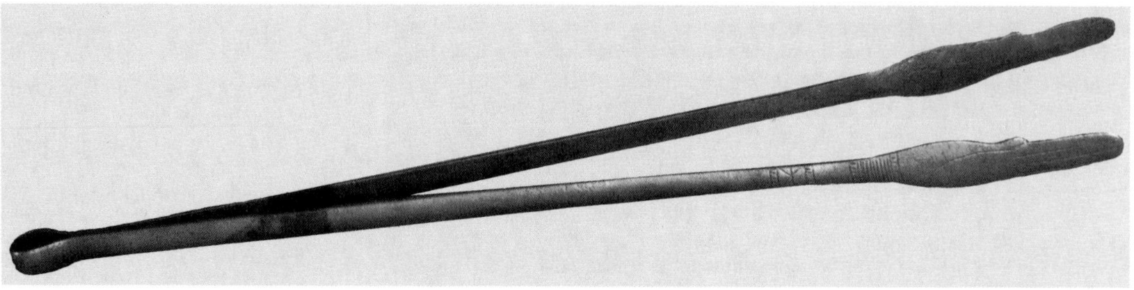

Bronze snuffers or tongs with ends shaped like human hands. From El-Amarna, Egypt. Length 35·56 cm. c. 1350 BC. (BM)

■ **SOBER**
See Self-control, Part 3.

■ **SODA**
See Nitre, Part 2.

■ **SODOM**
See Plain, cities of the, Part 3.

■ **SOIL CONSERVATION**
See Agriculture, Part 1.

2. *melqāḥayim*. These latter were 'tongs' (*cf.* Is. 6:6), but they are variously translated: 1 Ki. 7:49; 2 Ch. 4:21, 'tongs'; Ex. 37:23 'snuffers'; Ex. 25:38; Nu. 4:9, RSV 'snuffers', AV 'tongs'. See G. E. Wright, *Biblical Archaeology*, 1957, pp. 141f. D.W.G.

SO. By conspiring with 'So king of Egypt' *c.* 726/5 BC (2 Ki. 17:4), Hoshea brought Assyrian retribution upon Israel. If So is the proper name of an Egyp. king, he must be either the last shadowy Libyan pharaoh, Osorkon IV (Aa-kheper-rē') *c.* 727–716 BC, or the *de facto* W-Delta ruler Tefnakht, *c.* 727–720 BC, or some lesser and unidentified E-Delta kinglet. No mere kinglet could have helped Hoshea, nor can *Sô'* derive from Tefnakht's name; it is possible that *Sô'* could be an abbreviation for Osorkon (IV), as Egyp. *Sese* for Rameses (II).

Some identify So, vocalized *Siwe'* or *Sewe'*, with the Ethiopian Pharaoh Shabako (omitting formative *-ko*) who acted as army commander in Egypt before his accession. This is impossible in 726/5 BC, because the Ethiopians' W-Delta rivals, Tefnakht and Bekenranef (Bocchoris), held Lower Egypt until 716 BC. Others identify So/Siwe with 'Sib'e the *turtan* (army commander) of Egypt' whom Sargon II of Assyria defeated at Raphia in 720 BC. But So cannot be a king in 726/5 BC and then simply army commander in 720 BC, unless he were throughout a petty Delta kinglet acting as commander for Osorkon IV (or Tefnakht and Bekenranef). Therefore, if So is an Egyp. ruler's name, he would be either Osorkon IV abbreviated (but *not* Sib'e the *turtan*) or else a lesser kinglet and army commander under Osorkon IV, Tefnakht or Bekenranef.

S. Yeivin's suggestion in *VT* 2, 1952, pp. 164–168, that *Sô'* is not a proper name but merely a transcription of Egyp. *ṯ'*, 'vizier', then *sô' meleḵ miṣrayim* = 'the vizier of the king of Egypt' is phonetically unsuitable. The cuneiform name of the Egyp. commander of 720 BC, hitherto read as Sib'e, must now almost certainly be read as Re'e (R. Borger, *JNES* 19, 1960, pp. 49–53); this name cannot be identified with So as a proper name. It is possible that Re'e could be the name of the Egyp. vizier. H. Goedicke (*BASOR* 171, 1963, pp. 64–66) improbably read 'to (city) Sa(is), [to] the king of Egypt', with Tefnakht in mind. See K. A. Kitchen, *The Third Intermediate Period in Egypt*, 1972, pp. 182, 372–376. K.A.K.

SOAP. 'Soap' is the rendering in the EVV of Heb. *bōrîṯ* (Mal. 3:2; Je. 2:22), a word derived from *bārar*, 'to purify'. It probably means 'lye', a solution of potash (potassium carbonate) and soda (sodium carbonate) in water, which acts as a simple detergent. This is obtained by filtering water through vegetable ash, various alkaline salts being produced, of which potash is the principal. The Heb. term *bōr* is also best rendered 'lye' in Is. 1:25 and Jb. 9:30 (RVmg., RSV), though this is not observed by AV. (*ARTS AND CRAFTS, **III.** *h.*)

BIBLIOGRAPHY. R. Campbell Thompson, *A Dictionary of Assyrian Chemistry and Geology*, 1936, p. 14; M. Levey, *Chemistry and Chemical Technology in Ancient Mesopotamia*, 1959, p. 122. T.C.M.

SOCOH, SOCO. 1. A town SE of Azekah in the Shephelah, the scene of the Philistine defeat (1 Sa. 17; see G. A. Smith, *The Historical Geography of the Holy Land*[25], 1966, pp. 161–162, for tactical description). The name is preserved in Khirbet Suweike (Roman and Byzantine); slightly farther W, the Early Iron fortification Khirbet Abbad commands the Wadi es-Sunt (Vale of Elah) from the S. Here the Wadi es-Sur from the S is joined by wadis coming down from the hills W of Bethlehem. Either this or **2** below was fortified by Rehoboam and later taken by the Philistines (2 Ch. 11:7; 28:18). Socoh is one of the cities named on royal jar-handle stamps found at *Lachish and other sites, which probably points to its importance as a major Judaean administrative centre in the reign of Hezekiah (*WRITING).

2. A place in the highlands near Debir (Jos. 15:48; v. 35 refers to **1**); Khirbet Suweike, 3 km E of Dhahiriya (1 Ch. 4:18 probably refers to this place). **3.** A town in Solomon's tribute-area of Hepher (1 Ki. 4:10); probably the Bronze Age–Byzantine site Tell er-Ras by Suweike, N of Tulkarm in the plain of Sharon, and 24 km NW of Shechem (Tuthmosis III list no. 67).

BIBLIOGRAPHY. *LOB*, pp. 340–346; D. Ussishkin, *Tel Aviv*, 4, 1977. J.P.U.L.
G.I.D.

SOLOMON. The third king of Israel (*c.* 971–931 BC), son of David and Bathsheba (2 Sa. 12:24); also named Jedidiah ('beloved of the Lord') by Nathan the prophet (2 Sa. 12:25). Solomon (*šᵉlōmōh*, probably 'peaceful') does not figure in the biblical narrative until the last days of David (1 Ki. 1:10ff.) despite the fact that he was born (in Jerusalem; 2 Sa. 5:14) early in his father's reign.

I. The rise to power

Solomon's path to the throne was far from smooth. Absalom's opposition was carried on by David's oldest surviving son, Adonijah (2 Sa. 3:4), who made a strong bid for the throne during his father's last days (1 Ki. 1:5ff.). Supported by David's deposed general, Joab, who had slain Absalom (2 Sa. 18:14–15), and the influential priest Abiathar, Adonijah rallied support and actually held a corona-

Socoh (škwh) *is named on this jar-handle with royal stamp found at Lachish. 7th cent.* BC. (BM)

tion feast at Enrogel. But Solomon was not without allies. Benaiah, the son of Jehoiada, had his eye on the generalship; Zadok coveted a prominent priestly position. Their spokesman was Nathan the prophet, a confidant of David and Bathsheba (1 Ki. 1:11ff.). After Nathan and Bathsheba reminded David of his unexecuted promise concerning Solomon, the king gave instructions for Solomon's accession and sealed them with an oath (1 Ki. 1:28ff.).

The news of Solomon's coronation, for which David's storied bodyguard of Cherethites and Pelethites offered protection, broke up Adonijah's festivities (1 Ki. 1:41ff.) but not his stratagems to control the kingdom. He implored Bathsheba to influence Solomon to give him Abishag, David's handmaiden (1 Ki. 1:3–4), as wife (1 Ki. 2:13ff.). Solomon, apparently fearing that such a marriage would give Adonijah leverage with which to prise him from the throne, refused. Adonijah paid with his life for his rash proposal (1 Ki. 2:25); when Abiathar the priest was banished from office (1 Ki. 2:26–27) and Joab vengefully slain before the altar (1 Ki. 2:28ff.), Solomon reigned without a rival. The prominent role of the queen-mother in this whole intrigue is noteworthy. Bathsheba seems to have blazed the trail for other queen-mothers in Judah, for the author of Kings faithfully records the name of each king's mother (*e.g.* 1 Ki. 15:2, 10, *etc.*). The arbitrary manner in which Solomon was chosen boded ill for the future. The elders of Judah and Israel, on whose good-will true national harmony depended, were by-passed in the decision.

II. The master sage

Solomon was Israel's first *dynastic* ruler. Saul and David, like the judges, were chosen because God had given them a special measure of power: they were *charismatic* rulers. Although Solomon took office without God's *charisma*, he received it during his vision at Gibeon, when the Lord offered him his choice of gifts (1 Ki. 3:5ff.). Realizing the enormity of his task, Solomon chose an 'understanding heart' (v. 9). The story of the harlots' dispute over the baby (1 Ki. 3:16ff.) has become a classic display of Solomon's royal wisdom.

Surpassing his contemporaries in

Solomon's administrative districts as described in 1 Ki. 4:7–19.

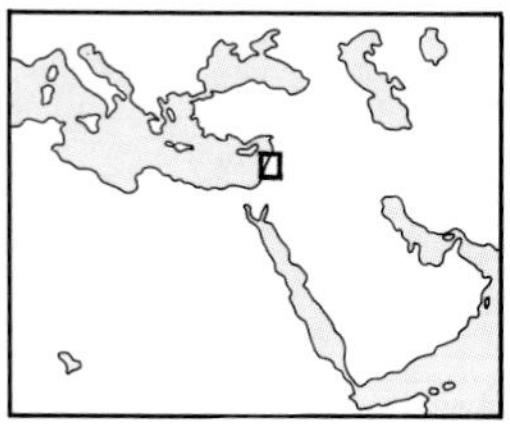

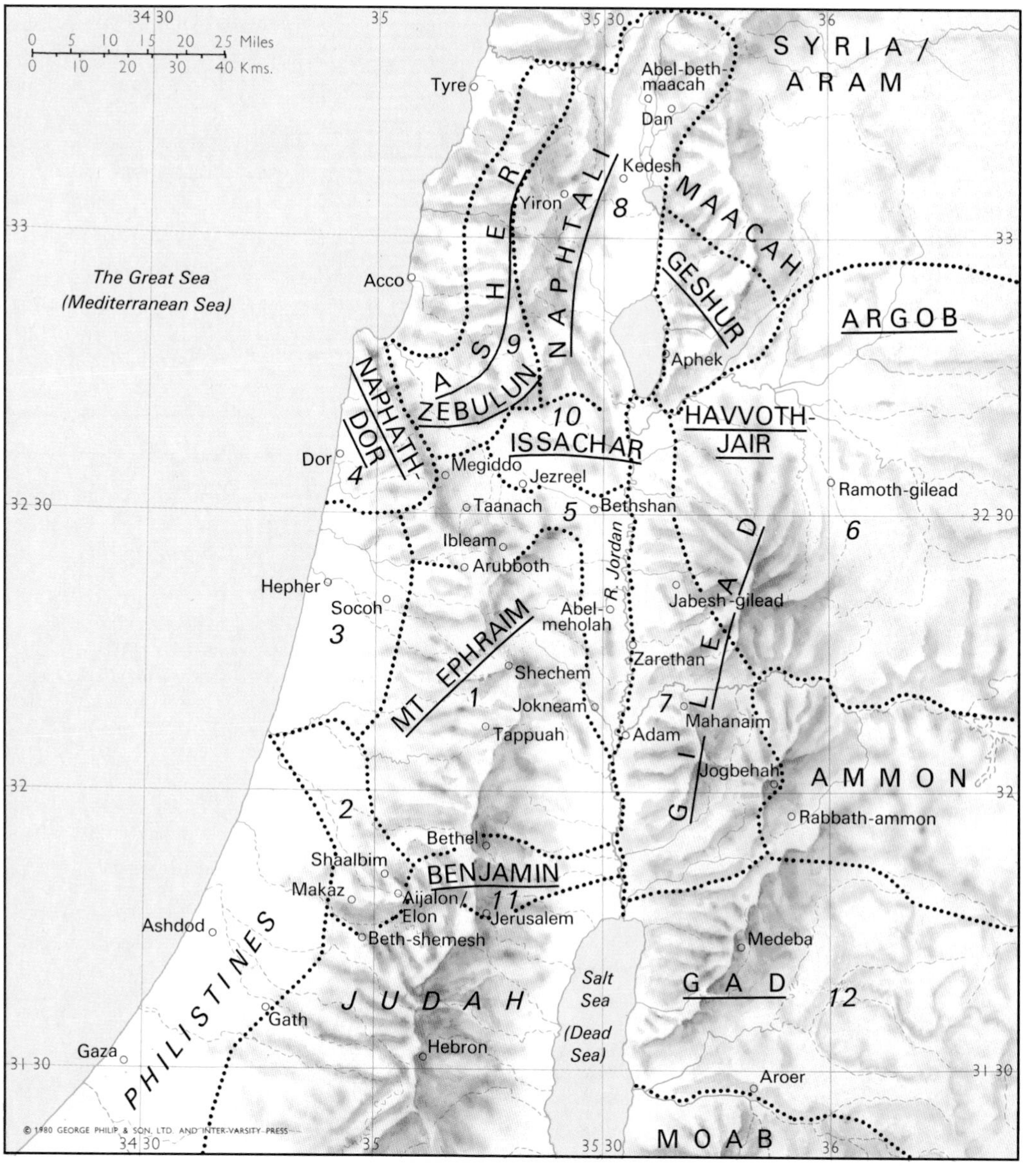

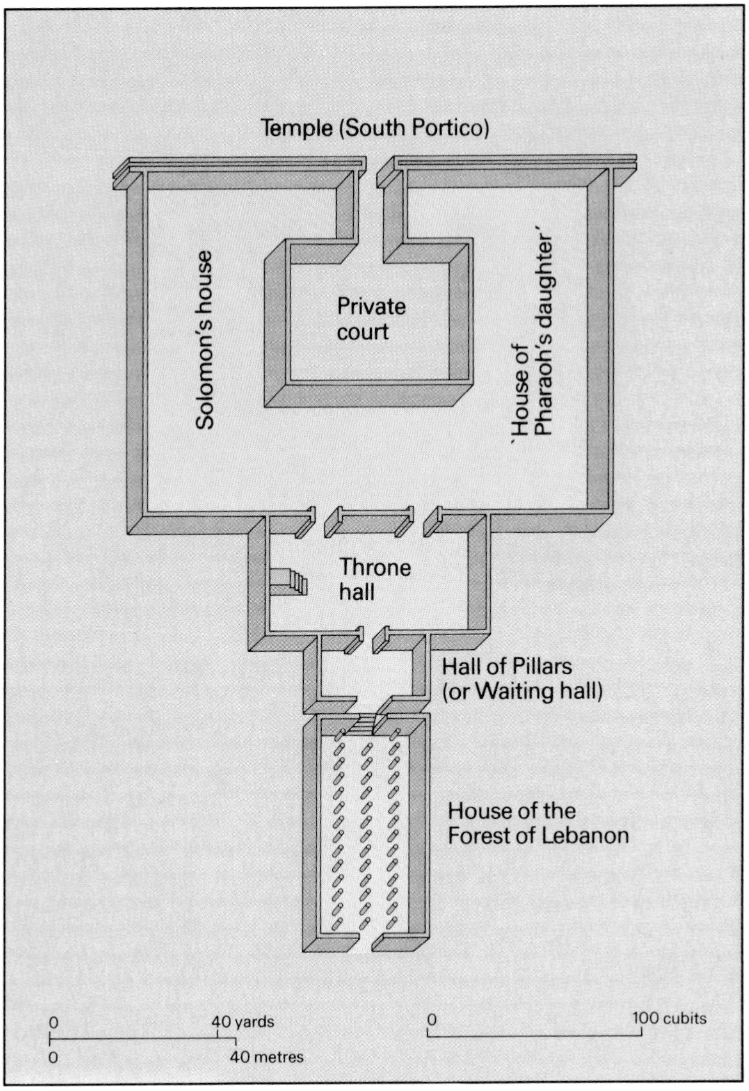

Suggested arrangement of the buildings of Solomon's palace at Jerusalem.

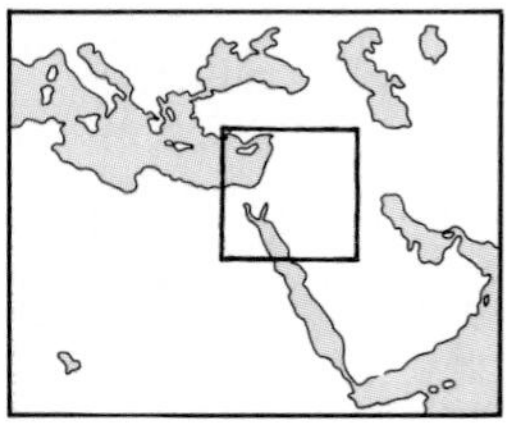

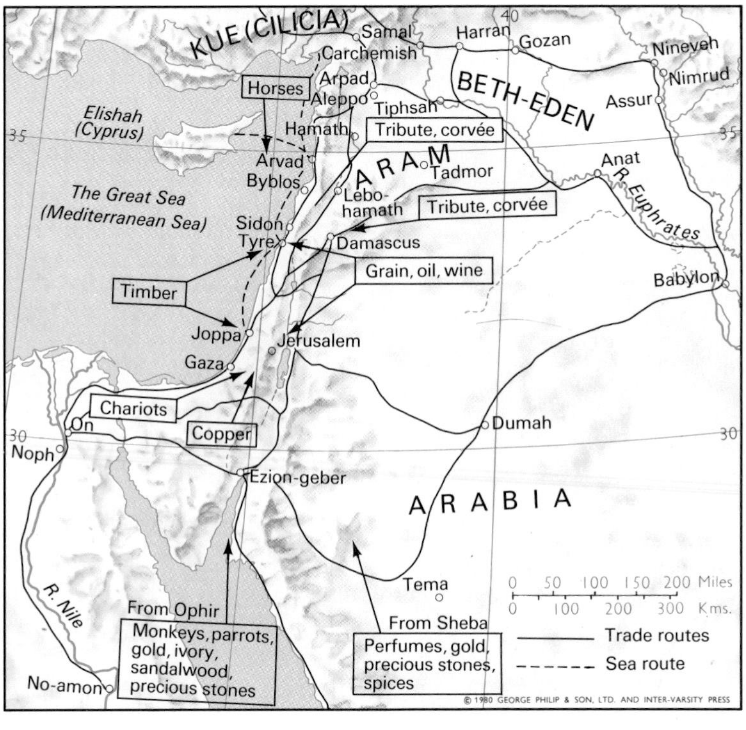

Trade routes in Solomon's time, showing principal imports and their sources.

Egypt, Arabia, Canaan and Edom in wisdom (1 Ki. 4:29ff.), Solomon became the great patron of Israel's *Wisdom literature. No other period of the Monarchy provided the combination of international contacts, wealth and relief from war necessary for literary productivity. Solomon took the lead in this movement, collecting and composing thousands of proverbs and songs (1 Ki. 4:32). The statement that he spoke of trees, beasts, *etc.* (1 Ki. 4:33) probably refers to his use of plants and animals in his proverbs rather than to accomplishments in botany and zoology, although close observation of these creatures would be necessary before he could use them in his sayings (*cf.* Pr. 30:24–31).

Two extensive collections in Proverbs (10:1–22:16; 25:1–29:27) are credited to him, and the entire collection bears his name as the chief contributor (1:1). Canticles and Ecclesiastes have traditionally been ascribed to him, although the latter does not mention his name. Though the final composition of these books seems to be much later than the 10th century BC, both may contain accurate descriptions of Solomon's glory and wisdom. Two psalms (72, a royal psalm; 127, a wisdom psalm) complete the list of canonical writings attributed to him. The relationship of *corporate personality* (the view that members of a clan are so inter-related that when one member acts the others may be viewed as taking part in the act) to problems of authorship is not clear: it is possible that some of the Solomonic writings are products of sages who felt their kinship with their intellectual father so strongly that they credited him with their work.

No hero of antiquity (with the possible exception of Alexander the Great) is so widely celebrated in folk literature. The Jewish, Arabian and Ethiopian tales about Solomon's intellectual prowess and magical powers are legion. (For collections of post-biblical tales about Solomon, see G. Salzberger, *Die Salomo-Sage*, 1907, and St J. Seymour, *Tales of King Solomon*, 1924.)

III. The iron ruler

Solomon's task was to maintain and control the expanse of territory bequeathed him by David. Further, he had to effect as smooth a transition as possible from the tribal confederacy which had characterized pre-Davidic political life to the strong central government which alone could maintain Israel's empire.

The traditional tribal boundaries were replaced by administrative districts: twelve in Israel (1 Ki. 4:7ff.) and perhaps one in Judah; *cf.* the problematic 4:19 in RSV. (See J. Bright, *A History of Israel*, 1960, p. 200, for the view that Jos. 15:20–62 contains the list of the twelve districts of Judah.) Each of these tax districts was obligated to provide support for the court for a month during the year (1 Ki. 4:7), which would appear an onerous task according to the list in 1 Ki. 4:22–23. (*FOOD, **I.** *d* (iii).)

In addition to this, Solomon began recruiting labourers from among the Israelites, a measure unpalatable to a people who relished freedom. There is an apparent contradiction between 1 Ki. 5:13ff. and 9:22, the former stating that Solomon used 30,000 Israelites in forced labour and the latter affirming that Israelites held positions in the army but were not slaves. It may be that 5:13ff. deals with events subsequent to the summary given in 9:15ff. When Canaanite labour proved insufficient for Solomon's enormous construction enterprises he was compelled to draft labourers from Israel. Further, there may be a technical difference between forced labour (*mas* in 5:13) and the more permanent slave-labour (*mas 'ōḇēḏ* in 9:21). The unpopularity of Solomon's policy is evidenced in the assassination of Adoniram, the superintendent of the labour crews (1 Ki. 4:6; 5:14; 12:18) and in the request for redress of grievances, the denial of which by Rehoboam led to the secession of the N kingdom (1 Ki. 12:4ff.).

Resentment was also engendered, in all probability, by Solomon's pledging of 20 Galilean cities to Hiram in return for financial aid (1 Ki. 9:10ff.). The fact that Hiram may have returned these later (as 2 Ch. 8:1–2 seems to hint) would not have completely relieved the resentment. Solomon had accomplished monumental tasks, including the building of the *Temple, but at an exorbitant price: the goodwill and loyalty of his people.

IV. The enterprising merchant

Trading was Solomon's forte. Knowing full well the significance of Israel's strategic control of the land-bridge between Egypt and Asia, he set out to exploit his position by controlling the major N–S caravan routes. His ties with Hiram of Tyre placed at his disposal fleets which enabled him to monopolize sea lanes as well.

Ezion-geber (*ELATH), his manufacturing centre and sea-port on the Gulf of Aqabah, was a main base of his trading activities. From here his fleet manned by Phoenicians (the Israelites apparently had neither love for nor knowledge of the sea) sailed to *Ophir carrying smelted copper. The phrase 'ships of *Tarshish' is probably to be translated 'refinery ships', *i.e.* ships equipped to carry smelted ore. In return, these ships brought back splendid cargo: gold, silver, hardwood, jewels, ivory and varieties of apes (1 Ki. 9:26–28; 10:11–12, 22; 'peacocks' in v. 22 should probably be translated 'baboons', as in RSVmg.).

The visit of the Queen of *Sheba (1 Ki. 10:1–13) may have had a commercial purpose. Solomon's control of the trade routes and his sea ventures in the south made him a serious financial threat to the Sabaeans, whose strategic position in SW Arabia enabled them to control trade in incense and spice. The queen's journey was successful, but she probably had to share her profits with Solomon, as did other Arabian monarchs (10:13–15).

Solomon's business acumen took advantage of Israel's location when he became the exclusive agent through whom the Hittites and Aramaeans had to negotiate in order to buy horses from Kue (Cilicia) or chariots from Egypt (1 Ki. 10:28–29). These and other enterprises made silver as common as stone and cedar as sycamore in Jerusalem, where the king lived in oriental splendour, in marked contrast to Saul's rustic simplicity in Gibeah. Although Israel's standard of living was undoubtedly raised, Israelites did not profit uniformly. The tendency towards centralization of wealth which brought the censure of the 8th-century prophets began during Solomon's golden reign.

V. The peaceful emperor

Solomon, who had inherited a large empire from his father, apparently conducted no major military campaigns. His task was to maintain Israel's extensive boundaries and to exploit his position of strength during the power-vacuum created by the temporary eclipse of Egypt and Assyria. The two main pillars of Solomon's foreign policy were friendly alliances, sometimes sealed by marriage, and the maintenance of a formidable army.

Among his wives Solomon numbered pharaoh's daughter, an accomplishment almost unprecedented among ancient oriental monarchs. Because of her high station, Solomon built a special wing on his palace for her (1 Ki. 3:1; 7:8). This alliance was profitable for Solomon, for pharaoh (probably one of the last members of the impotent Dynasty 21) gave him the frontier city of Gezer as a dowry (1 Ki. 9:16; see J. Bright, *op. cit.*, p. 191, n. 63, for the view that 'Gerar' is a preferable reading to 'Gezer'). In view of Solomon's numerous foreign marriages (1 Ki. 11:1–3), it is not surprising that Arabian, Jewish and especially Ethiopian traditions describe his amorous relations with the Queen of *Sheba, who according to the Ethiopians bore him a son, Menelik I, the traditional founder of their royal house.

Solomon made the most of his alliance with Hiram (*c.* 969–936 BC) of Tyre (1 Ki. 5:1–12). The Phoenicians, just entering their colonial heyday, supplied the architectural skill and many of the materials, especially the fine Lebanese woods, for Solomon's Temple and palaces; they designed and manned his ships; they provided a market for the Palestinian crops of wheat and olive oil. On at least one occasion Hiram came to Solomon's aid with a substantial loan (1 Ki. 9:11).

The backbone of Solomon's military defence was a ring of cities strategically located near the borders of Israel and manned by companies of charioteers (1 Ki. 9:15–19). His militia included 4,000 stalls for horses (40,000 in 1 Ki. 4:26 is apparently a scribal error; *cf.* 2 Ch. 9:25), 1,400 chariots, and 12,000 horsemen (1 Ki. 10:26). Several cities have yielded Solomonic remains in recent years, *e.g.* *Hazor, *Gezer and especially *Megiddo, where a ceremonial palace and casemate wall testify both to Solomon's prowess as builder and to the influence of Phoenician architecture on his work. See Y. Yadin, 'Megiddo' and 'Hazor' in *IDBS*, 1976.

Solomon's era of peace was marred by two recorded incidents, both of which are interpreted by the author of Kings in terms of

■ SOLOMON'S PORCH
See Temple, Part 3.

■ SOLOMON'S TEMPLE
See Temple, Part 3.

divine judgment (1 Ki. 11:14ff., 23ff.). Hadad, an Edomite prince, who had taken refuge in the court of Egypt during Joab's massacre of the Edomite males, returned to his homeland and apparently harassed Israel's S flank (1 Ki. 11:14–22, 25). Hadad's activities may have been confined to scattered skirmishes, for there is no indication that he posed a major threat to Solomon's S port, Ezion-geber. The zest with which the pharaoh courted Hadad's favour is further indication of the Egyptians' *penchant* for forming beneficial alliances during this period.

Solomon's second antagonist was Rezon, who wrested Damascus from Israel and set up an independent kingdom in the city which had been David's N headquarters (2 Sa. 8:6). Solomon's loss of this strategically located, commercially important Aramaean city greatly weakened his control of N and central Syria. The monolithic empire, which at the outset of Solomon's reign had stretched from the Gulf of Aqabah to the Orontes and Euphrates and from the Mediterranean coast to the Transjordan (*cf.* 1 Ki. 4:24), was in danger of crumbling. (See M. F. Unger, *Israel and the Aramaeans of Damascus*, 1957, pp. 47–57.)

VI. The fatal flaw

Marrying foreign wives was expedient politically, but not spiritually. The historian does not chide Solomon for sensuality but for disobedience to Israel's monotheistic ideal. Foreign marriages brought foreign religions, and the king compromised the convictions which he had expressed in his dedicatory prayer for the Temple (1 Ki. 8:23, 27) by engaging in syncretistic worship to placate his wives. This violent breach of Israel's covenant could not go unpunished. Though judgment was stayed during Solomon's lifetime for David's sake, the seeds of dissatisfaction sown among the people by Solomon's harsh policies of taxation and *corvée* were to bear bitter fruit during the reign of his son and successor, Rehoboam (1 Ki. 11:1–13).

BIBLIOGRAPHY. C. H. Gordon, *The World of the Old Testament*, 1958, pp. 180–189; A. Malamat, 'The Kingdom of David and Solomon in its Contact with Egypt and Aram Naharaim', *BA* 21, 1958, pp. 96–102; J. A. Montgomery, *ICC, Kings*, 1951, pp. 67–248; M. Noth, *The History of Israel*, 1958, pp. 201–223; J. Gray, *I and II Kings*², 1970; J. M. Myers, 'Solomon', in *IDB*, 4, pp. 399–408; D. F. Payne, 'Solomon', in *NIDNTT* 3, pp. 605–607. D.A.H.

SONG OF SOLOMON. 'Song of Songs' (*šîr haššîrîm*, 1:1) is a superlative denoting the best of songs. LXX *Asma Asmatōn* and Vulg. *Canticum Canticorum* (whence the alternative title 'Canticles') are literal translations of the Hebrew. The first of the five scrolls read at Jewish feasts, the Song is used at the Passover. Since analysis must depend on the particular theory of interpretation adopted (see below), no outline of contents is attempted here.

I. Canonicity

The Mishnah (*Yadaim* 3. 5) seems to indicate that the Song was not accepted without dispute. Following an affirmative verdict by Rabbi Judah and a negative opinion by Rabbi Jose, Rabbi Akiba affirms the canonicity of the Song in superlatives: 'the whole world is not worth the day on which the Song of Songs was given to Israel; all the Writings are holy, and the Song of Songs is the holy of holies'. His strong denial of any dispute may well serve as evidence for one.

Undoubtedly the opposition to canonizing the Song stemmed from its erotic nature. This objection was outweighed by the traditional Solomonic authorship and by rabbinic and Christian allegorical interpretations which lifted the poems above a sensual level.

II. Authorship and date

The traditional attribution to Solomon is based on the references to him (1:5; 3:7, 9, 11; 8:11), especially the title verse (1:1). The phrase *lišlōmōh* probably intimates authorship but can mean 'for Solomon'. Solomon's prowess as a song-writer is attested in 1 Ki. 4:32 (*cf.* Pss. 72; 127). The opinion expressed in *Baba Bathra* 15a that Hezekiah and his scribes wrote the Song of Songs is probably based on Pr. 25:1.

The presence of what seem to be Persian (*pardēs*, 'orchard', 4:13) or Greek (*'appiryôn* from *phoreion*, AV 'chariot', better RSV 'palanquin', 3:9) loan-words, a consistent (except for 1:1) use of *š* as the relative pronoun, and numerous words and phrases akin to Aramaic (see S. R. Driver, *Literature of the Old Testament*, p. 448) suggest to some that the final redaction of the book, if not its actual composition, took place after Solomon's time. It seems unnecessary, however, to date the composition as late as the Greek period (*c.* 300 BC) in view of the evidences for intercourse between Canaan and Ionia from the Solomonic period onwards. Likewise the presence of Aramaisms is no proof of a late date. S. R. Driver (*op. cit.*, p. 449) notes that the linguistic evidence, together with a number of geographical allusions (*e.g.* Sharon, 2:1; Lebanon, 3:9; 4:8, 11, 15, *etc.*; Amana, Senir, Hermon, 4:8; Tirzah, 6:4; Damascus, 7:4; Carmel, 7:5), points to a *northern* origin. But there is no provincialism here. The author is acquainted with the geography of Palestine and Syria from En-gedi, by the Dead Sea (1:14), to the mountains of Lebanon.

III. Literary qualities

The intensely personal speeches of Canticles take two main forms: dialogue (*e.g.* 1:9ff.) and soliloquy (*e.g.* 2:8–3:5). It is not easy to identify the participants in the conversation apart from the two lovers. Daughters of Jerusalem are mentioned (1:5; 2:7; 3:5, *etc.*), and brief responses have been credited to them (1:8; 5:9; 6:1, *etc.*). Statements have been attributed to citizens of Jerusalem (3:6–11) and Shulem (8:5). In highly figurative lyrical poetry it is possible that the central figures are reconstructing the responses of others (*e.g.* the Shulammite seems to quote her brothers in 8:8–9).

The power of the poetry lies in the intensity of love and devotion expressed and especially in the rich imagery which permeates the descriptions of the lovers and their love. If these descriptions are too intimately detailed to suit Western tastes we must remember that they are the product of a distant time and place. If some of the similes sound less than complimentary (*e.g.* teeth like ewes, neck like the tower of David, 4:2ff.), A. Bentzen's reminder is apposite: 'Orientals fix the eye on one single striking point, which according to our conceptions is perhaps not characteristic' (*IOT*, 1, p. 130). L. Waterman's opinion that the compliments are backhanded (*JBL* 44, 1925, pp. 179ff.) has not gained scholarly support. The pastoral qualities of the imagery have been noted frequently.

The poems abound in references to animals and especially plants. This fact has not gone unnoticed by those who find the source of the Song in pagan fertility rites (see below).

IV. Theories of interpretation

Interpretations of the Song have been legion, and there is little agreement among scholars as to its origin, meaning and purpose. The vividly detailed, erotic lyrics, the virtual absence of overt religious themes, and the vagueness of its plot make it a challenge to scholarship and a temptation to imaginative ingenuity. Indispensable to the study of the varieties of interpretation is H. H. Rowley's essay 'The Interpretation of the Song of Songs' in *The Servant of the Lord*, 1952.

The problem of accepting a group of love poems into the Canon was solved for rabbis and church Fathers by an *allegorical* method of interpretation. Traces of this method are found in the Mishnah and Talmud, while the Targum of the Song sees in the love-story a clear picture of God's gracious dealings with Israel throughout her history. Once the allegorical trail had been blazed, the rabbis vied with one another in attempts to expand and redirect it. Allusions to Israel's history were squeezed from the most unlikely parts of the Song. The church Fathers and many subsequent Christian interpreters baptized the Song into Christ, finding within it an allegory of Christ's love for the church or the believer. Various mediaeval writers followed the example of Ambrose in finding the Virgin Mary foreshadowed in the *Shulammite. Christian interpreters have yielded nothing to the rabbis in imaginative interpretation of details. The allegorical approach has been predominant in Protestant thought until recently, and includes as its advocates such stalwarts as Hengstenberg and Keil.

Closely related is the *typical* method which preserves the literal sense of the poem but also discerns a higher, more spiritual meaning. Avoiding the excesses in detailed interpretation of the allegorical method, typology stresses the major themes of love and devotion and finds in the story a picture of the love relationship between Christ and his believers. This approach has been justified by analogies from Arabic love-poems which may have esoteric meanings, by Christ's use of the story of Jonah (Mt. 12:40) or the serpent in the wilderness (Jn. 3:14), and by biblical analogies of spiritual marriage, *e.g.* Ho. 1–3; Je. 2:2; 3:1ff.; Ezk. 16:6ff.; 23; Eph. 5:22ff. Not a few modern conservatives have espoused the *typical* view, *e.g.* J. H. Raven (*Old Testament Introduction*, 1910), M. F. Unger (*Introductory Guide to the Old Testament*², 1956).

Though Jews and Christians have found devotional benefits in allegorical or typical approaches to the Song, the exegetical basis of these approaches is questionable. Both the abundance of details and the absence of clues as to deeper spiritual significance within the book itself speak against the finding of allegory or type in the Song.

The *dramatic* interpretation of Canticles, suggested by both Origen and Milton, was developed in the 19th century in two major forms. F. Delitzsch found two main characters, Solomon and the Shulammite girl. Taking her from her village home to Jerusalem, Solomon learnt to love her as his wife with an affection that rose above physical attraction. H. Ewald formulated an interpretation based on three main characters: Solomon, the Shulammite and her shepherd lover to whom she remains true despite the king's desperate efforts to win her. While Ewald's approach (called the *shepherd hypothesis*), which was accepted by S. R. Driver and refined by other scholars, avoids some of the difficulties of Delitzsch's view by explaining why the lover is pictured as a shepherd (1:7–8) and why the poem ends in a N pastoral setting, it has its own difficulties, *e.g.* the absence of dramatic instructions, the complexities involved in the dialogues when Solomon describes the Shulammite's beauty while she responds in terms of her shepherd lover. Dramatic interpretations face another difficulty: the scarcity of evidence for dramatic literature among the Semites, especially the Hebrews.

J. G. Wetzstein's study of Syrian marriage customs prompted K. Budde to interpret the Song as a collection of *nuptial songs* akin to those used in the week-long marriage feast in which the bride and groom are crowned as king and queen. Critics of this view have pointed out the danger of using modern Syrian customs to illustrate ancient Palestinian practices. Also, the Shulammite is not called by the name of 'queen' anywhere in the Song.

The view of T. J. Meek that the Song is derived from the *liturgical rites* of the *Tammuz cult (*cf.* Ezk. 8:14) has gained widespread attention. But it is unlikely that a pagan liturgy with overtones of immorality would be incorporated in the Canon without a thorough revision in terms of Israel's faith, and the Song bears the marks of no such redaction.

Leroy Waterman, who had originally supported Meek's theory (*JBL* 44, 1925), has recently returned to a historical basis for the Song. This he finds in the story of Abishag, David's *Shunammite maiden (1 Ki. 1:3), who allegedly refused Solomon's overtures in favour of her shepherd lover. This interpretation hangs on the conjectural connection between Shunammite and *Shulammite.

An increasing number of scholars have viewed Canticles as a collection of *love-poems* not necessarily connected with wedding festivities or any other specific occasion. Attempts to assign the various sections to different authors (*e.g.* W. O. E. Oesterley divided the Song into 28 distinct poems and emphatically denied the unity of the book; *Song of Songs*, 1936, p. 6b) have been resisted by a number of scholars, especially H. H. Rowley: 'The repetitions that occur leave the impression of a single hand . . .' (*op. cit.*, p. 212).

V. Purpose

If the Song is not an allegory or type conveying a spiritual message, what place does it have in the Canon? It serves as an object-lesson, an extended *māšāl* (*PROVERB), illustrating the rich wonders of human love. As biblical teaching concerning physical love has been emancipated from sub-Christian asceticism, the beauty and purity of marital love have been more fully appreciated. The Song, though expressed in language too bold for Western taste, provides a wholesome balance between the extremes of sexual excess or perversion and an ascetic denial of the essential goodness of physical love. E. J. Young carries the purpose one step further: 'Not only does it speak of the purity of human love, but by its very inclusion in the Canon it reminds us of a love that is purer than our own' (*IOT*, 1949, p. 327).

■ **SONG OF SONGS**
See Song of Solomon, Part 3.

BIBLIOGRAPHY. W. Baumgartner, in *OTMS*, pp. 230–235; J. C. Rylaarsdam, *Proverbs to Song of Solomon*, 1964; W. J. Fuerst, *Ruth, Esther, Ecclesiastes, The Song of Songs, Lamentations*, 1975; S. C. Glickman, *A Song for Lovers*, 1976; H. J. Schonfield, *The Song of Songs*, 1960; J. C. Exum, 'A Literary and Structural Analysis of the Song of Songs', *ZAW* 85, 1973, pp. 47–79; R. Gordis, *The Song of Songs*, 1954; L. Waterman, *The Song of Songs*, 1948. D.A.H.

SONS (CHILDREN) OF GOD.

I. In the Old Testament

a. Individuals of the class 'god'

'Son' (Heb. *bēn*, Aram. *bar*) is commonly used in Semitic languages to denote membership of a class, as 'son of Israel' for 'Israelite', 'son of might' for 'valorous'. 'Son of God' in Heb. means 'god' or 'god-like' rather than 'son of (the) God (Yahweh)'. In Jb. 1:6; 2:1; 38:7; Ps. 29:1; 89:6, the 'sons of God' form Yahweh's heavenly train or subordinates, though LXX Job calls them *angeloi* of God (*cf.* Dt. 32:8 LXX, whence RSV 'according to the number of the sons of God' supported by a Heb. Dead Sea Scroll text, 4Q Dt[q], against *MT* 'sons of Israel'). Similarly the 'son of the gods' in Dn. 3:25 is called the 'angel of the Jews' God' in 3:28.

In Gn. 6:1–2 the 'sons of God' are contrasted with human women in a way which seems to preclude their identification with the line of Cain. Many commentators treat these verses as pagan myth, hardly altered from a polytheistic background. Others argue that the phrase denotes demon-possessed men or fallen angels (*cf.* 1 Pet. 3:19–20; Jude 6). A more attractive interpretation falls into the next category.

b. Men who by divine appointment exercise God's prerogative of judgment

In Ex. 21:6; 22:8–9, 28, 'God' (Heb. *'ᵉlōhîm*) may stand for 'judges' (so AV, RVmg.), his deputies, exercising power of life and death (*cf.* 2 Ch. 19:6), as may be the case in Ps. 82:6.

Kings were titled 'son of god X' in the OT world, and in Israel in sense *c*, below. M. G. Kline has proposed that this usage be seen in Gn. 6:1–2, referring to rulers of the remote antediluvian era (*WTJ* 24, 1962, pp. 187–204).

c. Those who are related to Yahweh by covenant

Sonship of God chiefly denotes relationship by *covenant and is used (i) of Israel as a whole ('Israel is my first-born son', Ex. 4:22; *cf.* Ho. 11:1); (ii) of the Israelites generally ('You are the sons of the Lord your God', Dt. 14:1; *cf.* Ho. 1:10—of an individual Israelite in later Judaism, *e.g.* Wisdom 2:18); (iii) of the Davidic king, Yahweh's anointed, who will rule his people for ever ('You are my Son; today I have begotten you', Ps. 2:7). This relationship is not biological, though metaphors of birth, infancy and growth are sometimes used (Ho. 11:1; Dt. 32:6; Is. 1:2; 63:8) and conformity to the Father's character expected. But basically sonship is established by God through his covenant. Dt. 14:1–2 well illustrates the covenantal context of Israel's sonship. The Messiah-King, though called (like Israel with whom he is so closely identified) 'my first-born' (Ps. 89:27) and 'begotten' of Yahweh (Ps. 2:7), no less owes his status to God's covenant with him (Ps. 89:28; 2 Sa. 23:5). The terms of this covenant ('I will be his father, and he shall be my son', 2 Sa. 7:14) are parallel to the terms of the covenant with Israel ('I . . . will be their God, and they shall be my people', Je. 31:33). D.W.B.R. A.R.M.

II. In the New Testament

Both expressions, 'sons (Gk. *hyioi*) of God' and 'children (Gk. *tekna*) of God', occur in the NT, but without obvious distinction in meaning. The NT usage is based on one or other of the OT uses of 'sons of God'.

a. Lk. 20:36

This reference, 'they are equal to angels and are sons of God, being sons of the resurrection', reflects the use of 'sons of God' as in Pss. 29:1; 89:6; Dt. 32:8 (LXX), where it means non-terrestrial beings in the presence of God, in contrast to 'the sons of this age'. That the elect should have this destiny before them was already the belief of many Jews, but it was to acquire a more distinctive meaning in the light of Christ's resurrection.

b. Those who act like God

Lk. 6:35, 'you will be sons of the Most High', means little more than 'you will be like God'. 'Son of . . .' is an idiom for 'having the characteristics of' or 'doing the work of' (*cf.* the parabolic description of the apprentice son in Jn. 5:19), and the 'sons of God' in Mt. 5:9 and 5:45 belong to this category. Ps. 82:6, discussed by Jesus in Jn. 10:34–36, may be an OT example of this sense, judges being men who exercise God's power of life and death. Paul's simple metaphor in Eph. 5:1, 'be imitators of God, as beloved children', reflects this idiom, though it also presupposes a deeper relation between the 'children' and their Father.

c. The sonship of Israel

The collective sonship of Israel ('Israel is my first-born son', Ex. 4:22) is prominent in the thought of Paul (*e.g.* Rom. 9:4, 'they are Israelites, and to them belong the sonship . . .') and elsewhere in the NT. Sometimes this sonship is seen as represented and fulfilled in Jesus Christ, as in Mt. 2:15 and in the narratives of his baptism and temptation. However, even without a direct connection with Christ's sonship, 'sons (or children) of God' recalls the OT application of the term to God's covenant people who are to reflect his holiness. If Eph. 5:1 is little more than metaphorical, Phil. 2:15, 'children of God without blemish in the midst of a crooked and perverse generation', is based on the Song of Moses (Dt. 32:5–6, 18–20), and 2 Cor. 6:18 combines a number of covenantal passages (*e.g.* Is. 43:6; 2 Sa. 7:14). 'The children of God who are scattered abroad' in Jn. 11:52 are the lost sheep of the house of Israel (*cf.* 10:16). The idea is derived from Ezk. 34 and 37, though whether the reference in John is to Jewish believers only or all believers is a matter of debate.

The sonship of God's people is, however, linked with the special sonship of Jesus in Heb. 2:10–17. (A different word, *paidia*, is used for 'children' in the quotation in vv. 13–14.) Here, Jesus' sonship is that conferred on the Messiah-King, David's son (Ps. 2:7; 2 Sa. 7:14, quoted in Heb. 1:5), which itself is parallel to, and perhaps epitomizes, Israel's covenantal sonship. The 'many sons' are the 'descendants of Abraham' and 'children' by election even before Christ's incarnation. But they are brought 'to glory' through the Son sharing in their 'flesh and blood' in which he secured their salvation by his death.

d. Paul in Romans and Galatians

Though Paul acknowledges that 'the sonship' belongs to Israelites (Rom. 9:4), he insists that not all the offspring of Israel are 'Israel' in the true sense, and that therefore it is not 'the children of the flesh' but 'the children of the promise' who are 'children of God' and true partakers of the privilege (Rom. 9:6ff.).

By this test, Gentiles as well as Jews are included, 'for in Christ Jesus you are all sons of God, through faith' (Gal. 3:26). This doctrine of sonship is expounded in Rom. 8, where Paul invokes the idea of *hyiothesia*, usually rendered *'adoption'. But, though the term was used in contemporary Gk. to denote legal adoption of children (see *MM*), it is not clear how far this enters Paul's thought. Despite the contrast with a former status of slavery, both in Rom. 8:15 (where RSV renders *hyiothesia* as 'sonship') and Gal. 4:5, at least in the latter passage *hyiothesia* seems to correspond to the entering of a child on his inheritance at 'the date set by the father'. The primary model is the sovereign act of God's grace when he declared Israel, and then the Davidic king, to be his son. Neither Israel's sonship (Ex. 4:22) nor that of Messiah (Pss. 2:7; 89:27) was inconsistent with the recipient's being called God's 'first-born', and the *hyiothesia* of the believer is practically identical with the notion of spiritual generation. In Rom. 8:23 the *hyiothesia* is yet to come. Though again associated with the notion of 'redemption' (from slavery?), the positive act is really 'the revealing of the sons of God', showing them to be what they already are. This sonship is indissolubly linked with the sonship of Christ (Rom. 8:17), is attested and controlled by the Spirit (8:14, 16), and its ultimate nature disclosed when Christ's sonship is disclosed and when God's elect are seen as 'conformed to the image of his Son, in order that he might be the first-born among many brethren' (8:19, 29).

e. John

John's concept of 'children of God' differs only in emphasis from that of Paul, although he employs simply *tekna*, and reserves *hyios* exclusively for Christ. Westcott held that John deliberately avoided *hyios*, 'the name of definite dignity and privilege', to describe the relation of Christians to God, since 'he regards their position not as the result of an "adoption" (*hyiothesia*), but as the result of a new life which advances from the vital germ to full maturity'. However, Westcott overstated the case. While John undoubtedly exploits the imagery of natural birth and consequent relationship (*e.g.* 1 Jn. 3:9), he is also aware of the OT background where Israel became God's son by election and calling. We have already referred to Jn. 11:52. In Jn. 1:12 the 'children of God' may be interpreted as believing Israelites before the Word became flesh. In any case, they are described not only as being 'born of God' but also as becoming 'children of God' by having that status conferred on them: 'to them gave he the right to become children of God' (RV). Again in 1 Jn. 3 and 4 believers are described as 'born of God', with special reference to their reproducing God's character of love and righteousness; nevertheless the title 'children of God' is also a privilege bestowed through God's 'calling' (3:1). Though it 'may be seen' now who are children of God by their behaviour (3:10), their final form 'does not yet appear', but will be manifested in the day when the Son of God is manifested and they fully reflect the image of their Father (3:2); which image is in the Son.

BIBLIOGRAPHY. B. F. Westcott, *The Epistles of St. John*, 1883, pp. 94, 119ff.; Arndt, *s.v. hyios, teknon*; A. Richardson, *An Introduction to the Theology of the New Testament*, 1958, pp. 147ff., 263ff.; J. D. G. Dunn, *Jesus and the Spirit*, 1975, pp. 21–40.

D.W.B.R.

SOPATER, SOSIPATER, a believer from Beroea in Macedonia (Acts 20:4), was one of the missionary party which waited for Paul at Troas, and then accompanied him to Asia on his way to Syria. Sosipater is called, in Rom. 16:21, a kinsman (*syngenēs*) of Paul. His greeting was sent to the church at Rome.

Some consider that the references are to the same man. Perhaps Sopater was a fruit of Paul's preaching in Macedonia, and was therefore Paul's kinsman in Christ. He probably represented the Beroean church in the delegation which was about to set sail with Paul to carry the Gentile churches' contributions to Jerusalem.

C.H.D.

SOREK, VALLEY OF. The home of Delilah (Jdg. 16:4). There is little doubt that this may be equated with the Wadi al-Sarar, a large valley lying between Jerusalem—starting some 20 km from it—and the Mediterranean. It must always have offered a convenient route inland (it is today followed by the railway line). There is a ruin near the valley called Khirbet Surik, preserving the biblical name. Eusebius

SOOTHSAYER
See Divination, Part 1.

SOP
See Lord's supper, Part 2.

SORCERY
See Magic, Part 2.

The valley of Sorek (Nahal Soreq), home of Delilah. (RS)

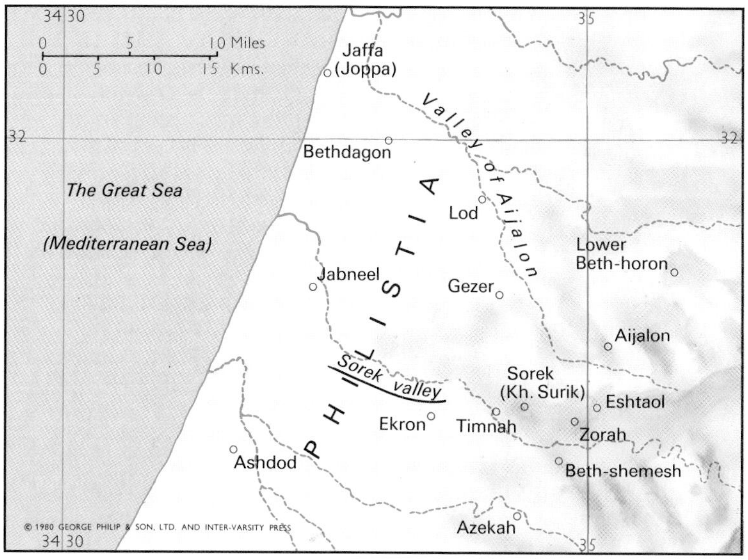

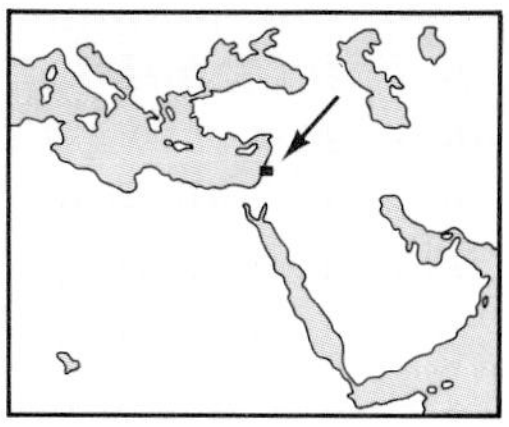

The Sorek valley.

SOSIPATER
See Sopater, Part 3.

SOWER, SOWING
See Agriculture, Part 1.

SPAN
See Weights and measures, Part 3.

SPARROW
See Animals, Part 1.

SPEAKING AGAINST
See Talebearing, Part 3.

SPEAKING IN TONGUES
See Tongues, gift of, Part 3.

SPEAR
See Armour, Part 1.

and Jerome made the same identification. D.F.P.

SOSTHENES. The chief ruler of the synagogue at Corinth, and successor (or possibly colleague) of the converted *Crispus. He was assaulted in court after Gallio disallowed a Jewish prosecution of Paul (Acts 18:17), either in an anti-Semitic demonstration by Greeks (as Western Text) or in Jewish spite against an unsuccessful or lukewarm spokesman.

The latter might indicate pro-Christian sympathy: did 'Paul sow, Apollos water' (*cf.* 1 Cor. 3:6)? 'Sosthenes the brother' is co-sender of 1 Corinthians (1:1), and Sosthenes is not the commonest of Gk. names. Paul's tact and modesty, in approaching a sensitive church in association with the ex-archisynagogue, then at Ephesus, best explain the allusion. Joint-authorship is not implied.

Sosthenes' inclusion in the Seventy (Clem. Alex., *Hyp.* 5, in Eus., *EH* 1. 12. 1–2) doubtless reflects his assumed participation in a canonical letter. A.F.W.

SOUL. 1. The usual Heb. word *nepeš* (*n^e^šāmâ*, Is. 57:16, is an exception) occurs 755 times in the OT. As is clear from Gn. 2:7, the primary meaning is 'possessing life'. Thus it is frequently used of animals (Gn. 1:20, 24, 30; 9:12, 15–16; Ezk. 47:9). Sometimes it is identified with the blood, as something which is essential to physical existence (Gn. 9:4; Lv. 17:10–14; Dt. 12:22–24). In many cases it stands for the life-principle. This sense is common in the book of Psalms, though not confined to it.

The numerous occurrences with a psychical reference cover various states of consciousness: (a) where *nepeš* is the seat of physical appetite (Nu. 21:5; Dt. 12:15, 20–21, 23–24; Jb. 33:20; Pss. 78:18; 107:18; Ec. 2:24; Mi. 7:1); (b) where it is the source of emotion (Jb. 30:25; Pss. 86:4; 107:26; Ct. 1:7; Is. 1:14); (c) where it is associated with the will and moral action (Gn. 49:6; Dt. 4:29; Jb. 7:15; Pss. 24:4; 25:1; 119:129, 167). In addition there are passages where *nepeš* designates an individual or person (*e.g.* Lv. 7:21; 17:12; Ezk. 18:4) or is employed with a pronominal suffix to denote self (*e.g.* Jdg. 16:16; Ps. 120:6; Ezk. 4:14). A remarkable extension of the latter is the application of *nepeš* to a dead body (*e.g.* Lv. 19:28; Nu. 6:6; Hg. 2:13). Usually the *nepeš* is regarded as departing at death (*e.g.* Gn. 35:18), but the word is never used for the spirit of the dead. Since Hebrew psychology lacked precise terminology, there is some overlapping in the use of *nepeš*, *lēḇ* (*lēḇāḇ*) and *rûaḥ* (*Heart, *Spirit).

2. Gk. *psychē*, the corresponding term to *nepeš* in the NT, occurs in the Gospels with similar meanings, but in certain instances, indicating life, more is implied than physical life, ceasing at death (Mt. 10:39; Mk. 8:35; Lk. 17:33; 21:19; Jn. 12:25). In all four Gospels *pneuma*, the equivalent of *rûaḥ*, sometimes denotes the principle of life, although in other cases it means the higher level of psychical life.

Of 12 occurrences in Paul, 6 represent life (Rom. 11:3; 16:4; 1 Cor. 15:45; 2 Cor. 1:23; Phil. 2:30; 1 Thes. 2:8), 2 are personal (Rom. 11:3; 13:1) and 4 are psychical, 3 of these representing desire (Eph. 6:6; Phil. 1:27; Col. 3:23), while the remaining one indicates emotion (1 Thes. 5:23). For the higher aspects of ordinary life and especially the higher life of a Christian he uses *pneuma*. In line with this is his use of the adjectives *psychikos* and *pneumatikos* (1 Cor. 2:14–15). When he employs *psychē* along with *pneuma* (1 Thes. 5:23) he is merely describing the same immaterial part of man in its lower and higher aspects.

Other NT writers provide examples of a somewhat heightened use of *psychē*. The Word of God can save it and recovery from error rescues it from death (Jas. 1:21; 5:20). The outcome of faith is the salvation of the *psychē* (Heb. 10:29; 1 Pet. 1:10), while fleshly desires are inimical to it (1 Pet. 2:11). Hope of what shall be firmly anchors it (Heb. 6:19). In the description of what follows the opening of the fifth seal, *psychē* is used with reference to the martyrs seen below the altar (Rev. 6:9). (*Spirit.)

Bibliography. A. R. Johnson, *The Vitality of the Individual in the Thought of Ancient Israel*, 1949; E. White, 'A Preface to Biblical Psychology', *JTVI* 83, 1951, pp. 51ff.; *idem*, 'The Psychology of St Paul's Epistles', *JTVI* 87, 1955, pp. 1ff.; J. Laidlaw, *The Bible Doctrine of Man*, 1879, pp. 49–96, 179–220; H. W. Robinson, *The Christian Doctrine of Man*[3], 1926, pp. 11–27, 104–111; G. Bertram *et al.*, *TDNT* 9, pp. 608–656; G. Harder, C. Brown, *NIDNTT* 3, pp. 676–689. W.J.C.

SPAIN. For the discussion of possible OT references to Spain, see *Tarshish. A series of Gk. commercial colonies founded from Massilia (Marseilles) introduced Spain into world history, and in the 3rd century BC it became a theatre for the long struggle between Carthage and Rome. By 197 BC, the Carthaginians being dispossessed, two Roman provinces, Hispania Citerior and Hispania Ulterior, were set up; but the forcible reconciliation of the Spanish tribes to Roman rule took almost 2 centuries more. Later, however, Spain developed, economically and culturally, perhaps faster than any other part of the empire. Augustus reorganized the peninsula into three provinces, Hispania Tarraconensis, Baetica and Lusitania: Vespasian extended Latin status to all the Spanish municipalities. The Senecas, Lucan, Quintilian, Martial and other prominent Latin writers of that age, as well as the emperors Trajan and Hadrian, were of Spanish birth.

These things show how forward-looking was Paul's plan to travel beyond Rome to Spain (Rom. 15:24, 28), a project in which he clearly expects the co-operation of the Roman Christians. Even if his first object was the Hellenized towns, 'it marks the beginning of an entirely new enterprise; behind it lies Gaul and perhaps Germany and Britain. He is about to pass over from the Greek into the distinctly Roman half of the civilized world' (J. Weiss, *History of Primitive Christianity*, 1, 1937, p. 359).

Whether *Paul achieved his ambition remains uncertain. The silence of the Pastorals may indicate a change of plan. Clement of Rome, *c.* AD 95, says that Paul reached 'the boundary of the West' (*1 Clem.* 5)—most naturally interpreted, not of Rome, but of the Pillars of Hercules. The 2nd-century *Acts of Peter* and the Muratorian Fragment are more explicit, but may reflect assumptions based on Rom. 15. The earliest surviving Spanish traditions are too late to help, and later Roman theory was interested in proving that all W churches were founded by Peter's lieutenants (Innocent, *Ep.* 25. 2, AD 416).

Bibliography. Strabo, 3; C. H. V. Sutherland, *The Romans*

Lady with a spindle, shown on a stone relief from Susa, Iran. Height 10 cm. Early 1st millennium BC. (MC)

SPECKLED BIRD
See Animals, Part 1.

SPEECH
See Tongue, Part 3.

SPELL
See Magic, Part 2.

SPELT
See Grain, Part 2.

SPICES
See Herbs, Part 2.

SPIDER
See Animals, Part 1.

SPINDLE
See Spinning, Part 3.

n Spain 217 BC–AD *117*, 1939; Ch. Zahn, *INT*, 1909, 2, pp. 61ff., 3ff.; P. N. Harrison, *The Problem f the Pastoral Epistles*, 1921, pp. 02ff.; F. F. Bruce, *Paul: Apostle of he Free Spirit*, 1977, pp. 445ff.

A.F.W.

SPECK. The word occurs in Mt. :3–5, and almost identically in the ucan parallel (Lk. 6:41–42 *bis*). The Gk. word is *karphos* (AV mote'), and is cognate with the erb *karphō*, 'to dry up'. The noun neans a small, dry stalk or twig, a ight piece of straw, or even of wool uch as might fly into the eye. Metaphorically it is used by Jesus o denote a minor fault. S.S.S.

SPINNING AND WEAVING. Two implements were used in spinning (Heb. *ṭāwâ*; Gk. *nēthō*). The listaff (Heb. *kîšôr*, Pr. 31:19; AV spindle'), on which were wound the inspun fibres, was held with the eft hand, while the spindle (Heb. *pelek*, Pr. 31:19; AV 'distaff') was vorked by the fingers and thumb f the right hand to twist the short atural fibres into yarn. The pindle had a wooden shank 23 to 0 cm long, with a heavy whorl of stone or clay part way down to give momentum to its rotation. A hook at one end held the yarn which, when spun, was twisted on to the spindle shank. A variety of fibres such as flax and wool (Lv. 13:47), goat hair (Ex. 35:26), and camel hair (Mt. 3:4) were used in spinning, though the blending of different kinds of yarn was forbidden, for ritual purity (Lv. 19:19).

In Israel the task of spinning belonged to women (Ex. 35:25; Pr. 31:19). For weaving (Heb. *'ārag*; Gk. *hyphainō*), however, both men (Ex. 35:35) and women (2 Ki. 23:7)

Spinners and weavers at work. Copy of a wall-painting in the tomb of Khnum-hotep, Beni Hasan. Height 55 cm. 2050–1800 BC. (MetNY)

were employed, and the existence of a guild of weavers is indicated in 1 Ch. 4:21. Whether the horizontal or the vertical loom was more common in Israel is uncertain, though the weaving of the sleeping Samson's hair (Jdg. 16:13) suggests the former in this instance at least. In Egypt horizontal looms were common and such are still in use among Bedouin and peasants in Palestine. Egyp. weavers seem to have been famed particularly for their white cloth (Is. 19:9).

The weaver's beam (*mānôr*), to which the massive shaft of Goliath's spear is compared (1 Sa. 17:7), was the means of raising and lowering the longitudinal warp threads (*š^{e}ṯî*) to allow the shuttle carrying the transverse woof thread (*'ēreḇ*, Lv. 13:48) to pass between them. The woof was then beaten tight by a stick or 'pin' (*yāṯēḏ*, Jdg. 16:14) to produce firm cloth.

The familiar art of weaving supplies some striking similes in the OT; the speed of the weaver's shuttle portrays the swift passing of man's life (Jb. 7:6), and death is likened to the cutting of finished cloth from the thrums (*dallâ*) attached to the loom (Is. 38:12). Spinning and weaving are singled out as examples of unremitting human toil from which the world of nature is free (Lk. 12:27, RSV mg.).

BIBLIOGRAPHY. R. J. Forbes, *Studies in Ancient Technology*, 4, 1956; A. Neuburger, *The Technical Arts and Sciences of the Ancients*, 1930.

G.I.E.

SPIRIT, HOLY SPIRIT. OT, Heb. *rûaḥ* 378 times (plus 11 Aramaic in Dn.); NT, Gk. *pneuma* 379 times.

I. Basic range of meaning of *rûaḥ* and *pneuma*

From earliest Heb. thought *rûaḥ* had various meanings, all more or less equally prominent. **1.** *Wind*, an invisible, mysterious, powerful force (Gn. 8:1; Ex. 10:13, 19; Nu. 11:31; 1 Ki. 18:45; Pr. 25:23; Je. 10:13; Ho. 13:15; Jon. 4:8), regularly with the notion of strength or violence present (Ex. 14:21; 1 Ki. 19:11; Pss. 48:7; 55:8; Is. 7:2; Ezk. 27:26; Jon. 1:4). **2.** *Breath* (*i.e.*, air on a small scale), or *spirit* (Gn. 6:17; 7:15, 22; Pss. 31:5; 32:2; Ec. 3:19, 21; Je. 10:14; 51:17; Ezk. 11:5), the same mysterious force seen as the life and vitality of man (and beasts). It can be disturbed or activated in a particular direction (Gn. 41:8; Nu. 5:14, 30; Jdg. 8:3; 1 Ki. 21:5; 1 Ch. 5:26; Jb. 21:4; Pr. 29:11; Je. 51:17; Dn. 2:1, 3), can be impaired or diminished (Jos. 5:1; 1 Ki. 10:5; Ps. 143:7; Is. 19:3) and revive again (Gn. 45:27; Jdg. 15:19; 1 Sa. 30:12). That is, the dynamic

Wooden tomb-model of a weaver's house with women preparing flax, spinning, and weaving on a horizontal loom. Warping frames are shown on right and on rear wall. From Egypt. Length 59 cm, width 35·5 cm, height 22 cm. 12th Dynasty. 1990–1780 BC. (MetNY)

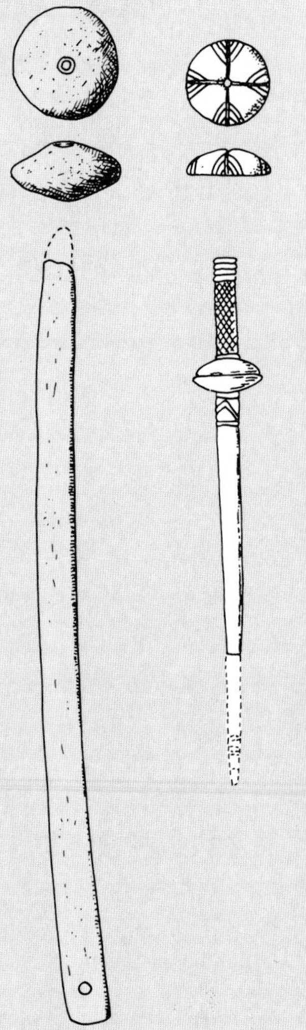

Bottom right:
Left: *A stone spindle whorl and a bone needle shuttle used in weaving. From Ghassul, Palestine. c. 3000 BC.*
Right: *A bone spindle whorl and a decorated bone spindle. From Megiddo. Late Bronze Age, c. 1500 BC.*

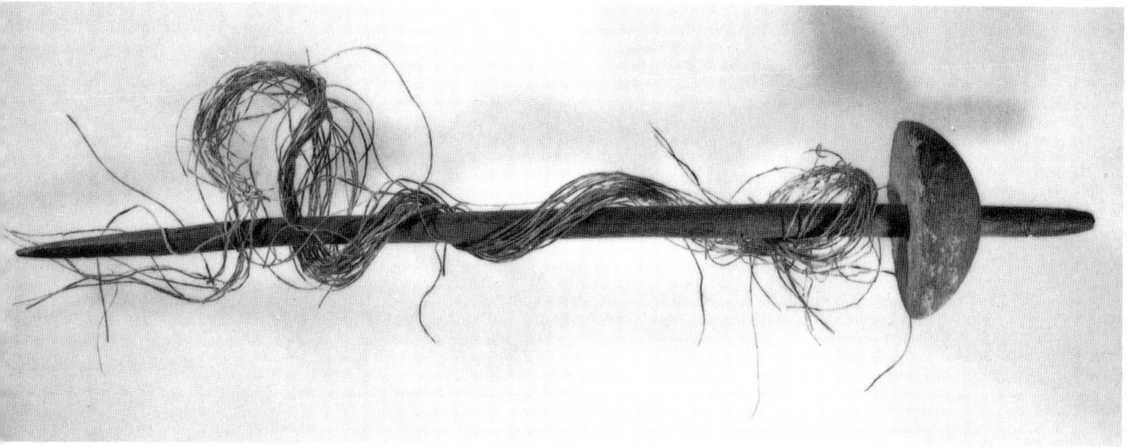

A spindle with original flaxen thread wound round it. From Egypt (Thebes?). Length c. 35 cm. New Kingdom or later. (BM)

force which constitutes a man can be low (it disappears at death), or there can be a sudden surge of vital power. **3.** *Divine power*, where *rûaḥ* is used to describe occasions when men seemed to be carried out of themselves—not just a surge of vitality, but a supernatural force taking possession. So particularly with the early charismatic leaders (Jdg. 3:10; 6:34; 11:29; 13:25; 14:6, 19; 15:14f.; 1 Sa. 11:6), and the early prophets—it was the same divine *rûaḥ* which induced ecstasy and prophetic speech (Nu. 24:2; 1 Sa. 10:6, 10; 19:20, 23f.).

These should not be treated as a set of distinct meanings; rather we are confronted with a spectrum of meaning where the different senses merge into each other. Note, *e.g.*, the overlap between **1** and **2** in Ps. 78:39, between **1** and **3** in 1 Ki. 18:12; 2 Ki. 2:16; Ezk. 3:12, 14, between **2** and **3** in Nu. 5:14, 30; 1 Sa. 16:14–16; Ho. 4:12, and between **1**, **2** and **3** in Ezk. 37:9. Initially at least these are all seen simply as manifestations of *rûaḥ*, and the meanings of *rûaḥ* are not kept strictly separate. In particular, therefore, we may not presuppose an initial distinction in Heb. thought between divine *rûaḥ* and anthropological *rûaḥ*; on the contrary, man's *rûaḥ* can be identified with God's *rûaḥ* (Gn. 6:3; Jb. 27:3; 32:8; 33:4; 34:14f.; Ps. 104:29f.).

It also becomes immediately evident that the concept *rûaḥ* is an existential term. At its heart is the *experience* of a mysterious, awesome power—the mighty invisible force of the wind, the mystery of vitality, the otherly power that transforms—all *rûaḥ*, all manifestations of divine energy.

In later usage the meanings human spirit, angelic or demonic spirit, and divine Spirit predominate and are more distinct. Thus in the NT *pneuma* is used nearly 40 times to denote that dimension of the human personality whereby relationship with God is possible (Mk. 2:8; Acts 7:59; Rom. 1:9; 8:16; 1 Cor. 5:3–5; 1 Thes. 5:23; Jas. 2:26). Slightly more frequent is the sense of unclean, evil, demonic spirit, a power which man experiences as an affliction, an injurious limitation to full relationship with God and with his fellows (chiefly in the Synoptic Gospels and Acts: Mt. 8:16; Mk. 1:23, 26f.; 9:25; Lk. 4:36; 11:24, 26; Acts 19:12f., 15f.; 1 Tim. 4:1; Rev. 16:13f.). Occasionally there is reference to heavenly (good) spirits (Acts 23:8f.; Heb. 1:7, 14), or to spirits of the dead (Lk. 24:37, 39; Heb. 12:23; 1 Pet. 3:19; *cf.* 1 Cor. 5:5). But by far the most frequent reference in the NT is to the Spirit of God, the Holy Spirit (more than 250 times). At the same time the earlier, wider range of meaning is still reflected in the ambiguity of Jn. 3:8; 20:22; Acts 8:39; 2 Thes. 2:8; Rev. 11:11; 13:15; and in particular there are several passages where it is not possible to decide with finality whether it is human spirit or divine Spirit that is meant (Mk. 14:38; Lk. 1:17, 80; 1 Cor. 14:14, 32; 2 Cor. 4:13; Eph. 1:17; 2 Tim. 1:7; Jas. 4:5; Rev. 22:6).

II. Pre-Christian usage

In the earliest understanding of *rûaḥ* there was little or no distinction between natural and supernatural. The wind could be described poetically as the blast of Yahweh's nostrils (Ex. 15:8, 10; 2 Sa. 22:16 = Ps. 18:15; Is. 40:7). And man's God-breathed *rûaḥ* was from the first more or less synonymous with his *nep̄eš* (soul) (especially Gn. 2:7). *rûaḥ* was the same divine, mysterious power which is to be seen most clearly in the wind or in the ecstatic behaviour of prophet or charismatic leader.

Initially also the *rûaḥ* of God was conceived more in terms of power than in moral terms, not yet as the (Holy) Spirit of God (*cf.* again Jdg. 14:6, 19; 15:14f.). A *rûaḥ* from God could be for evil as well as for good (Jdg. 9:23; 1 Sa. 16:14–16; 1 Ki. 22:19–23). At this early stage of understanding, God's *rûaḥ* was thought of simply as a supernatural power (under God's authority) exerting force in some direction.

The earliest leadership in the emergence of Israel as a nation rested its claim to authority on particular manifestations of *rûaḥ*, of ecstatic power—so with the judges (references above, **3**), Samuel who had the reputation of a seer and was evidently the leader of a group of ecstatic prophets (1 Sa. 9:9, 18f.; 19:20, 24), and Saul (1 Sa. 11:6; *cf.* 10:11f.; 19:24). Note the part apparently played by music in stimulating the ecstasy of inspiration (1 Sa. 10:5f.; 2 Ki. 3:15).

Various developments are evident in subsequent periods. We can recognize a tendency to open up a distinction between the natural and supernatural, between God and man. Just as the vivid anthropomorphisms of the earlier talk of God are abandoned, so *rûaḥ* becomes more clearly that which characterizes the supernatural and distinguishes the divine from the merely human (particularly Is. 31:3; so Jn. 4:24). So too a distinction between *rûaḥ* and *nep̄eš* begins to emerge: the *rûaḥ* in man retains its immediate connection with God, denoting the 'higher' or Godward dimension of man's existence (*e.g.* Ezr. 1:1, 5; Ps. 51:12; Ezk. 11:19), while *nep̄eš* tends more and more to stand for the 'lower' aspects of man's consciousness, the personal but merely human life in man, the seat of his appetites, emotions and passions (so regularly). Thus the way is prepared for the Pauline distinction between the psychical and the spiritual (1 Cor. 15:44–46).

Also evident is a tendency for the focus of authority to shift from the manifestation of *rûaḥ* in ecstasy to a more institutionalized concept. Possession of the Spirit of God is now conceived as more permanent, and capable of being passed on (Nu. 11:17; Dt. 34:9; 2 Ki. 2:9, 15). So presumably the anointing of the king was more and more thought of in terms of an anointing with Spirit (1 Sa. 16:13; and the implication of Ps. 89:20f.; Is. 11:2; 61:1). And prophecy tended to become more and more attached to the cult (the implication of Is. 28:7; Je. 6:13; 23:11; it is likely that some of the psalms began as prophetic utterances in the cult; Hab. and Zc. were quite probably cult prophets). This development marks the beginning of the tension within the Judaeo-Christian tradition between charisma and cult (see especially 1 Ki. 22:5–28; Am. 7:10–17).

The most striking feature of the pre-exilic period is the strange reluctance (as it would appear) of the classical prophets to attribute their inspiration to the Spirit. Neither the 8th-century prophets (Am., Mi., Ho., Is.) nor those of the 7th century (Je., Zp., Na., Hab.) refer to the Spirit to authenticate their message—with the possible exception of Mi. 3:8 (often regarded as a later interpolation for that reason). In describing their inspiration they preferred to speak of the word of God (especially Am. 3:8; Je. 20:9) and the hand of God (Is. 8:11; Je. 15:17). Why this was so we cannot tell: perhaps *rûaḥ* had become too much identified with the ecstatic both in Israel and in other near-Eastern religions (*cf.* Ho. 9:7); perhaps they were reacting against cult professionalism and abuse (Is. 28:7; Je. 5:13; 6:13; 14:13ff.; *etc.*; Mi. 2:11); or perhaps already emerging was the conviction that the work of God's *rûaḥ* would be primarily eschatological (Is. 4:4).

In the exilic and post-exilic period the work of the Spirit came to renewed prominence. The role of divine *rûaḥ* as inspirer of prophecy was reasserted (Pr. 1:23; *cf.* Is. 59:21—Spirit *and* word together; Ezk. 2:2; 3:1–4, 22–24; *etc.*—Spirit, word *and* hand). The inspiration of the earlier prophets too was freely attributed to the Spirit (Ne. 9:20, 30; Zc. 7:12; *cf.* Is. 63:11ff.). The sense that God is present through his Spirit, expressed for example in Ps. 51:11, appears also in Ps. 143:10; Hg. 2:5; Zc. 4:6. And 2 Ch. 20:14; 24:20 may reflect a desire to bridge the gap between charisma and cult.

The tradition which attributed the artistic skills and craftsmanship of Bezalel and others to the activity of the Spirit (Ex. 28:3; 31:3; 35:31) forged a link between the Spirit and more aesthetic and ethical qualities. It is perhaps with this in view, or since the Spirit is the Spirit of the holy and good God, that some authors specifically designate the Spirit as God's 'holy Spirit' (only 3 times in the OT—Ps. 51:13; Is. 63:10f.) or as God's 'good Spirit' (Ne. 9:20; Ps. 143:10).

Another infrequent emphasis is the association of the Spirit with the work of creation (Gn. 1:2; Jb. 26:13; Pss. 33:6; 104:30). In Ps. 139:7 *rûaḥ* denotes the cosmic presence of God.

Probably most important of all from a Christian perspective is the growing tendency in prophetic circles to understand the *rûaḥ* of God in eschatological terms, as the power of the End, the hallmark of the new age. The Spirit would effect a new creation (Is. 32:15; 44:3f.). The agents of eschatological salvation would be anointed with God's Spirit (Is. 42:1; 61:1; and later particularly *Psalms of Solomon* 17:42). Men would be created anew by the Spirit to enjoy a relationship with God much more vital and immediate (Ezk. 36:26f.; 37; *cf.* Je. 31:31–34), and the Spirit would be freely dispensed to all Israel (Ezk. 39:29; Joel 2:28f.; Zc. 12:10; *cf.* Nu. 11:29).

In the period between the Testaments the role attributed to the Spirit is greatly diminished. In Hellenistic Wisdom literature the Spirit is not given any prominence. In speaking about the divine/human relationship Wisdom is wholly dominant, so that 'spirit' is simply one way of defining Wisdom (Wisdom 1:6f.; 7:22–25; 9:17), with even prophecy ascribed to Wisdom rather than to the Spirit (Wisdom 7:27; Ecclus. 24:33). In Philo's attempt to merge Jewish theology and Gk. philosophy the Spirit is still the Spirit of prophecy, but his concept of prophecy is the more typically Gk. one of inspiration through ecstasy (*e.g.*, *Quis Rerum Divinarum Heres Sit* 265). Elsewhere in his speculation about creation the Spirit still has a place, but the dominant category of thought is the Stoic Logos (the divine reason immanent in the world and in men).

In the apocalyptic writings references to the human spirit outweigh those to the Spirit of God by nearly 3 : 1, and references to angelic and demonic spirits outweigh the latter by 6 : 1. In only a handful of passages is the Spirit spoken of as the agency of inspiration, but this is a role which is thought of as belonging to the past (*e.g.*, *1 Enoch* 91:1; *4 Ezra* 14:22; *Martyrdom of Isaiah* 5:14).

In rabbinic Judaism the Spirit is specifically (almost exclusively) the Spirit of prophecy. But here, even more emphatically, that role belongs to the past. With the rabbis the belief becomes very strong that Haggai, Zechariah and Malachi were the last of the prophets and that thereafter the Spirit had been withdrawn (*e.g.*, *Tosefta Sotah* 13:2; earlier expressions in Ps. 74:9; Zc. 13:2–6; 1 Macc. 4:46; 9:27; *2 Baruch* 85:1–3). Most striking is the way in which the Spirit to all intents and purposes is subordinated to the Torah (law). The Spirit inspired the Torah—a view of course also carried over into early Christianity (Mk. 12:36; Acts 1:16; 28:25; Heb. 3:7; 9:8; 10:15; 2 Pet. 1:21; *cf.* 2 Tim. 3:16). But for the rabbis this means that the law is now in effect the only voice of the Spirit, that the Spirit does not speak apart from the law. 'Where there are no prophets there is obviously no Holy Spirit' (*TDNT* 6, p. 382). Likewise in the rabbinic hope for the age to come Torah fills a far more prominent role than Spirit. This diminished role for the Spirit is reflected too in the Targums where other words denoting divine activity become more prominent (Memra, Shekinah); and in the Babylonian Talmud 'Shekinah' (glory) has more or less completely supplanted talk of the Spirit.

Only in the Dead Sea Scrolls does 'Spirit' come back into prominence in speaking of present experience (especially 1QS 3. 13–4. 26), reflecting a conviction of living in the last days not dissimilar to the eschatological consciousness of the first Christians.

III. The Spirit in the teaching of John the Baptist and ministry of Jesus

(1) *In early Judaism*, at the time of Jesus, God was tending to be thought of as more and more distant from man, the transcendent holy God, high and lifted up,

dwelling in unapproachable glory. Hence the hestitation even to speak the divine name and the increasing talk of intermediary figures, the name, angels, the glory, wisdom, *etc.*, these all being ways of speaking about God's activity in the world without compromising his transcendence. In early days the Spirit had been one of the chief ways of speaking about the presence of God (note, *e.g.*, the implication of 1 Sa. 16:13f. and 18:12, and of Is. 63:11f., that the Spirit of the Lord is the presence of the Lord). But now that consciousness of divine presence was lacking too (with the exception of Qumran). The Spirit, understood principally as the Spirit of prophecy, had been active in the past (inspiring prophet and Torah) and would be poured out in the new age. But in the present, talk of the Spirit had become wholly subordinate to Wisdom and Logos and Torah, and in particular with the rabbis, Torah was becoming more and more the exclusive focus of religious life and authority.

In this context John the Baptist created considerable excitement. Not that he himself claimed to have the Spirit, but he was widely recognized to be a prophet (Mt. 11:9f.; Mk. 11:32) and so to be inspired by the Spirit of prophecy (*cf.* Lk. 1:15, 17). More striking was his message, for he proclaimed that the outpouring of the Spirit was imminent—the one who was coming would baptize in Spirit and fire (Mt. 3:11; Lk. 3:16; Mk. 1:8 and Jn. 1:33 omit the 'and fire'). This vigorous metaphor was probably drawn partly from the 'liquid' metaphors for the Spirit familiar in the OT (Is. 32:15; Ezk. 39:29; Joel 2:28; Zc. 12:10), and partly from his own characteristic rite of water baptism—his drenching with or immersion in water was a picture of an overwhelming experience of fiery Spirit. It would be an experience of judgment (note the emphasis of John's message in Mt. 3:7–12 and particularly on fire in 3:10–12), but not necessarily wholly destructive, the fire could purge as well as destroy (Mal. 3:2f.; 4:1). The Baptist here was probably thinking in terms of 'the Messianic woes', the period of suffering and tribulation which would introduce the age to come—'the birth pangs of the Messiah' (Dn. 7:19–22; 12:1; Zc. 14:12–15; *1 Enoch* 62:4; 100:1–3; *Sibylline Oracles* 3. 632–651). The idea of entry into the new age by immersion in a stream of fiery *rûaḥ* which would destroy the impenitent and purify the penitent was not a strange or surprising one for John to formulate in view of the parallels in Is. 4:4; 30:27f.; Dn. 7:10; 1QS 4. 21; 1QH 3. 29ff.; *4 Ezra* 13:10f.

(2) *Jesus* created an even bigger stir, for he claimed that the new age, the kingdom of God, was not merely imminent but was already effective through his ministry (Mt. 12:41f.; 13:16f.; Lk. 17:20f.). The presupposition of this was clearly that the eschatological Spirit, the power of the End, was already working through him in unique measure, as evidenced by his exorcisms and successful deliverance of Satan's victims (Mt. 12:24–32; Mk. 3:22–29), and by his proclamation of good news to the poor (Mt. 5:3–6 and 11:5, echoing Is. 61:1f.). The Evangelists of course were in no doubt that Jesus' whole ministry had been in the power of the Spirit from the beginning (Mt. 12:18; Lk. 4:14, 18; Jn. 3:34; also Acts 10:38). For Matthew and Luke this special working of the Spirit in and through Jesus dates from his conception (Mt. 1:18; Lk. 1:35), with his birth in Luke announced by an outburst of prophetic activity heralding the beginning of the end of the old age (Lk. 1:41, 67; 2:25–27, 36–38). But all four Evangelists agree that at Jordan Jesus experienced a special empowering for his ministry, an anointing which was also evidently bound up with his assurance of sonship (Mt. 3:16f.; Mk. 1:10f.; Lk. 3:22; Jn. 1:33f.), hence in the subsequent temptations he is enabled to maintain his assurance and to define what sonship involves, sustained by the same power (Mt. 4:1, 3f., 6f.; Mk. 1:12f.; Lk. 4:1, 3f., 9–12, 14).

Jesus' emphasis in his message was significantly different from that of the Baptist, not just in his proclamation of the kingdom as present, but in the character he ascribed to the present kingdom. He saw his ministry in terms more of blessing than of judgment. In particular, his reply to the Baptist's question in Mt. 11:4f. seems deliberately to highlight the promise of blessing in the passages he there echoes (Is. 29:18–20; 35:3–5; 61:1f.) and to ignore the warning of judgment which they also contained (*cf.* Lk. 4:18–20). On the other hand, when he looked towards the end of his earthly ministry he did evidently speak of his death in terms probably drawn from the Baptist's preaching (Lk. 12:49–50, baptism and fire), probably seeing his own death as a suffering of the Messianic woes predicted by John, as a draining of the cup of God's wrath (Mk. 10:38f.; 14:23f., 36). He also held out the promise of the Spirit to sustain his disciples when they experienced tribulation and trial in their turn (Mk. 13:11; more fully in Jn. 14:15–17, 26; 15:26f.; 16:7–15). Otherwise, however, 'the Holy Spirit' in Lk. 11:13 is almost certainly an alternative to the less explicit 'good things' (Mt. 7:11); and the repetition of the Baptist's promise in Acts 1:5 and 11:16 is probably intended by Luke as a word of the risen Jesus (*cf.* Lk. 24:49; perhaps also Mt. 28:19).

IV. The Spirit in Acts, Paul and John

The main NT writers agree on their understanding of the Spirit of God, albeit with differing emphases.

a. The gift of the Spirit marks the beginning of the Christian life

In Acts the outpouring of the Spirit at Pentecost is the time when the disciples first experienced 'the last days' for themselves (the free dispensing of the eschatological Spirit being the hallmark of the new age), the time when their 'fully Christian' faith began (Acts 11:17). So in Acts 2:38f. the promise of the gospel to the first enquirers centres on the Spirit, and in other evangelistic situations it is the reception of the Spirit which is evidently seen as the crucial factor manifesting the respondents' acceptance by God (8:14–17; 9:17; 10:44f.; 11:15–17; 18:25; 19:2, 6).

Similarly in Paul the gift of the Spirit is the beginning of Christian experience (Gal. 3:2f.), another way of describing the new relation of justification (1 Cor. 6:11; Gal. 3:14; so Tit. 3:7). Alternatively expressed, one cannot belong to Christ unless one has the Spirit of Christ (Rom. 8:9), one cannot be united with Christ except through the Spirit (1 Cor. 6:17), one cannot share Christ's sonship without sharing his Spirit (Rom. 8:14–17; Gal. 4:6f.), one cannot be a member of the body of Christ except by being baptized in the Spirit (1 Cor. 12:13).

Likewise in John the Spirit from above is the power effecting new birth (Jn. 3:3–8; 1 Jn. 3:9), for the Spirit is the life-giver (Jn. 6:63), like a river of living water flowing from the Christ bringing life to him who comes and believes (7:37–39; so 4:10, 14). In 20:22 the language deliberately echoes Gn. 2:7; the Spirit is the breath of the life of the new creation. And in 1 Jn. 3:24 and 4:13 the presence of the Spirit is one of the 'tests of life'.

It is important to realize that for the first Christians the Spirit was thought of in terms of divine power clearly manifest by its effects on the life of the recipient; the impact of the Spirit did not leave individual or onlooker in much doubt that a significant change had taken place in him by divine agency. Paul refers his readers back to their initial experience of the Spirit again and again. For some it had been an overwhelming experience of God's love (Rom. 5:5); for others of joy (1 Thes. 1:6); for others of illumination (2 Cor. 3:14–17), or of liberation (Rom. 8:2; 2 Cor. 3:17), or of moral transformation (1 Cor. 6:9–11), or of various spiritual gifts (1 Cor. 1:4–7; Gal. 3:5). In Acts the most regularly mentioned manifestation of the Spirit is inspired speech, speaking in tongues, prophecy and praise, and bold utterance of the word of God (Acts 2:4; 4:8, 31; 10:46; 13:9–11; 19:6). This is why possession of the Spirit as such can be singled out as the defining characteristic of the Christian (Rom. 8:9; 1 Jn. 3:24; 4:13), and why the question of Acts 19:2 could expect a straightforward answer (*cf.* Gal. 3:2). The Spirit as such might be invisible, but his presence was readily detectable (Jn. 3:8).

The gift of the Spirit was thus not simply a corollary or deduction drawn from baptism or laying on of hands but a vivid event for the first Christians. It is most probably to the impact of this experience that Paul refers directly in passages like 1 Cor. 6:11; 12:13; 2 Cor. 1:22; Eph. 1:13; also Tit. 3:5f., though many refer them to baptism. And although Rom. 6:3 and Gal. 3:27 ('baptized into Christ') are usually understood as references to the baptismal act, they could as readily be taken as an abbreviation of the fuller allusion to the experience of the Spirit, 'baptized in Spirit into Christ' (1 Cor. 12:13). Certainly according to Acts the first Christians adapted their embryonic ritual in accordance with the Spirit rather than vice versa (Acts 8:12–17; 10:44–48; 11:15–18; 18:25–19:6). And though Jn. 3:5 probably links baptism ('water') and the gift of the Spirit closely together in the birth from above, the two are not to be identified (*cf.* 1:33) and birth by the Spirit is clearly the primary thought (3:6–8).

Acts, Paul and John know of many experiences of the Spirit, but they know of no distinctively second or third experience of the Spirit. So far as Luke is concerned Pentecost was not a second experience of the Spirit for the disciples, but their baptism in Spirit into the new age (Acts 1:5 and above, **III**), the birth of the church and its mission. Attempts to harmonize Jn. 20:22 with Acts 2 at a straightforwardly historical level may be misguided, since John's purpose may be more theological than historical at this point, that is, to emphasize the *theological* unity of Jesus' death, resurrection and ascension with the gift of the Spirit and mission (Pentecost, Jn. 20:21–23; *cf.* 19:30, literally, 'he bowed his head and handed over the spirit/Spirit'). Similarly in Acts 8, since Luke does not conceive of the coming of the Spirit in a silent or invisible manner, the gift of the Spirit in 8:17 is for him the initial reception of the Spirit (8:16, 'they had only been baptized in the name of the Lord Jesus'). Luke seems to suggest that their earlier faith fell short of commitment to Christ or trust in God (8:12—'they believed Philip'—as a description of conversion it would be without parallel in Acts).

b. The Spirit as the power of the new life

According to Paul the gift of the Spirit is also a beginning that looks to final fulfilment (Gal. 3:3; Phil. 1:6), the beginning and first instalment of a life-long process of transformation into the image of Christ which only achieves its end in the resurrection of the body (2 Cor. 1:22; 3:18; 4:16–5:5; Eph. 1:13f.; 2 Thes. 2:13; also 1 Pet. 1:2). The Spirit is the 'first fruits' of the harvest of resurrection, whereby God begins to exercise his claim over the whole man (Rom. 8:11, 23; 1 Cor. 3:16; 6:19; 15:45–48; Gal. 5:16–23).

Life for the believer is therefore qualitatively different from what it was prior to faith. His daily living becomes his means of responding to the Spirit's claim, enabled by the Spirit's power (Rom. 8:4–6, 14; Gal. 5:16, 18, 25; 6:8). This was the decisive difference between Christianity and rabbinic Judaism for Paul. The Jew lived by law, the deposit of the Spirit's revelatory work in past generations, an attitude which led inevitably to inflexibility and casuistry, since revelation from the past is not always immediately appropriate to the needs of the present. But the Spirit brought an immediacy of personal relationship with God, which fulfilled the ancient hope of Jeremiah (31:31–34) and which made worship and obedience something much more free, vital and spontaneous (Rom. 2:28f.; 7:6; 8:2–4; 12:2; 2 Cor. 3:3, 6–8, 14–18; Eph. 2:18; Phil. 3:3).

At the same time, because the Spirit is only a *beginning* of final salvation in this life, there can be no final fulfilment of his work in the believer so long as this life lasts. The man of the Spirit is no longer dependent on this world and its standards for his meaning and satisfaction, but he is still a man of human appetites and frailty and part of human society. Consequently to have the Spirit is to experience tension and conflict between the old life and the new, between flesh and Spirit (Rom. 7:14–25; 8:10, 12f.; Gal. 5:16f.; *cf.* Heb. 10:29). To those who saw the characteristic life of the Spirit in terms of visions, revelations and the like, Paul replied that grace comes to its full expression only in and through weakness (2 Cor. 12:1–10; *cf.* Rom. 8:26f.).

Luke and John say little of other aspects of the ongoing life of the Spirit (*cf.* Acts 9:31; 13:52), but focus attention particularly on the life of the Spirit as directed towards mission (Acts 7:51; 8:29, 39; 10:17–19; 11:12; 13:2, 4; 15:28; 16:6f.; 19:21; Jn. 16:8–11; 20:21-23). The Spirit is that power which bears witness to Christ (Jn. 15:26; Acts 1:8; 5:32; 1 Jn. 5:6–8; also Heb. 2:4; 1 Pet. 1:12; Rev. 19:10).

c. The Spirit of community and of Christ

A distinguishing feature of the Spirit of the new age is that he is experienced by all and works through all, not just the one or two (*e.g.*, Acts 2:17f.; Rom. 8:9; 1 Cor. 12:7, 11; Heb. 6:4; 1 Jn. 2:20). In Paul's teaching it is only this common participation (*koinōnia*) in the one Spirit that makes a group of diverse individuals one body (1 Cor. 12:13; 2 Cor. 13:14; Eph. 4:3f.; Phil. 2:1). And it is only as each lets the Spirit come to expression in word and deed as a member of the body that the body grows towards the maturity of Christ (1 Cor. 12:12–26; Eph. 4:3–16). This is why Paul both encourages a full range and free expression of the Spirit's gifts (Rom. 12:3–8; 1 Cor. 12:4–11, 27–31; Eph. 5:18f.; 1 Thes. 5:19f.; *cf.* Eph. 4:30) and insists that the community test every word and deed which claims the authority of the Spirit by the measure of Christ and the love he embodied (1 Cor. 2:12–16; 13; 14:29; 1 Thes. 5:19–22; *cf.* 1 Jn. 4:1–3).

The same twin emphasis on a worship which is determined by immediate dependence on the Spirit (rather than in terms of sacred place or sanctuary) and in accordance with the truth of Christ is present in Jn. 21:24 (*cf.* Rev. 19:10). Similarly John emphasizes that the believer may expect an immediacy of teaching by the Spirit, the Counsellor (Jn. 14:26; 16:12f.; 1 Jn. 2:27); but also that the new revelation will be in continuity with the old, a reproclaiming, reinterpretation of the truth of Christ (Jn. 14:26; 16:13–15; 1 Jn. 2:24).

It is this tie-in with Christ which finally distinguishes the Christian understanding of the Spirit from the earlier, less well-defined conception. The Spirit is now definitively the Spirit of Christ (Acts 16:7; Rom. 8:9; Gal. 4:6; Phil. 1:19; also 1 Pet. 1:11; *cf.* Jn. 7:38; 19:30; 20:22; Acts 2:33; Heb. 9:14; Rev. 3:1; 5:6), the other Counsellor who has taken over Jesus' role on earth (Jn. 14:16; *cf.* 1 Jn. 2:1). This means that Jesus is now present to the believer only in and through the Spirit (Jn. 14:16–28; 16:7; Rom. 8:9f.; 1 Cor. 6:17; 15:45; Eph. 3:16f.; *cf.* Rom. 1:4; 1 Tim. 3:16; 1 Pet. 3:18; Rev. 2–3), and that the mark of the Spirit is both the recognition of Jesus' present status (1 Cor. 12:3; 1 Jn. 5:6–12) and the reproduction of the character of his sonship and resurrection life in the believer (Rom. 8:11, 14–16, 23; 1 Cor. 15:45–49; 2 Cor. 3:18; Gal. 4:6f.; 1 Jn. 3:2).

The roots of subsequent Trinitarian theology are perhaps evident in Paul's recognition that the believer experiences through the Spirit a twofold relation, to God as Father (Rom. 8:15f.; Gal. 4:6) and to Jesus as Lord (1 Cor. 12:3).

(*Counsellor, *Angels, *Baptism, *Body of Christ, *Conversion, *Demons, *Eschatology, *Exorcism, *Guidance, *Inspiration, *Life, *Power, *Prophecy, *Spiritual Gifts, *Trinity, *Wind.)

Bibliography. H. Berkhof, *The Doctrine of the Holy Spirit*, 1965; F. D. Bruner, *A Theology of the Holy Spirit*, 1970; J. D. G. Dunn, *Baptism in the Holy Spirit*, 1970; *idem, Jesus and the Spirit*, 1975; *idem*, 'Spirit, Holy Spirit', *NIDNTT* 3, pp. 689–709; M. Green, *I Believe in the Holy Spirit*, 1975; G. S. Hendry, *The Holy Spirit in Christian Theology*, 1965; J. H. E. Hull, *The Holy Spirit in the Acts of the Apostles*, 1967; M. E. Isaacs, *The Concept of Spirit*, 1976; G. W. H. Lampe, 'Holy Spirit', *IDB*, 2, pp. 626–638; K. McDonnell (ed.), *The Holy Spirit and Power*, 1975; G. T. Montague, *The Holy Spirit: Growth of a Biblical Tradition*, 1976; D. Moody, *Spirit of the Living God*, 1968; E. Schweizer *et al.*, *TDNT* 6, pp. 332–451; T. S. Smail, *Reflected Glory: The Spirit in Christ and Christians*, 1975; A. M. Stibbs and J. I. Packer, *The Spirit within You*, 1967; L. J. Suenens, *A New Pentecost?*, 1975; J. V. Taylor, *The Go-Between God*, 1972. *On (human) spirit see:* H. W. Robinson, *The Christian Doctrine of Man*, 1926; W. D. Stacey, *The Pauline View of Man*, 1956.

J.D.G.D.

SPIRITS IN PRISON. The single explicit reference is 1 Pet. 3:19, with a possible hint at 4:6. The patristic exegesis of 3:19f. regarded the 'disobedient' of Noah's day as typical of sinners who before the incarnation had no chance of hearing the gospel and repenting. The interval between the death and resurrection of Jesus came later to be understood, especially in the Eastern church, as the occasion when Christ, by his *descent into their 'prison', offered these spirits life. Another suggestion for the meaning of this phrase (Reicke, Dalton) links it with the proclamation of Christ's victory after his passion (with or without the offer of life) to the *angels* who fell (*cf.* 2 Pet. 2:4f.; Jude 6; note also the possible influence of *1 Enoch*). This is supported by the unqualified use of *pneumata* ('spirits'), which is used elsewhere in the Bible only of supernatural beings, never of departed humans.

Bibliography. Bo Reicke, *The Disobedient Spirits and Christian Baptism*, 1946; E. G. Selwyn, *The First Epistle of St Peter*, 1946, pp. 314–362; W. J. Dalton, *Christ's Proclamation to the Spirits*, 1965.

S.S.S.

SPIRITUAL GIFTS.

I. Name and nature

The term 'spiritual gifts' represents the common rendering in Eng. of the Gk. neuter plural noun *charismata*, formed from *charizesthai* (to show favour, give freely), which is related to the noun *charis* (grace); they are the concrete expression of *charis*, grace coming to visible effect in word or deed. The singular form is used of God's gift of salvation through Christ (Rom. 5:15f.; 6:23) and of any special grace or mercy (Rom. 1:11; 1 Cor. 1:7; 7:7; 2 Cor. 1:11). The plural form is used chiefly in a technical sense to denote the extraordinary gifts of the Holy Spirit bestowed on Christians for special service, and in a few instances the singular form is similarly employed in a distributive or semi-collective sense (1 Tim. 4:14; 2 Tim. 1:6; 1 Pet. 4:10).

A general diffusion of the gifts of the Holy Spirit, marking the new dispensation, was foretold by the prophet Joel (2:28), and confirmed by the promises of Christ to his disciples (Mk. 13:11; Lk. 12:11f.; Jn. 14:12; Acts 1:8; *cf.* Mt. 10:1, 8 and parallels; Mk. 16:17f.). On the day of Pentecost these prophecies and promises were fulfilled (Acts 2:1–21, 33). Later, numerous spiritual gifts are frequently mentioned by Luke (Acts 3:6ff.; 5:12–16; 8:13, 18; 9:33–41; 10:45f., *etc.*), by Peter (1 Pet. 4:10), and by Paul (Rom. 12:6–8; 1 Cor. 12–14), who also describes them as 'spiritual things' (Gk. *pneumatika*, 1 Cor. 12:1; 14:1), and 'spirits', that is, different manifestations of the Spirit (Gk. *pneumata*, 1 Cor. 14:12). The gifts are distributed by the Holy Spirit according to his sovereign will (1 Cor. 12:11) and an individual believer may receive one or more of them (1 Cor. 12:8f.; 14:5, 13).

II. Purpose and duration

The purpose of these charismatic gifts is primarily the edification of the whole church (1 Cor. 12:4–7; 14:12), and, secondarily, the conviction and conversion of unbelievers (1 Cor. 14:21–25; *cf.* Rom. 15:18f.). A disputed question is whether they should be regarded as permanently bestowed on the church or only as a temporary endowment.

The once popular view that the *charismata* were given for the founding of the church and ceased during the 4th century when it

SPIRITUAL DEATH
See Death, Part 1.

became strong enough to continue without their assistance is contrary to historical evidence (B. B. Warfield, *Counterfeit Miracles*, 1972, pp. 6–21). Warfield himself held the view that the *charismata* were given for the authentication of the apostles as messengers of God, one of the signs of an apostle being the possession of those gifts and the power to confer them on other believers. The gifts gradually ceased with the death of those on whom the apostles had conferred them (*op. cit.*, pp. 3, 21ff.). W. H. Griffith Thomas saw the *charismata* as a testimony to Israel of the Messiahship of Jesus, becoming inoperative after the end of Acts when Israel had refused the gospel (*The Holy Spirit of God*, 1972, pp. 48f.; *cf.* O. P. Robertson, *WTJ* 38, 1975, pp. 43–53). Those holding these views naturally tend to deny the authenticity of subsequent allegedly charismatic manifestations.

On the other hand, strong evidence for the permanence of *charismata* in the church is found in 1 Cor. 13:8–12, where Paul envisages them as continuing to be manifest until the *parousia*. In that case their intermittent appearance in later history may have been affected by the fluctuating faith and spirituality of the church and by the sovereign purpose of the Spirit himself who distributes the gifts 'as he wills' (1 Cor. 12:11).

III. Individual gifts

The lists of *charismata* in the NT (Rom. 12:6–8; 1 Cor. 12:4–11, 28–30; *cf.* Eph. 4:7–12) are clearly incomplete. Various classifications of the gifts have been attempted, but they fall most simply into two main categories—those which qualify their possessors for the ministry of the word and those which equip them for practical service (*cf.* 1 Pet. 4:10f.).

a. Gifts of utterance

(i) * *Apostle* (Gk. *apostolos*, lit. 'one sent forth', envoy, missionary, 1 Cor. 12:28f.; *cf.* Eph. 4:11). The title of 'apostle' was originally given to the Twelve (Mt. 10:2; Lk. 6:13; Acts 1:25f.), but was later claimed by Paul (Rom. 1:1; 1 Cor. 9:1f., *etc.*), and applied in a less restricted sense to Barnabas (Acts 14:4, 14), Andronicus and Junias (or Junia) (Rom. 16:7), and possibly to Apollos (1 Cor. 4:6, 9), Silvanus and Timothy (1 Thes. 1:1; 2:6), and James the Lord's brother (1 Cor. 15:7; Gal. 1:19). The special function of an apostle was, as its meaning suggests, to proclaim the gospel to the unbelieving world (Gal. 2:7–9).

(ii) * *Prophecy* (Gk. *prophēteia*, Rom. 12:6; 1 Cor. 12:10, 28f.; *cf.* Eph. 4:11). The chief function of the NT prophet was to convey divine revelations of temporary significance which proclaimed to the church what it had to know and do in special circumstances. His message was one of edification, exhortation (Gk. *paraklēsis*) and consolation (1 Cor. 14:3; *cf.* Rom. 12:8), and included occasional authoritative declarations of God's will in particular cases (Acts 13:1f.), and rare predictions of future events (Acts 11:28; 21:10f.). His ministry was primarily directed to the church (1 Cor. 14:4, 22). Some prophets were itinerant (Acts 11:27f.; 21:10), but there were probably several attached to every church (Acts 13:1), as at Corinth, and a few of them are named (Acts 11:28; 13:1; 15:32; 21:9f.).

The ability to 'distinguish between spirits' (Gk. *diakriseis pneumatōn*, 1 Cor. 12:10; *cf.* 14:29) was complementary to that of prophecy, and enabled the hearers to judge claims to prophetic inspiration (1 Cor. 14:29) by interpreting or evaluating prophetic utterances (1 Cor. 2:12–16), thus recognizing successfully those of divine origin (1 Thes. 5:20f.; 1 Jn. 4.1–6), and distinguishing the genuine prophet from the false.

(iii) *Teaching* (Gk. *didaskalia*, Rom. 12:7; 1 Cor. 12:28f.; *cf.* Eph. 4:11). In contrast to the prophet, the teacher did not utter fresh revelations, but expounded and applied established Christian doctrine, and his ministry was probably confined to the local church (Acts 13:1; *cf.* Eph. 4:11). The 'utterance of knowledge' (Gk. *logos gnōseōs*, 1 Cor. 12:8), an inspired utterance containing or embodying knowledge, is related to teaching; but the 'utterance of wisdom' (Gk. *logos sophias*, 1 Cor. 12:8), expressing spiritual insight, may be related rather to the apostles and evangelists (*cf.* 1 Cor. 1:17–2:5, esp. 1:24–30), or to the prophets.

(iv) *Kinds of tongues* (Gk. *genē glōssōn*, 1 Cor. 12:10, 28ff.) and the *interpretation of* * *tongues* (Gk. *hermēneia glōssōn*, 1 Cor. 12:10, 30).

b. Gifts for practical service

(i) *Gifts of power*. **1.** Faith (Gk. *pistis*, 1 Cor. 12:9) is not saving faith, but a higher measure of faith by which special, wonderful deeds are accomplished (Mt. 18:19f.; 1 Cor. 13:2; Heb. 11:33–40). **2.** Gifts of healings (Gk. plural *charismata iamatōn*, 1 Cor. 12:9, 28, 30) are given to perform miracles of restoration to health (Acts 3:6; 5:15f.; 8:7; 19:12, *etc.*). **3.** Working of miracles (Gk. *energēmata dynameōn*, 1 Cor. 12:10, 28f.), lit. 'of powers'. This gift conferred the ability to perform other miracles of varied kinds (Mt. 11:20–23; Acts 9:36f.; 13:11; 20:9–12; Gal. 3:5; Heb. 6:5).

(ii) *Gifts of sympathy*. **1.** Helpers (Gk. *antilēmpseis*, lit. 'acts of helping', 1 Cor. 12:28) denotes the aid given to the weak by the strong (see LXX of Pss. 22:19; 89:19; the verb occurs in Acts 20:35), and refers to special gifts to care for the sick and needy. It probably includes **2.** the liberal almsgiver (Gk. *ho metadidous*, Rom. 12:8) and **3.** the one who performs works of mercy (Gk. *ho eleōn*, Rom. 12:8). **4.** The service (Gk. *diakonia*, Rom. 12:7; *cf.* Acts 6:1) of the deacon is doubtless in view (Phil. 1:1; 1 Tim. 3:1–13).

(iii) *Gifts of administration*. **1.** Administrators (Gk. *kybernēseis*, lit. 'acts of guidance, giving directions') enjoyed the gifts and authority to govern and direct the local church. **2.** The 'leader' (Rom. 12:8, NEB, Gk. *ho prohistamenos*) apparently shares the same gift (the Gk. word recurs in 1 Thes. 5:12; 1 Tim. 5:17), unless the term is to be translated (with RSV, Rom. 12:8), 'he who gives aid', in which case a gift of sympathy is indicated.

Some gifts, such as those of apostleship, prophecy and teaching, were exercised in regular ministry; other gifts like tongues and healing were manifested occasionally. In some instances the gifts appear to involve a release or enhancement of natural ability, for example, the gifts of teaching, helping or leadership; others are clearly a special endowment: faith, gifts of healing and the power to work miracles.

BIBLIOGRAPHY. A. Bittlinger, *Gifts and Graces*, 1967; *idem*, *Gifts and Ministries*, 1974; D. Bridge and D. Phypers, *Spiritual Gifts and the Church*, 1973; H. von Campenhausen, *Ecclesiastical Authority and Spiritual Power in the Church of the First Three Centuries*, 1969; H. Conzelmann, '*charisma*', *TDNT* 9, pp. 402–406; J. D. G. Dunn, *Jesus and the Spirit*, 1975; E. Schweizer, *Church Order in the New Testament*, 1961. W.G.P.

SPIRITUAL HOUSE
See House, Part 2.

SPITTING. From early times the Oriental gesture of spitting upon or in the face of a person conveyed deep enmity (Nu. 12:14). Christ submitted to this indignity as the suffering Servant (Is. 50:6; Mt. 26:67).

The Essenes punished spitting in their assembly with a 30-day penance (Jos., *BJ* 2. 147, and the Qumran *Manual of Discipline*, 7. 13).

'Saliva' (Gk. *ptysma*) was used by Christ to cure the blind (Mk. 8:23; Jn. 9:6) and a deaf mute (Mk. 7:33). It was probably placed in the mouth to facilitate speech in the latter case. Its use with clay in Jn. 9:6 was said by Irenaeus to be creative. The healing technique was common to both Jews and Greeks. Suetonius says Vespasian cured a blind man by spittle. The rabbis condemned its use when accompanied with incantations. The usage persisted with the word *ephphatha* in baptismal rites in Rome and Milan. See A. E. J. Rawlinson, *The Gospel according to St Mark*[5], 1942, p. 102. D.H.T.

SPOKESMAN. The *rhētōr* was a professional teacher of rhetoric, or, as Tertullus (Acts 24:1, AV 'orator') a speech-writer who might accept a barrister's brief himself. The extreme refinement of the rhetorical art, which formed the hallmark of higher education, and the difficulties of a hearing before a foreign court, made his services indispensable to the Jews. They were rewarded with a fine speech, notable for its ingratiating exordium. Paul, a master of the art himself, was able to reply in his own person. Elsewhere (1 Cor. 2:4) he disdained professional skill.

BIBLIOGRAPHY. G. A. Kennedy, *The Art of Rhetoric in the Roman World*, 1972. E.A.J.

STACHYS. A friend of Paul (Rom. 16:9) with an uncommon Gk. name (but see instances in Arndt). Lightfoot (*Philippians*, p. 174) finds one Stachys a *medicus* attached to the Imperial household near this time. (*AMPLIAS.) A.F.W.

STARS.

I. General use of the term

Stars (Heb. *kôkābîm*; Gk. (LXX, NT *asteres*) are nowhere in the Bible the subject of scientific curiosity. The term is used generally of any luminous non-terrestrial body, other than sun and moon. The great number of the stars is symbolic of God's prodigality (Ex. 32:13; Dt. 1:10; 10:22; 28:62; 1 Ch. 27:23; Ne. 9:23; Heb. 11:12). God promises Abram that his seed shall be numerous as the stars (Gn. 15:5; 22:17; 26:4). Pre-Christian astronomers (*e.g.* Hipparchus, 150 BC) mapped about 3,000 stars; not until the beginning of telescopic astronomy by Galileo in 1610 was it appreciated how many stars there were. This is, however, implied by the Bible references given above.

They are seen poetically as a majestic manifestation of God's 'otherness' in relation to men. He alone makes, controls, numbers them. Man's arrogant pride sometimes endeavours to usurp this authority (Gn. 1:16; Pss. 8:3; 136:9; 147:4; Am. 5:8; Jb. 9:7; Je. 31:35; Is. 14:13; Ob. 4; Na. 3:16; *cf.* Gn. 37:9). A constant temptation was to worship stellar deities; but the stars are insignificant compared with Yahweh himself (Dt. 4:19; Je. 7:18; Am. 5:26; Acts 7:43). He is at the zenith of the heavens (Jb. 22:12).

God's final acts of redemption and judgment are foreshadowed by astronomical signs. The prophets and our Lord foretell such signs; and in Revelation they are prominent (Is. 13:10; Ezk. 32:7; Dn. 8:10; Joel 2:10; 3:15; Mt. 24:29; Mk. 13:25; Lk. 21:25; Rev. 6:13; 8:10–12; 9:1).

The word 'star' is also used metaphorically without astronomical reference, usually to imply dignity, either innate or usurped (Jb. 38:7; Dn. 12:3; Rev. 1:16, 20; 2:1; 3:1; 12:1; 22:16).

II. Named constellations

A few constellations are mentioned in the Bible by name.

a. The Bear (AV 'Arcturus') (Jb. 9:9; 38:32). The prominent circumpolar constellation Ursa Major. Hence, 'with its children'—the seven main stars of the group. NEB renders 'Aldebaran'.

b. Mazzaroth (Jb. 38:32). Meaning obscure. Possibly the (twelve) zodiacal signs (so NEB), or the S ones only. (Aram. *Mazzaloth*, 'girdling stars', *i.e.* the Zodiacal circle.)

c. Orion (Jb. 9:9; 38:31; Am. 5:8). 'The Hunter'—an outstanding S constellation, containing the first magnitude stars Betelguese (top left, red) and Rigel (bottom right, blue). The range of colour and brightness of these and adjacent stars is an interesting illustration of 1 Cor. 15:41.

d. Pleiades (Jb. 9:9; 38:31; Am. 5:8). A compact cluster of seven faint stars in Taurus, constituting a connected system enveloped in nebulous material about 300 light-years from the sun. The expressions 'binding the chains' and 'loosing the cords' may refer to the supposed heralding of spring and autumn respectively by the Pleiades and Orion. An attractive but probably unacceptable alternative is that the 'binding' of the Pleiades by their mutual attraction, or (poetically) by the nebulosity surrounding them, is contrasted with the 'loosing' of Orion, the stars of which are physically unconnected, and associated for us only by our line of sight.

e. Chambers of the south (Jb. 9:9). Obscure; possibly the constellations which appear over the horizon as one travels S along the trade route to Arabia. NEB renders 'the circle of the southern stars'.

Particularly interesting is the NEB rendering of Jb. 9:12–15, with its twofold mention of the Dog-star and its description of dawn, 'when the light of the Dog-star is dimmed and the stars of the Navigator's Line go out one by one'—a rendering which makes sense of an otherwise unintelligible passage.

III. The star of Bethlehem

The star heralding the birth of Jesus is mentioned in Mt. 2 only, though seemingly foretold in Nu. 24:17; Is. 60:3. It has been explained in three ways.

a. It may have been Halley's Comet (11 BC) or another comet visible in 4 BC. This would have moved against the stars, and astrologers would have thought it significant. But would it have been visible long enough? And can the chronology be fitted in with the probable date of our Lord's birth?

b. It may have been a planetary conjunction. An interesting conjunction of Jupiter, Saturn and Venus took place early in 7 BC. Astrologers would certainly have noted this; but its duration would be brief, and such a phenomenon could not naturally be referred to as 'a star'.

c. It may have been a supernova. Novae occur regularly; a faint star becomes suddenly brighter, then slowly fades. Probably all stars do this at some stage of development.

SPORT
See Games, Part 1.

STADION
See Weights and measures, Part 3.

STAFF
See Rod, Part 3.

STAG
See Animals, Part 1.

STALL
See Manger, Part 2.

STAR OF JACOB
See Balaam, Part 1.

STATER
See Money, Part 2.

STATUE
See Art, Part 1.

STATUTE
See Decree, Part 1.

STEEL
See Mining, Part 2.

Supernovae, however, are very rare; there has not been one in our galaxy since telescopes were invented. Novae are not usually visible to the naked eye, but a supernova in our galaxy might temporarily dominate the night sky, and produce more light than all the other stars together. Novae and supernovae are entirely unpredictable. Chinese astronomers recorded a nova or supernova at about the right date to be 'the Magi's star'. The phrase *en tē anatolē*, 'at its rising' (Mt. 2:2), may possibly reflect the awe of the wise men at the first rising of this new star. Its position would convey to them an immediate astrological meaning. It is not unfitting that a billion times the light of the sun should be poured out to herald the birth of the Saviour of the world.

IV. Astronomy

There is no real 'astronomy' in the Bible and the scientific approach of, for example, the Babylonians, who by the 4th century BC could predict many astronomical events, is not found there. But a view of the universe is assumed which is not inconsistent with modern scientific cosmology. It is, of course, easy to find references to a primitive and unacceptable world-view comparable, for example, with the Babylonian creation myths. But to judge the Bible only by these is as uncritical as to judge our modern knowledge of the universe by our use of such terms as 'sunrise' and 'the canopy of heaven'. (*CREATION.)

We live in a gigantic star-system composed of perhaps a thousand million stars like the sun, arranged in a disc 60,000 light-years across. This is our 'universe'. But there are tens of millions of similar 'universes' or 'galaxies' visible up to a thousand million light-years away—the limit of present telescopes. Radio-astronomy presents a still more marvellous picture. The contrast between this cosmos and the three-decker universe of Semitic mythology is striking. The Bible is often closer to the former than the latter in spirit. For the universe of the biblical writers is rational, and of awe-inspiring immensity. Ps. 104, for example, speaks of a world which is completely rational, and depends entirely on God's laws; this is typical of the outlook of the biblical writers. In the promise to Abram, God couples the number of stars with the number of grains of sand. Only *c.* 3000 stars are visible to the naked eye, so on the face of it this is a feeble comparison. But the total number of stars in the galaxy *is* comparable with the number of grains of sand in all the world! The Bible is full of such implications of vastness quite beyond the knowledge of its day.

We assert, then, that the Bible consistently assumes a universe which is fully rational, and vast in size, in contrast to the typical contemporary world-view, in which the universe was not rational, and no larger than could actually be proved by the unaided senses. The books of I. Velikovsky (*Worlds in Collision*, 1950, *etc.*), though highly controversial, are written from a Jewish standpoint and are full of interest to the OT student who is also interested in astronomy.

BIBLIOGRAPHY. G. V. Schiaparelli, *Astronomy in the Old Testament*, 1905; O. Neugebauer, *The Exact Sciences in Antiquity*, 1958; E. A. Milne, *Modern Cosmology and the Christian Idea of God*, 1952; G. R. Driver and L. W. Clarke, 'Stars', *HDB*², 1963, pp. 936ff.; R. A. Rosenberg, 'The "Star of the Messiah" reconsidered', *Bib* 53, 1972, pp. 105ff.; W. Foerster, *TDNT* 1, pp. 503–505; D. A. Hagner, *NIDNTT* 3, pp. 734–736.

M.T.F.

STEPHANAS. A Corinthian, whose family, one of the few baptized by Paul himself (1 Cor. 1:16), was known for its exertions in voluntary Christian service; Paul, perhaps thinking of the Corinthian factions, bespeaks recognition of such leadership (1 Cor. 16:15ff.). The phrase 'the first converts of Achaia' (*cf.* Rom. 16:5) has been taken to indicate an Athenian origin (Acts 17:34), but it may rather indicate the first Christian *family* in the province, and thus the earnest of the church there (*cf.* Ramsay, *BRD*, pp. 385ff.). The link sometimes made with the apostolic ordination of their 'firstfruits' in *1 Clement* 42 is purely verbal.

Stephanas, with *Fortunatus and *Achaicus, delighted Paul with a visit at Ephesus (1 Cor. 16:17): no doubt they carried the Corinthians' letter and returned with 1 Cor. No connection with the 'household of *Chloe' is likely.

The name is a pet-form (from *Stephanēphoros*?). Two late MSS of Acts 16:27 identify him with the Philippian jailor. A.F.W.

STEPHEN (Gk. *stephanos*, 'crown'). Stephen was one of the seven men chosen by the disciples soon after the resurrection to look after the distribution of assistance to the widows of the church, so that the apostles themselves should be free for their spiritual tasks (Acts 6:1–6). All seven had Gk. names, which suggests that they were Hellenistic Jews (one of them indeed, Nicolas of Antioch, was a proselyte). Stephen is recorded as standing out from the others in faith, grace, spiritual power, and wisdom (6:5, 8, 10). He had time to do more than the special work assigned to him, for he was among those foremost in working miracles and preaching the gospel.

He soon fell foul of the Hellenistic synagogue, which brought him before the Sanhedrin on charges of blasphemy (6:9–14). Stephen, with angelic face, replied to the charges with a survey of the history of Israel and an attack upon the Jews for continuing in the tradition of their fathers and killing the Messiah (6:15–7:53). This brought upon him the fury of the council, and when he claimed to see Jesus standing at the right hand of God (probably as his advocate or witness in his defence) he was seized and stoned to death (7:54–60). He met his end courageously, as did his Master, on accusations by false witnesses of seeking to overthrow the Temple and law (*cf.* Mt. 26:59–61). He prayed as Jesus had done (Lk. 23:34) for his persecutors to be forgiven and committed his soul into Christ's keeping (*cf.* Lk. 23:46). Whether it was a legal execution or not, it seems that Pilate, who normally lived in Caesarea, turned a blind eye to it all.

There were striking consequences from Stephen's death. The persecution which followed (Acts 8:1) led to a more widespread preaching of the gospel (8:4; 11:19). Stephen's death was also undoubtedly a factor in bringing Saul of Tarsus to Christ (7:58; 8:1, 3; 22:20). But above all, Stephen's speech was the beginning of a theological revolution in the early church, as the principles of the universal mission were clearly stated for the first time. Luke records it at great length, and this surely indicates the importance he attached to it.

Stephen's theme in reviewing the history of Israel was that God's presence cannot be localized, and that the people have always re-

rebelled against the will of God. He showed first of all that Abraham lived a pilgrim life, not inheriting the land promised to him (7:2–8). Then he demonstrated how Joseph likewise left Canaan, sold by his brothers through jealousy (vv. 9–16). A long section deals with Moses, against whom Stephen was alleged to have spoken (vv. 17–43). Moses also was shown to have been rejected by his brethren when he came to deliver them. Yet God vindicated him by sending him back to Egypt to bring his people out. Again they turned aside to idolatry in the wilderness and refused to obey Moses. This idolatry continued until the Babylonian Exile owing to their desire to have visible gods.

The next section (vv. 44–50) deals with the tabernacle and the Temple. The tabernacle was mobile and went with God's people on their pilgrimage. The Temple was static and too easily gave rise to a localized view of God. But the Most High does not dwell in manufactured houses (*cf.* Mk. 14:58). The Jewish religion had become static and failed to move on towards the new Temple, the body of Christ.

The references to the tabernacle and the whole idea of the real but invisible Christian cultus is developed in the Epistle to the Hebrews, which has been seen to have close affinities with this speech. It is certain that Paul, too, worked out the principles stated by Christ and developed here by Stephen. When these principles were understood by the church there ensued a break with the old Temple worship (Acts 2:46). The Christians saw in practice that they were not just a sect of the old Israel. They were the new people of God, with the true temple, altar and sacrifice, living the truly pilgrim life, and rejected, as the prophets and as Jesus had been, by the Jews.

BIBLIOGRAPHY. M. Simon, *St Stephen and the Hellenists in the Primitive Church*, 1956; A. Cole, *The New Temple*, 1950; W. Manson, *The Epistle to the Hebrews*, 1951, pp. 25ff.; R. J. McKelvey, *The New Temple*, 1969; F. F. Bruce, *New Testament History*, 1969, pp. 206ff.

R.E.N.

STEPS (Heb. *ma‘alôṯ*, from *ma‘alâ*, 'a going up', 'ascent', *cf.* Lat. *gradus*; Gk. *bathmos*, 'a step' (so LXX), 'ascent'). That the shadow should go back ten steps was the sign by which the Lord confirmed to Hezekiah his recovery from mortal illness (2 Ki. 20:8–11; *cf.* Is. 38:8). Josephus (*Ant.* 10. 29) suggested that the stairs of the king's palace may have constituted a type of sun-dial, but for a detailed discussion of the whole incident and possible interpretations, see C. F. Keil, *The Books of the Kings*, 1854, pp. 463–465 and S. Iwry, 'The Qumrân Isaiah and the End of the Dial of Ahaz', *BASOR* 147, 1957.

The word is found also in the titles of Pss. 120–134, which in AV are called Songs of Degrees (RSV 'ascents') and said to have been sung by processions of pilgrims while ascending Mt Zion during the great Temple festivals (* PSALMS).

The term occurs once in the NT (1 Tim. 3:13), where the Gk. word denotes 'good standing'. According to Arndt, a technical term of the mysteries may be involved here, implying a 'step' in the soul's journey heavenward.

J.D.D.

STEWARD. In the OT a steward is a man who is 'over a house' (Gn. 43:19; 44:4; Is. 22:15, *etc.*). In the NT there are two words translated steward: *epitropos* (Mt. 20:8; Gal. 4:2), *i.e.* one to whose care or honour one has been entrusted, a curator, a guardian; and *oikonomos* (Lk. 16:2–3; 1 Cor. 4:1–2; Tit. 1:7; 1 Pet. 4:10), *i.e.* a manager, a superintendent—from *oikos* ('house') and *nemō* ('to dispense' or 'to manage'). The word is used to describe the function of delegated responsibility, as in the parables of the labourers, and the unjust steward.

More profoundly, it is used of the Christian's responsibility, delegated to him under 'Christ's kingly government of his own house'. All things are Christ's, and Christians are his executors or stewards. Christians are admitted to the responsibilities of Christ's overruling of his world; so that stewardship (*oikonomia*) can be referred to similarly as a dispensation (1 Cor. 9:17; Eph. 3:2; Col. 1:25).

C.H.D.

STOCKS (Heb. *mahpeḵeṯ*, 'pillory'; *saḏ*, 'fetters'; *ṣînōq*, 'a collar'). Referred to in later OT passages only, this instrument of punishment comprised two large pieces of wood into which were inserted the feet, and sometimes also the hands and neck, of the prisoner. The prophets Jeremiah (Je. 20:2–3; *cf.* 29:26) and Hanani (2 Ch. 16:10) were subjected to it, and Job uses the idea figuratively in mourning his affliction (Jb. 13:27; 33:11).

In the NT Gk. *xylon*, 'wood', is used in describing the Philippian incident when Paul and Silas were put in the stocks (Acts 16:24). (* PRISON.)

J.D.D.

STOICS. The Stoic school of philosophy derived its name from the Stoa Poikile, the portico in Athens where Zeno of Citium (335–263 BC) first taught its characteristic doctrines. His teaching was systematized and extended by Chrysippus (*c.* 280–207 BC), the 'second founder' of Stoicism. By the time when Paul encountered Stoics at Athens (Acts 17:18) their general attitude had been modified by elements taken from Platonism; of this more syncretist Stoicism Posidonius was a leading exponent.

Grappling with that same uncertainty of life which led the Epicureans to seek happiness in serene detachment, the Stoics sought salvation in aligning the will with the inherent Reason of the universe, * Logos. Man is happy when he does not want things to be any other than they are; let him, then, seek clear knowledge of the cycle of nature and cultivate a willing acceptance of it. Though a man must play his part willy-nilly in the outworking of universal Reason, for his own peace of mind it is essential that he do so consciously and willingly; he must seek out the things which befit his place in the natural order (*ta kathēkonta*) and pursue them not with desire, which might be disappointed, but with disinterested virtue. His fellow men he must serve not from love, which would make him suffer if service failed to help them, but from a pure recognition that the life of service is the 'natural' life for man. The universal Reason is God; traditional mythologies were given a symbolic interpretation in this sense.

All this seems very formal and austere, but individual Stoics, including the Roman emperor Marcus Aurelius, set a high standard of personal conduct. The form could, moreover, in part be adapted to receive a Christian content; much of Paul's language in the apologetic discourse on Mars' Hill

STOA
See Stoics, Part 3.

Stones were often used as weights, and sometimes inscribed with the appropriate measurement. These represent 8 shekels and nṣp *(a temple shekel, inscription not shown). From Lachish. Height 3·6 cm and 1·75 cm. 7th–6th cent.* BC. (BM)

(*AREOPAGUS) is drawn from that of Stoicism.

BIBLIOGRAPHY. H. von Arnim, *Stoicorum Veterum Fragmenta*, 1903–5; E. Bevan, *Stoics and Sceptics*, 1913; M. Pohlenz, *Paulus und die Stoa*, 1964. M.H.C.

STOMACH, BELLY. Principally, Heb. *beṭen* or *mēʿîm*; Gk. *koilia*. Indistinguishable from *bowels or *womb in OT and NT, these words being translated by 'stomach' or 'belly' generally when referring to eating, or wounding (Jdg. 3:21; Ezk. 3:3; Jon. 1:17; Lk. 15:16 [RSVmg.]; often translated 'body' in RSV [*e.g.* Nu. 5:21]).

Once in the NT the word *stomachos* is used (1 Tim. 5:23) of the stomach. In early Gk. usage it referred to an opening, or the *mouth (*stoma*), later the opening of the stomach, so having a more precise physiological reference than in the OT. B.O.B.

STOMACHER. The somewhat misleading AV translation of Heb. *p^{e}ṯîḡîl*, a word of uncertain meaning which occurs only in Is. 3:24 as an antithesis for 'a girding of sackcloth'. RSV 'a rich robe' seems to fit this requirement. J.D.D.

STONE. The chief biblical words are Heb. *'eḇen* and Gk. *lithos* and *akrogōniaios* ('cornerstone').

The common word 'stone' is used in the Bible with a variety of reference. Small stones made a convenient weapon (1 Sa. 17:40), were a means of attack and even execution (Nu. 35:17; *cf.* Jn. 8:59; Acts 7:58f.), formed a handy measure of weight (Lv. 19:36, where *'eḇen* is so translated), and were used, when sharpened, as knives (Ex. 4:25). Larger stones were used to cover wells (Gn. 29:2), to close the mouth of caves (Jos. 10:18) and of tombs (Mt. 27:60), to serve as a landmark (2 Sa. 20:8), as a memorial (Jos. 4:20ff.), and as a pillar or altar which had specifically religious associations (Gn. 28:18; Dt. 27:5). Stones were also, of course, a primary building material.

Figurative as well as literal uses of the term 'stone' occur in the Bible. Notably, the 'stone' image is used in the NT to describe the person of Jesus. In the Synoptic Gospels, for example, the parable of the vineyard (Mk. 12:1–11 and

Stone commemorative stele erected in honour of Adad-eṭir by his son Marduk-balaṭsu-iqbi, both of whom are depicted. Babylonian, Sippar. Height 40·64 cm. 9th cent. BC. (BM)

parallels) is followed by the Lord's citation of Ps. 118:22, which is obviously applied to himself ('The very stone which the builders rejected has become the head of the corner'). This provides us with an important clue to the self-understanding of Jesus. The meaning of 'head stone' (LXX, *eis kephalēn gōnias*) in this psalm is 'top stone' or 'coping stone', that is, the carefully chosen and perfectly made stone which completes a building (*cf.* Zc. 4:7). Probably the immediate reference here was to Israel herself, rejected by men but chosen by God. The real significance of the passage in its NT setting is made abundantly clear from Peter's quotation of Ps. 118:22, with reference to Jesus, during his speech before the Jewish court in Jerusalem (Acts 4:11). God has vindicated him whom the Jews cast out, and exalted him to the headship of the new Israel. In the *Epistle of Barnabas* (6:4) these words are quoted directly from the LXX (Ps. 118), and also applied to Christ.

The only OT occurrences of the phrase 'corner stone' are Jb. 38:6 (LXX *lithos gōniaios*) and Is. 28:16 (LXX *akrogōniaios*); and these are both figurative (*cf.* Ps. 144:12). But unlike 'head of the corner', the stone referred to here would seem to be part of the foundation of a building, and to bear its weight. This is evidently the meaning of *akrogōniaios* in 1 Pet. 2:6, where the writer quotes Is. 28:16 itself. Christ is now the corner-stone of the church, the location of which is the heavenly Zion (*cf.* Eph. 2:20, where the same Gk. word is used, and 1 Cor. 3:11). In v. 7 of the same passage, however, the writer goes on to quote the psalmic reference we have noted (118:22, echoed in v. 4), and he thus gives us the complementary truth that Christ is also the *head* of the church, exalted by God the Father to that position of vindication. In this exaltation, moreover, believers will share. The writer's use of *lithos* in v. 8 with reference to stumbling suggests a confusion of images; although it is possible, as J. Y. Campbell points out (*TWBR*, p. 53), that a stone at the corner of the foundation of a building might also form a stumbling-stone (*cf.* also Rom. 9:32f.). Christ is described in the same passage (v. 4) as a 'living stone' (*lithon zōnta*), alive and giving life to those who as believers are incorporated into him, and built up as *lithoi zōntes* into the spiritual building of his church for purposes of worship (v. 5) and witness (v. 9).

BIBLIOGRAPHY. J. R. Harris, *Testimonies*, 1, 1916, pp. 26–32; S. H. Hooke, 'The Corner-Stone of Scripture', *The Siege Perilous*, 1956, pp. 235–249; F. F. Bruce, 'The Corner Stone', *ExpT* 84, 1972–3, pp. 231–235; J. Jeremias in *TDNT* 4, pp. 268–280; W. Mundle *et al.*, *NIDNTT* 3, pp. 381–394. S.S.S.

STONING (Heb. *sāqal*, 'to stone', 'to be stoned'; Heb. *rāgam*, 'to collect or cast stones'; Gk. *katalithazō*, 'to stone (thoroughly)'; Gk. *lithazō*, 'to stone'; Gk. *lithoboleō*, 'to cast stones'). Stoning was the usual Heb. form of execution (Ex. 19:13; Lv. 20:27; Lk. 20:6; Acts 7:58, *etc.*). The prosecution witnesses (the law required at least two such) had to cast the first stone (Dt. 13:9f.; *cf.* Jn. 8:7), and afterwards if the victim still lived the spectators carried out the sentence, and the body was suspended until sunset (Dt. 21:23).

For an excellent summary of offences for which stoning was prescribed, and further details of the execution, see W. Corswant, *A Dictionary of Life in Bible Times*, E.T. 1960, p. 261. J.D.D.

STORE-CITIES. Towns (Heb. *'ᵃrê-miskᵉnôt*) where provisions, often revenue paid in kind (grain, oil, wine, *etc.*), and weapons were laid up in magazines or storehouses by the central government, for maintaining frontier and defence forces, and as reserve supplies, *etc.* The Hebrews had to labour on Pharaoh's store-cities Pithom and Ra'amses on the eve of the Exodus (Ex. 1:11). The Delta-residence Ra'amses (Egyp. *Pi-Ramessē*) was frequently boasted of in Egyp. texts as being in a region of plenty, with stores and treasuries abundantly filled (*ANET*, 1955, pp. 470–471; *JEA* 5, 1918, pp. 186f., 192, 194f.). Solomon had store-cities and depots in Israel and Hamath (1 Ki. 9:19; 2 Ch. 8:4–6). When summoned against Baasha of Israel by Asa of Judah, Ben-hadad I of Aram-Damascus smote stores in ('of') cities of Naphtali (2 Ch. 16:4). Jehoshaphat built store-cities in Judah (2 Ch. 17:12), and Hezekiah was proud of his well-filled storage-magazines for revenue in grain, wine and oil (2 Ch. 32:28). And likewise some of his contemporaries: Asitawanda king of Cilicia (*c.* 725 BC) 'filled the storehouses (or, depots) of (the city) Pa'ar' (*ANET*, p. 499; *cf.* Dupont-

STONEMASON
See Arts and crafts, Part 1.

STONE OF STUMBLING
See Stumbling-block, Part 3.

STONES, PRECIOUS
See Jewels, Part 2.

STOOL
See Health (Midwifery), Part 2.

STORAX
See Herbs, Part 2.

City storage-pit used for grain at Megiddo held c. 12,800 bushels. Depth 7 m, diameter at top 11 m. 780–650 BC. (OIUC)

View of a government storehouse excavated at Hazor. Built about the time of King Ahab (c. 850 BC). Goods were loaded and unloaded from pack animals in the central aisle, and stored in the chambers on either side. (YY)

STOREHOUSE
See Threshold, Part 3.

STORK
See Animals, Part 1.

STORM-GOD
See Hadad, Part 2.

STOVE
See Furnace, Part 1.

STRAIGHT STREET
See Damascus, Part 1.

STRAW
See Agriculture, Part 1.

STRING INSTRUMENTS
See Music, Part 2.

STRONG DRINK
See Wine, Part 3.

STUBBLE
See Agriculture, Part 1.

Sommer, *Oriens* 1, 1948, pp. 196–197). Remains, possibly those of government storehouses, have been excavated in Palestine. For remains at Beth-shemesh and Lachish, *cf.* Wright, *Biblical Archaeology*, 1957, p. 130. For Hazor and Samaria, *cf.* K. M. Kenyon, *Archaeology in the Holy Land*, 1960, pp. 271–272, 279, and Y. Yadin, *Hazor*, BM Exhibition Guide, 1958, p. 17 and fig. 30. K.A.K.

STORM. The more violent activities of nature are usually associated with rain- and hail-storms. Generally the incidence of violent rainstorms and cloud-bursts occurs at the commencement of the rainy season, or at the beginning of each renewed spell of rain during the cooler months. At Haifa, for example, on 9 December 1921, 28 cm fell in 24 hours. Thunder-storms are most frequent in Nov. and Dec. and occur most commonly in the Jordan Valley. Hail not infrequently accompanies thunder between Dec. and March. Scripture vividly describes its disastrous effects upon the growing crops (Ps. 78:47; Is. 28:2; Ezk. 13:13–14; Hg. 2:17). The wind-storms that sweep down upon the Sea of Galilee are vividly recorded in the events of Mk. 4:37ff., and perhaps in the parable of the badly founded house sited in some dried-up water-bed, when 'the rain fell, and the floods came, and the winds blew and beat against that house' (Mt. 7:27).

God spoke in the thunderstorm (Ex. 9:28; 19:16, 19; 1 Sa. 7:10; 12:18; Jb. 37:1–5; Pss. 18:13; 29:3–9; 104:7), as he judged in the earthquake (Je. 4:24–26; Na. 1:5). The Hebrews in conceiving how 'thy glory passed through the four gates of fire and earthquake and wind and ice' (2 Esdras 3:19) had to learn, however, that Yahweh was more revelatory to them in the Exodus than in storm and earthquake. This certainly was the experience of Elijah, who had the consciousness of 'the still small voice' as more expressive of the divine presence and power than earthquake, wind and fire (1 Ki. 19:11–13). (*EARTHQUAKE, *EUROCLYDON, *RAIN, *THUNDER, *WHIRLWIND, *WIND.) J.M.H.

STRANGLED (THINGS). Gk. *pnikta* (Acts 15:20, 29; 21:25) refers to animals killed without shedding their blood, to eat which was repugnant to Jews (*cf.* Lv. 17:13; Dt. 12:16, 23). For general principles involved, see *IDOLS, MEATS OFFERED TO. J.D.D.

STRIPES. The rendering of several Heb. and Gk. words, only one of which (Gk. *plēgē*) occurs more than twice. The Deuteronomic law limited to forty the number of blows which a judge could prescribe (Dt. 25:2–3). The punishment was generally carried out by a three-thonged scourge, and the executioner himself was punished if the stipulated number were exceeded. Thus, what Paul describes in his 'foolish boasting' (2 Cor. 11:24) was in fact the maximum penalty, for the forty strokes were in practice reduced by one on the principle of 'setting a hedge around the law'.

Stripes can be a symbol of salutary correction (Ps. 89:32; *cf.* Pr. 13:24) and a reminder of the Lord's sacrifice (Is. 53:5; 1 Pet. 2:24). (*SCOURGING.) J.D.D.

STUMBLING-BLOCK. In the OT the Heb. root *kāšal*, 'to stagger', 'to stumble', forms the basis of *mikšôl*, *makšēlâ*, 'that against which anyone stumbles' (Lv. 19:14). It is used figuratively of idols (Is. 57:14; Ezk. 7:19, 14:3–4; Zp. 1:3).

In the NT two Gk. words are used. *proskomma* (*tou lithou*), 'stone of stumbling' (Rom. 9:32–33; 14:13; 1 Cor. 8:9; 1 Pet. 2:8), is used of any form of barrier. *skandalon* (Rom. 11:9; 1 Cor. 1:23; Rev. 2:14), originally the trigger stick of a trap, is used in LXX to translate Heb. *mikšôl*, but also *môqēš*, 'a snare', 'a trap' (*cf.* Pss. 69:22; 140:5). *Cf.* also Mt. 16:23, 'you are a hindrance (*skandalon*; AV 'offence') to me'. See W. Barclay, *New Testament Wordbook*, 1955 (*s.v. skandalon, skandalizein*). J.B.Tr.

SUBURB. In AV and RV most commonly the equivalent of Heb. *migrāš*, more accurately rendered 'pasture lands' in RVmg. and 'common land' in RSV in Lv. 25:34. It is used specially, but not exclusively, with regard to the uncultivated land, suitable for the pasturing of cattle, surrounding the levitical cities; its alienation from levitical ownership was forbidden (Lv. 25:34, *etc.*).

In 2 Ki. 23:11, AV, the word 'suburbs' is the rendering of Heb. *parwārîm* (RV and RSV 'precincts'), a word of doubtful origin and meaning, but possibly derived, like 'Parbar' in 1 Ch. 26:18, from Old Persian *frabada*, 'forecourt'. F.F.B.

SUCCOTH. 1. First site on the journey of the Israelites during the Exodus, possibly equivalent to the Old Egyp. *ṯkw* (Pithom), which was in the E part of Wadi Tumilat (Ex. 12:37; 13:20; Nu. 33:5–6). This was the normal way in or out of Egypt for displaced persons. We find it mentioned in the Story of Sinuhe, in Papyrus Anastasi V and VI. (*ENCAMPMENT BY THE SEA, *PITHOM.)

2. City of the tribe of Gad (Jos. 13:27) in the Jordan Valley not far from a water passage (Jdg. 8:5, 16) and from Zarethan (1 Ki. 7:46). It is the modern Tell Akhsâs or Tell Dêr Allah.

The name Succoth is explained in Gn. 33:17, where it is connected with 'booths', since Jacob established himself there. C.D.W.

SUCCOTH-BENOTH. The name of an object made by Babylonians exiled in Samaria *c.* 722 BC and named among the pagan deities worshipped there (2 Ki. 17:30). The *MT sukkôṯ-bᵉnôṯ* implies an interpretation as 'booths of daughters' (*cf.* Gk. *sokchōthbenithei*). This has been explained either as places of prostitution or as shrines in which were carried images of female deities, *e.g.* Banitu (an epithet of the Babylonian goddess Ishtar).

The parallelism with Nergal of Cutha seems to require the name of a deity here also. Following Rawlinson, Zēr-bānīt (Zarpanitum) the consort of Marduk (* MERODACH) has been proposed, but this is very doubtful. D.J.W.

SUFFERING. In the Bible suffering is regarded as an intrusion into this created world. Creation was made good (Gn. 1:31). When sin entered, suffering also entered in the form of conflict, pain, corruption, drudgery and death (Gn. 3:15–19). In the new heaven and earth suffering has been finally abolished (Rev. 21:4; Is. 65:17ff.). The work of Christ is to deliver man from suffering, corruption and death (Rom. 8:21; 1 Cor. 15:26), as well as from sin (Mt. 1:21). Though Satan is regarded as having power to make men suffer (2 Cor. 12:7; Jb. 1:12; 2:6), they suffer only in the hand of God, and it is God who controls and sends suffering (Am. 3:6; Is. 45:7; Mt. 26:39; Acts 2:23).

The burden of suffering was always keenly felt by God's people (Gn. 47:9; 2 Sa. 14:14). Its presence often became a problem, since it was regarded as sent by God (Ps. 39:9), and thus had to be related to the fact of God's love and righteousness (Ps. 73). Therefore, in the midst of suffering, man was forced to decide how far he could live by faith, and resist the demand for a rational explanation. The problem was not so acute at times when the sense of solidarity within the community was strong, and the individual, as a responsible member of his tribe or family in all circumstances, was able to accept the judgment and suffering that fell on his people as his own responsibility (Jos. 7). But the problem became more urgent as the responsible relation of each individual to God was emphasized (Je. 31:29; Ezk. 18:2–4).

True faith, wrestling with the problem and burden of suffering, does not require an immediate and complete justification of God. It can wait in the darkness (Hab. 2:2–4).

It finds in the reality of God's presence and goodness a more decisive factor in the present situation than even the bitterness of pain (Ps. 73:21–23), and is willing to set against the distorted shape of things present the perfect new order of things in the kingdom of God, of which it has already received a foretaste (Ps. 73:24–26; Rom. 8:18; 2 Cor. 4:16–18). But the man of faith is not insensitive to the baffling nature of the problem. The book of Job shows him experiencing in an extreme degree the bitterness and perplexity of unexplained suffering, refusing to acquiesce in rational theories that make God's ways subject to simple human calculation, temporarily losing his balance, but able ultimately to recover, and finally, through an overwhelming vision of God himself, reaching a certainty in which he can triumph over all his difficulties even though he is not yet, and knows he never will be, able to provide a rational explanation for all circumstances in this life.

Though it is thus asserted that such solutions are inadequate when applied generally, yet sometimes definite understandable reasons are given for instances of suffering (*cf.* Ps. 37), and several lines of thought on the problem appear and converge. Suffering can be the harvest of sin (Ho. 8:7; Lk. 13:1–5; Gal. 6:8), both for the individual (Ps. 1) and for the community and nation (Am. 1–2). It can be regarded at times as a punishment administered by God, or a chastisement designed to correct the ways of his people (Pr. 3:12; Jdg. 2:22–3:6), or a means whereby men are tested or purified (Ps. 66:10; Jas. 1:3, 12; 1 Pet. 1:7; Rom. 5:3) or brought closer to God in a new relationship of dependence and fellowship (Ps. 119:67; Rom. 8:35–37). Thus suffering can be for good (Rom. 8:28f.), or it can have the opposite effect (Mt. 13:21).

In bearing their witness to the sufferings of the coming Messiah (1 Pet. 1:10–12) the OT writers are taught how God can give a new meaning to suffering. Their own experience of serving God in his redemptive purposes in Israel

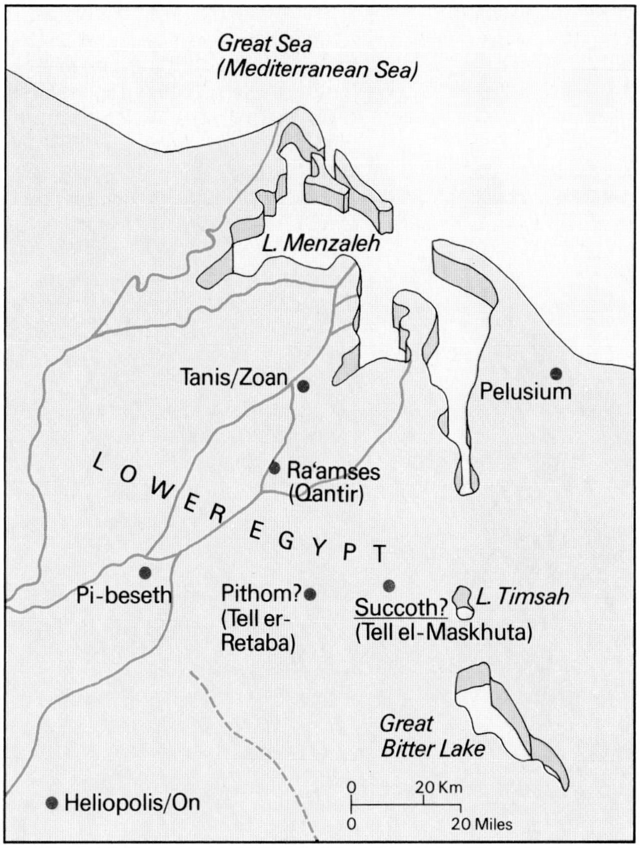

taught them that the love of God must involve itself in sharing the affliction and shame of, and in bearing reproach from, those he was seeking to redeem (Ho. 1–3; Je. 9:1–2; 20:7–10; Is. 63:9). Therefore his true Servant, who will perfectly fulfil his redeeming will, will be a *suffering Servant.* Such suffering will not simply arise as a result of faithfulness to God in pursuing his vocation, but will indeed constitute the very vocation he must fulfil (Is. 53). A new vicarious meaning and purpose is now seen in such unique suffering in which One can suffer in the place of, and as the inclusive representative of, all.

Suffering can have a new meaning for those who are members of the body of Christ. They can share in the sufferings of Christ (2 Cor. 1:5ff.; Mk. 10:39; Rom. 8:17), and regard themselves as pledged to a career or vocation of suffering (Phil. 1:29; 1 Pet. 4:1–2), since the members of the body must be conformed to the Head in this respect (Phil. 3:10; Rom. 8:29) as well as in respect of his glory. Whatever form the suffering of a Christian takes it can be regarded as a cross which may be taken up in following Christ in the way of his cross (Mt. 16:24; Rom. 8:28–29). Such suffering is indeed the inevitable way that

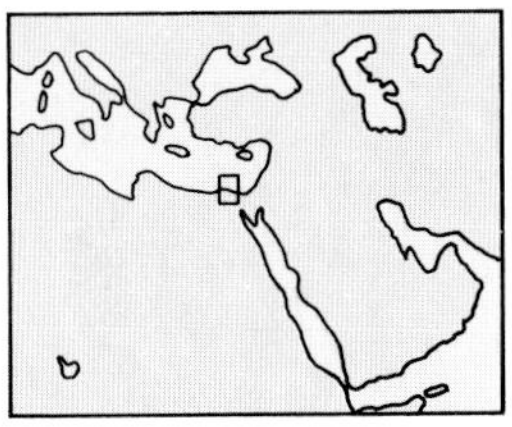

Possible location of Egyptian Succoth.

SUCKLING
See Nurse, Part 2.

leads to resurrection and glory (Rom. 8:18; Heb. 12:1–2; Mt. 5:10; 2 Cor. 4:17f.). It is by tribulation that men enter the kingdom of God (Acts 14:22; Jn. 16:21). The coming of the new age is preceded by birth pangs on earth, in which the church has its decisive share (Mt. 24:21–22; Rev. 12:1–2, 13–17; *cf.*, *e.g.*, Dn. 12:1; Mi. 4:9–10; 5:2–4). Since the sufferings of Christ are sufficient in themselves to set all men free (Is. 53:4–6; Heb. 10:14), it is entirely by grace, and not in any way by necessity, that the sufferings in which his people participate with him can be spoken of as filling up what is lacking in his affliction (Col. 1:24), and as giving fellowship in his vicarious and redemptive suffering.

BIBLIOGRAPHY. A. S. Peake, *The Problem of Suffering in the Old Testament*, 1904; S. R. Driver and G. B. Gray, *Job*, *ICC*, 1921; *ERE*; C. S. Lewis, *The Problem of Pain*, 1940; H. E. Hopkins, *The Mystery of Suffering*, 1959; W. Eichrodt, *Man in the Old Testament*, 1951; H. H. Rowley, *Submission in Suffering*, 1951; J. Scharbert and J. Schmidt, 'Suffering', in *EBT*, 3, 1970, pp. 890–897; J. Bowker, *The Problem of Suffering in the World Religions*, 1970; B. Gärtner, *NIDNTT* 3, pp. 719–726.

R.S.W.

SULPHUR
See Brimstone, Part 1.

Sumer, the S part of Babylonia.

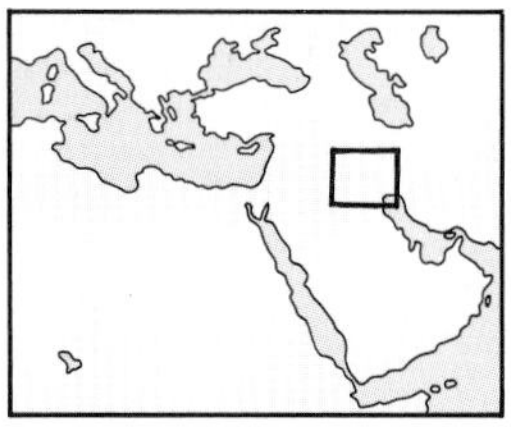

SUKKIIM (Egyp. *ṯktn*, *ṯk*). Libyan auxiliaries in the Egyp. army when *Shishak invaded Palestine (2 Ch. 12:3). They were employed as scouts from 13th to 12th centuries BC. See references in R. A. Caminos, *Late-Egyptian Miscellanies*, 1954, pp. 176–177, 180. K.A.K.

SUMER, SUMERIANS. The lower part of ancient Mesopotamia or S Iraq between the area of modern Baghdad and the Persian Gulf and S of the region was known as *Akkad. This flat area of *c.* 10,000 sq. m is traversed by the rivers *Tigris and *Euphrates. Although not directly referred to in OT it may be *Shinar (*šin'ar*; Sumerian *keñir* and *šumer*). The Sumerian civilization may lie behind the narratives of Gn. 1–11 (see **II**, below). The region was settled from *c.* 4500 BC by Sumerians until *c.* 1750 BC when they were finally absorbed by the Semites who inhabited the same area. The origin of the Sumerians is not known, though theories on this include migration from the E.

I. History

The history of the Sumerians falls into three periods: (*a*) Early Sumerian, 3000–2700 BC; (*b*) Classic Sumerian, 2700–2250 BC; (*c*) Neo-Sumerian, 2100–1960 BC. It is reconstructed in each of these respective periods chiefly from epic poems, scattered historic records and hundreds of thousands of business documents.

a. The first period was dominated by three major cities: Uruk, Aratta and Kish. The three leading figures, all rulers of Uruk, were Enmerkar, Lugalbanda and especially Gilgamesh, who is the most famous hero of all Sumerian history. Since the historical figures and events were recovered not from contemporaneous records but from later literary compositions, it is difficult to assign the events to a given archaeological level of any of the cities mentioned. Furthermore, very little of this period has been uncovered in either Kish or Uruk. The epoch is a shadowy one, from which come faint echoes of lusty deeds performed by a young and vigorous people.

b. The classic period centres chiefly on four cities: Ur, Kish, Umma and Lagash. The best-known rulers are Eannatum, Urukagina and Gudea of Lagash and Lugalzaggisi of Umma. By this time contemporaneous documents are extant bearing the names and recording some of the exploits of these rulers. We can therefore frequently identify many of the cities and even buildings to which reference is made in the documents. Rather more is known archaeologically than historically of Ur at this time. The names of the kings are known without reference to significant events. But the greatest treasure of all time from Mesopotamia belongs to this period—the fabulously rich 'royal tombs'. The first true historic document of any length also comes from this period and deals with strife between Umma and Lagash. Inscribed about 2400 BC at the time of Entemena of Lagash, it contains much economic and social data as well as history. But a later governor of Lagash, Gudea, is more widely known today, since scores of inscribed statues of him are extant, witnessing to the skill of sculpture in hard stone at this time. His inscriptions yield abundant data on economic and religious life. Lugalzaggisi, the last Sumerian king of the period, fell prey to the famous Semitic dynast Sargon of Agade.

c. Nearly 2 centuries later the Neo-Sumerian epoch with its capi-

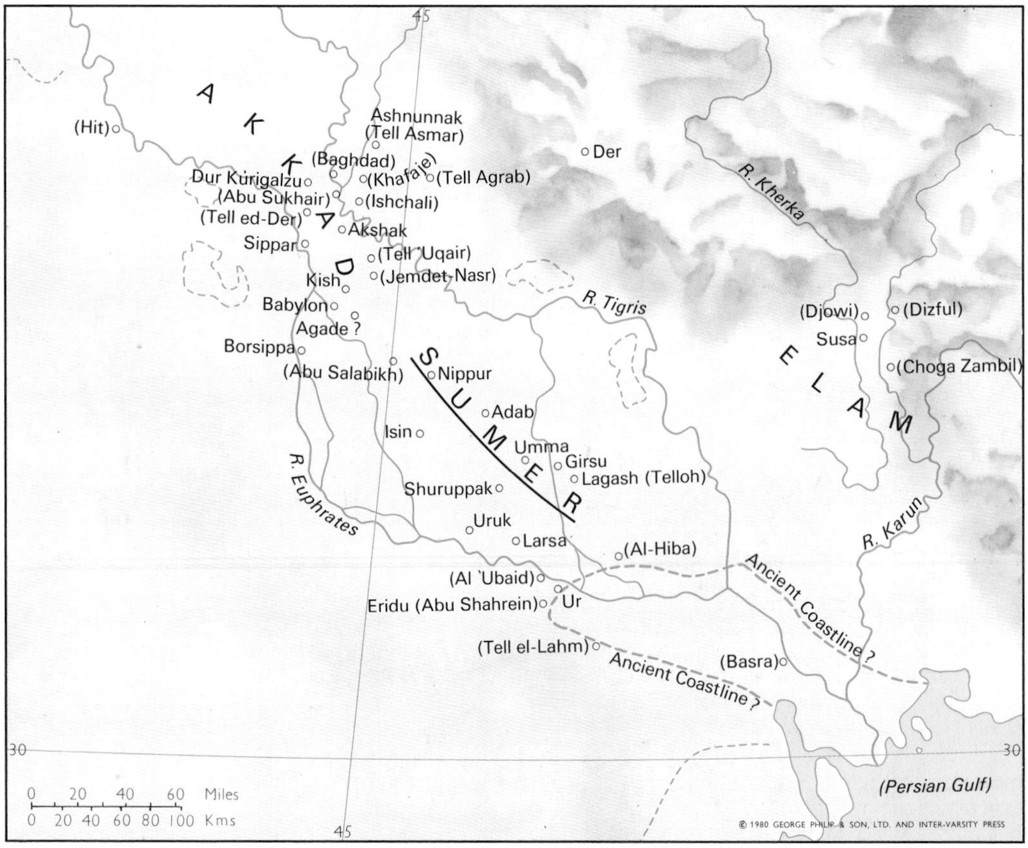

tal at Ur rose on the ruins of the Akkadian dynasty. But Sumerian blood had thinned drastically as a result of widespread immigration of other peoples, chiefly Amorites. Only the first two of Ur's five kings actually bore Sumerian names. Nevertheless, even after all Sumerians disappeared and the language was no longer spoken it was still the language of religion, science, business and law for many more centuries.

II. Literature

The invention of *writing *c.* 3200 BC, as known from texts at *Erech, is attributed to the Sumerians. The language, in several dialects including 'fine speech' (*eme.-sal*), is agglutinative in form and non-Semitic. It cannot be related reliably with any known language group, though it shares elements which feature in several. Originally developed for the purposes of recording legal transactions and economic and administrative texts which comprise 75% of all extant documents in Sumerian using the cuneiform script, it soon was employed for all types of literature as later known throughout the ancient Near East. The script and literary genres were adapted and developed by subsequent *Babylonians, *Assyrians, *Hittites, *Hurrians, *Canaanites and *Elamites.

Historiography includes building and votive inscriptions, military accounts of inter-state relations (Lagash–Umma; Stela of Vultures), king-lists, year formulae for dating, royal correspondence and significant detailed documents (Tummal) and poetic explanations of major events ('The Curse of Agade'). Epico-historic accounts of the exploits of *Sargon of Agade and Ur-Nammu and nine *Epic*-tales attest other forms of historiography. The latter reflect the relations of the city-states with their neighbours, *e.g.*, Enmerkar and Aratta, Lugalbanda with Enmerkar and Gilgamesh with Agga of Kish.

In Sumerian *myths* the heroes are deities and cover the themes of *creation ('Enlil and Ninlil: the birth of the Moon-god', 'The Creation of the Pick-axe', 'Enlil and Ninmah: the Creation of Man'); of civilization ('Enki and the World Order: the Organization of the earth and its Cultural Processes', 'Inanna and Enki: the transfer of the arts of Civilization from Eridu to Erech') and of a 'heroic age' ('Enlil and Ninhursag: the Sumerian Paradise Myth') as well as of man's failure ('Inanna and Shukalletuda: the Gardener's Mortal Sin'). The goddess Inanna (later *Ishtar) and Dummuzi (*Tammuz) play a leading role in myths about the descent of gods into the nether world. The *Flood, though known in Sumerian translation, may well be of Semitic literary origin (*cf.* Epic of Atrahasis). Similar themes occur in OT early historiography (Gn. 1–11).

The Sumerians also composed highly sophisticated *hymns* extolling gods, kings and temples and *lamentations* bewailing the destruction of city-states and cities (Ur, Nippur) or the death of the god Tammuz.

Other Sumerian genres comprise the beginning of the so-called

This statue of Gudea, ensi (*governor*) *of Lagash* (*modern Tell el-Hiba*), *is a fine example of the art of Sumer. Dolerite. Height 73·6 cm. c. 2143–2124* BC. (BM)

'wisdom' literature with collections of instructions, essays, fables, proverbs and riddles. All these gained a currency through their use in the educational system of schools where instruction covered writing, rhetoric, music and other forms, including examinations. The school 'contest' literature gives us the contrasts between the 'Summer and Winter', 'Pickaxe and Plough', *etc.* Other contests were used to describe the school system (*é.dub.ba*).

III. Culture

Originally Sumerian society appears to have grouped villages and towns around the larger cities into city-states controlled by a council of senators and young men of military status under the leadership of a 'lord' (*en*), later the *lugal*, 'chief man, king'. Alongside such institutions arose a bureaucracy of the temple and priests which also owned property and occasionally dominated this 'democratic' and highly organized society. Human government was thought to reflect on earth what happened in heaven. The king was but the vicegerent of the chief god of the city who both called him to office and required him to account for his stewardship in office as dispenser of law and justice. The king later ruled through provincial governors and through certain cities designated to control the economy in its relations with the surrounding nomads.

IV. Legacy

In addition to its literary heritage Sumer gave to later civilizations its concepts of law and government backed by a 'scientific technology'. The latter was based on empirical methods (data in lists) and practice. Astronomy and mathematics used both the decimal and sexagesimal systems, including the subdivision of time and area into degrees from which we derive our hours, minutes and linear measurements. The wheel was developed both for transport and for the *potter in his work. Architectural practices included the arch, vault, dome, niches, columns as well as the decorative techniques of stucco and inlay used on temple façades, the temple platform and the stepped pyramid (*ziggurat*). In art, the engraved stamp and cylinder *seal was closely associated with its long tradition of writing.

BIBLIOGRAPHY. S. N. Kramer, *The Sumerians: their history, culture and character*, 1963; T. Jacobsen, *Treasures of Darkness*, 1976; H. Ringgren, *Religions of the Ancient Near East*, 1975. For history see *CAH*^{3}, 1–2, pp. 190–195, and for texts *ANET*^{3}, 1969, pp. 37–39 (myths, epics), 159ff. (laws), 265ff. (historical texts), 455ff. (lamentations), 589ff. (proverbs), 575ff. (hymns).

F.R.S.
D.J.W.

SUMMON
See Call, Part 1.

The sun with its rays reaching to earth represents the sun-god Aton to whom King Akhenaton (c. 1363–1347 BC) and Queen Nefertiti make offerings. El-Amarna. Height 43·5 cm. (PAC)

SUN (Heb. *šemeš*; Gk. *hēlios*). In addition to many references which merely indicate the time of day, the Bible mentions natural effects of the sun, such as causing the fruits of the earth to grow (Dt. 33:14; 2 Sa. 23:4), withering growth that is insufficiently rooted (Mt. 13:6), producing physical injury (Ps. 121:6; Is. 49:10; Jon. 4:8; Rev. 7:16; 16:8, *etc.*), and inspiring the desire for life (Ec. 11:7). Such poetical allusions as 'a tabernacle for the sun' (Ps. 19:4) and the 'habitation'

The sun, the symbol of the god Shamash, portrayed on an Assyrian relief. Ashurnasirpal II stele, Nimrud. c. 876 BC. (DJW)

of the sun (Hab. 3:11) may have been suggested by the Heb. term for the setting sun, *bô'*, meaning literally 'to go in'. A parallel idea finds expression on certain Bab. seals, which represent the sun issuing from a gate. Sun-worship, which was expressly forbidden (Dt. 4:19; 17:3), assumed various forms in Judah (2 Ki. 23:11; Ezk. 8:16–17). Several passages indicate God's control of the sun (Jos. 10:12–14; 2 Ki. 20:8–11; Is. 38:7–8). Ahaz's sundial (2 Ki. 20:11; Is. 38:8) probably had the form of a stairway (* STEPS).

In the book of Psalms the sun is thrice mentioned as an emblem of constancy (Pss. 72:5, 17; 89:36) and God himself is said to be a sun (Ps. 84:11), implying that he is the source of spiritual light and gladness. The face of Jesus at the time of the transfiguration is compared to the shining sun (Mt. 17:2) and it appeared to John in Patmos 'like the sun shining in full strength' (Rev. 1:16). On the other hand the glory of God and of Christ is declared to be greater and more enduring than sunlight (Is. 24:23; 60:19; Acts 26:13; Rev. 21:23; 22:5). Malachi foretells that in the day of the Lord 'the sun of righteousness' shall rise with healing in its rays for them that fear God. In its context this implies that not only will the wicked be punished, but the justice of God will be vindicated and the desire for righteousness of person and environment fully met (Mal. 4:2). The Fathers understood the expression as referring to Christ, and the objection that *šemeš* is feminine cannot be pressed in view of its use in Ps. 84:11 (see above). Part of the imagery associated with 'the day of the Lord' in Scripture is an eclipse of the sun (Is. 13:10; Joel 2:10; 3:15; Am. 8:9; Mt. 24:29; Rev. 6:12), while a third of the sun ceases to function after the fourth trumpet sounds (Rev. 8:12).

W.J.C.

SUPERSCRIPTION (Lat. *superscriptio*, 'a writing on or above', = Gk. *epigraphē*, which it translates). The word is used on two occasions in the NT.

1. In Mt. 22:20 (Mk. 12:16; Lk. 20:24) it is used with the word *eikōn* to refer to the head of the emperor and accompanying inscription on the obverse of a silver *denarius* (* MONEY). The *denarius* then in circulation bore the *eikōn* of the head of Tiberius and the *epigraphē* TI. CAESAR DIVI AUG. F. AUGUSTUS ('Tiberius Caesar Augustus, son of the divine Augustus').

2. In Mk. 15:26 (Lk. 23:38) the superscription is the placard, consisting of a board smeared with white gypsum and bearing in black letters the name of a condemned criminal and the offence for which he was being executed. Hence Mt. 27:37 calls it an *aitia* (accusation): Jn. 19:19–20 uses the official Roman word *titulus*, calling it a *titlos*. This was usually hung about the criminal's neck on the way to execution, and subsequently affixed to the cross over his head. The superscription written by Pilate for Jesus in Hebrew, Greek and Latin was 'This is Jesus of Nazareth, the King of the Jews'.

D.H.W.

SUPH. In Dt. 1:1 this may be a place-name (so in RV, RSV, 'over against Suph') whose location is quite uncertain (*cf. GTT*, § 431, p. 255, n. 223). In rendering 'over against the Red Sea', AV understands Suph as standing for *yam-sûp̄*, referring to the Gulf of Aqabah, which is also possible (* RED SEA). In Nu. 21:14, Suph(ah), 'storm'(?), is perhaps an area in which Waheb is located, in the brief quotation from the *Book of the Wars of the Lord.* Its relation to Suph in Dt. 1:1 is uncertain. Musil suggested it might be Khirbet Sufah, some 6 km SSE of Madaba (*GTT*, § 441, pp. 261–262, n. 229 end). On Suph and Suphah, *cf.* also E. G. Kraeling, *JNES* 7, 1948, p. 201.

K.A.K.

SURETY. A surety is a person who undertakes responsibility for a debt, or the fulfilment of an engagement by another. The word is also used to describe a pledge deposited as a security against loss or damage. It means also 'certainty'. In the latter sense we find the word used in the AV of Gn. 15:13; 18:13; 26:9; Acts 12:11 (RSV translates variously: 'indeed', 'I am sure', *etc.*).

Scripture counsels extreme

SUN-DIAL
See Steps, Part 3.

SUPERNATURAL
See Magic, Part 2.

SUPPER
See Meals, Part 2.

SUPPER, LORD'S
See Lord's supper, Part 2.

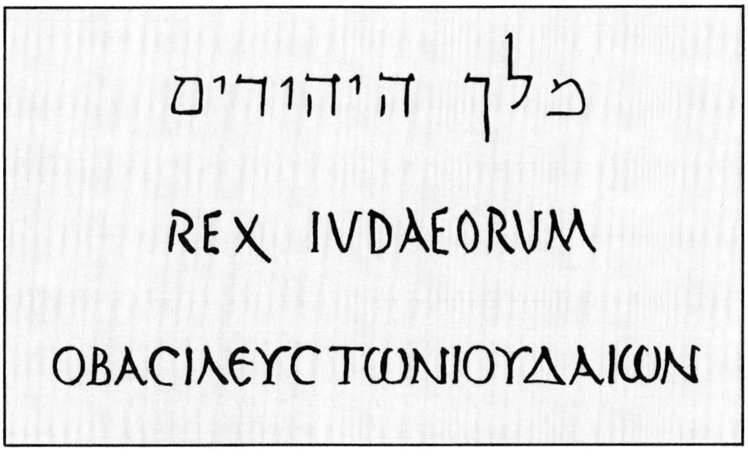

The superscription 'The King of the Jews', put on the cross, was written in Hebrew, Latin and Greek (Jn. 19:19–20). Here reproduced in letters of styles current in the 1st cent. AD. (ARM)

The superscription TI. CAESAR DIVI AUG. F. AUGUSTUS *on a silver* denarius *bearing the head of the Emperor Tiberius, similar to the coin used to test Christ (Mt. 22:17–21). Diameter 21·5 mm.* (RG)

caution in standing surety (Pr. 11:15; 17:18; 22:26–27). The phrase 'to strike hands' (AV) is equivalent to being surety (Pr. 6:1–2; 17:18).

Judah undertook to be a personal surety for Benjamin's safety (Gn. 43:9; 44:32). The giving of hostages (2 Ki. 18:23; Is. 36:8) is a similar idea. The word is used of our Lord (Heb. 7:22; *cf.* Ps. 119:122). M.R.G.

SUSA (AV Shushan), the ruins of which lie near the river Karun (*ULAI), SW Persia, was occupied almost continuously from prehistoric times until it was abandoned by the Seleucids. Here was the capital of *Elam, whose royal inscriptions of the 2nd millennium have been recovered. It maintained its importance under the Kassites and its independence until sacked in 645 BC by Ashurbanipal, who sent men of Susa (Susanchites) to exile in Samaria (Ezr. 4:9). Under the Achaemenids Susa flourished as one of the three royal cities (Dn. 8:2; Ne. 1:1). Darius I built his palace here, the ruins of which, restored by Artaxerxes I (Longimanus) and II (Mnemon), remain, with the Apadana, one of the outstanding Persian architectural features of the 5th century BC. This palace figures prominently in the book of *Esther (1:2, 5; 2:3; 3:15, *etc.*). (*AHASUERUS.) The site was first excavated by Loftus in 1851, and subsequently extensive operations have been undertaken there by the French.

BIBLIOGRAPHY. R. Ghirshman, *Iran*, 1963; E. M. Yamauchi, *Near East Archaeological Society Bulletin* 8, 1976, pp. 5–14.. D.J.W.

SYCHAR. The Samaritan town whence the woman came to fetch water from Jacob's well, where she met Jesus who taught her the nature of spiritual worship (Jn. 4). Sychar is commonly identified with Askar, a village 1 km N of Jacob's well, on the E slope of Mt Ebal. A.R.M.

SYENE (AV Sinim, Sinites). **1.** Heb. *sînîm.* A distant land from which the people will return (Is. 49:12), named with the N and W, so either in the far S or E (so LXX 'land of the Persians'). Scholars have looked for a connection with classical Sinae (China), but it is unlikely that Jews had settled in so distant a place by this period. Therefore Sin (Pelusium, Ezk. 30:15) or Sin in Sinai (Ex. 16:1) has been proposed. Most likely is identification with Syene of Ezk. 29:10; 30:6, on the far S border of Egypt. This is Egyp. *swn* 'market', Coptic *Suan*, modern *'Aswān.* A Jewish community living there in the 5th century BC has left us many Aram. papyri in which the place name is written *swn*, hence RV, RSV *Seveneh in Ezk. 29 and 30, better taken as 'to Seven'. 'From Migdol (AV, RV 'tower') to Syene' means from one

SUSIANS
See Dehavites, Part 1.

SWALLOW
See Animals, Part 1.

SWEET CANE
See Herbs, Part 2.

SWIFT
See Animals, Part 1.

SWINE
See Animals, Part 1.

SYCAMINE
See Trees (Poplar), Part 3.

SYCAMORE
See Trees (Sycomore), Part 3.

SYCHEM
See Shechem, Part 3.

SYCOMORE FIG
See Trees (Sycamine), Part 3.

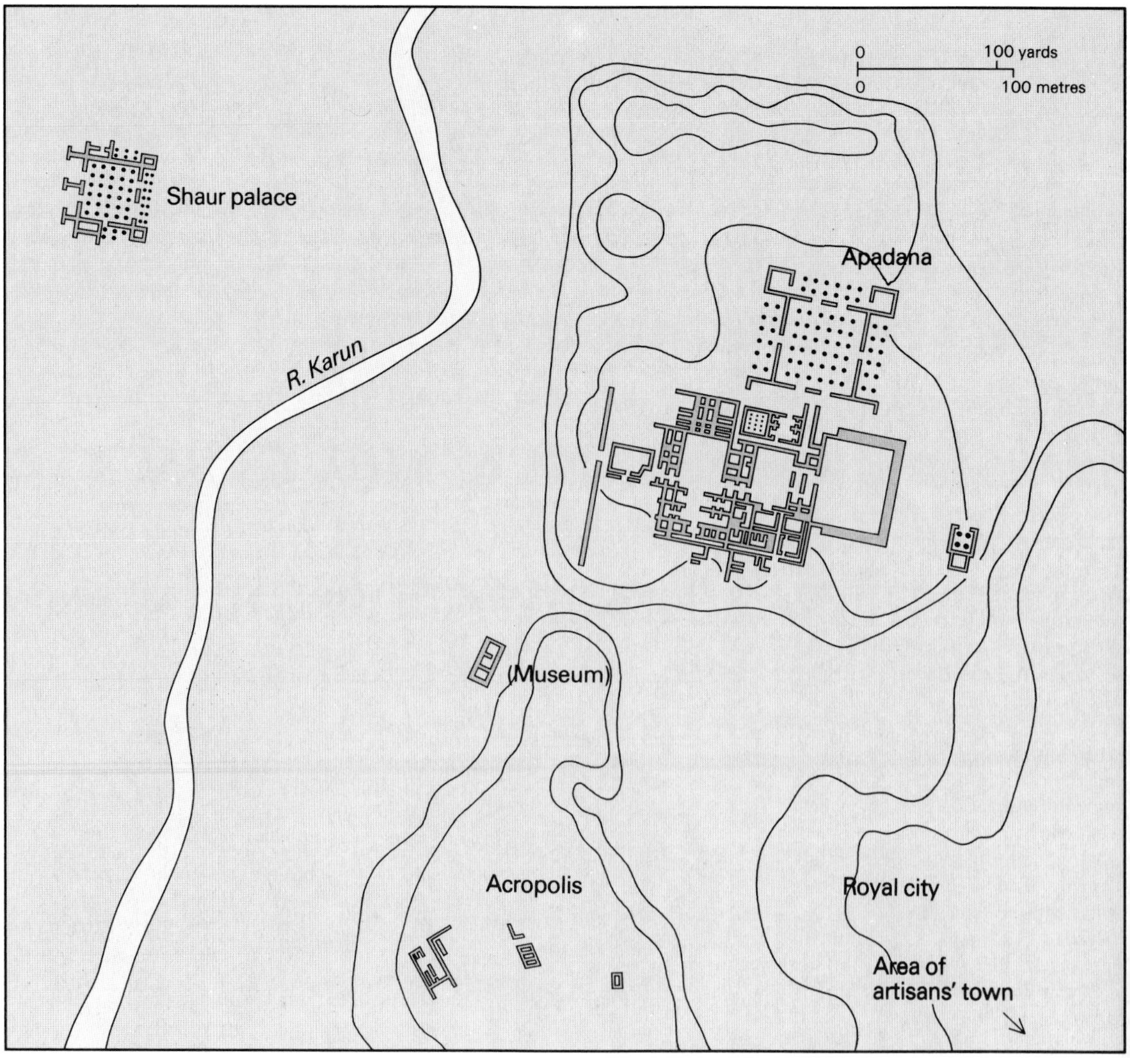

The site of Susa, Iran.

Enamelled bricks forming part of the wall of a palace staircase at Susa, built by Artaxerxes II, 404–358 BC. (MC)

end of Egypt to the other. Syene, on the first cataract of the Nile, was a fortress and base for expeditions into Nubia (Cush), a terminus for river traffic and a source of red granite for monumental buildings (syenite). The Qumran MS of Isaiah (1QIs[a]) suggests that 'Syenites' should replace *sînîm* (Is. 49:12); LXX has *Syene* for *Sin* in Ezk. 30:16.

2. Sinites (Heb. *sînî*) were a Canaanite people (Gn. 10:17; 1 Ch. 1:15), probably to be identified with a region, near Arqā, on the Lebanon coast, named in texts from * Mari and possibly * Ebla. The name survives in Nahr as-Sinn and is Ugaritic *syn*, Akkad. *siyanu*.

BIBLIOGRAPHY. E. G. Kraeling, *BA* 15, 1952, pp. 50–68; *The Brooklyn Museum Aramaic Papyri*, 1953, p. 21. D.J.W.

Bottom left: The modern well-head above 'Jacob's Well' at Sychar, near modern Nablus. (MEPhA)

SYMBOL. This word is not found in the Bible, but the use of symbols is common to all religions. The Gk. word *symbolon* had several uses, *e.g.* as a sign, pledge, token, and its importance derived from the fact that it was a representative object which guaranteed the reality of that which it symbolized. The *Concise Oxford Dictionary* defines a symbol as a 'thing regarded by general consent as naturally typifying or representing or recalling something (esp. an idea or quality) by possession of analogous qualities or by association in fact or thought'. This clear distinction between object and symbol is inevitable in analytical philosophy, but is not found in primitive thought. Malinowski emphasized that symbolism is founded, not in a relationship between an object and a sign, but in the influence that a sign or action has upon a receptive organism (*A Scientific Theory of Culture*, 1944). It is important to remember this when examining symbolism in the Bible.

View of the town-area excavations of Susa. Early 2nd millennium BC. (TCM)

Symbols of Assyrian gods: Shamash (sun with rays), Sin (the moon god, crescent moon), Sibitti (Pleiades, 7 dots), Nabu (wedge, stylus or astronomical sighting instrument), Marduk (spade), Adad (forked lightning), Enlil (divine horned head-dress) and Ashur (winged disc). The 'Joash' stele. Tell Rimah, Iraq. c. 796 BC. (BSAI)

I. In the Old Testament

a. Personal symbols

In early Israelite thought the clan or the family was the fundamental unit, not the individual. The life (*nep̄eš*) of the individuals made up the life of the group; the life of the group was extended through all the individuals. This psychological conception has been termed corporate personality (Wheeler Robinson) or group consciousness (Radcliffe Brown), and helps to explain how one person could symbolize a group of people (2 Sa. 18:3) or the presence of God (Ex. 7:1).

There is an expression, *'îš hā'ᵉlōhîm*, used more than 70 times and translated 'man of God', which could be translated 'divine man'. 27 times it refers to Elisha, and in the remaining instances to prophets such as Elijah and Samuel, or Moses and David. Elisha is credited with divine powers, such as restoring life (2 Ki. 4:35) and mind reading (2 Ki. 5:26). He stands in the place of God, does the works of God, and is the symbol of God's presence. Similarly, Moses was as God to Aaron (Ex. 4:15) and to pharaoh (Ex. 7:1), in word and deed (Ex. 14:16; 17:9). All the prophets spoke the word of God, and when the Israelites heard them they heard God himself; consequently, the person of the prophet was immune from harm. There is little evidence to show that the Israelite monarchy was regarded as divine, but it is possible that Solomon set himself up as a symbol of God.

b. Objective symbols

External objects were also used to symbolize the presence of God, in representative or conventional manner. The rainbow was accepted as the assurance that God's wrath had passed and that he would remember his covenant (Gn. 9:13). Moses made a bronze serpent, symbolizing the wisdom and healing power of God (Nu. 21:9); golden calves were made to symbolize the great power of God (Ex. 32 and 1 Ki. 12). More frequently objects were made without representing particular characteristics of God, one important example being the altar. The Heb. word *mizbēaḥ*, from the root *zbḥ* ('slaughter'), suggests the place where the animal was prepared for sacrifice. One should note, however, that in the earliest accounts the Patriarchs erected altars after an appearance by God, to mark the site and claim it for him for ever. In Israelite worship the altar symbolized the meeting-place of God with man, while the ark symbolized the presence of God because it contained the tablets of the Decalogue, and where the Word of the Lord was, there was the Lord himself.

When the Temple was built it symbolized the universal power of God. The Temple itself was a symbol of the earth, the brazen laver a symbol of the sea and the golden candlestick a symbol of the sun. It was necessary that a priest should be properly vested when he entered the tabernacle or Temple, and the vestments were clearly symbolic. They were made of linen (Ex. 28:39), which was regarded as having protective qualities (Lv. 6:8–12). Two reasons are possible. As the sacrifices were animal, the flax as vegetable conferred an immunity which would not have been found in woollen or leather garments. But it is more likely that, as in many folk stories, flax was regarded as the symbol of immortality or indestructibility. Jewish scholars have suggested symbolic meanings for the colours of the vestments, and for each separate item. The ephod and breastpiece symbolized the 12 tribes and judgment, and as the priest put them on they gave him power of judgment in the name of the Lord. His robe was decorated with pomegranates and bells—symbols of fertility and warnings to evil spirits. On his head was a mitre engraved with the words 'Holy to the Lord' (Ex. 28:36), which made the priest himself the extension of the presence of God—the divine symbol.

c. Acted symbols

These symbols were actions that were illustrative or purposive beyond their immediate context. They demonstrated or introduced new circumstances. They must be distinguished from magic, which was designed to compel a particular action from God. When an Israelite slave preferred to surrender himself to permanent slavery rather than accept his freedom, the owner pierced the slave's ear and fastened him to the doorpost to signify that the slave was from then on part of the household (Ex. 21:6). Other symbolic actions of a domestic nature were the surrender of a shoe to symbolize the surrender of all personal rights of inheritance (Ru. 4:7) and the cutting of hair to symbolize the offering of the mourner's life to a dead relative (Is. 22:12).

Among religious symbolic actions, *circumcision has always been a significant rite; originally connected with marriage, it was performed to avert the evil intentions of spirits that watch over the bridal chamber, but in Israel it was pushed back into childhood and then into infancy, and represents the dedication of the reproductive powers to divine guidance, and the incorporation of the child into the community.

The ceremony of the scapegoat by which the sins of the people were transferred to a goat on the Day of Atonement was a ritual of a type well known in many countries; it has been described as a clear instance of the principle of vicarious solidarity, here between priest, people and goat (C. Lattey, *VT* 1, 1951, p. 272).

Other instances of transference by symbolic action are the red heifer (Nu. 19), which transferred uncleanness, and anointing, which transferred spiritual power (*e.g.* 1 Sa. 16:13).

Special attention should be paid

to the importance of the symbolic actions of the prophets. These men not only proclaimed their message but performed actions to demonstrate what God would do, and thereby helped to bring about the result. They did not perform these actions to influence the will of God, but to prepare the way for that which he had decreed. Thus, Isaiah went about naked as a sign that God would bring poverty and exile upon Israel (Is. 20:2). Jeremiah buried a new girdle in damp earth and later dug it up, spoilt, to show how Israel, once so close to God, had now been rejected and would be despoiled (Je. 13). Ezekiel drew a city on a tile and set model siege-engines round it to demonstrate the destruction of Jerusalem which God had already decided (Ezk. 4:1–3). Other examples are in 1 Sa. 15:27; Je. 19:11; 28:11.

II. In the New Testament

Here the situation is quite different. There are no symbolic persons; Jesus Christ was not a symbol of God, for he *was* God, as he claimed in the words, 'I and my Father are one' (Jn. 10:30). Neither could one describe the disciples as symbols, because they were servants under discipline, not representatives.

But Jesus performed symbolic actions and approved them for the church. His healing miracles were not merely deeds of sympathy, but symbols or signs demonstrating the approach of the kingdom of God. Similarly, when he took the bread and the wine and gave them to the disciples, saying, 'Do this in remembrance of me', he was not simply exhorting them to good fellowship, but giving them a rite by which they could symbolize his presence eternally with his church. So the church has accepted the symbolism of the sacraments. In the bread and the wine the worshipper receives by faith the true body and blood of the Lord. In the waters of baptism sin is symbolically washed away and the person made a member of Christ's flock. In these actions the church symbolizes its faith; the *sacraments are not only illustrations but the appointed channels of divine grace.

In addition to the sacramental symbols, the church has used the symbol of the cross. This is a true symbol in that it is a pictorial representation of a historical fact, a visual summary of certain essential features of the Christian faith, and at the same time a means of grace to the worshipper. In the history of Christian art there have crystallized accepted pictorial symbols of the 12 apostles, *e.g.* the keys for St Peter and the symbols of the four Evangelists. At one time the fish was a popular symbol of the Christian faith as the letters of the Gk. word for fish, *ichthys*, formed the initials of words meaning 'Jesus Christ, son of God, Saviour'. The Christian church has never forbidden the use of symbols, because they are rooted in the nature and experience of man, but it has not encouraged them, lest in stressing the symbol the Christian should lose the Lord Jesus Christ himself.

BIBLIOGRAPHY. F. W. Dillistone, *Christianity and Symbolism*, 1955; G. Cope, *Symbolism in the Bible and the Church*, 1958; F. Herrmann, *Symbolik der Religionen* (vols. 3, 6, 7), 1960. A.A.J.

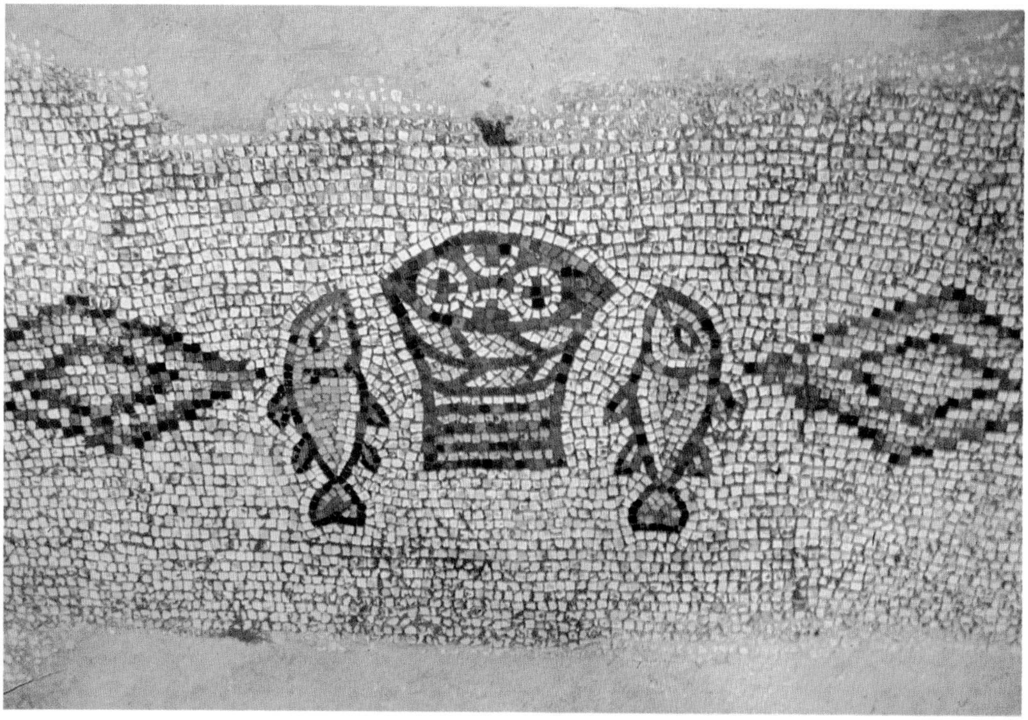

Two Christian symbols, the cross and the fish, depicted on a mosaic floor. The crosses are on loaves of bread in a basket. From the church at Tabgha in Galilee. 5th cent. AD. (MEPhA)

SYNAGOGUE. In the OT 'synagogue' occurs only in Ps. 74:8, AV (RSV 'meeting places'), where it is a translation of Heb. *mô'ēḏ*. It is not definite that the reference has its present connotation. The Gk. term *synagōgē* is used frequently in the LXX for the assembly of Israel, and occurs 56 times in the NT. The basic sense is a place of meeting, and thus it came to denote a Jewish place of worship. The Heb. equivalent of the Gk. noun is *kᵉnēseṯ*, a gathering of any persons or things for any purpose. In the Scriptures it is a gathering of individuals of a locality for worship or common action (Lk. 12:11; 21:12). It came to refer to the building in which such meetings were held.

I. Its significance

The importance of the synagogue for Judaism cannot be overestimated. More than any other institution it gave character to the Jewish faith. Here Judaism learnt its interpretation of the law. Ezk. 11:16, 'I have been a sanctuary to them for a while', was interpreted by Jewish authorities to mean that in world-wide dispersion Israel would have the synagogue as a sanctuary in miniature to replace the loss of the Temple. Unlike the Temple, it was located in all parts of the land, and put the people in touch with their religious leaders. A. Menes states: 'On the Sabbaths and holy days the loss of the Temple and the absence of the solemn sacrificial celebrations were keenly felt by the exiles . . . the synagogue . . . served as a substitute for the Temple. In the synagogue there was no altar, and prayer and the reading of the Torah took the place of the sacrifice. In addition the prayer house performed an important social function . . . it was a gathering point and a meeting place where the people could congregate whenever it was necessary to take counsel over important community affairs. The synagogue became the cradle of an entirely new type of social

The synagogue at Masada, built by the Zealots c. AD 70, had benches around the walls and a roof supported by two rows of columns. (JPK)

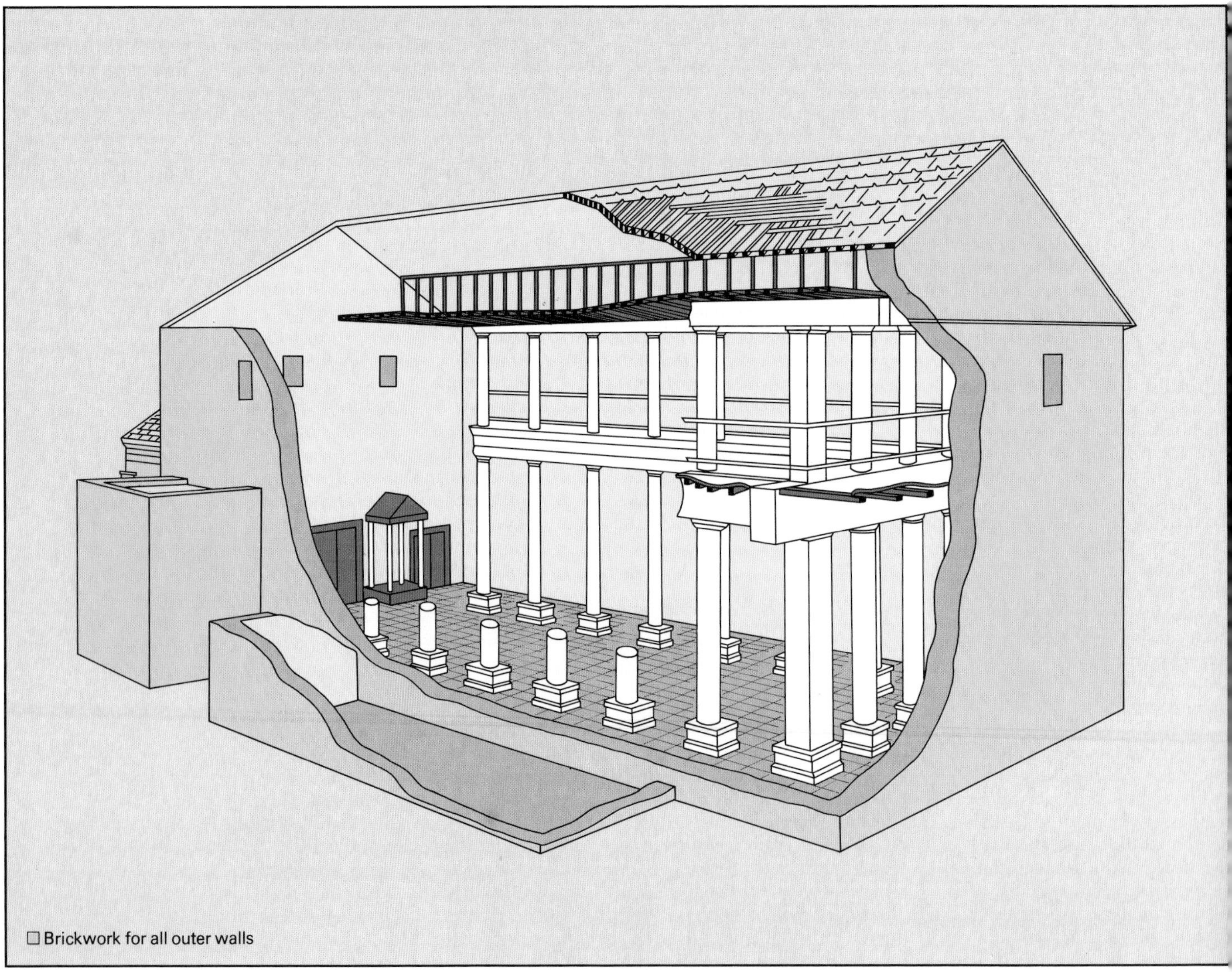

Reconstruction of the synagogue at Meiron, Palestine, showing the galleries and the Ark of the Law (at the far end) common in synagogue buildings. 3rd–4th cent. AD.

and religious life and established the foundation for a religious community of universal scope. For the first time Jewish monotheism emancipated itself in religious practice from its bonds to a specific and designated site. God was now brought to the people wherever they dwelt' ('The History of the Jews in Ancient Times', *The Jewish People*, 1, pp. 78–152). Today the synagogue is still one of the dominant institutions of Judaism, and the centre of the religious life of the Jewish community. The book of Acts indicates the significant role the synagogue played in the propagation of the new Messianic faith.

II. Its origin

Neither OT nor NT furnishes any definite information as to the origin of the synagogue. The situation is not altered by extra-biblical sources, for there is no reference to the institution in the Apocrypha. The Apocryphal books do not even mention the burning of the synagogues of the land during the persecutions of Antiochus Epiphanes in the 2nd century BC (although a reference to this has been seen in Ps. 74:8). Before the Babylonian captivity worship was centred at the Temple in Jerusalem. During the Exile, when worship at Jerusalem was an impossibility, the synagogue arose as a place for instruction in the Scriptures and prayer. Such is the general opinion. R. W. Moss maintains, however, that 'the Exile marks not the first stage in the origin of the synagogue, but an important modification of its functions, worship becoming thenceforward the principal though far from the sole occupation, and the administrative functions falling for a time into abeyance' ('Synagogue' in *DCG*).

Corinthian capital from the synagogue at Capernaum depicting the branched lampstand (menorah), *ram's horn* (shofar) *and incense shovel, common symbols in ancient Jewish art. Middle 4th cent. AD.* (JPK)

Characteristic Jewish synagogue ornament from Chorazin. Late Roman period. (JPK)

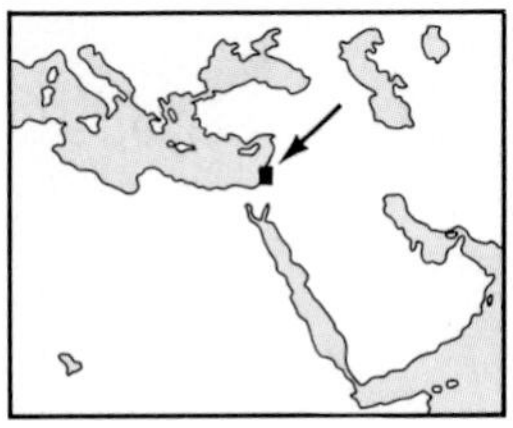

Sites of synagogues which were in use in Palestine during the 1st to 6th centuries AD, as known from archaeological exploration.

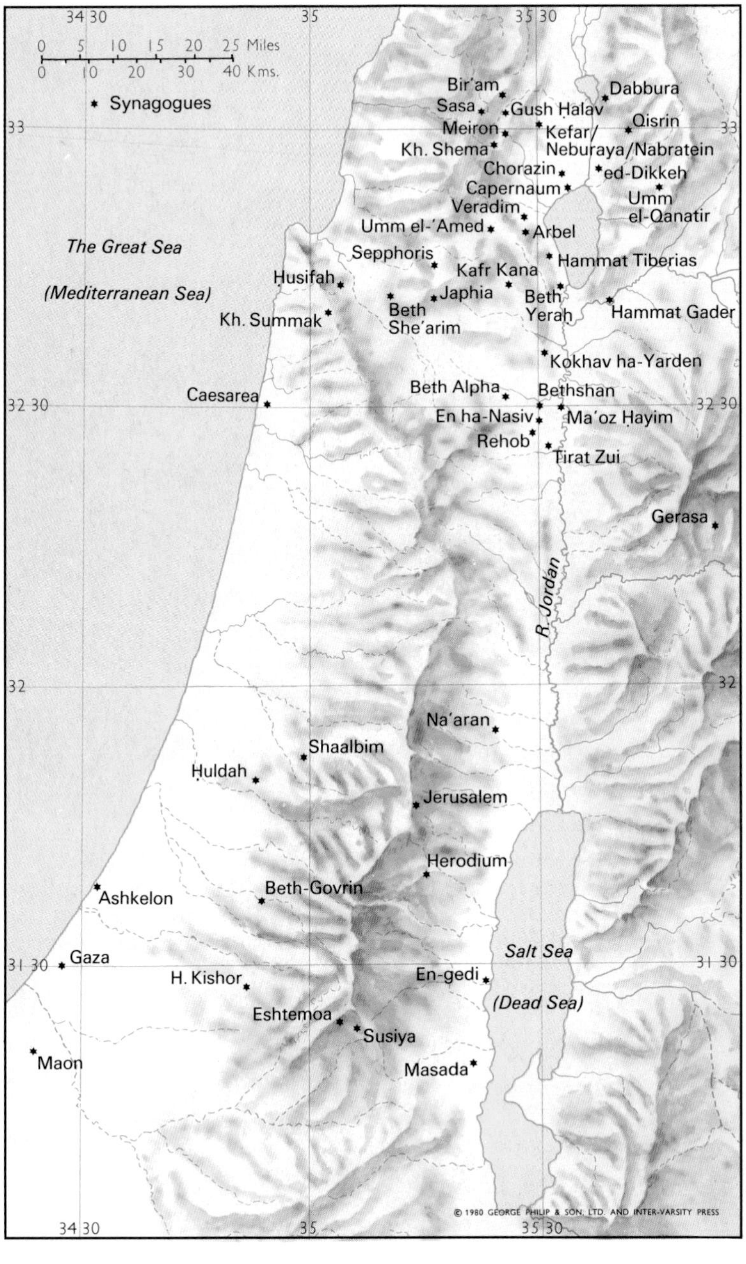

In any event a probable basis for the origin of the institution is to be found in Ezk. 14:1: 'Then came certain of the elders of Israel to me, and sat before me' (*cf.* Ezk. 20:1). Levertoff asserts without equivocation, 'It must have come into being during the Bab. exile' ('Synagogue' in *ISBE*).

III. General description

In the 1st century AD synagogues existed wherever Jews lived. *Cf.* Acts 13:5 (Salamis in Cyprus); 13:14 (Antioch in Pisidia); 14:1 (Iconium); 17:10 (Beroea). Large cities, such as Jerusalem and Alexandria, had numerous synagogues. One legend has it that there were 394 synagogues in Jerusalem when Titus destroyed the city in AD 70; another legend sets the number at 480.

The Gospels speak of the synagogues of Nazareth (Mt. 13:54; Lk. 4:16) and Capernaum (Mk. 1:21; Jn. 6:59) as places where our Lord ministered. The apostle Paul found them wherever he went in Palestine, Asia Minor and Greece. According to the Talmud (*Shabbath* 11a), it was required that synagogues be built on high ground or above surrounding houses. Archaeological evidence does not confirm such a practice for Palestine. In all probability the synagogues were constructed on the model of the Temple in Jerusalem. A. Edersheim states that the interior plan 'is generally that of two double colonnades, which seem to have formed the body of the Synagogue, the aisles E and W being probably used as passages. The intercolumnar distance is very small, never greater than $9\frac{1}{2}$ feet (3m)' (*The Life and Times of Jesus the Messiah*, 1, p. 435).

There was a portable ark in which the scrolls of the Law and the Prophets were kept (*M^{e}ḡillah* 3. 1). It faced the entrance of the building. On fast days the ark was carried in a procession. Before the ark and facing the worshippers were the 'chief seats' (Mt. 23:6, AV) for the religious and governing leaders of the synagogue. The Law was read from a *bēmâ* or platform (*M^{e}ḡillah* 3. 1). Ruins of such buildings can be seen at Tell Ḫum (probably the site of *Capernaum), Nebartim and other sites. The remains show the influence of a Graeco-Roman style. Synagogue ornaments were vine leaves, the seven-branched candlestick, the paschal lamb and the pot of manna. The seats near the reading-desk were the more honourable (Mt. 23:6; Jas. 2:2–3). Maimonides said, 'They put a platform in the middle of the house, so that he who reads from the Law, or he who speaks words of exhortation to the people, may stand upon it, and all may hear him.' Men and women were seated apart.

The Great Synagogue of tradition may have been organized by Nehemiah about 400 BC. It is said to have consisted of 120 members (*Pirqe Aboth* 1. 1), who occupied themselves with the study of the law of Moses and transmitted it. The Sanhedrin succeeded it (*Aboth* 10. 1). There is doubt as to the existence of the Great Synagogue, because neither the Apocrypha, nor Josephus, nor Philo mentions the body. Such silence, however, is not conclusive against the existence of such a council.

IV. Its purpose and practice

The synagogue served a threefold purpose of worship, education and government of the civil life of the community. Subject to the law of the land, the synagogue had its own government (Jos., *Ant.* 19. 291). The congregation was governed by elders who were empowered to exercise discipline and punish members. Punishment was by scourging and excommunication. The chief officer was the ruler of the synagogue (*cf.* Mk. 5:22; Acts 13:15; 18:8). He supervised the service to see that it was carried on in accord

Synagogue at Capernaum. These steps suggest that this was the synagogue seen by Egeria (c. AD *383), reached by an ascent of 'many steps'.* (JPK)

with tradition. The attendant (Lk. 4:20) brought the scrolls of Scripture for reading, replaced them in the ark, punished offending members by scourging and instructed children to read. Peritz has shown that 'the primary function of the synagogue assemblies was the popular instruction in the law' ('Synagogue' in *EBi*). The dispenser of alms received the alms from the synagogue and distributed them. Finally, a competent interpreter was required to paraphrase the Law and the Prophets into the vernacular Aramaic.

Those qualified were permitted to conduct the services (Christ, Lk. 4:16; Mt. 4:23; Paul, Acts 13:15). The Sabbath was the appointed day for public worship (Acts 15:21). The Mishnah (*Meḡillah* 4. 3) indicates that the service consisted of five parts. First, the *Shema'* was read. This prayer covers Dt. 6:4–9; 11:13–21; Nu. 15:37–41. Then synagogical prayers were recited, the most ancient and best known being the eighteen petitions and benedictions.

The first of the 'Eighteen Benedictions' reads: 'Blessed art Thou, the Lord our God, and the God of our fathers, the God of Abraham, the God of Isaac, and the God of Jacob: the great, the mighty and the terrible God, the most high God Who showest mercy and kindness, Who createst all things, Who rememberest the pious deeds of the patriarchs, and wilt in love bring a redeemer to their children's children for Thy Name's sake; O King, Helper, Saviour and Shield! Blessed art Thou, O Lord, the Shield of Abraham.'

Another prayer is worded: 'And to Jerusalem, Thy city, Thou wilt return in mercy and wilt dwell in her midst, as Thou hast said. And do Thou build her soon in our days an eternal building, and the throne of David Thou wilt speedily establish in the midst of her.'

The restoration of Israel to the land of their fathers, the return of the Shekinah glory to the Temple and rebuilt city of Jerusalem, and the re-establishment of the Davidic dynasty are recurring themes in the prayers.

These were followed by the reading of the Law. The Pentateuch, which is now read in the synagogues in annual cycles, was originally covered in 3 years. After the reading from the first portion of the OT Canon a selection from the Prophets was read. In the time of Christ this portion was not yet fixed, but the reader was permitted to make his own choice (Lk. 4:16ff.). The reading of Scripture was central. The portion of the Prophets was expounded, and an exhortation drawn from it. The benediction concluded the service. Later additions were the translation and exposition of the Scripture portions read. To conduct public worship in the synagogue ten adult males were required.

'Synagogue of the Libertines' (AV) (*libertinoi*, from Lat. *libertini*, *'freedmen', RSV) was the name given to worshippers in a synagogue in Jerusalem who disputed with Stephen (Acts 6:9). They were Jews who had been captured in Pompey's campaign, then were freed later by their masters. Thus the privileges of Roman citizenship were accorded them.

Reference is made in Rev. 2:9 and 3:9 to the 'synagogue of Satan'. Since the citations are general in character, it is impossible with certainty to identify those who are meant by John. A heretical party within the infant church would seem to be indicated.

BIBLIOGRAPHY. Articles in *JewE*, *HDB*, *EBi*, *EJ*; G. F. Moore, *Judaism*, 1, 1927, pp. 281–307; I. Abrahams, *Studies in Pharisaism and the Gospels*, 1, 1917; E. L. Sukenik, *Ancient Synagogues in Palestine and Greece*, 1932; C. W. Dugmore, *The Influence of the Synagogue upon the Divine Office*, 1944; A. E. Guilding, *The Fourth Gospel and Jewish Worship*, 1960; L. Coenen, *NIDNTT* 1, pp. 291–307. C.L.F.

SYNOPTIC GOSPELS
See Gospels, Part 2.

SYNTYCHE
See Euodia, Part 1.

Opposite page: Syria in NT times.

SYNZYGUS. Gk. *synzygos* (*syzygos*), 'yokefellow' (Phil. 4:3), is treated as a personal name by *WH* mg. and others, as though Paul meant 'Yokefellow by name and yokefellow by nature'. The word, however, is certainly to be taken as a common noun, the person addressed being (not Lydia, supposed by S. Baring-Gould and others to have been Paul's wife, but) possibly Luke, who seems to have stayed in Philippi for the 7 years separating the first 'we' section of Acts (ending 16:17) from the second (beginning 20:5). (This identification presupposes that the letter, or at least this part of it, was sent from Ephesus.) F.F.B.

SYRIAN ROCK HYRAX
See Animals, Part 1.

SYRIANS
See Syria, Part 3.

SYRACUSE. A city with a large harbour on the E coast of Sicily. Founded in 734 BC by Corinthian colonists, it had by the end of the 5th century BC become the most important city, politically and commercially, in Sicily, especially under the tyrants Gelon and Dionysius I. With its allies it was strong enough to defeat the great Athenian expedition to Sicily in 415–413 BC. The Romans captured it in 212 BC, in spite of a defence strengthened by the inventions of the great mathematician Archimedes, and made it the seat of government of the province of Sicily, which became one of the sources of grain for Rome. Syracuse continued to flourish down to the 3rd century AD.

On the last stage of his journey

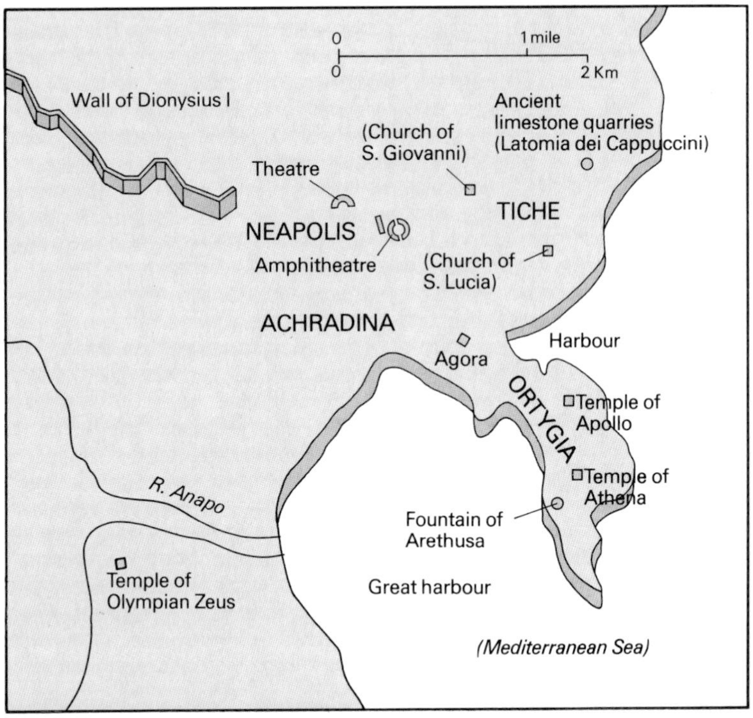

Plan of the site of Syracuse in Sicily, showing its double harbour. Paul stayed here for three days (Acts 28:12).

The Greek theatre at Syracuse in Sicily. (PP)

Opposite page: Syrian tribute-bearers on a wall-painting in the tomb of Sebekhotep, Thebes. c. 1420 BC. (BM)

to Rome Paul's ship stayed there for 3 days (Acts 28:12), presumably waiting for a suitable wind.

K.L.McK.

SYRIA, SYRIANS. 1. In the Eng. OT this merely denotes *Aramaeans.

2. The geographical entity Syria is bounded by the Taurus Mountains in the N, the W bend of the Euphrates river and the Arabian desert-edge from there to the Dead Sea in the E, the Mediterranean Sea on the W, and the Sinai isthmus at the extreme S (R. Dussaud, *Topographie Historique de la Syrie Antique et Médiévale*, 1927, pp. 1–2, *etc.*; see this work generally).

3. 'Syria' is a Gk. term; Nöldeke derived it from *Assyrios*, 'Assyria(n)', and this suggestion is open to the least objection. *Cf.* F. Rosenthal, *Die Aramaistische Forschung*, 1939, p. 3, n. 1.

4. Historically, ancient Syria existed as a political *unit* only during the period of the Hellenistic Seleucid monarchy, founded by Seleucus I (312–281 BC), who ruled over a realm that stretched from E Asia Minor and N Syria across Babylonia into Persia to the border of India; in 198 BC all 'Syria' belonged to this kingdom when Antiochus III finally gained Palestine from Ptolemy V of Egypt. But from 129 BC, with the death of Antiochus VII, everything E of the Euphrates was lost, and the Seleucids held Syria only. After this, internal dynastic strife disrupted the shrinking state until Pompey annexed the region for Rome in 64 BC. Syria as defined in **2** above constituted the Rom. province of Syria, with which Cilicia was closely associated (Judaea being separate from AD 70). *ANTIOCH (Syrian), *ANTIOCHUS, *UGARIT, *ALALAH, *etc.*, and also *CAH*.

K.A.K.

SYROPHOENICIAN. An inhabitant of Phoenicia, which in NT times was part of the Rom. province of Cilicia and Syria. It was a Syrophoenician woman (*syrophoinikissa*), a Greek from the region of Tyre and Sidon, who pleaded with Jesus to heal her daughter (Mk. 7:26; *cf.* Mt. 15:21–28). The parallel verse in Mt. 15:22 calls the woman a Canaanite, using the ancient name by which these people were known. The name Syrophoenician combines the area of Phoenicia

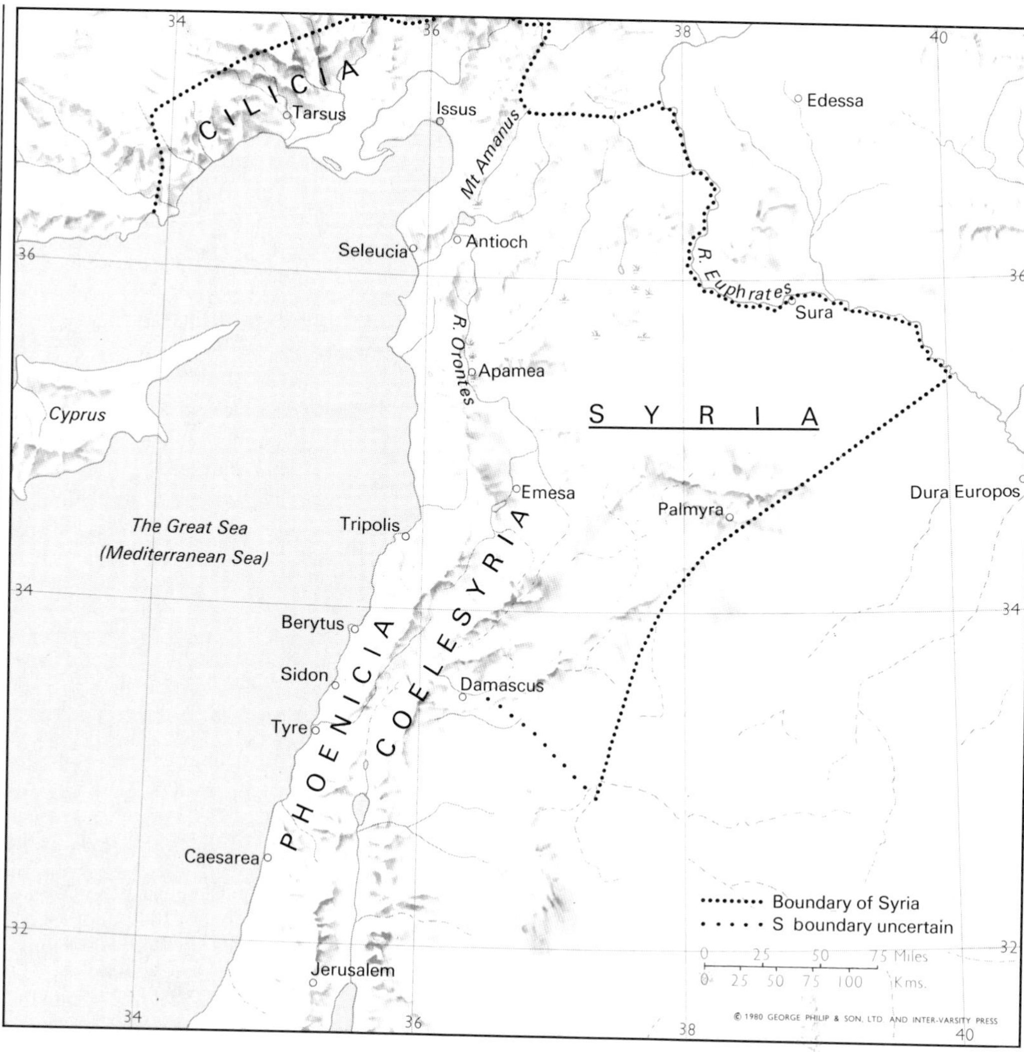

■ **SYRTIS**
See Quicksands, Part 3.

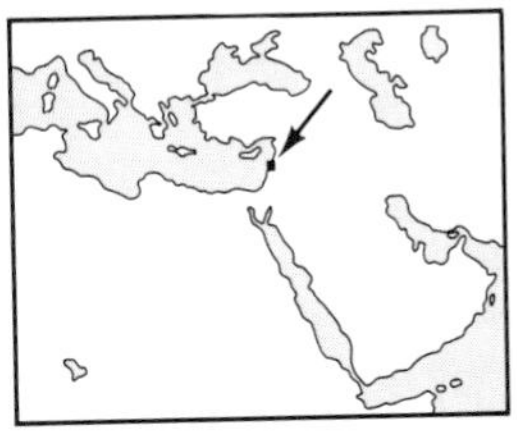

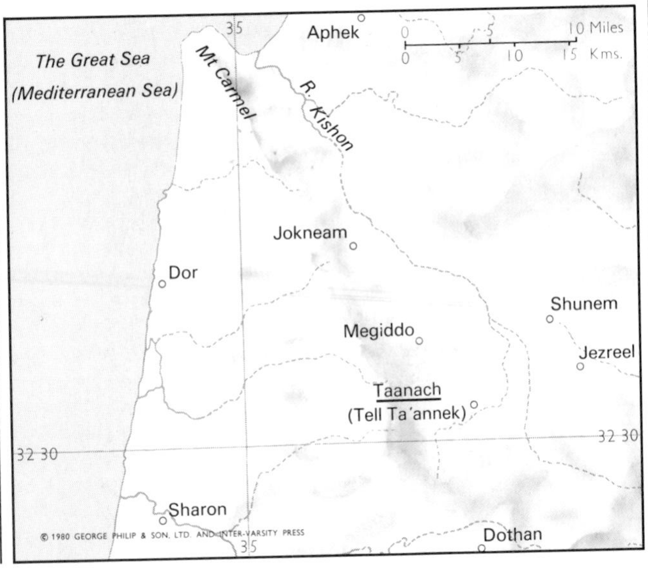

Taanach (Tell Ta'annek).

which included Tyre and Sidon, and the larger Rom. province of Syria. Phoenicians who lived in Carthage were called Libyphoenicians. J.A.T.

TAANACH. Modern Tell Ta‘annek on the S edge of the valley of Jezreel, guarding a pass across Mt Carmel following the Wadi Abdullah.

Thothmes III mentions Taanach in the account of his conquest of W Palestine (*c.* 1450 BC; *ANET*, pp. 234ff.), as does *Shishak. Amarna letter 248 complains of a raid by men of Taanach on Megiddo, which was loyal to Egypt. The Israelites defeated the king of this city, but the tribe to which it was allotted, Manasseh, was unable to take possession of it (Jos. 12:21; 17:11; Jdg. 1:27). It was one of the levitical cities (Jos. 21:25) and was also occupied by Issachar (1 Ch. 7:29). Taanach and Megiddo are closely associated in Solomon's administrative division of Israel (1 Ki. 4:12) and in the Song of Deborah, where 'Taanach, by the waters of Megiddo' (Jdg. 5:19) is the site of the Canaanite defeat. Excavations in 1901–4, 1963, 1966 and 1968 revealed an Early Bronze Age city, a Middle Bronze II occupation with typical glacis fortification, destroyed violently, and a prosperous town of Late Bronze I (14 Akkad. cuneiform tablets were found). At the end of the Late Bronze Age there was another destruction, perhaps the work of Deborah's men. In the debris a clay tablet inscribed in a Canaanite cuneiform alphabet was found. The Early Iron Age city, containing a supposed cultic building with stone stelae, numerous pig bones and an elaborate pottery incense-stand, appears to have been destroyed by Shishak. Thereafter the city declined.

BIBLIOGRAPHY. E. Sellin, *Tell Ta‘annek*, 1904; P. W. Lapp, *BA* 30, 1967, pp. 1–27; *BASOR* 173, 1964, pp. 4–44; 185, 1967, pp. 2–39; 195, 1969, pp. 2–49; D. R. Hillers, *BASOR* 173, 1964, pp. 45–50; A. Glock, *BASOR* 204, 1971, pp. 17–30. A.R.M.

TABERNACLE. 1. The tabernacle of the congregation (AV), more properly 'tent of meeting', as in RV, RSV: a small, provisional meeting-place of God and his people in use before the large tabernacle was built (Ex. 33:7–11). This tent of meeting was pitched outside the camp. Moses would enter it and the Cloud, marking the divine Presence, would descend and stand outside it at the door. In this the function of the tent resembled that of the cleft of the rock in which Moses was placed (Ex. 34:22–23), and that of the cave in which Elijah stood (1 Ki. 19:9–18), to be addressed by God while the glory of God passed by outside. The tabernacle, by contrast, was erected in the midst of the camp, and the Cloud of glory rested not outside but inside it, so that at first Moses had to stay outside (Ex. 40:34–35).

2. The tabernacle commonly so-called was the portable sanctuary in which God dwelt among the Israelites in the desert. After their entry into Canaan, it was stationed successively at Shiloh (Jos. 18:1), at Nob (1 Sa. 21) and at Gibeon (1 Ch. 16:39). Eventually Solomon brought it up to the Temple (1 Ki. 8:4). It is called simply *miškān* = 'dwelling' (EVV 'tabernacle'), as in Ex. 25:9; or *miškān YHWH* = 'dwelling of Yahweh' as in Lv. 17:4; or *miškān ha‘ēḏûṯ* = 'dwelling of the *covenant terms' (AV, RSV 'of the testimony'), because it housed the covenant tablets, as in Ex. 38:21; or *’ōhel mô‘ēḏ* = tent (AV 'tabernacle') of meeting', *i.e.* the appointed meeting-place between God and his people, as in Ex. 28:43; or *miškān ’ōhel mô‘ēḏ* = 'dwelling of the tent of meeting', as in Ex. 39:32; or *miqdāš* = 'sanctuary' as in Ex. 25:8; or *qôḏeš* = ' 'holy place' (AV, RSV 'sanctuary'), as in Ex. 38:24. It is also called *beṯ YHWH* = 'house of Yahweh', as in Ex. 34:26.

The materials used in its construction are listed at Ex. 25:3–7. The metal translated 'bronze' (AV 'brass') was more probably copper. The colour 'blue' was probably a violet-blue and the colour 'purple' a reddish-purple. The material translated 'goatskins' (RSV; AV 'badgers' skins') was probably dugong (or 'porpoise', NEB) skin.

I. Tabernacle, tent, coverings and frames

In its stricter technical meaning the term 'tabernacle' refers to a set of ten linen curtains, which when draped round a structure of wooden frames formed God's dwelling-place. The curtains were of linen with figures of cherubim woven into the violet-blue, reddish-purple and scarlet tapestry-work. Each measuring 28 cubits by 4, they were sewn together along their length into two sets of five, which when assembled were held together by fifty golden clasps (AV 'taches') passing through loops on the edge of each set (Ex. 26:1–6). The tabernacle was covered by eleven goats'-hair curtains, called in strict terminology 'the tent' (Ex. 26:7–15). They each measured 30 cubits by 4, were sewn together into two sets, one of five, the other of six, which when assembled were held together, like the tabernacle, by loops and clasps, only their clasps were of copper.

Over the tent went a covering of tanned (literally, 'reddened') rams' skins, and over that again (*cf.* NEB 'an outer covering'; AV, RV 'above') a covering of dugong skin (Ex. 26:14).

These curtains were spread over the top, back and two sides of a framework (Ex. 26:15–30) assembled from forty-eight units, each 10 cubits high and 1½ wide, called *qᵉrāšîm*. The most likely interpretation of these *qᵉrāšîm* is that given by A. R. S. Kennedy (*HDB*, 4, pp. 659–662); they were not solid boards (as AV, RV), nor planks (as NEB), but open frames, each consisting of two long uprights (*yāḏôṯ*: not 'tenons' as in most versions) joined by cross-rails somewhat like a ladder. Such frames would have three advantages over solid planks: they would be much lighter, less liable to whip, and instead of hiding the beautiful tabernacle curtains would allow them to be seen from the inside all round the walls. The feet of the two uprights in each frame stood in sockets made of silver obtained

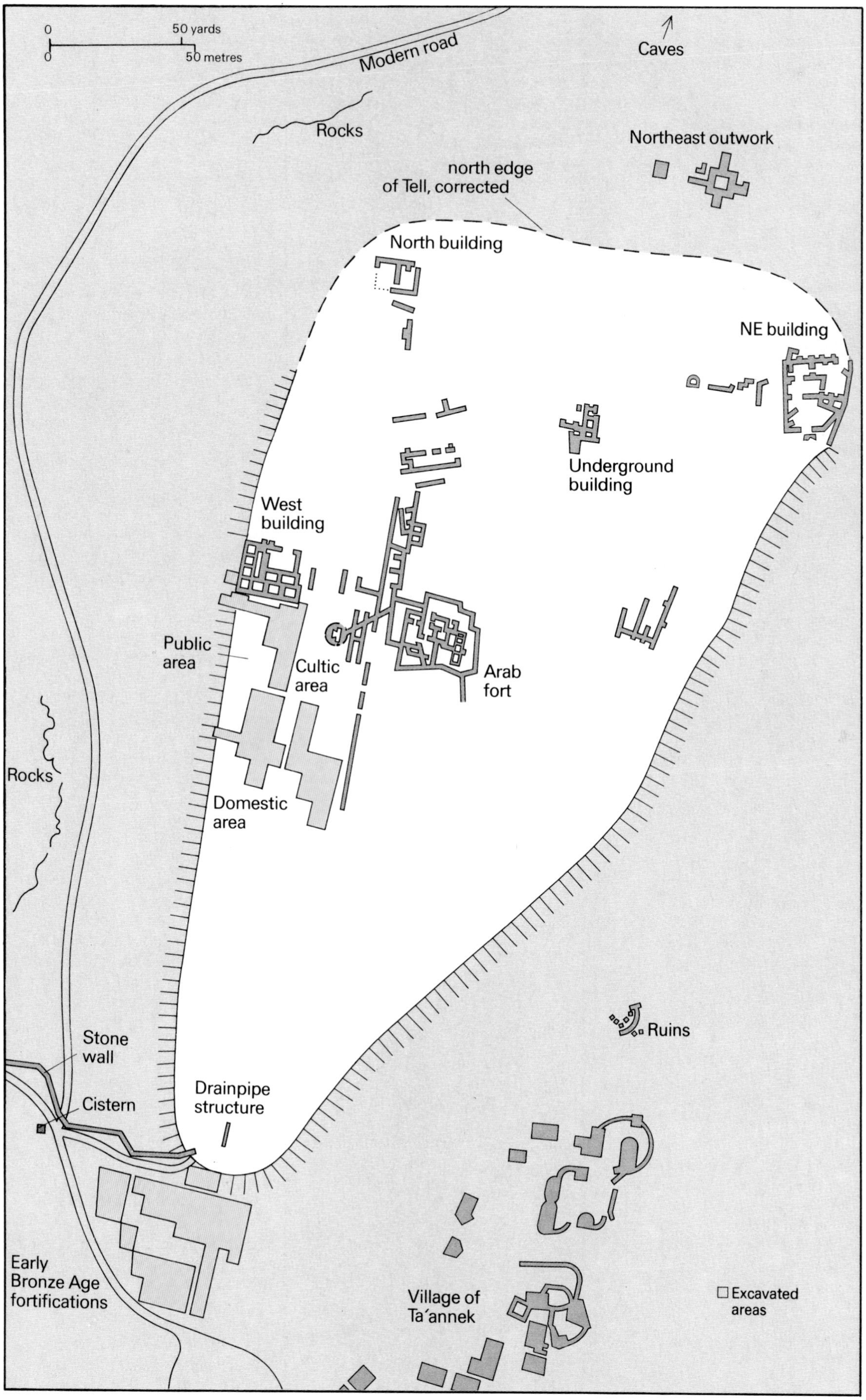

The mound of Taanach (Tell Ta'annek), showing excavated areas.

A reconstruction of the tabernacle, described in Exodus, showing, in the courtyard, the altar of burnt-offering and the laver and, behind the curtain, the incense-altar and the table for the showbread. The seven-branched lampstand and the ark of the covenant are not visible. (DWG)

from the census tax (Ex. 30:11–16; 38:25–27). Twenty frames in their sockets, stationed side by side, formed each side of the tabernacle; six formed the rear. In each corner at the rear was an extra frame. The purpose of these extra frames, to give rigidity to the whole structure, is clear; but the details of the specification are not. Perhaps the best explanation is that given by U. Cassuto: each corner frame was coupled (not 'separate' as RSV) at the bottom and the top so as to form a twin with the end frame in the side, and then clamped to its twin by means of a metal ring (translating v. 24 'into the one ring' and not 'at the first ring', as RSV). To keep the frames in alignment five bars ran along the sides and rear through gold rings attached to the cross-rails of each frame. The middle bar ran the whole length, the other four only part of the way. The frames and bars were made of acacia wood overlaid with gold.

When the frames were assembled the distance from the top of the frames at the front along the roof and down to the bottom of the frames at the rear was $20 \times 1\frac{1}{2} + 10 = 40$ cubits. The assembled tabernacle curtains measured 28 cubits by $10 \times 4 = 40$ cubits. They were spread over the frames so that the 40 cubits ran from the top front of the frames to the rear bottom. The assembled tent curtains measured 30 cubits by $11 \times 4 = 44$ cubits. When they were spread over the tabernacle curtains, the extra 2 cubits (30 as against 28) gave an overhang of 1 cubit on each side (Ex. 26:13). The extra 4 cubits in the other direction (44 as against 40) were disposed as follows: at the rear the tent extended 2 cubits beyond the tabernacle curtains (v. 12), and at the front the other 2 cubits were doubled back and, presumably, tucked under the tabernacle curtains all the way along the top and sides, so protecting what otherwise would have been an exposed edge of tabernacle curtain (v. 9). The word used for arranging the curtains over the frames is not the normal word for pitching a tent, *naṭâ*, but *pāraś*, which means 'to spread' (it is used of wrapping cloths round the furniture). The roof was flat. To prevent the curtains from sagging at the roof and so causing the frames to collapse inwards, there were probably (the text does not say so, but it omits many details which one would need to know to make a tabernacle) wooden struts running across the top of the framework from side to side (see, for comparison, the portable pavilion of Hetep-heres). J. Fergusson (*Smith's Dictionary of the Bible*, 3, pp. 1452–1454) and many others have argued unconvincingly that the curtains must have been spread over a ridge-pole. Some of their arguments presuppose that the sides and rear of the tabernacle were formed of solid planks; since they were formed not of planks but of open fragments, their arguments are invalid, and would lead to the impossible result of exposing the holy place and the most holy to view from the outside. Other arguments are invalidated by their failure to observe that the term 'tabernacle' in Ex. 26:1–13 refers not to the building in general but to the ten linen curtains.

II. The interior

The interior of the dwelling was divided into two compartments by a veil hung under (not 'from' as RSV) the clasps that joined the tabernacle curtains (Ex. 26:31–34). Hence we know that the first compartment was 20 cubits long, the second 10. The height of the frames, 10 cubits, gives us the second dimension, and in all probability the breadth of both compartments was 10 cubits likewise: for while the six frames at the back give a total breadth of 9 cubits, allowance must be made for the thickness of the side frames and corner frames. The first compartment is called 'the holy place', the second 'the holy of holies', *i.e.* the most holy place, or simply 'the holy place' (Lv. 16:2–3; Heb. 9:12; 10:19, RV. RSV 'sanctuary' in these latter two verses is misleading: entry into the holy of holies is intended). Again, the first compartment is sometimes called 'the first tabernacle' and the second 'the second tabernacle' (Heb. 9:6–7, AV, RV; RSV 'the outer tent' and 'the second' respectively). The dividing veil (*pārōḵeṯ*: a term used of no other hanging), made of the same material, colours and design as the tabernacle curtains, was hung by gold hooks on four acacia-wood pillars overlaid with gold and standing in silver sockets. The pillars had no capitals. At the door (= doorway) was a linen screen of violet-blue, reddish-purple and scarlet (but without cherubim). It hung by gold hooks on five acacia-wood pillars overlaid with gold standing in copper sockets. These pillars did have capitals and were overlaid with gold, as were their fillets (Ex. 26:36; 37:38). To distinguish the *pārōḵeṯ* from this screen, the *pārōḵeṯ* is sometimes called the second veil.

III. The furniture

In the most holy place stood the *ark of the covenant (Ex. 25:10–22). A slab (AV, RSV 'mercy seat') of pure gold with a cherub at each end rested on top. The name of this slab, *kappōreṯ*, means not 'lid' but 'propitiatory', *i.e.* place where the blood of propitiation was sprinkled. This is how the LXX (*hilastērion*) understood it, as does the NT (Heb. 9:5; RSV 'mercy seat').

The poles for carrying the ark ran through rings attached to the feet (not 'corners', as in AV) of the ark (Ex. 25:12). There is no implied discrepancy between Ex. 25:15 and Nu. 4:8. The latter verse indicates that to facilitate the covering of the ark for transport the poles were temporarily removed and immediately replaced: the former verse directs that at all other times the poles were to be left in their rings even when the ark was not travelling.

In the holy place in front of the veil was the incense-altar (Ex. 30:1–10). Made of acacia wood and overlaid with pure gold—hence its other name, 'the golden altar'—it was a cubit square and 2 cubits high, with horns projecting at the four corners and an ornamental gold moulding round the top. (For a pagan, stone incense-altar with horns, see *ALTAR.) For transport, two poles were shot through gold rings attached just under the moulding. The altar stood directly opposite the ark (note the emphasis of 30:6), and so was regarded as 'belonging to' the most holy place (*cf.* 1 Ki. 6:22 and Heb. 9:4, where 'golden altar of incense' and not 'censer' seems to be the right translation). With the position of the altar compare the position of the two incense-altars in the temple at Arad (*BA* 31, 1968, pp. 22ff.).

On the N side (Ex. 26:35) stood a table for the Bread of the Presence (AV 'shewbread'; *SHOWBREAD) (Ex. 25:23–29). One such table and a lampstand (see below) from Herod's Temple are represented on Titus' Arch at Rome. Some doubt is cast, however, on the accuracy of these sculptures, since on the lampstand's base various non-Jewish figures appear. The detail of v. 25 is uncertain. Some translators envisage an 8-cm wide horizontal border, some an 8-cm high vertical rim, or frame, running round the top of the table, others, in agreement with apparent vestiges on Titus' Arch, envisage 8-cm broad cross-struts between the legs of the table.

The vessels connected with the table were: plates, presumably for the bread; dishes (*kappōṯ*: for incense, so RSV; *cf. kap̄*, in Nu. 7:14 = AV 'spoon'); and flagons and bowls for drink-offerings (not as AV 'to cover withal').

On the S side (Ex. 26:35) stood the *lampstand, *m^e^nōrâh* (AV 'candlestick') (Ex. 25:31–40), in the form of a stylized tree. In strict technical parlance the base and central shaft form the lampstand proper; the six branches are then described as 'going out of the lampstand' (v. 33). In v. 31 the RSV's literal translation, 'its cups, its capitals, and its flowers', *i.e.* three items, is to be preferred to interpretative renderings such as that of NEB 'its cups, both calyxes and petals', *i.e.* one item made up of two parts. The capitals were round protuberances of some kind, in the arms and shaft of the lampstand (not, as 'capital' might suggest, on the ends of them). It is probable, but not completely certain, that the six branches rose to the same height as the central shaft. The seven lamps were presumably placed one on the end of each of the six branches and one on the central shaft. There were provided *snuffers and *trays.

Reconstruction of the portable pavilion of Hetep-heres shown without its coverings but with chair, bed and headrest placed in position. From Giza, Egypt. Height of pavilion 2·2 m, length 3·2 m, width 2·5 m. c. 2600 BC. (MFAB)

IV. Court

The tabernacle stood in the W half of a courtyard, 100 × 50 cubits, the long sides running N and S (Ex. 27:9–19). The tabernacle door faced E.

The courtyard was bounded by a linen screen (EVV 'hangings') 5 cubits high hung on pillars. There was an opening for a gate, 20 cubits wide, set centrally in the E end. The gate screen was linen, embroidered in violet-blue, reddish-purple and scarlet.

The pillars were apparently made of acacia wood (they are not mentioned in the list of copper articles, Ex. 38:29–31), and stood in copper sockets. They were stabilized by guy-ropes and pegs, and had capitals overlaid with silver, and silver bands, called fillets, round the neck.

Three main methods are advocated for spacing the pillars:

(1) On the basic assumption that there was one pillar per 5 cubits of hanging, and that no pillar was counted twice, sixty pillars in all are placed to make twenty spaces along the two long sides and ten spaces along the two ends. The gate screen then hangs on four of its own pillars and one of the others (see diagram below).

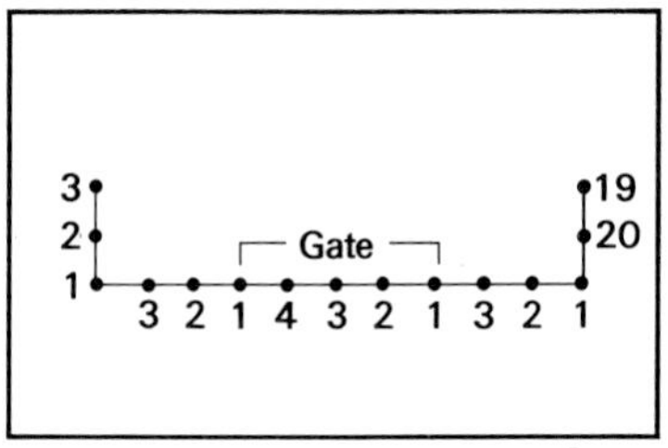

It is questionable whether this satisfies the direction for the 20 cubits of gate-screen '. . . *their pillars four* . . .'.

(2) The *Baraitha on the Erection of the Tabernacle*, 5, has it that the pillars stood in the middle of each imaginary space of 5 cubits and that there were no pillars in the corners. (For an attempted solution of the difficulties this would create at the corners and the gate, see M. Levine, *The Tabernacle*, 1969, pp. 76, 81.).

(3) Since the text nowhere says that the pillars were 5 cubits apart, maybe at the corners the two end pillars stood together. Or perhaps the corner pillars were counted twice (the text does not explicitly state that the total was sixty). The gate could then be recessed (or advanced: see diagram above). But this system gives very awkward measurements for the spaces between the pillars.

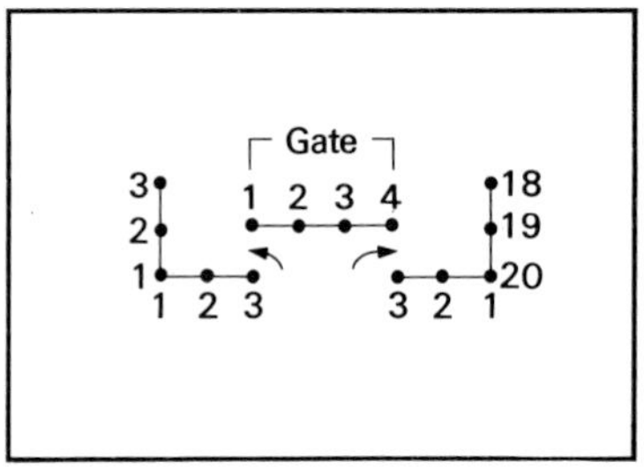

In the E half of the court stood an altar. It was called the copper altar from its covering material and the altar of burnt-offering from the chief *sacrifice offered on it (Ex. 27:1–8). It was a hollow framework of acacia wood, 5 cubits square and 3 high, with projecting horns at the top corners. The whole was overlaid with copper. Halfway up the altar, on the outside, was a horizontal ledge (AV 'compass') running all round. (For a stone altar of comparable dimensions with horns, see Y. Aharoni, *BA* 37, 1974, pp. 2–6; *ALTAR.) Running vertically all round from the ground up to the ledge (not 'extending halfway down the altar' as RSV) was a grating of copper network, on the four corners of which were the rings for the carrying-poles. The grating was not a hearth, and the altar was topless and hollow. Some suppose that in use it was filled with earth and stones, others that it acted like an incinerator, draught being supplied through the grating. Its service vessels were *pots for ashes, *shovels, *basins, *forks (AV *'fleshhooks') and *firepans.

Between the altar and the door of the tabernacle stood the laver (Ex. 30:17–21; 38:8; 40:29–32). It was a copper basin standing on a copper base. Nothing is told us of its size, shape and ornamentation (nor of its means of transport, though the absence of this detail from the *MT* of Nu. 4 may be accidental: LXX gives the expected information). It held water for the priests' ablutions.

In camp the tabernacle court was surrounded first by the tents of the priests and Levites, and outside them by those of the twelve tribes (Nu. 2; 3:1–30).

V. Problems arising

Revision of source-critical theories, particularly those relating to the so-called Priestly texts, together with archaeological discoveries have considerably modified the earlier arguments of the liberal school against the historicity of the tabernacle. See *e.g.* G. Henton-Davies, *IDB*, 3, pp. 503–506; Y. Aharoni, *Orient and Occident* (ed. H. A. Hoffner, Jr), 1973, p. 6; C. L. Meyers, *IDBS*, p. 586. Allegations that the instructions for the building of the tabernacle are in parts impracticable, and thus evidently the work of an idealist, would be valid only if the records were intended to be fully detailed blueprints. They are not that, of course, but records 'for our learning'. Hence many practical details of no aesthetic, symbolic or spiritual value are omitted. At the same time portable pavilions, employing practically the same constructional techniques as the tabernacle, are known to have been in actual use in Egypt long before the time of Moses; see K. A. Kitchen, *THB* 5–6, 1960, pp. 7–13. From the fact that the instructions for the making of the incense-altar stand in Ex. 30, and not as expected in Ex. 25, it used to be argued that its description is a late addition to Exodus and that the incense-altar was not introduced into Israel's worship until a comparatively late date. But since incense-altars have been discovered at Arad and at various Canaanite sites dating from the 10th century BC, it is highly improbable that Israel lacked one in the early period. Similarly, on the basis of the wide divergence of the LXX from the *MT* in Ex. 36–40, it used to be argued that the last chapters of Exodus in Heb. had not yet reached their final form when the LXX was translated, and that the LXX followed in part a Heb. tradition which knew of no incense-altar. But the argument is not valid: see D. W. Gooding, *The Account of the Tabernacle*, 1959.

VI. Significance

Theologically the tabernacle as a dwelling-place of God on earth is of immense importance, as being the first in the series: tabernacle, Temple, the incarnation, the body of the individual believer, the church. It follows from the fact that the tabernacle was built to God's design as 'a copy and shadow of heavenly things' (Heb. 8:5) that its symbols conveyed spiritual meaning to the Israelites of the time. What that meaning was is often stated explicitly, as with the ark and mercy seat (Ex.

Offerings	Bullocks and related cereal offerings▽	Rams and related cereal offerings○	Male lambs* and related cereal offerings☆	Male goats
Month of Tišri Day 15	(13 bullocks) $\frac{9}{10}$	(2 rams) $\frac{4}{10}$	(14 lambs) $\frac{4}{10}$	(1 goat)
Day 16	(12 bullocks) $\frac{6}{10}$	(2 rams) $\frac{4}{10}$	(14 lambs) $\frac{4}{10}$	(1 goat)
Day 17	(11 bullocks) $\frac{3}{10}$	(2 rams) $\frac{4}{10}$	(14 lambs) $\frac{4}{10}$	(1 goat)
Day 18	(10 bullocks)	(2 rams) $\frac{4}{10}$	(14 lambs) $\frac{4}{10}$	(1 goat)
Day 19	(9 bullocks) $\frac{7}{10}$	(2 rams) $\frac{4}{10}$	(14 lambs) $\frac{4}{10}$	(1 goat)
Day 20	(8 bullocks) $\frac{4}{10}$	(2 rams) $\frac{4}{10}$	(14 lambs) $\frac{4}{10}$	(1 goat)
Day 21	(7 bullocks) $\frac{1}{10}$	(2 rams) $\frac{4}{10}$	(14 lambs) $\frac{4}{10}$	(1 goat)
Day 22	(1 bullock) $\frac{3}{10}$	(1 ram) $\frac{2}{10}$	(7 lambs) $\frac{7}{10}$	(1 goat)
Totals	$\frac{3}{10}$		$\frac{5}{10}$	

Key
- □ 1 animal
- ▩ 10 animals
- ▢ 1 ephah
- ▨ 10 ephahs

▽ $\frac{3}{10}$ of an ephah for each bullock
○ $\frac{2}{10}$ of an ephah for each ram
☆ $\frac{1}{10}$ of an ephah for each lamb

*Yearlings without blemish

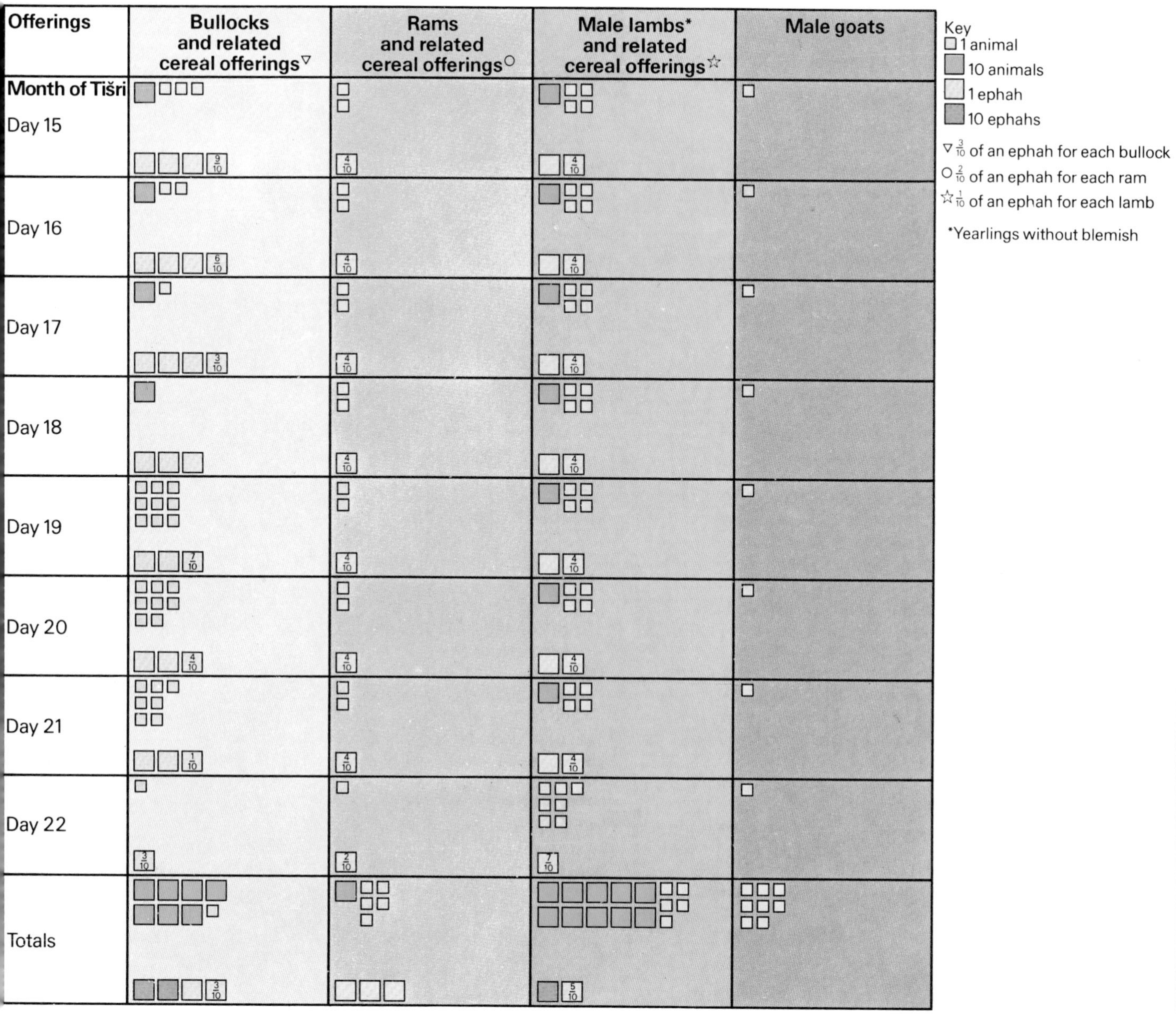

Chart showing the daily offerings during the Feast of Tabernacles (Nu. 29:12–35).

25:16, 22; Lv. 16:15–16), the veil and the two-compartment structure (Lv. 16:2; Heb. 9:8), the incense-altar (Ps. 141:2; *cf.* Lk. 1:10–13; Rev. 5:8; 8:3–4), the laver (Ex. 30:20–21), the copper altar (Lv. 1:3–9; 17:11); and where it is not stated explicitly, as with the table and the lampstand, it is self-evident from their declared function. How far these symbols were also types of spiritual realities later to be revealed to us is disputed. Understandably, the extravagant interpretations that from the early centuries have been placed upon the subject have brought it into disrepute. But the NT declares that the law had 'a shadow of the good things to come', which good things actually came with Christ (Heb. 10:1; 9:11). So Christ is said to have

entered through the veil (Heb. 6:19–20), and to be set forth as a propitiatory, or mercy seat (Rom. 3:25, *hilastērion*; *cf.* LXX Ex. 25:17–22; Lv. 16:15–16. RSV 'expiation' is scarcely exact); while the writer to the Hebrews indicates that he could have expounded in this fashion all the tabernacle vessels and not simply the one feature which was relevant to his immediate argument (Heb. 9:5).

BIBLIOGRAPHY. A. H. Finn, *JTS* 16, 1915, pp. 449–482; A. R. S. Kennedy, *HDB*, 4, pp. 653–668; M. Haran, *HUCA* 36, 1965, pp. 191–226; U. Cassuto, *A Commentary on the Book of Exodus*, 1967, pp. 319ff.; R. K. Harrison, *IOT*, 1970, pp. 403–410; R. P. Gordon, *An Old Testament Commentary* (ed. G. C. D. Howley), 1979. D.W.G.

TABERNACLES, FEAST OF.
Heb. *ḥaḡ hassukkôṯ*, 'festival of booths' (Lv. 23:34; Dt. 16:13), or *ḥaḡ hā'āsîp̄*, 'festival of ingathering' (Ex. 23:16; 34:22). This was one of the three great pilgrimage-festivals of the Jewish year; it was kept for 7 days from the 15th to the 22nd day of the 7th month. It came at the end of the year when the labours of the field were gathered in, and was one of the three annual festivals at which every male was required to appear (Ex. 23:14–17; 34:23; Dt. 16:16). It was a time of rejoicing (Dt. 16:14). The designation 'feast of booths (tabernacles)' comes from the requirement for everyone born an Israelite to live in booths made of boughs of trees and branches of palm trees for the

■ **TABITHA**
See Dorcas, Part 1.

■ **TABLES OF COVENANT**
See Ten Commandments, Part 3.

■ **TABLES OF TESTIMONY**
See Ten Commandments, Part 3.

■ **TABLETS**
See Table, Part 3.

A table laden for an Egyptian nobleman's feast. Wall-painting from the tomb of Nakht, Thebes. c. 1415 BC. (RS)

Opposite page: Right: A table being carried by an Assyrian servant. Relief from the palace of Sargon II at Khorsabad. c. 710 BC. (MC)

Opposite page: Left: Elaborately decorated table depicted on a relief of a banquet for King Ashurbanipal and his queen. Nineveh. Height 75 cm. c. 640 BC. (RS)

TABOO
See Ban, Part 1.

TABRET
See Music, Part 2.

TACHMONITE
See Jashobeam, Part 2.

TACKLING
See Cord, Part 1.

7 days of the feast (Lv. 23:42). Sacrifices were offered on the 7 days, beginning with thirteen bullocks and other animals on the 1st day and diminishing by one bullock each day until on the 7th seven bullocks were offered. On the 8th day there was a solemn assembly when one bullock, one ram and seven lambs were offered (Nu. 29:36). This is the last day, 'that great day of the feast', probably alluded to in Jn. 7:37. As a feast, divinely instituted, it was never forgotten. It was observed in the time of Solomon (2 Ch. 8:13), Hezekiah (2 Ch. 31:3; *cf.* Dt. 16:16), and after the Exile (Ezr. 3:4; Zc. 14:16, 18–19). The ceremony of water-pouring, associated with this festival in post-exilic times and reflected in Jesus' proclamation in Jn. 7:37f., is not prescribed in the Pentateuch. Its recognition of rain as a gift from God, necessary to produce fruitful harvests, is implied in Zc. 14:17 (*cf.* 1 Sa. 7:6).

This feast had a historical reference to the Exodus from Egypt and reminded the Jews of their wandering and dwelling in booths in the wilderness (Lv. 23:43). However, this is not evidence of the conversion of the agricultural festival to a historical one. Rather it points to the truth that Israel's life rested upon redemption which in its ultimate meaning is the forgiveness of sin.

This fact separates this feast from the harvest festivals of the neighbouring nations whose roots lay in the mythological activity of the gods.

BIBLIOGRAPHY. N. Hillyer, *TynB* 21, 1970, pp. 39–51. D.F.

TABLE. 1. A table as an article of furniture (Heb. *šulḥān*; Gk. *trapeza*). The table in the steppe, or wilderness (Pss. 23:5; 78:19), was a prepared area or skin laid out on the ground (Heb. *šlḥ*). Elsewhere the word is used, as its modern counterpart, for the table made of wood or metal which was a common item of furniture (2 Ki. 4:10). To eat 'at the king's table' was a signal honour (2 Sa. 9:7; *cf.* Lk. 22:21), while to eat at 'one's own table', as well as having its literal meaning, denoted living at one's own expense (1 Ki. 18:19; Ne. 5.17). 'The table of the Lord' (Mal. 1:7, 12; Ezk. 41:22; 44:16; 1 Cor. 10:21; *ALTAR) implies that at which he is the host. Ps. 69:22 is of uncertain meaning.

2. For AV 'table' standing for writing-tablet (RSV 'tablet', Lat. *tabula*) see *WRITING. The AV also has 'table' for Heb. *lûaḥ*, for a plank used in the construction of the altar (Ex. 27:8), a ship (Ezk. 27:5), a door (Ct. 8:9), and the metal plates at the base of Solomon's lavers (1 Ki. 7:36). All these were also potential surfaces for inscriptions. D.J.W.

Mount Tabor. (RS)

TABOR. If Jos. 19:22; Jdg. 8:18; and 1 Ch. 6:77 refer to the same place, Tabor was on the Zebulun–Issachar border: and it was presumably on or near Mt Tabor. The 'oak', or 'terebinth' (NEB), of 1 Sa. 10:3 must have been at a different Tabor, in Benjaminite territory. D.F.P.

TABOR, MOUNT. A notable mountain rising from the Plain of Jezreel to 588 m above sea-level. Its slopes are steep, and the views from the summit magnificent; hence it was considered worthy of comparison with Mt Hermon, in spite of the latter's much greater bulk and height (*cf.* Ps. 89:12). It was the scene of Barak's mustering (Jdg. 4:6) and of an idolatrous shrine in Hosea's day (*cf.* Ho. 5:1). In later times there was a town on the summit, which was taken and then fortified by Antiochus III in 218 BC. In 53 BC it was the scene of a battle between the Romans and Alexander the son of Aristobulus. Josephus, in his role as Jewish general, gave the town on the summit a defensive rampart in AD 66; remains of this wall can still be seen. The mountain also figured in the events of Crusader times.

Since the 4th century AD, and perhaps earlier, tradition has held that Mt Tabor was the scene of the transfiguration. This is not very likely; more probable is the view that Mt Tabor is intended in Dt. 33:19. The Arabs called the mountain Jabal al-Tur; the Israelis have given it its old Heb. name, *Har Tāḇôr*. D.F.P.

TADMOR. This place-name occurs twice in AV (1 Ki. 9:18; 2 Ch. 8:4), and is usually identified with mod. Tudmur, 'Palmyra', 200 km NE of Damascus; mentioned as *Tadmar* in Assyr. texts *c.* 1110 BC. Tadmor in AV in 1 Ki. 9:18 is based on *qᵉrē'* and the ancient versions. The *kᵉṯîḇ* is *tāmār*. The ancient versions have 'Palmyra' (Gk. for 'palm tree' = Heb. *tāmār*). The problem is

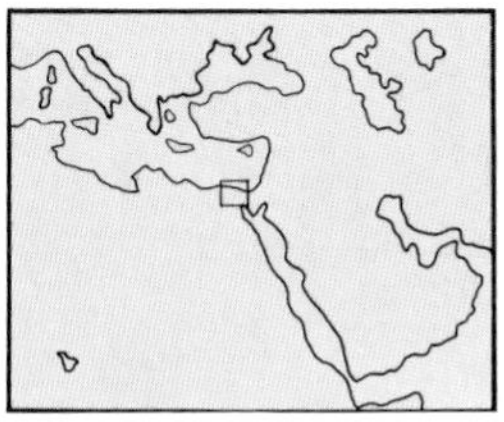

The location of Tahpanhes.

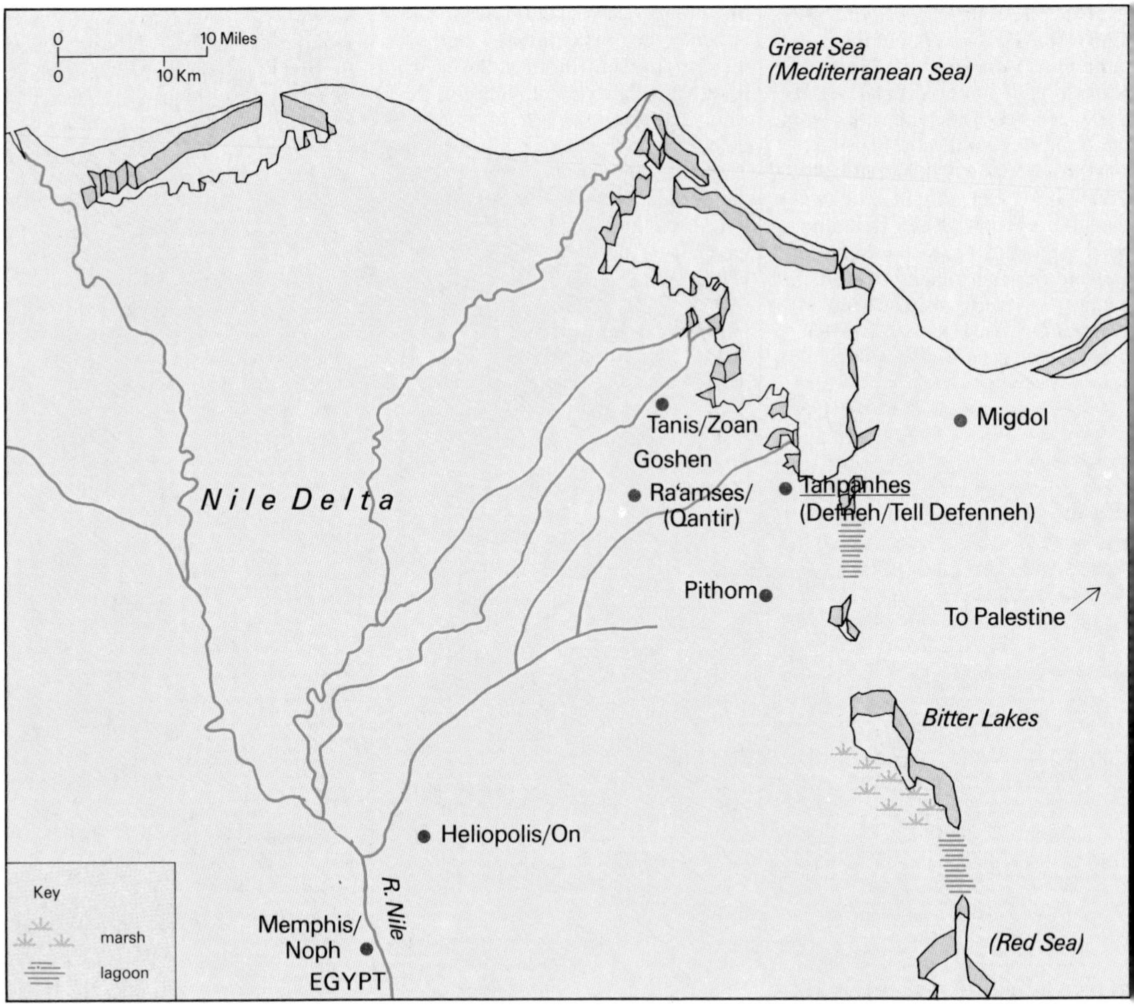

whether the Tamar of 1 Ki. 9:18 (RV, RSV) is identical with the Tadmor of 2 Ch. 8:4. The following solutions are proposed: **1.** Later in the time of the Chronicler, when the government of Solomon was idealized, the unimportant Tamar of the Judaean desert was changed to the then well-known, illustrious Tadmor in the Syrian desert. **2.** *Qᵉrē'* and the ancient versions are to be followed in identifying the place in 1 Ki. 9:18 with Tadmor, the later Palmyra in the Syrian desert. **3.** Tamar of 1 Ki. 9:18 and Tadmor of 2 Ch. 8:4 are different places. Tamar, the modern *Kurnub*, called *Thamara* in the *Onomasticon* of Eusebius, was situated on the route between Elath and Hebron. This city was fortified to protect the trade with S Arabia and the seaport Elath. Tadmor was the famous trading-centre NE of Damascus and could have been brought under Solomon's rule with the operations against the Syrian Hamath and Zobah.

The third solution is acceptable, because Tamar in 1 Ki. 9:18 is expressly called 'in the land' and thus in Israelite territory (*cf.* also Ezk. 47:19; 48:28).

BIBLIOGRAPHY. J. Starcky, *Palmyra*, 1952. F.C.F.

TAHPANHES. An important Egyptian settlement in the E Delta, named with Migdol, Noph (Memphis), *etc.* (Je. 2:16; 44:1; 46:14; Ezk. 30:18 as Tehaphnehes), to which certain Jews fled *c.* 586 BC, taking thither the prophet Jeremiah (Je. 43). The same consonantal spelling *Tḥpnḥs* recurs in a Phoen. papyrus letter of the 6th century BC found in Egypt (*cf.* A. Dupont-Sommer, *PEQ* 81, 1949, pp. 52–57). The LXX form Taphnas, Taphnais, probably equates Tahpanhes with the Pelusian Daphnai of Herodotus (2. 30, 107) where the 26th Dynasty pharaoh Psammetichus I (664–610 BC) established a garrison of Gk. mercenaries. On grounds of geographical location, the equivalence of Arabic Defneh with Daphnai, and the excavation at Defneh of Gk. pottery and other objects, Tahpanhes-Daphnai is located at modern Tell Defneh ('Defenneh'), about 43 km SSW of Port Said. The Egyptian for Tahpanhes is not inscriptionally attested, but may be *T'-ḥ(wt)-p'-nḥsy*, 'mansion of the Nubian', names compounded with *nḥsy*, 'Nubian', being known elsewhere in Egypt (so Spiegelberg).

'Pharaoh's house in Tahpanhes' and the 'brickwork' (RV) at its entry in which Jeremiah hid stones to presage Nebuchadrezzar's visitation there (Je. 43:9) may just possibly be the fortress of Psammetichus I, with traces of a brick platform on its NW side, excavated by Petrie (*Nebesheh (Am) and Defenneh (Tahpanhes)* bound with *Tanis II*, 1888). K.A.K.

TAHPENES. An Egyp. queen whose sister the pharaoh married off to Hadad of Edom (1 Ki. 11:19–20; *PHARAOH, **II.** 6). B. Grdseloff (*Revue de l'Histoire Juive en Égypte*, No. 1, 1947, pp. 88–90) took Heb. *tḥp̄ns* as a transcription of the Egyp. title *t(')-ḥ(mt)-p(')-ns(w)*,

TAHCHEMONITE See Jashobeam, Part 2.

'Royal Wife'. W. F. Albright (*BASOR* 140, 1955, p. 32) postulated an Egyp. name *T(')-ḥ(nt)-p(')-* (or *pr-*) *-ns(w)*, for which partial parallels exist. K.A.K.

TAHTIM-HODSHI. In 2 Sa. 24:6 a place in the N of David's realm, near the frontier with the kingdom of Hamath, mentioned in his census record. On the basis of LXX, *MT 'ereṣ taḥtîm ḥoḏšî* (AV 'the land of Tahtim-hodshi') has been very plausibly emended to *qāḏēš 'ereṣ ha-ḥittîm* (RSV 'Kadesh in the land of the Hittites'). (*KADESH; *HITTITES.) F.F.B.

TALE. The AV rendering of four Heb. words, each of which is thus translated once only. Three of them mean 'number': *mispār* (1 Ch. 9:28); *maṯkōneṯ*, 'measure', 'proper quantity' (Ex. 5:8); and *tōḵen*, 'a weight', 'measure' (Ex. 5:18).

In the fourth occurrence the Heb. word is *hegeh*, which could mean 'meditation' or 'utterance' and is found in the phrase 'as a tale that is told' (Ps. 90:9), a rendering much disputed. LXX and Vulg. read 'as a spider's web'. The literal translation is 'like a sigh', and this is retained by RSV. J.D.D.

TALEBEARING, SLANDER. These words translate, in the OT, expressions implying secrecy (Pr. 18:8, 'whisperer'), evil report (Nu. 14:36), the giving out (Ps. 50:20) or carrying (Pr. 11:13) of slander, or the (wrong) use of tongue (Ps. 101:5) or feet (2 Sa. 19:27). In the NT the words translate accusation (1 Tim. 3:11, *diabolos*), speaking against (2 Cor. 12:20; 1 Pet. 2:1, *katalalia*) or defaming (Rom. 3:8, *blasphēmeō*). All talebearing, whether false (*cf.* Mt. 5:11) or not (*cf.* Dn. 3:8), malicious (Ps. 31:13; Ezk. 22:9) or foolish (Pr. 10:18; *cf.* 18:8 = 26:22; Mt. 12:36), especially between neighbours (Je. 9:4) or brothers (Jas. 4:11), is condemned (Lv. 19:16) and punished (Ps. 101:5) by God, and causes quarrelling (Pr. 26:20). Slander springs from the heart (Mk. 7:22) of the natural man (Rom. 1:30), excludes from God's presence (Ps. 15:3), and must be banished from the Christian community (2 Cor. 12:20; Eph. 4:31; Col. 3:8; 1 Pet. 2:1; *cf.* [of women] 1 Tim. 3:11; Tit. 2:3), which itself suffers slander (Mt. 5:11; *cf.* Rom. 3:8). P.E.

TALITHA CUMI. 'Little girl, . . . arise.' Mk. 5:41 records these words spoken by Jesus in a Galilean Aramaic dialect to the daughter of Jairus, the Jewish leader. The word used for girl comes from a root meaning 'lamb' and is an affectionate term, like the Eng. 'lambkin'. MSS א, B, C read *koum* for *koumi.* This is due to the fact that the final vowel is not pronounced in some dialects. R.A.H.G.

TALMAI. 1. A descendant of 'Anaq, a 'giant' (*ANAK), resident in Hebron at the time of the Conquest (Nu. 13:22) but driven out by Caleb (Jos. 15:14). He is described as a Canaanite in Jdg. 1:10, which records his death.

2. The son of Ammihud and ruler of Geshur. David married his daughter Maacah, who bore Absalom (2 Sa. 3:3; 13:37; 1 Ch. 3:2). After the assassination of Amnon Absalom fled for refuge with Talmai in *Geshur (2 Sa. 13:37). The (Hurrian?) name Talmai occurs in texts from *Alalaḫ and *Ugarit of the 14th century BC and as a later Nabataean name. D.J.W.

TALMUD AND MIDRASH.

I. Talmud

The Talmud is composed of the *Mishnah*, the oral law which was in existence by the end of the 2nd century AD, and was collected by Rabbi Judah the Prince; and the *Gemara*, the comments of the Rabbis from AD 200 to 500 on the Mishnah. The Talmud contains *Halakhah*, legal enactments and precepts with the elaborate discussions whereby decisions were reached; and *Haggadah*, non-legal interpretations. The Talmud is the source from which Jewish law is derived. It is binding for faith and life on orthodox Jews. Liberal Jews do not consider it authoritative, though interesting and venerable. It is important for our knowledge of how the Jews interpreted the OT. It also throws light on portions of the NT.

The position is taken that the law of Moses had to be adapted to changing conditions in Israel. The claim is made that the 'Great Synagogue' (120 men) had such authority, but there is no proof to support the assertion. Rabbi Akiba (*c.* AD 110–35) or an earlier scholar made a comprehensive collection of traditional laws. Rabbi Judah the Prince utilized this material along with other portions in his edition of the Mishnah. The earliest collection of Mishnah may be assigned to the time of the noted schools of Hillel and Shammai, who flourished at the time of the second Temple.

The Mishnah is divided on three principles: (1) subject-matter; (2) biblical order; and (3) artificial devices, such as numbers. The Mishnah is found in six orders or main divisions (called *s*ᵉ*ḏārîm*), which contain the material of sixty treatises. The main categories are subdivided into tractates, chapters and paragraphs. The first order (*Seeds*) treats of agricultural laws and religious duties relating to cultivation of the land, including commandments concerning the tribute of agricultural products to be given to the priest, the Levite, and the poor. The second division (*Feasts*) sets forth the various festivals of the religious calendar, including the observance of the sabbath, with the ceremonies and sacrifices to be brought on those days. The third order (*Women*) deals with the laws of marriage, divorce, the levirate marriage, adultery and regulations for the Nazirite.

The fourth division of the Mishnah (*Fines*) handles civil legislation, commercial transactions of different kinds, legal procedures and a collection of the ethical maxims of the Rabbis. *Sacred Things*, the fifth order of the Mishnah, presents legislation concerning sacrifices, the first-born, clean and unclean animals, together with a description of Herod's Temple. The sixth part of the Mishnah (*Purifications*) lays down the laws touching levitical cleanness and uncleanness, clean and unclean persons and objects, and purifications. In all these portions it was the aim of Rabbi Judah to differentiate between current and obsolete law, and between civil and religious practices.

The Mishnah is marked by brevity, clarity and comprehensiveness, and was employed as a textbook in rabbinical academies. After the editing of the Mishnah, it soon became the official standard of the Academies of Palestine (Tiberias, Caesarea, Sepphoris and Lydda) and Babylonia (Sura, Pumbedita and Nehardea), resulting in the Palestinian Talmud and the Babylonian Talmud respec-

■ **TAMBOURINE**
See Music, Part 2.

■ **TANNER, TANNING**
See Arts and crafts, Part 1.

■ **TAPE WORM**
See Animals, Part 1.

tively. Discussion in these seats of learning became the nucleus for the study of the law, which became known as the Talmud.

The greater part of the discussions in the Talmud is in dialogue form. The dialogue introduces questions and seeks after causes and origins. There are numerous lengthy digressions into the Haggadah. This is actually a literary device to relieve the complexity and monotony of legal discussions. The extant Talmud is a commentary on only two-thirds of the Mishnah. It contains rejected as well as accepted decisions of the law. The observation of A. Darmesteter is amply justified: 'The Talmud, exclusive of the vast Rabbinic literature attached to it, represents the uninterrupted work of Judaism from Ezra to the sixth century of the common era, the resultant of all the living forces and of the whole religious activity of a nation. If we consider that it is the faithful mirror of the manners, the institutions, the knowledge of the Jews, in a word of the whole of their civilization in Judaea and Babylonia during the prolific centuries preceding and following the advent of Christianity, we shall understand the importance of a work, unique of its kind, in which a whole people has deposited its feelings, its beliefs, its soul' (*The Talmud*, p. 7).

II. Midrash

The term *midrash* derives from the Heb. root *dāraš*, 'to search out, investigate', that is, to discover a thought not seen on the surface. It has reference, then, to a didactic or homiletic exposition. It occurs twice in the OT, in 2 Ch. 13:22, where the 'story' (AV, RSV) or 'commentary' (RV) of the prophet Iddo is spoken of, and in 2 Ch. 24:27, where the 'story' (RV; RSV 'Commentary') of the book of the Kings is referred to. 'They were probably didactic developments of the historical narratives we possess, making use of these narratives to emphasize some religious truth; but nothing is known of them beyond their titles' (*HDB*, 1, p. 459).

Our term has received its widest usage in extra-biblical context. Midrash is sometimes used in contrast to Mishnah, in which case it denotes that branch of rabbinic learning which has especially to do with the rules of traditional law. It is impossible at this stage of our knowledge to state which is the older method of study, Midrash or Mishnah. (See G. F. Moore, *Judaism*, 1, pp. 150ff.) Suffice it to say, after the return of the Jews from Babylon with the activity of Ezra and his school on behalf of the law, exposition and commentary for the congregation became a necessity.

The oral form of these commentaries was later crystallized into writing. Since the greater portion of the important works is no longer extant in the original composition, the date of compilation is almost impossible to ascertain. Midrashic activity came to an end soon after the completion of the Babylonian Talmud. In time the Midrash was displaced by the disciplines of history, grammar and theology.

Midrashim are divided into expositional and homiletical. The former comment on the text of Scripture according to their present order, or join to them tales, parables and the like (H. L. Strack, *Introduction to Talmud and Midrash*, pp. 201–205). The latter deal with individual texts, mostly from the beginnings of Scriptural lections. Midrashim exist on the Pentateuch, the Five Rolls, Lamentations, the Psalms, Proverbs and other books.

BIBLIOGRAPHY. *HDB* (*s.v.* 'Commentary'); B. Cohen, 'Talmudic and Rabbinical Literature', *The Jewish People*, 3, pp. 54–79; G. F. Moore, *Judaism*, 3 vols., 1927–30; H. L. Strack, *Introduction to Talmud and Midrash*, 1931; *JewE* (*s.v.* 'Midrash'); *EJ* (*s.vv.* 'Midrash', 'Mishnah', 'Talmud'). C.L.F.

TAMAR (Heb. *tāmār*, 'palm'). **1.** The wife, first of Er the eldest son of Judah, then of *Onan (Gn. 38:6ff.). After Onan's death his father Judah, not recognizing Tamar, became by her the father of twins, Perez and Zerah. The story of Tamar reveals something of the marriage customs in early Israel. (*MARRIAGE, **IV**.)

2. Daughter of David, violated by Amnon her half-brother, and avenged by Absalom (2 Sa. 13:1ff.; 1 Ch. 3:9). **3.** A daughter of Absalom (2 Sa. 14:27). **4.** A city in SE Judah (Ezk. 47:19; 48:28), near the Dead Sea. For discussion of location, see *TADMOR. J.D.D.

TAMMUZ. The deity whose cult was characterized by ritual offerings and lamentations. In a vision Ezekiel saw women sitting in the N gate of the *Temple in Jerusalem weeping for 'the Tammuz' (8:14). The Tammuz cult is little known and it is by no means certain that mourning for this god was made in the 4th month of the Babylonian *calendar which was named after him.

Tammuz was a predeluvian Sumerian shepherd and ruler who married the goddess *Ishtar. When he died she followed him into the underworld to try for his release and all fertility ceased on the earth. It was once thought that the death and resurrection of Tammuz was reflected in the disappearance of the vegetation in June and its revival in the following spring.

However, it now seems to be more likely from textual evidence that he did not rise (*JSS* 7, 1962, p. 153), or if he did it was for no more than for half the year when his place below was taken by the goddess Geshtinanna (*BASOR* 183, 1966, p. 31), or he was but a ghost coming with others for the funerary offerings prepared for him (*JSS* 11, 1966, pp. 10–15). Babylonian sources provide hymns and lamentations for the god but little about his worship. Tammuz seems to have had devotees at Air and Arad (*BASOR* 208, 1970, pp. 9–13) and later in *Phoenicia and Syria where a similar legend is told of Adonis (identified in *Egypt with Osiris) and Aphrodite whose temple at Byblos (Gebal) was a centre of the cult in Hellenistic times.

BIBLIOGRAPHY. T. Jacobsen in W. L. Moran (ed.), *Towards the Image of Tammuz*, 1970, pp. 73–103; B. Alster, *Dumuzi's Dream*, 1972, pp. 9–15; *ANET*, 1969, pp. 637–642. D.J.W.

TAPPUAH ('quince'?). **1.** A village in the *Shephelah, E of Azekah (Jos. 15:34, 53, Beth-tappuah), sometimes identified with Beit Netif, *c.* 18 km W of Bethlehem. The place-name may derive from a Calebite from Hebron (1 Ch. 2:43). **2.** A town in Ephraim territory (Jos. 16:8) on the S border of Manasseh (Jos. 17:7–8), possibly mod. Sheikh Abu Zarad, *c.* 12 km S of Shechem. Its Canaanite king was defeated by Joshua (Jos. 12:17; *Test. Judah* 3:2; 5:6). If 2 Ki. 15:16 refers to this same place (so RSV, after LXX; *cf.* AV Tiphsah), it was later attacked by Menahem of Israel. D.J.W.

TARGUMS. The Heb. word *targum* (plural *targumîm*) denotes an Aram. translation or paraphrase of some part of the OT. Targums are extant for every book except Ezra, Nehemiah and Daniel.

I. Historical survey

Targums gradually came into being as the *synagogue evolved. After the Babylonian Exile, Aramaic came to predominate over Hebrew as the language of the Jews; in consequence it became customary for the reading of the Heb. scriptures to be followed by an oral rendering into Aramaic for the benefit of the worshippers. Perhaps *cf.* Ne. 8:8. No doubt such renderings were free and spontaneous at first, but they became more and more fixed and 'traditional' as time passed. The next stage was to commit such material to writing; the earliest extant targumic material is from the 2nd century BC, from Qumran.

In the 1st millennium AD Judaism had two chief centres, Babylonia and Palestine. It would seem that most if not all the traditional targumic material originated in Palestine; some of it was transmitted to Babylonia, where in due course Targum Onkelos for the Pentateuch and Targum Jonathan on the Prophets (see below) were given official status. (N.B. References to 'the Targum' without further definition are normally to Onkelos or Jonathan.) Onkelos is claimed by TB (*Megillah* 3. 1) to have been a 1st-century AD proselyte, while Jonathan ben Uzziel lived in the 1st century BC; but considerable doubt surrounds the appropriateness of both names (*cf.* M. McNamara, *Targum and Testament*, p. 174). Neither Targum is likely to be so early; but both were in final, standard form by the 5th century.

Meanwhile an independent targumic tradition developed inside Palestine, and some of it attained a semi-official status there. It is convenient to call this tradition 'the Palestinian Targum', in spite of its varied and rather disparate character. The dating of the various individual targums has been and remains much disputed; it is even more difficult to decide the date of origin of specific features within any targum.

II. General characteristics

At one extreme, Targum Onkelos is for the most part an accurate, word-for-word rendering of the Hebrew. In view of their synagogue purpose, however, it is not surprising that targums were used as a medium of interpretation and instruction. Even the more literal of them display interpretative traits: *e.g.* place-names are brought up to date, difficulties are smoothed over and obscurities clarified. In the more paraphrastic targums (*e.g.* Pseudo-Jonathan), the text is expanded to a marked degree. Not only can the whole sense of a verse or passage be altered, but a great deal of additional material ('midrash') may be incorporated. Thus a targum may be scarcely recognizable as a translation of the Heb. original (see, *e.g.*, the translation of Is. 53 in J. F. Stenning, *The Targum of Isaiah*, 1949).

III. List of Targums

The targums follow the divisions of the Heb. Bible (*CANON OF THE OT, III).

a. The Law

(i) Targum Onkelos (or Onqelos): the official version of Babylonian Jews, among whom it was authoritative no later than the 4th century.

(ii) The Palestinian Targum is extant in three recensions. The only complete version is Neofiti I, probably of the 3rd century AD, although its first editor has claimed a pre-Christian date. Incomplete are the Jerusalem Targums I and II (often known as 'Pseudo-Jonathan', due to a mediaeval error, and 'Fragment Targum' respectively). The former is very complex, at times identical with Onkelos, elsewhere extremely paraphrastic. Fragments of the Palestinian Targum on the Pentateuch are also extant among the Cairo Genizah scrolls.

b. The Prophets

(i) Targum Jonathan ben Uzziel: the official Babylonian version, authoritative from the 4th century AD.

(ii) The Palestinian Targum has not survived, apart from fragments and occasional citations.

c. The Writings

Separate targums are extant on Job–Psalms, Proverbs, the Five Scrolls and Chronicles. These, which were never official, were later in origin than those on the Law and Prophets. From Qumran there are fragments of a much earlier and totally different targum on Job (4Qtg Job; 11Qtg Job).

IV. Value

a. Language

Targumic material offers some of the major evidence for the vernacular speech of ancient Palestine. It is therefore of special importance for the study of the *ipsissima verba* of Jesus and of the Aramaic substratum of the NT as a whole. Major problems remain, however, in view of uncertainties about the date of the various targums, and the problem of the existence of various dialects within Palestine.

b. Text

The targums offer an important witness to the text of the OT, comparable in value with the LXX, Peshitta and Vulgate (*TEXTS AND VERSIONS, I). The evidence is much more reliable in literal than in paraphrastic targumic material, for obvious reasons. Occasionally NT quotations from the OT are closer to the targums than to other Versions or to the *MT*.

c. New Testament background

The targums bear witness to Jewish modes of expression, exegetical methods and current interpretations in the early Christian centuries. Many of them are reflected, whether directly or in a more diffuse way, in the NT. The targums therefore often throw light on the NT, although their evidence is not to be used in isolation from all other rabbinic sources.

BIBLIOGRAPHY. *Major texts:* A. Sperber, *The Bible in Aramaic*, 1957–73; A. Díez Macho, *Neophyti*, 1, 1968– . *Studies:* R. Le Déaut, *Introduction à la littérature targumique*, 1, 1966; E. Schürer, *HJP*, pp. 99–114; M. McNamara, *The New Testament and the Palestinian Targum to the Pentateuch*, 1966; *idem*, *Targum and Testament*, 1968; *idem*, *IDBS*, *s.v.* 'Targums'; J. Bowker, *The Targums and Rabbinic Literature*, 1969; R. Le Déaut, 'The Current State of Targumic Studies', *Biblical Theology Bulletin* 4, 1974, pp. 3–32. See also B. Grossfeld, *A Bibliography of Targumic Literature*, 1972; *Newsletter for Targumic Studies*, 1974– .

D.F.P.

TARSHISH. 1. A grandson of Benjamin, son of Bilhan (1 Ch. 7:10). **2.** One of the seven notable princes of Ahasuerus, ruler of Persia (Est. 1:14).

3. The son of Javan, grandson of Noah (Gn. 10:4; 1 Ch. 1:7). The

TARAH
See Terah, Part 3.

name Tarshish (*taršîš*), which occurs 4 times in AV as Tharshish (1 Ki. 10:22 (twice); 22:48; 1 Ch. 7:10), refers both to the descendants and to the land.

Several of the references in the OT are concerned with ships and suggest that Tarshish bordered on the sea. Thus Jonah embarked on a ship sailing to Tarshish (Jon. 1:3; 4:2) from Joppa in order to flee to a distant land (Is. 66:19). The land was rich in such metals as silver (Je. 10:9), iron, tin, lead (Ezk. 27:12), which were exported to places like Joppa and Tyre (Ezk. 27). A land in the W Mediterranean where there are good deposits of mineral seems a likely identification, and many have thought of Tartessus in Spain. According to Herodotus (4. 152), Tartessus lay 'beyond the Pillars of Hercules', and Plinius and Strabo placed it in the Guadalquivir Valley. Certainly the mineral wealth of Spain attracted the Phoenicians, who founded colonies there. Interesting evidence comes from Sardinia, where monumental inscriptions erected by the Phoenicians in the 9th century BC bear the name Tarshish. W. F. Albright has suggested that the very word Tarshish suggests the idea of mining or smelting, and that in a sense any mineral-bearing land may be called Tarshish, although it would seem most likely that Spain is the land intended. An old Semitic root found in Akkad. *rašāšu* means 'to melt', 'to be smelted'. A derived noun *taršīšu* may be used to define a smelting-plant or refinery (Arab. *ršš*, 'to trickle', *etc*., of liquid). Hence any place where mining and smelting were carried on could be called Tarshish.

There is another possibility as to the site of Tarshish. According to 1 Ki. 10:22 Solomon had a fleet of ships of Tarshish that brought gold, silver, ivory, monkeys and peacocks to Ezion-geber on the Red Sea, and 1 Ki. 22:48 mentions that Jehoshaphat's ships of Tarshish sailed from Ezion-geber for

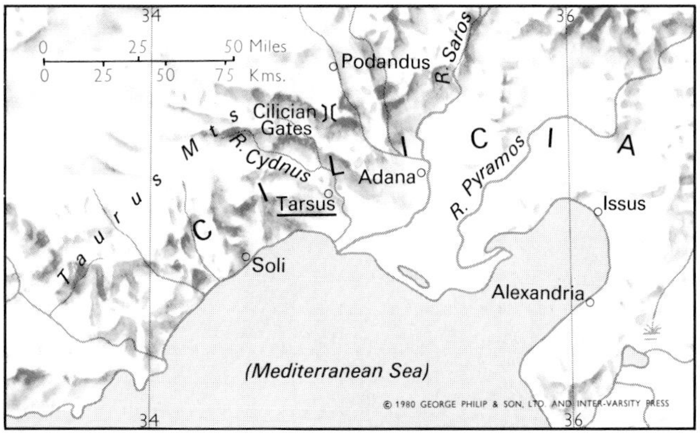

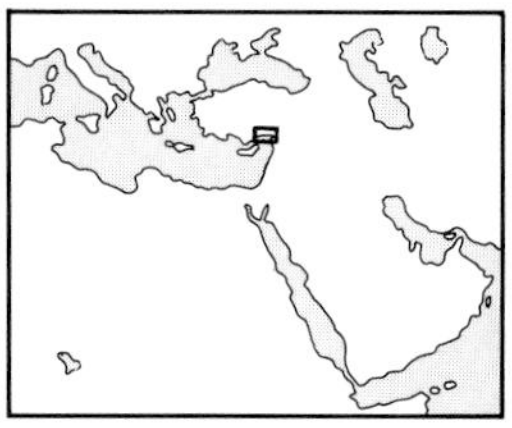

Tarsus, a city of Cilicia.

The Cilician Gates were a formidable pass on the main highway through the Taurus mountains. (SH)

Ophir. Further, 2 Ch. 20:36 says that these ships were made in Ezion-geber for sailing to Tarshish. These latter references appear to rule out any Mediterranean destination but point to a place along the Red Sea or in Africa. The expression *'ºnî taršîš*, navy of Tarshish or Tarshish fleet, may refer more generally to ships which carried smelted metal either to distant lands from Ezion-geber or to Phoenicia from the W Mediterranean. For the view that Tarshish vessels were deep seagoing vessels named after the port of Tarsus, or Gk. *tarsos*, 'oar' see *SHIPS AND BOATS.

These ships symbolized wealth and power. A vivid picture of the day of divine judgment was to portray the destruction of these large ships in that day (Ps. 48:7; Is. 2:16; 23:1, 14). The fact that Is. 2:16 compares the ships of Tarshish with 'the pleasant place' (RSV 'beautiful craft') suggests that whatever the original identification of Tarshish may have been, it became in literature and in the popular imagination a distant paradise from which all kinds of luxuries might be brought to such areas as Phoenicia and Israel.

BIBLIOGRAPHY. W. F. Albright, 'New Light on the Early History of Phoenician Colonization', *BASOR* 83, 1941, pp. 14ff.; 'The Role of the Canaanites in the History of Civilization', *Studies in the History of Culture*, 1942, pp. 11–50, esp. p. 42; C. H. Gordon, 'Tarshish', *IDB*, 4, pp. 517f. J.A.T.

TARSUS. A city on the Cilician plain, watered by the Cydnus, and some 16 km inland after the fashion of most cities on the Asia Minor coast. To judge from the extent of its remains, Tarsus must have housed a population of no less than half a million in Roman times. The lower Cydnus was navigable, and a port had been skilfully engineered. A major highway led N to the Cilician Gates, the famous pass through the Taurus range some 50 km distant.

Nothing is known of the foundation of Tarsus. It was probably a native Cilician town, penetrated at a very early date by Gk. colonists. The name of Mopsus is traditionally associated with Gk. settlement in Cilicia, and may indicate, as Ramsay believed (*The Cities of St. Paul*, 1907, pp. 116f.), early Ionian settlement. Gn. 10:4, 'The sons of Javan, Elishah, Tarshish . . .' may support this theory. Josephus' identification of Tarshish with Tarsus in this passage does not preclude a different interpretation in other contexts. The antiquity of Gn. 10 is a graver objection, but the words may be evidence of Ionian intrusion of very remote date.

Tarsus appears sporadically in history. It is mentioned in the Black Obelisk of Shalmaneser as one of the cities overrun by the Assyrians in the middle of the 9th century BC. Median and Persian rule followed, with that typically loose organization which permitted the rule of a Cilician subject-king. Xenophon, passing through in 401 BC, found Tarsus the royal seat of one Syennesis, ruling in such capacity. This petty king may have been deposed for his association with Cyrus' revolt which brought Xenophon and the Ten Thousand to Cilicia, for Alexander, in 334 BC, found the area in the hands of a Persian satrap. The coinage of the period suggests a mingling of Greek and Oriental influence, and gives no indication of autonomy. Ramsay professes to trace a decline of Greek influence under the Persian rule.

Nor did the Seleucid kings, who ruled after Alexander, promote the influence of the Greeks in Tarsus. Their general policy, here as elsewhere, was to discourage the Greek urge to city autonomy and its attendant liberalism. It is possible that the shock of the Roman defeat of Antiochus the Great and the peace of 189 BC reversed the process. The settlement limited the Syrian domain to the Taurus, and Cilicia became a frontier region. The fact seems to have prompted Syria to some reorganization, and the granting of a form of autonomy to Tarsus. The Tarsus of Paul, with its synthesis of East and West, Greek and Oriental, dates from this time.

A story in 2 Macc. 4:30–36 reveals the rapid growth of independence, and the reorganization of the city which a Tarsian protest won from Antiochus Epiphanes in 171 BC. The formation of a 'tribe' of Jewish citizens after the Alexandrian fashion may date from this time. (Antiochus' anti-semitism was against metropolitan recalcitrance.) Tarsian history in the rest of the 2nd century BC is obscure. The 1st century BC is better known. Roman penetration of Cilicia began in 104 BC, but Roman and Greek influence were both overwhelmed in Asia by the Oriental reaction under Mithridates (83 BC). Pompey's settlement in 65–64 BC reconstituted Cilicia as a 'sphere of duty', which is the basic meaning of 'province', rather than a geographical entity, and the governors, Cicero among them (51 BC), had a roving commission to pacify the pirate coast and hinterlands and to protect Roman interests.

In spite of Roman experimentation with the land at large, Tarsus flourished, played some part in the civil wars, was visited by Antony, and favoured by Augustus as the home town of Athenodorus, his teacher at Apollonia and life-long friend. The Roman citizenship of some Tarsian Jews dates probably from Pompey's settlement. E.M.B.

TARTAK. The name of an idol or deity (Heb. *tartāq*) worshipped by the men of *Avva who were settled in Samaria after its capture by the Assyrians in 722 BC (2 Ki. 17:31). The identification must remain open until the location of Avva itself is sure. TB (*Sanhedrin* 63b) ascribes the form of an ass to Tartak, but this is probably conjecture, as is the suggestion that the deity Atargatis is intended. D.J.W.

TARTAN. The title of a high Assyrian officer. Two are mentioned in the OT. The first was sent by Sargon II to besiege and capture Ashdod in 711 BC (Is. 20:1, AV). The second came from Sennacherib with other officials (*RABSARIS, *RABSHAKEH) and a military force to demand the surrender of Jerusalem in 701 BC (2 Ki. 18:17). In neither case is the personal name of the officer given. The Assyr. *turtanu* is listed in the Assyrian Eponym texts as the highest official after the king. He was also titular head of the province of which Harran was the capital. D.J.W.

TATTENAI (Heb. *tattᵉnai*; AV 'Tatnai'; *cf.* Gk. *Sisinnes*, 1 Esdras 6:3; 7:1, RSV). The Persian governor, successor of Rehum, of the Samaria district during the reign of Darius Hystaspes and Zerubbabel (Ezr. 5:3, 6; 6:6, 13). He investigated and reported in a sympathetic manner on complaints made from Jerusalem against Jews in his district. He is called 'Tat-

TARTAROS
See Hell, Part 2.

TASSELS
See Fringes, Part 1.

tanni, of the District across the River' (as Ezr. 5:6) in a cuneiform inscription from Babylon, dated 5 June 502 BC (*JNES* 3, 1944, p. 46), and appears to be under the satrap of Babylon Ushtani at this time. D.J.W.

TAVERNS, THREE (Lat. *Tres Tabernae*). This was a station about 50 km from Rome on the Via Appia, which led SE from the city. It is mentioned by Cicero in his correspondence with Atticus (2. 10). When the apostle Paul and his company were on their way from Puteoli to Rome, Christians came out of the city and met him here (Acts 28:15). B.F.C.A.

TAUNT-SONG
See Proverb, Part 3.

TAWNY OWL
See Animals, Part 1.

TAXATION
See Taxes, Part 3.

TAX COLLECTOR. The Gk. word *telōnēs* (AV 'publican') means a collector of tax or custom on behalf of the Romans, employed by a tax farmer or contractor. As early as 212 BC there existed in Rome a class of men (*ordo publicanorum*, Livy, 25. 3. 8–19) who undertook state contracts of various kinds. They were closely associated with, and supported by, the equestrian order; and at a later date were active in a number of provinces (Cicero, *In Verrem*, 2. 3. 11, §§ 27–28), where their work included the collection of tithes and various indirect taxes. The system was very open to abuse, and the *publicani* seem to have been prone to extortion and malpractice from the very beginning, so that while the grossest excesses were restrained by the government, and cases sometimes brought to justice, a generally bad reputation has come down to us. Cicero considered such occupations as that of customs officer vulgar on account of the hatred they incurred (*de Officiis*, 1. 42, § 150) and Livy records the opinion, expressed in 167 BC, that where there is a *publicanus* allies have not liberty (45. 18. 3–4). The central contractors were often foreign to the provinces whose taxes they farmed, though there was nothing to prevent their being natives, and they might employ native sub-contractors. (The expression *architelōnēs* in Lk. 19:2 seems to imply that Zacchaeus was the contractor for the whole of the taxes of Jericho and had collectors under him—*SB*, 2, p. 249.) But the collectors were usually from the native population, for they needed to know local people and their ways to avoid being deceived. Their generally extortionate practices (*cf.* what amounts to an admission in the words of Zacchaeus, Lk. 19:8, and the conditions implied by the counsel of John the Baptist, Lk. 3:13) made them an especially despised and hated class, so that our Lord could refer to them as typical of a selfish attitude (Mt. 5:46). For the strict Jew, however, this quite natural attitude of hatred was aggravated and altered in character by the religious consideration that the *telōnēs* was regarded as ceremonially unclean, on account of his continual contact with Gentiles, and his need to work on the sabbath. This uncleanness, and the rabbis' teaching that their pupils should not eat with such persons, account for the attitude evidenced by the expressions *tax collectors and sinners*

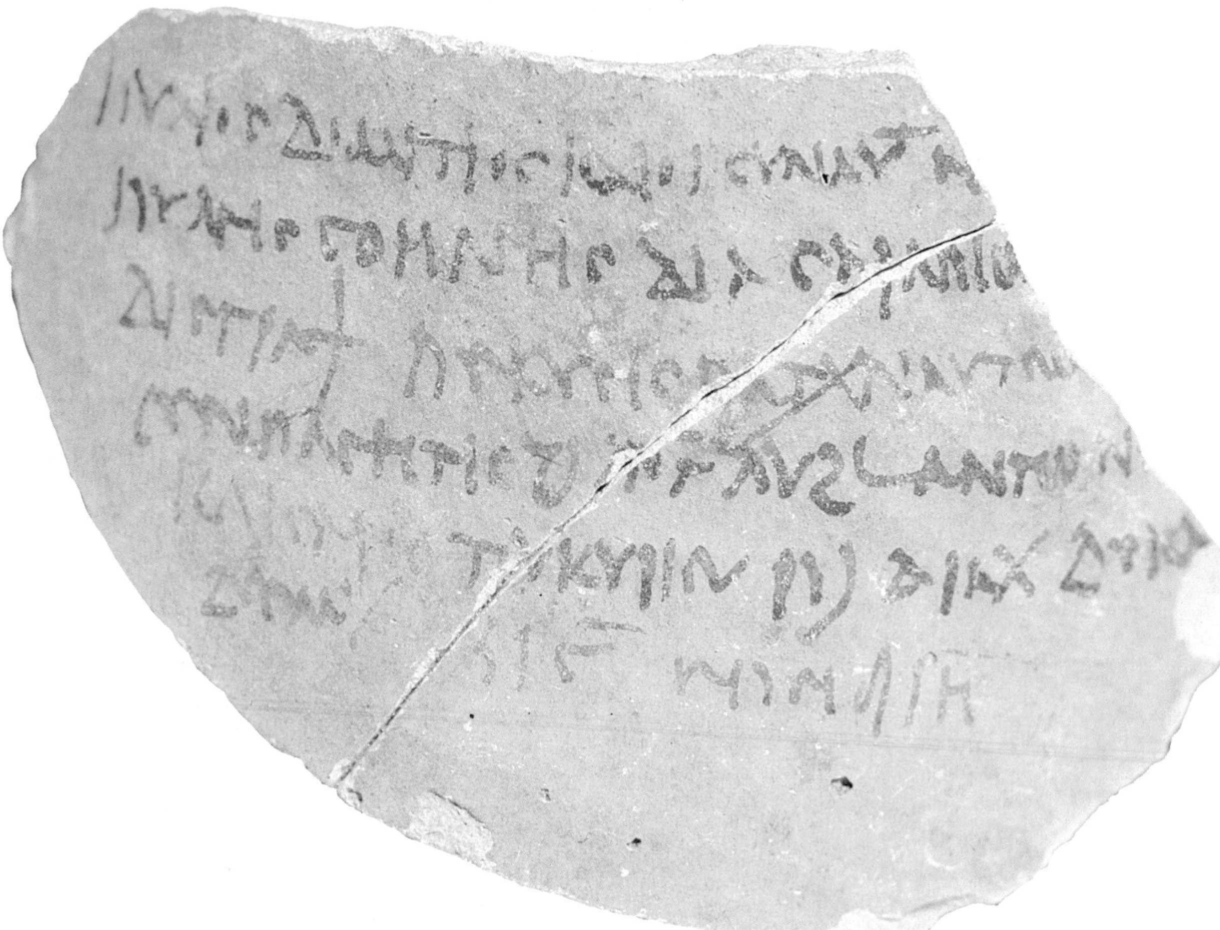

Receipt for poll-tax paid to officials of the Sacred Gate in Syene (Aswan). Written in Greek on a potsherd. Length 10·5 cm, width 7 cm. 12 July, AD 144. (ARM)

A defaulting Egyptian taxpayer is held against a post and beaten. Relief from the tomb of Mereruka, Saqqara. c. 2300 BC. (KAK)

Mt. 9:10f.; 11:19; Mk. 2:15f.; Lk. ·:30; 7:34; 15:1) and *tax collectors ·nd harlots* (Mt. 21:31), and for ·he questions of Mt. 9:10f.; 11:19; ·Mk. 2:15f.; Lk. 5:29f. (*cf. SB*, 1, ·p. 498f.), and indicates the inten·ion of the command of Mt. 18:17. ·This also lends point to both the ·egative and positive aspects of the ·lenunciation of the chief priests ·nd elders in Mt. 21:31b, to the ·tatement of Mt. 11:19; Lk. 7:34, ·nd to the story of the Pharisee and ·he tax collector, Lk. 18:10ff.

BIBLIOGRAPHY. Arndt; *OCD*, *s.vv. ·lecumae, portoria, publicani, vecti·alia*; E. Schürer, *HJP*, 1, 1973, ·p. 372ff.; *SB*, 1, pp. 377f., 498f., ·70f.; 2, p. 249; N. Hillyer, ·*NIDNTT* 3, pp. 755–759. J.H.H.

·AXES. Regular payments ex·racted from a state and its pro·inces by its own rulers are taxes, ·listinct from wealth received from conquered states which is *tribute.

In Israel's infancy the only taxes required were to maintain the tabernacle and its ministers, a practice renewed after the Exile (Dt. 18:1–5; 14:22–27, *etc.*; Ne. 10:32–39; *TITHES). With the Monarchy came heavier demands as listed by Samuel (1 Sa. 8:15, 17), comparable with the habits of all ancient kings. Occasionally there were exceptional levies to pay tribute to foreign conquerors (2 Ki. 15:19–20; 23:35).

In NT times Roman provinces paid regular taxes to Caesar in Roman coin, as Mt. 22:17; Mk. 12:14 are aware, whereas Herodian rulers collected dues in their realms (Mt. 17:24–27). In these passages Mt. and Mk. used Gk. *kēnsos*, borrowed from Lat. *censum*, 'poll-tax', while Lk. has the more general *phoros*, 'tribute, tax' (Lk. 20:22). (*CENSUS; *TAX COLLECTOR.)

BIBLIOGRAPHY. A. N. Sherwin-White, *Roman Society and Roman Law in the New Testament*, 1963, pp. 125–127; M. J. Harris, C. Brown, N. Hillyer, in *NIDNTT* 3, pp. 751–759. A.R.M.

TEKOA. 1. A town in Judah, about 10 km S of Bethlehem, the home of Amos (Am. 1:1). When Joab 'perceived that the king's heart went out to Absalom' he sent to Tekoa for a wise woman who might reconcile David and Absalom (2 Sa. 14:1f.). Rehoboam fortified the town (2 Ch. 11:6). Later, when Jehoshaphat was faced by Ammonites and Moabites, he consulted with the people in 'the wilderness of Tekoa' (2 Ch. 20:20). Jeremiah called for the blowing of a trumpet in Tekoa in the face of the advancing enemy (Je. 6:1). After the Exile the town was re-inhabited (Ne. 3:5, 27). In Maccabean and Roman times the place was known,

TEACHING OF JESUS
See Jesus Christ, life and teaching of, Part 2.

TEBETH
See Calendar, Part 1.

TEETH
See Grinder, Part 2.

TEHAPHNEHES
See Tahpanhes, Part 3.

TEIL TREE
See Trees (Terebinth), Part 3.

TELEM
See Telaim, Part 3.

TELL EL-AMARNA
See Amarna, Part 1.

TEMPERANCE
See Self-control, Part 3.

and the name lingers today as Khirbet Taqû'a, a ruined village of some 5 acres, which has not been excavated.

2. A descendant of Hezron, the grandson of Judah, belonging to the general Calebite stock (1 Ch. 2:24; 4:5).

BIBLIOGRAPHY. F. M. Abel, *Géographie de la Palestine*, 2, 1933, p. 478; D. Baly, *Geography of the Bible*², 1974, pp. 89, 182. J.A.T.

TELAIM. The place where Saul gathered his army before his attack on the Amalekites (1 Sa. 15:4). The incident described in 1 Sa. 15, in which Saul disobeyed God's word given by the prophet Samuel, provoked the severe rebuke of 1 Sa. 15:22–23, 'to obey is better than sacrifice'. Telaim (Heb. *ṭᵉlā'îm*) is identified by some with Telem (Jos. 15:24), in the Negeb. Some MSS allow of an occurrence of the word in 1 Sa. 27:8, and read 'they of Telaim' for 'of old'. J.A.T.

TELASSAR. A place inhabited by the 'children (sons) of Eden' and cited by Sennacherib's messengers to Hezekiah as an example of a town destroyed in previous Assyr. attacks (as also *GOZAN, *HARAN, *REZEPH). The name *tᵉla'śśār* (2 Ki. 19:12) or *tᵉlaśśār* (Is. 37:12) represents Tell Assur ('mound of Assur'). The *bᵉnê 'eḏen* probably lived in the area between the Euphrates and Baliḫ rivers, called in Assyr. Bît-Adini (Beth-Eden), but no Til-Assur has been found in this region, although the area does suit the context. A Til-Aššur named in the annals of Tiglath-pileser III and Esarhaddon appears to lie near the Assyr. border with Elam. The common form of the place-name means that it may not yet be identified. There is no need to emend to Tell Bassar (Basher), SE of Raqqa on the Euphrates (as L. Grollenberg, *Atlas of the Bible*, 1956, p. 164). D.J.W.

TEMA. The name (Heb. *tēmā'*) of the son and descendants of Ishmael (Gn. 25:15; 1 Ch. 1:30) and of the district they inhabited (Jb. 6:19). It is mentioned, with Dedan and Buz, as a remote place (Je. 25:23) and as an oasis in the desert on a main trade route through Arabia (Is. 21:14). Aramaic stelae of the 5th century BC were found in the ruins of Taima' about 400 km NNW of Medina in NW Arabia. The city (Bab. *Tema'*) is also named in documents recording its occupation by Nabonidus during his exile (*AS* 8, 1958, p. 80; *ANET*³, p. 562). D.J.W.

TEMAN. The grandson of Esau (Gn. 36:11; 1 Ch. 1:36), who may have given his name to the district, town or tribe of that name in N Edom (Je. 49:20; Ezk. 25:13; Am. 1:12). The inhabitants were renowned for wisdom (Je. 49:7; Ob. 8f.). Eliphaz the Temanite was one of Job's comforters (Jb. 2:11, *etc.*). A chief (*'allûp̄*) of Teman (*têmān*) is named among the chiefs of Edom (Gn. 36:15, 42; 1 Ch. 1:53), and Husham was one of the early rulers (Gn. 36:34). The prophets include Teman among Edomite towns to be destroyed (Je. 49:20; Ezk. 25:13; Am. 1:12; Ob. 9). Habakkuk in his great vision saw God the Holy One coming from Teman (Hab. 3:3).

N. Glueck (*The Other Side of Jordan*, 1940, pp. 25–26) identified it with Tawilân, since excavated to show a large Edomite town of the 8th to 6th centuries BC (*RB* 76, 1969, pp. 386ff.). R. de Vaux argued that it denoted S Edom (*RB* 77, 1969, pp. 379–385). J.A.T.

TEMPLE.

I. Historical background

Some of the earliest structures built by man were temples or shrines where he could worship his god in his 'house' (see K. M. Kenyon, *Archaeology in the Holy Land*, pp. 41, 51, for the Mesolithic and Neolithic shrines at Jericho). The Tower of *Babel is the first structure mentioned in the Bible which implies the existence of a temple (Gn. 11:4). Although this seems to have been intended as a place where man might meet God, it symbolized the self-confidence of man attempting to climb up to heaven, and for such pride it was doomed.

In Mesopotamia, which Abraham left, each city had a temple dedicated to its patron deity. The god was looked upon as the owner of the land, and if it was not blessed by him it would be unproductive, resulting in poor revenues for his temple. The local king or ruler acted as steward for the god.

There was no purpose in the semi-nomadic Patriarchs building one particular shrine for their God. He revealed himself as and where he pleased. Such occasions were sometimes the scene of a sacrificial *altar. They might be commemorated by a *pillar (Gn. 28:22).

After Israel had grown into nationhood a central shrine became a necessity, as a gathering-point for all the people, a symbol of their unity in the worship of their God. This need was supplied by the *tabernacle during the trek through the wilderness and by recognized shrines during the period of the judges (*e.g.* Shechem, Jos. 8:30ff.; 24:1ff.; Shiloh, 1 Sa. 1:3).

The nations of Canaan had their own temples, simply called 'Dagon's house' or the house of whoever the patron deity was (Heb. *bêṯ dāḡôn*, 1 Sa. 5:5; *bêṯ 'aštārôṯ*, 1 Sa. 31:10; *cf. bêṯ yhwh*, Ex. 23:19). A variety have been uncovered at Beth-shan, Hazor and other sites.

The lack of a shrine of Yahweh appeared invidious when David had consolidated his power and built a permanent palace for himself. The king said, 'I dwell in a house of cedar, but the ark of God dwells in a tent' (2 Sa. 7:2). It was not given to him to build the Temple because he was stained with the blood of his enemies, but he collected materials, gathered treasure and bought the site (1 Ch. 22:8, 3; 2 Sa. 24:18–25). Solomon began the actual construction in his 4th year, and the Temple was completed 7 years later (1 Ki. 6:37–38).

II. Solomon's Temple

a. The site

That it stood within the area now called 'Haram esh-Sherif' at the E side of the 'Old City' of *Jerusalem is undisputed. The precise location within the vast enclosure is less certain. The highest part of the rock (now covered by the building known as 'The Dome of the Rock') may have been the site of the innermost sanctuary or of the altar of burnt-offering outside (2 Ch. 3:1). This rock was presumably part of the threshing-floor of *Araunah, bought by David for a sum given as 50 silver shekels (2 Sa. 24:24) or 600 gold shekels (1 Ch. 21:25).

Nothing of Solomon's structure remains above ground, nor were any definite traces found in the diggings sponsored by the Palestine Exploration Fund. Indeed, it is likely that the work of levelling the rock and building up the great retaining walls for the courtyard of

Ierod's Temple obliterated earlier constructions.

. Description

The passages 1 Ki. 6–7 and 2 Ch. 3–4 must be the bases of any reconstruction of Solomon's Temple. These accounts, while detailed, do not cover every feature, are not entirely understood and contain some apparent discrepancies (*e.g.* Ki. 6:2 and 16f.). They may be supplemented by incidental references and by the description of Ezekiel's Temple, an elaborated version of Solomon's building Ezk. 40–43). The Temple proper was an oblong, orientated E and W. t is reasonable to assume that, like Ezekiel's Temple, it stood on a platform (*cf.* Ezk. 41:8). No dimensions are given for the surrounding area. Again following Ezekiel's plan, it seems that there were two courtyards, inner and outer; a suggestion supported by 1 Ki. 6:36; 7:12; 2 Ki. 23:12; 2 Ch. 4:9.

The bronze altar for burnt-offerings stood in the inner court (1 Ki. 8:22, 64; 9:25). It was 20 cubits square and 10 cubits high (2 Ch. 4:1). Between this and the porch was the bronze laver holding water for ritual washings (AV 'molten' or 'brazen sea', 1 Ki. 7:23–26). This great basin, 10 cubits in diameter, rested upon four groups of four bronze oxen orientated to the four compass-points. These were removed by Ahaz (2 Ki. 16:17).

At the dedication of the Temple, Solomon stood on a bronze 'scaffold' (2 Ch. 6:12f., Heb. *kîyyôr*, the word used for 'laver' elsewhere, Ex. 30:18, *etc.*; here it may denote an inverted basin), which has parallels

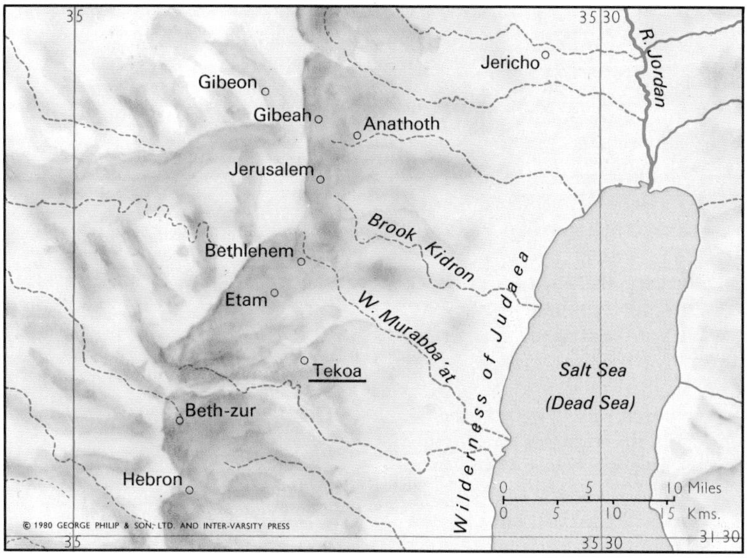

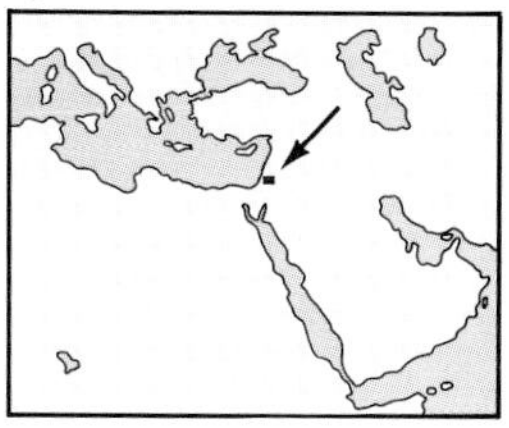

Tekoa in Judah.

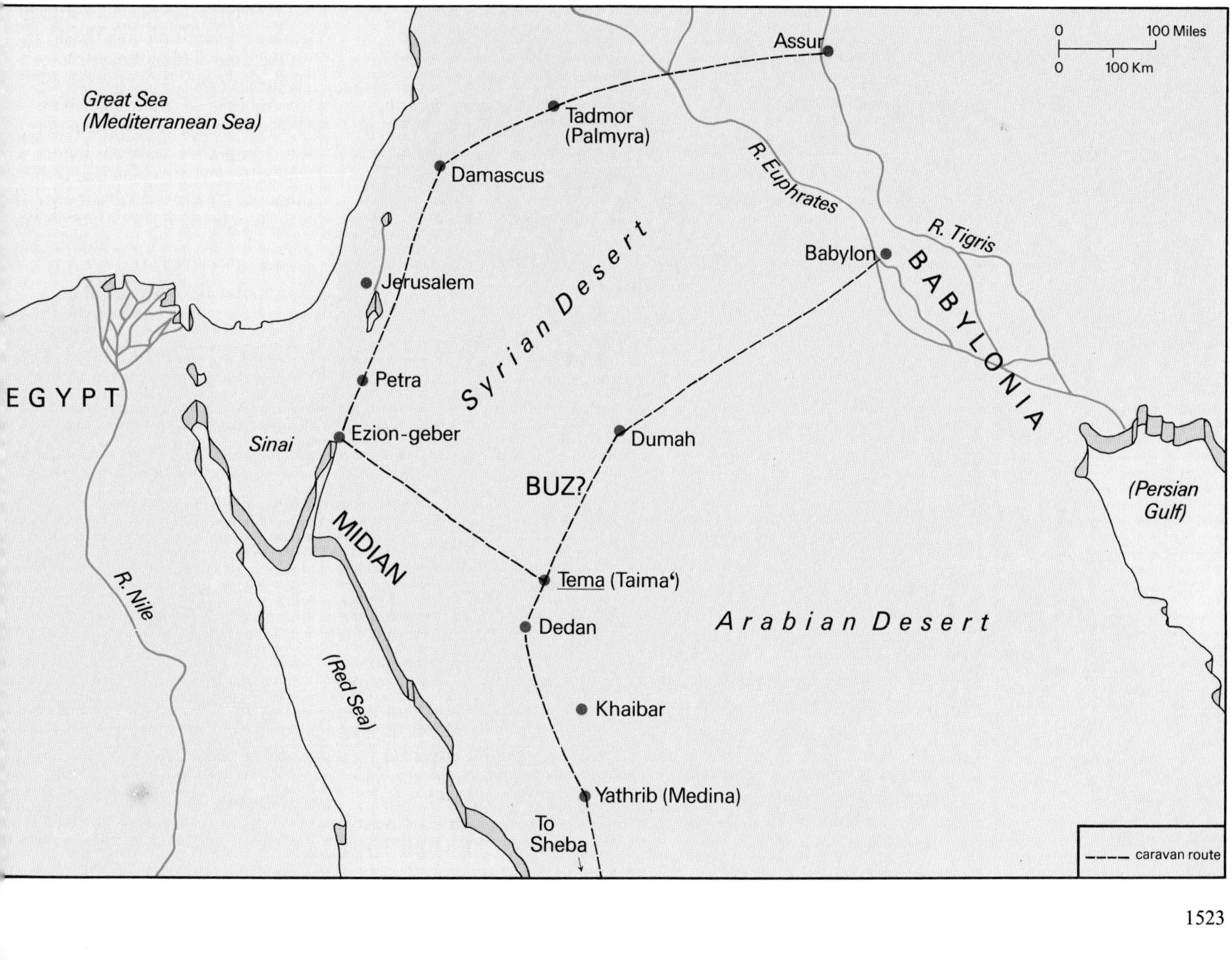

Tema, on a main Arabian trade route.

in Syr. and Egyp. sculptures and possibly in Akkadian (see W. F. Albright, *Archaeology and the Religion of Israel*[3], 1953, pp. 152–154).

A flight of steps would have led up from the inner court to the *porch (Heb. *'ûlām*). The entrance was flanked by two pillars, *Jachin and Boaz, with elaborately ornamented capitals. Their purpose remains indeterminate; they were not part of the structure. Gates probably closed the passage (*cf.* Ezk. 40:48).

The porch was 10 cubits long and 20 cubits wide (on the length of the cubit, see *WEIGHTS AND MEASURES). Its height is given as 120 cubits (2 Ch. 3:4), but this is surely erroneous, as the remainder of the building was only 30 cubits high. W of the porch was the large chamber in which the ordinary rituals were performed. This 'holy place' (AV 'temple'; Heb. *hêkāl*, a word derived through Canaanite from Sumerian *É. GAL*, 'great house') was 40 cubits long, 20 in breadth, and 30 high. It was shut off from the porch by double doors of cypress wood, each composed of two leaves. The statement that the doorposts were a fourth (Heb. *meẓûzôṯ mē'ēṯ reḇi'îṯ*, 1 Ki. 6:33; RSV 'in the form of a square' follows LXX) is difficult to explain. Possibly the doorway was 5 cubits wide, *i.e.* one-quarter of the width of the dividing wall, a proportion known in some other temples.

Latticed windows near the ceiling lighted the holy place (1 Ki. 6:4). Here stood the golden incense-*altar, the table for *showbread, and five pairs of *lampstands, together with the instruments of *sacrifice. The double doors of cypress leading to the inner sanctuary (Heb. *deḇîr*, 'innermost place'; AV 'oracle' is an unlikely rendering) were rarely opened, probably only for the high priest at the atonement ceremony. The doorposts and lintel are said to have been a fifth (Heb. *hā'ayil meẓûzôṯ ḥamiššîṯ*, 1 Ki. 6:31). As with the *hêkāl*, this may be explained as one-fifth of the dividing wall, 4 cubits.

The inner sanctuary was a perfect cube of 20 cubits. Although it might be expected that the floor was raised above the *hêkāl*, there is no hint of this. Within stood two wooden figures side by side, 10 cubits high. Two of their wings met in the centre above the *ark of the covenant, and the other wing of each touched the N and S walls respectively (1 Ki. 6:23–28; *CHERUBIM). In this most holy place the presence of God was shown by a cloud (1 Ki. 8:10f.).

Each room was panelled with cedar wood and the floor planked with cypress (or pine, Heb. *berôš*; *TREES). The walls and doors were carved with flowers, palm trees and cherubim, and overlaid with gold in the way approved for ancient temples, as inscriptions testify. No stonework was visible.

The outer walls of the inner sanctuary and the holy place were built with two offsets of 1 cubit to support the joists of three storeys of small chambers all around. Thus the ground-floor chambers were 5 cubits wide, those above 6, and the uppermost 7. A door in the S side gave access to a spiral staircase serving the upper floors. These rooms doubtless housed various stores and vestments, provided accommodation, maybe, for the priests in course, and sheltered the offerings of money and goods made by the worshippers.

Much has been made of the proximity of the royal palace to the Temple and the inference drawn that it was the 'Chapel Royal'. While admitting such a relationship (emphasized by the passage connecting the two buildings, 2 Ki. 16:18), it should be remembered that it was appropriate for the viceroy of Yahweh to reside near to the house of God; entry was not restricted to the king.

Solomon hired a Tyrian to take charge of the work and used Phoenician craftsmen (1 Ki. 5:10, 18; 7:13–14). It is not surprising to find parallels to the design of the Temple and its decoration in surviving examples of Phoenician or Canaanite handiwork. The ground plan is very similar to that of a small shrine of the 9th century BC excavated at Tell Tainat on the Orontes. This shows the three rooms, an altar in the innermost and two columns in the porch, but supporting the roof (for full report see R. C. Haines, *Excavations in the Plain of Antioch*, 2, 1971). At Hazor a Late Bronze Age shrine is also tripartite and was constructed with timbers between the stone-courses (Y. Yadin, *Hazor*, 1972, pp. 89–91; *cf.* 1 Ki. 5:18; 6:36). Numerous carved ivory panels (from the walls or furnishings of palaces) found throughout the ancient East are Phoenician work, often with Egyp. themes. Among the common subjects are flowers, palms and winged sphinxes, undoubtedly comparable with the carvings in the Temple. As with the Temple's panelling, these carvings were overlaid with gold and set with coloured stones.

c. Later history

Ancient temples generally served as state treasuries, emptied to pay tribute or filled and decorated with booty according to the power of the land. If, for some reason, a ruler paid little attention to the temple it would lose its revenue and rapidly fall into disrepair (*cf.* 2 Ki. 12:4–15). Solomon's Temple was no exception. The treasures which he had gathered in the Temple were raided in the reign of his son, Rehoboam, by Shishak of Egypt (1 Ki. 14:26). Later kings, including even Hezekiah, who had adorned the Temple (2 Ki. 18:15f.), used the treasure to purchase allies (Asa, 1 Ki. 15:18) or to pay tribute and buy off an invader (Ahaz, 2 Ki. 16:8). The idolatrous kings added the appurtenances of a Canaanite shrine, including the symbols of pagan deities (2 Ki. 21:4; 23:1–12), while Ahaz introduced an altar of foreign type, displacing the laver, at the time of his submission to Tiglath-pileser III (2 Ki. 16:10–17). By the time of Josiah (*c.* 640 BC), 3 centuries after its construction, the Temple was in need of considerable repair, which had to be financed by the contributions of the worshippers (2 Ki. 22:4). In 587 BC it was looted by Nebuchadrezzar and sacked (2 Ki. 25:9, 13–17). Even after the destruction men came to sacrifice there (Je. 41:5).

III. Ezekiel's Temple

The exiles were heartened in their grief (Ps. 137) by the vision of a new Temple granted to Ezekiel (Ezk. 40–43, *c.* 571 BC). More details are given of this than of Solomon's structure, although it was never built. The actual shrine was different in little other than its size (porch 20 cubits wide, 12 long; holy place 20 cubits wide and 40 long; inner sanctuary 20 cubits each way). The walls were again panelled and carved with palms and cherubim. The building was set on a platform mounted by ten steps which were flanked by two bronze pillars. Three tiers of rooms enfolded the inner sanctuary and the holy place. The vision gives a description of the surrounding area, something lacking from the account of the first Temple. An area of 500 cubits square was enclosed by a wall pierced by a single gateway on each of the N, E and S sides. Three more gates, opposite the former, led to an inner courtyard, where the altar of sacrifice stood before the shrine. All these gates were well fortified to prevent the entry of any but Israelites. There were various buildings in the courtyards for storage and for the use of the priests.

IV. The Second Temple

This stood for almost 500 years, longer than either the first or Herod's Temple. Yet it is only vaguely known from incidental references. The exiles who returned (*c*. 537 BC) took with them the vessels looted by Nebuchadrezzar, and the authorization of Cyrus for the rebuilding of the Temple. Apparently the site was cleared of rubble, an altar built and the laying of the foundations commenced (Ezr. 1; 3:2–3, 8–10). A stretch of walling on the W side of the present enclosure, abutting the Herodian stonework, may be a part of these foundations. When eventually finished it was 60 cubits long and 60 cubits high, but even the foundations showed that it would be inferior to Solomon's Temple (Ezr. 3:12). Around the shrine were store-places and priests' rooms. From some of these Nehemiah expelled the Ammonite Tobiah (Ne. 13:4–9). 1 Macc. 1:21; 4:49–51 give information about the furnishings. The ark had disappeared at the time of the Exile and was never recovered or replaced. Instead of Solomon's ten lampstands, one seven-branched candelabrum stood in the holy place with the table for showbread and the incense altar. These were taken by Antiochus IV Epiphanes (*c*. 175–163 BC), who set up the 'desolating sacrilege' (a pagan altar or statue) on 15 December 167 BC (1 Macc. 1:54). The triumphant * Maccabees cleansed the Temple from this pollution and replaced the furniture late in 164 BC (1 Macc. 4:36–59). They also turned the enclosure into a fortress so strong that it resisted the siege of Pompey for 3 months (63 BC).

V. Herod's Temple

The building of Herod's Temple, commenced early in 19 BC, was an attempt to reconcile the Jews to their Idumaean king rather than to glorify God. Great care was taken to respect the sacred area during the work, even to the training of 1,000 priests as masons to build the shrine. Although the main structure was finished within 10 years (*c*. 9 BC), work continued until AD 64.

As a basis for the Temple buildings and to provide a gathering-place, an area about 450 m from N to S and about 300 m from E to W was made level. In places the rock surface was cut away, but a large part was built up with rubble and the whole enclosed by a wall of massive stone blocks (normally about 1m high and up to 5 m long; *cf*. Mk. 13:1). At the SE corner, overlooking the Kidron ravine, the inner courtyard was about 45 m above the rock. Perhaps the parapet above this corner was the pinnacle of the Temple (Mt. 4:5). Stretches of this wall still stand. One gateway pierced the N wall (Tadi Gate), but was apparently never used, and one led through the wall on the E (under the present Golden Gate). Traces of the two Herodian gates on the S side are still visible beneath the Mosque of el-Aqsa. Ramps led upwards from these to the level of the court. Four gates faced the city on the W. They were approached by viaducts across the Tyropoeon valley (* JERUSALEM). At the NW corner the fortress of Antonia dominated the enclosure. This was the residence of the procurators when in Jerusalem, and its garrison was always at hand to subdue any unrest in the Temple (*cf*. Lk. 13:1; Acts 21:31–35). The high priest's robes were stored therein as a token of subjection.

The outer court of the Temple was surrounded by a portico, inside the walls. As described by Josephus (*Ant*. 15. 410–416), the S porch had four rows of columns and was called the Royal Porch. The porticoes of the other sides each had two rows. Solomon's Porch stretched along the E side (Jn. 10:23; Acts 3:11; 5:12). In these colonnades the scribes held their schools and debates (*cf*. Lk. 2:46; 19:47; Mk. 11:27) and the merchants and money-changers had their stalls (Jn. 2:14–16; Lk. 19:45–46). The inner area was raised slightly above the court of the Gentiles and surrounded by a balustrade. Notices in Gk. and Lat. warned that no responsibility could be taken for the probable death of any Gentile who ventured within. Two of these inscriptions have been found. Four gates gave access on the N and S sides and one on the E. This last had doors of Corinthian bronze-work and may be the Beautiful Gate of Acts 3:2.

The first court inside (Women's Court) contained the chests for gifts towards the expenses of the services (Mk. 12:41–44). Men were allowed into the Court of Israel, raised above the Court of the Women, and at the time of the Feast of Tabernacles could enter the innermost (Priests') Court to circumambulate the * altar. This was built of unhewn stone, 22 cubits away from the porch (*cf*. Mt. 23:35). The plan of the shrine copied Solomon's. The porch was 100 cubits wide and 100 cubits high. A doorway 20 cubits wide and 40 high gave entry, and one half that size led into the holy place. This was 40 cubits long and 20 cubits wide. A curtain divided the holy place from the inner sanctuary (the veil, Mt. 27:51; Mk. 15:38; *cf*. 2 Ch. 3:14). The inner sanctuary was 20 cubits square and, like the holy place, 40 cubits high. An empty room above the holy place and the inner sanctuary rose to the height of the porch, 100 cubits, thus making a level roof. Three storeys of chambers surrounded the N, S and W sides to a height of 40 cubits. Golden spikes were fixed on the roof to prevent birds from perching there.

The magnificent structure of cream stone and gold was barely finished (AD 64) before it was destroyed by the Rom. soldiery (AD 70). The golden candelabrum, the table of showbread and other objects were carried in triumph to Rome, as depicted on the Arch of Titus.

For organization of the Temple, see * Priests and Levites.

BIBLIOGRAPHY. The best summary is A. Parrot, *The Temple of Jerusalem*, 1957, with a comprehensive bibliography. For a detailed survey, see L. H. Vincent, *Jérusalem de l'Ancien Testament*, 1–2, 1954; J. Simons, *Jerusalem in the Old Testament*, 1952; T. A. Busink, *Der Tempel von Jerusalem*, 1970; L. H. Vincent, 'Le temple hérodien d'après la Mišnah', *RB* 61, 1954, pp. 1–35. For reconstructions of Solomon's Temple, see G. E. Wright, *BA* 18, 1955, pp. 41–44.

A.R.M.

VI. 'Temple' in the New Testament

Two Gk. words, *hieron* and *naos*, are translated 'temple'. The former refers to the collection of buildings which comprised the Temple at

Jerusalem, the latter refers more specifically to the sanctuary. Commentators draw attention to the fact that the word preferred by the NT writers to describe the church as the temple of God is *naos*. But the use of *naos* in Mt. 27:5 and Jn. 2:20 prevents one from making much of this fact. In the case of Mt. 27:5 the term is almost certainly to be understood in the sense of *hieron*, otherwise we have the formidable difficulty of explaining how Judas penetrated the area which was closed to all except priests. As for the Jews' statement in Jn. 2:20 that 46 years were spent in building the *naos*, it is unlikely that only the sanctuary was in mind. The use of *naos* as a synonym for *hieron* is also present in Herodotus (2. 170) and Josephus (*BJ* 5. 207–211).

With the literal use of 'temple' in the NT, *cf.* 'house' (*oikos*) and 'place' (*topos*). For a description of the Temple of Jerusalem in the time of our Lord, see section **V**, above. The metaphorical use of 'temple' should be compared with the metaphorical use of 'house', 'building' (*oikodomē*), 'tent' (*skēnē*), 'habitation' (*katoikētērion*; 'dwelling place').

a. 'Temple' in the Gospels

The attitude of Jesus to the Temple of Jerusalem contains two opposing features. On the one hand, Jesus greatly respected it; on the other hand, he attached relatively little importance to it. Thus, he called it the 'house of God' (Mt. 12:4; *cf.* Jn. 2:16). Everything in it was holy, he taught, because it was sanctified by God who dwelt in it (Mt. 23:17, 21). Zeal for his Father's house inspired him to cleanse it (Jn. 2:17), and thought of the impending doom of the holy city caused him to weep (Lk. 19:41ff.). In contrast are those passages in which Jesus relegated the Temple to a very subordinate position. He was greater than the Temple (Mt. 12:6). It had become a cover for the spiritual barrenness of Israel (Mk. 11:12–26 and parallels). Soon it would perish, for a terrible desecration would render it unfit to exist (Mk. 13:1f., 14ff.). See also Mk. 14:57f.; 15:29f. and parallels. These differing attitudes are not, however, without explanation.

At the beginning of his ministry Jesus addressed himself to the Jews and summoned all Israel to repentance. In spite of mounting opposition, we find him appealing to Jerusalem (Mk. 11:1ff. and parallels). The Temple was cleansed with a view to reforming the existing order (11:15ff. and parallels). But the Messianic implications of this action (Mal. 3:1ff.; *cf. Psalms of Solomon* 17:32ff.; Mk. 11:27ff.) engendered still greater hostility on the part of the religious leaders, and Judaism, persistently obdurate and unreformable, was in the end judged as unworthy of the divine presence (Mk. 12:1–12). So Jesus, who began by venerating the Temple, finally announced that his rejection and death would issue in its destruction. The accusation produced at the trial which asserted that Jesus had taught, 'I will destroy this temple that is made with hands, and in three days I will build another not made with hands' (Mk. 14:58; *cf.* 15:29) would therefore be a fitting peroration to the appeal of our Lord to Jewry. Mark attributes the saying, however, to false witnesses, and what constituted the falsity of the witness is a matter of conjecture among scholars. It is probably wisest to understand the charge as an unscrupulous combination of the prediction of Jesus that the Temple of Jerusalem

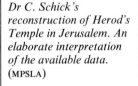

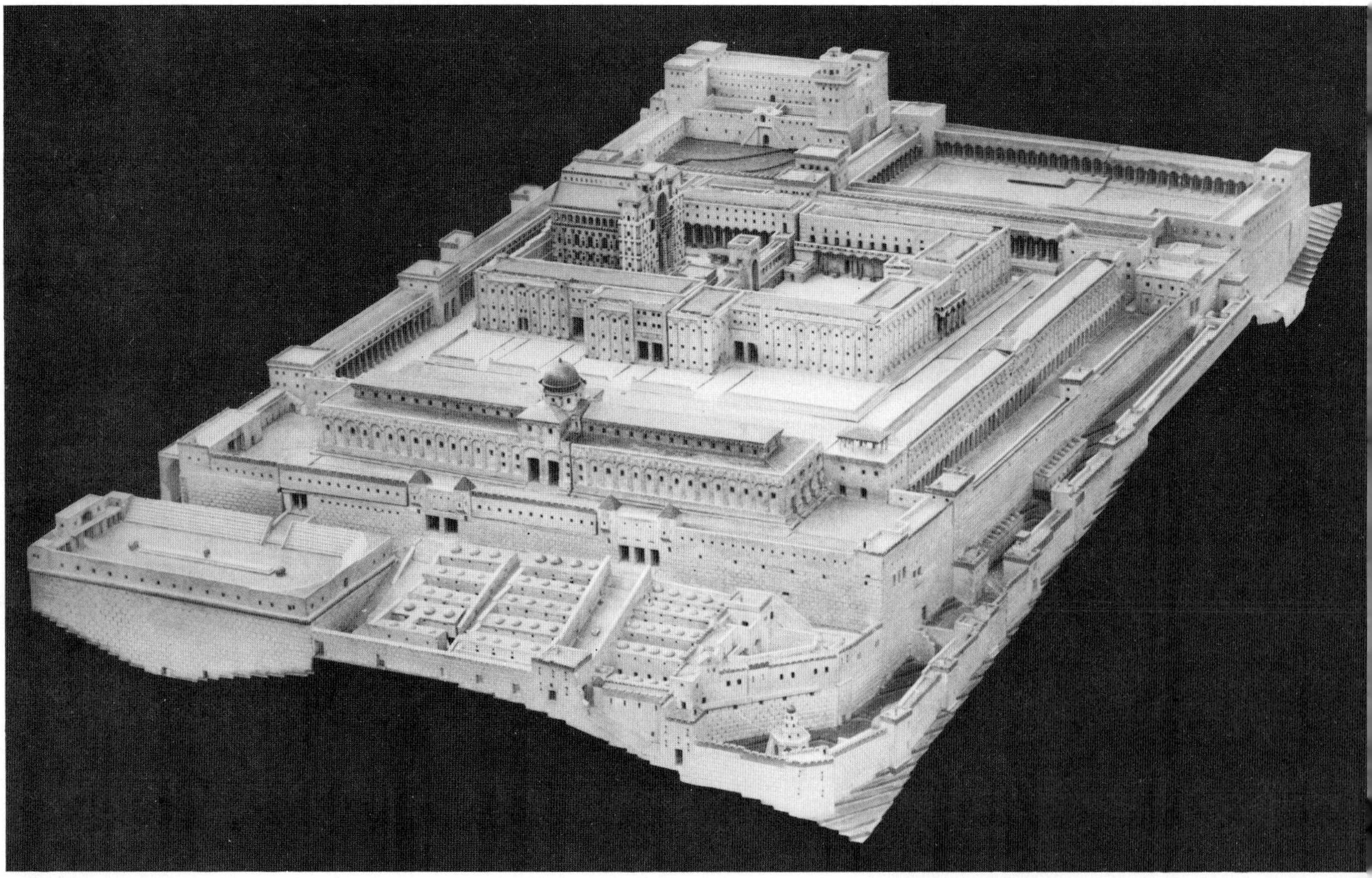

Dr C. Schick's reconstruction of Herod's Temple in Jerusalem. An elaborate interpretation of the available data. (MPSLA)

would be destroyed (Mk. 13:2 and parallels) and the logion that the Son of man would be destroyed and rise again on the 3rd day (Mk. 8:31; 9:31; 10:34 and parallels). That is to say, the falsity lay in misrepresentation of what Jesus actually had taught. One reason why Mark did not trouble to correct the misrepresentation may be due to the fact that the accusation was true in a deeper sense than the witnesses had in mind. The death of Jesus did in fact result in the supersession of the Temple of Jerusalem, and his resurrection put another in its place. The new temple was the eschatological congregation of Jesus Messiah (Mt. 18:20; *cf.* Jn. 14:23). Luke and John, therefore, made no reference to the false witness because when they wrote their Gospels the accusation was no longer seen to be groundless.

b. 'Temple' in the Acts of the Apostles

Some time elapsed, however, before the full ramifications of the work of Christ became apparent, and in the Acts we find the apostles continuing to worship at the Temple of Jerusalem (Acts 2:46; 3:1ff.; 5:12, 20f., 42; *cf.* Lk. 24:52). It appears

A model of the central part of Herod's Temple at Jerusalem, giving one possible interpretation of the available data. (RS)

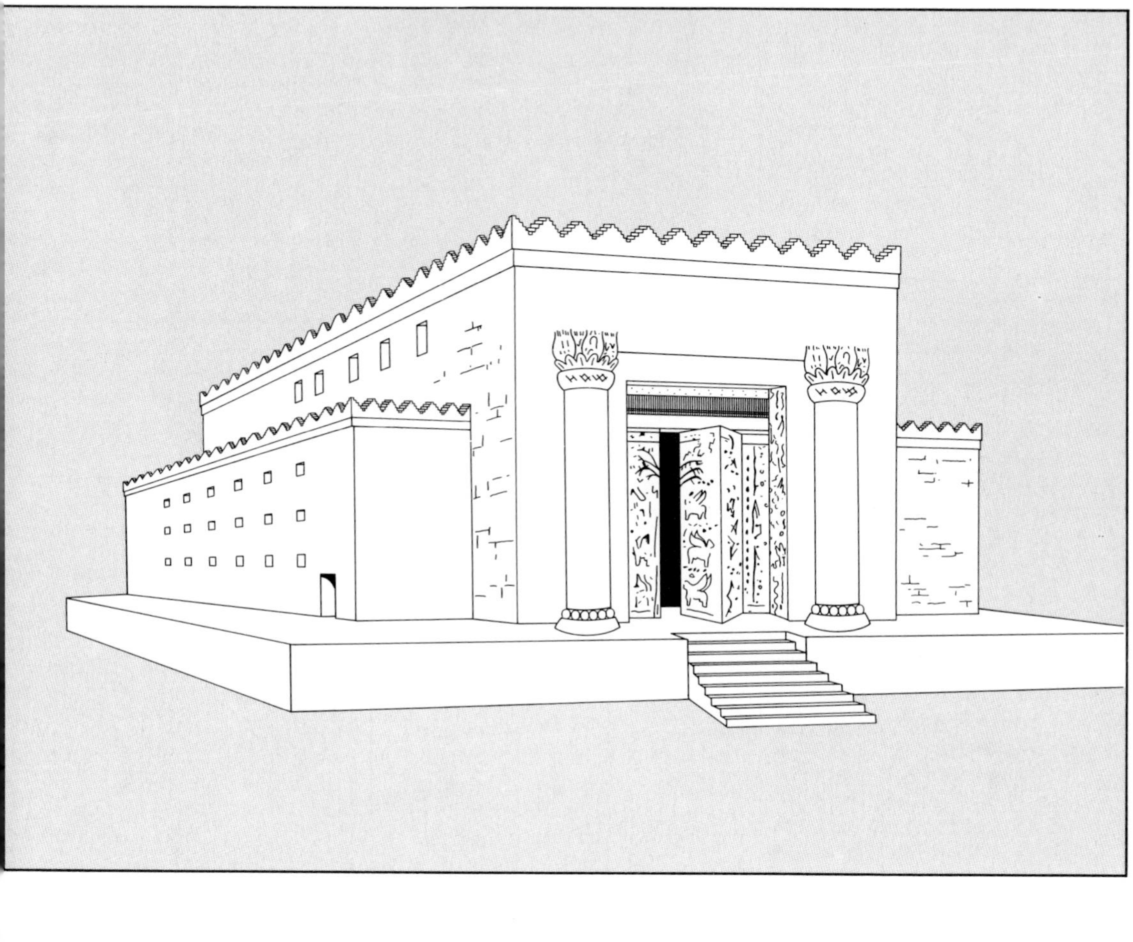

Steven's reconstruction of Solomon's Temple, showing the twin free-standing pillars (Jachin and Boaz), the vestibule porch and side storage-chambers.

Right and Opposite page Bottom: Notices in Greek and Hebrew warned non-Jews not to enter the inner court of Herod's Temple on pain of death (cf. Acts 21:28). One whole copy and part of another, in Greek, have been found. Standing in the time of Christ and the apostles. Jerusalem. Width of complete example 86·36 cm. c. 30 AD. (RS) (IsM)

that the Hellenistic-Jewish party represented by Stephen was the first to discover that belief in Jesus as Messiah meant the abrogation of the order symbolized by the Jerusalem Temple (Acts 6:11ff.). Accordingly, Stephen's defence became an attack on the Temple, or, more correctly, on the attitude of mind to which the Temple gave rise (Acts 7). But whether it is justifiable to find in Stephen's denunciation of the Temple a hint of the new temple made without hands, as some commentators do, is not at all certain. We are on firmer ground in Acts 15:13–18. The 'tabernacle of David' of Am. 9:11, to be sure, has the primary sense of dynasty or kingdom, but the use of this OT text in the eschatology of the Covenanters of Qumran to support their novel conception of a spiritual temple (CDC 3. 9) permits us to see here an adumbration of the doctrine of the church as God's new temple which is so common a feature of the Epistles.

c. 'Temple' in the Epistles

The doctrine of the church as the realization of the Messianic temple of OT and intertestamental eschatology is most prominent in the writings of Paul. See 1 Cor. 3:16–17; 6:19; 2 Cor. 6:16–7:1; Eph. 2:19–22. The appeal to prophecy is particularly strong in the case of 2 Cor. 6:16ff., where we have an OT couplet (Lv. 26:12; Ezk. 37:27) which was already in use in Jewish eschatology on the Messianic temple (*Jubilees* 1:17). Also characteristic of the temple image in 1 and 2 Cor. is its hortatory and admonitory application. Since Christians are the realization of the long-cherished hope of the glorious temple, they ought to live holy lives (2 Cor. 7:1; *cf.* 1 Cor. 6:18ff.). Unity is likewise enjoined upon them. Since God is one, there is only one habitation in which he can dwell. Schism is tantamount to profanation of the temple, and merits the same terrible penalty of death (1 Cor. 3:5–17). In Eph. the figure of the temple is employed in the interests of doctrinal instruction. Uppermost in the mind of the writer is the inter-racial character of the church. The language of the context of 2:19–22 makes it plain that the apostle borrowed liberally from the OT hope of the ingathering of Israel and the nations to the eschatological temple at Jerusalem. For example, the words 'far' and 'near' of vv. 13 and 17 (*cf.* Is. 57:19; Dn. 9:7) were rabbinic technical terms for the Gentiles and the Jews

Part of the cultic furniture of the Canaanite temple at Megiddo. This bronze stand depicts a priest or worshipper making an offering to a seated deity. Height c. 10 cm. c. 1050–1000 BC. (IM)

(*Numbers Rabbah* 8:4). Similarly, the 'peace' mentioned in vv. 14 and 17 is an allusion to the eschatological peace which was to prevail when Israel and the peoples were united in the one cult at Zion (Is. 2:2ff.; Mi. 4:1ff.; *Enoch* 90:29ff.). Paul undoubtedly regarded the fruits of his Gentile mission as the fulfilment of Jewish faith at its widest and most generous expression. He spiritualized the ancient hope of a reunited mankind, and represented Jews and Gentiles as the two walls of one building, joined by and resting upon Christ, the foremost cornerstone (Eph. 2:19–22). The statement that the building 'grows' (*auxein*) into a 'temple' introduces a different figure, *viz.* that of the body, and reveals a certain fusion of images. 'Temple' and 'body' are largely coterminous ideas of the church. Note the juxtaposition of the two conceptions in Eph. 4:12, 16.

Parallels for Paul's use of the metaphor in 1 and 2 Cor. are frequently sought in the writings of Philo and the Stoics, where the individual is called a 'temple'. The practice is scarcely justifiable, however. 1 Cor. 6:19–20 does indeed have the individual in mind, but only as a member of the community which corporately comprises the temple of God. Philo and the Graeco-Roman humanists

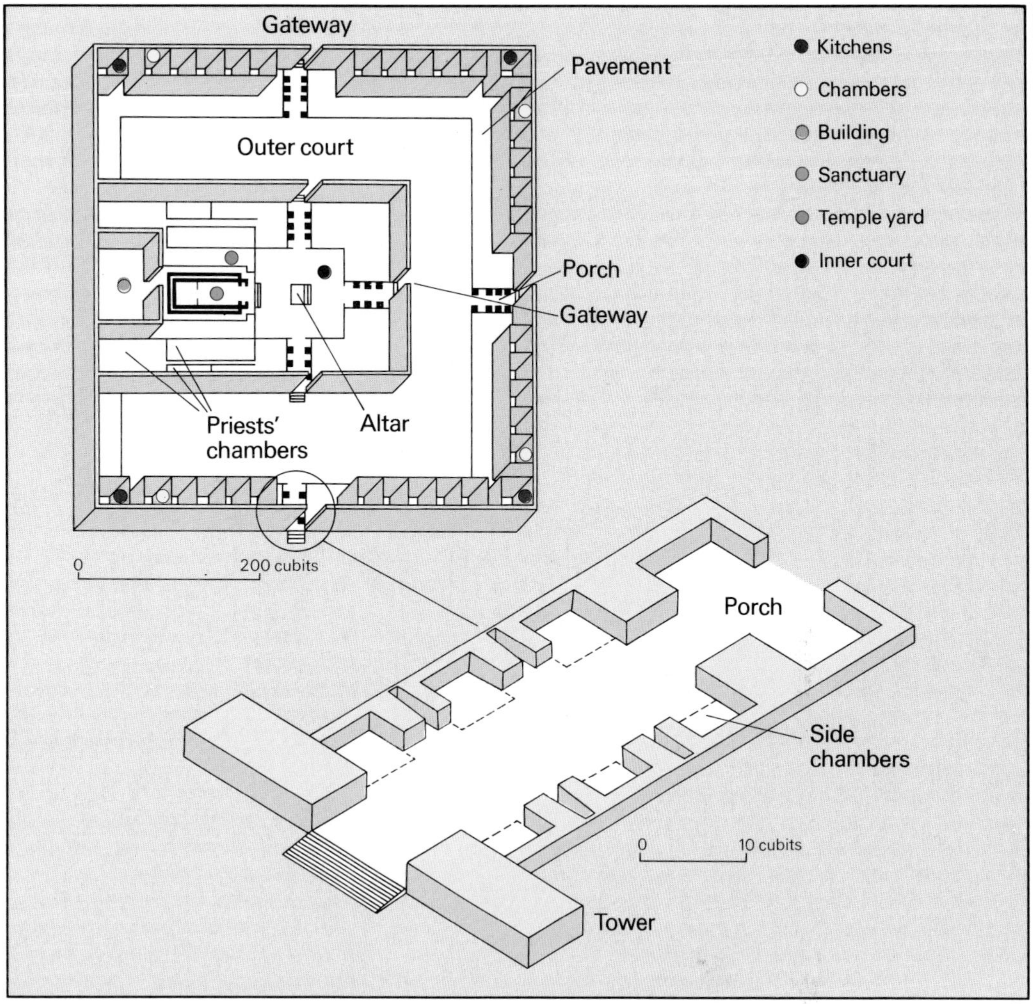

*Reconstruction of the layout of the Temple as seen by Ezekiel in his vision. Similar to Solomon's Temple at Jerusalem, the plan of the gates can be compared with Solomonic entrances excavated at the cities of *Hazor, *Megiddo and *Gezer.*

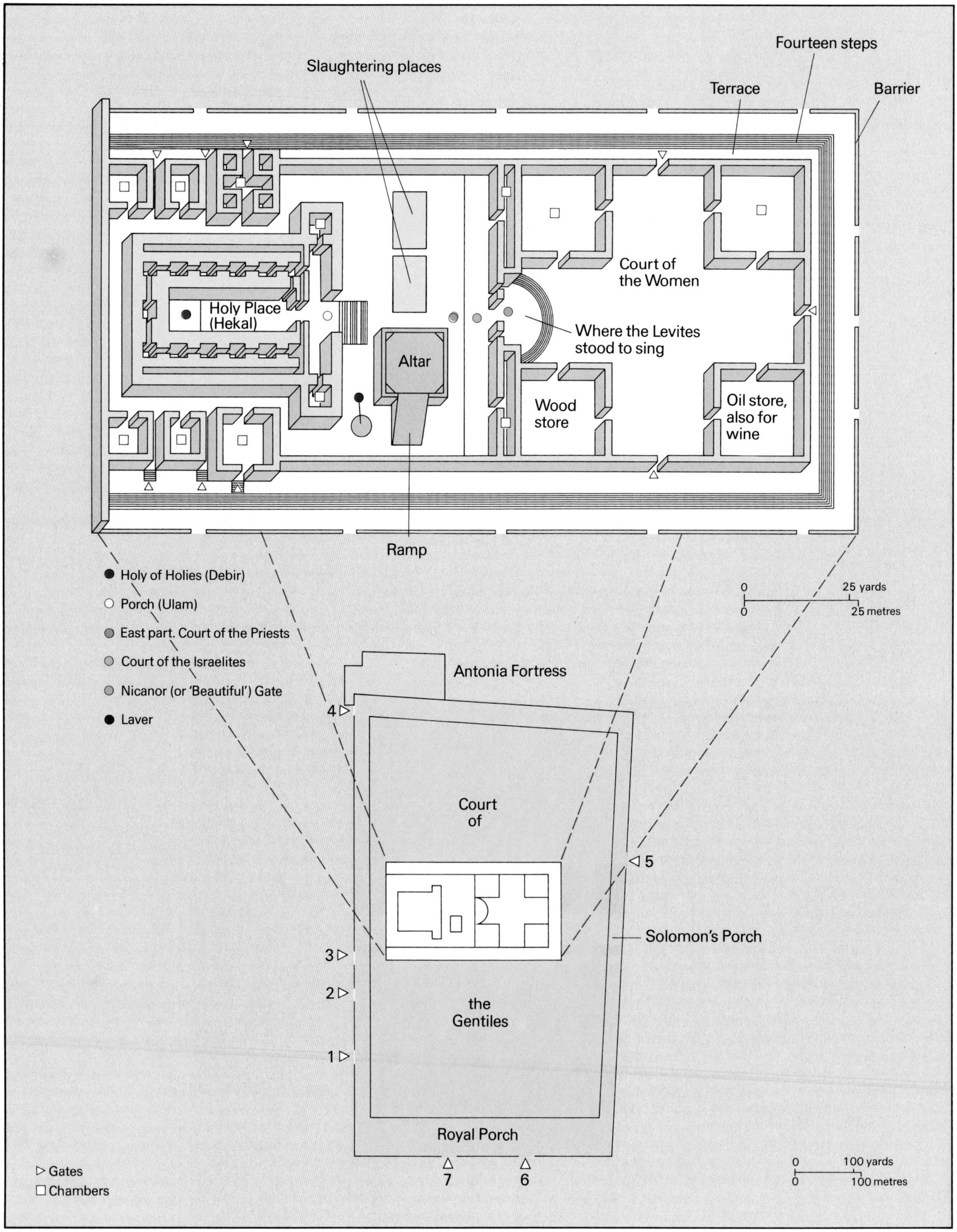
Slaughtering places
Fourteen steps
Terrace
Barrier
Court of the Women
Holy Place (Hekal)
Altar
Where the Levites stood to sing
Wood store
Oil store, also for wine
Ramp
Holy of Holies (Debir)
Porch (Ulam)
East part. Court of the Priests
Court of the Israelites
Nicanor (or 'Beautiful') Gate
Laver
0 25 yards
0 25 metres
Antonia Fortress
4
Court of
5
Solomon's Porch
3
2
the Gentiles
1
Royal Porch
7
6
Gates
Chambers
0 100 yards
0 100 metres

spiritualized the word 'temple' for the sake of anthropology, whereas Paul was occupied with ecclesiology and eschatology and had only a very secondary interest in anthropology. If comparisons are desired one may look for them with greater justification in the writings of the Covenanters of Qumran (CDC 5. 6; 8. 4–10; 9. 5–6).

With 'temple' in the Pauline corpus *cf.* 'house' in 1 Pet. 2:4–10, where it is manifest that the numerous allusions in the NT to the priestly and sacrificial character of Christian life stem from the conception of the church as God's sanctuary. See also 'house' in Heb. 3:1–6.

d. 'Temple' in Hebrews and Revelation

The idea of a heavenly temple, which was common among the Semites and which helped to sustain Jewish hope when the exigencies of the intertestamental period made it appear that the Temple of Jerusalem would never become the metropolis of the world, was adopted by the early Christians. Allusions to it are present in Jn. 1:51; 14:2f.; Gal. 4:21ff.; and possibly in Phil. 3:20. The 'building from God . . . eternal in the heavens' in the notoriously difficult passage 2 Cor. 5:1–5 may also bear some connection with the idea. The conception is, of course, most developed in Heb. and Rev.

According to the writer to the Hebrews the sanctuary in heaven is the pattern (*typos*), *i.e.* the original (*cf.* Ex. 25:8f.), and the one on earth used by Jewry is a 'copy and shadow' (Heb. 8:5). The heavenly sanctuary is therefore the true sanctuary (Heb. 9:24). It belongs to the people of the new covenant (Heb. 6:19–20). Moreover, the fact that Christ our High Priest is in this sanctuary means that we, although still on earth, already participate in its worship (10:19ff.; 12:22ff.). What is this temple? The writer supplies a clue when he says that the heavenly sanctuary was cleansed (9:23), *i.e.* made fit for use (*cf.* Nu. 7:1). The assembly of the first-born (Heb. 12:23), that is to say, the church triumphant, is the heavenly temple (*TABERNACLE).

The celestial temple in Rev. is part of the grand scheme of spiritualization undertaken by the author, and note should also be taken of the celestial Mt Zion (14:1; 21:10) and the new Jerusalem (3:12; 21:2ff.). In point of fact the prophet of Patmos was shown two temples, one in heaven and the other on earth. The latter is in mind in 11:1ff. The harassed militant church is depicted under the guise of the Temple of Jerusalem, or, more accurately, the sanctuary of the Temple of Jerusalem, for the forecourt, that is, the lukewarm who are on the fringe of the church, is excluded from the measurement. The imagery owes something to Zc. 2:5, and appears to have the same meaning as the sealing of the 144,000 in 7:1–8. Those measured, alias the numbered, are the elect whom God protects.

Similar spiritualizing is evident in the author's vision of the temple in heaven. On the top of Mt Zion he sees not a magnificent edifice, but the company of the redeemed (14:1; *cf.* 13:6). That John intends his readers to regard the martyr-host as taking the place of a temple is hinted at in 3:12: 'He who conquers, I will make him a pillar in the temple of my God.' The heavenly temple thus 'grows', like its earthly counterpart (see above on Eph. 2:21f.), as each of the faithful seals his testimony with martyrdom. The building will eventually be completed when the decreed number of the elect is made up (6:11). It is from this temple of living beings that God sends out his judgment upon impenitent nations (11:19; 14:15ff.; 15:5–16:1), just as he once directed the destinies of the nations from the Temple of Jerusalem (Is. 66:6; Mi. 1:2; Hab. 2:10).

The new Jerusalem has no temple (21:22). In a document like Rev. which follows the traditional images and motifs so closely, the

Opposite page: One proposed plan of Herod's Temple, with indication of its position within the Temple enclosure.

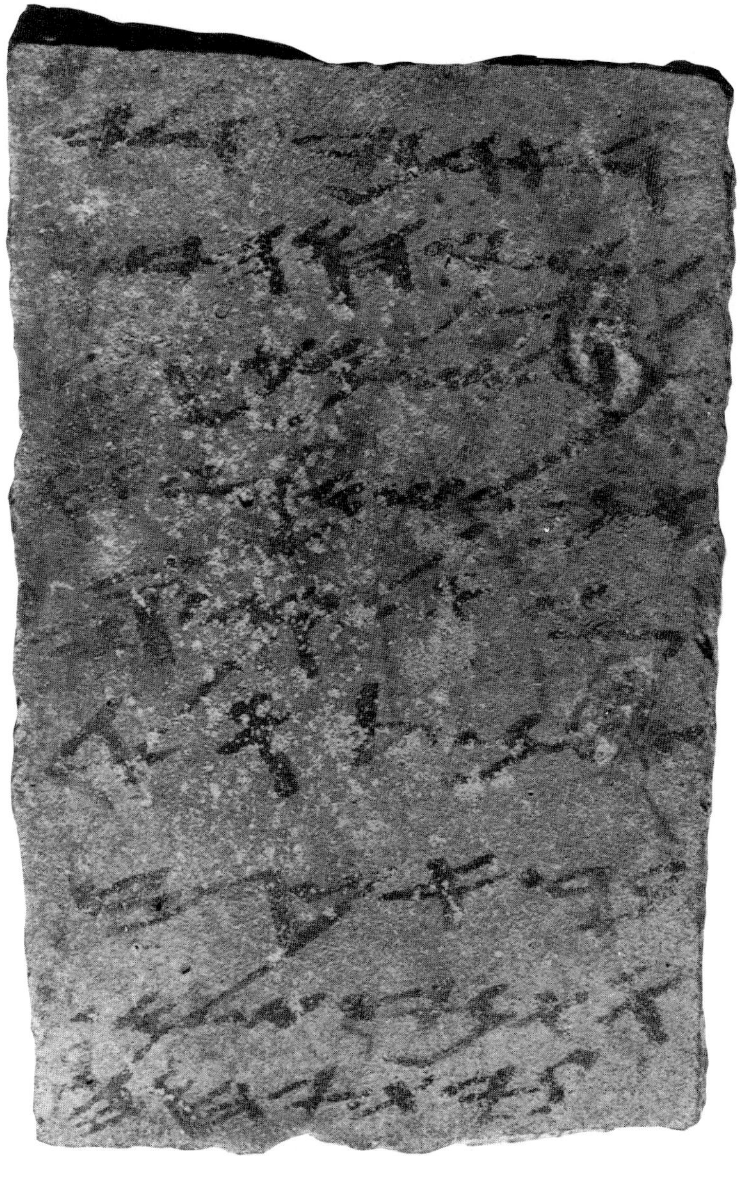

This Hebrew ostracon probably contains the earliest extra-biblical reference to the Temple. The last line visible reads 'the house of the Lord' (byt yhwh). *From Arad. Early 6th cent.* BC. (IM)

TEMPLE FURNITURE
See Ornaments, Part 2.

TEMPLE GUARD
See Guard, Part 2.

TEMPLE, LOSS OF
See Synagogue, Part 3.

TEMPLE SERVANT
See Nethinim, Part 2.

idea of a Jerusalem without a Temple is surely novel. John's statement that he 'saw no temple in the city' has been taken to mean that the whole city was a temple; note that the shape of the city is cubical (21:16), like the holy of holies in Solomon's Temple (1 Ki. 6:20). But that is not what John says. He states plainly that God and the Lamb is the Temple. What he very likely means is that in the place of the temple is God and his Son. Such indeed would appear to be the grand dénouement for which the writer prepares his readers. First he dramatically announces that the temple in heaven is opened and its contents laid bare for human eyes to see (11:19). Later he drops the hint that the divine dwelling may be none other than God himself (21:3; note the play on the words *skēnē* and *skēnōsei*). Finally, he states quite simply that the temple is the Lord God Almighty and the Lamb. One after another the barriers separating man from God are removed until nothing remains to hide God from his people. 'His servants . . . shall see his face' (22:3f.; *cf.* Is. 25:6ff.). This is the glorious privilege of all who enter the new Jerusalem.

The use made of the ancient motif of the ingathering and reunion of Israel and the nations at the eschatological temple by the author of Rev. is thus different from, although complementary to, that of Paul. Paul, as we noted above, applied it to the terrestrial church; John projects it into the heavenly realm and into the world to come. The difference is another illustration of the flexibility of the Temple image.

BIBLIOGRAPHY. P. Bonnard, *Jésus-Christ édifiant son Église*, 1948; A. Cole, *The New Temple*, 1950; Y. M. J. Congar, *The Mystery of the Temple*, 1962; M. Fraeyman, 'La Spiritualisation de l'Idée du Temple dans les Épîtres pauliniennes', *Ephemerides Theologicae Lovanienses* 23, 1947, pp. 378–412; B. Gärtner, *The Temple and the Community in Qumran and the New Testament*, 1965; R. J. McKelvey, *The New Temple*, 1969; M. Simon, 'Le discours de Jésus sur la ruine du temple', *RB* 56, 1949, pp. 70–75; P. Vielhauer, *Oikodomē*, dissertation, 1939; H. Wenschkewitz, 'Die Spiritualisierung der Kultusbegriffe Tempel, Priester und Opfer im Neuen Testament', *Angelos* 4, 1932, pp. 77–230; G. Schrenk, *TDNT* 3, pp. 230–247; O. Michel, *TDNT* 4, pp. 880–890; 5, pp. 119–130, 144–147; W. von Meding, C. Brown, D. H. Madvig, in *NIDNTT* 3, pp. 781–798.

R.J.McK.

TEMPTATION. The biblical idea of temptation is not primarily of seduction, as in modern usage, but of making trial of a person, or putting him to the test; which may be done for the benevolent purpose of proving or improving his quality, as well as with the malicious aim of showing up his weaknesses or trapping him into wrong action. 'Tempt' in AV means 'test' in this unrestricted sense, in accordance with older English usage. It is only since the 17th century that the word's connotation has been limited to testing with evil intent.

The Heb. noun is *massâ* (EVV 'temptation'); the Heb. verbs are *māsâ* (EVV usually 'tempt') and *bāḥan* (EVV usually 'prove' or 'try': a metaphor from metal refining). The LXX and NT use as equivalents the noun *peirasmos* and the verbs *(ek)peirazō* and *dokimazō*, the latter corresponding in meaning to *bāḥan*.

The idea of testing a person appears in various connections throughout the Bible.

1. Men test their fellow human beings, as one tests armour (1 Ki. 10:1; *cf.* 1 Sa. 17:39; *māsâ* both times), to explore and measure their capacities. The Gospels tell of Jewish opponents, with resentful scepticism, 'testing' Christ ('trying him out', we might say) to see if they could make him prove, or try to prove, his Messiahship to them on their terms (Mk. 8:11); to see if his doctrine was defective or unorthodox (Lk. 10:25); and to see if they could trap him into self-incriminating assertions (Mk. 12:15).

2. Men should test themselves before the Lord's Supper (1 Cor. 11:28: *dokimazō*), and at other times too (2 Cor. 13:5: *peirazō*), lest they become presumptuous and deluded about their spiritual state. The Christian needs to test his 'work' (*i.e.* what he is making of his life), lest he go astray and forfeit his reward (Gal. 6:4). Sober self-knowledge, arising from disciplined self-scrutiny, is a basic element in biblical piety.

3. Men test God by behaviour which constitutes in effect a defiant challenge to him to prove the truth of his words and the goodness and justice of his ways (Ex. 17:2; Nu. 14:22; Pss. 78:18, 41, 56; 95:9; 106:14; Mal. 3:15; Acts 5:9; 15:10). The place-name Massah was a permanent memorial of one such temptation (Ex. 17:7; Dt. 6:16). Thus to goad God betrays extreme irreverence, and God himself forbids it (Dt. 6:16; *cf.* Mt. 4:7; 1 Cor. 10:9ff.). In all distresses God's people should wait on him in quiet patience, confident that in due time he will meet their need according to his promise (*cf.* Pss. 27:7–14; 37:7; 40; 130:5ff.; La. 3:25ff.; Phil. 4:19).

4. God tests his people by putting them in situations which reveal the quality of their faith and devotion, so that all can see what is in their hearts (Gn. 22:1; Ex. 16:4; 20:20; Dt. 8:2, 16; 13:3; Jdg. 2:22; 2 Ch. 32:31). By thus making trial of them, he purifies them, as metal is purified in the refiner's crucible (Ps. 66:10; Is. 48:10; Zc. 13:9; 1 Pet. 1:6f.; *cf.* Ps. 119:67, 71); he strengthens their patience and matures their Christian character (Jas. 1:2ff., 12; *cf.* 1 Pet. 5:10); and he leads them into an enlarged assurance of his love for them (*cf.* Gn. 22:15ff.; Rom. 5:3ff.). Through faithfulness in times of trial men become *dokimoi*, 'approved', in God's sight (Jas. 1:12; 1 Cor. 11:19).

5. Satan tests God's people by manipulating circumstances, within the limits that God allows him (*cf.* Jb. 1:12; 2:6; 1 Cor. 10:13), in an attempt to make them desert God's will. The NT knows him as 'the tempter' (*ho peirazōn*, Mt. 4:3; 1 Thes. 3:5), the implacable foe of both God and men (1 Pet. 5:8; Rev. 12). Christians must constantly be watchful (Mk. 14:38; Gal. 6:1; 2 Cor. 2:11) and active (Eph. 6:10ff.; Jas. 4:7; 1 Pet. 5:9) against the devil, for he is always at work trying to make them fall; whether by crushing them under the weight of hardship or pain (Jb. 1:11–2:7; 1 Pet. 5:9; Rev. 2:10; *cf.* 3:10; Heb. 2:18), or by urging them to a wrong fulfilment of natural desires (Mt. 4:3f.; 1 Cor. 7:5), or by making them complacent, careless and self-assertive (Gal. 6:1; Eph. 4:27), or by misrepresenting God to them and engendering false ideas of his truth and his will (Gn. 3:1–5; *cf.* 2 Cor. 11:3; Mt. 4:5ff.; 2 Cor. 11:14; Eph. 6:11). Mt. 4:5f. shows that Satan can even quote (and misapply) Scripture for this purpose. But God promises that a way of deliverance will always be open when he allows Satan to tempt

Christians (1 Cor. 10:13; 2 Pet. 2:9; *cf.* 2 Cor. 12:7–10).

The NT philosophy of temptation is reached by combining these last two lines of thought. 'Trials' (Lk. 22:28; Acts 20:19; Jas. 1:2; 1 Pet. 1:6; 2 Pet. 2:9) are the work of both God and the devil. They are testing situations in which the servant of God faces new possibilities of both good and evil, and is exposed to various inducements to prefer the latter. From this standpoint, temptations are Satan's work; but Satan is God's tool as well as his foe (*cf.* Jb. 1:11f.; 2:5f.), and it is ultimately God himself who leads his servants into temptation (Mt. 4:1; 6:13), permitting Satan to try to seduce them for beneficent purposes of his own. However, though temptations do not overtake men apart from God's will, the actual prompting to do wrong is not of God, nor does it express his command (Jas. 1:12f.). The desire which impels to sin is not God's, but one's own, and it is fatal to yield to it (Jas. 1:14ff.). Christ taught his disciples to ask God not to expose them to temptation (Mt. 6:13), and to watch and pray, lest they should 'enter into' temptation (*i.e.* yield to its pressure) when at any time God saw fit to try them by it (Mt. 26:41).

Temptation is not sin, for Christ was tempted as we are, yet remained sinless (Heb. 4:15; *cf.* Mt. 4:1ff.; Lk. 22:28). Temptation becomes sin only when and as the suggestion of evil is accepted and yielded to.

BIBLIOGRAPHY. Arndt; H. Seeseman in *TDNT* 6, pp. 23–26; M. Dods in *DCG*; R. C. Trench, *Synonyms of the New Testament*[10], pp. 267ff.; W. Schneider, C. Brown, H. Haarbeck, *NIDNTT* 3, pp. 798–811. J.I.P.

TEN COMMANDMENTS. The 'ten words' (Heb. *dᵉḇārîm*; *cf.* Ex. 34:28; Dt. 4:13; 10:4) were originally uttered by the divine voice from Sinai in the hearing of all Israel (Ex. 19:16–20:17). Afterwards, they were twice written by the finger of God on both sides of two tables of stone (Ex. 31:18; 32:15–16; 34:1, 28; *cf.* Dt. 10:4). Moses shattered the first pair, symbolizing Israel's breaking of the covenant by the sin of the golden calf (Ex. 32:19). The second pair were deposited in the ark (Ex. 25:16; 40:20). Later, Moses republished the Ten Commandments in slightly modified form (Dt. 5:6–21).

The common designation of the contents of the two tables as 'the Decalogue', though it has biblical precedent, has tended to restrict unduly the general conception of their nature. To classify this revelation as law is not adequate; it belongs to the broader category of covenant. The terminology 'covenant' (Heb. *bᵉrîṯ*; Dt. 4:13) and 'the words of the covenant' (Ex. 34:28; *cf.* Dt. 29:1, 9) is applied to it. It is also identified as the 'testimony' (Heb. *'ēḏûṯ*; Ex. 25:16, 21; 40:20; *cf.* 2 Ki. 17:15), which describes the covenant order of life as one solemnly imposed and sworn to so that *'ēḏûṯ* becomes practically synonymous with *bᵉrîṯ*. The two tables are called 'the tables of the covenant' (Dt. 9:9, 11, 15) or 'testimony' (Ex. 31:18; 32:15; 34:29).

The historical occasion of the original giving of this revelation was the establishment of the theocratic covenant. The principles of Ex. 20:2–17 as elaborated and applied in casuistic form in the book of the covenant (Ex. 20:22–23:33) served as a legal instrument in the ratification of that covenant (Ex. 24:1–8). The later, Deuteronomic, version is part of a document of covenant renewal.

When, therefore, the Scripture designates the revelation of the two tables as 'the ten words', it clearly does so as *pars pro toto*. At the same time, this terminology and the preponderance of law content which it reflects indicates that the type of covenant involved is essentially the establishment of a kingdom order under the lordship of the covenant suzerain.

The covenantal character of the Decalogue is illuminated and corroborated by ancient international treaties of the type used to formalize the relationship of a suzerain and vassal (*COVENANT). Suzerainty treaties began with a preamble identifying the covenant lord, the speaker (*cf.* Ex. 20:2a), and a historical prologue recounting especially the benefits previously bestowed on the vassal through the favour and might of the lord (*cf.* Ex. 20:2b). The obligations imposed on the vassal, the longest section, followed. The foremost stipulation was the requirement of loyalty to the covenant lord or negatively the proscription of all alien alliances (*cf.* Ex. 20:3–17, the first and great principle of which is whole-hearted love of Yahweh, who is a jealous God). Another section enunciated the curses and blessings which the gods of the covenant oath would visit on the vassals in accordance with their transgressions or fidelity. These sanctions were sometimes interspersed among the stipulations (*cf.* Ex. 20:5b, 6, 7b, 12b). Among other parallels are the 'I–thou' style, the practice of placing a copy of the treaty in the sanctuaries of the two parties, and the administrative policy of renewing the covenant with the successive generations of the vassal kingdom. In covenant renewal documents, modification of the stipulations to meet new conditions was customary. That explains the various differences between the Ex. 20 and Dt. 5 forms of the Decalogue. For example, Dt. 5:21 adds 'his field' because of the relevance of land ownership to Israel's now imminent inheritance of Canaan.

In brief, the two tables contained the essence of the Sinaitic Covenant. Yahweh, Creator of heaven, earth, sea and all that is in them, is presented as covenant Suzerain. The theocratic covenant relationship is traced to Yahweh's redemptive election and deliverance, and its continuance to the thousandth generation is attributed to his faithful mercies. The covenant way of life is sovereignly dictated in ten commandments, the standard of Israel's consecration to her Lord.

The very fact that the law is embedded in divine covenant disclosure points to the religious principle of personal devotion to God as the heart of true fulfilment of the law. But there is no incompatibility between the divine demand communicated in concrete imperatives and the call of God to personal commitment to him in love. Yahweh describes the beneficiaries of his covenant mercy as 'those who love me and keep my commandments' (Ex. 20:6; *cf.* Jn. 14:15). The biblical ethic is rooted in biblical religion, and biblical religion is not shapeless mysticism but a structured order.

The revelation of the law in the context of redemptive covenant action indicates that conformity to the law must be a gracious accomplishment of Yahweh, saving from bondage. In this context even the preponderantly negative form of the Decalogue serves to magnify the grace of God, who presents this protest against man's sin not as a final condemnation but as a sum-

TEN
See Number, Part 2.

A tent, used by King Sennacherib near Lachish, Palestine, is supported by poles and cords. The upper canopy was designed to catch the cooling breezes, and imitates those built in Assyrian houses. Relief from Nineveh. 704–681 BC. (BM)

Typical bedouin tent made of goats' hair. (SH)

TENDER MERCIES
See Mercy, Part 2.

mons to the godliness which is the goal of restored covenantal communion. The negative form thus becomes a divine promise to the redeemed servants of perfect ultimate triumph over the demonic power that would enslave them in the hell of endless alienation from God. An ethic rooted in such religion possesses the dynamic of faith, hope and love.

The laws of the Decalogue are formulated in terms appropriate to the covenantal order for which it was the treaty-constitution. For example, the specific form of the sabbath law reflects the OT eschatological perspective and the promise appended to the fifth word (and elsewhere related to the entire law, *cf.* Dt. 5:33–6:3) employs the imagery of the contemporary, typical manifestation of God's kingdom. This does not mean the Ten Commandments are not normative for covenant life today; but in determining their precise application we must always reckon with our eschatological location.

As for the division into ten words, the Decalogue's parallelism with the suzerainty treaty structure shows the error of regarding the preamble and historical prologue as a commandment. Also, the variant forms of the prohibition of covetousness in Ex. 20:17 and Dt. 5:21 contradict the division of it into two commandments, and that obviates the associated error of combining into one what most Protestants, following the oldest tradition, have regarded as the first and second commandments. The customary division of the Decalogue into 'two tables' stems from failure to recognize the two tables as duplicate treaty texts.

Speculative higher criticism, though postulating an early (even Mosaic) Decalogue, regards the canonical form as the result of later expansive revisions. Such a reconstruction is incompatible with the form-critical identification of the treaty-nature of the Decalogue, for treaties were not subject to revisionary tampering. Moreover, the treaty form called for by the covenantal context of Sinai would be lost in the shrunken hypothetical original. The theory that Ex. 34:11–26 is a primitive cultic 'decalogue' rests on a mistaken identification of this passage with the 'ten words' mentioned in Ex. 34:28. The actual relation of Ex. 34:5–27 to the second two Decalogue texts (Ex. 34:1–4, 28) is akin to that of Ex. 20:22–23:33 to the original tables.

BIBLIOGRAPHY. C. Hodge, *Systematic Theology*, 3, 1940, pp. 271–465; G. Vos, *Biblical Theology*, 1954, pp. 145–159; M. G. Kline, *The Structure of Biblical Authority*, 1975.

M.G.K.

TENT. A collapsible structure of cloth or skins supported on poles, and often held firm by cords stretched from the poles to pegs or stakes fixed in the ground all round. Compare Is. 54:2, which mentions the curtains, cords, stakes or tent-pegs (but not the poles); the tent-cloth was often dark in colour (Ct. 1:5). Tents were among the earliest habitations made by man himself (Gn. 4:20; 9:21). They were the normal dwelling of both nomadic and semi-nomadic people. The Heb. Patriarchs lived in tents (Gn. 18:1, 6, 9–10, *etc.*); and the womenfolk sometimes had their own tents (Sarah, Gn. 24:67; Jacob, Leah, the maids, Rachel, Gn. 31:33), doubtless adjoining those of their husbands. On their journeyings from Egypt to Canaan, Israel lived in tents (Ex. 16:16; 33:8, 10; Nu. 16:26; 19:14), taking up more permanent dwellings when occupying Canaan. In the days of Jeremiah, the Rechabite sect held to the nomadic ideal of dwelling in tents and scorned the ways of sedentary life (Je. 35:7), but even the romantic ideal of independent tent-nomadism was not to be treasured above devotion to God (Ps. 84:10). Death is compared to packing up the tent in Jb. 4:21; *cf.* 2 Cor. 5:1.

Among other peoples, Scripture mentions the tents of the Midianites (Jdg. 6:5; 7:13), of Kedar (Ct. 1:5), and Cushan (Hab. 3:7, also Midian), all dwellers in the desert fringes of Transjordania and NW Arabia. Tents had specific uses in settled nations. Besides the peaceful shepherd tenting in his pastures (Ct. 1:8; Is. 38:12), kings and armies camped in tents in the field, *cf.* 1 Sa. 17:54 (David); 2 Ki. 7:7–8 (Aramaeans). Finally, 'tent' in ordinary speech came to be used of any kind of dwelling (not only literally; *cf.* 1 Ki. 8:66; 2 Ki. 13:5, both rendered 'homes' in RSV), perhaps because the tent was largely used in the summer by many town and village dwellers. The external data on tents illustrate that in Scripture. In the patriarchal period the Egyptian Sinuhe in Canaan had a tent and encampment and plundered that of his adversary (*ANET*, p. 20b, line 145). In the period following Israel's Exodus and initial settlement, Rameses III (*c.* 1192–1161 BC) records that he 'devastated Se'ir (*i.e.* Edom) among the nomadic tribes, and pillaged their tents (*'hr*, from Heb. *'ōhel*) of people and goods' (*ANET*, 262a). *Cf.* Midian, Cushan or Kedar. For pictures of Assyr. military tents (round, supported on poles and sticks), see *ANEP*, figs. 170–171, 374 (royal war-tent). Tents of patriarchal age, *cf.* D. J. Wiseman, in G. A. Cuttle (ed.), *Biblical and Near Eastern Studies* (Essays in Honor of W. S. LaSor), 1978. (*TABERNACLE.)

K.A.K.

TERAH. 1. The father of Abram, Nahor and Haran (Gn. 11:27; AV 'Thara', Lk. 3:34). Heb. *teraḥ* is usually taken as connected with the moon-god and compared with Turaḫi, a place near Harran. Terah emigrated from Ur of the Chaldees and settled in Harran, where he died long after Abram's departure (Acts 7:4 is an oral slip). In Jos. 24:2 he is described as an idolater.

2. An unidentified Israelite encampment in the wilderness between Tahath and Mithkah (Nu. 33:27–28; AV 'Tarah').

J.W.C.

TERAPHIM. These objects are mentioned in every OT period: the Patriarchs (Gn. 31:19); the judges (Jdg. 17:5–18:30); early and late Monarchy (1 Sa. 15:23; 19:13–16; 2 Ki. 23:24; Ho. 3:4; Ezk. 21:21; and post-exile (Zc. 10:2). When mentioned in Israelite contexts they are almost always condemned, directly (1 Sa. 15:23; 2 Ki. 23:24) or indirectly (Jdg. 17:6; Zc. 10:2). In their use, they are mostly associated with *divination: note the pairing of ephod and teraphim in the idolatrous religion of Micah (Jdg. 17:5, *etc.*); the association with divination by arrows and hepatoscopy (Ezk. 21:21), and with spiritist practices (2 Ki. 23:24). Nowhere are we told how they were consulted, nor even what their appearance was. While Gn. 31:34 suggests that they were small objects, 1 Sa. 19:13–16 suggests a life-size figure, or at least a life-size bust. However, it is possible that Michal placed the teraphim 'beside' rather than 'in' the bed, and that they were considered to have some prophylactic or curative propensity. W. F. Albright (*Archaeology and the Religion of Israel*, 1942, p. 114) reasonably urges that all available evidence is against the former view in that 'no "idols" of comparable size have ever been found in Palestine excavations'. He further suggests (*op. cit.*, p. 207) that, from a Canaanite *trp*, 'to wear out', the 'teraphim' in question here might not be any sort of figure but 'old rags', presumably used to simulate the recumbent figure of David.

These last two references (also Jdg. 17:5ff.) associate *t^erāp̄îm* with the home, and Laban, at least, considered them as household gods (Gn. 31:30). The suggestion that Rachel's theft of her father's gods (Gn. 31:19, 30–35) signified an inheritance claim on the basis of Nuzi custom can no longer be sustained, however. Possession of household gods at Nuzi probably indicated family headship, but such a privilege was given, not seized (see M. Greenberg, *JBL* 81, 1962, pp. 239–248; see further, M. J. Selman, *TynB* 27, 1976, pp. 123–124). Rachel's purpose can only be surmised, but examples from Mesopotamia suggest that she may have desired protection on the dangerous journey to Palestine.

Heb. *t^erāp̄îm* is a plural form, for which the corresponding singular is unknown. Possible derivations have been proposed from *rāp̄ā'*, 'to heal', or post-biblical *tōrep̄*, 'obscenity' (W. F. Albright, *From the Stone Age to Christianity*, 1957, p. 311), but the most likely association is with Hittite *tarpiš*, a type of spirit, sometimes evil, sometimes protective (H. A. Hoffner, *POTT*, pp. 215ff.; *JNES* 27, 1968, pp. 61–68). Other suggestions have connected *t^erāp̄îm* with ancestor worship (B. Stade, *Geschichte* 1, 1887, p. 467), perhaps in the form of an ancestor's mask (A. Phillips, *Ancient Israel's Criminal Law*, 1970, p. 61) or mummified human heads (H. L. Ellison on Ezk. 21:21 in *Ezekiel: The Man and his Message*, 1956).

BIBLIOGRAPHY. C. H. Gordon, 'Biblical Customs and the Nuzu Tablets', *BA* 3, 1940, pp. 1–12.

J.A.M.
M.J.S.

TERTIUS. The amanuensis who wrote Romans at Paul's dictation (Rom. 16:22); on the process, see B. M. Metzger, 'Stenography and Church History', in *TCERK*, 2, pp. 1060f., and references there. He appends his own greetings, perhaps at the point where he resumes his pen after Paul has written some personal greetings in autograph (*cf.* Gal. 6:11; Col. 4:18; 2 Thes. 3:17). This may suggest that he had Roman connections himself. The name is Latin and appears in a 1st-century inscription in the Roman cemetery of St Priscilla (cited in *MM*).

A.F.W.

TERTULLUS. A fairly common Rom. name, in origin a diminutive of Tertius. Nothing is known of the orator Tertullus who accused Paul before Felix except what can be deduced from Acts 24:1ff.

From his use of the first person in vv. 3–4 and 6–7 (although found only in the Western Text, v. 7 is undoubtedly genuine) it seems probable that Tertullus was a Jew. The words 'this nation' (v. 2) and 'the Jews' (v. 5) are not inconsistent with this deduction. It was not uncommon for Jews at this period to have Gentile names, and it was possible for a good Jew to be also a Roman citizen, with a Roman name, like Paul.

This small bronze figurine of the intercessory goddess Lama (arms missing) has been compared with the biblical teraphim *sometimes associated with the protection of the owner. From Ur. Height 10 cm. c. 2000* BC. (BM)

TENT PEG
See Nail, Part 2.

TEN WORDS
See Ten Commandments, Part 3.

TERROR
See Fear, Part 1.

The fulsome flattery of Felix in Tertullus' opening sentences is in accordance with the rhetorical fashion of the period, but the rest of the speech is unimpressive. Even in his précis Luke makes it clear that Tertullus was trying to cover up a weak case with rhetorical padding.

In addition to the real charge that Paul had attempted to 'profane the temple', Tertullus tries to represent him as one of the sedition-mongers and Messianist politicians who were so often a problem to the Rom. rulers of Palestine. K.L.McK.

TETRARCH. This title (Gk. *tetraarchēs*, contracted *tetrarchēs*) was used in classical Gk. to denote the ruler of a fourth part of a region, and especially applied to the rulers of the four regions of Thessaly. The Romans gave it to any ruler of part of an Oriental province. When Herod the Great, who ruled Palestine as a client-king under the Romans, died in 4 BC, his sons disputed their father's will. Appeal on their part to Augustus Caesar led to the division of the territory among three sons: Archelaus being appointed *ethnarch of Judaea,

Samaria and Idumaea; Antipas tetrarch of Galilee and Peraea; and Philip tetrarch of Batanea, Trachonitis, Ituraea, Gaulanitis and Auranitis, areas NE of the Sea of Galilee. In the NT the noun is used solely in reference to Herod Antipas (Mt. 14:1; Lk. 3:19; 9:7; Acts 13:1), though in Lk. 3:1 the cognate verb is applied to *Antipas, *Philip and *Lysanias, tetrarch of Abilene.

BIBLIOGRAPHY. E. Schürer, *HJP*, 1, 1973, pp. 336ff.; S. Perowne, *The Later Herods*, 1958. D.H.W.

TEXTS AND VERSIONS. Texts and versions provide the raw materials for the discipline known as textual criticism. The ultimate aim is to provide a text in the form intended by its author. Generally speaking, the greater the age of a document, the greater is its authority. There may be cases, however, where this does not hold; for instance, of two MSS, the older may have been copied from a recent and poor exemplar, while the other goes back to a very much earlier and better one. The history of a document must be taken into consideration before a verdict can be given on readings.

Documents are exposed to the ravages of time and the frailty of human nature, and the latter gives rise to most of our problems. The errors of scribes, however, seem to run in well-defined channels. Among common errors are: 1. *haplography* (failure to repeat a letter or word); 2. *dittography* (repeating what occurs only once); 3. *false recollection* (of a similar passage or of another MS); 4. *homoeoteleuton* (omission of a passage between identical words); 5. *line omission* (sometimes through homoeoteleuton); 6. *confusion of letters of similar form*; 7. *insertion into body of text of marginal notes*. The comparative study of texts can

The areas administered by the tetrarchs in Palestine.

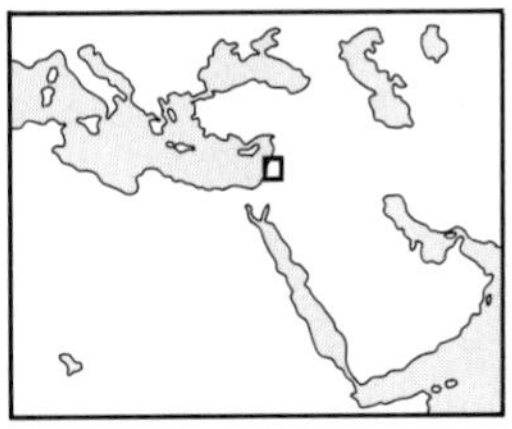

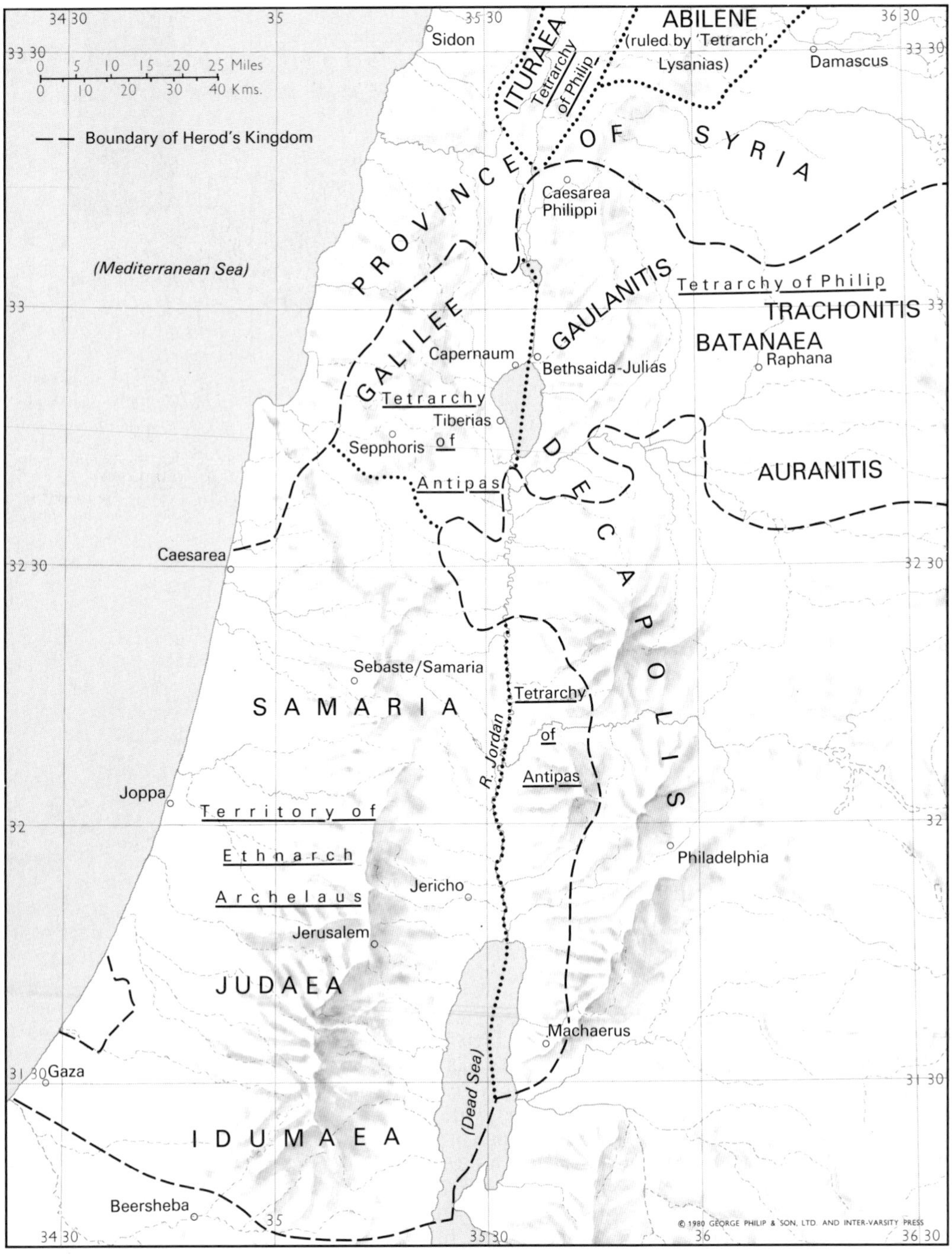

elp towards the elimination of cor-
uptions. Here numerical prepon-
lerance is not decisive: several rep-
esentatives of the same archetype
ount as only one witness. The
orm of textual transmission is best
epicted as a genealogical tree, and
he facts of the genealogical rela-
ions can be applied to the assess-
nent of evidence for any given
eading.

. OLD TESTAMENT: HEBREW

The documentary evidence for the OT text consists of Heb. MSS from rd century BC to 12th century AD, nd ancient versions in Aramaic, Greek, Syriac and Latin.

From earliest times the Jews had at their disposal the means of producing written records. The Semitic alphabet was in existence ong before the time of Moses *WRITING). Moses would have been familiar with Egyp. writing nd literary methods. He may, too, have been acquainted with cuneiform, for the El-*Amarna and other letters show that Akkadian was widely used during the 15th to 3th centuries BC as a diplomatic anguage. If the Bible did not expressly state that Moses was literate Nu. 33:2 and *passim*), we should be compelled to infer it from collateral evidence. There is, therefore, no need to postulate a period of oral tradition. Analogies drawn rom peoples of disparate culture, even if contemporary, are rrelevant. The fact is, that the peoples of the same cultural background as the Hebrews were literate from the 4th millennium BC onwards, and from the 3rd millennium men were being trained not merely as scribes but as expert copyists. It is unlikely that under Moses the Hebrews were less advanced than their contemporaries or that they were less scrupulous in the transmission of their texts than the Egyptians and Babylonians (*cf.* W. J. Martin, *Dead Sea Scroll of Isaiah*, 1954, pp. 18f.).

Before describing the sources at our disposal for the restoration of the text of the OT, it is important to recall the attitude of the Jews to their Scriptures. It can best be summed up in the statement by Josephus: 'We have given practical proof of our reverence for our own Scriptures. For, although such long ages have now passed, no one has ventured either to add, or to remove, or to alter a syllable; and it is an instinct with every Jew, from the day of his birth, to regard them as the decrees of God, to abide by them, and, if need be, cheerfully to die for them. Time and again ere now the sight has been witnessed of prisoners enduring tortures and death in every form in the theatres, rather than utter a single word against the laws and the allied documents' (*Against Apion* 1. 42f.).

That Josephus is merely expressing the attitude of the biblical writers themselves is clear from such passages as Dt. 4:2 ('You shall not add to the word which I command you, nor take from it, that you may keep the commandments of the Lord your God which I command you') or Je. 26:2 ('. . . all the words which I command you to speak to them; do not hold back a word'). There is no reason to suppose that the Jews ever abandoned these principles. Many of the divergences in texts may be due to the practice of employing the same scribes to copy both biblical texts and Targums. As the latter are frequently paraphrastic in their treatment of the text, this laxity could subconsciously easily affect the copyists.

I. The transmission of the text

Measures for the preservation of the text were already in use in the pre-Christian era, for in the Dead Sea Scroll of Isaiah (*e.g.* plate XXIX, lines 3 and 10) dots are put over doubtful words, just as the Massoretes did later. In NT times the scribes were too well established to be a recent innovation. It was doubtless due to their activity that terms such as *'jot' and 'tittle' owed their currency. The Talmud states that these scribes were called *sōp̄*^{e} *rîm* because they counted the letters in the Torah (*Qiddushin* 30a). Since their intensive preoccupation with the text of Scripture qualified them as exegetes and educationalists, the transmission of the text ceased to be regarded as their prime responsibility.

II. The Massoretes

The writing of the consonants only was sufficient as long as Heb. remained a spoken language. Where a word might be ambiguous 'vowel-letters' could be used to make the reading clear. These 'vowel-indicators' were in origin residual: they arose through 'waw' (*w*) and 'yod' (*y*) amalgamating with a preceding vowel and losing their consonantal identity, but they continued to be written, and in time came to be treated as representing long vowels. Their use was then extended to other words, where etymologically they were intrusive. Their insertion or omission was largely discretionary. Consequent variants have no significance. It was not until about the 7th century of our era that the Massoretes introduced a complete system of vowel-signs.

The Massoretes (lit. 'transmitters') succeeded the old scribes (*sōp̄*^{e} *rîm*) as the custodians of the sacred text. They were active from about AD 500 to 1000. The textual apparatus introduced by them is probably the most complete of its kind ever to be used. Long before their time, of course, others had given much thought to the preservation of the purity of the text. Rabbi Akiba, who died about AD 135, was credited with the saying, 'The (accurate) transmission is a fence for the Torah.' He stressed the importance of preserving even the smallest letter. In this he was by no means the first, as the statement in Mt. 5:18 shows: 'Till heaven and earth pass away, not an iota, not a dot, will pass from the law, until all is accomplished.'

The Massoretes introduced vowel-signs and punctuation or accentual marks into the consonantal text. Three systems of vocalization had been developed: two supralinear (Babylonian and Palestinian) and one infralinear, except for one sign. This system, called the Tiberian, supplanted the other two, and is the one now used in Heb. texts.

As it was the resolute purpose of the Massoretes to hand on the text as they had received it, they left the consonantal text unchanged. Where they felt that corrections or improvements should be made, they placed these in the margin. Here the word preferred and which they intended to be read (called the *Q*^{e}*rē*, 'that which is to be read') was placed in the margin, but its vowels were placed under the consonants of the word in the inviolable text (called the *K*^{e}*ṯîḇ*, 'the written'). It is possible that a form given in the margin (*Q*^{e}*rē*) was sometimes a variant reading. The view held in some quarters that the scribes or Massoretes boggled at giving variant readings, and in fact deliberately suppressed them, is contrary to what we know of the actual practice of the copyists.

The Massoretes retained, for instance, certain marks of the earlier scribes relating to doubtful words and listed certain of their conjec-

Opposite page: Bronze coin of Herod Antipas, appointed tetrarch of Galilee and Peraea in 4 BC. The coin shows a palm branch with the words 'of Herod the tetrarch' around, and the date, c. AD 29. Diameter 24 mm. (RG)

TESTAMENT
See Covenant, Part 1.

TESTIMONIA
See Quotations, Part 3.

TETRADRACHMON
See Money, Part 2.

TETRAGRAMMATON
See God, names of, Part 1.

tures ($s^e\underline{b}\hat{\imath}r\hat{\imath}n$). They used every imaginable safeguard, no matter how cumbersome or laborious, to ensure the accurate transmission of the text. The number of letters in a book was counted and its middle letter was given. Similarly with the words, and again the middle word of the book was noted. They collected any peculiarities in spelling or in the forms or positions of letters. They recorded the number of times a particular word or phrase occurred. Among the many lists they drew up is one containing the words that occur only twice in OT. Their lists finally included all orthographic peculiarities of the text.

The textual notes supplied by the Massoretes are called the *Massorah.* The shorter notes placed in the margin of the codices are referred to as the *Massorah Parva.* They were later enlarged and arranged into lists and placed at the top or bottom of the page. In this form they were called *Massorah Magna.* This fuller form may give, for instance, the references to the passages where a certain form occurs, whereas the shorter would give only the number of the occurrences. The notes provide the results of their analysis or textual peculiarities. They give variant readings from recognized codices, such as the Mugah and Hilleli (both now lost).

Among the names of Massoretes known to us is that of Aaron ben Asher, who was active in the first half of the 10th century AD. Five generations of his family seem to have worked on the Heb. text, and under Aaron the work reached a definitive stage. The best codex of this school is thought to be the one formerly in Aleppo, now in Israel. Another noted family of Massoretes was that of ben Naphtali, one of whom was apparently contemporary with Aaron ben Asher. The differences between them in their treatment of the text was largely confined to matters of vocalization. The 'Reuchlin' codex in Karlsruhe is a representative of the ben Naphtali approach.

The text edited by Jacob ben Chayyim for the second rabbinic Bible published by Daniel Bomberg in Venice in 1524–5 came to be accepted practically as a standard text. The text was eclectic in character, and scholars have been aware for some 250 years that it could be improved. It is significant, however, that M. D. Cassuto, a scholar who probably had a finer sense for Heb. than any other in this field, and who had an unrivalled knowledge at first hand of the Aleppo Ben Asher codex, evidently saw no reason for preferring this to the Ben Chayyim text, which he retained for his fine edition of the Hebrew Bible (Jerusalem, 1953). The non-expert might easily be misled by the somewhat hyperbolic language used of the extent of the differences to be found in the various MSS. They relate mostly to matters of vocalization, a not altogether indispensable aid in Semitic languages. Linguistically considered they are largely irrelevant minutiae, at the most of diachronistic interest. Belief in the golden age of the phoneme dies hard; it ranks with the naïveté that believes 'honour' is a better spelling than 'honor'. Vocalization in a Semitic language belongs primarily to orthography and grammar, and to exegesis, and only to a limited extent to textual criticism. There never was an original *vocalized* text to restore. It is clear that the Massoretic text is a single type which became recognized as authoritative after the Fall of Jerusalem in AD 70. All Hebrew Bible fragments found with relics of the Second Revolt (AD 132–135) in caves near the Dead Sea belong to it, in contrast to the situation at Qumran before AD 70 (see **III**, below).

III. The Dead Sea Scrolls

The discovery of biblical MSS, in caves to the W of the Dead Sea, has revolutionized the approach to the OT text by going some 800 years behind the Massoretic apparatus. It has also been a salutary reminder that the purpose of the discipline is the restoration of a consonantal text. The original find included one complete MS of Isaiah and another containing about one-third of the book. The later discoveries brought to light fragments of every book of the Bible, with the exception of Esther, as well as Bible commentaries and works of a religious nature.

The Dead Sea biblical MSS give us for the first time examples of Heb. texts from pre-Christian times, about 1,000 years earlier than our oldest MSS; thus they take us behind the alleged suppression of all divergent texts in AD 100. According to the Talmud, an attempt was made to provide a standard text with the help of three Scrolls formerly belonging to the Temple, by taking in cases of disagreement the reading that had the support of two (TJ, *Ta'anith* 4. 2; *Soferim* 6. 4; *Sifre* 356). The finds have helped to relegate questions of vocalization to their proper sphere, that of orthography and grammar, and have deprived of much of its pertinency the work done in the field of Massoretic studies by providing us with MSS much older than any hitherto at our disposal.

The Isaiah MSS provide us with a great variety of scribal errors, but all of them familiar to textual criticism. We find examples of haplography, dittography, harmonization (*i.e.* alteration to something more familiar), confusion of letters, homoeoteleuton, line omission and introduction into the text of marginal notes.

The great significance of these MSS is that they constitute an independent witness to the reliability of the transmission of our accepted text. There is no reason whatever to believe that the Qumran community would collaborate with the leaders in Jerusalem in adhering to any particular recension. They carry us back to an earlier point on the line of transmission, to the common ancestor of the great Temple scrolls and the unsophisticated scrolls from Qumran. Beside MSS close to the *MT*, fragments of others display Heb. texts that differ. Until all the material is published, it is hard to evaluate them; by their nature these have attracted most attention (see *DEAD SEA SCROLLS for details). That any are generally superior to *MT* or represent an older text is questionable; each passage has to be considered separately in the light of known scribal customs.

IV. The Cairo Genizah

The MSS discovered from 1890 onwards in the Genizah of the Old Synagogue in Cairo are of considerable importance for the vocalized text. (A Genizah was the depository for scrolls no longer considered fit for use.) The lack of uniformity in vocalization and the virtual absence of variations from the consonantal text show that the vocalization was secondary. Among the fragments of biblical MSS from this Genizah are some with supralinear vowel-signs. In the collection were also quantities of fragments of Targum and of rabbinic literature. Some of the MSS may be older than the 9th century.

V. The Hebrew Pentateuch of the Samaritans

The Heb. Pentateuch preserved by the *Samaritans is unquestionably derived from a very ancient text. The Samaritans, probably the descendants of the mixed population of Samaria, the result of a partial deportation of Jews by Sargon in 721 BC, followed by the plantation of foreigners (*cf.* 2 Ki. 17:24; 24:15–16), were refused a share in the rebuilding of the Temple by the Jews returning under Ezra and Nehemiah. The breach which followed (probably in the time of Nehemiah, *c.* 445 BC) led to the establishment of a separate Samaritan cultic centre at Mt *Gerizim, near Shechem. Contacts between the two communities virtually ceased during the 2nd century BC, and it is to this period that the distinctive Samaritan text form is assigned. It is probably a revision of a form current much earlier. All copies are written in a derivative of the 'Phoenician' alphabet akin to that on Jewish coins of the 2nd century BC, not the Aramaic 'square' script used for Hebrew after the Exile.

The oldest MS is in all probability the one traditionally accredited to Abishua, the great-grandson of Aaron (1 Ch. 6:3f.). The MS itself, written on thin vellum, is not uniformly old; the oldest part seems to be that from the end of Nu. onwards. Expert opinion would assign this scroll to the 13th century AD, or not much earlier than its alleged discovery by the high priest Phinehas in 1355.

The first copy of the Samaritan Pentateuch reached Europe in 1616 through Pietro della Valle, and in 1628 an account of it was published by J. Morinus, who claimed it to be far superior to the Massoretic text. This seems to be the case with every new discovery of documents, prompted either by a preference for the LXX or an innate hostility to the traditional Jewish text. There was in this instance another motive at work: the desire on the part of certain scholars to weaken the position of the Reformers in their stand for the authority of the Bible. Gesenius, probably Germany's greatest Hebrew scholar, brought this barren controversy to an end and demonstrated the superiority of the Massoretic text (1815). We are witnessing in our day an attempt to reinstate the Samaritan Pentateuch. Some of its protagonists betray by their faith in the trustworthiness of the Samaritan transmission an ingenuousness never surpassed by the most extreme conservatives. It is true that in some 1,600 places the Samaritan agrees with the LXX, but the disagreements are equally numerous. It is not easy to account for the agreements; one possibility is that when corrections had to be made in the Samaritan Hebrew Pentateuch an Aram. *targum was used (the Samaritan dialect and Aram. are practically identical, and the Samaritan version, that is, the translation of the Pentateuch into Samaritan, in places agrees verbatim with the Targum of Onkelos). There are numerous traces of the influence of the targums in the LXX.

For many of the variants a simple explanation can be given: the attempt to show that God had chosen Gerizim. After the Ten Commandments in Ex. 20 and in Dt. 5, the Samaritan inserts the passage Dt. 27:2–7 with 'Mount Ebal' replaced by 'Mount Gerizim', and Dt. 11:30 changes 'over against Gilgal' into 'over against Shechem'.

Many of the variants are due to a misunderstanding of grammatical forms or syntactical constructions. Others consist of gratuitous additions from parallel passages. Some stem from dialect influence. Many arise from their effort to remove all anthropomorphic expressions.

There is no evidence that the Samaritans ever had a body of trained scribes, and the absence of any proper collations of MSS, as attested by the numerous variations, is not compatible with any serious textual knowledge. Neither do the deliberate changes or superfluous additions distinguish them as conscientious custodians of the sacred text. Therefore, its variants must be treated with extreme caution. See the important survey by B. K. Waltke, in J. B. Payne (ed.), *New Perspectives on the Old Testament*, 1970, pp. 212–239.

BIBLIOGRAPHY. C. D. Ginsburg, *Hebrew Bible*, 1926– ; R. Kittel, *Biblia Hebraica*, 1952; C. D. Ginsburg, *Introduction to the Massoretico-Critical Edition of the Hebrew Bible*, 1897; F. Buhl, *Kanon und Text*, 1891; F. Delitzsch, *Die Lese- und Schreibfehler im Alten Testament*, 1920; O. Eissfeldt, *The Old Testament: An Introduction*, 1965; P. E. Kahle, *The Cairo Geniza*[2], 1959; F. G. Kenyon, *Our Bible and the Ancient Manuscripts*, 1939 (new edn., 1958); B. J. Roberts, *The Old Testament Text and Versions*, 1951; E. Würthwein, *The Text of the Old Testament*, 1957; *idem*, *Der Text des alten Testaments*[4], 1973; M. Burrows, *Dead Sea Scrolls of St. Mark's Monastery*, 1950; W. J. Martin, *Dead Sea Scroll of Isaiah*, 1954; F. M. Cross, *The Ancient Library of Qumran and Modern Biblical Studies*, 1958; P. E. Kahle, *Der hebräische Bibeltext seit Franz Delitzsch*, 1958; F. M. Cross, S. Talmon, *Qumran and the History of the Biblical Text*, 1975. W.J.M.
A.R.M.

2. THE SEPTUAGINT

The oldest and most important Gk. translations of OT books are to be found in the so-called Septuagint (commonly denoted by 'LXX').

I. Its varied contents and uncertain limits

The LXX is a collection of very varied works: it contains at least one translation into Gk. of each of the OT canonical books, and sometimes, as with Dn. and Ezr.–Ne., more than one. The translations were later radically revised, some more than once, and the LXX MSS now present varying mixtures of revised and unrevised translations. Some of the canonical books, such as Est. and Dn., are enlarged by the insertion of apocryphal material, though again not all MSS contain the same amount of insertion. Then, of course, the LXX nowadays contains many apocryphal books, though these do not coincide in number (it tends to have more), nor always in name, with the books of the English *Apocrypha. Moreover the early LXX codices do not themselves agree on the number of apocryphal books they include, and in consequence neither do the modern editions. Some of the latter even include Christian canticles and hymns. The apocryphal books likewise differ among themselves in that some are translations from an original Heb. (or Aram.), while some were originally composed in Gk. The date of all this varied material is equally varied: the translation of the Pentateuch was made in Alexandria in the first half of the 3rd century BC; the translation of Ec. is probably the work of Aquila, and if so, was done in Palestine in the 2nd century AD. Some scholars think that the Pss. may have first been translated in Palestine and then taken to Alexandria. Some believe that parts of Sa.–Ki. were originally translated in Ephesus, and some apocryphal books composed in Antioch. Originally this varied material would have stood as single books, or as groups of small books, on separate scrolls; nor was it even possible to collect it together in one volume until advancing technology (and wealth) made available to the Christians of the 2nd century AD onwards the large-codex format. The so-called LXX, then, is far from homogeneous: different accounts must be given of its different parts.

II. Origins

a. Pentateuch

The earliest source of information on the origin of the LXX Pentateuch is the Alexandrian Jewish philosopher, Aristobulus (*c.* 170 BC), the surviving fragments of whose writings have in recent years been proved authentic. Aristobulus asserts that a translation of the Law was made in the reign of Ptolemy II Philadelphus (285–247 BC), and we have no reason to doubt it. He adds that Demetrius of Phalerum made the arrangements for it. Since upon accession Philadelphus banished Demetrius, there is a discrepancy here, unless Aristobulus means that Demetrius had made some preliminary arrangements before being banished.

The next source is Aristeas, author of the so-called *Letter to Philocrates*. He purports to be a Greek who was present in Ptolemy's court when Demetrius suggested that the Jewish Law should be translated, and who was subsequently sent to request from the high priest at Jerusalem an accurate copy of the Law and 72 Jewish experts to translate it (whence in part has come the name Septuagint, which later generations applied to the whole Gk. OT). Aristeas, however, was not a Greek, but a Jew, and wrote not in the time of Philadelphus, but at some point between *c.* 170 and 100 BC. Despite the extravagantly unhistorical details of his story, his basic claim that the Law was translated in the reign of Ptolemy II agrees with that of Aristobulus, and is generally accepted.

Josephus relates Aristeas' story and so is not an independent witness. Philo (*Vit. Mos.* 2. 5ff.) may perhaps be independent of Aristeas; he likewise attributes the translation to Ptolemy II's reign, but adds miraculous details to the story.

Of the Christian fathers some soberly follow Aristeas' story, others follow Philo, and add yet more miraculous elements. Justin Martyr (*c.* AD 100–165) is the first to extend Aristeas' account to cover the whole OT; Augustine (AD 354–430) observes that it was customary in his day to call the translation 'the Septuagint'.

In the rabbinic literature the tradition persists that the translation of the Law was made in the time of a Ptolemy; but there is disagreement over the number of the translators: TB *Megillah* 9a gives it as 72, but *Massekhet Soferim* 1. 7–10 as five (though some scholars regard this as a scribal error).

Both Aristobulus and Aristeas assert that there had been earlier translations before the time of Ptolemy II. But Aristobulus' assertion is made in order to explain how, according to Aristobulus, Plato was able to incorporate material from Moses into his philosophy; while Aristeas asserts that, although there was an earlier translation, divine intervention had prevented any Gentile from ever citing it. This conflicting testimony is of little worth. Scholars nowadays leave open the question whether there may in fact have been earlier translations; but unlike Paul Kahle, whose theories were widely accepted in the 50s and 60s, they find no evidence of such translations either within the LXX MS tradition or without.

b. The other canonical books

From remarks made by Ben Sira's grandson in the Prologue to his translation of his grandfather's book, translations of 'the Law, the prophets and the rest of the books', *i.e.* of the whole of the OT, seem to have been in existence by the end of the 2nd century BC, though, as noted above, the translation of Ec. that now stands in the LXX comes from the 2nd century AD, and the revised and considerably enlarged edition of the Gk. Est. which we now have was introduced into Egypt, as we learn from the colophon, in the year 78–77 BC.

c. The non-canonical books

Dates of translation (or composition) vary widely from the 2nd century BC to the 1st century AD.

III. Revisions

The original translations (designated OGr. = Old Greek), were many of them subsequently subjected in whole or part to a series of revisions. The most important of these revisions were:

1. *The so-called kaige recension.* Made probably in Palestine, but perhaps in Alexandria, around the turn of the two eras, it aimed at making the Gk. represent the Heb. extremely literalistically. Its original extent is unknown, but it survives in parts of a number of books.

2. *Origen's recension.* Completed about 245 AD, Origen's edition was arranged in six parallel columns (hence the name Hexapla) containing: (1) the Heb. text; (2) the Heb. text transliterated into Gk. letters; (3) Aquila's translation; (4) Symmachus' translation; (5) the LXX as revised by Origen himself; (6) Theodotion's translation, or some other such as Quinta. Sometimes, as in the Minor Prophets, Theodotion's translation was placed in a 7th column. The chief purpose of the edition, which covered the whole OT, was to show where the LXX had material that was not in the Heb., and where the LXX lacked material present in the Heb.

3. *Hesychius' recension.* Little is known about this recension; some scholars even dispute its existence, while those who argue for it cannot identify it in many parts of the OT. Its author, a bishop in Egypt, died AD 311.

4. *The Lucianic recension.* Made by Lucian the martyr towards the end of the 3rd century AD, this recension has long been famous because in some books, notably Sa., it presents readings that appear to be based on a Heb. text of better quality than the *MT.* Nowadays however it is thought that these better readings were not supplied by Lucian, who in fact contributed little of importance, but were already present in the MSS on which he based his recension. The better readings may in fact be the OGr., and the variants in the other MSS the result of revisions. Unfortunately the Lucianic tradition, while prominent in some books, seems entirely absent or unidentifiable in others.

The results of these major, and many other minor, revisions are spread in varying mixtures throughout the surviving MSS, and in consequence care is needed in using popular editions of the LXX to check whether the printed text in any one place represents the OGr., translated in the 3rd–2nd century BC, or some later revision, ema-

.ating from Egypt, Palestine, or \sia Minor in the course of the .ext 3 centuries.

V. Character of the LXX translations

Iere two questions arise: (1) how .ccurately does the Gk. convey the neaning of its original Heb., and 2) how idiomatic is the Gk.? On oth counts the translations and evisions vary enormously. Nowhere is the Gk. of the translated ooks straightforward *koinē* Gk. \t its best it abounds with Hebaisms; at its worst it is little more han Heb. in disguise. The literalisic translations follow the Heb. so losely that the result would have een largely unintelligible to a Greek who knew no Heb. The nore idiomatic translations may, ike that of the Pentateuch, convey he meaning of the Heb. fairly ccurately, or may like Pr. be free paraphrase, including material and deas that never stood in the Heb. t all. However, even translators who normally follow their Heb. losely, on occasions deliberately lepart from the Heb. Sometimes everence dictates the change: *e.g.* n Ex. 24:10 'they saw the God of srael' has been altered to 'they saw he place where the God of Israel tood'. Sometimes the translator, or some subsequent reviser—it is not always possible to tell which—ubstitutes for straight translation a midrashic interpretation which patently goes beyond, or even contradicts, the plain meaning of the Ieb., and not seldom such midashic interpretations can be paralleled in later rabbinic literature. The strange interpretation of the limensions of width and height of he E end of the tabernacle court given in the Gk. of Ex. 27:14–16, or instance, is also to be found in TB *'Erubin* 2b and *Zebaḥim* 59b, where it arises not from some non-*MT*-type Heb. text, but from abbinic exegesis. Similarly in the nistorical books the characters of David, Solomon and Ahab are in he LXX 're-interpreted' to their advantage according to principles of exegesis which were later formally enunciated in talmudic schools. The mere fact that the Pentateuch was translated in Egypt is enough to account for some of its departures from the Heb. text. Egyp. influence is marked in Is., and in Lv. the technical terms for the various Temple sacrifices are inexactly and inconsistently rendered: perhaps in Alexandria, where such sacrifices could not be offered, accuracy and consistency were of no great importance. In addition to making deliberate alterations, the translators, when faced with Heb. words of which they did not know the meaning, were obliged to conjecture. The conjectures of course were not necessarily always correct.

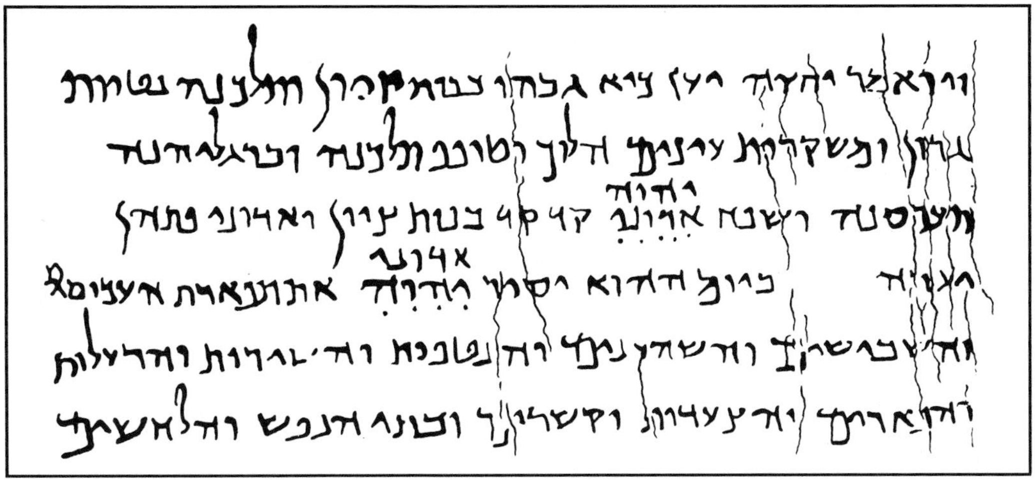

Is. 3:16–20 in the Dead Sea Scroll (1Q Is[a]) *showing alterations to the divine Name* (*from* 'aḏōnāy *to* Yahweh *in line 3 and from* Yahweh *to* 'aḏōnāy *in line 4*).

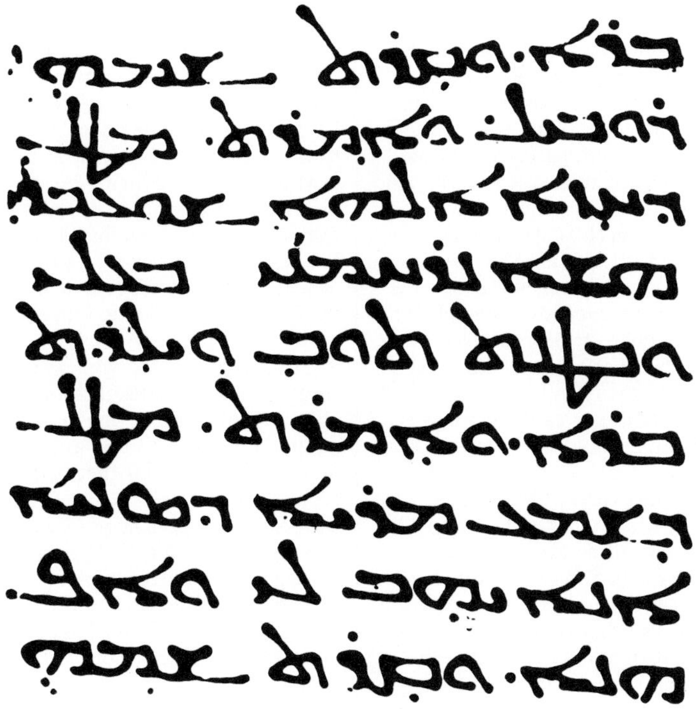

Gn. 29:32–33 in the Syriac Peshitta version. Vellum MS. *5th cent.* AD.

V. Status of the translations

This is a topic on which widely differing views have been, and still are, held. Philo, for instance, claims that the translators of the Law 'became as it were possessed, and under inspiration wrote, not each several scribe something different, but the same word for word, as though dictated to by an invisible prompter . . . the Gk. words used corresponded literally with the Chaldaean' (*Vit. Mos.* 2. 37–38). This exaggerated claim contrasts vividly with the realism of the earlier, Palestinian Jew, the grandson of Ben Sira. Recently arrived in Alexandria, and having experienced the difficulties involved in translating his grandfather's work into Gk., he remarks in the Prologue to his translation: 'For what was originally expressed in Heb. does not have exactly the same sense when translated into another language. Not only this work, but even the Law itself, the prophecies, and the rest of the books differ not a little as originally expressed.'

Aristeas, for his part, is aware

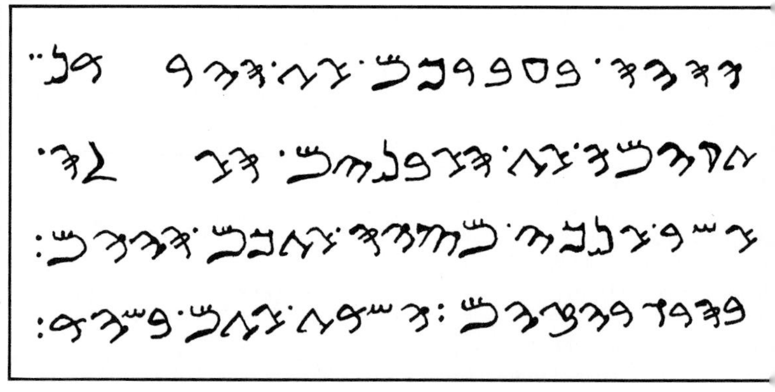

Dt. 27:4 from the Samaritan Pentateuch. Mt Gerizim is substituted for Mt Ebal at the beginning of line 4.

that the Heb. MSS circulating in Alexandria are not of the best quality (30), and he is doubtless aware also of criticisms that the Gk. translation is not everywhere accurate. He therefore invents a story designed to invest the Gk. translation of the Law, now already 100, perhaps 150 or more, years old, with supreme cultural authority, that of the reigning Ptolemy, with supreme religious authority, that of the high priest at Jerusalem, and with supreme academic authority, that of Demetrius of Phalerum (who he wrongly supposes was the head of the famous library at Alexandria). In saying moreover that the translation was done by 72 translators, six drawn from each of the twelve tribes, and that upon completion it was solemnly read before the assembled Jewish community along with their priests and elders, who received it with great acclaim and pronounced curses on any who should subsequently alter it, Aristeas, as H. M. Orlinsky has pointed out, is doubtless claiming canonicity for the translation. It is therefore the more remarkable that, unlike Philo, he does not claim that the translators produced their work by divine inspiration, but rather that they used the normal scholarly procedures, 'making all details harmonize by comparing their work each with the other' (302). Aristeas' story would hardly have convinced his near contemporary, Ben Sira's grandson; but his keenness to assert the authority of the translation of the Law suggests that it was currently the official translation used in the synagogues of Alexandria. For the translations of the other canonical books Aristeas makes no claim, even though by his time most, if not all, of them had been, or were in the process of being, translated. Of the exact origin and immediate purpose of these translations we know practically nothing. Were they scholarly products made in the course of study by historians and theologians? Or were they made primarily to serve as translations in the synagogues? Some may have had this latter purpose in mind, but others, like the translation of Pr., surely not. 1 Ki., even at the OGr. level, often reads more like a midrash than a Gk. targum. Its peculiar timetable of events, and its re-ordering of the book's contents to agree with that timetable, may well have originated in the discussions conducted in schools such as that led by the Alexandrian Jewish chronographer, Demetrius (early 2nd century BC).

It is almost unnecessary to say that the non-canonical books would never have been regarded as inspired even by Alexandrian Jews. 2 Macc., for instance, a confessedly uninspired book, composed directly in Gk., was aimed by Palestinian Jews at persuading their Alexandrian brethren to observe certain festivals, recently introduced in Palestine in connection with the Maccabean victories, in spite of the fact that they had no biblical authority. 1 Macc., likewise, was translated into Gk. to impress Gk.-speaking Jews with the devotion of the Hasmoneans to the Temple and the Law. But it freely admits that in certain matters they had been unable to decide what to do, since Scripture gave no guidance and they had no inspired prophet among them to direct them.

As early as the 2nd century BC Palestinian Jews became interested in the Gk. translations of the OT. Eupolemus, the friend of the Maccabees, seems in his history to be dependent on the Gk. translation of Ch. In the following 2 centuries it would seem that Palestine as well as Alexandria spent a good deal of effort on revising the Gk. translations to make them conform more closely to the Heb., which incidentally shows where the Jews as a whole considered the ultimate authority lay. When later the Christians began using the translations in their controversies with the Jews, the latter, already dissatisfied with the translations, eventually abandoned them and produced fresh versions of their own (see below). In the Talmud two attitudes to the LXX are to be found, one favourable and one hostile. They probably reflect the earlier and the later views of Judaism respectively.

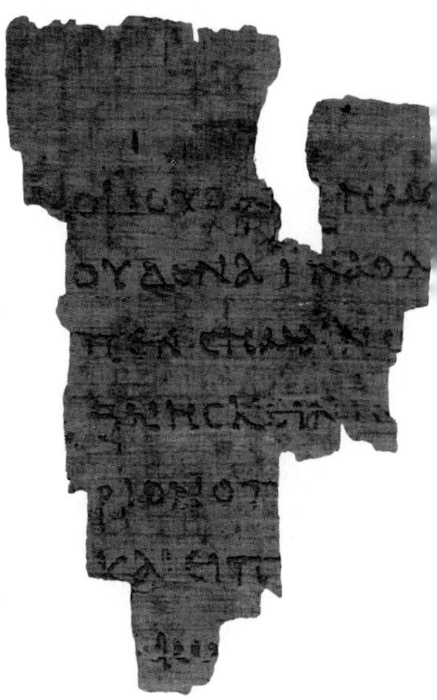

The earliest extant copy of any New Testament book. Part of a papyrus page from a copy of John's Gospel (18:31–33). Greek script of c. AD 125–150. (JR)

The NT writers frequently cite LXX-translations, particularly in formal quotations. But they do not quote them exclusively: when it suits them they cite other versions. In their day, in addition to the so-called LXX translation of Dn., there was available another, more exact, translation (later commonly, but wrongly, attributed to Theodotion). They cited the latter rather than the former. In later centuries, however, some church Fathers who could not read Heb. for themselves came to regard the LXX translations as equally inspired as the Heb. originals, and, in case of disagreement, to be preferred. In support of this claim (and to Jerome's great annoyance), they embroidered Aristeas' and Philo's stories with additional marvels and miracles, and extended them to cover not only the Law but the other canonical and non-canonical books as well. Jerome eventually discarded the Old Lat. versions of the LXX and made new Lat. translations of the canonical books direct from the Heb. It is these translations that stand today in the Vulgate.

VI. Other translations

a. Aquila. Produced in AD 128, Aquila's version was extremely literalistic: it was designed to express in Gk. the minutiae of the Heb. language which were important to the rabbinic exegesis of the time. Only fragments (though some are extensive) survive.

b. Theodotion. Traditionally associated with Ephesus, Theodotion, whoever he was, seems to have produced sometime towards the end of the 2nd century AD a version which was in reality merely a revision of an older version or revision, commonly called nowadays Ur-Theodotion. Opinions, however, differ on who this Ur-Theodotion may have been and on the extent of his work. Some think he belonged to Asia Minor and there translated a great deal of the OT which the Alexandrian Jews had not completed, but which they eventually took over from him. Others believe that he was a Palestinian and none other than Jonathan ben Uzziel, author of the kaige recension.

c. Symmachus. Produced towards the end of the 2nd century AD, or the beginning of the 3rd, Symmachus' version stands at the opposite extreme from Aquila's, being both idiomatic and elegant.

Of the origin and nature of other versions, known as Quinta, Sexta and Septima, little is known: indeed it is uncertain whether they were independent versions or merely revisions.

VII. History of the text

The LXX translations were themselves translated by the early Christian missionaries into Latin, Syriac, Coptic, Armenian, Ethiopic, Gothic, Georgian and Arabic. Moreover they were copiously cited by the Gk.-speaking church Fathers, and the Lat. version(s) by the Lat.-speaking Fathers. These translations and citations, together with the hundreds of LXX MSS, ranging in date from the 3rd century BC to the advent of printing, form the evidence from which we must try to reconstruct the history of the text. Ideally the prime aim should be to recover the text of the original translations as they left the pen of the translator(s), by removing all changes brought about either by error or by revision. In many books the aim is attainable, within reasonable limits. In some books, however, the text-history is exceedingly problematic, and it is doubtful if it will ever be possible to identify the original with any certainty, though the more limited and necessary task of showing what the text looked like at various major stages in its history may still be possible.

VIII. Importance

The LXX translations are valuable for four major reasons among others: (1) they are a witness to the influence of Hellenism on Judaism both in the Diaspora and in Palestine; (2) they form a linguistic bridgehead between the theological vocabulary of the OT and that of the NT; (3) they were the translations in which the church Fathers read their OT in the centuries when they were building their formal theologies; (4) they are an important part of the evidence for the reconstruction of the history of the text of the Heb. OT. The translators undoubtedly sometimes had before them a Heb. text superior to the *MT*; and the NT itself sometimes (*e.g.* in Heb. 11:21) follows the LXX rather than the *MT*. Moreover the Dead Sea Scrolls have shown us that the LXX's disagreements with the *MT* are more often based on non-*MT*-type Heb. MSS than some scholars had previously thought. On the other hand the fact that some ancient Heb. MS agrees with the LXX against the *MT*, does not necessarily mean that MS automatically represents the original better than the *MT* does. The matter still has to be decided by the ordinary canons of textual criticism. Moreover, where the LXX disagrees with the *MT* and no non-*MT* Heb. MS survives, the use of the LXX to reconstruct the original Heb. is fraught with difficulties. Obviously in books where the LXX translation is paraphrastic, it is almost impossible to be sure in any one place what stood in its Heb. But even in books where the translators have followed their Heb. closely, certainty in knowing what Heb. they had before them in any one place is for various reasons often more difficult to attain than might at first be thought. And even where the *MT* makes no sense and the LXX offers what seems to make very good sense, that does not necessarily mean that the LXX translators found their good sense in the Heb. MS before them: like modern scholars, faced with a Heb. text difficult to construe, and having to put something in their translation, they may have resorted to conjecture. And finally when one attempts to retrovert a Gk. word or phrase into Heb., it not seldom happens that more than one retroversion is possible. That does not mean that we should not call on the LXX's evidence; but we need to use it with great caution. Major problem areas are the OGr. text of Jb. (one-sixth shorter than the *MT*), of Je. (one-eighth shorter than the *MT* and with a different order of contents, finding some support in the Qumran Heb. MS 4Q Jer^b), of the last six chapters of Ex., and of parts of Sa.–Ki. Much more research needs to be done before we can properly understand and interpret the LXX evidence: and until it is done, it is ill-advised to fill new translations with disputable conjectures based on the LXX.

BIBLIOGRAPHY. S. Jellicoe, *The Septuagint and Modern Study*, 1968; S. P. Brock *et al.*, *A Classified Bibliography of the Septuagint*, 1973; *Bulletins of the International Organization for Septuagint and Cognate Studies* 1– , 1968– ; P. Walters, *The Text of the Septuagint*, 1973; R. A. Kraft (ed.), *Proceedings of IOSCS Symposium on Samuel–Kings*, 1972; E. Tov, *The LXX translation of Jeremiah and Baruch*, 1975; J. W. Wevers, *Text history of the Greek Genesis*, 1974; D. W. Gooding, *Relics of ancient exegesis*, 1975; *idem*, *TynB* 26, 1975, pp. 113–132; L. C. Allen, *The Greek Chronicles*, 1974; J. G. Janzen, *Studies in the text of Jeremiah*, 1973.

D.W.G.

3. THE SYRIAC VERSION

After the LXX, the oldest and most important translation of the Heb. Scriptures is the Syriac Version. This translation, used by the Syriac church, was described since the 9th century as the Peshitta (Syr. *pšiṭṭâ*) or 'simple' translation.

I. Origins

No direct information of the authorship or date of the version has been discovered, and as early as Theodore of Mopsuestia (died 428) details concerning its provenance were unknown.

Internal evidence, however, indicates its probable origin. Linguistic affinities have been noted between the Palestinian Aram. Targum and the Syriac translation of the Pentateuch, whereas Syriac (the name usually given to Christian Aram.) is an E Aram. language, and an explanation of this phenomenon offered by P. Kahle throws some light on the possible origin of the version.

These linguistic traces of W Aram., in a version otherwise in E Aram. dialect, reveal some acquaintance with a Palestinian Targum to the Pentateuch. Similarly, A. Baumstark has shown the direct agreement of the Peshitta text of Gn. 29:17 with a Genizah text and the Palestinian Targum as against Targum Onkelos and Pseudo-Jonathan ('Neue orientalische Probleme biblischer Textgeschichte', *ZDMG* 14, 1935, pp. 89–118). These facts suggest that the Peshitta Pentateuch originated in an E Aram. district which had some relationship with Jerusalem.

The ruling house of Adiabene was converted to Judaism about AD 40. Judaism spread among the people of Adiabene, and they needed the Heb. Scriptures in a language they could understand, *i.e.* Syriac, so it is probable that parts of the Syriac OT, and at first the Pentateuch, were introduced into the kingdom in the middle of the 1st century. The Palestinian Targum composed in the W Aram. dialect of Judaea was in current use at that time in Palestine, and we must suppose that this was transposed into the Aram. dialect spoken in Adiabene.

This, however, is not a complete solution, as Baumstark has shown that the original text of the Syriac version goes back even farther than the Palestinian Targum. The Palestinian Targum contains haggadic explanations which in general are not found in the Syriac Bible. On the other hand, the oldest preserved fragment of this Targum containing part of Ex. 21 and 22 does not possess any haggadic explanation, while the Syriac version of Ex. 22:4–5 follows the usual Jewish interpretation. Hence it is supposed that this fragment represents an older type of the Targum than that which might have been sent to Adiabene.

MSS of the Peshitta Pentateuch indicate the early existence of two recensions, one a more literal translation of the Heb. and the other a rendering, as has been described above, closely related to the Palestinian Targum. Many scholars think that the literal translation is the earlier as Syriac church Fathers show more familiarity with a text which followed the Heb. more closely than did the text in common use in the 6th century, *e.g.* W. E. Barnes, *JTS* 15, 1914, p. 38. However, against this view is the fact that Aphraates and Ephrem did not always quote the 'literal' translation.

It would seem that the literal translation made by Jewish scholars for the Jewish community was taken over by the Syriac church improved in style, and this text was accepted as standard about the 5th century AD. This Syriac church had taken root in the district of Arbela, the capital of Adiabene, before the end of the 1st century, and in the course of the 2nd century Edessa, E of the Upper Euphrates, was the centre of Mesopotamian Christianity.

When at the beginning of the 4th century the Christian faith was declared the official religion of the Roman empire, codices of the LXX were produced, and B. J. Roberts writes (*The Old Testament Text and Versions*, 1951, p. 222), 'It is reasonable to suppose that a similar development was taken with the Peshitta version. Thus it is held that an attempt was made to revise the Syriac version in order to bring it more into harmony with the LXX. It took place shortly after the NT Peshitta was revised, but it is obvious that the recension was not carried out in the same way for all the sacred books. Thus the Psalter and the Prophetic books, because of their relatively greater importance for the NT, were more carefully collated with the Gk. version. Job and Proverbs, on the other hand, were scarcely touched and the same may be said to be true, but to a lesser degree, of Genesis.'

An alternative view concerning origin is advanced by R. H. Pfeiffer (*IOT*, 1941, p. 120), quoting F. Buhl (*Kanon und Text dess Alten Testaments*, 1890, p. 187) that 'the Peshitta owed its origin to Christian efforts: in part older individual Jewish translations were utilized, in part the remainder was commissioned to Jewish Christians for translation'. Such a view is possible, as the Syriac Christians included a large Jewish element and came possibly from an originally Jewish congregation.

Concerning the influence of the LXX on the Peshitta, the conclusion of W. E. Barnes may also be quoted (*JTS* 2, 1901, p. 197): 'The influence of the Septuagint is for the most part *sporadic*, affecting the translation of a word here and of a word there. The Syriac translators must indeed have known that their knowledge of Hebrew was far in advance of the knowledge possessed by the Septuagint, and yet the stress of Greek fashion had its way now and again. The Syriac transcribers on the contrary were ignorant of Hebrew and ready to introduce readings found in a Greek version or recommended by a Greek Father. So the Peshitta in its later text has more of the Septuagint than in its earlier form. It is only in the Psalter (so it seems to me at the present stage of my work) that any general Greek influence bringing in a new characteristic is to be found. That characteristic is a dread of anthropomorphisms from which the Syriac translators of the Pentateuch were free.'

II. Language and translation

An examination of the character of the Syriac translation in the various books of the OT shows there is no uniformity of rendering between the various books, and this implies a variety of authors. Of the Peshitta of Samuel S. R. Driver has written (*Notes on the Hebrew Text and the Topography of the Books of Samuel*[2], 1913, p. lxxi): 'The Hebrew text presupposed by the Peshitta deviates less from the Massoretic text than that which underlies the LXX, though it does not approach it so closely as that on which the Targums are based. It is worth observing that passages not infrequently occur, in which Peshitta agrees with the text of *Lucian*, where both deviate from the Massoretic text. In the translation of the books of Samuel the Jewish element alluded to above is not so strongly marked as in that of the Pentateuch; but it is nevertheless present, and may be traced in certain characteristic expressions, which would hardly be met with beyond the reach of Jewish influence. . . .'

For the character of the translation in other books we may quote B. J. Roberts (*The Old Testament Text and Versions*, 1951, pp. 221f.): 'The book of Psalms, for example, is a free translation showing considerable influence of the Septuagint; Proverbs and Ezekiel closely resemble the Targumim. Isaiah and the Minor Prophets, for the most part, are again fairly freely translated. The book of Job, although a servile translation, is in parts unintelligible, due partly to textual corruption and partly to the influence of other translations. The Song of Songs is a literal translation, Ruth a paraphrase.

Chronicles more than any other book is paraphrastic, containing Midrashic elements and exhibiting many of the characters of a Targum. This book did not originally belong to the Syriac Canon, and it is conjectured that the Syriac version was composed by Jews in Edessa in the third century AD. Christian tendencies, perhaps emanating from an early Christian re-editing, are to be observed in the translation of many passages, prominent among them being Gn. 47:31; Is. 9:5; 53:8; 57:15; Je. 31:31; Ho. 13:14; Zc. 12:10. Many Psalms evidently derive their superscriptions from Christian origins, although in places they also embody some Jewish traditions. How far, however, these may be due to later redactoral activity cannot be determined.'

III. Later history of the Peshitta text

A schism in the Syriac church at the end of the 1st quarter of the 5th century resulted in Nestorius and his followers withdrawing E. Nestorius was expelled from the bishopric of Constantinople in 431 and he took with him the Peshitta Bible. Following the destruction of their school at Edessa in 489, the Nestorians fled to Persia and established a new school at Nisibis. The two branches of the church kept their own Bible texts, and from the time of Bar-Hebraeus in the 13th century others have been distinctive Eastern and Western. The

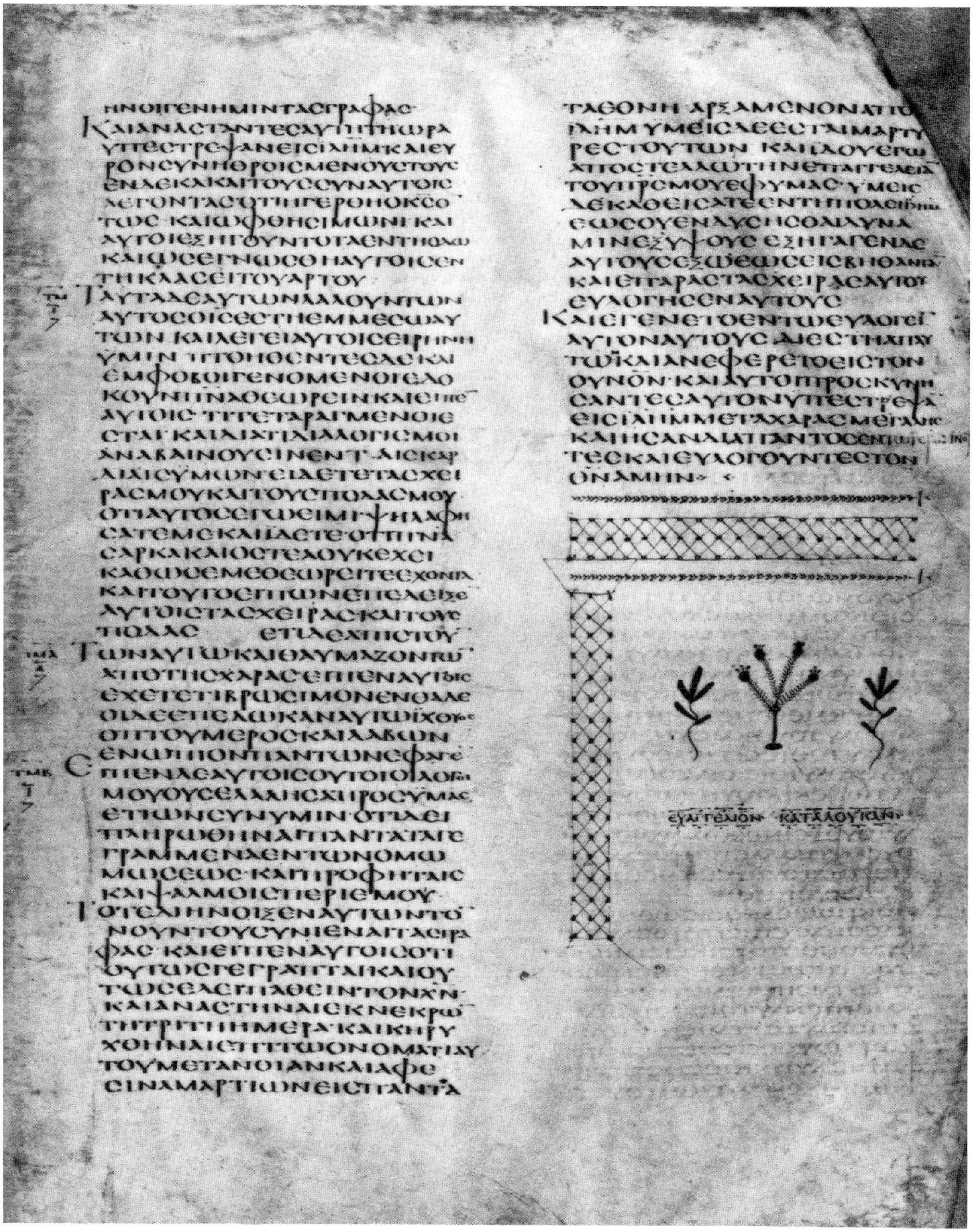

Page from the Codex Alexandrinus (Lk. 24:32–53), a 5th-century MS *in Greek of OT and NT books, probably originating from Constantinople (Istanbul).* (BL)

Opposite page: Greek papyrus of the Epistle to the Hebrews (9:2–10). 3rd cent. AD. (CBL)

Eastern, Nestorian, texts have undergone fewer revisions based on Heb. and Gk. versions on account of the more isolated location of this church.

IV. Other translations

Other Syriac translations were made at an early date, but there remains no complete MS evidence. Fragments exist of a Christian Palestinian Syriac (Jerusalem) translation, a version of the OT and NT dating from the 4th to the 6th centuries. This was made from the LXX and intended for the religious worship of the Melchite (Palestinian-Syriac) church. It is written in Syriac characters, and the language is Palestinian Aram.

Philoxenus of Mabbug commissioned the translation of the whole Bible from Gk. (*c.* AD 508); of this only a few fragments remain, giving portions of the NT and Psalter. Baumstark states that the extant remains are confined to fragments which are based on a Lucianic recension of the text of Is. These belong to the early 6th century AD.

Another Syriac version of the OT was made by Paul, Bishop of Tella in Mesopotamia, in 617 and 618. This follows the text of the Gk. and also keeps the Hexaplaric signs in marginal notes. Readings are given from Aquila, Symmachus and Theodotion. As this is really a Syriac version of the LXX column of Origen's Hexapla, it is known as the Syro-Hexaplaric text, and it is a valuable witness to the Hexaplar text of the LXX.

V. The manuscripts and editions of the Peshitta

The oldest *dated* biblical MS yet known, British Museum MS Add. 11425, dated AD 464, contains the Pentateuch except the book of Lv. (MS 'D'). Other extant MSS of Is. and Pss. date to the 6th century. The important W Syriac Codex Ambrosianus in Milan of the 6th or 7th century has been published photolithographically by A. M. Ceriani (*Translatio Syra Pescitto Veteris Testamenti*, 1867). This consists of the whole of the OT and is close to the *MT*.

The writings of the Syriac church Fathers, *e.g.* Ephrem Syrus (died AD 373) and Aphraat (letters dated 337–345), contain quotations from the OT, giving textual readings of an early date. The commentaries of Philoxenus, Bishop of Mabbug 485–519, give Jacobite readings. The most valuable authority for the text is the *'Auṣar Raze* of Bar-Hebraeus, composed in 1278.

The *editio princeps* of the Peshitta was prepared by a Maronite, Gabriel Sionita, for inclusion in the Paris Polyglot of 1645. He used as his main source the MS *Codex Syriaque* b in the Bibliothèque Nationale in Paris. This is an erratic 17th-century MS.

The Peshitta text in Brian Walton's Polyglot of 1657 is that of the Paris Polyglot; S. Lee's *Vetus Testamentum Syriace*, 1823, is essentially a reprint of the texts of the Paris and Walton Polyglots, although Lee had access to Codex B (the Buchanan Bible, 12th century) and three MSS, p, u and e, W Syriac MSS of the 17th century.

The Urmia edition was published in 1852, and in many places follows the readings of Nestorian MSS. In 1887–91 the Dominican monks at Mosul published both OT and NT, also depending upon an E Syriac tradition.

4. ARAMAIC

I. Aramaic text of the Old Testament

See * LANGUAGE OF THE OT, **II**.

II. Aramaic in the New Testament

From the time of the Exile Aram. spread as the vernacular language in Palestine, and was the commonly spoken language in the country in NT times, probably more so than Gk., introduced at the time of the conquests of Alexander the Great.

The Gospels record Christ's words in Aram. on three occasions: Mk. 5:41—* *Talitha cumi*; Mk. 7:34—*ephphatha*, representing a dialect form of *'iṯpattaḥ*; and his cry upon the cross, Mk. 15:34—* *Eloi, Eloi, lama sabachthani?* (*cf.* Mt. 27:46). When Jesus prayed in the Garden of Gethsemane he addressed God the Father as * *'Abbā'*, Aram. for 'father'.

In Rom. 8:15 and Gal. 4:6 Paul also uses this intimate form '*Abba*, Father', as an intimation that God has sent the Spirit of his Son into the hearts of believers in Christ when they pray, '*Abba*, Father'. Another Aramaism current in early churches, * *Maranatha* (*maranā ṯā'*), 'Our Lord, come!' is recorded by Paul in 1 Cor. 16:22. Other Aram. words found in the NT are * *Akeldama* ('field of blood', Acts 1:19), and several place-names and personal names.

Acts 26:14 mentions that Paul heard the risen Christ speaking to him 'in the Hebrew tongue', for which we should undoubtedly understand Aram. (see F. F. Bruce, *The Book of the Acts*, 1954, p. 491, n. 18), as also in Acts 22:2. See also * LANGUAGE OF THE NT.

5. OTHER VERSIONS

Of the other translations of the OT the Coptic is based on the LXX. It was probably made in the 3rd century AD. There are two versions: one in Bohairic, the dialect of Lower Egypt; the other and older in Sahidic, the dialect of Thebes.

The Ethiopic translation, apparently made from the LXX, is too late to be of any real value.

The best-known Arabic translation is that of Saadia ha-Gaon (892–942). It would be surprising if this was the first translation into such an important language as Arabic. A midrashic reference to an Arabic translation of the Torah may have been prompted by an existing one. Arabic translations known to us are all too late to provide material for the textual criticism of the OT.

BIBLIOGRAPHY. F. F. Bruce, *The Books and the Parchments*[3], 1963, pp. 54ff., 191ff. and bibliography pp. 268f.; P. Kahle, *The Cairo Geniza*, 1947, pp. 129ff., 179–197; R. H. Pfeiffer, *IOT*, 1941, pp. 120f.; B. J. Roberts, *The Old Testament Text and Versions*, 1951, pp. 214–228 and bibliography pp. 309f.; T. H. Robinson, 'The Syriac Bible', in *Ancient and English Versions of the Bible* (ed. H. Wheeler Robinson), 1940; E. R. Rowlands, 'The Targum and the Peshitta Version of the Book of Isaiah', *VT* 9, 1959, pp. 178ff.; H. H. Rowley (ed.), *OTMS*, pp. 257f.; E. Würthwein, *The Text of the Old Testament*, 1957, pp. 59ff. and bibliography p. 172; M. Black, *An Aramaic Approach to the Gospels and Acts*[3], 1967; G. H. Dalman, *The Words of Jesus*, 1902; *idem*, *Jesus–Jeshua*, 1929; C. C. Torrey, *Documents of the Primitive Church*, 1941; G. M. Lamsa (tr.), *The Holy Bible from Ancient Eastern Manuscripts*, 1957.

R.A.H.G.

6. THE NEW TESTAMENT

The NT has been handed down amidst many hazards encountered by all the literature of antiquity. The mistakes of the scribe and the corrections of the redactor have left their mark upon all the sources from which we derive our knowledge of its text (or wording). Before we may ascertain the original text, we have to apply to the prolific mass of material a series of disciplines, *viz.* (1) *Codicology*—the study of ancient documents and their interrelation, closely linked with palaeography, the science of ancient writing. In some cases stemmata (family trees) may be established: the stages of transmission ascertained (with or without stemmatic precision), and, in ideal conditions, an archetypal text. (2) *Rational criticism*—the method of informed choice between the variants of the documents or their archetypes where these differ uncompromisingly and cannot be explained in terms of simple error. (3) *Conjectural emendation* may be invoked where insoluble difficulties remain. In the text of the NT, there is much still to be done in the study of single documents and their interrelationship, although there has been much work of this kind: recent decades have laid greater stress on rational criticism as a way towards the original text. The sources of information are many and very few scholars seek recourse to conjectural emendation.

The Gk. sources are very numerous. The standard list of Gk. NT MSS begun by C. R. Gregory (*Die griechischen Hss. des NTs*, 1908, reprinted 1973), is superseded by K. Aland, *Kurzgefasste Liste der griechischen Hss. des N.T.*, 1963; *Materialien z. nt. Handschriftkunde*, 1, 1969, pp. 1–53; *Bericht der Stiftung z. Foerderung der nt. Textforschung*, 1972–4; *idem*, 1975–6. In this there now appear 88 papyri, 274 uncial MSS, 2,795 minuscule MSS, and 2,209 lectionary MSS. Here indeed is *embarras de richesse*. Moreover, besides sources in the original Gk., recourse may be had to the ancient translations (usually termed 'versions') in the languages of Christian antiquity and to the citations made by Christian writers from the Scriptures. Both these prove to be sources of the most important evidence for the establishment of the text and its history.

I. Manuscripts

Our primary source is in Gk. MSS, which are found in a number of different materials. The first of these is *papyrus*; this is a durable writing material made from reeds. It was used throughout the ancient world, but has been preserved mainly in the sands of Egypt. Among the most significant of the 88 listed papyri of the NT (indicated in the list of Gregory–von Dobschütz–

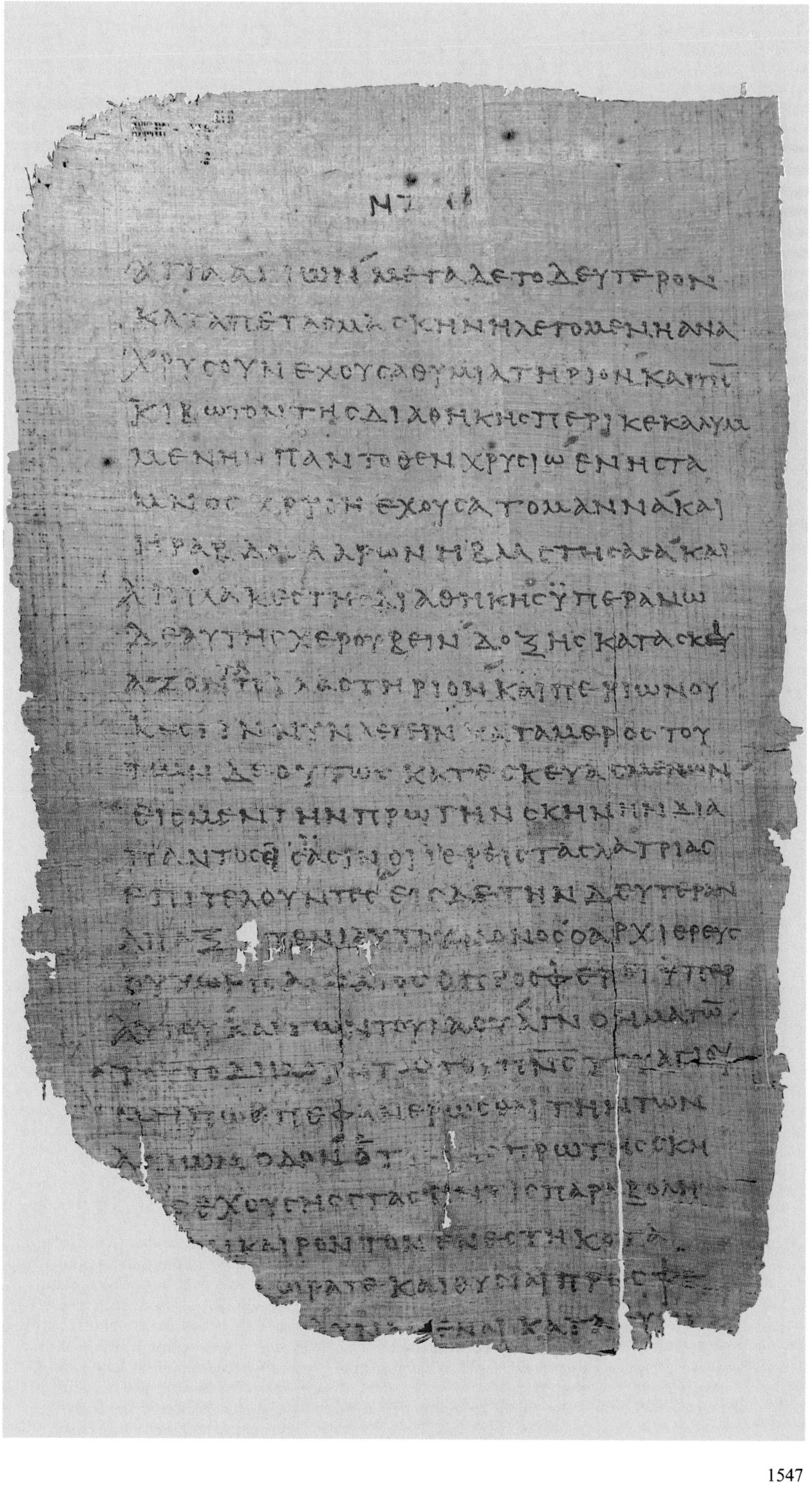

The Massoretic text of Je. 31:38–40. A scribal error (haśśārēmoṯ *for* haśśāḏēmot) *in verse 40 is corrected by a marginal note* (Q^{e}rē').

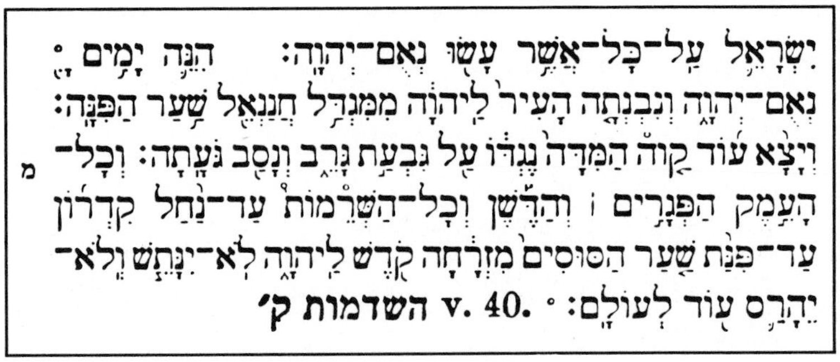
ישראל על־כל־אשר עשו נאם־יהוה׃ הנה ימים
נאם־יהוה ונבנתה העיר ליהוה ממגדל חננאל שער הפנה׃
ויצא עוד קוה המדה נגדו על גבעת גרב ונסב געתה׃ וכל־ מ
העמק הפגרים והדשן וכל־השרמות עד־נחל קדרון
עד־פנת שער הסוסים מזרחה קדש ליהוה לא־ינתש ולא־
יהרס עוד לעולם׃ v. 40. השדמות ק׳

The LXX *of Je. 38:40 (in MT Je. 31:40) from the Codex Sinaiticus. The translators have copied into Greek letters* (sarēmōth) *a Hebrew word which they did not understand because of a scribal error in the Hebrew* MS.

Aland by a 'p' in Gothic style, followed by a numeral) are the following.

(i) *Of the Gospels.* P^{45} (Chester Beatty papyrus of the Gospels, Dublin), *c.* AD 250, contains large parts of Lk. and Mk., somewhat less of Mt. and Jn.; P^{52} (John Rylands University Library, Manchester), *c.* AD 100–150, is our earliest fragment of the NT; P^{66} (Bodmer papyrus II, Geneva), *c.* AD 200, contains the Gospel of Jn., with some gaps in chs. 14–21; P^{75} (Bodmer papyrus XIV–XV), 2nd century, contains Lk. 3–14; Jn. 1–15.

(ii) *Of the Acts of the Apostles.* P^{38} (Michigan pap. 1571, Ann Arbor), dated by some in the 3rd century, by some in the 4th, contains Acts 18:27–19:6; 19:12–16; P^{45} (Chester Beatty, as above) contains parts of Acts 5:30–17:17; P^{48} (Florence) from the 3rd century, a single leaf containing Acts 23:11–29.

(iii) *Of the Pauline Epistles.* P^{46} (Chester Beatty papyrus of the Epistles, Dublin), *c.* AD 250, contains considerable parts of Rom., Heb., 1 and 2 Cor., Gal., Eph., Phil., Col., 1 Thes., in this order.

(iv) *Of the Catholic Epistles.* P^{72} (Bodmer papyrus VII–VIII), 3rd or 4th century, contains Jude, 1 Pet., 2 Pet. (mingled with apocryphal and hagiographical writings, and Pss. 33, 34).

(v) *Of the Revelation.* P^{47} (Chester Beatty papyrus of Rev., Dublin) contains Rev. 9:10–17:2.

All these papyri make significant contributions to our knowledge of the text. It should be particularly noted, however, that it is the age of these MSS, not their material or place of origin, which accords such significance to them. A late papyrus need not of necessity have any great importance.

The second material of which Gk. MSS were made is *parchment.* This was the skin of sheep and goats dried and polished with pumice; it made a durable writing material resistant to all climates. It was used from antiquity till the late Middle Ages, when paper began to replace it. The form of the manuscript book was originally the scroll, but few Christian writings survive in this form. The Christian book was usually the codex, *i.e.* the form of binding and pagination familiar to us. (*WRITING, IV.) Many parchment codices survive (the papyri are also in this form) and some are works of great beauty. Some were even 'de luxe' editions coloured with purple and written in gold or silver ink. At certain periods, however, parchment became scarce and the writing on old MSS would be erased and the parchment re-used. Such re-used MSS are called *palimpsests*: it is often the erased writing which is of importance to modern scholarship, in which case the use of chemical reagents, photography and other modern technical methods is frequently required before it can be deciphered.

The parchment MSS of the NT (together with the relatively few paper MSS of the 15th and 16th centuries) are divided by a threefold classification. The first main demarcation is that between MSS containing continuous texts and those arranged according to the lections for daily services and church festivals. The latter are termed lectionaries or *evangelistaria*; they are indicated in the Gregory–von Dobschütz–Aland list by the letter 'l' followed by a numeral ('1' alone indicates a gospel lectionary; 'l^{a}' indicates a lectionary of the Epistles; 'l + ^{a}', a lectionary containing both Gospels and Epistles). This group of MSS was formerly little studied in any systematic way: the series *Studies in the Lectionary Text of the Greek New Testament* (1933–1966), and R. E. Cocroft (*Studies and Documents* 32, 1968) have redressed much of the balance. The former group is further divided into two sub-groups distinguished by the style of writing employed in their execution and roughly consecutive in point of time. The relatively older group is that of the *Uncials*, *i.e.* MSS written in capital letters: the relatively younger group is that of the *Minuscules* or *Cursives*, *i.e.* MSS written in the stylized form of the lower case perfected by scribes of the 10th century and thereabouts, and perhaps popularized from the Stoudios monastery.

As in the case of the papyri it should be noted that an uncial MS is not *ipso facto* a better representative of the NT text than a minuscule. Some older uncials rightly occupy a chief place in critical apparatus; some younger are comparatively worthless. Similarly, minuscules, though later in date, may prove to be faithful copies of early MSS; such then have as great importance as uncials.

Uncials are indicated in the Gregory–von Dobschütz–Aland list by capital letters of the Lat. and Gk. alphabets or by a numeral preceded by a zero. Important among the uncials are the following: (1) Codex Sinaiticus (א or 01), a 4th-century MS of OT and NT; in addition to its intrinsically important text it contains a series of corrections made in the 6th century and probably to be connected with the critical work of Pamphilus of Caesarea. (2) Codex Vaticanus (B or 03), a MS of similar content, but lacking the latter part of the NT from Heb. 9:14 to the end of Rev. Both these MSS are probably of Egyp. origin. (3) Codex Alexandrinus (A or 02), a 5th-century MS containing OT and NT, probably of Constantinopolitan origin. (4) Codex Ephraemi Rescriptus (C or 04), a 5th-century palimpsest MS of OT and NT re-used in the 13th century for the works of Ephraem the Syrian in Gk. translation. (5) Codex Bezae (Cantabrigiensis) (D or 05), 4th or 5th century and of uncertain provenance—suggestions range from Gaul to Jerusalem; it presents a Gk. text on the left page, a Lat. on the right, and contains an incomplete text of the Gospels and Acts with a few verses of 1 Jn. (6) Codex Washingtonianus (the Freer Codex) (W or 032), probably a 4th-century MS, containing the Gospels of which the text-type varies considerably from place to place. (7) Codex Koridethianus (Θ or 038), which it is impossible to date, since it was apparently written by a scribe unaccustomed to Gk., probably a Georgian; the MS copied by him was apparently a late uncial of the 10th century. (8) Codex Laudianus (E^{a} or 08), a 6th-or 7th-century Graeco-Lat. MS of the Acts. (9, 10, 11) Codices Claromontanus, Boernerianus, Augiensis (D^{paul} or 06; G^{paul} or 012; F^{paul} or 010), a group of Graeco-Lat. MSS, the former of the 6th, the two latter of the 9th century, containing the Pauline Epistles. (12) Codex Euthalianus (H^{paul} or 015), 6th-century MS much fragmented and scattered, containing the Pauline Epistles connected, according to a colophon (*i.e.* appended note), with a MS in the library of Pamphilus of Caesarea.

These MSS give the varying text-types existing in the 4th century; it is around these that debate has centred in the last 100 years and on these MSS that critical texts have been based. As an exploratory investigation this is justifiable, but, as more recent discoveries have shown, the complexity of the data is greater than this procedure would imply.

The researches of Lake, Ferrar, Bousset, Rendel Harris, von Soden, Valentine-Richards and many others have made it abundantly plain that a fair proportion of minuscules of all dates contain in larger or smaller measure important ancient texts or traces of such texts: to give then even an approximate indication of all important minuscules is virtually impossible. The following remarks give some idea of the significance of this material. Two MSS numbered 33 and 579 in Gregory's list are very closely allied to the text of B; 579 has even been described as presenting a text older than B itself. The text of Θ, otherwise unknown in the uncials save in part of W, is also found in 565, 700 and some others; as such a text was known to Origen, these are of great significance. Closely allied texts are found in the minuscule families known as family 1 and family 13 and in MSS 21, 22 and 28. In the Acts some of the peculiarities of D and E are attested by various minuscules, pre-eminent among which are 383, 614 and 2147. In the Pauline Epistles the minuscule evidence has not been so thoroughly sifted yet, save in the unsatisfactory work of von Soden. However, 1739 has attracted much study, and with its congeners 6, 424, 1908, and the late uncials erroneously placed together as M^{paul}, proves to attest a text of equal antiquity and comparable significance to that of P^{46} and B. In Rev., 2344 is an ally of A and C, the best witnesses to the original text of that book.

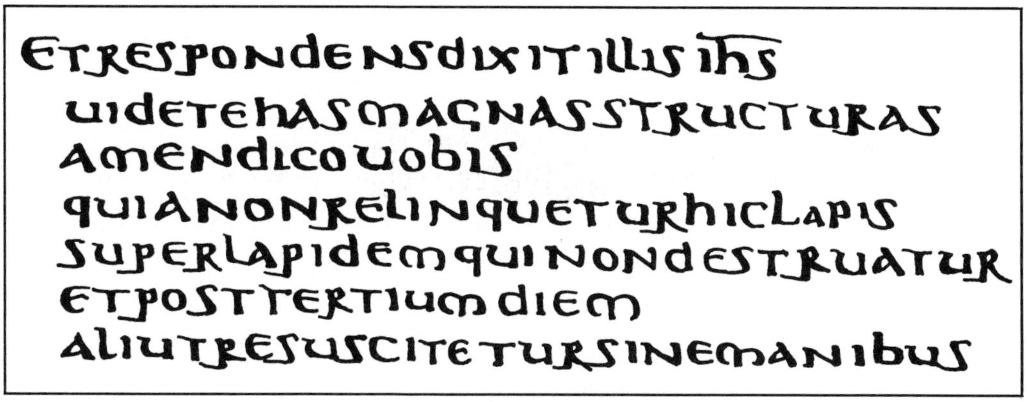
ET RESPONDENS DIXIT ILLIS IHS
UIDETE HAS MAGNAS STRUCTURAS
AMEN DICO UOBIS
QUIA NON RELINQUETUR HIC LAPIS
SUPER LAPIDEM QUI NON DESTRUATUR
ET POST TERTIUM DIEM
ALIUT RESUSCITETUR SINE MANIBUS

The Latin text of Mk. 13:2 with the addition 'and after three days another shall be raised up without hands'. From the Codex Bezae (D).

II. Versions

By the mid-3rd century parts at least of the NT had been translated from the Gk. original into three of the languages of the ancient world: Lat., Syriac and Coptic. From that time on, these versions were revised and expanded: and in their turn became the basis of other translations. Especially in the E, Bible translation became an integral part of the missionary work of both Gk.-speaking and Syriac-speaking Christians. As churches developed and theology flourished, versions would be revised to the standard of the Gk. text then prevalent. So, both by reason of their ultimate antiquity and by their contacts with the Gk. at various historical points, the versions preserve much significant material for textual criticism.

From this outline it will be plain that each version has a history. There is need, then, for internal textual criticism of any version before it can be used in the determination of the Gk. text; and in scarcely any case may we speak of 'such and such a version' but need to speak of such MSS or such a form or stage of the version in question. This, already observed for the Lat. and Syriac versions, should become the general rule.

In tracing the internal history of a version we have the advantage of the phenomenon of 'rendering' to aid us, which is not to be found in dealing with the Gk. text. In the Gk., text-types can be differentiated by variant readings alone: in any version even the same reading may be found differently rendered in particular MSS. Where this is so, different stages in the evolution of the version may be traced.

Difficulties are to be met, however, in the use of any version for the criticism of the Gk. text. These arise because no language can reproduce any other with complete exactness. This is so even in the case of cognates of Gk. such as Lat. or Armenian; it is more strikingly true of languages of other linguistic type such as Coptic or Georgian. Particles essential to the one are found to have no equivalent or no necessary equivalent in the other; verbs have no equivalent conjugation; nuances and idioms are lost. Sometimes a pedantic translator will maltreat his own language in order to give a literal rendering of the Gk.; in such a case we may have an almost verbatim report of the Gk. model. But in the earliest versions pedantry has no place and we encounter the difficulties of racy idiom and sometimes paraphrase. Nevertheless, the evidence of the versions needs to be mastered in the quest for the original text.

Some have claimed that an important factor in the history of many versions is the *Diatessaron*, a harmony of the four Gospels and some apocryphal source made *c.* AD 180 by Tatian, an Assyr. Christian converted in Rome and a disciple of Justin Martyr (*CANON OF THE NT). Unfortunately for research, no unequivocal evidence of it has been available, until recently, in Syriac, its probable original language. The most important witnesses to it are a commentary upon it by Ephrem the Syrian preserved in Armenian (a considerable portion of the Syriac original of this commentary came to light in 1957); a translation into Arabic extant in several MSS, but apparently much influenced before its translation by the text of the Syriac Peshitta; the Lat. Codex Fuldensis, similarly influenced by the Lat. Vulgate; and a fragment in Gk. found at Dura-Europos. Its widespread vogue and influence may be shown by the existence of harmonies in Old High German, Middle High German, mediaeval Dutch, Middle English, the Tuscan and Venetian dialects of mediaeval Italian, Persian and Turkish. It is quite clear that a *Diatessaron* lies beneath the oldest stratum of the Syriac, Armenian and Georgian versions, but the view that it influenced the Lat. has many flaws. These matters are still an area for research and debate.

The three basic versions made directly from Gk. are the Lat., Syriac and Coptic. Of none of these is the earliest stage certainly known. Tertullian usually translated directly from the Gk., with wide variety of rendering, in which his acquaintance with an early form of the Old Lat. translation shows itself. Our MS evidence for the pre-Vulgate stage of the Lat. consists of about 30 fragmentary MSS. These show a somewhat bewildering richness of variants well meriting the *bon mot* of Jerome, '*tot sunt paene* (*exemplaria*) *quot codices*'. Scholars usually distinguish two or three main types of text (*viz.* 'African', 'European' and sometimes 'Italian') in the various parts of the NT before Jerome; the Vetus Latina Institute of Beuron is presenting in its edition a more precise analysis with alphabetical sigla for text-types and sub-text-types.

But in the Gospels at least there is more interconnection between types than is usually thought: and even in the 'African' Lat. of MSS k and e there may be discerned more than one stage of translation and revision. Jerome undertook a revision of the Lat. Bible (normally known as the Vulgate) at the request of the Pope Damasus about AD 382. It is uncertain how far his revision actually extended. The latter books of the NT are probably very little revised. In the course of time this revision itself became corrupt and a number of attempts at purification figure in its history, most notably those of Cassiodorus, Alcuin and Theodulph.

The Syriac church, after using an apocryphal Gospel, was first introduced to the canonical Gospels in the form of the *Diatessaron*: this remained long in vogue, but was gradually supplanted by the separated Gospels in the form known to us in the Curetonian and Sinaitic MSS and in citations. This retained much of Tatian's language in a four-Gospel form. We have no MSS of a parallel version of the Acts and Epistles, but the citations made by Ephrem indicate its existence. Towards the end of the 4th century a revision was made of an Old Syriac base to a Gk. standard akin to Codex B of the Gk.; this was the Peshitta, which in course of time became the 'Authorized Version' of all the Syriac churches. Its author is unknown: more than one hand has been at work. The version comprises in the NT the canonical books apart from 2 Pet., 2 and 3 Jn., Jude and Rev. Later scholarly revisions—by Polycarp, at the command of Mar Xenaia (Philoxenus) of Mabbug (AD 508) and by Thomas of Harkel (AD 616) made good the omission. Few MSS of either remain, and the existence of a separate Harklean version (as distinct from the addition of scholarly marginal apparatus to the Philoxenian) is still a matter of debate. The version in the quite distinct Palestinian Syriac dialect is generally thought to be unconnected with this stream of translation, but otherwise its origins are at present obscure. Much of the NT is extant in lectionary form.

Biblical remains are found in several dialects of Coptic: the entire NT in Bohairic, the dialect of Lower Egypt and the Delta; almost the whole in Sahidic, the dialect of Upper Egypt; considerable fragments in Fayyumic and Achmimic; and the Gospel of John in sub-Achmimic. To trace in detail the history of the versions in these dialects and in the various parts of the NT is still an unaccomplished task: neither the dates of the versions nor the interrelations between them, if any, have yet been elucidated from the abundant materials to hand. The Sahidic is usually dated in the 3rd or 4th century, while for the Bohairic dates as diverse as the 3rd century and the 7th have been proposed. In the main these versions agree with the Gk. text-types found in Egypt: the Diatessaric element discerned in the Lat. and Syriac texts is scarcely present here, and it may be concluded that, whatever the internal relations of the versions in the different dialects, the Coptic as a whole stands in a direct relation to the Gk. text.

The majority of other versions are dependent on these. From the Latin come mediaeval versions in a number of W European languages: while these mainly reflect the Vulgate, traces of Old Lat. readings are to be found. Thus, Provençal and Bohemian versions preserve an important text of the Acts. The Syriac versions served as base for a number of others, the most important being the Armenian (from which the Georgian was in its turn translated), and the Ethiopic. These have complex internal history, their ultimate form conformed to the Gk., but their earlier stages less so. Persian and Sogdian versions derive from the Syriac, while the many Arabic versions and the fragmentarily preserved Nubian have both Syriac and Coptic ancestry. The Gothic and the Slavonic are direct translations from the Gk. in the 4th and 10th centuries respectively.

III. Patristic citations

For dating different text-types and for establishing their geographical location, we rely on the data provided by scriptural citations in early Christian writings. Much significant work has been done in this field, the most important results being in respect of Origen, Chrysostom and Photius among Gk. writers, of Cyprian, Lucifer of Cagliari and Novatian among the Latins, and of Ephrem and Aphraat among the Syrians. About the effects of the work of Marcion and Tatian on the NT text and concerning the text attested by Irenaeus—

all matters of great importance—we are still in some uncertainty.

The whole field is much complicated by the vagaries of human memory and customs of citation. We also find instances where the writer on changing his domicile changed his MSS or on the contrary took a particular text-type with him. For these reasons few would accept a reading attested in citation alone; yet F. Blass and M.-E. Boismard have dared to do this in works on the text of the Gospel of Jn.

IV. Analysis

In many cases of classical literature it is found that the material available for the establishment of the text may be analysed into one *stemma* or line of descent, leading down from the archetype which may be adequately reconstructed even where a careful transcript is not to be discovered among the MSS, as is often the case. The NT material is not patient of such analysis in spite of the efforts of a number of scholars to apply a genealogical method to it. Westcott and Hort used the criterion of conflate readings as the primary stage in such an analysis. In this way they established the inferiority of the text of the mass of the late MSS, a conclusion corroborated by their second criterion, the evidence of patristic citation. They were then faced, however, with two main types of text, *viz.* that attested by B ℵ and that attested by D lat. Between these texts of equal antiquity they were unable to decide by these two objective criteria, and so fell back on a third, inevitably somewhat subjective, namely, that of intrinsic probability. By this means they were enabled to follow the B ℵ text in most cases and to reject the D lat text.

H. von Soden's analysis of the same material arrived at a system of three recensions, all dating in his view from the 4th century: by a simple arithmetical procedure he thought himself able to arrive at a pre-recensional text, always allowing for the factor of harmonization which he considered all-pervasive (and due in the Gospels to the corrupting influence of the *Diatessaron*).

Neither theory has met with unqualified approval subsequently. Von Soden's methodology is open to criticism because of the sometimes artificial rigidity of his triple pattern, and his uncritical use of the Arabic *Diatessaron*. He is, in Lake's phrase, 'so often instructive, so rarely correct'. Hort's theory has a whole history of subsequent debate. Slavishly followed at first, it was then put in doubt by the growing knowledge of the Lat. and Syriac versions, and of minuscule families with early patristic links, both of which helped to create a picture of an early complex of 'mixed texts' rather than a simple clearcut twofold division of text-types. But more recently, anticipated by rational–critical approbation of the codex B and its allies by Lagrange and Ropes, new discoveries and fresh examination have resulted in a growing consensus that the P^{75}-B text in Lk. and Jn., the P^{46}-B text in the Pauline Epistles, is in most of its features an intrinsically good text. Presence of possible corruption within it is not, however, denied. Hort's fault was to suggest, whether intentionally or not, that the third criterion of intrinsic probability had the 'objectivity' of the genealogical method exemplified in the first and second. In fact, he was using rational criticism, and in many of his conclusions, although probably not in all, his judgment appears to have been sound. We need the analysis of text-types and their history and the definition of recensions if these existed: but the concluding stage of any search for the original text can only be pursued by rational criticism, *i.e.* the practice of scientific judgment by intrinsic probability. A number of objective criteria may be established for this purpose.

V. Criteria

In this matter sylistic and linguistic standards play a large part. In every part of the NT enough remains without serious variation to enable studies of the characteristic style and usage of individual writers to be made. In cases of textual doubt we may use such knowledge of the accustomed style of the book in question. Furthermore, we shall in the Gospels prefer variants where the influence of parallel Synoptic passages is absent; or those in which a strongly Aram. cast in the Gk. reveals the underlying original tradition. Throughout, we shall avoid constructions of Attic or Atticizing Gk., preferring those of the Hellenistic vernacular. In other places, factors from a wider sphere may be discerned. Palaeography can elucidate variants which derive from primitive errors in the MS tradition. The history or economics of the 1st century AD can sometimes show us the choice between variants by providing information on technical terms, value of currency, *etc.* Church history and the history of doctrine may reveal where variants show accommodation to later doctrinal trends.

It will be plain from the fact that such criteria can be applied that in spite of the profusion of material the text of the NT is fairly well and accurately preserved, well enough at least for us to make stylistic judgments about, *e.g.*, Paul or John, or to judge in what case doctrine has transformed the text. The text is in no instance so insecure as to necessitate the alteration of the basic gospel. But those who love the Word of God will desire the greatest accuracy in the minutest details, knowing the nuances of meaning made possible by word-order, tense, change of particle, *etc.*

VI. History of the text

In brief outline we may thus sketch the history of the NT text. Many of the factors earliest at work are those described in the history of the growth of the * Canon of the NT. The circulation of separate Gospels, but of the Pauline letters as a corpus; the chequered history of the Acts and Rev.; the overshadowing of the Catholic Epistles by the rest: all these are reflected in the textual data for the several books. During the period of the establishment of the Canon a number of factors were at work. There was a tendency as early as we can trace to attempt emendation of the Gk. according to prevailing fashions or even scribal whim; in the case of the Gospels a close verbal identity was sought, often at the expense of Mk. In some cases, 'floating tradition' was added; or items were taken away from the written word. Such heretical teachers as Marcion and Tatian left the mark of tendentious correction upon their editions of the text, and doubtless their opponents were not blameless in this. In the Acts, alterations were made perhaps for purely literary or popularizing motives. Nevertheless, good texts were to be found, whether preserved by miracle or by philology, although no text known is without some corruption. In the 2nd and 3rd centuries, we find a mixture of good and bad, in differing proportions, in all our evidence.

It has seemed to a number of scholars that at some time in the late 3rd or early 4th century attempts at recensional activity took place. But there is little direct evidence of this, and recent discovery and discussion have put a completely new look on the question. We now know from the close affinity of P^{75} and B that the text-type of the latter, known in the Alexandrian Fathers, was not a creation of the shadowy Hesychius (named, with Lucian, by Jerome in his letter to Damasus, as author of a recension), but existed in the 2nd century. Since, however, as we know from the papyri, other types were known in Egypt, scholarly work may have rescued that one which commended itself on traditional philological grounds. The Byzantine text has been associated with the name of Lucian, and this has been supported by the similarity of many of its features to those of the Lucianic recension of the LXX. That recension, however, may antedate Lucian, at least in some of its elements, and likewise in the NT we have some evidence of Byzantine readings in papyri earlier than his date. The so-called Caesarean text, which Streeter and Lake were confident to have found in the citations of Origen and Eusebius, and in codex Θ and various minuscules, has disintegrated upon closer examination. While there may be a recensional form in some of the witnesses adduced, there was a pre-recensional stage, known, for instance, in P^{45}. In other words, Christian scholars, where their activity may be discerned, were not creating new texts so much as choosing from a variety which already existed. In the Epistles their scope for choice was apparently less since only three forms (Alexandrian, Byzantine and 'Western') are found, but in Rev. there is a distinct fourfold pattern, yet one unrelated to the textual divisions of the Gospels. The data which earlier generations termed 'Western text' exemplify the way in which ancient readings could co-exist in specific traditions with material evidently secondary. It is the principles of choice utilized by the Christian scholars of the 3rd and 4th centuries which demand our scrutiny, and the general sobriety of Alexandrian judgment shows itself more and more. Yet no critic today would follow a single text-type alone, even if he were to give pride of place to one in particular.

In the Middle Ages the Alexandrian text seems to have suffered eclipse. Various forms of Caesarean and Byzantine wrestled for supremacy till about the 10th century. After this, the Byzantine text may be said to have been supreme in the sense that many MSS of nearly identical type were produced and have been preserved. But variants from even the earliest times are recrudescent in late MSS, and important MSS of other recensions and even of pre-recensional type come from very late dates, while some late MSS in fact change their allegiance in a bewildering fashion from text-type to text-type.

VII. Conclusion

Thus the task of NT textual criticism is vast and unfinished. Certainly, advances have been made since the material began to be collected and examined in the 17th century. Both Hort and von Soden present texts better than the printed texts of the Renaissance, and provide a sound basis upon which satisfactory exegesis may proceed. It is evident that many of the principles behind the Alexandrian text were sound. But it must be constantly borne in mind that even the best philological work of antiquity demands critical scrutiny if we seek the original text. The textual critic will be as the scribe discipled in the kingdom of heaven, bringing forth from his treasures things new and old. The busy textual projects of the post-war years should bring us nearer to the apostolic *ipsissima verba* than previous generations were favoured to come; yet we cannot but build on other men's foundations.

BIBLIOGRAPHY. P. Maas, *Textkritik*², 1950 (E.T. 1958); G. Pasquali, *Storia della Tradizione e Critica del Testo*², 1952; A. Dain, *Les Manuscrits*², 1964; C. Tischendorf, *Novum Testamentum Graece*, 8a Editio Maior, 1869–72; H. von Soden, *Die Schriften des neuen Testaments in ihrer aeltesten erreichbaren Textgestalt*, 1911–13; C. R. Gregory, *Textkritik des neuen Testaments*, 1900–9; F. H. A. Scrivener, *Introduction to the Criticism of the New Testament*⁴, 1894; A. Vööbus, *Early Versions of the New Testament*, 1954; B. F. Westcott and F. J. A. Hort, *The New Testament in the Original Greek*, 1881; K. Lake, *The Text of the New Testament*⁶, 1928; M.-J. Lagrange, *Critique Textuelle*, 2: *La Critique Rationelle*², 1935; G. D. Kilpatrick, 'Western Text and Original Text in the Gospels and Acts', *JTS* 44, 1943, pp. 24–36, and 'Western Text and Original Text in the Epistles', *JTS* 45, 1944, pp. 60–65; G. Zuntz, *The Text of the Epistles*, 1953; M. M. Parvis and A. P. Wikgren (eds.), *New Testament Manuscript Studies*, 1950; A. J. F. Klijn, *A Survey of the Researches into the Western Text of the Gospels and Acts*, 1, 1949; 2, 1969; J. Schmid, *Studien zur Geschichte des griechischen Apokalypse-Textes*, 1955; S. Éphrem, *Commentaire de l'évangile concordante, Texte syriaque édite et traduite par D. Louis Leloir*, 1963; C. M. Martini, *Il problema della recensionalità del codice B alla luce del papiro Bodmer XIV*, 1966; J. N. Birdsall, 'The New Testament Text', *Cambridge History of the Bible*, 1, 1970, pp. 308–377; K. Aland, *Die alten Übersetzungen des neuen Testaments, die Kirchenväterzitate u. Lektionare*, 1972; B. M. Metzger, *The Text of the New Testament*², 1968; *idem*, *A Textual Commentary on the Greek New Testament*, 1971; *idem*, *The Early Versions of the New Testament*, 1977.

Editions with select apparatus: *Novum Testamentum Graece et Latine* . . . edidit Augustinus Merk⁸, 1958; *Novum Testamentum Graece* . . . curavit E. Nestle²⁵, 1963; Η ΚΑΙΝΗ ΔΙΑΘΗΚΗ (ed. G. D. Kilpatrick), British and Foreign Bible Society, 1958.

J.N.B.

THADDAEUS. This name occurs only in the list of the 12 apostles (Mt. 10:3; Mk. 3:18). The equivalent in Lk. 6:16 is 'Judas the son of James' (*cf.* also Acts 1:13). AV in Mt. 10:3 reads 'Lebbaeus, whose surname was Thaddaeus'. Most textual critics now read simply 'Thaddaeus' and treat 'Lebbaeus' as an intrusion from the Western Text, though some have suggested 'Lebbaeus' to be correct and 'Thaddaeus' to have been introduced from Mk. 3:18. 'Thaddaeus' is probably derived from Aram. *taḏ*, meaning the female breast, and suggests warmth of character and almost feminine devotedness. 'Lebbaeus' comes from Heb. *lēḇ*, 'heart', and it may therefore be an explanation of the other name. Attempts have been made to derive 'Thaddaeus' from 'Judah' and 'Lebbaeus' from 'Levi'.

There seems little doubt that

The theatre at Ephesus, with its tiers of seats cut into the hillside, was commonly used as a place of city assembly (Acts 19:29). (RH)

Thaddaeus is to be identified with 'Judas of James' (see F. F. Bruce, *The Acts of the Apostles*, 1951, p. 73). The name 'Judas' would not be popular with the deed of Judas Iscariot in mind, and this may be why it is not used in Mt. and Mk. The post-canonical literature does not help us to obtain a clear picture, but Jerome says that Thaddaeus was also called 'Lebbaeus' and 'Judas of James', and that he was sent on a mission to Abgar, king of Edessa. Eusebius, on the other hand, reckoned him to be one of the Seventy. The mention of the Gospel of Thaddaeus in some MSS of the *Decretum Gelasii* is thought to be due to a scribal error. R.E.N.

THEATRE. Gk. theatres were usually cut in some naturally concave hillside such as might be afforded by the acropolis of the town concerned. There was thus no limit to size, provided the acoustic properties were adequate, and some theatres seated many thousands of persons. The seats rose precipitously in a single tier around the *orchēstra*, or dancing space. Behind this the theatre was enclosed by a raised stage, the *skēnē*. Together with the gymnasium, the theatre was the centre of cultural affairs, and might be used as a place for official assemblies, as at Ephesus (Acts 19:29). This particular theatre stood facing down the main thoroughfare of the city towards the docks, and as in most Gk. states remains the most substantial relic of the past. E.A.J.

THEBES (Heb. *No*, as AV). Once Egypt's most magnificent capital. Heb. *No* corresponds to the Egyp. *niw*(*t*), 'the City' *par excellence*, and No-Amon to the Egyp. phrase *niw*(*t*)-*'Imn*, 'the City of (the god) Amūn'. In Gk. it is called both Thebes, the usual term in modern writings, and Diospolis magna. Some 530 km upstream from Cairo as the crow flies, its site on the two banks of the Nile is marked on the

The temple of Queen Hatshepsut at Deir el Bahri is one of the major monuments of the necropolis at Thebes. (MEPhA)

THARA
See Terah, Part 3.

THARSHISH
See Tarshish, Part 3.

E side by the two vast temple-precincts of the god Amūn (*AMON), now known by the Arab. names Karnak and Luxor, and on the W side by a row of royal funerary temples from modern Qurneh to Medinet Habu, behind which extends a vast necropolis of rock-cut tombs.

Thebes first rose to national importance in the Middle Kingdom (early 2nd millennium BC), as the home town of the powerful pharaohs of the 12th Dynasty (*EGYPT, History); however, the land was then administered not from Thebes in the far S, but from the better-placed Itjet-Tawy just S of ancient *Memphis and modern Cairo. During the Second Intermediate Period Thebes became the centre of Egyp. opposition to the foreign Hyksos kings, and from Thebes came the famous 18th Dynasty kings, who finally expelled them and established the Egyp. empire (New Kingdom). During the imperial 18–20th Dynasties, *c.* 1550–1070 BC, the treasures of Asia and Africa poured into the coffers of Amūn of Thebes, now state god of the empire. All this wealth plus the continuing gifts of Late Period pharaohs such as *Shishak fell as spoil to the conquering Assyrians under Ashurbanipal in 663 BC amid fire and slaughter. In predicting mighty Nineveh's fall, no more lurid comparison could Nahum (3:8–10) draw upon than the fate of Thebes. The force of this comparison rules out attempts occasionally made to identify Nahum's No-Amon with a Lower Egyp. city of the same name. The Nile, Nahum's 'rivers', was truly Thebes' defence. The Late Period pharaohs made full use of its E Delta branches and irrigation and drainage canals as Egypt's first line of defence, with sea-coast forts at the Nile mouths and across the road from Palestine—perhaps alluded to in the phrase 'wall(s) from the sea' (coast inwards?). To this protection was added Thebes' great distance upstream, which invaders had to traverse to reach her. In the early 6th century BC Jeremiah (46:25) and Ezekiel (30:14–16) both spoke against Thebes. See C. F. Nims, *Thebes*, 1965. K.A.K.

THEBEZ (Heb. *tēḇēṣ*, 'brightness'). A fortified city in Mt. Ephraim, in the course of capturing which *Abimelech was mortally wounded by a millstone hurled down on him by a woman (Jdg. 9:50ff.; 2 Sa. 11:21). Thebez is the modern Tūbās, about 16 km N of Nablus, and NE

The location of some of the major tombs in the Valley of the Kings, Thebes.

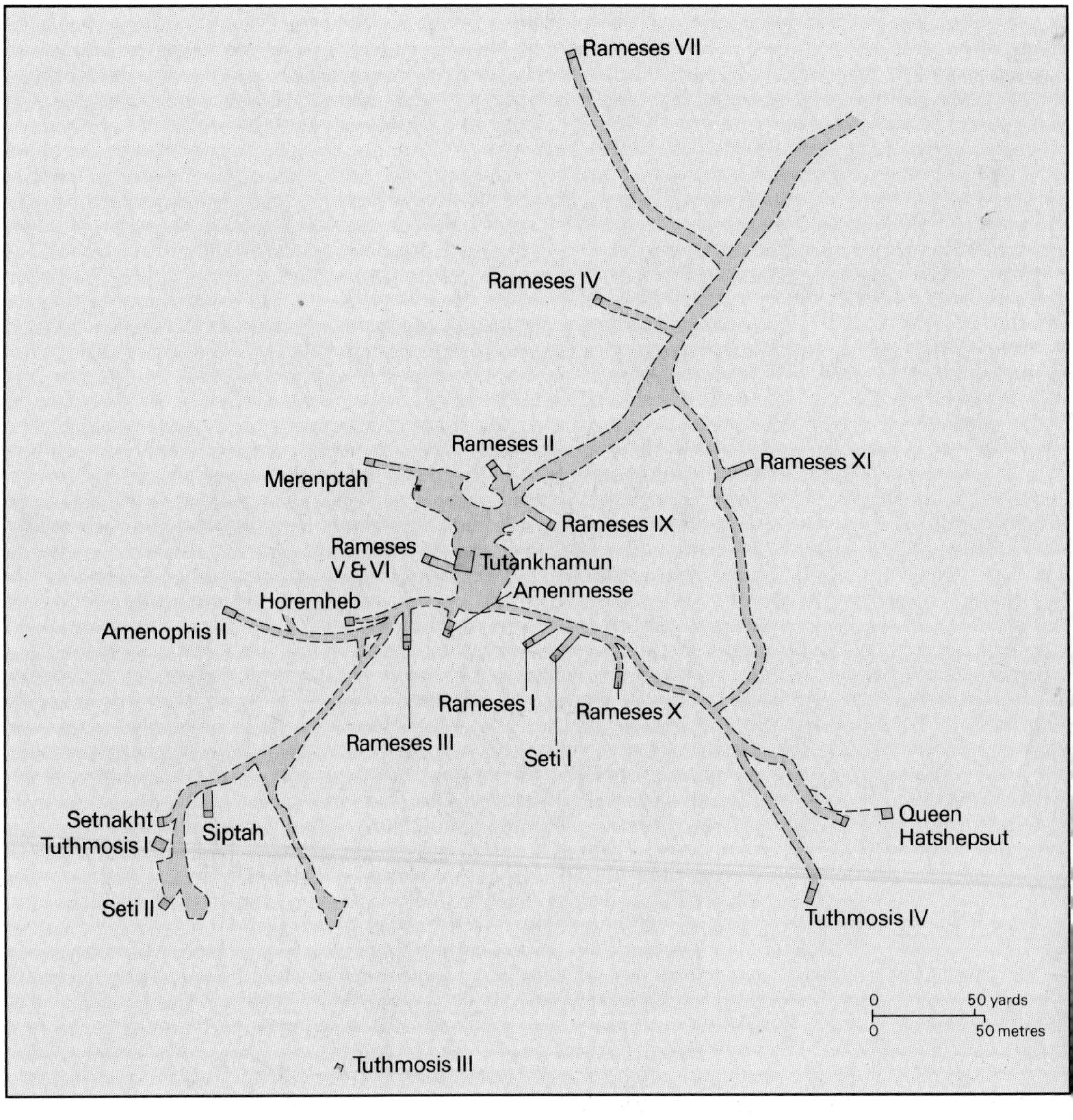

of Shechem on the road to Beth-shan. J.D.D.

THEOPHILUS (Gk. *theophilos*, 'dear to God', 'friend of God'), the man to whom both parts of Luke's history were dedicated (Lk. 1:3; Acts 1:1). Some have thought that the name indicates generally 'the Christian reader', others that it conceals a well-known figure, such as Titus Flavius Clemens, the emperor Vespasian's nephew (so B. H. Streeter, *The Four Gospels*, 1924, pp. 534ff.). But it is most probably a real name. The title 'most excellent' given to him in Lk. 1:3 may denote a member of the equestrian order (possibly in some official position) or may be a courtesy title (*cf.* Acts 23:26; 24:3; 26:25). Theophilus had acquired some information about Christianity, but Luke decided to supply him with a more orderly and reliable account. He may have been a representative of that class of Rom. society which Luke wished to influence in favour of the gospel, but scarcely the advocate briefed for Paul's defence before Nero (so J. I. Still, *St Paul on Trial*, 1923, pp. 84ff.). F.F.B.

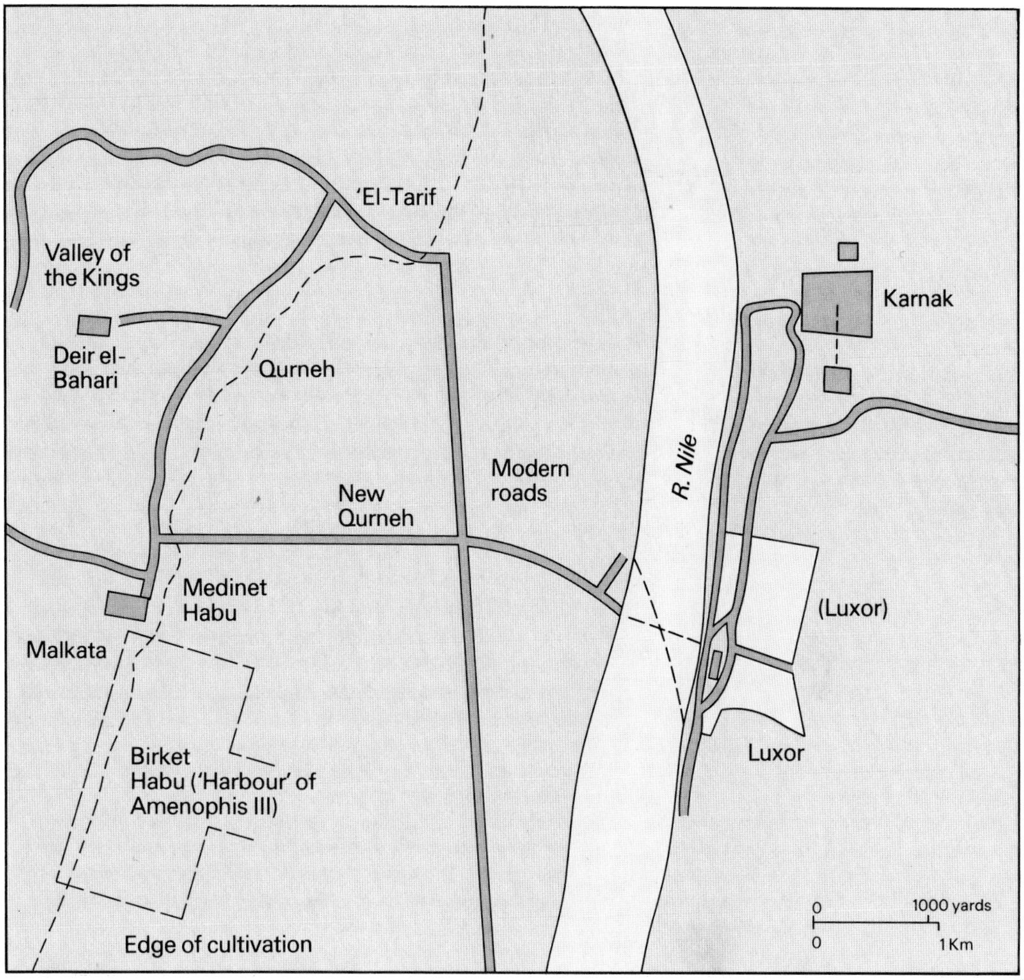

The site of Thebes on the banks of the R. Nile.

THESSALONIANS, EPISTLES TO THE.

I. Outline of contents

1 Thessalonians

a. Greeting (1:1).

b. Thanksgiving for the Thessalonian Christians' faith and steadfastness (1:2–10).

c. Paul's explanation of his recent conduct (2:1–16).

d. Narrative of events since he left Thessalonica (2:17–3:10).

e. His prayer for an early reunion with them (3:11–13).

f. Encouragement to holy living and brotherly love (4:1–12).

g. Concerning the parousia (4:13–5:11).

h. Some exhortations (5:12–22).

i. Prayer, final greeting and benediction (5:23–28).

2 Thessalonians

a. Greeting (1:1–2).

b. Thanksgiving and encouragement (1:3–12).

c. Events which must precede the day of the Lord (2:1–12).

d. Further thanksgiving and encouragement (2:13–3:5).

e. The need for discipline (3:6–15)

f. Prayer, final greeting and benediction (3:16–18).

II. Authorship

Both the Epistles to the Thessalonians are superscribed with the names of Paul, Silvanus (= Silas) and Timothy; but in both Paul is the real author, although he associates with himself his two companions who had recently shared his missionary work in Thessalonica. In 1 Thes. Paul speaks by name in the first person singular (2:18) and refers to Timothy in the third person (3:2, 6); in 2 Thes. he appends his personal signature (3:17) and is therefore to be identified with the 'I' of 2:5. His use of 'we' and 'us' when he is referring to himself alone is as evident in these Epistles as in others, especially so in 1 Thes. 3:1: 'we were willing to be left behind at Athens alone' (*cf.* Acts 17:15f.).

There has been little difficulty about the Pauline authorship of 1 Thes.; F. C. Baur's ascription of it to a disciple of Paul's who wrote after AD 70 to revive interest in the parousia is but a curiosity in the history of criticism.

Greater difficulty has been felt with 2 Thes. Its style is said to be formal as compared with that of the first Epistle; this judgment, based on such expressions as 'we are bound' and 'as is fitting' in 1:3, is not of great moment; it certainly needs no such explanation as that offered by M. Dibelius—that this Epistle was written to be read in church—for the same is true of the first Epistle (*cf.* 1 Thes. 5:27). More serious is the argument that the eschatology of 2 Thes. contradicts that of 1 Thes. The first Epistle stresses the unexpectedness with which the day of the Lord will arrive, 'like a thief in the night' (1 Thes. 5:2), whereas the second Epistle stresses that certain events will intervene before its arrival (2 Thes. 2:1ff.), and does so in a passage whose apocalyptic character is unparalleled in the Pauline literature.

A. Harnack accounted for the difference with the suggestion that 1 Thes. was written to the Gentile section of the church of Thessalonica, and 2 Thes. to the Jewish

THEOCRACY See Government, Part 2.

THEOLOGY See God, Part 1.

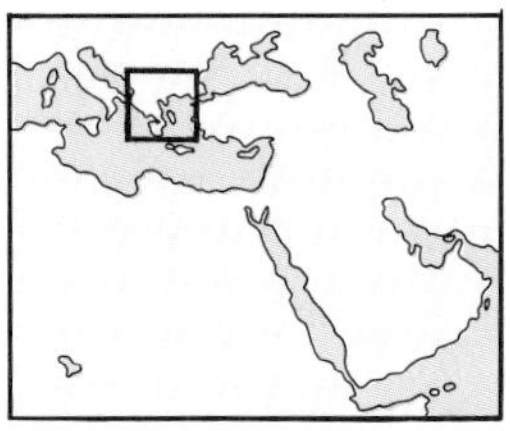

Thessalonica, a major city of Macedonia.

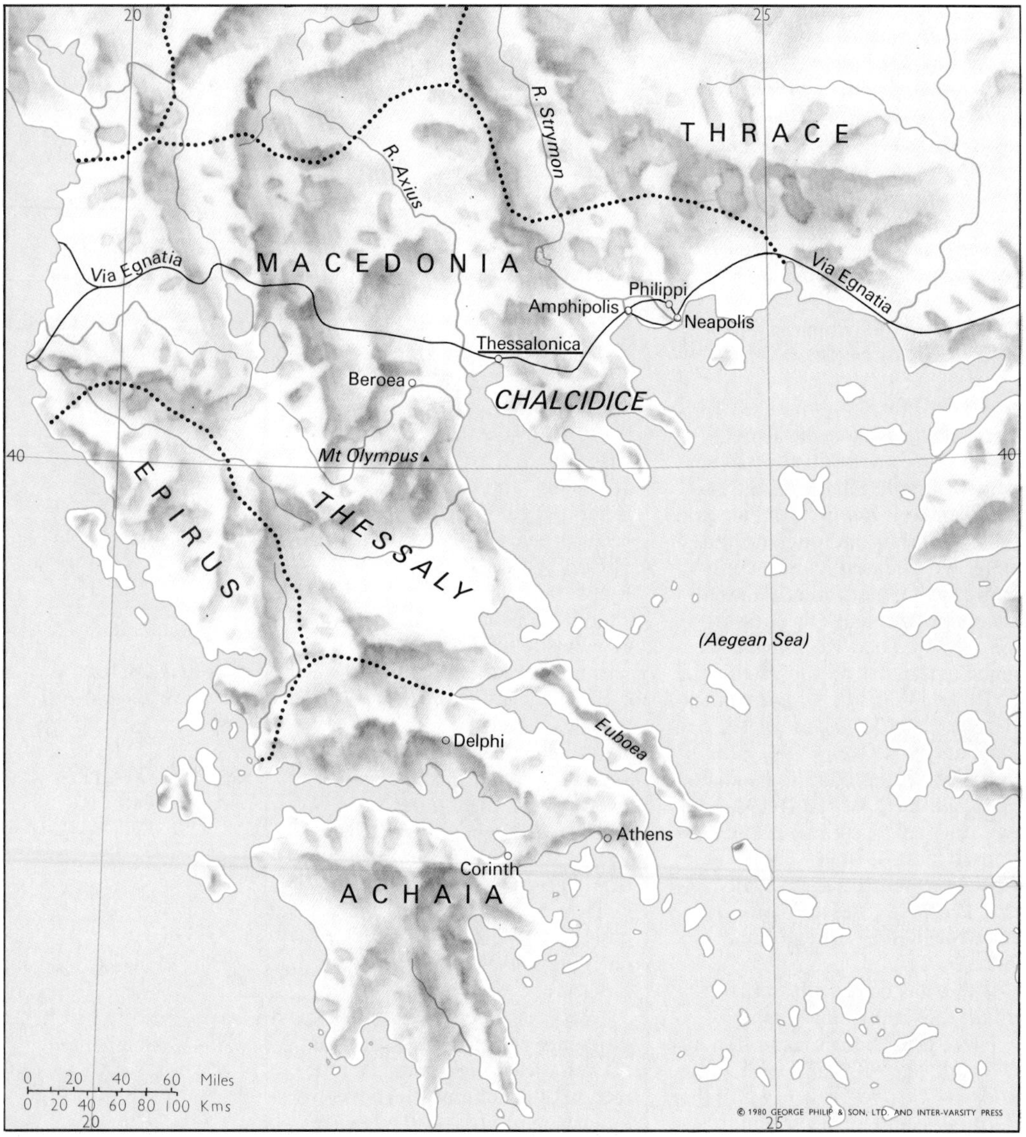

section. This is not only rendered improbable by the direction of 1 Thes. 5:27 that that Epistle be read to 'all the brethren' but is incredible in the light of Paul's fundamental insistence on the oneness of Gentile and Jewish believers in Christ. Equally unconvincing is F. C. Burkitt's supplement to Harnack's theory—that both Epistles were drafted by Silvanus and approved by Paul, who added 1 Thes. 2:18 ('I Paul') and 2 Thes. 3:17 in his own hand.

Alternative suggestions to the Pauline authorship of both letters raise greater difficulties than the Pauline authorship does. If 2 Thes. is pseudonymous, it was an unbelievable refinement of subtlety on the writer's part to warn the readers against letters forged in Paul's name (2:2); the salutation in 2 Thes. 3:17 is intelligible only as Paul's safeguard against the danger of such forged letters. The difficulties raised by the Pauline authorship can best be accounted for by considering the occasion and relation of the two letters. Both letters were included in the earliest ascertainable edition of the Pauline corpus.

III. Occasion

a. The First Epistle

Paul and his companions had to leave *Thessalonica hastily in the early summer of AD 50, after making a number of converts and planting a church in the city (Acts 17:1–10). The circumstances of their departure meant that their converts would inevitably be exposed to persecution, for which they were imperfectly prepared, because Paul had not had time to give them all the basic teaching which he thought they required. At the earliest opportunity he sent Timothy back to see how the Thessalonian Christians were faring. When Timothy returned to him in Corinth (Acts 18:5) he brought good news of their steadfastness and zeal in propagating the gospel, but reported that they had certain problems, some ethical (with special reference to sexual relations) and some eschatological (in particular, they were concerned lest at the parousia those of their number who had died should be at a disadvantage as compared with those who were still alive). Paul wrote to them immediately, expressing his joy at Timothy's good news, protesting that his recent abrupt departure from them was through no choice of his own (as his detractors urged), stressing the importance of chastity and diligence in daily work, and assuring them that believers who died before the parousia would suffer no disadvantage but would be raised to rejoin their living brethren and 'meet the Lord in the air' at his coming.

b. The Second Epistle

Before long, however, further news reached Paul which indicated that there were still some misapprehensions to be removed. He suspected that some of these misapprehensions might be due to misrepresentations of his teaching to the Thessalonian church. Some members of the church had inferred that the parousia was so imminent that there was no point in going on working. Paul explains that certain events must take place before the parousia; in particular, there will be a world-wide rebellion against God, led by one who will incarnate the forces of lawlessness and anarchy, which at present are being held in check by a power which he need not name in writing, since his readers know what he means. (The allusiveness of his reference to this power makes it likely that he had in mind the Roman empire, whose maintenance of law and order gave him cause for gratitude several times in the course of his apostolic service.) As for those who were disinclined to work, he speaks to them even more sharply than in the former Epistle; to live at the expense of others is unworthy of able-bodied Christians, who had seen an example of the worthier course in the conduct of Paul himself and his colleagues. Spongers and slackers must be treated by their fellow-Christians in a way that will bring them to their senses.

An attempt has sometimes been made to relieve the difficulties felt in relating the two Epistles to each other by supposing that 2 Thes. was written first (*cf.* J. Weiss, *Earliest Christianity*, 1, 1959, pp. 289ff.; T. W. Manson, *Studies in the Gospels and Epistles*, 1962, pp. 268ff.; R. G. Gregson, 'A Solution to the Problems of the Thessalonian Epistles', *EQ* 38, 1966, pp. 76ff.). But 2 Thes. does presuppose some previous correspondence from Paul (2:15), while the language of 1 Thes. 2:17–3:10 certainly implies that 1 Thes. was Paul's first letter to the Thessalonian Christians after his enforced departure.

IV. Teaching

With the possible exception of *Gal., the two Thessalonian letters are Paul's earliest surviving writings. They give us an illuminating, and in some ways a surprising, impression of certain phases of Christian faith and life 20 years after the death and resurrection of Christ. The main lines have already been laid down; the Thessalonian Christians (formerly pagan idolaters for the most part) were converted through hearing and accepting the apostolic preaching (1 Thes. 1:9f.); Jesus, in whom they had put their trust, is the Son of God who can be freely and spontaneously spoken of in terms which assume rather than assert his equality with the Father (*cf.* 1 Thes. 1:1; 3:11; 2 Thes. 1:1; 2:16); the gospel which has brought them salvation carries with it healthy practical implications for everyday life. The living and true God is holy, and he desires his people to be holy too; this holiness extends to such matters as relations with the other sex (1 Thes. 4:3) and the honest earning of their daily bread (1 Thes. 4:11f.; 2 Thes. 3:10–12). The apostles themselves had set an example in these and other matters (1 Thes. 2:5ff.; 2 Thes. 3:7ff.).

Both Epistles reflect the intense eschatological awareness of those years, and the unhealthy excesses to which it tended to give rise. Paul does not discourage this awareness (indeed, eschatology had evidently been prominent in his preaching at Thessalonica), but he teaches the Thessalonians not to confuse the suddenness of the parousia with its immediacy, and he impresses on them the ethical corollaries of Christian eschatology. He himself did not know then whether he would still be alive at the parousia; he hoped he would be, but he had received no assurance on the point. His prime concern was to discharge his appointed work so faithfully that the day would not find him unprepared and ashamed. So to his converts he presents the parousia as a comfort and hope for the bereaved and distressed, a warning to the careless and unruly, and for all a stimulus to holy living. The parousia will effect the ultimate conquest of evil; it will provide the universal manifestation of that triumph which is already guaranteed by the saving work of Christ.

BIBLIOGRAPHY. Commentaries on the Gk. text by G. G. Findlay, *CGT*, 1904; G. Milligan, 1908; J. Moffatt, *EGT*, 1910; J. E. Frame, *ICC*, 1913; B. Rigaux, *Études Bibliques*, 1956; on the Eng. text by J. Denney, *EB*, 1892; C. F. Hogg and W. E. Vine, 1914; E. J. Bicknell, *WC*, 1932; W. Neil, *MNT*, 1950; *idem*, *TBC*, 1957; W. Hendriksen, 1955; J. W. Bailey, *IB*, 11, 1955; L. Morris, *TNTC*, 1956; *idem*, *NLC*, 1959; A. L. Moore, *NCB*, 1969; D. E. H. Whiteley, *NClB*, 1969; E. Best, *BNTC*, 1972; also J. B. Lightfoot, *Biblical Essays*, 1893, pp. 235ff.; *idem*, *Notes on the Epistles of St Paul*, 1895, pp. 1ff.; K. Lake, *Earlier Epistles of St Paul*, 1911, pp. 61ff.; T. W. Manson, *Studies in the Gospels and Epistles*, 1962, pp. 259ff.

F.F.B.

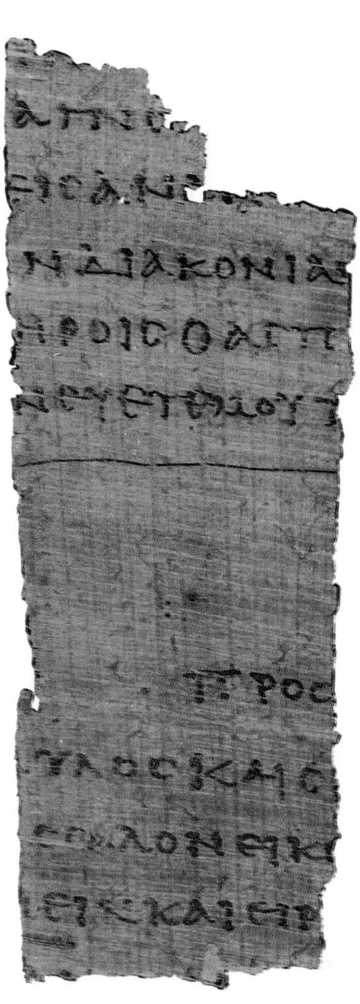

Fragment of a Greek papyrus book containing letters of Paul. Part of the end of Colossians (4:16–18) and the beginning of 1 Thessalonians (1:1). 3rd cent. AD. (CBL)

THESSALONICA. Founded after the triumph of Macedonia to grace her new position in world affairs, the city rapidly outstripped its older neighbours and became the principal metropolis of Macedonia. Situated at the junction of the main land route from Italy to the E with the main route from the Aegean to the Danube, her position under the Romans was assured, and she has remained a major city to this day. Thessalonica was the first place where Paul's preaching achieved a numerous and socially prominent following (Acts 17:4). His opponents, lacking their hitherto customary influence in high places, resorted to mob agitation to force the

Thessalonica was governed by 'politarchs' in the time of Paul. Six of these city officials are named in this Greek inscription which was incorporated into a Roman arch (the 'Gate of Vardar') at Thessalonica. White marble. Length 2·07 m. AD 143. (BM)

government's hand. The authorities, neatly trapped by the imputation of disloyalty towards the imperial power, took the minimum action to move Paul on without hardship to him. In spite of his success, Paul made a point of not placing himself in debt to his followers (Phil. 4:16f.; 1 Thes. 2:9). Not that they were themselves without generosity (1 Thes. 4:10); Paul was apparently afraid that the flourishing condition of the church would encourage parasites unless he himself set the strictest example of self-support (2 Thes. 3:8–12). The two Epistles to the *Thessalonians, written soon after his departure, reflect also his anxiety to conserve his gains from rival teachers (2 Thes. 2:2) and from disillusionment in the face of further agitation (1 Thes. 3:3). He need not have feared. Thessalonica remained a triumphant crown to his efforts (1 Thes. 1:8).

BIBLIOGRAPHY. E. Oberhummer, *RE*, *s.v.* 'Thessalonika'. E.A.J.

THEUDAS. 1. In Acts 5:36 an impostor (possibly a Messianic pretender) who some time before AD 6 gathered a band of 400 men, but he was killed and his followers dispersed. His activity was probably one of the innumerable disorders which broke out in Judaea after Herod's death in 4 BC. Origen (*Contra Celsum*, 1. 57) says he arose 'before the birth of Jesus', but that may simply be an inference from this passage, where Gamaliel speaks of his rising as having preceded that of *Judas.

2. In Josephus (*Ant.* 20. 97–99) a magician who led many followers to the Jordan, promising that the river would be divided at his command, so that they could cross it dry-shod. They were attacked by cavalry sent against them by the procurator Fadus (*c.* AD 44–46), and Theudas' head was brought to Jerusalem. F.F.B.

THIGH. Heb. *yārēḵ*, also translated 'side' in RSV, of altar or tabernacle (Nu. 3:29; 2 Ki. 16:14). The variant form *yar^{e}ḵâ* is almost always used of objects or places generally, mostly in the dual, *i.e.* derived from the thought of the two thighs. The other word translated 'thigh' in RSV (Ex. 29:22, 27) refers to the *leg. The Gk. *mēros* is used once (Rev. 19:16), where it probably refers to the locality of the inscription on the garment. (See *NBCR*, p.1304.)

The Heb. word is found in similar usage to *moṯnayim* or *ḥ^{a}lāṣayim* and Gk. *osphys*, 'loins', in respect of the parts of the body usually clothed (Ex. 28:42; *cf.* Is. 32:11), and especially of the position where a sword is worn (Ps. 45:3); also of the locality of the genital organs, and so by figure of speech to one's offspring (Gn. 46:26; *cf.* Gn. 35:11; Acts 2:30; *moṯnayim* is not used in this sense). The custom of making an oath by placing the hand under another's thigh (Gn. 24:2f.; 47:29ff.) signifies the association of the peculiar power of these parts, perhaps with the idea of invoking the support of the person's descendants to enforce the oath. For association in a particular form of oath, see Nu. 5:21ff.

Smiting upon the thigh is a sign of anguish (Je. 31:19). For a discussion of the custom of not eating the sinew of the thigh joint (Gn. 32:32), see *SINEW. B.O.B.

THIRD DAY
See Number, Part 2.

THIRD HEAVEN
See Heaven, Part 2.

THISTLE
See Plants, Part 3.

THOMAS. One of the twelve apostles. In the lists of the Twelve which are arranged in three groups of four each, Thomas occurs in the second group (Mt. 10:2–4; Mk. 3:16–19; Lk. 6:14–16; Acts 1:13). He is linked with Matthew in Mt. 10:3 and with Philip in Acts 1:13. The name comes from Aram. *t^{e}'ômā'*, meaning 'twin'; John three times uses the Gk. version of it, 'Didymus' (11:16; 20:24; 21:2). The question whose twin he was cannot be answered with certainty. Various traditions (Syriac and Egyp.) suggest that his personal name was Judas.

It is only in the Fourth Gospel that there are any personal references to Thomas. He was prepared to go with Jesus to the tomb of Lazarus and to possible death at the hands of the Jews (Jn. 11:16). He confessed himself unable to understand where Jesus was going when he warned the Twelve of his impending departure (Jn. 14:5). The chief incident for which he has always been remembered, and for which he has been called 'Doubting Thomas', is his disbelief in the resurrection. He missed the appearance of Christ to the other apostles (Jn. 20:24) and said that he needed

Throne-like chair from the tomb of Yuya and Thuya, the parents of Tiye, wife of Amenophis III. 18th Dynasty. (SI)

Tiglath-pileser III on his throne, with attendants during a royal audience. Wall-painting from the palace at Til Barsip (Tell Ahmar, Syria). 8th cent. BC. (AP)

visual and tactual proof of the resurrection (20:25). A week later Christ appeared again to the Eleven and he offered Thomas the opportunity to test the reality of his body.

Thomas' confession of faith, 'My Lord and my God' (20:28), marks the climax of the Fourth Gospel; blessing is promised to those who can come to faith without the aid of sight. R.E.N.

THORNS, CROWN OF. This was made by the Roman soldiers and placed on the head of Christ when he was mocked before the crucifixion (Mt. 27:29; Mk. 15:17; Jn. 19:2).

It was, with the sceptre of reed and the purple robe, symbolic of the fact that he had been said to be King of the Jews. The superscription on the cross likewise proclaimed this in mockery. Yet Christians have seen the life of Jesus as a royal road from the manger of Bethlehem to the cross of Calvary, and the very incidents in which he least seemed to be a king have won their allegiance more than anything else. For John especially the moment of Christ's humiliation is the moment of his glory (12:31–33; *cf.* Heb. 2:9).

It is uncertain exactly what plant is signified by *akantha.* There are a number of plants with sharp spines which grow in Palestine. Christians have seen the thorns as symbolic of the effects of sin (Gn. 3:18; Nu. 33:55; Pr. 22:5; Mt. 7:16; 13:7; Heb. 6:8).

H. St J. Hart (*JTS* n.s. 3, 1952, pp. 66ff.) suggests that the crown was made from palm leaves, which would be readily available. *Phoenix dactylifera* has sharp spines. The crown might thus have been intended to resemble the 'radiate crown' of a divine ruler, so that Christ was being mocked as 'God' as well as 'king'.

See also * PLANTS (Thorns).

R.E.N.

THRACE. A tribally organized region lying between Macedonia and the Gk. states of the Bosporus coast. It had always maintained a sturdy independence of Gk. control, and the Romans left it as an isolated enclave under its own dynasties until AD 44, when it was incorporated into the Caesarean province under a low-ranking procurator. Republican institutions were not widely developed before the 2nd century AD. There is no record of Christianity there in NT times.

BIBLIOGRAPHY. A. H. M. Jones, *Cities of the Eastern Roman Provinces*², 1970; J. Keil, *CAH*, 11, 1936, pp. 570–573. E.A.J.

THRESHOLD 1. *mip̄tān* is used for the threshold of the temple of Dagan at Ashdod (1 Sa. 5:4–5), the Jerusalem Temple (Ezk. 9:3; 10:4, 18) and Ezekiel's Temple (46:2; 47:1). Zephaniah alludes to an idolatrous practice of leaping over the threshold (1:9). An example of a threshold was found at Hazor (Y. Yadin, *Hazor*, 1972, pl. 22a).

2. *sap̄* (AV also as gate, door, doorpost) applies mainly to sacred buildings, although 1 Ki. 14:17 probably refers to Jeroboam's house, Est. 2:21; 6:2 to a palace, and Jdg. 19:27 to a house. Most references (2 Ki. 12:9; Is. 6:4; Am. 9:1) imply that the threshold indicated belongs to the sanctuary of the Jerusalem Temple, although in the Temple of Ezekiel (40:6–7) it refers to the single gateway in the outer wall. The threshold itself was made of stone and may have contained the cupped socks in which the door-posts swiveled.

3. *'ᵃsup̄îm* (Ne. 12:25), 'thresholds' (AV), is better 'storehouses' (RSV). C.J.D.

THRONE. Heb. *kissē'* may refer to any seat or to one of special importance (1 Ki. 2:19). Its root (Heb. *kāsâ*, 'to cover') suggests a canopied construction, hence a throne (*e.g.* Ex. 11:5; Ezk. 26:16). The throne symbolizes dignity and authority (Gn. 41:40; 2 Sa. 3:10), which may extend beyond the immediate occupant (2 Sa. 7:13–16). Since the king is Yahweh's representative, his throne is 'the throne of the kingdom of the Lord over Israel' (1 Ch. 28:5); it typifies Yahweh's throne in the heavens (1 Ki. 22:10, 19; *cf.* Is. 6:1). Right-

THOMAS JUDAS, ACTS OF
See New Testament apocrypha, Part 2.

THREE
See Number, Part 2.

THREE TAVERNS
See Taverns, three, Part 3.

Relief showing 'Sennacherib, king of Assyria, sitting upon his throne while the spoil from the city of Lachish passed before him' (inscription above figure to left of king). Nineveh. c. 690 BC. (BM)

A prince receives tribute, seated on a throne supported by winged cherubim (cf. 1 Sa. 4:4). Ivory from Megiddo. Height 4 cm. 8th cent. BC. (OIUC)

eousness and justice are therefore enjoined upon its occupants (Pr. 16:12; 20:28; *cf.* Is. 9:7; 2 Sa. 14:9). Although Yahweh's throne is transcendent (Is. 66:1; *cf.* Mt. 5:34), he graciously condescends to sit enthroned upon the cherubim (*e.g.* 1 Sa. 4:4). In the Messianic age 'Jerusalem shall be called the throne of the Lord' (Je. 3:17; *cf.* Ezk. 43:7).The thrones of judgment in Dn. 7:9ff. form a good introduction to the usual sense of the word in the NT.

Jesus receives 'the throne of his father David' (Lk. 1:32; *cf.* Acts 2:30; Heb. 1:5–9, all of which allude to 2 Sa. 7:12–16. *Cf.* also Heb. 8:1; 12:2). As Son of man, he will judge from his throne (Mt. 25:31ff.). In the world to come the disciples will have thrones and assist the Son of man (Mt. 19:28; *cf.* Lk. 22:30). The faithful are promised a seat on the throne of the Lamb (Rev. 3:21), and the pre-millennial judgment appears to be committed to them (20:4; *cf.* Dn. 7:9, 22). In the post-millennial judgment, however, there is only the great white throne (20:11). The disparity is more apparent than real, for Dn. 7 forms the background of each vision. Similarly, the vision of the august throne of God and the Lamb in Rev. 22:3 compares with Mt. 19:28 and Lk. 22:30, because John, in adding 'and they shall *reign* . . .' (22:5), undoubtedly has in mind the thrones of the faithful. *Cf.* 'throne of grace' (Heb. 4:16). R.J.McK.

THUMB. Heb. *bōhen*, in the OT equally and always together, of the thumb and big toe, differentiated by the designation, 'of the hand' or 'of the foot'. The root is related to an Arabic word meaning 'to cover' or 'shut', hence of that member which closes or covers the hand.

The practice of placing blood from the sacrificial beast upon the right thumb, great toe and also *ear of the priests probably indicated the dedication of the prominent organs of hearing, doing and walking, symbolizing the securing of the whole man (Ex. 29:20; Lv. 8:23, *etc.*). Similarly, the practice of cutting off the thumbs and great toes of a defeated enemy probably symbolized his being rendered powerless (Jdg. 1:6f.), and also ceremonially incompetent to discharge any sacral duties. B.O.B.

THUNDER. Most frequent during the winter season, thunder is vividly described in Jb. 37 and Ps. 29. The few rainstorms of summer are usually associated with thunder (*e.g.* 1 Sa. 12:17); the coincidence of this event with Samuel's message helped to deepen the warning to Israel when they desired a king. A desert thunderstorm seems the most plausible explanation for the narrative of 2 Ki. 3:4–27, when 'the country was filled with water', presumably as a result of a desert thunderstorm on the plateau E of the Zered valley. In another military campaign a thunderstorm decided the result of the battle between Israel and the Philistines (1 Sa. 7:10).

Thunder is frequently associated with the voice of God and is spoken of as a voice in Pss. 77:18; 104:7. The creative voice of God which bade the waters go to their appointed place (Gn. 1:9) is identified with thunder (Ps. 104:7). It was associated with the giving of the law at Sinai (Ex. 19:16; 20:18), and the voice out of heaven which answered Christ (Jn. 12:28f.) was identified by those present as a thunder-peal. Voices like thunder are referred to in the Apocalypse (Rev. 6:1; 14:2; 19:6), where they are even given articulate meaning (Rev. 10:3f.).

(*PLAGUES OF EGYPT.)

J.M.H.

THYATIRA. A city in the Roman province of Asia, in the W of what is now Asiatic Turkey. It occupied an important position in a low-lying 'corridor' connecting the Hermus and Caicus valleys. It was a frontier garrison, first on the W frontier of the territory of Seleucus I of Syria, and later, after changing hands, on the E frontier of the kingdom of Pergamum. With that kingdom, it passed under Roman rule in 133 BC. But it remained an important point in the Roman road-system, for it lay on the road from Pergamum to Laodicea, and thence to the E provinces. It was also an important centre of manufacture; dyeing, garment-making, pottery and brass-working are among the trades known to have existed there. A large town (Akhisar) still stands on the same site.

The Thyatiran woman Lydia, the 'seller of purple' whom Paul met at Philippi (Acts 16:14), was probably the overseas agent of a Thyatiran manufacturer; she may have been arranging the sale of dyed woollen goods which were known simply by the name of the dye. This 'purple' was obtained from the madder root, and was still produced in the district, under the name 'Turkey red', into the present century.

The Thyatiran church was the fourth (Rev. 1:11) of the 'seven

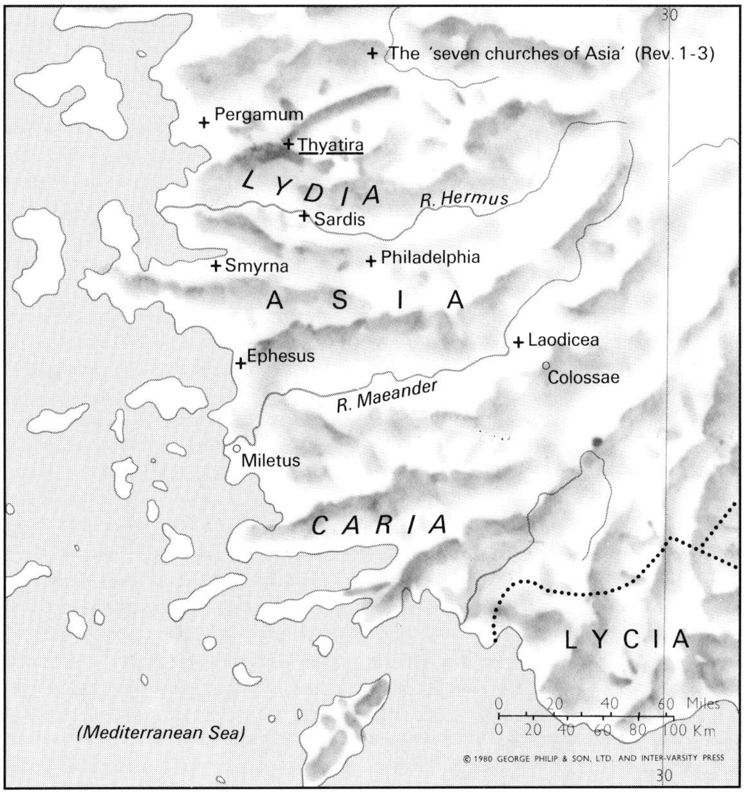

■ **THRUM**
See Spinning, Part 3.

■ **THRUSH**
See Animals, Part 1.

■ **THUMMIM**
See Urim, Part 3.

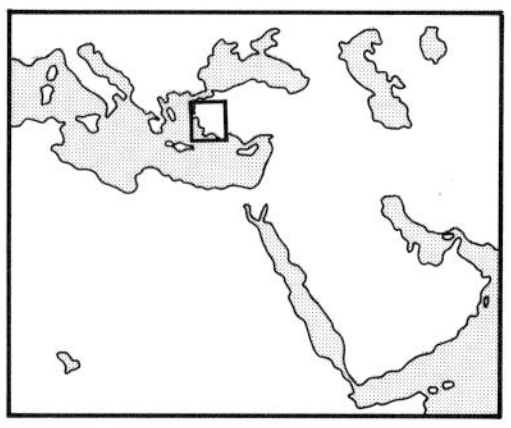

Thyatira, one of the 'seven churches of Asia' (Rev. 1–3).

churches of Asia'. Some of the symbols in the letter to the church (Rev. 2:18–29) seem to allude to the circumstances of the city. The description of the Christ (v. 18) is appropriate for a city renowned for its brass-working (*chalkolibanos*, translated 'fine brass', may be a technical term for some local type of brassware). The terms of the promise (vv. 26–27) may reflect the long military history of the city. 'Jezebel' (the name is probably symbolic) was evidently a woman who was accepted within the fellowship of the church (v. 20). Her teaching probably advocated a measure of compromise with some activity which was implicitly pagan. This is likely to have been membership of the social clubs or 'guilds' into which the trades were organized. These bodies fulfilled many admirable functions, and pursuance of a trade was almost impossible without belonging to the guild; yet their meetings were inextricably bound up with acts of pagan worship and immorality. (See W. M. Ramsay, *The Letters to the Seven Churches of Asia*, 1904, chs. 23–24; C. J. Hemer, *Buried History* 2, 1975, pp. 110–118.) M.J.S.R.
C.J.H.

THYINE WOOD See Trees, Part 3.

Bust of Tiberius, Emperor of Rome (AD *14–37*) *until a few years after the crucifixion* (*Lk. 3:1; Jn. 19:12, 15*). *Capri. Parian marble. Height c. 47 cm.* (BM)

TIBERIAS. A city on the W shore of the Sea of * Galilee which subsequently gave its name to the lake. It was founded by Herod Antipas about AD 20 and named after the emperor Tiberius. The principal factors influencing Herod's choice of site seem to have been: (1) a defensive position represented by a rocky projection above the lake; (2) proximity to some already-famous warm springs which lay just to the S. Otherwise, the site offered little, and the beautiful buildings of the city (which became Herod's capital) rose on ground that included a former graveyard, and so rendered the city unclean in Jewish eyes.

Tiberias is mentioned only once in the Gospels (Jn. 6:23; 'sea of Tiberias' appears in Jn. 6:1; 21:1), and there is no record of Christ ever visiting it. It was a thoroughly Gentile city, and he seems to have avoided it in favour of the numerous Jewish towns of the lake shore. By a curious reversal, however, after the destruction of Jerusalem it became the chief seat of Jewish learning, and both the Mishnah and the Palestinian Talmud were compiled there, in the 3rd and 5th centuries respectively.

Of the towns which surrounded the Sea of Galilee in NT times, Tiberias is the only one which remains of any size at the present day. J.H.P.

TIBERIUS. The stepson of Augustus Caesar, reluctantly adopted as his heir when all other hope of a direct succession was lost. On Augustus' death in AD 14, Tiberius at 56 years of age had a lifetime's experience of government behind him. It was nevertheless a momentous decision when the Senate transferred Augustus' powers bodily to him, thus recognizing that the *de facto* ascendancy of Augustus was now an indispensable instrument of the Roman state. For 23 years Tiberius loyally and unimaginatively continued Augustus' policies. His dourness gradually lost him the confidence of the nation, and he withdrew to a disgruntled retirement on Capri until his death. In his absence treason trials and the intervention of the praetorian guard set dangerous new precedents in Roman politics. He is referred to in Lk. 3:1 and indirectly wherever 'Caesar' is mentioned in the Gospels.

View of the surroundings of Tiberias on the W side of the Lake of Galilee. (MEPhA)

Bath house at Tiberias fed by warm springs. Byzantine, 1st cent. AD. (MEPhA)

Gold coin (aureus) *of Tiberius, Roman Emperor* AD *14–37. Diameter 19 mm.* (RG)

BIBLIOGRAPHY. R. Seager, *Tiberius*, 1972; B. M. Levick, *Tiberius the Politician*, 1976. E.A.J.

TIBHATH. A town in the Aramaean kingdom of Zobah (*ṣôḇâ*). After David defeated a composite force of Aramaeans, including men from Zobah and Damascus, he pressed on to the towns of Tibhath (*ṭiḇhaṯ*) and Chun, from which he took booty (1 Ch. 18:8). J.A.T.

TIDAL. One of four kings who subdued five kings of the cities of the plain (Sodom, Gomorrah, *etc.*), quelling their revolt 13 years later, in Abraham's time (Gn. 14:1–9). Heb. *tiḏ'āl* derives from the old Anatolian name *Tudḫali(y)a*, based on that of a sacred mountain (E. Laroche, *Les noms des Hittites*, 1966, pp. 191, 276, 283), attested also in the alphabetic texts at Ugarit as *tdġl*, *ttġl* (C. Virolleaud, *Palais royal d'Ugarit*, 2, 1957, pp. 64–66 [No. 39:21], 92 [No. 69:4]).

'Tidal king of *ḡōyîm*' (nations, groups) cannot be identified at present. The Hittite kings Tudkhalia II–IV (15th–13th centuries BC) are chronologically too late, likewise the Ugaritic occurrences. The name does go back, however, to the first half of the 2nd millennium BC. A possible Tudkhalia I (17th century BC?), father of Pusarruma, occurs in Hittite royal offering-lists ('C'; H. Otten, *Mitteilungen d. Deutsch. Orient-Gesellschaft* 83, 1951, pp. 62ff.; K. A. Kitchen, *Suppiluliuma and the Amarna Pharaohs*, 1962, p. 53, and Otten, *Die hethitischen historischen Quellen und die altorientalische Chronologie*, 1968, p. 26). In the story of the siege of Urshu, a little later, occurs back-reference to an official(?) named Tudkhalia (H. G. Güterbock, *ZA* 44, 1938, pp. 122/3:17; p. 135). Still earlier (*c.* 19th/18th centuries BC), Tudkhalia occurs at least twice as a private personal name in Old-Assyrian tablets from Cappadocia (Laroche, *op. cit.*, p. 191:1389:1; P. Garelli, *Les Assyriens en Cappadoce*, 1963, p. 160).

In the early 2nd millennium BC, alliances of kings are commonly attested in Mesopotamia; likewise in Anatolia then, the existence of paramount chiefs and their vassal-rulers—several such are solidly attested (A. Goetze, *Kleinasien*, 1957, p. 75; Garelli, *op. cit.*, pp. 61ff., 206, n. 4), but by no means exhaust the total of all that once existed. Therefore, it is a reasonable hypothesis that Tidal of Gn. 14 was some such Anatolian chief who (like Anum-hirbi) penetrated S into the Levant. *Cf.* also Kitchen, *Ancient Orient and Old Testament*, 1966, pp. 44–46, with references. K.A.K.

TIGLATH-PILESER, TILGATH-PILNESER. This king of Assyria is known by more than one name. *tiḡlaṯ-pil'eser* (2 Ki. 15:29; 16:7–10) is close to Assyr. *Tukulti-apil-Ešarra* ('My trust is in the son of Ešarra') and the Aram. *tgltpl'sr* (Zinjirli Stele; Ashur ostracon. The variant *tilgaṯ-piln'eser* (1 Ch. 5:6; 2 Ch. 28:20; LXX *Algathphellasar*) may be an inner-Hebrew form (*JSS* 21, 1976, p. 7). The king's other name, Pul, is given in both the OT (2 Ki. 15:19; 1 Ch. 5:26) and the Babylonian Chronicle (*Pulu*).

Tiglath-pileser III (745–727 BC) was a son of Adad-nirari III (*AfO* 3, 1926, p. 1, n. 2). The history of his reign is imperfectly known owing to the fragmentary nature of the extant inscriptions, mainly found at Nimrud (*CALAH), but the primary events are listed in the Assyrian Eponym canon.

The first campaign was directed against the Aramaeans in Babylonia, where Pul 'took the hands of Bel' and regained control until the rebellion of Ukīn-zēr in 731 and the siege of Sapia, following which the Chaldean chief Marduk-apla-iddina (*MERODACH-BALADAN)

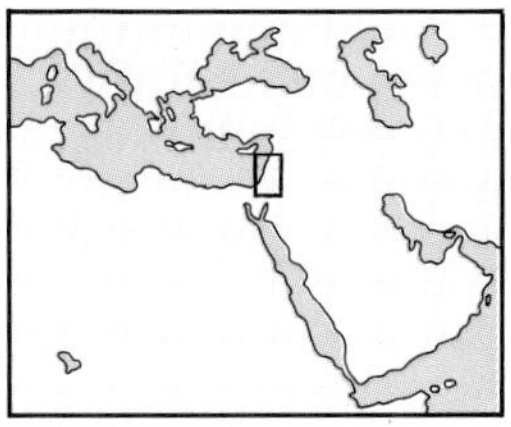

Provinces established by Tiglath-pileser III, king of Assyria, 745–727 BC.

submitted to the Assyrians. Other campaigns were directed against the Medes and Urartians (Armenia).

In 743 BC Tiglath-pileser marched to subdue the N Syrian city states which were under Urartian domination. During the 3-year siege of Arpad he received tribute from Carchemish, Hamath, *Tyre, Byblos, Rezin of Damascus and other rulers. Among those listed, *Menahem (*Menuhimme*) of Samaria, who was to die soon afterwards, raised his contribution by collecting 1 mina (50 shekels) from each of the 60,000 men of military age 'so that his hands (*i.e.* Tiglath-pileser's) would be with him to confirm the kingdom in his hands' (2 Ki. 15:19–20; *cf. Iraq* 18, 1956, p. 117).

While Tiglath-pileser himself was fighting Sarduri of Urarṭu, a revolt was instigated by 'Azriyau of Yaudi' (Annals). It would seem that when the Urartians imposed control on Carchemish, Bît-Adini (Beth-eden) and Cilicia, the weakened Aramaean states in S Syria came under the leadership of Azariah of Judah, who at this time was stronger than Israel. Azariah-Uzziah (the names *'zr* and *'zz* are variants; G. Brin, *Leshonenu* 24,

Tiglath-pileser III, king of Assyria (745–727 BC), standing in his chariot with driver and 'third man'. Relief from Nimrud. c. 740 BC. (BM)

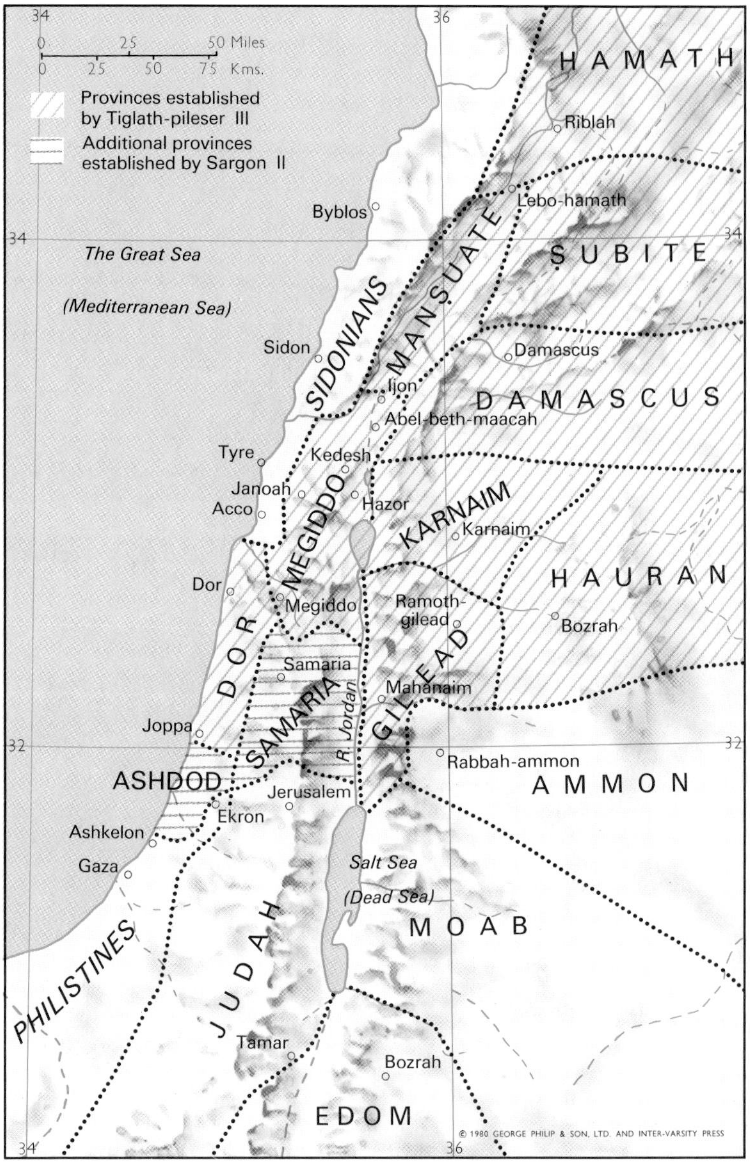

1960, pp. 8–14), however, died soon afterwards (2 Ki. 15:7), and 'Judaeans' are named among captives settled in Ullubu (near Bitlis). N Syria was organized into an Assyrian province (Unqi) under local governors.

When opposition to Assyria continued, Tiglath-pileser marched again to the W in 734. The Phoenician seaports were plundered and heavy tribute imposed on Ashkelon and on Gaza, whose ruler Hanun fled to Egypt. Statues of the Assyrian king were set up in their temples.

The army which had marched through the W border of Israel (Bit-Humri; the earlier reading of the names Galilee and Naphtali in these Annals is now disproved) turned back at the 'River of Egypt' (*naḫal-muṣur*). Rezin of Damascus, Ammon, Edom, Moab and (Jeho)ahaz of Judah (*Iauḫazi* [*mat*]*Iaudaia*) paid tribute to the king of Assyria. (2 Ch. 28:19–21).

Ahaz, however, received no immediate help from Assyria against the combined attacks of Rezin and Pekah of Israel, who, with Edomites and Philistines, raided Judah (2 Ch. 28:17–18). Jerusalem itself was besieged (2 Ki. 16:5–6) and relieved only by the Assyrian march on Damascus late in 733 BC. When Damascus fell in 732 BC, Metenna of Tyre also capitulated and Israel, including Ijon, Abel of Beth-Maachah, Janoah, Kadesh, Hazor, Gilead, Galilee and all Naphtali, was despoiled and captives were taken (v. 9). A destruction level at *Hazor is attributed to this period. Tiglath-pileser claims to have replaced Pekah (*Paqaḫa*) on the throne of Israel by Hoshea (*Ausi'*) and may well have plotted the murder of the former as described in 2 Ki. 15:30.

Ahaz paid for Assyrian help by becoming a vassal, which probably required certain religious concessions and practices to be observed (*cf.* 2 Ki. 16:7–16). Tiglath-pileser extended his control to include Samsi, queen of Aribi (Arabia), Sabaeans and Idiba'il (Adbeel of Gn. 25:13). With captive labour Tiglath-pileser III built himself a palace at Calah, from which have been recovered reliefs depicting the king himself and his campaigns. Although Tiglath-pileser I (1115–1077 BC) invaded Phoenicia, there is no reference to him in the OT.

BIBLIOGRAPHY. D. J. Wiseman in *Iraq* 13, 1951, pp. 21–24; *ibid.*, 18, 1956, pp. 117–129; H. W. F. Saggs in *Iraq* 19, 1957, pp. 114–154; *ZDPV*, 1974, pp. 38–49; R. D. Barnett and M. Falkner, *Sculptures of Tiglath-pileser III*, 1962; H. Tadmor, *Inscriptions of Tiglath-pileser III*, 1978. D.J.W.

TIGRIS. The Gk. name for one of the four rivers marking the location of Eden (*Hiddekel*; Gn. 2:14; Akkad. *Diglat*; Arab. *Dijlah*). It rises in the Armenian Mountains and runs SE for 1,900 km via Diarbekr through the Mesopotamian plain to join the river *Euphrates 64 km N of the Persian Gulf, into which it flows. It is a wide river as it meanders through Babylonia (Dn. 10:4) and is fed by tributaries from the Persian hills, the Greater

The source of the R. Tigris (Hiddekel) *inside a mountain was one goal of an Assyrian expedition. Bronze relief from the Balawat gates of Shalmaneser III. c. 845 BC.* (BM)

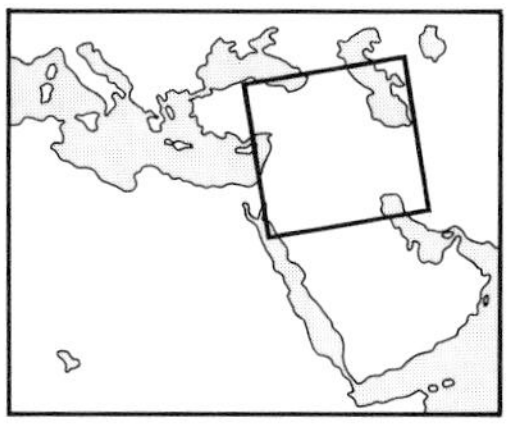

The course of the R. Tigris.

and Lesser Zab, Adhem and Diyala rivers. When the snows melt, the river floods in Mar.–May and Oct.–Nov. Nineveh, Calah and Assur are among the ancient cities which lay on its banks. D.J.W.

TILE, TILING. Ezekiel was commanded to scratch a representation of Jerusalem on a sun-dried brick (4:1; Heb. *l^e^ḇēnâ*, AV 'tile'). Plans engraved on clay tablets have been found (*e.g. ANEP*, no. 260). When Moses and the elders were given a vision of the God of Israel (Ex. 24:10) there was beneath him 'as it were a pavement of sapphire stone'. This may well be a comparison with the contemporary dais built for Rameses II at Qantir which was covered with blue glazed tiles; *cf.* 'Sapphire' under *JEWELS AND PRECIOUS STONES and W. C. Hayes, *Glazed Tiles from a Palace of Rameses II at Kantir*, 1937. Roof tiles were not used in ancient Palestine, so far as is known, so in Lk. 5:19 Gk. *keramos* should be translated more generally 'roofing'. (*HOUSE.) A.R.M.

TIMBREL
See Music, Part 2.

TIME. Biblical words for time are not in themselves a sound basis for reflection on biblical concepts of time. These must be gathered from the contexts in which the words are used.

I. Times and seasons

The Hebrews had their ways of measuring the passing of time (*CALENDAR) but the most frequent contexts for the words translated 'times' and 'seasons' suggest a concern for appointed times, the right time, the opportunity for some event or action. The commonest word is *'ēṯ* (*cf.* Ec. 3:1ff. for a characteristic use); *z^e^mān* has the same meaning. *mô'ēḏ* comes from a root meaning 'appoint' and is used of natural periods such as the new moon (*e.g.* Ps. 104:19) and of appointed festivals (*e.g.* Nu. 9:2). In particular, all these words are used to refer to the times appointed by God, the opportunities given by him (*e.g.* Dt. 11:14; Ps. 145:15; Is. 49:8; Je. 18:23). In NT the Gk. *kairos* often occurs in similar contexts, though it does not in itself mean 'decisive moment' (*cf.* Lk. 19:44; Acts 17:26; Tit. 1:3; 1 Pet. 1:11).

The Bible thus stresses not the abstract continuity of time but rather the God-given content of certain moments of history. This view of time may be called 'linear', in contrast with the cyclical view of time common in the ancient world; God's purpose moves to a consummation; things do not just go on or return to the point whence they began. But calling the biblical view of time 'linear' must not be allowed to suggest that time and history flow on in an inevitable succession of events; rather the Bible stresses 'times', the points at which God himself advances his purposes in the world (*DAY OF THE LORD).

God is sovereign in appointing these times, and so not even the Son during his earthly ministry knew the day and hour of the consummation (Mk. 13:32; Acts 1:7). God's sovereignty extends also to the times of an individual life (Ps. 31:15).

In the Aramaic of the book of Daniel the word *'iddān* refers to chronological periods of time (*e.g.* 2:9; 3:15), often apparently a year (*e.g.* 4:16; 7:25, though not all interpreters agree that years are meant). God's sovereignty is still stressed (2:21).

The word *chronos* sometimes refers in the NT, as in secular Gk., simply to the passing of time (*e.g.* Lk. 20:9; Acts 14:28). The context may give it the sense of 'delay', 'time of tarrying or waiting' (*e.g.* Acts 18:20, 23); this is probably the meaning of Rev. 10:6 rather than that 'time shall have an end'.

II. Eternity

Heb. has the words *'aḏ* and *'ôlām* for lengthy or remote time such as that which brings an end to man's life (*cf.* 1 Sa. 1:22, 28) or the age of the hills (Gn. 49:26). Above all, these words are applied to God, whose being is unlimited by any bound of time (Ps. 90:2). This absence of temporal limit also belongs to all God's attributes and to his grace towards his people (*cf.* Je. 31:3; 32:40; Ho. 2:19). To express more intensely the conviction that God is not limited to any fixed span Heb. uses a poetic intensive plural (*e.g.* Ps. 145:13; Dn. 9:24) or a double form (*e.g.* Ps. 132:14).

The NT usage of *aiōn* is similar; it can be used of a lifetime (1 Cor. 8:13, Phillips) or of a remote time in the past (Lk. 1:70) or future (Mk. 11:14). It is intensively used in phrases such as *eis tous aiōnas tōn aiōnōn* (*e.g.* Gal. 1:5); that such uses are intensive rather than true plurals envisaging a series of world periods, 'ages of ages', is suggested by Heb. 1:8, where the genitive is in the singular. God is also described as active *pro tōn aiōnōn*, 'before the ages' (1 Cor. 2:7).

These uses in both OT and NT correspond to the Eng. use of 'eternal, eternity' to point to that which always has existed and will exist; the language used in the Bible does not itself determine the philosophical questions concerning time and eternity, which are discussed briefly below.

The adjective *aiōnios* corresponds to the use of *aiōn* with reference to God, and therefore adds to its temporal sense of 'everlasting' a qualitative overtone of 'divine/immortal'. This tendency is helped by the

The plan of the Babylonian city of Nippur engraved on a clay tablet ('tile') (cf. Ezk. 4:1). The temple, walls, gates and canals are all labelled. 15 cm × 20 cm. c. 1500 BC. (UMUP)

An Egyptian device for calculating time. The shadow cast by the central block of this model shadow clock was read off along the upper surface. Limestone. Length c. 38 cm. (MNAC)

fact that in late Heb. *'ôlām* is used in the spatial sense of 'the world'; *cf.* the AV translation of *aiōn* in, *e.g.,* Mk. 10:30; Eph. 1:21.

III. The two ages

The NT picks out one of the times appointed by God as decisive. The first note of Jesus' preaching was 'The time is fulfilled' (Mk. 1:15). The life and work of Jesus mark the crisis of God's purposes (Eph. 1:10). This is the great opportunity (2 Cor. 6:2) which Christians must fully seize (Eph. 5:16; Col. 4:5). Within the period of Jesus' earthly ministry there is a further narrowing of attention to the time of his death and resurrection (*cf.* Mt. 26:18; Jn. 7:6).

It is the fact that this decisive time is in the past which makes the difference between the Jewish and Christian hopes for the future: the Jew looks for the decisive intervention of God in the future; the Christian can have an even keener expectation of the consummation of all things because he knows that the decisive moment is past 'once for all'. The last times are with us already (Acts 2:17; Heb. 1:2; 1 Jn. 2:18; 1 Pet. 1:20).

The NT makes a striking modification of the contemporary Jewish division of time into the present age and the age to come. There is still a point of transition in the future between 'this time' and 'the world to come' (Mk. 10:30; Eph. 1:21; Tit. 2:12–13), but there is an anticipation of the consummation, because in Jesus God's purpose has been decisively fulfilled. The gift of the Spirit is the mark of this anticipation, this tasting of the powers of the world to come (Eph. 1:14; Heb. 6:4–6; *cf.* Rom. 8:18–23; Gal. 1:4). Hence John consistently stresses that we now have eternal life, *zōē aiōnios* (*e.g.* Jn. 3:36). It is not simply that *aiōnios* has qualitative overtones; rather John is urging the fact that Christians now have the life into which they will fully enter by resurrection (Jn. 11:23–25). This 'overlapping' of the two ages is possibly what Paul has in mind in 1 Cor. 10:11.

IV. Time and eternity

Many Christian philosophers have maintained that the intensive time language of the Bible points to aspects of the Being of God which in philosophy can best be expressed in terms of an eternity in some way qualitatively different from time.

Others have held that any talk of God's Being as timeless is unscriptural; that our language is necessarily time-referring and that we cannot talk about timeless being without the risk of so abstracting it from the world that it cannot be thought to influence the world's life directly at all. Thus if the Christian view of God as active in history is to be preserved, we must adhere to biblical language rather than use any Platonist terminology which contrasts the world of time 'here' with a world of eternity 'there'. Nevertheless, the NT goes beyond a simple antithesis of this world and the next, 'now' and 'then', by its doctrine of anticipation.

Whatever the outcome of the philosophical debate, Scripture roundly asserts that God is not limited by time as we are, that he is 'the king of ages' (1 Tim. 1:17; *cf.* 2 Pet. 3:8).

BIBLIOGRAPHY. J. Barr, *Biblical Words for Time*, 1962; O. Cullmann, *Christ and Time*, 1951; H. Sasse, *TDNT* 1, pp. 197–209; H. W. Wolff, *Anthropology of the OT*, 1973, ch. 10; J. Guhrt, H.-C. Hahn, *NIDNTT* 3, pp. 826–850.

M.H.C.

TIMNA. 1. A concubine of Eliphaz the son of Esau, mother of Amalek (Gn. 36:12). **2.** A daughter of Seir and sister of Lotan (Gn. 36:22). **3.** A chief of Edom (1 Ch. 1:51; wrongly called 'Timnah' in Gn. 36:40, AV).

J.D.D.

TIMNAH (Heb. *timnâh*). **1.** A town on the N boundary of Judah, formerly counted as Danite (Jos. 15:10; 19:43). It changed hands more than once between Israelites and Philistines (Jdg. 14:1; 2 Ch. 28:18). Samson's first wife lived there. This may be the place Tamnā, later mentioned in the annals of Sennacherib, *c.* 701 BC (ii. 83). Tell Batashi, 9 km S of Gezer, is probably the site, though Khirbet Tibneh (4 km SE) has the name; see B. Mazar, *IEJ* 10, 1960, pp. 65–73.

2. S of Hebron (Gn. 38:12; Jos. 15:57); copper was mined here (B. Rothenberg, *Timna*, 1972; N. Glueck, *Rivers in the Desert*, 1968, p. 36).

J.P.U.L.

TIMNATH-HERES, TIMNATH-SERAH (Heb. *timnaṯ-ḥeres, timnaṯ-seraḥ*). The personal inheritance of Joshua, where he was buried (Jos. 19:50; 24:30; Jdg. 2:9). The Samaritans claimed Kafr Haris, 16 km SW of Shechem, as the site; but H. W. Hertzberg (*PJB* 22, 1926, pp. 89ff.) proposed Khirbet Tibneh, a Late Bronze and Early Iron site 27 km from Shechem and from Jerusalem. It lies on the S side of a deep ravine (*cf.* Jos. 24:30); the traditional tomb of Joshua, mentioned by Eusebius, is in the side of the valley towards the E.

ḥeres is a rare word for 'sun' (Jdg. 1:35; 8:13; Job. 9:7; Is. 19:18, where AV 'destruction' reads *ḥerem*). If it had idolatrous implications, the variant *seraḥ* ('extra') was perhaps intended to avoid them (G. F. Moore, *Judges*, *ICC*, 1895, on 2:9); but this leaves unexplained the retention of *ḥeres* in

2:9 and of *šemeš* in other place-names. See C. F. Burney, *Judges*, 1918, p. 32. J.P.U.L.

TIMOTHY. The son of a mixed marriage; his mother, who evidently instructed him in the Scriptures, was a Jewess and his father a Greek (Acts 16:1; 2 Tim. 1:5). He was a native of Lystra (Acts 16:1) and was highly esteemed by his Christian brethren both there and in Iconium (Acts 16:2). When he became a Christian is not specifically stated, but it is a reasonable inference that he was a convert of Paul's first missionary journey, which included Lystra in its itinerary, and that on that occasion he witnessed Paul's sufferings (2 Tim. 3:11). It is not certain when Timothy's mother Eunice became a Christian, perhaps before Timothy, but certainly before Paul's second missionary journey.

The apostle was strongly attracted to the young man and although he had only recently replaced Barnabas by Silas as his travelling companion he added Timothy to his party, perhaps as a substitute for John Mark whom he had refused to take (Acts 15:36f.). This choice appears to have had other endorsement, for Paul later refers to prophetic utterances which confirmed Timothy's being set apart for this work (*cf.* 1 Tim. 1:18; 4:14). He had received at this time a special endowment for his mission, communicated through the laying on of the hands of the elders and of Paul (1 Tim. 4:14; 2 Tim. 1:6). To allay any needless opposition from local Jews, Timothy was circumcised before setting out on his journeys.

He was first entrusted with a special commission to Thessalonica to encourage the persecuted Christians. He is associated with Paul and Silvanus in the greetings of both Epistles directed to that church, and was present with Paul during his preaching work at Corinth (2 Cor. 1:19). He is next heard of during the apostle's Ephesian ministry, when he was sent with Erastus on another important mission to Macedonia, whence he was to proceed to Corinth (1 Cor. 4:17). The young man was evidently of a timid disposition, for Paul urges the Corinthians to set him at ease and not to despise him (1 Cor. 16:10–11; *cf.* 4:17ff.). From the situation which resulted in Corinth (see 2 Cor.) Timothy's mission was not successful, and it is significant that, although his name was associated with Paul's in the greeting to this Epistle, it is Titus and not Timothy who has become the apostolic delegate. He accompanied Paul on his next visit to Corinth, for he was with him as a fellow-worker when the Epistle to the Romans was written (Rom. 16:21).

Timothy also went with Paul on the journey to Jerusalem with the collection (Acts 20:4–5) and is next heard of when Paul, then a prisoner, wrote Colossians, Philemon and Philippians. In the latter Epistle he is warmly commended and Paul intends soon to send him to them in order to ascertain their welfare. When the apostle was released from his imprisonment and engaged in further activity in the E, as the Pastoral Epistles indicate, it would seem that Paul left Timothy at Ephesus (1 Tim. 1:3) and commissioned him to deal with false teachers and supervise public worship and the appointment of church officials. Although Paul evidently hoped to rejoin Timothy, the fear that he might be delayed occasioned the writing of the first letter to him, and this was followed by another when Paul was not only re-arrested but on trial for his life. Timothy was urged to hasten to him, but whether he arrived in time cannot be ascertained. Later Timothy himself became a prisoner as Heb. 13:23 shows, but no details are given, and of his subsequent history nothing definite is known.

He was affectionate (2 Tim. 1:4) but very fearful (2 Tim. 1:7ff.), needing not a few personal admonitions from his father in the faith; he is warned not to give way to youthful lusts (2 Tim. 2:22) and not to be ashamed of the gospel (2 Tim. 1:8). Yet no other of Paul's companions is so warmly commended for his loyalty (1 Cor. 16:10; Phil. 2:19ff.; 2 Tim. 3:10ff.). It is fitting that the apostle's concluding letter should be addressed so affectionately to this almost reluctant successor, whose weaknesses are as apparent as his virtues. D.G.

TIMOTHY AND TITUS, EPISTLES TO. The two Epistles to Timothy and one to Titus, commonly grouped together as the *Pastoral Epistles, belong to the period at the close of Paul's life and provide valuable information about the great missionary apostle's thoughts as he prepared to pass on his tasks to others. They are addressed to two of his closest associates, and for that reason introduce a different kind of Pauline correspondence from the earlier church Epistles.

I. Outline of contents

1 Timothy

a. Paul and Timothy (1:1–20)

The need for Timothy to refute false teaching at Ephesus (1:3–11); Paul's experience of God's mercy (1:12–17); a special commission for Timothy (1:18–20).

b. Worship and order in the church (2:1–4:16)

Public prayer (2:1–8); the position of women (2:9–15); the qualifications of bishops and deacons (3:1–13); the church: its character and its adversaries (3:14–4:5); the church: Timothy's personal responsibilities (4:6–16).

c. Discipline within the church (5:1–25)

A discussion of the treatment suit-

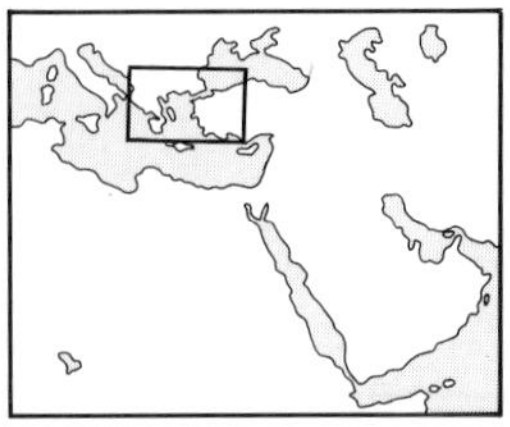

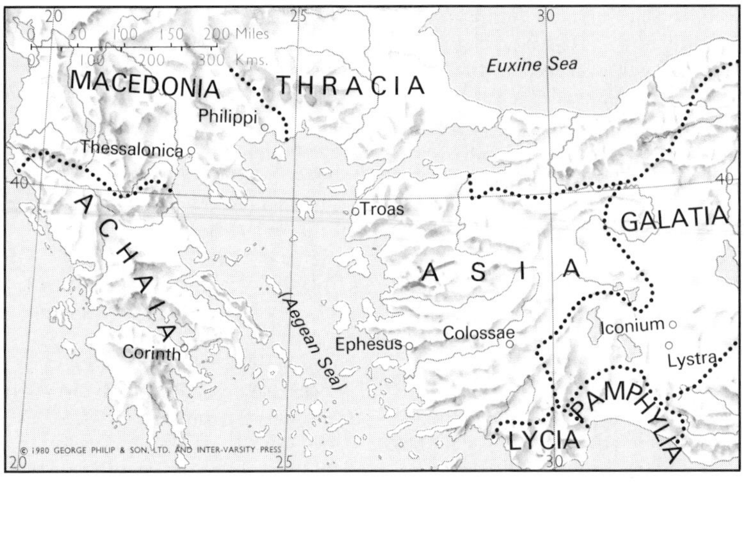

Places associated with the life of Timothy.

able for various groups, especially widows and elders.

d. Miscellaneous injunctions (6:1–19)

About servants and masters (6:1–2); about false teachers (6:3–5); about wealth (6:6–10); about the aims of a man of God (6:11–16); more about wealth (6:17–19).

e. Concluding admonitions to Timothy (6:20–21)

2 Timothy

a. Paul's special regard for Timothy (1:1–14)

Greeting and thanksgiving (1:1–5); exhortations and encouragements to Timothy (1:6–14).

b. Paul and his associates (1:15–18)

The disloyal Asiatics and the helpful Onesiphorus (1:15–18).

c. Special directions to Timothy (2:1–26)

Encouragements and exhortations (2:1–13); advice on the treatment of false teachers (2:14–26).

d. Predictions about the last days (3:1–9)

The times of moral deterioration to come.

e. More advice to Timothy (3:10–17)

A reminder of Paul's early experiences of persecution (3:10–12); an exhortation to Timothy to continue as he had begun (3:13–17).

f. Paul's farewell message (4:1–22)

A final charge to Timothy (4:1–5); a confession of faith (4:6–8); some personal requests and warnings (4:9–15); Paul's first defence and his future hope (4:16–18); greetings and benediction (4:19–22).

Titus

a. Paul's greeting to Titus (1:1–4)

The apostle's consciousness of his high calling.

b. The kind of men Titus must appoint as elders (or bishops) (1:5–9)

c. The Cretan false teachers (1:10–16)

Their character and the need to rebuke them.

d. Christian behaviour (2:1–10)

Advice about the older and younger people and about slaves.

e. Christian teaching (2:11–3:7)

What the grace of God has done for Christians (2:11–15); what Christians ought to do in society (3:1–2); how Christianity contrasts with paganism (3:3–7).

f. Closing admonitions to Titus (3:8–15)

About good works (3:8); about false teachers (3:9–10); about Paul's companions and his future plans (3:11–15).

II. The historical situation

It is difficult to reconstruct this period of Paul's life, because there is no independent court of appeal such as the Acts supplies in the case of the earlier Epistles. But certain data may be ascertained from the Epistles themselves. At the time of writing 1 Tim. and Tit., Paul is not in prison, but when 2 Tim. was written he is not only a prisoner (1:8; 2:9), but appears to be on trial for his life, with the probability that an adverse verdict is imminent which will result in his execution (4:6–8). From 1 Tim. 1:3 it is clear that Paul had recently been in the vicinity of Ephesus, where he had left Timothy to fulfil a specific mission, mainly of administration. The Epistle to Titus provides additional historical data, for from 1:5 it may be inferred that Paul had paid a recent visit to Crete, on which occasion he must have had opportunity to ascertain the condition of the churches and to give specific instructions to Titus for rectifying any deficiencies. At the conclusion of the letter (3:12) the apostle urges Titus to join him at Nicopolis for the winter, and it is fairly safe to assume that this was the city situated in Epirus, in which case it is the sole reference to Paul visiting that district. Titus is also instructed to help Zenas and Apollos on their journey (3:13), but the precise point of this allusion is obscure.

2 Tim. is much more specific in historical information. In 1:16 Paul refers to Onesiphorus as having sought him out while in Rome, which suggests that the writer is still in Rome as a prisoner. In 4:16 he mentions an earlier trial which is generally regarded as the preliminary examination preparing for the official trial before the Roman authorities. Paul makes an interesting request in 4:13 for a cloak which he had left behind at the house of Carpus at Troas, which would seem to imply that he had recently visited there. In the same passage Paul mentions that he recently left Trophimus sick at Miletus (4:20), while Erastus, an associate of his, had stayed behind at Corinth.

It is impossible to fit all these historical data as they stand into the Acts history, and there is therefore no alternative if their authenticity is to be maintained (see later discussion) but to assume that Paul was released from the imprisonment mentioned at the close of Acts, that he had a period of further activity in the E, and that he was rearrested, tried and finally executed in Rome by the imperial authorities. The data available from the Pastorals are insufficient to facilitate a reconstruction of Paul's itinerary, but further activity in Greece, Crete and Asia is at least certain. Some scholars, on the basis of Rom. 15:24, 28, have also fitted into this period a visit to Spain, and if this assumption is correct this W visit must have preceded Paul's return to the E churches. But if Col., Phm. and Phil. are assigned to the Roman imprisonment (see separate articles) it seems clear that Paul's face was turned towards the E and not the W at the time of his release. (*CHRONOLOGY OF THE NEW TESTAMENT.)

III. Purpose

Assuming therefore that all three of these Epistles were written within a comparatively short interval of time, it must next be noted that they have a common purpose. They are all designed to supply Paul's associates with exhortations and encouragements for both present and future responsibilities. There is a good deal of instruction about ecclesiastical administration, but it would be wrong to assume that such instruction wholly accounts for the underlying purpose of each. Of the three Epistles the motive for writing 2 Tim. is clearer than that of the others. The apostle is delivering his final charge to his timid successor, and in the course of it reminds Timothy of his early history (1:5–7) and exhorts him to act worthily of his high calling. Many times throughout the Epistle solemn exhortations are directed to him (1:6, 8, 13f.; 2:1, 22; 3:14; 4:1f.), which suggest that Paul was not too certain of his courage in face of the heavy responsibilities now falling upon him. The apostle yearns to see him again and twice urges him to come as soon as possible (4:9, 21), although the tone of the concluding part of the letter suggests that Paul is not convinced that circumstances will permit a reunion (*cf.* 4:6). There are warnings about ungodly men who cause trouble to the church both in the present and in the last days (3:1f.), and Timothy is urged to avoid these. He is to entrust to worthy men the task of passing on the traditions already received (2:2).

The purpose behind the other two Epistles is less plain, for in both instances Paul has only recently left the recipients, and the need for such detailed instructions is not immediately apparent. It would seem probable that much of the subject-matter had already been communicated orally, for in both Epistles detailed qualifications are given for the main office-bearers of the church, and it is inconceivable that until this time neither Timothy nor Titus had received any such instruction. In all probability the Epistles were intended to strengthen the hands of Paul's representatives in their respective tasks. Timothy appears to have had some difficulty in commanding respect (*cf.* 1 Tim. 4:12f.), while Titus had a particularly unenviable constituency in Crete according to Tit. 1:10ff. Both men are to have sober concern for sound doctrine and right conduct and to teach it to others (1 Tim. 4:11; 6:2; Tit. 2:1, 15; 3:8).

It is not to be expected that in these letters the apostle would present to his closest friends anything in the nature of a theological treatise. There was no need to dwell on the great Christian doctrines, oral expositions of which both Timothy and Titus must often have heard from their master's lips. But they did need to be reminded of the futility of wasting time with certain groups of false teachers whose teachings were dominated by irrelevances and wordy combats which led nowhere (see 1 Tim. 1:4; 4:1f.; 6:3f., 20). There does not appear to be any close connection between these heresies in the Ephesian and Cretan churches and that combated by Paul in his letter to Colossae, but they may have been different forms of the tendency which later developed into 2nd-century Gnosticism.

IV. Authenticity

Modern criticism has so much challenged the Pauline authorship of these Epistles that the attestation of the early church is of prime importance in a fair examination of the whole question. There are few NT writings which have stronger attestation, for these Epistles were widely used from the time of Polycarp, and there are possible traces in the earlier works of Clement of Rome and Ignatius. The omission of the Epistles from Marcion's Canon (*c.* AD 140) has been thought by some to be evidence that they were not known in his time, but, in view of his propensity to cut out what did not appeal to him or disagreed with his doctrine, this line of evidence can hardly be taken seriously. The only other possible evidence for the omission of the Epistles is the Chester Beatty papyri, but since these are incomplete it is again precarious to base any positive hypothesis upon their evidence, especially in view of the fact that the Epistles were known and used in the E at an earlier period than the papyri represent.

Objections to authenticity must therefore be regarded as modern innovations contrary to the strong evidence from the early church. These objections began seriously with Schleiermacher's attack on the genuineness of 1 Tim. (1807) and have been developed by many other scholars, among whom the most notable have been F. C. Baur, H. J. Holtzmann, P. N. Harrison and M. Dibelius. They have been based on four main problems. At different periods of criticism different difficulties have been given prominence, but it is probably the cumulative effect which has persuaded some modern scholars that these Epistles cannot be by Paul.

a. The historical problem

The historical situation cannot belong to the period of the Acts history and the consequent need for postulating Paul's release has caused some scholars to suggest alternative theories. Either all the personal references are the invention of the author, or else some of them are genuine notes which have been incorporated into the author's own productions. There has never been anything approaching unanimity among the advocates of the latter alternative as to the identification of the 'notes', which in itself raises suspicions against the theory. Moreover, the notion of a fiction-writer producing personal notes of such verisimilitude is improbable, and neither theory is necessary if the perfectly reasonable supposition that Paul was released from his first Roman imprisonment is maintained.

b. The ecclesiastical problem

It has been claimed that the ecclesiastical situation reflects a 2nd-century state of affairs, but this line of criticism has been widely influenced by the assumption that: (i) 2nd-century Gnosticism is combated in the Epistles, and (ii) the church organization was too developed for the primitive period. The force of the first assumption is reduced to nothing by the increasing modern recognition that Gnosticism had much earlier roots than was at one time imagined and that the form of heresy combated in these Epistles is far removed from developed Gnosticism. The second assumption is equally insecure in view of the fact that the church organization is certainly more primitive than in the time of Ignatius and betrays no anachronism with the period of the apostle.

c. The doctrinal problem

The absence of the great Pauline doctrinal discussions as found in the earlier letters and the presence of stereotyped expressions such as 'the faith' and 'sound doctrine', which suggest a stage of development when Christian doctrine had reached fixity as tradition, have given rise to further doubts about Pauline authorship. But the recognition of the mainly personal character of these communications and of the knowledge that both Timothy and Titus already had of Paul's main teaching is sufficient to account for the first objection, while the second may be annulled by the valid assumption that Paul as a far-sighted missionary pioneer, however creative and dynamic his earlier pronouncements may have been in his church Epistles, could not have been unmindful of the need to conserve true doctrine, and the aptness of the terms used for this purpose must be admitted.

d. The linguistic problem

These Epistles contain an unusually large number of words used nowhere else in the NT and a number not found anywhere else in Paul's writings, and these indications are claimed to demonstrate their un-Pauline character, especially when supported by the absence of many pronouns, prepositions, and particles used by the apostle. But word-counts of this kind can be effective only if sufficient data exist to serve as a fair basis of comparison, and this cannot be maintained in the case of the Pauline Epistles, where the total vocabulary does not exceed 2,500 different words. There appears to be no valid reason why the differences of vocabulary and style could not have taken place in the writings of one man. Some, who in all other respects regard the Epistles as genuine but find some difficulties in the linguistic problem, resort to the hypothesis that Paul used a different amanuensis.

In conclusion, it may be stated that these objections, even when cumulatively considered, do not provide adequate reason for discarding the acknowledged and unchallenged conviction of the Christian church until the 19th century that these three Epistles are genuine writings of the apostle Paul.

V. Value

Throughout the history of the church these Epistles have been used to instruct the ministers of Christ in their duties and demeanour, and have been invaluable in providing a pattern of practical behaviour. Yet their usefulness and appeal have not been restricted to this, for they contain many gems of spiritual encouragement and theological insight which have greatly enriched the devotional life of the church. Such passages as 1 Tim. 3:16 and Tit. 2:12ff.; 3:4ff., among many others, draw the reader's attention to some of the great truths of the gospel, while the last chapter of 2 Tim. preserves the moving swan-song of the great apostle.

BIBLIOGRAPHY. C. K. Barrett, *The Pastoral Epistles*, 1963; J. N. D. Kelly, *The Pastoral Epistles*, 1963; M. Dibelius and H. Conzelmann, *Die Pastoralbriefe*, 1955; B. S. Easton, *The Pastoral Epistles*, 1948; D. Guthrie, *The Pastoral Epistles, TNTC*, 1957; *idem*, *New Testament Introduction*[3], 1970; A. T. Hanson, *Studies in the Pastoral Epistles*, 1968; P. N. Harrison, *The Problem of the Pastoral Epistles*, 1921; W. Hendriksen, *Commentary on I & II Timothy and Titus*, 1957; J. Jeremias, *Die Briefe an Timotheus und Titus*, *NTD*, 1953; W. Michaelis, *Pastoralbriefe und Gefangenschaftsbriefe*, 1930; E. K. Simpson, *The Pastoral Epistles*, 1954; C. Spicq, *Les Épîtres Pastorales, Études Bibliques*, 1948.

D.G.

TIPHSAH (Heb. *tip̄saḥ*, 'a ford', 'a passage'). Probably Thapsacus, an important crossing on the W bank of the Middle Euphrates. At the NE boundary of Solomon's territory (1 Ki. 4:24), it was placed strategically on a great E–W trade route. J.D.D.

TIRAS (Heb. *tîrās*). A son of Japheth, and brother of Gomer, Madai, Javan and Muški (Gn. 10:2; 1 Ch. 1:5), all probably N peoples (*NATIONS, TABLE OF). The name is commonly identified with the Tursha (*Trš.w*) mentioned among the N invaders in the 13th century BC by Merenptah (*EGYPT). These are in turn often equated with the *Tyrrēnoi* (dialectal form of *Tyrrhēnoi*) of Gk. literature, connected by many with the Etruscans, though this identification is still questioned.

BIBLIOGRAPHY. A. H. Gardiner, *Ancient Egyptian Onomastica*, Text, 1, 1947, p. 196*; M. Pallottino, *The Etruscans*, 1955, pp. 55–56; see also *AS* 9, 1959, pp. 197ff.; N. K. Sanders, *The Sea Peoples*, 1978.

T.C.M.

TIRHAKAH. The pharaoh Taharqa of Egypt's 25th ('Ethiopian') Dynasty; he reigned 26 years, *c.* 690–664 BC. 2 Ki. 19:9 (= Is. 37:9) appears to indicate that Tirhakah led those Egyp. forces which *Sennacherib had to defeat at *Eltekeh in 701 BC while attacking Hezekiah of Judah. If so, Tirhakah was then only the army-commander, as he was not king until 11 years later. The epithet 'king of Ethiopia' is that of the source used in Is. and 2 Ki., and would date from 690 BC or after. An alternative view, namely that Sennacherib again invaded Palestine early in Tirhakah's actual reign (*c.* 688 BC?), requires two major assumptions: a second Palestinian campaign by Sennacherib, otherwise unknown, and a conflation of the two campaigns into one by the OT narrators; references in W. F. Albright, *BASOR* 130, 1953, pp. 8–9. The theory of M. F. L. Macadam (*Temples of Kawa*, 1, 1949, pp. 18–20) that Tirhakah was born *c.* 709 BC, and so could not command troops in 701 BC, is unnecessary and open to other objections; see J. Leclant and J. Yoyotte, *Bulletin de l'Institut Français d'Archéologie Orientale* 51, 1952, pp. 17–27; K. A. Kitchen, *The Third Intermediate Period in Egypt*, 1972, pp. 383–386, *cf.* pp. 154ff., 164ff. K.A.K.

TIRSHATHA. A title used of the governor of Judaea under the Persian empire (AV, Ezr. 2:63; Ne. 7:65, 70; 8:9; 10:1). It is probably a Persian form (*cf.* Avestan *taršta*, 'reverend') roughly equivalent to the Eng. 'His Excellency'. The title puzzled the Gk. translators, who either omit it or render it as a proper name, 'Athersastha', 'Attharates' or 'Atharias'. J.S.W.

TIRZAH. 1. The youngest daughter of Zelophehad (Nu. 26:33; 27:1; Jos. 17:3).

2. A Canaanite town noted for its beauty (Ct. 6:4) which lay in the N part of Mt Ephraim at the head of the Wadi Far'ah along which passed the road from Transjordan to the central hill country where Shechem, Samaria, Dothan and other towns lay. It was captured by Joshua (Jdg. 12:24) and was assigned to Manasseh (Jos. 17:2–3). Jeroboam I lived at Tirzah (1 Ki. 14:17) and the town became the capital of the N kingdom in the time of Baasha (1 Ki. 15:21, 23; 16:6), Elah and Zimri (1 Ki. 16:8–9, 15). Zimri burnt the palace over his own head when trapped there

TIN
See Mining, Part 2.

The figure of 'Tirhakah, king of Ethiopia', the ally of Hezekiah (2 Ki. 19:9), beneath the protection of the god Amun, shown as a colossal recumbant ram. Kawa. Grey granite. Height 63·5 cm. c. 675 BC. (BM)

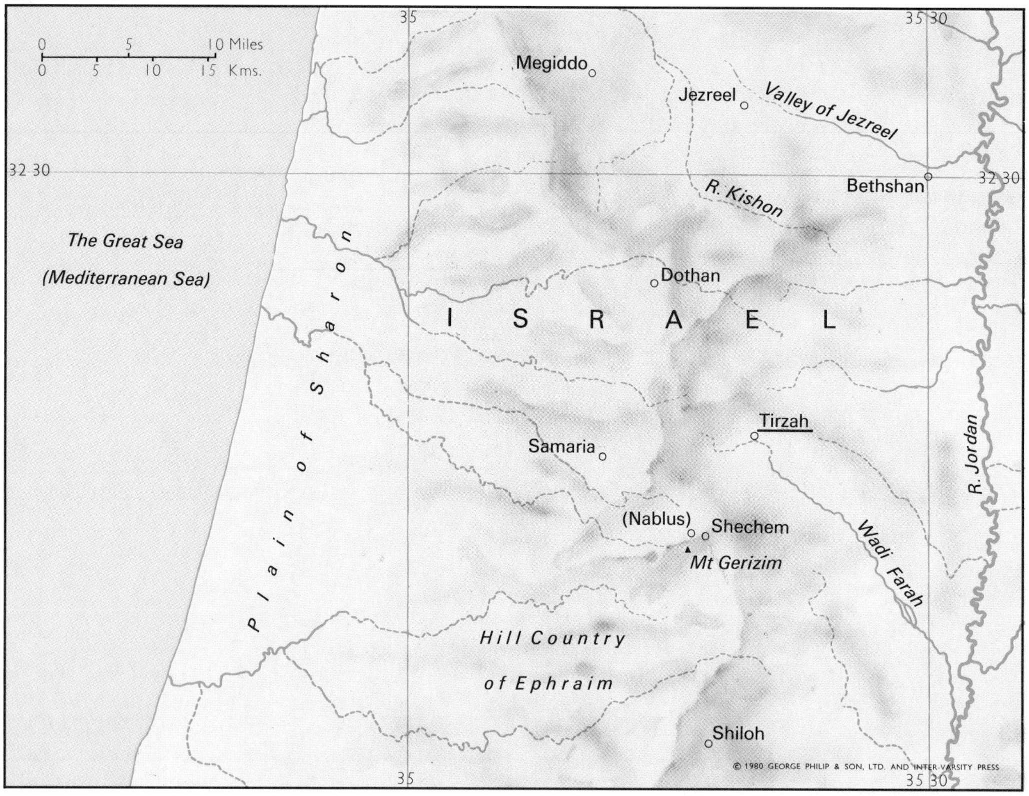

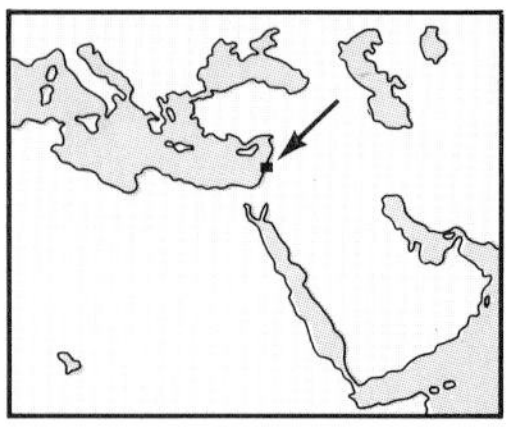

The location of Tirzah.

by Omri (1 Ki. 16:17–18). After 6 years Omri transferred the capital to Samaria which was more central and easier to defend. In *c.* 752 BC Menahem, a resident of Tirzah, was able to overthrow Shallum and usurp the throne (2 Ki. 15:14, 16).

De Vaux identified the large mound of Tell el-Far'ah, about 11 km NE of Nablus, as the site of Tirzah and over the course of several years excavation revealed the archaeological story of the site. There was continuous settlement here from Chalcolithic times, before 3000 BC, down to Assyrian times. The last period of the city's life (Level I) represents the years of Assyrian domination culminating in the destruction of the city at the end of the 7th century, possibly by Nebuchadrezzar. The Israelite occupation during the days of the N kingdom is represented by levels I to III. The 9th-century level showed a standard type of house over a wide area with one larger administrative building near the gate (Level III). By the 8th century there were several large houses, a great administrative building and a considerable number of very poor houses, confirming the picture drawn by the 8th-century prophets (Am. 5:11; Is. 9:8–10). This latter phase of the city ended with the Assyrian invasion of 723–721 BC (Level II).

BIBLIOGRAPHY. W. F. Albright, 'The site of Tirzah and the Topography of Western Manasseh', *JPOS* 11, 1931, pp. 241–251; R. de Vaux and A. M. Steve, several articles in *RB* from 1947 (Vol. 54) to 1962 (Vol. 69), especially Vol. 62, 1955, pp. 587–589; 'Tirzah' in *AOTS*, pp. 371–383; 'The Excavation at Tell el-Far'ah and the site of ancient Tirzah', *PEQ*, 1956, pp. 125–140; G. E. Wright, *BA* 12, 1949, pp. 66–68.

J.A.T.

TISHRI

See Calendar, Part 1.

TISHBITE, THE (Heb. *hattišbî*). An epithet of Elijah (1 Ki. 17:1; 21:17, 28; 2 Ki. 1:3, 8; 9:36). Generally seen as denoting one from a town Tishbeh in Gilead. N. Glueck read 1 Ki. 17:1 as 'Jabeshite, from Jabesh–Gilead'. A town Tishbeh in Gilead is not otherwise known (Tobit 1:2 places one in Naphthali), but tradition locates it at al-Istib, 12 km N of the Jabbok. The word has been read as *hattōš*^{e}*ḇî*, 'the sojourner', related to the following word 'settlers' (RSVmg.).

BIBLIOGRAPHY. N. Glueck, *AASOR* 25–28, 1951, pt. 1, pp. 218, 225–227; F. M. Abel, *Géographie de la Palestine*, 2, 1937, p. 486.

D.W.B.

TITHES. The custom of tithing did not originate with the Mosaic law (Gn. 14:17–20), nor was it peculiar to the Hebrews. It was practised among other ancient peoples. There are three main questions to consider.

1. What were the Hebrews required to tithe? The Torah legislated that 'the seed of the land' (crops), 'the fruit of the trees' and 'herds and flocks' (Lv. 27:30–32) were to be tithed. The manner of tithing livestock was as follows: the owner counted the animals as they passed out to pasture, and every tenth one was given to God. In this way there was no possibility of selecting inferior animals for the tithing of the flocks and herds (Lv. 27:32f.). If a Hebrew preferred to dedicate the tenth of his cereal and fruit yields in the form of their monetary value he was free to do so, but a fifth of that sum had to be added to it. He was not allowed to redeem the tenth of his flocks and herds in this way (Lv. 27:31, 33).

2. To whom were the tithes paid? They were to be given to the Levites (Nu. 18:21ff.). But in Heb.

View of the excavated remains of Tirzah (Tell el-Far'ah), capital of Israel under Baasha, Elah and Zimri. (GW)

Opposite page: The western part of Tirzah (modern Tell el-Far'ah), showing buildings of the Middle Bronze Age – Iron Age III.

7:5 it is said to be the sons of Levi 'who receive the priestly office' who are to be the recipients of the tithes. This departure from the Law may have been due to the Levites' unwillingness to fulfil their duties in Jerusalem after the return under Ezra (Ezr. 8:15ff.). The Levites, because of the nature of their status and functions in the community, had no means of income, livelihood or inheritance to ensure their support; therefore, and in return 'for their service which they serve, the service in the tent of meeting', they were to receive 'the tithe of the people of Israel' (Nu. 18:21, 24). This passage in Nu. 18 mentions only the tithing of cereal and fruit crops (v. 27). The Levites, however, were not allowed to keep the whole of the tenth. They were directed to present an offering which was to be taken out of the tenth, which represented 'a tithe of the tithe' (Nu. 18:26). This 'tithe of the tithe' was to be 'from all the best of them' (v. 29) and was to be given to the priests (v. 28; Ne. 10:39).

3. Where were the Hebrews to offer their tithes? They were to bring them to 'the place which the Lord your God will choose out of all your tribes, to put his name there' (Dt. 12:5f., 17f.); *i.e.* Jerusalem. And the offering of the tithes was to take the form of a ritual meal, in which the Levite was to share (Dt. 12:7, 12). If Jerusalem was a long way off from a man's village the transporting of the tithe of his crops might create a problem, but he could always take his tithe in the form of money (Dt. 14:22–27). Every third year the tithe was to be offered in each man's own locality (Dt. 14:28f.), although on these occasions he was still obligated to go up to Jerusalem to worship after the offering of his tithes in his home community (Dt. 26:12ff.).

To these comparatively simple laws in the Pentateuch governing tithing there were added a host of minutiae which turned a beautiful religious principle into a grievous burden. These complex additions are recorded in the Mishnaic and Talmudic literature. This unfortunate tendency in Israel undoubtedly contributed to the conviction that acceptance with God could be merited through such ritual observances as tithing (Lk. 11:42), without submitting to the moral law of justice, mercy and faith (Mt. 23:23f.).

The tithes paid by Abraham, the

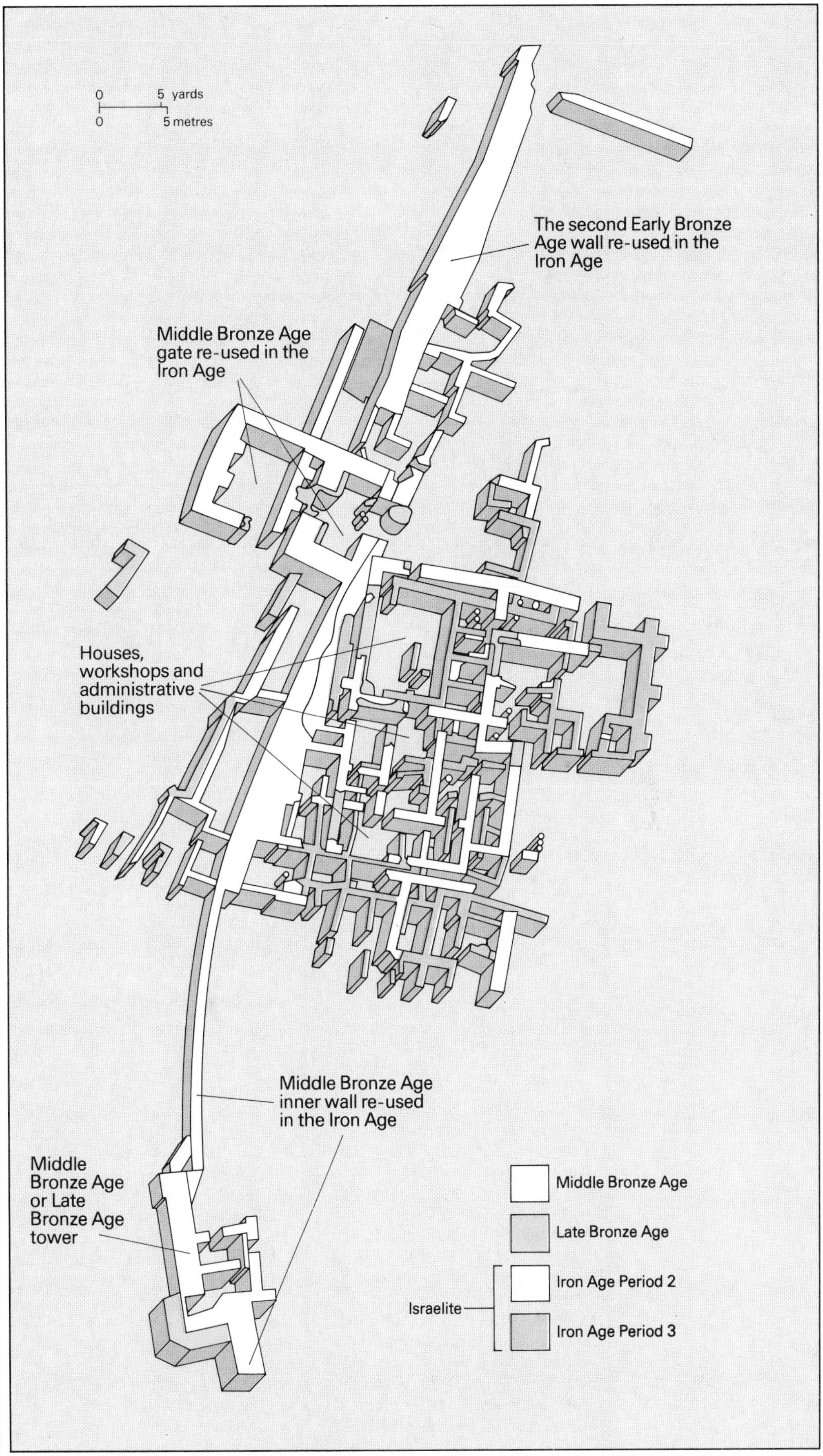

TITIUS
See Justus, Part 2.

TITLES OF JESUS CHRIST
See Jesus Christ, titles of, Part 2.

TITTLE
See Jot, Part 2.

TITUS, EPISTLE TO
See Timothy and Titus, Part 3.

TOBIJAH
See Tobiah, Part 3.

TOMBS, ROYAL
See Sepulchre of kings, Part 3.

TONGS
See Snuffers, Part 3.

ancestor of Israel and, therefore, of the Aaronic priesthood, to Melchizedek (Gn. 14:20), and his receiving the blessing of this priest-king (Gn. 14:19), signify in Heb. 7:1ff. that Melchizedek's priesthood was infinitely superior to the Aaronic or levitical priesthood. Why Abraham paid tithes to Melchizedek is not explained in Gn. 14:18–20.

The NT reference to the tithing of 'mint and dill and cummin' (Mt. 23:23; Lk. 11:42) illustrates a Talmudic extension of the Mosaic law, ensuring that 'everything that is eaten . . . and that grows out of the earth' must be tithed. J.G.S.S.T.

TITUS. Although not mentioned in Acts, Titus was one of Paul's companions in whom he placed a considerable amount of trust. He is first heard of at the time of the Gentile controversy when he accompanied Paul and Barnabas to Jerusalem (Gal. 2:1). He provided a test case, since he was a Gentile, but he was apparently not compelled to be circumcised (Gal. 2:3). Titus probably accompanied Paul on his subsequent journeys, but no definite information of his work is available until the time of the Corinthian crisis. He had evidently been acting as Paul's representative at Corinth during the year preceding the writing of 2 Cor. (*cf.* 8:16) with a special commission to organize the collection scheme there. The task was unfinished, for Titus is later urged by Paul to return to Corinth to see its completion (2 Cor. 8:6).

A more delicate task was the smoothing over of the tense situation which had arisen between Paul and the Corinthians, a task which clearly demanded a man of great tact and force of character. He appears to have been a stronger personality than Timothy (*cf.* 1 Cor. 16:10; 2 Cor. 7:15) and possessed ability as an administrator. A comparison of 2 Cor. 2 and 7 suggests that he carried a letter from Paul to the Corinthians which has since been lost (the 'severe letter') and in which the apostle took them to task with much anguish of heart for their high-handed attitude. Titus eventually rejoined Paul in Macedonia (2 Cor 7:6) with good news, and as a result 2 Cor. was written and was willingly carried by Titus (2 Cor. 8:16f.), who seems to have possessed a particular affection and serious concern for the Corinthians. He is described by the apostle as his 'partner and fellow worker' (8:23), who would not think of taking advantage of those entrusted to his care (12:18).

From the Epistle addressed to him it may be surmised that Titus accompanied Paul to Crete subsequent to the latter's release from the Roman imprisonment and was left there to consolidate the work (Tit. 1:5f.). The letter urges the use of authority in establishing a worthy ministry, in overcoming opposition, and in the teaching of sound doctrine. He was summoned to rejoin Paul at Nicopolis when relieved by either Artemas or Tychicus (Tit. 3:12), and may possibly have been further commissioned at Nicopolis for an evangelistic mission to Dalmatia on which he was engaged at the time when Paul wrote 2 Tim. (2 Tim. 4:10). Later tradition, however, assumed his return to Crete and described him as bishop there until his old age (Eusebius, *EH* 3. 4. 6). For the possibility that he was Luke's brother (which might explain the absence of his name from Acts), see W. M. Ramsay, *SPT*, p. 390. D.G.

TOB. The name of an Aramaean city and principality lying N of Gilead, mentioned in connection with Jephthah and David (Jdg. 11:3; 2 Sa. 10:6); the district named in 1 Macc. 5:13 is probably identical. The likely location of the city is al-Taiyiba (preserving the ancient name), some 20 km ENE of Ramoth-gilead. For its history, *cf.* B. Mazar, *BA* 25, 1962, pp. 98–120. D.F.P.

TOBIAH. 1. One of *Nehemiah's principal opponents, Tobiah is described by him as 'the servant (or 'slave', NEB), the Ammonite' (Ne. 2:10). 'Servant' may well be an honourable title for a high-ranking Persian official; 'Ammonite' could refer to his ancestry, though he seems at least half Jewish, since his name means 'Yahweh is good', his son is called Jehohanan ('Yahweh is merciful'; Ne. 6:18), and he has many important friends among the Jews (6:18f.; 13:4f.). Some have seen him as Persian governor of the sub-province of Ammon, or even governor of Jerusalem before Nehemiah's arrival (*cf.* Ne. 5:15), but his close association with Sanballat, governor of Samaria (4:7; 6:1) suggests rather that he was Sanballat's deputy. It is uncertain whether this Tobiah had any connection with the famous family of the Tobiads, who in the 3rd century BC ruled a large area of Ammon from their fortress at 'Araq el-Amir, 20 km NW of Heshbon, and were one of the most influential pro-Greek families in Jerusalem (Josephus, *Ant.* 12. 160–236). The inscription at 'Araq el-Amir mentioning a Tobiah is now thought to be no earlier than the 2nd century BC.

2. The name of a clan unable to prove its authentic Israelite ancestry at the time of the 6th-century return from exile (Ezr. 2:60; Ne. 7:62; 1 Esdras 5:37). The *Tobijah of Zc. 6:10, 14, a leading nobleman in Jerusalem, *c.* 520 BC, may perhaps belong to the Tobiah family.

BIBLIOGRAPHY. B. Mazar, *IEJ* 7, 1957, pp. 137–145, 229–238; C. C. McCown, *BA* 20, 1957, pp. 63–76; P. W. Lapp, *BASOR* 171, 1963, pp. 8–39. D.J.A.C.

TOGARMAH. The third son of Gomer, grandson of Japheth and brother of Ashkenaz and Riphath (Gn. 10.3; 1 Ch. 1:6). (Beth-) Togarmah, with Tubal, *Javan and *Meshech, supplied horses and mules to Tyre (Ezk. 27:14) and soldiers to *Gog (Ezk. 38:6). During the 2nd millennium BC Old Assyrian and Hittite texts locate Tegarama near Carchemish and Harran on a main trade-route. It was called Til-garimmu in the Annals of Sargon and Sennacherib, and was the capital of Kammanu on the border of Tabal (*TUBAL), until destroyed in 695 BC. Perhaps to be identified with classical Gauraena, modern Gürün, 120 km W of Malatya. D.J.W.

TOLA (Heb. *tôlā'*). **1.** A family name in a clan of Issachar (Gn. 46:13; Nu. 26:23; 1 Ch. 7:1–2). **2.** Tola ben Puah, of Shamir, an unknown village in Mt Ephraim, who was a national judge for 23 years after Abimelech's reign (Jdg. 10:1). Puah was also a family name in Issachar. J.P.U.L.

TONGUE. Heb. *lāšôn*, Gk. *glōssa*, both of the tongue of man and, by extension, of man's language. The Heb. is also used of the tongue of animals and reptiles (Jb. 20:16), with the still common misapprehension that the poison of a snake lies in its tongue. It is also used of tongue-shaped objects or phenomena, *e.g.* a wedge of gold (Jos. 7:21) or a bay of the sea (Jos. 15:2).

It was apparently believed in biblical times that dumbness was due to some paralysis or binding of the tongue or its cleaving to the palate (Ps. 137:6; Mk. 7:35; Lk. 1:64) (see *BODY for a statement on the apparent belief among the Hebrews that the organs functioned semi-independently).

The tongue is used in parallel with or interchangeably for *lip and *mouth, as the instruments of speech or related concepts, and is spoken of as good or evil (Ps. 120:2; Pr. 6:17; 10:20), taught (Is. 50:4), singing (Ps. 51:14) and speaking (Ps. 71:24). As the mouth can be said to contain something, so wickedness can be hidden under the tongue (Jb. 20:12).

The metaphor of a sharp tongue was used in OT times. The tongue was spoken of as being whetted like a sword (Ps. 64:3; *cf.* Ps. 140:3; Heb. 4:12; Rev. 1:16) and the simile of a bow and arrow is also used (Je. 9:3, 8). The tremendous influence of words for good or ill is expressed by attributing power to the tongue (Pr. 18:21; Jas. 3:5–6).

Famine and thirst are described as causing the tongue to cleave to the palate (La. 4:4), and it rots through disease (Zc. 14:12).

The tongue is used in Ps. 55:9 figuratively to refer to the confusion of language as at Babel (Gn. 11:1ff., where the word for language is 'lip', *śāpâ*; *cf.* Is. 19:18). The alienation of man from man due to the gulf created by language difference, cutting, as it does, across the whole area of instinctive feelings, common interests and co-operation, is attributed in the Gn. passage to the sinful pride of man, bringing upon them this form of visitation by God.

The word 'tongue' is thus used to describe the different nations, or tribes, which generally have distinctive languages (Is. 66:18; Rev. 5:9).

(*TONGUES, GIFT OF.) B.O.B.

TONGUES, GIFT OF. Speaking in tongues, or glossolalia (a 19th-century formation from Gk. *glōssa*, tongue, and *lalia*, speech), is a spiritual gift mentioned in Mk. 16:17, RSVmg.; Acts 10:44–46; 19:6, and described in Acts 2:1–13; 1 Cor. 12–14. The same phenomenon may lie behind such passages as 1 Thes. 5:19; Rom. 12:11.

When the assembled disciples were filled with the Holy Spirit on the day of Pentecost they began 'to speak in other tongues (*lalein heterais glōssais*), as the Spirit gave them utterance' (Acts 2:4), so that many Jews of the Dispersion were astonished to hear the praises of God in their own native languages (*glōssa*, v. 11; *dialektos*, vv. 6, 8). Although it is generally agreed that Luke intended the phrase 'to speak in other tongues' to mean that the disciples spoke in foreign languages, this explanation has not been universally accepted. From the days of the early Fathers some have seen in v. 8 evidence for a miracle of hearing performed on the audience. Gregory Nazianzen (*Orat.* 41. 10, *In Pentecosten*) rejected this view on the ground that it transfers the miracle from the disciples to the unconverted multitude. It also overlooks the fact that speaking in tongues began before there was any audience (v. 4; *cf.* v. 6) and some bystanders thought what they heard was drunken babbling (v. 13).

In the opinion of most modern scholars the glossolalia of Acts 2:1–13 was similar to that described in 1 Cor. 12–14, and consisted of unintelligible ecstatic utterances. They advance various theories to explain why Luke wrote instead about foreign languages. Some think he may have misinterpreted his sources and inserted 'other' (Acts 2:4) on his own initiative; others suggest that he may have interpolated the reference to foreign languages as a more favourable explanation when glossolalia fell into disrepute. Yet others regard his narrative as a dogmatic creation combining reports of ecstatic glossolalia with legends of the giving of the law at Sinai in the 70 languages of mankind (Midrash *Tanḥuma* 26c), the conception of Pentecost as a reversal of the curse of Babel (Gn. 11:1–9) and his own universalism. However, it is unlikely that Luke, a careful historian (Lk. 1:1–4) and close companion of Paul (who spoke in tongues, 1 Cor. 14:18), misunderstood the nature of glossolalia. If the disciples did not actually speak in foreign languages at Pentecost, then the most satisfactory explanation is that Luke records from his sources the convictions of those present who believed they had recognized words of praise to God in other languages. The straightforwardness of the narrative and the scorn of the mockers (v. 13) count against the mediating view that the disciples' speech was delivered from its peculiarities (v. 7; *cf.* Mk. 14:70) and made intelligible to their hearers, most of whom would probably know Greek or Aramaic.

Speaking 'in new tongues' (*glōssais kainais*) is mentioned in Mk. 16:17 (not an original part of the Gospel) as a sign following faith in Christ. It accompanied the outpouring of the Holy Spirit upon the first Gentile converts (Acts 10:44–46; 11:15), and was doubtless one of the manifestations among the earliest Samaritan believers (Acts 8:18). The isolated group of disciples at Ephesus, who may have been early believers in Christ unaware of Pentecost (N.B. Stonehouse, *WTJ* 13, 1950–1, pp. 11ff.) also spoke in tongues

TONGUES, CONFUSION OF
See Babel, Part 1.

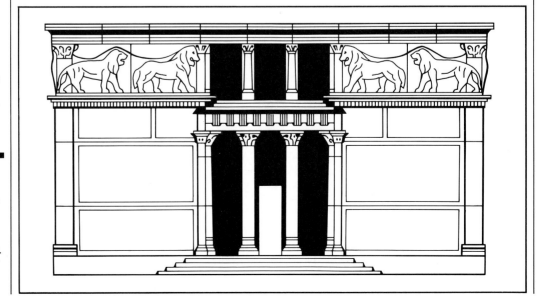

Reconstruction of the façade of a shrine built by the Tobiad family at Araq el-Emir, Jordan. c. 175 BC.

TOPAZ
See Jewels, Part 2.

TORTOISE
See Animals, Part 1.

TOWER OF BABEL
See Babel, Part 1.

TOWER OF SILOAM
See Siloam, Part 3.

when the Holy Spirit came on them (Acts 19:6). In each case spontaneous glossolalia was perceptible evidence of the repetition, in association with the ministry of an apostle (*cf.* 2 Cor. 12:12), of the initial bestowal of the Spirit at Pentecost, and apparently served to endorse the inclusion of new classes of believers into the cautious Jewish–Christian church (*cf.* Acts 10:47; 11:17–18). If tongues serve as a sign of covenantal judgment for Israel (Is. 28:10ff.; *cf.* Dt. 28:49; 1 Cor. 14:21ff.), and the tongues of Pentecost represent the taking of the kingdom from Israel and giving it to men of all nations (see O. P. Robertson, *WTJ* 38, 1975, pp. 43–53), the pattern of glossolalic occurrences in Acts emphasizes this transition.

Corinthian glossolalia differed in some respects from that described in Acts. In Jerusalem, Caesarea and Ephesus, whole companies on whom the Spirit fell immediately broke into tongues, whereas at Corinth not all possessed the coveted gift (1 Cor. 12:10, 30). Glossolalia in Acts appears to have been an irresistible and possibly temporary initial experience, whereas Paul's instructions to the Corinthians imply a continuing gift under the control of the speaker (1 Cor. 14:27–28). At Pentecost 'tongues' were understood by the hearers, but at Corinth the additional gift of interpretation was necessary to make them intelligible (1 Cor. 14:5, 13, 27). Only at Pentecost is speaking in foreign languages explicitly mentioned. On the other hand, glossolalia is everywhere represented as consisting of meaningful utterances inspired by the Holy Spirit and employed primarily for worship (Acts 2:11; 10:46; 1 Cor. 14:2, 14–17, 28).

The 'various kinds of tongues' (1 Cor. 12:10) may include unlearned languages, non-languages, or other forms of utterance (*cf.* S. D. Currie, *Int* 19, 1965, pp. 274–294). At Corinth they were apparently not foreign languages, which Paul denotes by a different word (*phōnē*, 14:10–11), because a special gift, not linguistic proficiency, was necessary to understand them; nor were they for him meaningless ecstatic sounds, though the mind was inactive (v. 14) and the utterances, without interpretation, unintelligible even to the speaker (v. 13), because words (v. 19) and contents (vv. 14–17) were recognized, and interpreted tongues were equivalent to prophecy (v. 5)..A definite linguistic form is suggested by the Gk. words for 'to interpret', which elsewhere in the NT, except Lk. 24:27, always mean 'to translate' (*cf.* J. G. Davies, *JTS* n.s. 3, 1952, pp. 228ff.; R. H. Gundry, *JTS* n.s. 17, 1966, pp. 299–307), and Paul probably regarded them as special heavenly languages not having ordinary human characteristics, inspired by the Holy Spirit for worship, for a sign to unbelievers (O. P. Robertson, *op. cit.*; J. P. M. Sweet, *NTS* 13, 1966–7, pp. 240–257), and, when interpreted, for the edification of believers. The Corinthians so overrated and abused glossolalia that Paul strictly limited its exercise in public (1 Cor. 14:27–28), and emphasized the superior value of prophecy for the whole church (1 Cor. 14:1, 5). Whilst it is uncertain how far later manifestations of glossolalia resemble the NT phenomenon, recent studies evaluate them as cadences of vocalization, not languages.

BIBLIOGRAPHY. J. Behm, *TNDT* 1, pp. 722–727; G. B. Cutten, *Speaking with Tongues*, 1927; J. D. G. Dunn, *Jesus and the Spirit*, 1975; A. A. Hoekema, *What about Tongue-Speaking?*, 1966; M. T. Kelsey, *Tongue Speaking*, 1973; J. P. Kildahl, *The Psychology of Speaking in Tongues*, 1972; W. J. Samarin, *Tongues of Men and Angels*, 1972; A. C. Thiselton, 'The "Interpretation" of Tongues? A new suggestion in the light of Greek usage in Philo and Josephus', *JTS* n.s. 30, 1979. W.G.P.

TOPHEL. Mentioned only in Dt. 1:1 as the locality where Moses addressed the Israelites. The identification with el-Tafileh, 25 km SE of the Dead Sea, is philologically unlikely (N. Glueck, *AASOR* 18–19, 1939, pp. 42–43). Tophel may well have been a stopping-place in the Israelites' wilderness itinerary. D.J.W.

TOPHETH (AV **TOPHET**). This was a 'high place' in the valley of *Hinnom just outside Jerusalem, where child sacrifices were offered by fire to a deity *Molech. Josiah defiled this idolatrous shrine (2 Ki. 23:10), and Jeremiah prophesied that the place would be used as a cemetery (Je. 7:32f.). The root of the noun seems to be the *tpt* of Aram. and Arab. denoting 'fireplace'. The vowels are artificial, taken from the Heb. noun *bōšeṯ*, 'shame'. D.F.P.

TORCH. The word is usually a translation of Heb. *lappîḏ* in OT and of Gk. *lampas* in NT. *lappîḏ* signifies the traditional torch consisting of a long pole with rags soaked in oil wrapped round the top of it. The word is translated as 'lightnings' in Ex. 20:18. *lampas* is normally translated 'torch' in Jn. 18:3 and Rev. 4:5; 8:10. In Acts 20:8, where the scene is a domestic one, translations generally render it as 'lamp' or 'light' (RSV). The other occurrences are all in Mt. 25:1–8, the parable of the wise and foolish maidens. While most translations favour the rendering 'lamp', it would probably be more appropriate to see a reference to the torches which were used in wedding processions. R.E.N.

TOWN CLERK. The *grammateus* (Acts 19:35) was frequently the secretary of a board of magistrates, responsible for the accurate recording of official decisions. At Ephesus he was clearly the president of the assembly. His punctilious regard for legal niceties, and anxiety about Roman intervention, mark him as a member of the Romanized aristocracy, among whom Paul found support (v. 31). His speech has been much admired as a little masterpiece of political *savoir faire*. E.A.J.

TRACHONITIS. The only biblical reference is Lk. 3:1, where, linked with *Ituraea, it is called the tetrarchy of Philip (the brother of Herod, tetrarch of Galilee). Trachonitis must have been the district around Trachon (Josephus uses both names); Trachon corresponds with the modern al-Laja', a pear-shaped area of petrified volcanic rock some 900 square km in area, to the E of Galilee and S of Damascus. It is on the whole extremely unproductive, but here and there are patches of fertile ground, with a spring or two. The cracked and broken nature of its terrain made it ideal for outlaws and brigands. Among others Varro (governor of Syria under Augustus), Herod the Great and Herod Agrippa I endeavoured to civilize the area, with varying success. Later on a Roman road was built through it. Targum Jonathan identifies the OT *Argob with Trachonitis. D.F.P.

TRADE AND COMMERCE.

I. In the Old Testament

*Palestine has always been the only natural bridge between Europe and Asia on the N and Africa on the S. This accounts for the fact that, although she was a poor country, she was constantly enriched by the trade and commerce that went through her land. Ezk. 27:12–25 presents a cross-section of the world commerce that passed through her territory.

Palestine's major contributions to commerce in OT times were agricultural products and metals. Phoenicia just to the N was a manufacturing area forced to import food. Israel supplied her with grain, oil and wine. Egypt to the S had a surplus of grain, but was short of olive oil and wine. As the desert peoples to the E became more influential after David's day they too absorbed Palestine's agricultural products.

Iron, which had been earlier introduced by the Philistines, appeared in such quantity after David's wide conquests in Syria that it could also be passed on to iron-hungry Egypt. Solomon traded down the Red Sea to the backward peoples of Arabia and Africa. These lands in return sent precious incense, spices and gold to the Mediterranean *via* Palestine as well as Egypt. This Arabian commerce in Palestine was at its peak in Nabataean times. During the intertestamental period the asphalt traffic from the Dead Sea was so important that this body of water was called the Asphalt Sea, and it entered into international politics. Perfumes and spices were always items of exchange, some varieties moving out of the country and others moving in. Both were more important in ancient times than today. Spices, for example, were a common method of varying a rather monotonous menu.

Palestine's flocks produced a surplus of wool, which was probably exported both in bulk and as manufactured goods. Moab was a major wool producer. The excavations at Tell beit Mirsim have shown that this was a manufacturing city devoted exclusively to weaving and dyeing of cloth. Flax was also used for clothing. If it was exported, then it was sent to Phoenicia, since

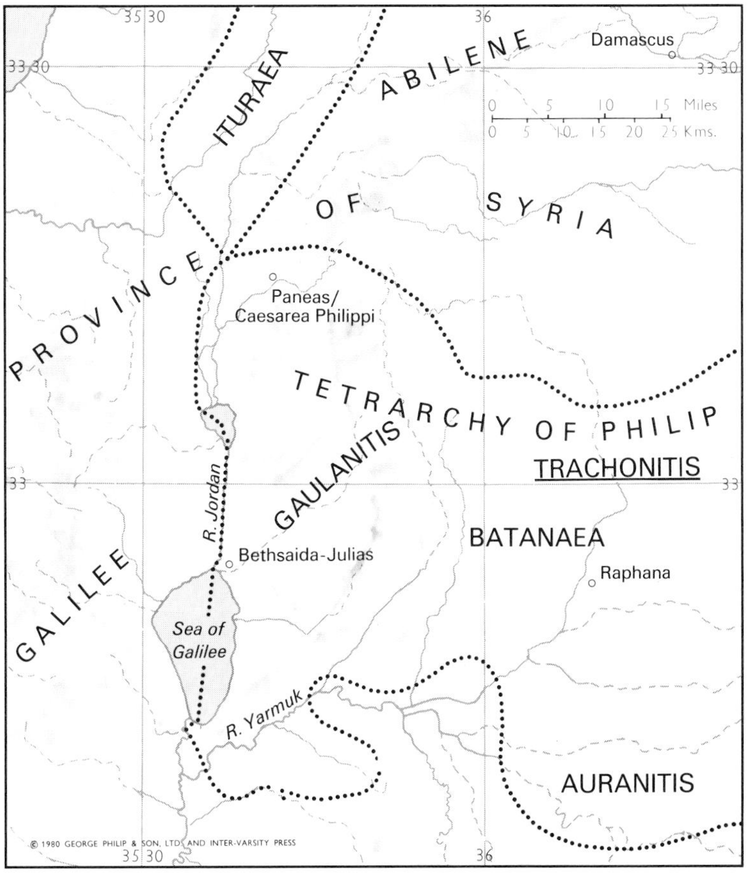

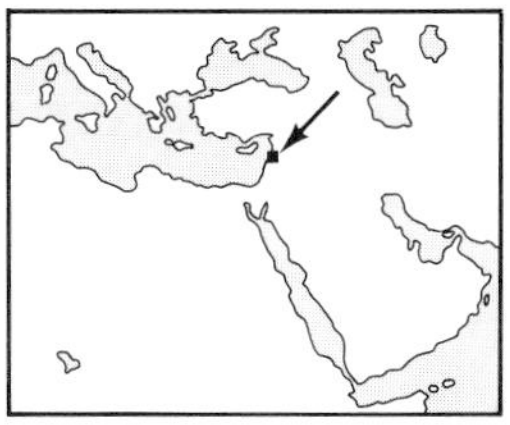

The area of Trachonitis in the territory of Philip.

Egypt was a heavy producer of linen. The wide distribution of expensive garments is shown by the finding of a Babylonian garment at the time of Joshua's conquest of Jericho, although that city was of minor importance. The value of good raiment is seen in the fact that it was commonly included in the list of booty taken in war.

*Egypt was the outstanding manufacturing nation along the Mediterranean in early days, but Phoenicia began to cut into her trade by imitating and modifying Egyp. craftsmanship. With Phoenicia's expanding manufacturing and shipping trade, Israel had a constantly increasing market for her agricultural products. Palestine itself entered the manufacturing field about the time of the written prophets. Indeed, much of their social criticism deals with the inevitable economic crises which come when any agricultural people shifts into full-scale manufacturing. An early date to Pentateuchal laws is demonstrated by the absence of any manufacturing code. Palestine used modern assembly-line techniques and standardization of forms and sizes. Their mass-production material was of good quality, although they were often using poorer materials and cheaper labour. Their manufactured goods, however, seemed to have been primarily for local consumption. Trade guilds came in at this time, and trade marks were used by the pottery manufacturers. (*ARTS AND CRAFTS.) In OT times agricultural taxes were largely paid in kind, and the government had its own potteries making official government standardized containers with the government seal stamped on the handles.

Coined *money came into Palestine towards the close of OT times. Previously gold and silver in ingots, bars and rings were weighed out. Jewels offered a more convenient and fairly safe method of investing and transporting larger sums than would be convenient in bullion. After Alexander the Great, coined money was common. During the intertestamental period, Jewish bankers came into prominence, and the synagogues of Asia Minor in NT times are in part due to Jewish influence in banking and commerce. During this same period Alexandria, which had become probably the greatest manufacturing city of the world, attracted a heavy Jewish population.

Only in the days of Solomon and

Opposite page: The trade routes through Palestine throughout Bible times.

Jehoshaphat did sea commerce play an important part in Palestinian trade, and both ventures were short-lived. Sea commerce was predominantly in the hands of foreigners, first Philistines and other sea peoples, then later Phoenicians and Greeks.

For land travel the ass was the beast of burden until about David's day, when the camel, previously used primarily for war, also became available for the caravan trade. Part of Palestine's commercial wealth came from these caravans, which purchased necessary supplies from farmers and craftsmen as they moved through the country. At the local market-place the population absorbed foreign news, and the efficacy of this news medium can be seen in the sermons of Amos, with their broad picture of world affairs. Ishmaelites and Midianites handled much of the early commerce on the desert fringe. Later the Ammonites took over from them and became the dominant camel-owning people before the Nabataeans, who brought desert commerce to its financial peak.

Ben-hadad and the Omri dynasty had business depots in each other's capital city, and this was probably common practice between adjacent nations. Israel and Phoenicia were normally on far better terms with each other than Israel and Syria. A good source of income for the government was the tax on commerce entering the country. This source of wealth, of course, was at its peak in the days of David and Solomon. But there was a second peak of prosperity under Jeroboam II in Israel and Uzziah in Judah.

The major trade routes of Palestine ran N and S. The most important came out of Egypt, crossed the Philistine plain, continued along the E edge of the plain of Sharon, crossed the Carmel ridge at Megiddo, and then went on to Dan either *via* Hazor of Galilee or *via* Beth-shan and the upland road just N of the Yarmuq river. The high ridge road *via* Beersheba, Hebron, Jerusalem, Shechem and Beth-shan handled more local traffic than through commerce. E of the Jordan valley was the King's Highway coming out of the Gulf of Aqabah and touching the key cities of Kir, Dibon, Medeba, *etc.*, along the centre of the populated areas. A second road followed a parallel track to the E of the King's Highway and just inside the desert fringe. Today a modern road follows the former and the railway the latter. These routes picked up the Arabian trade at such points as Petra, Amman and Edrei.

E and W roads were less profitable, except the most S one, where Arabian commerce came *via* Nabataean Petra to Gaza. Commerce also came out of the caravan city of Amman, down the Jabbok valley, up to Shechem and over to the Mediterranean. More commerce, however, probably came through the Hauran down to Beth-shan and up the plain of Esdraelon to the Mediterranean. The great grain fields of the Hauran sold their wheat down this route. A shorter road cut across Galilee from the Sea of Galilee to Accho. The major seaports used in OT times were Joppa, Dor and Accho. Ashkelon was the Philistine seaport, and Gaza was the Mediterranean outlet for the Nabataean trade.

BIBLIOGRAPHY. D. Baly, *The Geography of the Bible*[2], 1974; data from ancient Near East: *cf.* W. F. Leemans, H. Hirsch, in D. O. Edzard (ed.), *Reallexikon der Assyriologie*, 4, 1973, pp. 76–97; from Egypt: W. Helck, in Helck and Otto (eds.), *Lexikon der Ägyptologie*, 2, 1976, cols. 943–948.

J.L.K.

II. In the New Testament

Trade and commerce have no large place in the NT. The coast of Palestine is harbourless and swept with surf, and no natural port formed a cross-road for trade. The sea in Heb. metaphor is a barrier, not a pathway, and such an attitude was natural in a land which fronted the unbroken border of the waters. The ruins of artificial harbours are common enough, and suggest rather the futility than the success of man's attempts to tame the E end of the Mediterranean (see G. A. Smith, *The Historical Geography of the Holy Land*[25], 1931, pp. 127–144).

Caravan routes, on the other hand, naturally converged on Palestine, and the NT is aware of the activities of the trader. Such parables as those of the talents and the merchant who found 'a pearl of great price' were obviously meant to be understood by the audience to which they were addressed. But this was the petty trade of a small, poor and under-privileged land.

Major activities in trade and commerce, all through NT times, were in the hands of the Romans and Italians. State interference with the processes of trade, which became a sombre feature of late imperial times, was already visible in the 1st century. The legal machinery by which a 'mark in hand or head' could prevent the non-conformist from buying and selling (Rev. 13:16–17) was early apparent. The foreign trade of the empire was extensive and varied. There is also evidence that it was unbalanced, for the hoards of Rom. coins found commonly in India are clear indication of a perilous leakage of bullion, and one cause of the creeping paralysis of inflation.

Lat. and Gk. words in early Irish, German, Iranian, Indian and even Mongolian tongues are evidence of the wide influence of Rom. trade. Archaeology, especially on the S Indian coast, has a similar word to say. An excavation at Pondicherry has established the fact of a large Rom. trade with India in the 1st century. Rom. merchants, indeed, were ubiquitous. There was a Rom. market, the remains of which may still be seen, outside the sacred precincts at Delphi. Trade was no doubt brisk in amulets and souvenirs, and may have been typical of petty Italian enterprise abroad wherever crowds were gathered. Similar activity in the Temple of Jerusalem had been cannily kept in the hands of the Sadducean chief priests.

From the 2nd century before Christ a Rom. city stood on Delos, the Aegean centre of the slave-trade, and when Mithridates in 88 BC massacred the Italian residents of Asia Minor and the Aegean islands, 25,000 fell in Delos alone out of a total of 100,000 victims. They must have been mostly traders and the agents of commerce. The capital itself, whose population in the 1st century was something like one million, was a vast market, and a grim, satiric chapter in the Apocalypse (Rev. 18), constructed after the fashion of an OT 'taunt-song', and in imitation of Ezk. 27, speaks of the wealth and volume of Rome's luxury trade, and the economic disruption sure to follow the loss of a market so rich. Ostia, Rome's port, is full of warehouses.

Rom. trade extended far beyond the boundaries of the empire. The 'far country' of Mt. 25:14 is quite literal. Merchants from Italy carried their foods into unsubdued Germany, along the 'amber route' to the Baltic, to India and perhaps China. All this activity sprang from Rome's dominance, the peace which she policed, and above all from the absence of political frontiers over significant areas of the world. Petronius' Trimalchio, the *nouveau riche* of the *Satiricon*, could make fortunes and lose them, and make them again. Of Augustus the merchants said that 'through him they sailed the seas in safety, through him they could make their wealth, through him they were happy'.

The account of the last journey of Paul to Rome, so ably told by Luke, first in a ship of Adramyttium of Asia Minor, and then in an Alexandrian freighter, probably under charter to the Rom. government for the transport of Egyp. corn, gives a vivid picture of the hazards of trade and navigation.

Apart from the list of Rev. 18, which may have been deliberately selected in accordance with the polemic and satirical purpose of the passage, the commodities of export trade are not widely known. No cargo lists survive. Oysters came from Britain to Rome in barrels of sea-water. Cornish tin, no doubt, came down the same sea-route. N Gaul seems to have had the rudiments of an exporting textile industry, and Gaul certainly exported cheap Samian pottery. Underwater archaeology on wrecked ships has revealed that large cargoes of wine were carried. A monogram device of a double S in a trident seems to indicate that one such freighter, wrecked near Marseilles, was the property of one Severus Sestius, who occupied 'the House of the Trident' on Delos.

On the subject of mass production for such trade there is little information, and none on the business organization necessarily involved. Certain localities, however, became famous for special products, and the resultant commerce would have been in the control of specialist traders who would create and operate their own markets. A striking example is Lydia, 'a seller of purple goods', from the city of Thyatira in Asia Minor (Acts 16:14), whom Paul's party met at Philippi in Macedonia. Corinthian bronze, in ornaments and mirrors (1 Cor. 13:12), and the *cilicium* or goats'-hair cloth, which was either the product or the raw-material of Paul's tent-making (Acts 18:3), were probably distributed by similar private enterprise. The imagery of John's letter to Laodicea (Rev. 3:14–18) is partly derived from the trade and commerce of the town. Ramsay has established the exis-

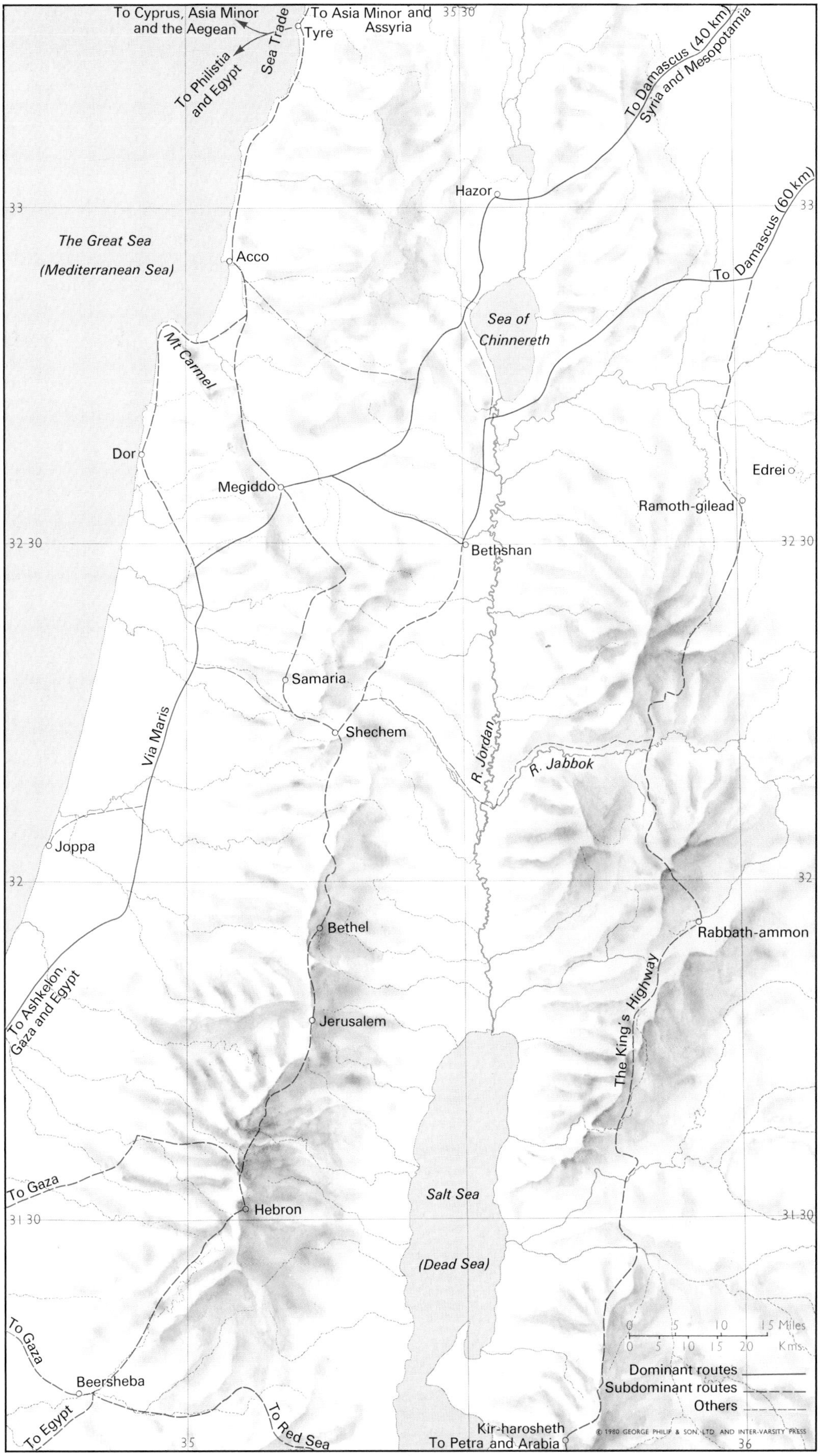

tence of a Laodicean trade in valuable black woollen garments. Laodicea and Colossae produced black fleeces, the evidence of which is still genetically apparent, it is said, in the sheep of the area today. There was also a Laodicean eye-salve, based probably on the kaolin of the thermal area at Hierapolis, 10 km away. Hence the taunt about 'white garments' and 'eye-salve' (see W. M. Ramsay, *The Letters to the Seven Churches of Asia*, chs. 29–30).

*Thyatira, of the earlier letter, was also a centre of trade and commerce, though probably without Laodicea's export emphasis. Lydia has already been mentioned, and archaeological evidence speaks of wool- and linen-workers, dyers, leather-workers, tanners, potters, slave-traders and bronze-smiths. The dyers, and Lydia was probably one of them, dealt in a purple dye made from the madder root, which undercut the expensive sea-dye from the murex shell.

It is curious to note that, in writing to Thyatira, John uses the figure of Jezebel, sign and symbol of Israel's compromising trade partnership with Phoenicia, to describe a local 'Nicolaitan'. 'Jezebel' of Thyatira had no doubt taught some form of compromise with the surrounding pagan world. In a town of brisk trade activity some such adjustment would appear more urgently necessary because of the power of the trade guilds.

These organizations were a source of major difficulty to Christians, who sought, in their daily converse with the pagan world around, to keep a clear conscience. The trade guilds or *collegia* appear in Acts 19 as a force of organized opposition to Christianity. An important trade commodity of Ephesus, now that the harbour was silting, and commerce was passing to Smyrna, was the manufacture of silver souvenirs and cult objects of Artemis, for sale to the pilgrims who visited the famous shrine. Ephesus saw the guilds concerned exercise sufficient pressure to end Paul's ministry. A famous letter of Pliny (*Ep*. 10. 96), which vividly describes the suppression of a vigorous church in Bithynia in AD 112, is also a clear indication of such influence. The guild of the butchers, alarmed at the falling sales of sacrificial meat, successfully stirred up official action against the church. It was difficult for Christians, whose trade depended upon a measure of goodwill, to carry on their daily activities if they obviously abstained from fellowship with their colleagues. On the other hand, since all the callings of trade and commerce were under the patronage of pagan deities, fellowship, and indeed membership of a trade *collegium*, involved the compromising act of libation or sacrifice at the guild dinner. Records exist of a considerable number of such organizations, and the strictures of Jude, Peter and John against the 'Nicolaitans', the 'followers of Balaam' and 'Jezebel', suggest that the simple functions of trade and commerce may have proved a source of deep division in the early church.

BIBLIOGRAPHY. G. A. Smith in *EBi* (*s.v.* 'Trade'); *BC*, 1, pp. 218ff.; M. Rostovtzeff, *The Social and Economic History of the Roman Empire*, 1926. E.M.B.

TRADE MARKS
See Trade and commerce, Part 3.

TRADES
See Arts and crafts, Part 1.

TRADITION (Gk. *paradosis*). That which is handed down, particularly teaching handed down from a teacher to his disciples. The concept is often present without the word being mentioned. The main references in the Gospels occur in Mt. 15 and Mk. 7, and concern Jewish tradition.

I. Jewish tradition

The word tradition does not occur in the OT, but between the Testaments much teaching in explanation of the OT was added by the rabbis. Tradition was handed down from teacher to pupil, and by Jesus' day had assumed a place alongside Scripture. This equation of human commentary with divine revelation was condemned by the Lord. By such tradition the Word of God was 'transgressed', 'made of none effect', laid aside, and rejected (Mt. 15:3, 6; Mk. 7:8–9, 13). The doctrines taught by tradition were 'the commandments of men' (Mt. 15:9; Mk. 7:6–7).

II. Christian tradition

Jesus placed his own teaching alongside the Word of God as an authoritative commentary, which he handed down to his disciples. Thus in the Sermon on the Mount Jesus quoted from the Law, but put beside it his own words, 'but I say to you' (Mt. 5:22, 28, 32, 34, 39, 44; *cf*. 6:25). His justification for so doing is found in his Person. As the Spirit-anointed Messiah, the Word made flesh, he alone could make a valid and authoritative commentary on the Spirit-inspired Word of God. Likewise the Epistles emphasize the Person of Christ in contrast to tradition. In Col. 2:8 Paul warns against falling prey to 'philosophy and empty deceit . . . according to human tradition . . . and not according to Christ'. So in Gal. 1:14, 16 Paul abandoned the elders' tradition when God revealed his Son in him; Christ not only created the true tradition but constitutes it.

Christian tradition in the NT has three elements: (*a*) the facts of Christ (1 Cor. 11:23; 15:3; Lk. 1:2, where 'delivered' translates *paredosan*); (*b*) the theological interpretation of those facts; see, *e.g*., the whole argument of 1 Cor. 15; (*c*) the manner of life which flows from them (1 Cor. 11:2; 2 Thes. 2:15; 3:6–7). In Jude 3 the 'faith . . . once for all delivered' covers all three elements (*cf*. Rom. 6:17).

Christ was made known by the apostolic testimony to him; the apostles therefore claimed that their tradition was to be received as authoritative (1 Cor. 11:2; 2 Thes. 2:15; 3:6). See also Eph. 4:20–21, where the readers had not heard Christ in the flesh but had heard the apostolic testimony to him. Christ told the apostles to bear witness of him because they had been with him from the beginning; he also promised the gift of the Spirit who would lead them into all truth (Jn. 15:26–27; 16:13). This combination of eyewitness testimony and Spirit-guided witness produced a 'tradition' that was a true and valid complement to the OT. So 1 Tim. 5:18 and 2 Pet. 3:16 place apostolic tradition alongside Scripture and describe it as such.

One influential form-critical school of theology questions the historical validity of NT tradition saying that in this tradition Christians were concerned with proclaiming the Christ of faith rather than passing on facts of history. This concern in turn led to their account being coloured by their belief, and therefore the biblical scholar's task is seen as identifying that which originally belonged to Christ and that which was added by early believers. B. Gerhardsson challenges the validity of this form-critical presupposition. He points out that the very thorough methods of transmission of tradition in the rabbinic schools later can be traced back to NT times. Methods such as learning by heart, memorizing the actual words of the teacher, condensing the material into short texts and the use of notebooks were common in the days of Christ. The apostles and the early church were also seriously concerned with a conscious handing down of a valid tradition of Christ and not just with an unconscious transmission of a diluted tradition through preaching. When the uniqueness of Jesus in the eyes of the early church is also taken into account, the likelihood of additions to the story becomes even more suspect.

Gerhardsson's work provoked strong reaction, which questioned the reading back of later rabbinic methods into the early church period and pointed to the distinctiveness of Christian teaching over against contemporary Jewish teaching. Although Gerhardsson may have overstated his case, he has shown that the environment in which the Gospels were written was deeply concerned for the correct handing on of tradition and not as interested in supplementing fact with imagined improvement, as some scholars believe. The exhortations of Paul regarding the 'tradition' gain added significance in this context. The apostolic office was limited to eyewitnesses, and, as only eyewitnesses could bear a faithful witness to Christ as he lived and died and rose again, true tradition must also be apostolic. This was recognized by the church in later years when the Canon of the NT was eventually produced on the basis of the apostolic nature of the books concerned. Apostolic tradition was at one time oral, but for us it is crystallized in the apostolic writings containing the Spirit-guided witness to the Christ of God. Other teaching, while it may be instructive and useful and worthy of serious consideration, cannot claim to be placed alongside OT and NT as authoritative without manifesting the same defects as condemned Jewish tradition in the eyes of our Lord.

BIBLIOGRAPHY. O. Cullmann, 'The Tradition', in *The Early Church*, 1956, pp. 59ff.; B. Gerhardsson, *Memory and Manuscript*, 1961, especially pp. 122–170; *idem*, *Tradition and Transmission in Early Christianity*, 1964; R. P. C. Hanson, *Tradition in the Early Church*, 1962; Y. M. J. Congar, *Tradition and Traditions*, 1966; F. F. Bruce, *Tradition Old and New*, 1970.

D.J.V.L.

TRANCE. The Gk. word *ekstasis* (lit. 'standing outside' or 'being put outside', *i.e.* of one's normal state of mind) is rendered 'trance' in Acts 10:10; 11:5; 22:17, where it forms the condition of a vision. The trance state has never been fully explained, but it involves an overriding of normal consciousness and perception. In the only two occurrences of the strange Heb. word *sanwērîm*, translated 'blindness' in Gn. 19:11 and 2 Ki. 6:18, it is clear that a trancelike state of hypnotic suggestibility is indicated.

J.S.W.

TRANSFIGURATION. The transfiguration is recorded in Mt. 17:1–8; Mk. 9:2–8; Lk. 9:28–36. Its absence from John is usually accounted for on the ground that the whole of Christ's life was a manifestation of the divine glory (Jn. 1:14; 2:11, *etc*.). There is also a reference to it in 2 Pet. 1:16–18.

In the Synoptic Gospels the event takes place about a week after Peter's confession of the Messiahship of Jesus. He took his three closest disciples, Peter, James and John, up to a mountain (probably Hermon, which rises to a height of 2,814 m above sea-level). There he was transformed (rather than changed in appearance) and his garments shone with heavenly brightness. Moses and Elijah then appeared and talked to him, and Peter suggested making three tents for them. A voice then came from a cloud declaring Christ's Sonship and his authority, after which the vision ended. The narrative suggests that the whole event was objective, though many modern scholars have sought to describe it in terms of a subjective experience of Jesus or of Peter.

The transfiguration marks an important stage in the revelation of Jesus as the Christ and the Son of God. It is an experience similar to his baptism (Mt. 3:13–17; Mk. 1:9–11; Lk. 3:21f.). Here his glory is revealed not just through his deeds, but in a more personal way. The glory denotes the royal presence, for the kingdom of God is in the midst of his people.

There are many features about the account which derive significance from the OT. Moses and Elijah represent the Law and the Prophets witnessing to the Messiah and being fulfilled and superseded by him. Each of them had had a vision of the glory of God on a mountain, Moses on Sinai (Ex. 24:15) and Elijah on Horeb (1 Ki. 19:8). Each of them left no known grave (Dt. 34:6; 2 Ki. 2:11). The law of Moses and the coming of Elijah are mentioned together in the last verses of the OT (Mal. 4:4–6). The two men at the empty tomb (Lk. 24:4; Jn. 20:12) and at the ascension (Acts 1:10) and the 'two witnesses' (Rev. 11:3) are sometimes also identified with Moses and Elijah. The heavenly voice, 'This is my beloved Son; listen to him' (Mk. 9:7), marks Jesus out not only as the Messiah but also as the Prophet of Dt. 18:15ff.

The cloud symbolizes the covering of the divine presence (Ex. 24:15–18; Ps. 97:2). There is a cloud to receive Christ out of his disciples' sight at the ascension (Acts 1:9). The return of Christ will be with clouds (Rev. 1:7).

In Luke we are told that the subject of their conversation was the *exodos* which he was to accomplish at Jerusalem. This seems to mean not simply his death but the great facts of his death and resurrection as the means of redemption of his people typified by the OT Exodus from Egypt.

The transfiguration is therefore a focal point in the revelation of the kingdom of God, for it looks back to the OT and shows how Christ fulfils it, and it looks on to the great events of the cross, resurrection, ascension and parousia. Peter was wrong in trying to make the experience permanent. What was needed was the presence of Jesus alone and attention to his voice.

BIBLIOGRAPHY. G. H. Boobyer, *St Mark and the Transfiguration Story*, 1942; A. M. Ramsey, *The Glory of God and the Transfiguration of Christ*, 1949.

R.E.N.

TRAVAIL. 17th-century English made no distinction between the words 'travel' and 'travail', the two spellings being employed indiscriminately for the two ideas in the earlier editions of the AV. Later editions have, on the whole, conformed to the changing usage, as does RSV. The Eng. word translates a number of Heb. and Gk. words, all of which are normally connected with childbirth. The word is sometimes employed metaphorically, notably in Rom. 8:22 and Gal. 4:19, and in simile as in Ps. 48:6 and Mi. 4:9–10.

BIBLIOGRAPHY. G. Bertram,

TRANSJORDAN
See Gilead, Part 1.

TRANSPORT
See Ships and boats, Part 3.

The Appian Way ran SE from Rome to Capua. The Christians of Rome came out along this road to greet Paul, meeting him at Appii Forum (Acts 28:15). (SH)

TDNT 9, pp. 667–674; R. K. Harrison, *NIDNTT* 3, pp. 857f.

G.W.G.

TRAVEL IN BIBLICAL TIMES. Travel in the world of biblical times was governed by the available land and water routes. Early in the history of the ancient Near East, especially in Mesopotamia and Egypt, rivers and coastal waters provided the best means for trade or travel. Bridle tracks developed to link villages and villages grew up at crossroads in a continuing double process. As trade developed international sea and land routes came into being. The Mediterranean world was greatly privileged for sea travel because of its climate, coastal pattern and access to other areas (*cf.* 1 Ki. 9:26ff.; Paul's journeys). Palestine was a vital land-bridge between Eurasia and Africa for both sea and land travellers, and so played an important role in communication and *trade. With the establishment of the Roman peace and road system, travel in the biblical world was greatly facilitated, playing an important part in the spread of the gospel.

I. Old Testament times

Land travel in the early OT period was relatively restricted, caravans and military forces being the main groups on the move. Although individuals tended to remain in their home areas so as not to lose their status as citizens, there is evidence of group migrations during the Middle Bronze age. The relatively widespread trade empire of *Ebla in the latter 3rd millennium, from the Mediterranean to the Persian Gulf, indicates reasonable communications and the possibility of travel in the Near East well before the patriarchal age.

A number of Heb. words are used for roads or paths. Of these *dereḵ*, that which is trodden underfoot, and *m^esillâh*, the levelling and filling of a track, suggest best the nature of ancient roads. Although the evidence is not final, it does appear that properly constructed

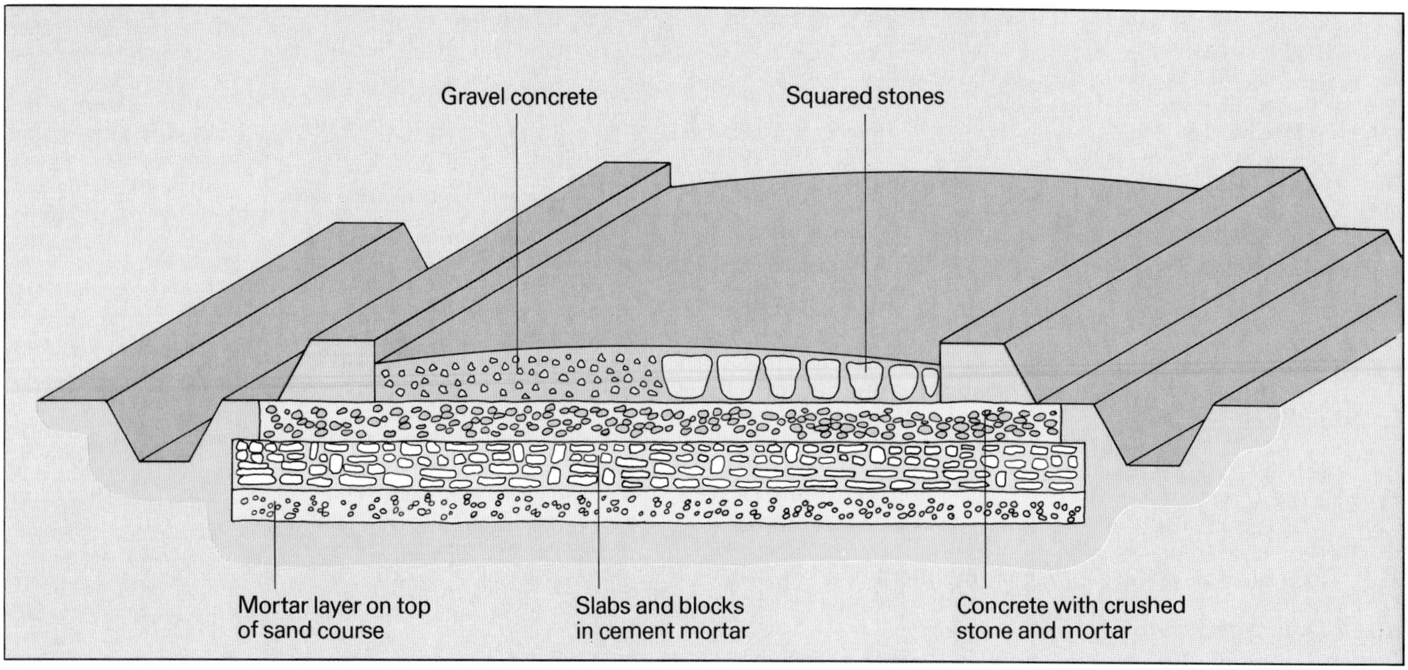

roads were unknown before the Roman road system. Prior to this roads were paths followed regularly by men and animals. Some tracks were better maintained, such as to provincial centres or the cities of refuge (Dt. 19:3), but this meant essentially the clearing of stones and limited levelling (*cf.* Is. 40:3; 62:10). Tiglath-pileser I (1115–1077 BC) of *Assyria used engineers to lay bridges and level tracks for carts and siege-engines. An Egyp. writer, a century earlier, described Palestinian roads as 'filled with boulders and pebbles, . . . overgrown with reeds, thorns and brambles' (*ANET*, p. 478a). Such references indicate unpaved roads but tracks which could be maintained. Even the royal roads of the Persians, including the 2,600 km major link between Sardis and Susa, were probably formed but not paved except perhaps in immediate city areas. Paved streets seem to have been limited to some towns (*e.g.* Nineveh, Babylon). Travellers, caravans, official messengers and armies would use these tracks, travellers normally going with caravans for safety (*cf.* Jdg. 5:6).

Usually travellers would walk, although the ass was used for both riding and as a pack animal from early times. Chariots and horses were used for military purposes. The ox wagon carried heavy loads and probably people (Gn. 46:5). In later times the camel was also utilized. Throughout river and coastal traffic remained very important modes of travel. Little is known of resting-places, but it seems that the traveller prior to Roman times needed to provide and fend for himself (Jos. 9:3–14). People would travel mainly to trade, sometimes to attend religious festivals, and on occasions when migrating due to war, famine or similar reasons.

Roads may be classified as international or internal routes. Often local roads linked international highways, as the E–W roads of Palestine sometimes ran between the 'way of the sea' (Is. 9:1; the so-called Via Maris) and the 'King's Highway' (Nu. 20:17). The former ran from Egypt along the coast of Palestine then inland to Megiddo where it divided, although the main route continued N to Damascus and on to Mesopotamia. The *'King's Highway' also ran N–S between Bozrah in Edom to Damascus, linking both Arabia and Egypt with the N. Lesser N–S roads in Palestine followed the Jordan Valley and the central mountain ridge. Numerous latitudinal roads linked these highways, including the road from Jerusalem to Jericho (see *LOB*). Sea travel was not normally a feature of Israelite life, although ships traversed the coast of Palestine and sailed from Ezion-geber on the Gulf of Aqabah. Jonah's flight illustrates that some individuals did travel on cargo ships in OT times (*SHIPS AND BOATS; *TRADE AND COMMERCE).

International land routes linked important cities of Egypt, Mesopotamia, Syria and Asia Minor. The two highways through Palestine linked Arabia and Egypt with Damascus. From thence one road ran to Babylon via Tadmor (2 Ch. 8:4) and Mari; another went N to Carchemish, W to Haran and Ashur, then S to Babylon and the Persian Gulf. Finally a road N from Carchemish linked up with the Hittite city of Kanish in Asia Minor.

II. New Testament times

By NT times the Roman peace and authority had made travel relatively safe and constant. The simple acceptance in the Gospels and Acts of both short and long journeys as normal demonstrates this. Although some classical writers give the impression that travel, especially by sea, was to be avoided, those who really knew the world of their day, like Pliny and Philo, confirm the NT picture. Extensive plans for travel by land and sea were made and executed, and assurances given of return visits despite the distances involved (*e.g.* Rom. 15:24–25; Acts 15:36; 18:18–21). Such journeys were within the Roman empire: travel in foreign lands, although not unknown, was exceptional.

Within Palestine the Gospels indicate regular movement of people, including annual visits to Jerusalem for the Passover (Lk. 1:39; 2:3–5, 41ff.; Jesus' ministry). These journeys were usually made on foot and lasted a number of days, *e.g.* 5 from Nazareth to Jerusalem. As the Roman road system was not extended to Palestine until late in the 1st century AD, such internal travel would have been on the older road system (*IEJ* 1, 1950, pp. 54ff.). Journeys were also made to or from Palestine (Mt. 2:1, 13–15). Most significant are the extensive travels of *Paul. He utilized to the full the free access to travel within the Roman world. The government's support for shipping, the extermination by Augustus of pirates at sea and much brigandage on land, and the extensive road system leading to Rome, all helped the early Christian traveller. In fact, Christianity first spread directly along the great roads which led to Rome. The great E road illustrates this, with the diversion to Macedonia through divine guidance as a corollary (Acts 16:6–10); the route ran from Caesarea via Syrian Antioch, Tarsus, Derbe, Iconium, Pisidian Antioch, Laodicea, Ephesus, by sea to Corinth, and then to Brundisium or Puteoli, and by land along the Appian Way to Rome.

Begun in 312 BC the Appian Way was the first great Roman highway built. These roads, well planned and constructed, running as much as possible on a straight course, provided ready travel unequalled until the coming of the railway many centuries later. Major roads were paved over a width of 6–8 m; minor roads surfaced with sand or gravel were cambered to ditches 6 m or 3 m apart. Because of their strategic importance it was the army that often built these roads, although Augustus appointed permanent road boards in 22 BC. Josephus records that Vespasian had road-surveyors with his army during the 1st Jewish Revolt (*BJ* 3. 118). Milestones set at 1,000 paces (1,480 m) recorded the distance from the road-head or nearest city. These are valuable sources of information today. Maps of roads, and certainly lists of resting-places and distances both by land and sea were available for travellers to plan their journeys. Such itineraries, more or less complete, have been found belonging to post-NT times, but they must have existed earlier as Strabo (64 BC–AD 19) and other geographers obviously drew information from them.

Apart from the army the road system was used for the imperial post and by other travellers. The royal courier service not only handled communications but also provided transport for officials. Ordinary travellers had to make their own arrangements; so did private persons wishing to send correspondence to others, as in Paul's case. Resting-places with fresh horses were provided at cities or every 25 Roman miles, with prob-

Opposite page: Diagrammatic cross-section of a typical Roman road showing the principal parts of its construction. Either squared stones or gravel concrete were normally used for the top layer.

ably two intermediary stops in between. Again only couriers and officials were catered for. The ordinary traveller could stay at inns run by private owners. Some provided food and lodging; some lodgings only. Those in the E provinces seem to have been superior in quality, but the over-all picture of inns and innkeepers suggests a generally poor standard. Many were little removed from brothels. Hence the stress in early Christian literature on providing *hospitality. Normal distances travelled would be 16 Roman miles a day by foot, and about 25 by horse or carriage. On some occasions couriers or officials covered 100 miles a day, but on the other hand letters to Cicero from Syria took respectively 50 and 100 days for delivery. Winter months hampered or stopped travel, especially in mountainous regions or plateaux, just as most shipping ceased between mid-November and mid-March at least, preferring to sail between 26 May and 14 September (Acts 27:9ff.). Prevailing winds also determined the courses followed by the ships. Paul used trading ships, whose movements were regulated by considerations of freight, and seems to have avoided ships apparently especially provided for Jews of the Dispersion to go to Jerusalem for the Passover (Acts 20:1ff.). His final journey to Rome was by two grain ships (*SHIPS AND BOATS).

Travel on land would have been similar to that in OT times. Most would go by foot. Officials with permits could use the facilities of the courier system, both horses and carriages. Various light carriages were used (*cf.* Acts 8:29—a travelling chariot?) and some ordinary travellers rode on the heavier ox-wagons, both open and covered. There was even a drive-yourself carriage, the *essedum*! The horse, with a cloth but no saddle, was used by messengers, troops (with Paul, Acts 23:23f., 32) and some travellers; the ass continued its burden-bearing task as it does today. Both personal and group travel were common in NT times. People moving around the empire included government officials, traders, workers seeking employment, especially in large cities, students going to centres of study and the infirm seeking healing sanctuaries. In particular people in large numbers would attend games and great religious festivals. These included not only the Jewish feasts but major events in Greece and Italy. Not least among the travellers were the early Christians using the facilities provided by Rome as they spread the Gospel and corresponded with one another.

Asiatics in a caravan driving a donkey with loaded panniers. From Egypt. Beni Hasan tomb. c. 1890 BC. (PAC)

These Judaeans, on a cart pulled by oxen and leading a loaded camel, illustrate some of the ancient means of travel. Nineveh, Lachish relief. c. 700 BC. (BM)

BIBLIOGRAPHY. *LOB*; M. Avi-Yonah, 'The Development of the Roman Road System in Palestine', *IEJ* 1, 1950–1; C. Singer *et al.* (ed.), *A History of Technology*, 1, 1967; 2, 1972; D. Baly, *The Geography of the Bible*, 1967; L. Casson, *Travel in the Ancient World*, 1974. G.G.G.

TRAYS. Heb. *maḥtôṯ* (AV 'snuff dishes') were vessels made of gold, used for removing the trimmings from the lamps in the tabernacle and Temple (Ex. 25:38; 37:23; Nu. 4:9). To be distinguished from the copper firepans and censers, likewise called *maḥtôṯ* (Ex. 27:3; Nu. 16:6). D.W.G.

TREASURE, TREASURY. 'Treasure' usually refers to valuables, such as silver or gold. 'Treasures of darkness' (Is. 45:3) are hoarded riches; 'treasures of wickedness' (Mi. 6:10; *cf.* Pr. 10:2) are ill-gotten gains. In Mt. 2:11 'treasures' are boxes containing valuables.

'Treasury' and 'treasure house' frequently signify a place where treasure is stored, generally attached to a sanctuary (Jos. 6:19, 24; 1 Ki. 7:51; Dn. 1:2) or belonging to a king (2 Ki. 12:18; Est. 3:9). In Ezr. 2:69; Ne. 7:70f., 'treasury' is a fund for rebuilding the Temple. In Mk. 12:41; Lk. 21:1 it refers to the thirteen trumpet-shaped offertory boxes placed in the Court of the Women in the Temple; it is apparently used of the vicinity of these boxes in Jn. 8:20.

'Treasure' also has the wider meaning of a store. In 2 Ki. 20:13 'treasure house' is a storage place in the palace (*cf.* v. 15). In Mt. 13:52 it is a store-room.

The Bible uses 'treasure' and 'treasury' metaphorically too. Yahweh keeps sin in the treasuries of his memory (Dt. 32:34). Wisdom is to be treasured in the mind, *i.e.* valued and taken to heart (Pr. 2:1; 7:1). Awe of Yahweh is Zion's treasure (Is. 33:6). The sky is Yahweh's 'good treasury' containing rain (Dt. 28:12); in poetry, snow, hail (Jb. 38:22) and the wind (Ps. 135:7; Je. 10:13; 51:16) also have 'storehouses' or treasuries. In Zc. 11:13 *MT hayyôṣēr*, 'potter' (RSVmg.), has been emended to *hā'ôṣār*, 'treasury' with Pesh., but it is possible that *MT* can mean 'foundry worker' (*cf.* LXX, NEBmg. 'foundry').

In the Synoptic Gospels Jesus often uses 'treasure' figuratively. Since God rewards whole-hearted service in the hereafter, it is termed laying up treasure in heaven, which is contrasted with money-making in Mt. 6:19f.; Mk. 10:21 and parallels; Lk. 12:33 (*cf.* Mt. 19:21; Lk. 18:22). As the storehouse of either good or evil the heart controls conduct (Mt. 12:35; Lk. 6:45). A man's heart is where his treasure is (Mt. 6:21; Lk. 12:34), *i.e.* his interests are determined by what he values most.

Paul's phrase 'treasure in earthen vessels' (2 Cor. 4:7) contrasts the glory of the divine gospel with the weakness of its human ministers. Wisdom and knowledge are treasures to be found only in Christ (Col. 2:3).

'Peculiar treasure' was the AV and RV rendering of *s^eḡullâ* in Ex. 19:5; Ps. 135:4; Ec. 2:8. The RV also translated it thus in Mal. 3:17 (AV 'jewels'). The Heb. word occurs with 'people' in Dt. 7:6; 14:2; 26:18. It means 'personal property', and the RSV generally renders one's 'own possession' or the like. Apart from 1 Ch. 29:3; Ec. 2:8, where it is used literally of kings' possessions (RSV 'treasure'), *s^eḡullâ* is applied to Israel as Yahweh's very own people. Tit. 2:14; 1 Pet. 2:9 and possibly Eph. 1:14 use the LXX equivalents of the new Israel.

BIBLIOGRAPHY. Arndt; L. Koehler, *Lexicon in Veteris Testamenti Libros*, 1953. L.C.A.

TREES. Comments in the article on *PLANTS concerning the uncertainty of identifications apply equally to the trees.

Trees and timber are frequently mentioned in the Bible. The Holy Land itself can never have been thickly afforested, though woodlands are known to have occurred in areas now devoid of trees. Deciduous oaks covered parts of the Plain of Sharon, while evergreen oaks occurred on much of the hill country, including Carmel where remnants still exist. Aleppo pines also grew on suitable soils in the hills. Bashan and Lebanon were important sources of timber and the cedar of Lebanon is famous. Timber was required for buildings (although rough branches would suffice for humbler dwellings), ships, wooden musical instruments, farm implements, household items and even idols.

Acacia (Heb. *šiṭṭim*, AV shittah, shittim). Several species of acacia (*Acacia albida*, *A. tortilis*, *A. iraqensis*) occur in the desert wadis of Sinai and the hot Jordan valley, where the place Shittim was named after them (Jos. 2:1). The hard timber was used by the Israelites for the ark and parts of the *tabernacle or tent of meeting (Ex. 25). These spreading, thorny trees were some of the few available in Sinai and likely to produce pieces of wood of sufficient size.

Algum (Heb. *'algûmmîm*, 2 Ch. 2:8; 9:10–11). Apparently a tree native to Lebanon, and possibly the coniferous tree called the Cilician fir (*Abies cilicia*). The eastern savin or Grecian juniper (*Juniperus excelsa*) and the evergreen cypress (*Cupressus sempervirens*) have also been suggested. A doubtful suggestion is that the algum is identical with the almug tree of Ophir and that it was re-exported to Judah from Lebanon and thought by the Chronicler to be native there. The reference to 'algum trees' in 2 Ch. 9:10–11 appears to be an example of metathesis, or it may be simply an alternative form.

Almond. The almond (*Prunus dulcis* or *Amygdalus communis*) blooms in the Holy Land as early as Jan. Its Heb. name, *šāqēḏ*, 'waker', suggests the first of the fruit trees to awake after the winter. Blossoms are pink-flushed white, demonstrating an analogy with the hoary-headed patriarch (Ec. 12:5). The almond's beauty was often copied in ornamental work (Ex. 25:33–34). As well as being oil-producing, the kernel was a favourite food in Palestine, and an acceptable gift when sent by Jacob to Egypt (Gn. 43:11). It is probably denoted in Gn. 30:37, where AV renders 'hazel', and is mentioned in Je. 1:11–12, where a play on the words (*šāqēḏ* and *šōqēḏ*) illustrates God's prompt fulfilment of his promises. See A. Goor and M. Nurock, *Fruits of the Holy Land*, 1968, pp. 241–254.

Almug (Heb. *'almûggîm*, 1 Ki. 10:11–12). Imported into Judah with gold from Ophir. The location of Ophir remains a matter of conjecture, and the identity of the tree is uncertain. The traditional identification is with red sandal-wood (*Pterocarpus santalinus*), a large leguminous tree native to India and Ceylon. Others argue, however, that *'algûmmîn* and *'almûggîm* should both be identified with a Lebanese tree.

Apple (Heb. *tappûaḥ*). Referred to chiefly in Canticles, this fruit's identity has long been discussed in view of the (untenable) objection that Palestine is too hot and dry to

TREE OF LIFE
See Fruit, Part 1.

The cypress (Cupressus sempervirens) *and a branch of the tree.* (FNH)

allow satisfactory cultivation of the true apple (*Malus pumila* or *Pyrus malus*). The Heb. and Arab. words, however, favour this reading; the tree affords good shade, the fruit is sweet (Ct. 2:3) and the perfume is much appreciated (Ct. 7:8). The cultivated apple may have originated in the Caucasus area and it certainly grows well in cultivation in parts of the Holy Land. Though most of these attributes apply also to the apricot (*Armeniaca vulgaris* or *Prunus armeniaca*), about which the image in Pr. 25:11 concerning 'apples of gold' would be more apposite, it is questionable whether the apricot was established in Palestine at this time. This objection is even more serious in the case of the Chinese citron (*Citrus medicus*), a third suggestion. A W Asiatic fruit, the quince (*Cydonia oblonga*), has been proposed also, but its taste is somewhat bitter, and the Mishnah renders it by a different Heb. word. See Goor and Nurock, *op. cit.*

Cedar (Heb. *'erez*; Gk. *kedros*). *Cedrus libani*, the cedar of Lebanon, a large spreading coniferous tree formerly abundant in Mt Lebanon where it is now reduced to scattered remnants and is protected. The wood was highly esteemed for its durability and was used, for example, for building David's house (2 Sa. 5:11, *etc.*), Solomon's Temple (1 Ki. 5:6–10, *etc.*) and the new Temple built after the Babylonian Exile (Ezr. 3:7). Extra-biblical texts speak of Nebuchadrezzar's exploitation of the Lebanese forests (*cf.* Hab. 2:17). Solomon had chariots, or more probably sedans (Heb. *'appiryôn*), made of cedar (Ct. 3:9). Cedars may attain a height of 40 m and OT writers used them as a figure of stature in man (Ezk. 31:3; Am. 2:9), grandeur (Ps. 92:12) and majesty (2 Ki. 14:9). The meaning of Heb. *'ezrāḥ* in Ps. 37:35 is obscure (AV 'bay tree', RSV 'cedar of Lebanon'), but elsewhere in OT means 'native', and a plant indigenous to Palestine is indicated here.

The cedar-wood burnt by a priest during levitical cleansing (Lv. 14:4–6, 49–52; Nu. 19:6) would not have been the cedar of Lebanon but a small tree of the Sinai desert, the Phoenician juniper, *Juniperus phoenicea*, which is fragrant when burnt. See **Pine**, below.

Cypress. A tree (*Cupressus sempervirens*) with a dense habit 13–20 m high, with numerous branchlets having scale leaves and providing excellent timber. Often planted in Mediterranean cemeteries as the columnar variety (var. *pyramidalis*). RSV renders as 'cypress' the Heb. *b^erôš* (Is. 41:19; 55:13; AV 'fir'), yet the variant *b^erôṯîm* (Ct. 1:17) is taken to be 'pine'. Evidence favours cypress as being Heb. *t^e'aššûr* (Is. 41:19; 60:13; AV 'box tree'). The reference in Ho. 14:8 to an 'evergreen cypress' (RSV) or 'green fir tree' (AV) continues with a mention of its

Acacia trees flourish in the desert. They provided the Israelites with timber for the tabernacle or 'tent of meeting' during their wanderings in Sinai. (FNH)

fruit, which is presumably edible. This is probably the stone pine (*Pinus pinea*), which has a spreading crown and edible seeds in the cone.

Ebony (Heb. *hoḇnîm*, Ezk. 27:15; Egyp. *hbny*). The reddish black heart-wood of *Dalbergia melanoxylon*, a leguminous tree of the drier parts of tropical Africa. It was used extensively in ancient Egypt for fine furniture, valuable vessels, veneers, sceptres and idols. Only later was this Egyp. word transferred to the jet black timbers of the genus *Diospyros* obtained from tropical Africa, and now especially to *D. ebenum* of Ceylon. See A. Lucas and J. R. Harris, *Ancient Egyptian Materials*[4], 1962, pp. 434–435; F. N. Hepper, 'On the transference of plant names', *PEQ* 109, 1977, pp. 129f.

Fir. The RSV renders Heb. *b^erôš*, *b^erôṯîm* as 'cypress' and 'fir', which popularly applies to coniferous trees in general. Heb. scholars accept these names as applying to the tall Grecian juniper, *Juniperus excelsa*, of which the timber was imported from Lebanon for the construction of Solomon's house and Temple (1 Ki. 5:8, 10), from Senir (Hermon) for ship boards (Ezk. 27:5) and also for musical instruments (2 Sa. 6:5).

Holm (Heb. *tirzâ*, Is. 44:14). A wood used for making a heathen idol. If the 'holm tree' of RSV indicates the timber of the evergreen holm oak (*Quercus ilex*) of the central Mediterranean area, it would have had to be imported. But an indigenous tree, such as one of the native oaks, is evidently intended by the context. AV renders the Heb. word as 'cypress' (*Cupressus sempervirens*), other versions as 'plane-tree' (*Platanus orientalis*); both are native in Palestine. The Heb. word *tirzâ* is similar to the Ugaritic *tisr* for cypress.

Oak (Heb. *'allôn*, *ēlôn*). In Palestine there are three species of oak (*Quercus*). The kermes oak (*Q. coccifera*, also known as *Q. calliprinos*) is evergreen and inhabits the hills where it is often

The almond tree (Prunus dulcis) *in blossom. It is the earliest to flower in spring. In the Bible it is associated with Aaron, whose almond rod flowered and fruited overnight.* (FNH)

The cedar of Lebanon (Cedrus libani) *growing at the foot of Jebel Makhmal in Lebanon. Solomon used cedar timber in his principal buildings.* (VI)

Bottom right: Tamarisk (Tamarix aphylla) *growing beside the R. Nile. Abraham planted a tamarisk at Beersheba (Gn. 21:33).* (FNH)

One of the three species of oak, the deciduous Quercus aegilops, *which occur in Palestine, here growing near Dan.* (FNH)

A shoot of the evergreen laurel or bay-tree (Laurus nobilis) (*Ps. 37:35*, AV). *Its leaves were used for athletes' crowns.* (FNH)

seen as a shrub, although the Palestinian variety may form a rounded tree with a stout trunk when protected. One of the deciduous oaks (*Q. infectoria*) is unlikely to be referred to in the Bible owing to its limited occurrence at high altitudes. The other one, the Vallonea or Tabor oak (*Q. aegilops*, also known as *Q. ithaburensis*), occurs in lowland Palestine, but extensive felling has eliminated the woodlands that used to cover the Sharon Plain. Oaks are sturdy, hardwood trees which live to a great age, and the fruit, or acorn, is set in a cup. There is some confusion with the terebinth which has a similar stature and Heb. name, although botanically it is distinct.

An oak was a favourite tree under which to sit (1 Ki. 13:14), or to bury the dead (Gn. 35:8; 1 Ch. 10:12). Solitary trees were landmarks (1 Sa. 10:3, AV 'plain'). Its timber is seldom mentioned: it is hard and was used for oars (Ezk. 27:6). Bashan was renowned for its oaks (Is. 2:13; Ezk. 27:6; Zc. 11:2), and to this day there are many finely grown trees of *Q. aegilops* in that region. The scarlet or crimson dye, used in Heb. rites (Ex. 25:4; 26:1; Heb. 9:19, *etc.*), was obtained from a scale-insect that covered branchlets of the kermes oak. Absalom was caught by his hair in an oak (2 Sa. 18:9–10).

The sycomore fig tree (Ficus sycomorus) *favours warm conditions. Zacchaeus climbed such a tree in a street in Jericho in order to see Jesus* (*Lk. 19:4*). (FNH)

The plane tree (Platanus orientalis) *occurs naturally in N Palestine.* (FNH)

The pine (Pinus halepensis)*, here at Olympia in Greece, was an important timber tree in biblical times.* (FNH)

Top right: Poplars planted by a stream at the foot of Mt Sinai. (FNH)

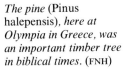

The ebony wood of ancient Egypt was obtained from the leguminous tree Dalbergia melanoxylon. (FNH)

Heb. *'*^{a}*šērâ* is translated in AV (following LXX *alsos*) as an idolatrous 'grove' or a 'high place' (Ex. 34:13; Dt. 16:21; 2 Ki. 17:16, *etc.*) since it was thought to refer to a clump of oaks. But recent scholarship holds that the reference is not to trees but to an image or cult-pole of the Canaanite goddess Asherah, consort of El, hence the RSV use of 'Asherah' and 'Asherim'. However, trees were often involved, too: 'You shall not plant any tree as an asherah' (Dt. 16:21); 'They sacrifice . . . under oak, poplar, and terebinth, because their shade is good' (Ho. 4:13). To this day 'sacred' groves of oaks and terebinths may be seen in various parts of Palestine.

Palm (Heb. *tāmār*, Gk. *phoenix*). The date palm, *Phoenix dactylifera*, a tall, slender, unbranched tree with a tuft of feather-like leaves 3–4 m long at its crown. The male and female flower clusters among the leaves are borne on separate trees. It flourishes in groves in the hot Jordan valley and appears, from the numerous references, to have been commonly planted as an isolated tree (Jdg. 4:5) in biblical times, although the fruit from highland trees was of poor quality. The palm often gave its name to the place where it grew, *e.g.* Tamar (Ezk. 47:18–19; 48:28); Hazazon-tamar (Gn. 14:7, *etc.*). Jericho was called 'the city of palm trees' (2 Ch. 28:15). The palm typified grace, elegance and uprightness (Ps. 92:12; Je. 10:5), and Tamar was used as a woman's name (2 Sa. 13:1; 14:27). It was also a symbol of victory and rejoicing, and the use of palm leaves ('branches') during Jesus' entry into Jerusalem (Jn. 12:13) was significant (*cf.* Rev. 7:9). The form of the palm was used in architectural ornamentation (1 Ki. 6:29, 32; Ezk. 40:31). See Goor and Nurock, *op. cit.*, pp. 121–151.

Pine. There is reason to believe that Heb. *'ōren* of Is. 44:14 applies to the Aleppo pine (*Pinus halepensis*), and not the cedar (RSV) or ash (AV). This pine occurs on the Palestinian hills where the soil is suitable. It is a tall slender tree with pairs of needle leaves and soft, workable timber.

Plane (Heb. *'armôn*, Gn. 30:37; Ezk. 31:8). A large deciduous tree, the plane (*Platanus orientalis*) grows in rocky stream beds in N Palestine. It has digitate leaves and round hanging flower-heads. In AV the Heb. is rendered 'chesnut' (chestnut), which is not native to that region.

Pomegranate (Heb. *rimmôn*). A small tree or bush (*Punica granatum*) growing wild in some E countries, but much prized and cultivated from earliest times, several places in Palestine bearing its name, *e.g.* Rimmon (Jos. 15:32), Gath-rimmon (Jos. 19:45), En-rimmon (Ne. 11:29). It has numerous spreading branches, dark green deciduous leaves, occasional thorns, large persistent calyx and bright red flowers. When fully ripe the apple-shaped fruit is a mixture of yellow, brown and maroon in

Fir trees depicted on a relief in the palace of Sennacherib, Nineveh. c. 690 BC. (BM)

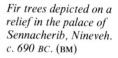

Date palms (Phoenix dactylifera) *beside a river in Babylonia, felled by Assyrian soldiers. Drawing from a relief in the palace of Sennacherib at Nineveh. c. 704–681 BC.*

Willows (Salix acmophylla) *growing in a stream on the Carmel range. The 'willows of Babylon' were probably poplars.* (FNH)

colour, and contains multitudinous seeds covered with thin skin and surrounded by watery pink pulp. There are two varieties, sweet and acid. A refreshing drink is made from the juice, a syrup (grenadine) from the seeds and an astringent medicine from the blossoms. Ornamental pomegranates decorated the high priest's robe (Ex. 28:33), the capitals of Solomon's Temple pillars (1 Ki. 7:20) and the silver shekel of Jerusalem in circulation 143–135 BC. See Goor and Nurock, *op. cit.*, pp. 70–88.

Poplar (Heb. *libneh*; *bᵉkā'îm*, 2 Sa. 5:23–24; 1 Ch. 14:14–15; RSV 'balsam tree', AV 'mulberry'). Rods of poplar, almond and plane were peeled in Jacob's deception of Laban (Gn. 30:37). The poplar tree (*Populus euphratica*) is tall with rustling leaves (2 Sa. 5:23–24; 1 Ch. 14:14–15) and, like willow (see below), grows beside the Jordan and streams where its branches root easily (Ho. 14:5). It is therefore unlikely to be found on the top of mountains as one of the shady trees under which sacrifices and offerings were made (Ho. 4:13) and this may refer to the storax (*Styrax officinalis*) which has leaves white on the lower surface. The 'ben-tree' of Gn. 49:22 (NEBmg.) is thought to have been the Euphratean poplar.

Sycamine (Gk. *sykaminos*, Lk. 17:6). The black mulberry or sycamine (*Morus nigra*), a small, sturdy tree with blood-red, edible fruits, is cultivated in Palestine. Some consider this may refer to the sycomore fig, but there is no reason to doubt that the black mulberry had been introduced by NT times.

Sycomore (Heb. *šiqmâ*, Gk. *sykomōraia*). The sycomore-fig (sycamore, RSV), *Ficus sycomorus*, a sturdy tree 10–13 m high, with a short trunk, widely spreading branches and evergreen leaves. It was, and still is, planted in Egypt and the lowlands of Palestine (1 Ki. 10:27; 2 Ch. 1:15; 9:27). Its timber was important in Egypt, where trees were scarce, for the construction of coffins and other wooden objects. The fruits are edible and were sufficiently important for King David to appoint an overseer to look after the olive-trees and sycomore-trees (1 Ch. 27:28) and for the psalmist to regard the destruction of the sycomores by frost as a calamity for the Egyptians comparable with the destruction of their vines (Ps. 78:47). In Am. 7:14 the AV translation, 'a gatherer of sycomore fruit', is incorrect, since the Heb. means a dresser or tender of the fruit. This is the operation of cutting the top of each fig to ensure its ripening as clean, insect-free fruit. Zacchaeus climbed a sycomore to see Jesus pass (Lk. 19:4); sycomore trees are still to be seen as street trees in some Palestinian towns. This should not be confused with the European sycamore (*Acer pseudoplatanus*) or the N American plane (*Platanus*) also known as sycamore.

Tamarisk (Heb. *'ēšel*, Gn. 21:33; 1 Sa. 22:6; 31:13; AV 'grove', 'tree'). A soft-wooded tree of desert wadis with numerous slender branchlets, scale-like leaves and small tassels of pink or white flowers. Several similar species grow in Palestine (*Tamarix aphylla*, *T. nilotica*, *T. pentandra*, *T. tetragyna*) especially around Beersheba where Abraham planted one. (* MANNA.)

Terebinth, turpentine tree (Heb. *'ēlâ*, Is. 6:13, AV 'teil tree'; Ho. 4:13, 'elm'). The Palestine terebinth (*Pistacia terebinthus* var. *palestina*, or *P. palestina*) is a small tree occurring very frequently in the hills. The much larger Atlantic terebinth (*P. atlantica*) of hotter drier places resembles an oak and having a similar name may be confused with it in OT. The terebinth was one of the trees under which sacrifice and offerings were made 'because their shade is good' (Ho. 4:13).

Thyine Wood (Gk. *thyinos*, Rev. 18:12, RSV 'scented wood'). Timber from the sanderac-tree (*Tetraclinis articulata*), a small coniferous tree native to NW Africa. The wood is dark, hard and fragrant, and was valued by the Greeks and Romans for cabinet-making. Another name for it is citron wood (botanically unrelated to *Citrus*), and some versions use that name here; others identify it with the almug tree.

Willow (Heb. *ʿᵃrāḇîm, ṣap̄ṣāp̄â*). Willows (*Salix acmophylla* and other species) are commonly found beside perennial streams in the Middle East, and in the biblical references are usually linked with their habitat (Jb. 40:22; Is. 25:7; 44:4; Ezk. 17:5). They are shrubs or small trees forming thickets. The 'willows of the brook' (Lv. 23:40) and the 'willows' of Babylon (Ps. 137:2) are now usually regarded as being poplar (*Populus euphratica*). Indeed M. Zohary (*Flora Palaestina*, 1, 1966, p. 29) states that in post-biblical literature the Heb. names for willow and poplar were exchanged.

The 'green withs' or new ropes used by Delilah to bind Samson (Jdg. 16:11) may have been willow bark or the fibrous twigs of the desert shrub *Thymelaea hirsuta*.

F.N.H.

TRIAL OF JESUS. The arrest of our Lord in the garden is followed, in the Synoptic tradition, by his removal to a meeting of the Jewish leaders (Mk.14:53). Jn. 18:12–13 preserves an independent account of a preliminary examination before Annas, the father-in-law of the high priest Caiaphas. There follows an interrogation concerning his disciples and his teaching, which is inconclusive because Jesus refuses to answer direct questions put by the high priest (Jn. 18:19). He is abused (Jn. 18:22) and sent as a prisoner to Caiaphas (Jn. 18:24).

The reference to 'the high priest' in Jn. 18:19 has raised a difficulty. If the Lord is questioned by Caiaphas in 18:19, why does Annas remit him to the same person in 18:24? It is tempting to see in this preliminary investigation the first of the two Jewish 'trials' which are described in Mk. 'The high priest' in Jn. 18:19 will then be Caiaphas, but the enquiry will be of an informal character. Its chronological placing will be the evening of the arrest. Jn. 18:24, which records the official appearance before Caiaphas and the full Sanhedrin, will be dated the following morning (*cf.* Jn. 18:28) and be parallel with the consultation of Mk. 15:1.

John, however, makes no mention of the issues which are so prominent in the Synoptic report of the first 'trial': the question of Jesus' Messiahship and the accusation of blasphemy.

Mk. 14:53–65 describes an appearance of the prisoner before an assembly of 'all the chief priests and the elders and the scribes' (Mk. 14:53), under the presidency of the high priest. The gravamen of the charge is the witnesses' statement that Jesus had prophesied the destruction of the Jerusalem sanctuary (*cf.* Mk. 13:2; Acts 6:13–14) and the establishment of a new temple. The claim to be the builder of a new temple seems to be the equivalent to the claim to Messiahship, according to contemporary Jewish expectation. But it was the new temple of his body, the church (Jn. 2:19; 1 Cor. 3:16; Eph. 2:21), that he had in view. (See R. J. McKelvey, *The New Temple*, 1969.)

The incriminating challenge of the high priest, 'Are you the Christ, the Son of the Blessed?' drew from him the reply, 'I am,' according to Mk. 14:62. Further, his use of the title 'the Son of man' and his quotation of Ps. 110:1 and Dn. 7:13 are an unmistakable claim to his unique status and destiny, which Caiaphas was quick to grasp and interpret as overt blasphemy. 'It was not blasphemy to claim to be the Messiah, but to speak with assurance of sharing the throne of God and of the fulfilment of Daniel's vision in himself and his community was blasphemy indeed' (Vincent Taylor).

The symbolic action of the high priest's tearing of his clothes, as laid down in the Mishnah, is the prelude to the verdict, 'guilty of death' (Mk. 14:64), and the horseplay of the officers (14:65).

A second meeting of the Sanhedrin the following morning was necessary if, with Vincent Taylor, we take Mk. 14:64 to record a condemnation of Jesus as deserving of death but not the judicial verdict which was required to be passed by 'the whole council' (15:1). The prisoner is then led away to the Roman governor Pilate for the sentence of death to be pronounced. Whether the Jewish council had the power to pronounce and carry out the death sentence on religious grounds (as Juster and Lietzmann believe) or not (so Jn. 18:31: see Barrett's full note) is a complicated question. There is evidence for the view that the Jewish leaders had the power to carry out death sentences at this time. For example, in the Mishnah the tractate *Sanhedrin* gives a variety of regulations for the different types of execution. The warning inscription on Herod's Temple, promising death to any foreigner who is caught inside the barrier and fence around the sanctuary, does not read like an idle threat. Stephen is put to death following a session of the Jewish Sanhedrin. These pieces of evidence seem hardly to harmonize with the admission of Jn. 18:31: 'It is not lawful for us to put any man to death'. E. C. Hoskyns in his commentary (pp. 616f.) sees in the use of the verb 'put to death' (*apokteinai*) a veiled and subtle reference to death by crucifixion as distinct from the customary method of capital punishment for blasphemy, *viz.* stoning. The Jewish admission, then, that they cannot carry out a judicial sentence by crucifixion is recorded by the Evangelist who means his readers to see in it (v. 32) the way in which it fulfilled unconsciously yet providentially God's age-old plan adumbrated in such verses as Dt. 21:23; Ex. 12:46; Nu. 9:12; *cf.* Jn. 19:36. See G. D. Kilpatrick's brochure, *The Trial of Jesus*, 1953; T. A. Burkill in *VC* 10, 1956, and 12, 1958.

Before Pilate the allegation turns on Jesus' claim to kingship (Mk. 15:2; Lk. 23:2) which the Jews would wish Pilate to construe in a political sense. Thus the main charge preferred is one of *majestas* or treason against the Roman imperial authority. See Jn. 19:12. Pilate, however, from the first, is suspicious of these charges and sees through the accusers' motives (Mk. 15:4, 10). He tries to extricate himself in three separate ways from the task of sentencing Jesus to death. He tries to pass the responsibility to Herod (Lk. 23:7ff.); then to offer to punish Jesus by flogging and release him (Lk. 23:16, 22); finally to release Jesus as an act of clemency at the feast (Mk. 15:6; Jn. 18:39). All these expedients fail. Herod sends him back; the fickle and disappointed crowd will not be content with any punishment less than the death sentence (Lk. 23:18, 23); and Barabbas, a condemned murderer, is preferred to Jesus the Christ. And, in spite of the repeatedly confessed innocence of the prisoner (Lk. 23:14–15, 22), he is sentenced to the death of the cross by the judgment of the procurator (Mk. 15:15), and as the

TRIAL
See Temptation, Part 3.

The tribes of Israel.

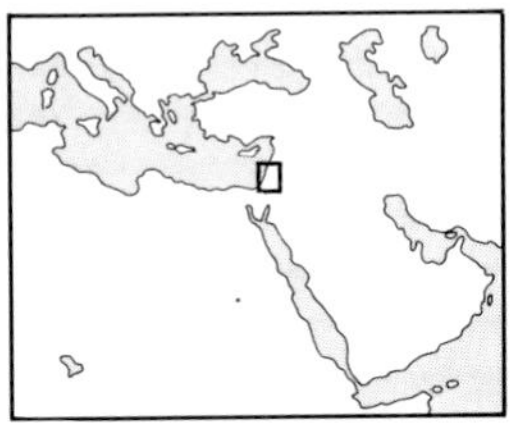

Lord himself had foreseen (Jn. 12:33; 18:32).

BIBLIOGRAPHY. A. N. Sherwin-White, *Roman Society and Roman Law in the New Testament*, 1963; J. Blinzler, *The Trial of Jesus*, 1959; P. Winter, *On the Trial of Jesus*, 1961; W. R. Wilson, *The Execution of Jesus*, 1970; D. R. Catchpole, *The Trial of Jesus*, 1971; G. S. Sloyan, *Jesus on Trial*, 1973 (bibliography); P. W. Walasky, *JBL* 94, 1975, pp. 81–93. R.P.M.

TRIBES OF ISRAEL. When the Israelites entered Canaan they entered as twelve tribes, and portions of the land were assigned to each of the twelve (*cf.* Jos. 13:1ff.). These twelve tribes were descended from the twelve sons of Jacob who had gathered themselves about their father and heard his prophecies uttered concerning them and their future (Gn. 49).

According to certain modern theories the biblical picture of the origin of the tribes cannot be accepted. The Bible states that the entire nation was in Egypt, but some of these theories hold that not all of the tribes had been in Egypt. Basic to these theories is the idea that there was a dualism or separation between the Leah and the Rachel tribes, and that the Leah tribes had settled in the cultivated land earlier than had the tribes descended from Rachel. It is sometimes held that the cult of Yahweh was brought into the land by the Joseph tribes, and then adopted by the Leah tribes. In the worship of Yahweh there arose a religious confederacy or amphictyony, somewhat akin to the amphictyonies of the old Greek states. It was thus the worship or cult of Yahweh which bound the tribes together.

According to the Pentateuchal narrative, however (Nu. 32:33–42; 34:1–35:8), Moses had already made a division between tribes to inhabit the E and those to inhabit the W side of the Jordan river. On the E side portions were allotted to the tribes of Reuben and of Gad, together with the half-tribe of Manasseh. This last was to occupy the territory S of the Sea of Galilee, including the villages of Jair together with Ashtaroth and Edrei. Gad was to occupy the land immediately S of that of Manasseh extending to the N end of the Dead Sea, and S of this section was the territory of Reuben, which reached as far S as Aroer and the Arnon.

On the W side of the Jordan in Canaan proper the remainder of the tribes were to settle. Their inheritance was to be determined by lot, save that to the tribe of Levi no inheritance was to be given. Eventually the tribes became divided into N and S, represented respectively by Ephraim and Judah. The N kingdom came to be designated by the term Israel.

In the S territory was allotted to Simeon, who appears to have occupied land in the Negeb. Above him was the allotment of Judah, including the Judaean hill country and extending as far N as to include Bethlehem and almost to the city of Jerusalem itself. Immediately above the territory of Judah and extending E to the Jordan was the territory of Benjamin. This section reached to the N only a few kilometres and only as far W as the edge of the hill country. To its W was the small section given to the tribe of Dan.

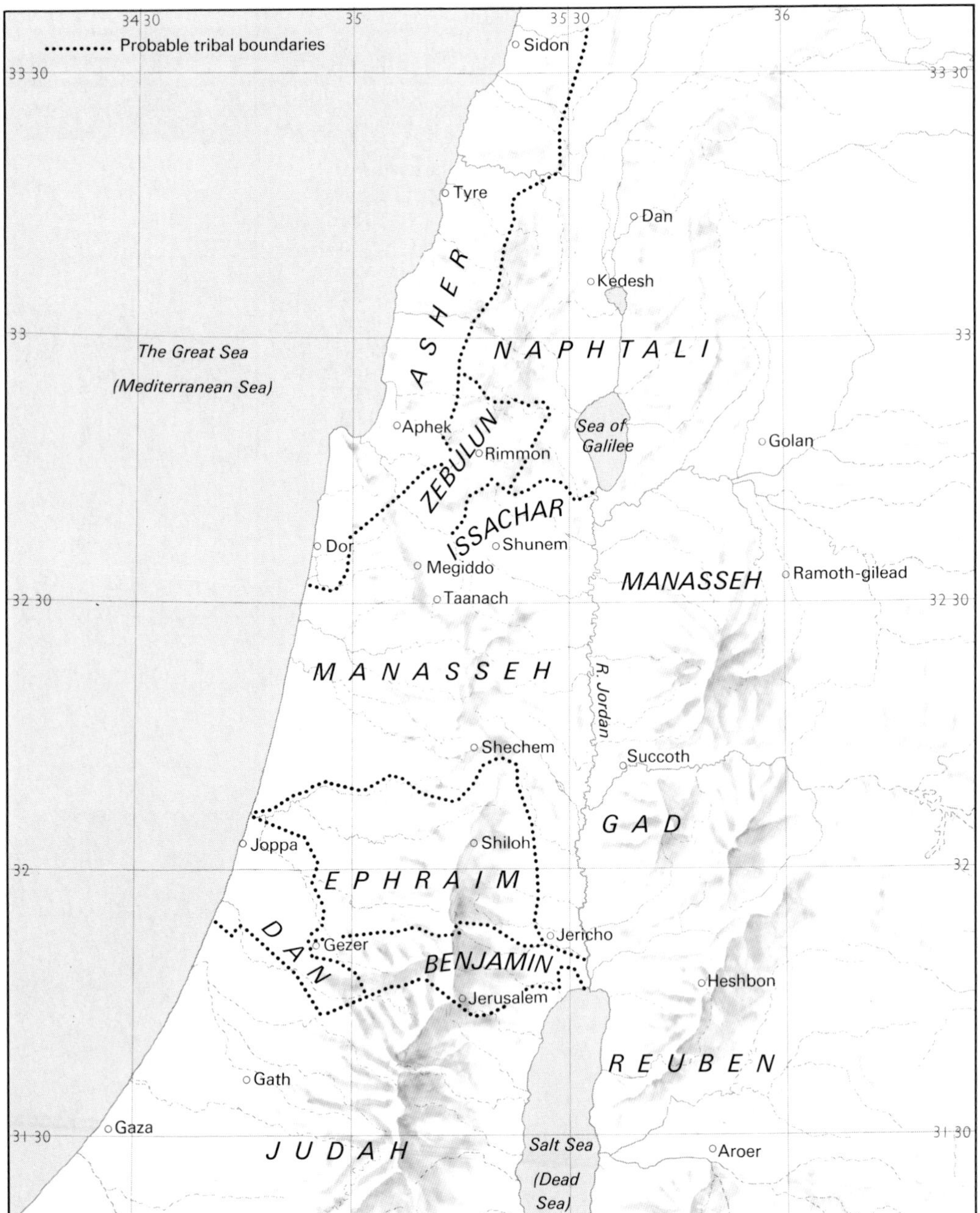

Above the two tribes of Dan and Benjamin was the territory which had been allotted to Ephraim which reached as far N as the river Kanah and Shechem. Then came the large section assigned to the half-tribe of Manasseh, comprising everything between the Mediterranean and the Jordan river and extending N to Megiddo. Above Manasseh was Issachar and Zebulun, and on the sea-coast, reaching N from Carmel, the territory of Asher.

As time went on the tribe of Judah gained more and more in significance, for it really embraced Benjamin, and Jerusalem became the capital. In the N the tribal distinctions seemed to become less important than at first, and the N kingdom as such became the enemy of Judah. The N tribes, Zebulun and Naphtali, were first carried into captivity, and then in 722 BC Samaria itself fell. Nebuchadrezzar finally conquered Jerusalem in 587 BC, and the entire nation ceased its existence as such. Tribal distinctions became of less and less significance, and practically disappeared after the Exile.

BIBLIOGRAPHY. J. Bright, *History of Israel*², 1972, pp. 130–175; M. Noth, *The History of Israel*², 1960, pp. 53–138; M. Weippert, *The Settlement of the Israelite Tribes in Palestine*, 1971. E.J.Y.

TRIBULATION. The Heb. word most commonly translated as tribulation in the Eng. Bible is *ṣārā* and its cognates. The root meaning is 'narrow' (*cf.* Nu. 22:26) or 'compressed' (Jb. 41:15) from which arises the figurative sense of straitened circumstances, and hence, affliction, distress or tribulation (Dt. 4:30; Jb. 15:24; Ps. 32:7; Is. 63:9; Jon. 2:2). The LXX uses *thlipsis* (vb. *thlibō*) to translate all the Heb. terms within this area of meaning. The basic idea here is 'severe constriction', 'narrowing' or 'pressing together' (as of grapes) (*cf.* Mt. 7:14; Mk. 3:9). Similar notions underlie the Lat. *tribulum* (a threshing sledge), which is the source of the Eng. word tribulation. The great bulk of the biblical references to tribulation are to sufferings endured by the people of God. The central and dominating factor in the biblical understanding of such suffering however is the mystery of the *thlipsis* of the *Messiah (Col. 1:24; Rev. 1:9; *cf.* Is. 63:9). All the tribulations of the Messianic people stand in this light.

1. The tribulation of the Christ is the pattern and norm for the experience of the Christian community. Thus tribulation is inevitable and to be anticipated (Mt. 13:21; Jn. 16:33; Acts 14:22; Rom. 8:35; 12:12; 1 Thes. 3:3f.; 2 Thes. 1:4; Rev. 1:9). The tribulation of Israel under the old testament finds its counterpart in the tribulation of the church under the new (Heb. 11:37; 12:1). This tribulation is particularly the lot of the apostles who exemplify in a special manner the path of suffering discipleship (Acts 20:23; 2 Cor. 1:4; 4:8, 17; 6:4; Eph. 3:13).

2. The tribulation of the people of Christ is in some sense a participation in the sufferings of Christ (Col. 1:24; *cf.* 2 Cor. 1:5; 4:10f.; Phil. 3:10; 1 Pet. 4:13). Underlying the NT teaching here may be the notion of the so-called 'afflictions of the Messiah', a tally of suffering to be endured by the righteous before the consummation of the redemptive purpose of God (*cf.* SB, 1, p. 95).

3. The tribulations of the people of Christ are instrumental in promoting their moral transformation into the likeness of Christ (Rom. 5:3f.; 2 Cor. 3:18 with 4:8–12, 16f.). In particular the experience of tribulation promotes the upbuilding of the community through enabling the comforting of others in similar experiences (2 Cor. 1:4f.; 4:10f.; Col. 1:24; 1 Thes. 1:6f.).

4. The tribulations of the people of Christ are eschatological; *i.e.* they belong to the last age, the kingdom of the end time. As such they are a witness to the inbreaking and presence of the kingdom (Mt. 24:9–14; Rev. 1:9; 7:14). A certain intensification of these tribulations will prelude the return of Christ and the consummation of the kingdom (Mt. 24:21; Mk. 13:24; 2 Thes. 1:5–6; 2 Tim. 3:1f.). B.A.M.

TRIBUTE. Tribute in the sense of an impost paid by one state to another, as a mark of subjugation, is a common feature of international relationships in the biblical world. The tributary could be either a hostile state or an ally. Like deportation, its purpose was to weaken a hostile state. Deportation aimed at depleting the man-power. The aim of tribute was probably twofold: to impoverish the subjugated state and at the same time to increase the conqueror's own revenues and to acquire commodities in short supply in his own country. As an instrument of administration it was one of the simplest ever devised: the subjugated country could be made responsible for the payment of a yearly tribute. Its non-arrival would be taken as a sign of rebellion, and an expedition would then be sent to deal with the recalcitrant. This was probably the reason for the attack recorded in Gn. 14.

There are already in Sumerian literature references to tribute, although a specific term does not yet seem to be in use. The scene on the reverse of the 'Standard' of Ur is in all probability a tribute scene, as the carriers are identical in appearance with the enemies depicted on the obverse (Woolley, *Ur Excavations*, 2, pp. 266ff.). In ancient Egypt, too, the payment of tribute is often referred to. For instance, in the inscriptions of the Theban tomb of *Tnn* we read: 'The bringing of imposts from *Rtnw* (Syria, *etc.*), and the deliveries of the northern lands: silver, gold, malachite, precious stones, of the land of the god, from the great ones of all lands, as they came to the good god (*i.e.* the king) to supplicate, and to ask for breath' (*Urkunden des äg. Altertums*, 4, 1007, 8ff.). The Egyp. kings, however, are not above representing gifts as tribute. Tuthmosis III reports having received tribute from the Assyrians, but we know that he made a reciprocal gift of 20 talents of gold to Ashur-nadin-ahi (EA 16, 21).

It is in Assyria that the role of tribute assumed its greatest importance. One of the earliest references to tribute is by Shamshi-Adad I in the 18th century BC. It continues to be mentioned down to Neo-Babylonian times. Cyrus claims that all the kings from the Mediterranean to the Persian Gulf brought him tribute.

From the Assyrian sources we learn that Israel, too, was compelled to pay tribute. Shalmaneser III (858–824 BC) exacted tribute of Jehu. On one of the panels of the Black Obelisk, Jehu is shown prostrating himself before the Assyrian king. Adad-nirari III (810–782) claims that Israel was among a number of states (Tyre, Sidon, Edom and Philistia) from whom he received tribute (*DOTT*, p. 51). Tiglath-pileser III (745–727) received tribute from Menahem of Israel and from Ahaz (called by him Jehoahaz). He later states that

Tribute including a tray of fruit, tin, silver, gold, golden cups and buckets, a golden vase, carried by Israelites to Shalmaneser III of Assyria on behalf of Jehu of Israel. Black obelisk, Nimrud. c. 840 BC. (BM)

Tribute of gold from Nubia. Wall-painting from tomb at Thebes. c. 1400 BC. (MH)

he deposed Pekah, and put Hoshea on the throne (as a puppet king), and received tribute of gold and silver (*DOTT*, pp. 54ff., and 2 Ki. 15:17–30; 16:7–18). Sargon II (722–705) not only exacted tribute from Israel but deported part of the population of Samaria (2 Ki. 17:6, 24–34; 18:11). The most detailed list of a tribute payment is that given by Sennacherib (705–681). It consists not only of large quantities of gold and silver but also of rich inlaid furniture and even musicians sent by Hezekiah (*DOTT*, p. 67). Manasseh, king of Judah, is mentioned as a tributary of Esarhaddon (681–669) and Ashurbanipal (668–627).

There are a number of terms in the OT denoting taxes in general, but none seems to be confined exclusively to the meaning of tribute. *'eškār*, used only twice (Ps. 72:10; Ezk. 27:15), could have the meaning of tribute, at least in the Psalm. *mas* occurs 22 times, but seems generally to have the meaning of corvée (*cf.* Ex. 1:11 or 1 Ki. 5:13); in a passage like Esther 10 it would refer to tribute. *maśśā'* twice seems to mean impost or tax (Ho. 8:10 and 2 Ch. 17:11). *'ōneš* in 2 Ki. 23:33, and possibly also in Pr. 19:19, denotes tribute, but the verb from the same root can mean to impose a fine (*cf.* Ex. 21:22). *meḵes*, translated 'tribute' in the AV in Nu. 31:28, 37–41, was a levy on the spoils of war. *b^{e}lô* (Aram.), as it is used of a group in the community, cannot refer to 'tribute' in the strict sense (Ezr. 4:13, 20; 7:24). *middâ*, used in both Heb. and Aram. contexts (Ezr. 4:13, 20; 6:8; 7:24; Ne. 5:4), may refer to tribute.

In several passages the Heb. *minḥâ* may refer to tribute, as RSV at 2 Sa. 8:2, 6, brought by conquered Moabites and Syrians to David, or 2 Ki. 17:4, sent by Egypt to Assyria, but it is clearly a gift in 2 Ki. 20:12, for *Merodach-baladan was no vassal of Hezekiah.

That tribute is not given greater prominence in the OT may be due to the fact that Israel, being a small nation, had few opportunities of imposing tribute. The gifts that Hiram, king of Tyre, brought to Solomon were the gifts of an ally and a friend, and it was probably taken for granted that Solomon would reciprocate (1 Ki. 5:10 and *passim*; 9:11).

(*TAX; *TEMPLE; *MONEY; *TREASURE.)

BIBLIOGRAPHY. W. J. Martin, *Tribut und Tributleistungen bei den Assyrern*, 1936; J. N. Postgate, *Neo-Assyrian Royal Grants and Decrees*, 1969, pp. 9–16; J. Nougayrol, *PRU*, 3, pp. 31–32. W.J.M.
A.R.M.

TRINITY. The word Trinity is not found in the Bible, and though used by Tertullian in the last decade of the 2nd century, it did not find a place formally in the theology of the church till the 4th century. It is, however, the distinctive and all-comprehensive doctrine of the Christian faith. It makes three affirmations: that there is but one God, that the Father, the Son and the Spirit is each God, and that the Father, the Son and the Spirit is each a distinct Person. In this form it has become the faith of the church since it received its first full formulation at the hands of Tertullian, Athanasius and Augustine.

I. Derivation

Though it is not a biblical doctrine in the sense that any formulation of it can be found in the Bible, it can be seen to underlie the revelation of God, implicit in the OT and explicit in the NT. By this we mean that though we cannot speak confidently of the revelation of the Trinity in the OT, yet once the substance of the doctrine has been revealed in the NT, we can read back many implications of it in the OT.

a. In the Old Testament

It can be understood that in ages when revealed religion had to hold its own in the environment of pagan idolatry, nothing that would imperil the oneness of God could be freely given. The first imperative, therefore, was to declare the existence of the one living and true God, and to this task the OT is principally dedicated. But even in the opening pages of the OT we are taught to attribute the existence and persistence of all things to a threefold source. There are passages where God, his Word and his Spirit are brought together, as, for example, in the narrative of the creation where Elohim is seen to create by means of his Word and Spirit (Gn. 1:2–3). It is thought that Gn. 1:26 points in the same direction, where it is stated that God said: 'Let us make man in our image, after our likeness', followed by the statement of accomplishment: 'So God created man in his own image', a striking case of plural and singular interchanged, suggesting plurality in unity.

There are many other passages where God and his Word and Spirit are brought together as 'co-causes of effects'. In Is. 63:8–10 we have the three speakers, the covenant God of Israel (v. 8), the angel of the presence (v. 9) and the Spirit 'grieved' by their rebellion (v. 10). Both the creative activity of God and his government are, at a later stage, associated with the Word personified as 'Wisdom' (Pr. 8:22; Jb. 28:23–27), as well as with the Spirit as the Dispenser of all blessings and the source of physical strength, courage, culture and government (Ex. 31:3; Nu. 11:25; Jdg. 3:10).

The threefold source revealed in creation becomes still more evident in the unfolding of redemption. At an early stage there are the remarkable phenomena connected with the angel of Yahweh who receives and accepts divine honour (Gn. 16:2–13; 22:11–16). Not in every OT passage in which it appears does the designation refer to a divine being, for it is clear that in such passages as 2 Sa. 24:16; 1 Ki. 19:35, the reference is to a created angel invested with divine authority for the execution of a special mission. In other passages the angel of Yahweh not only bears the divine name, but has divine dignity and power, dispenses divine deliverance, and accepts homage and adoration proper only to God. In short, the Messiah has deity ascribed to him, even when he is regarded as a person distinct from God (Is. 7:14; 9:6).

The Spirit of God is also given prominence in connection with revelation and redemption, and is assigned his office in the equipment of the Messiah for his work (Is. 11:2; 42:1; 61:1), and of his people for the response of faith and obedience (Joel 2:28; Is. 32:15; Ezk. 36:26–27). Thus the God who revealed himself objectively through the Angel-Messenger revealed himself subjectively in and through the Spirit, the Dispenser of all blessings and gifts within the sphere of redemption. The threefold Aaronic blessing (Nu. 6:24) must also be noted as perhaps the prototype of the NT apostolic blessing.

b. In the Gospels

By way of contrast it must be remembered that the OT was written before the revelation of the doctrine of the Trinity was clearly given, and the NT after it. In the

TRIGON
See Music, Part 2.

NT it was given particularly in the incarnation of God the Son, and the outpouring of the Holy Spirit. But however dim the light in the old dispensation, the Father, Son and Spirit of the NT are the same as in the OT.

It can be said, however, that preparatory to the advent of Christ, the Holy Spirit came into the consciousness of God-fearing men in a degree that was not known since the close of Malachi's prophetic ministry. John the Baptist, more especially, was conscious of the presence and calling of the Spirit, and it is possible that his preaching had a trinitarian reference. He called for repentance toward God, faith in the coming Messiah, and spoke of a baptism of the Holy Spirit, of which his baptism with water was a symbol (Mt. 3:11).

The special epochs of trinitarian revelation were as follows.

(i) *The annunciation.* The agency of the Trinity in the incarnation was disclosed to Mary in the angelic annunciation that the Holy Spirit would come upon her, the power of the Most High would overshadow her and the child born of her would be called the Son of God (Lk. 1:35). Thus the Father and the Spirit were disclosed as operating in the incarnation of the Son.

(ii) *The baptism of Christ.* At the baptism of Christ in the Jordan the three Persons can be distinguished, the Son being baptized, the Father speaking from heaven in recognition of his Son and the Spirit descending in the objective symbol of a dove. Jesus, having thus received the witness of the Father and the Spirit, received authority to baptize with the Holy Spirit. John the Baptist would seem to have recognized very early that the Holy Spirit would come from the Messiah, and not merely with him. The third Person was thus the Spirit of God and the Spirit of Christ.

(iii) *The teaching of Jesus.* The teaching of Jesus is trinitarian throughout. He spoke of the Father who sent him, of himself as the one who reveals the Father, and the Spirit as the one by whom he and the Father work. The interrelations between Father, Son and Spirit are emphasized throughout (see Jn. 14:7, 9–10). He declared with emphasis: 'I will pray the Father, and he will give you another counsellor (Advocate), to be with you for ever, even the Spirit of truth' (Jn. 14:16–26). There is thus a distinction made between the Persons, and also an identity. The Father who is God sent the Son, and the Son who is God sent the Spirit, who is himself God. This is the basis of the Christian belief in the 'double procession' of the Spirit. In his disputation with the Jews, Christ claimed that his Sonship was not simply from David, but from a source that made him David's Lord, and that he had been so at the very time when David uttered the words (Mt. 22:43). This would indicate both his deity and his pre-existence.

(iv) *The commission of the Risen Lord.* In the commission given by Christ before his ascension, instructing his disciples to go into the whole world with his message, he made specific reference to baptism as 'in the name of the Father and of the Son and of the Holy Spirit'. It is significant that the name is one, but within the bounds of the one name there are three distinct Persons. The Trinity as tri-unity could not be more clearly expressed.

c. The New Testament writings

The evidence of the NT writings, apart from the Gospels, is sufficient to show that Christ had instructed his disciples on this doctrine to a greater extent than is recorded by any of the four Evangelists. They whole-heartedly proclaim the doctrine of the Trinity as the threefold source of redemption. The outpouring of the Spirit at Pentecost brought the personality of the Spirit into greater prominence and at the same time shed light anew from the Spirit upon the Son. Peter, in explaining the phenomenon of Pentecost, represents it as the activity of the Trinity: 'This Jesus . . . being . . . exalted at the right hand of God, and having received from the Father the promise of the Holy Spirit, he has poured out this which you see and hear' (Acts 2:32–33). So the church of Pentecost was founded on the doctrine of the Trinity.

In 1 Cor. there is mention of the gifts of the Spirit, the varieties of service for the same Lord and the inspiration of the same God for the work (1 Cor. 12:4–6).

Peter traces salvation to the same triunal source: 'destined by God the Father and sanctified by the Spirit for obedience to Jesus Christ' (1 Pet. 1:2). The apostolic benediction: 'The grace of the Lord Jesus Christ and the love of God and the fellowship of the Holy Spirit be with you all' (2 Cor. 13:14), not only sums up the apostolic teaching, but interprets the deeper meaning of the Trinity in Christian experience, the saving grace of the Son giving access to the love of the Father and to the communion of the Spirit.

What is amazing, however, is that this confession of God as One in Three took place without struggle and without controversy by a people indoctrinated for centuries in the faith of the one God, and that in entering the Christian church they were not conscious of any break with their ancient faith.

II. Formulation

Although Scripture does not give us a formulated doctrine of the Trinity, it contains all the elements out of which theology has constructed the doctrine. The teaching of Christ bears testimony to the true personality of each of the distinctions within the Godhead, and also sheds light upon the relations existing between the three Persons. It was left to theology to formulate from this a doctrine of the Trinity. The necessity to formulate the doctrine was thrust upon the church by forces from without, and it was, in particular, its faith in the deity of Christ and the necessity to defend it, that first compelled the church to face the duty of formulating a full doctrine of the Trinity for its rule of faith. Irenaeus and Origen share with Tertullian the responsibility for the formulation which is still, in the main, that of the church catholic. Under the leadership of Athanasius the doctrine was proclaimed as the faith of the church at the Council of Nicea (AD 325), and at the hands of Augustine, a century later, it received a formulation enshrined in the so-called Athanasian Creed that is accepted by Trinitarian churches to this day. After it had received a further elucidation at the hands of John Calvin (for which see B. B. Warfield, *Calvin and Augustine*, 1956, pp. 189–284), it passed into the body of the reformed faith.

In the relationship between the Persons there are recognizable distinctions.

a. Unity in diversity

In most formularies the doctrine is stated by saying that God is One in his essential being, but that in his being there are three Persons, yet so as not to form separate and distinct individuals. They are three modes or forms in which the divine essence exists. 'Person' is, however, an imperfect expression of the truth inasmuch as the term denotes to us a separate rational and moral individual. But in the being of God there are not three individuals, but three personal self-distinctions within the one divine essence. Then again, personality in man implies independence of will, actions and feelings leading to behaviour peculiar to the person. This cannot be thought of in connection with the Trinity. Each person is self-conscious and self-directing, yet never acting independently or in opposition. When we say that God is a Unity we mean that, though God is in himself a threefold centre of life, his life is not split into three. He is one in essence, in personality and in will. When we say that God is a Trinity in Unity, we mean that there is a unity in diversity, and that the diversity manifests itself in Persons, in characteristics and in operations.

b. Equality in dignity

There is perfect equality in nature, honour and dignity between the Persons. Fatherhood belongs to the very essence of the first Person and it was so from all eternity. It is a personal property of God 'from whom every family in heaven and on earth is named' (Eph. 3:15).

The Son is called the 'only begotten' perhaps to suggest uniqueness rather than derivation. Christ always claimed for himself a unique relationship to God as Father, and the Jews who listened to him apparently had no illusions about his claims. Indeed they sought to kill him because he 'called God his own Father, making himself equal with God' (Jn. 5:18).

The Spirit is revealed as the One who alone knows the depths of God's nature: 'For the Spirit searches everything, even the depths of God . . . No one comprehends the thoughts of God except the Spirit of God' (1 Cor. 2:10f.). This is saying that the Spirit is 'just God himself in the innermost essence of his being'.

This puts the seal of NT teaching upon the doctrine of the equality of the three Persons.

c. Diversity in operation

In the functions ascribed to each of the Persons in the Godhead, especially in man's redemption, it is clear that a certain degree of subordination is involved (in relation, though not in nature); the Father first, the Son second, the Spirit third. The Father works through the Son by the Spirit. Thus Christ can say: 'My Father is greater than I.' As the Son is sent by the Father, so the Spirit is sent by the Son. As it was the Son's office to reveal the Father, so it is the Spirit's office to reveal the Son, as Christ testified: 'He will glorify me, for he will take what is mine and declare it to you' (Jn. 16:14).

It has to be recognized that the doctrine arose as the spontaneous expression of the Christian experience. The early Christians knew themselves to be reconciled to God the Father, and that the reconciliation was secured for them by the atoning work of the Son, and that it was mediated to them as an experience by the Holy Spirit. Thus the Trinity was to them a fact before it became a doctrine, but in order to preserve it in the credal faith of the church the doctrine had to be formulated.

III. Implications of the doctrine

The implications of the doctrine are vitally important not only for theology, but for Christian experience and life.

a. It means that God is revealable

Revelation is as natural for God as it is for the sun to shine. Before there had been any created being, there was self-revelation within the Trinity, the Father revealing to the Son, the Father and the Son revealing to the Spirit, and the Spirit communicating that revelation within the Being of God. When God willed to create a universe it implied no change in God's behaviour; it meant letting his revelation shine outwards to his creation. And this he did by his revealing Spirit.

b. It means that God is communicable

As the sun shines it communicates its light and heat and energy. So if God is a fellowship within himself he can let that fellowship go out to his creatures and communicate himself to them according to their capacity to receive. This is what happened supremely when he came to redeem men: he let his fellowship bend down to reach outcast man and lift him up. And so because God is a Trinity he has something to share: it is his own life and communion.

c. It means that the Trinity is the basis of all true fellowship in the world

Since God is within himself a fellowship, it means that his moral creatures who are made in his image find fullness of life only within a fellowship. This is reflected in marriage, in the home, in society and above all in the church whose *koinōnia* is built upon the fellowship of the three Persons. Christian fellowship is, therefore, the divinest thing on earth, the earthly counterpart of the divine life, as Christ indeed prayed for his followers: 'That they may all be one; even as thou, Father, art in me, and I in thee, that they also may be in us' (Jn. 17:21).

d. It gives variety to the life of the universe

There is, as we have seen, diversity in the life of God. God the Father designs, God the Son creates, God the Spirit quickens; a great diversity of life and operation and activity. For that reason we can realize that if the universe is a manifestation of God, we can expect a diversity of life within the whole of the created universe. We think that the so-called uniformity of nature is utterly untrue. All the wonders of creation, all the forms of life, all the movement in the universe, are a reflection, a mirroring, of the manifold life of God. There is no monotonous sameness, no large-scale uniformity of pattern, for nature reflects the many-sidedness of the nature and character of the living God.

BIBLIOGRAPHY. J. R. Illingworth, *The Doctrine of the Trinity*, 1909; C. W. Lowry, *The Trinity and Christian Devotion*, 1946; A. E. Garvie, *The Christian Doctrine of the Godhead*, 1925; H. Bavinck, *The Doctrine of God*, 1951, pp. 255–334; B. B. Warfield in *ISBE* (*s.v.* 'Trinity'); R. S. Franks, *The Doctrine of the Trinity*, 1953; K. Barth, *Church Dogmatics*, E.T. 1936, 1, pp. 339ff.; D. Lamont, *Christ and the World of Thought*, 1934, pp. 221–247.

R.A.F.

TROAS. The principal seaport of NW Asia Minor, established some 20 km SSW. of the site of Troy (Ilium) by the successors of Alexander the Great, and named Alexandria after him. 'Troas' was originally a distinguishing epithet, but it became the usual designation

TROY
See Troas, Part 3.

TRUST
See Faith, Part 1.

TRUSTEE
See Governor, Part 2.

Troas, the principal seaport of NW Asia Minor at the time of Alexander the Great.

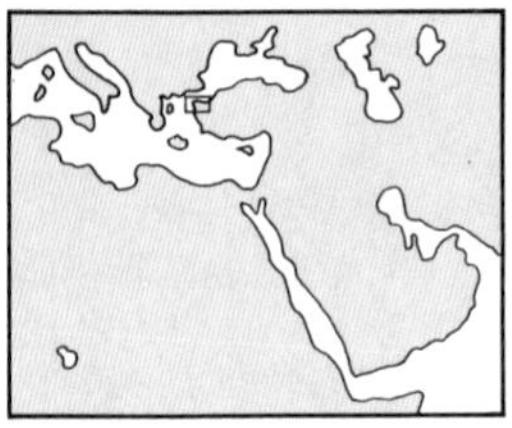

of the city after Augustus made it a Roman colony. The place grew rapidly around its artificial harbour-basins, which provided necessary shelter from the prevailing northerlies at a focal meeting-point of sea-routes, close to the mouth of the Hellespont (Dardanelles). Troas was the port for the crossing to *Neapolis in Macedonia for the land-route to Rome. Though rarely mentioned in secular literature, it had a strategic function in the Roman system of communication, and its importance emerges clearly from unobtrusive references both in Acts and the Epistles. It was the scene of the vision of the 'man of Macedonia' (Acts 16:8–11) and of the raising of Eutychus (Acts 20:5–12). The former incident was the occasion of the coming of the gospel from Asia to Europe, though this aspect is not stressed in Acts. Perhaps this also marks the meeting of Paul with Luke, for the 'we-passages' begin at Acts 16:10. Later Paul found an 'open door' at Troas (2 Cor. 2:12), and again stayed there as long as possible when in haste to reach Jerusalem (Acts 20:6, 13). Paul's urgent request in 2 Tim. 4:13 may reflect a hurried departure from Troas under arrest. Ignatius, too, after sending three of his epistles from Troas, had to sail in haste for Neapolis as a prisoner bound for Rome (*Ep. to Polycarp* 8), when the weather permitted.

The site of Troas at Dalyan is now deserted, but there are remains of the harbour, baths, stadium and other buildings, and several kilometres of the walls may be traced.

BIBLIOGRAPHY. C. J. Hemer, 'Alexandria Troas', *TynB* 26, 1975, pp. 79–112.

C.J.H.

TROGYLLIUM (or Trogyllia). A promontory of the W coast of Asia Minor between Ephesus and Miletus, and reaching to within 2 km of Samos. Paul's delay there (Acts 20:15) was no doubt due to the difficulty of navigating a strait in darkness. The Alexandrian text omits reference to this delay at Trogyllium, but is almost certainly at fault here.

K.L.McK.

TROPHIMUS. An Ephesian Christian who evidently accompanied Paul to Europe after the Ephesian riot, later re-crossing and awaiting Paul at Troas for the journey to Jerusalem—doubtless as one of the delegates of the Asian churches with the collection (Acts 20:1–5; *cf.* 1 Cor. 16:1–4). In Jerusalem, however, Jewish pilgrims from Asia recognized him in Paul's company, and afterwards, finding Paul in the Temple with four others, jumped to the false conclusion that he had introduced Trophimus there (Acts 21:27ff.). Trespass beyond the Court of the Gentiles would for Trophimus be to risk the death penalty. The incident issued in a riot, and Paul's arrest.

2 Tim. 4:20 states that Paul left Trophimus sick at Miletus. This was near Trophimus' own city; but if Timothy was himself in the Ephesus area it may seem strange that he needed this information. The circumstances and intention of the verse are, however, uncertain: it may be connected with greetings, like the immediate context, or perhaps Paul's mind has reverted to the diminution of his band of helpers (*cf.* vv. 10–12). P. N. Harrison (*Problem of the Pastoral Epistles*, 1921, pp. 118ff.) argues that Paul was *en route* for Troas (*cf.* 2 Cor. 2:12) when he left Trophimus; G. S. Duncan (*St. Paul's Ephesian Ministry*, 1929, pp. 191ff.) that he was returning from Corinth to Asia (*cf.* 2 Cor. 1:8). Preferable to these intricate hypotheses is the view that Paul was heading W, destined for his second Roman imprisonment.

A.F.W.

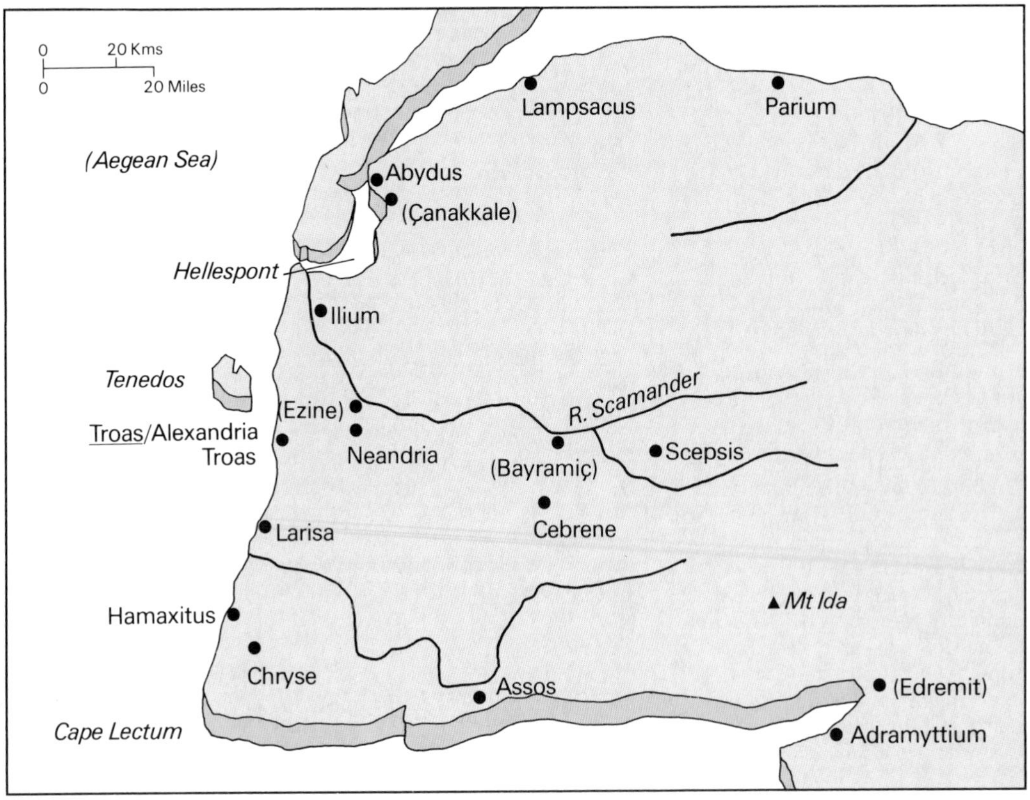

TRUMPETS, FEAST OF. 'Day of blowing the trumpets' (Heb. *yôm* t^{e}*rûʿâ*, Nu. 29:1) or 'memorial of blowing of trumpets' (Lv. 23:24). The 7th month in the Jewish *calendar, *tišri* (Sept./Oct.), was the beginning of the civil year. The first day of the month was to be 'a day of solemn rest', in which 'no laborious work' was to be done. The LXX of Nu. 29:1 renders the phrase *yôm* t^{e}*rûʿâ* by *hēmera sēmasias*, 'a day of signalling', but the Mishnah and traditional Jewish practice have understood by this the use of the *šôp̄ār*, usually, though not always, made of ram's horn. Tradition is not clear as to what precisely was meant by the trumpet-blowing, which was accompanied by reading of relevant passages of Scripture (H. G. Friedmann, *JQR* 1, 1888, pp. 62ff.).

BIBLIOGRAPHY. N. H. Snaith, *The Jewish New Year Festival*, 1947.

T.H.J.

TRUTH. Truth, like its relation *knowledge, is used in the OT in two senses: (1) the intellectual, of facts which may be ascertained to be true or false (Dt. 17:4; 1 Ki. 10:6); (2) far more commonly, the

existential and moral, of truth as the attribute of a person. Joseph's brothers are detained in prison 'that your words may be tested, whether there is truth in you' (Gn. 42:16), *i.e.* whether they are dependable, consistent, of reliable character. It is significant that of the Heb. words translated 'truth' (*'^{e}meṯ*, *'^{e}mûnâ*), the latter is sometimes rendered by the EVV as 'faithfulness' (Dt. 32:4; Ho. 2:20) (*AMEN). The OT thinks much more of the basis of truth in a reliable person than of the mere facts of the case. This reliability is basically an attribute of God (Ps. 31:5; Je. 10:10), whose truth 'reaches to the clouds' (Ps. 108:4). The God of the Bible is thus very far removed from the capricious pagan deities. He is true, *i.e.* consistent, both in his loving care for his children (Gn. 32:9f.) and in his implacable hostility against sin (Ps. 54:5).

It is no far cry from truth as an attribute of God himself to one of his activity. So he judges truly (Ps. 96:13), and sends truth forth (Ps. 57:3, AV). His word is true in the sense that it is permanently valid. 'As Thou art truth, so is Thy word truth, for it is written "Thy word, O God, stands fast in heaven" (Ps. 119:89)' (Exodus Rabbah on 29:1). Truth is demanded of man as his response to God in obedience to the law (Ps. 119:151) and in his inmost nature (Ps. 51:6), and is the bedrock of all human relationships (Ex. 20:16; Dt. 5:20).

In Gk. literature, the words for truth (*alētheia, alēthēs, alēthinos*) do not have the same personal and moral connotation. Rather, truth is intellectual. It is 'the full or real state of affairs . . . As in judicial language the *alētheia* is the actual state of affairs to be maintained against different statements, so historians use it to denote real events as distinct from myths, and philosophers to indicate real being in the absolute sense' (R. Bultmann, *TDNT* 1, p. 238).

In the NT these Gk. words occur commonly, and bring with them both their OT and their classical and Hellenistic Gk. meanings, so that it is often an extremely delicate matter to decide which nuance predominates. It is possible, however, to distinguish three broad senses in which the words are used, even though these may overlap.

1. Dependability, truthfulness, uprightness of character (the Heb. sense predominating). This applies to God (Rom. 3:7; 15:8) and to men (2 Cor. 7:14; Eph. 5:9) alike. The use of the actual word 'truth' in this sense is not common, but the thought of a God who can be trusted to keep his word is implicit throughout the NT.

2. Truth in the absolute sense of that which is real and complete as opposed to what is false and wanting (Mk. 5:33; Eph. 4:25). The Christian faith in particular is the truth (Gal. 2:5; Eph. 1:13). Jesus claimed that he was truth personified (Jn. 14:6; *cf.* Eph. 4:21). He mediates the truth (Jn. 1:17) and the Holy Spirit leads men into it (Jn. 16:13; *cf.* 14:17; 1 Jn. 4:6), so that Jesus' disciples know it (Jn. 8:32; 2 Jn. 1), do it (Jn. 3:21), abide in it (Jn. 8:44), and their new birth as God's children rests upon it (Jas. 1:18). This truth is more than a credal formula, it is God's active word which must be obeyed (Rom. 2:8; Gal. 5:7).

3. The adjective *alēthinos* especially sometimes carries the 'Platonic' sense of something real as opposed to mere appearance or copy. The Christ is thus a minister of the true tabernacle (Heb. 8:2) in contrast with the shadows of the levitical ritual (Heb. 8:4f.). In clear allusion to the words of institution of the Lord's Supper, Jesus declares that he is the true bread (Jn. 6:32, 35) and the true vine (Jn. 15:1), *i.e.* that he is the eternal reality symbolized by the bread and wine. Similarly, the true worshippers (Jn. 4:23) are not so much sincere as real. Their worship is a real approach to God who is spirit, in contrast to the ritual which restricts God to Jerusalem or Mt Gerizim (Jn. 4:21), and which can at best symbolize and at worst distort him.

BIBLIOGRAPHY. R. Bultmann, *TDNT* 1, pp. 232–251; C. H. Dodd, *The Interpretation of the Fourth Gospel*, 1953, pp. 139f., 170–178; D. J. Theron, '*Aletheia* in the Pauline Corpus', *EQ* 26, 1954, pp. 3–18; A. C. Thiselton, *NIDNTT* 3, pp. 874–902. F.H.P.

TRYPHAENA AND TRYPHOSA. Two women, probably—from the manner of mentioning them and

The Feast of Trumpets was marked by the blowing of the ram's horn (šôp̄ār). (MEPhA)

TRY
See Temptation, Part 3.

TUBAL
See Meshech, Part 2.

TUMBLEWEED
See Plants, Part 3.

TURBAN
See Dress, Part 1.

TURIN SHROUD
See Burial and mourning, NT, Part 1.

TURN THE BACK
See Neck, Part 2.

TURN TO GOD
See Conversion, Part 1.

TURTLE
See Animals, Part 1.

TURTLE DOVE
See Animals, Part 1.

TUTOR
See Schoolmaster, Part 3.

TWELVE FOUNDATIONS
See Jewels, Part 2.

TWELVE GATES
See Jewels, Part 2.

TWIN
See Thomas, Part 3.

TWIN BROTHERS
See Castor and Pollux, Part 1.

TWO
See Number, Part 2.

TWO WAYS
See Way, Part 3.

TYPE
See Typology, Part 3.

the similarity of their names—sisters, and possibly twin sisters, greeted in Rom. 16:12. Like other women addressed there (Mary, v. 6; Persis, v. 12), they were noted for 'work'—the recurrence of this term may indicate some regular form of service (*cf.* W. Sanday and A. C. Headlam, *Romans*, *ICC*, 1902, p. xxxv). The names ('Delicate' and 'Dainty') were widely used, including in Rome, where Lightfoot (*Philippians*, pp. 175f.) pointed to several examples in 'Caesar's household' in Paul's time. Another contemporary Tryphaena was the daughter of Polemon I of Pontus, mother of three kings, who appears in the *Acts of Paul and Thecla*.
A.F.W.

TUBAL-CAIN. The son of Lamech by Zillah (Gn. 4:22) and half-brother of *Jabal and *Jubal. In the words of AV he was 'an instructer of every artificer in brass and iron', but this could be as well translated 'a hammerer of every cutting tool of copper or iron', and could mean either that he was a metal-smith, the most commonly held view, or that he discovered the possibilities of cold forging native copper and meteoric iron, a practice attested archaeologically from the pre-historic times. T.C.M.

TYCHICUS. An Asian—the 'Western' Text says an Ephesian—who accompanied Paul to Jerusalem, doubtless as a delegate of his church, with the collection (Acts 20:4; *cf.* 1 Cor. 16:1–4). He was the apostle's personal representative—probably (taking 'sent' as an epistolary aorist) the bearer of the letters—to the Colossians (Col. 4:7–9) and Ephesians (Eph. 6:21–22), and, should *Ephesians be a circular letter, to other Asian churches as well. Paul seems to have considered him a possible relief for Titus in Crete (Tit. 3:12), and to have sent him to Ephesus (bearing 2 Tim.?) just when Timothy was needed elsewhere (2 Tim. 4:12). These commissions reflect that trustworthiness which Paul commends (Eph. 6:21; Col. 4:7). His designation as a 'minister' in these contexts probably relates to service to the church, possibly to service to Paul, most improbably to the status of *deacon. Some who have questioned the authenticity of Eph. have connected Tychicus with its origin (*cf.* W. L. Knox, *St. Paul and the Church of the Gentiles*, 1939, p. 203; C. L. Mitton, *Epistle to the Ephesians*, 1950, p. 268). A.F.W.

TYPOLOGY (Gk. *typos*, 'seal-impression'). A way of setting forth the biblical history of salvation so that some of its earlier phases are seen as anticipations of later phases, or some later phase as the recapitulation or fulfilment of an earlier one.

I. In the Old Testament

There are two archetypal epochs in the OT which are repeatedly presented in this way: the creation and the Exodus from Egypt. The Exodus is viewed as a new creation, or at least as a repetition of the original creative activity. He who in the beginning constrained the unruly sea within bounds, saying, 'Thus far shall you come, and no farther' (Gn. 1:9f.; Jb. 38:8–11), manifested the same power when he restrained the waters of the sea of reeds at the Exodus (Ex. 14:21–29). This parallelism is specially emphasized when the Creator's overthrow of the primeval symbols of chaos, *Rahab and the dragon (Jb. 26:12f.), is taken up and applied to his victory at the Exodus (Pss. 74:12–14; 89:8–10). Rahab becomes a 'type' of Egypt (*cf.* Is. 30:7) and the dragon (Leviathan) of Pharaoh (*cf.* Ezk. 29:3).

The restoration of Israel from the Babylonian captivity is portrayed as both a new creation and a new exodus. The verbs which are used of the Creator's workmanship in Gn. 1 and 2 (Heb. *bārā'*, *yāṣar*, *'āśâ*) are used of his activity in the restoration of the exiles (*cf.* Is. 43:7, where all three verbs appear together). The dragon-typology of creation, which had already been taken over as a picture of Yahweh's victory at the Exodus, now became a means of describing this new victory. When the arm of Yahweh is called upon to 'awake . . . as in days of old', when it 'cut Rahab in pieces' and 'didst pierce the dragon' (Is. 51:9), God is being urged to repeat in this new situation the mighty acts of creation and Exodus. If at the Exodus he saved his people by making 'a way in the sea, a path in the mighty waters' (Is. 43:16), so he will be with the returning exiles when they pass through the waters (Is. 43:2), making 'a way in the wilderness and rivers in the desert' (Is. 43:19). As the Exodus generation was led by a pillar of cloud by day and fire by night, which moved behind them when danger threatened from the back, so the exiles receive the promise: 'The Lord will go before you, and the God of Israel will be your rear guard' (Is. 52:12). Of the later generation as of the earlier it would be true that 'they thirsted not when he led them through the deserts; he made water flow for them from the rock' (Is. 48:21).

In the language of typology, the earlier series of events constituted a 'type' of the later; the later series was an 'antitype' of the earlier. Or it may be said that the successive epochs of salvation-history disclose a recurring pattern of divine activity, which the NT writers believed to have found its definitive expression in their own day.

II. In the New Testament

The typological relation between the two Testaments was summed up in Augustine's epigram: 'In the OT the NT lies hidden; in the NT the OT stands revealed.' In the NT the Christian salvation is presented as the climax of the mighty works of God, as the 'antitype' of his 'typical' mighty works in the OT. The Christian salvation is treated as a new creation, a new exodus, a new restoration from exile.

a. New creation. 'It is the God who said, "Let light shine out of darkness," who has shone in our hearts to give the light of the knowledge of the glory of God in the face of Christ' (2 Cor. 4:6). The Fourth Gospel perhaps provides the clearest instance of creation typology, with its exordium 'In the beginning . . .' echoing the opening words of Gn.: the divine Word which called the old creation into being has now become flesh to inaugurate a new creation. Those who are 'in Christ', according to Paul, constitute a 'new creation' (2 Cor. 5:17; Gal. 6:15). Paul and the seer of Patmos join in seeing the curse of the primordial fall reversed by the redemptive work of Christ (Rom. 8:19–21; Rev. 22:1–5). The gospel establishes 'new heavens and a new earth in which righteousness dwells' (2 Pet. 3:13; *cf.* Rev. 21:1).

b. New exodus. The exodus typology is particularly pervasive in the NT. Matthew seems to view the infancy of Jesus as a recapitulation of the early experiences of Israel, which went down to Egypt and came up again (Mt. 2:15). John, by the chronology of his Gospel and otherwise, implies that Christ is the antitypical Passover lamb (*cf.* Jn. 19:14, 36). Peter's language points in the same direction (1 Pet. 1:19), while Paul makes the thought explicit: since 'Christ, our paschal lamb, has been sacrificed', the ensuing festival should be celebrated by his people 'with the unleavened bread of sincerity and truth' (1 Cor. 5:7f.). As the Israelites passed through the Sea of Reeds, so Christians have been baptized into Christ; as the Israelites received bread from heaven and water from the rock, so Christians have their distinctive 'supernatural food and drink' (1 Cor. 10:1–4). As, despite all those blessings, the Exodus generation died in the wilderness because of unbelief and disobedience and so failed to enter the promised land, Christians for their part are exhorted to take warning lest they fall (1 Cor. 10:5–12; *cf.* Heb. 3:7–4:13; Jude 5). For these things befell the Israelites 'as a warning (*typikōs*), but they were written down for our instruction, upon whom the end of the ages has come' (1 Cor. 10:11). This typology has an intensely ethical and paraenetic emphasis.

c. New restoration. The very word 'gospel' (*euangelion*) and its cognates are probably derived by the NT writers from their occurrences in Is. 40–66 to denote the 'good tidings' of return from Exile and rebuilding of Zion (Is. 40:9; *cf.* 52:7; 61:1). No stretch of OT prophecy has provided such a fertile 'plot' of gospel *testimonia*, from the 'voice' of Is. 40:3 through the ministry of the Servant in Is. 42–53 to the new heavens and new earth of Is. 65:17; 66:22.

d. Typical persons. In Rom. 5:14 Adam is called 'a type (*typos*) of the one who was to come' (*i.e.* of Christ, the last Adam). Adam, as head of the old creation, is an obvious counterpart to Christ, head of the new creation. All humanity is viewed as being either 'in Adam', in whom 'all die', or 'in Christ', in whom all are to 'be made alive' (1 Cor. 15:22).

No other OT character is expressly called a *typos* of Christ in the NT. But other OT characters typify him in some degree, by comparison or contrast—Moses, as prophet (Acts 3:22f.; 7:37), Aaron, as priest (Heb. 5:4f.), David, as king (Acts 13:22). The writer to the Hebrews, taking his cue from Ps. 110:4, sees in Melchizedek a specially apt counterpart of Christ in his priestly office (Heb. 5:6, 10; 6:20ff.). He also hints that the details of the apparatus and services of the wilderness tabernacle might yield typical significance although, from what he says in Heb. 9:6–10, this significance would involve the difference rather than the resemblance between that order and the new order introduced by Christ. It is only in the light of the antitype that the relevance of the type can be appreciated.

III. Post-biblical developments

The post-apostolic age witnessed the beginning of a more unfettered Christian typology. From the first half of the 2nd century the *Epistle of Barnabas* or Justin's *Dialogue with Trypho* illustrates the length to which the typological interpretation of OT episodes could be carried in the absence of exegetical controls. The result was that the OT acquired its chief value in Christian eyes as a book of anticipatory pictures of the person and work of Christ—pictures presented in words and even more in visible art. Perhaps the most impressive example in art is Chartres Cathedral, where the sculptures and windows on the N side depict a wealth of OT analogies to the NT story depicted by their counterparts on the S side. Thus Isaac carrying the wood is a counterpart to Christ carrying his cross, the sale of Joseph for 20 pieces of silver is a counterpart to Christ's being sold for 30 pieces, and so forth. The whole OT is thus made to tell the Christian story in advance, but not on principles which the biblical writers themeslves would have recognized.

What was spontaneous in the early Middle Ages tends to become studied and artificial when attempts are made to revive it at the present day. 'If the appeal to Scripture is to be maintained in its proper sense, and Christian doctrine is to be set on a less unstable foundation than the private judgment of ingenious riddle-solvers, some attempt is urgently needed to establish a workable criterion for the legitimate use of the typological method, and so to smooth the path of biblical theology' (G. W. H. Lampe, *Theology* 56, 1953, p. 208).

BIBLIOGRAPHY. A. Jukes, *The Law of the Offerings*, 1854; *idem*, *Types of Genesis*, 1858; P. Fairbairn, *The Typology of Scripture*[6], 1880; C. H. Dodd, *According to the Scriptures*, 1952; H. H. Rowley, *The Unity of the Bible*, 1953; G. W. H. Lampe and K. J. Woollcombe, *Essays on Typology*, 1957; S. H. Hooke, *Alpha and Omega*, 1961; D. Daube, *The Exodus Pattern in the Bible*, 1963; A. T. Hanson, *Jesus Christ in the Old Testament*, 1965; G. von Rad, *Old Testament Theology*, 2, 1965, pp. 319–409; F. F. Bruce, *This is That*, 1968; *idem*, *The Time is Fulfilled*, 1978; J. W. Drane, *EQ* 50, 1978, pp. 195–210. F.F.B.

TYRANNUS. There is no known reference to Tyrannus apart from Acts 19:9, in which Paul at Ephesus is said to have reasoned daily in the *scholē* of Tyrannus. The word *scholē* (AV 'school', RSV 'hall') means a group or place where lectures are given and discussed. It is not known whether Tyrannus was the founder of the lecture-hall or its owner at the time of Paul's stay. The word translated 'one' in AV, which would support the latter view, is not in the best MSS. D.R.H.

TYRE, TYRUS. The principal seaport on the Phoenician coast, about 40 km S of Sidon and 45 N of Akko, Tyre (mod. Ṣûr; Heb. *ṣôr*; Assyr. *Ṣur(r)u*; Egyp. *Ḏaru*; Gk. *Tyros*) comprised two harbours. One lay on an island, the other 'Old' port on the mainland may be the Uššu of Assyrian inscriptions. The city, which was watered by the river Litani, dominated the surrounding plain, in the N of which lay Sarepta (*ZAREPHATH).

I. History

According to Herodotus (2. 44), Tyre was founded *c.* 2700 BC, and is mentioned in Execration Texts from *Egypt (*c.* 1850 BC) and in a Canaanite poem (Keret, *ANET*, pp. 142f.) from Ras Shamra (*UGARIT). It took an early and active part in the sea-trade in trade and luxuries with Egypt which led to the Egyptian campaigns to control the Phoenician coast. During the Amarna period the local ruler of Tyre, Abimilki, remained loyal, writing to Amenophis III of the defection of surrounding towns and requesting aid against the Amorite Aziru and king of Sidon. When the Philistines plundered Sidon (*c.* 1200 BC) many of its inhabitants fled to Tyre, which now became the 'daughter of Sidon' (Is. 23:12), the principal Phoenician port. By the late 2nd millennium BC it was counted as a strongly defended city on

Bronze coin from Tyre depicting a war galley. Diameter 22 mm. AD 3. (RG)

Tribute for Assyria is being ferried from the fortified island-city of Tyre across to the Phoenician mainland. Bronze band from the gates of Shalmaneser III at Balawat (near Calah). 858–824 BC. (BM)

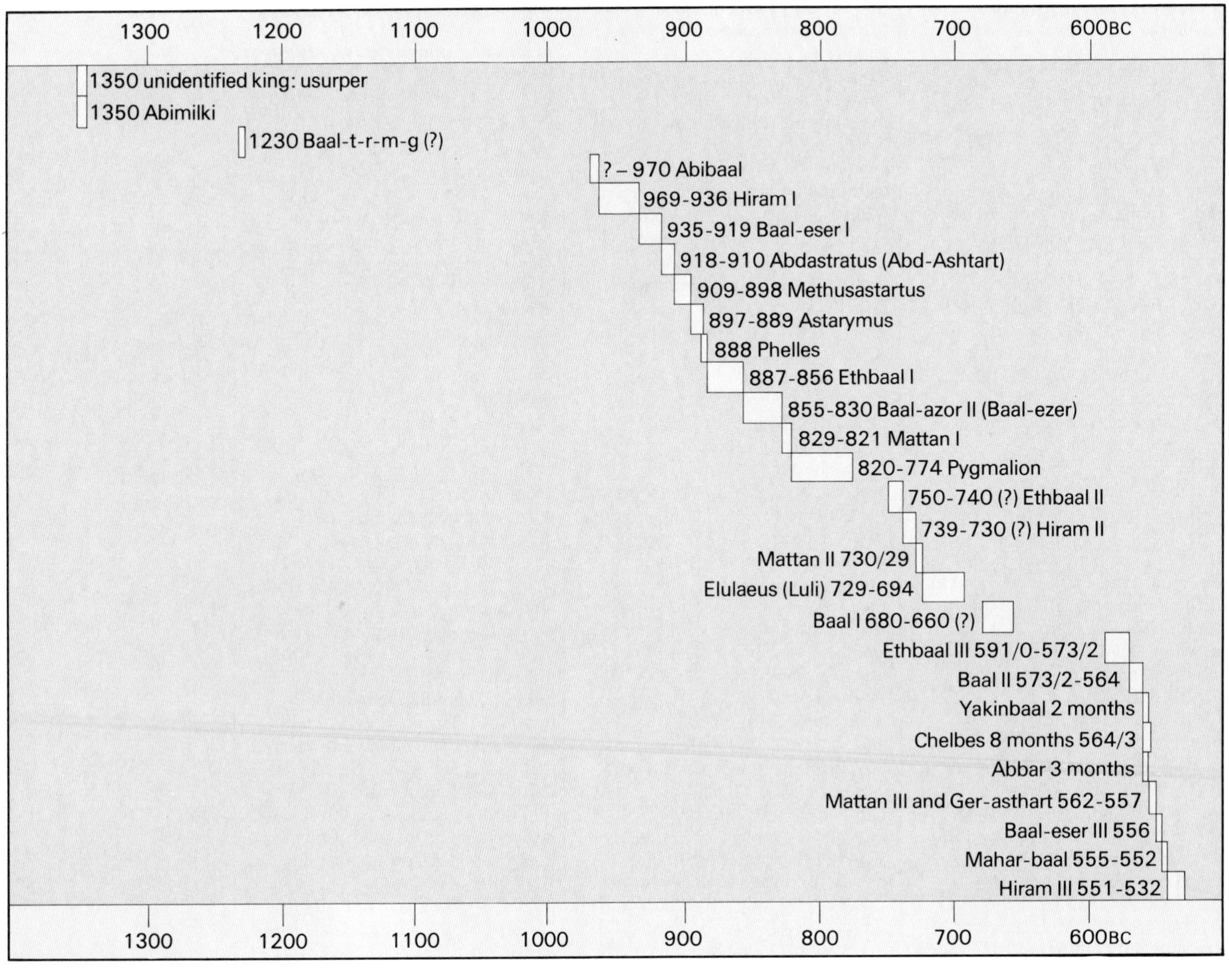

Kings and rulers of ancient Tyre (according to H. J. Katzenstein).

the border of the land allocated to Asher (Jos. 19:29), and this reputation continued (2 Sa. 24:7; RSV 'fortress').

With the decline of Egypt Tyre was independent, its rulers dominating most of the Phoenician coastal cities, including the Lebanon hinterland. Hiram I was a friend of David and supplied materials for building the royal palace at Jerusalem (2 Sa. 5:11; 1 Ki. 5:1; 1 Ch. 14:1), a policy he continued during the reign of Solomon, when he sent wood and stone for the construc-

tion of the Temple (1 Ki. 5:1–12; 2 Ch. 2:3–16) in return for food supplies and territorial advantages (1 Ki. 9:10–14). Tyrians, including a bronze-caster also named Hiram, assisted in Solomon's projects (1 Ki. 7:13–14). During his reign Hiram I linked the mainland port with the island by an artificial causeway and built a temple dedicated to the deities Melqart and Astarte. As part of his policy of colonial expansion and trade he assisted Solomon's development of the Red Sea port of Ezion-geber for

Kings and rulers of ancient Tyre:

- 1350 unidentified king: usurper
- 1350 Abimilki
- 1230 Baal-t-r-m-g (?)
- ? – 970 Abibaal
- 969-936 Hiram I
- 935-919 Baal-eser I
- 918-910 Abdastratus (Abd-Ashtart)
- 909-898 Methusastartus
- 897-889 Astarymus
- 888 Phelles
- 887-856 Ethbaal I
- 855-830 Baal-azor II (Baal-ezer)
- 829-821 Mattan I
- 820-774 Pygmalion
- 750-740 (?) Ethbaal II
- 739-730 (?) Hiram II
- Mattan II 730/29
- Elulaeus (Luli) 729-694
- Baal I 680-660 (?)
- Ethbaal III 591/0-573/2
- Baal II 573/2-564
- Yakinbaal 2 months
- Chelbes 8 months 564/3
- Abbar 3 months
- Mattan III and Ger-asthart 562-557
- Baal-eser III 556
- Mahar-baal 555-552
- Hiram III 551-532

S voyages (1 Ki. 9:27), his ships reaching distant places (1 Ki. 9:28; *OPHIR). From this time, often called 'the golden age or Tyre', the people became the merchant princes of the E Mediterranean (Is. 23:8), and were henceforth noted for their seafaring prowess (Ezk. 26:17; 27:32). The primary trade was in their own manufactured *glass and the special scarlet-purple dyes, called 'Tyrian', made from the local *murex* (*ARTS AND CRAFTS; *PHOENICIA).

The Canon of Ptolemy is still a primary source for the king list, though, despite correlations with Assyrian and Hebrew history, there remains a divergence of about 10 years in the chronology of the earlier rulers. Thus Hiram I is dated *c.* 979–945 BC (*cf.* Albright, Katzenstein, *c.* 969–936 BC). His successor Baal-eser I (= Balbazeros) was followed by Abd-Ashtart, who was murdered by his brothers, the eldest of whom, Methus-Astartus, usurped the throne. Phelles, who succeeded Astarymus *c.* 897 BC, was overthrown by the high priest Ethbaal (Ithobal), whose daughter Jezebel was married to Ahab of Israel to confirm the alliance made between their countries (1 Ki. 16:31). Ethbaal was also a contemporary of Ben-hadad I. His success against Phelles may have been connected with the invasion of Ashurnasirpal II of Assyria, who took a heavy tribute from Tyre.

The port suffered another blow in 841 BC, when, in his 18th regnal year, Shalmaneser III of Assyria received tribute from Ba'alimanzar at the same time as Jehu paid him homage at the Nahr-el-Kelb (*Sumer* 7, 1951, 3–21). Baalezer II was followed by Mattan I (*c.* 829–821) and by Pygmalion (Pu'm-yaton), in whose 7th year (825 BC; others 815 BC) Carthage was founded from Tyre.

Assyrian pressure on Phoenicia continued, and Tyre paid tribute to Adad-nirari III of Assyria in 803 BC and its king Hiram II sent gifts to Tiglath-pileser III, who claims that his *Rab-shakeh took 150 talents of gold from Mattan II, the next king of Tyre (*c.* 730 BC; *ANET*, p. 282). By peaceful submission the city retained a large measure of autonomy. According to Josephus (*Ant.* 9. 283), Shalmaneser V of Assyria (whose own records are wanting) laid siege to Tyre in 724, and the city fell with Samaria into the hands of Sargon II in 722 BC. Local Assyrian officials supervised the return of taxes in kind to Nineveh, but considerable unrest was fomented from Egypt, to whom the Tyrians turned for help. This led to denunciation of Tyre by the Heb. prophets who followed Isaiah and by Joel (3:5–6) for their selling them as slaves to the Greeks. Tyre came under the domination of Sidon, and when Sennacherib approached its ruler Luli (Elulaeus) fled and died in exile. This saved the city from assault, for the Assyrians installed their nominee Tuba'alu (Ethbaal III) in 701 BC.

Esarhaddon, who was keeping the route open to attack Egypt, executed Abdi-milkitti of Sidon (*c.* 677 BC) and set Ba'ali (I) on the throne, binding him by treaty to Assyria. However, Tyre, instigated by Tirhakah of Egypt, rebelled and Esarhaddon besieged the port, which did not, however, fall since Ba'ali submitted. His influence and independence must have been great in Phoenicia, since he retained the throne throughout his life. When he rebelled again in 664 BC the city fell to Ashurbanipal, who made Azi-Baal king, taking his sisters and many officials as hostages to Nineveh.

With the decline of Assyria at the end of the reign of Ashurbanipal (*c.* 636–627 BC), Tyre regained her autonomy and much of her former sea-trade. Nevertheless, Jeremiah prophesied Tyre's subjection to the Babylonians (25:22; 27:1–11), as did Ezekiel later (26:1–28:19; 29:18–20) and Zechariah (9:2ff.). Nebuchadrezzar II besieged Tyre for 13 years, *c.* 587–574 BC (Jos., *Ant.* 10. 228; *JBL* 51, 1932, pp. 94ff.), but no contemporary record of this remains (*cf.* Ezk. 29:18–20). The city (under Ba'ali II) eventually recognized Babylonian suzerainty, and a number of Babylonian contracts confirm this and give the names of the local Babylonian officials. For a decade the city was ruled by 'judges' (*špṭ*).

In 332 BC Alexander the Great laid siege to the island port for 7 months and captured it only by building a mole to the island fortress. Despite heavy losses, the port soon recovered under Seleucid patronage. Herod I rebuilt the main temple, which would have been standing when our Lord visited the district bordering Tyre and Sidon (Mt. 15:21–28; Mk. 7:24–31). People of Tyre heard him speak (Mk. 3:8; Lk. 6:17), and he cited Tyre as a heathen city which would bear less responsibility than those Galilaean towns which constantly witnesses his ministry (Mt. 11:21–22; Lk. 10:13–14). Christians were active in Tyre in the 1st century (Acts 21:3–6), and there the scholar Origen was buried (AD 254).

II. Archaeology

The main extant ruins date from the fall of the Crusader city in AD 1291, but excavations from 1921 (*Syria* 6, 1922), and from 1937 in the harbour, have traced some of the earlier foundations. The many coins minted in Tyre from the 5th century BC onwards, found at sites throughout the ancient Near East and Mediterranean, attest its greatness.

The 'ladder of Tyre' (Jos., *BJ* 2. 188), which marked the division between Phoenicia and Palestine proper (1 Macc. 11:59), is identified with the rocky promontory at Ras en-Naqara or Ras el-'Abyad.

BIBLIOGRAPHY. N. Jidejian, *Tyre through the Ages*, 1969; H. J. Katzenstein, *The History of Tyre*, 1973.

D.J.W.

UGARIT, RAS SHAMRA. This important trade centre flourished as the capital of a city-state in N Syria throughout the second millennium BC. It is mentioned in the *Mari and *Amarna letters, though not in the OT. The site, known as Ras Shamra ('Fennel Hill'), lies *c.* 1 km from the Mediterranean coast, and *c.* 15 km N of Latakia. Excavations were begun in 1929 after a peasant had uncovered a tomb on the sea coast in what

UCAL
See Ithiel, Part 2.

Tyre, the principal seaport of Phoenicia.

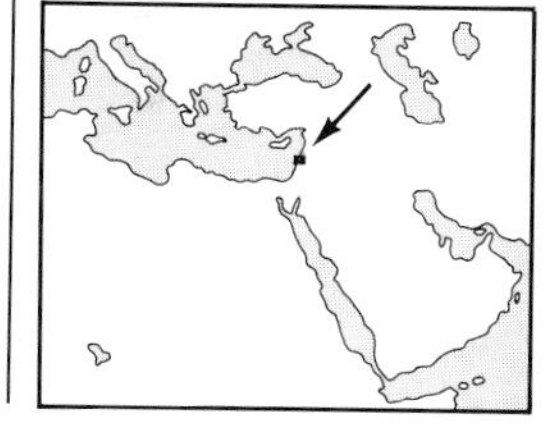

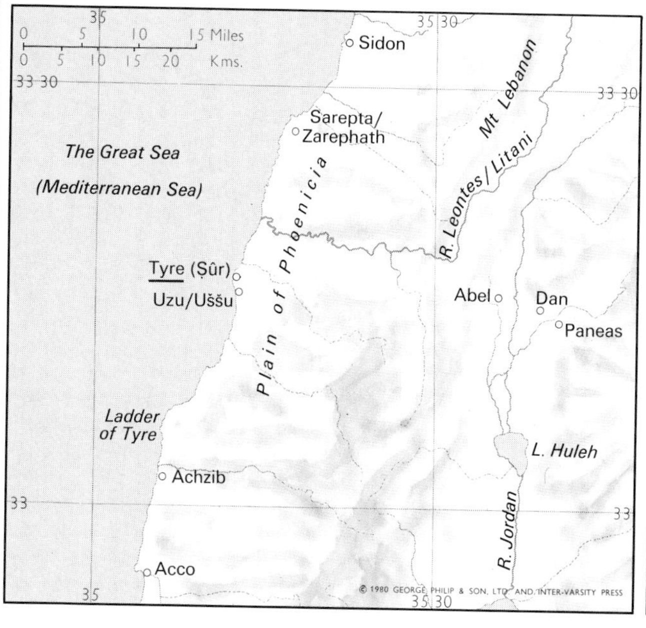

proved to be the port of Ugarit, ancient Ma'hadu (now Minet el-Beida). C. F. A. Schaeffer directed a team of French archaeologists for many years (1929–39, 1948–73), and the work continues. Occupation from pre-pottery Neolithic (*c.* 6500 BC) to Roman times has been traced in fifteen levels. Among major buildings cleared are two temples, one dedicated to El (at first thought to be Dagan's) founded in Level II, *c.* 2100 BC and associated by the excavator with the *Amorites. An enormous palace, over 900 m square, was the major building of the Late Bronze Age (*c.* 1550–1180 BC). Houses of officials, scribes, and a high priest living in the same time were also uncovered. The city had been sacked, perhaps by theSea People

One of the many tablets, written in an alphabetic cuneiform script, found at Ugarit (Ras Shamra). This mentions King Danel, who was cured of sterility by the gods Baal and El, and had a son, Aqhat. 13th cent. BC. (MC)

Statue of a seated goddess from Ugarit (Ras Shamra). Height 24·8 cm. 19th–17th cent. BC. (MC)

A bronze tripod decorated with pomegranates, used as a support for a ritual vessel. Part of an offering made to the high priest of Ugarit by a bronzesmith. Height 12 cm. 15th–14th cent. BC. (MC)

(*PHILISTINES) soon after 1200 BC, so many objects lay buried in the ruins.

A vivid picture of Ugarit's wealth and trading connections can be built up on the evidence of pottery and ivory carvings imported from Crete and Greece, of Egyptian and Babylonian products and things from Asia Minor and Cyprus, as well as the first local 'Canaanite' work in gold and silver, bronze and stone so far unearthed. Most important of all is the large number of written documents recovered from the palace and various houses. Egyptian, Cypriot and Hittite *writing systems were all known in the city, but Babylonian cuneiform was the most commonly used. The scribes learnt this writing in Ugarit, and some of their exercises and reference books survive. They copied Babylonian literature, or composed their own variations of it. Examples include an account of the *Flood (Atrahasis), a story about Gilgamesh, and a unique version of the 'Babylonian Job'. There are also proverbs, riddles, and love-lyrics. A hymn in Hurrian has notes which provide clues to its musical accompaniment (*RA* 68, 1974, pp. 69–82). Babylonian was not the scribes' native language, so beside the standard lists of Sumerian and Akkadian words, they compiled others giving equivalents in their own W Semitic language ('Ugaritic') and in Hurrian, another current tongue. These lists are of great value for our understanding of the lesser-known languages. Babylonian was used in daily life for business and administration in the temples, the palace and the big houses. It was the international diplomatic language, so was used

Plan of the mound of Ugarit (Ras Shamra), showing where excavation has been undertaken and some of the main buildings uncovered.

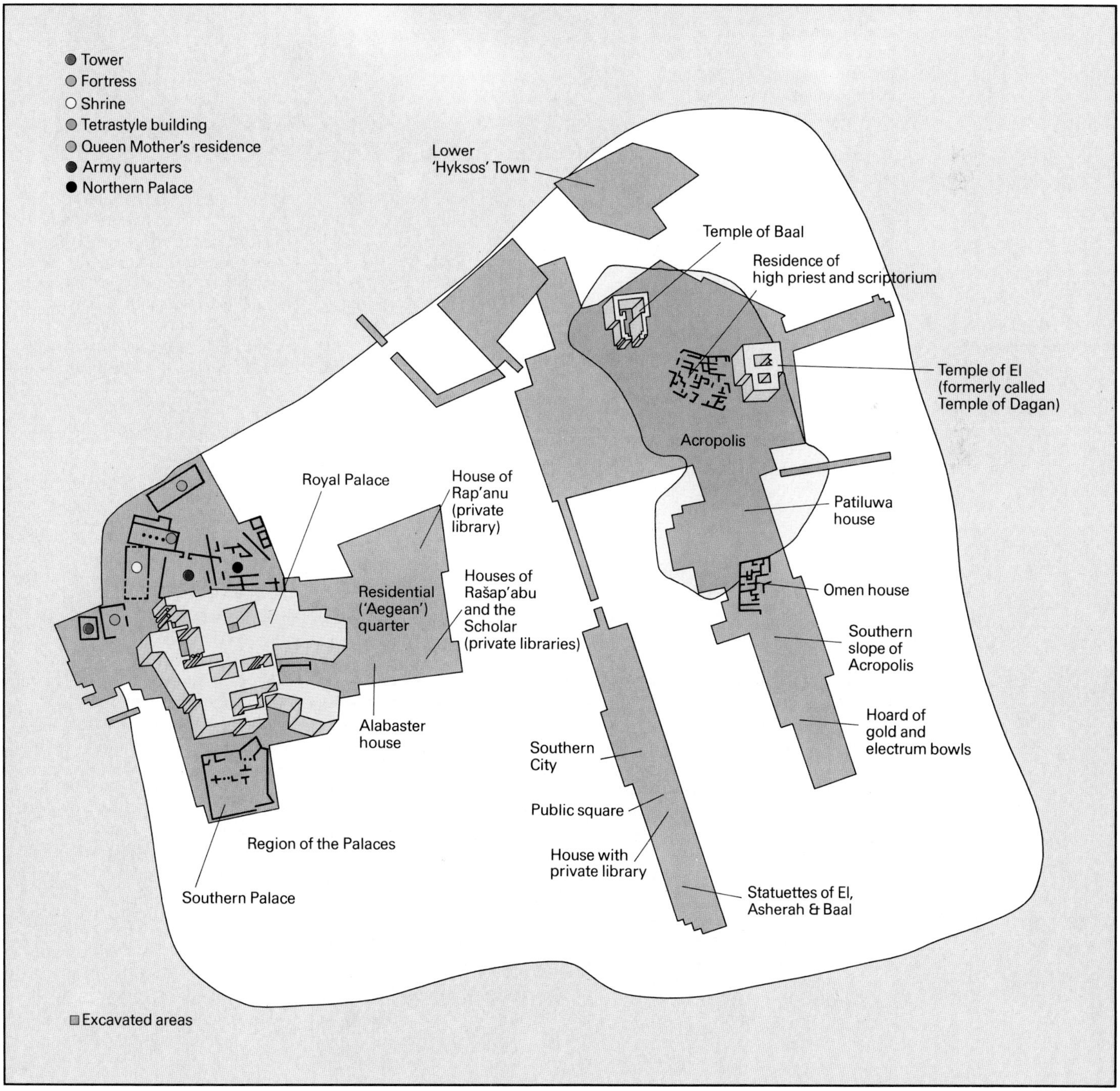

Gold plate from Ugarit (Ras Shamra) depicting a hunting scene. Diameter 19 cm. 14th cent. BC. (MC)

for writing treaties. The kings of Ugarit in the 14th and 13th centuries BC traced their dynasty back to an ancestor who ruled the city *c.* 1850 BC. The later kings were subject to the *Hittites, and several treaties made with them, or at their suggestion, are available for study. In those texts elements of the pattern displayed by *Hittite treaties and the OT *covenant texts appear.

In order to write their own language, the scribes of Ugarit imitated the idea of the alphabet which had been invented by the Canaanites to the S. Instead of using signs based on pictures (*WRITING), they combined wedges to make 29 cunieform letters, each representing one consonant. The letters were learnt in an order which is the same as the Hebrew, with additions. Over 1,300 inscriptions in this alphabet, dating from 1400 BC onwards, have been found at Ugarit, a few dozen at a site called Ras Ibn Hani to the S. and one at Tell Sukas farther down the coast. A shorter form of this alphabet, having only 22 letters, was more widely known. Beside three examples from Ugarit, single inscriptions have been unearthed at *Kadesh in Syria, Kamid el-Loz and *Zarephath in Lebanon, and *Beth-shemesh, *Taanach, and near Mt Tabor in Palestine.

Ugaritic is closely related to Hebrew and has broadened appreciation of the *language of the OT in many ways. It is necessary to realize, however, that the languages are not identical, so what is true of one may not be applied automatically to the other. There is similarity between the terminology of the elaborate Ugaritic ritual system and that in Leviticus. Thus the whole burnt-offering (Ugaritic *kll*; Dt. 33:10), burnt-(*šrp*), communion- (*šlmn*), trespass-(*'asm*), and tribute- or gift- (*mtn*) offerings, and offerings made by fire (*'est*) are named, though their use differs from OT spirit and practice (*SACRIFICE AND OFFERING). These epics, myths and hymns have a distinct poetic style, with irregular metre, repetitions and parallelisms, which have led Albright and his students to argue for a date of 13th–10th century BC or earlier for some Hebrew poetic passages, *e.g.* for the Songs of Miriam (Ex. 15; *JNES* 14, 1955, pp. 237–250), and Deborah (Jdg. 5); the blessing of Moses (Dt. 33; *JBL* 67, 1948, pp. 191–210) and Pss. 29 and 58 (*HUCA* 23, 1950–1, pp. 1–13). Many phrases which occur in Heb. poetry are found in these texts; a few examples may be cited: 'flashing (*ysr*) his lightning to the earth', as Jb. 37:2 is to be read; 'the dew of heaven and the fat (*smn*) of the earth' (*cf.* Gn. 27:28, 39; 'LTN the swift . . . the crooked serpent' is the Leviathan of Is. 27:1; Jb. 26:13. In this way the meaning and exegesis of a number of difficult Hebrew passages can be elucidated. The 'fields of offerings' of 2 Sa. 1:21 (AV) is rather the Ugaritic 'swelling of the deep', and the Ugaritic root *spsg*, 'glaze', helps to translate Pr. 26:23 correctly as 'like glaze upon a potsherd.' The study of Ugaritic grammar and syntax, especially of such prepositions and particles as *b*, *l*, *'el*, *k*(*i*), has shown that many of the old emendations proposed for the *MT* are unnecessary.

Texts in the alphabetic script include a number of epics or myths, several hundred lines in length. Ever since their discovery, their significance has been disputed, some

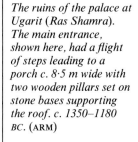

The ruins of the palace at Ugarit (Ras Shamra). The main entrance, shown here, had a flight of steps leading to a porch c. 8·5 m wide with two wooden pillars set on stone bases supporting the roof. c. 1350–1180 BC. (ARM)

arguing they are dramas acted in the cult, some claiming a basis in the annual cycle of seasons for the *Baal Epics*, others seeing a seven-year cycle. The *Baal Epics* tell how that god met his rivals Yam ('Sea') and Mot ('Death') and overcame them with the weapons fashioned by the craftsman god Ktr(whss). These were probably thunder (a mace or drumstick) and lightning (a lance or thunderbolt), as shown on bronze statuettes of the god Baal found there. Following a successful war in which Baal's sister Anat, probably to be identified with the Phoenician Ashtart, a goddess of war, love and fertility, played a major part, the craftsman-god built Baal a temple at the command of El. Mot later rebelled and Baal appears to have journeyed to the underworld to stay for half a year while the earth wilted until he was rescued by the Sun-goddess.

The *Keret* legend tells of a godly king who had no heir until El appeared to him in a dream and told him to march to besiege Udm to win Huriya, the daughter of King Pabil. In time he had sons and daughters by her but, failing to repay a vow to the goddess Atherat, he fell sick and died. During this time his eldest son Yassib was disinherited in favour of the younger (*cf.* Gn. 25:29–34). The *Aqhat* texts record the doings of the pious hero King Danel (*cf.* Ezk. 14:20) who died following a misunderstanding about the bow of the goddess Anat he had acquired and refused to give up in answer to a promise of wealth and immortality.

The texts show the degrading results of the worship of these deities; with their emphasis on war, sacred prostitution, sensuous love and the consequent social degradation. They reveal aspects of Canaanite religious thought and practice, but care should be taken in estimating any influence they may have had on the Hebrews. The same applies to the use of Ugaritic in the clarification of the OT text. Other deities met here include the 'Lady of the Sea' (*ASHERAH, *Aššuratum*). She was the chief goddess of Tyre, where she was known also as *Qudšu*, 'Holy'. Her name was sometimes used for 'goddess' in general and linked with Baal (*cf.* Jdg. 3:7). Among the prayers to Baal is one in which the worshipper pleads for deliverance for his city: '. . . . "the bulls for Baal we will consecrate, we will fulfil the vows made to Baal; we will dedicate the first-born to Baal; we will pay tithes to Baal; we will go up to the sanctuary of Baal; we will go up the path to the temple of Baal." Then Baal will hear your prayer; he will drive away the strong one from your gate, the warrior from your walls.'

Lists of gods, Babylonian, Hurrian and Ugaritic, in both cuneiform scripts, give more than 250 names, but of these only some 15–28 were classified in the primary pantheon. This was headed by *'l ib* ('god of the fathers or spirits'), followed by El, Dagan (*DAGON), Ba'al of the heights and seven Baals. In the second rank were the sun, moon (Yerih), Reshef (Hab. 3:5) and several goddesses, including Baalat, Anat, Pidriya, and 'Athirat of the grove. Since several of the gods listed have foreign associations, there were probably frequent cases of syncretism.

The alphabetic script was used as freely as the Babylonian for writing letters, business documents, magical spells and every sort of document, even medical prescriptions for horses. It fell into oblivion with the city of Ugarit; its recovery is one of the major landmarks of 20th-century archaeology.

BIBLIOGRAPHY. General: C. F. A. Schaeffer, *Mission de Ras Shamra*, 1–18, 1929–78 includes *Ugaritica*, 1–7. Alphabetic texts: A. Herdner, *Corpus des tablettes en cunéiformes alphabétiques découvertes à Ras Shamra de 1929–1939*, 1963; *Ugaritica*, 2, 6–7. Cuneiform (Akkadian) texts: J. Nougayrol, *Palais royal d'Ugarit*, 3, 1955; 4, 1956; 6, 1970; *Ugaritica*, 5, 1968, pp. 1–446. See also *Syria*; *UF* 1, 1969; *ANET*, pp. 129–155; M. Dietrich *et al.*, *Ugarit-Bibliographie 1928–1966*, 1973; J. Gray, *The Legacy of Canaan*, 1965. D.J.W.

ULAI. The canal or river flowing E of Susa in Elam (SW Persia) where Daniel heard a man's voice (Dn. 8:16). The river (Heb. *'ûlāi*; Assyr. *Ulai*; classical *Eulaeus*) has changed its course in modern times, and the present Upper Kherkhah and Lower Karun (Pasitigris) rivers may then have been a single stream flowing into the delta at the N of the Persian Gulf. The river is illustrated in the Assyrian reliefs showing Ashurbanipal's attack on Susa in 646 BC (R. D. Barnett, *Assyrian Palace Reliefs*, 1960, plates 118–127). D.J.W.

UNBELIEF. Expressed by two Gk. words in the NT, *apistia* and *apeitheia*. According to *MM*, the word *apeitheia*, together with *apeitheō* and *apeithēs*, 'connotes invariably disobedience, rebellion, contumacy'. So Paul says that the Gentiles have obtained mercy through the rebellion of the Jews (Rom. 11:30). See also Rom. 11:32; Heb. 4:6, 11. This disobedience springs from *apistia*, 'a want of faith and trust'. *apistia* is a state of mind, and *apeitheia* an expression

UKNAZ
See Kenaz, Part 2.

UMMAH
See Ptolemais, Part 3.

UMPIRE
See Mediator, Part 2.

The Elamite inhabitants of Susa (Persia) escaping across the R. Ulai as Assyrian troops march on the city. Relief from the palace of Ashurbanipal, Nineveh. c. 640 BC. (BM)

of it. Unbelief towards himself was the prime sin of which Christ said that the Spirit would convict the world (Jn. 16:9). Unbelief in all its forms is a direct affront to the divine veracity (*cf.* 1 Jn. 5:10), which is why it is so heinous a sin. The children of Israel did not enter into God's rest for two reasons. They lacked faith (*apistia*, Heb. 3:19), and they disobeyed (*apeitheia*, Heb. 4:6). 'Unbelief finds its practical issue in disobedience' (Westcott on Heb. 3:12).

BIBLIOGRAPHY. O. Becker, O. Michel, in *NIDNTT* 1, pp. 587–606.

D.O.S.

UNCTION. In its three NT occurrences, *i.e.* 1 Jn. 2:20, 27 (twice), AV renders Gk. *chrisma*, 'unction', and RSV has 'anointed', *'anointing'. Christians who, by virtue of their 'unction' (vv. 20, 27), are all able to discern schism (v. 19) and heresy (denial of the incarnation, v. 22) are exhorted to adhere to the apostolic message (v. 24), which led them to confess the Father and the Son. Grammatically, 'unction' must be either (*a*) 'that which is smeared on' (so B. F. Westcott, *The Epistles of John*, 1892); or (*b*) 'the act of anointing' (so A. E. Brooke, *ICC*, 1912); but in either case the word refers to the gift of the Holy Spirit, of which baptism is the outward sign, and whose sensible reception, leading to awareness of dangers to the church, is the consequence of true incarnational faith. This exegesis is compatible with, though not necessarily proving, the belief that the anointing of the Spirit leads to spoken prophecy within the church.

BIBLIOGRAPHY. W. Grundmann, *TDNT* 9, p. 372; D. Müller, *NIDNTT* 1, pp. 121–124; I. H. Marshall, *The Epistles of John*, *NIC*, 1978, pp. 153–156.

M.R.W.F.

UNKNOWN GOD (Gk. *agnōstos theos*). In Acts 17:23 Paul refers to an Athenian altar-dedication 'To the unknown God' which forms the text of his *Areopagus address. Pausanias (*Description of Greece*, 1. 1. 4) says that in Athens there are 'altars of gods called unknown' and Philostratus (*Life of Apollonius of Tyana*, 6. 3. 5) similarly speaks of 'altars of unknown divinities' as

UNCHASTITY
See Marriage, Part 2.

UNCIRCUMCISED
See Circumcision, Part 1.

UNEDUCATED
See Ignorance, Part 2.

UNFIT
See Reprobate, Part 3.

UNITY OF GOD
See Trinity, Part 3.

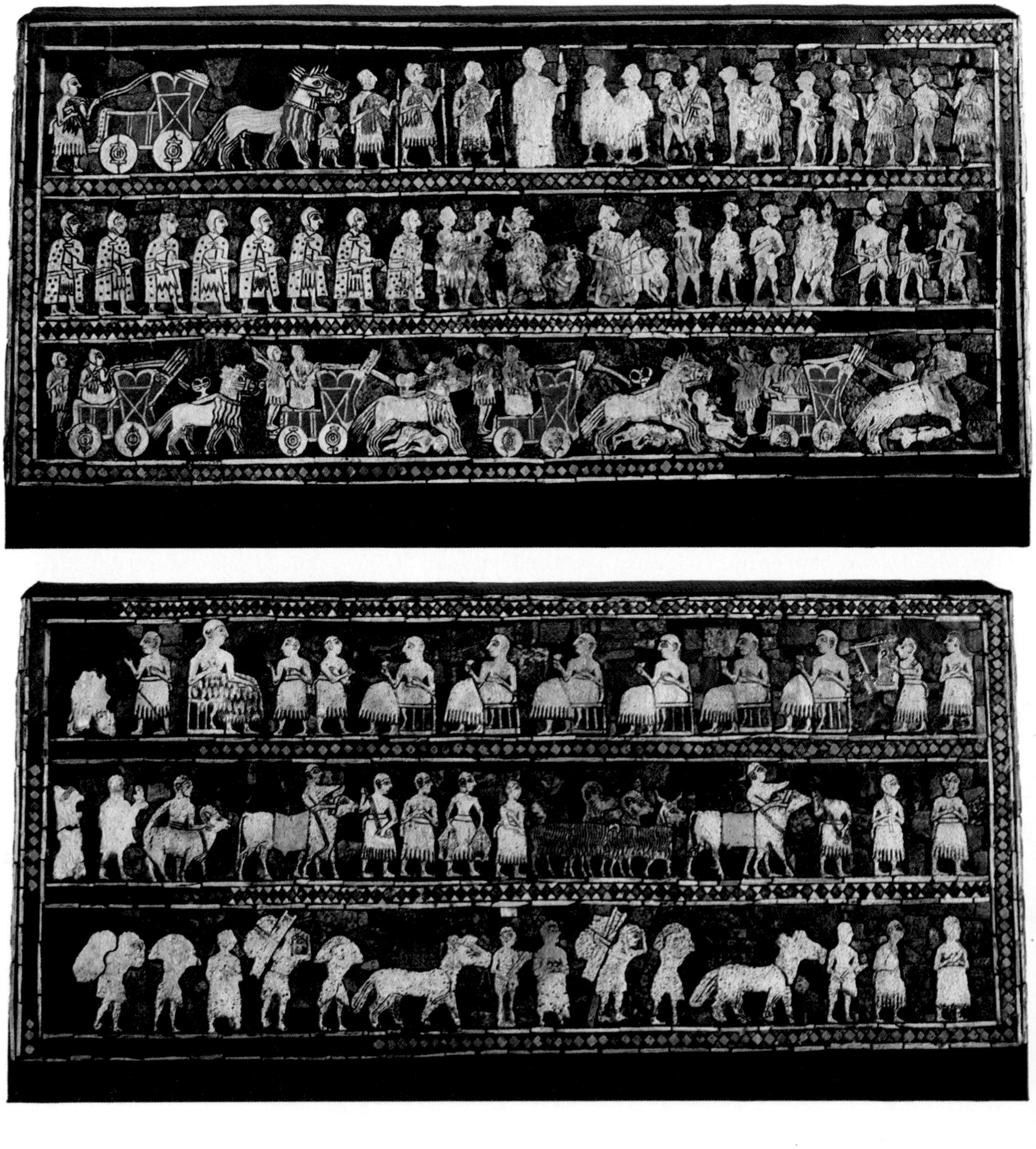

From the royal tombs at Ur comes this standard depicting war and (on reverse) peace. The mosaic was made of lapis lazuli and shell set in bitumen on wood. Length 48·3 cm, height 21·6 cm. c. 2500 BC. (BM)

set up there. They are frequently associated with a story told by Diogenes Laertius (*Lives of Philosophers*, 1. 110) about the setting up of 'anonymous altars' in and around Athens on one occasion to avert a pestilence. Similar dedications are attested elsewhere, if the name of a local deity was uncertain or the wording of an original dedication had become lost.

BIBLIOGRAPHY. E. Norden, *Agnostos Theos*, 1912; K. Lake, 'The Unknown God', in *BC*, 5, pp. 240–246; B. Gärtner, *The Areopagus Speech and Natural Revelation*, 1955, pp. 242ff.; E. Haenchen, *The Acts of the Apostles*, 1971, pp. 516ff. F.F.B.

UPHAZ. An unidentified location from which came fine gold (Je. 10:9; Dn. 10:5). It may, however, be a technical term for 'refined gold' itself (so 1 Ki. 10:18, *mûp̄āz*; *cf. mippāz*, Is. 13:12) similar to the definition 'pure gold' (*zāhāḇ ṭāhôr*; 2 Ch. 9:17). Others, with some support from VSS, read *'ûp̄îr* (*OPHIR; *cf.* Je. 10:9) for *'ûp̄āz* owing to the similarity of Heb. *z* and *r*. D.J.W.

UR OF THE CHALDEES. The city which Terah and Abram left to go to Harran (Gn. 11:28, 31; 15:7; Ne. 9:7). Considered by Stephen to be in Mesopotamia (Acts 7:2, 4). An old identification of Heb. *'ûr* with Urfa (Edessa), 32 km NW of Harran, is unlikely on philological grounds, and *Ura'* is the name of several places known in Asia Minor. Moreover, such an identification would require Abraham to retrace his steps E before setting out W towards Canaan. This identification requires that the 'Chaldea' which identifies the location must be equated with Ḫaldai (part of ancient Armenia). The *Chaldeans were a Semitic people known in Babylonia from at least the end of the 2nd millennium BC, but there are no references to their presence in N Mesopotamia. LXX wrote 'the land (*chōra*) of the Chaldees', perhaps being unfamiliar with the site. However, Eupolemus (*c.* 150 BC) refers to Ur as a city in Babylonia called Camarina ('the moon') or Ouria. The Talmudic interpretation of Ur as Erech is unlikely since the latter is distinguished in Gn. 10:10.

The most generally accepted identification is with the ancient

Gold vessel from the grave of Queen Pū-abi at Ur. c. 2500 BC. (BM)

UPHARSIN
See Mene, mene, Part 2.

UPPER EGYPT
See Pathros, Part 3.

Excavations at Ur uncovered this figure of a goat decorated with gold, silver, lapis and shell. Probably used as an incense- or offering-stand. From the royal graves at Ur. Height c. 46 cm. c. 2500 BC. (BM)

Silver rein-ring with electrum donkey from the sledge-chariot of Queen Pū-abi. From the royal graves at Ur. c. 2500 BC. (BM)

site of Ur (*Uri*), modern Tell el-Muqayyar, 14 km W of Nasiriyeh on the river Euphrates in S Iraq. Excavations at this site in 1922–34 by the joint British Museum and University Museum, Philadelphia, expedition under Sir C. L. Woolley traced the history of the site from the 'Al 'Ubaid period (5th millennium BC) until it was abandoned about 300 BC. Many spectacular discoveries were made, especially in the royal cemeteries of the early Dynastic 3 period (*c.* 2500 BC). Beneath these a layer of silt was at first equated with the flood of the Epic of Gilgamesh and Genesis (see now *Iraq* 26, 1964, pp. 65ff.). The ruins of the temple tower (*ziggurat*) built by Ur-Nammu, the founder of the prosperous 3rd Dynasty (*c.* 2150–2050 BC) still dominate the site (*BABEL). The history and economy of the city is well known from thousands of inscribed tablets and the many buildings found at the site. The principal deity was Nannar (Semitic Sin or Su'en), who was also worshipped at Harran. The city was later ruled by the Neo-Babylonian (Chaldean) kings of Babylonia.

BIBLIOGRAPHY. C. L. Woolley, *Excavations at Ur*, 1954; H. W. F. Saggs, 'Ur of the Chaldees', *Iraq* 22, 1960; C. J. Gadd, 'Ur', *AOTS*, 1967, pp. 87–101; *CAH*, 1/2, 1971, pp. 595–617; *Orientalia* 38, 1969, pp. 310–348. D.J.W.

URBANUS. Latin servile (*cf.* A. Deissmann, *Bible Studies*², 1909, pp. 271ff.) recurrent in inscriptions of the imperial household (*e.g. CIL*, 6. 4237)—perhaps the Urbanus greeted in Rom. 16:9 (AV, Urbane) belonged to it (*cf.* Phil. 4:22; Lightfoot, *Philippians*, p. 174). 'Our fellow-worker' need not imply service with Paul personally. Paul, exact with pronouns, uses '*my* fellow-worker' for companions (*cf.* Rom. 16:3, 21). (*AMPLIAS.) A.F.W.

URIAH (Heb. *'ûriyyâ, 'ûrriyyāhû*, 'Yahweh is my light'). **1.** A Hittite whose name may be Hurrian *Ariya* conformed to Heb. Uriah, one of several non-Israelites among David's mighty warriors (2 Sa. 23:39; 1 Ch. 11:41). While Uriah was away with the army besieging *Rabbah, David committed adultery with his wife *Bathsheba in Jerusalem (2 Sa. 11:1–4; *cf.* 1 Ki. 15:5). In order to legalize this relationship, David had Uriah placed in a vulnerable position in battle so that he was killed (2 Sa. 11:6–21). He is mentioned in the genealogy of Jesus as the husband of Bathsheba, mother of Solomon (Mt. 1:6).

2. A priest and one of two 'reliable witnesses' to the prophecy concerning Maher-shalal-hash-baz (Is. 8:2). He aided *Ahaz in introducing a foreign-inspired altar and in making other unorthodox changes in the cult (2 Ki. 16:10–16).

3. A prophet from Kiriath-jearim, whose message supported his contemporary, Jeremiah. Flight to Egypt to escape Jehoiakim's wrath, which his prophecies had incited, did not protect him since he was extradited to Judah and executed there (Je. 26:20–24).

4. Father of Meremoth, a priest during the time of Ezra (Ezr. 8:33; *cf.* N. 8:4). D.W.B.

URIEL (Heb. *'ûrî'ēl*, 'God is my light'). **1.** Chief of the Kohathites in the reign of David. He assisted in the bringing up of the ark from the house of Obed-edom (1 Ch. 15:5, 11). He is perhaps the same as in 1 Ch. 6:24. **2.** The maternal grandfather of Abijah (2 Ch. 13:2). M.A.M.

URIM AND THUMMIM. In association with the office of high priest, God made a provision for giving guidance to his people (Dt. 33:8, 10) but particularly to the

Opposite page: The sacred enclosure of Ur, in which stood temples, the ziggurat and the royal tombs.

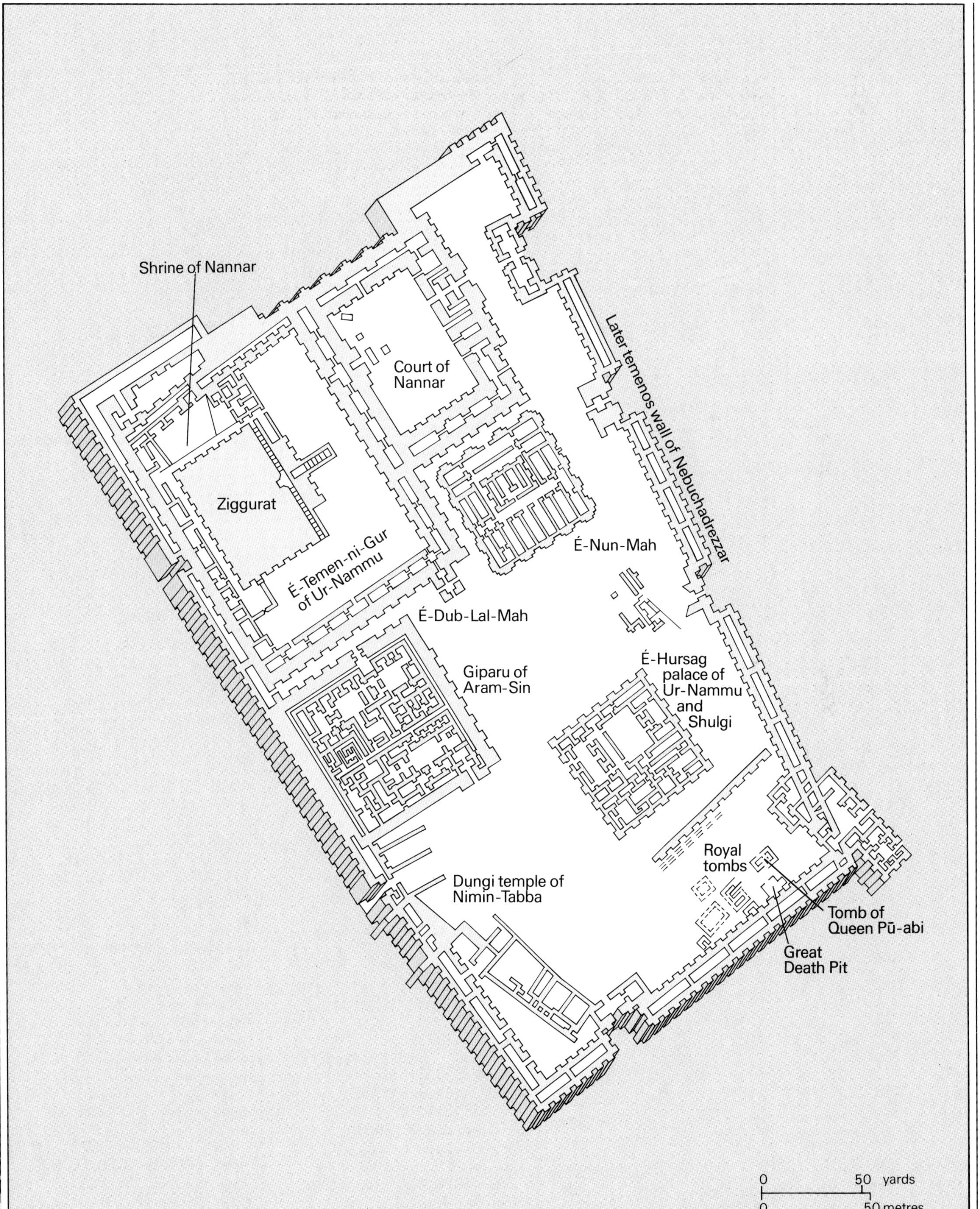
Shrine of Nannar
Court of Nannar
Later temenos wall of Nebuchadrezzar
Ziggurat
É-Temen-ni-Gur of Ur-Nammu
É-Nun-Mah
É-Dub-Lal-Mah
Giparu of Aram-Sin
É-Hursag palace of Ur-Nammu and Shulgi
Royal tombs
Dungi temple of Nimin-Tabba
Tomb of Queen Pū-abi
Great Death Pit
0 50 yards
0 50 metres

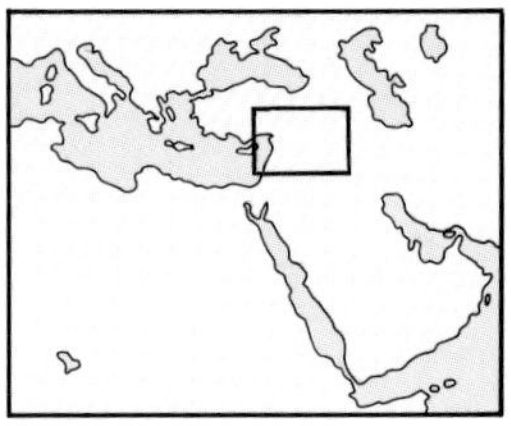

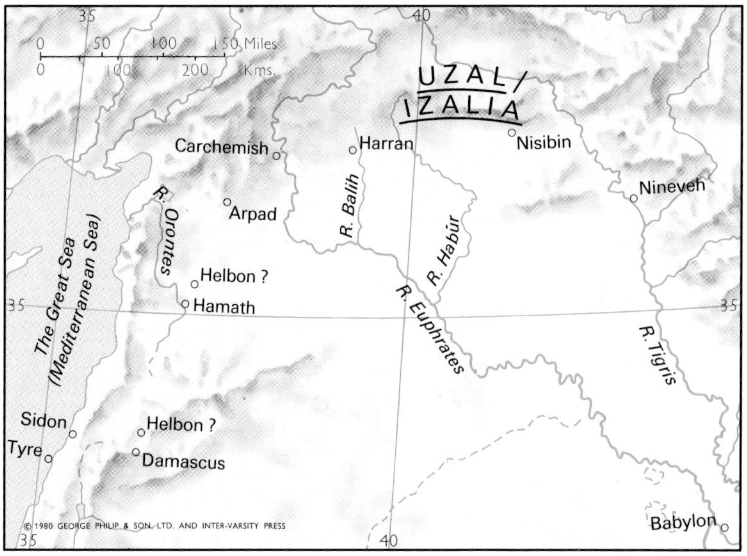

The location proposed for Uzal.

USURY
See Debt, Part 1.

UTTERANCE
See Spiritual gifts, Part 3.

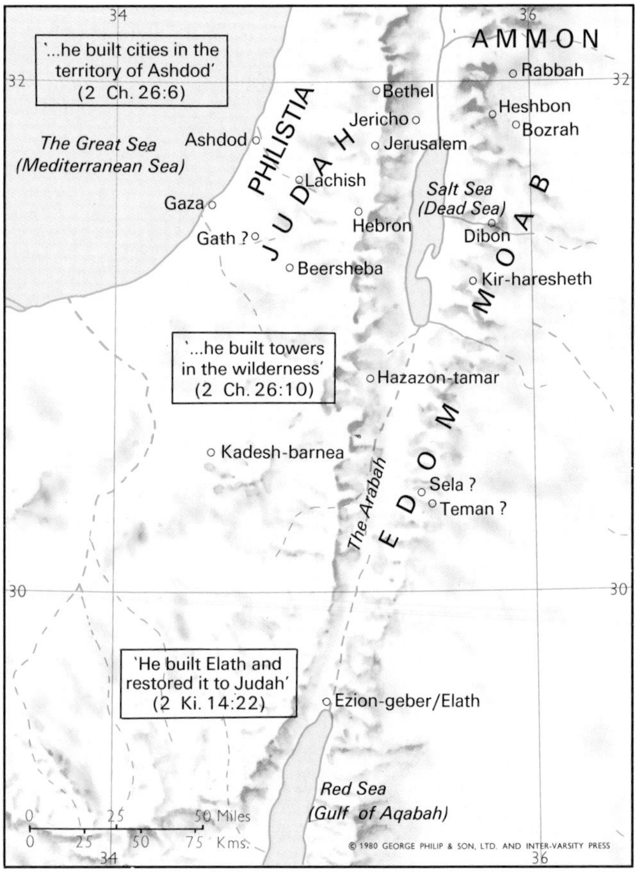

Uzziah's expansion of the territory dominated by Judah.

leaders of his people (Nu. 27:21, *cf.* below). Almost everything, however, about this provision remains unexplained. The words Urim and Thummim have received no satisfactory etymology and the technique whereby guidance was made plain has not been recorded. A further mystery is the apparent disappearance of the Urim and Thummim from national life between the early monarchy (*e.g.* 1 Sa. 23:6) and some revival of the usage envisaged in Ezr. 2:63; Ne. 7:65.

Three passages are of particular interest. Abiathar came to David (1 Sa. 23:6) with the 'ephod'. It is reasonable to assume that this was the high-priestly ephod, not the ordinary ephod of priestly wear (1 Sa. 22:18), for otherwise why should it be mentioned? In the light of the remainder of the story we must assume that 'ephod' here acts as a comprehensive term for that whole unit of high-priestly garb: ephod-breastpiece-Urim (*cf.* Ex. 28:28–30; see 1 Sa. 14:18, where 'ark' [LXX reads 'ephod'] seems similarly to summarize the oracular equipment of the priest). David (1 Sa. 23:9–12) asks direct questions and elicits affirmative answers. In point of fact no examples of negative answers are anywhere recorded. The second passage is 1 Sa. 14 and it presents similarities: *cf.* 14:3, 41 with 23:6, 9; note the identical title in 14:41; 23:10 (a customary formula?). According to *MT* Saul requests: 'Give perfect things' (*tāmîm*, related, presumably, to Thummim). RSV accepts the reconstruction of the text here, helped by LXX, and reads 'If this guilt is in me or in Jonathan . . . give Urim . . . if this guilt is in thy people . . . give Thummim.' The third passage shows that the Urim and Thummim could not be compelled to give an answer: 1 Sa. 28:6; *cf.* 14:36–37.

It is extremely difficult if not impossible to offer a coherent suggestion on the basis of this evidence. H. H. Rowley conjectures that Urim (related to *'ārar*, to curse) gives the negative answer and Thummim (related to *tāmam*, to be perfect) gives the affirmative. On the assumption that the Urim and Thummim were two flat objects each with a 'yes' side and each with a 'no' side, then on being taken or tossed out of the pouch (*cf.* Pr. 16:33) a 'yes' (two Thummim) and 'no' (two Urim) and a 'no reply' (one Urim and one Thummim) were all possible. This is intriguing and plausible but, of course, must rest in part on the reconstruction of 1 Sa. 14:41 and ignore the lack of evidence for negative replies.

BIBLIOGRAPHY. H. H. Rowley, *The Faith of Israel*, 1956, pp. 28ff.; *VT* 12, 1962, pp. 164ff.; Josephus, *Ant.* 3. 214–218; S. R. Driver, *Notes on the Hebrew Text of the Books of Samuel*, 1913, p. 117; J. Mauchline, *I and II Samuel*, 1971.

J.A.M.

UZ. 1. Son of Aram and grandson of Shem (Gn. 10:23). In 1 Ch. 1:17 Uz (Heb. *'ûṣ*, perhaps related to Arab. *'Awḍ*, the name of a deity) is named among the sons, *i.e.* descendants, of Shem. **2.** Son of Nahor and Milcah and brother of Buz (Gn. 22:21, where AV reads Huz). **3.** Son of Dishan and grandson of Seir, the Horite (Gn. 36:28).

4. The land of Uz was Job's homeland (Jb. 1:1; *cf.* Je. 25:20 and La. 4:21), the location of which is uncertain. Of the numerous suggestions (*e.g.* near Palmyra, near Antioch, or in N Mesopotamia) the two most likely are Hauran, S of Damascus, and the area between Edom and N Arabia. The former is supported by Josephus (*Ant.* 1. 145) and both Christian and Muslim traditions. On this view (favoured by F. I. Andersen, *Job*, 1976) Uz is the land settled by the son of Aram.

Many modern scholars (*e.g.* E. Dhorme, *Job*, E.T. 1967) incline towards the more S location. Job's friends seem to have come from the vicinity of Edom, *e.g.* Eliphaz the Temanite (Jb. 2:11). Uz appears to have been accessible both to Sabaean bedouin from Arabia and Chaldean marauders from Mesopotamia (Jb. 1:15, 17). The postscript to the LXX locates Uz 'in the regions of Idumaea and Arabia', but partly on the basis of a spurious identification of Job with Jobab (Gn. 36:33). Uz in Je. 25:20 is coupled with Philistia, Edom, Moab and Ammon, while La. 4:21 indicates that the Edomites were occupying the land of Uz.

However, the LXX omits Uz in both of these passages, and the identity of this land of Uz with Job's is not certain. The fact that Job is numbered with the people of the E (1:3; *cf.* Jdg. 6:3, 33; Is. 11:14; Ezk. 25:4, 10) seems to substantiate a location E of the great rift (Arabah) in the area where Edom and W Arabia meet.
D.A.H.

UZAL. 1. Heb. *'ûzāl* in Gn. 10:27 and 1 Ch. 1:21 signifies an Arabian descendant of Joktan, perhaps connected with 'Azal, given by Arab historians as the ancient name of San'a in Yemen.

2. Ezk. 27:19, AV translates 'Dan also and Javan going to and fro occupied in thy fairs' from Heb. *w^{e}ḏān w^{e}yāwān m^{e}'ûzzāl b^{e}'izbônayiḵ nāṯānû*, which RVmg. renders 'Vedan and Javan traded from Uzal for thy wares', while RSV reads 'and wine from Uzal they exchanged for your wares' (following LXX). Uzal may be identified with Izalla in NE Syria, whence Nebuchadrezzar obtained wine (S. Langdon, *Neubabylonische Königsinschriften*, no. 9, I, l. 22; *cf.* l. 23 'wine from *Ḫilbunim*' with Helbon of Ezk. 27:18). The alteration of *w^{e}yāwān* to *w^{e}yayin*, 'and wine', is very slight. Although *w^{e}ḏān* may be omitted as a scribal error due to the proximity of Dedan (v. 20), it might be a cognate of Akkad. *dannu* (and Ugaritic *dn*), 'a large jar or vat used for storing wine or beer'. This would lead to a translation, 'and vat(s) of wine from Uzal they exchanged for your wares'; *cf.* NEB.

See A. R. Millard, *JSS* 7, 1962, pp. 201–203.
A.R.M.

UZZA (Heb. *'uzzā'*). **1.** A descendant of Ehud, a Benjaminite (1 Ch. 8:7). **2.** A son of Merari (1 Ch. 6:29). **3.** The head of a family of Nethinim who returned from the Exile (Ezr. 2:49). **4.** A son of Abinadab, probably a Levite (*cf.* 1 Sa. 7:1), who drove the new cart carrying the ark when it was removed from Kiriath-jearim (2 Sa. 6:3). When the oxen stumbled he 'put out his hand to the ark of God and took hold of it', for which irreverent handling of the ark he was struck dead by God (2 Sa. 6:6–7). **5.** The otherwise unknown owner of a garden in which Manasseh and Amon were buried (2 Ki. 21:18, 26).
M.A.M.

UZZI. A priest in the line of descent from Eleazar (1 Ch. 6:5; Ezr. 7:4), probably contemporary with *Eli. For others of the same name in Benjaminite families, see 1 Ch. 7:7; 9:8; in Issachar, 1 Ch. 7:2–3; and Levites (Ne. 11:22; 12:19, 42).
D.J.W.

UZZIAH (Heb. *'uzziyyâ, 'uzziyāhû*, 'Yahweh is my strength'. An alternative form is Azariah, *'^{a}zaryâ, '^{a}zaryāhû*, 'Yahweh has helped', the difference in spelling is one letter in Heb. The two words, 'strength' and 'help', became almost synonymous, and they were apparently interchangeable.

1. Son of *Amaziah who was made tenth king of Judah by the people upon the assassination of his father (*c.* 767 BC; 2 Ki. 14:18–21; 2 Ch. 25:27–26:1). He was probably co-regent from *c.* 791 BC when his father was imprisoned (*cf.* 2 Ki. 14:13; 2 Ch. 25:23). Although this is not explicit in the text, it is required by the *chronology in the light of his 52-year reign (2 Ki. 15:2; 2 Ch. 26:3).

Uzziah extended Judah's borders, regaining control of the Red Sea port of Elath and rebuilding it (2 Ki. 14:22), as well as successfully campaigning against the Philistines, Arabs and Ammonites (2 Ch. 26:6–8). For his internal security he strengthened the fortifications of Jerusalem, perhaps introducing new defensive techniques (vv. 9–15; Y. Yadin, *The Art of Warfare in Biblical Lands*, 1963, p. 326), and maintaining a standing army. A king Azriyau who is mentioned by *Tiglath-pileser III as leader of a revolt against Assyria has been identified with Azariah-Uzziah (*DOTT*, pp. 54–56; *ANET*, p. 282; H. Tadmor, *Scripta Hierosolymitana* 8, 1961, pp. 232–271), but a more recent examination of

A limestone plaque, found in Jerusalem, inscribed in Aramaic, 'Hither were brought the bones of Uzziah, king of Judah. Not to be opened'. Probably to be dated in the 1st cent. AD *at a time of reburial of the bones. Height 35 cm.* (IM)

This fortress at 'Ain el Qudeirat (Kadesh-barnea) may have been built by Uzziah (2 Ch. 26:10). Some date this, however, to the 9th cent. BC.

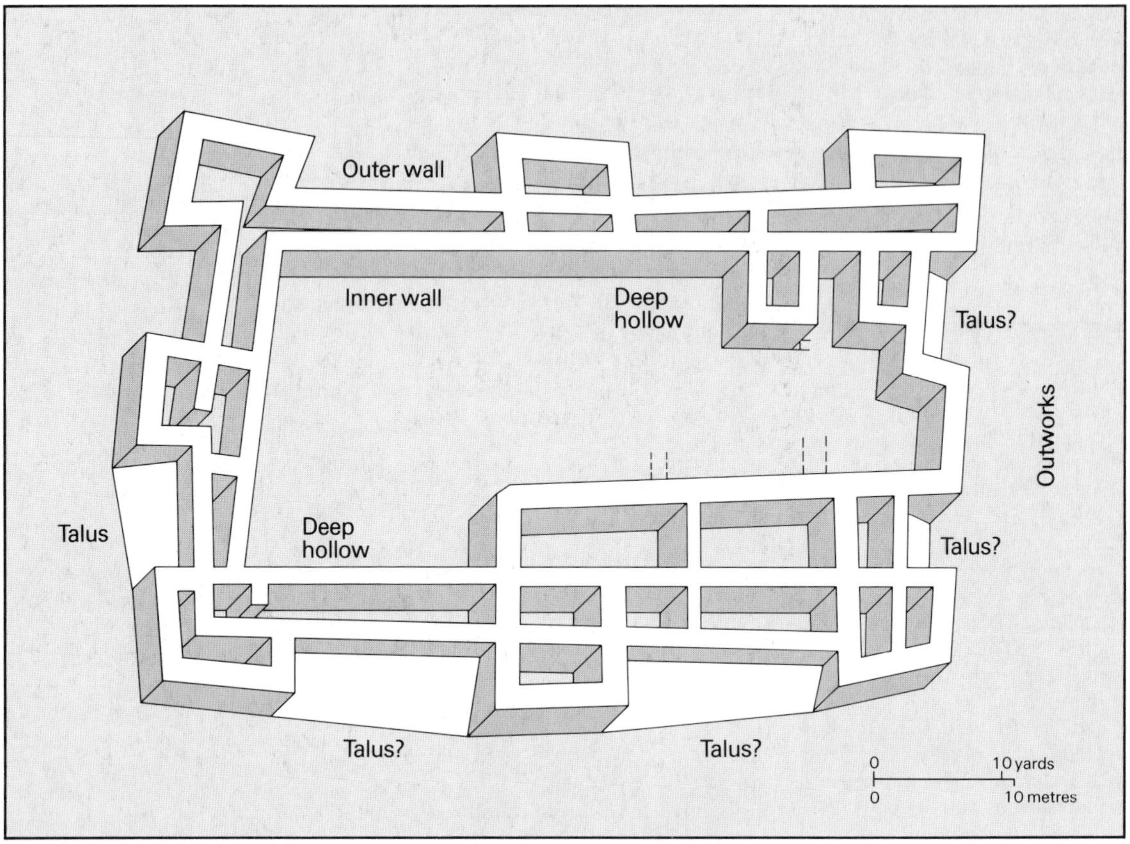

VAIN
See Vanity, Part 3.

VALLEY OF DECISION
See Decision, valley of, Part 1.

VALLEY OF JEHOSHAPHAT
See Jehoshaphat, valley of, Part 2.

VALLEY OF SALT
See Salt, valley of, Part 3.

VALLEY OF SHAVEH
See Shaveh, valley of, Part 3.

VALLEY OF SOREK
See Sorek, Part 3.

VAMPIRE
See Animals, Part 1.

the sources throws considerable doubt on this (N. Na'aman, *BASOR* 214, 1974).

For a cultic misdemeanour, Uzziah was struck with leprosy, and his son Jotham became co-regent (2 Ch. 26:16–21). Josephus (*Ant.* 9. 225) retains a tradition that the earthquake occurred at that moment which was long remembered (Am. 1:1; Zc. 14:5).

A stone slab found in Jerusalem bears an Aramaic notice of the 1st century AD recording the re-burial of the king's remains: 'Hither were brought the bones of Uzziah, king of Judah—do not open!'

2. A Kohathite Levite (1 Ch. 6:24 = Azariah, v. 36). **3.** A Judaean who lived in Jerusalem after the exile (Ne. 11:4). D.W.B. A.R.M.

UZZIEL (Heb. *'uzzî'ēl*, 'God is my strength'). **1.** A Levite, son of Kohath and father of *Mishael, *Elzaphan and Sithri (Ex. 6:22). **2.** The founder of a levitical family subdivision (Nu. 3:19, 30), twice called Uzzielites (Nu. 3:27; 1 Ch. 26:23) whose members helped David bring the ark to Zion and were subsequently assigned responsibility in the Temple (1 Ch. 23:12, 20; 24:24). D.W.B.

VAGABOND. In RSV only at Pr. 6:11, where the sluggard is warned that poverty will come upon him like a vagabond (AV 'as one that travelleth'). 'Highwayman' is apt (C. H. Toy, *Proverbs*, *ICC*, 1899). Vagabond occurs in AV for (1) Heb. *nûḏ*, 'to wander', to describe Cain's lot after God's sentence, Gn. 4:12, 14; *cf.* *NOD; (2) *nûa'*, 'to wander about' (like beggars), Ps. 109:10; (3) Gk. *perierchomai*, 'to go around', to refer to Jewish exorcists, Acts 19:13 (RV, NEB 'strolling'; RSV 'itinerant'; *cf.* Lat. *vagari*, 'to wander'). N.H.

VALE, VALLEY. In Palestine, where rain falls only at a certain time of year, the landscape is cut by many narrow valleys and stream-beds (wadis), wet only in the rainy season (Heb. *naḥal*; Arab. *wadī*). Often water may be found below ground in such wadis during the dry months (*cf.* Gn. 26:17, 19). Perennial rivers flow through wider valleys and plains (Heb. *'ēmeq*, *biq'â*) or cut narrow gorges through the rock. Heb. *šᵉp̄ēlâ* denotes low ground, especially the coastal plain (*SHEPHELAH); *gay'* is simply a valley. For geographical details, see under proper names: *HINNOM; *JEHOSHAPHAT; *SALT (VALLEY OF); *etc.* A.R.M.

VANITY, VAIN. The three main Heb. words translated in EVV 'vanity' are distributed broadly as follows: *hebel*, Pss., Ec., Je.; *šāw'*, Jb., Ezk.; *tōhû*, Is. *heḇel*, lit. 'a vapour', 'a breath' (*cf.* Pss. 78:33; 94:11; Is. 57:13, *etc.*), indicates the fruitlessness of human endeavours. Such is man's natural life (Jb. 7:3; Ps. 39:5). Figuratively *heḇel* conveys the idea of unsubstantial, worthless, thus 'the vanity of idols' (*cf.* Je. 10:15; 51:18, AV). The worship of such is consequently unprofitable (Dt. 32:21; 1 Sa. 15:23; Pss. 4:2; 24:4, *etc.*). Unprofitable, too, are those who turn to such vain things (1 Sa. 12:21; 2 Ki. 17:15; Is. 41:29; 44:9). Idolatry is the worship of a 'no-god', by which God is provoked (Dt. 32:21; 1 Ki. 16:13, 26, *etc.*), in contrast with the true worship of God (*cf.* Is. 30:7; 40). Because idols and their worship raise vain hopes, worthless likewise must be the proclamation of false prophets (Je. 23:16; Ezk. 13:1–23; Zc. 10:2). A 'vain offering' (Is. 1:13) is ritual without righteousness. Wealth got by vanity dwindles (Pr. 13:11; LXX, Vulg., 'in haste'; *cf.* 21:6). *heḇel* has reference

Valley cutting through the rock in Sinai. Dry for most of the year. (RS)

to man's human life: 'man at his best estate' (Heb. 'standing firm') is 'a few handbreadths' (Pss. 39:5; *cf.* v. 11; 62:9; 78:33, *etc.*). This *heḇel* of all human existence is fully treated in the book of Ecclesiastes.

With *šāw'* the idea of 'foul', 'unseemly', 'evil' is introduced. Jb. 31:5 illustrates this with reference to behaviour; Pss. 12:2; 41:6; Ezk. 13:8 to speech; Ezk. 13:6, 9 (*cf.* v. 23); 21:29; 22:28 to sight. The word *'āwen* meaning 'breath' is also translated 'vanity' (*e.g.* Jb. 15:35; Ps. 10:7; Pr. 22:8; Is. 41:29; 58:9; Zc. 10:2). It inclines, however, more to the idea of iniquity, and is thus translated by such terms as 'deceit', 'iniquity', 'calamity', 'delusion', 'wickedness', 'nonsense', in the RSV. *tōhû*, lit. 'a waste' (*cf.* Gn. 1:1; Dt. 32:10, *etc.*), then figuratively 'emptiness', 'uselessness'; so God the Lord regards the nations (Is. 40:17, *cf.* v. 23). Ps. 4:2; Hab. 2:13 have the word *rîq*, translated 'vanity' in EVV, lit. 'emptiness' (*cf.* Je. 51:34), in the figurative sense a useless thing.

In the NT the word vanity occurs three times only in the AV, but not at all in the RSV, where the purely biblical and ecclesiastical *mataiotēs* is used (LXX for *heḇel* and *šāw'*). (1) In Eph. 4:17 (RSV 'futility') it refers to behaviour and there 'includes moral as well as intellectual worthlessness or fatuity. It is of all that is comprehended under the word *nous*, the understanding of the heart, that this vanity is predicated. Everything included in the following verses respecting the blindness and depravity of the heart is therefore comprehended in the word vanity' (C. Hodge, *The Epistle to the Ephesians*, 1856, *ad loc.*). (2) In Pet. 2:18 (RSV 'folly') the reference is to speech with the idea of 'devoid of truth', 'inappropriate'. (3) In Rom. 8:20 (RSV 'futility') the thought is 'frailty', 'want of vigour' (*cf.* use of verb in Rom. 1:21 'to make empty', 'foolish'). 'The idea is that of looking for what one does not find—hence of futility, frustration, disappointment. Sin brought this doom on creation; it made a pessimistic view of the universe inevitable. *hypetagē*: the precise time denoted is that of the Fall, when God pronounced the ground cursed for man's sake' (J. Denney in *EGT*).

Heathen deities are vanities, vain things (Acts 14:15; *cf.* Je. 2:5; 10:3, *etc.*). Cognate with the word 'vanity' is 'vain', literally 'devoid of force or purpose'. Our Lord pronounced Gentile worship and Pharisaic piety so (Mt. 6:7; 15:9; Mk. 7:7); so too Paul estimated pagan philosophy (Rom. 1:21; Eph. 5:6, *etc.*). It is possible through faithlessness in Christian service to become so (*cf.* 1 Cor. 9:15; 2 Cor. 6:1; 9:3; Phil. 2:16; 1 Thes. 3:5). Where Christ's resurrection is denied, preaching is 'false' (1 Cor. 15:14) and faith without force (1 Cor. 15:17). Allegiance to the law robs faith of its worth (Rom. 4:14), and Christ's death of its effect (Gal. 2:21). Yet faith without works is as vain as works without faith (Jas. 2:20).

BIBLIOGRAPHY. E. Tiedtke, H.-G. Link, C. Brown, *NIDNTT* 1, pp. 546–553. H.D.McD.

VASHNI. According to AV, following the *MT* of 1 Ch. 6:28, Vashni was the elder son of Samuel. RV and RSV following the Syriac, and Lagarde's recension of the LXX and the parallel text 1 Sa. 8:2 supply Joel as the name of Samuel's elder son; the Hebrew letters of 'Vashni' are then repointed with 'the' inserted to give the meaning 'and the second' Ahijah. R.A.H.G.

VEGETABLES (Heb. *zērō'îm*, 'seeds', AV 'pulse', Dn. 1:12; *zērᵉ'ōnîm*, seeds, RVmg. 'herbs', Dn. 1:16). A general term for something that is sown, but usually denoting edible seeds which can be cooked, such as lentils, beans, *etc.* In the biblical context the word is used of the plain vegetable food sought by Daniel and his friends, instead of the rich diet of the king's table.

The Heb. word *pôl* (2 Sa. 17:28) denotes the beans brought for David and his men. Ezk. 4:9 refers to them as a substitute for grain meal in famine bread. Ezekiel's bread probably did not break the levitical law against mixing diverse kinds (see *ICC*, *ad loc.*) The Mishnah uses the same word with the national adjective for Egyptian beans, as do the Greek writers with *kyamos*. The precise species is open to question since the modern

VEDAN
See Uzal, Part 3.

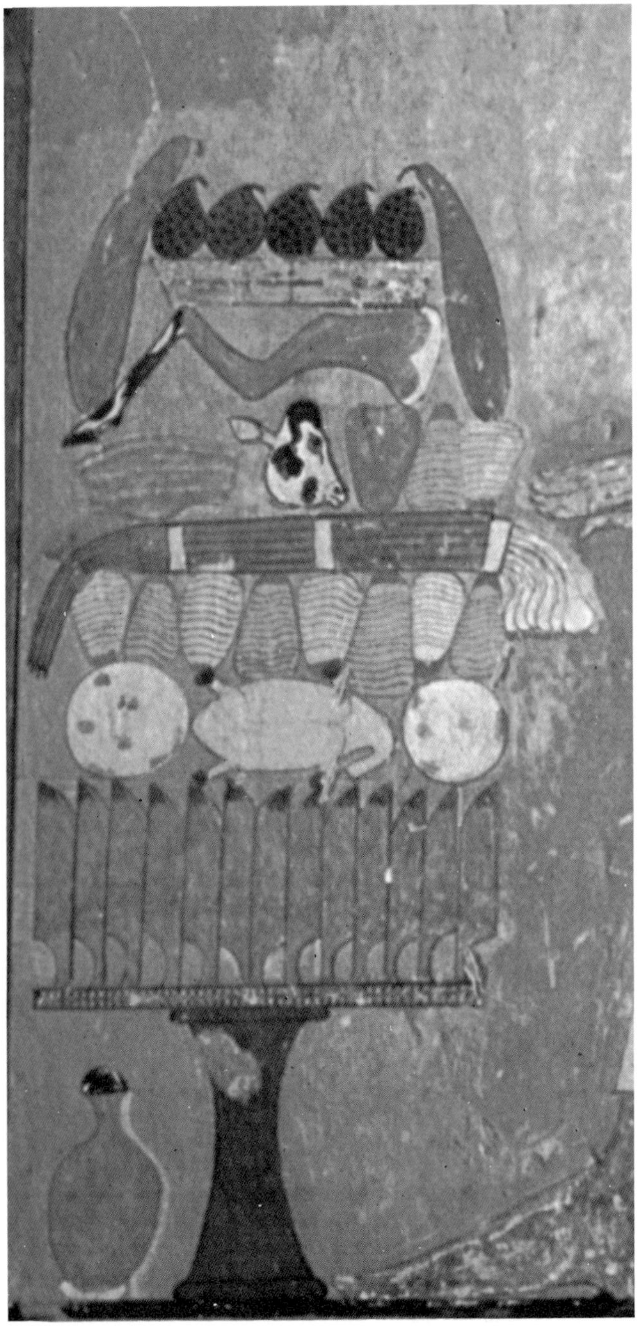

Onions and other vegetables and fruit on a table, probably as an offering to the gods. Wall-painting from tomb 35 at Elephantine. Early 2nd millennium BC. (RS)

Top right:
Lentils (Lens culinaris), *a leguminous crop grown in dry countries. These carbonized seeds came from a tomb at Saqqara. Esau sold his birthright to Jacob for a meal of lentil stew (Gn. 25:29–34).* (FNH)

Arabic word has wide scope, but there were several plants of the pea family available in biblical times, such as broad bean (*Vicia faba*), chick pea (*Cicer arietinum*) and lentil (*Lens culinaris*).

Vegetables were grown in gardens (Dt. 11:10, 1 Ki. 21:2), and other crops such as leeks, onions and melons were cultivated. Many wild plants were gathered for use as vegetables and *herbs. See also *AGRICULTURE.

Cucumber (Heb. *qiššu'îm*). One of the articles of food which made the discontented Israelites, wandering in the wilderness of Paran, hanker after the pleasures of Egypt (Nu. 11:5). This is most likely to have been the snake cucumber, *Cucumis melo*, which was well known in ancient Egypt, rather than the present-day cucumber, *Cucumis sativus*, which is a native of India and reached the Mediterranean area much later.

The 'lodge' referred to in Is. 1:8 as being in 'a cucumber field' (Heb. *miqšâ*) was a crude wooden hut on four poles or other rough booth. It sheltered the watchman who protected the plants, but after the season was over it was abandoned and allowed to disintegrate, presenting a picture of utter desolation.

Garlic (Heb. *šûmîm*). A kind of onion well known in ancient Egypt and craved after by the wandering Israelites (Nu. 11:5). Garlic (*Allium sativum*) differs from other onions in having scales ('cloves') instead of the usual tunicated bulb; it never sets seeds and is unknown in the wild state.

Leeks (Heb. *ḥāṣîr*, 'herb'). Only in Nu. 11:5; the Heb. word is elsewhere translated 'grass' or 'herb'. The leek of ancient Egypt, judging by samples from the tombs, was the salad leek (*Allium kurrat*) with grass-like leaves narrower than those of the familiar common larger leek (*A. porrum*). Both are evidently cultivated varieties of the wild *A. ampeloprasum*.

Lentils (Heb. *ᵃḏāšîm*). A small pea-like plant (*Lens culinaris*, formerly called *L. esculenta* or *Ervum lens*) of the pea family, lentils are easily grown and are still a favourite food throughout the Near East.

The broad bean (Vicia faba) *was an important vegetable in biblical times.* (FNH)

Garlic (Allium sativum) *was popular in ancient Egypt and was craved after by the wandering Israelites (Nu. 11:5). Its bulb, shown here, has separate scales or 'cloves'.* (FNH)

The parched seeds are regarded as the best food to carry on a long journey or in an emergency (*cf.* Ezk. 4:9). Lentils formed the 'pottage' associated with Esau (Gn. 25:29–34), and were among the foods offered to David at Mahanaim (2 Sa. 17:28). A field of lentils is mentioned in 2 Sa. 23:11–12 as the scene of an Israelite warrior's doughty deeds against the Philistines. See D. Zohary, 'The wild progenitor and the place of origin of the cultivated lentil', *Economic Botany* 26, 1972, pp. 326–332.

Melons (Heb. *’^{a}ḇaṭṭiḥîm*). Mentioned in Nu. 11:5. The reference is to the water-melon (*Citrullus vulgaris*), a member of the marrow family *Cucurbitaceae*, with white or red flesh of the fruit, cultivated from the earliest times in Egypt and the Orient, and seeds of which have been frequently found in Egyp. tombs.

Onions (Heb. (*b^{e}ṣālîm*). The onion (*Allium cepa*) is mentioned only once in the Bible (Nu. 11:5). It has always been a common and much appreciated food, and regarded, moreover, as possessing medicinal qualities. Cultivated by the Egyptians from the earliest times, the onion is represented on some of their tomb-paintings.

F.N.H.

VERVET MONKEY
See Animals, Part 1.

VESSELS. Before the invention of pottery (during the 6th millennium BC) vessels were containers made from skins, rushes, wood and stone. These, made of perishable materials, have seldom survived. The dry sands of Egypt have preserved some leather and basketry (see S. Cole, *The Neolithic Revolution*, BM (Natural History), 1959, Plate XI). The peculiar geological conditions at Jericho have resulted in the preservation of a quantity of wooden dishes and trays in tombs of the mid-2nd millennium BC (K. M. Kenyon, *Jericho* 2, 1965). Such wooden vessels, together with leather containers, baskets and sacks, all widely used by the modern Palestinian peasants, were probably as important as pottery in daily life (*cf.* Lv. 11:32). Bottles for carrying both water and wine were simply skins sewn up tightly (Heb. *’ōḇ*, Jb. 32:19; *ḥēmeṯ*, Gn. 21:14; *n^{e}’ōḏ*, Jos. 9:4; *nēḇel*, 1 Sa. 1:24; Gk. *askos*, Mt. 9:17). Soft stones, limestone, alabaster, basalt and even obsidian were cut and ground into shape as bowls, jars, dishes, *etc.* After the introduction of metal tools (*ARCHAEOLOGY) elaborately carved stone vessels were produced, and these often formed part of the equipment of a temple (*e.g.* at Hazor, see Y. Yadin, *Hazor*, 1958, plates 21,

Opposite page: Bottom right: Chives, similar to the ancient Egyptian leek for which the wandering Israelites longed (Nu. 11:5), had narrower leaves than the stout leek of the present day. (FNH)

Pottery vessel of characteristic Khirbet Kerak ware. Beth Yeraḥ (Khirbet Kerak, Galilee). Early Bronze Age III, c. 2500 BC. (IM)

A golden bowl inscribed in Persian cuneiform with the name and title of Darius, 'the great king'. This fluted and embossed style is typical of some metal vessels found at this period throughout Palestine and the Ancient Near East. Hamadan. Diameter 21 cm. 5th cent. BC. (MetNY)

23). Large jars of stone or earthenware were used for storing liquids. The porous earthenware of which the vessels were made absorbed a little of the liquid, thus hindering evaporation and keeping the contents cool (Heb. *kad̲*, 'pitcher', Gn. 24:14; *cf.* 1 Ki. 17:12ff., AV 'barrel'; Gk. *lithinai hydriai*, 'stone water-jars', Jn. 2:6). The rich could afford vessels of metal, glass and ivory (Jb. 28:17; Rev. 18:12). Metal vessels are rarely found in Palestine, but bronze bowls of Phoenician workmanship found at Nimrud (H. Frankfort, *Art and Architecture of the Ancient Orient*, 1954, plates 141–143) show the type in use during the Monarchy. Gold and silver vessels were a convenient method of storing wealth before the introduction of coined money, and formed the bulk of temple and royal treasures and payments of tribute (see *DOTT*, p. 48, c). Some metal shapes were imitated in pottery. *Glass and *ivory were mainly used for small cosmetic flasks and toilet instruments (see *BA* 20, 1957; *IEJ* 6, 1956).

Definition of the various Heb. terms describing vessels is not usually possible. Many containers, although differently named, could serve the same purpose (1 Sa. 2:14).

A skin water-container is used to give a drink to a child. A companion holds a typical pointed-base vessel over her shoulder. Relief from the palace of Sennacherib, Nineveh. c. 690 BC. (BM)

Jar, with lid, of the type in which a 'Dead Sea scroll' of Scripture was stored. Khirbet Qumran. Height 70 cm. 1st cent. AD. (BM)

VESTMENTS
See Vesture, Part 3.

For the types and proposed identifications of earthenware vessels, see *POTTER. The following terms seem to describe metal vessels only, mostly used in the tabernacle and the Temple: **1.** Heb. *'ᵃgarṭāl* (Ezr. 1:9), a large bowl; **2.** *gullâ* (Zc. 4:2; *cf.* 1 Ki. 7:41), a round bowl for holding the oil in a lamp, in Ec. 12:6 perhaps a hanging lamp; **3.** *kap̄* (Nu. 7:14), a shallow open dish for holding incense; **4.** *kᵉp̄ôr* (1 Ch. 28:17), a small bowl; **5.** *mᵉnaqqiyyâ* (Ex. 25:29), the golden bowl from which libations were poured; **6.** *merqāḥâ* (Jb. 41:31), an apothecary's compounding jar, possibly pottery; **7.** *mizrāq* (Ex. 27:3), a large basin used at the altar of burnt-offering, probably to catch the blood, and also a large banqueting bowl (Am. 6:6); **8.** *ṣinṣeneṯ* (Ex. 16:33), the golden jar in which the specimen of manna was kept (*cf.* Heb. 9:4); **9.** *qᵉ'ārâ* (Ex. 25:29; Nu. 7:13), a plate; **10.** *qaśwâ* (Ex. 25:29), the golden pitcher containing wine for libations. For Heb. *dûḏ*, *sîr* and *qallaḥaṯ* translated 'caldron', see *POTTER; in Jb. 41:20 Heb. *'aḡmôn* is not 'caldron' but possibly 'rushes' (*cf.* Is. 58:5 where *'aḡmôn* is 'rush').

The Gk. *chalkion* (Mk. 7:4) is simply any bronze vessel. Heb. *kᵉlî*, Aram. *mā'n*, Gk. *skeuos* are general words for implements, equipment (1 Sa. 8:12; Acts 9:15) and hence, in many contexts, vessels both actual (1 Sa. 9:7; Jn. 19:29) and metaphorical (1 Pet. 3:7).

BIBLIOGRAPHY. J. L. Kelso, *The Ceramic Vocabulary of the Old Testament*, *BASOR* Supplementary Studies 5–6, 1948. A.R.M.

VESTURE. An archaic word denoting *dress used once in RSV for the obscure *sûṯ*, which appears only in Gn. 49:11 (AV 'clothes', JB 'coat', NEB 'robes'). In AV 'vesture' translates: Heb. *beḡeḏ*, 'cloak', 'garment', 'covering' (Gn. 41:42); Heb. *kᵉsûṯ*, 'a covering' (Dt. 22:12, *FRINGES); Heb. *lᵉḇûš*, 'clothing', 'dress', 'attire' (Pss. 22:18; 102:26); Gk. *himation*, 'an outer garment' (Rev. 19:13, 16), possibly a large square piece of cloth which could be used as a shawl or as a cloak (so rendered in Mt. 5:40; 'raiment' in Lk. 9:29); Gk. *himatismos*, 'dress', 'apparel' (Mt. 27:35; Jn. 19:24); Gk. *peribolaion*, 'what is thrown round one' (Heb. 1:12).

In 2 Ki. 10:22 there is a reference to the one who was over the 'vestry' (*meltāḥâ*; *cf.* 'keeper of the wardrobe', 2 Ki. 22:14), who cared for the 'vestments' (*malbûš*) or sacred dresses used by priests in the temple of Baal. J.D.D.

VIAL. 1. Heb. *paḵ*, 'a flask'. A vial of oil was used in anointing Saul (1 Sa. 10:1) and Jehu (2 Ki. 9:1, 3, AV *'box', RSV 'flask'). **2.** Gk. *phialē*, a broad shallow 'bowl' (RSV) used for incense and drink offering. The word is translated by AV as 'vial' eight times in Revelation (Rev. 5:8, *etc.*). (*POTTER.) J.D.D.

VICTORY. The primary biblical assertion is that victory belongs to God (Jon. 2:9; 1 Cor. 15:54–57; Rev. 7:10). This is succinctly expressed in the phrase 'the battle is the Lord's' (1 Sa. 17:47), *i.e.* victory belongs exclusively to the Lord: it is his to bestow at will.

There are three special features of the Lord's victory which enable us to glimpse its inner character. In the first place, sometimes the Lord's victory is the defeat of his people (*e.g.* Jdg. 2:14; Is. 42:24–25; Je. 25:8–9). The Lord's victory is the exercise of holy sovereignty in the course of history. 'Victory' is another way of saying that the government of the world rests in the hands of a holy God, who orders all things according to inflexible principles of morality, so that sometimes his holiness must be asserted against his people, and becomes 'his strange deed' (Is. 28:21).

Secondly, this holy government of the world will issue in the great victory of the eschatological *'Day of the Lord'. The power of victory is annexed to the holy rule of the only God. Therefore the issue of that conflict is not in doubt. Just as, at creation, there was no possibility of opposing the Creator's will, so, at the new creation, he will speak and it shall be done (Ezk. 38–39; Rev. 19).

Thirdly, the people of God enter upon victory by the obedience of faith: *i.e.* they experience victory in God's victory (Ex. 14:13–14; Dt. 28:1–14; Ps. 20; Eph. 6:16; 1 Jn. 5:4–5). As the Lord Jesus said, only the Son can set men free (Jn. 8:36); those who abide in his word know the truth, and the truth sets them free (Jn. 8:31–32).

The OT associates *'peace', *'righteousness' and *'salvation' with victory. The peace of the victor (*e.g.* 1 Ki. 22:28; Is. 41:3, Heb. text) is not simply cessation of hostilities—even the defeated have that! It is the enjoyment of total well-being which victory brings. Salvation is, positively, the personal enlargement, and negatively, the deliverance, which victory effects (1 Sa. 14:45; Jdg. 6:14). Righteousness is the personal quality which guarantees victory (Is. 59:16–17). All these cluster in a unique way round the cross of the Lord Jesus Christ, the supreme victory of God: peace (Eph. 2:14ff.), salvation (Tit. 3:4–7) and righteousness (Rom. 1:17; 3:21–27).

BIBLIOGRAPHY. J. Pedersen, *Israel*, 1–4, 1926–40, Index *s.v.* 'Victory'; J.-J. von Allmen, *Vocabulary of the Bible*, 1958, *s.v.* 'Victory'. J.A.M.

VILLAGE. The biblical village was usually, as today, a small group of dwellings, distinct from a *city (Lv. 25:29, 31, *etc.*) in being unwalled and without defences (Ezk. 38:11). Many OT and NT 'cities' (so RSV, NIV, AV) could well be translated 'village' in the British sense. However, the distinction between town and village is not always maintained, *e.g.* Bethlehem is called a town (Gk. *polis*) in Lk. 2:4 and a village (*kōmē*) in Jn. 7:42. A village might be enlarged into a town or city (1 Sa. 23:7).

Villages were often grouped as 'daughters' (lit. Heb.; Nu. 21:25, *etc.*) around the city on which as agricultural communities they depended politically and economically (Jos. 15:13–63). The inhabitants would retreat within the nearest city defences in time of war. The common Semitic word for village (Heb. *kāp̄ār*; Akkad. *kapru*) may not necessarily relate to this 'protection' so much as denote a hamlet or village set in open country (hence *prz* of Jdg. 5:7, 11 (see AV); *cf.* Est. 9:19), farmsteads or suburban settlement around a city. Nomadic camps were also designated 'villages' (Gn. 25:16; Is. 42:11), and names like *Havvoth-jair may reflect this. A village might have its own local government of elders (Ru. 4:2), and sometimes a shrine or sacred place.

D.J.W.

VINE, VINEYARD. The common grape-vine, *Vitis vinifera* L., is a slender plant which trails on the ground or climbs supports by

The town or village of Madaktu shows the typical use of natural protection afforded by the river. The high structure on the roof may be either an upper room or air-vent. Relief from the palace of Ashurbanipal, Nineveh. c. 640 BC. (BM)

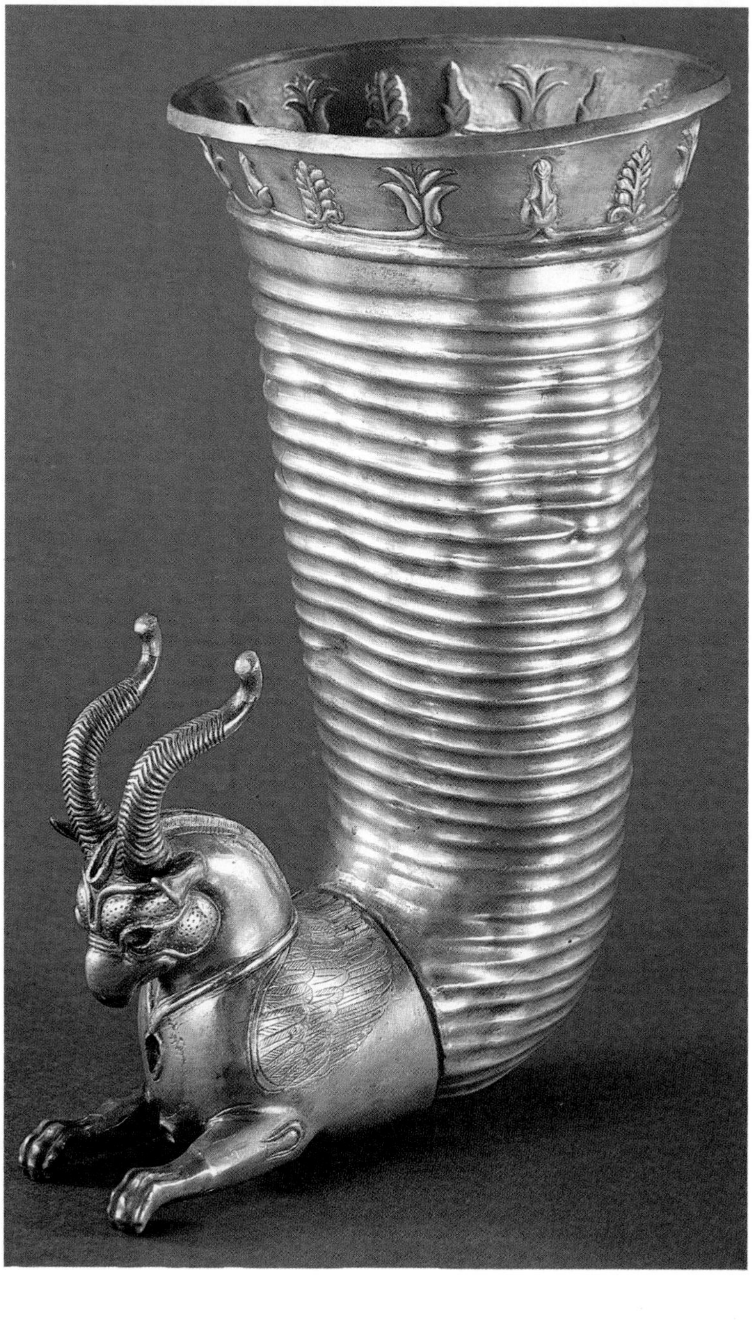

Gold vessel with handle. From the tomb of Queen Pū-abi at Ur. c. 2500 BC. (BM)

means of tendrils. It is mentioned throughout Scripture, frequently in a symbolic sense. First named in connection with Ararat (Gn. 9:20), perhaps its original habitat, it was also cultivated in ancient Egypt. Paintings found on the walls of Egyp. tombs depicted the various stages of wine-making, while inscriptions and sculptures attested to the importance of the vine.

Viticulture was practised in Canaan prior to the Hebrew invasion, as is indicated by the provisions set out by Melchizedek (Gn. 14:18), the report of the spies (Nu. 13:20, 24) and the references of Moses to the Promised Land (Dt. 6:11). That Judah was already renowned for its viticulture may be inferred from the blessing of Jacob (Gn. 49:11). The valley of Eshcol ('grape-cluster') then as now was a particularly productive locality, as

A silver and gilt drinking vessel (rhyton). *There is a small pouring-hole in the chest of the crouching, horned griffin. From Erzincan, Iran. Height 25 cm. Achaemenid, 5th cent.* BC. (BM)

A vine laden with grapes growing in the royal garden. Relief from the palace of Ashurbanipal at Nineveh. c. 640 BC. (BM)

was the valley of Sorek in the Philistine plain (Jdg. 14:5; 15:5; 16:4). The En-gedi vineyards were also notable (Ct. 1:14), as were those of Sibmah (Je. 48:32), for whose ruin Jeremiah lamented. Ezekiel recorded that the wine of Helbon was exported to Tyre (Ezk. 27:18), while Hosea referred to the scent of the wine of Lebanon (Ho. 14:7). The ideal of the invading nomadic Israelite was realized when sedentary occupation made it possible for every man to sit 'under his vine and under his fig tree' (1 Ki. 4:25).

The preparation of a vineyard (Is. 5:1ff.; Mk. 12:1) usually involved terracing the hillsides and clearing the stones. These were used for the retaining walls, which were thicker than necessary if the stones were abundant, with still more piled in heaps (*cf.* Ho. 12:11). A living hedge of boxthorn (*Lycium*)—in modern times the American *Opuntia* cactus was substituted and then *Acacia farnesiana*—was planted, or a low wall built and topped with dead spiny burnet (*Poterium spinosum*) to deter animals and thieves. A watch-tower or stone hut served as a cool shelter during the summer when the labourers lived in the vineyards. The enclosed area of ground was dug over carefully, and when the soil was friable young vines were planted. Normally they were arranged in rows about 2·5 m apart, and when the fruit-bearing branches developed they were raised above the ground on supports (Ezk. 17:6). The vines were pruned each spring (Lv. 25:3; Jn. 15:2) by means of pruning-hooks (Joel 3:10). The vine-dressers, who pruned and cultivated the vines, appear to have belonged to the poorer classes (Is. 61:5). A covered wooden structure, the watchtower, was erected on an elevation overlooking the vineyard (Mk. 12:1), where the householder and his family kept a watch throughout the vintage period (Jb. 27:18; Is. 1:8).

When the grapes had reached maturity they were gathered in baskets and taken to the wine-presses (Ho. 9:2), which were hewn out of the solid rock. The grapes were trodden out by helpers (Am. 9:13), who shouted and sang together (Is. 16:10; Je. 25:30). The fermenting wine was stored in strong new goatskin bags (Mt. 9:17) or in large pottery containers. Tax-collectors claimed their share of the produce (*cf.* Is. 3:14), and accumulated debts were often discharged in terms of wine (2 Ch. 2:10). Exemption from military service was granted to men engaged in the vintage. No other plants were to be sown in a vineyard (Dt. 22:9), and the vines were allowed to lie fallow every 7th year (Ex. 23:11; Lv. 25:3). When the harvest had been gathered in, the poor were permitted to enter the vineyard to glean any remaining bunches (Lv. 19:10; Dt. 24:21). When a vineyard had become completely unproductive it was abandoned (*cf.* Is. 16:8) and the dry vines used for fuel and making charcoal (Ezk. 15:4; Jn. 15:6).

Apart from their use in the form of wine, grapes constituted an important item in the diet of the Hebrews, supplying iron and other essential minerals. A certain proportion of the harvest was preserved in the form of raisin cakes. Raisins (Heb. *ṣimmûqîm*, 'dried fruits') have from earliest times been a staple food in biblical lands (*cf.* Nu. 6:3). The grapes were laid out, often on house-tops, to dry in the hot sun (Pliny, *NH* 16). A welcome food for the hungry, being full of energizing sugars (1 Sa. 30:12; 1 Ch. 12:40), raisins were an easily carried and acceptable gift (1 Sa. 25:18; 2 Sa. 16:1).

Used symbolically, the vine was the emblem of prosperity and peace among the ancient Hebrews. More particularly it symbolized the chosen people. They were the vine which God had taken out of Egypt (Ps. 80:8–14; Is. 5:1–5) and planted in a particularly choice land. They had been given all the attention necessary for the production of outstanding fruit, but instead yielded only wild grapes. For this they were to be abandoned to the depredations of their enemies.

No fewer than five parables of Jesus related to vines and their culture. These were the fig in the vineyard (Lk. 13:6–9); labourers in the vineyard (Mt. 20:1–16); new wine in old wineskins (Mt. 9:17); the two sons (Mt. 21:28–32); and the wicked husbandmen (Mt. 21:33–41; Mk. 12:1–11; Lk. 20:9–18). Particularly significant was Christ's description of himself as the true vine (Jn. 15:1ff.), with whom all true believers are in organic relationship. At the Last Supper the fruit of the vine symbolized Christ's atoning blood, becoming the sacramental wine of the Christian Communion service. In Christian art the fruitful vine has often symbolized the union of Christ with his followers.

BIBLIOGRAPHY. A. I. Perold, *Treatise on Viticulture*, 1927; H. N. and A. L. Moldenke, *Plants of the Bible*, 1952, pp. 28ff., 239f.; A. Goor, 'The history of the grape-vine in the Holy Land', *Economic Botany* 20, 1966, pp. 46–66; A. Goor and N. Nurock, *Fruits of the Holy Land*, 1968, pp. 18–45.

R.K.H.
F.N.H.

VINEGAR (Heb. *ḥōmeṣ*, Gk. *oxos*). A sour liquid resulting from acetous fermentation in wine or other strong drink. The acid nature of vinegar is indicated in Pr. 10:26; 25:20, while a reference in Ps. 69:21 not merely attests to its nauseous flavour but implies that it was used in punishment.

The vinegar of Ru. 2:14 is typical of the fermented acid drinks enjoyed by labourers in wine-growing countries. The *posca* of the Romans was very similar in nature, and formed part of the soldiers' rations. It was this which was offered to the crucified Christ as refreshment (Mk. 15:36; Jn. 19:29–30), and was different from the myrrh-flavoured anodyne which he had refused earlier (Mt. 27:34; Mk. 15:23). Wine or vinegar was prohibited to Nazirites (Nu. 6:3), hence the gravity of the offence in Am. 2:12.

R.K.H.

VIRGIN. Heb. *bᵉṯûlâ* comes from a root meaning 'to separate' and is the common word for a woman who has never had sexual intercourse (Gk. *parthenos*). Metaphorically it is used of nations and place-names, *e.g.* the virgin of Israel (Je. 18:13; 31:4, 21; Am. 5:2); the virgin daughter of Zion (Is. 37:22); Judah (La. 1:15); Sidon (Is. 23:12); Babylon (Is. 47:1); Egypt (Je. 46:11). *'almâ* derives from a root meaning 'to be sexually mature', and refers to a woman of marriageable age who has not yet borne children, though she may be married. It occurs seven times and is translated 'young woman' (Gn. 24:43; Is. 7:14), 'maiden' (Ct. 1:3; 6:8; Pr. 30:19; Ps. 68:25) and 'girl' (Ex. 2:8). The Gk. equivalent is usually *neanis*, 'a young woman', but in Gn. 24:43 (of Rebekah) and in Is. 7:14 *parthenos* is used. As a result, the Isaiah passage has been regarded since early Christian times as a prophecy of the *virgin birth of Christ (Mt. 1:23).

The primary meaning of Isaiah's sign to Ahaz is probably that in less than 9 months (reading RSVmg., 'with child and shall bear') the tide would turn in such a way that a child would be given the name of Immanuel, 'God is with us'. The Messianic interpretation is based on the coincidence of the name Immanuel, which expressed so well the early Christians' belief in the deity of the Christ, and the LXX rendering 'the virgin (*hē parthenos*) shall be with child and shall bear a son', which is a legitimate translation of the Heb. words but which imports into the sign to Ahaz the implication that the mother of Immanuel was a specific woman who was at the time of writing still a virgin (*i.e.* in at least 9 months' time a son would be called Immanuel). The door is thus left open for Matthew and the early church to see a remarkable verbal correspondence with what happened at the birth of Jesus Christ. For a fuller study of this passage, and a different viewpoint, see *IMMANUEL.

BIBLIOGRAPHY. R. E. Brown, *The Birth of the Messiah*, 1977; G. Delling, *TDNT* 5, pp. 826–837; O. Becker, C. Brown, *NIDNTT* 3, pp. 1071–1073; H. A. Hoffner, *TDOT* 1, pp. 287–291. On the various explanations of Paul's teaching on virgins in 1 Cor. 7:25–38, see L. Morris, *I Corinthians*, *TNTC*, 1958; F. F. Bruce, *1 & 2 Corinthians*, *NCB*, 1971. (*MARRIAGE.) J.B.Tr.

VIRGIN BIRTH. By virgin birth the Protestant means virginal conception. The Roman Catholic believes both in the virginal conception and in a miraculous virgin birth, whereby the baby passed out of Mary's body in such a way as to leave her medically still a virgin. This idea in the *Protevangelium of James* (late 2nd century) became a standard doctrine as part of the idea of the perpetual virginity of *Mary. It is unlikely in view of Luke's quotation of 'every male that opens the womb' (2:23) and Matthew's statement that Joseph 'knew her not *until* she had borne a son . . . Jesus' (1:25), which seems to rule out the view that Joseph and Mary abstained permanently from normal marital relations (*BRETHREN OF THE LORD). In this article we use virgin birth as the equivalent of virginal conception.

The two accounts of the birth of Jesus in Matthew and Luke are clearly independent of one another, and both record that he was born through the direct action of the Holy Spirit without a human father (Mt. 1:18–25; Lk. 1:34). If it were not for the miracle involved, anyone would accept the record as adequate.

There is supporting evidence in the rest of the NT. Although a person may not say directly what he believes, he shows his belief by a turn of phrase. Thus Mark has no birth narrative, since he starts where the preachers in Acts start, namely, with the baptism by John. Yet in 6:3 he alone of the Synoptists quotes objectors as saying, 'Is not this the carpenter, the son of Mary?' By contrast Mt. 13:55 has 'the carpenter's son', and Lk. 4:22 'Joseph's son'.

John also begins Christ's earthly ministry with the Baptist. Later he indicates that there were rumours about the illegitimacy of Jesus when in 8:41 the Jews declared, '*We* (emphatic pronoun and emphatic position) were not born of fornication.' Less evidential, although accepted by some Christian writers from Tertullian onwards, and by Douglas Edwards in *The Virgin Birth in History and Faith*, is the reading in the Verona Latin codex of Jn. 1:13, which has the singular, 'who was born not of blood, nor of the will of the flesh, but of God'. (This reading is attested in no Gk. MS.)

Paul, the companion of Luke, uses language that implies accep-

VINE OF SODOM
See Plants, Part 3.

VINEYARD
See Vine, Part 3.

VIOL
See Music, Part 2.

VITICULTURE
See Vine, Part 3.

VIZIER
See So, Part 3.

VOLE
See Animals, Part 1.

VOTIVE PLAQUES
See Art, Part 1.

tance of the virgin birth. When he speaks of the coming, or birth, of Jesus Christ, he uses the general verb, *ginomai*, not *gennaō*, which tends to associate the husband (*e.g.* Rom. 1:3; Phil. 2:7). This is particularly marked in Gal. 4:4, where 'God sent forth his Son, coming (*genomenon*) from a woman'. By contrast in 4:23 Ishmael 'was born', *gegennētai* (from *gennaō*).

In 1 Cor. 15:45–48 a fair interpretation is to see both Adam and Christ coming miraculously from the hand of God. Irenaeus links this with the virgin birth.

Silence about the fact of the virgin birth may have been partly to keep the good name of Mary from gossip. Moreover how rarely do preachers actually mention the virgin birth in their sermons, however often they speak of the incarnation. After AD 100 the virgin birth is accepted by Ignatius, Aristides, Justin, Irenaeus and others.

Objections are in two forms. Even though some call attention to poorly supported variants in single texts, none of these overthrows the description of the fact in all MSS.

Theologically it has been argued that the reason given for the title 'the Son of God' in Lk. 1:35 cannot be reconciled with the idea of the eternal Son of God of the Epistles. This argument assumes that Mary and Joseph would have been given a full theological statement. The two records give the contents of what they were told, namely, that Mary was to be the mother of the promised Messiah, the Son of God and 'God with us'. In our carol services we start with the simple birth and go on to the depths of the incarnation without any contradiction. The fact that Matthew and Luke do not here reflect later theology is a further argument for the authenticity of their records.

In fact genetic considerations may with caution be used to show that the incarnation necessitated the virgin birth. If a child had first been conceived through the act of Joseph and Mary, there would have been a potential and complete man from the beginning. God could not then *become* this man, but would either have to attach himself in some way as an extra (Nestorianism), or be content to fill him spiritually as the Holy Spirit filled holy men of old. Neither of these concepts fits the biblical picture. It is since the rejection of the incarnation and of the virgin birth that all sorts of new theories have emerged as to how Jesus Christ was God.

We now know that the female ovum contains half the forty-six chromosomes that are in every other cell of the human body. The male sex cell adds the other twenty-three, and immediately the two cells, now one, begin to divide, and build up a complete body, mind and spirit. If without irreverence we ask how the ultimate mystery of the incarnation can be linked to the physical, it would seem that, in order that the Second Person of the Trinity might become man, the Holy Spirit fashioned the necessary genes and chromosomes that could be the vehicle of Christ's person in uniting with those in the body of the virgin. We can begin to see how the Christian definitions rightly describe him as one person, since he was conceived by the union of cells by which a single person is produced, and of two natures, since the cell which united with the human ovum was of divine, and not human, origin.

BIBLIOGRAPHY. L. Sweet, *The Birth and Infancy of Jesus Christ*, 1906; J. Orr, *The Virgin Birth of Christ*, 1907; J. G. Machen, *The Virgin Birth of Christ*, 1930; D. Edwards, *The Virgin Birth in History and Faith*, 1943; T. Boslooper, *The Virgin Birth*, 1962; R. E. Brown, *The Birth of the Messiah*, 1977; J. Stafford Wright, 'The Virgin Birth as a Biological Necessity', *FT* 95, 1966–7, pp. 19–29.

J.S.W.

VIRTUE. The word used in the OT is Heb. *ḥayil*, 'ability', 'efficiency', often involving moral worth, as in Ru. 3:11; Pr. 12:4; 31:10 (*'ēšeṯ ḥayil*, 'a woman of worth', 'a virtuous woman'); *cf.* Pr. 31:29 (*'āśâ ḥayil*, 'to do worthily').

In the NT AV renders two words as 'virtue'. **1.** Gk. *aretē*, meaning any excellence of a person or thing (1 Pet. 2:9, RSV 'wonderful deeds', AV 'praises'; 2 Pet. 1:3, 5). In Homer the word is used especially of manly qualities (*cf.* Phil. 4:8). In the LXX it is the equivalent of Heb. *hôḏ*, 'splendour', 'majesty' (of God, Hab. 3:3), and *tᵉhillâ*, 'praise' (Is. 42:12; 43:21, quoted in 1 Pet. 2:9). **2.** *dynamis*, 'power', 'influence' Mk. 5:30; Lk. 6:19; 8:46), is used of the healing influence proceeding from our Lord. The word is commonly translated 'power' (*e.g.* 2 Cor. 12:9; Heb. 11:11).

D.O.S.

VISION. The border-line between vision and dream or trance is difficult, if not impossible, to determine. This is reflected in the biblical vocabulary of 'vision'.

Heb. *ḥāzôn* comes from a root used to describe the beholding of a vision by the seer while in an ecstatic state (Is. 1:1; Ezk. 12:27); while the word *mar'â*, from the ordinary root 'to see', means vision as a means of revelation (Nu. 12:6; 1 Sa. 3:15). The NT uses two words in this connection: *horama* (Acts 9:10, 12; 10:3, 17, 19) and *optasia* (Lk. 1:22; Acts 26:19; 2 Cor. 12:1). They signify 'appearance' or 'vision'.

The emphasis here seems to be upon the ecstatic nature of the experience, and the revelatory character of the knowledge, which came to the biblical prophets and seers. The experience points to a special awareness of God shared by saintly men (*e.g.* Je. 1:11; Dn. 2:19; Acts 9:10; 16:9), and to God's readiness to reveal himself to men (Ps. 89:19; Acts 10:3).

The circumstances in which the revelatory visions came to the seers of the Bible are varied. They came in men's waking hours (Dn. 10:7; Acts 9:7); by day (Acts 10:3) or by night (Gn. 46:2). But the visions had close connections with the dream-state (Nu. 12:6; Jb. 4:13).

In the OT the recipients of revelatory visions were the prophets, 'writing' (Is. 1:1; Ob. 1; Na. 1:1) and 'non-writing' (2 Sa. 7:17; 1 Ki. 22:17–19; 2 Ch. 9:29). But the outstanding examples were Ezekiel and Daniel.

In the NT Luke manifests the greatest interest in visions. He reports, *e.g.*, the visions of Zechariah (Lk. 1:22), Ananias (Acts 9:10), Cornelius (10:3), Peter (10:10ff.) and Paul (18:9); although Paul treated visions with much reserve (2 Cor. 12:1ff.). The supreme set of visions in the NT is that in the book of the *Revelation.

Biblical visions concerned both immediate situations (Gn. 15:1f.; Acts 12:7) and the 'far-off divine event' of the kingdom of God, as the writings of Isaiah, Daniel and John testify. In this connection the passages in 1 Sa. 3:1; Pr. 29:18 are especially relevant.

BIBLIOGRAPHY. J. M. Lower, 'Vision', *ZPEB*, 5, p. 889; R. Schnackenburg, 'Vision of God', *EBT*, 3, pp. 947–952; K. Dahn, *NIDNTT* 3, pp. 511–518.

J.G.S.S.T.

VOW. The idea of 'vow' in Semitic thought may well have been derived from the name of a deity. If so, it illustrates the fact that in biblical usage a vow is always used with reference to God and offers a new interpretation for such passages as Je. 32:35: they must then be construed as the sacrificing of children, not 'to Molech' (*mōleḵ*), but 'as a *mōleḵ*', *i.e.* a votive or 'vowed' offering. On Jdg. 11:30f., see *Jephthah. A vow may be either to perform (Gn. 28:20ff.) or abstain from (Ps. 132:2ff.) an act in return for God's favour (Nu. 21:1–3) or as an expression of zeal or devotion towards God (Ps. 22:25). It is no sin to vow or not to vow, but, if made—presumably uttered (Dt. 23:23)—a vow is as sacredly binding as an *oath (Dt. 23:21–23). Therefore, a vow should not be made hastily (Pr. 20:25); for the person vowing, *e.g.* to offer a sacrifice, then enters into 'the sphere of the offering' and is released only when the sacrifice is made (Pedersen). To have this fulfilment is the state of the happy man (Jb. 22:27), and the character of Israel's future blessedness (Na. 1:15). On the other hand, to substitute a blemished animal for the one vowed reveals a sin and brings God's curse (Mal. 1:14).

What is already the Lord's (*e.g.* firstlings, tithes (Lv. 27:26)), or an abomination to the Lord (Dt. 23:18), cannot be vowed or consecrated; but since a first-born child might be redeemed (Lv. 27; Nu. 3:44ff.), it is proper for Hannah to give Samuel to the Lord as a *Nazirite (1 Sa. 1:11). A vow has no virtue in itself (Ps. 51:16ff.), and may be only the pious pretence of a treacherous (2 Sa. 15:7ff.) or immoral (Pr. 7:14) person. Thus, in the NT the religionist's vow of Corban is condemned by Christ (Mk. 7:11). Paul's (probably not Aquila's) vow (*euchē*) no doubt was a temporary Nazirite vow—a sincere and proper expression of the ancient Hebrew faith (Acts 18:18, *cf.* 21:23).

Bibliography. A. R. Johnson, *Sacral Kingship in Ancient Israel*, 1955, p. 40 n.; J. Pedersen, *Israel, Its Life and Culture*, 4, 1959, pp. 265f., 324–330; R. de Vaux, *Ancient Israel*, 1961, pp. 465ff. E.E.E.

WAFER. Heb. *rāqîq*, 'thin cake', refers to home-made *bread, named from its thinness (Ex. 29:2; Nu. 6:15, *etc.*; *cf.* Arab. *warak*, 'foliage', 'paper'). Heb. *ṣappîḥiṯ*, 'a cake', appears once only (Ex. 16:31). J.D.D.

WAGES. Basically the payment made for services rendered. The frequency of the term in the Bible is somewhat obscured in that the Heb. and Gk. terms are sometimes translated 'reward' or 'hire'.

In OT society the hired labourer was not common. The family worked the farm. The family group included slaves and relatives whose wages would be in kind, *e.g.* those of Jacob as he worked for Laban. But a Levite received money as well as his keep for his service as family priest (Jdg. 17:10). And when Saul consulted Samuel, the seer, he first planned to pay the fee in kind, but finally resolved on a monetary fee (1 Sa. 9:7–8).

In primitive communities the employer had great power in fixing wages, and Jacob could complain that Laban had changed his wages ten times (Gn. 31:41). But the OT legislated to protect the wage-earner. Unscrupulous employers must not take advantage of his economic weakness. He must be given a fair wage, and paid promptly each day (Dt. 24:14–15).

Men working for wages meet us in the NT, both in actuality (Mk. 1:20) and in parable (Mt. 20:1–2; Lk. 15:17, 19; Jn. 10:13, *etc.*). The principle is laid down in the maxim, 'the worker earns his pay' (Lk. 10:7, NEB). Paul makes use of this to lay bare the essential truth at the heart of the gospel. 'To one who works,' he says, 'his wages (Gk. *misthos*) are not reckoned as a gift but as his due' (Rom. 4:4). Then he goes on to point out that men are saved, not by working for a heavenly wage but by trusting 'him who justifies the ungodly' (Rom. 4:5). By contrast the lost receive an exact if grim wage, for 'the wages of sin is death' (Rom. 6:23; *cf.* 2 Pet. 2:13, 15).

There is a sense in which the preachers of the gospel receive wages from those to whom they preach (*misthos* is used in this connection in Lk. 10:7; 2 Cor. 11:8; 1 Tim. 5:18). Our Lord himself enjoined the principle that 'those who proclaim the gospel should get their living by the gospel' (1 Cor. 9:14; *cf.* D. L. Dungan, *The Sayings of Jesus in the Churches of Paul*, 1971, pp. 3–80). This must not be misinterpreted, however, for in both OT and NT those who teach for the sake of money are castigated (Mi. 3:11; Tit. 1:7; 1 Pet. 5:2).

There are many passages which speak of God as giving wages or reward for righteousness (*e.g.* Lk. 6:23, 35; 1 Cor. 3:14; 2 Jn. 8). The metaphor is striking, but Scripture makes it clear that we are not to think of any rewards that God may give as merited in any strict sense. They are the acts of grace of a beneficent God who delights to give his people all things richly to enjoy. The knowledge of these gratuitous rewards is given to us in order to strengthen our perseverance in the way of righteousness. D.B.K.

WALK. Of the very many occasions when this verb is used in Scripture, the vast majority have the strictly literal sense of moving along or making one's way. It was the normal activity of men, but where the ability to walk had been lost it was capable of being restored by Christ. This outward healing corresponded to an inward renewal which Jesus claimed to be able to effect (Mk. 2:9). Jesus is further represented in the Gospels as walking and enabling others to walk under conditions not normally given to men (Mk. 6:48). Here again, as Matthew's Gospel makes clear, the physical act has a spiritual significance (Mt. 14:31). Walking can be understood as representative of the whole range of human activity to which an impotent man is restored (Acts 3:6).

The term is used in an anthropomorphic sense of God who walks in the garden in the cool of the evening (Gn. 3:8), and metaphorically it is applied to the heart (Jb. 31:7), to the moon (Jb. 31:26), to the tongue of the wicked (Ps. 73:9) and to the pestilence (Ps. 91:6). More frequently it stands for the whole manner of a man's life and conduct, and to the attitude which God takes up towards him, so that God can say: 'If you . . . walk contrary to me, then I also will walk contrary to you' (Lv. 26:23–24).

On occasion the term can be used in a more limited sense, referring to specific laws and observances enjoined upon men (Acts 21:21; *cf.* Heb. *hᵃlāḵâ*, 'rule', lit. 'walk'), while in John's Gospel it sometimes assumes the connotation of unwearied activity (Jn. 11:9), and sometimes of public

VULGAR FELLOW
See Raca, Part 3.

VULTURE
See Animals, Part 1.

WAILING
See Burial and mourning, Part 1.

appearance (Jn. 7:1). Metaphorically it denotes a studied observance of the new rule of life, and it is this sense which dominates the usage of all the forms in the Epistles, where there is a frequent contrasting of the walk which was characteristic of believers in their unregenerate days, and that to which they are called through faith in Christ. Baptism is to mark decisively the dividing-point between these two (Rom. 6:4), which is as clear as the distinction between the life of Christ before and after his resurrection. This renewal of life can equally well be expressed as walking in the spirit in contrast to walking according to the flesh. The word *stoicheō*, which appears once in Acts and four times in the Pauline Epistles, is used of the setting of plants in rows, and of soldiers walking in file, but the choice of verb appears to have no special significance.

BIBLIOGRAPHY. G. Ebel, *NIDNTT* 3, pp. 933–947. F.S.F.

WAND
See Rod, Part 3.

WALLS. To build his earliest houses, man used any available stone or lumps of unbaked mud, roughly shaped, *e.g.* Jarmo in E Iraq (*Antiquity* 24, 1950, pp. 185–195), Jericho (*PEQ* 88, 1956, plates X–XI). In Palestine stone foundations were often surmounted by brick walls. The enormous city walls of the mid-2nd millennium BC consisted of a strong stone footing to contain a sloping rampart which was smoothed over with plaster, with thick brick walls, sometimes containing chambers inside them, rising above (for those at Jericho, see *ANEP*, no. 715; *PEQ* 84, 1952, plate XVI. 1; see also P. J. Parr, *ZDPV* 84, 1968, pp. 18–45).

Wooden baulks were frequently incorporated into brickwork; in Egypt at least, this served to prevent warping as the mud-brick structure dried out, and to bind the whole (Petrie, *Egyptian Architecture*, p. 9). In Asia Minor, the Aegean and N Syria such beams were commonly inserted on stone foundations under or in mud-brick or stone walls (R. Naumann, *Architektur Kleinasiens*, 1955, pp. 83–86, 88–104, and figs. 63–66, 72–89)—so in houses of 14th–13th centuries BC at Canaanite Ugarit (Schaeffer, *Ugaritica*, 1, 1939, plate 19, with pp. 92–96 and fig. 90). This widespread and venerable use of brick upon wood over stone is apparently referred to in 1 Ki. 6:36; 7:12, as used by Solomon in buildings at Jerusalem. This technique was actually found at the Israelite Megiddo of Solomon or Ahab's day (Guy, *New Light from Armageddon*, Oriental Institute Communication No. 9, 1931, pp. 34–35; *cf.* building illustrated in Heaton, *Everyday Life in Old Testament Times*, 1956, fig. 106 opposite p. 207. See also H. C. Thomson, *PEQ* 92, 1960, pp. 57–63).

(*ARTS AND CRAFTS; *BRICK; *FORTIFICATION AND SIEGECRAFT; *HOUSE.) A.R.M. K.A.K.

WAR. Heb. *milḥāmâ*, 313 times in the OT from *lāḥam*, 'to fight'; *cf.* Arab. *laḥama*, 'fit close together', denoting the army in battle array (*BDB*). NT Gk. *polemos*, used 18 times.

I. Strategic importance of Palestine

The position of Palestine in relation to Mesopotamia and Egypt was truly axial. And the existence of the great Arabian desert between these two ancient centres of civilization further ensured that contact was almost always via Palestine. This contact was frequently of an inimical sort, so that Palestine could not avoid being the theatre of war—and a prize of war—for considerable periods during the last two millennia BC. Added to this was the fact that the people of Israel secured a kingdom for themselves only by embarking on a war of conquest and that, once established, they had to engage in defensive wars to fend off the Philistines who were challenging their claim to the title-deeds of Canaan. Neither were David's territorial gains

A corner-stone with blocks used as retaining walls for less skilfully set materials. Israelite masonry at Hazor. 8th cent. BC. (DJW)

made without military engagements beyond the borders of Israel. The imperial era was short-lived, however, and the divided kingdoms of Israel and Judah are soon to be seen defending themselves against their immediate neighbours, and finally against the unrelenting might of Assyria and Babylonia. It is no wonder, then, that war so stalks the pages of the OT.

II. War and religion

In the Near East generally war was a sacred undertaking in which the honour of the national god was very much at stake. The OT writers' conception of Israel's wars bears a superficial resemblance to this. The difference was that the God of Israel was transcendent and did not rise and fall with the fortunes of his people. For all that, he is 'the God of the armies of Israel' (1 Sa. 17:45) and far more involved in the struggles of his people than Marduk or Asshur were ever thought to be (*cf.* 2 Ch. 20:22). God himself is described as a 'man of war' (Ex. 15:3; Is. 42:13) and one of his titles is 'Lord of hosts'. This latter may refer to heavenly hosts (1 Ki. 22:19) or to Israelite armies (1 Sa. 17:45). It was God who led the armies of Israel into battle (Jdg. 4:14) so that the earliest account of Israelite triumphs was called 'the Book of the *Wars of the Lord' (Nu. 21:14). Indeed, at every stage in preparations for battle Israel's dependence upon God was acknowledged. First, enquiry was made as to whether this was the propitious moment for attack (2 Sa. 5:23–24); then sacrifice had to be offered. So vital did the latter preliminary seem that Saul in desperation arrogated priestly privilege to himself, lest battle be joined before the favour of the Lord had been sought (1 Sa. 13:8–12).

The battle cry had a religious significance (Jdg. 7:18, 20) and, further, acclaimed the presence of God as symbolized in the *ark of the covenant (1 Sa. 4:5–6; *cf.* the manner in which the arrival of the ark in Jerusalem was greeted, 2 Sa. 6:15). Because of the divine presence the Israelites could join battle in confidence of victory (Jdg. 3:28; 1 Ch. 5:22), even if the forces of nature had to be invoked to secure the victory (Jos. 10:11–14).

After battle it often happened that the Israelites observed a *'ban' (*ḥērem*), which meant that a whole city or country, people and possessions, would be set apart for God. No Israelite was permitted to appropriate for personal needs anything or anyone belonging to a place which had been put under a ban; failure in this matter met with the direst consequences (Jos. 7; 1 Sa. 15). Sometimes the ban might not be so comprehensive as in the case of Jericho (Jos. 6:18–24), but always the right of God to the fruit of victory was being asserted. The ban was God's way of dealing with 'the iniquity of the Amorites' (Gn. 15:16) and is central to the OT concept of 'the holy war'. Moreover, if pagan tendencies were discovered among the Israelites themselves, the offending community was likewise to be put under a ban (Dt. 13:12–18). And if the whole nation incurred God's displeasure, as they often did, then the agents of retribution could be the very pagans whom God had previously repudiated (Is. 10:5–6; Hab. 1:5–11). The ultimate is reached at the end of the monarchical period, when God announces his intention of himself fighting against Judah and on the side of the Babylonians (Je. 21:5–7). For a considerable time, however, the prophetic community had enjoyed the assurance of a better hope—nothing less than the eradication of war from the earth and the inauguration of a new era of peace by a Davidic 'Prince of Peace' (Is. 9:6; *cf.* Is. 2:4; Mi. 4:3).

III. Method of warfare

In the days before Israel had a standing army the national militia was summoned for action by means of the trumpet (Jdg. 3:27) or by messenger (1 Sa. 11:7). When on the offensive the Israelites set much store by military intelligence (Jos. 2; 2 Ki. 6:8–12); since there was no such thing as a declaration of war, the advantage for the assailant was all the greater. Usually expeditions were undertaken in spring when the roads were suitable (2 Sa. 11:1). Tactics naturally depended on the terrain and on the numbers involved, but in general the Israelite commanders were able, in defensive engagements at least, to exploit their superior knowledge of local geography. When it was a case of a head-on confrontation, as between Josiah and Pharaoh Neco at Megiddo, the Israelites do not seem to have fared so well. As well as the trumpet, signalling could be done by means of fires—to which practice one of the *Lachish ostraca bears testimony. The conventional methods of warfare are all represented in the OT; foray (1 Sa. 14), siege (1 Ki. 20:1) and ambush (Jos. 8) figure alongside the set piece. (*ARMOUR; *ARMY.)

IV. War in the New Testament

Extending Christ's kingdom by military means is clearly not part of the ideal of the NT. 'My kingship is not of this world; if my kingship were of this world, my servants would fight' (Jn. 18:36) was the principle enunciated by our Lord

Guard-room entrance to part of Solomon's buildings at Megiddo. (FNH)

The horror and casualties of war are clearly shown in this relief depicting the defeat of Tammaritu, king of Elam, and his son by Ashurbanipal, king of Assyria, at the battle of Ulai in 653 BC. Nineveh. (BM)

Reconstruction of the watchtowers in Jerusalem named Phasael, Hippicus and Mariamne (left to right) erected by King Herod to protect his palace. 37–4 BC. (JPK) (HC)

when he stood before Pilate. And his words to Peter as recorded in Mt. 26:52 cast a certain shadow on the use of force whatever the circumstances may be. But the Christian is a citizen of two worlds and has duties to both; tension between the conflicting demands is inevitable, especially since the secular powers have been ordained by God and do not 'bear the sword in vain' (Rom. 13:4). Paul availed himself not only of Roman citizenship but also of the protection of Roman troops, as when his life was threatened in Jerusalem (Acts 21). Piety was not regarded as incompatible with the pursuit of a military career, moreover, and those soldiers who inquired of John the Baptist as to their higher duty were not encouraged to desert (see Acts 10:1–2; Lk. 3:14). We are to assume, on the other hand, that the cause which bound together Matthew the tax collector and Simon the Zealot in the original Twelve required *both* to abandon their erstwhile occupations. In the early church a military career for the Christian was generally frowned upon; Tertullian is representative in his view that the two callings were incompatible, though he made allowances for those already committed to military service before conversion.

The Christian's warfare is preeminently a spiritual warfare and he has been equipped with all the armour necessary if he is to obtain victory (Eph. 6:10–20). It follows that he should be under military discipline, and to this end the NT abounds in injunctions couched in military terms (*cf.* 1 Tim. 1:18; 1 Pet. 5:9) and in military metaphors generally (*cf.* 2 Tim. 2:3–4; 1 Pet. 2:11). The critical battle was won at Calvary (Col. 2:15) so that the emphasis in a passage like Eph. 6:10–20 is not so much on the gaining of new ground, but on the holding of what has already been won. Victory ultimate and complete will come when Christ is revealed from heaven at the end of the age (2 Thes. 1:7–10). The final clash between Christ and the minions of darkness is depicted in chs. 16, 19 and 20 of Revelation. A decisive battle is fought at a place called *Armageddon (or Har-Magedon) according to Rev. 16:16. The most likely explanation of the name is that which links it with the hill (Heb. *har*) of Megiddo(n). Megiddo was the scene of many great battles in history (*cf.* 2 Ch. 35:22) and its appearance in an apocalyptic context is most fitting. For the enemies of Christ this encounter will mean destruction (Rev. 19:17–21). But thus will Ps. 110 and a host of OT passages find their fulfilment as the era of Messianic rule begins. The harbingers of that blessed age will indeed be 'wars and rumours of wars' (Mt. 24:6), but when Messiah reigns 'of the increase of his government and of peace there will be no end' (Is. 9:7).

V. The Qumran War Scroll

Among the first *Dead Sea Scrolls to be discovered was one which has become known as 'The War of the Sons of Light against the Sons of Darkness'. It is undoubtedly a product of the community which was once installed at Qumran and it issues directions to the community in anticipation of a protracted war between the forces of good—represented by the sectaries—and the forces of evil. The war will be fought in accordance with all the laws of warfare which Moses laid down, and although victory is predetermined by God there will be serious setbacks. Prominent among the 'sons of darkness' are the 'Kittim', and these are almost certainly to be identified as the Romans. It would seem that this scroll was one of the more exotic products of the age of Rom. domination of Palestine, an age when apocalyptic was at a premium and Messianic expectation at fever pitch.

BIBLIOGRAPHY. G. von Rad, *Der heilige Krieg im alten Israel*, 1951; Y. Yadin, *The Scroll of the War of the Sons of Light against the Sons of Darkness*, 1962; *idem*, *The Art of Warfare in Biblical Lands*, 1963; R. de Vaux, *Ancient Israel*², 1965, pp. 247–267; C. Brown, J. Watts, 'War', *NIDNTT* 3, pp. 958–967; M. Langley, 'Jesus and Revolution', *NIDNTT* 3, pp. 967–981. R.P.G.

WARS OF THE LORD, BOOK OF THE. A document mentioned and quoted in Nu. 21:14f. The quotation ends with the word 'Moab' (v. 15), but possibly fragments of poetry in vv. 17–18 and 27–30 come from the same source. The work was evidently a collection of popular songs commemorating the early battles of the Israelites. The name indicates that the Israelites viewed Yahweh virtually as their commander-in-chief, and credited him with their victories. Another similar work was probably the Book of Jashar of 2 Sa. 1:18; it is evident that this document was compiled after the time of David, and probably the Book of the Wars of the Lord appeared at the same period. A few scholars, following the LXX, would emend the text of Nu. 21:14 to excise the reference to any such document. D.F.P.

WASHBASIN (Heb. *sîr raḥaṣ*). Probably a wide, shallow bowl in which the feet were washed. The word is applied in triumphant scorn to Moab's inferiority (Pss. 60:8; 108:9; AV 'washpot'). A.R.M.

WATCH. 1. The 'guard' (RSV) of soldiers (Gk. *koustōdia*) mentioned in Mt. 27:65 as being deputed to watch over our Lord's tomb.

2. A measure of time into which the 12 hours of the night were divided. In Israelite times the division was threefold (Jdg. 7:19). In NT times the Rom. division into four watches seems to have been used (*cf.* Mk. 6:48).

BIBLIOGRAPHY. H.-G. Schütz, C. Brown, in *NIDNTT* 2, pp. 132–137. J.D.D.

WATCHMAN, WATCH-TOWERS. Watchman is in Heb. *ṣōpeh* and *šōmēr*, in Gk. *phylax* and *tērōn*; watch-tower is in Heb. *miṣpâ*, *migdāl* and *baḥan*. Watch-towers were used for two different purposes in biblical times:
(1) Towers were built from the earliest times (*cf.* Gn. 35:21) in the pastures to protect cattle and sheep against wild animals and thieves (*cf.* 2 Ch. 26:10; Mi. 4:8). It is possible that towers were erected in vineyards and cornfields for protection against thieves (*cf.* Is. 27:3).
(2) Towers of a more complex structure were built in the defence works of larger cities. The oldest Israelite tower of this kind as yet known was excavated by W. F. Albright at Tell el-Ful, the citadel of Saul. It is a corner tower which forms part of a casemate wall.

Important is the discovery by Albright at Tell beit Mirsim in S Palestine of a gate tower with a rectangular court. This court gives access to six paved rooms probably for guests (*ARCHITECTURE). Excavations at Tell en-Nasbeh show that towers were constructed in the city's defence wall at distances of

WARDROBE
See Vesture, Part 3.

WARRIOR
See Giant, Part 1.

WARSHIP
See Ships and boats, Part 3.

WASHING
See Clean, Part 1.

WASHING FEET
See Foot, Part 1.

WASHING HANDS
See Meals, Part 2.

WASHPOT
See Washbasin, Part 3.

WASP
See Animals, Part 1.

WATER HEN
See Animals, Part 1.

WATER POTS
See Vessels, Part 3.

WATER-SHAFT
See Siloam, Part 3.

WAX
See Panag, Part 2.

about 30 m apart and extending about 2 m to the outside. Square towers were built in early Israelite times, but later round ones were favoured. Herod erected in *Jerusalem three massive towers, called Hippicus, Phasael and Mariamne. The ground structure of the so-called 'tower of David' is possibly that of Phasael (8 m × 40 m). The *miḡdāl* and *millô'* (Jdg. 9:6, 20; 2 Sa. 5:9; 1 Ki. 9:15) were citadels or a kind of acropolis in a walled city. This citadel was used as a final place of refuge after the city was conquered. A good example of a *miḡdāl* was excavated at Beth-shean (*cf.* C. Watzinger, *Denkmäler*, 2, 1935, plates 19–21).

In the watch-towers were watchmen on the alert for hostile action against the city. They were also there to give word to the king of any person approaching the city wall (*e.g.* 2 Sa. 18:24–27; 2 Ki. 9:17–20). In time of hostility the dangers of the night were especially feared and the watchmen eagerly looked forward to the break of day (Is. 21:11). (*FORTIFICATION AND SIEGECRAFT.) F.C.F.

WATER (Heb. *mayim*, Gk. *hydōr*). In a part of the world where water is in short supply, it naturally features significantly in the lives of the people of the Bible. Nothing is more serious to them than absence of water (1 Ki. 17:1ff.; Je. 14:3; Joel 1:20; Hg. 1:11), and conversely rainfall is a sign of God's favour and goodness. An equally serious menace to life is water that has been polluted or rendered undrinkable. This was one of the plagues of Egypt (Ex. 7:17ff.). The Israelites found the water at Marah bitter (Ex. 15:23), and the well at Jericho was unpleasant in Elisha's day (2 Ki. 2:19–22).

It was common practice in time of warfare for an invading army to cut off the water-supply of beleaguered cities, as did Jehoshaphat with the wells of Moab (2 Ki. 3:19, 25), and Holofernes at Bethulia (Judith 7:7ff.). Hezekiah averted this danger by the construction of the tunnel which exists to this day in Jerusalem, running from the Virgin's fountain (Gihon), outside the city walls of his day, to the Pool of *Siloam (2 Ch. 32:30). Under conditions when water had to be rationed (La. 5:4; Ezk. 4:11, 16), the phrase 'water of affliction' could fittingly be used (Is. 30:20), but the context usually suggests punishment (1 Ki. 22:27; 2 Ch. 18:26).

Frequently water is symbolical of God's blessing and of spiritual refreshment, as in Ps. 23:2; Is. 32:2; 35:6–7; 41:18, *etc.*, and the longing for it indicates spiritual need (Pss. 42:1; 63:1; Am. 8:11). In Ezekiel's vision of God's house (47:1–11) the waters that poured out from under the threshold represented the unrestricted flow of Yahweh's blessings upon his people (*cf.* Zc. 14:8). Jeremiah describes Yahweh as 'the fountain of living waters' (2:13; 17:13), a phrase that is echoed in Jn. 7:38 of the Holy Spirit. In the NT water is connected with eternal life as the supreme blessing that God gives (Jn. 4:14; Rev. 7:17; 21:6; 22:1, 17), but in Eph. 5:26; Heb. 10:22, the predominant idea is that of baptismal cleansing for forgiveness of sins.

The idea of cleansing comes next to that of refreshment. In the ceremonial system washing was a prominent feature. Priests were washed at their consecration (Ex. 29:4); Levites too were sprinkled with water (Nu. 8:7). Special ablutions were demanded of the chief priest on the Day of Atonement (Lv. 16:4, 24, 26), of the priest in the 'water of separation' ritual (Nu. 19:1–10), and of all men for the removal of ceremonial defilement (Lv. 11:40; 15:5ff.; 17:15; 22:6; Dt. 23:11). The laver before the *tabernacle was a constant reminder of the need for cleansing in the approach to God (Ex. 30:18–21). A developed form of this ritual ablution was practised by the Qumran sect and by a variety of Jewish baptist sects which flourished before and after the turn of the Christian era. These provide the background to John's baptism of repentance and to the Christian *baptism of cleansing, initiation and incorporation into Christ.

A third aspect is that of danger and death. The story of the Flood, the drowning of the Egyptians in the Red Sea, and the general fear of the sea and deep waters expressed by the psalmist (18:16; 32:6; 46:3; 69:1ff., *etc.*) indicate that water could in Yahweh's hands be an instrument of judgment, although at the same time there was the thought of salvation through danger for the faithful people of God (*cf.* Is. 43:2; 59:19). It is hard to say to what extent these ideas were moulded by the Canaanite myths of the contest of Baal with the tyrannical waters of the sea, recounted in the Ras Shamra texts. Scandinavian scholars and Hooke's 'Myth and Ritual' school saw in these OT references, especially in the Psalms, a clue to the existence in Israel of an annual kingly festival at which the victory of Yahweh, personified by the king, was re-enacted. That Heb. thought and poetry echoed the language of Near Eastern mythology is clear (*cf.* the references to Rahab, Leviathan, the dragon, *etc.*), but to hold that the Canaanite rituals themselves or the doctrinal beliefs underlying them were taken over by the religion of Israel goes beyond the evidence. The views of Gunkel, Mowinckel and others are well discussed by A. R. Johnson in the chapter on 'The Psalms' in *OTMS*, 1951.

BIBLIOGRAPHY. O. Böcher, R. K. Harrison, in *NIDNTT* 3, pp. 982–993. J.B.Tr.

WAY. 1. OT usage. Apart from the obvious literal uses, there are a number of closely linked metaphorical ones. They derive from the fact that one on a public path becomes known and his goal and purposes are revealed by the road he takes. Most important is the sense of God's purposes and will, *e.g.* Ex. 33:13; Jb. 21:14, 31; Ps. 67:2; Pr. 8:22; Ezk. 18:25. There follows the idea of God's commandments, *cf.* especially Ps. 119. 'Way' is used generally of man's conduct, good or bad, and even of that of animals, *e.g.* Ps. 1:1, 6; Pr. 30:19–20. These usages are common in the Qumran literature.

2. NT usage. There are two developments of OT usage that call for comment. In Mt. 7:13–14 (*cf.* Lk. 13:24) we have the two ways in which man can walk contrasted. The earliest evidence for this thought is found at Qumran (1QS 3. 13–4. 26); it is common in rabbinic literature and was developed in the *Didache*, the *Epistle of Barnabas* and later patristic writings. From Acts 9:2; 19:9, 23; 22:4; 24:14, 22 we learn that 'the Way' was the oldest designation of the Christian church for itself. This is partly an extension of a use already found in the OT; *cf.* Is. 40:3 with 40:10–11, where God's people are seen being led along God's way. It can also be explained from Mt. 7:14 as the Way to salvation. Probably Jn. 14:6 was most influential of all, for here Christ claims to be the summing up of all 'the Way' means in relationship to God.

BIBLIOGRAPHY. E. Repo, *Der 'Weg' als Selbstbezeichnung des Urchristentums*, 1964; G. Ebel, *NIDNTT* 3, pp. 933–947. H.L.E.

WAYMARK. A conspicuous mark, monument or sign, usually made of a heap of stones, to mark a track (Je. 31:21, plural; AV 'high heaps'). The meaning is clear from the context and parallelism: Heb. *ṣiyyûn*, *cf.* Arab. *ṣuwwah*, 'guide-stone'; Syr. *ṣwāyâ*, 'stone-heap'. The same Heb. word is used of a monument or pile of stones used to mark the burial-place of the dead (Ezk. 39:15, 'sign'; 2 Ki. 23:17, AV 'title'). The standing stone over Rachel's grave may have been such a marker (Gn. 35:20; *PILLAR). D.J.W.

WEALTH. The view of the OT and of the NT is that wealth is a blessing from God. Abraham is a typical example of a wealthy God-fearing man (Gn. 13:2). The psalmists celebrate material blessings. The godly man flourishes 'like a tree planted by streams of water' (Ps. 1:3). 'Wealth and riches' are in the house of the man that 'fears the Lord' (Ps. 112:1, 3). God is beneficent, and material wealth is a consequence of his bounty: 'God . . . richly furnishes us with everything to enjoy' (1 Tim. 6:17).

The possession of wealth, however, brings with it the duty of generous liberality towards those in need (1 Tim. 6:18; 2 Cor. 8 and 9). (*ALMS.) Such is Christ's own example, 'Though he was rich, yet for your sake he became poor, so that by his poverty you might become rich' (2 Cor. 8:9). Faithfulness in the use of riches brings spiritual reward (Lk. 16:11); for true wealth and true riches are the spiritual blessings which God gives, rather than his material blessings (Lk. 12:33; 16:11).

The Bible recognizes that the possession of material wealth brings with it great dangers. For example, there is the danger of failing to acknowledge that God is the source of the blessing (Dt. 8:17–18; Ho. 2:8). There is the related danger of trusting in riches (Ps. 52:7). This danger of trusting in riches is so great that our Lord said that it was extremely difficult for a rich man to enter the kingdom of heaven, explaining the hard saying by the paraphrase 'those who have riches'. The disciples rightly concluded that all men have this besetting sin; to which our Lord replied that God alone can change the heart (Mk. 10:23, 27). Another spiritual danger associated with riches is materialism, that is, making riches the centre of one's interest. This was the case of the wealthy farmer in Lk. 12:21, who was not rich towards God; and of the church of Laodicea (Rev. 3:17). This temptation that wealth brings is described in the parable of the sower (Mt. 13:22), where the deceitfulness of riches chokes the word, so that it becomes unfruitful in the life. (*MAMMON.)

Covetousness, or the desire to be rich, is an evil against which the Scriptures frequently warn. The love of money is described as the root of all kinds of evil (1 Tim. 6:9–10). Consequently a spirit of contentment with such things as God has given is a virtue inculcated in both Testaments (Ps. 62:10; 1 Tim. 6:8; Heb. 13:5).

Because of the dangers of riches into which the possessor so frequently falls, rich men are, as a class, denounced in several passages of the Scriptures, *e.g.* Lk. 6:24f. and Jas. 5. Blessings are, however, pronounced on the poor (Lk. 6:20ff.); for poverty should quicken faith in God, which riches so frequently in practice deadens.

BIBLIOGRAPHY. J. Eichler *et al.*, *NIDNTT* 2, pp. 829–853.

D.B.K.

WEASEL
See Animals, Part 1.

WEAVER'S BEAM
See Spinning, Part 3.

WEAVING
See Spinning, Part 3.

WEDGE OF GOLD
See Money, Part 2.

WEEPING
See Burial and mourning, Part 1.

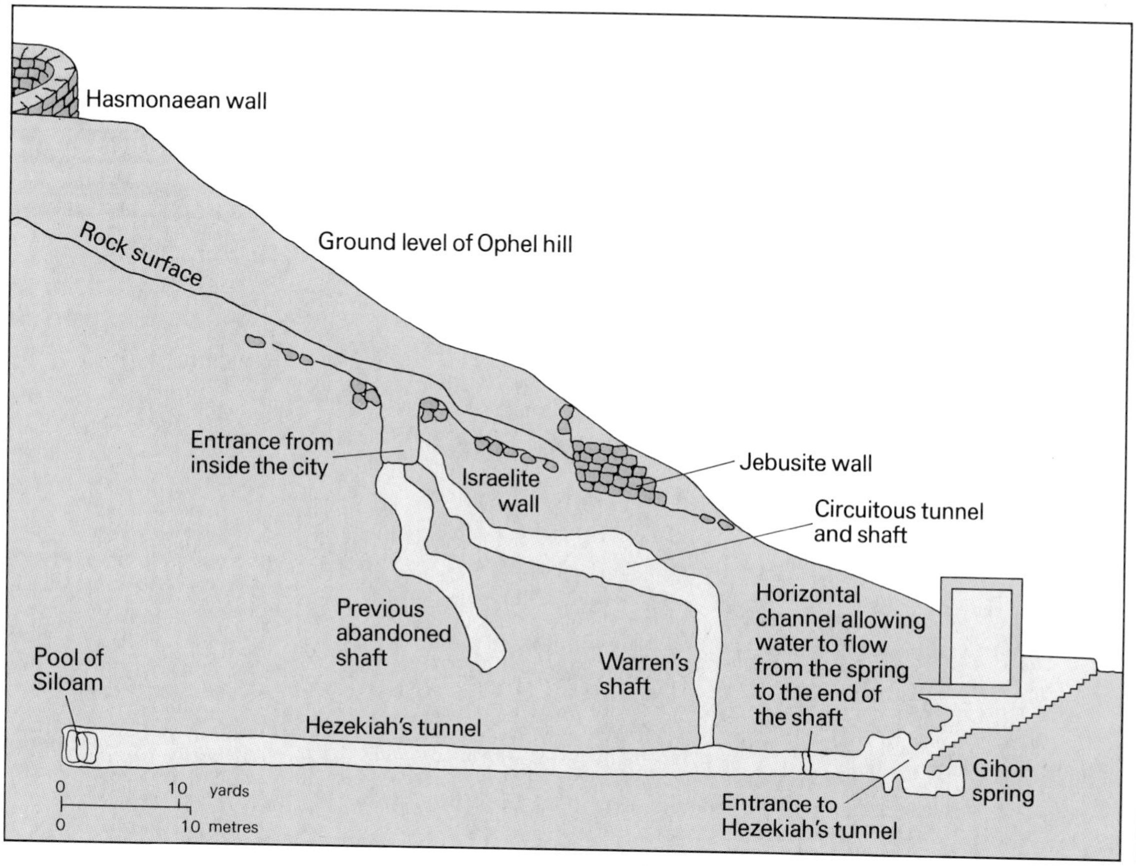

Cross-section of the water-system of ancient Jerusalem, including Hezekiah's tunnel.

WEIGHTS AND MEASURES.

1. IN THE OLD TESTAMENT

Metrology, an exact science, requires legal sanction to enforce the authority granted to any particular system. In the ancient Near East standards varied between districts and cities, and there is no evidence that Israel had or used an integrated system. David (2 Sa. 14:26) and Ezekiel (45:10) pronounced certain basic standards of weight and measurements. Rabbinic tradition that standard measures were deposited in the Temple is unverified (*cf.* 1 Ch. 23:29). The law, however, prescribed that the Hebrew keep a just weight, measure and balance (Lv. 19:35–36; Ezk. 45:10). The prophets spoke against those merchants who, by increasing or decreasing their weights (Dt. 25:13), or using deceitful weights (Mi. 6:11) or false balances (Pr. 11:1; 20:23), defrauded their fellows. Since ancient balances had a margin of error of up to 6% (*PEQ* 74, 1942, p. 86), and few Heb. weights yet found of the same inscribed denomination have proved to be of exactly identical weight, the importance of this exhortation can be seen. These, and other variants, mean that ancient weights and measures can be given only their approximate equivalent in modern terms.

I. Weights

Ancient weights were stones (Heb. *'eḇen*) carved in shapes, usually with a flat base, which made them easy to handle or recognize (*e.g.* turtles, ducks, lions). They were often inscribed with their weight and the standard followed. Weights were carried in a pouch or wallet (Dt. 25:13; Mi. 6:11; Pr. 16:11) in order that the purchaser could check with the 'weights current among the merchants' at a given place (Gn. 23:16).

a. Talent (Heb. *kikkār*, 'a round'; Akkad. *biltu*, 'a burden'; Gk. *talanton*, 'a weight'). This was the largest unit, probably named after the characteristic shape in which large metal lumps were moulded, as in the lead cover of the ephah (Zc. 5:7). It was used to weigh gold (2 Sa. 12:30, *etc.*), silver (1 Ki. 20:39), iron (1 Ch. 29:7) and bronze (Ex. 38:29). 666 talents of gold were included in Solomon's annual revenue (1 Ki. 10:14).

The 30 talents of gold paid by Hezekiah as tribute (2 Ki. 18:14) corresponds with the amount Sennacherib claims to have received (Annals), implying a similar talent in use in Judah and Assyria at this time. This might be the 'light' talent of about 30 kg, as inscribed Babylonian duck-weights of this value range 29·76–30·27 kg. A weight found at Tell Beit Mirsim (4,565 gm) has been interpreted as this talent of 30·43 kg or, more likely, of 28·53 kg (*i.e.* 8 minas of 570·6 gm = 8 × 50 shekels of 11·41 gm; see below).

Other Babylonian weights show that a 'heavy' or double standard talent was also in use, weighed examples ranging from 58·68 to 59·82 kg, *i.e.* about 60 kg.

b. Mina (AV 'maneh'; Heb. *māneh*; Akkad. *manû*) was a weight used to measure gold (1 Ki. 10:17), silver (Ezr. 2:69; Ne. 7:71–72) and other commodities. The talent was subdivided into 60 minas of 50 shekels or 50 minas of 60 shekels. There is some evidence that in Palestine, as at Ras Shamra, the 50-shekel mina was in use in pre-exilic times. The payment by 603,550 men of a poll-tax of ½ shekel (see *f. beka*) produced 100 talents, 1,775 shekels, *i.e.* 3,000 shekels to the talent (as at Ras Shamra), but could be interpreted by either standard. However, multiples of 50 shekels (*e.g.* 400—Gn. 23:15; 500—Ex. 30:24; 5,000—1 Sa. 17:5; 16,750—Nu. 31:52) seem to be conclusive evidence for the use of a 50-shekel mina.

Ezekiel's metrological reforms included the redefinition of the mina to 60 shekels (45:12, *MT*, 20 + 25 + 15). Thus the new Heb. mina at 20 (gerahs) × 60 (shekels) kept the value of the mina unchanged in relation to the Babylonian, which comprised 24 (*girū*) × 50 (*šiqlu*) = 1,200 gerahs.

c. The *shekel* (Heb. *šeqel*; Akkad. *šiqlu*; Aram., Ugar. *ṯql*) was common to all Semitic metrologies and was the basic weight (*šāqal*, 'to weigh'). Its value varied considerably at different times and areas:

(i) The royal shekel, set by 'the king's weight' (2 Sa. 14:26), was a standard known also in Babylonia. This was probably the 'heavy shekel' of Ras Shamra (*kbd*). Analysis of weights discovered at Gibeon, Gezer, Megiddo and Tell en-Nasbeh show a 'heavy' shekel of 12·5–12·88 gm, *i.e.* about 13 gm (0·457 oz).

(ii) The common shekel was often used to weigh metal objects (1 Sa. 17:5; Goliath's armour of 5,000 shekels = 56·7 kg or 125 lb), foodstuffs (2 Ki. 7:1; Ezk. 4:10), and commonly gold and silver, thus implying its use as a means of payment. Silver shekel coins (*sigloi*) first appeared in the reign of Darius I (* MONEY).

Some fifty inscribed weights of a shekel or multiples upwards show a variation 11·08–12·25; average 11·38 gm. This compares well with calculations based on the inscribed weights of smaller denominations (see below), which confirm a possible devaluation in post-exilic times to about 11·7–11·4 gm (0·401 oz) for the shekel.

Inscriptions on the weights use the symbols I : II : III : 𐤄 : Λ : IΛ : IIΛ : T : TΛ : — : = : ≡ : ×. Interpreted by Y. Yadin (*Scripta Hierosolymitana* 8, 1961, pp. 1–62) as 1, 2, 3, 4, 5, 6, 7, 8, 9, 10, 20, 30, royal (*lmlk*). Others (Scott, Aharoni) however equate these markings as the equivalent of the shekel in terms of Egyp. weights, 8 shekels = 1 *deben* = 10 *qedets* (1 *deben* = about 91 gm). Thus Egyp. hieratic numerals were engraved on the weights to show their value; I and II for 1 and 2 shekels, 4 and 8 shekel weights bearing the numbers 5 and 10 (𐤄 and Λ), then values in *qedets*.

(iii) The temple shekel or 'shekel of the sanctuary' (Ex. 30:13; Lv. 5:15, *etc.*) was related to a *beqa'* or ½ shekel (RSV 'beka', AV 'bekah', Ex. 38:26) and 20 gerahs (Ezk. 45:12), though later with revaluation it equalled ⅓ shekel (Ne. 10:32). This shekel is believed to be the *nṣp* (see *d.* below), of which examples have been discovered weighing 9·28–10·5 gm, *i.e.* about 10 gm (0·353 oz) depreciating to about 9·8 gm (0·349 oz).

d. nṣp or 'part' was ⅚ shekel. Thirteen examples give it a weight of about 10 gm (see *c.* above).

e. pim (Heb. *pîm* or *payim*) is mentioned only in 1 Sa. 13:21 (AV 'Yet they had a file [with mouths]') which should be translated 'and the charge was a *pim* for the ploughshares . . .' (so RSV). This weight was ⅔ of a unit (*cf.* Akkad. [*šini*]*pu*), probably of the common shekel, since twelve inscribed *pim* weights (from Lachish, Jerusalem, Gezer, Tell en-Nasbeh, *etc.*) average 7·8 gm.

f. beka (Heb. *beqa'*, 'fraction, division', AV 'bekah') was used for weighing gold (Gn. 24:22) and for paying the poll-tax said to be the equivalent of 'half a shekel, after

Figure holding scales and a bag of weights. Fragment of a Neo-Hittite stele from Marash. 8th cent. BC. (MC)

the shekel of the sanctuary' (Ex. 38:26). Since seven inscribed weights inscribed *bqʿ* or abbreviated as *b* have been found (at Lachish, Jerusalem, Gezer and Beth-zur), this enables a check to be made of the value of the shekel. These *bqʿ* have an average weight of 6·02 gm.

g. ḥmš, '$\frac{1}{5}$' was inscribed on a turtle-shaped weight from Samaria weighing 2·499 gm. This compares with another inscribed '$\frac{1}{4}$ *nṣp*, $\frac{1}{4}$ *šql*', implying a subdivision of the Ezekiel shekel.

h. gerah (Heb. *gērâ*; Assyr. *girû*). This was defined as $\frac{1}{20}$ shekel (Ex. 30:13; Ezk. 45:12).

i. Other weights. The *peres* (Aram. pl. *parsin*) of Dn. 5:25, 28 was a subdivision of the shekel in use at Babylon (*cf.* Old Bab. *paras*), and like the *parisu* (Alalaḫ) possibly equal to $\frac{1}{2}$ shekel since a term for any weight (here 'fraction') had a precise value. Thus the writing on the wall superficially implied a statement of weight 'Mina, mina, shekel, half-shekel'. The *q^{e}šîṭâ* (*qesitah*, RSVmg., Gn. 33:19; Jos. 24:32; Jb. 42:11) appears to be a unit of as yet unknown weight. A stone weight of Darius II is inscribed 120 *krš* = 20 mina.

The table on p. 1638 indicates the relation of these weights to each other and gives approximate modern equivalents, which should be used with caution owing to the varying standards in use in antiquity.

II. Linear measures

Linear measures were based on the 'natural' units which could be easily applied.

a. The *reed* (*qāneh*), though often denoting a measuring instrument rather than a measure (*ARTS AND CRAFTS), was of 6 cubits length and exact enough to be reckoned as a unit of length (Ezk. 40:5; *cf.* 'rod', Rev. 21:15).

Duck-shaped weight in diorite, with inscription stating that its weight, 5 minas, had been guaranteed by the king. From Ur. 2090 BC. (SI)

b. The *cubit* (Heb. *'ammâ*; Akkad. *ammātu*; Lat. *cubitus*) was the distance from elbow to finger tip. This 'natural' cubit (AV 'cubit of a man', RSV 'common cubit', Dt. 3:11) was used to indicate the general size of a person (4 cubits the height of a man; *cf.* 1 Sa. 17:4; 1 Ch. 11:23) or object (Est. 5:14; Zc. 5:2). It described depth (Gn. 7:20) or distance (Jn. 21:8).

A more precisely defined cubit was used for exact measurement. This *standard Hebrew cubit* was 17·5 inches (44·45 cm), slightly shorter than the common Egyp.

Assyrians weighing tribute in a balance. From the black basalt obelisk of Ashurnasirpal II, Nimrud. c. 880 BC. (BM)

cubit of 17·6 inches (44·7 cm). This generally accepted figure compares closely with the length given for the Siloam tunnel as '1,200 cubits', equivalent to a measured 1,749 feet (533·1 m), giving a cubit of 17·49 inches or 44·42 cm. Excavated buildings at Megiddo, Lachish, Gezer and *Hazor reveal a plan based on multiples of this measure. Also Solomon's bronze laver of 1,000 *bath* capacity (*i.e.* 22,000 litres; 1 Ki. 7:23–26; 2 Ch. 4:2, 5), when calculated for the capacity of a sphere, gives a cubit of 17·51 inches or 44·48 cm (R. B. Y. Scott, *JBL* 77, 1958, pp. 210–212).

The *long* or 'royal' *cubit* was a handbreadth ('palm') longer than the standard cubit of 6 palms (Ezk. 40:5), *i.e.* 20·4 inches or 51·81 cm. With this compare the Babylonian cubit of 50·3 cm (of 30 fingers length marked on a statue of Gudea) which was '3 fingers' shorter than the Egyp. cubit of 52·45 cm (Herodotus, *Hist.* 1. 178).

c. The *gōmeḏ* (AV, RSV 'cubit') occurs only in Jdg. 3:16, where it measures a weapon, probably a dagger rather than a sword, and has thus been interpreted as a subdivision (perhaps $\frac{2}{3}$) of the cubit, or as the short cubit of 5 palms mentioned in the Mishnah.

d. The *span* (*zereṯ*), or outstretched hand from the thumb to the little finger (Vulg. wrongly *palmus*), was a half-cubit (1 Sa. 17:4; Ex. 28:16; Ezk. 43:13), though 'half a cubit' could be expressed literally (Ex. 25:10).

e. The *palm* (*ṭep̄aḥ*; *ṭōp̄aḥ*) or 'handbreadth' was the width of the hand at the base of the 4 fingers (hence Vulg. *quattuor digitis*), *i.e.* 7·37 cm. Thus was measured the thickness of the bronze laver (1 Ki. 7:26 = 2 Ch. 4:5), the edge of the tabernacle table (Ex. 25:25; 37:12), and of that in Ezekiel's Temple (40:5; 43:13). A man's life is but (a few) handbreadths in length (Ps. 39:5).

f. The *finger* or digit (*'eṣba'*) was a $\frac{1}{4}$ handbreadth (Je. 52:21), and the smallest subdivision of the cubit in common use in Palestine, as in Egypt and Mesopotamia. It is generally taken to be 1·85 cm.

g. Distance, as opposed to the measurement of objects, was in pre-exilic times reckoned by equation with a known average. It is reck-

Babylonian polished haematite weights ranging from 25·57 to 83·70 g. Range of lengths 3·5 cm–11 cm. Warka. 18th cent. BC. (BM)

Bronze lion-weights, some of which are inscribed in Aramaic and Assyrian cuneiform with the name of the king for whom they were made, and their weights (from 3 shekels to 15 minas). Nimrud. Lengths 25·4 cm–5·08 cm. 8th cent. BC. (BM)

oned as a 'bowshot' (Gn. 21:16), the length of a ploughed furrow (1 Sa. 14:14), 'a day's journey' (Nu. 11:31; 1 Ki. 19:4), or 'a journey of three days' (Gn. 30:36; Ex. 3:18; Jon. 3:3). It is not proved that the latter is to be taken merely as general indication of 'a long distance' (*cf.* 'a seven days' journey', Gn. 31:23), for exact standards were used by the Babylonians; *e.g. bēru*, 'double-hour' march of 10·692 km (*AfO* 16, 1953, p. 20, n. 138).

The step (*peśa'*) in 1 Sa. 20:3 was used metaphorically rather than in the exact manner of the contemporary Assyrian 'foot' (= 32·92 cm). Similarly the 'stretch of the ground' (*kiḇraṯ hā'āreṣ*, RSV 'some distance', Gn. 35:16; 48:7; 2 Ki. 5:19) was only a vague indication of distance.

In Maccabean times Hellenistic measures were introduced. Thus Beth-zur was about 5 *schoinoi* from Jerusalem (2 Macc. 11:5, RSV 'leagues'), *i.e.* 30·5 km at the Ptolemaic value of a *schoinos* of 6·1 km. The Alexandrian *stadion* of 184·9 m was employed. Jerusalem to Scythopolis was 600 *stades* (2 Macc. 12:29, RSVmg.), which corresponds well with the known distance of 110 km between these two cities.

III. Measures of area

Superficial areas were not specifically expressed but described by giving the necessary dimensions. Thus the square was of four sides of equal dimension (*m^e^rubbā'aṯ*, AV 'foursquare', 1 Ki. 7:31; Ezk. 40:47; 45:2), the circumference of a circle (1 Ki. 7:23) and the diameter the distance 'from brim to brim' (2 Ch. 4:2).

The area of land was calculated empirically. Thus vineyards (Is. 5:10) or a field (1 Sa. 14:14) could be measured by the *ṣemeḏ* ('acre'), *i.e.* the area a pair of yoked animals could plough in a day (*cf.* Arab. *faddan*). In Babylonia this was defined as 6,480 square cubits = $\frac{2}{5}$ acre (1,618 sq m). This in later times was the Lat. *jugum, jugerum* of 28,800 square Rom. feet = $\frac{5}{8}$ acre (2,529 sq m). Another method was to estimate the area by the amount of seed (*s^e^'â*) required to sow it (Lv. 27:16; 1 Ki. 18:32). In the Hellenistic period this was $3\frac{3}{5}$ seahs to a *jugerum* of land, *i.e.* 0·173 acre (700 sq m) per seah or 5·19 acres (2·1 hectares) per homer of 30 seahs (*JBL* 64, 1945, p. 372), which seems to have improved to 0·193 and 5·79 acres respectively by the 2nd century AD.

The specific measurement of the pastures round the levitical cities (Nu. 35:4–5) presents difficulties. It may have been an area 2,000 cubits square (v. 5), the centres of the sides of which were also reckoned as at a radius of 1,000 cubits from the city walls (v. 4).

IV. Dry measures of capacity

The terms used derive originally from the receptacles which contained an agreed amount and thus served as a measure.

a. Homer (Heb. *ḥōmer*; Akkad. *imēr*), 'a donkey load', was commonly used throughout Asia S of Anatolia and W of Euphrates in the 2nd millennium and thereafter as a measure for cereals. The *homer* is older than the *kor* (*RA* 67, 1973, p. 78); *cf.* Lv. 27:16; Ezk. 45:13. The collection of 10 homers of quails (Nu. 11:32) implied gluttony, whereas the return of only an ephah of wheat from a homer of seed was a picture of failure (Is. 5:10), there being 10 ephahs to the homer, which equalled about 220 litres (48·4 gallons).

b. Kor (RSV 'cor') (Heb. *kōr*; Sum. *gur*; Akkad. *kurru*) was a large dry measure equal to the homer (Ezk. 45:14) used of fine flour (*sōleṯ*), meal (*qemaḥ*, 1 Ki. 4:22), wheat and barley (2 Ch. 2:10; 27:5). It also appears as a liquid measure for oil (Ezk. 45:14), though 2 Ch. 2:10 and Gk. reads *bath* (*cf.* the parallel passage, 1 Ki. 5:11).

c. Half-homer (Heb. *leṯeḵ*) occurs only in Ho. 3:2 as a measure for barley. As it is mentioned after the homer, Aq., Sym. and Vulg. interpret as $\frac{1}{2}$ *kōr* or $\frac{1}{2}$ homer, but there is no confirmatory evidence for this. The *leṯeḵ* may be a Phoenician measure.

d. Ephah (Heb. *'ēp̄â*; Egyp. *ipt*) is the name of a vessel large enough to hold a person (Zc. 5:6–10), and thence of an exact measure (Lv. 19:36). Used only of cereals, and with subdivision of $\frac{1}{6}$ (Ezk. 45:13; 46:14) or $\frac{1}{10}$ (Lv. 5:11), it was in common use from an early period (Jdg. 6:19). The ephah must never be diminished (Am. 8:5) but always be of equal (just) measure (Dt. 25:14; Pr. 20:10). The ephah was equal to the liquid measure *bath*, both being $\frac{1}{10}$ of a homer (Ezk. 45:11).

e. Seah (Heb. *s^e^â*; Akkad. *sûtu*) was also a measure for flour and cereals (Gn. 18:6; 1 Ki. 18:32).

f. Omer (Heb. *'ōmer*, *cf.* Arab. *'umar*, 'a small bowl') occurs only in the account of the collection of manna (Ex. 16), being used both of the measure itself (vv. 18, 32–33) and of the amount measured (vv. 16, 22). The *'ōmer* was equal to $\frac{1}{10}$ ephah (v. 36).

g. A '*tenth* deal' (AV; Heb. *'iśśārôn*) was a measure used for flour (Ex. 29:40; Nu. 15:4) equal to $\frac{1}{10}$ ephah (Nu. 28:5), and therefore equal to the omer.

h. Cab (Heb. *qaḇ*), a measure of capacity which occurs only in 1 Ki. 6:25, where among the inflated prices at the siege of Samaria $\frac{1}{4}$ *qaḇ* of carob pods was sold for 5 (shekels) of silver. The cab = 4 log = $\frac{1}{5}$ seah = $\frac{1}{6}$ hin = about 2 litres.

i. The 'measure' (Heb. *šālîš*) of Ps. 80:5; Is. 40:12 is literally '$\frac{1}{3}$', but no unit is expressed, so that the measure of capacity is unknown. It will be noted that these dry

Old Testament measures

Length		Metric*
	1 finger	= 1.85 cm
4 fingers =	1 palm	= 7.40 cm
12 fingers 3 palms =	1 span	= 22.25 cm
24 fingers 6(7) palms 2 spans =	1 cubit	= 44.5 cm (1 royal cubit (Ezk.) = 51.81 cm)
12 spans 6 cubits (7 royal cubits) =	1 reed	= 2.67 metres (1 reed (Ezk.) = 3.1 metres)

Capacity – dry and liquid		Metric*
	1 log †	= 0.3 litres
4 logs =	1 cab	= 1.2 litres
	1 omer (ʿiśśārôn)	= 2.4 litres
12 logs 2½ cabs =	1 hin †	= 3.6 litres
24 logs 5 cabs 2 hins =	1 seah	= 7.3 litres
72 logs 15 cabs 10 omers 6 hins 3 seahs =	1 ephah (bath) †	= 22 litres
360 logs 75 cabs 50 omers 30 hins 15 seahs 5 ephahs =	1 half-homer (*leṯeḵ*)	= 110 litres
720 logs 150 cabs 100 omers 60 hins 30 seahs 10 ephahs 2 half-homers =	1 homer (kor) ††	= 220 litres

† liquid measure only   †† dry and liquid measure

Weights		Metric*
	1 gerah	= 0.5 gm
10 gerahs =	1 beka	= 5 gm
13.3 gerahs 1.33 bekas =	1 pim	= 7 gm
20 gerahs 2 bekas 1.5 pims =	1 shekel	= 10 gm
1000 gerahs 100 bekas 75 pims 50 shekels =	1 mina	= 500 gm
60 000 gerahs 6000 bekas 4500 pims 3000 shekels 60 minas =	1 talent	= 30 kg

New Testament measures

Length		Metric*
	1 cubit	= 44.5 cm (Roman) 52.5 cm (Palestinian)
4 cubits =	1 fathom	= 2.10 metres 1.8 metres (Greek)
100 fathoms =	1 stade	= 185 metres
8 stades =	1 mile	= 1478.5 metres

Capacity – dry		Metric*
	1 choinix	= 1 litre
48 choinikes =	1 medimnos	= 52.5 litres
10 medimnoi =	1 koros	= 525 litres

Capacity – liquid		Metric*
	1 sextarius	= 500 cc
16 sextarii =	1 modius	= 8.75 litres
72 sextarii or 4.5 modii =	1 batos or 1 metrētēs	= 39.5 litres
6 modii =	1 medimnos	= 52.5 litres

*approximate metric equivalent

Two examples of measurements in proportion

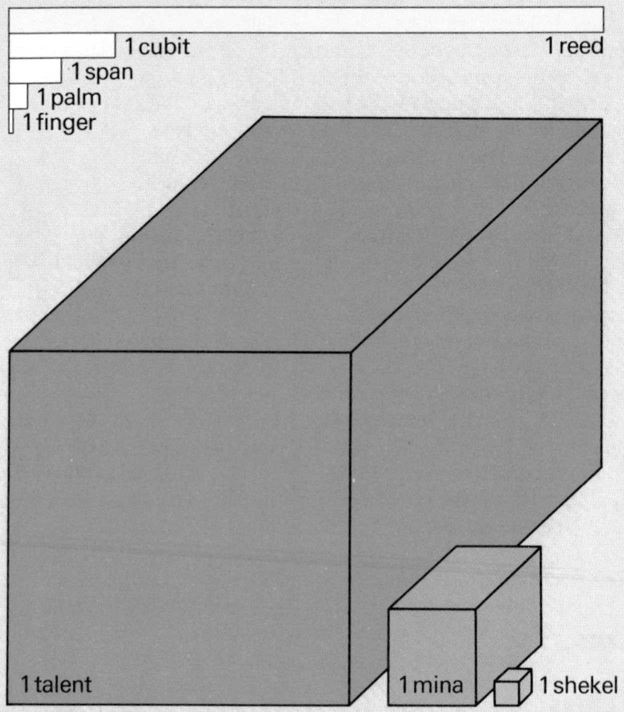

measures combine the Babylonian sexagesimal reckonings (1 *kur* = 30 *sutu* = 180 *qa*) with the decimal system (also employed by the Assyrians). See table on p. 1638.

V. Liquid measures of capacity

a. Bath (Heb. *baṯ*; Gk. *batos*, Lk. 16:6 only) was the equivalent in liquid of the ephah (Ezk. 45:11, 14). It was used to measure water (1 Ki. 7:26), wine (Is. 5:10) and oil (2 Ch. 2:10; so also 1 Ki. 5:11). It was an exact and standard measure (Ezk. 45:10, about 22 litres).

b. Hin (Heb. *hîn*; Egyp. *hnw*, 'a pot') was used of the vessel employed as a measure (Lv. 19:36) and of the measure of water (Ezk. 4:11), oil (Ex. 29:40) or wine (Lv. 23:13). According to Josephus (*Ant.* 3. 197; 4. 234), the *hin* was equal to $\frac{1}{6}$ *bath.*

c. Log (Heb. *lōg̅*) is used only in Lv. 14:10 as a measure of oil in the ceremony for the purification of the leper. According to the Talmud, this was equal to $\frac{1}{12}$ *hin.*

The values of these liquid measures depend upon that of the *bath*. This is uncertain, since the only inscribed vessels marked *bt* (Tell beit Mirsim) and *bt lmlk* (Lachish) are fragmentary and cannot be reconstructed with certainty; thus the value of the *bath* has been variously calculated between 20·92 and 46·6 litres. On the assumptions that the *bath* measure was half the size of the 'royal *bath*' and that these inscriptions denoted the full capacity of the vessels, the proposal of 22 litres in biblical times (Albright) and 21·5 litres in Hellenistic times is usually adopted as a basis for calculation, since it receives some support from the comparison with the capacity of Solomon's laver, which held 1,000 *baths* = 22,000 litres. For weights in the Talmud, see *EJ*, 16, 1971, pp. 388–392.

BIBLIOGRAPHY. A. E. Berriman, *Historical Metrology*, 1953; A. H. Gardiner, *Egyptian Grammar*³, 1957, pp. 197–200 (for Egyp. metrology); R. de Vaux, *Ancient Israel*, 1961, pp. 195–209; R. B. Y. Scott, 'Weights and Measures of the Bible', *BA* 22, 1951, pp. 22–40; *PEQ* 97, 1965, pp. 128–139; Y. Aharoni, *BASOR* 184, 1966, pp. 13–19.

D.J.W.

2. IN THE NEW TESTAMENT

I. Weights

Only two weights are mentioned in the NT. The *litra* of Jn. 12:3; 19:39 (*cf.* Lat. *libra*: 'pound'—from this weight we have our abbreviation *lb* for pound) was a Rom. measure of weight equivalent to 327·45 gm. In Rev. 16:21 the adjective *talantiaios*, 'weighing a talent'; RSV 'hundredweight', is used to describe hailstones: Arndt maintains that this talent equalled 125 librae, and so would be about 41 kg in weight, but *HDB* calculates it as weighing about 20·5 kg.

II. Linear measures

a. The *cubit*. As in OT times, measurements were related to the parts of the body, and the basic unit was still the *pēchys* ('forearm') or cubit. Under the Rom. empire there were two different measurements for a cubit: the Rom. cubit of 6 handbreadths of 74 mm = 44·4 cm, and the Philetarian cubit of 52·5 cm. Julian of Ascalon relates that the latter system of measurement was customary in Palestine and Egypt (Jeremias, p. 11n.), and this is probably the length indicated in Jn. 21:8; Rev. 21:17. In Mt. 6:27; Lk. 12:25 the term is also used.

b. The *orgyia* ('fathom', Acts 27:28) was the length of the outstretched arms, and so was approximately 1·8 m. This was a Gk. unit of measure, derived from the verb *oregō*, 'I stretch'. Herodotus (2. 149) says that it equalled 6 Gk. feet or 4 Gk. cubits.

c. The *stadion* ('furlong' AV, Lk. 24:13; Jn. 6:19; 11:18; Rev. 14:20; 21:16) was 100 *orgyiai* and equalled about 185 m. As the race-course at Olympia was supposed to be exactly a stade long, the word was used for an arena, as in 1 Cor. 9:24—hence the English 'stadium'.

d. The *milion* ('mile', Mt. 5:41) was a Gk. transliteration of the Rom. measurement *mille passuum*, 'a thousand paces'. This was 1,478·5 m, or 8 stades, and was calculated on the basis of 5 Rom. feet (each of 29·57 cm) to the pace (1·48 m).

e. The sabbath day's journey mentioned in Acts 1:12 was not a proper measurement, but rather the product of rabbinical exegesis of Ex. 16:29 and Nu. 35:5 (*cf.* Lumby in *CGT*, *ad loc.*). It was fixed at 2,000 cubits (Talmud *'Erubin* 51a) and was called *tᵉḥûm ha-šabbāṯ*—the limit of the sabbath.

III. Measures of area

None is used in the NT, but the basic unit under the Rom. empire was the *jugerum*, or acre, calculated on the amount of land a yoke of oxen could plough in a day. This was estimated at one *actus*, or furrow (36·6 m), by two (73·2 m); so the *jugerum* was the equivalent of 2 square *actus*, or 0·27 hectares, about $\frac{2}{3}$ acre.

IV. Dry measures of capacity

a. The *choinix* ('quart', Rev. 6:6), is variously estimated at 1½–2 pints, and the best calculation would be just over 1 litre. It was a Gk. measure, and Herodotus (7. 187) narrates that it was the daily ration of grain per man in Xerxes' invasion army.

b. The *saton* (Aram. *sā'ṯâ*, Heb. *sᵉ'â*) was the *sᵉ'â* of OT times: Josephus (*Ant.* 9. 85) rates this as equivalent to 1½ *modii* (see below). It is the measure mentioned in Mt. 13:33; Lk. 13:21, where leaven is added to 3 *sata* of wheat-flour: each would be about 12·3 litres.

c. The *koros* of Lk. 16:7 (a 'measure of wheat') was Heb. *kōr*. Josephus (*Ant.* 15. 314) equates it to 10 Attic *medimnoi*, and, as the *medimnos* contained 48 *choinikes*, this would rate the *koros* at 525 litres. Since Ezk. 45:11 rates the *baton* as the tenth of a *koros*, it is generally regarded that Josephus here mistook the *medimnos* for the *metrētēs*, and that the *koros* contained 10 *metrētai*, about 395 litres. It was used for both dry and liquid measure.

d. The *modios* ('bushel') of Mt. 5:15; Mk. 4:21; Lk. 11:33 was Lat. *modius*, and all three references use the word to denote the vessel used to measure this amount. It was a grain measure containing 16 *sextarii*: 6 *modii* equalled the Gk. *medimnos* (Cornelius Nepos, *Attica* 2). Thus the *modius* contained 8 *choinikes* and was about 8·75 litres.

V. Liquid measures of capacity

a. The *xestēs* of Mk. 7:4 (RSV 'pot') is again a reference to the vessel used for measuring this capacity, and is taken by most scholars (but see Moulton and Howard, *Grammar of New Testament Greek*, 2, 1929, p. 155) to be a corruption of the Lat. *sextarius*. This was a liquid and dry measure of $\frac{1}{16}$ *modius*, about 500 cc.

b. The *batos* ('measure' of oil in Lk. 16:6) is a Gk. form of Heb. *baṯ* (see above). According to Josephus (*Ant.* 8. 57), it contains 72 *sextarii* or 4½ *modii*—about 39·5 litres.

c. The *metrētēs* mentioned in Jn. 2:6 (AV 'firkin') was a Gk. liquid measure approximately equivalent

Opposite page: Old and New Testament measures with modern equivalents.

The well at Beersheba, built c. 12th–11th cent. BC, continued in use until Hellenistic times. Curved stone slabs formed its upper part, the lower being a circular shaft cut into the rock just outside the city gate. Depth 35–40 m, diameter 2 m. (TAU)

to the *bat*, and so containing about 39·5 litres. Thus the stone water-pots used in the wedding-feast at Cana held between 80 and 120 litres each.

BIBLIOGRAPHY. R. G. Bratcher, 'Weights, Money, Measures and Time', *BTh* 10.4, 1959; J. Jeremias, *Jerusalem in the Time of Jesus*, 1969. D.H.W.

WELL. 1. An artificial shaft sunk to reach underground water, percolating or collected (Heb. *b^e'ēr*; Arab. *bir*; Gk. *phrear*), whereas a spring (Heb. and Arab. *'ayin*; Gk. *pēgē*) is the work of nature. AV confusion of terminology is due to the same confusion in 17th-century English, reflected also in Milton. Heb. and Gk. are unambiguous.

2. An artificial shaft sunk to reach a natural underground spring—a fusion of concepts in which the terms could be interchanged correctly. There is a reasonable presumption that the well from which Rebekah drew (Gn. 24) was of this type—likewise Jacob's well at Shechem, where Jesus met the woman of Samaria (Jn. 4). This would explain satisfactorily the puzzling alternation of words in these two chapters.

3. A *cistern or pit, large or small, public or private, for collecting rain-water: Heb. *bôr*; Gk. *lakkos*. The well at Bethlehem (1 Ch. 11:17–18) was probably an example.

WELL OF SIRAH
See Sirah, well of, Part 3.

WESTERN RIVER
See Nile, Part 2.

WET-NURSE
See Nurse, Part 2.

The earliest type of wheel was made of wooden planks pegged together. This limestone fragment from Ur shows a two-wheeled chariot. Mid-3rd millennium BC. (UMUP)

4. A shaft, dry or with miry clay, used as a dungeon, for which the same Heb. word is used (Gn. 37:24; Ps. 40:2; Je. 38:6, *etc.*). The praise of the well of living water in folk-song is reflected in Nu. 21:17–18.

In the arid parts of the E *water may become as precious as gold. Wells were, and still remain, the subjects of fierce disputes and even strife (*cf.* Gn. 21:25, *etc.*). They became hereditary, and were exploited by human monopolies at an earlier date than land.

R.A.S.

WHEEL. The earliest attested wheels (Heb. *galgal*, *'ôp̄ān*) are clay models of chariot wheels and fragments of a potter's wheel (*cf.* Je. 18:3, Heb. *'oḇnayim*) of the 4th millennium BC (see C. L. Woolley, *Ur Excavations*, 4, 1956, p. 28, plate 24). Early wheels were made from wooden planks pegged together, with leather tyres (see *ANEP*, nos. 163, 169, 303), but with the displacement of the ass by the horse *c.* 1500 BC lighter spoked wheels came into use (see *ANEP*, nos.

Well in the NW palace of Ashurnasirpal II (c. 876 BC) at Calah (Nimrud) during excavation. The well is built from specially prepared and shaped kiln-fired bricks, some inscribed (e.g. upper left of ladder). The well was cut 25·4 m down into the conglomerate and supplied the citadel. (DJW)

Chariot-wheels found buried in a tomb at Susa. The oldest known type of wheel, they were made of three solid wooden planks clamped together with wooden struts, and studded with copper nails for 'tyres'. Sumero-Elamite. Diameters c. 83 cm and c. 66 cm. c. 2500 BC. (MC)

WHISPERER
See Talebearing, Part 3.

WHITE
See Colours, Part 1.

WHITE OF EGG
See Food, Part 1.

WHITE STORK
See Animals, Part 1.

WHITSUN
See Pentecost, Part 3.

167–168, 183–184). The bronze stands made for Solomon's Temple were miniature chariot wheels, with axles, rims, spokes and hubs (1 Ki. 7:33). Daniel saw the Ancient of Days seated on a throne with wheels of fire (7:9), and Ezekiel gives a description of the wheels in his visions of the chariot of God (1; 10). The rumble of chariot wheels betokened the approach of an enemy (Je. 47:3; Na. 3:2), but all those hostile to God's people will be blown away like whirling dust (Ps. 83:13; Is. 17:13). In later Heb. *galgal* is used *pars pro toto* for wagon (Ezk. 23:24; 26:10). Wheels were also used as part of the machinery for drawing water (Ec. 12:6). On the wheel of birth (Jas. 3:6, AV 'course of nature'), see R. V. G. Tasker, *James*, *TNTC*, 1956, pp. 75f. A.R.M.

WHIRLWIND. The Eng. translation of Heb. *sûpâ* applies loosely to any violent storm and is not restricted to a rotary movement of air (Jb. 37:9; Pr. 1:27; 10:25; Is. 5:28; 17:13; 21:1; 66:15; Je. 4:13; Am. 1:14; Na. 1:3). In AV it is translated 'storm' in other passages (Jb. 21:18; Ps. 83:15; Is. 29:6). *s^e'ārâ* is used synonymously, translated 'whirlwind' when it stands alone (*e.g.* 2 Ki. 2:1; Jb. 38:1; 40:6; Is. 40:24; 41:16) but sometimes 'storm' (Ps. 107:29). RV uses the expression only once in its technical sense (Je. 23:19).

The whirlwind is used aptly as a figure for the sudden attack of the invader (Is. 5:28; Je. 4:13; Dn. 11:40; Am. 1:14f.). It also symbolizes divine judgment because of its sudden motion (Ps. 18:10; Na. 1:3) and divine wrath (Ps. 58:9; Pr. 10:25; Is. 17:13; 28:17; 66:15; Ho. 8:7). It is similarly used of the Messianic wrath, described in Mt. 7:24–27. (*WIND.) J.M.H.

WICKED. In the OT, Heb. *rāšā'*, 'wicked, ungodly', and *ra'*, 'evil', are most common; Gk. *ponēros*, 'bad, malignant', as contrasted with *chrēstos*, is the usual NT word, although *athesmos*, *anomos* and *kakos* are also used. While the term is often used in the general sense of 'wrong' (Ps. 18:21), it refers more specifically to evil, not in its moral or judicial sense, but in its active form, *i.e.* mischief (Nu. 16:26). As such, it denotes perversity of mind (Pr. 15:26; Rom. 1:29) by which the natural man surrenders himself to evil impulses (Ps. 10:1–11). Wickedness has its seat in the heart (Je. 17:9; Mk. 7:21–23), and is inspired by Satan (Mt. 13:19; 1 Jn. 3:12). It is progressive (Gn. 6:5) and contagious (1 Sa. 24:13) in its manifestation. The wicked man is utterly perverse, finding unholy delight in the infliction of injury (Pr. 21:10). Jesus often characterized the *sin of his contemporaries as wickedness (Mt. 16:4), while Peter declares that wicked men crucified the Saviour (Acts 2:23).

The Psalms frequently contrast the righteous and the wicked, raising the question of the prosperity of the wicked, and offering suggestions which provide a partial answer (Pss. 37:35–36; 9:15, *et passim*). But this question, which is part of the general problem of evil, is insoluble in the light of the OT revelation. Throughout the Scriptures there is a strong insistence on the certainty of punishment for all who are wicked (Ps. 9:17; Je. 16:4; Mt. 13:49). It is significant to note that *ponēros* is never applied to believers; in 1 Cor. 5:13 the reference is to a nominal member of the Christian community. It is by wicked works that unbelievers are alienated from God (Col. 1:21), but those who are progressing in faith have overcome 'the wicked one' (1 Jn. 2:13), for the shield of faith is a sure defence against his attack (Eph. 6:16). A.F.

Spoked wheels with rims of layered wood. Detail from an Assyrian relief of an ox-drawn cart. Palace of Ashurbanipal, Nineveh. c. 640 BC. (MC)

WIDOW.

I. In the Old Testament

Heb. legislation has always been solicitous for widows and, together with the fatherless and strangers, made special provision for them (*e.g.* Ex. 22:21f.; Dt. 14:29; 16:11, 14; 24:17; *cf.* Je. 7:6). Even in pre-Mosaic times there was recognition of the predicament of the childless widow and arrangements made for her (Gn. 38; *MARRIAGE, **IV**), and these were formally enjoined under Moses (Dt. 25:5ff.; *KIN).

Since the bearing of children was accounted a great honour, and one still more enhanced later when the nation looked for Messiah (Is. 11:1), widowhood in such as were not past the age of childbearing, as well as *barrenness, was reckoned a shame and a reproach (Is. 4:1; 54:4). The widows of kings, however, continued in their widowhood, and were the property, though not always the wives, of the new king. To ask any of them in marriage was tantamount to a claim to the kingdom (1 Ki. 2:13ff.).

As widows are often overlooked by men, God has a peculiar concern for them (Pss. 68:5; 146:9; Pr. 15:25), and kindness to them was commended as one of the marks of true religion (Jb. 29:13; Is. 1:17).

The oppression and injury of widows, on the other hand, would incur dire punishment (Ps. 94:6; Mal. 3:5). Jerusalem and Babylon are likened in their desolation to widows (La. 1:1; Is. 47:8), and the effect of violent death compared to that of wives becoming widows (La. 5:3; Ezk. 22:25). (*ORPHAN.)

II. In the New Testament

The Christian church inherited from Judaism the duty of providing for the widow. The Jewish–Christian author of James states categorically that to give assistance to widows in their distress is a mark of the kind of religion with which God can find no fault (1:27). Even if widows were left comparatively well-off, they needed to be protected from the unscrupulous. One of the things that Jesus condemned in some Pharisees was that they 'devoured widows' houses' (Mk. 12:40); and he was probably drawing an illustration from contemporary life when he told the story of the widow who by her persistence in demanding justice was wearing out the judge! (Lk. 18:1–5). More often widows were left in penury. One of the earliest good works that engaged the attention of the church at Jerusalem was an organized daily distribution of alms to widows in need; and seven men were appointed to see that the Gk.-speaking widows were not overlooked in favour of those who spoke Aramaic (Acts 6:1–4). Acts also gives a striking illustration of charity shown by one individual when, after the death of Tabitha, it records that 'all the widows' at Joppa assembled to testify before Peter to the kindness she had shown to them (9:39).

Paul told the Corinthians that he thought it good that widows should not marry again, but he was far from making this a rule. Remarriage, however, should be within the Christian fellowship (see 1 Cor. 7:8–9, 39). On the other hand, in writing to Timothy, he expresses his desire that *young* widows should marry again; and urges that widows 'in the full sense', *i.e.* those who have no relatives to support them, and who are regular in their religious duties, should be given a special status and be a charge upon the church. A roll should be kept of these, and only those should be placed upon it who were over 60 years of age and who had given evidence of their good works, by caring for children, by hospitality or by rendering service to those of God's people who were in distress (1 Tim. 5:9–10).

In Rev. 18:7 'widow' is used metaphorically of a city bereaved of its inhabitants and stricken by plague and famine.

BIBLIOGRAPHY. S. Solle, *NIDNTT* 3, pp. 1073–1075.

J.D.D.
R.V.G.T.

WILDERNESS. In Scripture the words rendered 'wilderness' or 'desert' include not only the barren deserts of sand dunes or rock that colour the popular imagination of a desert, but also steppe-lands and pasture lands suitable for grazing livestock.

The commonest Heb. word is *miḏbār*, a word already well-attested in Canaanite epics from Ugarit (14th century BC, going back to earlier origin) as *mdbr* (Gordon, *Ugaritic Manual*, 3, 1955, p. 254, No. 458). This word can indicate grassy pastures (Ps. 65:12; Joel 2:22), supporting sheep (*cf.* Ex. 3:1), sometimes burnt up by the summer droughts (Je. 23:10; Joel 1:19–20), as well as denoting desolate wastes of rock and sand (Dt. 32:10; Jb. 38:26). The same applies to Gk. *erēmos* in the NT; note that the 'desert' (AV; RSV 'lonely place') of Mt. 14:15 does not lack 'much grass' (Jn. 6:10).

The Heb. *y^ešîmôn*, sometimes rendered as a proper name 'Jeshimon', is used of relatively bare wildernesses in Judaea in 1 Sa. 23:19, 24; 26:1, 3. The wilderness viewed from Pisgah (Nu. 21:20; 23:28; *cf.* Dt. 34:1ff.) would doubtless include the marly waste-lands on either side of the Jordan's channel before it entered the Dead Sea, the slopes of Pisgah and its range into the Jordan valley, and perhaps the edges of the Judaean wilderness opposite, behind Jericho and N and S of Qumran. For general references, *cf.* Dt. 32:10; Ps. 107:4; Is. 43:19. Besides its use as a proper name for the long rift valley from the Dead Sea to the Gulf of Aqabah, the term *ʿ^arāḇâ* can be used as a common noun for steppe or scrubland where wild creatures must seek out their food (Jb. 24:5; Je. 17:6) or else of barren desert (Jb. 39:6 in parallel with saltflats). The words *ṣiyyâ*, 'dry lands' (Jb. 30:3; Ps. 78:17) and *tōhû*, 'empty waste' (Jb. 6:18;12:24; Ps. 107:40) likewise refer to barren, uninhabitable deserts. K.A.K.

WILDERNESS OF WANDERING.

I. Limits

After leaving Egypt by crossing the Sea of Reeds (Ex. 14:10–15:27), and until they finally by-passed Edom and Moab to reach the Jordan (Nu. 20ff.), Israel spent long years in the intervening territory, comprising (1) the peninsula of Sinai flanked by the Gulfs of Suez and Aqabah and separated from the Mediterranean on the N by the dusty 'way of the land of the Philistines' that linked Egypt to Palestine, (2) the long Arabah rift-valley extending S from the Dead Sea to the Gulf of Aqabah, and (3) the wilderness of Zin S of Beersheba.

II. Physical features

The road from Egypt by 'the way of the land of the Philistines' to Raphia (Rafa) and Gaza, runs roughly parallel with the Mediterranean coast, passing through and along the N fringes of a barren sandy desert—the wilderness of *Shur—which lies between the line of the modern Suez Canal and the Wadi el-ʿArish (River of *Egypt), and then through cul-

WILD ASS
See Animals, Part 1.

WILD BOAR
See Animals, Part 1.

WILD BULL
See Animals, Part 1.

WILD CAT
See Animals, Part 1.

The 'wilderness' regions round the Dead Sea.

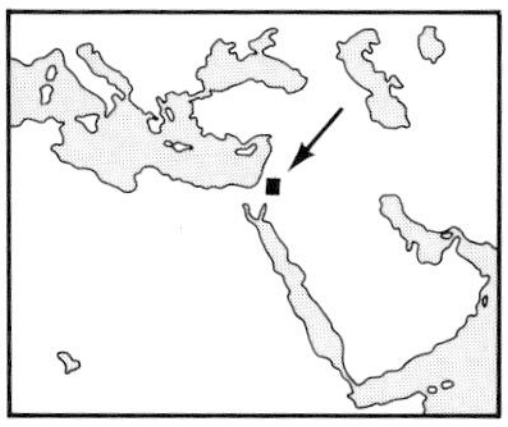

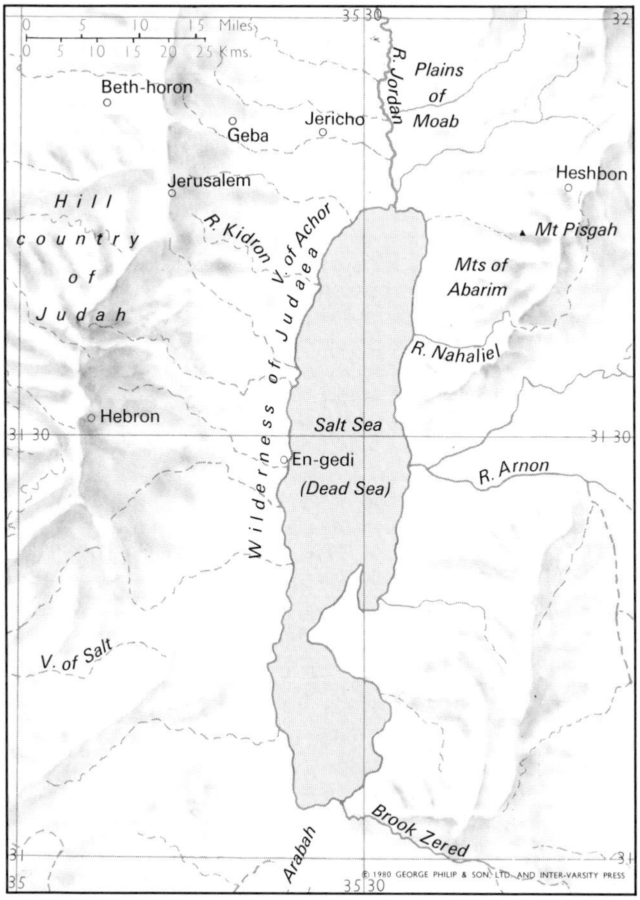

tivable land which becomes more evident between El-'Arish and Gaza (* NEGEB; *cf.* A. H. Gardiner, *JEA* 6, 1920, pp. 114–115; C. S. Jarvis, *Yesterday and Today in Sinai*, 1931, p. 107); 30–60 km S of the coast road tuns the 'way of the wilderness of Shur', from Egypt to the region of Kadesh and NE to Beersheba. S of this road there gradually rise the hills and wadis of the limestone plateau of Et-Tih which, from a 'base-line' N of a line drawn between the heads of the Suez and Aqabah Gulfs, occupies a great semicircle projecting into the peninsula of Sinai. Across the plateau to Aqabah ran an ancient trade-route. S of the plateau is a triangular-shaped area of granite, gneiss and other hard, crystalline rocks forming mountain ranges, which include the traditional Mt Sinai, several peaks rising to 2,000 m. This region is separated at its NW and NE corners from the limestone plateau by sandstone hills containing deposits of copper ores and turquoise. In the E the limestone plateau of Et-Tih gives way to the jumbled rocks and wadis of the S Negeb, bounded by the Rift Valley of the Arabah between the Dead Sea and the Gulf of Aqabah.

There are wells and springs at intervals of a day's journey all down the W coast from the Suez region to Merkhah; the water-table is usually close to the gravelly ground-surface. The wadis usually have some kind of scanty vegetation; where more permanent streams exist, notably in the broad Wadi Feiran (the finest oasis in Sinai), the vegetation flourishes accordingly. There is a 'rainy season' (up to 20 days) during winter, with mists, fogs and dews.

In the past, there has been much and persistent wholesale destruction of tamarisk and acacia groves for firewood and charcoal, there being a steady export of the latter to Egypt in the 19th century (Stanley, *Sinai and Palestine*, 1905 edn., p. 25). Thus, in ancient times the Sinai peninsula may have had more vegetation in its wadis and consequently better rains; but there has apparently been no fundamental climatic change since antiquity.

III. The route of the journeyings

The precise route taken by Israel from the Sea of Reeds (between Qantara and Suez; * RED SEA) to the edges of Moab is still conjectural, as almost none of the names of Israelite stopping-places has survived in the late, fluid and descriptive Arabic nomenclature of the peninsula of Sinai. Various stopping-places were named by the Israelites in relation to events that occurred on their travels, *e.g.* Kibroth-hattaavah, 'graves of craving' (Nu. 11:34), and they left no sedentary population behind to perpetuate such names. Furthermore, the traditions attaching to the present Mt Sinai (Gebel Musa and environs) have not been traced back beyond the early Christian centuries; this does not of itself prove those traditions wrong, but permits of no certainty. The traditional route ascribed to the Israelites is certainly a possible one. From the wilderness of * Shur they are usually considered to have passed S along the W coast-strip of the Sinai peninsula, Marah and Elim often being placed at 'Ain Hawarah and Wadi Gharandel respectively. That the camp after Elim (Ex. 16:1) is 'by the *yam sûp̄*' (Heb. of Nu. 33:10), *i.e.* the Sea of Reeds, or here by extension the Gulf of Suez (*cf.* * RED SEA), indicates clearly that Israel had kept to the W side of the Sinai peninsula and not gone N (the way of the Philistines). The Gulf of Aqabah is too far away to be the *yam sûp̄* in this passage. Somewhat later, Israel encamped at Dophkah. This name is sometimes considered to mean 'smeltery' (G. E. Wright, *Biblical Archaeology*, 1957, p. 64; Wright and Filson, *Westminster Historical Atlas of the Bible*, 1957 edn., p. 39) and so to be located at the Egyp. mining centre of Serabit el-Khadim. For copper and especially turquoise mining in that area, see Lucas, *Ancient Egyptian Materials and Industries*, 1962, pp. 202–205, 404–405; J. Černý, A. H. Gardiner and T. E. Peet, *Inscriptions of Sinai*, 2, 1955, pp. 5–8.

As Egyp. expeditions visited this region only during January to March (rarely later), and did not live permanently at the mines (*cf.* Petrie, *Researches in Sinai*, 1906, p. 169), the Israelites would not meet them there, as they left Egypt in the month Abib (Ex. 13:4), *i.e.* about March (*cf.* * PLAGUES OF EGYPT), and left Elim a month later (Ex. 16:1), *i.e.* about April. However, Dophkah could be any copper-mining spot in the metalliferous sandstone belt across S-central Sinai (which favours a S route for Israel in any case). Rephidim is sometimes identified with Wadi Feiran, sometimes with Wadi Refayid, and Mt Sinai with the summits of Gebel Musa (or, less likely, Mt Serbal near Feiran). See the works of Robinson, Lepsius, Stanley and Palmer (Bibliography below). Beyond Mt Sinai, Dhahab on the E coast might be Di-zahab (Dt. 1:1; so Y. Aharoni, *Antiquity and Survival*, 2. 2/3, 1957, pp. 289–290, fig. 7); if so, Huderah on a different road is less likely to be the Hazeroth of Nu. 11:35; 33:17–18. The next fixed points are Kadesh-

The barrenness of 'the wilderness of wandering' was relieved by oases such as the Wadi Feiran in Sinai. (MEPhA)

barnea (* KADESH) on the borders of the wilderness(es) of Zin and Paran (Nu. 12:16; 13:26) at 'Ain Qudeirat or 'Ain Qudeis and the surrounding region, including 'Ain Qudeirat, and Ezion-geber at the head of the Gulf of Aqabah (Nu. 33:35f.).

For the phenomenon of the earth swallowing up Korah, Dathan and Abiram (Nu. 16), a most interesting explanation was offered by G. Hort, *Australian Biblical Review* 7, 1959, pp. 2–26, especially 19–26. She would locate this incident in the Arabah Rift Valley between the Dead Sea and the Gulf of Aqabah. Here are to be found mudflats known as *kewirs*. A hard crust of clayey mud overlying layers of hard salt and half-dry mud, about 30 cm thick, eventually forms over the deep mass of liquid mud and ooze. When this crust is hard it may be walked on with impunity, but increased humidity (especially rainstorms) will break up the crust and turn the whole into gluey mud. Dathan, Abiram and Korah's adherents withdrew from the main camp probably to one of these deceptively level, hard mudflats. From his long years of experience in Sinai and Midian (Ex. 2–4), Moses had probably learnt of this phenomenon, but not so the Israelites. When a storm approached he saw the danger and called the Israelites away from the tents of the rebels. The crust broke up and the rebels, their families and their possessions were all swallowed up in the mud. Then the storm broke, and the 250 men with censers were struck by lightning—smitten down by the fire of the Lord.

Miss Hort thought that this incident occurred at Kadesh-barnea, and therefore that Kadesh should be located in the Arabah. But there are possible reasons for locating * Kadesh in the region of 'Ain Qudeis and 'Ain Qudeirat, and in fact Nu. 16 does *not* state that the revolt(s) of Korah, Dathan and Abiram occurred at Kadesh. It should be noted that it is the whole, unitary account of the twin rebellions in Nu. 16 and their awesome end that alone makes sense and fits the physical phenomena in question; the supposed sources obtained by conventional documentary literary analyses severally yield fragmentary pictures that correspond to no known realities.

The long list of names in Nu. 33:19–35 fall into the 38 years of wandering, and cannot be located at present. The precise route past Edom (Nu. 20:22ff.; 21; 33:38–44) is also obscure. Some of the incidents in these long journeys reflect the natural phenomena of the area. The repeated phenomenon of water coming from the smitten rock (Ex. 17:1–7; Nu. 20:2–13) reflects the water-holding properties of Sinai limestone: an army NCO once produced quite a good flow of water when he accidentally hit such a rock face with a spade! See Jarvis, *Yesterday and Today in Sinai*, 1931, pp. 174–175. The digging of wells as recorded in Nu. 21:16–18 (*cf.* Gn. 26:19) reflects the known occurrence of sub-surface water in various regions of Sinai, the Negeb and S Transjordan (see references above, and N. Glueck, *Rivers in the Desert*, 1959, p. 22). The references to the catching of quail (Ex. 16:13; Nu. 11:31–35) have been interpreted by some as requiring a N route for the Exodus along the Mediterranean (*e.g.* Jarvis, *op. cit.*, pp. 169–170; *cf.* J. Bright, *A History of Israel*, 1960, p. 114, after J. Gray, *VT* 4, 1954, pp. 148–154; G. E. Wright, *Biblical Archaeology*, 1957, p. 65). But that route was explicitly forbidden to Israel (Ex. 13:17f.), and in any case the quails land on the Mediterranean coast of Sinai (from Europe) only in the *autumn* and at dawn, whereas Israel found them in the *spring* in the evening, in or following Abib, *i.e.* March (Ex. 16:13), and a year and a month later (Nu. 10:11; 11:31). These two points exclude the Mediterranean coast from Israel's route on these two occasions, and directly favour the S route by the Gulfs of Suez and Aqabah *via* 'Mt Sinai'. The quails return to Europe in the spring—the season when Israel twice had them—across the upper ends of the Gulfs of Suez and Aqabah, and in the evening (Lucas, *The Route of the Exodus*, 1938, pp. 58–63 and refs., and p. 81, overstressing Aqabah at the expense of Suez).

A minority view would make Israel cross the Sinai peninsula more directly to the head of the Gulf of Aqabah and locate Mt Sinai in Midian. Among the best advocates of such a view is Lucas (*The Route of the Exodus*, 1938) who does not invoke non-existent active volcanoes as some have done. However, this view is no freer of topographical difficulties than any other, and fails entirely to account for the origin of the traditions of the Christian period that attached themselves to the peninsula now called Sinai and not to Midian or NW Arabia.

For a good comparative table of the data on the route and stopping-places on Israel's wanderings in Exodus–Numbers, Nu. 33 and Deuteronomy, see J. D. Davis and H. S. Gehman, *WDB*, pp. 638–639; literary background, *cf.* G. I. Davies, *TynB* 25, 1974, pp. 46–81; Bronze Age sites in Sinai, *cf.* T. L. Thompson, *The Settlement of Sinai and the Negev in the Bronze Age*, 1975.

IV. The numbers of the Israelites

When Israel left Egypt there went '600,000 men on foot' besides their families and the mixed multitude, while from a census of the men from the tribes other than Levi held at Sinai comes the total of 603,550 men over 20 who could bear arms (Nu. 2:32). These figures are commonly held to imply a total number of Israelites—men, women and children—of somewhat more than two million. That the slender resources of Sinai were of themselves insufficient to support such a multitude is indicated by the Bible itself (as well as suggested by exploration) in that Israel's chief sustenance came from God-given * manna (Ex. 16; *cf.* vv. 3–4, 35). Israel never went wholly without (Dt. 2:7), although the water-supply sometimes nearly failed them (*e.g.* at Rephidim, Ex. 17:1; Kadesh, Nu. 20:2). In any case, they would soon learn to subsist on very little water per head indeed, as illustrated by Robinson's guide in Sinai, who was able to go without water for a fortnight by living on camel's milk, while sheep and goats as well as camels can sometimes go without water for 3–4 months if they have had fresh pasture (E. Robinson, *Biblical Researches*, 1, 1841 ed., p. 221).

Furthermore, it is wholly misleading to imagine the Israelites marching in long 'columns of four' up and down Sinai, or trying to encamp all together *en masse* in some little wadi at each stop. They would be spread out in their tribal and family groups, occupying a variety of neighbouring wadis for all their scattered encampments; after they left Sinai with the ark and tabernacle (as baggage when on the move), the sites where these were successively lodged would be the focus of the various tribal camps, as in Nu. 2. In various parts of Sinai the water-table is

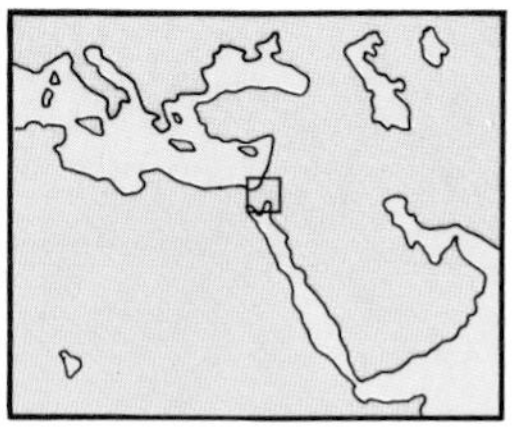

The 'wilderness' or desert through which Israel wandered during the Exodus.

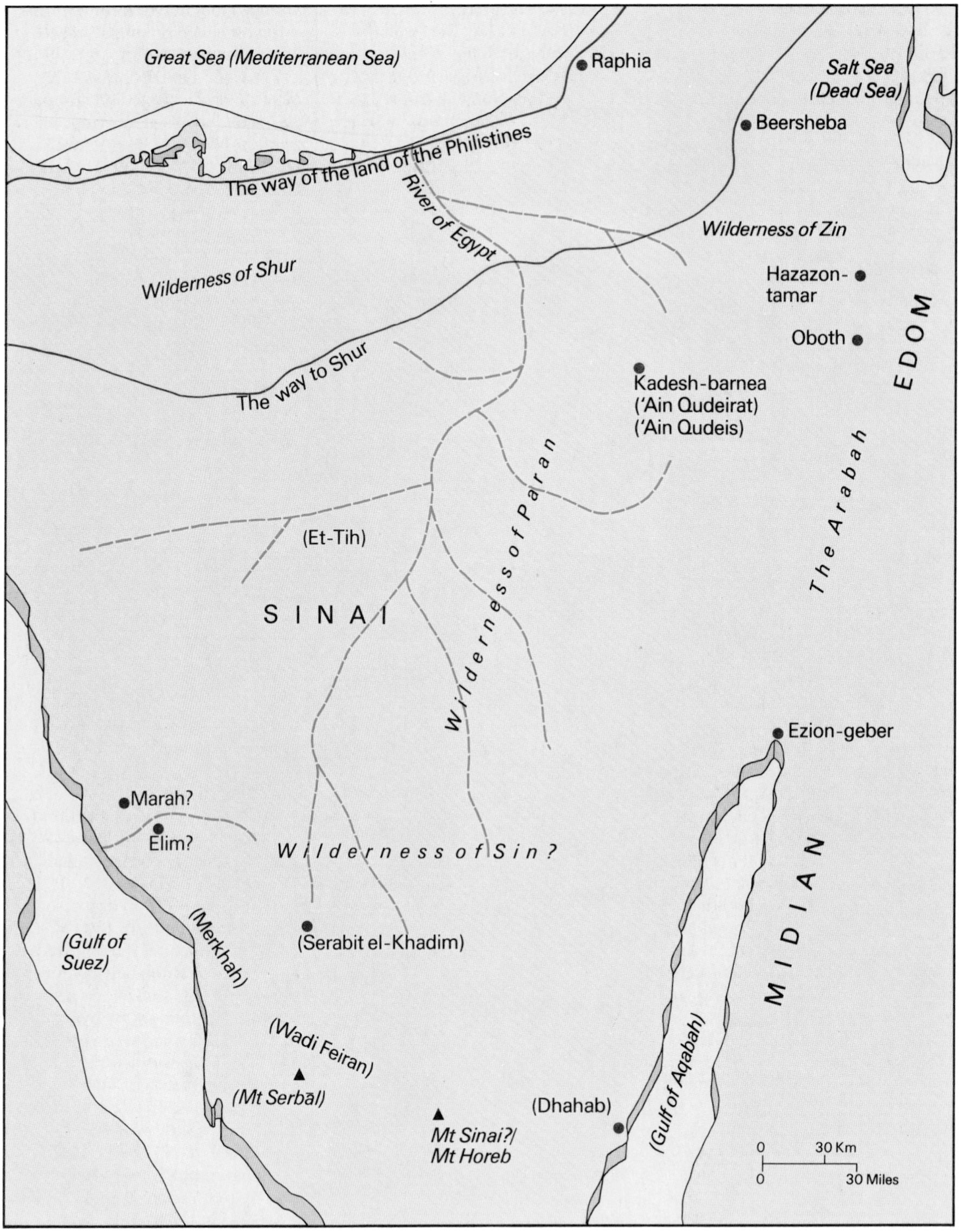

near the ground-surface; the scattered Israelite encampments would thus often get the little they needed by digging small pits over an area. *Cf.* Robinson, *Biblical Researches*, 1, 1841, pp. 100 (general observations), 129; Lepsius, *Letters, etc.*, 1853, p. 306; Currelly in Petrie, *Researches in Sinai*, 1906, p. 249; Lucas, *The Route of the Exodus*, 1938, p. 68.

There have been many attempts down the years to interpret the census-lists in Nu. 1 and 26 and related figures in Ex. 12:37; 38:24–29, besides the levitical reckoning (Nu. 4:21–49) and other figures (*e.g.* Nu. 16:49), in order to gain from the Heb. text a more modest total for the number of the people of Israel involved in the Exodus from Egypt through Sinai to Palestine. For recent attempts, see R. E. D. Clark, *JTVI* 87, 1955, pp. 82–92 (taking *'lp* as 'officer' instead of '1,000' in many cases); G. E. Mendenhall, *JBL* 77, 1958, pp. 52–66 (taking *'lp* as a tribal sub-unit instead of '1,000'), who refers to earlier treatments; and J. W. Wenham, *TynB* 18, 1967, pp. 19–53, esp. 27ff., 35ff. While none of these attempts accounts for all the figures involved, they indicate several possible clues to a better understanding of various apparently high figures in the OT. The fact is that these records must rest on some basis of ancient reality; the apparently high figures are beyond absolute disproof, while no alternative interpretation has yet adequately accounted for all the data involved. (* NUMBER.)

V. Later significance

Theologically, the wilderness period became the dual symbol of God's leading and providing and of man's rebellious nature typified by the Israelites (*cf.*, *e.g.*, Dt. 8:15–16; 9:7; Am. 2:10; 5:25 (*cf.* Acts 7:40–44); Ho. 13:5–6; Je. 2:6; Ezk. 20:10–26, 36; Pss. 78:14–41; 95:8–11 (*cf.* Heb. 3:7–19); 136:16; Ne. 9:18–22; Acts 13:18; 1 Cor. 10:3–5).

BIBLIOGRAPHY. E. Robinson, *Biblical Researches in Palestine, Mount Sinai and Arabia Petraea*, 1, 1841 edn., pp. 98–100, 129, 131, 179; C. R. Lepsius, *Letters from Egypt, Ethiopia and the Peninsula of Sinai*, 1853, pp. 306–307; A. P. Stanley, *Sinai and Palestine*, 1905 ed., pp. 16–19, 22, 24–27; E. H. Palmer, *The Desert of the Exodus*, 1, 1871, pp. 22–26; W. M. F. Petrie and C. T. Currelly, *Researches in Sinai*, 1906, pp. 12, 30, 247–250, 254–256 (Feiran), 269; C. L. Woolley and T. E. Lawrence, *Palestine Exploration Fund Annual*, 3, 1915, p. 33; C. S. Jarvis, *Yesterday and Today in Sinai*, 1931, p. 99; A. E. Lucas, *The Route of the Exodus*, 1938, pp. 19, 44–45, 68; W. F. Albright, *BASOR* 109, 1948, p. 11 (El-'Arish rains; scrub vegetation in N). For Sinai scenery, see G. E. Wright, *Biblical Archaeology*, 1957, pp. 62–64, figs. 33–35; or L. H. Grollenberg, *Shorter Atlas of the Bible*, 1959, pp. 76–77; Petrie, *Researches in Sinai*, 1906, *passim*; B. Rothenberg, *God's Wilderness*, 1961, *passim*. K.A.K.

WIND (Heb. *rûaḥ*). **1.** The Hebrews conceived of climate as influenced by the four winds from the four corners of the earth (Je. 49:36; Dn. 7:2; Rev. 7:1). The wind may be a source of blessing or a curse, according to its source. Its vast power suggests the wind is the breath of God (Is. 40:7), controlled by him (Ps. 107:25; Pr. 30:4; Mk. 4:41), created by him (Am. 4:13) and creative for his purposes (Gn. 1:2; Ezk. 37:9).

2. As compound names for winds are impossible in Hebrew, the four cardinal points are used freely to describe other directions (Ezk. 37:9; Dn. 8:8; Zc. 2:6; Mt. 24:31; Rev. 7:1).

a. The N wind (*rûaḥ ṣāpôn*) is associated with cold conditions, the NE wind dispersing the rain (Jb. 37:9, 22; Pr. 25:23).

b. The S wind (*rûaḥ dārôm*) is variable in its effects, whether tempestuous (Is. 21:1; Zc. 9:14) or gentle (Acts 27:13). The sirocco, usually associated with the S wind, is particularly hot and desiccating, a katabatic wind which descends from the highlands of Sinai and Arabia (Jb. 37:16–17; Je. 4:11; Ho. 12:1; Lk. 12:55). But the katabatic effects can be caused wherever there is a sudden change of gradient, so that its effects are also described as E winds (Is. 27:8; Ezk. 17:10; Ho. 13:15; Jon. 4:8). It destroys the grass, and all vegetation wilts (Ps. 103:16; Is. 40:6–8; Jas. 1:11).

c. The E wind (*rûaḥ qāḏîm*) is similarly described as a dry wind from the wilderness (Jb. 1:19; Je. 4:11; 13:24), strong and gusty (Ex. 14:21; Jb. 27:21; 38:24; Je. 18:17) and with scorching heat (Am. 4:9; Ho. 13:15), affecting the vegetation (Gn. 41:6, 23, 27; Ezk. 17:10; 19:12).

d. The W wind (*rûaḥ yām*) is in Arabic described as 'the father of rain' (1 Ki. 18:44–45; Lk. 12:54). Distinction, however, should be made between the diurnal sea breezes which are a marked feature of the coast in summer, bringing down the high temperatures, and the westerlies which blow strongly in winter, exposing all anchorages to NW gales. The wind is symbolic of nothingness (Is. 41:29) and of the transitoriness of man (Ps. 78:39), and is used also in connection with the Spirit of God (Jn. 3:8; Acts 2:2; * SPIRIT, HOLY).

e. Euraquilo (RV, rightly, for AV 'Euroclydon'), a hybrid formation from Gk. *euros*, 'east wind', and Lat. *aquilo*, 'north wind', and probably a nautical term, is the name given to the typhonic storm described at Paul's shipwreck (Acts 27:14). J. Smith has made a strong case for the wind being the 'north-easter' (so RSV, NEB), and that the shipwreck was, in fact, off the coast of * Malta. Recently, A. Acworth argued that the shipwreck was situated off Mljet in the Adriatic and that the wind was a south-easter. This has been conclusively challenged by C. J. Hemer, who reaffirms the location off Malta. Maltese sailors use the term 'gregale' to refer to violent winds, accompanied by sea-storms in the winter season, associated with depressions over Libya or the Gulf of Gabes. A small Rom. ship, caught in such a storm, having crossed Sicily, would welcome the sighting of the Maltese islands. For there stretched another 320 km or more of open sea between them and safety on the Tunisian coast.

BIBLIOGRAPHY. J. Smith, *Voyage and Shipwreck of St. Paul*[4], 1880, pp. 287–291; see also A. Acworth, 'Where was St. Paul shipwrecked? A re-examination of the evidence', *JTS* n.s. 24, 1973, pp. 190–192; C. J. Hemer, 'Euraquilo and Melita', *JTS* n.s. 26, 1975, pp. 100–111. J.M.H.

WINE AND STRONG DRINK.

I. In the Old Testament

Among a considerable number of synonyms used in the OT the most common are *yayin* (usually translated 'wine') and *šēḵār* (usually translated 'strong drink'). These terms are frequently used together, and they are employed irrespective of whether the writer is commending wine and strong drink as desirable or warning against its dangers. A third word, *tîrôš*, sometimes translated 'new' or 'sweet wine', has often been regarded as unfermented and therefore unintoxicating wine, but an example such as Ho. 4:11, together with the usage of the Talmud, makes clear that it is capable of being used in a bad sense equally with the others. Furthermore, while there are examples of the grapes being pressed into a cup and presumably used at once (Gn. 40:11), it is significant that the term 'wine' is never applied to the resultant juice.

The term 'new wine' does not indicate wine which has not fermented, for in fact the process of fermentation sets in very rapidly, and unfermented wine could not be available many months after the harvest (Acts 2:13). It represents rather wine made from the first drippings of the juice before the winepress was trodden. As such it would be particularly potent and would come immediately to mind as a probable explanation of what seemed to be a drunken state. Modern custom in Palestine, among a people who are traditionally conservative as far as religious feasts are concerned, also suggests that the wine used was fermented. It may be said, therefore, that the Bible in employing various synonyms makes no consistent distinction between them.

WILD GOAT
See Animals, Part 1.

WILD VINE
See Plants, Part 3.

WILLOW
See Trees, Part 3.

WIND INSTRUMENTS
See Music, Part 2.

Grapes being picked in an Egyptian vineyard. Copy of a wall-painting in the tomb of Nakht, Thebes. Original c. 1420 BC. (NDGD)

Naturally in a land and climate particularly suited to the cultivation of the vine, we find that wine was often associated with grain, and together they stand for a full and adequate supply of food and of the good gifts of life. They can be promised therefore as the tokens of the blessing of God (Gn. 27:28), and they are acceptable to him when offered back upon the altar (Ex. 29:40). As a discipline, however, they are on occasion to be dispensed with, as when a man engages in priestly service (Lv. 10:9), or in the case of a *Nazirite during the course of his vow (Nu. 6:3). The abstinence of the *Rechabites falls within a different category, for it was in an attempt to preserve the nomadic life that they dwelt in tents, and their refusal of wine was not on account of the dangers of its abuse, but because they were associated with the planting of vineyards, the sowing of seed and the building of houses (Je. 35:7). Evidence is by no means lacking, however, that even to those who accepted the agricultural way of life the dangers of strong drink were apparent. The warnings of the book of Proverbs are clear, and in the time of Isaiah even the priests fell into the snare.

These two aspects of wine, its use and its abuse, its benefits and its curse, its acceptance in God's sight and its abhorrence, are interwoven into the fabric of the OT so that it may gladden the heart of man (Ps. 104:15) or cause his mind to err (Is. 28:7), it can be associated with merriment (Ec. 10:19) or with anger (Is. 5:11), it can be used to uncover the shame of Noah (Gn. 9:21) or in the hands of Melchizedek to honour Abraham (Gn. 14:18).

In metaphorical usage the same characteristics are to be observed. Wine may represent that which God himself has prepared (Pr. 9:5), and which he offers to as many as will receive it from his hand (Is. 55:1); yet, on the other hand, it may equally well represent the intoxicating influence of Babylonian supremacy which brings ruin (Je. 51:7).

II. In the New Testament

In the NT the common word is Gk. *oinos* (*cf.* Heb. *yayin*). Once we find *sikera*, 'strong drink' (Lk. 1:15), a loan-word from Semitic (*cf.* Heb. *šēḵār*), and once *gleukos*, 'new wine' (Acts 2:13). This last word means literally 'sweet wine'; the vintage of the current year had not yet come, but there were means of keeping wine sweet all year round.

The references in the NT are very much fewer in number, but once

Drinking wine or beer from a communal vessel through pipes or 'straws' is shown on a lapis-lazuli cylinder-seal (and its impression) from Ur. Height 4·5 cm. c. 2500 BC. (BM)

more the good and the bad aspects are equally apparent, and many of the points which we noticed in the OT have their counterpart in the NT. John the Baptist is to abstain from wine in view of his special commission (Lk. 1:15), but this does not imply that of itself wine is evil, for Jesus is not only present at the wedding in Cana of Galilee, but when the wine fails he replenishes the supply in extraordinarily ample measure, and later his readiness to eat and drink with publicans and sinners draws forth the accusation that he is gluttonous and a wine-bibber. The refusal of Jesus to drink the wine offered to him in accordance with Jewish custom at his crucifixion (Mk. 15:23) was not based upon an objection to wine as such, but was due to a determination to die with an unclouded mind. Later he accepted the wine (vinegar) which was the ordinary drink of labourers in the field and of the lower class of soldiers.

On more than one occasion Jesus used wine to illustrate his teaching. Mk. 2:22 points to the current practice of putting new wine into new skins and emphasizes the impracticality of doing otherwise. Commentators differ regarding the interpretation of this parable. For, while the new wine clearly points to the lively and powerful working of Christ's new teaching, the skins which are broken may equally well refer to certain conventional forms or to the whole Judaistic system or to the human heart, all of which need to be recast in accordance with the challenge of the new age which has arrived. Unfortunately the Pharisees were unwilling to face the changes which would have been involved, and obstinately clung to the system upon which their livelihood depended (Lk. 5:39).

Metaphorically in the NT the word 'wine' is again used in both a good and a bad sense. The latter is found several times in Revelation, where the inhabitants of the earth are depicted as having been made drunk by the fornication of Babylon (Rev. 17:2) while she herself is drunk with their blood (Rev. 17:6). On the other hand, Paul exhorts his readers to be filled with the Spirit (Eph. 5:18) in contrast with their being intoxicated with wine. There are, of course, certain similarities between the two conditions, a consideration which may well have led Paul to express himself in this way. Certainly on the Day of Pentecost there were many who took the evidences of the Spirit to be nothing else than the result of strong drink. This same interpretation had been placed long before upon the movement of the lips of Hannah as she prayed in the presence of Eli, a supposed fault which Eli was quicker to rebuke in her than in his own sons (1 Sa. 1:14).

Timothy is exhorted by Paul to take a little wine because of its medicinal properties (1 Tim. 5:23; *cf.* its application in a different form in the story of the good Samaritan), but in the Pastoral Epistles there is a recognition of the grave dangers of excess, and those who bear office or in any way give leadership within the Christian community, both men and women, are specifically warned against this fault, which would unfit them for

The processes of making bread and beer depicted on an Egyptian relief from Saqqara. The grain is pounded, mixed into a dough and kneaded into loaves. The beer is made from a fermented mash, strained, and stored in jars. 2700–2200 BC. (RVO)

their task (1 Tim. 3:8; Tit. 2:3). This abuse is particularly unfitting within the church, for if it is true that drunkenness is in general a sign of heedlessness in spiritual matters, and a disregard of the imminent return of Christ (Rom. 13:13), how much more is it to be deplored at the Lord's table, where it reveals not only a spirit of complete indifference towards God but a spirit of utter thoughtlessness in regard to those who stand together within the Christian fellowship (1 Cor. 11:21).

To sum up, then, it may be said that while wine is not condemned as being without usefulness, it brings in the hands of sinful men such dangers of becoming uncontrolled that even those who count themselves to be strong would be wise to abstain, if not for their own sake, yet for the sake of weaker brethren (Rom. 14:21). If it is argued that there are many other things which may be abused besides wine, the point may be immediately conceded, but wine has so often proved itself to be peculiarly fraught with danger that Paul names it specifically at the same time as he lays down the general principle. That this principle has application within the setting of modern life is beyond dispute among those who take their Christian responsibility seriously.

BIBLIOGRAPHY. C. Seltman, *Wine in the Ancient World*, 1957; J. P. Free, *Archaeology and Bible History*, 1950, Appendix II, pp. 351ff.; 'Wine' in *TWBR*; 'Food' in *HDB*, 2, p. 32; C. Brown, *NIDNTT* 3, pp. 918–923. F.S.F.

WIRE-WORM
See Animals, Part 1.

WISDOM.

I. In the Old Testament

Like all Heb. intellectual virtues, wisdom (generally *ḥoḵmâ*, though other words are used; *e.g.*: *bînâ*, 'understanding', Jb. 39:26; Pr. 23:4; *t*[e]*ḇûnâ*, 'insight', Ps. 136:5; *śeḵel* or *śēḵel*, 'prudence', Pr. 12:8; 23:9) is intensely practical, not theoretical. Basically, wisdom is the art of being successful, of forming the correct plan to gain the desired results. Its seat is the heart, the centre of moral and intellectual decision (*cf.* 1 Ki. 3:9, 12).

Those who possess technical skill are called wise: Bezalel, chief artisan of the tabernacle (Ex. 31:3; RSV 'ability'); artificers of idols (Is. 40:20; Je. 10:9); professional mourners (Je. 9:17); navigators or shipwrights (Ezk. 27:8–9). Practical wisdom may take on a sinister aspect, as in Jonadab's crafty advice (2 Sa. 13:3).

Kings and leaders were in special need of wisdom. On them hung the responsibility for correct decisions in political and social affairs. Joshua (Dt. 34:9), David (2 Sa. 14:20), Solomon (1 Ki. 3:9, 12; 4:29ff.) were granted wisdom to enable them to deal with their official duties. The Messianic King predicted by Isaiah (11:2) was to be equipped with wisdom to judge impartially. 'Wonderful Counsellor' (9:6) avers that his advice would be amazingly successful. See N. W. Porteous, 'Royal Wisdom', in *Wisdom in Israel and in the Ancient Near East*.

A special class of wise men (or women, *cf.* 2 Sa. 14:2) seems to have developed during the Monarchy. By Jeremiah's time they had taken their place beside prophets and priests as a major religious and social influence. Their task was to formulate workable plans, to prescribe advice for successful living (Je. 18:18). For the view that 'wise men' described not a professional class but persons of uncommon intelligence whose wisdom was sought after by their fellow citizens, see R. N. Whybray, *The Intellectual Tradition in the Old Testament* (1974). The wise man or counsellor stood in a parental relationship to those whose well-being hinged on his advice: Joseph was a 'father' to the pharaoh (Gn. 45:8); Deborah, a 'mother' in Israel (Jdg. 5:7). See P. A. H. de Boer, 'The Counsellor' in *Wisdom in Israel and in the Ancient Near East*.

Wisdom in the fullest sense belongs to God alone (Jb. 12:13ff.; Is. 31:2; Dn. 2:20–23). His wisdom is not only completeness of knowledge pervading every realm of life (Jb. 10:4; 26:6; Pr. 5:21; 15:3) but also 'consists in his irresistible fulfilment of what he has in his mind' (J. Pedersen, *Israel: Its Life and Culture*, 1–2, p. 198). The universe (Pr. 3:19f.; 8:22–31; Je. 10:12) and man (Jb. 10:8ff.; Ps. 104:24; Pr. 14:31; 22:2) are products of his creative wisdom. Natural (Is. 28:23–29) and historical (Is. 31:2) processes are governed by his wisdom, which includes an infallible discrimination between good and evil and is the basis for the just rewards and punishments which are the lot of the righteous and the wicked (Pss. 1; 37; 73; Pr. 10:3; 11:4; 12:2, *etc.*). Such wisdom is inscrutable (Jb. 28:12–21): God in his grace must reveal it if man is going to grasp it at all (Jb. 28:23, 28). Even wisdom derived from natural abilities or distilled from experience is a gracious gift, because God's creative activity makes such wisdom possible.

Biblical wisdom is both religious and practical. Stemming from the fear of the Lord (Jb. 28:28; Ps. 111:10; Pr. 1:7; 9:10), it branches out to touch all of life, as the extended commentary on wisdom in Proverbs indicates. Wisdom takes insights gleaned from the knowledge of God's ways and applies them in the daily walk. This combination of insight and obedience (and all insight must issue in obedience) relates wisdom to the prophetic emphasis on the knowledge (*i.e.* the cordial love and obedience) of God (*e.g.* Ho. 2:20; 4:1, 6; 6:6; Je. 4:22; 9:3, 6; and especially Pr. 9:10).

Pagan wisdom, though it, too, may be religious, has no anchor in the covenant-God and, therefore, is doomed to failure, as the prophets frequently point out (Is. 19:11ff.; Ezk. 28:2ff.; Ob. 8). When secularism, materialism and disdain of the covenant-ideals squeezed the fear of God out of Israel's wisdom, it became practical atheism, as vapid as its pagan counterpart, and drew Isaiah's fire: 'Woe to those who are wise in their own eyes' (5:21; *cf.* 29:14; Je. 18:18).

A special problem is the personification of wisdom in Pr. 8:22ff. Jb. 28 anticipates this personification by depicting wisdom as a mystery inscrutable to men but apparent to God. In Pr. 1:20–33 wisdom is likened to a woman crying in the streets for men to turn from their foolish ways and to find instruction and security in her (*cf.* also Pr. 3:15–20). The personification continues in Pr. 8 and reaches its climax in vv. 22ff., where wisdom claims to be the first creation of God and, perhaps, an assistant in the work of creation (8:30; *cf.* 3:19; the difficult *'āmôn*, 'as one brought up' in AV, should be translated 'master workman', as in RV, RSV; see W. F. Albright in *Wisdom in Israel and in the Ancient Near East*, p. 8). The purpose of wisdom's recitation of her credentials is to attract men to pay her rightful heed, as 8:32–36 indicates. Therefore, caution must be exercised in reading into this passage a view of hypostatization, *i.e.* that wisdom is depicted as having an independent existence. The Hebrews' characteristic resistance to speculation and abstraction frequently led their poets to deal with inanimate objects or ideals as though they had personality. See H. W. Robinson, *Inspiration and Revelation in the Old Testament*, 1946, p. 260; H. Ringgren, *Word and Wisdom*, 1947. For the influence of the personification of wisdom on the Logos idea of the Fourth Gospel, see *LOGOS.

II. In the New Testament

By and large NT wisdom (*sophia*) has the same intensely practical nature as in the OT. Seldom neutral (although *cf.* 'the wisdom of the Egyptians', Acts 7:22), it is either God-given or God-opposing. If divorced from God's revelation it is impoverished and unproductive at best (1 Cor. 1:17; 2:4; 2 Cor. 1:12) and foolish or even devilish at worst (1 Cor. 1:19ff.; Jas. 3:15ff.). Worldly wisdom is based on intuition and experience without revelation, and thus has severe limitations. The failure to recognize these limitations brings biblical condemnation on all (especially the Greeks) who haughtily attempt to cope with spiritual issues by human wisdom.

The truly wise are those to whom God has graciously imparted wisdom: Solomon (Mt. 12:42; Lk. 11:31), Stephen (Acts 6:10), Paul (2 Pet. 3:15), Joseph (Acts 7:10). One of Christ's legacies to his disciples was the wisdom to say the right thing in times of persecution and examination (Lk. 21:15). A similar wisdom is necessary for understanding the apocalyptic oracles and enigmas (Rev. 13:18; 17:9). Wisdom is essential not only for leaders of the church (Acts 6:3) but for all believers that they may perceive God's purposes in redemption (Eph. 1:8–9) and may walk worthily of God (Col. 1:9; Jas. 1:5; 3:13–17) and discreetly before unbelievers (Col. 4:5). As Paul has taught his hearers in all wisdom (Col. 1:28), so they who are mature enough to understand this spiritual wisdom (1 Cor. 2:6–7) are to instruct others in it (Col. 3:16).

God's wisdom is clearly demonstrated in his provision of redemption (Rom. 11:33), which is manifested in the church (Eph. 3:10). It is supremely revealed 'not in some esoteric doctrine . . . addressed to . . . initiates of some secret cult, but in action, God's supreme action in Christ on the Cross' (N. W. Porteous, *op. cit.*, p. 258). This wisdom, previously veiled to human minds, brooks no philosophical or practical rivals. The best attempts of men to untangle the problems of human existence are shown to be foolishness in the light of the cross.

The incarnate Christ grew in wisdom (Lk. 2:40, 52) as a boy and astonished his audiences by his wisdom as a man (Mt. 13:54; Mk. 6:2). His claims included wisdom (Mt. 12:42) and a unique knowledge of God (Mt. 11:25ff.). Twice he personifies wisdom in a manner reminiscent of Proverbs: Mt. 11:19 (= Lk. 7:35) and Lk. 11:49 (Mt. 23:34ff.). In both passages Christ may be alluding to himself as 'Wisdom', although this is not certain, especially in the latter instance. (See Arndt for suggested interpretations.) Paul's wisdom Christology (1 Cor. 1:24, 30) was probably influenced both by Christ's claims and by the apostolic consciousness (grounded in Christ's teachings in Matthew) that Christ was the *new Torah*, the complete revelation of God's will, replacing the old law. Since the commandments and wisdom are linked in Dt. 4:6, and especially in Jewish thought (*e.g.* Ecclus. 24:23; *Apocalypse of Baruch* 3:37ff.), it is not unexpected that Paul would view Jesus, the *new Torah*, as the wisdom of God. That Paul saw in Christ the fulfilment of Pr. 8:22ff. seems apparent from Col. 1:15ff., which strongly reflects the OT description of wisdom.

Paul's wisdom Christology is a dynamic concept, as is shown by the emphasis on Christ's activity in creation in Col. 1:15ff. and in redemption in 1 Cor. 1:24, 30. The latter verses affirm that in the crucifixion God made Jesus our wisdom, a wisdom further defined as embracing righteousness, sanctification and redemption. As the slain yet exalted Lord of the church, he is lauded for wisdom (Rev. 5:12). 'Receive' in this verse implies acknowledgment of attributes which are already Christ's; for in him 'are hid all the treasures of wisdom' (Col. 2:3).

BIBLIOGRAPHY. W. D. Davies, *Paul and Rabbinic Judaism*, 1948, pp. 147–176; E. Jacob and R. Mehl in *Vocabulary of the Bible*, ed. J.-J. von Allmen, 1958; M. Noth and D. W. Thomas (eds.), *Wisdom in Israel and in the Ancient Near East*, 1955; H. Conzelmann, 'Wisdom in the NT', *IDBS*, 1976, pp. 956–960; J. L. Crenshaw (ed.), *Studies in Ancient Israelite Wisdom*, 1976; G. von Rad, *Wisdom in Israel*, E.T. 1972; R. L. Wilken (ed.), *Aspects of Wisdom in Judaism and Early Christianity*, 1975; J. Goetzmann *et al.*, in *NIDNTT* 3, pp. 1023–1038. D.A.H.

WISDOM LITERATURE. A family of literary *genres* common in the ancient Near East in which instructions for successful living are given or the perplexities of human existence are contemplated. There are two broad types: proverbial (*PROVERB) wisdom—short, pithy sayings which state rules for personal happiness and welfare (*e.g.* Proverbs), and speculative wisdom—monologues (*e.g.* Ecclesiastes) or dialogues (*e.g.* Job) which attempt to delve into such problems as the meaning of existence and the relationship between God and man. This speculative wisdom is practical and empirical, not theoretical. Problems of human existence are discussed in terms of concrete examples: 'There was a man . . . whose name was Job.'

The roots of wisdom literature are probably to be found in short, crisp popular sayings which express rules for success or common observations concerning life. OT examples are found in 1 Ki. 20:11; Je. 23:28; 31:29, *inter al.* The transition from oral to literary wisdom took place in Egypt *c.* 2500 BC (*e.g. Instruction of the Vizier Ptah-Hotep*) and in Sumer shortly after. Throughout the Near East, a class of scribes or wise men arose whose highly honoured task was to create or collect and polish sagacious sayings (Ec. 12:9), usually under the patronage of court or temple. The sources of these sayings may have been clan wisdom, instruction in schools or sayings circulated among the nobility. Two of Israel's kings are credited with important contributions in this area: Solomon (1 Ki. 4:29–34) and Hezekiah (Pr. 25:1). By the 7th century BC the wise man (*ḥāḵām*) had assumed sufficient prominence in Judah to be classed with prophet or priest (Je. 8:8–9; 18:18), although there is some question as to whether he was yet viewed as a professional or merely as an unusually wise citizen. As the phenomenon of prophecy faded in the Persian and Greek periods, the wise men gained in stature, as the important apocryphal works, Ecclesiasticus and Wisdom of Solomon, and the Mish-

WISE MEN
See Magi, Part 2.

WITCHCRAFT
See Magic, Part 2.

naic tractate *Pirqe Aboth* (Sayings of the Fathers), show.

The wise men employed several literary devices as aids to memory. The most frequent device was the use of poetic parallelism of either a synthetic (*e.g.* Pr. 18:10) or antithetic (*e.g.* Pr. 10:1) type. Comparisons are common (*e.g.* Pr. 17:1), as are numerical sequences (*e.g.* Pr. 30:15ff.). Alliteration and acrostic patterns (*e.g.* Ps. 37; Pr. 31:10–31) are employed occasionally. Riddles (Jdg. 14:12ff.; *cf.* 1 Ki. 10:1), fables (*e.g.* Jdg. 9:7–15; Ezk. 17:3ff.; 19:1ff.), parables, which are extensions of the comparisons mentioned above (*e.g.* 2 Sa. 12:1–4; Is. 28:4), and allegories (*e.g.* Is. 5:1–7) are part of the wise man's repertoire. This sampling testifies to the impact made by wisdom literature on historical and prophetic writings. H. Gunkel has categorized certain psalms as wisdom poetry: Pss. 127; 133 (simple proverbial type); Pss. 1; 37; 49; 73; 112; 128. S. Mowinckel has called these psalms examples of 'learned psalmography'. Whether stories that teach responsible conduct as a key to success like those of Joseph (Gn. 37;39–50), the succession narrative (2 Sa. 9–20; 1 Ki. 1f.), Esther and Daniel bear wisdom's stamp is still under debate. *Cf.* R. N. Whybray, *The Intellectual Tradition in the Old Testament*, 1974; *contra* J. L. Crenshaw, 'Method in Determining Wisdom Influence upon "Historical" Literature', *JBL* 88, 1969, pp. 129–142). Wisdom's contribution is most readily discernible when its peculiar vocabulary, techniques and didactic content are all present in a text. Such influence is detectable in the NT, both in the teaching methods of Christ, who as the Master Sage employs parables and proverbs, and also in the Epistle of James (*e.g.* 1:5ff.; 3:13ff.).

Though an international phenomenon, as the OT freely recognizes (Edom in 1 Ki. 4:31; Ob. 8; Je. 49:7; and Egypt in Gn. 41:8; 1 Ki. 4:30; Is. 19:11–15 were particularly renowned), wisdom literature has not escaped Israel's peculiar stamp. Israel's sages confessed that true wisdom stemmed from God (*cf.* Jb. 28). The impact of Israel's prophets upon her sages cannot be ignored. H. Wheeler Robinson (*Inspiration and Revelation in the Old Testament*, 1946, p. 241) goes so far as to define the wisdom movement as '*the discipline whereby was taught the application of prophetic truth to the individual life in the light of experience*'.

At the same time prophets like Amos, Isaiah and Jeremiah occasionally used the forms, techniques and teachings of wisdom literature to enrich and reinforce their oracles, as S. Terrien ('Amos and Wisdom', in *Israel's Prophetic Heritage*, ed. B. W. Anderson and W. Harrelson, 1962, pp. 108–115), H. W. Wolff (*Amos, the Prophet: the Man and His Background*, E.T. 1973) and J. W. Whedbee (*Isaiah and Wisdom*, 1970) have shown.

BIBLIOGRAPHY. J. Wood, *Wisdom Literature*, 1967; G. von Rad, *Wisdom in Israel*, E.T. 1972; J. L. Crenshaw, 'Wisdom', in *Old Testament Form Criticism*, ed. J. H. Hayes, 1974, pp. 225–264; *idem*, 'Wisdom in the OT', *IDBS*, 1976, pp. 952–956; R. E. Murphy, *Seven Books of Wisdom*, 1960; W. McKane, *Prophets and Wise Men*, 1965; R. B. Y. Scott, *The Way of Wisdom in the Old Testament*, 1971; M. Noth and D. W. Thomas (eds.), *Wisdom in Israel and in the Ancient Near East*, 1955; O. S. Rankin, *Israel's Wisdom Literature*, 1936; H. Ranston, *The Old Testament Wisdom Books and Their Teaching*, 1930; J. C. Rylaarsdam, *Revelation in Jewish Wisdom Literature*, 1946.

D.A.H.

WITNESS. In EVV 'to witness', 'to bear witness', a 'witness', 'to testify', 'testimony' (with a few minor additional renderings) represent a somewhat arbitrary and not always consistent rendering of the following Heb. and Gk. words. In the OT: *'ānâ* (lit. 'to answer'), *'ûḏ* (verb), *'ēḏ*, *'ēḏâ*, *'ēḏûṯ*, *t^{e}'ûḏâ*; in the NT: *martyreō* (verb) and compounds, *martys*, *martyria*, *martyrion*. Though 'to witness' is used with a wide range of connotations, the forensic often being virtually forgotten, it never occurs in the frequent modern Eng. usage as a synonym of 'to see'.

'ēḏ and its rare synonym *'ēḏâ* always refer to the person or thing bearing witness, examples of the latter being Gn. 31:48, 52; Jos. 22:27–28, 34; 24:27; Is. 19:20. The NT equivalent, *martys*, is used only of persons, there being no example of a thing as bearer of witness.

Heb., disliking abstracts, rarely speaks of witness in the sense of evidence given. In the three cases it does (Ru. 4:7; Is. 8:16, 20) it uses *t^{e}'ûḏâ*. Gk. uses the conception frequently, but distinguishes between *martyria*, the act of testifying or the testimony, and *martyrion*, that which may serve as evidence or proof or the fact established by evidence.

'ēḏûṯ, always rendered 'testimony' except in the AV of Nu. 17:7–8; 18:2; 2 Ch. 24:6, where it is 'witness', has lost its forensic meaning completely and is a technical religious term (*COVENANT), rendered by *KB* 'monitory sign, reminder, exhortation'. The outstanding example of *'ēḏûṯ* is the tables of the Ten Commandments (Ex. 16:34; 25:16, 21, *etc.*). Hence the ark which contained them became 'the ark of the testimony' (Ex. 25:22, *etc.*), the tent which sheltered them, 'the tent of the testimony' (Nu. 17:7), and the veil dividing off the Holy of holies, 'the veil of the testimony' (Lv. 24:3). The term is then enlarged to cover the law as a whole, *e.g.* Pss. 78:5; 119:2 and frequently. The meaning in 2 Ki. 11:12 is doubtful (see *ICC*, *ad loc.*).

AV translation 'martyr' in Acts 22:20; Rev. 2:13; 17:6 (in the last of these also RV, RSV) is hardly justified, though *martys* quickly developed this meaning; *cf.* Arndt, p. 495b.

BIBLIOGRAPHY. L. Coenen, A. A. Trites, in *NIDNTT* 3, pp. 1038–1051; A. A. Trites, *The New Testament Concept of Witness*, 1977; H. Strathmann, *TDNT* 4, pp. 474–514.

H.L.E.

WOE. The rendering of the Gk. interjection *ouai*, meaning 'Alas for'. When Jesus says 'Woe unto you', he is not so much pronouncing a final judgment as deploring the miserable condition in God's sight of those he is addressing. Their wretchedness lies not least in the fact that they are living in a fool's paradise, unaware of the misery that awaits them. The state of the materially-minded blinded by wealth to their spiritual needs, of the self-satisfied, of the impenitent and unsympathetic, and of those who are universally popular is declared by Jesus to be wretched (Lk. 6:24–26). Similarly, the woeful condition of the Pharisees and scribes (Lk. 'lawyers') lies, Jesus tells them, in the hypocritical zeal, the lack of proportion, the love of display and the self-complacency which disfigure their religion (Mt. 23:13–33; Lk. 11:42–52). When Jesus addresses the words 'Woe to you' to the unrepentant cities Chorazin and Bethsaida, he follows them with a prophecy of the doom that awaits them (Mt. 11:21) as they are in a woeful state for having refused the gospel. Paul says he would be in a woeful state if he failed to preach it (1 Cor. 9:16). The seer in the Revelation uses the word *ouai* as an interjection in his dirge over fallen Babylon (Rev. 18:10–16), and as a noun to describe three 'woes', a comprehensive term covering various plagues and disasters which will herald the final judgment (Rev. 9:12; 11:14).

BIBLIOGRAPHY. N. Hillyer, *NIDNTT* 3, pp. 1051–1054.

R.V.G.T.

WOMAN (Heb. *'iššâ*, Gk. *gynē*). Woman, with man, was 'made in the image of God': 'male and female he created them' (Gn. 1:27). She is man's helper (Gn. 2:20). (*EVE.)

From the Heb. laws we see that the mother was to be honoured (Ex. 20:12), feared (Lv. 19:3) and obeyed (Dt. 21:18ff.). She was to be reckoned with in her household, naming the children and being responsible for their early education. The same sacrifice was offered for cleansing, whether the new-born child was male or female (Lv. 12:5f.). She attended the religious gatherings for worship, and brought her offerings for sacrifice. The Nazirite vow was taken by her as she sought to dedicate herself specially to the worship of Yahweh (Nu. 6:2).

The woman was exempt from sabbath labour (Ex. 20:10), and if sold as a slave was freed like the man in the 7th year. If there were no male heirs, the woman could inherit and become a landowner in her own right.

Young men were exhorted to marry within the tribe lest their womenfolk wooed them away from their service of Yahweh.

Monogamy was regarded as the ideal state, although polygamy was common, and the relationship of Yahweh and Israel was often compared with that of a man and wife.

There are many examples of women of stature playing their part in the life of the people, *e.g.* Miriam, Deborah, Huldah, and being in a direct personal relationship with Yahweh. On the other hand, one sees the tremendous influence wielded against Yahweh by women such as Jezebel and Maacah.

As time went on there was a tendency, under rabbinical teaching, to make the man more prominent and to assign to women an inferior role.

Of greatest importance in the NT is our Lord's attitude to women and his teaching concerning them.

*Mary, the mother of Jesus, was described as 'Blessed . . . among women' (Lk. 1:42) by her kinswoman Elizabeth. Anna, the prophetess at the Temple, recognized the baby's identity (Lk. 2:38). There was much concerning her Son that Mary did not understand, but she 'kept all these things, pondering them in her heart' (Lk. 2:19), until the time to make public the details of his birth and boyhood. As he was on the cross Jesus commended her to the care of a disciple.

The Gospel narratives abound with instances of Jesus' encounters with women. He forgave them, he healed them, he taught them, and they in their turn served him by making provision for his journeys, by giving hospitality, by deeds of love, by noting his tomb so that they could perform the last rites for him, and by becoming eyewitnesses of his resurrection.

Jesus included them in his teaching illustrations, making it clear that his message involved them. By thus honouring them he put woman on an equality with man, demanding the same standard from both the sexes and offering the same way of salvation.

After the resurrection the women joined 'in prayer and supplication' with the other followers of Jesus, in entire fellowship with them (Acts 1:14). They helped to elect Matthias (Acts 1:15–26), and received the power and gifts of the Holy Spirit on the Day of Pentecost (Acts 2:1–4, 18).

It was the home of Mary, the mother of John Mark, which became a centre of the church at Jerusalem (Acts 12:12). Paul's first convert in Europe was the woman Lydia (Acts 16:14). Priscilla with her husband taught the great Apollos the full truths of the gospel. The four daughters of Philip 'prophesied' (Acts 21:9). Many others, as, for example, Phoebe, were active Christians and wholly engaged in the service of the gospel.

Paul dealt with the local situation in the churches by requiring that the conventions of the time be observed. Meanwhile he laid down the principle that 'God shows no partiality' and that in Christ 'there is neither male nor female', since Christians 'are all one in Christ Jesus' (Gal. 3:28).

BIBLIOGRAPHY. H. Vorländer *et al.*, in *NIDNTT* 3, pp. 1055–1078; K. Stendahl, *The Bible and the Role of Women*, 1966; P. K. Jewett, *Man as Male and Female*, 1975. M.B.

WOMB. Heb. *beṭen*, *mē'îm* and *reḥem* or *raḥam*; Gk. *gastēr*, *koilia* or *mētra*, the former two in both cases being used also of the belly generally, indicating the Heb. vagueness about the internal physiology (*STOMACH, *BOWELS). The reference is generally to the place or time of life's beginning (Jb. 1:21; Is. 49:1), and so figuratively of the origin of anything (Jb. 38:29). The formation of the babe in the womb is a wonderful mystery to the biblical writers, who, understandably enough, attribute it to the direct action and care of God (Jb. 31:15; Ec. 11:5). The presence of the living babe in the womb some time before birth is mentioned in the NT (Lk. 1:41). *Barrenness is attributed to the closing up of the womb, sometimes specifically stated to be done by God (1 Sa. 1:5). This is a great cause of sorrow and shame to the woman concerned (v. 6). The *first-born, referred to as that which opens the womb, is regarded as holy (Ex. 13:2; Lk. 2:23). B.O.B.

WOOL. The high value set upon wool as the basic fabric for clothing (Jb. 31:20; Pr. 31:13; Ezk. 34:3) is reflected in its inclusion among the first fruits to be offered by the priests (Dt. 18:4) and as an important item in Mesha's tribute (2 Ki. 3:4). Damascus wool was prized at Tyre market (Ezk. 27:18); the LXX compares its quality to that of Miletus which was famous in the ancient world (Pliny 8. 73). The reason for the Mosaic prohibition against wearing cloth made of a mixture of wool and linen (Dt. 22:11) is not clear. Josephus (*Ant.* 4. 208) claims that garments of wool and linen mixture were reserved for priests, but gives no evidence. Static electricity in such a mixture would be uncomfortable to the wearer (*NBCR*, p. 223). The brilliant whiteness of wool after thorough washing is used to illustrate purity (Is. 1:18) and beautiful teeth (Ct. 4:2) and is likened to snowflakes (Ps. 147:16). N.H.

WOLF
See Animals, Part 1.

WOMEN IN CHURCH
See Deaconess, Part 1.

WOMEN, SEALS OF
See Seal, Part 3.

WOOD-WORM
See Animals, Part 1.

The long woollen skirt typical of Sumerian dress is clearly shown on this stone statue of the scribe Dudu. Height 39 cm. c. 2500 BC. (SAOB)

WORD. In the OT 'the word (*dāḇār*) of God' is used 394 times of a divine communication which comes from God to men in the form of commandment, prophecy, warning or encouragement. The usual formula is 'the word of Yahweh came (lit. was) to . . .' but sometimes the word is 'seen' as a vision (Is. 2:1; Je. 2:31; 38:21). Yahweh's word is an extension of the divine personality, invested with divine authority, and is to be heeded by angels and men (Ps. 103:20; Dt. 12:32); it stands for ever (Is. 40:8), and once uttered it cannot return unfulfilled (Is. 55:11). It is used as a synonym for the law (*tôrâ*) of God in Ps. 119, where alone its reference is to a written rather than a spoken message.

In the NT it translates two terms, * *logos* and *rhēma*, the former being supremely used of the message of the Christian gospel (Mk. 2:2; Acts 6:2; Gal. 6:6), though the latter also bears the same meaning (Rom. 10:8; Eph. 6:17; Heb. 6:5, *etc.*). Our Lord spoke of the word of God (in the parable of the sower, Lk. 8:11; see also Mk. 7:13; Lk. 11:28), but in the Synoptic Gospels he always used the plural of his own message ('my words', Mt. 24:35 and parallels; Mk. 8:38; Lk. 24:44). In the Fourth Gospel, however, the singular is often found. To the early church the word was a message revealed from God in Christ, which was to be preached, ministered and obeyed. It was the word of life (Phil. 2:16), of truth (Eph. 1:13), of salvation (Acts 13:26), of reconciliation (2 Cor. 5:19), of the cross (1 Cor. 1:18).

BIBLIOGRAPHY. H. Haarbeck *et al.*, in *NIDNTT* 3, pp. 1078–1146; A. Debrunner *et al.*, in *TDNT* 4, pp. 69–143. J.B.TR.

WORK. The main words here are the Heb. *ma'ᵃśeh* (181 times), 'an act', 'a doing' (*cf.* Gn. 5:29; Ex. 5:4, *etc.*, and especially in the Psalms of God's act, see Pss. 8:3, 6; 19:1, *etc.*); *mᵉlā'ḵâ* (117 times; *cf.* Gn. 2:2–3; Ex. 20:9, *etc.*); *pō'al* (30 times), 'a deed' (*cf.* Dt. 32:4, *etc.*). Gk. *ergon* (142 times) is found frequently in Jn., Heb., Jas. and Rev. Less frequent is the abstract *energeia*, literally 'energy' (EVV 'working'). This is a specific Pauline word (Eph. 1:19; 3:7; 4:16; Phil. 3:21; Col. 1:29; 2 Thes. 2:9). Note should be taken also of the Heb. *yᵉgî'â*, 'labour', 'weariness', and *'āmāl*, 'labour', 'misery'; *cf.* Gk. *kopiaō*, 'to labour', 'to be wearied out' (*cf.* Mt. 11:28; Jn. 4:38, *etc.*), and *ergatēs*, 'a worker' (Mt. 9:37–38; 20:1–2, 8; Lk. 10:2, 7; Jas. 5:4).

In classical Gk. the verb *kopiaō* has reference to the weariness which labour produces (*cf. LSJ*, *ad loc.*), but in the NT it signifies the toil itself (*cf.* Mt. 6:28; 11:28; Lk. 5:5; 12:27; Jn. 4:38). The word *ergatēs* has reference to the business or the trade by which men gain their subsistence (Acts 19:25), and it is also used to denote the profit which results from their activity (Acts 16:16, 19) as well as the toil which the pursuit of their gain involves. *ergasia* occurs in an ethical sense in Eph. 4:19 and means literally 'to make a trade of'; *cf.* 'worker' (*ergatēs*) in Lk. 13:27; 2 Cor. 11:13; Phil. 3:2, and in a good sense Mt. 10:10; 2 Tim. 2:15. Luke's usage of the Latinism *dos ergasian*, 'make an effort' (AV 'give diligence') (Lk. 12:58), to emphasize Christ's warning concerning reconciliation with an adversary is thought by some to be derived from his medical studies, where the term had reference to the making of some mixture, the mixture itself, and the work of digestion, and of the lungs, *etc.* (*cf.* W. K. Hobart, *The Medical Language of St Luke*, 1882, p. 243). The phrase, however, occurs in the LXX (*cf.* Wisdom 13:19) with which Luke was familiar.

I. The general sense

It is clear from the interchangeable use of certain words to indicate God's activity and man's that work is itself a God-ordained thing. Work was from the beginning God's purpose for men, and is set forth in Ps. 104:19–24 and Is. 28:23–29 as a provision of the divine wisdom. Creation itself 'works' (*cf.* Pr. 6:6–11). The fact of work as forming an integral part of the pattern of the divine purpose for man is implied in the fourth commandment. But the entrance of sin changed work from a joy to a toil (*cf.* Gn. 3:16–19). Work has thus become a burden instead of a blessing, and, although not bad in itself, it has lost its true value. It has become an occasion for sin; idolatry results when it becomes an end in itself (*cf.* Ec. 2:4–11, 20–23; Lk. 12:16–22). By some it has become the means of exploitation and oppression (*cf.* Ex. 1:11–14; 2:23; Jas. 5:4). But in redemption, work is again transformed into a means of blessing. From the beginning Christianity has condemned idleness even when this has been indulged in in the name of religion (*cf.* 1 Thes. 4:11; also Eph. 4:28; 1 Tim. 5:13). Our Lord, working as a carpenter (Mk. 6:3), has sanctified common toil, and Paul set an example in honest labour (Acts 18:3). He virtually established a law of social economics in his announcement in 2 Thes. 3:10: 'this we commanded you, that if any would not work, neither should he eat'. On the other side the principle proclaimed by our Lord remains the basis of society, 'the labourer deserves his wages' (Lk. 10:7).

In the experience of grace human tasks are given a new value and become more worth while. They are performed for the sake of the Name. And in their fulfilment in this context they are thrice blessed. The one who works is himself blessed in his reception of divine grace to carry through his labours for the glory of God; those who receive the results of such tasks done in a new spirit and with a new quality are benefited also; and in all God is himself glorified. Such work is done 'in' and 'for' the Lord (*cf.* Rom. 14:7–8; Eph. 6:5–9; Col. 3:23–24). In this way man becomes a steward of God's riches (1 Cor. 4:1–2; *cf.* Mt. 25:14–30) and a servant of his neighbour (Mt. 25:40; Gal. 5:13; 1 Pet. 4:10). The genuineness of man's faith is proved in the end by the quality of his works (*cf.* Mt. 16:27, *praxis*). Yet in the end the acceptance of the labourer will be an act of divine grace (*cf.* 1 Cor. 3:8–15; note especially v. 10).

II. The spiritual and ethical reference

The word 'work' is used with reference to God's act of creation and providence. In the Psalms this note is given special emphasis. God's work or works are great and manifold (*cf.* Pss. 92:5; 104:24; 111:2, *etc.*). They give him everlasting praise (*cf.* Ps. 145:4, 9–10), declare his righteousness (145:17) and bring him joy (104:31). It is the same in the NT (*cf.* Heb. 4:10; Jn. 1:3; Acts 13:41; Rev. 15:3). The term is used also for the work of salvation committed by the Father to the Son. This is specifically a Johannine idea.

The Son has come to do the Father's work (*cf.* Jn. 4:34; 5:36; 9:4; 10:25, 37, *etc.*), which work he has finished (Jn. 15:24; 17:4). This means that nothing can be added to the work he has done, since it is once and for all. *Salvation is therefore not a matter of works or merit but of *grace. But the redeemed man will work and serve and labour and thus commend himself in the Lord. He will be fruitful in every good work (Col. 1:10; *cf.* Gal. 6:4; 2 Thes. 2:17; 2 Tim. 2:21; *etc.*). Those who undertake special work for God are to be esteemed for their work's sake (*cf.* 1 Thes. 5:13; also Phil. 2:29). Yet no work for God can be done apart from the inworking of his grace (*cf.* Eph. 2:10; 3:20; Phil. 2:13; Col. 1:29, *etc.*). Such is the 'work of faith, and labour of love' (1 Thes. 1:3; *cf.* 2 Thes. 1:11).

BIBLIOGRAPHY. J. Calvin, *Institutes*, 3. 7; A. Richardson, *The Biblical Doctrine of Work*, 1952; J. Murray, *Principles of Conduct*, 1957, pp. 82–106; H.-C. Hahn, F. Thiele, in *NIDNTT* 3, pp. 1147–1159. H.D.McD.

WORKS. The three main uses of this term, although distinct, are essentially related: the works of God, the works of Jesus Christ and the works of man in relation to faith.

1. In the OT the works of God are presented as evidence of God's supreme power, authority, wisdom and benevolence. The OT defines the Deity not by abstract terms such as omnipotence, but by his activity. Moses adduced the works of God as evidence of his unique distinction from other gods (Dt. 3:24). In the Psalms the works of God are frequently proclaimed as providing confidence in his power and authority and his sole right to receive worship. These works are his creative activity (Ps. 104:24) and his sovereign acts in relation to his redeemed people (Ps. 77:11–20) and to the nations (Ps. 46:8–10).

2. It was by his works that Jesus revealed that he was both Messiah and Son of God, exemplified by his answer to John the Baptist (Mt. 11:2–5). John's Gospel records the significant activity of Jesus with set purpose to reveal his Messiahship and deity so as to induce faith in his Person (Jn. 20:30–31). Frequently Jesus pointed to his works as evidence that he was sent by the Father (Jn. 5:36; 10:37–38). Being the very works of God (Jn. 9:3–4), his works are sufficient ground for faith in him as being uniquely related to the Father (Jn. 10:38; 14:10–11). It was through equating his work with that of God that he was accused of blasphemy in identifying himself with God (Jn. 5:17–23). His death completed that work (Jn. 17:4; 19:30).

3. The believer also demonstrates by his good works the divine activity within him (Mt. 5:16; Jn. 6:28; 14:12). Conversely, the man who has no faith demonstrates by his evil works his separation from God (Jn. 3:19; Col. 1:21; Eph. 5:11; 2 Pet. 2:8, *etc.*). Good works are therefore the evidence of living faith, as James emphasizes in opposition to those who claim to be saved by faith alone without works (Jas. 2:14–26). James is in harmony with Paul, who also repeatedly declared the necessity for works, *i.e.* for behaviour appropriate to the new life in Christ following our entry into it by faith alone (Eph. 2:8–10; 1 Cor. 6:9–11; Gal. 5:16–26, *etc.*). The works rejected by Paul are those which men claim as earning God's favour and securing their discharge from the guilt of sin (Rom. 4:1–5; Eph. 2:8–9; Tit. 3:5). Since salvation is given by God in grace, no degree of works can merit it. The good works of the heathen are therefore unavailing as a means of salvation, since the man himself relies on the flesh and not on the grace of God (Rom. 8:7–8). J.C.C.

WORLD. The Gk. word *kosmos* means by derivation 'the *ordered* world'. It is used in the NT, but not in LXX, sometimes for what we should call the 'universe', the created world, described in the OT as 'all things' or 'heaven and earth' (Acts 17:24). The 'world' in this sense was made by the Word (Jn. 1:10); and it was this 'world' of which Jesus was speaking when he said it would not profit a man anything if he gained the whole of it and lost his soul in the process (Mt. 16:26).

But, because mankind is the most important part of the universe, the word *kosmos* is more often used in the limited sense of human beings, being a synonym for *hē oikoumenē gē*, 'the inhabited earth', also translated in the NT by 'world'. It is into this 'world' that men are born, and in it they live till they die (Jn. 16:21). It was all the kingdoms of this world that the devil offered to give to Christ if he would worship him (Mt. 4:8–9). It was this world, the world of men and women of flesh and blood, that God loved (Jn. 3:16), and into which Jesus came when he was born of a human mother (Jn. 11:27).

It is, however, an axiom of the Bible that this world of human beings, the climax of the divine creation, the world that God made especially to reflect his glory, is now in rebellion against him. Through the transgression of one man, sin has entered into it (Rom. 5:18) with universal consequences. It has become, as a result, a *disordered* world in the grip of the evil one (1 Jn. 5:19). And so, very frequently in the NT, and particularly in the Johannine writings, the word *kosmos* has a sinister significance. It is not the world as God intended it to be, but '*this* world' set over against God, following its own wisdom and living by the light of its own reason (1 Cor. 1:21), not recognizing the Source of all true life and illumination (Jn. 1:10). The two dominant characteristics of '*this* world' are *pride*, born of man's failure to accept his creaturely estate and his dependence on the Creator, which leads him to act as though he were the lord and giver of life; and *covetousness*, which causes him to desire and possess all that is attractive to his physical senses (1 Jn. 2:16). And, as man tends in effect to worship what he covets, such covetousness is idolatry (Col. 3:5). Accordingly, worldliness is the enthronement of something other than God as the supreme object of man's interests and affections. Pleasures and occupations, not necessarily wrong in themselves, become so when an all-absorbing attention is paid to them.

'*This* world' is pervaded by a spirit of its own, which has to be exorcized by the Spirit of God, if it is not to remain in control over human reason and understanding (1 Cor. 2:12). Man is in bondage to the elements which comprise the world (Col. 2:20) until he is emancipated from them by Christ. He cannot overcome it till he is himself 'born of God' (1 Jn. 5:4). Legalism, asceticism and ritualism are this world's feeble and enfeebling substitutes for true religion (Gal. 4:9–10); and only a true knowledge of God as revealed by Christ can prevent men from relying upon them. It was because the Jews relied upon them that they did not recognize either the Christ in the days of his flesh (Jn. 1:11) or his followers (1 Jn. 3:1). Similarly, false prophets who advocate such things, or anti-christs who are antinomian in their teaching, will always be listened to by those who belong to this world (1 Jn. 4:5).

Christ, whom the Father sent to be the Saviour of this world (1 Jn. 4:14), and whose very presence in it was a judgment upon it (Jn. 9:39), freed men from its sinister forces by himself engaging in mortal combat with its 'prince', the perpetual instigator of the evil within it. The crisis of this world came when Jesus left the upper room and went forth to meet this prince (Jn. 14:30–31). By voluntarily submitting to death, Jesus brought about the defeat of him who held men in the grip of death, but who had no claims upon himself (Jn. 12:31–32; 14:30). On the cross, judgment was passed on the ruler (AV 'prince') of this world (Jn. 16:11); and faith in Christ as the Son of God, who offered the sacrifice which alone can cleanse men from the guilt and power of sin (a cleansing symbolized by the flow of water and blood from his stricken side, Jn. 19:34), enables the believer to overcome the world (1 Jn. 5:4–6), and to endure the tribulations which the world inevitably brings upon him (Jn. 16:33). The love of a Christian for God, the Father of Jesus Christ his Redeemer, who is the propitiation for the sins of the whole world (1 Jn. 2:2), acts with the expulsive power of a new affection; it makes it abhorrent to him to set his affections any longer upon 'this world', which, because it is severed from the true source of life, is transitory and contains within itself the seeds of its own decay (1 Jn. 2:15–17). A man who has come to experience the *higher* love for God, and for Christ and his brethren, must abandon the lower love for all that is contaminated by the spirit of the world: friendship of the world is of necessity enmity with God (Jas. 4:2).

Jesus, in his last prayer in the upper room, did not pray for the world, but for those whom his Father had given him out of the world. By this 'gift', these men whom Jesus described as 'his own' ceased to have the characteristics of the world; and Jesus prayed that they might be kept safe from its evil influences (Jn. 17:9), for he knew that after his own departure they would have to bear the brunt of the world's hatred which had hitherto been directed almost entirely against himself. As the risen and ascended Christ he still limits his intercessions to those who draw near to God through him (Heb. 7:25); and he continues to manifest himself not to the world but to his own that are in the world (Jn. 14:22).

But it is very certain that Christ's disciples cannot and must not attempt to retreat from this world. It is into this world, *all* the world (Mk. 16:15), that he sends them. They are to be its light (Mt. 5:14); and the 'field' in which the church is to do its work of witnessing to the truth as it is in Jesus is no less comprehensive than the world itself (Mt. 13:38). For the world is still God's world, even though at present it lies under the evil one. In the end, 'earth's true loveliness will be restored'; and, with all evil destroyed and the sons of God manifested, the whole creation will be 'set free from its bondage to decay and obtain the glorious liberty of the children of God' (Rom. 8:21). Then God will be 'everything to every one' (1 Cor. 15:28); or, 'present in a total manner in the universe' (J. Héring in *Vocabulary of the Bible*, 1958). The seer of Rev. envisages the day when great voices in heaven will proclaim: 'The kingdom of the world has become the kingdom of our Lord and of his Christ, and he shall reign for ever and ever' (Rev. 11:15). R.V.G.T.

WORM
See Animals, Part 1.

WORMWOOD
See Plants, Part 3.

WORSHIP. The vocabulary of worship in the Bible is very extensive, but the essential concept in Scripture is 'service'. Heb. *'aḇôḏâ* and Gk. *latreia* both originally signified the labour of slaves or hired servants. And in order to offer this 'worship' to God his servants must prostrate themselves—Heb. *hištaḥawâ* or Gk. *proskyneō*—and thus manifest reverential fear and adoring awe and wonder.

In the OT there are instances of individual worship (Gn. 24:26f.; Ex. 33:9–34:8). But the emphasis is upon worship in the congregation (Ps. 42:4; 1 Ch. 29:20). In tabernacle and Temple worship ritual was prominent. Apart from the daily morning and evening sacrifices, the celebration of Passover and the observance of the Day of Atonement would be highlights in the Jewish religious calendar. The ritual acts of shedding of blood, presenting incense, pronouncing the priestly blessing, *etc.*, would tend to emphasize the ceremonial to the detriment of the spiritual aspects of worship, and even tend to introduce a sense of tension or conflict between the two attitudes (Pss. 40:6; 50:7–15; Mi. 6:6–8). But many in Israel would be able to take the public praise (*e.g.* Pss. 93; 95–100) and prayers (*e.g.* Pss. 60; 79; 80), and use them to express their love and gratitude to God (Dt. 11:13) in a real act of inward spiritual worship.

This highly-developed public worship offered in the tabernacle and Temple is a far cry from earlier times when the Patriarchs believed that the Lord could be worshipped wherever he had chosen to reveal himself. But that public worship in the Temple was a spiritual reality is clear from the fact that when the sanctuary was destroyed, and the exiles found themselves in Babylon, worship remained a necessity, and to meet this need the synagogue service, consisting of (1) the *Shema'*, (2) prayers, (3) Scripture readings and (4) exposition, was 'created'. But later in the second Temple the daily services, the sabbath, the annual festivals and fasts, and the praises of the hymn-book (book of Psalms) of this second Temple ensured that worship remained a vital factor in Jewish national life.

In the NT Temple and synagogue worship are again found. Christ participated in both, but he always inculcated the worship that is the love of the heart towards a heavenly Father. In his teaching the approach to God through ritual and priestly mediation is not merely unimportant, it is now unnecessary. At last 'worship' is true *'aḇôḏâ* or *latreia*, a service offered to God not only in terms of temple worship but of service to one's fellows (Lk. 10:25ff.; Mt. 5:23f.; Jn. 4:20–24; Jas. 1:27). At the beginning, however, the church did not abandon Temple worship; and probably Christians continued to attend the synagogue services too. And when the break between Judaism and the church finally came Christian worship may have been modelled on the synagogue service.

The great contributory factor in the break away from the Jewish sabbath, Temple, ritual, *etc.*, was the bitter antagonism of the Jews against the church. But so far as the NT is concerned our notions of Christian worship are very vague. Clearly the main day of worship was the Lord's Day (Acts 20:7), although we do hear of daily services at the beginning (Acts 2:46). There is no mention in the NT of services commemorating the Lord's resurrection and the Spirit's coming at Pentecost. Worship would be conducted in believers' homes. In such circumstances official ministrants would be unnecessary. Simplicity would be the keynote of these house-church worship services, consisting for the most part of *praise (Eph. 5:19; Col. 3:16), *prayer, reading from the Scriptures and exposition. In the church at Corinth we hear of 'speaking in tongues' (1 Cor. 14). The love-feast, followed by the Lord's Supper (1 Cor. 11:23–28), were also common features of Christian worship. But the emphasis throughout would be upon the Spirit, and the inner love and devotion of the heart.

Bibliography. J. V. Bartlett in *ERE*; R. Martin-Achard in J.-J. von Allmen (ed.), *Vocabulary of the Bible*, 1958, pp. 471–474; R. Abba, *Principles of Christian Worship*, 1957; R. P. Martin, *Worship in the Early Church*², 1974. J.G.S.S.T.

WRATH. The permanent attitude of the holy and just God when confronted by sin and evil is designated his 'wrath'. It is inadequate to regard this term merely as a description of 'the inevitable process of cause and effect in a moral universe' or as another way of speaking of the results of sin. It is rather a personal quality, without which God would cease to be fully righteous and his love would degenerate into sentimentality. His wrath, however, even though like his love it has to be described in human language, is not wayward, fitful or spasmodic, as human anger always is. It is as permanent and as consistent an element in his nature as is his love. This is well brought out in the treatise of Lactantius, *De ira Dei*.

The injustice and impiety of men, for which they have no excuse, *must* be followed by manifestations of the divine wrath in the lives both of individuals and of nations (see Rom. 1:18–32); and the OT contains numerous illustrations of this, such as the destruction of Sodom and Gomorrah and the downfall of Nineveh (see Dt. 29:23; Na. 1:2–6). But until the final 'day of wrath', which is anticipated throughout the Bible and portrayed very vividly in Rev., God's wrath is always tempered with mercy, particularly in his dealings with his chosen people (see, *e.g.*, Ho. 11:8ff.). For a sinner, however, to 'trade' upon this mercy is to store up wrath for himself 'on the day of wrath when God's righteous judgment will be revealed' (Rom. 2:5). Paul was convinced that one of the main reasons why Israel failed to arrest the process of moral decline lay in their wrong reaction to the forbearance of God, who so often refrained from punishing them to the extent they deserved. They were presuming upon 'the riches of his kindness and forbearance and patience', and failed to see that it was intended to lead them to repentance (Rom. 2:4).

In their unredeemed state men's rebellion against God is, in fact, so persistent that they are inevitably the objects of his wrath (Eph. 2:3), and 'vessels of wrath made for destruction' (Rom. 9:22). Nor does the Mosaic law rescue them from this position, for, as the apostle states in Rom. 4:15, 'the law brings wrath'. Because it requires perfect obedience to its commands, the penalties exacted for disobedience render the offender more subject to the divine wrath. It is, to be sure, only by the merciful provision for sinners made in the gospel that they can cease to be the objects of this wrath and become the recipients of this grace. The love of God for sinners expressed in the life and death of Jesus is the dominant theme of the NT, and this love is shown not least because Jesus experienced on man's behalf and in his stead the misery, the afflictions, the punishment and the death which are the lot of sinners subject to God's wrath.

Consequently, Jesus can be described as 'the deliverer from the wrath to come' (see 1 Thes. 1:10); and Paul can write: 'Since, therefore, we are now justified by his blood, much more shall we be saved by him from the wrath of God' (Rom. 5:9). On the other hand, the wrath of God remains upon all who, seeking to thwart God's redemptive purpose, are disobedient to God's Son, through whom alone such justification is rendered possible.

Bibliography. R. V. G. Tasker, *The Biblical Doctrine of the Wrath of God*, 1951; G. H. C. Macgregor, 'The Concept of the Wrath of God in the New Testament', *NTS* 7, 1960–1, pp. 101ff.; H.-C. Hahn, *NIDNTT* 1, pp. 105–113.

R.V.G.T.

WRITING. Throughout the ancient Near East, from at least *c.* 3100 BC onwards, writing was a hallmark of civilization and progress. In the 2nd millennium BC there were several experiments which led to the development of the alphabet, with a consequent general increase in literacy. Although the number of documents from the pre-exilic period found in Palestine is small when compared with the many thousands from Egypt, Mesopotamia and Syria, they show it is reasonable to assume that proximity to other cultural centres stimulated the art of writing there through all periods. The commonest words for writing (Heb. *kāṯaḇ*; Aram. *kᵉṯaḇ*; Gk. *graphō*) occur more than 450 times in OT and NT.

I. Biblical references

Moses is said to have written (Ex. 17:14) the Decalogue (Ex. 24:12; 34:27), the words of Yahweh (Ex. 24:4), the Law (Torah, Jos. 8:31), and spoken about a written copy of it (Dt. 27). He also wrote all the statutes (Dt. 30:10) and judgments (Ex. 34:27; *cf.* 2 Ki. 17:37), as well as legal enactments (Dt. 24:1; Mk. 10:4), details of the journeys made by the Israelites (Nu. 33:2), and the words of the victory song (Dt. 31:19, 22). In these he was helped by officials (probably literate *šōṭᵉrîm*, Nu. 11:16, 'officers'; *cf.* Akkad. *šaṭāru*, 'to write') who, by reason of their ability to record decisions, were closely connected with the judiciary (Dt. 16:18; 1 Ch. 23:4; Jos. 8:33). During the Exodus wanderings priests also wrote down curses (Nu. 5:23) and names of objects (17:3). Joshua wrote a copy of the Ten Commandments (Jos. 8:32) and of the renewed covenant (24:26).

Samuel wrote down the charter of the newly created kingship of Saul (1 Sa. 10:25). David wrote letters to his commander Joab (2 Sa. 11:14) and details of the Temple administration, as did his son Solomon (2 Ch. 35:4), who corresponded with Hiram of Tyre in writing (2 Ch. 2:11). The king of Syria wrote a letter to the king of Israel about Naaman (2 Ki. 5:5). As in all periods, court *scribes were frequently employed to write lists of persons (1 Ch. 4:41; 24:6; see also Nu. 11:26; Is. 10:19; Je. 22:30; Ne. 12:22).

Isaiah the prophet wrote (2 Ch. 26:22; Is. 8:1) and dictated to a

WORTHLESS FELLOWS
See Raca, Part 3.

scribe (30:8). In his time Hezekiah both wrote letters (*'iggereṯ*) to Ephraim and Manasseh (2 Ch. 30:1; *cf.* Is. 38:9 entitled 'the writing [*mikṯāḇ*] of Hezekiah') and received them from the Assyr. king Sennacherib (Is. 37:14; 39:1; 2 Ch. 32:17). Jeremiah dictated to his amanuensis Baruch (Je. 30:2; 36:27; 45:1), as probably did Hosea (8:12) and Malachi (3:16), for the written word was an important part of prophecy (2 Ch. 21:12), its value being emphasized also by Job (19:23).

Daniel and the Babylonian savants could read, and therefore presumably could themselves write, Aramaic (Dn. 5:24f.). There was an active correspondence within the empire as in earlier periods (* RUNNERS, * ASSYRIA, * BABYLONIA). Nehemiah wrote down the covenant (Ne. 9:38), while his opponents in Samaria wrote to the Persian king (Ezr. 4:6–7), as did other district-governors (Ezr. 5:7; 6:2). Ezra himself was a scribe who wrote decrees or state documents in the local dialects (8:34), in the style of court officials, including Mordecai, on behalf of the king (Est. 9:28f.), who affixed his * seal (Dn. 6:25).

Jesus Christ and his apostles made constant reference to the written Scriptures (*e.g.* 'it is written'—*gegraptai*—occurs 106 times). Our Lord himself was literate (Jn. 7:14–15), reading (Lk. 4:16–19) and writing publicly on at least one occasion (Jn. 8:6). Zechariah the priest wrote on a wax-covered writing-board (Lk. 1:63), and the Roman governor Pilate had a trilingual inscription written to be placed on the cross (Jn. 19:19, 22).

John (21:24), Luke (1:3; Acts 1:1), and Paul himself (Gal. 6:11; Phm. 19; Rom. 15:15), though often using an amanuensis such as Tertius (Rom. 16:22), wrote the historical records and letters which have come down to us. Through to Rev. there is constant reference to writing in its use for letters, legal evidence and record (Rev. 1:11; 21:5). Since writing, by its nature, is a means of communication, declaration and testimony, it is used to illustrate the impression, written in (*engraphō*, 2 Cor. 3:2f.) or upon (*epigraphō*, Heb. 8:10; 10:16) the mind and heart (*cf.* Je. 31:33; Pr. 3:3) by the Holy Spirit.

II. Materials

Almost any smooth surface was used for writing.

a. Stone

Inscriptions were carved on stone or rock surfaces (Jb. 19:24), monumental texts being cut on a prepared stele, obelisk or cliff-face (*e.g.* Heb. tomb inscription, * SHEBNA, *IBA*, fig. 53, *cf.* 43, 48). The softer or more rugged surfaces could be covered with a plaster coating, before inscription, as in Egypt, and on the altar stones (Jos. 8:32; Dt. 27:2f.). Stone tablets were normally used for royal, commemorative or religious texts or public copies of legal edicts (* HAMMURAPI). Such rectangular stone tablets, apparently no larger than 45 × 30 cm, were used for the Ten Commandments (Ex. 32:16). These tablets (*lûḥōṯ*: AV, RSV 'tables') were 'written with the finger of God' or 'the writing of God' (*mikṯāḇ 'ᵉlōhîm*), usually taken to be a clear well-written script in contrast to the mere scratches of man. The word 'tablet' (*lûaḥ*) probably describes the (rectangular) form rather than the material, and there is no certainty that in the OT it denotes a clay tablet, though the use of these in Palestine in the 2nd millennium BC is known (see *c*, below).

b. Writing-boards

The tablets used by Isaiah (30:8) and Habakkuk (2:2) may have been writing-boards made of wood or ivory with a recess to hold a wax surface (Akkad. *lê'u*). Such writing-boards, usually hinged to form a diptych or polyptych, could be used for writing in any script. The individual leaf was called a 'door', a term also used for a column of writing (Je. 36:23, AV 'leaves'). The earliest yet found, at Nimrud, Assyria, is inscribed with a long composition of 6,000 lines dated *c.* 705 BC (*Iraq* 17, 1955, pp. 3–13) and is a type also shown on the sculptures in use by scribes for field notes (*IBA*, fig. 60). Similar writing-boards, the forerunner of the school slate, were frequently used in Gk. and Rom. times (Lk. 1:63; *pinakidion*, a small writing-tablet, AV 'table').

c. Clay tablets (see also **IV**. *a*).

The 'brick' (*lᵉḇēnâ*) used by Ezekiel (4:1) was probably of clay similar to the tablets used for plans and surveys in Babylonia, though the word could be used to describe any flat tile. The great 'tablet' on which Isaiah had to write with the 'pen of a man' (as opposed to that of a skilled scribe?) was a sheet or 'blank surface' of an unspecified material (Is. 8:1, *gillāyôn*).

d. Papyrus

Papyrus is not directly mentioned in the OT as a writing-material (Egyp. *ni*[*t*]*r*[*w*]; Akkad. *ni'aru*). It was, however, obtainable from Phoenicia, Lake Huleh and the Jordan (* PAPYRI) from the 11th century BC onwards, and its use is attested by the marks on the backs of seal impressions originally attached to this perishable substance (*e.g.* the reverse of the seal of * GEDALIAH). One example of ancient Heb. writing on papyrus was found in a cave near the Dead Sea (see Gibson, 1, pp. 31ff.). Papyrus (from which the Eng. word 'paper' is derived) was also known to the Assyrians and Babylonians in the 7th century (R. P. Dougherty, 'Writing on Parchment and Papyrus among the Babylonians and the Assyrians', *JAOS* 48, 1928, pp. 109–135). Used extensively in Egypt in all periods, papyri were found among the * Dead Sea Scrolls of the 2nd century BC–2nd century AD period. Isaiah's 'paper reed' (19:7 [AV], *'ārôṯ*), though possibly an indirect reference to papyri, is better interpreted as 'bare place'. The 'paper' used by John (2 Jn. 12) was probably papyrus (Gk. *chartēs*).

e. Leather and parchment

Leather was sometimes used in Egypt for working records because the ink could be washed off and the surface re-used (K. A. Kitchen, *TynB* 27, 1976, p. 141). During at least the Persian period skins were prepared for writing in Babylonia where papyrus did not grow. Skins of goats and sheep would have been available to the Israelites, and their use for copies of the biblical texts by the NT period (* DEAD SEA SCROLLS) may reflect earlier practice.

f. Ostraca

Potsherds or ostraca were another common writing material, since their low cost and availability made them especially useful for the writing of short memoranda with pen or brush and ink. Such potsherds have been recovered in considerable quantity from Palestine, being all but indestructible unless the ink was rubbed. About 240 have been found from the period of the Monarchy. See A. Lemaire, *Inscriptions Hebräiques*, 1, *Les Ostraca*, 1977

(*PAPYRI AND OSTRACA).

Pottery sometimes had characters inscribed on it before or after firing. They usually give the owner's name or the content or capacity of the vessel (*PEKAH; *SEAL, **I.** *f*).

III. Writing implements

1. Metal chisels and gravers were readily available for inscribing stone, metal, ivory or clay (*ARTS AND CRAFTS; *SEAL). The 'stylus' (*ḥereṭ*) or 'pen' (*'ēṭ*) used by Jeremiah (17:1) with its 'iron' point has been interpreted either as used for writing with a soft 'nib' or as a hard (emery?) point for use on iron, lead or other hard surface (Is. 8:1, Vulg. *stylus*; see also Jb. 19:24). None of the many pointed instruments so far excavated can be identified beyond question as used for writing a linear script. The 'pen of the scribes' (Je. 8:8) used for writing with ink on ostraca, papyrus or other smooth surfaces was a reed, split or cut to act as a brush. In ancient Egypt such pens were cut from rushes (*Juncus maritimus*) 15–40 cm long, the end being cut to a flat chisel shape so that the thick or thin strokes might be made with the broad or narrow edges. In Graeco-Roman times reeds (*Phragmites communis*) were cut to a point and split like a quill-pen (A. Lucas, *Ancient Egyptian Materials and Industries*, 1948, p. 417). This type of pen was the *kalamos* used in NT times (3 Jn. 13). The stylus used for writing the cuneiform script was a square-ended reed. For a discussion of the shape, method of use and illustrations of scribes with pens, chisels and styli, see G. R. Driver, *Semitic Writing*[3], 1976, pp. 17ff.

2. Ink was usually a black carbon (charcoal) mixed with gum or oil for use on parchment or with a metallic substance for papyrus. It was kept as a dried cake on which the scribe would dip his moistened pen. The ink of the Lachish ostraca was a mixture of carbon and iron (as oak-galls or copperas). The Romans also used the juice of cuttle-fish (Persius, *Satires* 3. 13), which, like most inks, could easily be erased by washing (Nu. 5:23) or by scratching with the 'penknife' (Je. 36:23, Heb. *ta'ar sōp̄ēr*, 'scribe's knife') normally used for trimming or cutting pens or scrolls. It has been suggested that Heb. d^e*yô*, 'ink' (Je. 36:18), should be emended to r^e*yô* (= Egyp. *ryt*, 'ink'; T. Lambdin, *JAOS* 73, 1953, p. 154), but this is not certain. The ink used by Paul (2 Cor. 3:3) and John (2 Jn. 12) is simply designated 'black' (*melan*).

The 'inkhorn' (Ezk. 9:2–3, 11; Heb. *qeseṯ*) may be the palette (Egyp. *gsti*), the narrow rectangular wooden board with a long groove to hold the rush pens and circular hollows for the cakes of black and red ink. For illustrations of these palettes, *etc.*, see W. C. Hayes, *The Sceptre of Egypt*, 1, 1953, pp. 292–296; J. B. Pritchard, *The Ancient Near East*, 1958, figs. 52, 55; *IBA*, p. 32, fig. 27. Similar palettes were in use in Syria, being carried by the scribe 'by his side' (Ezk. 9:2–3, 11), as shown on the Aram. stele of Bar-Rekub (*ANEP*, p. 460).

IV. Forms of documents

a. Tablets

The clay documents on which cuneiform script was inscribed vary in size (about 6 mm square to 45 × 30 cm) according to the amount of space required for the text. The inscription from left to right ran in lines (sometimes ruled) down the obverse (flat) side along the lower edge, then on down the reverse (convex) side, the upper and left edges. Where more than one tablet was needed to complete a work each text in the series was linked by a catchline and colophon (see **VI**, below) to indicate its correct place.

Contracts were often enclosed in a clay envelope on which the text was repeated and the *seals of the witnesses impressed. Larger historical or commemorative inscriptions were written on clay prisms or barrel-shaped cylinders which were often placed as foundation deposits. Wooden tablets or writing-boards varied both in size and in the number of leaves as required.

b. The roll

The usual form of the 'book' in Bible times was a roll or scroll (m^e*ḡillâ*) of papyrus, leather or parchment in which the text was written 'within' (recto) and, when necessary, continued 'without' on the back (verso) as described by Ezekiel (2:10). This was sometimes called the 'roll of a book' (m^e*ḡillaṯ sēp̄er*; Ps. 40:8; Ezk. 2:9); the LXX (B) of Je. 36:2, 4 (*chartion biblion*) implies the use of papyrus. The term for scroll (*cf.* Bab. *magallatu*) is not necessarily a late one in Heb. (*BDB*) and it is likely that the Jewish tradition requiring copies of the law to be made on a leather roll (*Soferim* 1. 1–3) reflects earlier practice.

The Heb. *sēp̄er*, usually translated 'book' in AV, could refer to a roll or scroll (so AV Is. 34:4, correctly). It denotes any parchment or papyrus document (R. P. Dougherty, *op. cit.*, p. 114) and means a 'writing, document, missive, or book' (*cf.* Akkad. *šipru*). It is synonymous with the term for 'letter' (*'iggereṯ*, Est. 9:25), being also used for a letter or order from the king (2 Sa. 11:14; 2 Ki. 5:10; 10:1; Is. 37:14) or published decree (Est. 1:22).

These cuneiform tablets lie fallen from shelves in the 'archive room' at Ebla (Tell Mardikh), Syria. c. 2400–2252 BC. (PM)

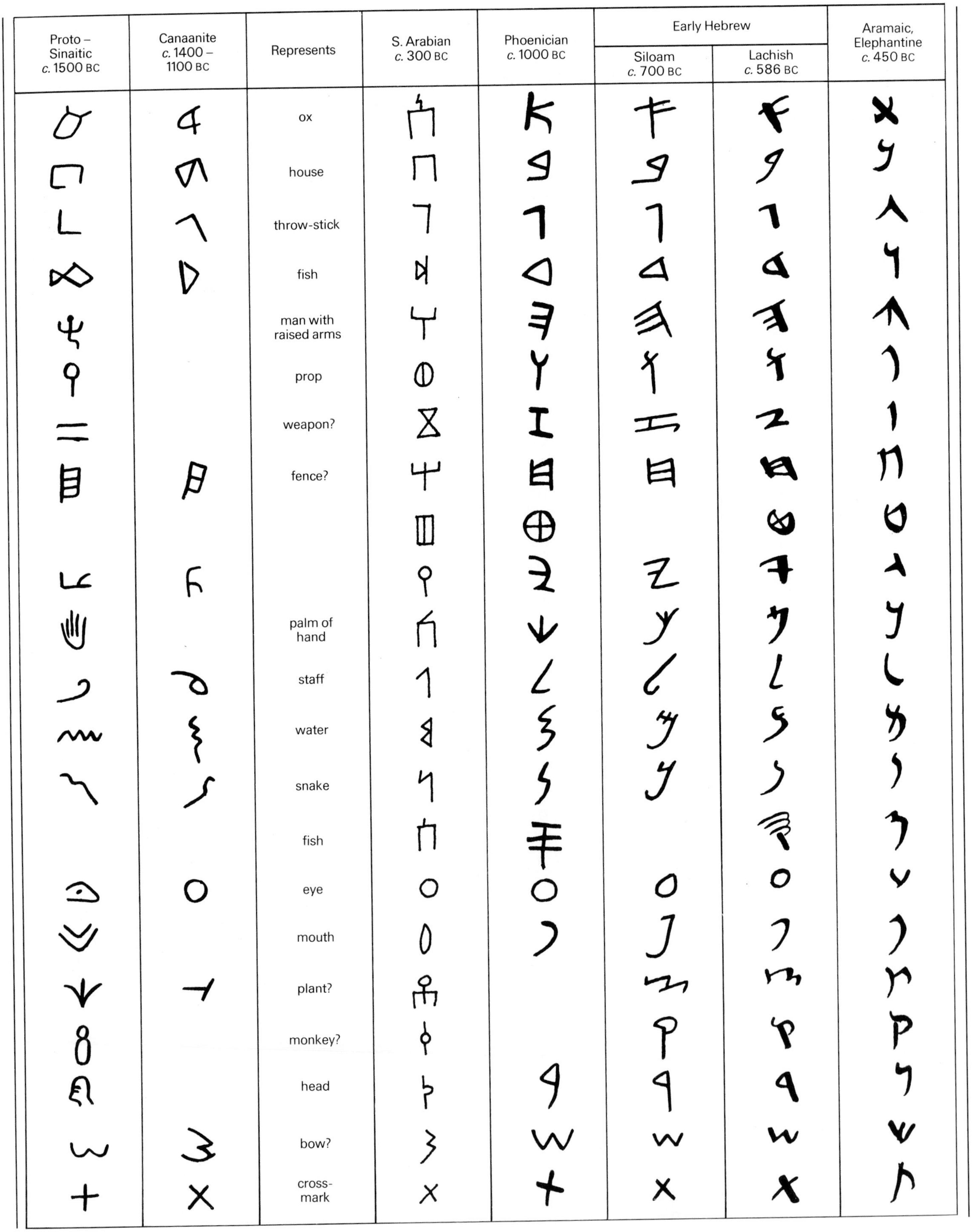
Proto – Sinaitic c. 1500 BC
Canaanite c. 1400 – 1100 BC
Represents
S. Arabian c. 300 BC
Phoenician c. 1000 BC
Early Hebrew
Siloam c. 700 BC
Lachish c. 586 BC
Aramaic, Elephantine c. 450 BC
ox
house
throw-stick
fish
man with raised arms
prop
weapon?
fence?
palm of hand
staff
water
snake
fish
eye
mouth
plant?
monkey?
head
bow?
cross-mark

Hebrew 1st cent. AD	Hebrew name	Phonetic value	Early Greek 8th cent. BC	Classical Greek: Athens 5th cent. BC	Greek name	Roman
א	'alep̄	ʾ	A	A	alpha	A
ב	bêṯ	b	B	B	bēta	B
ג	gîmel	g	Γ, (	Γ	gamma	G
ד	dāleṯ	d	Δ	Δ	delta	D
ה	hē	h	E	E	epsilon	E
ו	waw	w	F	Y	(digamma) upsilon	F Y
ז	zayin	z	I	Z	zēta	Z
ח	ḥêṯ	ḥ	B	H	ēta	H
ט	ṭêṯ	ṭ	⊕	⊙	thēta	
י	yôḏ	y	≀, I	I	iota	I
כ	kap̄	k	K	K	kappa	K
ל	lāmeḏ	l	L, Γ	L	lambda	L
מ	mēm	m	M	M	mu	M
נ	nûn	n	N	N	nu	N
ס	sāmeḵ	s	Ξ	Ξ	xi	
ע	'ayin	ʿ	O	O	omicron	O
פ	pê'	p	Γ	Γ	pi	P
צ	ṣaḏê	ṣ	M		(san)	
ק	qôp̄	q	Ϙ		(koppa)	Q
ר	rêš	r	P, R	P	rhō	R
ש	šîn	š	Σ, Σ	Σ	sigma	S
ת	taw	t	T	T	tau	T

Chart showing the development of the alphabet in various scripts in use in ancient Palestine.

sēp̄er, as a general term for writing, is used of the communication from a prophet (Je. 25:13; 29:1; Dn. 12:4); a legal certificate of divorce (Dt. 24:1; Je. 3:8; Is. 50:1); a contract for the purchase of real estate (Je. 32:11); or an indictment (Jb. 31:35). It also denotes a general register (Ne. 7:5; Gn. 5:1), a covenant (Ex. 24:7) or law book (Dt. 28:61; Jos. 8:31), a book of poems (Nu. 21:14; Jos. 10:13) as well as collections of historical data (1 Ki. 11:41; 14:19; 1 Ch. 27:24; 2 Ch. 16:11; 25:26). Once 'the books' (plural *s^e^p̄ārîm*) refers to the canonical scriptures of the time (Dn. 9:2). It refers to the divine records (Pss. 69:28; 139:16; Mal. 3:16; Ex. 32:32; Dn. 12:1) and once to book-learning in general (Is. 29:11; *cf.* Dn. 1:4). The word and its cognates were current with similar meanings in the texts of * Ugarit, and *sēp̄er*, 'scribe', appears as a loan word in Egypt during the 13th century BC.

The scroll, as the writing-boards and clay tablets, was inscribed in as many columns (*d^e^lāṯôṯ*), and therefore of any length, as required (Je. 36:23).

In NT times the 'book' (*biblion*) was a roll as used for the law (Mk. 12:26; Lk. 4:17–20). It formed a scroll (Rev. 6:14) made up of sections of * papyrus, the inner bark of which (*byblos*) was used. Like the Heb. *sēp̄er*, the Gk. *biblion* could be used of any (or unspecified) form of written document, including registration lists (Phil. 4:3; Rev. 13:8). 'The books' (plural *ta biblia*; Jn. 21:25; 2 Tim. 4:13, hence our 'Bible') came to be a term for the collected Scriptures. Where a small scroll was in mind *biblaridion* was used (Rev. 10:2, 8–10).

Scribes record booty taken by Tiglath-pileser III. They write with a stylus on a clay tablet in the cuneiform script, and with a brush-pen on a papyrus or leather scroll in Aramaic. Nimrud. Height c. 40 cm. c. 740 BC. (BM)

Hittite hieroglyph inscription naming the Great King Tudhaliyas IV, son of Hattusilis III (c. 1250–1220 BC*). From the Karakuyu dam, c. 125 km NE of Kayseri.* (JDH)

Part of a series of Assyrian ivory writing-boards originally linked with gold hinges and bearing traces of the wax overlay, inscribed with a series of astrological omens. Nimrud. Height 38 cm. 715 BC. (BM)

Two Egyptian wooden writing-palettes. A *has 14 depressions for colours, and mentions the royal steward Meryre and his scribe Tenen. Length c. 35·5 cm. 1570–1546 BC.* B *has depressions containing red and black ink, a stick for mixing them, and a number of rush brushes. It is inscribed with the names of Ahmose I (18th Dynasty). Length 28·5 cm. c. 1420 BC.* (BM)

Top right:
An early form of cuneiform writing still resembling pictograph can be seen on this account of fields, crops and commodities. Jemdet Nasr (near Kish). c. 7·8 cm × 7·3 cm. Pre-dynastic, c. 3100 BC. (BM)

Bottom right:
The earliest Sumerian writing employed pictographs. The order of reading these signs is still disputed. From Kish (near Babylon). Limestone. c. 6·5 cm × 7 cm. c. 3300 BC. (SAOB)

c. The codex

About the 2nd century AD the roll began to be replaced by the codex, a collection of sheets of writing-material folded and fastened together at one edge and often protected by covers. This was an important step in the development of the modern 'book', and was based on the physical form of the writing-tablet.

At first these papyrus or parchment notebooks were little used for pagan literature, but were used in Palestine (Mishnah, *Kelim* 24. 7), and especially in Egypt, for biblical writings where the adaptation of 'the codex form to receive all texts both OT and NT used in Christian communities . . . was complete, as far as our present evidence goes, before the end of the 2nd century, if not earlier'. Outside Christian circles the codex form was generally accepted by the 4th century AD. It has even been suggested, but not proved, that this form was developed by the early Christian church because of the ease of transport and reference. Certainly the *membranai* requested by Paul (2 Tim. 4:13) could have been a papyrus notebook of his own addresses or other writings or, more likely, an early Christian writing, perhaps the second Gospel or the Book of Testimonies, an anthology of OT passages used to support the Christian claim. These writings were a contrast to 'books' (*ta biblia*), in general probably rolls (of the LXX?). For the significance of the early codices in the history of the *Canon of Scripture, see C. H. Roberts in P. R. Ackroyd (ed.), *Cambridge History of the Bible*, 1, 1970, p. 57.

V. Scripts

a. Hieroglyphs

(i) *Egyptian.* The native script of pharaonic Egypt appears in three forms: hieroglyphic (Gk. *hieros*, 'sacred', and *glyphē*, 'carving'), hieratic (Gk. *hieratikos*, 'priestly'), and demotic (Gk. *demotikos*, 'popular').

1. The *hieroglyphic* system. The Egyp. hieroglyphs are pictorial signs, originally pictures to express the things they represent; many of them were soon used to express

sounds—specifically the consonants of the Egyp. word for the thing represented by the picture-hieroglyph. Such a sign could then be used to stand for the same consonants in spelling out other words. Some of these phonetic signs came to stand for just one such consonant, becoming thus the world's first alphabetic signs. However, the Egyptians never isolated these as a separate alphabet as did their W Semitic neighbours. After most Egyp. words as spelt out by phonetic or sound signs, there comes a picture-sign or 'determinative' which signifies the general class into which the word falls. However, in very many cases it would be more accurate to say that the phonetic signs were actually added in front of the picture-sign (so-called 'determinative') as complements to determine the precise reading or sound of the latter, and thus its correct meaning, rather than that the picture-sign acted as classifier to the phonetically written word (*cf.* H. W. Fairman, *Annales du Service des Antiquités de l'Égypte* 43, 1943, pp. 297–298; *cf.* P. Lacau, *Sur le Système hiéroglyphique*, 1954, p. 108). Where a phonetic sign could have more than one sound-value, supplementary alphabetic signs could be added to show which reading was intended, though these were sometimes added even where no ambiguity existed.

2. *Hieratic and demotic.* The other two Egyp. scripts, hieratic and demotic, are adaptations of the hieroglyphic script which retained its splendid pictorial shapes throughout Egyp. history. The hieratic script is a cursive form of hieroglyphic script, written with pen and ink on papyrus, reduced to formal symbols no longer pictorial, for ease of rapid writing. Hieratic is to hieroglyphs what our long-hand script is to printed characters. The hieroglyphs first appear in Egypt just before the foundation of the pharaonic monarchy (1st Dynasty) *c.* 3000 BC, and hieratic came into use soon after. The third form of Egyp. script, demotic, is simply an even more rapid and abbreviated form of hieratic handwriting that first appears about the 7th century BC, and like the other two scripts lasted until the 5th century AD.

3. *Decipherment.* The ancient scripts of Egypt finally passed out of use in the 4th (hieroglyphic) and the 5th (demotic) centuries AD, and remained a closed book for 13 centuries until the discovery of the Rosetta Stone in 1799 during Napoleon's Egyptian expedition made possible the decipherment of Egypt's ancient scripts and language. The Rosetta Stone is a bilingual decree of Ptolemy V, 196 BC, in Gk. and Egyp., the latter in both hieroglyphic and demotic scripts. This and the Bankes obelisk eventually enabled the Frenchman, J. F. Champollion, to achieve the basic decipherment of the Egyp. hieroglyphs in 1822, showing that they were largely phonetic in use and that the Egyp. language was in fact simply the parent of Coptic, the language of the native Egyp. church.

4. *Scope.* From the very beginning, the Egyp. hieroglyphs were used for all purposes: historical records, religious texts and the mundane purposes of administration. They were accordingly drawn on papyrus or ostraca, carved on stone monuments, and engraved in wood or metal wherever inscriptions were required. However, from early in the 3rd millennium, the more rapid cursive script—hieratic—became customary for writing on papyrus, and so for all the records of daily life and administration, while hieroglyphs continued in use for all formal texts, stone inscriptions and monumental purposes. Eventually, from the 7th century BC, demotic largely replaced hieratic as the script of business and administration, and hieratic from the 10th century BC onwards became largely the script of religious papyri.

BIBLIOGRAPHY. On the Egyp. scripts, see A. H. Gardiner, *Egyptian Grammar*, 1957, pp. 5–8. On the hieroglyphs themselves as pictures, see N. M. Davies, *Picture Writing in Ancient Egypt*, 1958, illustrated in colour. On the origin and early development of the hieroglyphic system, see S. Schott, *Hieroglyphen: Untersuchungen zum Ursprung der Schrift*, 1950, and P. Lacau, *op. cit.* For the Rosetta Stone, see BM brochure *The Rosetta Stone*, and, for its discoverer, W. R. Dawson, *JEA* 43, 1957, p. 117, with *ibid.*, 44, 1958, p. 123. On the decipherment of the hieroglyphs, see F. Ll. Griffith, *JEA* 37, 1951, pp. 38–46, or A. H. Gardiner, *op. cit.*, pp. 9–11; *Egypt of the Pharaohs*, 1961, pp. 11–14, 19–26.

(ii) *Hittite.* The system of hieroglyphs used by the Hittites in Anatolia and Syria, mainly in the latter half of the 2nd millennium BC, was deciphered in 1946 (see *AS*

Sarcophagus of Eshmunazer, king of Sidon, with a Phoenician inscription. Length 2·51 m. 5th cent. BC. (MC)

Opposite page: Top left: Inscription, written in the old Aramaic script, on a funerary stele of Sin-zēr-ibni. Found at Nerab, Syria. Height 93 cm. 6th cent. BC. (MC)

3, 1953, pp. 53–95) and this script is now being studied in detail and used for comparison with the Hittite dialects written in the cuneiform script. It is a series of simple syllables (*ba*, *da*, *etc.*) with word-signs for common nouns (earth, king); see E. Laroche, *Les Hiéroglyphes Hittites*, 1, 1960.

b. Cuneiform scripts

(i) *Akkadian.* In Babylonia pictographs were used for writing on clay and stone from *c.* 3100 BC onwards. It was, however, soon found difficult to draw curved lines on clay, and the pictograph was gradually replaced by its representation made by a series of wedge-shaped incisions. A further change for convenience from writing down columns from right to left resulted in the classical script being written horizontally in columns, the lines running from left to right. In a major development, word-signs (ideograms) were used to represent words with the same sounds but differing meanings (*e.g.* meat, meet) or syllables in other words (*e.g.* meat, metre). Certain signs were also used as determinatives placed before or after words of a distinct class (*e.g.* deities, personal and place-names, animals, wooden objects, *etc.*). By 2800 BC the cuneiform script had fully developed, though the forms of signs were modified at different periods (for a table illustrating this development see *IBA*, fig. 22).

From the 3rd millennium BC, the cuneiform, using at least 500 different signs, was widely in use outside Mesopotamia (where it was employed for the Sumerian, Bab. and Assyr. languages). It was adapted for writing other languages, notably W Semitic dialects, Hurrian, the various Hittite tongues. During the 15th–13th centuries BC in Palestine the chief cities used it for diplomacy and administration. Cuneiform tablets have been found at *Taanach (12), Shechem (2), Aphek (3), Tell el-Hesi, Gezer, Hazor, Jericho. The discovery of a copy of part of the Epic of Gilgamesh at Megiddo in 1955 (*'Atiqot* 2, 1959, pp. 121–128) shows that at this period the few scribes trained in this script had readily available the major Bab. literary texts and reference works.

(ii) *Ugaritic.* At Ras Shamra scribes employed cuneiform Akkadian for international correspondence and some economic texts in the 15th–13th centuries BC. Parallel with this, however, a unique system of writing was developed. It combined the simplicity of the existing Canaanite (Phoenician) alphabet with the Mesopotamian system of writing with a stylus on clay, thus transcribing the consonantal alphabet by means of cuneiform writing. Since it was employed for both Semitic and non-Semitic (Hurrian) languages, 29 signs were developed (by the addition of a few wedges in a simple pattern bearing little or no relation to Akkadian) to represent the consonant and three *'ālep̄* signs with variant vowels ('a 'i 'u). A number of scribal practice tablets give the order of the alphabet which prefigured the Hebrew order (C. Virolleaud, *Palais royal d'Ugarit*, 2, 1957).

This script was used for both religious, literary (mythological) and administrative texts and for a few letters. Although easier to learn than Akkadian, there is as yet little evidence of it being widely used; but a few examples of a variant form have been found as far afield as Beth-Shemesh, Tabor and Taanach in Palestine, and places in S Syria. The invention appears to have come too late to oust the already established and simplified Phoenician linear script. For a general survey, see C. H. Gordon, *Ugaritic Textbook*, 1967.

(iii) *Old Persian.* By the late 7th century BC the Aramaic alphabetic script had largely displaced the cuneiform script, except in a few traditional centres and types of temple documents for which, as at Babylon until AD 75, the Bab. cuneiform script continued to be used.

Under the Achaemenid Persians a special system, derived from the cuneiform of Babylonia, was employed alongside the Aramaic script for their Indo-Iranian (Aryan) language. This simplified cuneiform is mainly known from historical texts of the reigns of Darius I and Xerxes. An inscription of the former written on a rock at Behistun in Old Persian, Bab. and Elamite provided the key to the decipherment of the cuneiform scripts, the Old Persian version being deciphered soon after Rawlinson's copy of 1845 had been published. This cuneiform script comprises 3 vowel signs, 33 consonantal signs with inherent vowel plus 8 ideograms and 2 word dividers. A variant form of cuneiform script was used for the Elamite (SW Persia) language in its earliest forms, and later for more than 2,000 economic texts from Persepolis *c.* 492–460 BC (G. G. Cameron, *Persepolis Treasury Tablets*, 1948; R. T. Hallock, *Persepolis Fortification Tablets*, 1969).

c. Linear scripts

(i) Wide use of Egyp. hieroglyphs and Bab. cuneiform in Syro-Palestine from the 3rd millennium BC on (*e.g.* *EBLA) stimulated the production of simpler writing systems for local languages. At Byblos (*GEBAL) a system of about 100 syllabic signs flourished during the 2nd millennium BC, but they are as yet not fully understood. At the same time Linear A and Linear B scripts arose in Crete with a related

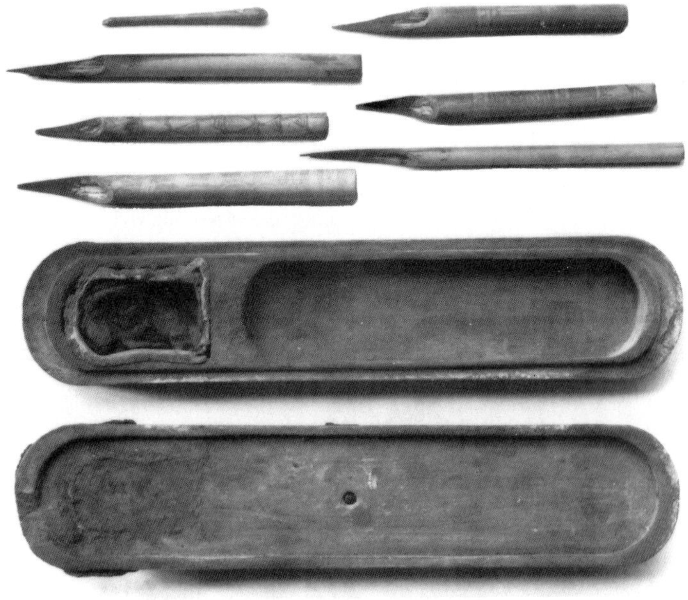

Writing with reed pens was common in the Roman period. These examples, which have been cut to the required shape, are stained with black ink which was found in the well of the wooden pen-case, here shown with lid. From Egypt. Length c. 23 cm. After 30 BC. (BM)

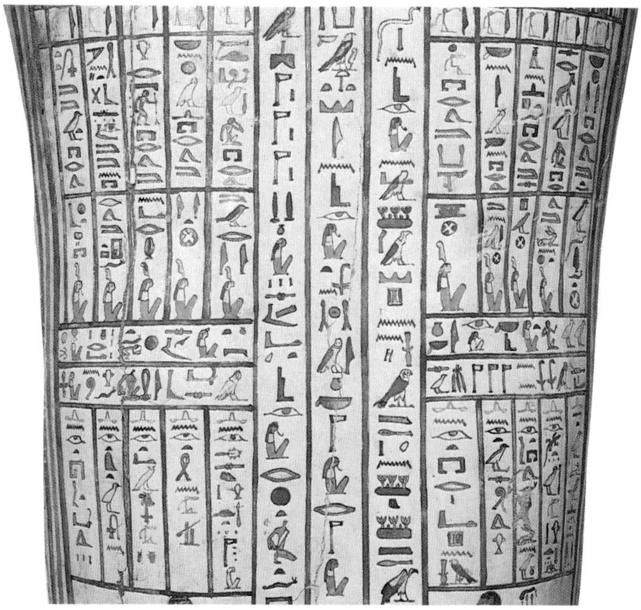

script in Cyprus of which examples have been found at Ugarit (Cypro-Minoan). Isolated discoveries attest the existence of other scripts at this period, notably three clay tablets from Tell Deir 'Alla in the Jordan valley, and a stele from Balu'ah in Moab.

(ii) *Alphabetic*. Early in the 2nd millennium BC, it would seem that a scribe living in Syro-Palestine, perhaps at Byblos, realized that his language could be represented by many fewer signs than any of the current more cumbrous syllabaries employed; each consonant could be shown by one symbol. The symbols adapted were pictures on the Egyp. model. The hieroglyphic script included pictures which stood for the initial sounds of their names only, *e.g. r'* 'mouth' for *r*. The value of the alphabetic principle lay in reducing the number of symbols until

Formal Egyptian writing in hieroglyphs, painted on this wooden coffin of Pa-sen-hor, son of Shakshak and Amenhotep. Third Intermediate Period: 22nd–23rd (Libyan) Dynasties (8th cent. BC). (BM)

Bronze plaque inscribed with raised Himyaritic characters. Dedicated by Yusup and family to the god Ilmaqah for hearing their prayers. From S. Arabia. Height 25 cm. c. 1st cent. AD. (BM)

The demotic script, an abbreviated and modified form of Egyptian hieratic. One of the three sections of text written on the Rosetta Stone. Rashid, Egypt. Length 1·14 m. 195 BC. (BM)

Top right: Writing in cuneiform (Assyrian script) on clay with a square-ended wooden stylus (modern reconstruction). (DJW)

Cuneiform writing of the Old Babylonian period. Purchase of an office, dated 39th year of Rim-Sin. From Larsa? c. 1711 BC. (DJW)

there was only one for each consonantal sound in the language. Vowels were not separately represented until the Greeks took over the alphabet. It is probable that the symbols were treated initially as consonants plus appropriate vowel (*e.g. ba, du, gi*). With this outstanding invention mankind gained a simple means of recording which eventually broke the monopoly of the *scribes and placed literacy within the reach of everyone (see **VI**, below).

Examples of this ancestor of all alphabets have been found in Palestine and can be dated shortly before 1500 BC. These exhibit a few signs only, probably personal names, scratched on pottery and metal. The full range of signs—about thirty—appears in the only early group of texts written in a form of this alphabet recovered so far, the 'Proto-Sinaitic' inscriptions. These are short prayers and dedications scratched on the surfaces by Canaanites employed in the Egyp. turquoise mines at Serbit el-Khadim in SW Sinai during the 16th century BC. During the next 500 years the signs were simplified, losing their pictorial form. Examples from sites in Canaan show widespread use and growing standardization (*e.g.* potsherds from Lachish, Hazor, arrowheads from near Bethlehem and the Lebanon; see A. R. Millard, *Kadmos* 15, 1976, pp. 130–144).

The order of the letters is attested by the cuneiform alphabet of Ugarit (13th century BC), an early imitator, by an ostracon from 'Izbet Ṣarṭah, near Aphek (*c.* 1100 BC; M. Kochari, *Tel Aviv* 4, 1977, pp. 1–13). Heb. acrostics also display it (Na. 1:2–14; Pss. 9, 10, 25, 34, 37, 111, 112, 119, 145; La. 1–4; Pr. 31:10–31; Ecclus. 5:13, 29). The Greeks borrowed the letters in the same order. The reason for the arrangement is uncertain. Mnemonic needs and similarities in names or the nature of sounds expressed have been suggested (Driver, *op. cit.*, pp. 180–185, 271–273).

(iii) *Phoenician–early Hebrew.* In the main from 1000 BC onwards we can trace the history of the letters clearly, although there are few specimens written between 1000 and 800 BC. The direction of the writing was standardized, from right to left, as in Egypt. Most

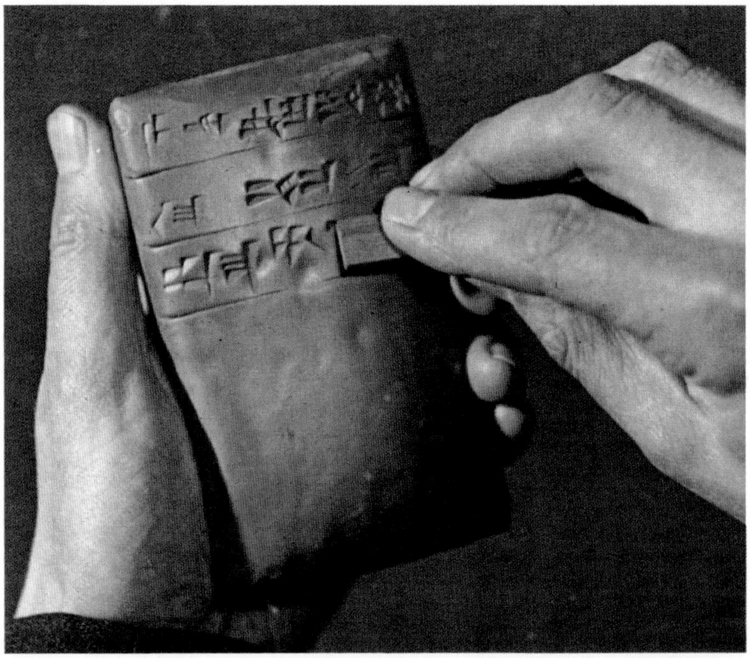

Page from a Greek codex (Acts 17:9–17) written in 'Rustic capitals'. 3rd cent. AD. (CBL)

documents were made of papyrus and so have perished in the damp soil. Those that survive, on stone, pottery and metal, prove the ready acceptance of the script for all purposes. It was evidently well established before the end of the 2nd millennium BC, a ready tool for the Israelites to employ in recording and teaching the laws of God and the history of his works on their behalf (see A. R. Millard, *EQ* 50, 1978, pp. 67 ff.).

1. The major *monumental* inscriptions for the study of Heb. epigraphy are: (*a*) The agricultural calendar from * Gezer, variously attributed to an archaic or unskilled hand and dated to the 10th century BC (*DOTT*, pp. 201–203). (*b*) The stele of Mesha', king of Moab (* MOABITE STONE). This 34-line inscription is important historically and as an example of the development of the monumental Heb. script in use in a remote place *c.* 850 BC. The well-cut letters already show a tendency to become cursive. This is further seen in (*c*) the * Siloam Inscription (*IBA*, fig. 56), dating from the reign of Hezekiah, *c.* 710 BC, and (*d*) the Tomb inscription of the Royal Steward from Siloam of about the same date (* SHEBNA; *IBA*, fig. 53). For the lapidary form of the script, see * seals. By this time Phoenician and Aram. letters had taken their own distinctive forms.

2. The *cursive* hand which the OT writers would have originally employed is seen in the inscribed arrow-heads and other smaller writings of *c.* 1000 BC. The earliest body of texts is 75 ostraca from Samaria, some assigned to the reign of Jeroboam II (*c.* 760 BC; Y. Yadin, *Studies in the Bible*, 1960, pp. 9–17; *DOTT*, pp. 204–208). These show a clear, flowing script written by scribes long practised in the art. The unvocalized words are divided by small dots. A few scattered sherds from Jerusalem, Beth-shemesh, Tell el-Hesi, Megiddo and Ezion-geber show that the script is close to that on the Siloam tunnel inscription and changed only a little in outward form by the time of the * Lachish letters dated to *c.* 590–587 BC, and most of the ostraca from * Arad at the end of Judah's history, which show a more advanced stage of the current hand (*DOTT*, pp. 212–215; *ANET*, pp. 568–569; A. Lemaire, *op. cit.*).

(iv) *Aramaic.* Aramaeans adopted the Canaanite alphabet as they settled in Syria and gradually gave it distinctive features. The earliest texts (*c.* 850–800 BC) are the partly illegible Melqart Stele of Bar-hadad (* BEN-HADAD; *DOTT*, pp. 239–241, but note the second line cannot be read 'son of Tab-rimmon'), and two pieces of ivory bearing the name of * Hazael. Soon after 800 BC Zakkur, king of * Hamath, erected a stele with 46 lines of inscription, and about 750 BC a treaty between the unknown Bar-ga'ayah and Mati'-el of * Arpad was recorded on three stelae. An increasingly cursive style is attested by the Bar-rakkab Stele (*ANEP*, p. 460). As Aramaic spread, the alphabet quickly took root in Assyria and Babylonia, to the disadvantage of the cuneiform script. Papyrus documents have perished, but a list of names on a sherd from Nimrud (* CALAH) in Assyria of the early 7th century BC (J. B. Segal, *Iraq* 19, 1957, pp. 139–145), notes scratched on clay tablets, and a long letter written on a potsherd and sent from Erech to Ashur about 650 BC, show its use. Papyrus documents found in Egypt show the script developing from *c.* 600 BC (letter from Philistia to Egypt) until the end of the Persian period, notably in the 5th-century documents from Elephantine (*DOTT*, pp. 256–269) and other places (G. R. Driver, *Aramaic Documents of the Fifth Century BC*, 1954).

(v) *Early Jewish scripts.* The discoveries of MSS from the Wadi

Opposite page: Bottom right: The 30 characters of the Ugaritic alphabet inscribed in order on a clay tablet, possibly a school exercise. Ras Shamra. 14th cent. BC. (DM)

An example of Assyrian cuneiform writing on stone (gypsum). Part of the historical annals of Ashurnasirpal II. Nimrud. c. 865 BC. (DJW)

Fragment of an inscription of Xerxes I, king of Persia (485–465 BC) in Old Persian cuneiform naming the god Ahuramazda. Persepolis XPb. Height 35·5 cm, width c. 84 cm. (BM)

Qumran (*DEAD SEA SCROLLS), Judaean caves (especially the dated texts from Murabba'at) and inscribed ossuaries from the Jerusalem area have produced a wealth of material for the study of the formal and cursive Palaeo-Hebrew and early Jewish scripts from the 3rd century BC to the 2nd century AD. The fall of the Persian empire and the displacement of the common Aramaic of the imperial court led to many local variations.

1. The Archaic or proto-Jewish script of Judah, *c.* 250–150 BC, as reflected in the Qumran MSS, shows a formal hand derived from the Persian Aramaic which, by the late 3rd century, is a cross between the formal and cursive scripts and close to the common Aramaic scripts of Palmyra and Nabataea which also emerged at this time. While these national scripts cannot yet be more precisely dated, formal, semi-formal and true cursive hands can sometimes be distinguished. This script is also to be seen on coins of the period.

2. The Hasmonean period (*c.* 150–30 BC) saw the development of the formal, squarer and more angular hand seen in its first stages in the Nash Papyrus, now dated *c.* 150 BC.

3. The Herodian period (30 BC–AD 70) was a time of swift development, and texts can thus be closely dated.

4. The post-Herodian period (after AD 70) is now well known from dated commercial and legal documents. The cursive script is not a literary but highly involved hand. The development of all these Jewish hands is illustrated and discussed in detail by F. M. Cross (*The Bible and the Ancient Near East*, ed. G. E. Wright, 1961, pp. 133–202). Study of early Heb. writing, the scribes' habits and letter forms, is of especial value in considering how errors may, or may not, have crept into the OT text.

(vi) *Greek*. The Gk. alphabet was by tradition attributed to a Phoenician trader Cadmus (Herodotus, *Hist*. 5. 58–59) and, by comparison between the early Gk. alphabets at Athens, Crete, Thera, Corinth and Naxos and dated Phoenician texts (see above), this view is justified. It would seem probable from the form of the letters that the Greeks had by the middle of the 9th century BC adapted the script to the needs of their Indo-European language. They used the Phoenician symbols for sounds which they did not possess (ʼ h ḥ ʻ u̯ [w] y), for the vowel sounds they required (a e ē o y i respectively), and thus created the first true alphabet in which consonants and vowels were represented by distinct signs.

The abundance of monumental and manuscript evidence makes the study of Gk. epigraphy and palaeography an important and exact science for the background of the biblical Gk. texts. From W Greece the alphabet reached the Etruscans, and thus through the Roman script entered Europe.

(vii) *Other scripts*. As well as the development of the Phoenician script for use in the Gk., and thence Roman and subsequently European scripts, the early Canaanite script was developed for writing S Semitic dialects. Examples have been found in S Palestine and S Babylonia from *c.* 600 BC, and from S Arabian sites from slightly later.

VI. Literacy and literary methods

Evidence for the degree of literacy, which varied according to time and place, is small. Gideon was able to lay hands on a young man of Succoth in Jordan who wrote down a list of the city elders (Jdg. 8:14; Heb., RSV, AVmg., RVmg. 'write', AV, RV, unjustifiably 'describe'). Such ability among the young to write (Is. 10:19) was enhanced by the advent of the alphabet and by the establishment of *schools for scribes attached to temples and shrines. Every Israelite householder had to write the words of the Law (Dt. 6:9; 11:20). Writing, though not so well attested in the West as in Babylonia, was certainly widespread in Syria and Palestine by the 2nd millennium, when at least five scripts were in use, *viz*. Egyp. hieroglyphs, Byblian syllabary, Canaanite alphabet, Akkad. cuneiform and the Ugaritic alphabetic cuneiform (see above).

Writing was generally undertaken by trained *scribes. who could be drawn from any class of the population (*contra* E. Nielsen, *Oral Tradition*, 1954, pp. 25, 28), though most higher officials in administration were literate. The mass of cuneiform tablets, ostraca and papyri so far found shows the prominent place of the written word throughout the ancient Near East. A percentage is difficult to estimate owing to the incompleteness of the records, but the six scribes to a population of about 2,000 at Alalaḫ in Syria in *c.* 1800–1500 BC is probably indicative of the literacy in important towns (D. J. Wiseman, *The Alalakh Tablets*, p. 13). Recent studies show that scribes may have learnt their Akkadian at main 'university' centres such as Aleppo in Syria or Babylon itself.

Documents were stored in baskets, boxes or jars (Je. 32:14) and laid up in the local temple (1 Sa. 10:25; Ex. 16:34; *cf.* 2 Ki. 22:8) or special archive stores (Ezr. 6:1). Specific reference books were held by scribes (as, *e.g.*, at Nippur, *c.* 1950 BC). Tiglath-pileser I (*c.* 1100 BC) at Assur and Ashurbanipal (*c.* 650 BC) at Nineveh collected copies of texts or had them written for their libraries. When copying texts a scribe would often quote the source, giving the condition of the document from which he copied, and stating whether the text had been checked with the original document, or only copied down from oral tradition, which was considered a less reliable method (J. Læssøe, 'Literacy and Oral Tradition in Ancient Mesopotamia', *Studia Orientalia Ioanni Pedersen*, 1953, pp. 205–218). Oral tradition was conceived as existing alongside the written word but not taking the place of primary authority. The colophon (both Akkadian and Egyp.) would also give the title or catchline which designated the work; but authorship was often, though not invariably, anonymous. It is likely that the Heb. writers used similar methods.

BIBLIOGRAPHY. See references given in text above; also, for a full description, G. R. Driver, *Semitic Writing*³, 1976; I. J. Gelb, *A Study of Writing*², 1963; D. Diringer, *The Alphabet*, 1948; J. Černý, *Paper and Books in Ancient Egypt*, 1952. For books in the ancient world, see *Cambridge History of the Bible*, 1, 1970, pp. 30–66; J. C. L. Gibson, *Syrian Semitic Inscriptions*, 1, *Hebrew*, 1971; 2, *Aramaic*, 1975.

D.J.W.
K.A.K.
A.R.M.

YARN. In the Bible the yarns mentioned are goats' hair, camels' hair, cotton (Heb. *karpas*; Est. 1:6; *cf.* *EBi*, 1, p. 915), linen and silk (Ezk. 16:10; Rev. 18:12). Cotton, from the lint around the seeds produced by the shrub *Gossypium herbaceum*, originated in ancient India, but spread E only in the Gk. period. The 'linen yarn' in the AV of 1 Ki. 10:28 and 2 Ch. 1:16 is due to a misunderstanding of the Heb. text. The correct translation, referring to a country called Kue (*i.e.* *CILICIA), is to be found in the RSV.

F.N.H.

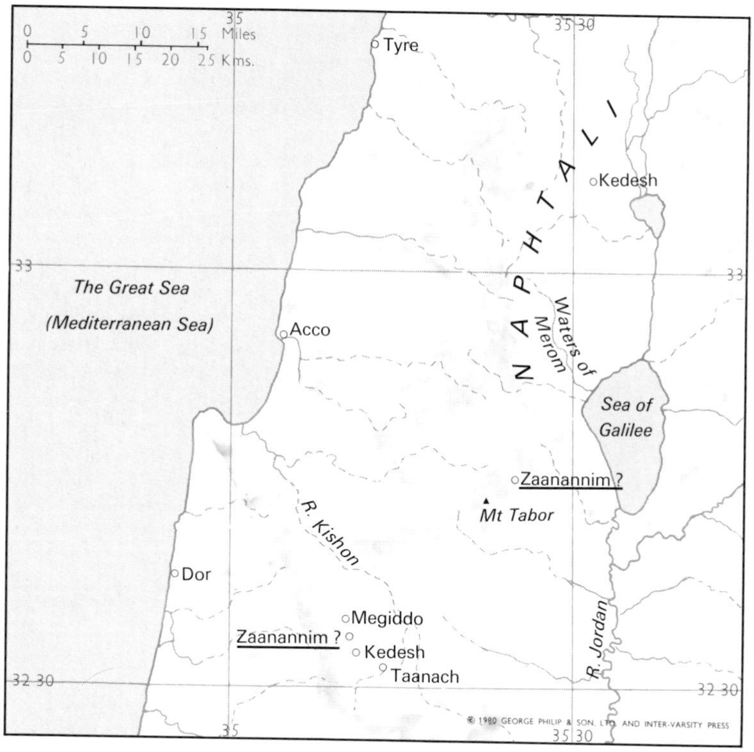

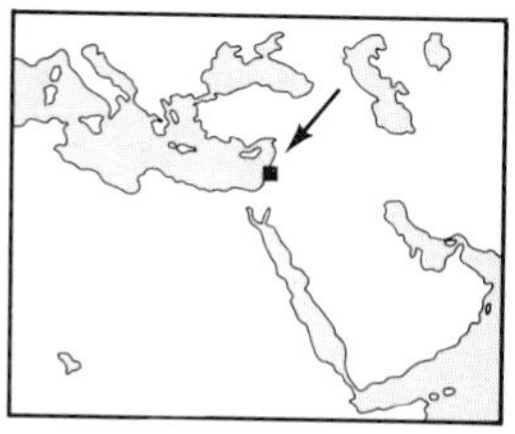

Proposed locations for Zaanannim.

YOKE. The rendering of several Heb. and Gk. words, used either literally for the wooden frame joining two animals (usually oxen), or metaphorically as describing one individual's subjection to another. The words are *môṭ* (Na. 1:13) and *môṭâ* (Is. 58:6; Je. 27:2, *etc.*), 'a bar'; *'ōl* (Gn. 27:40; La. 1:14, *etc.*), 'a yoke'; *ṣemeḏ* (1 Sa. 11:7; Jb. 1:3, *etc.*), 'yoke of oxen'; *zeugos* (Lk. 14:19), 'a pair'; *zygos* (Mt. 11:29; 1 Tim. 6:1, *etc.*), 'a yoke', 'a balance' (*AGRICULTURE).

In 2 Cor. 6:14 Paul uses *heterozygeō*, 'to be yoked with one of another kind'. For the 'yoke-fellow' of Phil. 4:3 see *SYNZYGUS.

J.D.D.

ZAANAN. A place mentioned in Mi. 1:11, the inhabitants of which remained in their city when invading forces passed through the land. It may be identical with Zenan in the Shephelah of Judah listed in Jos. 15:37.

J.D.D.

ZAANANNIM, ZAANAIM (Heb. *ṣa'ᵃnannîm*). On the S border of Naphtali, near Kedesh (Jos. 19:33); Heber the Kenite camped there (Jdg. 4:11; AV, *Kᵉṯîḇ* 'Zaanaim'); the place-name may have been Elon ('Oak')-in-Zaanannim, *cf.* G. F. Moore, *ICC*, 1903, and C. F. Burney, *Judges*, 1918, *ad loc.*

Khan et-Tuggar, 4 km NE of Tabor, preserves the name in its Arabic equivalent ('traveller'). Khan Leggun near Tell abu Qedeis, 4 km N of Taanach, has been suggested as a more likely refuge for Sisera (Jdg. 4:17), but would have been the wrong side of the flooded Kishon.

J.P.U.L.

ZABAD. 1. An Ephraimite (1 Ch. 7:21). **2.** A man of Judah, of the lineage of Hezron (1 Ch. 2:36f.). **3.** One of David's mighty men (1 Ch. 11:41), probably to be equated with **2**; note the name Ahlai in the parentage of both. **4.** A conspirator against Joash (2 Ch. 24:26). The correct form of the name is *Jozachar. *Cf.* 2 Ki. 12:21. **5, 6, 7.** Three laymen who put away their foreign wives, as directed by Ezra (Ezr. 10:27, 33, 43).

D.F.P.

ZABBAI. Possibly a shortened form of Heb. *zāḇaḏyâ*, 'The Lord bestowed upon' (W. Rudolph).

YOM KIPPUR
See Atonement, Day of, Part 1.

Opposite page: An example of cursive Hebrew writing is given by this ostracon from Lachish. It lists nine Hebrew names, seven of which are compounded with Yhwh. *It is datable to the time of Jeremiah. c. 590–587 BC.* (IA)

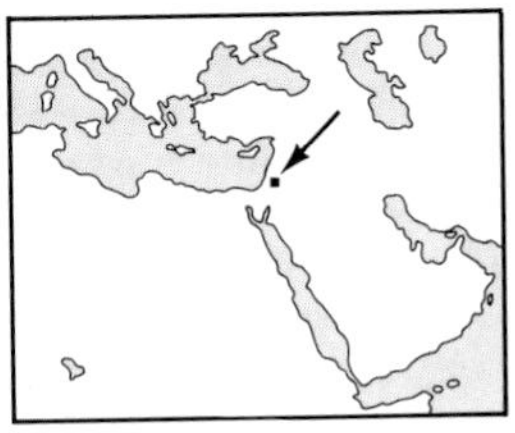

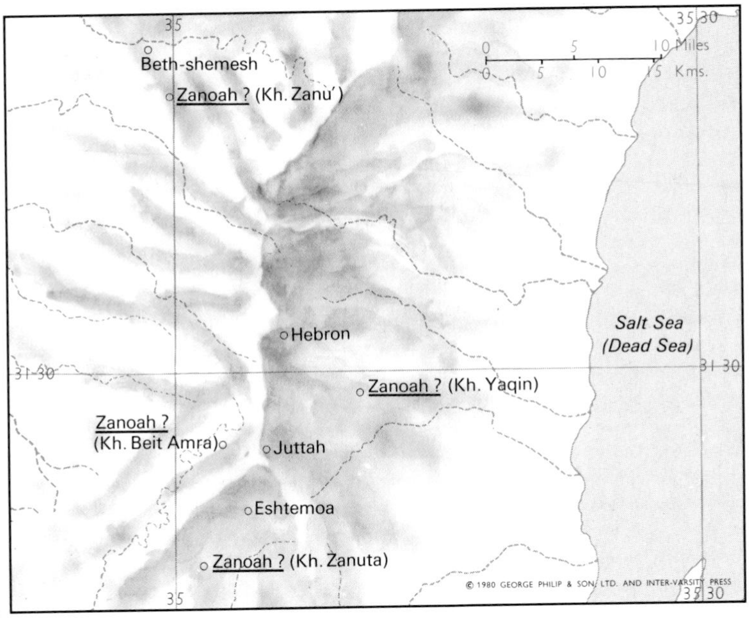

Proposed sites for Zanoah.

ZACHARIAH, ZACHARIAS See Zechariah, Part 3.

ZAKKAI See Zabbai, Part 3.

This name is found in Ezr. 10:28 and Ne. 3:20. Zabbai was forced by Ezra, according to Ezr. 10:28, to put away his foreign wife. Zabbai in Ne. 3:20 is problematic. He was the father of Baruch who helped with the rebuilding of the walls of Jerusalem. Either he is the same person as in Ezra, or a different person with the same name, or Zabbai must be replaced by Zakkai (*cf.* Ezr. 2:9 and various MSS, Vulg. and Syr.). F.C.F.

ZABDI. 1. The grandfather of Achan who took some of the devoted spoil at Jericho (Jos. 7:1, 17–18). He is also called Zimri (1 Ch. 2:6). **2.** A Benjaminite (1 Ch. 8:19). **3.** An officer of David's vineyards (1 Ch. 27:27). **4.** A Levite (Ne. 11:17), also called Zichri (1 Ch. 9:15). R.A.H.G.

ZACCHAEUS, from Heb. and Aram. *Zakkai*, a reduced form of Zechariah. A chief tax-collector at Jericho who became a disciple of Christ (Lk. 19:1–10). He was probably the general tax-farmer of Jericho and undoubtedly had abused his position on occasions to enrich himself. Being a small man, he climbed a tree to see Jesus, who then asked to stay at his house. Zacchaeus welcomed him and showed practical repentance in giving half his goods to the poor and fourfold compensation to any whom he had defrauded. Christ said that this showed him to be a true son of Abraham and declared that salvation had come, not only to him, but to his house. The self-righteous in the crowd were critical of Jesus' action, but he declared his mission to be the seeking and saving of the lost.

BIBLIOGRAPHY. J. D. M. Derrett, *Law in the New Testament*, 1970, pp. 278–285. R.E.N.

ZADOK (Heb. *ṣāḏôq*, 'righteous'?). **1.** Son of Ahitub, who was, according to 1 Ch. 6:1ff., 50ff., a descendant of Eleazar, third son of Aaron. He was priest at David's court along with Abiathar (2 Sa. 8:17) and had charge of the ark (2 Sa. 15:24f.); he took part in the anointing of Solomon as David's successor when Abiathar supported Adonijah (1 Ki. 1:7ff.). He and his descendants discharged the chief-priestly duties in Solomon's Temple until its destruction in 587 BC. Ezekiel restricts the priestly privileges in his new commonwealth to the Zadokite family on the ground that they alone were innocent of apostasy under the Monarchy (Ezk. 44:15ff.). In the second Temple the Zadokites retained the high priesthood continuously until 171 BC, when it was transferred to Menelaus by Antiochus IV; even after that a Zadokite priesthood presided over the Jewish temple at Leontopolis in Egypt until Vespasian closed it soon after AD 70. The Qumran community remained loyal to the Zadokite priesthood and looked forward to its restoration.

2. A descendant of Zadok, grandfather of Hilkiah (1 Ch. 6:12; 9:11; Ne. 11:11). **3.** Father-in-law of King Uzziah and grandfather of Jotham (2 Ki. 15:33; 2 Ch. 27:1). **4, 5.** Two builders of the wall under Nehemiah (Ne. 3:4, 29); one or the other of these may be the same as Zadok, a signatory to the covenant (Ne. 10:21), and 'Zadok the scribe' (Ne. 13:13).

BIBLIOGRAPHY. H. H. Rowley, 'Zadok and Nehushtan', *JBL* 58, 1939, pp. 113ff.; *idem*, 'Melchizedek and Zadok' in *Festschrift für A. Bertholet* (ed. W. Baumgartner), 1950, pp. 461ff.; R. de Vaux, *Ancient Israel*, 1961, pp. 372–405; J. R. Bartlett, 'Zadok and his successors at Jerusalem', *JTS* n.s. 19, 1968, pp. 1–18. F.F.B.

ZAIR. 2 Ki. 8:21 records that King Joram passed over to Zair to crush a revolt of the Edomites, hence its probable location was on the border of Edom. Some MSS of the LXX read here Z(e)ior, and Zair may possibly be identical with *Zior, listed in Jos. 15:54, in the Judaean hill-country. R.A.H.G.

ZALMON. 1. A personal name. One of David's mighty men, said to be an Ahohite (2 Sa. 23:28). He is called Ilai in 1 Ch. 11:29.

2. The name of a mountain in the vicinity of the tower of Shechem (Jdg. 9:48). Its identification is far from certain; both Gerizim and Ebal have been suggested.

3. Another mountain, mentioned in Ps. 68:14 (spelt Salmon in AV). Some have equated it with the foregoing, but this mountain would appear to have been to the E of the Jordan and is usually identified with Jebel Ḥaurân. D.F.P.

ZAMZUMMIM (*zamzummim*, meaning uncertain; possibly 'whisperers', 'murmurers', from a root known in Arabic). The name given by the *Ammonites to the people (known also as *Rephaim) whom they themselves displaced from their territory in central Transjordan (Dt. 2:20–23). It is at present difficult to associate them with any particular archaeological remains but, assuming that the Ammonites settled in the 13th century BC, one might consider these people as the Middle Bronze/Late Bronze Age occupants of the region, whose presence is attested by a few recent discoveries (*cf. IDBS*, p. 20). Whether the *Zuzim in Gn. 14:5 are the same people remains uncertain. J.G.G.N. G.I.D.

ZANOAH (Heb. *zānôaḥ*). **1.** A town in the Shephelah (Jos. 15:34; Ne. 3:13; 11:30); Khirbet Zanu', 3 km S of Beth-shemesh, W of modern Zanoah. **2.** A town in the hills near Juttah (Jos. 15:56; 1 Ch. 4:18); may be Khirbet Beit Amra, overlooking the Wadi el-Halil (W Hevron), part of which is called Wadi Abu Zenah (Grollenberg, Abel); or Khirbet Zanuta, SW of Eshtemoa (Rudolph, *Chronikbücher*, 1955, *ad loc.*; Israeli Survey); or Khirbet Yaqin, 6 km SE of Hebron (Noth, *Josua*, *ad loc.*, citing LXX to read 'Zanoah of Kain'; but the readings are doubtful). J.P.U.L.

ZAPHENATH-PANEAH. An Egyp. name bestowed by the pharaoh upon Joseph at his investiture (Gn. 41:45). The search for its Egyp. original has produced many widely divergent suggestions. Steindorff's *D̠(d)-p'-nt̠(r)-ìw.f-'nḫ* is phonetically good, but is circumstantially inappropriate in meaning and of too late a date. Most other suggestions are either phonetically unacceptable or else lack any real Egyp. parallels. However, the Heb. consonantal form *ṣ-p-n-t p-'-n-ḥ* may, with one slight change (for euphony in Heb.) to *ṣ-t-n-p p-'-n-ḥ*, stand for (*yôsēp̄*) *d̠d-n.f 'Ip-'nḫ* '(Joseph), who is called 'Īp'ankh'; *d̠d-n.f* would be the well-known construction introducing a second name, the name itself being 'Ip'ankh, a common name in the Middle Kingdom and Hyksos periods, *i.e.* in the patriarchal and Joseph's age. K.A.K.

ZAPHON. A town referred to in Jos. 13:27 and Jdg. 12:1, lying in Gadite territory in the Jordan valley. TJ identifies it with the Amathus of Josephus, which is to be located at Tell 'Ammatah; but this is improbable. Other proposed locations for Zaphon are Tell al-Sa'idiya and Tell al-Qos. D.F.P.

ZAREPHATH ('smelting place'). Akkad. *ṣariptu*; *cf.* *ṣarāpu*, 'to refine (metals), to fire (bricks)'. A small Phoenician town (mod. Sarafand), originally belonging to *Sidon, it appears in late 13th century Papyrus Anastasi 1 (*ANET*[3], p. 477). It was captured by Sennacherib in 701 BC (Zarebtu, *ANET*[3], p. 287) and by Esarhaddon, *c.* 680–669 BC, who gave it to Ba'ali, king of Tyre (J. B. Pritchard, 'Sarepta in History and Tradition', in J. Reumann (ed.), *Understanding the Sacred Text*, 1971, pp. 101–114).

Situated about 13 km S of Sidon on the Lebanese coast on the road to *Tyre, it is mentioned in 1 Ki. 17:9ff. as the place to which *Elijah went during the drought in Ahab's reign and where he restored life to the son of the widow with whom he lodged. Lk. 4:26 refers to this incident, the town there being called by the Gk. and Lat. name, Sarepta.

Obadiah prophesied that in the Day of the Lord those of the children of Israel who were deported by Sargon after the fall of Samaria should possess Phoenicia as far as Zarephath.

For excavations begun in 1969, see *AJA* 74, 1970, p. 202; 76, 1972, p. 216; *Archaeology* 24, 1971, pp. 61–63; J. Pritchard, *Sarepta*, 1975. R.A.H.G.

ZARETHAN. This town is spelt variously Zaretan, Zartanah and Zarthan in AV; and the name appears as Zeredah (AV Zeredathah) in 2 Ch. 4:17. Zarethan is mentioned in connection with Beth-shean, Adam and Succoth, and lay in the Jordan valley, near a ford over the river. Its exact site has been debated, but it almost certainly lay W of the Jordan. One suggested location, Qarn Sartaba, perhaps recalls the name Zarethan; but most authorities prefer Tell al-Sa'idiya. (Excavated by J. B. Pritchard, 1964–7; see *Expedition* 6–11, 1964–1968.) Tell Umm Ḥamâd is another possibility. D.F.P.

ZEAL. In modern Eng. usage, fervour in advancing a cause or in rendering service. But the corresponding Heb. and Gk. words in the Bible can have a bad sense. Thus *qānā'* (verb), *qin'â* (noun), are often rendered *'envy', 'envious' (as in Gn. 26:14; Ps. 37:1), or *'jealous', 'jealousy' (Gn. 37:11; Jb. 5:2), and once 'passion' (Pr. 14:30), as well as 'zeal' in a positive sense (2 Sa. 21:2).

The phrase 'the zeal of the Lord (of hosts)' occurs several times (2 Ki. 19:31; Is. 9:7; 37:32; *cf.* Is. 26:11; 63:15) and means his jealous concern for his own people and their welfare: their relationship to him is as a wife to a husband, hence NEB's 'jealous anger' in Is. 59:17 (Heb. *qin'â*; RSV 'fury').

Similarly, in NT the Gk. terms *zēloō* (verb) and *zēlos* (noun) can have a bad or a good sense, according to context. Thus RSV gives 'jealous' (Acts 7:9), 'jealousy' (Acts 5:17) and 'covet' (Jas. 4:2), but translates in a good sense as 'earnestly desire' (1 Cor. 12:31), 'make much of' (Gal. 4:17) or 'zeal' (2 Cor. 7:7). But 'jealous' can have a positive meaning. In 2 Cor. 11:2 Paul is 'jealous' (*zēloō*) over his converts 'with a divine jealousy' (*zēlos*), not meaning the human jealousy of selfish possessiveness or a concern for his own reputation, but the jealousy which a lover feels for his beloved; and a 'divine' jealousy because it is as felt by God himself for his own people, who stand as in the marriage relationship to him (*cf.* Ex. 20:5; 34:14; Dt. 5:9, *etc.*).

zēlōtēs, *'zealot', is applied to the apostle Simon (Lk. 6:15; Acts 1:13), called in Mt. 10:4 and Mk. 3:18 Simon the Cananean, where *ho kananaios* may translate Aram. *qan'ān*, 'zealot'. *zēlōtēs* also occurs in 1 Cor. 14:12, where Paul's readers who are zealots (RSV 'eager') for manifestations of the Spirit are bidden to strive (*zēteō*) to excel in building up the church, *i.e.* to realize that the purpose of spiritual gifts is communal and not for selfish ends. Elsewhere *zēlōtēs* is translated by RSV as 'zealous' (Acts 21:20; 22:3; Gal. 1:14; Tit. 2:14; 1 Pet. 3:13).

The verb *spoudazō* is translated 'zealous' (2 Pet. 1:10, 15; 3:14), but also 'eager' (Gal. 2:10; Eph. 4:3; 1 Thes. 2:17), 'do your best' (2 Tim. 2:15; 4:9, 21; Tit. 3:12), 'strive'

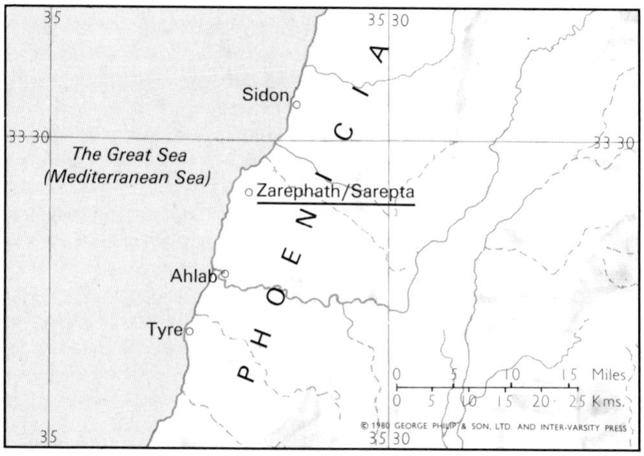

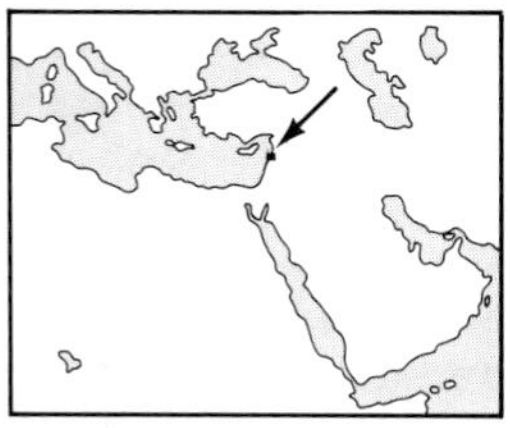

Zarephath (Sarepta), a town in Phoenicia.

Drawing of a stamp seal-impression bearing the name of Zarephath (Sarepta) in Phoenician script (ṣrpt). *Width c. 1·9 cm. Late 5th cent. BC.*

ZARETAN
See Zarethan, Part 3.

ZARTANAH
See Zarethan, Part 3.

ZARTHAN
See Zarethan, Part 3.

(Heb. 4:11). The adjective *spoudaios* occurs in 2 Cor. 8:17, 22 ('earnest'), and the adverb *spoudaiōs* in Lk. 7:4 ('earnestly'), Phil. 2:28; 2 Tim. 1:17 ('eagerly'), Tit. 3:13 ('do your best'). RSV renders *spoudē* as 'zeal' (Rom. 12:8, 11; 2 Cor. 7:12), 'haste' (Mk. 6:25; Lk. 1:39), 'eagerness' (2 Cor. 8:7–8, 16; Heb. 6:11), 'effort' (2 Pet. 1:5).

BIBLIOGRAPHY. H.-C. Hahn, *NIDNTT* 3, pp. 1166–1168; A. Stumpf, *TDNT* 2, pp. 877–888; G. Harder, *TDNT* 7, pp. 559–568.

N.H.

ZEALOT (Gk. *zēlōtēs*). One of the twelve apostles is called Simon the Zealot (Lk. 6:15; Acts 1:13), either because of his zealous temperament or because of some association with the party of the Zealots (*CANANAEAN). Paul speaks of himself as having been a religious zealot (Acts 22:3; Gal. 1:14), and the many members of the church of Jerusalem are described as all 'zealots for the law' (Acts 21:20).

The party of the Zealots, described by Josephus as the 'fourth philosophy' among the Jews (*BJ* 2. 117; *Ant*. 18. 23), was founded by *Judas the Galilean, who led a revolt against Rome in AD 6 (*CENSUS). They opposed the payment of tribute by Israel to a pagan emperor on the ground that this was treason to God, Israel's true King. They were called Zealots because they followed the example of Mattathias and his sons and followers, who manifested zeal for the law of God when Antiochus IV tried to suppress the Jewish religion (1 Macc. 2:24–27), and the example of Phinehas, who showed comparable zeal in a time of apostasy in the wilderness (Nu. 25:11; Ps. 106:30f.). When the revolt of AD 6 was crushed they kept its spirit alive for 60 years. Members of Judas's family were Zealot leaders; two of his sons were crucified by the procurator Alexander *c*. AD 46 (Jos., *Ant*. 20. 102), and a third, Menahem, attempted to seize the leadership of the anti-Roman revolt in AD 66 (Jos., *BJ* 2. 433). Zealots were active throughout the war of AD 66–73; the last Zealot stronghold, Masada, fell in May AD 74, but even then the Zealot spirit was not completely quenched. (*ASSASSINS.)

BIBLIOGRAPHY. F. J. Foakes-Jackson and K. Lake, 'The Zealots', in *BC*, 1, 1920, pp. 421ff.; W. R. Farmer, *Maccabees, Zealots*

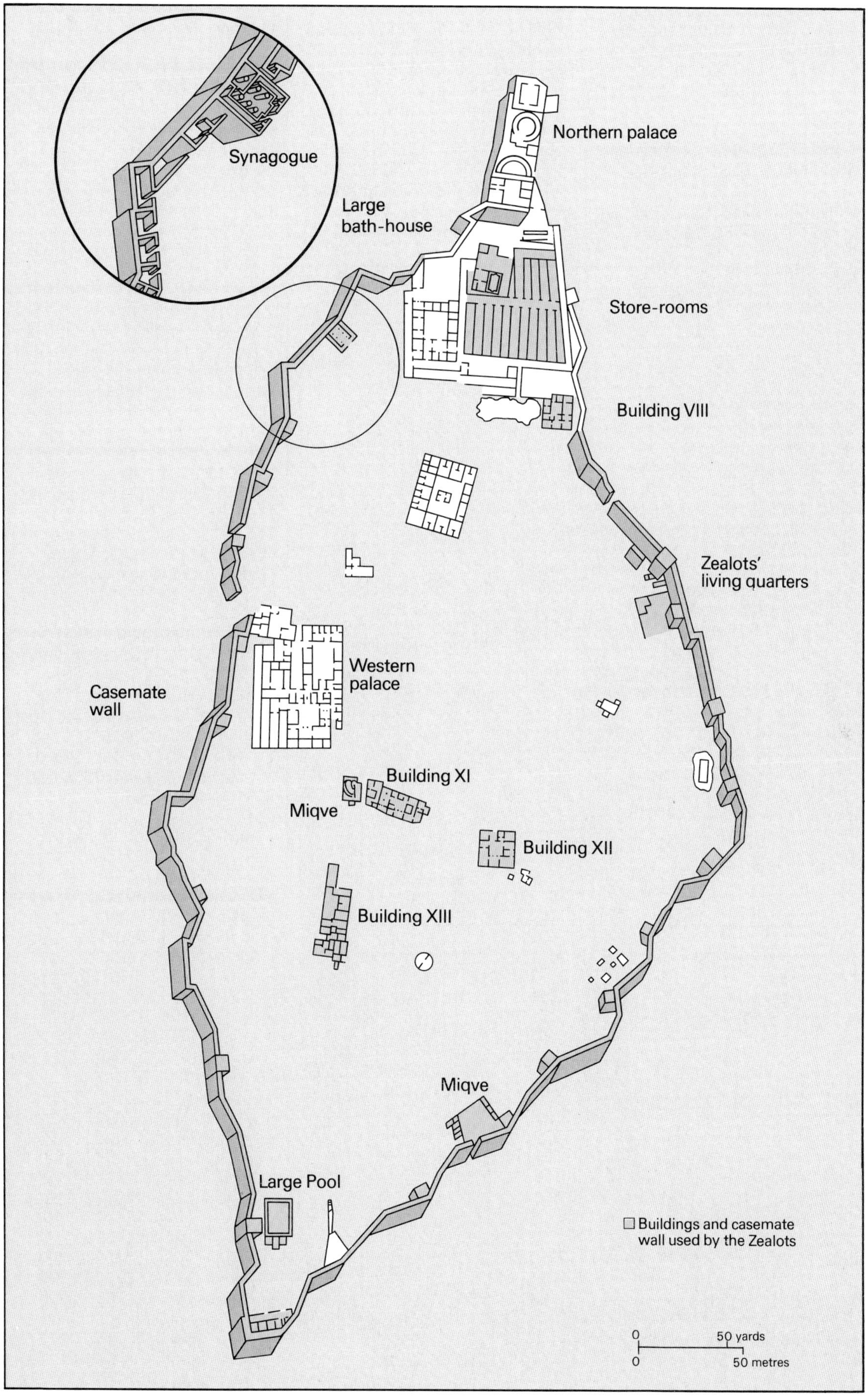

Plan of Masada, showing the buildings defended by the Zealots when it fell in AD 73.

Opposite page:
The Zealots hid in caves such as these at Arbela, Galilee. (RP)

and Josephus, 1956; M. Hengel, *Die Zeloten*, 1961; Y. Yadin, *Masada: Herod's Fortress and the Zealots' Last Stand*, 1966; O. Cullmann, *Jesus and the Revolutionaries*, 1970.

F.F.B.

ZEBAH (Heb. *ze***b***aḥ*, 'slaughter', 'sacrifice'). One of two kings of Midian who raided Palestine in the days of Gideon the judge. Some of Gideon's people had been slain in a Midianite raid (Jdg. 8:18f.). Gideon carefully selected 300 and pursued the raiders. The people of Succoth and Penuel refused to help him and were later punished. At Karkor (v. 10) Gideon captured the two chiefs Zebah and Zalmunna and slew them. Following this exploit, Gideon was invited to be king over Israel, but refused (Jdg. 8:22–23). In Ps. 83:1–12 this incident finds a place among the list of victories God gave his people.

J.A.T.

ZEBEDEE (Gk. *Zebedaios* from Heb. *zi***b***diyāhû*, 'the gift of Yahweh'). The father of the apostles James and John (Mk. 1:19) and husband of Salome (Mt. 27:56; Mk. 15:40). A Galilean fisherman, probably of some means (*cf.* Mk. 1:20); he evidently lived at or near Bethsaida.

J.D.D.

ZEBOIIM (NEB **ZEBOYIM**). One of the cities of the plain (Gn. 14:2) eventually destroyed with * Sodom and Gomorrah (Dt. 29:23). Its location seems to have been in the vicinity of * Admah.

D.F.P.

ZEBOIM. 1. A valley near Michmash in Benjaminite territory (1 Sa. 13:18), modern Wadi Abu Daba'. The Heb. phrase means 'ravine of hyenas' (*gê ṣ*[e]***b****ō'îm*). **2.** A Benjaminite town of post-exilic times, near Lydda (Ne. 11:34).

D.F.P.

ZEBUL (Heb. *z*[e]***b****ûl*, 'exalted', *i.e.* prince, or height). Ruler of Shechem under the self-styled 'king' Abimelech, whom he rescued from Gaal's revolt (Jdg. 9:26–41). In Ugaritic, *zbl* (I), 'prince', is used of Baal, lord of the earth, while *zbl* (II) is 'sick (man)'; *cf.* (*e.g.*) C. H. Gordon, *Ugaritic Textbook*, 3, 1965, p. 393, Nos. 815–816.

K.A.K.

ZEBULUN. The tenth son of

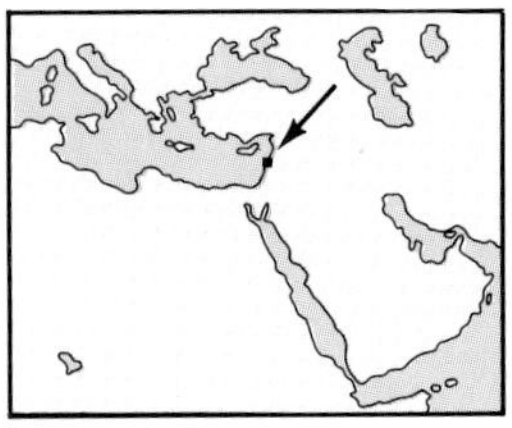

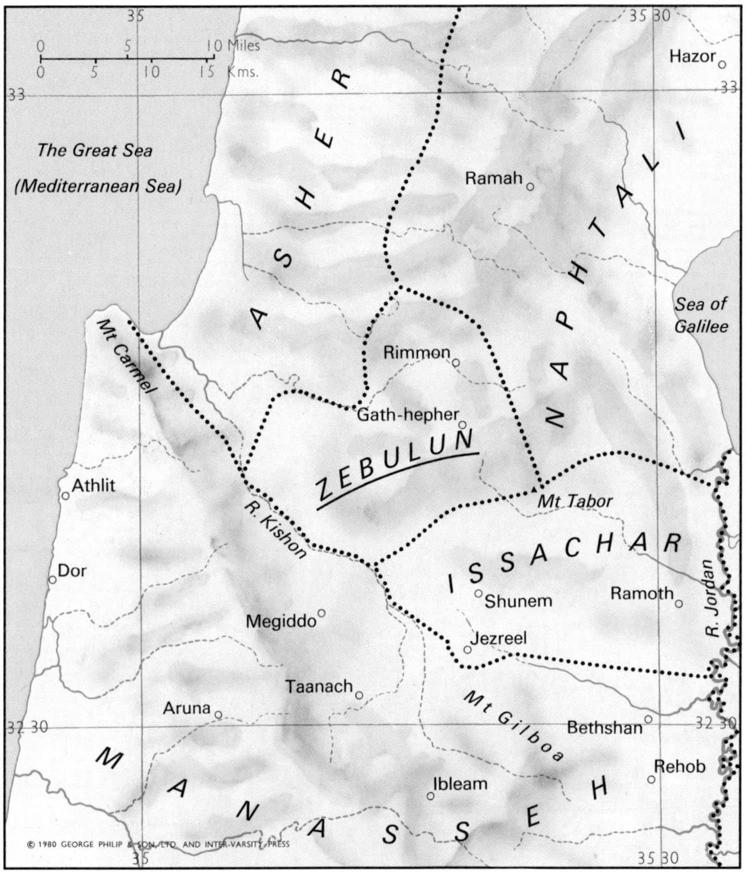

The territory of Zebulun with approximate boundaries.

ZEBOYIM
See Zeboiim, Part 3.

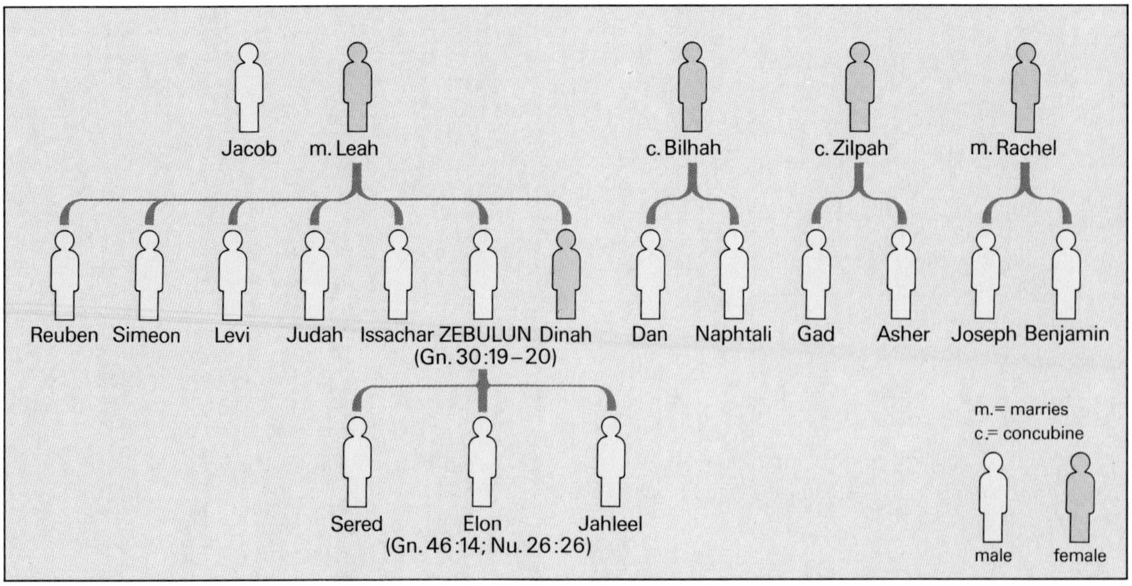

The genealogy of Zebulun.

Jacob and the sixth son of Leah (Gn. 30:19f.). The original form of the name may have been Zebulon or Zebul, the name of Abimelech's lieutenant (Jdg. 9:26–41). In the account of his birth a double derivation is suggested: *zāḇal* to 'honour' and *zāḇaḏ* to 'endow' or 'bestow'. Similar forms are found in Egyp., Akkad. and Canaanite sources. Before the descent into Egypt Zebulun had three sons, Sered, Elon and Jahleel (Gn. 46:14), founders of their respective tribal clans.

Zebulun was able to possess more of its allotted territory than most of the tribes, possibly because it comprised largely virgin country, with no great cities (Jos. 19:10–16). Kitron (perhaps the Kattath of Jos. 19:15) and Nahalol are mentioned as incompletely conquered (Jdg. 1:30). Generally speaking, Zebulun occupied a broad wedge in S Galilee between Asher and Naphtali with Manasseh to the SW and Issachar to the SE. The S boundary was probably the river Kishon in the Valley of Esdraelon, which gave Zebulun, like Issachar, control over the trade routes. The Blessing of Jacob (Gn. 49:13) promises Zebulun access to the sea, although it is not clear whether Galilee or the Mediterranean is meant. In either case this was never realized, but the reference may be to the strategic commercial position shared with Issachar (*cf.* Dt. 33:18f.). These tribes also shared the same holy mountain (Dt. 33:19), probably Tabor (*cf.* Jdg. 4:6), on the fringe of Zebulun's territory. Although one of the smaller tribal areas, it was fertile, being exposed to the rain-bearing W winds. With 57,400 and 60,500 warriors respectively in the two census lists (Nu. 1:31; 26:27), it was the fourth largest tribe.

In the great covenant-renewal ceremony at Shechem, Zebulun was assigned an inferior place with Reuben and the 'handmaiden' tribes (Dt. 27:13). But in the Judges period it distinguished itself in the conflicts against the Canaanites and Midianites (Jdg. 4:6, 10; 5:14, 18; 6:35). One of the minor judges, Elon, came from Zebulun (Jdg. 12:11). When David became king over a united Israel, considerable initial military and economic support was supplied (1 Ch. 12:33, 40). The prophet Jonah was a Zebulunite from Gath-hepher (2 Ki. 14:25; *cf.* Jos. 19:18). Zebulun suffered severely in the Assyr. invasion under Tiglath-pileser (2 Ki. 15:29; *cf.* Is. 9:1), many of its inhabitants were deported and its territory was assimilated into the Assyr. empire. However, its tribal identity survived, and its inhabitants are included among the participants in Hezekiah's Passover (2 Ch. 30:10–22). In the NT, apart from the quotation in Mt. 4:13–16, Zebulun is mentioned only in Rev. 7:8, but Nazareth, where Jesus spent his early years, was within its traditional borders.

BIBLIOGRAPHY. *LOB*, pp. 200, 212, 233, 237. A.E.C.

ZECHARIAH, ZACHARIAH, ZACHARIAS. Some 28 men bear this name in the Bible, most of them mentioned only once or twice, including the last king of Jehu's line (2 Ki. 14:29; 15:8, 11). The best known is the prophet, who is mentioned with Haggai in Ezr. 5:1; 6:14, and whose prophecies are found in the book that bears his name. As these two prophets were enthusiasts for the rebuilding of the Temple in 520 BC, one must account for their silence during the period 536–520 BC, when the Temple building was neglected. Either their parents had brought them as infants in the return in 537 BC or they did not return until about 520 BC; in this case also they must have been infants in 537 BC, or their enthusiasm would have brought them back then. This means that Zechariah was a young man when he began to prophesy, and indeed it may be he, and not the man with the measuring line, who is referred to as 'this young man' in Zc. 2:4. It is likely that the second part of his book belongs to his old age (*ZECHARIAH, BOOK OF).

In the NT Zechariah is the father of John the Baptist (Lk. 1:5, *etc.*). There is also a mention of 'Zechariah son of Barachiah, whom you murdered between the sanctuary and the altar' (Mt. 23:35; *cf.* Lk. 11:51). Since the prophet Zechariah was the son of Berechiah (Zc. 1:1), it is possible that he was martyred, although there is no independent record of this. Others suppose that the reference is to the martyrdom of Zechariah the son of Jehoiada in 2 Ch. 24:20–22, and that the error of the father's name is due either to the Evangelist, or, since it does not occur in the best MSS of Lk., to a copyist's addition. Since Chronicles is the last book in the Heb. Bible, the naming of Abel and Zechariah in this verse would be the equivalent of our phrase 'from Genesis to Revelation'. There is also a Zechariah the son of Jeberechiah, who is called as a witness in Is. 8:2, but there is no reason to suppose that he is the one referred to by Christ. J.S.W.

ZECHARIAH, BOOK OF.

I. Outline of contents

a. Prophecies dated between 520 and 518 BC, during the rebuilding of the Temple, 1:1–8:23

(i) Introduction. Zechariah in the line of the true prophets (1:1–6).

(ii) First vision. Angelic riders are told that God will restore Jerusalem (1:7–17).

(iii) Second vision. Four destroying horns are destroyed by four smiths (1:18–21).

(iv) Third vision. The new Jerusalem cannot be contained by walls, but will be the home of Jews and Gentiles (2:1–13).

(v) Fourth vision. Joshua the high priest, accused by Satan, is vindicated by God, given access to his presence and made a type of the Branch-Messiah (3:1–10).

(vi) Fifth vision. A seven-branched candlestick, or lamp, fed by two branches (probably Joshua and Zerubbabel), from two olive trees. A special word of encouragement to Zerubbabel (4:1–14).

(vii) Sixth vision. An immense flying scroll carries God's words of condemnation of sin (5:1–4).

(viii) Seventh vision. A woman in an ephah measure, symbolizing sin, is removed to the unclean land of Babylon, the place of exile (5:5–11).

(ix) Eighth vision. Four chariots go out through the earth as God's executives (6:1–8).

(x) Joshua is crowned as a symbol of the Branch-Messiah who builds the Temple, and who rules as Priest-King (6:9–15).

(xi) A question about observing fasts that had been instituted to commemorate the fall of Jerusalem in 587 BC. Fasts will become feasts, and all nations will share the blessing (7:1–8:23).

b. Undated prophecies, which could be from a later period in Zechariah's ministry, 9:1–14:21

(i) The judgment of Israel's enemies is seen in the light of the coming of the Prince of Peace (9:1–17).

(ii) Evil shepherds give place to

God's Leader, who gathers in his people (10:1–12).

(iii) The Good Shepherd confounds the evil shepherds, but is rejected by the flock, who consequently suffer under yet another evil shepherd (11:1–17).

(iv) Jerusalem in distress looks to the One whom her people have pierced, and repents with true sorrow (12:1–14).

(v) Jewish prophecy ceases when the Good Shepherd is smitten and opens the fountain that cleanses from sin (13:1–9).

(vi) The distress of Jerusalem is followed by the blessings and judgments of God's kingdom (14:1–21).

II. Authorship and unity

Throughout chs. 1–8 Zechariah is named as the author, and the period is that of Ezr. 5–6. This claim is generally accepted, though occasionally attempts have been made to distinguish the Zechariah of the prophecies from the Zechariah of the visions (*e.g.* by S. B. Frost, *Old Testament Apocalyptic*, 1952).

The problem of chs. 9–14 is more complicated, and many hold that these chapters are neither to be ascribed to Zechariah nor are a unity in themselves. A moderate view, adopted by, *e.g.*, H. L. Ellison in *Men Spake from God*, 1952, is that three anonymous prophecies have been added at the end of the Minor Prophets, each introduced by the phrase, 'The burden of the word of the Lord'. The three are Zc. 9:1–11:17; Zc. 12:1–14:21; Mal. 1:1–4:6. Others (*e.g.* W. O. E. Oesterley and T. H. Robinson, *Introduction to the Books of the Old Testament*, 1934) find in these chapters fragments from various dates.

The main arguments against Zechariah's authorship are: (i) the difference of atmosphere between 1–8 and 9–14. The former are full of hope and promise; the latter show bad leadership and threat of attack. There is no reference to the recent rebuilding of the Temple. (ii) There is a reference in 9:13 to Greece as the dominant power, not Persia as in the days of Zechariah. (iii) The derogatory reference to prophecy in ch. 13 and apocalyptic pictures in ch. 14 are marks of a late date.

The first two contentions assume that, if the chapters are by *Zechariah, they must belong to approximately the same period as 1–8.

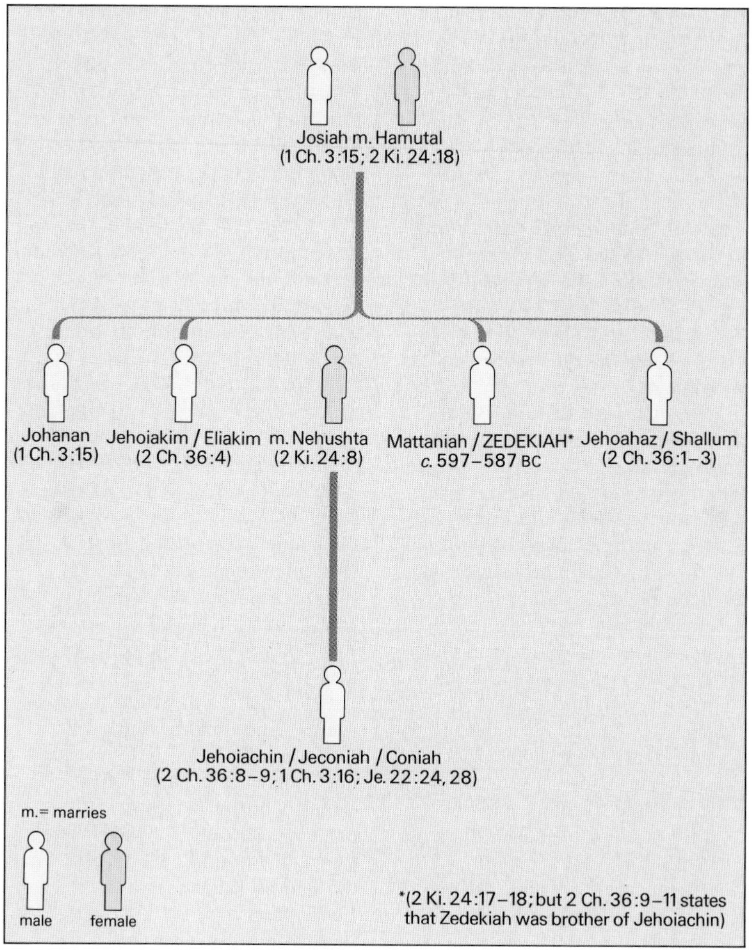

An interpretation of Zedekiah's family tree.

We have no means of knowing the length of Zechariah's prophetic ministry, but there are indications that he was a young man when he was first called to prophesy in 520 BC. Jeremiah prophesied for over 40 years, and Isaiah for over 50. If these chapters were uttered in Zechariah's old age they would be drawing near to the time of Malachi, Ezra and Nehemiah, and perhaps Joel, when the atmosphere of first enthusiasm had given place to coldness, formality, poor leadership and fear of attack.

The reference to Greece is not, then, a serious objection, even if one does not give any weight to belief in divine prediction, which is certainly present in the King and the Shepherd references in these chapters. Greece, or Javan, is named by Ezk. 27:13, 19, and also by Is. 66:19, as one of the places to which missionaries will go to declare God's glory. It is worth noting for the sake of the argument that many commentators would make 'Trito-Isaiah' (Is. 56–66) a contemporary of the actual Zechariah who wrote 1–8. It is probable that Zechariah had seen the vision of the chariots going 'toward the west country' (6:6), and in 8:7 he foresees captives returning from the W. Later Joel 3:6 refers to Jews who had been sold by the Phoenicians as slaves to the Greeks.

From about 520 BC onwards the Greeks in Asia Minor were a continual source of trouble to Darius, and in 500 BC a great Ionian revolt occurred. In 499 BC the Athenians burnt the Persian stronghold of Sardis, and in 490 BC and 480 BC the Persians, in a full-scale invasion of Greece, were defeated at Marathon and Salamis. From a purely human point of view, Zechariah could have looked to Greece as a power that would harass the countries in the Persian empire whose seaboard looked towards the W. Indeed, there may already have been raids on the coasts of Palestine. It should, however, be noted that Javan is only one out of several powers who are dealt with in ch. 9.

The contention about the derogatory reference to prophecy in ch. 13 reads too much into the passage. The writer cannot be belittling prophecy, since he is himself professing to be a prophet. In the context the thought is of the pierced Shepherd, whose death opens the fountain for sin, as being the climax of prophecy, so that true prophecy ceases, and any professed prophecy that remains is only false.

The contention about the later apocalyptic imagery of ch. 14 is a subjective opinion. It should be realized that the dating of eschatological and apocalyptic passages in the OT is based largely on opinion. Because there is much apocalyptic in the intertestamental period, it is assumed that similar pictures in the prophets, *e.g.* Isaiah and Zechariah, must be given a late date.

From the positive standpoint, there are certain definite links between 1–8 and 9–14; *e.g.* the need for repentance and cleansing (1:4; 3:3–4, 9; 5:1–11; 7:5–9; 9:7; 12:10; 13:1, 9); Jerusalem as the head (1:16–17; 2:11–12; 12:6; 14:9f.); the return of the nation (2:6, 10; 8:7–8; 9:12; 10:6–12); Israel's enemies are to be subdued (1:21; 12; 14) and converted (2:11; 8:20–23; 9:7; 14:16–19). There are also some similarities of style: *e.g.* the fondness for the number 'two' (4:3; 5:9; 6:1; 11:7; 13:8); the vocatival address (2:7, 10; 3:2, 8; 4:7; 9:9, 13; 11:1–2; 13:7); the phrase 'pass through nor return' occurs in 7:14 and 9:8 (AV; RSV 'to and fro') and nowhere else in the OT.

It is not possible to prove the unity of the book, but one should not too readily abandon it. It is not necessary to look for contemporary figures in 9:8, 16–17 and 12:10, though upholders of the later date suggest various priestly characters of the Maccabean age. If contemporary identifications were needed, the conservative commentator would be bound to say that we know nothing about the leaders in Judaea between 516 and 458 BC, and personal intrigues and assassinations were as likely then as in Maccabean times.

BIBLIOGRAPHY. H. G. Mitchell, *ICC*, 1912; C. H. H. Wright, *Zechariah and his Prophecies*, 1878; M. F. Unger, *Zechariah*, 1963; J. G. Baldwin, *Haggai, Zechariah, Malachi, TOTC*, 1972; L. G. Rignell, *Die Nachtgesichte des Sacharja*, 1950; P. Lamarche, *Zacharie IX–XIV*, 1961; B. Otzen, *Studien über Deuterosacharja*, 1964; F. F. Bruce, 'The Book of Zechariah and the Passion Narrative', *BJRL* 43, 1960–1, pp. 336ff.; R. K. Harrison, *IOT*, 1968. J.S.W.

ZEDAD. One of the sites on the N border of the promised land (Nu. 34:8), mentioned also in Ezekiel's vision of the limits of restored Israel (Ezk. 47:15). There are two main candidates for identification with it, corresponding to the two views that are taken about the line of the N border described in these texts as a whole. The dominant view (*e.g.* Aharoni) sees the name as preserved at Ṣadad, *c.* 110 km ENE of Byblos; this accords well with the preferred location for the 'entrance of *Hamath', the adjacent point on the boundary. A minority of scholars advocate a more S position, at Kh. Ṣerādā, a few miles N of Dan, reading the name as Zerad, with LXX and the Samaritan text.

BIBLIOGRAPHY. G. B. Gray, *Numbers*, 1903, p. 459; G. A. Cooke, *Ezekiel, ICC*, 1936, p. 527; Y. Aharoni, *LOB*, pp. 65–67.

R.A.H.G.
G.I.D.

ZEDEKIAH (Heb. *ṣiḏqiyyāhû—ṣiḏqiyyâ*, only in 1 Ki. 22:11; Je. 27:12; 28:1; 29:3—'Yahweh is (my) righteousness'). **1.** One of 400 court prophets under *Ahab who lied by prophesying his victory over Syria (1 Ki. 22:1–12; 2 Ch. 18:1–11). When Micaiah revealed the truth, Zedekiah symbolically called him a liar by striking his cheek (1 Ki. 22:13–28; 2 Ch. 18:12–27).

2. A false prophet among the exiles in Babylon whose death at the hand of Nebuchadrezzar is foretold by Jeremiah (Je. 29:21–23).

3. A prince of Judah who heard the scroll of Jeremiah read during the reign of Jehoiachin (Je. 36:11–13).

4. The twenty-first, and last, king of Judah (*c.* 597–587 BC). The third son of Josiah (1 Ch. 3:15), he was placed on the throne by Nebuchadrezzar in the place of *Jehoiachin, his nephew. His name was also changed from Mattaniah, showing his vassalage to Babylon (2 Ki. 24:17). Enthroned at the age of 21, he reigned for 11 years (v. 18; 2 Ch. 36:11).

Since the leading citizens had been deported with Jehoiachin (2 Ki. 24:14–16), Zedekiah was left with the undesirables, whose advice, which he was not able to refuse, finally led to Yahweh's punishment (Je. 24:8–9; 29:16–19; Ezk. 11:14–21). Rebellion in Babylonia in *c.* 594 BC (A. K. Grayson, *Assyrian and Babylonian Chronicles*, 1975, p. 102, Ezk. 11:21–24) gave the W vassals an opportunity to conspire to throw off their subjugation, sending to Judah, where there was evidence of an anti-Babylonian faction (Je. 28:1–10), for support (27:3). Jeremiah saw the Babylonian overlordship as divinely ordained (Je. 27; *cf.* 28:12–14). Zedekiah went to Babylon in 593 BC, possibly to allay suspicion concerning his involvement in the plot (Je. 51:59).

Zedekiah finally did revolt (2 Ki. 24:20), breaking a covenant with Babylon (Ezk. 17:12–13). This was possibly related to the arrival of the pharaoh Hophra (Apries; Je. 44:30), whose aid, as indicated by Lachish Letter 3, might have been sought by Judah (*DOTT*, p. 214). In 588 BC, Nebuchadrezzar and his army invaded Judah and laid siege to Jerusalem. The siege was lifted for a period to meet the approaching Egyptians (Je. 37:5) but, as Jeremiah predicted (vv. 6–10; 34:21–22), the siege was resumed. When the famine inside the city had reached its peak, the wall was breached in July, 586 BC, and the city fell (2 Ki. 25:3–4; Je. 52:6–7). The Temple was plundered and burnt and people exiled (2 Ki. 25:17–20). Zedekiah fled towards the Jordan, where he was captured and taken to Nebuchadrezzar's military headquarters at Riblah. There his sons were executed before him. He was then blinded and led off to Babylon (2 Ki. 25:4–7; Je. 52:7–11). D.W.B.

This Babylonian Chronicle text tells how Nebuchadrezzar appointed 'a king of his own choice', i.e. Zedekiah (Mattaniah), instead of Jehoiachin after the Babylonian capture of Jerusalem in March 597 BC. Clay. (BM)

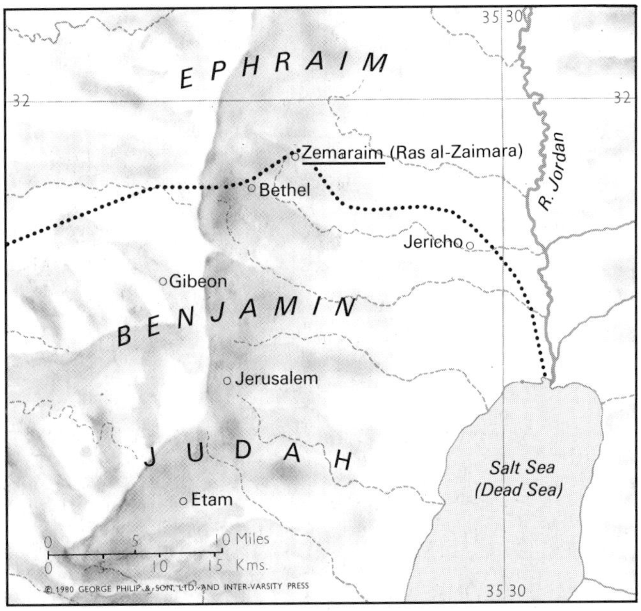

A possible location for Zemaraim.

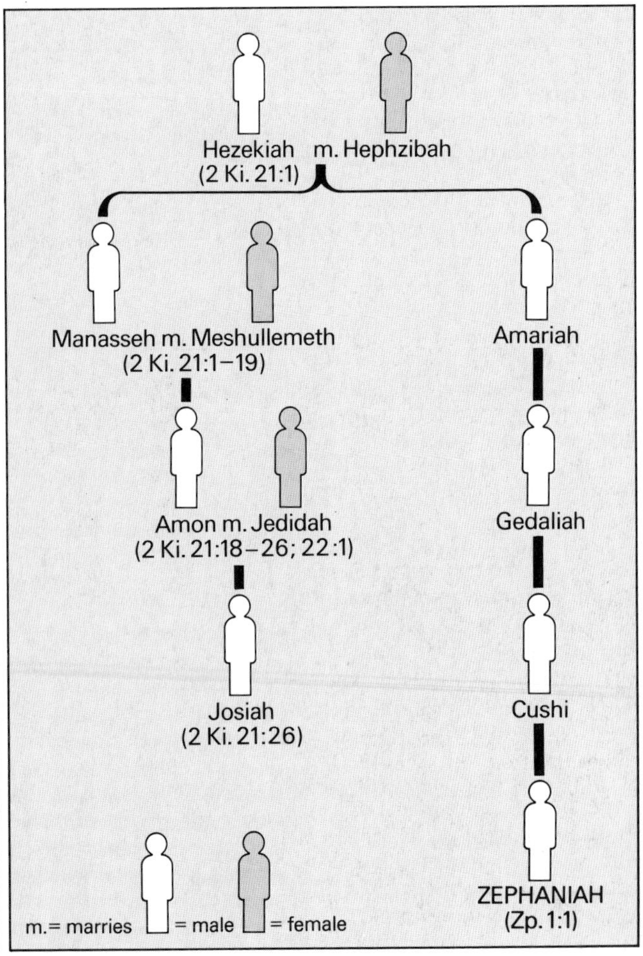

The genealogy of Zephaniah, based on the assumption that 'Hezekiah' (Zp. 1:1) was King Hezekiah of Judah.

ZELOPHEHAD. The son of Hepher, grandson of Gilead of the tribe of Manasseh, father of five daughters (Nu. 26:33; Jos. 17:3; 1 Ch. 7:15). After his death in the wilderness wanderings, because he was without male issue, his daughters successfully claimed the inheritance before Moses and Eleazar (Nu. 27:1, 7). Thus originated the law whereby the property of a man without a male heir should pass first to his daughters (v. 8). This is evidence of a custom, attested in Syria, Babylonia and Elam from early times, whereby property could be transmitted through daughters in the absence of male heirs. They had to marry within their own family and so keep the line within the tribe to which their father belonged (Nu. 36:2–9). (See Z. Ben-Barak, *JSS* 24, 1979.) The Gileadite chiefs later made the further request that the women should marry only within their own tribe to ensure the continuity of possession of such inheritances within the same tribe. This, being granted, also became Heb. law (Nu. 36:2–9).

D.J.W.

ZELZAH. After Samuel had anointed Saul 'prince over his people Israel' (1 Sa. 10:1), one of the signs given to Saul was that he would meet 'two men by Rachel's tomb . . . at Zelzah' (1 Sa. 10:2). LXX translates Zelzah by 'leaping furiously' (from *ṣōlᵉḥîm*), and the Vulgate 'in the south'. The village Beit Jala between Bethel and Bethlehem, to the W, may be the location.

R.A.H.G.

ZEMARAIM. 1. A Benjaminite town, listed with Beth-arabah and Bethel (Jos. 18:22). Proposed locations are Khirbet al-Samra, Ras al-Zaimara and Ras al-Tâḥûna.

2. A mountain in the hill country of Ephraim (2 Ch. 13:4). Bethel was presumably in the same general locality (*cf.* v. 19), so probably the mountain was near to, and named after, the town Zemaraim.

D.F.P.

ZEMARITES. A Canaanite tribe, mentioned in Gn. 10:18 and 1 Ch. 1:16. In both instances the name is listed between Arvadites and Hamathites. The tribe's home was the Ṣumur of the Tell el-Amarna letters, the Ṣimirra of Assyr. texts. Its modern name is Sumra, and it lies on the Mediterranean coast N of Tripoli (Tarablus).

D.F.P.

ZENAS. Gk. pet-name from Zenodorus (*cf.* Lightfoot on Col. 4:15); a lawyer (*nomikos*), accompanying Apollos to an unknown destination: Titus was to provide them with supplies and a good send-off (Tit. 3:13). They doubtless brought Titus Paul's letter (*cf.* Zahn, *INT*, 2, p. 49). Despite the association with Apollos, *nomikos* here probably does not refer to expertise in the Torah. Zenas' proficiency was probably in Roman law: *nomikos* is used of eminent jurists like Mucius Scaevola (Plutarch, *Sulla* 36) or of humble notaries (*cf.* examples in *MM*).

An *Acts of Titus* (5th century) claims his authority, and menologies include him in the Seventy.

A.F.W.

ZEPHANIAH. The only biographical reference to Zephaniah appears in the first verse of the book which bears his name. The genealogy of the prophet is carried back four generations to Hezekiah. Although this Hezekiah is not identified as the Judaean king of that name, the unusual form of Zephaniah's genealogy is best explained on that assumption.

The name of Zephaniah, 'Yahweh has hidden', may indicate that the prophet was born during the time of the atrocities perpetrated by Manasseh, who 'shed very much innocent blood' (2 Ki. 21:16).

Zephaniah prophesied during the reign of his kinsman, Josiah, the great-grandson of Hezekiah. Josiah came to the throne at the age of 8 (640 BC) and was largely influenced by Hilkiah the high priest. It may be presumed that Zephaniah also had an influence for godliness on King Josiah. In his 18th year the young king ordered the renovation of the Temple during which the 'book of the law of Yahweh' was found. When read before the king and the people of Jerusalem, this Scripture brought about a reformation in the life of the nation.

Zephaniah probably ministered early in the reign of Josiah. He speaks of the 'remnant of Baal' in Jerusalem (Zp. 1:4), and other idolatrous customs which were abandoned after the discovery of the law (1:5; *cf.* 2 Ki. 22:1–23:25; 2 Ch. 34:1–7).

Nahum, who prophesied the destruction of Nineveh, which took place in 612 BC, was probably a contemporary of Zephaniah, as was Jeremiah, who lived to see the destruction of Jerusalem (587 BC). The length of the ministry of Zephaniah is not known.

C.F.P.

ZEPHANIAH, BOOK OF. This book is the ninth of the Minor Prophets. It is pre-eminently concerned with the Day of Yahweh, which had earlier appeared as a factor in the prophecies of Amos (Am. 5:18–20).

Zephaniah, however, made the Day of Yahweh his central message. The visions of the Day of Yahweh subsequently played a conspicuous part in apocalyptic literature.

I. Outline of contents

a. Warning of the impending Day of Yahweh, 1:1–2:3

(i) Superscription (1:1).
(ii) The destruction of all things (1:2–3).
(iii) Judgment on Judah and Jerusalem (1:4–13).
(iv) Judgment described (1:14–18).
(v) Judgment may be avoided (2:1–3).

b. Judgment on foreign nations, 2:4–15

(i) Philistia (2:4–7).
(ii) Moab and Ammon (2:8–11).
(iii) Egypt (2:12).
(iv) Assyria (2:13–15).

c. Judgment on Jerusalem and subsequent blessing, 3:1–20

(i) The sins of Jerusalem judged (3:1–8).
(ii) The remnant of Judah blessed (3:9–20).

II. Historical background

The religious state of the kingdom of Judah deteriorated markedly following the death of Hezekiah. Manasseh, his son, rebuilt the altars to Baal which Hezekiah had destroyed (2 Ch. 33:1–11). Religion was debased to the level of crass externalism. The revival of idolatrous worship, common in the days of Ahaz (2 Ki. 16:3–4), was from the prophetic viewpoint a rejection of Israel's covenant with Yahweh.

Scythian invaders attacked Assyria in 632 BC. Josiah was able to carry out his reforms without fear of Assyr. interference. The Scythians moved into W Asia and reached the Egyp. border where they were bought off by pharaoh Psammetichus I. They do not appear to have attacked Israel, although the ferocity of their assault provided a background against which Zephaniah pictured the wrath of Yahweh.

III. Message of the book

Zephaniah's prophecies begin with a message of gloom. The prophet denounced the idolatry which he saw in Jerusalem, where there had been no spiritual revival since the days of Hezekiah. Zephaniah declared that God's judgment was imminent both on Judah's idolatrous neighbours (2:4–15) and on Judah and Jerusalem (1:4–18; 3:1–7).

The prophet, however, is not a pessimist. Beyond the impending doom he sees a better day. God must bring his people through the afflicting fires in order to prepare them to be a means of blessing to all mankind.

Some of the abuses denounced by Zephaniah were removed in Josiah's reformation (621 BC).

BIBLIOGRAPHY. J. M. P. Smith *et al.*, in *ICC*, 1912; G. G. Stonehouse, *WC*, 1929; C. L. Taylor in *IB*, 6, 1956; J. H. Eaton, *Obadiah, Nahum, Habakkuk, Zephaniah, TBC*, 1961; J. D. W. Watts, *Joel, Obadiah, Jonah, Nahum, Habakkuk and Zephaniah, CBC*, 1975.

C.F.P.

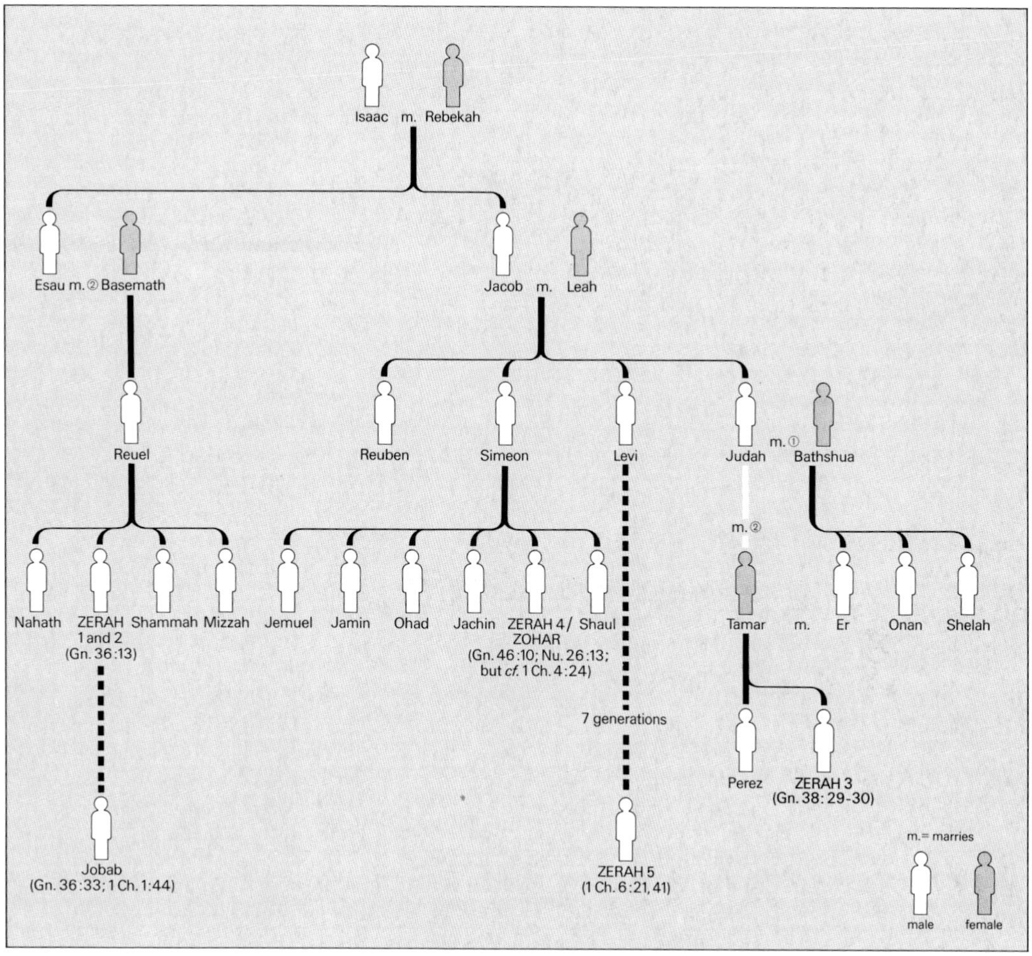

Four (or five) of the biblical Zerahs are shown on this family tree.

ZEPHATHAH (Heb. *ṣ^ep̄aṯâh*). 'The valley of Zephathah at (*l^e*) Mareshah', 2 Ch. 14:10 (v. 9 *MT*). The LXX apparently read *baggai miṣṣāp̄ôn* ('in the valley to the north') for *b^eḡê' ṣ^ep̄aṯâh*. Complex re-entrants in gently-sloping country lie N and S of *Mareshah.

J.P.U.L.

ZER. A fortified city in the territory of Naphtali (Jos. 19:35). It is not necessary to adopt the LXX reading *Tyros, i.e.* Tyre, which presupposes a Heb. reading *ṣōr* instead of *MT ṣēr*.

J.D.D.

ZERAH. From Heb. *zāraḥ*, 'to rise, shine/come forth', especially of the sun.

1. Son of Reuel son of Esau and Basemath (Gn. 36:4, 10, 13, 17; 1 Ch. 1:35, 37), who might be same as: **2.** Father of Jobab, second of the early kings of Edom (Gn. 36:33; 1 Ch. 1:44).

3. Son of Judah by Tamar, and twin of Perez (Gn. 38:29–30; 1 Ch. 2:4); progenitor of the Judaean clan

ZENAN
See Zaanan, Part 3.

ZERAD
See Zedad, Part 3.

Opposite page: The family of Zerubbabel according to (1) Ezra, Haggai and Matthew; (2) 1 Ch. 3:17–20.

ZEREDAH
See Zarethan, Part 3.

ZEREDATHAH
See Zarethan, Part 3.

ZERUIAH
See Nahash, Part 2.

ZICHRI
See Zabdi, Part 3.

ZIDON
See Sidon, Part 3.

The most probable location of Ziklag.

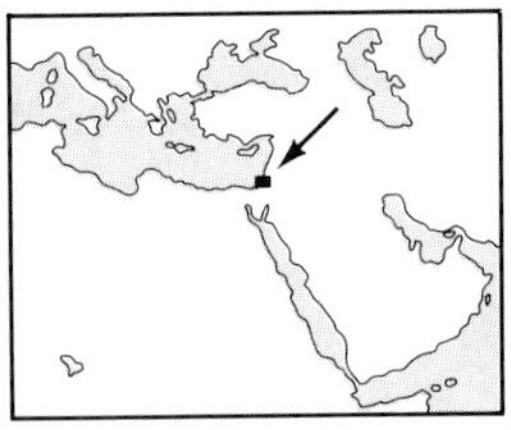

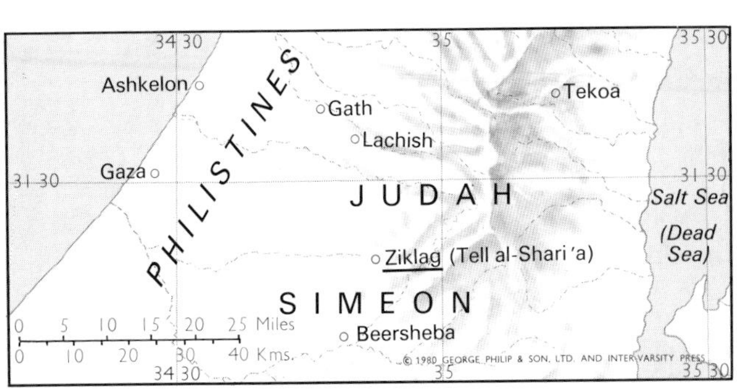

of Zerahites (Nu. 26:20), among whom was Achan who sinned at Jericho (Jos. 7:1, 17–18, 24; 22:20; 1 Ch. 2:6), besides others (1 Ch. 9:6; Ne. 11:24).

4. Son of Simeon and progenitor of a Simeonite clan of Zerahites (Nu. 26:13; 1 Ch. 4:24); the Zohar of Gn. 46:10; Ex. 6:15. **5.** Descendant of Levi through Gershom (1 Ch. 6:21, 41).

6. An Ethiopian who invaded Judah with large Ethiopian and Libyan forces (2 Ch. 14:9–15; 16:8) and was routed in battle at Mareshah by Asa in his 14th year, *c.* 897 BC (*cf.* 2 Ch. 15, especially v. 10, and E. R. Thiele, *The Mysterious Numbers of the Hebrew Kings*[2], 1965, pp. 58–60, on 2 Ch. 15:19; 16:1). Whether Zerah's starting-point was Egypt or Arabia is disputed. The only point favouring Arabia is the Semitic form of the name Zerah. His retreat by Gerar might hint, and the presence of Libyans in his forces strongly indicates, that Zerah had come from Egypt. Note that Zerah is *not* called king; hence he cannot be the Libyan pharaoh Osorkon I (*c.* 924–889 BC) in whose reign the battle occurred. The clear difference between Heb. *ḥ* and Egyp. *k* probably excludes identification of the names Zerah, *zrḥ*, and Osorkon, (*w*)*srk*(*n*); no convincing Egyp. or Ethiopian original for Zerah's name is yet forthcoming. Zerah would therefore probably be an Ethiopian army-commander leading the Egyp. forces on behalf of Osorkon I, who was seeking to follow up the success of his father Shishak; Zerah's ignominious defeat is unlikely to appear in the scanty Egyp. records of the period. K.A.K.

ZERED, a mountain-torrent (Heb. *naḥal*) or wadi crossed by the Israelites on their journey round the frontiers of Edom and Moab (Nu. 21:12; Dt. 2:13f.). In Nu. it is mentioned as a camping-ground, which accords with the order to 'rise up' in Dt. 2:13. Its identification is disputed; probably it is mod. Wadi el-Hesâ, which runs into the Dead Sea from the SE. The comments which follow in Dt. 2:14ff. show that its crossing was regarded as an important stage in the journey. G.T.M.

ZERUBBABEL. The exact meaning of the name is uncertain; perhaps it is from Akkad. *zeru-Babili*, 'seed of Babylon'. He was the son of Shealtiel, or Salathiel, and thus grandson of King Jehoiachin (Ezr. 3:2; Hg. 1:1; Mt. 1:12). In 1 Ch. 3:19 the Heb., though not LXX, makes him the son of Pedaiah, Shealtiel's brother. If this is not a copyist's error, there may have been a levirate marriage. It is most unlikely that Zerubbabel is to be identified with *Sheshbazzar, since the account given in the letter sent to Darius (Ezr. 5:6–17) is hardly intelligible unless Sheshbazzar was dead at the time of the interview which it records, whereas Zerubbabel is actively building the Temple. Sheshbazzar may have been Zerubbabel's uncle, Shenazzar (1 Ch. 3:18), but, whoever he was, he was more of a figurehead, while Zerubbabel and Joshua were the active leaders. Zerubbabel returned with the main party under Sheshbazzar in 537 BC, and laid the foundations of the Temple (Ezr. 3). Ezra records that the work was hindered until 520 BC, when a fresh beginning was made, with Zerubbabel and Joshua again in the lead (Ezr. 5–6; Hg. 1–2). In Hg. 1:1; 2:2 Zerubbabel is called 'governor'.

The visions of Zechariah encourage both Joshua and Zerubbabel in their work, and Zc. 4:6–10 promises that the mountain of opposition (probably that of Ezr. 5) will be removed, and Zerubbabel will complete the work. It is often held that the crowning of Joshua in Zc. 6:9–15 was really the crowning of Zerubbabel, but there is no MS evidence for this, and in 3:8 it appears to be Joshua who is the type of the Messianic Branch, as here. Since E. Sellin in 1898 it has been increasingly assumed, on the basis of the crowning and the promise of protection in Hg. 2:20–23, that Haggai and Zechariah induced the Jews to crown Zerubbabel as king, though this act of rebellion was speedily crushed by Persia. There is no shred of evidence for or against this theory.

BIBLIOGRAPHY. L. E. Browne, *Early Judaism*, 1929; A. C. Welch, *Post-Exilic Judaism*, 1935; J. S. Wright, *The Building of the Second Temple*, 1958; P. R. Ackroyd, *Exile and Restoration*, 1968. J.S.W.

ZERUIAH (Heb. *ṣ*ᵉ*rûyâ*, *ṣ*ᵉ*ruyâ*; possibly from Arab. root, either (1) 'run blood, bleed', or (2) the name of an odoriferous tree, or its gum). The mother of Abishai, Joab and Asahel, David's officers (1 Sa. 26:6; 2 Sa. 2:18; 8:16, *etc.*). Her husband is never mentioned, for which there are several explanations. He may have died young, or she may have been the more significant character. It may reflect the ancient custom of tracing kinship through the female line, or she may have married a foreigner, remaining in her own clan, her children being reckoned as belonging to that clan. She was also David's sister (1 Ch. 2:16), though 2 Sa. 17:25 may imply that she was strictly a step-sister, Jesse's wife being earlier married to Nahash; however, the text of this verse is uncertain. J.G.G.N.

ZEUS. The Gk. deities, *Zeus* and **Hermēs* (Acts 14:12), rendered in AV by their Roman equivalents, Jupiter and Mercurius, presumably in turn represent unknown local gods, whom the Lycaonian-speaking people of Lystra recognized in Barnabas and Paul. Why a miraculous healing should have prompted this particular identification is not clear. Hermes, the divine wayfarer and messenger of Zeus, suggested himself for Paul 'because he was the chief speaker'. The fact that there was a local cult of Zeus (v. 13) may have clinched the identity of Barnabas. The two gods were associated as wanderers on earth in the tale of Philemon and Baucis (Ovid, *Metamorphoses* 8. 618–724), who secured their favour by being the only ones to give them hospitality. This possibly explains the anxiety of the Lycaonians not to miss their opportunity.

Paul and Barnabas were naturally greatly distressed and managed only with difficulty to divert the people from their plan to offer sacrifice to them. But Paul also improved the occasion with remarkable dexterity: rising to his role of Hermes, he takes up the familiar picture of Zeus as the god of the sky who displays himself in the phenomena of the weather, and with delicacy and restraint reinterprets it to display the principles of the gospel.

BIBLIOGRAPHY. A. B. Cook, *Zeus*, 1914–40; W. K. C. Guthrie, *The Greeks and their Gods*, 1950.

E.A.J.

ZIBA (Heb. *ṣîḇā'*, *ṣiḇā'*, 'a post'). A servant of Saul (2 Sa. 9:2) who introduced Mephibosheth to David when he desired to honour Jonathan's memory. When Mephibosheth was given a place at court, Ziba was appointed steward of Saul's estates bestowed on Mephibosheth (2 Sa. 9). When David was driven out by Absalom's rebellion Ziba brought him food and also falsely accused Mephibosheth of deserting the king. David accepted his story, did not ascertain the other side, and gave the property to Ziba (2 Sa. 16:1–4). On David's return, Ziba hastened to meet him (2 Sa. 19:7), but later his treachery was revealed. David, in a difficult position, divided the property between them, and Mephibosheth was seemingly content (2 Sa. 19:24–30).

J.G.G.N.

ZIKLAG. Ziklag appears in Jos. 15:31 as being near the Edomite boundary, in the S of Judah. It was apportioned to the Simeonites, but later fell into Philistine hands. David, when a Philistine vassal, ruled it and was later able to retain and incorporate it in his own realm. It remained in the hands of Judah in both pre-exilic and post-exilic times. At least four locations have been proposed, of which Tell al-Shari'a (Tel Sera'), *c.* 25 km SE of Gaza, seems the most probable.

D.F.P.

ZILPAH. The handmaid of Jacob's first wife Leah, given to Leah by her father Laban (Gn. 29:24). Leah later gave her to Jacob as a concubine, and she bore him Gad and Asher.

J.D.D.

ZIMRAN (Heb. *zimrān*, meaning uncertain). Possibly derives from *zimrâ*, 'song, fame', thus 'the celebrated one', *i.e.* in song or fame. Alternatively, it may derive from *zemer*, 'mountain-sheep or goat'. A son of Abraham by the concubine Keturah (Gn. 25:2; 1 Ch. 1:32).

J.D.D.

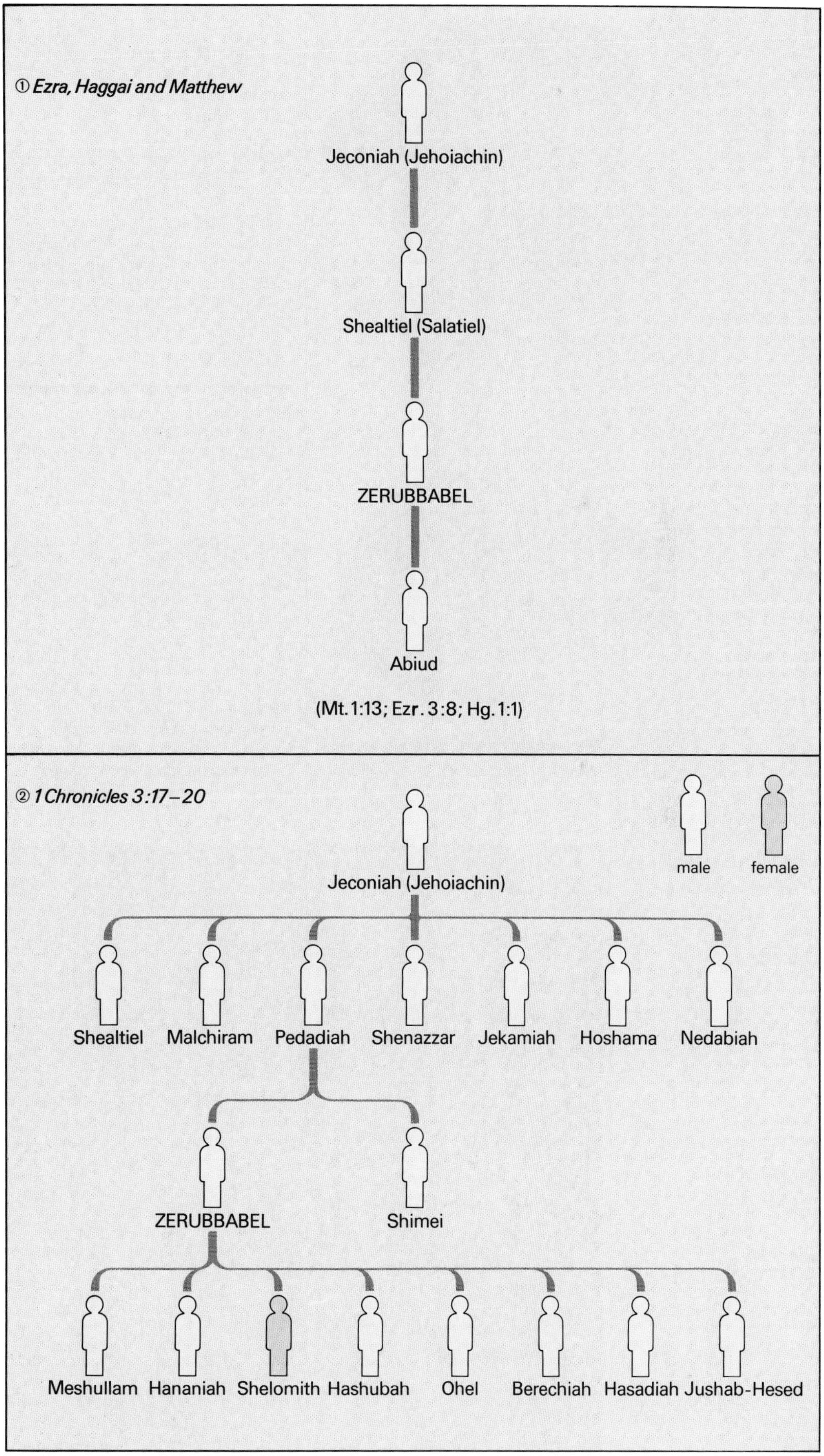

Jar-handle from Ziph bearing a seal-impression with the word lmlk, *'Belonging to the king', and the name of the town* (zp). *Late 7th cent.* BC. (BM)

ZIMRI (Heb. *zimrî*). **1.** A Simeonite prince (Nu. 25:6–15) who was put to death by Phinehas, the grandson of Aaron, for his audacious wickedness in bringing a Midianitess into the camp in contempt of the general spirit of penitence among the Israelites for the apostasy of *Baal-peor.

2. King of Israel *c.* 876 BC (1 Ki. 16:9–20). He reigned in Tirzah for only a week following his assassination of Elah in fulfilment of the prophecy against the dynasty of Baasha (1 Ki. 16:1–4). He lacked popular support, the majority following Omri, who immediately laid siege to Tirzah. When the city fell, Zimri burnt down the palace over his own head. J.C.J.W.

ZIN (Heb. *ṣin*). A name loosely applied to the Wilderness of Zin traversed by the Israelites in the Exodus, close to the borders of Canaan (Nu. 13:21). It refers to the extensive area between the camping-place of the Israelites at the oasis of Kadesh-barnea in NE Sinai, to the Ascent of Aqrabbim or Scorpion Pass constituting the limit between Edom and Judah (Jos. 15:1–4; *cf.* Nu. 34:1–5). The wilderness of Paran lay to the S of it, though Kadesh appears to have been included in both territories, and the two wildernesses occur within the broader term *'Negeb'.

BIBLIOGRAPHY. C. L. Woolley and T. E. Lawrence, *The Wilderness of Zin*, 1936. J.M.H.

Opposite page: The great temple enclosure at Tanis (Egypt). The city is identified with the biblical Zoan.

ZIONISM
See Promised land, Part 3.

ZIW
See Calendar, Part 1.

A wadi (Zin) in the wilderness of Zin, part of the desert of the Negeb. (PP)

ZIOR. A city listed in Jos. 15:54 in the Judaean hill-country NE of Hebron and allocated to the tribe of Judah; modern Si'ir (*ZAIR). J.D.D.

ZIPH. 1. A town in S Judah, near the Edomite boundary (Jos. 15:24), perhaps to be located at al-Zaifa. **2.** A town in the hill-country of Judah (Jos. 15:55), associated with David and with Rehoboam, who fortified it. It is identified with Tell Zif, 7 km SE of Hebron. Named on royal jar-handle stamps found at *Lachish and other sites, which probably points to its importance as a major Judaean administrative centre in the reign of Hezekiah. The adjoining area was known as the Wilderness of Ziph. **3.** A man of Judah (1 Ch. 4:16). D.F.P.

ZIPPOR (Heb. *ṣippôr*, *ṣippōr*, 'little bird', perhaps 'sparrow'). Father of Balak, the Moabite king who suborned Balaam to curse Israel (Nu. 22:2, 4, 10, 16; 23:18; Jos. 24:9; Jdg. 11:25). Some think the name implies totemistic associations. J.G.G.N.

ZIPPORAH. Daughter of Jethro priest of Midian and wife of *Moses. She apparently opposed the circumcision of their second son Gershom, but felt compelled to perform the duty herself when Moses' life was endangered because of its omission (Ex. 4:24–26). M.A.M.

ZIZ. The name of an ascent used by the Moabites and Ammonites in a campaign against Jehoshaphat of Judah (2 Ch. 20:16). Their army lay previously at Engedi, on the W shore of the Dead Sea; and they reached the wilderness of Tekoa. These details make the Wadi Hasasa, just N of Engedi, a virtually certain identification. D.F.P.

ZOAN. Ancient city, Egyp. *ḏ'n(t)* to which Heb. *ṣō'an* exactly corresponds. The Gk. Tanis and modern site of Ṣan el-Ḥagar near the S shore of Lake Menzaleh in NE Delta. The curious note in Nu. 13:22 that Hebron was built 7 years before Zoan in Egypt may indicate a refounding of Zoan in the Middle Kingdom (*c.* 2000–1800 BC); or

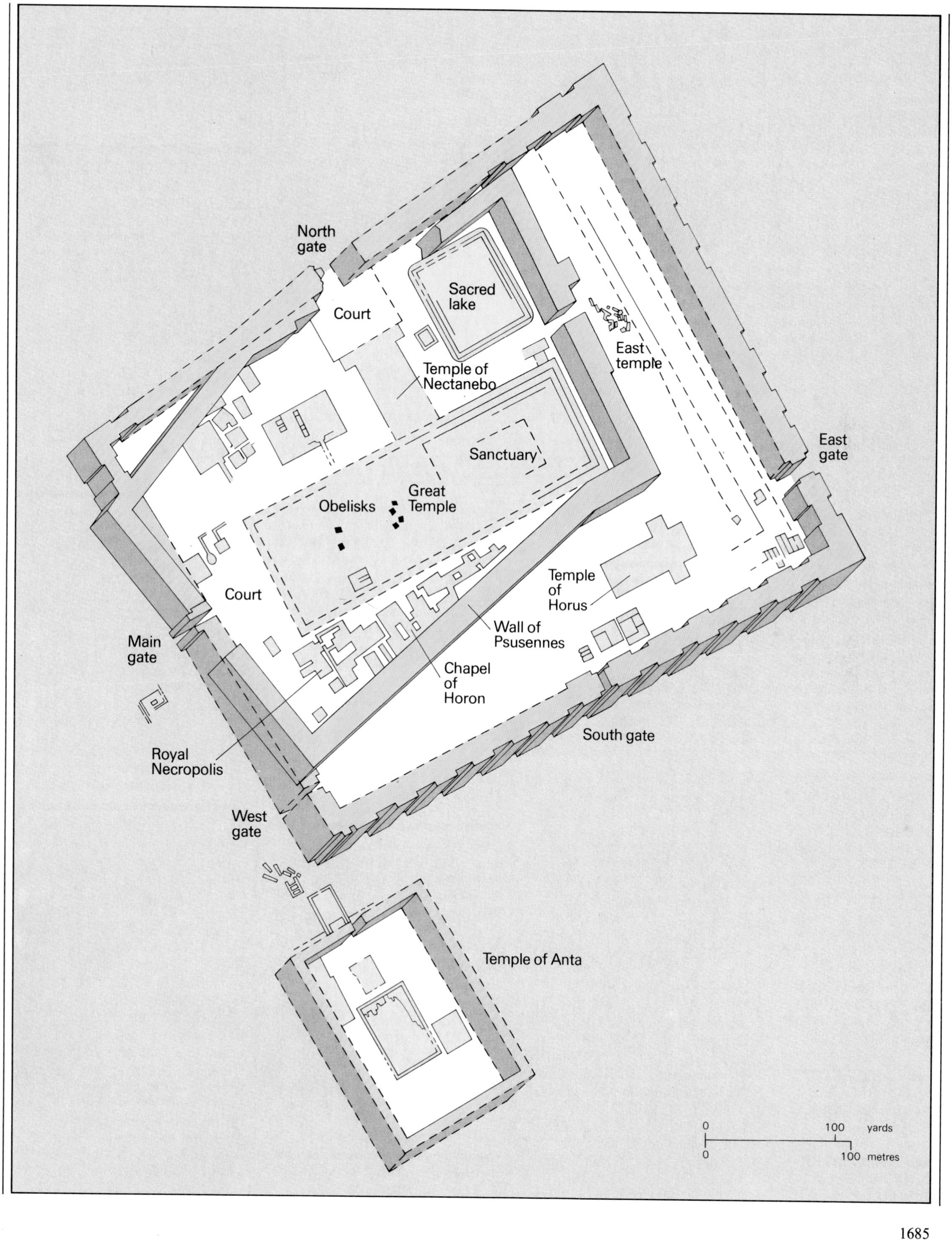
North gate
Court
Sacred lake
Temple of Nectanebo
East temple
East gate
Sanctuary
Great Temple
Obelisks
Court
Temple of Horus
Wall of Psusennes
Main gate
Chapel of Horon
Royal Necropolis
South gate
West gate
Temple of Anta
0 100 yards
0 100 metres

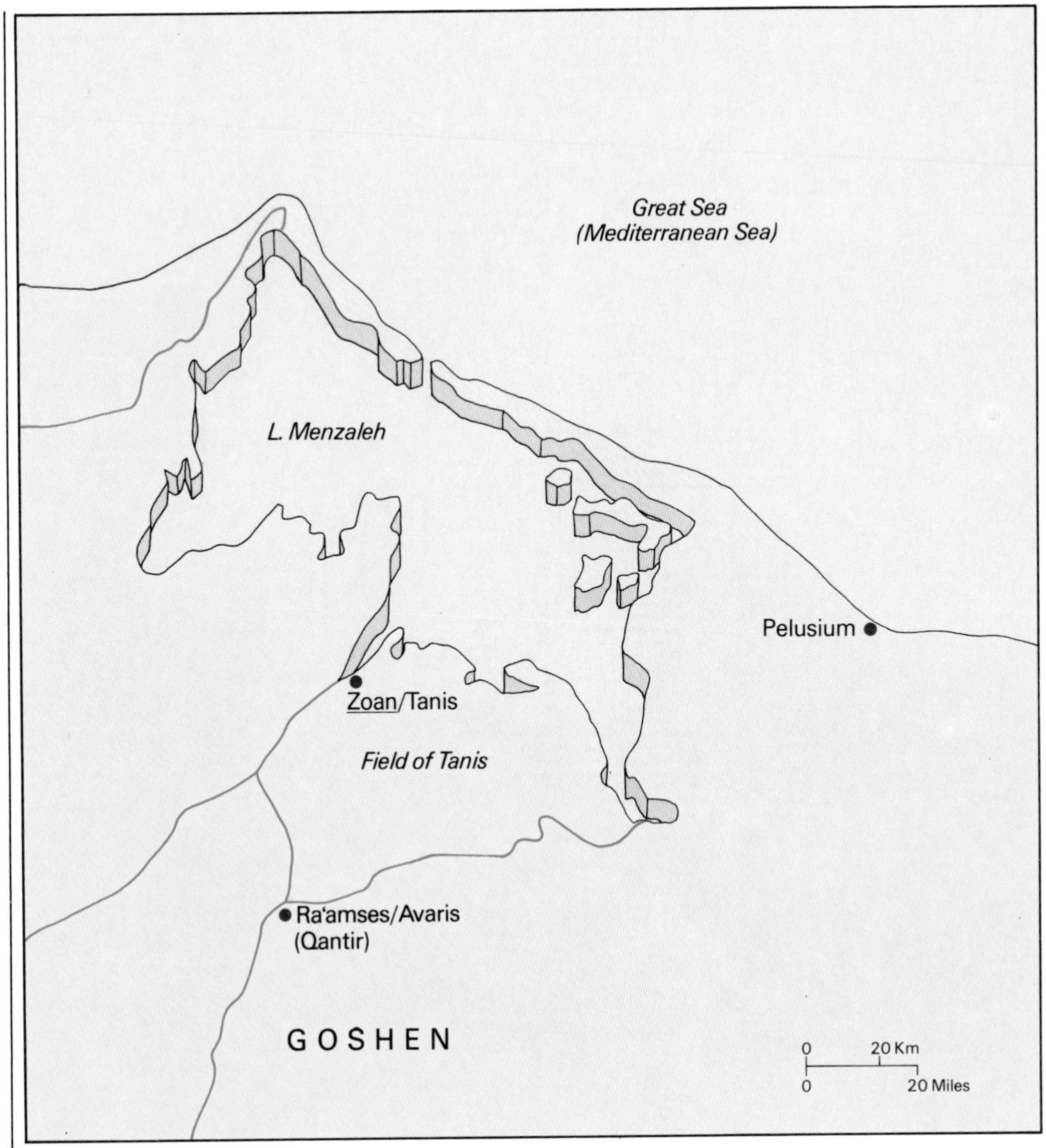

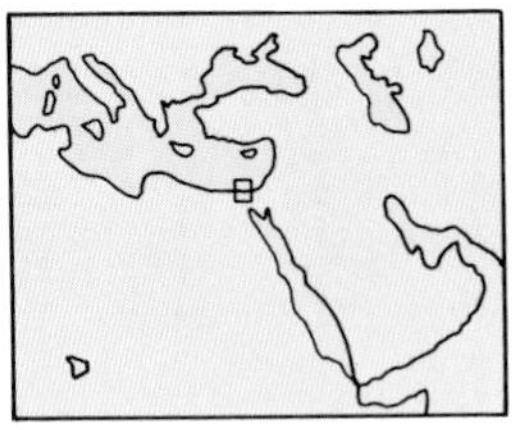

Zoan in Egypt.

more probably by the Hyksos kings in the 16th century BC, whose N capital Avaris Zoan may possibly be. For the era of Tanis, see *Chronology of the Old Testament, **III.** *b*. Ps. 78:12, 43 places the Exodus miracles in 'the field of Zoan', precisely the Egyp. *sḫt ḏ'(nt)*, 'field of Dja'(ne)', a term apparently applied to the region near Zoan; the possible identity of Zoan and *Ra'amses is now unlikely. From 1100 BC until about 660 BC, Zoan was the effective capital of Egypt in the 21st to 23rd Dynasties, and the N base of the Ethiopian 25th Dynasty. Hence the prominence of Zoan as the seat of pharaoh's counsellors and princes (Is. 19:11, 13; 30:4) and among Egypt's great cities in Ezekiel's (30:14) word of judgment. On Zoan/Tanis, see A. H. Gardiner, *Ancient Egyptian Onomastica*, 2, 1947, pp. 199*–201*, and P. Montet, *Les Énigmes de Tanis*, 1952; H. Kees, *Tanis*, 1964. K.A.K.

ZOAR
See Plain, cities of the, Part 3.

ZOHELETH, STONE OF
See Serpent's stone, Part 3.

ZOROASTER
See Persia, Part 3.

ZOBAH. An Aramaean kingdom which flourished during the early Heb. Monarchy, and which took the field against Saul and David. One of its kings was Hadadezer (2 Sa. 8:3). It lay between Hamath, to its N, and Damascus to its S, and at its height its influence reached these cities. It is unnecessary to postulate two Zobahs, one of them S of Damascus, merely because it is listed with Beth-rehob and Maacah in 2 Sa. 10:6 (both S of Damascus).

BIBLIOGRAPHY. J. Bright, *A History of Israel*², 1972, pp. 198–200. D.F.P.

ZOPHAR. The third of the friends of *Job was Zophar the Naamathite (Jb. 2:11). We have no knowledge where his home was, except that it was presumably E of Jordan. He is distinguished by the brutality of his commonsense position. He speaks in chs. 11, 20, and possibly in 27:13–23. H.L.E.

ZOPHIM. This place-name comes from Heb. *ṣōp̄îm*, 'watchers'. The location of 'the field of the watchers' (Nu. 23:14, AV) is difficult to determine. It must have been on a high part of the Pisgah Mts, from which Balaam could see the encampment of the Israelites at Shittim. Some propose to take the Heb. *śāḏeh* here in the meaning of the Akkad. *šâdû*, 'mountain' ('the mountain of the watchers'). The word 'watcher' is sometimes used in the sense of prophet (*cf.* Is. 52:8; 56:10) and is thus especially applicable to Balaam (*cf.* Ramathaim-zophim; Ramah, 1 Sa. 1:1). F.C.F.

ZORAH. A town in the lowlands of Judah (Jos. 15:33), closely connected with the Samson stories. Its site is Ṣar'a, on the N side of the Wadi al-Ṣarar, the biblical valley of Sorek. The Tell el-Amarna letters refer to it as Zarkha. It was fortified by Rehoboam (2 Ch. 11:10) and reoccupied after the Babylonian Exile (Ne. 11:29). The references to Hebron and Beersheba in these two passages, however, may suggest that there was another similarly named city a considerable distance S of Samson's territory. D.F.P.

ZUZIM (Heb. *zûzîm*; Gk. *ethnē ischyra*, 'strong peoples'). A people, conquered by Chedorlaomer, whose territory lay E of Jordan (Gn. 14:5). Their principal city, Ham, is probably to be identified with the modern village of the same name NE of the Gilboa Mts in N Jordan. Tristram (*Moab*, pp. 182ff.) and others, however, have sought to identify them with the Moabite village of Ziza, between Bozra and Lejūn. Because the Zuzim are mentioned in parallel with the Rephaim and Emim, it may be that it is descriptive of the inhabitants (so LXX) rather than a tribal name. For this reason some equate them with *Zamzummim who are identified with, or described as, Rephaim (Dt. 2:20), whose territory was later overrun by Ammonites. D.J.W.

Acknowledgments

Acknowledgment of the sources of illustrations

The publishers have made every effort to trace the copyright holders of illustrations in this book. Should any have been inadvertently missed, copyright holders are asked to contact the publishers.

Diagrams, charts, line drawings and town plans

All diagrams, charts, line drawings and town plans in **The Illustrated Bible Dictionary** have been specially prepared for this work. The publishers are glad to acknowledge their indebtedness to a variety of sources as indicated below.
In acknowledging the source, 'After' indicates that the material remains essentially as it appears in the source acknowledged but has been redrawn. 'Based on' means that the substance of the source material has been retained but reinterpreted.
For abbreviations see pp.xii-xvi.

PERGA, p.1192
Based on *ACA*, p.216.

PERGAMUM, p.1193
Based on *ACA*, p.206.

PERSIA, p.1196 (Plan)
Based on J. Hawkes, *Atlas of Ancient Archaeology* (William Heinemann, 1974), p.192.

PERSIA, p.1197 (Rulers)
Based on E. Porada, *The art of Ancient Iran* (Holle Verlag, Baden-Baden, 1965), p.256.

PHILIPPI, p.1214
Based on *ACA*, p.176.

PILLAR, p.1233
After *PEQ*, 109 (1977), p.48, figs. 6:1 and 6:2.

PTOLEMY, p.1302
Based on *CAH*, vol.7, table 3.

QUMRAN, p.1310
Based on R. de Vaux, *Archaeology and the Dead Sea Scrolls* (Oxford University Press, 1973), pl.39.

RABBAH, p.1315
Based on *EAEHL*, vol.4, p.990.

ROME, p.1350
Based on T. G. Tucker, *Life in the Roman World* (Macmillan), fig.17.

SACRIFICE AND OFFERING, pp.1363-5
Based on A. R. S. Kennedy, *Leviticus and Numbers, CB*, 1910, p.349.

SALAMIS, p.1369
Based on *ACA*, p.187.

SALT, CITY OF, p.1371
Based on R. de Vaux, *Archaeology and the Dead Sea Scrolls* (Oxford University Press, 1973), pl.3.

SAMARIA, p.1377
Based on *IDB*, vol.4, p.182 and W. G. Dever and S. M. Paul, *Biblical Archaeology* (Keter Publishing House, Jerusalem, 1973), p.22.

SAMOTHRACE, p.1382
Based on *ACA*, p.179.

SANCTUARY, p.1389
Based on *EAEHL*, vol.3, p.833.

SARDIS, p.1393
Based on J. Hawkes, *Atlas of Ancient Archaeology* (William Heinemann, 1974), p.144 and C. H. Greenwalt, *BASOR* 233, 1979, p.2.

SARGON, p.1395
Based on A. Parrot, *Nineveh and Babylon* (Thames and Hudson, 1961), p.10.

SEPULCHRE OF THE KINGS, p.1416
Based on *Atlas of Jerusalem* (Jewish History Publications, 1973), map 3:2 and Y. Yadin (ed.), *Jerusalem Revealed* (Israel Exploration Society and Yale University Press, 1976), pp.5 and 64.

SHARON, p.1428.
Based on Y. Karmon, *Israel; a regional geography* (John Wiley and Sons Ltd, 1971), p.17.

SHECHEM, p.1432 (Plan)
Based on *EAEHL*, vol.4, p.1083.

SHECHEM, p.1433 (Reconstruction)
After material provided by C. J. Davey.

SHECHEM, p.1433 (Plan)
Based on G. E. Wright, *Shechem* (Gerald Duckworth, 1964), fig.41.

SIDON, p.1449
Based on A. Poidebard and J. Lauffray, *Sidon aménagements antiques du port de Saida* (République Libanaise, Ministère des travaux publiques, Beyrouth, 1951), p.3, fig.1.

SILOAM, p.1452
Based on Y. Yadin (ed.), *Jerusalem Revealed* (The Israel Exploration Society, Jerusalem and Yale University Press, 1976), p.76.

SOLOMON, p.1470
Based on *IDB*, vol.2, p.657.

SPINNING AND WEAVING, p.1478
After C. Singer, E. J. Holmyard and A. R. Hall (eds.), *A History of Technology* (Oxford University Press, 1954), vol.1, p.433, fig.273.

SUSA, p.1496
Based on J. Hawkes, *Atlas of Ancient Archaeology* (William Heinemann, 1974), p.194.

SYNAGOGUE, p.1500
After E. M. and C. L. Meyers and J. F. Strange, *AASOR*, vol.43, p.87.

SYRACUSE, p.1504
Based on *ACA*, p.82.

TAANACH, p.1507
Based on *EAEHL*, vol.4, p.1140.

TEMPLE, p.1530
Based on information from J. Wilkinson, *Jerusalem as Jesus knew it* (Thames and Hudson, 1978), pp.71 and 84.

THEBES, p.1554 (Tombs)
Based on L. V. Grinsell, *Barrow, Pyramid and Tomb* (Thames and Hudson, 1975), p.134.

THEBES, p.1555 (Site)
Based on J. Hawkes, *Atlas of Ancient Archaeology* (William Heinemann, 1974), p.155.

TIRZAH, p.1573
Based on *EAEHL*, vol.2, p.398.

TRAVEL, p.1582
Based on C. Singer, E. J. Holmyard, A. R. Hall and T. I. Williams (eds.), *A History of Technology* (Oxford University Press, 1957), vol.2, p.503.

UGARIT, p.1607
Based on *IDBS*, p.929.

UR, p.1613
Based on J. Hawkes, *Atlas of Ancient Archaeology* (William Heinemann, 1974), p.173.

UZZIAH, p.1616
Based on B. Rothenberg *et al.*, *God's Wilderness* (Thames and Hudson, 1961), p.123.

WATER, p.1633
Based on W. G. Dever and S. M. Paul, *Biblical Archaeology* (Keter Publishing House, Jerusalem, 1973), p.132, fig.b.

WRITING, pp.1660-1
After information provided by A. R. Millard.

ZAREPHATH, p.1673
After J. B. Pritchard, *Recovering Sarepta, a Phoenician city* (Princeton University Press, 1978), p.103, fig.102.

ZEALOT, p.1675
Based on *EAEHL*, vol.3, p.795.

ZOAN, p.1685
Based on J. Hawkes, *Atlas of Ancient Archaeology* (William Heinemann, 1974), p.158.

Photographs

The photographs in **The Illustrated Bible Dictionary** are reproduced by permission of the following persons or agencies. The initials provide a cross-reference from the captions. The numbers in the list are page references to the text.

AMM
A. M. Morris, p.1244.

AN
A. Northedge, p.1315.

AP
A. Parrot, p.1559.

ARM
A. R. Millard, pp.1232, 1406, 1416, 1495, 1520, 1608.

BAV
Biblioteca Apostolica Vaticana, p.1206.

BL
Reproduced by permission of the British Library
Hebrew MSS=Or 4445, f. 106a, p.1182.
Cott. Claud B VIII (page indicating Dt. 4:32-40), p.1380.
Royal I.O. VIII, f. 4lv, p.1545.

BM
Reproduced by Courtesy of the Trustees of the British Museum, pp.1156, 1179, 1195, 1197, 1198, 1225, 1229, 1249(2), 1250, 1252(2), 1253(3), 1257, 1273, 1291, 1304, 1309, 1312, 1315, 1344, 1359, 1364, 1398, 1401, 1402, 1403, 1406, 1407(2), 1408(3), 1409(4), 1411, 1415, 1427, 1431, 1437, 1440, 1441, 1444(2), 1451, 1468, 1469, 1479, 1488(2), 1493, 1505, 1534, 1535, 1557, 1560, 1562, 1564, 1565, 1571, 1584, 1591, 1596, 1604, 1609, 1610, 1611(2), 1612, 1621(2), 1623(3), 1624, 1630, 1636(2), 1637, 1648, 1662, 1663(2), 1664, 1666, 1667(3), 1670, 1679, 1684.

BrM
Courtesy of The Brooklyn Museum
(218) Charles Edwin Wilbour Fund, p.1420.
(273) Gift of Miss Theodora Wilbour, p.1465.

BSAI
British School of Archaeology in Iraq, p.1498.

CBL
Chester Beatty Library, pp.1218, 1337, 1347, 1547, 1557, 1669.

DAA
Department of Antiquities, Amman, p.1314.

DJW
D. J. Wiseman, pp.1243, 1343, 1390, 1404, 1407, 1495, 1628, 1641, 1668(2), 1669.

DM
Damascus Museum, p.1668.

DWG
D. W. Gooding, p.1508.

ELS
From *Megillot Genuzot* by E. L. Sukenik (Jerusalem, 1948), plate 10. Published by Mosad Bialik, Jerusalem, p.1296.

FNH
F. N. Hepper, pp.1236(2), 1239(4), 1240(3), 1241(4), 1242(3), 1246, 1443, 1586(2), 1587(2), 1588(2), 1589(3), 1590(3), 1592, 1618(2), 1619(2), 1629.

GHG
From Gesenius' *Hebrew Grammar,* ed. E. Kautzsch and A. E. Cowley (Clarendon Press, Oxford, 1910, reprinted 1956) after p.x, p.1453.

GW
G. Wenham, p.1572.

HC
The Holyland Corporation.
Photo taken on the site of the reconstruction of Jerusalem at the time of the 2nd Temple (or Herod's time) in the grounds of the Holyland Hotel, Jerusalem, Israel, p.1630.

HW
H. Williamson, p.1453.

IA
Institute of Archaeology. By permission of the Wellcome Trust, p.1670.

IM
Israel Museum, pp.1220, 1221, 1248, 1375, 1378, 1421, 1528, 1531, 1615, 1620.

IsM
Istambul Museum, pp.1528, 1529.

JCL
J. C. Lennox, p.1365.

JDH
J. D. Hawkins, pp.1248, 1662.

JGM
J. G. McMillan, p.1159.

JPK
J. P. Kane, pp.1246, 1500, 1501(2), 1503, 1630.

JR
John Rylands Library, p.1542.

KAK
K. A. Kitchen, pp.1305(2), 1521.

MAIC
Missione Archeologica Italiana a Cesarea, p.1229.

MC
Maurice Chuzeville/Louvre Museum, pp.1164, 1275, 1363, 1422, 1440, 1447, 1477, 1497, 1513, 1606(3), 1608, 1635, 1641, 1642, 1664, 1665.

MELM
From *Nimrud and its Remains* by M. E. L. Mallowan (Collins), 2 vols, p.1426.

MEPhA
Middle East Photographic Archive, London, pp.1303, 1308, 1311, 1379, 1432, 1453, 1497, 1499, 1553, 1563(2), 1601, 1644.

MetNY
Metropolitan Museum of Art, New York.
Photography by the Egyptian Expedition, p.1274.
'Rogers Fund' 1933, p.1477.
Anonymous Gift, 1930, p.1478.
54.3.1 ANE Metalwork-Gold—Iranian Bowl of Darius I or II, p.1620.

MFAB
From Giza, Egypt. 38.873, No Fund. Courtesy, Museum of Fine Arts, Boston, p.1509.

MH
M. Holford, pp.1425, 1442, 1443, 1596.

MNAC
Museum of National Antiquities, Cairo, p.1567.

MPSLA
Matson Photo Service, Los Angeles, p.1526.

NDGD
From *The Tomb of Nakht at Thebes* by Norman D. G. Davies (New York, 1917), plate 26. Published by the Metropolitan Museum of Art, New York, pp.1265, 1467, 1648.

NMMH
The National Maritime Museum Haifa, p.1440.

OIUC
Oriental Institute, University of Chicago, pp.1221, 1324, 1489, 1560.

PAC
P. A. Clayton, pp.1220, 1403, 1420, 1446, 1451, 1494, 1584.

PM
P. Matthiae.
Missione Archeologica Italiana in Siria, p.1659.

PP
Picturepoint, London, pp.1193, 1215, 1369, 1467, 1504, 1684.

RG
Ray Gardner, pp.1156, 1214, 1305, 1412, 1495, 1536, 1563, 1604.

RH
Robert Harding Picture Library, pp.1190, 1191, 1340, 1553.

RM
Rockefeller Museum, p.1354.

RP
R. Pitt, p.1674.

RS
Ronald Sheridan's Photo-Library, pp.1195, 1208, 1259, 1307, 1309, 1311, 1343, 1357, 1371, 1381, 1438, 1441, 1445, 1460, 1475, 1512(2), 1513, 1527, 1528/9, 1617, 1618.

RVO
Courtesy of Rijksmuseum van Oudheden, Leiden, Netherlands, p.1649.

SAOB
The State Antiquities Organisation, Baghdad, pp.1439, 1653, 1664.

SH
Sonia Halliday Photographs, pp.1211, 1227, 1230, 1254, 1392, 1452, 1518, 1534, 1582.

SI
Foto Scala Firenze, Italy, pp.1558, 1635.

SMB
Staatliche Museen zu Berlin/DDR Ägyptisches Museum, p.1387.

TAU
Institute of Archaeology, Tel-Aviv University/Avraham Hay, p.1640.

TCM
T. C. Mitchell, p.1497.

UMUP
Reproduced by permission of The University Museum, University of Pennsylvania, pp.1421, 1566, 1640.

VI
Vision International, p.1351.
(407) Photo Paolo Koch, p.1588.

WM
W. MacQuitty, pp.1314, 1405.

YY
From *Hazor* by Yigael Yadin (Weidenfeld and Nicolson, 1975), p.216, pp.1181, 1446, 1490.

ZR
Zev Radovan, p.1232.

Index

Alphabetical order

The index has been arranged on a letter-by-letter basis, not word-by-word. Explanatory words, placed in brackets, have been ignored, but 'and' and 'the' are included in the letter-by-letter classification, for example:

Adam
Adam (place)
Adamah
Adam and Christ
Adam and Eve

Maps, diagrams and photographs

There is no separate index of maps, diagrams and photographs, but references are distinguished by the use of different styles of type, divided by semi-colons.

References in bold roman type indicate an article under that title.

References in ordinary roman type indicate significant appearances of the word(s) in the body of the Dictionary.

References in bold italic type indicate maps and serve as a gazetteer.

References in ordinary italic type indicate diagrams, charts, line drawings or photographs.

An abbreviated key appears at the head of each page.

Asterisks

Asterisks mean 'see' or 'see also', referring the reader to other index entries.

Compilation

The index was compiled under the direction of the Rev. Norman Hillyer with the assistance of a large team of helpers.

A

Aalders, G. Ch. 1185, 1187
Aaron **1;** 225f., 330, 631, 660, 674, 889, 944, 1013, 1447; *1028*
Aaron's descendants 546, 1266ff.
Aaron's rod **1f.;** 934, 1344; *1*
Ab ***Calendar**
Abacus 1226
Abaddon **2;** 1436
Abana R. **2;** 355; ***2, 355f.;*** *2*
Abarim **2**
Abba **3;** 774, 910, 1546
Abda 1106
Abdon **3**
Abednego **3**
Abel (location) **3**
Abel (person) **3;** 10, 1358, 1677
Abel-Beth-maacah ***Abel of Beth-maacah**
Abel-keramim 3
Abel-maim 3
Abel-meholah **3;** 441; ***443***
Abel-mizraim 3
Abel of Beth-maacah **3;** 925; ***2, 1180***
Abel-shittim 1446; ***860***
Aber 626
Abi-albon ***Abiel**
Abiathar **3;** 49
Abiel **3**
Abiesdri 977
Abiezer **3f.**
Abigail (sister of David) **4;** 1048
Abigail (widow of Nabal) **4;** *367*
Abihail **4**
Abihu **4;** *1028*
Abijah, Abijam (king of Judah) **4;** 187, 464, 824, 925, 1308; *273, 857*
Abijah (others) **4**
Abilene **4;** 102; *1536*
Abimael 806
Abimelech (Philistine kings) **4;** 6, 552
Abimelech (son of Gideon) **4;** 154, 531, 955, 1370, 1433, 1554; *836*
Abimilki *1604*
Abinadab *761, 1398*
Abinoam 175
Abiram (son of Eliab) **4;** *1332*
Abiram (son of Hiel) **4**
Abishag **4f.;** 179, 1473
Abishai **5;** 41, 735, 789
Abishalom ***Absalom**
Abishur 4
Abital *367*
Abitub 675
Abner **5;** 128, 366, 634, 789, 936, 1244
Abomination **5;** 657, 680
Abomination of desolation ***Desolating sacrilege**
Abraham **5ff.;** 4, 20, 33, 43, 163, 181ff., 231, 269f., 288f., 328, 356, 419, 435ff., 440, 464, 496, 500f., 506, 536, 549, 599, 626, 654f., 658, 691f., 697f., 730, 810, 844, 915f., 940, 957, 986f., 1019f., 1025, 1051, 1094, 1160ff., 1262, 1359; *7, 271*
Abraham, Apocalypse of 74
Abraham's bosom **8;** 51 ***Lazarus and Dives**
Abram 5, 46, 187, 976f., 1051, 1162, 1485 ***Abraham**
Abrech **8**
Absalom (son of David) **8;** 26f., 39, 154, 366, 554, 600, 789, 1063, 1232; *367*
Absalom (others) **8**
Absolution 1255f.
Abuse 201
Abyss **8f.;** 1410
Abyssinia 484
Acacia **1585;** *1587*
Acanthus 122
Accad, Akkad **9;** 154, 162, 1088; ***9, 1565;*** *9*
Accadian ***Akkadian**
Acceptance **9f.**
Access to God **10;** 17, 972
Accho ***Acco**
Accidents 331
Acco, Accho 98, 1303, 1578; ***1579*** ***Ptolemais**
Accusation 1495
Accuser ***Satan**
Aceldama ***Akeldama**
Achaemenes *1197*
Achaemenids 166; *1197*
Achaia **10f.;** 12, 147, 282f., 302, 313, 592, 921, 1076, 1294, 1345; ***10, 592;*** *314*
Achaicus **11;** 318
Achan **11;** 171, 211, 349, 500
Achar ***Achan**
Achish **11;** 28, 542f., 925, 1221
Achmetha ***Ecbatana**
Achor **11;** ***10***
Achsah **11;** 956
Achshaph **11**
Achzib **11**
Acre 1637
Acre (location) ***Acco** ***Ptolemais**
Acrocorinth 313
Acropolis 108; *108, 146*
Acrostic 414, 869, 1245, 1291, 1652, 1668
Actian games 1085
Actium 642
Acts and Galatians 1168f.
Acts, Apocryphal ***NT Apocrypha**
Acts, Book of the **11ff.;** 243f., 919f., 1168f., 1351; *280f.*
Acts of Andrew 243
Acts of John 243, 1083
Acts of Paul 243, 1083, 1303
Acts of Peter 1083, 1455
Adad 168, 947
Adad-nirari III 184, 258, 356, 752, 790, 970
Adah **14;** 177, 398
Adaiah ***Iddo**
Adam (location) **14;** ***811***
Adam (person) **14ff.;** 374, 471ff.
Adamah **16**
Adam and Christ 15f., 988, 1107, 1457ff., 1603
Adam and Eve 15, 1299
Adamant ***Jewels**
Adam, Apocalypse of 567, 1084
Adami-nekeb **16**
Adar ***Calendar**

B

Baal **153;** 24, 94, 166, 171, 218, 226, 234, 253, 382, 423, 559f., 597, 680, 709, 788f., 833, 862, 967, 980, 1225; *153*
Baalah 185, 860
Baal-berith **153f.;** 1433
Baale-judah 860
Baal-gad **154;** 218, 641, 810
Baal-Hazor **154**
Baal-hermon 641
Baali ***Ishi**
Baalis 42, 545, 706
Baal-melqart 253, 440f., 1018, 1375
Baal-meon **154;** 1017
Baal of Hadad 92
Baal of Tyre 140
Baal-peor ***Peor**
Baal, prophets of 253
Baal-shalishah 1426
Baal-worship 711
Baal-zebub, Beelzebul **154**
Baal-zephon **154**
Baanah 675
Baasha **154;** 26, 184, 432, 711, 720; *273, 857*
Babel **154ff.;** *155ff.*
Babylon **157ff.;** 183, 352, 361, 605, 652, 1198; ***9, 164, 1198;*** *158ff., 353, 981*
Babylon as name for Rome 162, 1202
Babylon, church at 1202
Babylonia **162ff.;** 1355; ***9, 142;*** *passim esp. 165ff., 252, 271ff.*
Babylonian Chronicle 169; *167, 759*
Babylonian creation myths 335
Babylonian crown 345
Babylonian flood story 511; *513*
Babylonian Job 144, 1607
Babylonian language 1607, 1666
Babylonian Talmud 1515f.
Babylon, Jews in 389
Baca, valley of **170**
Bacchides 193
Bachelor ***Marriage**
Bactrian camel 53, 228; *229*
Badge 520
Badgers' skins **170**
Bag **170**
Bagpipe ***Music**
Bahurim **170**
Baker 814
Balaam **170f.;** 36f., 50ff., 171, 933, 935, 986
Baladan ***Merodach-baladan**
Balak **171;** 170
Balawat 144
Bald locust 65
Baldness 211, 442, 601
Balih R. ***passim esp. 609***
Balm **637**
Balm of Gilead 639
Balsam tree 1592
Balthasar, Baltasar 183
Bamah, Bamoth, Bamoth-Baal **171**
Ban **171;** 48, 332, 897, 1629
Band ***Army**
Bani 439, 1055
Bank ***Fortification**
Bank, banker **171;** 1023, 1577
Banner **171f.;** *172, 1421*
Banquet **172;** 476, 967f.; *172*
Baptism **172ff.;** 313, 502, 590, 763, 889, 1205, 1325, 1357, 1410f., 1632
Baptism in the Spirit 1482
Baptism of Jesus 173, 278, 763, 1423, 1598
Barabbas **175**
Barachel 440
Barachiah ***Zechariah**
Barada R. 355
Barak **175;** 116, 610, 726, 833, 836, 847, 984; *272*
Barbarian **175**
Barbary dove 63
Barbary sheep 57
Barber 600
Bar-Jesus **175;** 1286
Bar-Kokhba 373
Barley **590f.;** 20f., 206, 224f., 967, 1019, 1138, 1235; *514*
Barn **175**
Barnabas **175f.;** 70, 80, 102, 282, 284f., 302, 628, 952, 1454
Barnabas, Epistle of 176, 1166, 1603
Barnabas, Gospel of 176
Barrel 1621
Barrenness **176;** 1653
Barsabbas 830
Barter 1018
Bartholomew **176;** 1055
Bartimaeus **176**
Baruch **176f.;** *177*
Baruch, Apocalypse of 176, 1300
Baruch, Book of 74, 77, 176
Baruch, Rest of the Works of 176
Barzillai **177**
Basalt 1109, 1136
Basemath **177**
Bashan **177;** 1136; ***177***
Basilisk 64
Basin 1004, 1244
Basket **177ff.;** 1142, 1619; *178*
Bas-relief 120, 1125
Bat **60;** 68
Batanaea 177; ***1577***
Bath, bathing **179;** 101; *178*
Bathroom 672
Bathsheba **179;** 16, 1308, 1469; *367*
Bathshua 179; *822*
Battering-ram 106, 523, 525f.; *523*
Battle ***Fortification**
Battle-axe 115
Battle-cry 1629
Battlement ***Fortification**
Baur, F. C. 198, 1173ff.
Bay tree 1586
Bdellium **179;** 409
Beans 20, 22; *514*
Bear **58f.;** 674, 1485
Beard **179;** 211, 555, 638; *179*
Bearded vulture **61**
Beast **179f.;** 182, 409, 475, 993, 1338, 1450
Beast (Apocalyptic) **180**
Beating the air 542
Beatitudes 483, 1031, 1418f.
Bed 126, 672
Bedding 672
Bede, Venerable 446f.; *448*
Bee **66;** 515; *66*
Beelzebub, Beelzebul ***Baal-zebub**
Beer (drink) 513, 515, 517
Beer (location) **180**
Beer-lahai-roi **180**
Beersheba **180ff.;** 36, 96, 255, 387, 524, 572; ***368, 1133;*** *99, 180f.*
Beeshterah ***Ashtaroth**
Beetle 68
Beggar, begging 33
Behemoth **182;** 61
Beka (h) 1634; *1638*
Bel **182;** 161, 168
Bela ***Plain, cities of the**
Bel and the Dragon 76
Belial, Beliar **182;** 733
Belief ***Faith**
Believer 226, 389, 1575
Bell **182;** 1039; *183, 1032*
Bellows 126; *1003ff.*
Bel Marduk 1395
Beloved 778
Beloved disciple 804
Belsham, Thomas 455; *449*
Belshazzar **183;** 85, 160, 258, 360f., 935, 980; *183, 273, 981*
Belteshazzar **183**
Benaiah **183;** 109, 789
Ben-ammi **183;** *915*
Bene-berak **183f.**
Benedicite 76
Benediction 40, 589 ***Blessing**
Benedictus **184;** 676, 1275
Benefactor **184;** 852
Bene-jaakan **184**
Ben-geber 545
Ben-hadad I **184f.;** 1320; *273*
Ben-hadad II **184f.;** 1376; *184, 273*
Ben-hadad III **184f.;** *273*
Ben-hur ***Hur (others)**
Benjamin (son of Jacob) **185f.;** 27, 440, 501, 1043, 1051, 1353; *731*
Benjamin (tribe) **185f.;** 114f., 544, 546, 557f., 563, 615, 710, 751, 755, 997, 1013, 1166, 1594f.; ***709***
Benjamin gates 185
Benjaminites 27, 111, 185, 366, 834, 946, 1013 ***Benjamin (tribe)**
Benoni 1051
Ben-Sira (Sirach), Joshua 77, 361, 492, 873, 1378, 1404, 1540
Beon 154
Beor ***Balaam**
Beracah **186;** 741
Berea ***Beroea**
Berenice 1306; *643*
Beriah 87, 270, 410, 626
Berkeley version 456; *449*
Bernice **186;** 1064
Berodach-baladan ***Merodach-baladan**
Beroea, Berea **186;** 928
Beryl **783;** *785*
Berytus (Beirut) ***892***
Best man ***Friend of the bridegroom**

D

F

G

H

I

J

James ('The younger' or 'less', son of Alphaeus) 732; 208
James, Apocalypse of 1084
James, Apocryphon of 1084
James, Epistle of 732f.; 196, 243f., 254, 466, 888, 1655
Jamnia 238, 726, 1194, 1209
Jannes and Jambres 733f.
Janoah 734; *1180*
Janobah 463
Japheth 734f.; 392, 1056f.; *734, 1057*
Japhethites 970
Japhia (descendant of David) *367*
Japhia (king of Lachish) 865
Jar 1619, 1621 ***Pottery**
Jareb 735; 458
Jar-handle *558, 1409, 1469*
Jarmuth 735
Jashar, Book of 735
Jashobeam 735
Jason 735
Jason (high priest) 541
Jasper 781, 783; *785*
Jattir 735; 697
Javan 735f.; *1059;* *734*
Javelin 112f., 234
Jazer 736
Jealousy 736f.; 459, 955
Jealousy offering 591
Jeberechiah 1677
Jebusi 737
Jebusite 737; 93, 754f., 758, 852, 1453; *736*
Jeconiah *Jehoiachin
Jedaiah 633, 760
Jediael 185
Jeduthun, Jedithun 737; 545, 1268
Jehdeiah 984
Jehiel 925
Jehoahaz 737
Jehoahaz (Ahaz) 737; 25, 139; *737*
Jehoahaz (Ahaziah) 737; 26; *740*
Jehoahaz (son of Jehu) 737; 361
Jehoahaz (son of Josiah) 737; *273, 739, 1678*
Jehoash *Joash
Jehohanan 705, 794
Jehoiachin 737f.; 267, 277, 548, 744, 1274, 1409; *273, 439, 738f., 857, 1678, 1683*
Jehoiada (chief priest) 738; 20, 147, 264, 741, 790; *740*
Jehoiada (father of Benaiah) 738; 183
Jehoiada (son of Benaiah) 738; 27
Jehoiada (others) 738
Jehoiakim 738ff.; 165, 360, 425, 744, 1130, 1416; *739, 1678*
Jehonadab (son of Rechab) 741; 1321
Jehonadab (son of Shimeah) 740
Jehoram, Joram (king of Israel) 741; 276, 442, 546, 611, 742, 788f.; *273, 740, 1117*
Jehoram (king of Judah) 741; 85, 146, 411, 618, 620; *273, 740*
Jehoram (others) 741
Jehoshabeath, Jehosheba 741; 738, 790; *740*
Jehoshaphat (king of Judah) 741; 85, 434, 824, 1282; ***740, 851;*** *273, 740*
Jehoshaphat, valley of 741; 379, 850
Jehovah passim esp. 571ff.
Jehovah-jireh 573
Jehovah-nissi 172, 573
Jehovah-shalom 573
Jehovah-shammah 573
Jehovah-tsidkenu 573
Jehozerah 1409
Jehu (king of Israel) 742; 226, 402, 611, 711, 788f., 824, 1321, 1426; *273, 707, 742, 857, 1427*
Jehu (of Anathoth) 741; 49
Jehu (prophet) 741
Jehudi 742
Jekabzeel *Kabzeel
Jephthah 742f.; 834f., 852, 943, 1383
Jephunneh 222, 848
Jerah 743
Jerahmeel (ancestor of Jerahmeelites) 743; 222
Jerahmeel (son of Kish) 743
Jerahmeel ('the king's son') 743
Jerahmeelites 707, 743, 1048
Jerash *Gerasa
Jerboa 60
Jeremiah (prophet) 743ff.; 24, 77, 176, 215, 290, 394, 563, 607, 868, 871, 1019, 1258, 1280ff.; *273, 743, 1277*
Jeremiah, Book of 195, 746f., 859, 1144; *239*
Jeremiah, Epistle of 76f., 373, 874, 1147
Jeremiah, Paralipomena of 1299
Jeremoth 1054
Jericho 748ff.; 14, 20, 94, 100f., 104, 176, 275, 522f., 671f., 810, 1136, 1247; ***passim esp. 750;*** *26, 297, 525, 671, 748ff., 1130f.*
Jeroboam I (king of Israel) 751f.; 26, 649, 679f., 710, 1268, 1270; *273, 707, 857*
Jeroboam II (king of Israel) 752; 44, 139, 662f., 711, 1408; ***752;*** *273, 707, 753, 857*
Jerome 200, 246, 795, 1081, 1206, 1212, 1550
Jerubbaal, Jerubbesheth *Gideon
Jeruel 752
Jerusalem 752ff.; 11ff., 100, 185, 228, 276f., 293, 366, 492, 524, 531, 644, 651, 719, 737, 766f., 771, 1070ff., 1131, 1276, 1370, 1416f., 1452f.; ***passim esp. 8, 227, 295, 650, 754f., 765, 851, 1071, 1133, 1416, 1452;*** *227f., 292f., 650, 756ff., 851, 1073, 1308, 1452f., 1470f., 1526f., 1530*
Jerusalem above, New Jerusalem 296ff., 391, 754, 760, 1232
Jerusalem Bible 456; *449*
Jerusalem, church in 11, 284ff., 794, 1643
Jerusalem Council *Council of Jerusalem
Jerusalem, fall of (587 BC) 682, 743, 746, 755; *273*
Jerusalem, fall of (AD 70) 756, 816, 964; *281*
Jeshimon 760; 1141
Jeshua 760
Jeshurun 760; 735
Jesse 760f.; 1048; *367, 761*
Jesus, burial of 212, 767
Jesus Christ, Deity of *Incarnation
Jesus Christ, life and teaching of 761ff.; 277ff., 581, 854f., 1417ff., 1598, 1649; ***765;*** *227, 280f., 295*
Jesus Christ, titles of 771ff.
Jesus, in the name of 173
Jesus Justus *Justus
Jesus, language of 950
Jesus' ministry, length of 279
Jesus, name of 772, 777f., 1052
Jesus, Sayings of 1150
Jether 39, 721
Jethro, Reuel 780; 655, 848, 1027; *1028*
Jeû, books of 1084
Jeush 1109
Jew 780f.; 461, 627, 1258; *780* ***Judaism**
Jewels and precious stones 781ff.; 127, 179, 1020, 1577; *120, 207, 781ff., 1123f.*
Jewish apocalyptic 471
Jewish canon 238, 240; *239*
Jewish coinage *Money
Jewish exorcists 1272
Jewish War, History of 816
Jewry 780
Jews and Gentiles, relationship of 71, 218 ***Council of Jerusalem**
Jezaniah 788; 725
Jezebel ('prophetess') 788; 1008, 1287
Jezebel (wife of Ahab) 788; 24, 321f., 440f., 933; *788, 1117*
Jezreel (location) 788f.; 476f., 708ff.; ***443, 476, 789;*** *476, 789*
Jezreel (son of Hosea) 789; 663
Joab 789; 411, 525, 634, 661, 971, 1314
Joanna 789
Joash (Benjaminite warrior) 790
Joash (father of Gideon) 790; 559
Joash, Jehoash (king of Israel) 790; 39, 184, 192, 356, 442, 755; *273, 707, 790, 1117*
Joash, Jehoash (king of Judah) 790; 39, 42, 147, 738, 821, 824; *273, 740, 826*
Joash ('son of Ahab') 790
Job (person) 790f.; 396, 617, 624, 933, 971, 1355, 1396
Jobab 204, 1056; *1057*
Job, Book of 791f.; 624, 1491, 1651; *239*
Job's well 458
Job, Testament of 1299
Jochebed 792; 270, 1011, 1026; *1028*
Joel (prophet) 741, 1188; *273, 1277*
Joel, Book of 792ff.
Jogbehah 794; *561*
Johanan, Jehohanan 794; 494, 705f.; *796, 1678*
John (apostle) 794f.; 283f., 462, 509, 1055, 1159, 1337f., 1370; *281*
John, Acts of *Acts of John
John, Apocryphon of 567, 1080, 1084
John, Epistles of 797ff.; *241*
John, Gospel of 799ff.; *241, 582f., 802, 1149* ***Gospels**
John Hyrcanus 100, 412, 554, 714, 927, 1209, 1416; *274, 926*
John Mark *Mark, John
John, Revelation of *Revelation, Book of
John Rylands Papyrus 1148
John the Baptist 795ff.; 172f., 518, 520, 644f., 761ff., 800, 816, 853f., 868f., 1199, 1239, 1274, 1285f., 1370, 1480f.; ***795;*** *280*
John the Elder 389
John the Hasmonaean 130, 926; *926*
Joiada 494

K

Kiriath-jearim 860f.; 111, 185, 263, 724; ***861***
Kiriath-sanna 377
Kiriath-sepher 861; 11, 377; ***861***
Kir of Moab, Kir Hareseth 861; ***1014, 1579***
Kish 861f.; 169, 259, 512, 1398; ***1492;*** *513, 861f., 1398*
Kishon R. 862f.; 210; ***789, 862***
Kiss 863; 555, 594, 665
Kitchen equipment 671f.
Kite 61
Kittim 863; 350, 597, 735
Kneading-trough 863
Knee, kneel 863; 555
Knife 863; 124, 658; *863*
Knossos 338; ***338;*** *337*
Knowledge 863f.; 305, 409, 690, 797, 801, 1374, 1484, 1600
Knox, R. A. 456; *449*
Koa 864
Kohath, Kohathites 864; 189, 557, 1266f., 1447; *731, 1028*
Koine Greek 878f., 950, 1149f.
Kolaiah 24
Korah, Korahites 864; 403, 1109
K source 1184

L

Laadan 270
Laban 864f.; 199, 537, 608, 678, 728, 1013, 1244, 1535; *7, 1316*
Labourers in the vineyard, parable of 589, 667
Lachish 865ff.; 34, 38f., 96ff., 106, 122, 524, 526, 556, 632, 670, 1220, 1249, 1315; ***43, 415;*** *107, 743, 866ff., 1147, 1670*
Lachmann, C. 582
Ladan 900
Ladanites 554
Lagash 162
Lahmi 868; 439
Laish (city) 358
Laish (person) 997
Lake of fire and brimstone 475, 1436
Lake of Galilee, Gennesaret *Galilee, Sea of
Lamb, bride of 298, 907, 957
Lamb of God 868f.; 55, 779, 1052, 1337, 1367, 1423, 1532
Lamb, sacrificial 54, 175, 489, 1028, 1157, 1364, 1502
Lamb's book of life 203, 474
Lamech 869; 14, 547, 954
Lament 211f., 1244f.
Lamentations, Book of 869ff.; 236, 238; *869*
Lammergeier 61
Lamp, lampstand, lantern 871ff.; 248, 672, 1110f., 1467, 1524, 1576; *870ff., 1111, 1501*
Lance 112, 127
Landmark 873
Land of promise *Promised land
Language 1574ff., 1607
Language of Palestine 762, 1517
Language of the Apocrypha 873f.; *875*
Language of the NT 878ff.; 1147ff.
Language of the OT 874ff.; 232, 1608; *877*
Laodicea 881f.; 102, 135, 304, 459, 647f., 1079, 1104, 1172, 1337, 1579f., 1633; ***648, 881, 1172, 1337;*** *882*
Lapis lazuli 121, 784f.; *782, 785, 787*
Lappidoth 882
Large numbers in OT 257, 491, 1097, 1646
Lasea 882; 337
Lasha 882; 231
Lasharon 882
Last days 470, 1116f., 1338
Last hour 470, 668
Last judgment 203, 474f., 532
Last supper *Lord's Supper
Last things 470
Latin 882; 879, 950; *883*
Latin versions 196, 1550
Latter prophets 195
Latter rains 20, 1317f.; *223*
Laurel 542; *1589*
Laver 906, 1523f.
Law 882ff.; 45, 51, 110, 235ff., 300, 311, 384f., 436, 474, 482f., 493f., 578f., 588f., 746f., 764, 827, 829, 840, 896, 899, 1029, 1072f., 1101f., 1282f., 1325, 1346, 1350, 1388f., 1391, 1404, 1419, 1456f., 1533, 1580; *385, 884, 889*
Law and gospel 888
Law-codes 331, 652
Lawgiver 889
Lawlessness 1456f.
Law of Moses 1181ff. ***Ten Commandments**
Law of sin 1350
Law, prophets' view of 330
Laws of Hammurapi 606; *889*
Laws of nature 380
Lawsuits 315, 330
Lawyer 889; 1264
Laying on of hands 889f.; 173, 310, 382, 1121, 1361, 1482
Lazarus and Dives 890; 8, 595f., 907
Lazarus of Bethany 890f.; 212, 622, 958f., 1330
Lead 1002, 1004
Leader 251, 1273
Leah 891; 130, 388, 500, 547, 620, 720, 728, 822, 895, 955f., 1104, 1333; *731, 1316*
Leah tribes 1594
Leather 55, 111, 114, 127, 1580, 1619, 1658f.
Leaven 891; 206, 516, 1157f., 1639
Lebanon 891ff.; 231, 651f., 1136, 1586; ***892;*** *893f.*
Lebbaeus 830, 1552 ***James**
Leb-kamai 894
Lecanomancy 934f.
Lechaeum 313
Lectionary 1181
Leda 254
Leech 68
Leeks 513, 1618; *514, 1618*
Lees 894; 891
Leg 894; 343; *623*
Legalism 484, 705, 829
Legate 1294
Legion 894; 117; *895*
Lehabim 894f.; 1014
Lehi 895; 458, 1383
Lemuel 895; 414, 960
Lending 379
Lentils 1618f.; 20, 22, 206, 513; *514, 1618*
Lentulus, letter of 1083
Leontes, Litani R. ***892, 1605***
Leontopolis 713
Leopard 59; 664
Leper 300, 1110, 1360, 1363
Leprosy 179, 299f., 546, 618, 622
Letter *Writing
Letters for numbers 1096
Letter-writing 1172
Leucian Acts 1082f.
Levi 895f.; 1f., 33, 46, 388, 548, 554, 864, 982
Leviathan 896; 65, 180, 591, 933, 1317 ***Serpent**
Levirate law 957
Levirate marriage 500, 692, 851 ***Marriage**
Levites 1, 8, 131, 267f., 291, 372, 558, 560, 692, 896 ***Priests and Levites**
Levitical cities 464, 533, 634, 676, 806, 847, 936, 1267, 1318, 1432, 1506, 1637; ***290, 1269*** ***Cities of refuge**
Leviticus, Book of 896ff.; 268, 1183
Levi, tribe of 896, 1026, 1266ff., 1270f., 1594
Lex talionis 291, 341, 652, 886
Libertines, synagogue of the 898
Liberty 898ff.; 315, 681
Libnah 900; 865
Libni 900
Libya, Lubim, Libys 900; 19, 275; ***18, 900***
Libyans 895
Lice 67, 1235
Lictors 1215, 1247
Lie, lying 900f.
Life 901ff.; 203, 334, 615, 801, 1325
Life after death 49, 473 ***Resurrection**
Light 904f.; 872f.
Light and shade 307
Lightning 905; 1435
Lights, festival of 380, 505; *504*
Likeness 941
Lilies of the field 1238; *1239*
Lilith 905
Lily 1238; *72*
Lily-work 1238
Lime, limestone 905; 388, 1002, 1132, 1143, 1243, 1308, 1619; ***905***
Lindisfarne Gospels 447; *450*
Line 905f.
Linear A and B 338
Linear measures 1635ff.
Linear scripts 350, 1666
Linen 906f.; 211f., 215, 1451, 1653; *906f.*
Linen yarn 1671
Line omission 1536
Lintel 248, 1125

M

N

O

P

Q

R

S

T

U

V

X

Y

Z